# Contents

KT-487-172

ECONOMICS

THIRD EDITION

REFERENCE ONLY

ALAIN ANDERTON

Causeway Press

Original cover design by Susan and Andrew Allen, third edition by Tim Button

Cover drawing by Pete Turner, provided by The Image Bank

Cartoons by Brick

Graphics by Caroline Waring-Collins, Elaine Marie Sumner and Chris Collins

Photography by Andrew Allen and Dave Gray

Edited by Dave Gray

Acknowledgements

The author and publishers wish to thank the following for permission to reproduce photographs and copyright material. Other copyright material is acknowledged at source.

Asea Brown Boveri 2, Body Shop 414, Cadbury Schweppes 304, Cambus Litho 65, Corel 20, 172, Courtlands 2, Digital Vision 75, Digital Stock 97, 125, 467, *Financial Times* 68, Ford 215, 304, HSBC 205, Kwik Save 287, Mike Gibbons 63, Nestlé 724,725, Photobiz 459, 461, Photodisc 15, 21, 46, 65, 71, 75, 81, 99, 105, 117, 119, 140, 146, 161, 179, 255, 266, 270, 308, 312, 333, 382, 383, 395, 449, 453, 465, 466, 467, 482, 486, 505, 512, 549, 553, 555, 636, 691, Popperfoto 11,228, Rex Features 7, 8, 11, 15, 73, 102, 150, 275, 287, 313, 328, 348, 349, 391, 393, 394, 427, 432, 452, 491, 497, 524, 588, 625, 715, Royal Mint 552, Ian Sager 111, 244, 580, Ian Traynor 254, Topham Picturepoint 15, 36, 80, 98, 119, 127, 150, 174, 189, 190, 348, 402, 415, 489, 510, 543, 551, 603, 651, 685, 715.

Office for National Statistics material is Crown Copyright, reproduced with the permission of the Controller of Her Majesty's Stationery Office.

Every effort has been made to locate the copyright owners of material used in this book. Any omissions brought to the notice of the publisher are regretted and will be credited in subsequent printings.

British Library Cataloguing in Publication Data

A catalogue record for this book is available from the British Library.

ISBN 1 902796 10 1

Causeway Press Limited
PO Box 13, Ormskirk, Lancs, L39 5HP
© Alain Anderton
Published 1991 (reprinted 3 times)
Second edition 1995 (reprinted 4 times)
Third edition 2000, reprinted 2000, 2001

Typesetting by Caroline Waring-Collins (Waring Collins Limited), Ormskirk, L39 2YT.
Printed and bound by Legoprint, Italy.

Preface

Teachers and students of economics are critical groups of people. Constantly dissatisfied with the materials that they use, they face the problems of limited resources, a wide variety of needs and a constantly changing world. This book is intended to go some way to resolving this example of the basic economic problem.

The book has a number of distinctive features.

Comprehensive The book contains sufficient material to satisfy the demands of students taking a wide range of examinations including AS/A Level and Higher Grade economics.

Flexible unit structure The material is organised not into chapters but into shorter units. This reflects the organisation of a number of GCSE textbooks, and therefore students should be familiar with this style of presentation. The unit structure also allows the teacher greater freedom to devise a course. Economics teachers have a long tradition of using their main textbooks in a different order to that in which they are presented. So whilst there is a logical order to the book, it has been written on the assumption that teachers and students will piece the units together to suit their own teaching and learning needs. Cross referencing has been used on occasions to further aid flexibility. This approach also means that it is relatively easy to use the book for a growing number of courses which encompass part of an AS/A Level specification, such as professional courses with an economics input. To allow flexibility in course construction **Economics AS Level** is also available. It provides the AS Level units in a separate book.

Accessibility The book has been written in a clear and logical style which should make it accessible to all readers. Each unit is divided into short, easily manageable sections. Diagrams contain concise explanations which summarise or support the text.

A workbook The text is interspersed with a large number of questions. These are relatively short for the most part, and, whilst some could be used for extended writing work, most require relatively simple answers. They have been included to help teachers and students assess whether learning and understanding has taken place by providing immediate application of content and skills to given situations. I hope that many will be used as a basis for class discussion as well as being answered in written form. **Economics Teachers' Guide (Third Edition)** provides suggested answers to questions that appear in the book.

Applied economics as well as economic theory Many economics courses require teachers and students to have a book covering economic theory **and** an applied economic text. In this book, a systematic approach to applied economics has been included alongside economic theory. Each unit has an applied economics section and some units deal only with applied economics. It should be noted that many of the questions also contain applied economics material, and where sufficiently significant, this has been referred to in the index.

Use of data Modern technology has allowed much of the book to proceed from manuscript to book in a very short period. This has meant that we have been able to use statistics which were available in early 2000. Most statistical series therefore go up to 1999, although some were only available for earlier years. At the same time, experience has shown that too many current stories quickly date a book. Materials have therefore been chosen, particularly for the macro-economic section of the book, from throughout the post-war era, with particular emphasis on the turbulent times of the 1970s, 1980s and 1990s. This approach will help candidates to answer questions which require knowledge of what has happened 'in recent years' or 'over the past decade'.

Study skills and assessment The last two units of this book provide guidance on effective study and the methods of assessment used in economics.

Key terms Many units contain a key terms section. Each section defines new concepts, which appear in capitals in the text of the unit. Taken together, they provide a comprehensive dictionary of economics.

Presentation Great care has been taken with how this book is presented. It is hoped that the layout of the book, the use of colour and the use of diagrams will make learning economics a rewarding experience.

Thanks

I have many thanks to make. When preparing the first edition, Rosalind Levačić provided invaluable comments on sections of the book. Ronald Bramham greatly improved the readability of the text. For the second edition, my colleague at Codsall High School, Andrew Cawthera, reviewed the new manuscript. Peter Chapman, who reviewed the first edition, also reviewed the second edition. Mike Kidson carried out the unenviable task of proof reading all three editions. Dave Gray has been a superb editor and, as always, has been an enormous pleasure to work with. Not least, I would like to thank my wife who has performed a variety of tasks, in particular putting up with the stresses and strains of the production of such a large volume. All mistakes in the book, however, remain my own responsibility.

Finally, I would like to thank all those who read this book. It is an enormous privilege to be able to explore the world of economics with you. Causeway Press and I always welcome your comments, whether critical or otherwise. I hope you find the subject as exciting, stimulating and rewarding as I have always found it.

Alain Anderton

Summary

1. Nearly all resources are scarce.
2. Human wants are infinite.
3. Scarce resources and infinite wants give rise to the basic economic problem - resources have to be allocated between competing uses.
4. Allocation involves choice and each choice has an opportunity cost.
5. The production possibility frontier (PPF) shows the maximum potential output of an economy.
6. Production at a point inside the PPF indicates an inefficient use of resources.
7. Growth in the economy will shift the PPF outwards.

Scarcity

It is often said that we live in a global village. The world's resources are finite; there are only limited amounts of land, water, oil, food and other resources on this planet. Economists therefore say that resources are SCARCE.

Scarcity means that economic agents, such as individuals, firms, governments and international agencies, can only obtain a limited amount of resources at any moment in time. For instance, a family has to live on a fixed budget; it cannot have everything it wants. A firm might want to build a new factory but not have the resources to be able to do so. A government might wish to build new hospitals or devote more resources to its foreign aid programme but not have the finance to make this possible. Resources which are scarce are called ECONOMIC GOODS.

Not all resources are scarce. There is more than enough air on this planet for everyone to be able to breathe as

much as they want. Resources which are not scarce are called FREE GOODS. In the past many goods such as food, water and shelter have been free, but as the population of the planet has expanded and as production has increased, so the number of free goods has diminished. Recently, for instance, clean beaches in many parts of the UK have ceased to be a free good to society. Pollution has forced water companies and seaside local authorities to spend resources cleaning up their local environment. With the destruction of the world's rain forests and increasing atmospheric pollution, the air we breathe may no longer remain a free good. Factories may have to purify the air they take from the atmosphere, for instance. This air would then become an economic good.

Infinite wants

People have a limited number of NEEDS which must be satisfied if they are to survive as human beings. Some are material needs, such as food, liquid, heat, shelter and clothing. Others are psychological and emotional needs such as self-esteem and being loved. People's needs are finite. However, no one would choose to live at the level of basic human needs if they could enjoy a higher standard of living.

This is because human WANTS are unlimited. It doesn't matter whether the person is a peasant in China, a mystic in India, a manager in the UK or the richest individual in the world, there is always something which he or she wants more of. This can include more food, a bigger house, a longer holiday, a cleaner environment, more love, more friendship, better relationships, more self-esteem, greater fairness or justice, peace, or more time to listen to music, meditate or cultivate the arts.

The basic economic problem

Resources are scarce but wants are infinite. It is this which gives rise to the BASIC ECONOMIC PROBLEM and which forces economic agents to make choices. They have to allocate their scarce resources between competing uses.

Question 1

Time was when people used to take their car out for a Sunday afternoon 'spin'. The novelty of owning a car and the freedom of the road made driving a pleasant leisure pursuit. Today, with 22 million cars registered in the UK, a Sunday afternoon tour could easily turn into a nightmare traffic jam.

Of course, many journeys are trouble free. Traffic is so light that cars do not slow each other down. But most rush hour journeys today occur along congested roads where each extra car on the road adds to the journey time of every other car. What's more, traffic concentration greatly increases the amount of pollution created by cars. Our ecosystem can cope with low levels of emissions, but, as cities like Paris and Athens have discovered, high levels of traffic combined with the right weather conditions can lead to sharp increases in pollution levels.

Explain whether roads are, in any sense, a 'free good' from an economic viewpoint.

Question 2

Draw up a list of minimum human needs for a teenager living in the UK today. How might this list differ from the needs of a teenager living in Bangladesh or sub-Saharan Africa?

Economics is the study of this allocation of resources - the choices that are made by economic agents. Every CHOICE involves a range of alternatives. For instance, should the government spend £10 billion in tax revenues on nuclear weapons, better schools or greater care for the elderly? Will you choose to become an accountant, an engineer or a vicar?

These choices can be graded in terms of the benefits to be gained from each alternative. One choice will be the 'best' one and a rational economic agent will take that alternative. But all the other choices will then have to be given up. The benefit lost from the next best alternative is called the OPPORTUNITY COST of the choice. For

instance, economics may have been your third choice at 'A' level. Your fourth choice, one which you didn't take up, might have been history. Then the opportunity cost of studying economics at 'A' level is studying history at 'A' level. Alternatively, you might have enough money to buy just one of your two favourite magazines - *Melody Maker* or the *New Musical Express*. If you choose to buy the *Melody Maker*, then its opportunity cost is the benefit which would have been gained from consuming the *New Musical Express*.

Free goods have no opportunity cost. No resources need be sacrificed when someone, say, breathes air or swims in the sea.

Question 3

In the 1990s, university students came under increasing financial pressure. Traditionally, the government had paid for all student tuition fees. It also gave a grant to cover living expenses. This grant was means tested according to the income of parents. In the 1990s, the government froze student grants and introduced a system of subsidised student loans to allow students to make up for the falling real value of the grants. In 1998 students for the first time were charged for part of their tuition fees. The amount they had to pay each year was set at £1 000. In 1999 maintenance grants were replaced by loans.

What might be the opportunity cost of the £1 000 fees:
(a) to parents if they pay them on behalf of their sons or daughters;
(b) to students if they have to borrow the money to pay them.

Production possibility frontiers

Over a period of time, resources are scarce and therefore only a finite amount can be produced. For example, an economy might have enough resources at its disposal to be able to produce 30 units of manufactured goods and 30 units of non-manufactures. If it were now to produce more manufactured goods, it would have to give up some of its production of non-manufactured items. This is because the production of a manufactured item has an opportunity cost - in this case the production of non-manufactures. The more manufactures that are produced, the less non-manufactures can be produced.

This can be shown in Figure 1.1. The curved line is called the PRODUCTION POSSIBILITY FRONTIER (PPF) - other names for it include PRODUCTION POSSIBILITY CURVE or BOUNDARY, and TRANSFORMATION CURVE. The PPF shows the different combinations of economic goods which an economy is able to produce if all resources in the economy are fully and efficiently employed. The economy therefore could be:
- at the point C on its PPF, producing 30 units of manufactured goods and 30 units of non-manufactures;
- at the point D, producing 35 units of manufactured goods and 20 units of non-manufactures;

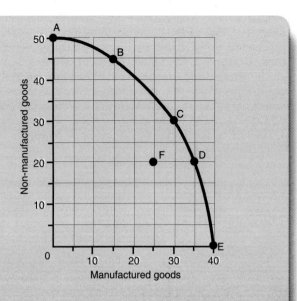

Figure 1.1 *The production possibility frontier*
*ABCDE is a production possibility frontier. It shows the
different combinations of goods which can be produced if all
resources are fully and efficiently utilised. For instance, the
economy can produce no manufactured goods and 50 units of
non-manufactures, 30 units of manufactured goods and 30 units
of non-manufactures, or 40 units of manufactured goods but no
non-manufactures.   .*

- at the point A, devoting all of its resources to the
  production of non-manufactured goods;
- at the points B or E or anywhere else along the line.
The production possibility frontier illustrates clearly the

principle of opportunity cost. Assume that the economy is
producing at the point C in Figure 1.1 and it is desired to
move to the point D. This means that the output of
manufactured goods will increase from 30 to 35 units.
However, the opportunity cost of that (i.e. what has to be
given up because of that choice) is the lost output of non-
manufactures, falling from 30 to 20 units. The opportunity
cost at C of increasing manufacturing production by 5
units is 10 units of non-manufactures.

   The production possibility frontier for an economy is
drawn on the assumption that all resources in the
economy are fully and efficiently employed. If there are
unemployed workers or idle factories, or if production is
inefficiently organised, then the economy cannot be
producing on its PPF. It will produce within the
boundary. In Figure 1.1 the economy could produce
anywhere along the line AE. But because there is
unemployment in the economy, production is at point F.

   The economy cannot be at any point outside its existing
PPF because the PPF, by definition, shows the maximum
production level of the economy. However, it might be
able to move to the right of its PPF in the future if there is
economic growth. An increase in the productive potential
of an economy is shown by a shift outwards of the PPF. In
Figure 1.2 economic growth pushes the PPF from PP to
QQ, allowing the economy to increase its maximum level
of production say from A to B. Growth in the economy
can happen if:
- the quantity of resources available for production
  increases; for instance there might be an increase in the
  number of workers in the economy, or new factories
  and offices might be built;
- there is an increase in the quality of resources;
  education will make workers more productive whilst
  technical progress will allow machines and production
  processes to produce more with the same amount of
  resources.

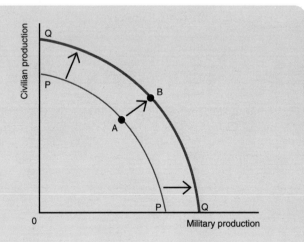

Figure 1.2 *Economic growth*
*Economic growth in the quantity or quality of the inputs to the
production process means that an economy has increased its
productive potential. This is shown by a shift to the right of the
production possibility frontier from PP to QQ. It would enable
the economy to move production, for instance, from point A to
point B.*

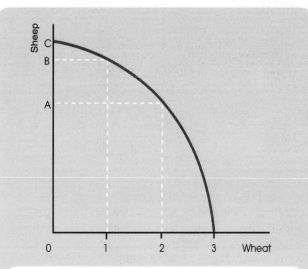

Figure 1.3 *Opportunity costs*
*The production possibility frontier is concave, showing that the
opportunity cost of production rises as more of a good is
produced.*

The production possibility frontiers in Figures 1.1. to 1.2 have been drawn concave to the origin (bowing outwards) rather than as straight lines or as convex lines. This is because it has been assumed that not all resources in the economy are as productive in one use compared to another.

Take, for instance, the production of wheat in the UK. Comparatively little wheat is grown in Wales because the soil and the climate are less suited to wheat production than in an area like East Anglia. Let us start from a position where no wheat is grown at all in the UK. Some farmers then decide to grow wheat. If production in the economy is to be maximised it should be grown on the land which is most suited to wheat production (i.e. where its opportunity cost is lowest). This will be in an area of the country like East Anglia. As wheat production expands, land has to be used which is less productive because land is a finite resource. More and more marginal land, such as that found in Wales, is used and output per acre falls. The land could have been used for another form of production, for instance sheep rearing. The more wheat is grown, the less is the output per acre and therefore the greater the cost in terms of sheep production.

In Figure 1.3 only sheep and wheat are produced in the economy. If no wheat is produced the economy could produce OC of sheep. If there is one unit of wheat production only OB of sheep can be produced. Therefore the opportunity cost of the first unit of wheat is BC of sheep. The second unit of wheat has a much higher opportunity cost - AB. But if the economy produces wheat only, then the opportunity cost of the third unit of wheat rises to OA of sheep.

The PPF by itself gives no indication of which combination of goods will be produced in an economy. All it shows is the combination of goods which an economy could produce if output were maximised from a given fixed amount of resources. It shows a range of possibilities and much of economics is concerned with explaining why an economy, ranging from a household economy to the international economy, chooses to produce at one point either on or within its PPF rather than another.

Question 4

Draw a production possibility frontier. The scale on both axes is the same. The economy is currently producing at point A on the frontier which is at the mid point between the vertical axis (showing public sector goods) and the horizontal axis (showing private sector goods). Mark the following points on your drawing.
Point B - a point which shows production following the election of a government which privatises many public sector services but maintains full and efficient employment.
Point C - where unemployment is present in the economy.
Point D - where the state takes over production of all goods and services in the economy.
Now draw two new production possibility frontiers.
PP - which shows the position after a devastating war has hit the economy.
QQ - where there is an increase in productivity in the economy such that output from the same amount of resources increases by 50 per cent in the public sector but twice that amount in the private sector.

key terms

Choice - economic choices involve the alternative uses of scarce resources.
Economic goods - goods which are scarce because their use has an opportunity cost.
Free goods - goods which are unlimited in supply and which therefore have no opportunity cost.
Needs - the minimum which is necessary for a person to survive as a human being.
Opportunity cost - the benefits foregone of the next best alternative.
Production possibility frontier - (also known as the production possibility curve or the production possibility boundary or the transformation curve) - a curve which shows the maximum potential level of output of one good given a level of output for all other goods in the economy.
Scarce resources - resources which are limited in supply so that choices have to be made about their use.
The economic problem - resources have to be allocated between competing uses because wants are infinite whilst resources are scarce.
Wants - desires for the consumption of goods and services.

Applied economics

Work and leisure

Paid work

Time is a scarce resource. There are only 24 hours in a day and 365 days in a year. Average life expectancy for a male born in 2000 was 75. For a female it was 80. So people have to make choices about how to allocate their time.

One fundamental choice is how to divide time between work and leisure. Work can narrowly be defined as paid work. Table 1.1 shows that there has been little change in the average number of hours worked per week in recent years. On the other hand, holiday entitlements have shortened the working year. Most workers are now entitled to at least 3-4 weeks paid holiday each year plus bank holidays. In 1970, the average was only 2 weeks.

Males have also been choosing to shorten their working life. Figure 1.4 shows activity rates for males and females, comparing 1971 with 1997. The activity rate is the percentage of the population in work or seeking work (i.e. officially unemployed). For instance

98 per cent of males aged 25-44 were in work or seeking work in 1971. In contrast, only 52 per cent of women of the same age were in work. Figure 1.4 shows that there was a fall in the activity rates of males aged 16-24 between 1971 and 1997. More males have chosen to remain in education in the early part of their life. There has been a large fall in the proportion of men working in their 50s and 60s. Far more are now taking early retirement, either through choice or because their employers are forcing them into retirement. Females, on the other hand, have seen a large increase in their activity rates. More and more women have been choosing to remain in employment between the ages of 25 and 54, rather than staying at home.

People work for a variety of motives, including the satisfaction of doing a job and enjoying being part of a team. However, the primary motivator is pay. When workers retire, they might choose to undertake voluntary work, or do jobs about the house which previously they would have paid someone else to do. Rarely will they put the time or energy into these activities that they put into their previous paid job. Over time, the opportunity cost of not working has been rising because wages have been rising. Since 1945, earnings have roughly been doubling every 30 years in real terms (i.e. after inflation has been taken into account). Workers today can buy far more goods and services than their parents or grandparents at a similar age. If a 40 year old doesn't work today, he or she will have to forego the purchase of far more goods and services than, say, 30 years ago. This is arguably the most important reason why more and more women are choosing to stay in work rather than give up work to stay at home to bring up their families.

For those taking early retirement, the opportunity cost of leisure time is far less than for other workers. When people retire, they receive a pension. Hence, the money foregone is only the difference between what they would have earned and their pension. Tax, National Insurance contributions and work related payments, like pension contributions or costs of commuting to work, all

Table 1.1 *Average weekly hours of full-time employees*

	1986	1999
Males	41.8	41.4
Females	37.3	37.5

Source: adapted from *Annual Abstract of Statistics*, Office for National Statistics.

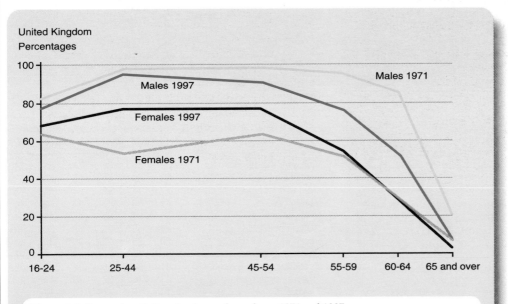

Figure 1.4 *Economic activity rates: by gender and age, 1971 and 1997*
Source: adapted from *Social Trends*, Office for National Statistics.

help to reduce the monetary value of a wage. Hence, many workers taking early retirement find that their new retirement income is not that much below their old take home pay. Many workers in their 50s and 60s therefore find early retirement an attractive proposition. The benefits of the extra leisure time they can gain far outweigh the losses in terms of the goods and services they could buy had they stayed in work.

Non-paid work

Paid work is not the only type of work undertaken by individuals. People also have to work at home, cooking and looking after others, particularly children, the sick and the elderly. Table 1.2 shows that women tend to spend more time on such domestic work than men. Consequently, they end up with less free time each week which can be used for leisure.

Leisure

Individuals spend their leisure time in a variety of ways. Table 1.3 shows participation rates in the main home-based leisure activities and how they have changed over time. The most popular leisure activity is watching television. Nearly everybody had watched some television in the four weeks prior to being interviewed for the survey. Equally, seeing friends or relatives is a highly popular activity. Table 1.3 shows that there are gender differences between leisure activities. Men are far more likely to do DIY and gardening, whilst women are more likely to do dressmaking, needlework and knitting.

Table 1.4 shows participation in leisure activities outside the home. The most popular leisure activity is going to a pub, whilst less than 10 per cent on average visited a betting shop.

Individuals have to allocate their scarce resources of time and money between different leisure pursuits.

Children tend to be time rich but financially poor. 45 year olds tend to be the reverse, time poor but financially better off. Old age pensioners are time rich but less financially well off than when they were working. Their health may also prevent them from taking part in activities, such as certain sports. These constraints could be represented on a production possibility frontier. For instance, a diagram could be drawn showing the trade off between home based leisure pursuits and leisure activities away from the home. The more time spent in the pub means that less time is available to watch television at home or gardening. Equally, a production possibility diagram could be used to illustrate the trade-off between work and leisure. The more time spent at work, the less leisure time is available.

Table 1.3 *Participation in home-based leisure activities: by gender*

Great Britain   Percentages

	1977	1980	1986	1990-91	1996-97
Males					
Watching TV	97	97	98	99	99
Visiting/entertaining friends or relations	89	90	92	95	95
Listening to records/tapes/CDs	64	66	69	78	79
Reading books	52	52	52	56	58
DIY	51	53	54	58	58
Gardening	49	49	47	52	52
Dressmaking/needlework/knitting	2	2	3	3	3
Females					
Watching TV	97	98	98	99	99
Visiting/entertaining friends or relations	93	93	95	97	97
Listening to records/tapes/CDs	60	62	65	74	77
Reading books	57	61	64	68	71
DIY	22	23	27	29	30
Gardening	35	38	39	44	45
Dressmaking/needlework/knitting	51	51	48	41	37

Source: adapted from *Social Trends*, Office for National Statistics.

Table 1.2 *Time use: by age, May 1995*

Great Britain   Hours and minutes

	Males			Females		
	16-44	45 and over	All aged 16 and over	16-44	45 and over	All aged 16 and over
Average daily hours spent on						
Sleep	8.25	8.54	8.40	8.33	9.03	8.48
Free time	5.22	6.48	6.06	4.54	6.15	5.35
Education/paid work	5.13	2.39	3.54	3.15	1.23	2.18
Domestic work	0.33	0.51	0.42	2.03	2.45	2.24
Personal care	0.37	0.42	0.39	0.46	0.49	0.47
Household maintenance	0.36	1.11	0.54	0.16	0.34	0.25
Free time per weekday	4.44	6.07	5.24	4.28	6.11	5.20
Free time per weekend day	7.32	8.56	8.19	6.02	9.42	6.22

Source: adapted from *Social Trends*, Office for National Statistics.

Table 1.4 *Participation in selected leisure activities away from home: by age, 1997-98*

Great Britain   Percentages

	16-24	25-34	35-44	45-59	60 and over	All 16 & over
Visit a public house	82	85	81	74	55	74
Meal in a restaurant (not fast food)	63	69	65	75	70	69
Meal in a fast food restaurant	77	74	55	34	11	48
Library	41	38	43	37	43	40
Cinema	65	51	31	23	11	34
Historic building	24	30	35	39	30	32
Short break holiday	39	35	27	26	30	31
Disco or night club	68	47	20	9	3	27
Spectator sports event	31	34	36	22	11	26
Museum or art gallery	21	18	27	26	19	22
Theatre	14	18	15	18	17	17
Theme park	29	22	23	10	5	17
Camping or caravanning	17	11	15	13	6	12
Bingo	11	6	7	11	16	11
Visit a betting shop	9	10	7	11	8	9

Source: adapted from *Social Trends*, Office for National Statistics.

Production possibility frontiers

The Third World debt crisis

In the 1970s and early 1980s, many Third World countries borrowed heavily from the West. The money was used for a combination of economic development, military spending and excessive consumption on the part of ruling elites. The borrowing, for the most part, stopped in 1982 when Mexico announced that it could no longer keep up with repayments on debts. Western banks, afraid that other countries would also default on their debts, stopped new lending to many countries. African countries were particularly badly affected. The money borrowed had been poorly used and they were faced with having to make considerable repayments each year. The result was deteriorating living standards. Governments cut back on social spending such as education and health care. Infrastructure such as roads and rail networks deteriorated.

Table 1.5 *Average annual growth in real national income and population, selected developing countries, 1980-98*

Percentages

		1980-90	1990-98
Argentina	National income	-0.4	5.3
	Population	2.5	1.5
Haiti	National income	-0.2	-2.5
	Population	3.6	2.4
Mozambique	National income	-0.1	5.7
	Population	3.4	2.6
Niger	National income	-0.1	1.9
	Population	6.0	3.9
Peru	National income	-0.3	5.9
	Population	3.6	2.0

Source: adapted from World Bank, *World Development Report*.

Kosovo

In 1999 the Serbian military forced ethnic Albanians living in Kosovo (a part of Serbia) to leave the province. The troops destroyed ethnic Albanians' houses and forcibly transported people to the border. Nato aircraft bombed Serbia's military infrastructure, including bridges and oil storage facilities, in an attempt to end this 'ethnic cleansing' and to put pressure on the Serbian government to remove its troops from the province.

The oil crises of the 1970s

In 1973-4 and 1978-80, there were substantial increases in the price of oil. In 1973-4, oil prices quadrupled whilst in 1978-80 they more than doubled. The initial cause of the oil price increase in both cases was political, but the members of OPEC, the Organisation of Petroleum Exporting Countries, contrived to maintain high prices by restricting oil supplies. These enormous increases in price had a substantial impact on economies throughout the world. In the industrialised countries of the world it made a considerable amount of equipment obsolete. For instance, a large new oil fired electricity power station on the Isle of Grain near London, built in 1972 and 1973, has never been used except as a reserve power station because the electricity it generates is so expensive. Oil fired heating systems were scrapped at an earlier date than they would otherwise have been, with gas or electric heating systems installed in their place. Scarce resources were used to develop engines which would use less petrol.

The break-up of Eastern Europe

When communism in Eastern Europe was replaced by more democratic systems of government in the early 1990s, there was a move away from state control of

Table 1.6 *National income, selected countries in Eastern Europe, 1999 as % of 1989*

	%
Poland	122.4
Hungary	100.1
Bulgaria	71.1
Russia	54.5
Ukraine	39.0

Source: adapted from United Nations, *Economic Survey of Europe*.

the economy towards a market-led economy. Before, the state had often decided which factories were to produce what products, and would issue instructions about who was to buy the resulting output. In the new market-led system, factories had to find buyers for their products. The result was that many factories closed down. Consumers often preferred to buy foreign made goods, or were unable to carry on buying because they had been made redundant from closing enterprises. Factories making goods for the defence industry were particularly badly affected as governments cut their spending on defence. Some attempted to transfer their skills to making civilian goods, but it often proved impossible to make the jump from making fighter jets to making washing machines. Countries such as Poland and Hungary, with governments which took strong action to sell off state owned firms and other assets and create a legal framework for private firms to prosper, suffered the least long term damage. Other countries, such as Russia, Bulgaria and the Ukraine, which implemented reforms slowly, were poorer in 2000 than they were in 1990.

Markets in Eastern Europe after trade liberalisation.

Former Yugoslavia

The collapse of communism in Eastern Europe was a mixed blessing for some. In Yugoslavia, it led to the break-up of the federation of states which formed the country. Serbia, which considered itself the most important part of the federation, strongly resisted the process. Slovenia, the state nearest to Austria and furthest from Serbia, was allowed to become independent but Serbia, which effectively inherited most of the armed forces of the former Yugoslavia, fought a war with Croatia in 1992 and over-ran part of the country, which today still remains in Serbian hands. The Serbs also prevented Bosnia-Herzegovina from gaining independence by starting a civil war in the state. The war in Croatia and Bosnia was marked by ethnic cleansing, atrocities committed against civilian populations and a breakdown in economic links within the countries and with outside countries. Much of the infrastructure, such as houses and factories, in war zones was destroyed. In the meantime, an embargo on trade with Serbia, imposed by the United Nations, led to severe shortages.

1. **What is a production possibility frontier for an economy?**
2. **Explain, illustrating your answer with examples from the data, why a production possibility frontier might shift inwards.**

3. **A peace group has put forward a proposal that the UK should halve its spending on defence, including giving up its nuclear capability. Using production possibility frontiers, evaluate the possible economic implications of this proposal.**

2 The function of an economy

Summary

1. An economy is a social organisation through which decisions about what, how and for whom to produce are made.
2. The factors of production - land, labour, capital and entrepreneurship - are combined together to create goods and services for consumption.
3. Specialisation and the division of labour give rise to large gains in productivity.
4. The economy is divided into three sectors, primary, secondary and tertiary.
5. Markets exist for buyers and sellers to exchange goods and services using barter or money.
6. The main actors in the economy, consumers, firms and government, have different objectives.

Consumers, for instance, wish to maximise their welfare whilst firms might wish to maximise profit.

What is an economy?

Economic resources are scarce whilst human wants are infinite. An economy is a system which attempts to solve this basic economic problem. There are many different levels and types of economy. There is the household economy, the local economy, the national economy and the international economy. There are free market economies which attempt to solve the economic problem with the minimum intervention of government and command economies where the state makes most resource allocation decisions. Although these economies are different, they all face the same problem.

Question 1

Consider your household economy.
(a) What is produced by your household (e.g. cooking services, cleaning services, accommodation, products outside the home)?
(b) How is production organised (e.g. who does the cooking, what equipment is used, when is the cooking done)?
(c) For whom does production take place (e.g. for mother, for father)?
(d) Do you think your household economy should be organised in a different way? Justify your answer.

Economists distinguish three parts to the economic problem.
- **What** is to be produced? An economy can choose the mix of goods to produce. For instance, what proportion of total output should be spent on defence? What proportion should be spent on protecting the environment? What proportion should be invested for the future? What proportion should be manufactured goods and what proportion services?
- **How** is production to be organised? For instance, are hi-fi systems to be made in the UK, Japan or Taiwan? Should car bodies be made out of steel or fibreglass? Would it better to automate a production line or carry on using unskilled workers?
- **For whom** is production to take place? What proportion of output should go to workers? How much should pensioners get? What should be the balance between incomes in the UK and those in Bangladesh?

An economic system needs to provide answers to all these questions.

Economic resources

Economists commonly distinguish three types of resources available for use in the production process. They call these resources the FACTORS OF PRODUCTION.

LAND is not only land itself but all natural resources below the earth, on the earth, in the atmosphere and in the sea. Everything from gold deposits to rainwater and natural forests are examples of land.

NON-RENEWABLE RESOURCES, such as coal, oil, gold and copper, are land resources which once used will never be replaced. If we use them today, they are not available for use by our children or our children's children. RENEWABLE RESOURCES on the other hand can be used and replaced. Examples are fish stocks, forests, or water. Renewable resources can sometimes be over-exploited by man leading to their destruction.

LABOUR is the workforce of an economy - everybody

from housepersons to doctors, vicars and cabinet ministers. Not all workers are the same. Each worker has a unique set of inherent characteristics including intelligence, manual dexterity and emotional stability. But workers are also the products of education and training. The value of a worker is called his or her HUMAN CAPITAL. Education and training will increase the value of that human capital, enabling the worker to be more productive.

CAPITAL is the manufactured stock of tools, machines, factories, offices, roads and other resources which is used in the production of goods and services. Capital is of two types. WORKING or CIRCULATING CAPITAL is stocks of raw materials, semi-manufactured and finished goods which are waiting to be sold. These stocks circulate through the production process till they are finally sold to a consumer. FIXED CAPITAL is the stock of factories, offices, plant and machinery. Fixed capital is fixed in the sense that it will not be transformed into a final product as working capital will. It is used to transform working capital into finished products.

Sometimes a fourth factor of production is distinguished. This is ENTREPRENEURSHIP. Entrepreneurs are individuals who:

- organise production - organise land, labour and capital in the production of goods and services;
- take risks - with their own money and the financial capital of others, they buy factors of production to produce goods and services in the hope that they will be able to make a profit but in the knowledge that at worst they could lose all their money and go bankrupt.

It is this element of risk taking which distinguishes entrepreneurs from ordinary workers. There is much controversy today about the role and importance of entrepreneurs in a modern developed economy.

Question 2

Table 2.1 *Factors of production: selected statistics*

	1989	1998
Production of coal (million tonnes)	98.2	40.0
Number of students gaining a degree qualification	74 953	233 610
Net investment in new physical fixed capital at 1995 constant prices (£ million)	50 766	59 634

Source: adapted from *Annual Abstract of Statistics*, Office for National Statistics.

(a) Explain what is meant by the 'factors of production'. Illustrate your answer from the data.

Specialisation

When he was alone on his desert island, Robinson Crusoe found that he had to perform all economic tasks by himself. When Man Friday came along he quickly

abandoned this mode of production and specialised. SPECIALISATION is the production of a limited range of goods by an individual or firm or country in co-operation with others so that together a complete range of goods is produced.

Specialisation can occur between nations. For instance, a country like Honduras produces bananas and trades those for cars produced in the United States. Specialisation also occurs within economies. Regional economies specialise. In the UK, Stoke-on-Trent specialises in pottery whilst London specialises in services.

Specialisation by individuals is called THE DIVISION OF LABOUR. Adam Smith, in a passage in his famous book An Enquiry into the Nature and Causes of the Wealth of Nations (1776), described the division of labour amongst pin workers. He wrote:

A workman not educated to this business ... could scarce ... make one pin in a day, and certainly could not make twenty. But in the way in which this business is now carried on, ... it is divided into a number of branches ... One man draws out the wire, another straightens it, a third cuts it, a fourth points, a fifth grinds it at the top for receiving the head; to make the head requires two or three distinct operations; to put it on is a peculiar business, to whiten the pins is another; it is even a trade by itself to put them into the paper.

He pointed out that one worker might be able to make 20 pins a day if he were to complete all the processes himself. But ten workers together specialising in a variety of tasks could, he estimated, make 48 000 pins.

This enormous increase in LABOUR PRODUCTIVITY (output per worker) arises from a variety of sources.

- Specialisation enables workers to gain skills in a narrow range of tasks. These skills enable individual workers to be far more productive than if they were jacks-of-all-trades. In a modern economy a person could not possibly hope to be able to take on every job which society requires.
- The division of labour makes it cost-effective to provide workers with specialist tools. For instance, it would not be profitable to provide every farm worker with a tractor. But it is possible to provide a group of workers with a tractor which they can then share.
- Time is saved because a worker is not constantly changing tasks, moving around from place to place and using different machinery and tools.
- Workers can specialise in those tasks to which they are best suited.

The division of labour has its limits. If jobs are divided up too much, the work can become tedious and monotonous. Workers feel alienated from their work. This will result in poorer workmanship and less output per person. Workers will do everything possible to avoid work - going to the toilet, lingering over breaks and reporting sick for instance. The size of the market too will limit the division of labour. A shop owner in a village might want to specialise in selling health foods but finds that in order to survive she has to sell other products as well.

Over-specialisation also has its disadvantages. For

instance, the North, Wales, Scotland and Northern Ireland have paid a heavy price in terms of income and unemployment for their over-dependence on heavy manufacturing industry. Shipyard, steel and textile workers have all found that the division of labour can exact a heavy price if their skills are no longer wanted. Another problem with specialisation is that a breakdown in part of the chain of production can cause chaos within the system. Small falls in the supply of oil on world markets in the past have resulted in major shocks to the world economy. Equally, anyone dependent upon rail transport knows that a rail strike can cause chaos.

Question 3

(a) Explain, with the help of the photographs, what is meant by 'specialisation'.
(b) What might be some of the (i) advantages to firms and (ii) disadvantages to workers of the division of labour shown in the photographs?

Sectors of the economy

Economies are structured into three main sectors. In the PRIMARY SECTOR of the economy, raw materials are extracted and food is grown. Examples of primary sector industries are agriculture, forestry, fishing, oil extraction and mining. In the SECONDARY or MANUFACTURING SECTOR, raw materials are transformed into goods. Examples of secondary sector industries are motor manufacturing, food processing, furniture making and steel production. The TERTIARY or SERVICE SECTOR produces services such as transport, sport and leisure, distribution, financial services, education and health.

Most firms tend to operate in just one of these sectors, specialising in producing raw materials, manufactured goods or services. Some very large firms, such as BP Amoco,

operate across all three sectors, from the extraction of oil to its refining and sale to the public through petrol stations.

Money and exchange

Specialisation has enabled people to enjoy a standard of living which would be impossible to achieve through self-sufficiency. Specialisation, however, necessitates exchange. Workers can only specialise in refuse collecting, for instance, if they know that they will be able to exchange their services for other goods and services such as food, housing and transport.

Exchange for most of history has meant **barter** - swopping one good for another. But barter has many disadvantages and it would be impossible to run a modern sophisticated economy using barter as a means of exchange. It was the development of **money** that enabled trade and specialisation to transform economies into what we know today. Money is anything which is widely accepted as payment for goods received, services performed, or repayment of past debt. In a modern economy, it ranges from notes and coins to money in bank accounts and deposits in building society accounts.

Markets

There must be a buyer and a seller for exchange to take place. Buyers and sellers meet in the market place. For economists, markets are not just street markets. Buying and selling can take place in newspapers and magazines, through mail order or over the telephone in financial deals in the City of London, or on industrial estates as well as in high street shopping centres. A MARKET is any convenient set of arrangements by which buyers and sellers communicate to exchange goods and services.

Economists group buyers and sellers together. For instance, there is an international market for oil where large companies and governments buy and sell oil. There are also national markets for oil. Not every company or government involved in the buying and selling of oil in the UK, say, will be involved in the US or the Malaysian oil markets. There are also regional and local markets for oil. In your area there will be a small number of petrol filling stations (sellers of petrol) where you (the buyers) are able to buy petrol. All these markets are inter-linked but they are also separate. A worldwide increase in the price of oil may or may not filter down to an increase in the price of petrol at the pumps in your local area. Equally, petrol prices in your area may increase when prices at a national and international level remain constant.

How buyers and sellers are grouped together and therefore how markets are defined depends upon what is being studied. We could study the tyre industry or we could consider the market for cars and car components which includes part but not all of the tyre industry. Alternatively, we might want to analyse the market for rubber, which would necessitate a study of rubber purchased by tyre producers.

Many Western economists argue that specialisation, exchange and the market lie at the heart of today's economic prosperity in the industrial world. Whilst it is likely that the market system is a powerful engine of prosperity, we shall see that it does not always lead to the most efficient allocation of resources (☞ units 15-23).

Question 4

(a) Who are the major buyers and sellers in the UK market for shoes?
(b) What is the relationship between this market and the market for (i) sports equipment and (ii) leather goods?

The objectives of economic actors

There are four main types of economic actors in a market economy - consumers, workers, firms and governments. It is important to understand what are the economic objectives of each of these sets of actors.

Consumers In economics, consumers are assumed to want to maximise their own **economic welfare**, sometimes referred to as UTILITY or **satisfaction**. They are faced with the problem of scarcity. They don't have enough income to be able to purchase all the goods or services that they would like. So they have to allocate their resources to achieve their objective. To do this, they consider the utility to be gained from consuming an extra unit of a product with its opportunity cost. If there is 30p to be spent, would it best be spent on a Mars Bar, a newspaper or a gift to a charity? If you could afford it, would you prefer to move to a larger but more expensive house, or spend the money on going out more to restaurants, or take more holidays abroad? Decisions are made at the **margin**. This means that consumers don't look at their overall spending every time they want to spend an extra 30p. They just consider the alternatives of that decision to spend 30p and what will give them the highest utility with that 30p.

Sometimes it is argued that economics portrays consumers as being purely selfish. This isn't true. Consumers do spend money on giving to charity. Parents

spend money on their children when the money could be spent on themselves. 17 year old students buy presents for other people. What this shows, according to economists, is that the utility gained from giving money away or spending it on others can be higher than from spending it on oneself. However, individuals are more likely to spend money on those in their immediate family than others. This shows that the utility to be gained from paying for a holiday for your child is usually higher than paying for a holiday for a handicapped person you do not know.

Workers Workers are assumed in economics to want to maximise their own welfare at work. Evidence suggests that the most important factor in determining welfare is the level of pay. So workers are assumed to want to maximise their earnings in a job. However, other factors are also important. Payment can come in the form of fringe benefits, like company cars. Satisfaction at work is also very important. Many workers could earn more elsewhere but choose to stay in their present employment because they enjoy the job and the workplace.

Firms The objectives of firms are often mixed. However, in the UK and the USA, the usual assumption is that firms are in business to maximise their PROFITS. This is because firms are owned by private individuals who want to maximise their return on ownership. This is usually achieved if the firm is making the highest level of profit possible. In Japan and continental Europe, there is much more of a tradition that the owners of firms are just one of the STAKEHOLDERS in a business. Workers, consumers and the local community should also have some say in how a business is run. Making profit would then only be one objective amongst many for firms.

Governments Governments have traditionally been assumed to want to maximise the welfare of the citizens of their country or locality. They act in the best interests of all. This can be very difficult because it is often not immediately obvious what are the costs and benefits of a decision. Nor is there often a consensus about what value to put on the gains and losses of different groups. For instance, in the 1990s the UK government brought the motorway building programme to a virtual halt following the growing feeling that motorways were destroying the environment and were therefore an economic 'bad' rather than a 'good'. However, many, particularly in industry, would argue that the environmental costs of new motorway building are vastly exaggerated and that the benefits of faster journey times more than outweigh any environmental costs.

Governments which act in the best interests of their citizens face a difficult task. However, it can also be argued that governments don't act to maximise the welfare of society. Governments are run by individuals and it could be that they act in their own interest. For instance, there is a tradition in government that bribery determines what decisions are made. Certain Third World countries have immense economic problems because their governments are not impartial, but are run for the monetary benefit of the few that can extort bribes from citizens. There is equally a long tradition of 'pork barrel politics'. This is where politicians try to stay in power by giving benefits to those groups who are important at election times. In the UK, it is expected that MPs (Members of Parliament) will fight for the interests of their constituents even if this clearly does not lead to an overall increase in welfare for the country as whole.

So governments may have a variety of motives when making decisions. In an ideal world, governments should act impartially to maximise the welfare of society. In practice they may fall short of this.

Question 5

The government, through local authorities, became a major owner of homes in post-war Britain. Council houses were built to provide affordable homes for a nation which had suffered bombing during the war. A growing population too put pressure on existing housing stock, much of which was sub-standard. Occasionally, a scandal would hit the headlines about councillors or council officials taking bribes or receiving 'kick backs' from construction projects. In the 1980s, the government instituted a policy of selling council houses to their occupants. This policy achieved notoriety in the 'Home for Votes' scandal in Westminster borough. The Conservative leader of Westminster Council, Dame Shirley Porter, was accused of rigging the sale of council houses in key wards in the borough in a way which would ensure that Conservative voters bought the homes.

(a) Suggest what might motivate a consumer to buy rather than rent a property.
(b) What might motivate government in its housing policies?

key terms

Division of labour - specialisation by workers.

Factors of production - the inputs to the production process: land, which is all natural resources; labour, which is the workforce; capital, which is the stock of man-made resources used in the production of goods and services; entrepreneurs, individuals who seek out profitable opportunities for production and take risks in attempting to exploit these.

Fixed capital - economic resources such as factories and hospitals which are used to transform working capital into goods and services.

Human capital - the value of the productive potential of an individual or group of workers. It is made up of the skills, talents, education and training of an individual or group and represents the value of future earnings and production.

Labour productivity - output per worker.

Market - any convenient set of arrangements by which buyers and sellers communicate to exchange goods and services.

Non-renewable resources - resources, such as coal or oil, which once exploited cannot be replaced.

Primary sector - extractive and agricultural industries.

Profits - the reward to the owners of a business. It is the difference between a firm's revenues and its costs.

Renewable resources - resources, such as fish stocks or forests, which can be exploited over and over again because they have the potential to renew themselves.

Secondary sector - production of goods, mainly manufactures.

Specialisation - a system of organisation where economic units such as households or nations are not self-sufficient but concentrate on producing certain goods and services and trading the surplus with others.

Stakeholders - groups of people which have an interest in a firm, such as shareholders, customers, suppliers, workers, the local community in which it operates and government.

Tertiary sector - production of services.

Utility - the satisfaction derived from consuming a good.

Working or circulating capital - resources which are in the production system waiting to be transformed into goods or other materials before being finally sold to the consumer.

Applied economics

Sport and leisure

Different markets

The sport and leisure market is made up of many different markets. For instance, there is a market for travel and tourism, a market for football, a television entertainment market and a restaurant market. Some of these markets overlap. A Japanese visitor to the UK might eat in a restaurant in London, and so the tourism and the 'eating out' markets overlap. Some markets are closely linked. Pubs near a football stadium are likely to benefit from increased trade on the day of matches.

Economic resources

Each market uses land, labour and capital to produce services. For instance, a visit to a National Trust property utilises land as a factor. There is likely to be a house built on land and the gardens too use land as their basic resource. Labour is needed for the upkeep of the property and to provide services to the visitor, including volunteers on the door and in the tea shop. Buildings on the property represent capital.

There are many examples of entrepreneurs in the market. Andrew Lloyd Webber, for instance, is an entrepreneur putting on musical shows for the mass market. Rich owners of football clubs are entrepreneurs too.

Objectives of participants in the market

In a market there are buyers and sellers. The objectives of consumers are to maximise their welfare or utility when buying sport and leisure services. They consider whether they will get more satisfaction per pound spent from going to a pub or going to a nightclub, for instance. They have to choose between spending on sport and leisure services and all other goods and services, like clothes or consumer durables. They also have to choose between different sport and leisure services.

There is a number of different types of suppliers to the market. First there are firms whose aim is to maximise profit. A travel company, for instance, is likely to be owned by shareholders to whom the directors of the company are accountable. There are many much smaller travel companies owned perhaps by one individual entrepreneur. That individual too is motivated by profit.

Second, there are many examples of charities and trusts in the market. The largest is The National Trust. Charities and trusts do not necessarily have the same objectives, but few are likely to have profit maximisation as their principle objective. The National Trust has as its primary aim to 'preserve places of historic interest and natural beauty permanently for the nation to enjoy'. Financially, it must break even over time to survive. But it is unlikely to see maximising profits or revenues as its priority. For instance, there are restrictions on the number of visitors to some properties that it owns because more visitors would lead to unacceptable levels of wear and tear.

Third, government is a major provider of services. As Table 2.2 shows, it owns some of Britain's most popular tourist attractions including the British Museum, the Tower of London and London Zoo. The management of these tourist attractions want to maximise resources available to them, particularly by securing larger grants from government. However, government itself is often interested in minimising spending on such bodies because of conflicting objectives. Government may prefer to spend more money on the National Health Service than on museums. The arts and sport have tended to be subsidised by government. Concerning the arts, there is a belief that 'culture' is important to the health of the nation. Hence, the Royal Opera House is heavily subsidised, whilst an Andrew Lloyd Webber production like The Phantom of the Opera receives no subsidy. Some would argue that there is no difference between a Mozart opera like The Marriage of Figaro and The Phantom of the Opera. Indeed, The Phantom of the Opera might be a better case for subsidy because more foreign tourists are likely to see it than a Royal Opera House production. Tourism brings money into the country and creates prosperity.

The same arguments apply to sport. There is an argument that everyone should have access to sporting facilities. Traditionally, local authorities have subsidised swimming pools, leisure centres and sports facilities. Sometimes government is swayed by lobbying from a particular part of the country for spending on the arts or leisure. Local MPs fight for grants for new theatres or recreational facilities. So government is likely to be motivated by a variety of factors when deciding on spending on sport and leisure.

Table 2.2 *Visits to the most popular tourist attractions*

Great Britain							Millions
	1981	1991	1997		1981	1991	1997
Museums and galleries				**Historic houses and monuments**			
British Museum	2.6	5.1	5.6	Tower of London	2.1	1.9	2.6
National Gallery	2.7	4.3	4.8	Edinburgh Castle	0.8	1.0	1.2
National History Museum	3.7	1.6	1.9	Windsor Castle	0.7	0.6	1.5
Tate Gallery	0.9	1.8	2.2	Roman Baths, Bath	0.6	0.8	0.9
Science Museum	3.8	1.3	1.6	Warwick Castle	0.4	0.7	0.8
Theme parks				**Wildlife parks and zoos**			
Blackpool Pleasure Beach	7.5	6.5	7.1	London Zoo	1.1	1.1	1.1
Alton Towers	1.6	2.0	2.8	Chester Zoo	..	0.9	0.9
Pleasureland, Southport	..	1.8	2.1	Knowsley Safari Park	..	0.3	0.5
Chessington World of Adventures	0.5	1.4	1.7	Edinburgh Zoo	..	0.5	0.5
Legoland, Windsor	..	..	1.5	London Aquarium	..	..	0.7

Source: adapted from *Social Trends*, Office for National Statistics.

DATA QUESTION

The oil industry

Oil production
in the North Sea

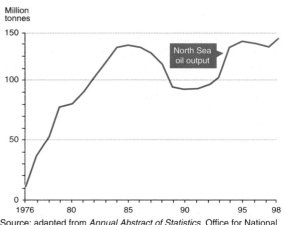

Source: adapted from *Annual Abstract of Statistics*, Office for National Statistics.

Figure 2.1 *North Sea oil output*

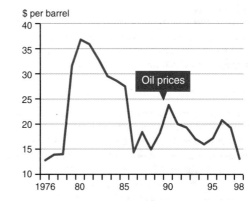

Source: adapted from *BP Statistical Survey of World Energy*.

Figure 2.2 *Oil prices, Brent $ per barrel*

A plastics factory
and a petrol station.

Table 2.3 *Petroleum products by end use, 1998*   Thousand tonnes

	Butane and propane	Naphtha (LDF) and Middle Distillate Feedstock	Motor spirit	Kerosene		Gas/diesel oil		Fuel oil	Bitumen	Lubric-ating oils	Total
				Aviation turbine fuel	Burning oil	Derv fuel	Other				
1998	2 368	3 643	21 848	9 221	2 698	15 160	7 244	2 907	813	1 967	71 944

Source: adapted from *Monthly Digest of Statistics*, Office for National Statistics.

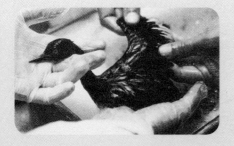

1. Explain the following economic concepts in the context of the UK oil industry:
   (a) economic resources; (b) specialisation; (c) money and exchange; (d) markets.
2. North Sea oil companies face a problem about how to dispose of redundant oil rigs. Environmental groups are concerned that companies will either leave then to rot where they stand or sink them, rather than dismantle them on land. What criteria do you think should be used to decide whether scarce resources should be used to dismantle redundant oil rigs?

Summary

1. Economic data are collected not only to verify or refute economic models but to provide a basis for economic decision making.
2. Data may be expressed at nominal (or current) prices or at real (or constant) prices. Data expressed in real terms take into account the effects of inflation.
3. Indices are used to simplify statistics and to express averages.
4. Data can be presented in a variety of forms such as tables or graphs.
5. All data should be interpreted with care given that data can be selected and presented in a wide variety of ways.

The collection and reliability of data

Economists collect data for two main reasons.

- The scientific method requires that theories be tested. Data may be used to refute or support a theory. For instance, an economist might gather data to support or refute the hypothesis that 'Cuts in the marginal rate of income will increase the incentive to work', or that 'An increase in the real value of unemployment benefit will lead to an increase in the number of people unemployed'.
- Economists are often required to provide support for particular policies. Without economic data it is often difficult, if not impossible, to make policy recommendations. For instance, in his Budget each year the Chancellor of the Exchequer has to make a statement to the House of Commons outlining the state of the economy and the economic outlook for the next 12 months. Without a clear knowledge of where the economy is at the moment it is impossible to forecast how it might change in the future and to recommend policy changes to steer the economy in a more desirable direction.

Collecting economic data is usually very difficult and sometimes impossible. Some macro-economic data - such as the balance of payments figures or the value of national income - are collected from a wide variety of sources. The figures for the balance of payments on current account are compiled from returns made by every exporter and importer on every item exported and imported. Not surprisingly the information is inaccurate. Some exporters and importers will conceal transactions to avoid tax. Others will not want to be bothered with the paper work.

Other macro-economic data such as the Index of Retail Prices (used to measure inflation) are based on surveys. Surveys are only reliable if there is accurate sampling and measuring and are rarely as accurate as a complete count.

Some macro-economic data are very reliable statistically but do not necessarily provide a good measure of the relevant economic variable. In the UK the unemployment level is calculated each month at benefit offices throughout the country. It is extremely accurate but no economist would argue that the figure produced is an accurate measure of unemployment. There is general agreement that some people who claim benefit for being unemployed are not unemployed and conversely there are

Question 1

In November 1998, the Office for National Statistics (ONS) suspended publication of one of the most important economic series it compiles. The average earnings index was found to be giving inaccurate information. The average earnings index is a measure of how much earnings in the whole of the UK are rising. It is calculated monthly by taking data from thousands of returns from businesses. They report on whether or not they have given any pay rises during the previous month and if so, by how much.

Problems arose because of different ways of calculating the average. In October 1998, the ONS launched a new series for average earnings which used a different way of calculating the average than before. But as Figure 3.1 shows, this revised series gave very different figures than the original series used before. It also didn't fit in very well with what other economic indicators were showing at the time.

A government enquiry found that the revised series was based on inadequate statistical methods which gave too much importance to large changes in earnings by small businesses. In March 1999, a new series was published which followed more closely the old series.

(a) The three lines in Figure 3.1 should show the same data: the percentage change in average earnings. Give ONE time period when the original series showed an upward movement in earnings when the revised series showed a downward movement.

(b) Why do the three sets of statistics differ in their estimate of changes in average earnings?

(c) Explain TWO reasons why it is important for economic statistics, like growth in average earnings, to be measured accurately.

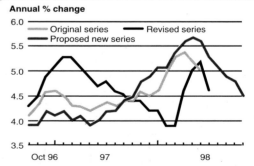

Figure 3.1 *Estimates of growth in average earnings*
Source: adapted from Office for National Statistics.

many unemployed people who are not claiming benefit.

In micro-economics use is again made of survey data, with the limitations that this implies. Economists also make use of more experimental data, gathering evidence for case studies. For instance, an economist might want to look at the impact of different pricing policies on entry to sports centres. He or she might study a small number of sports centres in a local area. The evidence gathered would be unlikely decisively to refute or support a general hypothesis such as 'Cheap entry increases sports centre use'. But it would be possible to conclude that the evidence **tended** to support or refute the hypothesis.

In economics it is difficult to gather accurate data and, for that reason, academic economists mostly qualify their conclusions.

Real and nominal values

There are many different **measures** in use today such as tonnes, litres, kilograms and kilometres. Often, we want to be able to compare these different measures. For instance, an industrialist might wish to compare oil measured in litres, and coal measured in kilograms. One way of doing this is to convert oil and coal into therms using gross calorific values. In economics, by far the most important measure used is the value of an item measured in **monetary terms**, such as pounds sterling, US dollars or French francs. One problem in using money as a measure is that inflation (the general change in prices in an economy) erodes the purchasing power of money.

For instance, in 1948 the value of output of the UK economy (measured by gross domestic product at market prices) was £11.8 billion. Half a century later in 1999 it was £814.2 billion. It would seem that output had increased about 69 times - an enormous increase. In fact, output increased by only a fraction of that amount. This is because most of the measured increase was an increase not in output but in prices. Prices over the period rose about 20 times. Stripping the inflation element out of the increase leaves us with an increase in output of 3.5 times.

Values unadjusted for inflation are called NOMINAL VALUES. These values are expressed AT CURRENT PRICES (i.e. at the level of prices existing during the time period being measured).

If data are adjusted for inflation, then they are said to be at REAL VALUES or at CONSTANT PRICES. To do this in practice involves taking one period of time as the BASE PERIOD. Data are then adjusted assuming that prices were the same throughout as in the base period.

For instance, a basket of goods costs £100 in year 1 and £200 in year 10. Prices have therefore doubled. If you had £1 000 to spend in year 10, then that would have been equivalent to £500 at year 1 prices because both amounts would have bought 5 baskets of goods. On the other hand, if you had £1 000 to spend in year 1, that would be equivalent to £2 000 in year 10 prices because both would have bought you 10 baskets of goods.

Taking another example, the real value of UK output in 1948 at 1948 prices was the same as its nominal value (i.e. £11.8 billion). The real value of output in 1999 at 1948 prices was £41 billion. It is much lower than the nominal 1999 value because prices were much higher in 1999.

Table 3.1 *Nominal and real values*

| Nominal value | Inflation between year 1 and 2 | Real values | |
		Value at year 1 prices	Value at year 2 prices
Example 1 £100 in year 1	10%	£100	£110
Example 2 £500 in year 1	50%	£500	£750
Example 3 £200 in year 2	20%	£166.66	£200
Example 4 £400 in year 2	5%	£380.95	£400

Note: £100 at year 1 prices is worth £100 x 1.1 (i.e. 1+10%) in year 2 prices. £200 at year 2 prices is worth £200 ÷ 1.2 in year 1 prices.

On the other hand, at 1999 prices, the real value of output in 1948 was £234.4 billion, much higher than the nominal value because prices in 1999 were much higher than in 1948. Further examples are given in Table 3.1.

Prices can be adjusted to any base year. UK government statistics expressed in real terms are adjusted every 5 years. In 1999, figures were expressed at 1995 prices. In 2005, they will be readjusted to 2000 prices.

Question 2

Table 3.2 *Components of final demand at current prices*

| | 1995=100 | £ billion | | |
	Index of prices	Households' expenditure	Government expenditure	Investment
1995	100	438	140	116
1996	102.4	468	146	126
1997	105.6	499	147	134
1998	109.3	523	152	145

Source: adapted from *Monthly Digest of Statistics*, Office for National Statistics.

Using a calculator or a spreadsheet, work out for the period 1995 -1998 the values of: (i) households' expenditure; (ii) government expenditure; and (iii) investment: (a) at constant 1995 prices and (b) at constant 1998 prices.
Present your calculation in the form of two tables, one for each set of real prices.

Indices

It is often more important in economics to compare values than to know absolute values. For instance, we might want to compare the real value of output in the economy in 1989 and 1999. Knowing that the real value of output (GDP at market prices at 1995 prices) in 1989 was £654.3 billion and in 1999 was £788.5 billion is helpful, but the very large numbers make it difficult to see at a glance what, for instance, was the approximate percentage increase. Equally, many series of statistics are averages.

The Retail Price Index (the measure of the cost of living) is calculated by working out what it would cost to buy a typical cross-section or 'basket' of goods. Comparing say £458.92 in one month with £475.13 the next is not easy.

So, many series are converted into INDEX NUMBER form. One time period is chosen as the base period and the rest of the statistics in the series are compared to the

Table 3.3 *Converting a series into index number form*

Year	£ millions	Index number if base year is:		
		year 1	year 2	year 3
1	500	100.0	83.3	62.5
2	600	120.0	100.0	75.0
3	800	160.0	133.3	100.0

Note: The index number for consumption in year 2, if year 1 is the base year, is (600 ÷ 500) x 100.

value in that base period. The value in the base period is usually 100. The figure 100 is chosen because it is easy to work with mathematically. Taking the example of output again, if 1948 were taken as the base year, then the value of real output in 1948 would be 100, and in 1999 would be 351.2. Alternatively if 1999 were taken as the base year, the value of output would be 100 in 1999 and 28.5 in 1948. Or with 1989 as the base year, the value of output in 1948 would be 34.3 whilst in 1999 it would be 120.5. Further examples are given in Table 3.3.

The interpretation of data

Data can be presented in many forms and be used both to inform and mislead the reader. To illustrate these points, consider inflation figures for the UK economy. Inflation is the general rise in prices in an economy. If there has been 2 per cent inflation over the past year, it means that prices on average have increased by 2 per cent. One way in which inflation figures can be presented is in **tabular form** as in Table 3.5.

Question 3

Table 3.4 *Consumers' expenditure*

£ billion

	Food	Vehicles	Energy products
1995	49.3	20.7	27.1
1996	52.5	23.5	28.8
1997	53.2	26.8	28.7
1998	53.9	28.5	28.6

Source: adapted from *Monthly Digest of Statistics*, Office for National Statistics.

Using a calculator or a spreadsheet, convert each category of expenditure into index number form using as the base year: (a) 1995 and (b) 1998.
Present your calculations in the form of two tables, one for each base year.

The data could also be presented in **graphical form** as in Figure 3.2 (a). Graphs must be interpreted with some care. Figure 3.2 (b) gives a far more pessimistic view of inflation between 1996 and 1998 than Figure 3.2 (a) at first glance.

Table 3.5 *UK inflation*

Year	Inflation, %
1986	3.4
1987	4.2
1988	4.9
1989	7.8
1990	9.4
1991	5.9
1992	3.8
1993	1.6
1994	2.5
1995	3.4
1996	2.4
1997	3.2
1998	3.4
1999	1.5

Source: adapted from *Economic Trends Annual Supplement*, Office for National Statistics.

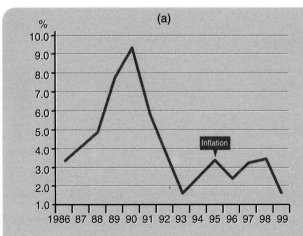

(a)

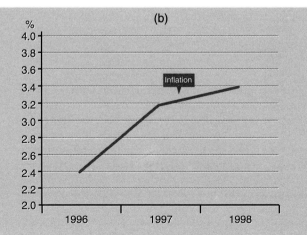

(b)

Figure 3.2 UK inflation
Source: adapted from *Economic Trends Annual Supplement*, Office for National Statistics.

Question 4

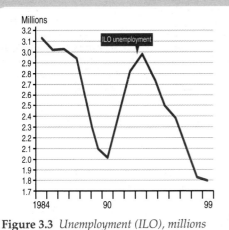

Figure 3.3 *Unemployment (ILO), millions*

Millions axis: 0, 0.5, 1.0, 1.5, 2.0 with years 1998 and 1999

ILO unemployment

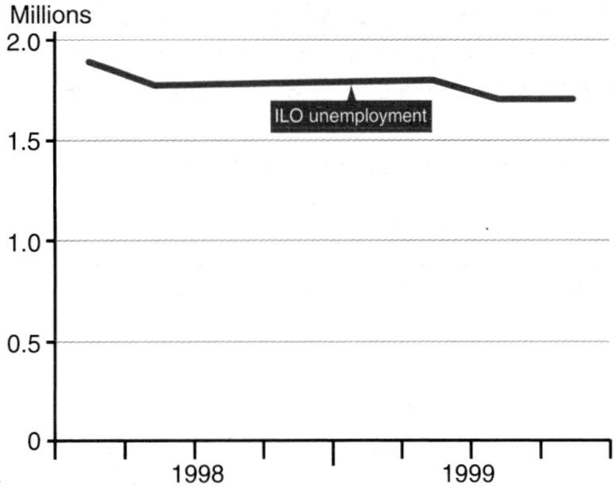

Figure 3.4 *Unemployment (ILO), millions*

Source: adapted from *Economic Trends Annual Supplement*, Office for National Statistics.

Consider each graph in turn.
(a) What does each show?
(b) Explain why each seems to give a different picture of unemployment in the UK.

One reason is that Figure 3.2 (b) is taken out of the context of its surrounding years. Figure 3.1 (a) would suggest that inflation between 1996-98 was relatively low for the whole period shown. Figure 3.2 (b) suggests the opposite, a dramatic increase in inflation. Another reason why Figure 3.2 (b) suggests a dramatic increase in inflation is because the line is drawn very steeply. This has been achieved through the scales used on the axes. The vertical axis in Figure 3.2 (b) only covers 2-4 per cent. In Figure 3.2 (a), in contrast, the vertical axis starts at zero and rises to 10 per cent over the same drawn height. The gradient of the line in Figure 3.2 (b) could have been been even steeper if the length of the horizontal time axis had been drawn shorter.

Graphs are sometimes constructed using log scales for the vertical axis. This has the effect of gradually compressing values on the vertical axis as they increase. The vertical distance between 0 and 1, for instance, is larger per unit than between 999 and 1 000.

Data can also be expressed in **verbal form**. It shows that inflation rose between 1986 and 1990, fell to 1993 and then fluctuated between 1 and 4 per cent. When expressing data in verbal form, it can become very tedious to describe each individual change. For instance, it would be inappropriate to say 'Inflation in 1986 was 3.4 per cent. Then it rose to 4.2 per cent in 1987. In 1988 it rose to 4.9 per cent in 1988 and then rose again to 7.8 per cent in 1989 etc.' When describing data in verbal form, it is important to pick out the main trends and perhaps give a few key figures to illustrate these trends.

key terms

Base period - the period, such as a year or a month, with which all other values in a series are compared.
Index number - an indicator showing the relative value of one number to another from a base of 100. It is often used to present an average of a number of statistics.
Nominal values - values unadjusted for the effects of inflation (i.e. values **at current prices**).
Real values - values adjusted for inflation (i.e. values at **constant prices**).

Applied economics

Tourism

Spending on tourism

Tourism is a major industry in the UK. Is it growing in size? There is a number of ways in which growth can be measured. Table 3.6 shows how total spending on tourism has grown between 1989 and 1998. It divides tourists into three categories - UK tourists who take a holiday within the country, foreign tourists who come to the UK and UK tourists who take holidays abroad. The figures in Table 3.6 are expressed at current prices. This means that inflation is not taken into account. If there had been very high inflation over the period 1989-98, the volume of tourism could have declined given the data in Table 3.6. In fact, consumer prices over the ten year period rose 41 per cent. So real growth in spending is that which is greater than a 41 per cent rise.

Table 3.6 *Spending on tourism at current prices, £ million*

	£ millions at current prices		
	Spending on holidays by UK citizens in the UK	Spending in the UK by foreign visitors	Spending on foreign holidays by UK residents
1989	10 865	6 945	9 357
1993	12 430	9 487	12 972
1998	14 030	12 671	23 871

Source: adapted from *Annual Abstract of Statistics*, Office for National Statistics.

Table 3.7 shows the figures in Table 3.6 expressed at constant 1995 prices, i.e. after the inflation element has been stripped out and adjusted to the level of prices in 1995. Taking 1995 as the reference year for prices means that the 1989 and 1993 data at current prices increase as numbers when they become data at constant prices, whilst the 1998 numbers fall.

Table 3.8 shows the figures in Table 3.7 in index number form. This has the advantage that it is much easier to see which of the three areas of tourism has grown more quickly. At a glance, it can be seen that the value of

Table 3.7 *Spending on tourism at constant 1995 prices, £ million*

	£ millions at constant 1995 prices		
	Spending on holidays by UK citizens in the UK	Spending in the UK by foreign visitors	Spending on foreign holidays by UK residents
1989	14 076	9 567	12 861
1993	13 191	10 188	13 184
1998	12 840	11 573	21 847

Source: adapted from *Annual Abstract of Statistics*, Office for National Statistics.

domestic tourism fell 8 per cent whilst spending on foreign holidays by UK citizens grew by 70 per cent. Foreign visitors to the UK spent 21 per cent more. Because these are index numbers, it is not possible to say how important is the 20 per cent rise in spending by foreign visitors to the total domestic tourist industry. For instance, if foreign tourists accounted for just 1 per cent of total spending, a 20 per cent rise would have almost no impact on tourism. This illustrates one of the disadvantages of using index numbers. To assess the relative impact of the increase in foreign tourists, we have to look back to Table 3.7. Total spending on tourism in the UK at constant 1995 prices rose from £23.6 billion to £24.4 billion, a 3 per cent increase, over the period 1989 to 1998. A 3 per cent change over ten years is an insignificant change and so it can be concluded that, broadly, the increase in spending by foreigners was cancelled out by a fall in spending by UK citizens.

Table 3.8 *Spending on tourism at constant 1995 prices, 1989 = 100*

	1989=100		
	Spending on holidays by UK citizens in the UK	Spending in the UK by foreign visitors	Spending on foreign holidays by UK residents
1989	100	100	100
1993	93.7	106.5	102.5
1998	91.2	121.0	169.9

Source: adapted from *Annual Abstract of Statistics*, Office for National Statistics.

Employment in tourism

Spending on tourism within the UK grew by 3 per cent between 1989 and 1998. Employment in tourism related industries also grew, but by 19 per cent as shown in Table 3.9. It is easier to see the increase in each sector by converting these figures into index number form as in Table 3.10.

The 70 per cent increase in the amount spent by UK citizens on holidays abroad is reflected in a 70 per cent rise in the number of workers amongst travel agents and tour operators. The 3 per cent rise in spending on tourism is matched by an 11 per cent rise in the number of workers in hotels and other tourist accommodation. The 46 per cent rise in numbers employed in restaurants, cafes, etc. will not have just been due to tourism. It should be remembered that Tables 3.9 and 3.10 refer to tourism **related** industries. Much of the increase in employment in restaurants etc. will have come from an increase in non-tourist demand for meals out. Similarly, much of the employment in libraries, museums and culture, and sport and recreation will be non-tourist related.

Trips and prices

Data for UK domestic tourism, trips made by British citizens within Great Britain, reveal some very interesting aspects of tourism. Table 3.11 shows that the number of trips made increased by 13 million between 1989 and 1998. The fall in 1993 from 1989 was probably due to the fact that in 1993 the UK was only just coming out of a deep recession, in which unemployment had doubled and many workers had seen hardly any pay increases. Each trip, though, was shorter. In 1989, the average number of nights spent was 4 but in 1998 had fallen to 3.6. Spending per trip at constant prices also fell.

Table 3.11 therefore shows that between 1989 and 1998, people went on more holidays in Britain, but they were shorter and they spent less per trip in real terms. This is an indication that 'short breaks' have become far more popular. More people are now taking a weekend holiday for instance. These will be less expensive than longer holidays. The fall in spending per trip could also be an indication that the price of holidays has fallen relative to all other prices in the economy. For instance, the 1990s saw the building of chains of budget hotels which helped reduce the average cost of hotel accommodation in Britain.

Table 3.9 *Employment in tourism related industries, Great Britain, thousands at June in each year*

Thousands, not seasonally adjusted

	Hotels and other tourist accommodation	Restaurants, cafes etc operators	Bars, pubs clubs culture	Travel agents, tour operators	Libraries, museums, culture	Sport and other recreation	Total employment in tourist related industries
1989	299.2	283.4	428.2	64.9	82.8	294.7	1 644.2
1993	317.6	298.0	370.6	69.3	75.6	316.5	1 643.6
1998	332.6	413.7	467.3	110.0	86.4	357.8	1 951.7

Source: adapted from *Annual Abstract of Statistics*, Office for National Statistics.

Table 3.10 *Employment in tourism related industries, Great Britain, 1989=100 at June in each year*

1989=100

	Hotels and other tourist accommodation	Restaurants, cafes etc operators	Bars, pubs clubs culture	Travel agents, tour operators	Libraries, museums, culture	Sport and other recreation	Total employment in tourist related industries
1989	100	100	100	100	100	100	100.0
1993	106.1	105.2	86.5	106.8	91.3	107.4	100.0
1998	111.1	146.0	109.1	169.5	104.3	121.4	118.7

Source: adapted from *Annual Abstract of Statistics*, Office for National Statistics.

Table 3.11 *UK domestic tourism*

	Number of trips, millions	Number of nights spent, millions	Average nights spent	Average expenditure per trip at current prices	Average expenditure per trip trip at constant 1995 prices
1989	109.6	443.2	4.0	99.1	128.2
1993	90.9	375.9	4.1	136.7	147.2
1998	122.3	437.6	3.6	114.7	105.0

Source: adapted from *Annual Abstract of Statistics*, Office for National Statistics.

Cinema data

Table 3.12 *Cinema exhibitor statistics, GB*

	Number of sites	Number of screens	Number of admissions, millions	at current prices			at constant 1995 prices		
				Gross box office takings, £ millions	Revenue per admission, £	Revenue per screen, £ 000	Gross box office takings, £ millions	Revenue per admission, £	Revenue per screen, £ 000
1987	492	1 035	66.8	123.8	1.85	118.7	181.2	2.70	173.70
1993	495	1 591	99.3	271.3	2.73	171.0	287.5	2.89	181.23
1998	481	1 975	123.4	449.5	3.64	227.6	411.4	3.33	208.30

Source: adapted from *Annual Abstract of Statistics*, *Monthly Digest of Statistics*, Office for National Statistics.

Table 3.13 *Cinema exhibitor statistics, GB*

1987=100

	Number of sites	Number of screens	Number of admissions	at current prices			at constant 1995 prices		
				Gross box office takings	Revenue per admission	Revenue per screen	Gross box office takings	Revenue per admission	Revenue per screen
1987	100.0	100.0	100.0	100.0	100.0	100.0	100.0	100.0	100.0
1993	100.6	153.7	148.7	219.1	147.6	144.1	158.7	106.6	104.3
1998	97.8	190.8	184.7	363.1	196.8	191.7	227.0	122.9	119.9

Source: adapted from *Annual Abstract of Statistics*, Office for National Statistics.

1. **Describe the main trends in cinema admissions shown in the data.**
2. **Explain the advantages and disadvantages of using index numbers to present data. Illustrate your answer from the data.**
3. **'Revenues per admission and the number of screens cannot carry on rising.'**
   (a) To what extent does this data support this statement for the period 1987-1998?
   (b) Discuss whether it is likely to be true in the future.

Summary

1. **Demand** for a good is the quantity of goods or services that will be bought over a period of time at any given price.
2. Demand for a good will rise or fall if there are changes in factors such as incomes, the price of other goods, tastes, and the size of the population.
3. A change in price is shown by a movement along the demand curve.
4. A change in any other variable affecting demand, such as income, is shown by a shift in the demand curve.
5. The market demand curve can be derived by horizontally summing all the individual demand curves in the market.

Demand

A market exists wherever there are buyers and sellers of a particular good (☞ unit 2). Buyers **demand** goods from the market whilst sellers **supply** goods on to the market.

DEMAND has a particular meaning in economics. Demand is the quantity of goods or services that will be bought at any given price over a period of time. For instance, approximately 2 million new cars are bought each year in the UK today at an average price of, say, £8 000. Economists would say that the annual demand for cars at £8 000 would be 2 million units.

Demand and price

If everything else were to remain the same (this is known as the **ceteris paribus** condition ☞ unit 45), what would happen to the quantity demanded of a product as its price changed? If the average price of a car were to fall from £8 000 to £4 000, then it is not difficult to guess that the quantity demanded of cars would rise. On the other hand, if the average price were £35 000 very few cars would be sold.

This is shown in Table 4.1. As the price of cars rises, then ceteris paribus, the quantity of cars demanded will fall. Another way of expressing this is shown in Figure 4.1. Price is on the vertical axis and quantity demanded over time is on the horizontal axis. The curve is downward sloping showing that as price falls, quantity demanded rises. This DEMAND CURVE shows the quantity that is

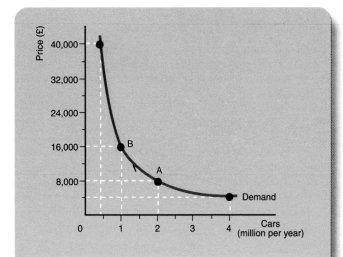

Figure 4.1 *The demand curve*
The demand curve is downward sloping, showing that the lower the price, the higher will be the quantity demanded of a good. In this example, only 0.4 million cars per year are demanded at a price of £40 000 each, but a reduction in price to £4 000 increases quantity demanded to 4 million units per year.

demanded at any given price. When price changes there is said to be a **movement along** the curve. For instance, there is a movement along the curve from the point A to the point B, a fall of 1 million cars a year, when the price of cars rises from £8 000 to £16 000.

It is important to remember that the demand curve shows EFFECTIVE DEMAND. It shows how much would be bought (i.e. how much consumers can afford to buy and would buy) at any given price and not how much buyers would like to buy if they had unlimited resources.

Economists have found that the inverse relationship between price and quantity demanded - that as price rises, the quantity demanded falls - is true of nearly all goods. In unit 10 we shall consider the few examples of goods which might have upward sloping demand curves.

Table 4.1 *The demand schedule for cars*

Price (£)	Demand (million per year)
4 000	4.0
8 000	2.0
16 000	1.0
40 000	0.4

Question 1

Stagecoach operates both bus and train services. It charges different prices to different passengers for the same journeys depending, for instance, on when they travel, their age, whether they are making a single or return journey or whether they have a season ticket. Using a demand curve diagram, explain what happens when:
(a) children are charged half price for a bus journey instead of being charged full price;
(b) old age pensioners are given a free bus pass paid for by the local authority rather than having to pay the full fare;
(c) Stagecoach increases its prices on a route by 5 per cent;
(d) passengers can get a 60 per cent reduction by buying a day return if they travel after 9.30 compared to having to pay the full fare.

Demand and income

Price is not the only factor which determines the level of demand for a good. Another important factor is income. Demand for a normal good rises when income rises. For instance, a rise in income leads consumers to buy more cars. A few goods, known as inferior goods, fall in demand when incomes rise (☞ unit 10).

The effect of a rise in income on demand is shown in Figure 4.2. Buyers are purchasing OA of clothes at a price of OE. Incomes rise and buyers react by purchasing more clothes at the same price. At the higher level of income they buy, say, OB of clothes. A new demand curve now exists passing through the point S. It will be to the right of the original demand curve because at any given price

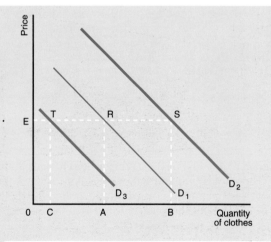

Figure 4.2 *A change in income*
An increase in income will raise demand for a normal good. At a price of OE, for instance, demand will rise from OA to OB. Similarly, at all other prices, an increase in income will result in a level of demand to the right of the existing demand curve. So the demand curve will shift from D_1 to D_2. A fall in income will result in less being demanded at any given price. Hence the demand curve will shift to the left, from D_1 to D_3.

more will be demanded at the new higher level of income.

Economists say that a rise in income will lead to an **increase in demand** for a normal good such as clothes. An increase in demand is shown by a SHIFT IN THE DEMAND CURVE. (Note that an **increase in quantity demanded** would refer to a change in quantity demanded resulting from a change in price and would be shown by a movement along the curve.) In Figure 4.2, the original demand curve D_1 shifts to the right to its new position D_2. Similarly, a fall in income will lead to a **fall in demand** for a normal good. This is shown by a **shift** to the left of the demand curve from D_1 to D_3. For instance, at a price of OE, demand will fall from OA to OC.

Two points need to be made. First, the demand curves in Figure 4.2 have been drawn as straight lines. These demand curves drawn show a hypothetical (or imaginary) position. They are drawn straight purely for convenience and do not imply that actual demand curves for real products are straight. Second, the shifts in the demand curves are drawn as parallel shifts. Again this is done for convenience and neatness but it is most unlikely that a rise or fall in income for an actual product would produce a parallel shift in its demand curve.

Question 2

Table 4.2

Quantity demanded (million tyres)	Price (£)
10	20
20	16
30	12
40	8
50	4

Table 4.2 shows the demand curve facing a tyre manufacturer.
(a) Draw a demand curve for tyres from the above data.
(b) An increase in income results in an increase in quantity demanded of tyres of: (i) 5 million; (ii) 10 million; (iii) 15 million; (iv) 25 million. For each of these, draw a new demand curve on your diagram.
(c) Draw a demand curve for tyres which would show the effect of a fall in incomes on the original demand for tyres.
(d) Draw a demand curve for tyres which would show that no products were demanded when their price was £8.

The price of other goods

Another important factor which influences the demand for a good is the price of other goods. For instance, in the great drought of 1976 in the UK, the price of potatoes soared. Consumers reacted by buying fewer potatoes and replacing them in their diet by eating more bread, pasta and rice.

This can be shown on a demand diagram. The demand curve for pasta in Figure 4.3 is D_1. A rise in the price of

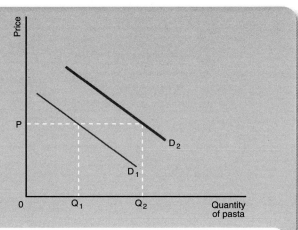

Figure 4.3 *A rise in the price of other goods*
A rise in the price of potatoes will lead to a rise in the demand for substitute goods. So the demand for pasta will increase, shown by a shift to the right in the demand curve for pasta from D_1 to D_2.

potatoes leads to a rise in the demand for pasta. This means that at any given price a greater quantity of pasta will be demanded. The new demand curve D_2 will therefore be to the right of the original demand curve.

Not all changes in prices will affect the demand for a particular good. A rise in the price of tennis balls is unlikely to have much impact on the demand for carrots for instance. Changes in the price of other goods as well may have either a positive or negative impact on demand for a good. A rise in the price of tennis rackets is likely to reduce the demand for tennis balls as some buyers decide that tennis is too expensive a sport. On the other hand, the demand for cinema places, alcoholic drink or whatever other form of entertainment consumers choose to buy instead of tennis equipment, will increase. The effect on the demand for one good of changes in price of other goods is considered in more detail in unit 7.

Question 3

Between 1973 and 1975, the US dollar price of crude oil quadrupled from approximately $3 to $12 a barrel provoking what came to be called 'the energy crisis'. Businesses and consumers expected oil prices to remain high after 1975. Explain, using demand diagrams, what effect you would expect this to have had on the demand in the UK for:
(a) oil tankers;
(b) coal;
(c) ice cream;
(d) gas-fired central heating systems;
(e) luxury cars with low-mileage petrol consumption;
(f) rail travel.

Other factors

There is a wide variety of other factors which affect the demand for a good apart from price, income and the prices of other goods. These include:

- changes in population - an increase in population is likely to increase demand for goods;
- changes in fashion - the demand for items such as wigs or flared trousers or black kitchen units changes as these items go in or out of fashion;
- changes in legislation - the demand for seat belts, anti-pollution equipment or places in old-people's homes has been affected in the past by changes in government legislation;
- advertising - a very powerful influence on consumer demand which seeks to influence consumer choice.

Question 4

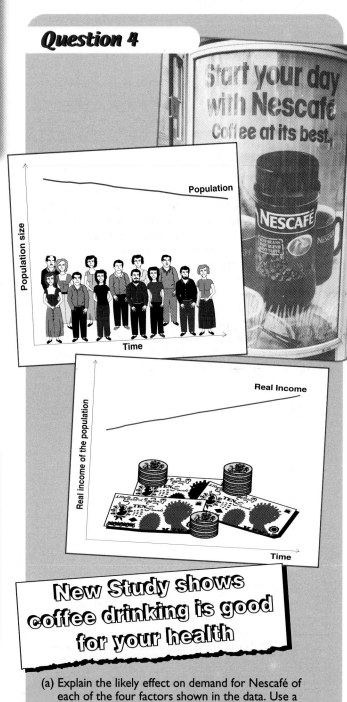

(a) Explain the likely effect on demand for Nescafé of each of the four factors shown in the data. Use a separate demand diagram for each factor to illustrate your answer.

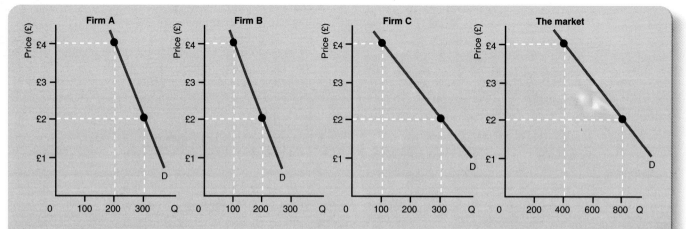

Figure 4.4 *Individual and market demand curves*
The market demand curve can be derived from the individual demand curves by adding up individual demand at each single price. In this example, for instance, the market demand at a price of £2 is calculated by adding the demand of firm A, B and C at this price.

A summary

It is possible to express demand in the form of a **functional** relationship. The quantity demanded of good N (Q_n) varies according to (i.e. is a function of) the price of good N (P_n), income (Y), the price of all other goods ($P_1,...P_{n-1}$) and all other factors (T). Mathematically, this is:

$$Q_n = f\,[P_n\,,\,Y,\,(P_1\,,...\,P_{n-1}),\,T]$$

At this stage, this mathematical form of expressing the determinants of demand is a convenient shorthand but little else. The major tools for dealing with demand at this level are either the written word or graphs. At a far more advanced level, the algebraic formula for demand is often the most powerful and useful tool in analysing demand.

Individual and market demand curves

So far, it has been assumed that demand refers to demand for a product in a whole market (i.e. MARKET DEMAND). However, it is possible to construct individual demand curves and derive market demand curves from them. An INDIVIDUAL DEMAND CURVE is the demand curve of an individual buyer. This could be a consumer, a firm or government.

The determinants of demand for an individual are no different from those of the market as a whole. When price rises, there is a fall in the quantity demanded of the product; when income rises, assuming that the product is a normal good, demand will increase, etc.

Question 5

$$Q = 20 - \tfrac{1}{2}\,P$$

where Q is the monthly quantity demanded of compact discs (CDs) in millions and P is their price.
(a) Draw the demand curve given by this equation between CD prices of £1 and £20.
(b) A new format results in a fall in demand of CDs of 5 million per month at any given price. (i) What is the new formula for quantity demanded of CDs?
(ii) Plot the new demand curve on your diagram.
(c) A rise in consumer incomes results in consumers being less price sensitive than before when buying CDs. As a result, instead of monthly demand falling by half a million when price is increased by £1, monthly demand now falls only by 400 000. Assume that the original equation for demand is as in (a). (i) What is the new formula for quantity demanded of CDs?
(ii) Plot the new demand curve on your diagram.

Question 6

Table 4.3

Price (£)	Quantity demanded of good X (000 units)		
	Firm A	Firm B	Firm C
100	500	250	750
200	400	230	700
300	300	210	650
400	200	190	600
500	100	170	550

There are only three buyers of good X, firms A, B and C.
(a) Draw the individual demand curves for each firm.
(b) Draw the market demand curve for good X.
(c) A fourth business, firm D, enters the market. It will buy 500 at any price between £100 and £500. Show the effect of this by drawing a new market demand curve for good X.
(d) Firm B goes out of business. Draw the new market demand curve with firms A, C and D buying in the market.

Figure 4.4 shows a situation where there are three and only three buyers in a market, firms A, B and C. At a price of £2, firm A will buy 300 units, firm B 200 units and firm C 300 units. So the total market demand at a price of £2 is 300 + 200 + 300 or 800 units. At a price of £4, total market demand will be 200 + 100 + 100 or 400 units. Similarly, all the other points on the market demand curve can be derived by summing the individual demand curves. This is known as **horizontal summing** because the figures on the horizontal axis of the individual demand curves are added up to put on the market demand curve. But the figures on the vertical axis of both individual and market demand curves remain the same.

Consumer surplus

The demand curve shows how much buyers would be prepared to pay for a given quantity of goods. In Figure 4.5, for instance, they would be prepared to pay 10p if they bought 1 million items. At 8p, they would buy 2 million items. As the price falls, so buyers want to buy more.

This can be put another way. The more buyers are offered, the less value they put on the last one bought. If there were only 1 million units on offer for sale in Figure 4.5, buyers would be prepared to pay 10p for each one. But if there are 3 million for sale, they will only pay 6p. The demand curve, therefore, shows the value to the buyer of each item bought. The first unit bought is worth almost 12p to a buyer. The one millionth unit is worth 10p. The four millionth unit would be worth 4p.

The difference between the value to buyers and what they actually pay is called CONSUMER SURPLUS. Assume in Figure 4.5 that the price paid is 6p. The buyers who would have paid 10p for the millionth unit have gained a consumer surplus of 4p (10p - 6p). Those who would have paid 8p for the 2 millionth unit would gain 2p. So the total consumer surplus at a price of 6p is the shaded triangular area in Figure 4.5.

Adam Smith, writing in the 18th century, was puzzled why consumers paid high prices for goods such as diamonds which were unnecessary to human existence, whilst the price of necessities such as water was very low. Figure 4.5 explains this **paradox of value**. If there are few goods available to buy, as with diamonds, then consumers are prepared to pay a high price for them. If goods are plentiful, then consumers are only prepared to pay a low price. This doesn't mean to say that they don't place a high

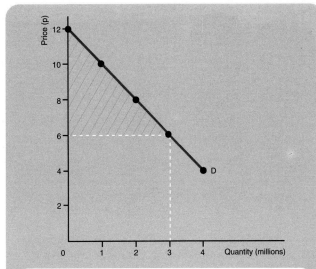

Figure 4.5 *Consumer surplus*
The demand curve shows the price that the buyer would be prepared to pay for each unit. Except on the last unit purchased, the price that the buyer is prepared to pay is above the market price that is paid. The difference between these two values is the consumer surplus. It is represented by the shaded area under the demand curve.

Question 7

Demand for a good is zero at £200. It then rises to 50 million units at £100 and 75 million at £50.
(a) Draw the demand curve for prices between 0 and £200.
(b) Shade the area of consumer surplus at a price of £60.
(c) Is consumer surplus larger or smaller at a price of £40 compared to £60? Explain your answer.

value on necessities when they are in short supply. In famine times, diamonds can be traded for small amounts of food. If diamonds were as common as water, buyers would not be prepared to pay much for the last diamond bought. Consumers enjoy large amounts of consumer surplus on water because the price is low and large amounts are bought. Far less consumer surplus is enjoyed by consumers on diamonds because far fewer diamonds are bought.

key terms

Consumer surplus - the difference between how much buyers are prepared to pay for a good and what they actually pay.
Demand curve - the line on a price-quantity diagram which shows the level of effective demand at any given price.
Demand or effective demand - the quantity purchased of a good at any given price, given that other determinants of demand remain

unchanged.
Individual demand curve - the demand curve for an individual consumer, firm or other economic unit.
Market demand curve - the sum of all individual demand curves.
Shift in the demand curve - a movement of the whole demand curve to the right or left of the original caused by a change in any variable affecting demand except price.

Applied economics

The demand for housing

Housing tenure

The housing market is not a single market because there are different forms of **tenure** in the market.

Owner-occupied housing Figure 4.6 shows that most homes today are owner-occupied. This means that they are owned by at least one of the people who live in the house.

Rented from local authorities The single largest group of landlords in the UK are local councils. In the 1980s and 1990s, their importance has declined as local authority housing has been sold off.

Rented from housing associations Housing associations are organisations set up to provide housing for rent. They have no shareholders and are not in business to make a profit. Their aim is to serve the needs of their customers. Much of their funding for building new houses comes from the government in the form of grants. Housing associations grew in importance in the 1980s and 1990s because the government increasingly channelled grants for house building in the rented sector away from local authorities and towards housing associations.

Rented from private landlords Private landlords are in business to make a profit from renting property. They might be companies with shareholders or they might be individuals. In the 1950s, 1960s and 1970s, the numbers of houses offered for rent from private landlords declined, mainly because government controls on rents made it more difficult to make a profit by renting out property. In the 1980s and 1990s, the government removed some of these controls. With higher rents, more private property has come onto the market.

The price of owner-occupied housing

Economic theory suggests that the higher the price, the less will be demanded of a good. In the owner-occupied market, rising house prices should lead to less demand and vice versa. However, Figures 4.7 and 4.8 show no evidence of this. In fact, rising house prices in the 1980s was associated with rising sales, whilst falling prices in the first half of the 1990s saw falling house sales.

One explanation is that the price of a house is arguably the wrong price to consider when looking at the demand for homes. Most houses are bought with a mortgage. This is a loan used to buy property. When potential buyers look at the price of the transaction, they tend to look at the value of the monthly repayments on the **mortgage** rather than the actual house price. In the short term, the value of monthly repayments is more influenced by interest rates than house prices. If interest rates rise, mortgage repayments rise and vice versa.

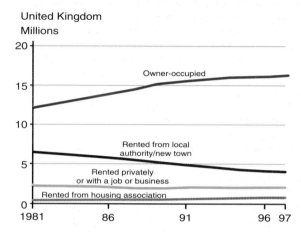

Figure 4.6 *Stock of dwellings by tenure*
Source: adapted from *Social Trends, Annual Abstract of Statistics*, Office for National Statistics.

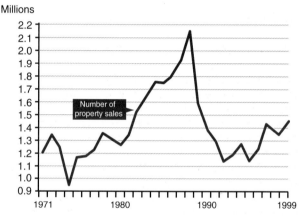

Figure 4.7 *Number of property sales: England and Wales (millions)*
Source: adapted from *Social Trends, Annual Abstract of Statistics*, Office for National Statistics.

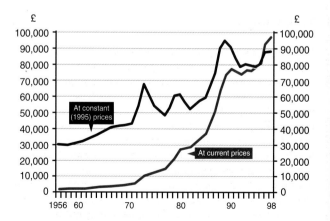

Figure 4.8 *Average UK house prices, £ at current and constant (1995) values*[1]
1. Average price of new dwellings with mortgages approved.
Source: adapted from *Economic Trends Annual Supplement*, Office for National Statistics.

Figure 4.9 shows changes in bank base rates, which are the most important influence on banks and building societies when they set their own mortgage rates. For instance, between 1985 and 1987, interest rates were falling, making repayments lower. This was associated with rising house purchases. Between 1988 and 1990, interest rates rose sharply and this led to the sharp fall in the number of houses being bought.

In the 1970s and 1980s, the government subsidised borrowing to buy a house through giving tax relief on the interest paid. This effectively reduced the monthly repayment cost of the mortgage. Starting in 1987, the value of mortgage tax relief was progressively reduced by the government and was finally abolished in 1999. This increased the cost of borrowing to buy a house and was one factor which dampened the demand for owner occupied housing in the 1990s.

Even so, not all houses are purchased using a mortgage. Higher priced houses in particular tend to be bought outright or with mortgages which only account for a fraction of the buying price. So other factors must also be important in determining the demand for owner-occupied housing.

Incomes

Real incomes (incomes after inflation has been taken into account) have been rising at an average of 2.5 per cent over the past 40 years in the UK. Figure 4.10 shows how the average real personal disposable income (income after income tax and National Insurance contributions have been deducted) of households has changed since 1971. Rising income has led to a rising demand for housing. When growth in income slowed or fell, as in the early 1980s and early 1990s, this was associated with slowdowns or falls in housing prices.

The increase in owner-occupation compared to renting is also probably due to rising income. Households in the UK prefer to own their own homes rather than renting them. Rising incomes makes home ownership more affordable to more people.

Population trends

Population trends have also been important in increasing the demand for housing. As Table 4.4 shows, the population of the UK is growing over time. However, the number of households is growing at a much faster rate. A household is defined as a group of people living together in a dwelling. Households have been getting smaller over time. More people are living longer and pensioners tend to live on their own. Divorce rates have increased whilst there are more one parent families than before. Fewer young people want to live at home with their parents once they have left school. So the number of dwellings needed to accommodate households has been rising and is predicted to carry on rising to 2050.

Other factors

Other factors may affect the demand for housing apart

from prices, income and population trends. One factor which influenced house buying in the 1970s and 1980s was speculation. Because house prices rose consistently during the 1950s and 1960s, many saw housing more as an investment rather than as a place to live. In the property booms of the early 1970s and late 1980s, higher house prices were encouraging people to buy houses in the hope that their value would go up even further. The 1990s saw far less speculative activity because house price increases remained relatively subdued.

The end of the housing boom in the late 1980s saw a reverse effect to this. Millions of households in the early

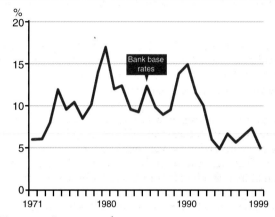

Figure 4.9 *Interest rates*[1]
1. Bank base rates, at 30 June of each year.
Source: adapted from *EconomicTrends Annual Supplement*, Office for National Statistics.

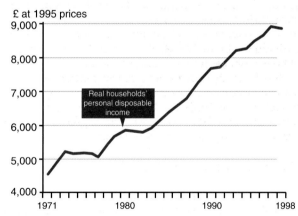

Figure 4.10 *Real households' disposable income at 1995 prices*
Source: adapted from *Economic Trends Annual Supplement*, Office for National Statistics.

Table 4.4 *Population and number of households: UK*

Millions

	Population	Number of households
1961	52.8	16.3
1971	55.9	18.6
1981	56.4	20.2
1991	57.8	22.4
1998	59.0	23.6

Source: adapted from *Social Trends*, Office for National Statistics.

1990s were caught in the negative equity trap. They bought houses at the top of the property boom in 1988 and 1989, borrowing almost all the money needed for the purchase. House prices fell in the early 1990s. This meant that many owed more money on their mortgage than their house was worth. Hence they had 'negative equity'. This discouraged people from buying houses because it was feared that house prices might fall even further, leading to equity losses. Moreover, due to very high interest rates and high unemployment, many fell behind with their mortgage payments and eventually saw their houses repossessed by their lenders. This experience discouraged households from overborrowing throughout the rest of the 1990s.

In the rented housing market, important legal changes led to changes in demand. In 1980, the government gave tenants of council houses the right to buy their homes at very low prices. Over the next two decades, more than one and half million council houses were sold to their tenants. So this legal change led to a rise in demand for owner occupied housing.

Another important legal change occurred in 1988. The government introduced a new type of tenancy called assured tenancy where rents were not regulated by the state and where landlords were able to repossess properties at the end of a period of time specified by the tenancy agreement. Existing laws dating from the 1960s had given tenants the right to ask council officials to fix a rent and effectively gave them the right to stay in the property for life. The result of the 1998 change was a rise in rents as landlords converted their tenancies wherever possible to the new assured tenancy agreements. This should have led to a fall in the quantity demanded for rented accommodation in the 1990s. However, two other factors more than outweighed this effect. First, some households decided to rent rather than buy because of the experience of negative equity. Second, more and better quality housing for rent came onto the market as a result of the 1988 changes. This again encouraged some households to rent rather than to buy.

The relative importance of different factors

In the long term, rising incomes and an increasing number of households are pushing up the demand for both owner-occupied and rented housing in the UK. In the short term, other factors have had a significant impact on the demand for housing, including property speculation, changes in the law, the ending of mortgage tax relief and changes in interest rates.

Millennium holidays

Millennium holiday prices are set to be slashed after a slump in demand for breaks over Christmas and the New Year. The UK's biggest holiday company, Thomson, yesterday admitted that demand had all but dried up. The company is already offering some half price deals and bigger discounts are likely. Only last week Airtours, the second largest player, said bookings for the Millennium period were lower than those for a normal winter. Some hotel groups are complaining that many consumers are failing to take advantage of one of the biggest excuses for a party in 1,000 years.

Excessive prices appear to have scared off would-be holiday makers. Brochure prices for a fortnight in the Mediterranean, for instance, were hiked to £600 per person - about £200 higher than in a normal year. However, both Airtours and Thomson said that long haul bookings to destinations such as Australia and the US had sold well, as have packages at the upper end of the price range.

A spokesman for Thomson said: 'We don't think people are frightened of flying over the Millennium - although our planes won't be in the air at midnight as we think passengers will want to be celebrating on the ground. There just seems to a general reluctance to travel. People have decided they want to stay at home with their families.'

Source: adapted from *The Guardian*, 26.11.1999.

1. Using a demand curve diagram, explain why Thomson cut its prices on Millennium holidays in November 1999.

2. Suggest other factors, apart from price, that were likely to have affected demand for Millennium holidays from Thomson.

3. Using a diagram, discuss the amount of consumer surplus a holiday maker is likely to have enjoyed if the holiday had been booked at full price in June 1999 or had been booked at half price in December 1999.

Summary

1. A rise in price leads to a rise in quantity supplied, shown by a movement along the supply curve.
2. A change in supply can be caused by factors such as a change in costs of production, technology and the price of other goods. This results in a shift in the supply curve.
3. The market supply curve in a perfectly competitive market is the sum of each firm's individual supply curves.

Supply

In any market there are buyers and sellers. Buyers **demand** goods whilst sellers **supply** goods. SUPPLY in economics is defined as the quantity of goods that sellers are prepared to sell at any given price over a period of time. For instance, in 1998 UK farmers sold 6.5 million tonnes of potatoes at an average price of £121 per tonne, so economists would say that the supply of wheat at £121 per tonne over the 12 month period was 6.5 million tonnes.

Supply and price

If the price of a good increases, how will producers react? Assuming that no other factors have changed, they are likely to expand production to take advantage of the higher prices and the higher profits that they can now make. In general, quantity supplied will rise if the price of the good also rises, all other things being equal.

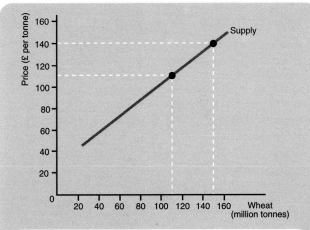

Figure 5.1 *The supply curve*
The supply curve is upward sloping, showing that firms increase production of a good as its price increases. This is because a higher price enables firms to make profit on the increased output whereas at the lower price they would have made a loss on it. Here, an increase in the price of wheat from £110 to £140 per tonne increases quantity supplied from 110 million tonnes to 150 million tonnes per year.

This can be shown on a diagram using a **supply curve**. A supply curve shows the quantity that will be supplied over a period of time at any given price. Consider Figure 5.1 which shows the supply curve for wheat. Wheat is priced at £110 per tonne. At this price only the most efficient farmers grow wheat. They supply 110 million tonnes per year. But if the price of wheat rose to £140 per tonne, farmers already growing wheat might increase their acreage of wheat, whilst other non-wheat growing farmers might start to grow wheat. Farmers would do this because at a price of £140 per tonne it is possible to make a profit on production even if costs are higher than at a production level of 110 million units.

A fall in price will lead to a **fall in quantity supplied**, shown by a **movement along** the supply curve. At a lower price, some firms will cut back on relatively unprofitable production whilst others will stop producing altogether. Some of the latter firms may even go bankrupt, unable to cover their costs of production from the price received.

An upward sloping supply curve assumes that:
● firms are motivated to produce by profit - so this model does not apply, for instance, to much of what is produced by government;
● the cost of producing a unit increases as output increases (a situation known as rising marginal cost) - this is not always true but it is likely that the prices of factors of production to the firm will increase as firms

Question 1

Table 5.1

Price (£)	Quantity supplied (million units per year)
5	5
10	8
15	11
20	14
25	17

(a) Draw a supply curve from the above data.
(b) Draw new supply curves assuming that quantity supplied at any given price:
(i) increased by 10 units; (ii) increased by 50 per cent; (iii) fell by 5 units; (iv) halved.

bid for more land, labour and capital to increase their output, thus pushing up costs.

Costs of production

The supply curve is drawn on the assumption that the general costs of production in the economy remain constant (part of the **ceteris paribus** condition). If other things change, then the supply curve will shift. If the costs of production increase at any given level of output, firms will attempt to pass on these increases in the form of higher prices. If they cannot charge higher prices then profits will fall and firms will produce less of the good or might even stop producing it altogether. A rise in the costs of production will therefore lead to a decrease in supply.

This can be seen in Figure 5.3. The original supply curve is S_1. A rise in the costs of production means that at any given level of output firms will charge higher prices. At an output level of OA, firms will increase their prices from OB to OC. This increase in prices will be true for all points on the supply curve. So the supply curve will **shift** upwards and to the left to S_2 in Figure 5.3. There will have been a **fall in supply**. (Note that a fall in **quantity supplied** refers to a change in quantity supplied due to a change in price and would be shown by a movement along the supply curve.) Conversely a fall in the costs of production will lead to an increase in supply of a good. This is shown by a shift to the right in the supply curve.

Technology

Another factor which affects supply of a particular good is

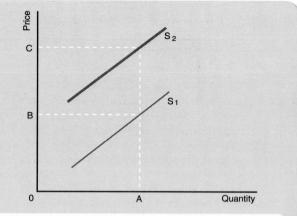

Figure 5.3 *A rise in the costs of production*
A rise in the costs of production for a firm will push its supply curve upwards and to the left, from S_1 to S_2. For any given quantity supplied, firms will now want a higher price to compensate them for the increase in their costs.

the state of technology. The supply curve is drawn on the assumption that the state of technology remains unchanged. If new technology is introduced to the production process it should lead to a fall in the costs of production. This greater **productive efficiency** will encourage firms to produce more at the same price or produce the same amount at a lower price or some combination of the two. The supply curve will shift downwards and to the right. It would be unusual for firms to replace more efficient technology with less efficient technology. However, this can occur at times of war or natural disasters. If new technical equipment is destroyed, firms may have to fall back on less efficient means of production, reducing supply at any given price, resulting in a shift in the supply curve to the left.

The prices of other goods

Changes in the prices of some goods can affect the supply of a particular good. For instance, if the price of beef increases substantially there will be an increase in the quantity of beef supplied. More cows will be reared and slaughtered. As a result there will be an increase in the supply of hides for leather. At the same price, the quantity of leather supplied to

Question 2

%
25

20

15

Change in average earnings

10

5

0
1977   80   85   90   95   98

Source: adapted from *Economic Trends Annual Supplement*.
Figure 5.2 *Annual average percentage change in earnings*

(a) Explain how a change in earnings can shift the supply curve of a product to the left.
(b) Discuss in which years the supply curves for goods made in the UK are likely to have shifted (i) furthest and (ii) least far to the left according to the data.

Question 3

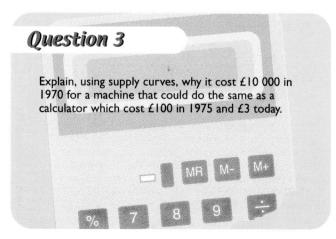

Explain, using supply curves, why it cost £10 000 in 1970 for a machine that could do the same as a calculator which cost £100 in 1975 and £3 today.

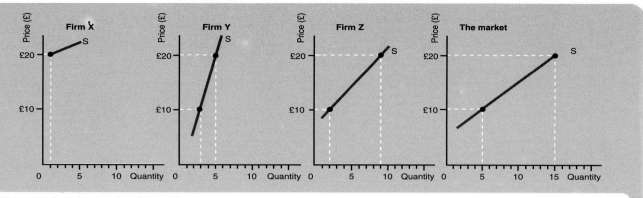

Figure 5.4 *Individual and market supply curves*
The market supply curve is calculated by summing the individual supply curves of producers in the market. Here the market supply at £20, for instance, is calculated by adding the supply of each individual firm at a price of £20.

the market will increase. An increase in the price of beef therefore leads to an increase in the supply of leather. On the other hand, an increase in cattle rearing is likely to be at the expense of production of wheat or sheep farming. So an increase in beef production is likely to lead to a fall in the supply of other agricultural products as farmers switch production to take advantage of higher profits in beef.

Other factors

A number of other factors affect supply. These include:
- the goals of sellers - if for some reason there is a change in the profit levels which a seller expects to receive as a reward for production, then there will be a change in supply; for instance, if an industry such as the book retailing industry went from one made up of many small sellers more interested in selling books than making a profit to one where the industry was dominated by a few large profit-seeking companies, then supply would fall;
- government legislation - anti-pollution controls which raise the costs of production, the abolition of legal barriers to setting up business in an industry, or tax changes, are some examples of how government can change the level of supply in an industry;
- expectations of future events - if firms expect future

prices to be much higher, they may restrict supplies and stockpile goods; if they expect disruptions to their future production because of a strike they may stockpile raw materials, paying for them with borrowed money, thus increasing their costs and reducing supply;
- the weather - in agricultural markets, the weather plays a crucial role in determining supply, bad weather reducing supply, good weather producing bumper yields.

Individual and market supply curves

The MARKET SUPPLY CURVE can be derived from the INDIVIDUAL SUPPLY CURVES of sellers in the market (this assumes that supply is not affected by changes in the demand curve as would happen under monopoly or oligopoly. Consider Figure 5.4. For the sake of simplicity we will assume that there are only three sellers in the market. At a price of £10 per unit, Firm X is unwilling to supply any goods. Firm Y supplies 3 units whilst Firm Z supplies 2 units. So the market supply at a price of £10 is 5 units. At a price of £20, Firm X will supply 1 unit, Firm Y 5 units and Firm Z 9 units. So the market supply at a price of £20 is 15 units. The rest of the market supply curve can be derived by **horizontally summing** the level of output at all other price levels.

Producer surplus

The supply curve shows how much will be supplied at any given price. In Figure 5.5, firms will supply 10 million units at 10p whereas they will supply 25 million units at 20p. Assume that the price that firms receive is actually 20p. Some firms will then receive more than the lowest price at which they are prepared to supply. For instance, one firm was prepared to supply the 10 millionth unit at 10p. The firm receives 20p, which is 10p more. This 10p is PRODUCER SURPLUS. It is the difference between the market price which the firm receives and the price at which it is prepared to supply. The total amount of producer surplus earned by firms is shown by the area between the supply curve and horizontal line at the market price. It is the sum of the producer surplus earned at each level of output.

Question 4

Explain, using diagrams, how you would expect supply of the following goods to be affected by the events stated, all other things being equal.
(a) Petrol, 1998. In 1998, the price of crude oil fell from $15 a barrel to $8 a barrel.
(b) Computers, 2000. In 2000, new generations of more powerful microchips reached the stage of mass production.
(c) Cardamom, 1998. Poor weather conditions in Guatemala, the source of 90 per cent of exports of the spice, meant that the total Guatemalan crop fell from 18 000 tonnes in 1997-98 to 8 000 tonnes in 1998-1999.

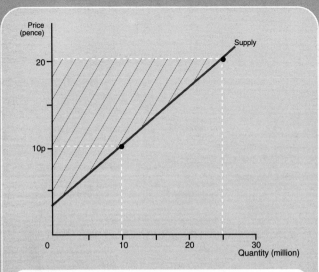

Figure 5.5. *Producer surplus*
The supply curve shows how much will be supplied at any given price. Except on the last unit supplied, the supplier receives more for the good than the lowest price at which it is prepared to supply. This difference between the market price and lowest price at which a firm is prepared to supply is producer surplus. Total producer surplus is shown by the shaded area above the supply curve.

Question 5

Table 5.2

Quantity supplied (million units)			Price (£)
Firms in area A	Firms in area B	Firms in area C	
10	2	0	1
12	5	3	2
14	8	6	3
16	11	9	4
18	14	12	5

Firms in areas A, B and C are the sole suppliers in the market and the market is perfectly competitive.

(a) Draw the market supply curve.
(b) What is supply at a price of (i) £1 and (ii) £3.50?
(c) One firm in area A decides to increase production by 5 million units at every given price. Draw the new market supply curve on your diagram.
(d) Explain what would happen to the market supply curve if new technology in the industry led to greater productive efficiency amongst individual firms.

terms

Individual supply curve - the supply curve of an individual producer.
Market supply curve - the supply curve of all producers within the market. In a perfectly competitive market it can be calculated by summing the supply curves of individual producers.

Producer surplus - the difference between the market price which firms receive and the price at which they are prepared to supply.
Supply - the quantity of goods that suppliers are willing to sell at any given price over a period of time.

Applied economics

The supply of housing

There is a number of different markets within the housing market, each of which has its own supply. Within the **owner occupied** market, there is a market for buying and selling second hand dwellings. There is also a market for new housing. Within the rented sector, local authorities, housing associations and the private sector supply housing to the market. Supply has changed in different ways in these different markets in the UK, as can be seen from Figure 5.6. The broad trend has been for owner occupation to increase whilst renting has declined.

The owner occupied market

Figures 5.7 and 5.8 give two different measures of

supply to the housing market. The first includes the total number of new houses built for sale to the private sector. The second shows the total number of property transactions per year. This includes both sale of the new houses and of existing houses which are sold second hand. Economic theory would suggest that the higher the price, the higher the quantity supplied. The experience of the past 30 years would tend to support this relationship in the housing market. Figure 5.9 shows that periods of high increases in house prices, as in 1972-73 and 1986-89, coincided with both high levels of new house completions and total number of property transactions. Slumps in property prices, as in 1990-93, occurred at the same time as falls in the number of sales of both new and existing houses.

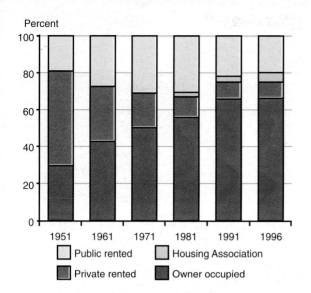

Figure 5.6 *Housing stock by tenure: 1951-1996*
Source: adapted from Department of the Environment, *Transport and the Regions*, *Housing and Construction Statistics*.

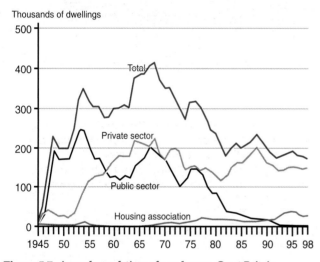

Figure 5.7 *Annual completions of new houses, Great Britain*
Source: adapted from Department of the Environment, *Transport and the Regions*, *Housing and Construction Statistics*.

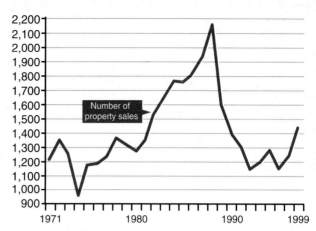

Figure 5.8 *Number of property sales: England and Wales (millions)*
Source: adapted from *Economic Trends Annual Supplement*, Office for National Statistics.

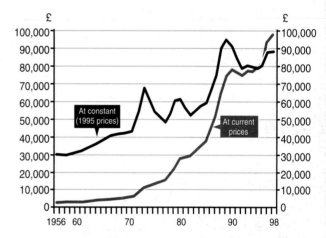

Figure 5.9 *Average UK house prices, £ at current and constant (1995) values[1]*
1. Average price of new dwellings with mortgages approved.
Source: adapted from *Economic Trends Annual Supplement*, Office for National Statistics.

Supply can also be influenced by other factors. One is cost. Increases in costs will push the supply curve upwards. The main cost in house building today in most areas of the UK is the cost of land. Typically, half the cost of a property represents the cost of the land on which it is built. The rest is made up of labour costs and materials. Figure 5.10, over the page, shows how the price of land and the average hourly earnings of male manual workers in the construction industry increased between 1986 and 1996 and how they correlate with increases in prices of new housing during the same period.

Another factor which has been very important in influencing the supply of housing is government regulation. The government and local authorities have restricted the supply of new housing, particularly through green belt regulations. In order to build new houses, construction firms have to obtain planning permission from the local authority. When the housing market has been buoyant, as in the late 1990s, construction firms have wanted to build more new houses than local authorities have permitted. This has driven up the cost of building land as construction companies have competed to buy scarce sites. The higher cost of building land has then reduced the supply of new housing. This has been particularly true in areas like the South East of England where the population has been growing relatively fast.

There has also been a significant flow of houses into the owner-occupied sector from sales of council houses.

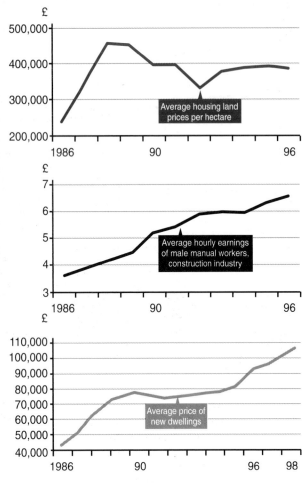

Figure 5.10 *Housing land prices, average earnings in the construction industry and price of new houses*
Source: adapted from Department of the Environment, Transport and the Regions, *Housing and Construction Statistics.*

In 1980, the government gave council house tenants the right to buy their homes at extremely advantageous prices. Figure 5.11 shows that over one and a half million homes have become owner occupied since then as a result.

Other factors have arguably not been significant in influencing the supply of houses in the UK. For instance, there have been no significant technological changes in building and the goals of building firms have not changed.

Renting from local authorities

The supply of local authority housing for rent is not determined by market forces but by political factors. In the 1950s, 1960s and 1970s, the government gave substantial grants to local authorities to build council houses. Each year, as Figure 5.7 shows, between 100 000 and 250 000 houses were completed. However, the government of Margaret Thatcher, which came into power in 1979, was ideologically opposed to council housing. It wanted to create a 'nation of homeowners'

and believed that local authorities were poor managers of their housing stocks. The government achieved its aims partly by introducing its right to buy legislation in 1980 which led to the sale of council houses to tenants shown in Figure 5.11. The stock of council housing was further reduced by sales of complete estates to housing associations by some councils. The other part of government policy was to cut off funding for new council house building. As Figure 5.7 shows, in 1978, 108 000 new council houses were built. In 1980, this had fallen to 86 000. By 1990, only 16 600 new council houses were built and in 1997 this was a mere 300.

With continued sales to tenants and insignificant new house building, the supply of council houses declined in the 1980s and 1990s as Figure 5.7 shows and likely to continue to decline in the future.

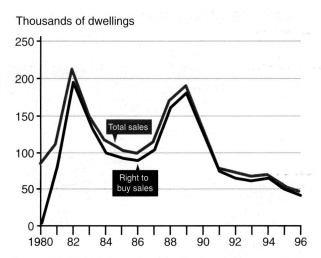

Figure 5.11 *Right-to-buy sales of dwellings owned by council sector*
Source: adapted from Department of the Environment, *Transport and the Regions, Housing and Construction Statistics.*

Table 5.3 *Number of privately rented houses and average rents, England*

	Number of private rented properties, millions	Average rent, £ per week	
		Shorthold assured tenancy	Regulated with registered rent
1988	1.81	-	18
1990	1.79	63	24
1994/95	2.19	83	36
1996/97	2.28	94	42

Source: adapted from Department of the Environment, Transport and the Regions, *Housing and Construction Statistics.*

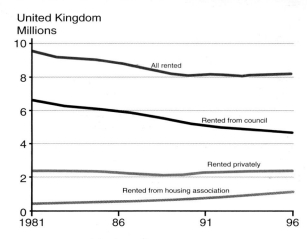

Figure 5.12 *Rented dwellings: by type*
Source: adapted from *Social Trends*, Office for National Statistics.

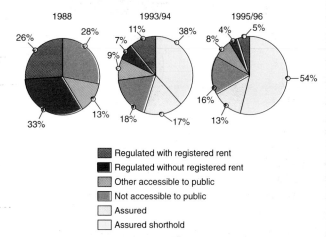

Regulated with registered rent
Regulated without registered rent
Other accessible to public
Not accessible to public
Assured
Assured shorthold

Figure 5.13 *Private tenancy by tenancy type, England*
Source: adapted from Department of the Environment, *Transport and the Regions, Housing and Construction Statistics.*

Housing associations

Housing associations are organisations which exist to provide housing at affordable rents. Throughout the 1950s, 1960s and 1970s, with the help of government grants, they built between 1 000 and 15 000 houses a year, a relatively small addition to the total supply of housing in the UK. However, in the 1980s and 1990s, the government increasingly channelled grants away from local authorities and to housing associations for social housing. By the mid-1990s, housing associations were building nearly 40 000 houses a year.

Like council housing, the supply of homes from housing associations is determined mainly not by markets but by political decisions about where grants for house building should be given.

The private rented market

The supply of private rented accommodation fell in the 1950s, 1960s and 1970s. This was mainly because the rent or price that landlords received was too low and

hence there was a movement down the supply curve. Increasing numbers either buying their own home or renting from a local authority put downward pressure on private rents. More important, though, from the mid 1960s there was legislation which gave tenants considerable rights including the right to a 'fair' or regulated rent. The legislation also made it very difficult for a landlord to evict a tenant if they wanted to stop renting the property. As a consequence, landlords withdrew from the housing market and the supply of private rented accommodation fell.

Since 1988, however, the private rented sector has begun to expand again as Figure 5.12 and Table 5.3 shows. This was because legislation passed in that year gave landlords the freedom to set their own rents and made it much simpler to evict tenants. These new 'assured' tenancy contracts quickly came to dominate the private rented market, as can be seen in Figure 5.13. Becoming a private landlord is now more profitable with higher rents as Table 5.3 shows.

Coffee

Colombian earthquake pushes up coffee prices

Last Monday's earthquake shook the heart of the coffee producing region of Colombia. Fears that there would be substantial damage to this year's crop sent coffee prices rising on London International Financial Futures and Options Exchange. Colombia is the world's largest coffee producer after Brazil. Half of Colombia's production comes from the area affected by the earthquake.

Source: adapted from the *Financial Times*, 27.1.1999.

Coffee prices plummet as rain hits Brazil

Coffee prices plunged yesterday amid signs that Brazil's weather pattern had returned to the seasonal normal. Widespread rainfall this week appears to have ended the dry spell that has damaged Brazil's coffee crop this year. Brazil is the world's largest producer of coffee.

Source: adapted from the *Financial Times*, 10.12.1999.

Venezuelan coffee industry perks up

Price liberalisation finally seems to be paying off as the Venezuelan coffee industry achieved record production this year. In 1992, Foncafe, the state coffee fund, relinquished its monopoly on distributing coffee and fixing prices. The result was that coffee growers could now get a higher price by selling their coffee into the market by themselves. Coffee growers who aimed at the export market were able to secure particularly large increases in price. However, coffee for export has to be of higher quality than much of that produced for the domestic market.

Source: adapted from the *Financial Times*, 10.3.1999.

Venezuelan coffee producers to receive further help

The record harvest of coffee in 1999 is set to be boosted by further help from the government. It is proposing to boost the agricultural sector of the economy through a series of measures. These include infrastructure projects which should lower the cost of production and of getting agricultural goods to market. The government is also proposing to offer cheap loans to farmers to invest. This will cut the cost of borrowing.

Source: adapted from the *Financial Times*, 10.3.1999.

1. **Explain, using a diagram, how a change in the price of coffee affects its supply. Illustrate your answer with an example from the data.**

2. **What other factors might affect the supply of coffee according to the data? Illustrate how these factors shift the supply curve for coffee.**

Summary

1. The equilibrium or market clearing price is set where demand equals supply.
2. Changes in demand and supply will lead to new equilibrium prices being set.
3. A change in demand will lead to a shift in the demand curve, a movement along the supply curve and a new equilibrium price.
4. A change in supply will lead to a shift in the supply curve, a movement along the demand curve and a new equilibrium price.
5. Markets do not necessarily tend towards the equilibrium price.
6. The equilibrium price is not necessarily the price which will lead to the greatest economic efficiency or the greatest equity.

Equilibrium price

Buyers and sellers come together in a market. A price (sometimes called the **market price**) is struck and goods or services are exchanged. Consider Table 6.1. It shows the demand and supply schedule for a good at prices between £2 and £10.

Table 6.1

Price (£)	Quantity demanded (million units per month)	Quantity supplied (million units per month)
2	12	2
4	9	4
6	6	6
8	3	8
10	0	10

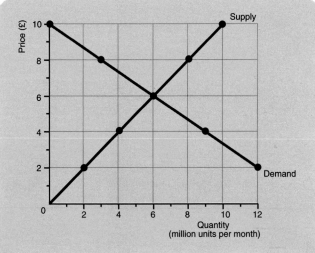

Figure 6.1 *Equilibrium*
At £6, the quantity demanded is equal to the quantity supplied. The market is said to be in equilibrium at this price.

- If the price is £2, demand will be 12 million units but only 2 million units will be supplied. Demand is greater than supply and there is therefore EXCESS DEMAND (i.e. too much demand in relation to supply) in the market. There will be a **shortage** of products on the market. Some buyers will be lucky and they will snap up the 2 million units being sold. But there will be a 10 million unit shortfall in supply for the rest of the unlucky buyers in the market. For instance, it is not possible to buy some luxury cars without being on a waiting list for several years because current demand is too great.
- If the price is £10, buyers will not buy any goods. Sellers on the other hand will wish to supply 10 million units. Supply is greater than demand and therefore there will be EXCESS SUPPLY. There will be a **glut** or surplus of products on the market. 10 million units will remain unsold. A sale in a shop is often evidence of excess supply in the past. Firms tried to sell the goods at a higher price and failed.
- There is only one price where demand equals supply. This is at a price of £6 where demand and supply are both 6 million units. This price is known as the EQUILIBRIUM PRICE. This is the only price where the planned demand of buyers equals the planned supply of sellers in the market. It is also known as the MARKET-CLEARING price because all the products supplied to the market are bought or cleared from the market, but no buyer is left frustrated in his or her wishes to buy goods.

An alternative way of expressing the data in Table 6.1 is shown in Figure 6.1. The equilibrium price is where demand equals supply. This happens where the two curves cross, at a price of £6 and a quantity of 6 million units. If the price is above £6, supply will be greater than demand and therefore excess supply will exist. If the price is below £6, demand is greater than supply and therefore there will be excess demand.

Question 1

Table 6.2

Price (£)	Quantity demanded (million units)	Quantity supplied (million units)
30	20	70
20	50	50
10	80	30

(a) Plot the demand and supply curves shown in Table 6.2 on a diagram.
(b) What is the equilibrium price?
(c) In what price range is there (i) excess demand and (ii) excess supply?
(d) Will there be a glut or a shortage in the market if the price is: (i) £10; (ii) £40; (iii) £22; (iv) £18; (v) £20?

Changes in demand and supply

It was explained in units 4 and 5 that a change in price would lead to a change in quantity demanded or supplied, shown by a movement along the demand or supply curve. A change in any other variable, such as income or the costs of production, would lead to:

• an **increase** or **decrease** in demand or supply and therefore
• a **shift** in the demand or supply curve.

Demand and supply diagrams provide a powerful and simple tool for analysing the effects of changes in demand and supply on equilibrium price and quantity.

Consider the effect of a rise in consumer incomes. This will lead to an increase in the demand for a normal good. In Figure 6.2 (a) this will push the demand curve from D_1 to D_2. As can be seen from the diagram, the equilibrium price rises from P_1 to P_2. The quantity bought and sold in equilibrium rises from Q_1 to Q_2. The model of demand and supply predicts that an increase in incomes, all other things being equal (the **ceteris paribus** condition) will lead to an increase both in the price of the product and in the quantity sold. Note that the increase in income **shifts** the

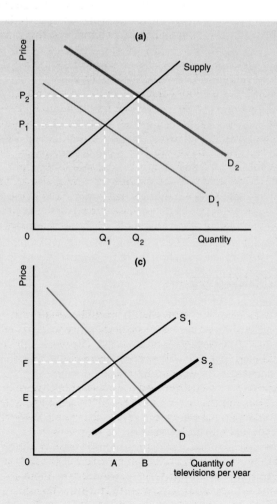

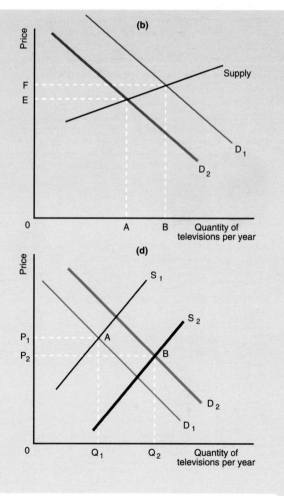

Figure 6.2 *Shifts in demand and supply curves*
Shifts in the demand or supply curves for a product will change the equilibrium price and the equilibrium quantity bought and sold.

demand curve and this then leads to a **movement along** the supply curve.

Figure 6.2 (b) shows the market for black and white televisions. In the early 1970s, both the BBC and Independent Television started to broadcast programmes in colour for the first time. Not surprisingly there was a boom in sales of colour television sets and a slump in sales of black and white ones. In economic terms the demand for black and white sets fell. This is shown by a shift to the left in the demand curve. The equilibrium level of sales in Figure 6.2 (b) falls from OB to OA whilst equilibrium price falls from OF to OE. Note again that a shift in the demand curve leads to a movement along the supply curve.

Prices of both black and white and colour television sets tended to fall in the 1970s and 1980s. The main reason for this was an increase in productive efficiency (☞ unit 16) due to the introduction of new technology, enabling costs of production to fall. A fall in costs of production is shown by the shift to the right in the supply curve in Figure 6.2 (c). At any given quantity of output, firms will be prepared to supply more television sets to the market. The result is an increase in quantity bought and sold from OA to OB and a fall in price from OF to OE. Note that there is a shift in the supply curve which leads to a movement along the demand curve.

So far we have assumed that only one variable changes and that all other variables remain constant. But in the real world, it is likely that several factors affecting demand and supply will change at the same time. Demand and supply diagrams can be used to some extent to analyse several changes. For instance, in the 1970s and 1980s the demand for colour television sets increased due to rising real incomes (☞ unit 3 for a definition of 'real' values). At the same time, supply increased too because of an increase in productive efficiency. Overall, the price of television sets fell slightly. This is shown in Figure 6.2 (d). Both the demand and supply curves shift to the right. This will lead to an increase in quantity bought and sold. In theory, depending upon the extent of the shifts in the two curves, there could be an increase in price, a fall in price or no change in the price. Figure 6.2 (d) shows the middle of these three possibilities.

Do markets clear?

It is very easy to assume that the equilibrium price is either the current market price or the price towards which the market moves. Neither is correct. The market price could be at any level. There could be excess demand or excess supply at any point in time.

Nor will market prices necessarily tend to change to equilibrium prices over time. One of the most important controversies in economics today is the extent to which markets tend towards market-clearing prices.

The argument put forward by neo-classical free market economists is that markets do tend to clear. Let us take the example of the coffee market. In this market, there are many producers (farmers, manufacturers, wholesalers and retailers) that are motivated by the desire to make as large a profit as possible. When there is excess demand for coffee (demand is greater than supply), coffee producers will be able to increase their prices and therefore their profits and still sell all they produce. If there is excess

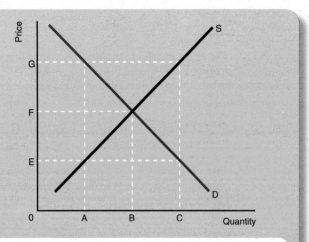

Figure 6.3 *The operation of market forces in the coffee market Market pressure will tend to force down coffee prices when there is excess supply, such as at price OG, but force up coffee prices when there is excess demand such as at price OE.*

supply (supply is greater than demand), some coffee will remain unsold. Producers then have a choice. Either they can offer coffee for sale at the existing price and risk not selling it or they can lower their price to the level where they will sell everything offered. If all producers choose not to lower their prices, there is likely to be even greater

pressure to reduce prices in the future because there will be unsold stocks of coffee overhanging the market. Therefore when there is excess demand, prices will be driven upwards whilst prices will fall if there is excess supply.

This can be shown diagrammatically. In Figure 6.3, there is excess demand at a price of OE. Buyers want to purchase AC more of coffee than is being supplied. Shops, manufacturers and coffee growers will be able to increase their prices and their production and still sell everything they produce. If they wish to sell all their output, they can increase their prices to a maximum of OF and their output to a maximum OB, the market-clearing prices and production levels. This they will do because at higher prices and production levels they will be able to make more profit. If there is excess supply, coffee producers will be left with unsold stocks. At a price of OG, output left unsold will be AC. Producers in a free market cannot afford to build up stocks forever. Some producers will lower prices and the rest will be forced to follow. Production and prices will go on falling until equilibrium output and price is reached. This is usually referred to as a **stable equilibrium** position.

These pressures which force the market towards an equilibrium point are often called FREE MARKET FORCES. But critics of the market mechanism argue that free market forces can lead away from the equilibrium point in many cases. One example of **unstable equilibrium**, the Cobweb theory, is explained in unit 12. In other markets, it is argued that market forces are too weak to restore equilibrium. Many Keynesian economists cite the labour market as an example of this. In other markets, there are many forces such as government legislation, trade unions and multi-national monopolies which more than negate the power of the market.

Points to note

Equilibrium is a very powerful concept in economics but it is essential to remember that the equilibrium price is unlikely to be the most desirable price or 'right' price in the market. The most desirable price in the market will depend upon how one defines 'desirable'. It may be, for instance, the one which leads to the greatest economic efficiency, or it may be the one which leads to greatest equity. Alternatively it may be the one which best supports the defence of the country.

Demand can also equal supply without there being equilibrium. At any point in time, what is actually bought must equal what is actually sold. There can be no sellers without buyers. So actual demand (more often referred to as **realised** or **ex post** demand in economics) must always equal actual (or realised or ex post) supply. Equilibrium occurs at a price where there is no tendency to change. Price will not change if, at the current price, the quantity that consumers wish to buy (called **planned** or **desired** or **ex ante** demand) is equal to the quantity that suppliers wish to sell (called planned or desired or ex ante supply).

Therefore only in equilibrium will planned demand equal planned supply.

Question 3

The 1990s were a terrible time for the Australian wool industry. The problems started with the collapse of the Soviet Union. At the end of the 1980s, the Soviet Union bought about 19 per cent of Australian wool exports. By 2000, it bought nothing, unable to afford the product. Sales to the rest of the world stagnated in the 1990s, not helped by competition from synthetic fibres, and were badly affected by the Asian crisis of 1997-99. Asian countries such as Thailand, South Korea and Indonesia were rocked by a financial crisis which resulted in sharp falls in their purchasing power in world markets. Exports to these countries slumped, including wool. With stockpiles of wool hanging over the market throughout the decade, prices fell. For instance, as a result of the Asian crisis, prices fell from A$6 to A$3 between June 1997 and October 1998. Not surprisingly, there has been a sharp fall in production over the decade. Greasy wool production fell by nearly half in the 1990s and sheep numbers at about 120 million were back to their 1950s levels. The numbers of specialist wool producers fell by half.

Source: adapted from the *Financial Times*, 4.3.1999.

(a) Prices for Australian wool fell during the 1990s. Explain, using a diagram, whether this was associated with excess demand or excess supply for wool.
(b) Many Australian wool producers went bankrupt during the decade. Explain: (i) why this happened; and (ii) what was its impact on the supply of Australian wool.

key terms

Equilibrium price - the price at which there is no tendency to change because planned (or desired or ex ante) purchases (i.e. demand) are equal to planned sales (i.e. supply).
Excess demand - where demand is greater than supply.
Excess supply - where supply is greater than demand.
Free market forces - forces in free markets which act to reduce prices when there is excess supply and raise prices when there is excess demand.
Market clearing price - the price at which there is neither excess demand nor excess supply but where everything offered for sale is purchased.

Applied economics

Demand and supply in the passenger transport market

The quantity demanded and supplied of passenger transport in the UK over the past 30 years has more than trebled, as Figure 6.4 shows. Almost all of this growth is accounted for by a rise in demand for car travel. Rail travel has remained broadly constant, whilst bus and coach travel has declined. Air travel has grown significantly, from 1 billion passenger kilometres in 1961 to 7 billion in 1998, but today only accounts for approximately 1 per cent of the total passenger miles travelled in the UK.

Demand and income

The main reason for the growth in demand for passenger transport has been rising incomes. As Table 6.3 shows, real personal households' disposable income (the average income per household after income tax and inflation has been accounted for) more than doubled between 1965 and 1998. Consumers have tended to spend a relatively high proportion of increases in income on transport. As a result, spending on transport as a proportion of household expenditure has risen from 9.7 per cent in 1965 to 16.7 per cent in 1998. Spending on car transport has risen faster than spending on other types of passenger transport. In 1965, there were 6.2 million cars and light vans on the road as Table 6.4 shows. 41 per cent of households had the use of at least one car whilst spending on cars and their running costs accounted for three quarters of total household spending on transport. By 1998, there were 24.5 million cars and light vans on the roads. 72.0 per cent of households had use of at least one car and spending on motor transport accounted for 85.0 per cent of total transport spending.

Rising income seems to have had little effect on overall rail travel. Between 1945 and 1985, the number of passenger journeys fell as shown in Table 6.5. Since then, there has been a modest rise in the number of journeys and distances travelled. The decision to travel by train seems to be dependent on other factors than income.

As for bus and coach travel, Table 6.6 shows that the number of passenger kilometres travelled has fallen in recent years. This is part of a longer term trend. In 1952, 92 billion passenger kilometres were travelled. By 1997, this had fallen more than 50 per cent. With rising incomes over the period, it could be argued that passengers have

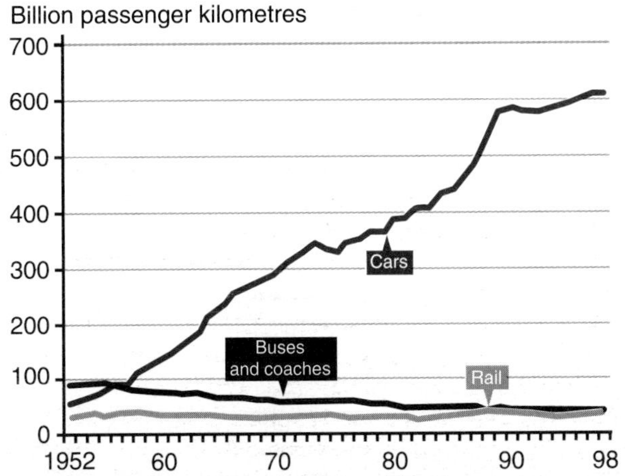

Figure 6.4 *Passenger transport use*
Source: adapted from *Transport Statistics*.

Table 6.3 *Disposable income and household expenditure on passenger transport*

	Personal households' disposable income per head, £, at 1995 prices	Household expenditure on transport, £, average per week at 1995 prices	Household expenditure on transport as a percentage of total household expenditure %	Motoring expenditure as a percentage of all household expenditure on transport %
1965	4 161	26.58	9.7	74.5
1970	4 494	31.22	10.2	77.2
1975	5 180	32.51	13.8	80.2
1980	5 818	34.88	14.6	81.2
1985	6 298	38.07	15.2	84.4
1990	7 626	47.31	16.2	84.5
1995	8 439	43.16	15.1	85.7
1998	8 867	50.15	16.7	85.0

1. Figures for expenditure for 1995 are 1995/6 and for 1998 are 1997/8.
Source: adapted from *Economic Trends Annual Supplement*, Office for National Statistics; Department for the Environment, Transport and the Regions, *Transport Statistics*.

Table 6.4 *Car ownership*

Year	Number of private cars licensed, millions	Households with regular use of car(s) %			
		no car	1 car	2 cars	3 or more
1965	7.7	59	36	5	-
1970	9.8	48	45	6	1
1975	12.5	44	45	10	1
1980	14.7	41	44	13	2
1985	16.5	38	45	15	3
1990	19.7	33	44	19	4
1995	20.5	30	45	21	4
1998	22.1	28	44	23	5

Source: Department for the Environment, Transport and the Regions, *Transport Statistics.*

Table 6.5 *Rail statistics*

Year	National rail, passenger journeys (million)	Passenger kilometres (billion)
1946	1 266	47.0
1960	1 037	34.7
1985/86	686	30.4
1990/91	809	33.2
1995/6	761	30.0
1998/9	892	35.1

Source: Department for the Environment, Transport and the Regions, *Transport Statistics.*

Table 6.6 *Bus and coach travel*

Year	Number of kilometres travelled by passengers on buses and coaches (bn)	Number of buses and coaches on UK roads (000)	Number of kilometres travelled by buses and coaches (bn)	Index of prices (1995=100) bus and coach fares	All consumer expenditure (RPI) 1995=100
1965	67	-	3.9	5.7	10.0
1970	60	-	3.6	8.0	12.4
1975	60	76.9	3.2	15.3	22.9
1980	52	69.9	3.5	36.5	44.9
1985	49	67.9	3.7	52.8	63.5
1990	46	71.9	4.6	73.8	84.6
1995	44	75.7	4.7	100.0	100.0
1997	43	76.2	5.0	110.0	109.3

Source: adapted from Department for the Environment, *Transport and the Regions*, *Transport Statistics.*

Table 6.7 *Passenger transport: consumer price indices (1995=100)*

Year	Motor vehicles Total	of which net purchase	Rail	Bus and coach	All transport	All consumer expenditure (RPI)
1965	9.4	11.6	6.7	5.7	9.1	10.0
1970	12.0	13.6	8.5	8.0	11.7	12.4
1975	22.6	23.8	17.4	15.3	22.0	22.9
1980	47.1	55.4	39.6	36.5	45.8	44.9
1985	65.1	70.8	50.7	52.8	62.7	63.5
1990	79.4	87.8	72.3	73.8	84.6	84.6
1995	100.0	100.0	100.0	100.0	100.0	100.0
1998	119.9	104.7	110.6	110.0	108.7	109.3

Source: adapted from *Economic Trends Annual Supplement*, Office for National Statistics; Department for the Environment, Transport and the Regions, *Transport Statistics.*

deserted buses and coaches for cars. Bus and coach travel would then be an inferior good.

Demand and prices

The average price of transport has risen broadly in line with the average increase in all prices in the economy, as can be seen from Table 6.7. However, Table 6.7 shows that the price of travelling by rail, bus and coach rose substantially faster than that of travelling by car in the 1980s and early 1990s. This was because the Conservative government of the time reduced subsidies for public transport and also privatised the bus industry. The fall in the price of motoring relative to bus and train travel was one factor accounting for the relative decline in demand for bus and train services during the period.

Since 1993, the government has sharply increased taxes on petrol each year in its Budget. This is reflected in the sharp rise in the cost of motoring compared to the average increase in prices for the whole economy. Government policy is driven by two objectives. First, it wishes to reduce traffic congestion by restricting the growth of motor transport. Second, it wants to reduce the pollution and damage to the environment that the motor car causes. The problem with the policy is that the demand for motor transport is fairly unresponsive

to increases in the price of petrol (i.e. demand is fairly **inelastic** ☞ unit 8). Petrol is only one cost in motor transport and once a car has been purchased, insured and taxed, petrol costs are usually less than the cost of any similar journey under public transport. What's more, most journeys could not be made with any convenience using public transport. For many motorists, there is no alternative to using the car.

Other factors affecting the demand for transport

Demand for transport has grown for a number of other reasons apart from rising income. The population of the UK has increased. In 1951, it was 52.7 million; in 1971 it had increased to 55.9 million and in 1998 was 59.0 million. Population-led increases in demand are set to continue with an estimated UK figure of 62.2 million by 2021.

Planning policies have led to a greater separation of housing and places of work. In Victorian England, workers tended to live within walking distance of their work. Planning regulations over the past 50 years, though, have created distinct zones within urban areas and, as a result, most people are no longer within walking distance of their place of work.

Improvements in infrastructure and advances in

technology have created their own demands. Building a new motorway or bypass reduces journey times and encourages people to live further away from their place of work. Faster roads or rail links also encourage greater leisure travel. Equally, improvements in car design have made motoring more reliable and comfortable. One reason why railways failed to attract more passengers in the second half of the twentieth century was that there was not a similar increase in quality of service. For instance, the shortest journey time from London to Birmingham was longer in 1999 than it was in 1979 and rolling stock had barely improved.

The supply of transport

There is no 'supply curve' for transport in general or for parts of the transport industry. For instance, there is no supply curve for motor vehicle transport because no single firm or industry provides this service. There are, though, supply curves for some of the components of the service such as petrol or servicing of cars. Nor is there a supply curve for rail travel. Until 1995, the rail industry was operated by a single company, British Rail, which was a monopoly (i.e. only) supplier and there is no supply curve under monopoly. Since 1995, the industry has been privatised but the key companies in the industry, such as Railtrack or Virgin, are still monopolies in their areas of service.

However, it could been argued that there has been a supply curve for bus and coach travel since 1980 (for coaches) and 1985 (for buses) when the industry was **deregulated** (☞ unit 18). Before deregulation, the government issued licences, and in general only one licence was offered on a route, establishing monopolies. After deregulation, any firm could set up and offer regular bus services in the UK. Table 6.6 shows that there was an increase in the number of buses on the roads during the 1980s and 1990s, travelling more kilometres. This was despite a fall in the number of kilometres travelled by passengers. The demand curve for bus transport has therefore probably been shifting to the left as more people switch to cars. The supply curve, however, has shifted to the right with new companies coming into the market and existing companies expanding their services. Opposing this rightward shift has been a fall in government subsidies to bus companies, which all other things being equal would have shifted the supply curve to the left.

Price determination

The supply and demand model cannot be used in industries where there is no supply curve in the market. In the rail industry, for instance, prices are fixed by the rail companies influenced by the actions of the rail regulator. In the bus industry, where arguably there is a supply curve, the 1980s and 1990s have seen fares rise by more than the general rate of inflation. As Table 6.7 shows, fares between 1980 and 1998 rose roughly three fold, whilst prices in general only roughly doubled. Falls in demand for bus travel due to increased demand for car travel, and an increase in supply as evidenced by the increased number of bus companies and buses, should have led to a relative fall in bus fares. Instead they rose, almost certainly due to the cuts in government subsidies during the period.

Gold

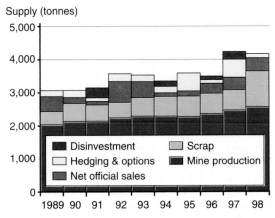

Figure 6.5 *Supply (tonnes)*
Source: adapted from Gold Fields Mineral Services, Gold Survey 1999.

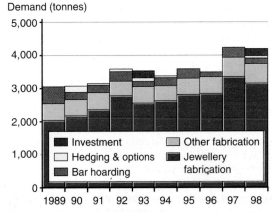

Figure 6.6 *Demand (tonnes)*
Source: adapted from Gold Fields Mineral Services, Gold Survey 1999.

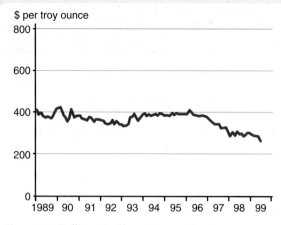

Figure 6.7 *Bullion price ($ per troy ounce)*
Source: adapted from Primark Datastream.

Demand

The main demand for gold comes from jewellery fabrication. In 1998, this amounted to roughly three quarters of purchases. Much of the rest tends to be taken up by demand from other fabrication such as coins, electronic bits and tooth fillings. Remaining demand comes from investment and speculation. Gold is bought, particularly in India and the Middle East, as a form of saving. The problem with it is that holding gold fails to generate interest, as money might in a savings account. Indeed, banks will charge customers to hold gold if they want it kept safe in bank vaults. So, investors must rely on rising prices to make a return on their investment. During the 1980s and 1990s, gold tended to fall in price. The fall was even larger if inflation is taken into account.

Supply

The main supply of gold comes from mine production. This typically accounts for between half and two thirds of sales. The second largest source of gold tends to be recycled gold. For instance, jewellery may be melted down and resold. The rest comes from hedging, options and disinvestment. Hedging and options are complicated financial instruments used by gold mining companies and others to fix the price of gold forward. Most contracts do not lead to the sale of any physical gold, but some do and hence they are a source of supply.
Disinvestment comes partly from private investors selling gold. However, in the 1990s, central banks have also been sellers of gold. These are the 'net official sales' in Figure 6.5. Central banks of countries have traditionally held gold. Until relatively recently, gold was money. Central banks, though, have increasingly come to believe that they could earn more on their financial holdings by selling their gold and buying financial assets on which they could earn interest. In 1999, for instance, the Bank of England announced that it would be selling 415 tonnes of its gold reserves. The price of gold fell sharply as a result of this news.

1. Outline the trends in the demand for and supply of gold since 1989.
2. During the 1980s and 1990s, fewer and fewer investors in the Western world considered gold to be a good investment. Why might this explain what happened to the gold price over this period?
3. Discuss THREE possible causes of a sustained rise in the price of gold in the future.

Summary

1. Some goods are complements, in joint demand.
2. Other goods are substitutes for each other, in competitive demand.
3. Derived demand occurs when one good is demanded because it is needed for the production of other goods or services.
4. Composite demand and joint supply are two other ways in which markets are linked.

Partial and general models

A model of price determination was outlined in unit 6. It was explained that the price of a good was determined by the forces of demand and supply. This is an example of a **partial model**. A partial model is an explanation of reality which has relatively few variables (☞ unit 45). But a more **general model** or wider model of the market system can be constructed which shows how events in one market can lead to changes in other markets. In this unit we will consider how some markets are interrelated.

Complements

Some goods, known as COMPLEMENTS, are in JOINT DEMAND. This means that, in demanding one good, a consumer will also be likely to demand another good. Examples of complements are:
● tennis rackets and tennis balls;
● washing machines and soap powder;
● strawberries and cream;
● video tapes and video recorders.
  Economic theory suggests that a rise in the quantity demanded of one complement will lead to an increase in the demand for another, resulting in an increase in the price and quantity bought of the other complement. For instance, an increase in the quantity demanded of strawberries will lead to an increase in demand for cream too, pushing up the price of cream.
  This can be shown on a demand and supply diagram. Assume that new technology reduces the cost of production of washing machines. This leads to an increase in supply of washing machines shown by a shift to the right of the supply curve in Figure 7.1 (a). As a result there is a fall in price and a rise in the quantity demanded of washing machines, shown by a movement along the demand curve. This in turn will increase the demand for automatic soap powder, shown by a shift to the right in the demand curve in Figure 7.1 (b). This leads to a rise in the quantity purchased of automatic soap powder and also an increase in its price.

Substitutes

A SUBSTITUTE is a good which can be replaced by another good. If two goods are substitutes for each other, they are said to be in COMPETITIVE DEMAND. Examples of substitutes are:
● beef and pork;
● Coca-cola and Pepsi-cola;
● fountain pens and biros;
● gas and oil (in the long term but not particularly in the short term).

Figure 7.1 *Complements*
An increase in supply and the consequent fall in price of washing machines will lead to a rise in the quantity of washing machines and a rise in demand (shown by a shift in the demand curve) for a complementary good such as automatic washing powder.

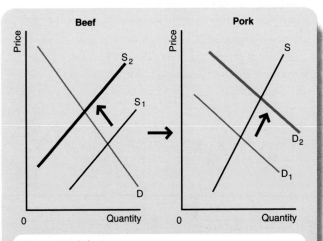

Figure 7.2 *Substitutes*
A fall in the supply of beef leading to a rise in its price will lead to a fall in the quantity demanded of beef and an increase in the demand for a substitute product such as pork.

Economic theory predicts that a rise in the price of one good will lead to an increase in demand and a rise in price of a substitute good.

Figure 7.2 shows a rise in the price of beef, due to a fall in its supply. This leads to a fall in the quantity demanded of beef as the price of beef rises. In turn, there will be an increase in the demand for pork as consumers substitute pork for beef. The demand for pork will increase, shown by a shift to the right in the demand curve for pork. This leads to a rise in the price of pork and a rise in quantity purchased.

Many substitute goods are not clearly linked. For instance, a rise in the price of foreign holidays will lead some consumers to abandon taking a foreign holiday. They may substitute a UK holiday for it, but they may also decide to buy new curtains or a new carpet for their house, or buy a larger car than they had originally planned.

Question 1

(a) It could be argued that the following pairs of products are both complements **and** substitutes. Explain why.
   (i) Electricity and gas.
   (ii) Tea and milk.
   (iii) Bus journeys and train journeys.
   (iv) Chocolate bars and crisps.
(b) (i) For each pair of products, explain whether you think they are more likely to be complements or substitutes.
   (ii) Show on a demand and supply diagram the effect on the price of the first product of a rise in price of the second product.

Derived demand

Many goods are demanded only because they are needed for the production of other goods. The demand for these goods is said to be a DERIVED DEMAND.

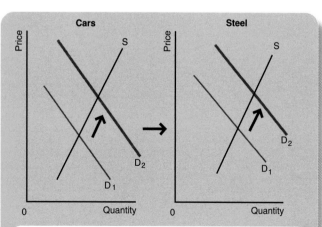

Figure 7.3 *Derived demand*
An increase in the demand for cars will lead to an increase in demand for steel. Steel is said to be in derived demand from cars.

For instance, the demand for steel is derived in part from the demand for cars and ships. The demand for flour is derived in part from the demand for cakes and bread. The demand for sugar is in part derived from demand for some beverages, confectionery and chocolate.

Figure 7.3 shows an increase in the demand for cars. This leads to an increase in quantity bought and sold. Car manufacturers will increase their demand for steel, shown by a rightward shift of the demand curve for steel. The price of steel will then increase as will the quantity bought and sold. Economic theory therefore predicts that an increase in demand for a good will lead to an increase in price and quantity purchased of goods which are in derived demand from it.

Question 2

The price of bauxite was depressed in 1998 and 1999 by the depressed demand for aluminium. Bauxite is the main raw material used to manufacture aluminium. The problem was part of a larger pattern of depressed demand for all metals resulting from the Asian crisis which hit the world in 1998. Financial problems in countries such as Thailand, South Korea and Indonesia led to a sharp fall in lending, with a knock on effect on demand. Output in the countries worst affected fell by up to 10 per cent. These countries had been the powerhouse of growth in Asia in the 1980s and 1990s and their economic crises led to sharp falls in their demand for imports. Hence, sales of raw materials such as aluminium to these countries, used in their industries to manufacture everything from cars to disposable food containers to window frames, fell. In the longer term, the future for the bauxite industry is uncertain. Aluminium is increasingly coming under threat from glass as a raw material for drinks containers. On the other hand, aluminium could replace steel in the manufacture of car bodies because of its lightness.

(a) Explain, with the help of diagrams and the concept of derived demand, the effect of the Asian crisis of 1998 on demand for bauxite.
(b) What might happen to the demand for bauxite in the future?

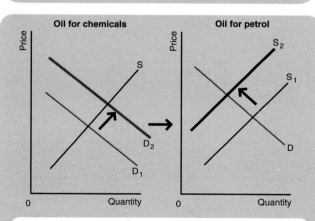

Figure 7.4 *Composite demand*
An increase in the demand for oil from chemical producers will result in a fall in the supply of oil to the petrol market because oil is in composite demand.

Composite demand

A good is said to be in COMPOSITE DEMAND when it is demanded for two or more distinct uses. For instance, milk may be used for yoghurt, for cheese making, for butter or for drinking. Land may be demanded for residential, industrial or commercial use. Steel is demanded for car manufacturing and for shipbuilding.

Economic theory predicts that an increase in demand for one composite good will lead to a fall in supply for another. Figure 7.4 shows that an increase in the demand by the chemical industry for oil will push the demand curve to the right, increasing both the quantity sold and the price of oil. With an upward sloping supply for oil as a whole, an increase in supply of oil to the chemical industry will reduce the supply of oil for petrol. This is shown by a shift upwards in the supply curve in Figure 7.4. The price of oil for petrol will rise and the quantity demanded will fall.

Economic theory therefore predicts that an increase in demand for a good will lead to a rise in price and a fall in quantity demanded for a good with which it is in composite demand.

Joint supply

A good is in JOINT SUPPLY with another good when one good is supplied for two different purposes. For instance, cows are supplied for both beef and leather. An oil well may give both oil and gas.

Economic theory suggests that an increase in demand for one good in joint supply will lead to an increase in its price. This leads to an increase in the quantity supplied. The supply of the other good therefore increases, leading to a fall in its price. Figure 7.5 shows that an increase in demand for beef leads to an increase in both price and quantity bought and sold of beef. More beef production will lead, as a by-product, to greater supply of leather. This is shown by a shift to the right in the supply curve for leather. The price of leather will then fall and quantity demanded, bought and sold will increase.

Question 3

Market forces could end the old tradition of kissing under the mistletoe. The price of mistletoe has been rising in recent years as supply falls. This has occurred because of what has been happening in the apple market. Mistletoe grows on apple trees, feeding off the sap of the tree. The past twenty years have not been good for British apple growers. Fierce competition from foreign producers has resulted in many traditional apple orchards being 'grubbed out,' with half of British apple trees disappearing since 1973. What's more, parasitic mistletoe is not allowed to grow on trees in new orchards. As old orchards disappear, so too will the mistletoe.

With the help of a diagram and the concept of joint supply, explain why the price of mistletoe has been rising in recent years.

key terms

Competitive demand - when two or more goods are substitutes for each other.
Complement - a good which is purchased with other goods to satisfy a want.
Composite demand - when a good is demanded for two or more distinct uses.
Derived demand - when the demand for one good is the result of or derived from the demand for another good.
Joint demand - when two or more complements are bought together.
Joint supply - when two or more goods are produced together, so that a change in supply of one good will necessarily change the supply of the other goods with which it is in joint supply.
Substitute - a good which can be replaced by another to satisfy a want.

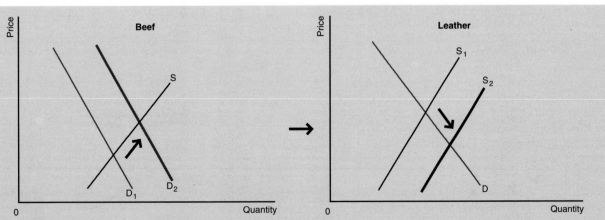

Figure 7.5 *Joint supply*
An increase in the demand for beef, which leads to more beef being produced, results in an increase in the supply of leather. Beef and leather are said to be in joint supply.

Applied economics

Commercial transport

Derived demand

Commercial transport, the transporting of goods in the UK from factory to shop for instance, is a derived demand. It is ultimately derived from the purchase of consumer goods and services. The movement of coal from a coal pit to an electricity power station is part of the long chain of production in the eventual consumption of, say, a packet of cornflakes.

Demand for commercial transport

Demand for commercial transport has grown over time as consumer incomes have risen and more goods and services have been consumed. Table 7.1 shows, however, that the growth in tonnage of goods moved has been relatively small since the 1960s. Much of this is due to the fact that goods have got lighter and less bulky. Far more plastic and far less metal are used today, for instance. So whilst more consumer goods are purchased, the total weight and volume have only increased a little. In contrast, Table 7.2 shows that there has been a significant growth over the same period in the number of tonne kilometres travelled. Each tonne is travelling a longer distance today than 40 years ago. This is the result of greater specialisation between regions and firms. In turn, this has been encouraged by the growth of the motorway network in the UK, which has allowed much faster journey times.

Substitutes

Different modes of transport are substitutes for each other. Both Tables 7.1 and 7.2 and Figure 7.6 indicate that there has been a switch away from rail transport to other modes, particularly road transport. In the early 1950s, railways carried slightly more freight than the roads. By the 1960s, rail had already lost much of its market share to road haulage and by the 1990s accounted for less than 10 per cent of freight transport by distance travelled and less than 5 per cent of total freight tonnage. Pipeline traffic has increased, mainly due to growth of gas consumption and North Sea oil production. The sudden increase in the share of water transport between 1976 and 1985 was entirely due to the growth of the North Sea oil industry.

Complements

The privatisation of British Rail led to an increase in the amount of rail freight carried. The private freight companies have proved more flexible than British Rail and have been able to drive down costs

and win orders. However, the future of rail transport lies mainly as a complement to road transport. Lorries and vans will take goods to railway collection depots. The goods will then be transported by rail before being taken away again by lorry. Loading and unloading from one mode of transport to another is relatively expensive. Therefore rail transport has proved to be

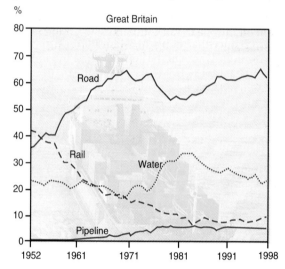

Source: adapted from Department for the Environment, *Transport and the Regions, Transport Statistics.*

Figure 7.6 *Commercial transport: by mode, distance transported*

Table 7.1 *Goods: total transported in millions of tonnes*

	Road	Rail	Water: coastwise oil	Water: other	Pipelines	Total
1961	1 295	249	57		6	1 607
1965	1 634	239	64		27	1 964
1970	1 610	209	58		39	1 916
1975	1 602	176	48		52	1 878
1980	1 383	154	54	83	83	1 757
1985	1 452	122	50	92	89	1 805
1990	1 749	152	44	108	121	2 163
1995	1 701	101	47	98	168	2 115
1998	1 727	102	55	94	148	2 126

Source: adapted from Department for the Environment, Transport and the Regions, *Transport Statistics.*

Table 7.2 *Goods: distance transported, total tonne kilometres (billions)*

	Road	Rail	Water: coastwise oil	Water: other	Pipelines	Total
1961	85.6	16.4	3.2	0.6	0.4	106.2
1965	108.0	15.8	3.7	0.6	1.8	129.8
1970	85.0	26.8	23.2	0.01	3.0	138.1
1975	95.3	23.5	18.3	0.1	5.9	143.1
1980	92.4	17.6	38.2	15.9	10.1	174.2
1985	103.2	15.3	38.9	18.7	11.2	187.3
1990	136.3	15.8	32.1	23.6	11.0	218.8
1995	149.6	13.3	31.4	11.1	11.1	226.6
1998	159.5	17.4	36.4	20.8	11.2	245.3

Source: adapted from Department for the Environment, Transport and the Regions, *Transport Statistics.*

economic mainly when journeys of over 300-400 miles are made by rail or when a dedicated rail link can take goods door to door, for instance from a pit head to a power station. The number of dedicated rail links could decrease in the immediate future if the electricity industry burns more gas and imported coal and less domestic coal. The Channel Tunnel, on the other hand, provides the rail industry with a long term commercial opportunity to gain export traffic away from the roads. The Channel Tunnel, for instance, is ideally suited for the transport of goods such as new cars being transported from manufacturing plants to dealers in other countries. The future success of rail freight is dependent on European rail companies becoming more flexible, substantially reducing journey times and cutting costs.

Composite demand

Roads are in composite demand with commercial transport and passenger transport. At present, there is no pricing mechanism for the road system. Most roads are free from congestion at all times of day. A minority of roads suffer from congestion at certain times of the day. This is a problem of scarce resources. Some potential road users react by either not travelling or travelling by an alternative mode of transport. Commuters in the London area, for instance, may choose to travel by rail, underground or bus because the opportunity cost of travelling by car is too high. Some commuters arrive earlier or later to their place of work to avoid the rush hour. Other road users accept that their road journey times will be longer in the rush hour than at other times of the day.

The more cars on the road, the greater the potential for congestion and longer journey times for freight transport. Road pricing could help the freight industry if car users were discouraged from travelling. Road pricing is when cars and lorries are charged for the use of a road, as for instance with motorway tolls in France. However, any road pricing system is likely to place charges on lorries as well as cars. Journey times for lorries might be reduced, lowering costs, but road tolls will increase freight costs. If the tolls are high enough to increase overall costs, they could act as an incentive for firms to switch some freight from road to rail. Indeed, some environmentalists have argued that revenues from road tolls should be used to subsidise rail freight to create a large shift from road to rail.

Land usage

The cost of planning restrictions

Planning restrictions have increased the price of housing land. The price of farming land, for instance, is often one-thirtieth or one-fortieth of what it is when housebuilding is allowed. Hence, there are plenty of farmers willing to sell their land for residential use. A 1994 study commissioned by the Department for the Environment, however, pointed out that this is a misleading comparison because the cost of preparing farming land for housing or industrial purposes is high. Instead, it estimated the opportunity cost of housing land by looking at the price in Barnsley, where there is no shortage of housing land available for sale. The cost of planning restrictions could then be calculated. For instance, in Reigate, prime commuter country in Surrey in the South of England, land prices were 3.6 times their opportunity cost. Even in Beverley in Yorkshire, the ratio was 2.2.

Nimbyism

A 'Nimby' is someone who says 'not in my backyard'. The word came into fashion in the 1980s to describe people who were all in favour of better facilities, better roads, more housing and more places of work to reduce unemployment so long as none of this happened in their local area.

It has often been justified by high-sounding references to preserving rural England, maintaining local amenities and protecting areas of natural beauty. Every new bypass or road upgrade seems to run through a patch of land which is the habitat of some rare species of plant or animal. However, in practice, the vast majority of Nimbys are motivated solely by the losses that they might incur if development went ahead. For instance, building a new housing estate next door is unlikely to help the property prices of existing houses in the area.

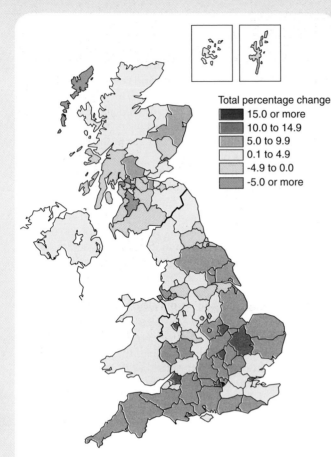

Total percentage change
- 15.0 or more
- 10.0 to 14.9
- 5.0 to 9.9
- 0.1 to 4.9
- -4.9 to 0.0
- -5.0 or more

Figure 7.7 *Projected population change by area, 1997-2011*
Source: adapted from *Regional Trends*, Office for National Statistics.

Table 7.3 *Changing population and number of households, England*

Millions

	1971	1981	1991	2011
Population	43.4	46.8	48.2	50.8
Number of households	15.9	17.3	19.2	22.8

Source: adapted from *Social Trends*, Office for National Statistics.

Greenbelt policies

Britain's greenbelts were established after the Second World War. They were intended to throw a cordon around urban areas to prevent their spread into the countryside. Within the greenbelt, planning restrictions are very strict about development. No new housing or industrial development is permitted. Greenbelt policies have severely restricted the supply of new land for housing and industry in the UK and contributed to the relatively high price of land in urban areas. This increases the costs of living for urban dwellers, the vast majority of people in the UK. Not only are house prices and rents much higher than they would otherwise be but the cost of services from supermarkets to cinemas is much higher. This is because high land prices paid by industry have to be paid for in the form of higher prices by consumers.

Households

The number of households in the UK is growing at a much faster rate than the slow growth in the overall population. The growth is coming partly from changes in society. The increase in divorce has created many one-person households and rising incomes mean that more young single people now have the choice between living at home with their parents or getting their own accommodation. Growth is also coming from demographic changes. There is an increasing number of elderly people who are living longer and living alone. The number of households with two parents and several children is declining.

New land for housing

New land for building houses comes from a variety of sources. 'Windfall sites' are those which come from homeowners selling part of their garden for development, or housebuilders buying a large old house, knocking it down and replacing it with a small estate of smaller houses. Another source is 'brownfield sites'. These are sites which have already been used for commercial or other urban purposes but now have a higher value as housing land. Third, and most controversially, new land can be found by small scale easing of greenbelt and other restrictions, usually amounting to just a few tens of acres in a specific locality.

1. Explain the following.
   (a) The demand for land is a derived demand.
   (b) Land is in composite demand.
   (c) Land is in joint supply.
   (d) Land is in joint demand with buildings.
2. Explain the economic relationships in the UK between land use and:
   (a) a growing population;
   (b) a shifting population geographically;
   (c) increasing affluence.
3. Do you think greenbelt regulations should be loosened to allow more house building in the UK? In your answer, consider the costs and benefits of such a change in policy. This will include an analysis of the effects on the price of houses, industrial property and agricultural land.

Summary

1. Elasticity is a measure of the extent to which quantity responds to a change in a variable which affects it, such as price or income.
2. Price elasticity of demand measures the responsiveness of quantity demanded to a change in price.
3. Price elasticity of demand varies from zero, or infinitely inelastic, to infinitely elastic.
4. The value of price elasticity of demand is determined by the availability of substitutes and by time.

The meaning of demand elasticity

The quantity demanded of a good is affected by changes in the price of the good, changes in price of other goods, changes in income and changes in other relevant factors. Elasticity is a measure of just how much the quantity demanded will be affected by a change in price or income etc.

Assume that the price of gas increases by 1 per cent. If quantity demanded consequently falls by 20 per cent, then there is a very large drop in quantity demanded in comparison to the change in price. The price elasticity of gas would be said to be very high. If quantity demanded falls by 0.01 per cent, then the change in quantity demanded is relatively insignificant compared to the large change in price and the price elasticity of gas would be said to be low.

Different elasticities of demand measure the responsiveness of quantity demanded to changes in the variables which affect demand. So price elasticity of demand measures the responsiveness of quantity demanded to changes in the price of the good. Income elasticity measures the responsiveness of quantity demanded to changes in consumer incomes. Cross elasticity measures the responsiveness of quantity demanded to changes in the price of another good. Economists could also measure population elasticity, tastes elasticity or elasticity for any other variable which might affect quantity demanded, although these measures are rarely calculated.

Price elasticity of demand

Economists choose to measure responsiveness in terms of percentage changes. So PRICE ELASTICITY OF DEMAND - the responsiveness of changes in quantity demanded to changes in price - is calculated by using the formula:

$$\frac{\text{percentage change in quantity demanded}}{\text{percentage change in price}}$$

Table 8.1 shows a number of calculations of price elasticity. For instance, if an increase in price of 10 per cent leads to a fall in quantity demanded of 20 per cent, then the price elasticity of demand is 2. If an increase in price of 50 per cent leads to a fall in quantity demanded of 25 per cent then price elasticity of demand is $\frac{1}{2}$.

Elasticity is sometimes difficult to understand at first. It is essential to memorise the formulae for elasticity. Only then can they be used with ease and an appreciation gained of their significance.

Table 8.1

Change in price (%)	Change in quantity demanded (%)	Elasticity
10	20	2
50	25	$\frac{1}{2}$
7	28	4
9	3	$\frac{1}{3}$

Question 1

Table 8.2

| | Percentage change in | |
	quantity demanded	price
(a)	10	5
(b)	60	20
(c)	4	8
(d)	1	9
(e)	5	7
(f)	8	11

Calculate the price elasticity of demand from the data in Table 8.2.

Alternative formulae

Data to calculate price elasticities are often not presented in the form of percentage changes. These have to be worked out. Calculating the percentage change is relatively easy. For instance, if a consumer has 10 apples and buys another 5, the percentage change in the total number of apples is of course 50 per cent. This answer is worked out by dividing the change in the number of apples she has (i.e. 5) by the original number of apples she possessed (i.e. 10) and multiplying by 100 to get a percentage figure. So the formula is:

$$\text{percentage change} = \frac{\text{absolute change}}{\text{original value}} \times 100\%$$

Price elasticity of demand is measured by dividing the percentage change in quantity demanded by the percentage change in price. Therefore an alternative way of expressing this is $\Delta Q/Q \times 100$ (the percentage change in quantity demanded Q) divided by $\Delta P/P \times 100$ (the percentage change in price P). The 100s cancel each other out, leaving a formula of:

$$\frac{\Delta Q}{Q} \div \frac{\Delta P}{P} \quad \text{or} \quad \frac{\Delta Q}{Q} \times \frac{P}{\Delta P}$$

This is mathematically equivalent to:

$$\frac{P}{Q} \times \frac{\Delta Q}{\Delta P}$$

Examples of calculations of elasticity using the above two formulae are given in Figure 8.1.

Question 2

Table 8.3

	Original values		New values	
	Quantity demanded	Price (£)	Quantity demanded	Price (£)
(a)	100	5	120	3
(b)	20	8	25	7
(c)	12	3	16	0
(d)	150	12	200	10
(e)	45	6	45	8
(f)	32	24	40	2

Calculate the price elasticity of demand for the data in Table 8.3.

Elastic and inelastic demand

Different values of price elasticity of demand are given special names.

- Demand is price ELASTIC if the value of elasticity is greater than one. If demand for a good is price elastic then a percentage change in price will bring about an even larger percentage change in quantity demanded. For instance, if a 10 per cent rise in the price of tomatoes leads to a 20 per cent fall in the quantity demanded of tomatoes, then price elasticity is 20÷10 or 2 and therefore the demand for tomatoes is elastic. Demand is

Example 1
Quantity demanded originally is 100 at a price of £2. There is a rise in price to £3 resulting in a fall in demand to 75.
Therefore the change in quantity demanded is 25 and the change in price is £1.
The price elasticity of demand is:

$$\frac{\Delta Q}{Q} \div \frac{\Delta P}{P} = \frac{25}{100} \div \frac{1}{2} = \frac{1}{2}$$

Example 2
Quantity demanded originally is 20 units at a price of £5 000. There is a fall in price to £4 000 resulting in a rise in demand to 32 units.
Therefore the change in quantity demanded is 12 units resulting from the change in price of £1 000.
The price elasticity of demand is:

$$\frac{P}{Q} \times \frac{\Delta Q}{\Delta P} = \frac{5000}{20} \times \frac{12}{1000} = 3$$

Figure 8.1 *Calculations of elasticity of demand*

said to be **infinitely elastic** if the value of elasticity is infinity (i.e. a fall in price would lead to an infinite increase in quantity demanded whilst a rise in price would lead to the quantity demanded becoming zero).
- Demand is price INELASTIC if the value of elasticity is less than one. If demand for a good is price inelastic then a percentage change in price will bring about a smaller percentage change in quantity demanded. For instance, if a 10 per cent rise in the price of commuter fares on British Rail Southern Region resulted in a 1 per cent fall in rail journeys made, then price elasticity is 1÷10 or 0.1 and therefore the demand for BR commuter traffic is inelastic. Demand is said to be **infinitely inelastic** if the value of elasticity is zero (i.e. a change in price would have no effect on quantity demanded).
- Demand is of UNITARY ELASTICITY if the value of elasticity is exactly 1. This means that a percentage change in price will lead to an exact and opposite change in quantity demanded. For instance, a good would have unitary elasticity if a 10 per cent rise in price led to a 10 per cent fall in quantity demanded. (It will be shown in unit 9 that total revenue will remain constant at all quantities demanded if elasticity of demand is unity.)

This terminology is summarised in Table 8.4.

Question 3

Explain whether you think that the following goods would be elastic or inelastic in demand if their price increased by 10 per cent whilst all other factors remained constant: (a) petrol; (b) fresh tomatoes; (c) holidays offered by a major tour operator; (d) a Ford car; (e) a Mars Bar; (f) the music magazine, *Melody Maker*.

Table 8.4 *Elasticity: summary of key terms*

	Verbal description of response to a change in price	Numerical measure of elasticity	Change in total outlay as price rises[1]
Perfectly inelastic	Quantity demanded does not change at all as price changes	Zero	Increases
Inelastic	Quantity demanded changes by a smaller percentage than does price	Between 0 and 1	Increases
Unitary elasticity	Quantity demanded changes by exactly the same percentage as does price	1	Constant
Elastic	Quantity demanded changes by a larger percentage than does price	Between 1 and infinity	Decreases
Perfectly elastic	Buyers are prepared to purchase all they can obtain at some given price but none at all at a higher price	Infinity	Decreases to zero

1. This is explained in unit 9.

Graphical representations

Figure 8.2 shows a straight line graph. It is a common mistake to conclude that elasticity of a straight line demand curve is constant all along its length. In fact nearly all straight line demand curves vary in elasticity along the line.

- At the point A, price elasticity of demand is infinity. Here quantity demanded is zero. Putting Q = 0 into the formula for elasticity:

$$\frac{\Delta Q}{Q} \div \frac{\Delta P}{P}$$

we see that zero is divided into ΔQ. Mathematically there is an infinite number of zeros in any number.
- At the point C, price elasticity of demand is zero. Here price is zero. Putting P = 0 into the formula for elasticity, we see that P is divided into ΔP giving an answer of infinity. Infinity is then divided into the fraction ΔQ÷Q. Infinity is so large that the answer will approximate to zero.
- At the point B exactly half way along the line, price elasticity of demand is 1.

Worth noting is that the elasticity of demand at a point can be measured by dividing the distance from the point to the quantity axis by the distance from the point to the price axis, BC ÷ AB. In Figure 8.2, B is half way along the line AC and so BC = AB and the elasticity at the point B is 1.

Two straight line demand curves discussed earlier do not have the same elasticity all along their length.

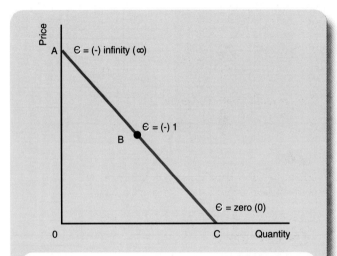

Figure 8.2 *Price elasticity along a straight demand curve*
Price elasticity varies along the length of a straight demand curve, moving from infinity, where it cuts the price axis, to half way along the line, to zero where it cuts the quantity axis.

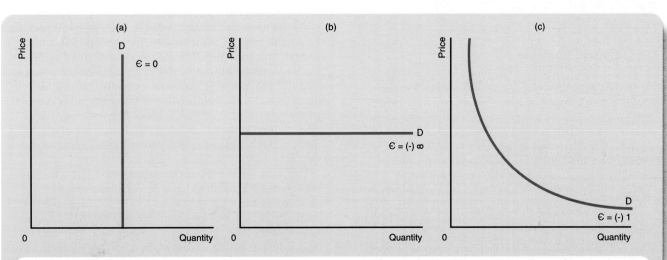

Figure 8.3 *Perfectly elastic and inelastic demand curves and unitary elasticity*
A vertical demand curve (a) is perfectly inelastic, whilst a horizontal demand curve (b) is perfectly elastic. A curve with unitary elasticity (c) is a rectangular hyperbola with the formula PQ = k where P is price, Q is quantity demanded and k is a constant value.

Figure 8.3(a) shows a demand curve which is perfectly inelastic. Whatever the price, the same quantity will be demanded.

Figure 8.3(b) shows a perfectly elastic demand curve. Any amount can be demanded at one price or below it whilst nothing will be demanded at a higher price.

Figure 8.3(c) shows a demand curve with unitary elasticity. Mathematically it is a rectangular hyperbola. This means that any percentage change in price is offset by an equal and opposite change in quantity demanded.

Question 4

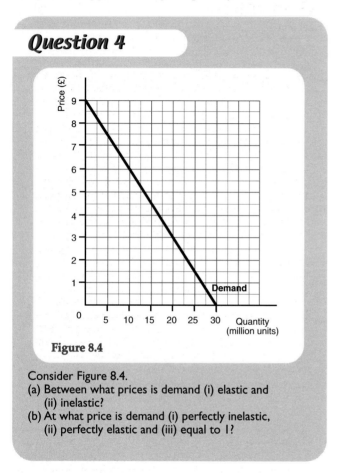

Figure 8.4

Consider Figure 8.4.
(a) Between what prices is demand (i) elastic and (ii) inelastic?
(b) At what price is demand (i) perfectly inelastic, (ii) perfectly elastic and (iii) equal to 1?

Two technical points

So far we have written of price elasticity of demand as always being a positive number. In fact any downward sloping demand curve always has a negative elasticity. This is because a rise in one variable (price or quantity) is always matched by a fall in the other variable. A rise is positive but a fall is negative and a positive number divided by a negative one (or vice versa) is always negative. However, economists find it convenient to omit the minus sign in price elasticity of demand because it is easier to deal in positive numbers whilst accepting that the value is really negative.

A second point relates to the fact that elasticities over the same price range can differ. For example, at a price of £2, demand for a good is 20 units. At a price of £3, demand is 18 units. Price elasticity of demand for a rise in price from £2 to £3 is:

$$\frac{P}{Q} \times \frac{\Delta Q}{\Delta P} = \frac{2}{20} \times \frac{2}{1} = \frac{1}{5}$$

But price elasticity of demand for a fall in price from £3 to £2 is:

$$\frac{P}{Q} \times \frac{\Delta Q}{\Delta P} = \frac{3}{18} \times \frac{2}{1} = \frac{1}{3}$$

The price elasticity for a rise in price is therefore less than for a fall in price over the same range. This is not necessarily a problem so long as one is aware of it. One way of resolving this is to average out price and quantity. In the formulae, P becomes not the original price but the average price (i.e. the original price plus the new price divided by 2) and Q becomes the average quantity demanded (i.e. the original quantity demanded plus the new quantity demanded divided by 2). In the above example, the average price is £(2+3)/2 or £2½. The average quantity demanded is (20+18)/2 or 19. Price elasticity of demand is then:

$$\frac{P}{Q} \times \frac{\Delta Q}{\Delta P} = \frac{2½}{19} \times \frac{2}{1} = \frac{5}{19}$$

As you would expect, this value is in between the two price elasticities of ⅕ and ⅓.

The determinants of price elasticity of demand

The exact value of price elasticity of demand for a good is determined by a wide variety of factors. Economists, however, argue that two factors in particular can be singled out: the availability of substitutes and time.

The availability of substitutes The better the substitutes for a product, the higher the price elasticity of demand will tend to be. For instance, salt has few good substitutes. When the price of salt increases, the demand for salt will change little and therefore the price elasticity of salt is low. On the other hand, spaghetti has many good substitutes, from other types of pasta, to rice, potatoes, bread, and other foods. A rise in the price of spaghetti, all other food prices remaining constant, is likely to have a significant effect on the demand for spaghetti. Hence the elasticity of demand for spaghetti is likely to be higher than that for salt.

The more widely the product is defined, the fewer substitutes it is likely to have. Spaghetti has many substitutes, but food in general has none. Therefore the elasticity of demand for spaghetti is likely to be higher than that for food. Similarly the elasticity of demand for boiled sweets is likely to be higher than for confectionery in general. A 5 per cent increase in the price of boiled sweets, all other prices remaining constant, is likely to lead to a much larger fall in demand for boiled sweets than a 5 per cent increase in the price of all confectionery.

Time The longer the period of time, the more price elastic is the demand for a product. For instance, in 1973/74 when the price of oil quadrupled the demand for oil was initially little affected. In the short term the demand for oil was price inelastic. This is hardly surprising. People still needed to travel to work in cars and heat their houses whilst industry still needed to operate. Oil had few good substitutes. Motorists couldn't put gas into their petrol tanks whilst businesses could not change oil-fired systems to run on gas, electricity or coal. However, in the longer term motorists were able to and did buy cars which were more fuel efficient. Oil-fired central heating systems were replaced by gas and electric systems. Businesses converted or did not replace oil-fired equipment. The demand for oil fell from what it would otherwise have been. In the longer run, the demand for oil proved to be price elastic. It is argued that in the short term, buyers are often locked into spending patterns through habit, lack of information or because of durable goods that have already been purchased. In the longer term, they have the time and opportunity to change those patterns.

It is sometimes argued that **necessities** have lower price elasticities than **luxuries.** Necessities by definition have to be bought whatever their price in order to stay alive. So an increase in the price of necessities will barely reduce the quantity demanded. Luxuries on the other hand are by definition goods which are not essential to existence. A rise in the price of luxuries should therefore produce a proportionately large fall in demand. There is no evidence, however, to suggest that this is true. Food, arguably a necessity, does not seem to have a lower elasticity than holidays or large cars, both arguably luxuries. Part of the reason for this is that it is very difficult to define necessities and luxuries empirically. Some food is a necessity but a significant proportion of what we eat is unnecessary for survival. It is not possible to distinguish between what food is consumed out of necessity and what is a luxury.

It is also sometimes argued that goods which form a relatively low proportion of total expenditure have lower elasticities than those which form a more significant proportion. A large car manufacturer, for instance, would continue to buy the same amount of paper clips even if the price of paper clips doubled because it is not worth its

while to bother changing to an alternative. On the other hand, its demand for steel would be far more price elastic. There is no evidence to suggest that this is true. Examples given in textbooks, such as salt and matches, have low price elasticities because they have few good substitutes. In the case of paper clips, manufacturers would long ago have raised price substantially if they believed that price had little impact on the demand for their product.

Question 5

Smoking is on the increase again in industrialised countries. In the 1970s and 1980s the numbers of smokers tended to decline. However, the 1990s have seen the start of a reversal of the trend mainly because of an increase in the number of teenage smokers, particularly girls. There seems to be only a weak link between prices and tobacco smoking. In the UK, for instance, between 1980 and 1986, a large increase in real cigarette prices coincided with a small decline in the number of cigarettes that smokers consumed. Other factors seem to be more important in determining smoking. The fall in consumption in the early 1980s, for instance coincided with a deep recession in the economy when unemployment rose from 1.5 million to 3 million. Rising awareness of health risks has also cut smoking, particularly amongst professional middle aged workers. Some have argued that the way forward is to deregulate the nicotine market. The main health hazards come not from nicotine but from tar and carbon monoxide associated with the smoking of cigarettes. At the moment, only tobacco companies and manufacturers of patches, gums and inhalers are licensed to sell nicotine based products. If any company could develop and sell nicotine products, there is a chance that one would come up with a safe nicotine delivery system which could compete with the cigarette.

Source: adapted from the *Financial Times*, 21.6.1998.

(a) Explain what, according to the article, is the price elasticity of demand of cigarettes.
(b) What might be the effect on price elasticity of demand for cigarettes if a manufacturer sold a nicotine based product which proved a satisfactory alternative to cigarettes?

key terms

Elastic demand - where the price elasticity of demand is greater than 1. The responsiveness of demand is proportionally greater than the change in price. Demand is infinitely elastic if price elasticity of demand is infinity.
Inelastic demand - where the price elasticity of demand is less than 1. The responsiveness of demand is proportionally less than the change in price. Demand is infinitely inelastic if price elasticity of demand is zero.

Price elasticity of demand - the responsiveness of changes in quantity demanded to changes in price, measured by the formula:

$$\frac{P}{Q} \times \frac{\Delta Q}{\Delta P}$$

Unitary elasticity - where the value of price elasticity of demand is 1. The responsiveness of demand is proportionally equal to the change in price.

Applied economics

The elasticity of demand for oil

Throughout the 1950s and 1960s oil was a cheap fuel. Indeed, the price of oil fell from approximately $1.70 a barrel in 1950 to $1.30 a barrel in 1970 as supply increased at a faster rate than demand. The early 1970s saw a reversal of this trend. Demand increased more rapidly than supply as the world economy boomed and policy makers became increasingly convinced that oil would remain a cheap and an efficient energy source. By 1973, the price of a barrel of oil had risen to approximately $3.

In November 1973, politics in the Middle East was to catapult the oil market into the world headlines. The Egyptians launched an attack on Israel on the day of Yom Kippur, the Jewish equivalent to Christmas. Other Middle Eastern states, such as Saudi Arabia, gave support to their Arab neighbours by threatening to cut off oil supplies to any country which gave support to Israel. With an existing tight market, the result was an explosion in the price of oil. The war was soon over but its economic fall-out was not lost on OPEC, the Organisation for Petroleum Exporting Countries. OPEC, whose members at the time supplied over 60 per cent of world demand for oil, organised a system of quotas amongst themselves, fixing limits on how much each member could produce. By slightly cutting back on pre-1973 production levels, they were able to increase the average price of oil to $10.41 a barrel in 1974, as shown in Figure 8.5.

The reason why OPEC could engineer this massive price rise was because the demand for oil was price inelastic in the short run. Oil consumers had invested heavily in capital equipment such as oil-fired heating systems and petrol-driven cars. In the short term, there were no cheap alternative substitutes. Car owners, for instance, did not suddenly change their cars for more fuel efficient models because the price of petrol at the pumps increased. Hence the near quadrupling of the price of oil (a 300 per cent increase) only led to a 5 per cent fall in world demand for oil (i.e. the price elasticity of demand for oil in the short term was 0.016).

In the longer term, consumers were able to replace oil-powered equipment. Cars became far more fuel-efficient.

Homeowners insulated their houses. In the UK, the bottom dropped out of the market for oil-fired heating systems. As a consequence, when the demand for oil began to grow again in 1976, it was at a slower rate than in the early 1970s.

In 1978, the Shah of Iran was toppled and was replaced by an Islamic fundamentalist government led by the Ayatollah Khomeini. Iran was a major oil producer and the Islamic revolution and subsequent war between Iran and Iraq severely disrupted supplies from these two countries. OPEC used this opportunity to tighten supply again. With highly inelastic demand, the price rose from $13.03 a barrel in 1978 to $35.69 a barrel in 1980. Total world demand, which peaked in 1979 at approximately 63 million barrels per day, fell to a low of 58 million barrels per day in 1982 before resuming its growth.

In August 1990, political events in the Middle East yet again rocked the world price of oil. Iraq invaded Kuwait and oil sanctions were immediately applied to the output of both countries by oil consuming countries. Other oil producing countries quickly increased production to fill the gap but the fear of a major shortage had driven oil prices up from $18 a barrel to $40. Prices fell back as it became clear that overall supply had not fallen. The successful counter attack by US and other forces in 1991 to retake Kuwait saw the price drop back to below $20 a barrel. For much of the rest of the 1990s, the oil price fluctuated in the $15-$20 a barrel range. However, the short term inelasticity of demand for oil was shown again between 1997 to 2000. At the end of 1997, OPEC decided to expand its production. Prices in 1996 to 1997 had been relatively firm, touching $25 a barrel for a

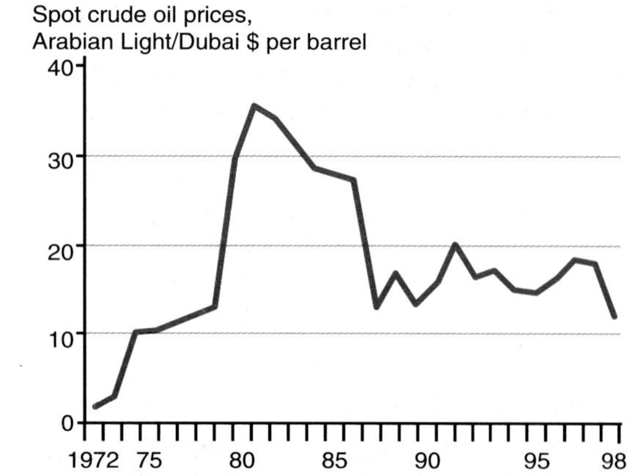

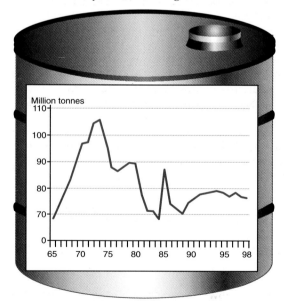

Spot crude oil prices, Arabian Light/Dubai $ per barrel

Source: adapted from *BP Statistical Review of World Energy*.

Figure 8.5 *Oil prices*

Million tonnes

1. Demand for oil in the UK was artificially increased in 1984 and 1985 by the miners' strike when oil was burnt instead of coal in power stations.

Source: adapted from Department of Trade and Industry.

Figure 8.6 *Oil consumption, UK*

short period, and demand for oil had continued growing at a slow but steady rate. The move proved disastrous. The winter of 1997-98 proved to be relatively mild, dampening demand. The Asian crisis of 1998, when a number of Far Eastern countries experienced severe downturns in their economy, further reduced demand. The Japanese economy remained in recession. The result was that world demand grew by just 0.1 per cent compared to, for instance, 2.2 per cent in 1996 and 2.6 per cent in 1997. There followed a sharp fall in the price of oil. By the end of 1998, despite three successive cuts in production quotas by OPEC, oil prices fell below $10 a barrel. The market then pushed the price back up but it went beyond its 1990s long term range of $15-$20 a barrel. The episode shows how very small fluctuations in demand or supply can lead to large fluctuations in price because of the short term price inelasticity of demand for oil.

Figure 8.6 shows what has happened to the UK demand for oil since 1965. The longer term rises and falls in demand follow the sharp changes in the price of oil in the 1970s and 1980s. The 1990s, with its greater stability in the price of oil, saw small, more stable growth in demand for oil.

The impact of rising incomes on demand in the UK can be excluded by calculating the amount of oil used per £1 000 of income (as measured by GDP at market prices). This rose from 0.19 tonnes of oil in 1965 to 0.24 tonnes in 1972, reflecting the fall in the price of oil over the period. Demand then fell sharply and by 1987 had halved to 0.12 tonnes, a fall of 50 per cent in response to an approximate 900 per cent rise in price. Between 1987 and 1998, when prices were broadly in the $15-$20 a barrel range, demand too was broadly constant. In 1998, it was 0.1 tonnes per £1 000 of GDP. The evidence would suggest, therefore, that whilst demand is extremely inelastic over a 12 month period, over a longer period of 5-10 years it is much higher.

Companies pay 'high price' for transatlantic business air fares

British companies are paying up to 76 per cent more for transatlantic business air fares than their counterparts elsewhere in Europe, according to a study published yesterday by American Express, the world's largest travel agent. This was calculated on a cost-per-mile basis using a basket of full business class fares from 10 other European departure points. For instance, a business traveller flying from London to New York would pay £3 230 - 55 per cent more than a business class ticket from Frankfurt and 46 per cent more than the fare from Paris. The gap is also widening. Over the past 5 years, international business class fares from the UK have risen by 35 per cent, while those from France have gone up by only 12 per cent.

British Airways (BA) rejected suggestions that, as the largest transatlantic operator, it was exploiting business travellers. 'Business class fares are a product of market demand, not any exploitation. We compete with 11 airlines (from London) ... across the Atlantic each day and we face considerably more competition at Heathrow than any other European airline does at its home hub' said the airline.

However, many argue that the problem is the restricted access of airlines to London Heathrow. The airport is the most important airline hub in Europe. A 'hub' is an airport which many passengers use to change planes to fly onto another destination. For instance, a traveller from New York to Zurich may not fly direct, but change at Heathrow. There is only a fixed number of landing and takeoff 'slots' from Heathrow, which is used to 100 per cent capacity, unlike most other European airports. These slots have already been allocated to airlines. So it is not possible for a company like British Midland to set up at Heathrow offering transatlantic flights. In practice, transatlantic flyers only have a choice of BA, Virgin Atlantic, American Airlines and United Airlines.

The 3 per cent fare increase announced by BA at the start of this month is further evidence that the airlines have a stranglehold on the market. Passengers could vote with their feet and fly to the US via Amsterdam or Paris, but this would involve much longer journey times and the discomfort of changing planes. Given business travellers rarely pay for their own ticket since they are paid for by their employers, travellers will continue to want to fly out of Heathrow whatever the cost.

Source: adapted from the *Financial Times*, 10.2.2000.

1. Why is Heathrow a relatively more popular airport for transatlantic flights than other European airports?
2. Compare the price elasticity of demand from Heathrow for transatlantic flights with other European airports such as Amsterdam or Paris.
3. To what extent do you think prices would fall from Heathrow if its capacity were expanded and the number of flights to the US were allowed to rise?

Summary

1. Income elasticity of demand measures the responsiveness of quantity demanded to changes in income.
2. Cross elasticity of demand measures the responsiveness of quantity demanded of one good to the change in price of another good.
3. Price elasticity of supply measures the responsiveness of quantity supplied to changes in price.
4. The value of elasticity of supply is determined by the availability of substitutes and by time factors.
5. The price elasticity of demand for a good will determine whether a change in the price of a good results in a change in expenditure on the good.

Income elasticity of demand

The demand for a good will change if there is a change in consumers' incomes. INCOME ELASTICITY OF DEMAND is a measure of that change. If the demand for housing increased by 20 per cent when incomes increased by 5 per cent, then the income elasticity of demand would be said to be positive and relatively high. If the demand for food were unchanged when income rose, then income elasticity would be zero. A fall in demand for a good when income rises gives a negative value to income elasticity of demand.

The formula for measuring income elasticity of demand is:

$$\frac{\text{percentage change in quantity demanded}}{\text{percentage change in income}}$$

So the numerical value of income elasticity of a 20 per cent rise in demand for housing when incomes rise by 5 per cent is +20/+5 or +4. The number is positive because both the 20 per cent and the 5 per cent are positive. On the other hand, a rise in income of 10 per cent which led to a fall in quantity demanded of a product of 5 per cent would have an income elasticity of -5/+10 or $-\frac{1}{2}$. The minus sign in -5 shows the fall in quantity demanded of the product. Examples of items with a high income elasticity of demand are holidays and recreational activities, whereas washing up liquid tends to have a low income elasticity of demand.

Just as with price elasticity, it is sometimes easier to use alternative formulae to calculate income elasticity of demand. The above formula is equivalent to:

$$\frac{\Delta Q}{Q} \div \frac{\Delta Y}{Y}$$

where Δ is change, Q is quantity demanded and Y is income. Rearranging the formula gives another two alternatives:

$$\frac{Y}{Q} \times \frac{\Delta Q}{\Delta Y} \quad \text{or} \quad \frac{\Delta Q}{Q} \times \frac{Y}{\Delta Y}$$

Examples of the calculation of income elasticity of demand are given in Table 9.1.

Table 9.1 *Calculation of income elasticity of demand*

Original quantity demanded	New quantity demanded	Original income (£)	New income (£)	$\frac{\Delta Q}{Q} \div \frac{\Delta Y}{Y}$	Numerical value
				Income elasticity of demand	
20	25	16	18	5/20 ÷ 2/16	+2
100	200	20	25	100/100 ÷ 5/20	+4
50	40	25	30	-10/50 ÷ 5/25	-1
60	60	80	75	0/60 ÷ -5/80	0
60	40	27	30	-20/60 ÷ 3/27	-3

Question 1

Table 9.2

£

	Original		New	
	Quantity demanded	Income	Quantity demanded	Income
(a)	100	10	120	14
(b)	15	6	20	7
(c)	50	25	40	35
(d)	12	100	15	125
(e)	200	10	250	11
(f)	25	20	30	18

Calculate the income elasticity of demand from the data in Table 9.2.

Cross elasticity of demand

The quantity demanded of a particular good varies according to the price of other goods. In unit 8 it was argued that a rise in price of a good such as beef would increase the quantity demanded of a substitute such as pork. On the other hand, a rise in price of a good such as cheese would lead to a fall in the quantity demanded of a complement such as macaroni. CROSS ELASTICITY OF DEMAND measures the responsiveness of the quantity demanded of one good to changes in the price of another. For instance, it is a measure of the extent to which demand for pork increases when the price of beef goes up; or the extent to which the demand for macaroni falls when the price of cheese increases.

The formula for measuring cross elasticity of demand for good X is:

$$\frac{\text{percentage change in quantity demanded of good X}}{\text{percentage change in price of another good Y}}$$

Two goods which are substitutes will have a positive cross elasticity. An increase (positive) in the price of one good, such as gas, leads to an increase (positive) in the quantity demanded of a substitute such as electricity. Two goods which are complements will have a negative cross elasticity. An increase (positive) in the price of one good such as sand leads to a fall (negative) in demand of a complement such as cement. The cross elasticity of two goods which have little relationship to each other would be zero. For instance, a rise in the price of cars of 10 per cent is likely to have no effect (i.e. 0 per cent change) on the demand for Tipp-Ex.

As with price and income elasticity, it is sometimes more convenient to use alternative formulae for cross elasticity of demand. These are:

$$\text{Cross elasticity of good X} = \frac{\Delta Q_X}{Q_X} \div \frac{\Delta P_Y}{P_Y}$$

or

$$\frac{P_Y}{Q_X} \times \frac{\Delta Q_X}{\Delta P_Y}$$

Question 2

Explain what value you would put on the cross elasticity of demand of: (a) gas for electricity; (b) tennis shorts for tennis rackets; (c) luxury cars for petrol; (d) paper for tights; (e) compact discs for audio cassettes; (f) Sainsbury's own brand baked beans for Tesco's own brand baked beans; (g) Virgin Cola for Coca Cola.

Price elasticity of supply

Price elasticity of demand measures the responsiveness of changes in quantity demanded to changes in price. Equally, the responsiveness of quantity supplied to changes in price can also be measured - this is called PRICE ELASTICITY OF SUPPLY. The formula for measuring the price elasticity of supply is:

$$\frac{\text{percentage change in quantity supplied}}{\text{percentage change in price}}$$

This is equivalent to:

$$\frac{\Delta Q}{Q} \div \frac{\Delta P}{P}$$

or

$$\frac{P}{Q} \times \frac{\Delta Q}{\Delta P}$$

where Q is quantity supplied and P is price.

The supply curve is upward sloping (i.e. an increase in price leads to an increase in quantity supplied and vice versa). Therefore price elasticity of supply will be positive because the top and bottom of the formula will be either both positive or both negative.

As with price elasticity of demand, different ranges of elasticity are given different names. Price elasticity of supply is:

- **perfectly inelastic** (zero) if there is no response in supply to a change in price;
- **inelastic** (between zero and one) if there is a less than proportionate response in supply to a change in price;
- **unitary** (one) if the percentage change in quantity supplied equals the percentage change in price;
- **elastic** (between one and infinity) if there is a more than proportionate response in supply to a change in price;
- **perfectly elastic** (infinite) if producers are prepared to supply any amount at a given price.

These various elasticities are shown in Figure 9.1.

It should be noted that any straight line supply curve passing through the origin has an elasticity of supply equal to 1. This is best understood if we take the formula:

$$\frac{P}{Q} \times \frac{\Delta Q}{\Delta P}$$

$\Delta Q / \Delta P$ is the inverse of (i.e. 1 divided by) the slope of the line, whilst P/Q, assuming that the line passes through the origin, is the slope of the line. The two multiplied together must always equal 1.

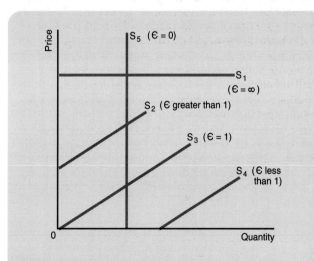

Figure 9.1 *Elasticity of supply*
The elasticity of supply of a straight line supply curve varies depending upon the gradient of the line and whether it passes through the origin.

Question 3

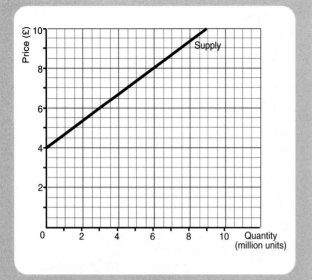

Figure 9.2
Calculate from Figure 9.2 the elasticity of supply of a change in price from: (a) £4 to £6; (b) £6 to £8; (c) £8 to £10; (d) £9 to £7; (e) £7 to £5.

Determinants of elasticity of supply

As with price elasticity of demand, there are two factors which determine supply elasticity across a wide range of products.

Availability of substitutes Substitutes here are not consumer substitutes but producer substitutes. These are goods which a producer can easily produce as alternatives. For instance, one model of a car is a good producer substitute for another model in the same range because the car manufacturer can easily switch resources on its production line. On the other hand, carrots are not substitutes for cars. The farmer cannot easily switch from the production of carrots to the production of cars. If a product has many substitutes then producers can quickly and easily alter the pattern of production if its price rises or falls. Hence its elasticity will be relatively high. But if a product has few or no substitutes, then producers will find it difficult to respond flexibly to variations in price. If there is a fall in price, a producer may have no alternative but either to carry on producing much the same quantity as before or withdrawing from the market. Price elasticity of supply is therefore low.

Time The shorter the time period, the more difficult firms find it to switch from making one product to another. During the late 1970s when skateboarding first became a craze, the supply of skateboards was relatively inelastic. Suppliers were overwhelmed with orders and were initially unable to expand production sufficiently to cope with demand. Supply elasticity was therefore low. In the longer term new firms came into the market, existing firms expanded their production facilities and price elasticity of supply rose. This has also been the case with videos, personal stereos and CD players.

Price elasticity of demand and total expenditure

Price elasticity of demand and changes in total expenditure on a product are linked. Total expenditure can be calculated by multiplying price and quantity:

Total expenditure = quantity purchased x price

For instance, if you bought 5 apples at 10 pence each, your total expenditure would be 50 pence. If the price of apples went up, you might spend more, less, or the same on apples depending upon your price elasticity of demand for apples. Assume that the price of apples went up 40 per cent to 14p each. You might react by buying fewer apples. If you now buy 4 apples (i.e. a fall in demand of 20 per cent), the price elasticity of demand is $20 \div 40$ or $\frac{1}{2}$. Your expenditure on apples will also rise (from 50 pence to 56 pence). If you buy two apples (i.e. a fall in quantity demanded of 60 per cent), your elasticity of demand is $60 \div 40$ or $1\frac{1}{2}$ and your expenditure on apples will fall (from 50 pence to 28 pence).

These relationships are what should be expected. If the percentage change in price is larger than the percentage change in quantity demanded (i.e. elasticity is less than 1, or inelastic), then expenditure will rise when prices rise. If the percentage change in price is smaller than the percentage change in quantity demanded (i.e. elasticity is greater than 1 or elastic), then spending will fall as prices rise. If the percentage change in price is the same as the change in quantity demanded (i.e. elasticity is unity), expenditure will remain unchanged because the percentage rise in price will be equal and opposite to the percentage fall in demand.

key terms

Cross elasticity of demand - a measure of the responsiveness of quantity demanded of one good to a change in price of another good. It is measured by dividing the percentage change in quantity demanded of one good by the percentage change in price of the other good.
Income elasticity of demand - a measure of the responsiveness of quantity demanded to a change in income. It is measured by dividing the percentage change in quantity demanded by the percentage change in income.
Price elasticity of supply - a measure of the responsiveness of quantity supplied to a change in price. It is measured by dividing the percentage change in quantity supplied by the percentage change in price.

Question 4

Table 9.3 *Estimates of price elasticities of demand for selected household foods*

	Estimated price elasticity
Milk and cream	-0.19
of which:	
liquid wholemilk and low fat milks, full price	-0.29
Cheese	-1.20
Carcass meat	-1.37
Other meat and meat products	-0.49
of which:	
bacon and ham, uncooked	-0.70
broiler chicken, uncooked	-0.13
other poultry, uncooked	-0.85
frozen convenience meat and meat products	-0.94
Sugar and preserves	-0.24
Fresh potatoes	-0.21
Fresh green vegetables	-0.58
Other fresh vegetables	-0.27
Processed vegetables	-0.54
of which:	
Frozen peas	-1.12
Frozen chips and other frozen convenience potato products	-0.29
Processed fruit and fruit products	-1.05
of which:	
fruit juices	-0.80
Bread	-0.09
Other cereals and cereal products	-0.94
of which:	
cakes and pastries	-0.37
frozen convenience cereal foods	-0.07

Source: adapted from HMSO, *Household Food Consumption and Expenditure.*

(a) Suggest reasons why the demand for some foods in Table 9.3 is more price elastic than the demand for others.
(b) An increase in the price of which foods would be most likely to lead to
  (i) the greatest and
  (ii) the least change in household expenditure?
Explain your answer.

Applied economics

Cross elasticities of demand for food

Many foods are substitutes for each other. Tea is a substitute for coffee; oranges are substitutes for apples; butter is a substitute for margarine. Economic theory would suggest that these goods would therefore have a positive cross elasticity of demand. An increase in the price of one good would lead to an increase in demand of the substitute good, whilst a fall in price of one good would lead to a fall in demand of another.

Evidence from the General Household Survey gives some support for this. Table 9.4 shows estimates of the cross elasticity of demand for 10 foods, grouped into four categories. The estimates are based on UK data for 1981-88. The cross elasticities are shown in black.

The cross elasticities of demand of butter for margarine and margarine for butter are 0.06 and 0.08 respectively. So a 10 per cent increase in the price of margarine will lead to a 0.6 per cent increase in the demand for butter, whilst a 10 per cent increase in the price of butter will lead to a 0.8 per cent increase in the demand for margarine.

Of the three fruits in Table 9.4, apples and pears have a relatively high cross elasticity. Pears seem to be a good substitute for apples. A 10 per cent increase in the price of apples leads to a 2.8 per cent rise in the quantity demanded of pears. Interestingly though, apples are less

good a substitute for pears since a 10 per cent increase in the price of pears results in only a 0.5 per cent increase in the demand for apples. The data would suggest that apples and oranges are not substitutes at all since their cross elasticities are negative at - 0.22 and - 0.09. Similarly pears and oranges have negative cross elasticities.

One explanation of the negative cross elasticities in Table 9.4 would be in terms of income and substitution effects. For instance, a rise in the price of coffee will lead to more tea being demanded because tea is now relatively cheaper (the substitution effect of the price rise). However, the real income of consumers (what they can buy with their money income) will have declined. Hence they buy less coffee (a drop of 1.4 per cent for every 10 per cent rise in price) but also less tea (the income effect). The data would suggest that this income effect is more significant than the substitution effect in the case of tea when the price of coffee increases.

Table 9.4 also shows (in red) the price elasticities of demand for the 10 food products. The demand for butter, margarine, tea, instant coffee and apples is price inelastic, whilst the demand for beef and veal, mutton and lamb, pork, oranges and pears is price elastic.

Table 9.4 *Estimates of price and cross-price elasticities of demand for certain foods, 1981-1988*

	Elasticity with respect to the price of	
	Tea	Instant coffee
Tea	-0.33	-0.01
Instant coffee	-0.01	-0.14

	Elasticity with respect to the price of		
	Beef and veal	Mutton and lamb	Pork
Beef and veal	-1.23	0.04	0.02
Mutton and lamb	0.10	-1.75	-0.11
Pork	0.05	-0.11	-1.57

	Elasticity with respect to the price of	
	Butter	Margarine
Butter	-0.38	0.06
Margarine	0.08	-0.29

	Elasticity with respect to the price of		
	Oranges	Apples	Pears
Oranges	-1.44	-0.22	-0.11
Apples	-0.09	-0.19	0.05
Pears	-0.28	0.28	-1.70

Source: adapted from HMSO, *Household Food Consumption and Expenditure.*

Leisure goods and services

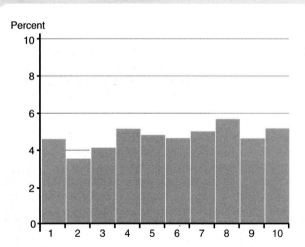

Figure 9.3 *Expenditure on leisure goods as a percentage of total expenditure by gross income decile group*
Source: adapted from *Family Spending 1997-98*, Office for National Statistics.

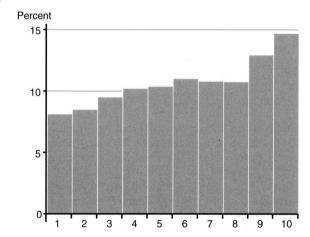

Figure 9.4 *Expenditure on leisure services as a percentage of total expenditure by gross income decile group*
Source: adapted from *Family Spending 1997-98*, Office for National Statistics.

Table 9.5 *Leisure goods and leisure services as a percentage of total household expenditure.*

	1990	1995-96	1997-98
Leisure goods	5	5	5
Leisure services	9	11	12

Source: adapted from *Family Spending 1997-98*, Office for National Statistics.

Decile groups
A population can be split into ten equal groups. These are called decile groups. In Table 9.6 the groups are households, which are split according to their gross income. So the first decile group is the tenth of households which have the lowest income. The fifth decile group is the tenth of households between 40 and 50 per cent of the total, whilst the tenth decile group is made up of the highest 10 per cent of households by gross income. Data for the other 7 deciles groups is available but is not printed here in order to simplify the data.

Table 9.6 *Household expenditure on leisure goods and services by gross income decile group, 1997-98*

	average weekly expenditure £		
	First decile	**Fifth decile**	**Tenth decile**
Leisure goods	4.40	13.00	38.20
Book, maps and diaries	0.20	1.00	4.30
Newspapers	1.10	2.00	2.80
Magazines and periodicals	0.30	8.00	1.60
TVs, videos, computers and audio equipment	1.50	4.60	15.70
Sports and camping equipment	0.10	0.50	2.00
Toys and hobbies	0.60	1.30	3.40
Photography and camcorders	0.20	0.50	3.80
Horticultural goods, plants	0.40	2.30	4.60
Leisure services	7.90	27.60	107.20
Cinema and theatre	0.20	0.60	2.40
Sports admissions and subscriptions	0.30	1.60	5.60
TV, video and satellite rental, television licences	2.00	3.50	4.30
Miscellaneous entertainments	0.20	0.90	3.10
Educational and training	0.40	1.80	23.00
Hotel and holiday in UK	0.40	2.90	5.50
Hotel and holiday abroad	1.00	4.70	30.90
Other incidental holiday	0.00	2.70	12.50
Gambling payments	1.60	4.50	4.90
Cash gifts, donations	1.10	4.40	15.00
Household income	less than £88	£254-329	£847+

Source: adapted from *Family Spending 1997-98*, Office for National Statistics.

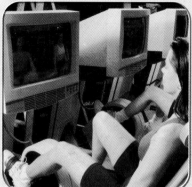

Measuring income elasticity of demand

Income elasticity of demand is measured by dividing the percentage change in quantity demanded of a good or a basket of goods by the percentage change in income of consumers. Quantity demanded is a physical number, like 100 washing machines or 1 000 shirts. However, when data for quantity is not available, a good proxy variable is expenditure. This is quantity times price. If prices remain the same as expenditure changes, then the percentage change in quantity will be the same as the percentage change in expenditure.

1. Describe how spending on leisure goods and services (a) has changed over time and (b) varies with income.
2. (a) Using Table 9.5 and Figures 9.3 and 9.4, explain whether leisure goods or leisure services are likely to have the higher income elasticity of demand.
   (b) Using Table 9.6, explain which leisure goods or services are likely to have the highest income elasticity.
3. A newspaper company is considering diversifying by buying a smaller company which publishes books. Discuss (a) whether books have a better long term sales future than newspapers and (b) whether the newspaper side of the company might soon be less important than the book publishing side.

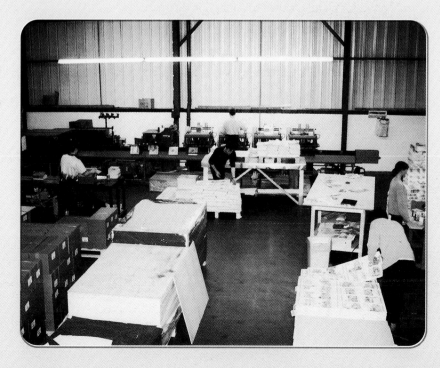

Summary

1. An increase in income will lead to an increase in demand for normal goods but a fall in demand for inferior goods.
2. Normal goods have a positive income elasticity whilst inferior goods have a negative elasticity.
3. A Giffen good is one where a rise in price leads to a rise in quantity demanded. This occurs because the positive substitution effect of the price change is outweighed by the negative income effect.
4. Upward sloping demand curves may occur if the good is a Giffen good, if it has snob or speculative appeal or if consumers judge quality by the price of a product.

Normal and inferior goods

The pattern of demand is likely to change when income changes. It would be reasonable to assume that consumers will increase their demand for most goods when their income increases. Goods for which this is the case are called NORMAL GOODS.

However, an increase in income will result in a fall in demand for other goods. These goods are called INFERIOR GOODS. There will be a fall in demand because consumers will react to an increase in their income by purchasing products which are perceived to be of better quality. Commonly quoted examples of inferior goods are:

● bread - consumers switch from this cheap, filling food to more expensive meat or convenience foods as their incomes increase;
● margarine - consumers switch from margarine to butter, although this has become less true recently with greater health awareness;
● bus transport - consumers switch from buses to their own cars when they can afford to buy their own car.

A good can be both a normal and an inferior good depending upon the level of income. Bread may be a normal good for people on low incomes (i.e. they buy more bread when their income increases). But it may be an inferior good for higher income earners.

Normal and inferior goods are shown on Figure 10.1. D_1 is the demand curve for a normal good. It is upward sloping because demand increases as income increases. D_2 is the demand curve for an inferior good. It is downward sloping, showing that demand falls as income increases. D_3 is the demand curve for a good which is normal at low levels of income, but is inferior at higher levels of income.

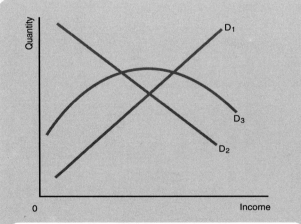

Figure 10.1 *Normal and inferior goods*
On the quantity-income diagram, a normal good such as D_1 has an upward sloping curve, whilst an inferior good such as D_2 has a downward sloping curve. D_3 shows a good which is normal at low levels of income but is inferior at higher levels of income.

Question 1

Table 10.1 *Estimated household food consumption in Great Britain*

	Grammes per person per week			
	1985	1990	1995	1997
Sugar	238	171	136	128
Chicken	196	226	237	254
Bananas	80	125	176	195
Bread	878	797	756	746
Pickles and sauces	61	67	80	92
Butter	80	46	36	38

Source: adapted from *Annual Abstract of Statistics*, Office for National Statistics.

Household incomes rose between each of the years 1985, 1990, 1995 and 1997. Assuming that all other factors remained constant, which of the goods shown in Table 10.1 are normal goods and which are inferior goods?

Inferior goods and income elasticity

Inferior goods can be distinguished from normal goods by their income elasticity of demand. The formula for measuring income elasticity is:

$$\frac{\text{percentage change in quantity demanded}}{\text{percentage change in income}}$$

A normal good will always have a positive income elasticity because quantity demanded and income either both increase (giving a plus divided by a plus) or both decrease (giving a minus divided by a minus). An inferior good, however, will always have a negative elasticity because the signs on the top and bottom of the formula will always be opposite (a plus divided by a minus or a minus divided by a plus giving a minus answer in both cases).

For instance, if the demand for bread falls by 2 per cent when incomes rise by 10 per cent then it is an inferior good. Its income elasticity is -2/+10 or -0.2.

Giffen goods

A GIFFEN GOOD is a special sort of inferior good. Alfred Marshall (1842-1924), an eminent economist and author of a best selling textbook of his day, claimed that another eminent economist, Sir Robert Giffen (1837-1910), had observed that the consumption of bread increased as its price increased. The argument was that bread was a staple food for low income consumers. A rise in its price would not deter people from buying as much as before. But 'poor' people would now have so little extra money to spend on meat or other luxury foods that they would abandon their demand for these and instead buy more bread to fill up their stomachs. The result was that a rise in the price of bread led to a rise in the demand for bread.

Another way of explaining this phenomenon is to use the concepts of INCOME and SUBSTITUTION EFFECTS. When a good changes in price, the quantity demanded will be changed by the sum of the substitution effect and the income effect.

● **Substitution effect**. If the price of a good rises, consumers will buy less of that good and more of others because it is now relatively more expensive than other goods. If the price of a good falls, consumers will buy more of that good and less of others. These changes in quantity demanded solely due to the relative change in prices are known as the substitution effect of a price change.
● **Income effect**. If the price of a good rises, the real income of consumers will fall. They will not be able to buy the same basket of goods and services as before. Consumers can react to this fall in real income in one of two ways. If the good is a normal good, they will buy less of the good. If the good is an inferior good, they will buy more of the good. These changes in quantity demanded caused by a change in real income are known as the income effect of the price change.

For a normal good the substitution effect and the income effect both work in the same direction. A rise in price leads to a fall in quantity demanded because the relative price of the good has risen. It also leads to a fall in quantity demanded because consumers' real incomes have now fallen. So a rise in price will always lead to a fall in quantity demanded, and vice versa.

For an inferior good, the substitution effect and income effect work in opposite directions. A rise in price leads to a fall in quantity demanded because the relative price of the good has risen. But it leads to a rise in quantity demanded because consumers' real incomes have fallen. However, the substitution effect outweighs the income effect because overall it is still true for an inferior good that a rise in price leads to an overall fall in quantity demanded.

A Giffen good is a special type of inferior good. A rise

in price leads to a fall in quantity demanded because of the substitution effect but a rise in quantity demanded because of the income effect. However, the income effect outweighs the substitution effect, leading to rises in quantity demanded. For instance, if a 10p rise in the price of a standard loaf leads to a 4 per cent fall in the demand for bread because of the substitution effect, but a 10 per cent rise in demand because of the income effect, then the net effect will be a 6 per cent rise in the demand for bread. The relationship between normal, inferior and Giffen goods and their income and substitution effects is summarised in Table 10.2.

Giffen goods are an economic curiosity. In theory they could exist, but no economist has ever found an example of such a good in practice. There is no evidence even that Sir Robert Giffen ever claimed that bread had an upward sloping demand curve - it crept into textbooks via Alfred Marshall and has remained there ever since!

Type of good	Effect on quantity demanded of a rise in price		
	Substitution effect	Income effect	Total effect
Normal good	Fall	Fall	Fall
Inferior good	Fall	Rise	Fall because substitution effect > income effect
Giffen good	Fall	Rise	Rise because substitution effect < income effect

Table 10.2 *Substitution and income effects on quantity demanded of a rise in price for normal, inferior and Giffen goods*

Question 2

Table 10.3

Good	Change in price (pence per unit)	Change in quantity demanded as a result of	
		income effect	substitution effect
Bacon	+10	+5%	-8%
Bus rides	+15	+7%	-5%
Jeans	-100	+1%	+5%
Baked beans	-2	-1%	+4%
Compact discs	-150	+4%	+3%

An economist claims that she has observed the effects detailed in Table 10.3 resulting solely from a change in price of a product. Which of these products are normal goods, which are inferior and which are Giffen goods?

Upward sloping demand curves

Demand curves are usually downward sloping. However, there are possible reasons why the demand curve for some goods may be upward sloping.

Giffen goods Giffen goods, a type of inferior good, have been discussed above.

Goods with snob appeal Some goods are bought mainly because they confer status on the buyer. Examples might be diamonds, fur coats or large cars. The argument is that these goods are demanded because few people can afford to buy them because their price is high. If large numbers of people could afford to buy them, then the demand (the quantity buyers would buy) would be low. This might be true for some individual consumers, but economists have not found any proof that it is true for markets as a whole. Whilst some might buy diamonds only because they are expensive, the majority of consumers would buy more diamonds if their price fell because they like diamonds. So there must be some doubt as to whether snob appeal does give rise to upward sloping demand curves.

Speculative goods Throughout most of 1987, stock markets worldwide boomed. Share prices were at an all time high and the demand for shares was high too. But in October 1987 share prices slumped on average between 20 and 30 per cent. Overnight the demand for shares fell. This could be taken as evidence of an upward sloping demand curve. The higher the price of shares, the higher the demand because buyers associate high share prices with large speculative gains in the future. However, most economists would argue that what is being seen is a shift in the demand curve. The demand curve is drawn on the assumption that expectations of future gain are constant. When share prices or the price of any speculative good fall, buyers revise their expectations downwards. At any given share price they are willing to buy fewer shares, which pushes the demand curve backwards to the left.

Quality goods Some consumers judge quality by price. They automatically assume that a higher priced good must be of better quality than a similar lower priced good. Hence, the higher the price the greater the quantity demanded. As with snob appeal goods, this may be true for some individuals but there is no evidence to suggest that this is true for consumers as a whole. There have been examples where goods that have been re-packaged, heavily advertised and increased in price have increased their sales. But this is an example of a shift to the right in the demand curve caused by advertising and repackaging rather than of an upward sloping demand curve.

In conclusion, it can be seen that there are various reasons why in theory demand curves might be upward sloping. But few, if any, such goods have been found in reality. The downward sloping demand curve seems to be true of nearly all goods.

Question 3

Stock market analysts made redundant after the crash.

Before the Stock Market crash of October 1987 which wiped out approximately 25 per cent of the value of shares on the London Stock Exchange, the number of shares traded was considerably more than after the crash. For instance, on 29 September 1987, the FT ordinary share index (a measure of the average price of shares listed on the Stock Exchange) stood at 1853.7 and 731.7 million shares were bought and sold. On 27 September 1990, the Ordinary Share Index had fallen to 1535.7 whilst the number of shares traded was 376.7 million.

To what extent can this data be used as evidence to support the existence of an upward sloping demand curve for shares?

key terms

Giffen good - a special type of inferior good where demand increases when price increases.
Income effect - the impact on quantity demanded of a change in price due to a change in consumers' real income which results from this change in price.
Inferior good - a good where demand falls when income increases (i.e. it has a negative income elasticity of demand).
Normal good - a good where demand increases when income increases (i.e. it has a positive income elasticity of demand).
Substitution effect - the impact on quantity demanded due to a change in price, assuming that consumers' real incomes stay the same (i.e. the impact of a change in price excluding the income effect).

Applied economics

Income elasticities and inferior goods

Table 10.4 gives estimates of the income elasticity of demand for food in the UK. The top half of the table refers to 1985-87, the bottom half to 1995-97. The columns refer to quintiles. A quintile is simply one fifth. Statisticians also often use quartiles. A quartile is one fourth. In Table 10.4, individuals have been ranked in order of magnitude of average income per person in a household. The poorest 20 per cent or fifth by income per person form the lowest quintile. The richest 20 per cent or fifth by income per person form the highest quintile. This is illustrated in Figure 10.2. The quintile boundaries referred to in Table 10.4 occur at the intersection of each quintile. With five quintiles, there are four boundaries. In 1985-87, the average income per person earned in a household at the lowest boundary was £56.20 (expressed at December 1997 prices to remove the distorting effect of inflation). One fifth of individuals lived in households where average income per person was less than £56.20. Fourth fifths of individuals therefore living in households whose income per person was more than £56.20. At the top boundary, one fifth of individuals averaged income of more than £138.38, whilst fourth fifths earned less.

The data show that income elasticity of demand for food tends to decline as income increases. For instance, in 1995-97, the income elasticity of demand for milk and cream fell from 0.16 for those on the bottom quintile income boundary to -0.02 for those at the top quintile income boundary. Over time there were also changes. The income elasticity of milk and cream was 0.26 in 1985-87 for those whose average income was £56.20 per week, but this fell to 0.16 in 1995-97 for the same bottom quintile boundary with an average income of £69.41. The exception to this trend seems to be the behaviour of those at the highest quintile income boundary in 1995-97, where income elasticities of demand tend to be higher for certain products, such as fish and vegetables, than for lower income groups.

Most foods seem to be normal goods although their income elasticity of demand is very low. A 10 per cent increase in income, for instance, will only increase demand for, say, cheese by 2.5 per cent for those on £69.41 per week in 1995-97. A number of foods, however, are inferior goods. Eggs and sugar and preserves, for instance, were inferior goods for the highest three of the four quintile boundary groups in 1995-97.

Table 10.4 *Estimated income elasticities at quintile boundaries[1] of income per person*

	Elasticity			
1985-87				
Milk and cream	0.26	0.19	0.03	-0.14
Cheese	0.38	0.34	0.30	0.21
Meat and meat products	0.31	0.28	0.17	0.15
Fish	0.38	0.39	0.21	0.11
Eggs	0.18	0.15	-0.12	-0.23
Fats and oils	0.26	0.22	0.01	-0.24
Sugar and preserves	0.21	0.17	-0.16	-0.48
Vegetables (inc. potatoes)	0.22	0.18	0.13	0.10
Fruit	0.44	0.48	0.41	0.32
Cereals (inc. bread)	0.19	0.17	0.06	0.01
Beverages	0.36	0.32	0.12	-0.06
Miscellaneous	0.31	0.28	0.16	0.13
All food	0.28	0.25	0.13	0.07
Quintile boundaries of income £/person/wk at December 1997 prices	56.20	70.11	94.63	138.38
1995-97				
Milk and cream	0.16	0.06	-0.02	-0.02
Cheese	0.25	0.23	0.18	0.22
Meat and meat products	0.21	0.19	0.17	0.22
Fish	0.20	0.16	0.17	0.34
Eggs	0.06	-0.01	-0.19	-0.18
Fats and oils	0.15	0.02	-0.07	-0.03
Sugar and preserves	0.10	-0.12	-0.30	-0.33
Vegetables (inc. potatoes)	0.20	0.18	0.15	0.28
Fruit	0.35	0.33	0.29	0.35
Cereals (inc. bread)	0.15	0.13	0.07	0.19
Beverages	0.29	0.21	0.11	0.01
Miscellaneous	0.20	0.25	0.23	0.40
All food	0.20	0.17	0.13	0.21
Quintile boundaries of income £/person/wk at December 1997 prices	69.41	97.51	135.64	196.37

1. quintile income boundaries divide households into lowest 20%, 40%, 60% and 80% of income per person.

Source: adapted from MAFF, *National Food Survey* 1997.

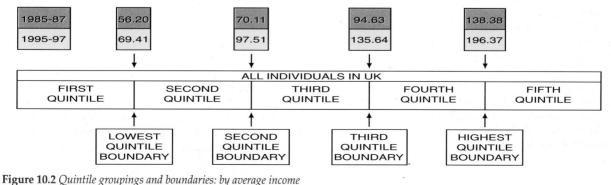

Income (£ per week per person at Dec 1997 prices)

| 1985-87 | 56.20 | 70.11 | 94.63 | 138.38 |
| 1995-97 | 69.41 | 97.51 | 135.64 | 196.37 |

ALL INDIVIDUALS IN UK

| FIRST QUINTILE | SECOND QUINTILE | THIRD QUINTILE | FOURTH QUINTILE | FIFTH QUINTILE |

LOWEST QUINTILE BOUNDARY · SECOND QUINTILE BOUNDARY · THIRD QUINTILE BOUNDARY · HIGHEST QUINTILE BOUNDARY

Figure 10.2 *Quintile groupings and boundaries: by average income*

DATA QUESTION

Tourism

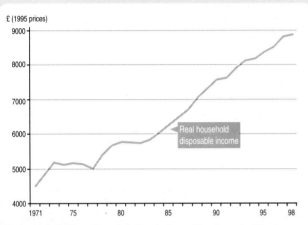

£ (1995 prices)

Real household disposable income

Source: adapted from *Economic Trends Annual Supplement.*, Office for National Statistics.

Figure 10.3 *Real household disposable income per head at 1995 prices*

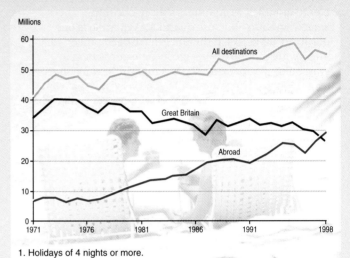

Millions

All destinations

Great Britain

Abroad

1. Holidays of 4 nights or more.
Source: adapted from *Social Trends*, Office for National Statistics.
Figure 10.4 *Holidays[1] taken by Great Britain residents: by destination*

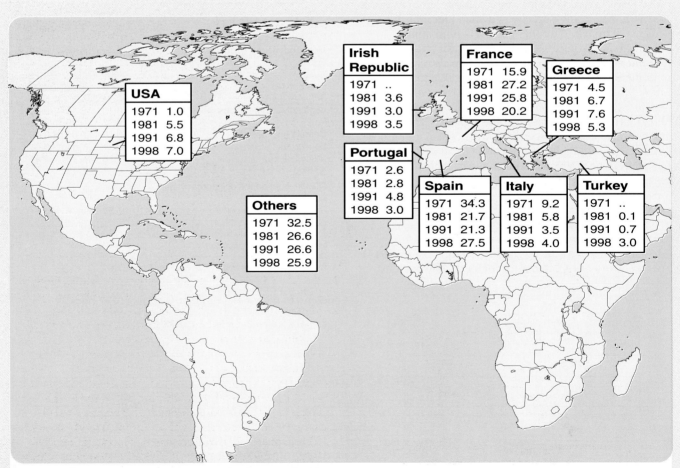

USA	
1971	1.0
1981	5.5
1991	6.8
1998	7.0

Irish Republic	
1971	..
1981	3.6
1991	3.0
1998	3.5

France	
1971	15.9
1981	27.2
1991	25.8
1998	20.2

Greece	
1971	4.5
1981	6.7
1991	7.6
1998	5.3

Portugal	
1971	2.6
1981	2.8
1991	4.8
1998	3.0

Others	
1971	32.5
1981	26.6
1991	26.6
1998	25.9

Spain	
1971	34.3
1981	21.7
1991	21.3
1998	27.5

Italy	
1971	9.2
1981	5.8
1991	3.5
1998	4.0

Turkey	
1971	..
1981	0.1
1991	0.7
1998	3.0

Source: adapted from *Social Trends*, Office for National Statistics.   1. Holidays of four nights or more taken by British residents; percentages.
Figure 10.5 *Holidays abroad[1] by destination, percentages*

Table 10.5 *Visits to the most popular tourist attractions*

Great Britain	1981	1991	1998		1981	1991	1998 Millions
Museums and galleries				**Historic houses**			
British Museum	2.6	5.1	5.6	**and monuments**			
National Gallery	2.7	4.3	4.8	Edinburgh Castle	0.8	1.0	1.2
Natural History Museum	3.7	1.6	1.9	Stonehenge	0.5	0.6	0.8
Tate Gallery	0.9	1.8	2.2				
Theme parks				**Wildlife parks and zoos**			
Blackpool Pleasure Beach	7.5	6.5	7.1	London Zoo	1.1	1.1	1.1
Alton Towers	1.6	2.0	2.8	Chester Zoo	..	0.9	0.9
Pleasure Beach, Great Yarmouth	..	2.5	1.4	Knowsley Safari Park	..	0.3	0.5

Source: adapted from *Social Trends*, Office for National Statistics.

Table 10.6 *Holiday taking: by social grade, 1995*

Great Britain			Percentages[1]
	Holidays in Britain	Holidays abroad	No holiday
AB	44	59	18
C1	37	47	31
C2	38	32	38
DE	28	20	57

1. Percentage of people in each social grade taking holidays in each location. Percentages do not sum to 100 because some people take holidays in Britain and abroad.
Source: adapted from *Social Trends*, Office for National Statistics.

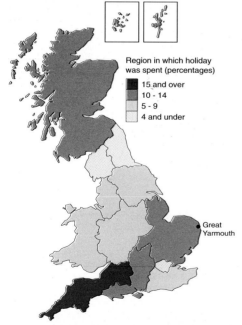

Region in which holiday was spent (percentages)
- 15 and over
- 10 - 14
- 5 - 9
- 4 and under

Great Yarmouth

1. Holidays of four nights or more taken by adults aged 16 and over.
Source: adapted from *Social Trends*, Office for National Statistics.

Figure 10.6 *Domestic holidays[1] taken by Great Britain residents: by destination 1998*

1. Describe the main trends in tourism shown in the data.
2. Using Figure 10.3, explain what you would expect to have happened to the number of holidays taken by UK residents and visits to tourist destinations since 1971, assuming that tourism is a normal good.
3. What evidence is there in the data that some tourist destinations and attractions are inferior goods?
4. Firms associated with tourism in the Great Yarmouth area are concerned that they are losing out in the expansion of tourism in the UK and abroad. (a) Suggest THREE reasons why a tourist might prefer to go to places such as Alton Towers, Cornwall, Spain or Florida rather than Great Yarmouth. (b) Discuss THREE strategies which stakeholders in the tourist industry in the Great Yarmouth area could adopt to make the income elasticity of demand more favourable to themselves.

Summary

1. Indirect taxes can be either ad valorem taxes or specific taxes.
2. The imposition of an indirect tax is likely to lead to a rise in the unit price of a good which is less than the unit value of the tax.
3. The incidence of indirect taxation is likely to fall on both consumer and producer.
4. The incidence of tax will fall wholly on the consumer if demand is perfectly inelastic or supply is perfectly elastic.
5. The incidence of tax will fall wholly on the producer if demand is perfectly elastic or supply is perfectly inelastic.

Indirect taxes and subsidies

An indirect tax is a tax on expenditure. The two major indirect taxes in the UK are VAT and excise duties.

VAT is an example of an AD VALOREM tax. The tax levied increases in proportion to the value of the tax base. In the case of VAT, the tax base is the price of the good. Most goods in the UK carry a $17\frac{1}{2}$ per cent VAT charge. Excise duties on the other hand are an example of a SPECIFIC or UNIT tax. The amount of tax levied does not change with the value of the goods but with the amount or volume of the goods purchased. So the excise duty on a bottle of wine is the same whether the bottle costs £5 or £500, but the VAT is 100 times more on the latter compared to the former. The main excise duties in the UK are on alcohol, tobacco and petrol. They should not be confused with customs duties which are levied on imports.

A SUBSIDY is a grant given by government to encourage the production or consumption of a particular good or service. Subsidies, for instance, may be given on essential items such as housing or bread. Alternatively they may be given to firms that employ disadvantaged workers such as the long term unemployed or handicapped people. Or they may be given to firms manufacturing domestically produced goods to help them be more competitive than imported goods.

The incidence of tax

Price theory can be used to analyse the impact of the imposition of an indirect tax on a good. Assume that a specific tax of £1 per bottle is imposed upon wine. This has the effect of reducing supply. Sellers of wine will now want to charge £1 extra per bottle sold. In Figure 11.1, this is shown by a vertical shift of £1 in the supply curve at every level of output. However many bottles are produced, sellers will want to charge £1 more per bottle and therefore there is a parallel shift upwards of the whole supply curve from S_1 to S_2.

The old equilibrium price was £3.30, at which price 60 million bottles were bought and sold. The introduction of

Question 1

The price of a litre of unleaded petrol at the pumps is made up as follows:

	pence
Petrol cost before tax	12.3
Excise duty	47.2
	59.5
VAT @ $17\frac{1}{2}$%	10.4
Price at the pumps	69.9

Calculate the new price of petrol if:
(a) an increase in the cost of crude oil pushed up the cost of petrol before tax from 12.3p to 12.8p.
(b) the government increased excise duty from 47.2 to 57.7p;
(c) VAT was reduced from 17.5 per cent to 15 per cent;
(d) the government subsidised the cost before tax by 2p a litre.
(For each part, assume that the price at the pumps is initially 69.9p.)

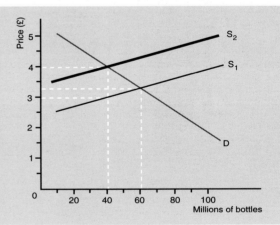

Figure 11.1 *The incidence of a specific tax*
The imposition of an indirect tax of £1 per unit on wine will push up the supply curve from S_1 to S_2. The vertical distance between the two supply curves at any given output is £1. As a consequence equilibrium price will rise from £3.30 to £4. The consumer therefore pays an extra 70p per bottle of wine. The other 30p of the tax is paid by the producer because the price it receives per bottle before tax falls from £3.30 to £3.

the £1 tax will raise price and reduce quantity demanded. The new equilibrium price is £4, at which price quantity demanded falls to 40 million bottles.

This result might seem surprising. The imposition of a £1 per bottle tax has only raised the price of a bottle by 70p and not the full £1 of the tax. This is because the INCIDENCE OF TAX is unlikely to fall totally on consumers. The incidence of tax measures the burden of tax upon the taxpayer. In this case the consumer has paid 70p of the tax. Therefore the other 30p which the government receives must have been paid by producers.

Question 2

In March 1999, Britain's aggregates producers lobbied the government to abandon plans to introduce a tax on extraction from quarries. Aggregates are materials such as stone used in construction. 40 per cent of all aggregates are bought by the government, mainly for road building and maintenance. The government argued that extraction led to substantial environmental costs. If a tax were imposed, it could lead to reductions in noise, dust, visual intrusion and damage to wildlife habitats as demand and production fell. The producers argued that the tax would fail in its objectives. Tarmac, the UK's largest aggregates producer, stated that: 'Aggregates are not a luxury. You cannot screw down demand just by imposing a tax.'

Source: adapted from the *Financial Times*, 5.3.1999.

(a) Explain, using a diagram, what would happen to supply if the government imposed a tax on aggregates.
(b) What, according to Tarmac, would be the impact on demand of the tax? Use your diagram to illustrate your answer.
(c) Explain who would end up paying most of the tax if Tarmac is correct in its assessment of the market.

Tax revenues

Using Figure 11.1 we can also show the change in total expenditure before and after imposition of the tax as well as the amount of tax revenue gained by the government. The government will receive total tax revenue of £1 x 40 million (the tax per unit x the quantity sold); hence tax revenues will be £40 million. Consumers will pay 70p x 40 million of this, whilst producers will pay 30p x 40 million. Consumers will therefore pay £28 million of tax whilst producers will pay £12 million. Total spending on wine will fall from £198 million (£3.30 x 60 million) to £160 million (£4 x 40 million). Revenues received by producers will fall from £198 million (£3.30 x 60 million) to £120 million (£3 x 40 million).

Ad valorem taxes

The above analysis can be extended to deal with ad valorem taxes. The imposition of an ad valorem tax will lead to an upwards shift in the supply curve. However, the higher the price, the greater will be the amount of the tax. Hence the shift will look as in Figure 11.2. Consumers will pay FG tax per unit whilst the incidence of tax on producers per unit will be HG.

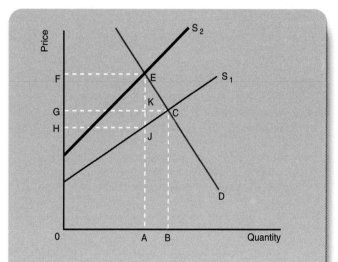

Figure 11.2 *The incidence of an ad valorem tax*
The imposition of an ad valorem tax will push the supply curve upwards from S_1 to S_2. The following gives the key facts about the change:
(a) original equilibrium price and quantity, OG and OB;
(b) new equilibrium price and quantity, OF and OA;
(c) incidence of tax per unit on consumers, GF;
(d) incidence of tax per unit on producers, HG;
(e) tax per unit in equilibrium, HF;
(f) total tax paid by consumers, GKEF;
(g) total tax paid by producers, GHJK;
(h) total tax revenue of government, FHJE;
(i) change in producers' revenue, OBCG - OAJH;
(j) change in consumers' expenditure, OBCG - OAEF.

Question 3

Table 11.1

Price (£)	Quantity demanded	Quantity supplied
4	16	4
6	12	6
8	8	8
10	4	10
12	0	12

(a) Draw the demand and supply curves from the data in Table 11.1.
(b) What is the equilibrium quantity demanded and supplied?
The government now imposes Value Added Tax of 50 per cent.
(c) Show the effect of this on the diagram.
(d) What is the new equilibrium quantity demanded and supplied?
(e) What is the new equilibrium price?
(f) What is the incidence of tax per unit on (i) the consumer and (ii) the producer?
(g) What is (i) the tax per unit and (ii) total government revenue from the tax?
(h) By how much will the before tax revenue of producers change?

Subsidies

A subsidy on a good will lead to an increase in supply, shifting the supply curve downwards and to the right. This is shown in Figure 11.3. It should be noted that a subsidy of AC will not lead to a fall in price of AC. Part of the subsidy, AB, will be appropriated by producers because of the higher unit cost of production of higher levels of output (shown by the upward sloping supply curve). Prices to consumers will only fall by BC.

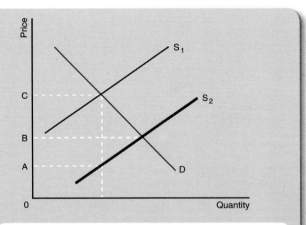

Figure 11.3 *The effect of a subsidy on price*
A subsidy of AC per unit will push the supply curve down from S_1 to S_2. The price to the consumer will fall by BC (i.e. less than the value of the subsidy per unit given).

Taxes and elasticity

The extent to which the tax incidence falls on consumers rather than producers depends upon the elasticities of demand and supply. Figure 11.4 shows a situation where either the supply curve is perfectly elastic or the demand curve is perfectly inelastic. In both cases, the vertical shift in the supply curve, which shows the value of the tax per unit, is identical to the final price rise. Therefore, all of the tax will be paid by consumers.

Figure 11.5, on the other hand, shows two cases where

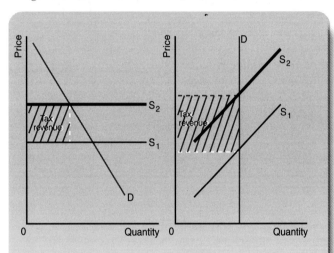

Figure 11.4 *Where the incidence of tax falls wholly on the consumer*
If supply is perfectly elastic or demand perfectly inelastic, then it can be seen from the graphs that the incidence of tax will fall wholly on consumers.

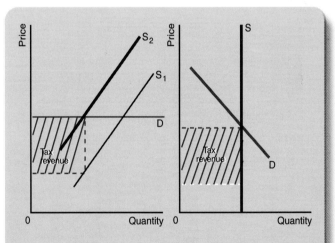

Figure 11.5 *Where the incidence of tax falls wholly on the producer*
If supply is perfectly inelastic or demand perfectly elastic, then it can be seen from the graphs that the incidence of tax will fall wholly on producers.

the incidence of tax falls totally on the producer. Producers will find it impossible to shift any of the tax onto consumers if the demand curve is perfectly elastic. Consumers are not prepared to buy at any higher price than the existing price. If the supply curve is perfectly inelastic, then the supply curve after imposition of the tax will be the same as the one before. Equilibrium price will therefore remain the same and producers will have to bear the full burden of the tax.

Generalising from these extreme situations, we can conclude that the more elastic the demand curve or the more inelastic the supply curve, the greater will be the incidence of tax on producers and the less will be the incidence of tax on consumers. So far as the government is concerned, taxation revenue will be greater, all other things being equal, the more inelastic the demand for the product taxed. For instance, if demand were perfectly elastic, the imposition of an indirect tax would lead to quantity demanded falling to zero and tax revenue being zero. At the opposite extreme, if demand were perfectly inelastic, consumers would buy the same quantity after imposition of the tax as before. Hence revenue will be equal to the tax per unit times the quantity demanded before imposition. If the price elasticity of demand lies between these two extremes, the imposition of a tax will lead to a fall in quantity demanded. The higher the elasticity, the larger will be the fall in quantity demanded and hence the lower will be the tax revenue received by government. Hence, it is no coincidence that in the UK excise duties are placed on alcohol, tobacco and petrol, all of which are relatively price inelastic.

key terms

Ad valorem tax - tax levied as a percentage of the value of the good.
Incidence of tax - the tax burden on the taxpayer.
Specific or unit tax - tax levied on volume.
Subsidy - a grant given which lowers the price of a good, usually designed to encourage production or consumption of a good.

Question 4

Table 11.2

	Price elasticity of demand
Food	- 0.52
Durables	- 0.89
Fuel and light	- 0.47
Services	- 1.02

Source: John Muellbauer, 'Testing the Barten Model of Household Composition Effects and the Cost of Children', *Economic Journal*.

The government wishes to raise VAT on selected goods, all these goods and services being zero-rated at present. Which categories of goods does the data suggest would yield (a) the most and (b) the least revenues? (Assume that at present the average price and the quantity demanded of goods in each category is identical.) Explain your reasoning carefully.

Applied economics

Taxes on petrol

In its April 1993 Budget, the government committed itself to raising taxes on petrol by 3 per cent per year in real terms for the foreseeable future, a figure which it increased to 5 per cent in its December 1993 Budget. It justified this by pointing out that petrol was cheaper in real terms in 1993 than it was in the early 1980s as can be seen in Figure 11.6. This was because the cost of oil had fallen sharply over the period. More importantly, the government was committed to reducing the level of carbon dioxide emissions by the year 2000 to the level that they were at in 1990. Fuel is a major source of carbon dioxide emissions in the UK. Hence, discouraging fuel use could help the UK achieve its internationally agreed target.

Raising the level of tax on petrol has also come to have a second objective. Britain's roads are becoming increasingly congested. As Figure 11.7 shows, the number of kilometres travelled by Britain's cars, lorries and buses has been rising over time with no prospect of any levelling off. This is not surprising given rising real incomes. The motor car has a relatively high income elasticity of demand. Rising real incomes also mean that consumers can afford to buy more goods, which accounts for part of the growth in freight transport. Given that the government has virtually brought to a halt its new road building programme, more and more vehicles are having to travel along the same total length of roads. The government sees price as one way of reducing demand for car journeys. Imposing road tolls is one way of achieving a reduction in road transport in the future. For the present, increasing tax on fuel is a simple way of increasing the cost per mile travelled.

The extent to which the government will achieve its objective depends, in part, upon the price elasticity of demand for petrol. If it is perfectly inelastic, then the shift to the left in the supply curve of 5 per cent per year in real terms will result in a movement up a vertical demand curve. The government will collect 5 per cent more revenue but there will be no change in demand for fuel. If demand is relatively inelastic, as is probably the case, the percentage fall in demand will be less than 5 per cent per year, with most of the increase in tax being paid by the consumer rather than absorbed by the producer.

Motorists may also respond to rising taxes on petrol by switching to more fuel efficient cars. For instance, diesel cars have become more popular in the 1990s. Having more fuel efficient cars helps the UK achieve its emission targets, but does nothing to help with congestion problems.

Finally, it could be argued that the government has little interest in reducing fuel consumption. If fuel is highly price inelastic, rises in tax on fuel simply lead to large increases in tax revenues for the government. It can then use this either to lower other taxes from what they would otherwise have been, or to pay for increased government spending. If voters prefer lower income taxes but higher fuel taxes to higher income taxes but lower fuel taxes, then there is an incentive for the government to raise fuel taxes. For a government wishing to maximise its votes, this is a very sensible policy to pursue, especially if it can appeal to the environmental lobby as well.

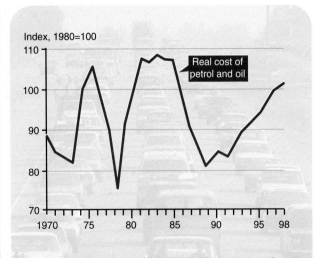

Source: adapted from *Labour Market Trends*, Office for National Statistics.
Figure 11.6 *Real cost of petrol and oil, UK, 1980 = 100*

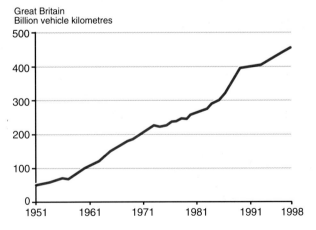

1. Includes cars, lorries and buses, but excludes two-wheeled traffic.
Figure 11.7 *Rise in road traffic[1]*
Source: adapted from *Social Trends*, Office for National Statistics.

VAT on domestic fuel

VAT imposed on domestic fuel

In 1994, the government imposed VAT for the first time on domestic fuels - gas, electricity, coal and oil - used to heat and light homes. Initially, the VAT rate was 8 per cent which was to rise to 17.5 per cent in 1995. However, the government was defeated in its attempt to raise the VAT rate in the House of Commons. In 1997, the incoming Labour government fulfilled its manifesto commitment to reduce the VAT rate to 5 per cent.

Norman Lamont, the Chancellor who decided to impose VAT on domestic fuels, justified the decision on environmental grounds. It was necessary to encourage households to economise on fuel consumption if environmental targets for emissions were to be met. Critics of the Chancellor argued that the move would hit poor people disproportionately hard. Pensioners in particular would suffer. To counter this, in 1994 the government increased the state pension by enough to cover the extra cost of fuel consumed by the typical pensioner household.

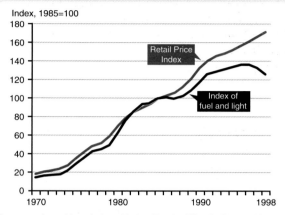

Source: adapted from *Labour Market Trends*, Office for National Statistics.

Figure 11.8 *Index of fuel and light and the Retail Price Index, 1985 = 100*

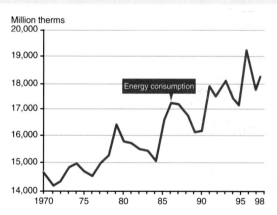

Source: adapted from *Annual Abstract of Statistics*, Office for National Statistics.

Figure 11.9 *Energy consumption of households*

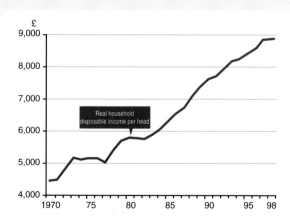

Source: adapted from *Economic Trends Annual Supplement*, Office for National Statistics.

Figure 11.10 *Real household disposable income per head at 1995 prices*

Table 11.3 *Energy consumption by class of consumer*

					Percentage
	Domestic	Road transport	Industry	Other[1]	Total
1980	28.0	19.5	34.9	17.6	100.0
1985	29.6	21.5	30.4	18.5	100.0
1990	27.9	26.5	26.7	19.9	100.0
1995	28.1	25.8	26.1	20.0	100.0
1998	29.4	25.7	23.2	21.7	100.0

1. Railways, water transport, public administration, commercial and other services.

Source: adapted from *Annual Abstract of Statistics*, Office for National Statistics.

1. From the data shown, outline the trends in (a) prices and consumption of domestic fuels, (b) incomes and (c) general price changes.

2. Using a demand curve diagram, explain what economic theory would predict would happen to the energy consumption of households (a) as their income rises and (b) if the price of energy becomes cheaper relative to all other goods.

3. (a) Using a demand and supply diagram, explain what economic theory would predict would happen when (i) VAT at 8 per cent was imposed on domestic fuel in 1994; (ii) VAT was reduced to 5 per cent in 1997. (b) Do the data support the conclusions of economic theory?

4. Some still argue that domestic fuel should be taxed more highly to discourage consumption on environmental grounds. Discuss whether raising VAT on domestic fuel to 17.5 per cent would increase economic welfare. In your answer, discuss (a) the likely impact on consumption of domestic fuel and its impact on the environment and (b) the possible effects on poorer households.

Summary

1. The cobweb theorem is a dynamic model of price and output determination.
2. It assumes that suppliers base their output decisions on the price received in the previous time period.
3. Cobwebs can be divergent, convergent or stable.
4. The cobweb theorem predicts that markets do not necessarily converge to their long term equilibrium position.

Static market models

A static model is one where time is not a variable. Time is said to be an **exogenous variable**, a variable which is not determined within the model. The theory of demand, supply and price outlined in unit 6 is an example of a static model.

However it was pointed out that there is a tendency for people who use this model to make a hidden assumption: that there are market forces at work which will move the market from a point where demand does not equal supply to an equilibrium position where the two are equal. To make this assumption explicit would require a more complicated **dynamic** model of price determination, one where time was an **endogenous variable** (i.e. included in the model).

Economists have devised many dynamic models of the market, but in this unit we will consider only one such model, called the COBWEB THEORY.

The assumptions of the cobweb model

The cobweb theory was devised by an American economist, Mordecai Ezekial, in the 1930s. He used it to try to explain why there were price oscillations in the pig market in Chicago.

He postulated that farmers based their supply decisions upon the price they received in the previous time period. Mathematically this can be expressed as:

$$Q_t = f(P_{t-1})$$

This says that the quantity supplied (Q_t) in time period t is a function of (i.e. varies with) the price received (P_{t-1}) in the previous time period t-1.

The cobweb diagram

The market for carrots can be used to illustrate the workings of the cobweb model. It takes time to plant and grow carrots for sale on the market. Because of this time lag, farmers are assumed within the model to base their decision as to how many carrots to grow this season on the price they received last season. So the supply in 1998 would be dependent upon the prices received by farmers in 1997.

In Figure 12.1, the market is in long run equilibrium at a price of P_0 and quantity Q_0. Assume that in year 1 a severe attack of carrot fly destroys much of the crop such that only Q_1 is available for sale. Consumers will pay a price of P_1 for Q_1 of carrots (remember the demand curve shows how much buyers will purchase at any given price). At the beginning of year 2 farmers have to decide how many carrots to grow. According to the cobweb theorem, they will base their decision on last year's prices. Hence, given that the price was P_1 last year and given that the supply curve S remains unchanged, farmers in year 2 will decide to grow Q_2 of carrots. But when they come to sell them they will find that buyers are not prepared to buy Q_2 of carrots at a price of P_1. Farmers cannot store carrots for several years. They have to sell them within 12 months or destroy them. Therefore the price of carrots will have to

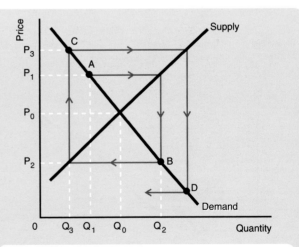

Figure 12.1 *A divergent cobweb*
Output is based upon price received in the previous time period. So short term equilibrium, starting at the point A, moves to B, then to C and then to D, steadily moving away from the stable equilibrium price of P_0.

Question 1

Supply is given by the following equation:

$$Q_t = 0.5 P_{t-1} - 10$$

where Q_t is quantity supplied in time period t, and P_{t-1} is price in time period t-1.

What would be the level of quantity supplied in 2000 if price in 2001 were:
(a) £60; (b) £100; (c) £300; (d) £250?

fall to P_2 to clear the market of Q_2 carrots. At the beginning of year 3, farmers will base their planting decision on the very low price of P_2 obtained the previous year. They will therefore only plant Q_3 of carrots and be pleasantly surprised at the end of the year to receive a price of P_3 for them. In year 4, carrot planting will be higher than in any of the previous years and consequently prices will plummet at harvest time.

The path shown in Figure 11.1, from point A through to point D, shows a market which is moving further and further away from the long term equilibrium price of P_0 and quantity Q_0. This is called a **divergent cobweb**. However, cobwebs can also be either **convergent** or **stable**. A convergent cobweb is shown in Figure 12.2.

Here market forces do act to restore a market to its long run equilibrium position where demand and supply are equal. Figure 12.3 shows a stable cobweb. The market has regular cycles of high prices followed by low prices and there is no tendency for the market either to move nearer the point where demand and supply are equal or to move away from it.

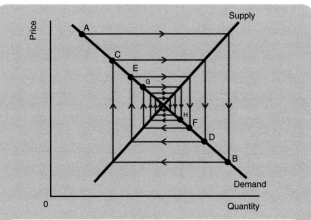

Figure 12.2 *A convergent cobweb*
With a convergent cobweb, price and output move nearer and nearer to the long term equilibrium where demand equals supply. Starting at A, the market moves from B to C and so on.

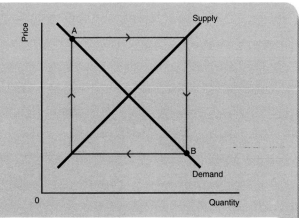

Figure 12.3 *A stable cobweb*
With a stable cobweb, the market neither converges towards equilibrium nor moves farther away from it over time.

Question 2

Demand and supply are given by the equations:

$$D = 30 - 0.75 P_t$$
$$S = P_{t-1} - 10$$

where D is quantity demanded, S is quantity supplied, P is price and t is time period t.

(a) Draw the demand and supply curves within the quantity range 0 to 30 and the price range 0 to 40.
(b) Will these equations produce a convergent, divergent or stable cobweb?
(c) (i) Draw two new supply curves which would make the cobweb different to your answer in (b).
    (ii) What would be the equation for each of the new supply curves?

Realism of the model

The theory does not suggest that a convergent cobweb is any more likely to occur than a divergent or stable cobweb. However, empirical evidence suggests that divergent cobwebs are not common. Farmers operating in free markets do not base their planting decisions solely on the basis of last year's price. If they did, they would soon learn that it was an inaccurate predictor of current prices. They use more sophisticated techniques, using both past prices and estimates of future supplies from other farmers. Even so, these techniques are unlikely to lead to accurate predictions, especially given the vagaries of the weather and other factors which affect output. Cycles do seem to exist but they are for the most part either stable or convergent. Anyway, many agricultural product markets are regulated by the state in industrialised countries, from rice in Japan to wheat in the USA to beef in the European Union. Such regulation destroys any cobweb-type relationship that might have existed in these markets.

Apart from farming, cobweb-type cycles seem to occur most in highly capital intensive industries. These are industries such as chemicals, paper or semi-conductor manufacturing, where a significant part of the cost of production is plant and machinery rather than raw materials or labour. High prices lead to over-investment in new plant and machinery. This leads to over-production, falling prices and cutbacks in investment. Supply shortages as a result drive up prices leading to a rapid expansion in investment. The cycle then starts all over again.

key terms

Cobweb theorem - a dynamic model of price determination which assumes that output decisions are based upon price received in the previous time period.

Applied economics

Semiconductors

The manufacture of semiconductor chips has long been subject to gluts and shortages. The pattern has been for strong sales leading to strong prices and high profits. Manufacturers have then invested heavily, leading to an oversupply of productive capacity in the industry. This leads to a sharp fall in the prices of semiconductor chips. Investment in new production facilities is cancelled. Supply falls from what it would otherwise have been, but this leads to shortages in the medium term. This pattern could be an example of a cobweb cycle.

Figure 12.4 shows that there was a fall in sales of semiconductor chips between 1995 and 1998. During the mid-1990s there was a shortage of commodity chips called D-Rams. This pushed up their prices, as Figure 12.5 shows, and profits soared. Between 1993 and 1995, the industry was making $2 billion profit a month on 16mb D-Ram chips. Companies in the USA, Japan, Europe and South Korea launched ambitious plans to expand capacity. Each new production facility, called a 'fab', cost an average $2 billion to build. However, there is a long lead time of two years from a decision to the full production of a fab.

By 1996, the industry was suffering from overproduction and D-Ram prices fell sharply. In 1998, the industry was further hit by a fall in demand for D-Rams from Asian countries caught in the Asian crisis of that year. The Asian crisis, caused by the failure of financial systems in a number of fast growing Asian countries, led to a sharp recession in Asia. Manufacturers initially reacted by continuing to produce and invest, in the hope that the crisis would be short lived. However, with losses estimated at $1.5 billion per month, the industry was forced to cut back. In 1998, about $28 billion of fab investments were deferred or cancelled. This included a new production facility in South Wales by LG, a South Korean firm.

By 1999, prospects were much brighter. Demand continued to grow strongly in Europe and the United States. Asian economies were recovering much faster than had been predicted. On the supply side, the industry had reduced capacity.

Analysts believed, though, that it was only a matter of time before the industry experienced another sharp downturn. The profits made in the first years of the 21st century would have encouraged overinvestment, leading to the next fall.

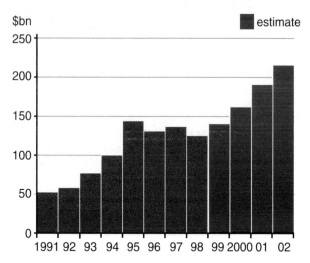

Figure 12.4 *World semiconductor industry sales*
Source: adapted from Semiconductor Industry Association, GartnerGroup's Dataquest.

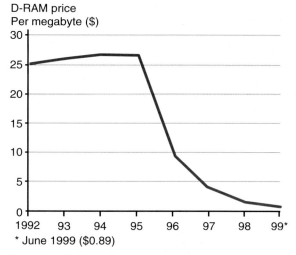

* June 1999 ($0.89)

Figure 12.5 *D-Ram prices*
Source: adapted from Semiconductor Industry Association, GartnerGroup's Dataquest.

Pig meat prices stuck in a trough

Pig prices are at a twenty year low. Factors outside the control of farmers are partly to blame. The Asian crisis of 1998 reduced exports from Europe to the region. The Russian financial crisis in the same year saw exports to Russia, which bought one third of all the EU's pig exports in 1997, collapse.

However, much of the problem can be laid at the door of farmers. In 1997 and the first part of 1998, pig herds expanded in the EU. In part this was a response to an outbreak of swine fever in the Netherlands. Competitors hoped to be able to take up the slack left by the fall in supply from that country.

The UK is also much more affected by trends in production in Europe and the USA than before. In 1998, the US pig market was in a trough, with farmers losing large amounts of money and cutting their herds. The slaughter of unwanted pigs increased the supply of pork in the US and therefore international markets, forcing prices down further. In future, hog cycles in Europe and the US are likely to move more in step than ever before. As a result, the hog cycle could be more volatile.

Source: adapted from the *Financial Times*, 28.12.1998.

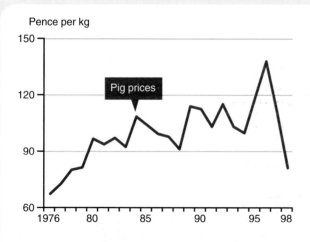

Source: adapted from *Annual Abstract of Statistics*, Office for National Statistics.

Figure 12.6 *Pig prices*

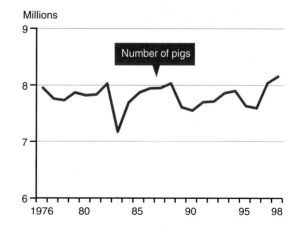

Source: adapted from *Annual Abstract of Statistics*, Office for National Statistics.

Figure 12.7 *Total number of pigs on UK farms*

1. Explain (a) what is meant by 'the pig cycle' and (b) using diagrams, what might cause the cycle.
2. To what extent does the evidence in Figures 12.6 and 12.7 support the view that a pig cycle exists in the UK?

3. As a farmer, how might a knowledge of the pig cycle affect your decisions about pig rearing?

Summary

1. In the labour market, the price of labour is the wage paid to workers. It is determined by the demand for and supply of workers.
2. In money markets, money is borrowed and lent. The price of money, the rate of interest, is determined by the demand for and supply of borrowed funds in a money market.
3. In foreign exchange markets, one currency is used to purchase another currency. The price of a currency, like the pound, euro or dollar, is determined by the demand for and supply of that currency at a point in time.

Different markets

In units 3-12, the demand and supply model has been used to explain the workings of goods markets. The term 'goods' in economics is used to describe both goods and services - everything from coal and steel to television sets to holidays and meals out. However, the demand and supply model can equally be used to explain the workings of other markets, such as factor markets, money markets and exchange rate markets.

Factor markets

The **factors of production** are land, labour, capital and entrepreneurship (☞ unit 2). These factors can either be bought and sold, or hired. Land, for instance, can be **rented**. Labour can be **hired** for a wage. The forces of demand and supply in these markets determine the equilibrium price. Take the labour market as an example.

The demand curve The demand curve for labour is downward sloping. This is because employers demand less labour as its price increases. One reason is that the higher the price of labour, the more incentive there is to substitute capital for labour. Another reason is that the higher the wage, the higher the cost of production. This is likely to lead to higher prices for the good being produced. Higher prices will lead to less demand for the good and hence less demand for the workers that produce the good.

The supply curve The supply curve of labour is upward sloping. The higher the wage, the more workers want to be employed. For instance, they might be attracted from other industries. They might be currently not be working, but be attracted back into the labour force by the high wages on offer. In the longer term, new entrants to the labour force may train to work in that occupation, increasing supply.

Equilibrium The equilibrium wage is shown in Figure 13.1. When demand equals supply, the wage rate is OA and the level of employment is OB.

Excess demand and supply If the wage rate is different to this, then market forces act to return the market to equilibrium. For instance, assume that the wage rate is OF, above the equilibrium wage rate OG in Figure 13.2.

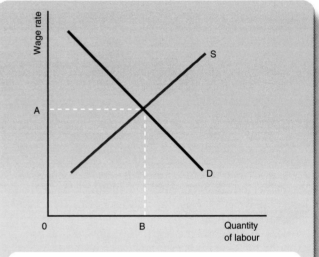

Figure 13.1 *The demand for and supply of labour*
The equilibrium wage rate of OA in a labour market is fixed by the forces of demand and supply. In equilibrium OB labour will be demanded and supplied.

There is then excess supply of labour to the market of AB. Some workers, OA, have got jobs. But AB workers are not employed in this market and want a job. They may be unemployed or they could be working in another industry, for instance at a lower rate of pay. With AB workers wanting a job, employers will be able to offer lower wages and still attract workers to work for them. If, however, they cut wages below OG, there will then be excess demand. Employers will want to employ more workers than want to work at that wage rate. Only at OG does demand equal supply.

Shifts in the demand and supply curves The demand and supply curves for labour can shift. For instance, the demand curve for computer programmers has shifted to the right over the past 20 years as the computer industry has expanded. At any given wage rate, more computer programmers are now demanded. A substantial increase in the number of workers entering the workforce can shift the supply curve of labour to the right. In many Third World countries, very high birth rates have resulted in ever increasing numbers of young workers entering the workforce.

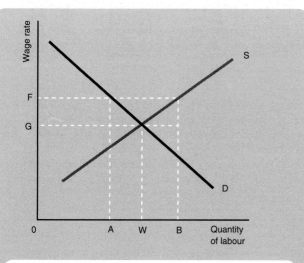

Figure 13.2 *Disequilibrium in the labour market*
If wages are OF, there is disequilibrium in the labour market because there is excess supply of labour. Wages will be bid down to the equilibrium wage of OG.

Elasticity The elasticity of demand and supply affects how shifts in demand and supply will change equilibrium wages and the levels of employment. For instance, if the supply of labour is highly inelastic, then an increase in demand shown by a shift to the right in the demand curve will bring large increases in wages, but only a small increase in employment. If the demand for labour is highly elastic, an increase in the supply of labour will only decrease wages slightly but there will be a large increase in employment.

Market imperfections Most labour markets are not perfectly free markets. For instance, trade unions attempt to restrict the supply of labour, minimum wage legislation prevents firms from paying below a certain wage and some employers are the sole employers of certain types of workers. These can affect the ways in which the forces of demand and supply determine wages.

Money markets

Money can be borrowed and lent. The price of money is the rate of interest which is charged on the borrowing and lending. There is a large number of different money markets, each with its own rate of interest. For instance, there is the mortgage market where borrowers are individuals wanting to buy a home and lenders are banks and building societies.

The demand curve The demand curve for borrowed money is downward sloping. For instance, the higher the interest rate, the higher the cost of the monthly repayments on a mortgage. Higher interest rates therefore mean that some potential borrowers can no longer afford the repayments, whilst others choose not to borrow because they think the cost is now too high. This discourages some potential house buyers from the market, fewer houses are bought and sold and fewer mortgages

Question 1

The public sector in the UK is experiencing a shortage of economists. The Bank of England, for instance, only managed to recruit 13 of its budgeted 20 economists for monetary analysis between the time it was made independent in May 1997 and June 1999. The Treasury and university departments have equally found it difficult to recruit appropriate staff. Pay has been a key factor. The Bank of England has a starting salary of £21 000 - £23 000 for economists with a masters degree. But the City of London is prepared to pay these sums for ordinary economics graduates with flair. By their mid-20s, they can expect to earn £35 000 a year, rising to around £100 000 a year or more on retirement.

The shortage of economists has been caused by rising demand for economists at a time when the supply of graduates has at best been static. The numbers of economics graduates has failed to rise in the 1990s as it has lost out to subjects such as Business Studies, described as a 'soft option' by Dame Sheila Masters, a member of the Bank of England's ruling court. At PhD level, there are now hardly any British citizens doing PhDs in economics. British universities have had to recruit foreign students to fill places whilst their British counterparts prefer to take well paid jobs in the City. As Gus O'Donnel, Chief Economist at the Treasury and head of the government economics services, said: 'More and more students are doing Business Studies. They are doing so because they think it is easier and they think it will be more useful. They are right about the former but not about the latter.'

Source: adapted from the *Financial Times*, 23.6.1999, *The Guardian*, 23.6.1999 and 5.7.1999.

(a) In the 1990s, demand for economics graduates has been rising whilst supply has been static. Using a demand and supply diagram, explain why this has led to increases in the starting salaries of economists.
(b) Examine whether there is an excess demand for economists in the UK according to the data.
(c) Discuss whether the recruitment shortage for economists in the UK could be solved if the institutions in the public sector, such as the Bank of England or the Treasury, considerably increased the pay they offered to economists.

are taken out.

The supply curve The supply curve for borrowed funds is upward sloping. For instance, the higher the rate of interest in the mortgage market, all other things being equal, the more profitable it is for lending institutions to lend to potential house buyers, rather than for business loans or personal loans.

Equilibrium price The equilibrium price or rate of interest is where demand equals supply at OA in Figure 13.3. If there is excess demand for mortgages, banks and building societies will switch funds from other money markets. New mortgage lenders will also be attracted into the market increasing the supply of funds. If there is excess supply, banks and building societies will switch funds out of the mortgage market to other money markets.

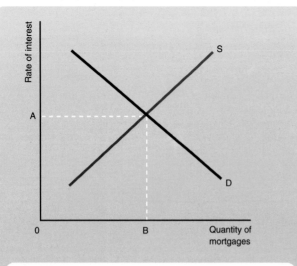

Figure 13.3 *Money markets*
The price of money is the rate of interest. In the market for mortgages, the equilibrium rate of interest is that which equals the demand for and supply of mortgages at OA.

Some mortgage lenders may leave the market because they can't do enough business at a profit.

Elasticities Elasticities vary from market to market. For instance, the supply of money to the mortgage market is relatively elastic. Banks and building societies can easily switch funds from other money markets into the mortgage market if they are able to earn higher rates of interest in the mortgage market. The elasticity of demand for mortgages is more difficult to estimate. However, if the elasticity of supply is elastic, large increases in mortgage lending will take place when there is a housing boom with

Question 2

Recent rises in interest rates have done little to slow the pace of the housing market so far, said the Halifax. House price rises hit a ten year high of 16 per cent in the year to January. It was the fastest rate of growth since July 1989. However, house prices are still relatively cheap compared to the last housing boom in the 1980s. Then, the housing boom was brought to a standstill by an increase in interest rates from 7.5 per cent to 14 per cent within a space of just one year. With interest rates having only increased a couple of per cent to less than 7 per cent over the past 12 months, it is perhaps not surprising that borrowers are not being particularly hard hit.

Source: adapted from the *Financial Times*, 4.2.2000.

(a) If there is a housing boom, what is likely to be happening to the demand for mortgages?
(b) What does the data suggest about the price elasticity of demand for mortgages?

relatively little effect on mortgage interest rates. The supply of mortgage finance is not a constraint to house buying.

Foreign exchange markets

Money can be bought and sold for other currencies (other forms of money). So dollars can be bought with yen, euros with pounds, and roubles with pesos. The price at which one currency can be bought for another is the EXCHANGE RATE. This is determined by the demand for and supply of currencies on foreign exchange markets.

Demand for a currency Demand for a currency comes from three major sources. There are those who want to buy currency in order to pay for purchases of goods and services. For instance, a British firm might buy US dollars to pay for goods it is buying from a US company. Currency is also demanded for saving and investment purposes. Nissan might want to buy pounds sterling to finance expansion of its British car plants, for instance. Or a UK pension fund might want to buy US dollars to take advantage of higher interest rates on bank deposits in the United States. Third, currency is demanded for speculative reasons. Traders buy and sell currencies hoping to make a profit on the difference between the buying price and the selling price.

The demand curve for a currency is downward sloping. The higher the price of a currency, the more expensive it becomes for foreigners to buy goods and services and hence less currency is demanded.

Supply of a currency The supply of a currency comes from those wanting to buy foreign goods and services, savers and investors wanting to invest abroad and currency speculators. The supply curve of a currency is upward sloping. The higher the price of a currency, the cheaper it becomes for businesses and individuals to buy goods from foreigners. Hence, more domestic currency is supplied.

Equilibrium price The equilibrium price of a currency occurs where demand equals supply. The equilibrium price of currencies such as the US dollar and Japanese yen is constantly changing because their prices are set by free markets where there is second by second trading. The demand and supply curves of currencies are shifting all the time, mainly because of speculation. However, this is not true for all currencies. Within the euro, for instance, the price of currencies was fixed on 1 January 1999. Central banks of countries within the euro zone agreed to supply any amount of their currency for another euro currency at a fixed price. So the supply curve of one euro currency for another was perfectly elastic and hence its price did not change as demand changed. However, the price of the euro against non-euro currencies like the pound or the US dollar was constantly changing according to the forces of demand and supply.

Question 3

The European Central Bank raised interest rates by 0.25 percentage points yesterday, a move apparently intended to boost the value of the euro against other major currencies such as the dollar and the pound. The rise, which took some buyers and sellers in the foreign exchange rate markets by surprise, gave a slight boost to the euro. It rose from $0.97 to $0.985 at the close of dealing. However, some economists thought that the rise would have little effect in the longer term. If speculators felt that the euro was going to fall further, a quarter per cent rise would not stop them from selling the euro short. What was needed was greater confidence that the euro would rise.

Source: adapted from the *Financial Times*, 4.2.2000.

(a) 'The exchange rate is a price.' Explain what this means, illustrating your answer from the data.
(b) Why might a change in interest rates in Europe affect the value of the euro?
(c) 'What was needed was greater confidence that the euro would rise.' Why might confidence affect the value of the euro?

key terms

Exchange rate - the price at which one currency is exchanged for another.

Applied economics

Female wages

Statistics show that women earn on average less than men. In research conducted by the London School of Economics, women's earnings over a lifetime were compared with those of men. Table 13.1 shows that under different circumstances, the lifetime gap varied from £143 000 to £482 000. There is a number of different reasons why females earn less than males on average and most are to do with the traditional role of women as child carers.

One is that when women take time out of their career to bring up children, they lose training, skills and experience. What's more, this is at an age when workers tend to be most likely to gain promotion. When women come back to work, they often have to start off at the bottom in their chosen career. Even worse, they may be unable to get a job in their previous occupation and have to start again in another career. Losing skills and experience affects the demand for female workers. The greater the loss, the less employers are prepared to pay for a worker.

Another aspect of female employment is that child carers often take on part time work. In Spring 1999, there were 5.5 million female part time workers compared to just 1.4 million male part time workers. Not only do women lose wages because they work part

time rather than full time, but also part-time jobs tend to be concentrated at the bottom of any occupational structure. This again is a demand side factor. Employers are unwilling to offer better jobs to part time workers because there is a perception that such jobs can only be done by full time workers.

A third problem facing women is that female employment is concentrated amongst low wage industries or occupations. For instance, nearly all secretaries are women, but secretaries are not particularly well paid on average. It could be argued that this is a supply side factor. Women are attracted disproportionately into 'women's jobs' which happen to be less well paid than typical 'men's jobs'. On the other hand, it could be an example of discrimination. Employers offer lower wages for those jobs where they think most employees will be women.

Table 13.1 shows that low skilled women suffer a greater loss of earnings than more highly skilled women. High skilled women are less likely to be trapped in lower wage, mainly female, occupations. However, they still are likely to suffer some discrimination. Parenthood affects low skilled women the most because they are most likely to take time out to bring up children and are most likely then to become part time workers.

Table 13.1 *The pay divide*

	Mrs Low-skill, left school with no qualifications, e.g. works as a shop assistant.	Mrs Mid-skill has O levels/GCSEs and works in a clerical job, e.g. as a secretary.	Mrs High-skill is a graduate and a professsional, e.g. a teacher.
The female forfeit - how much less the woman would earn in a lifetime than a man with similar qualifications, even if she had no children.	£197 000	£241 000	£143 000
	Marries at 21 and has first child at 23 and second at 26. Takes nine years in all out of the labour market and works part-time for a further 26 years.	Marries at 26 and has first child at 28 and second at 31. Out of the labour market altogether for just two years and works part time for a further 12.	Marries at 28, has a first child at 30 and second at 33. Works part time for just a year, working full time for the rest of her working life.
The mother gap - how much less the woman would earn in a lifetime than a woman with similar qualifications but no children.	£285 000	£140 000	£19 000
The parent gap - how much less the woman would earn than a man with similar qualifications, i.e. the female forfeit and mother gap combined.	£482 000	£381 000	£162 000

Source: adapted from *The Guardian*, 21.2.2000.

Vacancy signs as hotels lose staff

The sign outside says Investors in People - which certifies that this place excels in the training and development of its staff - but it seems that the five-star Langham Hotel in central London is lacking in the people to invest in. Like hotels and catering businesses across the country, it is suffering a recruitment shortage.

There are in excess of 100 000 vacancies within the industry and many of them look like they will remain empty for a very long time. Unemployment is at its lowest level for 20 years, while the number of people in work is at an all-time high of 27.5 million.

The industry is now finding it has to pay more. Andy Westwood, Director of Development at the Employment Policy Institute, points to what he calls the industry's star performers, such as the coffee bars that have opened over the past year and taken staff away from the larger hotels. 'The cappuccino economy has really taken off. Rather than go and be a silver service waiter in a big hotel, you can go and be a varista in Starbucks and become someone who knows which kind of coffee bean to grind for which coffee' he said. 'That's a recruitment tactic: they are paying a decent wage and they are trying to make it a skill to be in the service sector'.

Kevin Brett, Executive Assistant Manager of the Langham, said: 'The hours are perceived as unsocial and the salaries and packages we are paying don't compare to the more glamorous and high paying vacancies elsewhere in London'.

Source: adapted from *The Guardian*, 22.2.2000.

1. Describe the problem that hotels in central London face over recruitment of staff.
2. Explain, using a demand and supply diagram, why these hotels might be able to recruit more staff if they raised wages.
3. Discuss the impact a shortage of staff might have on a luxury hotel.

unit 14 International markets

Summary

1. If one country has lower costs of production for a good than another country, then it is said to have an absolute advantage in the production of that good.
2. International trade will take place even if a country has no absolute advantage in the production of any good. So long as it has a comparative advantage in the production of one good, international trade will be advantageous.
3. Transport costs will limit any welfare gain from international trade. However, economies of scale in production will increase the gains from trade.
4. The terms of trade (the ratio of export prices to import prices) will determine whether trade is advantageous for a country.
5. David Ricardo thought that comparative advantage existed because of differences in labour costs between countries. In the Heckscher-Ohlin model, comparative advantage is explained by differences in factor endowments.
6. The theory of comparative advantage argues that international trade takes place because of differences in the price of products. However, much world trade is the result of non-price competition between countries. Design, reliability, availability and image are some of the factors which determine purchases of foreign goods.
7. In the theory of preference similarity, it is argued that trade takes place because consumers demand more choice than can be provided by domestic producers.

International trade

Many goods and services are traded internationally. For instance, there are international markets in oil, motor vehicles and insurance. There is a number of reasons why international trade takes place.

Availability Some goods can only be produced in specific locations around the world. For instance, Saudi Arabia is oil rich whilst there are almost no known oil reserves in Japan. Fruits like bananas are tropical and so are not grown in the UK.

Price Some countries can produce goods at a relatively cheaper cost than other countries. This may be because of the availability of natural resources, the skills of the workforce or the quality of the physical capital in the economy. Much of the rest of this unit explains this in more detail.

Product differentiation Many traded goods are similar but not identical. For instance, a small hatchback car from one motor manufacturer is very much the same as another. It will, for instance, have four wheels, four seats and an engine. However, the differences mean that some consumers in one country will want to buy a car made in another country, even if domestically produced cars are available at exactly the same price. International trade allows consumers much wider choice about the product they buy. The same basic goods or service can differ in a wide variety of ways. Specifications might be slightly different. There may be different deals on finance available. Delivery times can vary. One product may be better quality than another. Much of world trade is driven by a combination of these factors.

Economists in the 18th and 19th century developed theories centred around why differences in costs led to international trade. These theories, which will now be considered, are as relevant today as they were then.

Absolute advantage

Adam Smith, in his famous example of a pin making factory, explained how specialisation enabled an industry to increase the production of pins from a given quantity of resources (☞ unit 2). In an economy, specialisation exists at every level, from the division of labour in households to production at international level.

Consider Table 14.1. Assume that there are only two countries in the world, England and Portugal. They produce only two commodities, wheat and wine. Labour is the only cost, measured in terms of man hours to produce 1 unit of output. Table 14.1 shows that it costs more in man hours to produce a unit of wine in England than in Portugal. Portugal is said to have an ABSOLUTE ADVANTAGE in the production of wine. It can produce both goods but is more efficient in the production of wine. On the other hand, it costs more in man hours to produce wheat in Portugal than in England. So England has an absolute advantage in the production of wheat. It is clear that it will be mutually beneficial for England to specialise in the production of wheat and for Portugal to specialise in the production of wine and for the two countries to trade.

Table 14.1

| | Cost per unit in man hours | |
	Wheat	Wine
England	10	15
Portugal	20	10

The same conclusion can be reached if we express relative costs in terms of absolute output. If Portugal could produce either 5 units of wheat or 10 units of wine, or some combination of the two, the relative cost of wheat to wine would be 2:1 as in Table 14.1. If England could produce either 9 units of wheat or 6 units of wine, the relative cost would be 3:2 as in Table 14.1. Hence, Portugal could produce wine more cheaply and England wheat more cheaply.

Question 1

Table 14.2

	UK			France	
	Cars	Computers		Cars	Computers
(a)	10	OR	100	9	OR	108
(b)	5	OR	10	4	OR	12
(c)	20	OR	80	25	OR	75
(d)	5	OR	25	4	OR	30
(e)	6	OR	18	8	OR	16

Two countries with identical resources, UK and France, using all these resources, can produce either cars or computers or some combination of the two as shown above. Assuming constant returns to scale, state which country has an absolute advantage in the production of (i) cars and (ii) computers in each of (a) to (e) above.

Comparative advantage

David Ricardo, working in the early part of the 19th century, realised that absolute advantage was a limited case of a more general theory. Consider Table 14.3. It can be seen that Portugal can produce both wheat and wine more cheaply than England (i.e. it has an absolute advantage in both commodities). What David Ricardo saw was that it could still be mutually beneficial for both countries to specialise and trade.

Table 14.3

	Cost per unit in man hours	
	Wheat	Wine
England	15	30
Portugal	10	15

In Table 14.3, a unit of wine in England costs the same amount to produce as 2 units of wheat. Production of an extra unit of wine means foregoing production of 2 units of wheat (i.e. the opportunity cost of a unit of wine is 2 units of wheat). In Portugal, a unit of wine costs 1½ units of wheat to produce (i.e. the **opportunity cost** of a unit of wine is 1½ units of wheat in Portugal). Because relative or comparative costs differ, it will still be mutually advantageous for both countries to trade even though Portugal has an absolute advantage in both commodities. Portugal is relatively better at producing wine than wheat: so Portugal is said to have a COMPARATIVE ADVANTAGE in the production of wine. England is

relatively better at producing wheat than wine: so England is said to have a comparative advantage in the production of wheat.

Table 14.4

	Production before trade Wheat Wine		Production after trade Wheat Wine	
England (270 man hours)	8	5	18	0
Portugal (180 man hours)	9	6	0	12
Total	17	11	18	12

Table 14.4 shows how trade might be advantageous. Costs of production are as set out in Table 14.3. England is assumed to have 270 man hours available for production. Before trade takes place it produces and consumes 8 units of wheat and 5 units of wine. Portugal has fewer labour resources with 180 man hours of labour available for production. Before trade takes place it produces and consumes 9 units of wheat and 6 units of wine. Total production between the two economies is 17 units of wheat and 11 units of wine.

If both countries now specialise, Portugal producing only wine and England producing only wheat, total production is 18 units of wheat and 12 units of wine. Specialisation has enabled the world economy to increase production by 1 unit of wheat and 1 unit of wine. The

Table 14.5

	Output		
	Good X		Good Y
Country A	20	OR	40
Country B	50	OR	100

Question 2

Table 14.6

	Cost per unit in man hours Meat	Bread
UK	5	10
France	3	4

(a) Which country has comparative advantage in the production of (i) meat and (ii) bread?
(b) The UK has a total of 300 man hours available for production whilst France has a total of 200. Before any trade took place, the UK produced and consumed 38 units of meat and 11 units of bread. France produced and consumed 20 units of meat and 35 units of bread. How much more could the two countries produce between them if each specialised and then traded?
(c) How would the answer to (a) be different, if at all, if the cost of meat and bread in France were: (i) 4 and 4; (ii) 3 and 7; (iii) 3 and 6; (iv) 6 and 12; (v) 6 and 15; (vi) 1 and 3?

theory of comparative advantage does not say how these gains will be distributed between the two countries. This depends upon the wheat/wine exchange rate, a point discussed below.

The THEORY OF COMPARATIVE ADVANTAGE states that countries will find it mutually advantageous to trade if comparative costs of production differ. If, however, comparative costs are identical, there can be no gains from trade. Table 14.5 shows the maximum output of two countries, A and B of two products, X and Y. The Table shows that country A, for instance, can either produce 20 units of good X or 40 units of good Y or some combination of both. The comparative costs or the opportunity cost of production is identical in both countries: one unit of X costs two units of Y. Hence there can be no gains from trade.

The assumptions of the theory of comparative advantage

The simple theory of comparative advantage outlined above makes a number of important assumptions.
- There are no transport costs. In reality, transport costs always exist and they will reduce and sometimes eliminate any comparative cost advantages. In general, the higher the proportion of transport costs in the final price to the consumer, the less likely it is that the good will be traded internationally.
- Costs are constant and there are no economies of scale. This assumption helps make our examples easy to understand. However, the existence of economies of scale will tend to reinforce the benefits of international specialisation. In Table 14.4 the gains from trade will be more than 1 unit of wheat and 1 unit of wine if England can lower the cost of production of wheat by producing more and similarly for Portugal.
- There are only two economies producing two goods. Again this assumption was made to simplify the explanation. But the theory of comparative advantage applies equally to a world with many economies producing a large number of traded goods. Table 14.7 shows that Chile has no absolute advantage in any product. However, it has a comparative advantage in the production of copper. Portugal has a clear comparative advantage in the production of wine whilst England has a comparative advantage in the production of apples. Exactly what and how much will be traded depends upon consumption patterns in all three countries. For instance, if neither Portugal or Chile consume apples, England will not be able to export apples to these countries.

Table 14.7

	Apples	Wine	Wheat	Copper
England	10	15	20	50
Portugal	15	10	30	60
Chile	20	20	50	70

Cost per unit in man hours

- The theory assumes that traded goods are homogeneous (i.e. identical). Commodities such as steel,

copper or wheat are bought on price. But a Toyota car is different from a Ford car and so it is far more difficult to conclude that, for instance, the Japanese have a comparative advantage in the production of cars.
- Factors of production are assumed to be perfectly mobile. If they were not, trade might lead to a lowering of living standards in a country. For instance, assume the UK manufactured steel but then lost its comparative advantage in steel making to Korea. UK steel making plants are closed down. If the factors of production employed in UK steel making are not redeployed, then the UK will be at less than full employment. It might have been to the UK's advantage to have kept the steel industry operating (for instance by introducing quotas) and producing something rather than producing nothing with the resources.
- There are no tariffs or other trade barriers (☞ unit 40).
- There is perfect knowledge, so that all buyers and sellers know where the cheapest goods can be found internationally.

The terms of trade

In Table 14.4 it was shown that England and Portugal could benefit from trade. Whether trade takes place will depend upon the TERMS OF TRADE between the two countries. From the cost data in Table 14.3, England could produce 2 units of wheat for every 1 unit of wine. It will only trade if it receives more than a unit of wine for every 2 units of wheat. Portugal on the other hand can produce 2 units of wheat for every $1\frac{1}{3}$ units of wine. It will only trade if it can give England less than $1\frac{1}{3}$ units of wine for 2 units of wheat. Hence trade will only take place if the terms of trade are between 2 units of wheat for 1 unit of wine and 2 units of wheat and $1\frac{1}{3}$ units of wine (i.e. between 2:1 and 2:1$\frac{1}{3}$).

This is shown in Figure 14.1. The cost ratios of wine for two units of wheat are drawn. England will only gain from trade if the international price of wine for wheat is to the right of its existing domestic cost line. Portugal on the other hand will only gain if the international price is to the left of its domestic cost line. Hence trade will only be mutually advantageous if the terms of trade are somewhere

Question 3

Table 14.8

	Tapes	Sweaters	Beefburgers	Chocolate
England	20	10	8	20
Portugal	30	8	12	30
Chile	40	8	4	25

Cost per unit in man hours

(a) Which country has an absolute advantage in the production of (i) tapes; (ii) sweaters; (iii) beefburgers; (iv) chocolates?
(b) Which country has a comparative advantage in the production of (i) tapes; (ii) sweaters; (iii) beefburgers; (iv) chocolates?

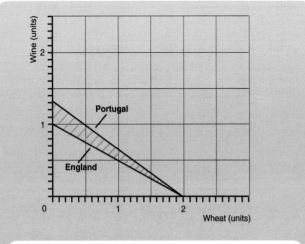

Figure 14.1 *The terms of trade*
England will find it advantageous to trade only if its terms of trade are at least 1 unit of wine for every two units of wheat exported. Portugal will only trade if it can receive at least 2 units of wheat for every 1⅓ units of wine exported. Therefore the terms of trade between the two countries will lie somewhere in the shaded area on the graph.

between the two lines, the area shaded on the graph.

The terms of trade is defined as the ratio between export prices and import prices:

$$\text{Index of terms of trade} = \frac{\text{Index of export prices}}{\text{Index of import prices}} \times 100$$

It is an **index** (☞ unit 3) because it is calculated from the weighted average of thousands of different export and import prices.

Why comparative advantage exists

David Ricardo believed that all costs ultimately could be reduced to labour costs. This belief is known as the **labour theory of value**. Hence the price of a good could accurately be measured in terms of man-hours of production. Following on from this, he argued that differences in comparative costs reflected differences in the productivity of labour.

There is an element of truth in this idea. The theory suggests that high labour productivity countries would have a comparative advantage in the production of sophisticated high technology goods whilst low labour productivity countries would have a comparative advantage in the production of low technology goods. Looking at the pattern of world trade, it is true for instance that developing countries export low technology textiles whilst developed countries export high technology computer equipment.

However, neo-classical price theory suggests that labour is not the only source of differing opportunity costs of production. For instance, the price of a piece of agricultural land can increase several times overnight if planning permission is given for residential building. This

increase in value has little to do with man-hours of production. Prices and costs are, of course, linked to quantities of labour inputs, but they are also linked to forces of scarcity which can drive prices up or down.

Heckscher and Ohlin, two Swedish economists working in the inter-war period, suggested that different costs were the result not just of different labour endowments between countries but also of different capital and land endowments. If an economy, such as India, has a large quantity of unskilled labour but little capital, then the price of capital relative to labour will be high. If, on the other hand, an economy like the USA has a large stock of capital relative to labour, then capital will be relatively cheap. Hence India will have a comparative advantage in the production of goods which can be made using unskilled labour. The USA will have a comparative advantage in the production of goods which require a relatively high capital input. Saudi Arabia is much more richly endowed with oil than France. France, on the other hand, has a rich abundance of skilled labour and capital equipment in the defence industry. Hence the theory would suggest that Saudi Arabia will specialise in producing oil, France in producing defence equipment and that the two countries will trade one product for the other.

Non-price theories of trade

The theory of comparative advantage provides a good explanation of world trade in commodities such as oil, wheat or copper. Countries with relatively rich endowments of raw materials or agricultural land specialise in the production of those commodities. It also provides a good explanation of the pattern of trade between First and Third World countries. Third World countries tend to export commodities and simple manufactured goods whilst importing more technologically sophisticated manufactures and services from the First World. However, the theory does not account for much of that half of world trade which occurs between the rich developed economies of the world.

Commodities are **homogeneous** products. There is nothing to choose between one grade of copper from Chile and the same grade from Zambia. Therefore the main determinant of demand is price. Manufactured goods and services tend to be **non-homogeneous**. Each product is slightly different. So when a consumer buys a car, price is only one amongst many factors that are considered. Reliability, availability, image, colour, shape and driving performance are just as important, if not more so. There is a wide variety of cars to choose from on the market, some produced domestically but many produced abroad. **Preference similarity theory** suggests that many manufactured goods are imported not because they are relatively cheaper than domestic goods but because some consumers want greater choice than that provided by domestic manufacturers alone. Domestic manufacturers, however, should have a competitive edge because they should be more aware of the needs of their domestic customers. This limits the extent to which foreign manufacturers can penetrate the home market.

Question 4

Look again at the data in Table 14.6.
(a) Show on a graph the price ratios of meat for bread in the two countries before trade.
(b) Would both countries find it mutually advantageous to trade if the international trade price ratio were 1 unit of meat for: (i) 4 units of bread; (ii) 3 units of bread; (iii) $1^1/_2$ units of bread; (iv) 1 unit of bread; (v) $^1/_2$ unit of bread; (vi) 2 units of bread; (vii) $1^1/_3$ units of bread?

key terms

Absolute advantage - exists when a country is able to produce a good more cheaply in absolute terms than another country.
Comparative advantage - exists when a country is able to produce a good more cheaply relative to other goods produced domestically than another country.
Terms of trade - the ratio of export prices to import prices.
Theory of comparative advantage - countries will find it mutually advantageous to trade if the opportunity cost of production of goods differs.

Question 5

For much of the first half of the 1990s, European alcoholic drinks producers saw their domestic markets as mature markets, producing little or no growth in sales. They looked to exports to grow in size. Developing a brand across international markets is a costly business. There need to be good distribution links established so that the product is available when the customer wants to buy it. Advertising, too, is essential to make customers aware of the value of the brand. Individual products are sold at premium prices. Cutting prices in times of difficulty would devalue the brand in the eyes of customers. After all, those buying Johnnie Walker whisky, Martell cognac or Pernod do so partly because they wish to show that they can afford the best drinks on the market.

In the second half of the 1990s, international drinks manufacturers were hard hit by the Asian crisis, caused by major problems in the financial systems of countries like South Korea and which led to sharp falls in GDP. For instance, Diageo saw its sales fall 40 per cent in the region. The economic rebound in 1999 and 2000 saw a sharp rise in sales, however.

Source: adapted from the *Financial Times*, 7.10.1999.

(a) Suggest why there is a market for expensive imported alcoholic drinks in countries such as Thailand, South Korea or India when there are locally produced substitutes sold at a fraction of the price.
(b) When sales fell during the Asian crisis, suggest why European drinks producers didn't respond by severely cutting prices.

Applied economics

UK trade flows

Table 14.9 *UK exports and imports of traded goods and services*

£ billion

	Exports		Imports		GVA[1]
	Goods	Services	Goods	Services	
1955	3.1	1.0	3.4	1.0	17.4
1965	5.0	1.6	5.2	1.7	32.7
1975	19.5	7.4	22.7	6.0	99.5
1980	47.5	15.0	46.2	11.3	208.5
1985	78.3	23.6	81.7	17.0	321.0
1990	102.3	31.2	121.0	27.2	499.7
1995	153.7	48.7	165.5	39.8	634.1
1998	163.7	61.8	184.3	49.1	741.6

1. Gross value added at factor cost, a measure of national income.
Source: adapted from *Economic Trends Annual Supplement, Monthly Digest of Statistics*, Office for National Statistics.

Total exports and imports

The UK trades in both goods and services. Table 14.9 shows that since 1955 exports of goods have accounted for approximately three quarters of total exports whilst exports of services have accounted for one quarter. Foreign trade has increased at a slightly faster rate than that of national income. In 1955, total exports accounted for 24 per cent of national income. By 1998, this had risen to 30.4 per cent.

Visible trade

Although the proportion of trade in goods to services has remained broadly the same in the post-war era, there have been some significant shifts in the composition of trade in goods. Table 14.10 gives a

Table 14.10 *Exports and imports by commodity (% of total value)*

		1955	1965	1975	1985	1998
Food, beverages	Exports	6.0	6.6	7.1	6.3	6.2
and tobacco	Imports	36.9	29.7	18.0	10.6	8.8
Basic materials	Exports	3.9	4.0	2.7	2.7	1.5
	Imports	29.0	19.3	8.4	6.0	3.0
Fuels	Exports	4.9	2.7	4.2	21.5	4.6
	Imports	10.6	10.6	17.5	12.8	2.6
Total food and	Exports	14.8	13.3	14.0	30.5	12.3
raw materials	Imports	76.5	59.6	43.9	29.4	14.4
Semi-	Exports	36.9	34.6	31.2	25.6	26.5
manufactured	Imports	17.9	23.8	23.9	24.8	24.4
Finished	Exports	43.5	49.0	51.0	41.2	60.0
manufactured	Imports	5.3	15.4	29.9	44.0	60.1
Total	Exports	80.4	83.6	82.2	66.8	86.5
manufactures	Imports	23.2	39.2	53.8	68.8	84.5
Unclassified	Exports	4.8	3.1	3.8	2.7	1.2
	Imports	0.3	1.2	2.7	1.8	1.1

Source: adapted from *Annual Abstract of Statistics, Monthly Digest of Statistics*, Office for National Statistics.

breakdown of visible trade (trade in goods) by commodity.

- Exports of fuel, nearly all of which is oil and related products, grew from less than 5 per cent in 1975 to 21.5 per cent of total visible exports by 1985. This was due to North Sea oil which first came on stream in 1976. Since the mid-1980s, the importance of oil to exports has declined. Partly this is because volumes of oil extracted from the North Sea have remained relatively static whilst other export volumes have been growing at over 3 per cent per year. Partly it is because real oil prices have fallen. In the first half of the 1980s, it could be claimed that the UK was a petro-economy. Today, North Sea oil does not play an especially significant role in the UK economy.
- Imports of food and raw materials have declined from 76.5 per cent of the total in 1955 to 14.4 per cent in 1998. In the Victorian age, Britain was known as the 'workshop of the world', importing raw materials and exporting manufactured goods. This fall would suggest that the UK has lost comparative advantage in the production of manufactured goods.
- This loss of comparative advantage in manufactured goods is clear from import figures for manufactures. In 1955, manufacturers accounted for only 23.2 per cent of imports. By 1998, this had risen to 84.5 per cent.

The decline of British manufacturing industry relative to its industrial competitors' goes back 100 years. At the turn of the 20th century, many commentators were pointing out how French, German and US manufacturers were overtaking UK firms on both price and quality. In the 1960s and 1970s, industries such as the motor cycle industry and electrical goods were decimated by competition from Japan. Britain's textile industry, once one of the country's most important exporters, has shrunk due to competition, first from

Europe and then from Third World countries. In contrast, there have been some success stories such as pharmaceuticals. Inward investment in the 1970s, 1980s and 1990s has also transformed the competitiveness of industries such as motor manufacturing and electrical goods.

The theory of comparative advantage is often expressed in terms of relative costs of production. Whilst it is clear that the UK's loss of competitiveness in industries such as textiles has been due to higher relative costs, this is less obvious in industries such as motor manufacturing. Here, poor quality, unreliability, poor design and long delivery dates were key to the destruction of the industry in the 1970s and 1980s. Equally, high quality, reliability and good design were an essential part of the story of the revival of the British motor manufacturing industry in the 1990s.

The loss of UK competitiveness in manufactured goods could be argued to be unimportant if manufacturers can be replaced by services. However, as Table 14.9 shows, growth in trade in services in the post-war period has been roughly the same as growth in trade in goods. Table 14.9 also shows that for every 1 per cent fall in exports in goods, services exports need to grow by 3 per cent to fill the gap. This would be very difficult to achieve over a period of time. So exports of goods, particularly manufactures, are the most important way in which imports are financed and are likely to remain so.

Trade in services

Table 14.11 shows the composition and change in trade in services since 1975. In 1998, the UK ran deficits on transport and tourism. For instance, UK citizens spent more on foreign holidays than foreigners taking a holiday in the UK. However, the UK has a significant comparative advantage in financial services. These are mainly the services provided by the financial markets in the City of London including insurance. London is one of the world's leading financial centres, the other two arguably being New York and Tokyo. At present it is by far the most important financial centre in Europe, although Britain's refusal to adopt the euro threatens that position.

Table 14.11 *Trade in services*

£ billion

		1975	1985	1998
Transport	Exports	3.4	6.1	11.4
	Imports	3.3	6.4	13.5
Travel	Exports	1.2	5.4	14.4
	Imports	0.9	4.9	20.0
Financial and	Exports	2.9	12.1	35.9
other services	Imports	1.5	4.6	15.6

Source: adapted from The Blue Book, *National Income Accounts Quarterly*, Office for National Statistics.

Income and current transfers

There is a third type of flow which forms part of the

Table 14.12 *Income and current transfers*

£ billion

		1975	1985	1998
Income	Credits	7.3	57.4	114.1
	Debits	6.7	57.4	98.4
Current transfers	Credits	1.0	7.5	15.3
	Debits	1.3	8.5	21.6

Source: adapted from *Economic Trends and Economic Trends Annual Supplement*, Office for National Statistics.

current account of the balance of payments. This is income and current transfers.

- Income is interest, profits and dividends on overseas assets. Foreigners own assets in the UK and take out income from the UK. This is a debit on the current account. Equally, UK firms and individuals own assets abroad and bring back income to the UK. This is a credit on the current account. Assets include financial assets, such as loans or shareholdings, or physical assets such as property or factories.
- Current transfers are transfers of income. This is made up of payments and receipts between the UK government and other bodies and the European Union (EU). For instance, all customs duties collected in the UK are paid to the EU. On the other hand, the EU pays large subsidies to UK farmers. The EU Social Fund gives grants to deprived regions of the UK.

Table 14.12 shows the UK has tended to receive more in income and current transfers than it has paid out. Income is in fact vitally important for the UK and in the late 1990s was the single most important contributor to the financing of the large deficit in the trade in goods that the UK tends to record. In 1998, income was one third of the value of all credits on the current account (i.e. the value of traded exports of goods and services, income and current transfers) and 28 per cent of all debits. It is as if a household paid 28 per cent of its income in mortgage repayments whilst receiving one third of its income from interest on money saved.

The direction of trade in goods

Table 14.13 shows how the direction of trade in goods has changed over time. In 1955, the UK was still to a a great extent following trading patterns established during the Victorian era, buying raw materials from developing countries and selling them manufactured goods. By 1998, UK trade had shifted dramatically. Over half of exports and imports were now with EU countries. Markets in the Third World were relatively unimportant. Note too that trade with Japan, classified under 'other developed countries', is very small in relation to the total, but has grown significantly over time. It has been argued by Eurosceptics that the UK could withdraw from the EU and rely more on its US trading connections. The UK would become the equivalent of Hong Kong or Singapore, a free trading

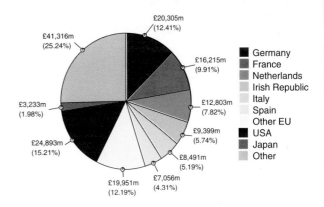

Figure 14.2 *The UK's main trading partners, exports 1998*
Source: adapted from *Annual Abstract of Statistics*, Office for National Statistics.

nation benefiting from its geographical location. The problem with this idea, as Figure 14.2 and Table 14.13 show, is that the USA is a relatively unimportant trading partner with the UK. Assume that the UK left the EU and as a result the EU imposed higher tariffs and quotas on the UK. If Britain lost just 10 per cent of its exports to the EU as result, it would have to increase exports by one third to the United States to compensate for this. It is most unlikely that UK exporters have such a comparative advantage that they could achieve this. Certainly from a trade viewpoint, Europe is vital to UK economic interests and is likely, if anything, to increase in importance over time.

Table 14.13 *Visible trade by area*

Percentage of total

		1955	1975	1995	1998
EU[1]	Exports	26.8	41.1	58.3	57.6
	Imports	25.9	45.1	55.9	53.5
Other Western Europe	Exports	3.8	6.8	4.2	4.8
	Imports	2.4	6.0	6.3	5.5
North America	Exports	11.3	12.1	13.2	15.2
	Imports	19.8	13.5	13.6	15.2
Other developed countries *of which*	Exports	15.3	9.6	6.0	5.5
	Imports	12.4	8.0	8.4	8.3
Japan	Exports	0.5	1.6	2.4	2.0
	Imports	0.6	2.8	5.7	5.1
Rest of the world	Exports	42.7	30.4	17.9	16.9
	Imports	39.5	27.4	15.8	17.6
of which Eastern Europe	Exports	1.3	3.4	1.3	1.5
	Imports	2.7	2.4	1.2	1.5
Oil exporting countries	Exports	5.1	11.6	4.1	4.6
	Imports	9.2	13.6	1.9	1.9

1. Includes all 1998 EU countries in 1955, 1975 and 1995 percentages.

Raleigh shuts frame plant

Raleigh is one of the symbols of British manufacturing. In its heyday, it employed 7 000 people in Nottingham making bicycles for Britain and its empire. In the 1950s it invented the 'sit-up-and-beg' bike, whilst in the 1970s it was responsible for bringing the Chopper bike to the market.

However, like all British manufacturing, it came under increasingly fierce foreign competition from the 1960s onwards. Sales fell as low-wage, low-cost imports rose, first from Europe and then from the Far East. Raleigh was also caught by the decline in demand for bicycles in the post-war period as adults left their old cycles in the shed for newly acquired motor cars.

Today, Raleigh produces around half a million bicycles a year from their Nottingham factory. However, the company is now only a 'kit-maker'. In December 1999, it closed down its last major manufacturing facility when it stopped making cycle frames. It now buys in all the components, many from the Far East, assembles them, paints them and puts the Raleigh brand on the finished bicycle.

Source: adapted from *The Guardian*, 11.12.1999.

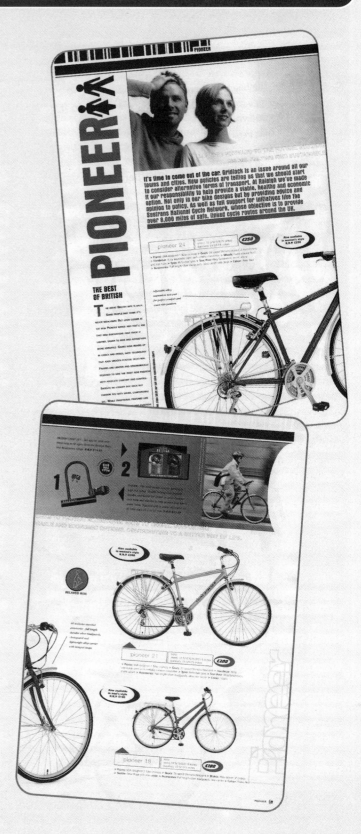

1. **Explain what is meant by comparative advantage, illustrating your answer from the data.**
2. **Suggest why Raleigh might today have a comparative advantage in the assembly and distribution of bicycles, but not in the manufacture of bicycle components.**

Summary

1. The market is a mechanism for the allocation of resources.
2. In a free market, consumers, producers and owners of the factors of production interact, each seeking to maximise their returns.
3. Prices have three main functions in allocating resources. These are the rationing, signalling and incentive functions.
4. If firms cannot make enough profit from the production of a good, the resources they use will be reallocated to more profitable uses.

The role of the market

Adam Smith, in his book *An Enquiry into the Nature and Causes of the Wealth of Nations*, attacked the economic system of his day. It was a system founded upon protectionism, economic restrictions and numerous legal barriers. He presented a powerful case for a free market system in which the 'invisible hand' of the market would allocate resources to everyone's advantage. There are three main types of actor or agent in the market system. Consumers and producers interact in the **goods markets** of the economy. Producers and the owners of the factors of production (land, labour and capital) interact in the **factor markets** of the economy.

The main actors in the market

The consumer In a pure free market system it is the consumer who is all powerful. Consumers are free to spend their money however they want and the market offers a wide choice of products. It is assumed that consumers will allocate their scarce resources so as to maximise their welfare, satisfaction or utility.

The firm In a pure free market, firms are servants of the consumer. They are motivated by making as high a profit as possible. This means maximising the difference between revenues and costs.

- **Revenues**. If they fail to produce goods which consumers wish to buy, they won't be able to sell them. Consumers will buy from companies which produce the goods they want. Successful companies will have high revenues; unsuccessful ones will have low or zero revenues.
- **Costs**. If firms fail to minimise costs, then they will fail to make a profit. Other more efficient firms will be able to take their market away from them by selling at a lower price.

The price of failure - making insufficient profit to retain resources and prevent factor owners from allocating their resources in more profitable ways - will be the exit of the firm from its industry. On the other hand, in the long run firms cannot make higher than average levels of profit. If they did, new competitors would enter the industry attracted by the high profits, driving down prices and profits and increasing output.

Owners of the factors of production Owners of land, labour and capital - rentiers, workers and capitalists - are motivated by the desire to maximise their returns. A landowner wishes to rent her land at the highest possible price. A worker wishes to hire himself out at the highest possible wage, all other things being equal. A capitalist wishes to receive the highest rate of return on capital. These owners will search in the market place for the highest possible reward and only when they have found it will they offer their factor for employment. Firms, on the other hand, will be seeking to minimise cost. They will only be prepared to pay the owner the value of the factor in the production process.

Question 1

(a) 'In a free market, consumers have no choice about what they can buy. Firms simply impose their wishes on the consumer.' Use the photograph to explain why this is incorrect.

The function of prices in the market

In a market, there are buyers who demand goods and sellers who supply goods. The interactions of demand

and supply fix the price at which exchange takes place. Price has three important functions in a market.

Rationing Consumer wants are infinite, but we live in a world of scarce resources (☞ unit 1). Somehow, those scarce resources need to be allocated between competing uses. One function of price in a market is to allocate and ration those resources. If many consumers demand a good, but its supply is relatively scarce, then prices will be high. Limited supply will be rationed to those buyers prepared to pay a high enough price. If demand is relatively low, but supply is very high, then prices will be low. The low price ensures that high numbers of goods will be bought, reflecting the lack of scarcity of the good.

Signalling The price of a good is a key piece of information to both buyers and sellers in the market. Prices come about because of the transactions of buyers and sellers. They reflect market conditions and therefore acts as a signal to those in the market. Decisions about buying and selling are based on those signals.

Incentive Prices act as an incentive for buyers and sellers. Low prices encourage buyers to purchase more goods. For consumers, this is because the amount of satisfaction or utility gained per pound spent increases relative to other goods. Higher prices discourage buying because consumers get fewer goods per pound spent. On the supply side, higher prices encourage suppliers to sell more to the market. Firms may have to take on more workers and invest in new capital equipment to achieve this. Low prices discourage production. A prolonged fall in prices may drive some firms out of the market because it is no longer profitable for them to supply.

To illustrate how these functions help allocate resources, consider two examples.

Example 1 Assume that lobbying from animal welfare groups changes consumers' tastes. In the market for fur coats, fewer fur coats will be purchased. In the short run, companies are likely to cut prices to boost demand. The fall in price is a signal that market conditions have changed. It also acts as a disincentive to production. At the new low prices, profits fall. So in the long run, some firms will leave the industry, reducing supply. When the price is in long run equilibrium, it will ration supply amongst those customers prepared to pay the new price. Factors markets too will be affected. The demand by firms in the fur industry for workers, equipment and animals will fall. So wages of fur workers may fall. This fall in wages, the price of labour, acts as a signal to workers. The incentive to work in the industry will have fallen so fewer workers will want jobs in the fur trade. Some workers will now leave the industry and get jobs elsewhere in the economy. This is the operation of the rationing function. Meanwhile, consumers will have increased their spending on other goods, for instance on imitation furs. In the short term, the price of imitation furs may rise. This acts as a signal and an incentive for existing firms to expand output and new firms to enter the market. With increased supply, there will be an increase in resources used in the production of imitation furs, an example of the rationing function of prices.

Example 2 There is a large increase in the number of young workers in the population. This increased supply of young workers will force their wages, the price of labour, down. The wage fall acts as a signal to firms that labour is now cheaper. It also acts as an incentive to employ more young workers because they are cheaper. Thus, the allocation of resources changes. Lower wage costs should reduce the costs of firms, which in turn may be passed on to the consumer in the form of lower prices. These lower prices will act as a signal to consumers and provide an incentive for them to increase purchases of goods, again altering the allocation of resources.

Maximising behaviour

In the market mechanism, everyone is assumed to be motivated by self interest. Consumers are motivated by the desire to maximise their welfare or utility. Producers wish to maximise profits. Workers, rentiers and capitalists seek to maximise the returns from the factor that they own. This maximising behaviour determines the way in which resources are allocated.

Consumers, for instance, will spend to maximise their satisfaction or utility. They cast spending 'votes' between different products and different firms. If consumer tastes change so that they want more ice cream and fewer hot dogs, then they will spend more on ice cream and less on hot dogs. Ice cream manufacturers will collect more money from the sale of ice cream which they will use to expand production. Manufacturers of hot dogs will be forced to lay off staff, buy fewer raw materials and in the long term shut factories.

Profit and not revenue is the signal to firms to change levels of production. When consumers demand more ice cream, firms will expand production only if it is profitable to do so. Hot dog manufacturers will shut down manufacturing plant only if these resources could be used at higher profit levels elsewhere. In a free market, changes in consumer demand are met by changes in patterns of production by firms because of their desire to maximise profit.

Judging the market

Markets are one way of allocating resources. There are alternatives. For instance, the government could allocate resources as it does with defence, education or the police. Economists are interested in knowing how to judge whether markets are the best way of allocating resources. There are two main ways in which they do this.

First, they consider whether markets are **efficient** (☞ unit 16) ways of allocating resources. By this, we mean whether firms produce at lowest cost and are responsive to the needs of consumers as in the ice cream and hot dog example above. Second, they consider issues of **equity** (☞ units 16 and 20). Efficiency takes income distribution for granted. But is income and wealth in society distributed in an acceptable way?

If resources are allocated inefficiently and inequitably, then there may be a case for governments to intervene, either by altering conditions in the market or by removing production from the market mechanism altogether. Units 16-22, consider these complex issues.

Question 2

In 1998 and 1999, the price of semi-conductors - the chips that power personal computers - fell sharply. Partly, this was because of demand factors. In 1998, the fast growing economies of East Asia suffered economic collapse. They had over-borrowed and expanded their industries too fast. When a Thai bank defaulted on its debts, the shock waves swept throughout the region. The result was a slump in the economies of the region, with output down by over 10 per cent. As a consequence, demand for computers and other devices containing micro-chips fell and so too did the demand for semi-conductors. However, sharp falls in the price of semi-conductors were also the result of over-expansion of supply. Firms, including those in East Asian countries such as South Korea, had invested heavily in new micro-chip production plants. Falling prices helped to increase demand outside of Asia for computers. But they also led companies to close down semi-conductor manufacturing plants. Siemens, for instance, closed its plant in the North of England and LG (Lucky Gold, a Korean

company) failed to complete a much publicised plant in South Wales.

Explain how prices in the semi-conductor industry have:
(a) rationed resources;
(b) acted as signals to the market;
(c) provided incentives to consumers and firms to allocate their resources.

Question 3

In April 1999, Marks & Spencer announced that it was to close all of its 38 stores in Canada. The company established its first store in the country in 1974, but had made losses in 24 out of the 25 years of operations. In the year to March 1998, M&S Canada incurred operating losses of £8.3 million on revenues of £44.3 million. The company blamed its inability to make profits in Canada on tough competition in the local retail market. In the

late 1990s, this had been intensified by the arrival and rapid growth of Wal-Mart Stores, the US discount store operator that is by far the world's biggest retailer.

Source: adapted from the *Financial Times*, 29.4.1999

(a) Explain, using M&S as an example, the role of profit in allocating resources.

Applied economics

Motor cars

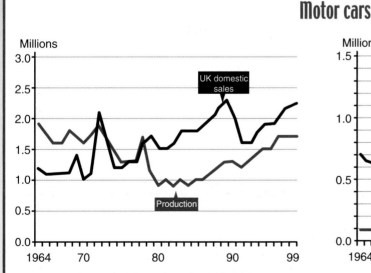

Figure 15.1 *Annual production and sales of cars, UK (millions)*
Source: adapted from *Economic Trends Annual Supplement*, Office for National Statistics.

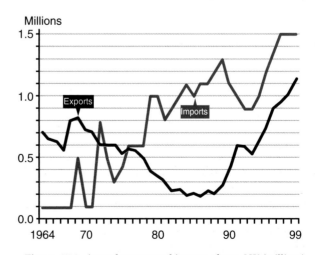

Figure 15.2 *Annual exports and imports of cars, UK (millions)*
Source: adapted from *Economic Trends Annual Supplement*, Office for National Statistics.

The history of the UK motor car industry in recent decades is a good example of how markets allocate resources. In the 1950s and 1960s, the British market was insulated to a great extent from foreign competition. The British motorist bought cars made in British factories, even if some of these factories were owned by foreign companies such as Ford. It was largely a sellers' market, with demand constrained by the ability of consumers to obtain credit for the purchase of cars.

However, the car industry suffered two major weaknesses at the time. First, it failed to address problems of quality. In a sellers' market, firms were under no pressure to manufacture world beating cars. Second, there was underinvestment by the industry. This was perhaps not surprising given the poor profitability of some companies. For instance, the original Mini car produced by what is now Rover failed to make a profit in its first five years of production because its price was set too low. Poor profitability led to rationalisation, with companies being taken over by others, and production was streamlined. However, the necessary investment in new production processes and facilities lagged behind the UK's main overseas competitors.

The weakness of the British motor industry became apparent in the 1970s and 1980s as shown in Figures 15.1 and 15.2. Imports soared, whilst exports declined. Domestic production fell from a peak of 1.9 million cars per year in 1972 to 0.9 million by 1984. What happened was that UK consumers increasingly wanted to buy foreign cars because they were better built, more reliable and, in the case of Japanese cars, more keenly priced. Equally, foreign customers turned away from British cars, reducing exports to a third of their 1960s levels. British car manufacturers responded by closing factories, laying off workers and reducing orders for components. The reduction in demand for British made cars resulted in a fall in demand for the factors of production used to manufacture those cars.

The mid-1980s was a turning point for British motor manufacturing. Arguably the most important factor in forcing change was the arrival of Japanese manufacturers in the UK. Honda established a working partnership with Rover and also built an engine plant in Swindon. Nissan built a new car plant in the North East of England, following by Toyota which set up in Derby. They came to the UK because they wanted to sell more cars in Europe. At the time, they were prevented from selling as many cars as they wanted because European countries had fixed limits on Japanese imports to protect their own car manufacturers from competition. England was in the European Union and so there would be unlimited access into Europe for Japanese cars built in the UK.

Japanese car producers lifted car production numbers in the UK simply by establishing plants here. But they also had an important effect on US and European car manufacturers. Japanese cars were increasingly popular with customers across the globe. Companies like General Motors and Ford could see that unless they could produce cars to the same quality and price as Japanese competitors, they would be driven out of the market. They responded by changing the way in which they designed and built cars. They adopted Japanese production methods such as just-in-time deliveries of components to factories. Workers were given far greater skills. New investment and new models were given to car plants which could show that they had high levels of productivity. British factories in particular were given a choice. Either they adopted new ways of working or they would be starved of investment and eventually closed. If British factories could not supply the right goods, the market would force them to shut down.

Market forces also played a part in the decision by the Japanese to come to the UK. In the first half of the 1980s, the government of Margaret Thatcher pursued **supply side policies** (☞ unit 38) which attracted foreign investment. Trade union power was curbed. Taxes on company profits were cut. Higher rates of tax paid by company executives were slashed. Finally, taxes paid by employers on their workers fell. The poor performance of the UK economy in the 1960s and 1970s relative to other European countries also meant that wages in the UK were now often lower than in Germany or France. Low taxes and low wages acted as powerful incentives for the Japanese and other foreign countries to set up in the UK.

In the 1990s, as Figures 15.1 and 15.2 show, the UK car industry has made a substantial recovery. Imports have stabilised to some extent whilst exports and production have grown. The profitability of UK car manufacturing plants has ensured continued investment by the multinational car producers. The long term future of the car industry in the UK seems secure.

The market for sportswear

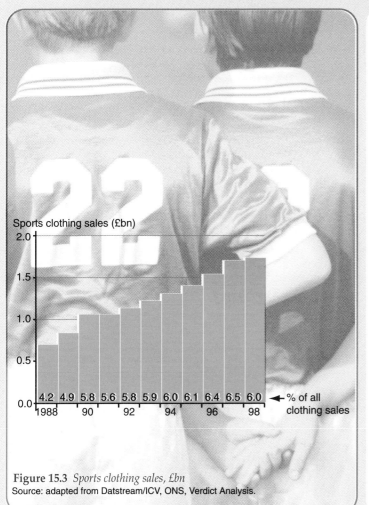

Sports clothing sales (£bn)

2.0	
1.5	
1.0	
0.5	
0.0	4.2 4.9 5.8 5.6 5.8 5.9 6.0 6.1 6.4 6.5 6.0 ◄— % of all clothing sales
	1988 90 92 94 96 98

Figure 15.3 *Sports clothing sales, £bn*
Source: adapted from Datstream/ICV, ONS, Verdict Analysis.

Buyers perusing the racks in sportswear shops along the UK's high streets are in retail heaven. Prices of most popular leisurewear, football kit and sports shoe brands were cut before Christmas. Now ailing retailers, overflowing with stock, have trimmed prices even lower. Analysts have feared for some time that the attractions of expensive sportsgear had peaked. Statistics show that sportswear sales are falling as a portion of the total clothes market. Verdict, the retail consultants, predicts that the percentage will drop to 5.7 per cent in 1999, 5.5 per cent in 2000 and 5.3 per cent in 2001. Replica football kits have been hardest hit; 'The bubble has burst. Consumers are becoming bored of big-branded sportswear and will no longer pay the high prices which used to be part of the attraction. Fashion has shifted to other leisurewear brands not catered for in most sportswear stores' says one analyst.

Source: adapted from the *Financial Times*, 3.2.1999.

Share prices of sports retailers fell throughout 1998. Analysts predict that some will have to close down stores with lower sales whilst some smaller unlisted chains and independents will go out of business. Some sports retailers have started to reposition themselves in the market. For instance, Duncan Sharpe, managing director of JJB Sports, said his group was increasing sales of sports equipment, which offers higher profit margins, and was expanding into women's and children's clothing. JD Sports has 'introduced exclusive and casual ranges and focused on high quality fashionwear' according to its finance director Peter Cowgill. Simon Bently, chief executive and chairman of Blacks, said his group's spread of businesses meant that it was less vulnerable than its competitors. Its smaller chains, Blacks Outdoors and Active Venture, were slightly removed from the sportswear market because they were outdoor specialists.

Source: adapted from the *Financial Times*, 3.2.1999.

1. **Describe the trends in the sportswear market.**
2. **What problems did sportswear retailers face in the late 1990s as a result of these trends?**

3. **Giving examples from the data, analyse how prices and profits influence the allocation of resources in the clothing and retailing industries.**

Summary

1. **Static efficiency refers to efficiency at a point in time. Dynamic efficiency concerns how resources are allocated over time so as to promote technical progress and economic growth.**
2. **Productive efficiency exists when production is achieved at lowest cost.**
3. **Allocative efficiency is concerned with whether resources are used to produce the goods and services that consumers wish to buy.**
4. **All points on an economy's production possibility frontier are both productively and allocatively efficient.**
5. **Free markets tend to lead to efficiency.**
6. **Market failure occurs when markets do not function efficiently. Sources of market failure include lack of competition in a market, externalities and missing markets.**

Efficiency

The market mechanism allocates resources, but how well does it do this? One way of judging this is to consider how **efficiently** it resolves the three fundamental questions in economics of how, what and for whom production should take place (☞ unit 2). Efficiency is concerned with how well resources, such as time, talents or materials, are used to produce an end result. In economic terms, it is concerned with the relationship between scarce inputs and outputs. There are a number of different forms of efficiency which need to be considered.

Static vs dynamic efficiency

STATIC EFFICIENCY exists at a point in time. An example of static efficiency would be whether a firm could produce 1 million cars a year more cheaply by using more labour and less capital. Another example would be whether a country could produce more if it cut its unemployment rate. Productive and allocative efficiency (discussed below) are static concepts of efficiency. Economists use them to discuss whether more could be produced **now** if resources were allocated in a different way. These concepts can be used, for instance, to discuss whether industries dominated by a monopoly producer might produce at lower cost if competition were introduced into the industry (☞ unit 18). Or they might be used to discuss whether a firm should be allowed to pollute the environment (☞ unit 19).

DYNAMIC EFFICIENCY is concerned with how resources are allocated **over a period of time**. For instance, would there be greater efficiency if a firm distributed less profit over time to its shareholders and used the money to finance more investment? Would there be greater efficiency in the economy if more resources were devoted to investment rather than consumption over time (☞ unit 27)? Would an industry invest more and create more new products over time if it were a monopoly than if there were perfect competition (☞ unit 18)?

Productive efficiency

PRODUCTIVE EFFICIENCY exists when production is achieved at lowest cost. There is productive inefficiency

when the cost of production is above the minimum possible given the state of knowledge. For instance, a firm which produces 1 million units at a cost of £10 000 would be productively inefficient if it could have produced that output at a cost of £8 000.

Productive efficiency will only exist if there is TECHNICAL EFFICIENCY. Technical efficiency exists if a given quantity of output is produced with the minimum

Question 1

Table 16.1

		Units
Output	Minimum input levels	
	Labour	Capital
10	4	1
20	8	2
30	11	3
40	14	4
50	16	5

(a) Firm A uses 21 units of labour and 6 units of capital to produce 60 units of output. A competing firm uses 19 units of labour and 6 units of capital to produce the same output. Explain whether Firm A is more technically efficient than the competing firm.
(b) Firm B uses 24 units of labour and 7 units of capital to produce 70 units of output. Firm B pays £10 000 to employ these factors. A competing firm employs the same number of factors to produce the same level of output but only pays £8 000 for them. Explain whether Firm B is more productively efficient.
(c) Now look at Table 16.1.
From the table, which of the following combinations are: (i) technically efficient and (ii) productively efficient if the minimum cost of a unit of labour is £100 and of a unit of capital is £500?
(1) 8 units of labour and 2 units of capital to produce 20 units of output at a cost of £1 800. (2) 15 units of labour and 4 units of capital to produce an output of 40 units at a cost of £3 500. (3) 4 units of labour and 1 unit of capital to produce 10 units of output at a cost of £1 000.

number of inputs (or alternatively, if the maximum output is produced with a given number of units). For instance, if a firm produces 1 000 units of output using 10 workers when it could have used 9 workers, then it would be technically inefficient. However, not all technically efficient outputs are productively efficient. For instance, it might be possible to produce 1 000 units of output using 9 workers. But it might be cheaper to buy a machine and employ only 2 workers.

Equally, Firm A might be using a machine and two workers to produce a given output. However, if it is paying £100 000 a year for this, whilst a competing business is paying only £80 000 a year for the same factor inputs, then Firm A is productively inefficient.

Allocative efficiency

ALLOCATIVE or ECONOMIC EFFICIENCY is concerned with whether resources are used to produce the goods and services that consumers wish to buy. For instance, if a consumer wants to buy a pair of shoes, are the shoes available in the shops? If a consumer wants schooling for her child, is education available?

There are many examples of where allocative efficiency is not present. In the Second World War, a system of rationing in the UK limited what consumers could buy. They were not free to buy more food and less clothing because both food and clothing could only be bought using coupons issued by the government. In the Soviet Union (now Russia), there were constant chronic shortages of consumer goods. What was available was often distributed via queuing mechanisms. Consumers did not

have the power to choose between shoes and food because shoes might be unavailable in the shops at the time.

Allocative efficiency occurs when no-one could be made better off without making someone else worse off. In the Second World War, for instance, some people would have preferred to buy more clothes and consume less food. Others wanted more food and fewer clothes. Allocative efficiency would have been greater if people had been allowed to trade their clothes coupons for food coupons because both groups would have gained.

Efficiency and the production possibility frontier

The various concepts of efficiency can be illustrated using a **production possibility frontier** or **PPF** (☞ unit 1). A production possibility frontier shows combinations of goods which could be produced if all resources were fully used (i.e. the economy were at full employment).

There is productive efficiency in an economy only if it is operating on the PPF. To understand why, consider an economy where all industries except the shoe industry are productively efficient. This means that the shoe industry is not operating at lowest cost and is using more resources than is necessary for its current level of output (i.e. it is technically inefficient). If the shoe industry became technically efficient, it could produce more shoes without reducing the output of the rest of the economy. Once the shoe industry is productively efficient, all industries are productively efficient and output cannot be increased in one industry without reducing it in another industry. But this is true about any point on the PPF. In Figure 15.1, the economy is initially at B, within the PPF. The shoe industry is productively inefficient because YZ more shoes could be produced without affecting the output, OX, of the rest of the economy. At A, the shoe industry cannot produce any more shoes without taking away resources from other industries and causing their output to fall. Hence the shoe industry must be productively efficient at A.

Question 2

In some areas of the country, some state schools are over-subscribed. This means that there are more children wanting to come to the school than there are places available. In such circumstances schools have to choose their children according to admission rules. Typically, these are based on catchment areas. Children who live close to the school get in. Those who live further away do not. This might not be the most efficient way of allocating places. Some economists have advocated giving each child in the country a voucher worth £x which is handed over to their school and then cashed in to pay for the expenses of running the school. Oversubscribed schools could charge fees over and above the value of the voucher. The size of the fee would be fixed to limit the number of entrants to the school to the number of places offered. Just as in, say, the market for second hand cars, if some cars are more popular than others then car sellers can charge higher prices, so would be the case in the education market. Resources will thus be efficiently allocated.

(a) Why might it be argued that there is allocative inefficiency in areas where some schools are oversubscribed?
(b) What might be the advantages and disadvantages to introducing a voucher and fee system in education?

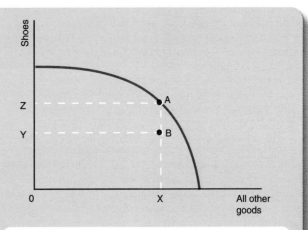

Figure 16.1 *Efficiency and the production possibility frontier*
At B, the economy is productively inefficient because more shoes could be produced without affecting the amount of all other goods available. All points on the PPF are productively efficient and allocatively efficient.

Question 3

Privatisation (the transfer of ownerships of assets from the government to the private sector) in the UK in the 1980s and 1990s led to a considerable reduction in the number of workers employed in the industries that were privatised. In electricity, gas, the railways and water, fewer workers were employed after privatisation to produce the same amount of goods and services. In the case of coal, the output of coal and the number of miners employed declined substantially after privatisation as coal mines found that demand for UK coal fell. The main customer for coal, the electricity industry, switched to gas fired power stations and also increased its imports of cheaper foreign coal.

(a) Using a production possibility diagram, explain the effect of privatisation on productive efficiency in the UK.
(b) Using a production possibility diagram and labelling the axes 'coal' and 'all other goods', explain how privatisation coincided with a change in allocative efficiency.

All points on the PPF are productively efficient because at any point, production must be taking place using the least amount of resources. All points are also allocatively efficient. Points to the right of the PPF are not obtainable. If production takes place within the PPF, it is possible to gain both more shoes and more of all other goods which can be distributed to consumers. So consumers don't have to give up shoes in order to get more of all other goods. On the frontier, a trade-off has to be made. So at any point on the frontier, a movement to another point would involve giving up one good for another. It is not possible to say which point is the most socially desirable because we would need information about social preferences to make this judgment.

The market and economic efficiency

Markets often lead to an efficient allocation of resources. In a market where there are many buyers and sellers, competition forces producers to produce at lowest cost. If they fail to do so, buyers will purchase their goods from lower cost firms. So competitive markets tend to lead to productive efficiency. Markets also tend towards allocative efficiency. Customers are able to cast their spending 'votes' in the market. This determines what is produced. If consumers want to buy more shoes and fewer garden chairs, then shoe firms will expand production, whilst manufacturers of garden chairs will cut back on their production. Free markets allow this transfer of productive resources from one use to another.

Market failure

Markets, though, do not necessarily lead to economic efficiency. MARKET FAILURE, where markets lead to economic inefficiency, can occur for a number of reasons. These will be considered in detail in units 18 to 22. However, market failure occurs for a number of reasons.

Lack of competition in a market (☞ unit 18) Economic efficiency is likely to be present in a market where there are many buyers and sellers. But in many markets, there are either only a few buyers or a fewer sellers. In the rail transport industry, for instance, most travellers have no choice about which company to use on a particular journey. In the water industry, households are forced to buy their water from one company. In the UK soap powder market, two firms dominate sales. In the defence industry, the UK government is the only UK buyer of goods. Trade unions would like to be in a position where only union members work in a place of work. Where there is **imperfect competition**, there is likely to be market failure. Firms which dominate their markets, for instance, will attempt to charge high prices in order to make greater profit. But they can only do this by restricting supply to the market, denying customers the ability to buy as much as they would have done if the market had been competitive. This leads to allocative inefficiency. Trade unions can push up costs to firms if they are successful in getting higher wages for their members than the market rate. This leads to productive inefficiency.

Externalities (☞ unit 19) Prices and profits should be accurate signals, allowing the actors in the market mechanism to allocate resources efficiently. In reality, prices and profits can be very misleading. This is because actual prices and profits may not reflect the true prices and profits to society of different economic activities. For instance, in Brazil it makes commercial sense to cut down the rain forest to provide grazing land for cattle sold to the West as meat for hamburgers. But this could lead to economic catastrophe in the long term because of the effects of global warming. The market is putting out the wrong signals and leading to economic inefficiency and a misallocation of resources.

Missing markets (☞ unit 20) The market, for a variety of reasons, may fail to provide certain goods and services. Some goods such as defence (called **public goods**) will not be provided by the market. Other goods, called **merit goods**, will be underprovided. Health care and education are two examples of merit goods. Part of the reason for underprovision is that the market mechanism can be poor at dealing with risk and providing information to agents in the market.

Factor immobility Factors of production (land, labour and capital, ☞ unit 2) may be immobile. This means that they are difficult to transfer from one use to another. For instance, a train once built is only useful as a train. It cannot be changed into a car or a plane. As for labour, workers can be immobile. A coal miner made redundant might have few skills to offer in other types of work. So he or she may find it difficult to get a job. An unemployed worker in a high unemployment area might be unable or not be willing to move to a job in a low unemployment area. For instance, it may be impossible to find housing at an affordable rent or price in the low unemployment area. Or the worker might not want to leave family and friends in the local area. The greater the immobility of factors, the more time it will take for markets to clear when there is a shock to the economic system. Factor immobility was one of the reasons why the North of England, Wales, Scotland and Northern Ireland suffered above average unemployment rates during the 1960s, 1970s and 1980s. Traditional heavy primary and manufacturing industries were concentrated in these areas. As they declined, workers were made redundant. However, new industry with new capital was not created in sufficient volume to compensate for the decline of old industries. Unemployed workers found it hard, if not impossible, to get jobs. But neither were sufficient workers prepared to leave these regions to find employment in low unemployment areas of the UK.

Inequality Market failure is not just caused by economic inefficiency. It can also be caused by **inequality** in the economy. In a market economy, the ability of individuals to consume goods depends upon the income of the household in which they live. Household income comes from a variety of sources.
- Wages are paid to those who work outside the

household. In the labour market, different wages are paid to different workers depending on factors such as education, training, skill and location.
- Interest, rent and dividends are earned from the wealth of the household. Wealth may include money in bank and building society accounts, stocks and shares, and property.
- Private pensions are another type of unearned income. Private pensions represent income from a pension fund which can be valued and is a form of wealth.
- Other income includes state benefits such as unemployment benefit, child benefit and state pensions.

The market mechanism may lead to a distribution of income which is undesirable or unacceptable. For instance, income levels may be so low that a household is unable to afford basic **necessities** (☞ unit 1) such as food, shelter or clothing. If healthcare is only provided by the private sector, a household may not be able to afford medical care. The state may then need to intervene, either to provide income in the form of benefits, or goods and services such as healthcare to increase consumption levels.

key terms

Allocative or economic efficiency - occurs when resources are distributed in such a way that no consumers could be made better off without other consumers becoming worse off.
Dynamic efficiency - occurs when resources are allocated efficiently over time.
Market failure - where resources are inefficiently allocated due to imperfections in the working of the market mechanism.
Productive efficiency - is achieved when production is achieved at lowest cost.
Static efficiency - occurs when resources are allocated efficiently at a point in time.
Technical efficiency - is achieved when a given quantity of output is produced with the minimum number of inputs.

Applied economics

The Common Agricultural Policy (CAP)

When the European Union (EU), formerly the European Community, was first formed there was a commitment to free trade between member countries. This found its first major expression in 1962 in the Common Agricultural Policy, a Community-wide policy which aimed to harmonise the agricultural policies of the original six member countries (☞ unit 21). One of the implicit aims of CAP was to increase efficiency in the market for agricultural products. To what extent has this been achieved?

Productive efficiency has certainly increased. Table 16.3 shows that the number of small, relatively inefficient, farms has declined over time whilst the number of large farms over 50 hectares with lower overall costs has increased. There has been a substantial fall in employment in the agricultural sector as Table 16.4 shows. At the same time, due to more intensive farming methods, more use of fertilizers and machinery and higher yielding crop and animal strains, output has risen.

However, European agriculture is not fully productively efficient. There are still far too many small farmers producing on marginal land, such as in Wales or the French Alps. In 1995, the average size of a farm ranged from 8.7 hectares in Portugal, to 19.1 hectares in Belgium, 38.5 hectares in France and 69 hectares in the UK. Small farmers are unable to exploit the economies of scale enjoyed by large farms and consequently their costs of production are much higher.

But it could be argued that the difference in productivity between farms in Europe is not as important an issue as the difference in the cost of production between the EU and the rest of the world. World prices for many agricultural commodities, such as wheat or butter, have been considerably below those maintained by the complex system of tariffs, quotas and intervention prices in the EU.

Consumers lose out because of these high domestic prices. Their loss can be calculated by multiplying the amount they purchase by the difference between domestic and world farm gate prices.

However, farmers worldwide also tend to be supported by the taxpayer. Figure 16.2 shows the extent of the subsidies paid to farmers throughout the world. In the EU, for instance, farmers receive an average 40 per cent of the market value of what they produce in subsidies. The EU operates a variety of agricultural support schemes. 1997/8 details are shown in Table 16.5. Part is structural aid, helping farmers to leave the land or improve their productivity. Part is income support, paying farmers an income irrespective of output, as for instance in the case of set-aside for wheat. The single largest cost, though, is on price support, raising the price of agricultural products, for instance by purchasing them when prices reach a low enough level.

The agricultural market is not just productively inefficient. It is arguably allocatively inefficient in terms of the MC = price criterion. The fact that taxpayers throughout the developed world are having to subsidise farmers means that the marginal cost of production far exceeds the price consumers are prepared to pay. Allocative efficiency could therefore be increased by shifting resources out of agriculture into other industries.

Over the past ten years, there has been an increasing awareness of the costs of CAP and other agricultural support systems. In the Uruguay Round of trade talks completed in 1994, the USA, Australia and New Zealand pressed for a complete abolition of all subsidies. The EU resisted and in the end only agreed to reduce but not eliminate farm subsidies. This was because the abolition of CAP would produce losers as well as gainers. EU land owning farmers would be the main losers. Land prices would plummet because prices for produce would fall substantially. Marginal farmers too would lose because their land would not be productive enough to support them in business. The experience of New Zealand, which almost abolished farm subsidies in the 1980s, suggests, however, that farm profits would remain roughly constant. There would be lower prices and less state handouts. But equally, the costs of production, particularly rents on farms, would fall too leaving most farmers on good farming land with broadly similar incomes.

Table 16.3 *Number of holdings by size, 000*

	Total	0-5ha	5-10ha	10-20ha	20-50ha	>50ha
EUR-10						
1970	7 667	4 257	1 244	1 115	850	201
1987	5 005	2 320	813	719	780	373
EUR-12						
1987	6 920	3 402	1 163	936	946	473
1993	7 226	4 234	930	747	783	534

Source: adapted from European Commission, *European Economy, EC Agricultural Policy for the 21st Century*, Number 4, 1994; European Commission, *The Agricultural Situation in the European Union 1997*.

Table 16.4 *Changes in the agricultural labour force*

	Millions				% of total civilian employment
	1970	1980	1990	1996	1998
Greece	1.3	1.0	0.9	0.8	20.3
Spain	3.7	2.2	1.5	1.1	8.6
France	2.8	1.8	1.4	1.1	4.8
Germany	2.3	1.4	1.1	1.0	3.2
UK	-	0.6	0.6	0.5	2.0
EU12	-	11.9	8.9	7.0	5.0
EU15	-	12.7	9.5	7.5	5.1

Source: European Commission, *The Agricultural Situation in the European Union 1997*.

Table 16.5 *Main institutional prices and aids applicable for 1997/98 marketing year* ECU/tonne

	1997/98
Arable crops	
Compensatory payment	
- Cereals	54.34
- Rapeseed, sunflower and soya (reference amounts in ECU/ha)	433.50
- Peas, fieldbeans and sweet lupins	78.49
- Non-fibre flax seed	105.10
- Set aside	68.83
Additional compensatory payment for durum wheat (ECU/ha)	
- Traditional zones	358.60
- Non-traditional zones	138.90
Cereals	
- Intervention price	119.10
Rice	
- Intervention price	333.45
Potato starch	
- Minimum price	209.78
- Compensatory payment	86.94
- Industry premium	22.25
Sugar	
- Basic price for sugar beet	47.67
- Intervention price for white sugar (ECU/q)	63.19
Olive oil	
- Production target price	3 837.70
- Intervention price	1 751.60
- Representative market price	295.00
- Production aid	1 422.00
- Consumption aid	120.70
Dried fodder	
- Fixed aid	68.83
Lentils, chick peas, vetches	
- Fixed aid (ECU/ha)	146.51
Fibre flax	
- Fixed aid (ECU/ha)	815.86
Hemp	
- Fixed aid (ECU/ha)	716.63
Silkworms	
- Aid per box	133.26
Cotton	
- Guide price	1 063.00
- Minimum price	1 009.90
Milk products	
(a) Target price for milk	309.80
(b) Intervention price	
- Butter	3 282.00
- Skimmed-milk powder	2 055.20
Beef/Veal	
- Intervention price for adult bovine animals (carcase weight - category R3)	3 475.00
Sheepmeat	
- Basic price (slaughter weight)	5 040.70

Pigmeat
- Basic price (slaughter weight)   1 509.39

Table wine		
- Guide price type	RI (ECU/%/hl)	3.828
	RII (ECU/%/hl)	3.828
	RIII (ECU/hl)	62.15
	AI (ECU/%/hl)	3.828
	AII (ECU/hl)	82.81
	AIII (ECU/hl)	94.57

Tobacco (premiums)		
- I	Flue cured	2 709.65
- II	Light air cured	2 167.48
- III	Dark air cured	2 167.48
- IV	Fire cured	2 383.62
- V	Sun cured	2 167.48
- VI	Basmas	3 754.15
- VII	Katerini	3 185.41
- VIII	Kaba koulak	2 276.15

Source: European Commission, *The Agricultural Situation in the European Union 1997*.

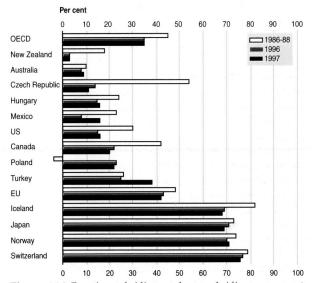

Figure 16.2 *Farming subsidies: producer subsidies as a percentage of value of farm production.*
Source: adapted from *Agricultural Policies in OECD Countries*, OECD, 1998.

Car pricing

Treasure Island

Motor manufacturers unofficially referred to the UK as 'Treasure Island' in the second half of the 1990s. This was because car manufacturers were able to charge some of the highest prices in Europe to their UK dealers for new cars. In 1998, for instance, European Commission figures showed that the UK was responsible for the highest prices in 57 of 76 models surveyed, with the cost up to 45 per cent more than in the cheapest EU countries.

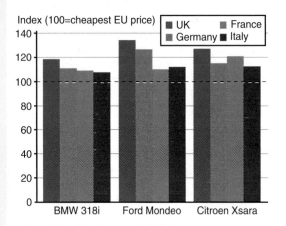

Figure 16.3 *Selected car prices: EU comparison*
Source: adapted from European Commission.

The block exemption

In 1985, car makers were given an exemption to competition rules by the European Union. This 'block exemption' enables them to decide who is to distribute their cars. In practice, the car makers have set up dealer networks. The car makers limit the number of dealers in an area, effectively giving dealers local monopolies. Dealers are only allowed to sell one make of car in the exclusive contracts they sign with car manufacturers.

The block exemption prevents the sort of competition that is standard in other markets. For instance, car manufacturers are legally entitled to refuse to supply cars to any business other than their dealers. This means that supermarkets, for instance, can't sell cars. Equally, parts retailers like Halfords could not set up a car selling business. It also means that car manufacturers can prevent car dealers from offering more than one make of car on their premises. For instance, a car dealer cannot sell both Ford and Vauxhall cars from the same site.

Buying abroad

Since the introduction of the block exemption, individual car buyers in the UK have, in theory, been able to buy a left-hand drive car from any dealer in the EU at the same pre-tax price as a right-hand drive car from the same dealer. In practice, few motorists did this. Indeed, few motorists were even aware of the fact that they could save money by buying abroad.

Even when motorists have been aware of this possibility, they have faced difficulties. One major obstacle has been that would-be car drivers have had to travel to the Continent to place their order in person. They have to put down a large deposit with a dealer who they know little or nothing about. Then they have to collect the car in person.

Another obstacle is that few continental dealers will accept an order for a left-hand drive car. Partly this is because the car manufacturers have, in contravention of EU law, essentially refused to supply left-hand drive cars to continental dealers. When dealers do accept orders, it might take months or even years to deliver, or the dealer might cancel the order and return the deposit. Again, this has tended to be because of illegal pressures from motor manufacturers. UK buyers are not the only victims of this. In 1998, for instance, Volkswagen was fined £71.6 million for ordering its Italian dealers not to sell cars to buyers from outside Italy. VW wanted to stop Austrian and German citizens from buying its cars in Italy where they were around 30 per cent cheaper.

In 1999, following much publicity, a number of organisations, including the Consumers Association and the Virgin Group, announced they would be setting up schemes which would allow individuals to buy cars from the Continent with their help. The motorist would pay a small fee for the service. The motor manufacturers will find it much more difficult to refuse to supply high-profile organisations than the lone motorist.

Dealers

Car manufacturers argue that exclusive dealer franchises benefit the consumer. Dealers must have facilities to repair and service cars according to minimum standards. Buying and running a car involves important safety issues. Only a franchised dealer network can maintain the standards needed to ensure that cars on the road are safe. Dealers must also carry stocks of parts. This provides an important service to customers who want their cars repaired quickly.

Critics point to surveys which show that motorists tend to be dissatisfied with garages. Franchised dealer garages come out no better than other garages. Franchised dealers certainly tend to be more expensive than non-franchised garages.

As for buying new cars, many firms have expressed interest in setting up car sale operations. Supermarket chains, for instance, argue that they could be highly successful by offering much lower prices. They could buy in bulk, arrange for pre-delivery work to be done at low cost, and deliver cars to the customer's door. They argue that franchised dealers, with low volume sales, large premises and staff to pay, are an inefficient part of the car distribution chain.

Source: adapted from *The Guardian*, 21.7.1999; the *Financial Times*, 12.11.1998.

1. **Distinguish between productive and allocative efficiency. Use examples from the data to illustrate your answer.**
2. **Explain what types of market failure might have existed in the UK car market in the second half of the 1990s.**
3. **Evaluate whether economic efficiency would occur if the block exemption for car manufacturers in the EU were abolished.**

Competition and efficiency

Summary

1. Competitive markets tend to be characterised by a number of different firms, none of which is able to control the market, producing homogeneous or weakly branded goods, in a market where there are low barriers to entry and there is perfect knowledge.

2. Firms in competitive markets are likely only to earn normal profit in the long run. In a perfectly competitive industry, firms will operate where their average costs are at a minimum.

3. Firms in perfectly competitive markets are likely to be economically efficient in that they produce at lowest cost and are unable to earn abnormal profits in the long run. In an imperfectly competitive market, prices are likely to be higher because firms are unlikely to produce at the lowest average cost possible and may be able to earn abnormal profits.

Market structure

No two markets are the same. The market for sports shoes is different from the market for steel or holidays abroad. This is because the MARKET STRUCTURE is different in each market. The market structure is those characteristics of the market which influence the way in which firms in the market behave. A **competitive market** has a number of different characteristics.

A number of different firms in the industry In a competitive industry there are at least two firms in the industry. In the most competitive industries, where there is PERFECT COMPETITION, there is a large number of firms, none of which is large enough to have any economic power over the industry. In farming, for instance, there are large numbers of farms. Even the largest farm in the UK still produces only a very small fraction of total farming output. In other industries, there is IMPERFECT COMPETITION, i.e. there is not full competition in the market. In some imperfectly competitive industries, there are large numbers of small firms. In most, though, a few firms tend to dominate the industry. In the grocery retailing industry in the UK, for instance, the largest four supermarket chains sell over 50 per cent of all goods (i.e. their MARKET SHARE is more than 50 per cent). In the soap powder industry, two firms have over 80 per cent of the market.

Entry to the industry New firms are constantly being set up. Existing firms may expand their product range and enter new markets. In some markets, it is easier to set up and enter than in others. The obstacles to setting up are called BARRIERS TO ENTRY. There are many types of barrier to entry (☞unit 18 for a more detailed discussion). For instance, it may be so costly to set up that only very large firms could consider entering the industry. Car manufacturing is an example. On the other hand, it is relatively cheap to set up in business as a grocery store. The law may be another barrier to entry. For instance, to set up a pharmacy in the UK, you have to have a licence. When setting up as a book publisher, you cannot print any books where the copyright is owned by another publisher. No firm in the UK is

legally allowed to enter the drugs trade. Costs of production might be another barrier to entry. In industries like car manufacturing or bulk chemical production it is very expensive to produce in small quantities. Producing in large quantities drives down the average cost. In these industries there are considerable **economies of scale** (☞unit 18). In a perfectly competitive industry, barriers to entry are very low. It is very easy, for instance, to enter the retail industry. In some imperfectly competitive industries, barriers to entry are low too, but in others they can be very high. This would then be a reason why competition was imperfect, because high barriers reduce competition in the market.

Product homogeneity and branding For there to be perfect competition, customers must be able to have a wide choice of supplier, all of whom are selling the same product. This means the goods being sold must be HOMOGENEOUS. In farming, for instance, carrots are a standard product. No farmer can claim that his or her carrots are different from those of another farmer. The same is true for products such as steel, oil, basic chemicals and copper.

In an imperfectly competitive market, however, the product of one firm is different from that of another. Persil washing powder is different from Ariel. A Vauxhall Vectra is different from a Ford Escort. Firms are then said to BRAND their products.

Knowledge In a perfectly competitive industry, there is PERFECT KNOWLEDGE. This means that all firms have access to the same information. They can all find out what is the current market price. There are no trade secrets. All firms have access to the same information about production techniques. In an imperfectly competitive industry, there might be perfect knowledge. However, knowledge may be imperfect for a number of reasons. For instance, firms may have secret formulations which make their products unique. The formula for Coca Cola, for instance, is known only to a few at Coca Cola itself. Firms may keep knowledge about methods of production to themselves, not allowing rivals to see how a good is manufactured.

Question 1

Barclaycard announced yesterday that it was to cut 1 100 jobs over the next three years due to increasing competition. Launched in 1966, it has always been the market leader in the UK market. But whereas it had 35 per cent of the market in 1992, this had now fallen to 25 per cent. Today, consumers have the choice of thousands of different cards. All the large banks and building societies offer their own cards and run cards on behalf of organisations ranging from gas companies to motoring organisations to Oxford colleges. Any organisation can, through a bank, issue its own card. Most card holders stay loyal to one card in the short term despite there being enormous differences in charges, interest rates and benefits between cards. However, as Barclaycard has found to its cost, over a number of years, customers do tend to change and move towards cards which offer low costs or give benefits like cashbacks or money off telephone or gas bills. Consumers are reluctant to change, partly because of the time cost in so doing but also because they are often unaware of just how expensive is their card to run compared to the best on the market.

Source: adapted from *The Times*, 23.9.1999.

(a) To what extent is the credit card market competitive?

Prices, profits and costs in competitive markets

In perfectly competitive markets, like farming or copper mining:
- there are large numbers of small firms in the industry;
- there is freedom of entry to the market;
- firms produce identical or homogeneous goods;
- perfect knowledge exists throughout the industry.

This market structure affects the way in which firms behave. Because there is freedom of entry to a market where firms produce identical goods, all firms will charge the same price in equilibrium. To understand why, consider what would happen if a firm charged a higher price than other firms. Customers would then switch their demand to other firms because other firms are offering identical products. The firm charging the higher price will lose all its sales and go out of business. If a firm charged a lower price than all other firms, then buyers would switch away from other firms and they would all lose their customers. So they would have to cut their prices to stay in the industry.

Competition will not drive prices down to zero. In the long term, firms will only supply a good if they can make a profit. The minimum profit that a firm must make to prevent it from moving its economic resources to production of another good is called NORMAL PROFIT. If firms in a perfectly competitive industry are able to make ABNORMAL PROFITS, profit which is greater than normal profit, then new firms will be attracted into the industry. They will want to take advantage of being able to earn higher than normal profit. However, their entry will increase supply and drive prices down. The long run equilibrium price will be the one where prices are just high enough for firms to make normal profits, so no firms

are being forced out of the industry, but equally no firms are being attracted into the industry.

Firms in a perfectly competitive industry will also produce at lowest average cost. Assume that one firm was a higher cost producer than other firms in the industry. It would have to charge the same price as other firms or risk losing all its customers. But then its profits would be lower than those of other firms because its costs were higher. Since all other firms are only earning normal profit, it would be making less than normal profit, the minimum profit needed to persuade the owners of the firm to keep their resources in that industry. So this firm would leave the industry because it was not sufficiently profitable.

On the other hand, assume that a firm could produce at lower cost than other firms and was making abnormal profit. Then other firms would be able to find out why this firm had lower costs because there is perfect knowledge in the industry. If it is because the firm has adopted new production methods, then these production methods will be taken up by other firms. If it is because the firm has a particularly productive factor of production, other firms will attempt to buy it, raising its price and hence its cost. For instance, if success is due to a very successful managing director, then other firms will attempt to employ him or her by offering a higher salary. In the long term, costs will be become the same across the industry. They will be the minimum cost possible.

In imperfectly competitive industries:
- there may be many small firms in the industry or it could be dominated by just a few firms;
- there might be relatively free entry to the industry or there might be barriers to entry;
- firms produce branded goods;
- there may or may not be perfect knowledge.

This market structure limits competition. Because each firm is producing a slightly different branded product, it is

Question 2

No frills airlines are a fact of life today. Debonair, Virgin Express, Ryanair and Easyjet are just some of the companies operating out of the UK. They offer rock bottom prices in return for a minimalist service. There are usually no free meals or drinks, limited or no refunds if you don't turn up for the flight and you may have to fly from less popular airports like Luton or Stansted. However, there is a big market for the product. Since Ryanair started flying from London to Dublin in 1985, the market has grown from 1 million flights per year to 4 million. Because these air companies operate at such low prices, profit margins are wafer thin. With more companies entering the market each year, it is likely that there will be some casualties in the future. Sharp unexpected falls in demand for a season, caused for instance by a fear of terrorist attack, could knock out the weakest companies. Even so, no frills airlines are here to stay, which is good news for the budget traveller.

Source: adapted from the *Financial Times*, 22.10.1999.

(a) Why are no frills airlines unlikely to earn abnormal profits despite a growing market?

able to some extent to decide on what price it will charge. If other firms charge lower prices, it is likely to still keep some of its customers who will remain loyal to buying its branded good. Market power will increase the fewer the number of competitors and the higher the barriers to entry. If entry barriers are very high, firms will be able to charge higher prices without worrying that new entrants will come in and take away market share. So in imperfect competition it could be that competitive pressures are strong enough to force profits down to a normal level in the long run. However, it is more likely that firms will be charging high enough prices to earn abnormal profit.

Competition and efficiency

Perfect competition is likely to lead to economic efficiency (☞ unit 16). First, firms in a perfectly competitive industry will, in the long run, be productively efficient. As explained above, competitive pressures will ensure that firms produce at lowest average cost. If they fail to do so, they will be driven out of the industry. Second, firms in a perfectly competitive industry are likely to be allocatively efficient (☞ unit 16). Customers will be able to buy at the lowest price that is possible because firms are only able to make normal profit.

In contrast, firms in imperfectly competitive industries are likely to be neither productively or allocatively efficient. There is no pressure to produce at lowest average cost because firms produce branded goods. This gives them some control over how much they wish to sell, i.e. it gives them some control over where on the demand curve they sell. Firms will choose to sell where profit is maximised and this is unlikely to be the minimum average cost point. Hence, imperfectly competitive firms are unlikely to be productively efficient.

They are unlikely to be allocatively efficient either. Production would be greater and prices lower if the industry were perfectly competitive. Firms in imperfect competition are likely to earn abnormal profits. If they earned only normal profit, they would have to cut prices and expand their production. Hence, in imperfect competition, firms restrict supply in order to exploit the customer for abnormal profit. Even where firms earn only normal profit, output is still likely to be lower and prices higher than if the industry were perfectly competitive. This is because firms will choose to produce where profit is maximised, in this case where they are earning just normal profit, and not where average costs are lowest.

Productive and allocative efficiency are aspects of static efficiency (efficiency at a point in time ☞ unit 16). Perfect competition is likely to lead to productive and allocative efficiency, whilst imperfect competition is not. Therefore perfect competition is likely to lead to static efficiency, whilst imperfect competition is not. However, perfect competition may not lead to greater **dynamic efficiency**. There is no incentive to innovate over time in a perfectly competitive industry. Because there is perfect knowledge in the industry, discoveries and inventions by one firm will become quickly available for use by all other firms. There is therefore no point in spending large amounts on research and development. In imperfect competition where firms can protect innovation, for instance through patents and copyrights, they have an incentive to be innovative. If they can develop a new product which customers like, they can sell it at a high price and earn abnormal profit on it.

Question 3

When Bill Good, managing director of Sterling Tubes, joined the company in the mid-1980s, it employed more than 600 workers. By 1996 this had fallen to a little over 400 and now only 300 are employed. These changes have in part been forced on the company by price pressures. Since 1995, the average price of its finished products has fallen by about 30 per cent before inflation, pushing the company into loss. Admittedly, the main raw material cost, steel itself, has also fallen by 30 per cent. However, to return to profitability the company has been forced to find ways of cutting all its other costs by 30 per cent. It has done that by cutting labour, investing in new machinery, changing production practices and imposing price cuts on suppliers. The company has also attempted to add value to products, to make its products superior to competitors. But there seems to be no halt to the price reductions in the industry. Competition is getting fiercer, especially as new suppliers emerge in the Far East. Only further cost cutting will enable Sterling Tubes to survive.

Source: adapted from the *Financial Times*, 18.2.1999.

(a) How has competition led to (i) productive efficiency and (ii) allocative efficiency in the steel market?
(b) How has Sterling Tubes attempted to increase its dynamic efficiency?

key terms

Abnormal profit - the profit over and above normal profit.
Barriers to entry - factors which make it difficult or impossible for firms to enter an industry and compete with existing producers.
Branded good - a named good which in the perception of its buyers is different from other similar goods on the market.
Homogeneous goods - goods which are identical.
Imperfect competition - a market structure where there are several firms in the industry, each of which has the ability to control the price that it sets for its products.
Market share - the proportion of sales in market taken by a firm or a group of firms.
Market structure - the characteristics of a market which determine the behaviour of firms within the market.
Normal profit - the profit that the firm could make by using its resources in their next best use. Normal profit is an economic cost.
Perfect knowledge or information - exists if all buyers in a market are fully informed of prices and quantities for sale, whilst producers have equal access to information about production techniques.

Applied economics

Financial services

The 1990s saw an explosion of competition in the financial services sector. First it was the building societies greatly expanding their product range to compete with the banks. Then other players entered the market. In the late 1990s, the large supermarket chains each launched saving and borrowing facilities. They wanted to capitalise on the trust that their customers placed in them, spreading their brand name and image across a wider range of products. Then insurance companies decided that they too could offer financial services other than their traditional insurance and long term savings products. In October 1998, the Prudential Bank launched its Egg savings account which promised to pay a high rate of interest until at least 2000. Its interest rate was so high and the product so successful that in April 1999, having gained half a million customers in just 6 months, it closed its doors to new customers other than those who were prepared to operate their account through the internet.

The financial services market has become a highly competitive market for a number of reasons. Traditionally, there has been a large number of firms in the market, but in the past they tended to specialise in offering a narrow range of products. Changes to the law in the 1980s deregulated the market giving much greater freedom to financial institutions to enter new markets. Barriers to entry are fairly low. It is, for instance, very cheap for a building society to offer pension products to its customers, or for an insurance company to offer a savings account. Companies entering the market typically use a respected brand name to increase access to the market. For instance, Sainsbury's, Virgin, Halifax and Direct Line have all used their names to launch financial services. Access to knowledge in the industry is relatively easy. Many new entrants have chosen to buy into industry knowledge by teaming up with an established firm in the market. Sainsbury's, for instance, uses the Royal Bank of Scotland to run its financial services.

There are economies of scale to be gained for those companies like Virgin or Egg which have proved successful. At the same time, the marginal or extra cost of offering a service which, in fact, has not proved particularly successful is fairly low. Successful products, therefore, tend to be ones which genuinely offer value for money to the customer. This might a high rate of interest on savings, as with Egg, a generous bonus scheme for use of a credit card as with Goldfish or low car insurance premiums as with Direct Line. These all cost money. So to make a profit, these providers have to have low costs and therefore they have to be productively efficient. In the short term, they might be so successful, as was the case with Direct Line, that they can earn abnormal profit.

But in the longer term, success tends to lead to other firms launching copycat products, driving down profits and ensuring that there is allocative efficiency. The financial services market can also be argued to be dynamically efficient in that over time it has launched new products geared to customer needs. Cash machines, telephone insurance and internet banking are just some of the innovations seen over the past twenty years.

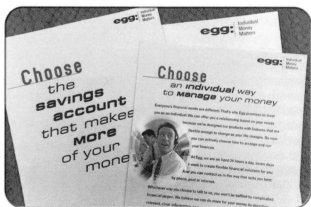

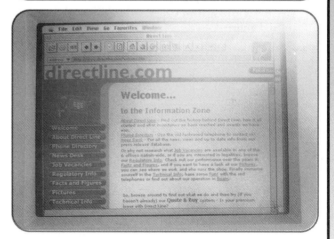

The cinema market

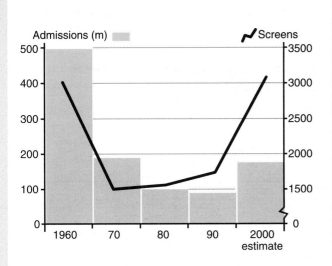

Figure 17.1 *The UK cinema market*
Source: adapted from HMSO.

Bolton in Lancashire became the first battlefield for the new multiplexes in Britain. In 1998, Virgin launched a new multiplex just a few miles away from Warner Village's. Virgin claimed in 1999 that the multiplex had met its sales targets but admitted that these were not as high as would have been the case had there not been another multiplex in the area.

In January 1999, Virgin opened a multiplex cinema in Crawley, Sussex. With 15 screens, a cafe bar and a milk bar, it is part of multi-million pound investment by Virgin countrywide to expand its range of cinemas. Rival chains, such as Warner Village and United Cinemas International, are investing equally heavily in the belief that more people will visit cinemas if they have access to clean, comfortable multiplexes rather than scruffy fleapits.

Source: adapted from the *Financial Times*, 23.1.1999.

Cinemas tend to compete on facilities and films rather than on price. Cinema admissions in any year are highly dependent on the new films launched in that year and outside events. In 1998, for instance, cinema admissions fell because, apart from Titanic, there were no particularly strong films. Cinemas also had to compete with the World Cup in that summer. Cinema operators increasingly want their customers to see going to the cinema as part of a wider leisure experience, including eating out and buying merchandise. In some complexes, there are book and CD stores as well as food outlets. This enables cinemas to increase profits on every visit.

Source: adapted from the *Financial Times*, 23.1.1999.

1. (a) Describe the trends in cinema admissions shown in the data.
   (b) What factors might determine cinema attendance in any one year?
2. Analyse how firms such as Virgin and Warner Village compete in the cinema market.
3. To what extent does this competition lead to economic efficiency in the market?

Summary

1. Monopolies exist because of legal and resource barriers to entry to an industry, natural cost advantages and uncompetitive practices.
2. Natural monopolies exist because of large scale economies in an industry. Economies of scale include purchasing economies, marketing economies, technical economies, managerial economies and financial economies.
3. Monopolies tend to earn abnormal profit by choosing a price higher than would be the case if the industry was competitive.
4. Monopolies are productively efficient if they are natural monopolies exploiting economies of scale and dynamically efficient if their existence leads to technological innovation.
5. Monopolies are allocatively inefficient if they exploit customers by charging higher prices than would be the case under competition.
6. Governments can intervene to correct market failure caused by monopoly activity through taxes and subsidies, prices controls, nationalisation and privatisation, deregulation, breaking up the monopolist or reducing entry barriers.

Monopoly

A MONOPOLY exists where there is only one firm or supplier in an industry. For instance, the Royal Mail has a monopoly on the delivery of certain letters in the UK. Transco has a monopoly on UK gas pipelines. Railtrack has a monopoly on UK rail infrastructure. In practice, firms which have a dominant share of the market tend to be referred to as monopolists as well. For instance, Microsoft, with 90 per cent of the world's PC operating systems market, could be seen as a monopolist.

Firms gain monopoly powers in the long run because of **barriers to entry** (☞ unit 17) to the industry. There are various barriers to entry which can create monopolies.

Legal barriers The government can create monopolies through the legal system. It can make competition illegal in an industry. For instance, in the UK only pharmacies can sell prescription drugs by law. The government has granted GNER a monopoly to run train services on the East Coast main line railway.

Resource barriers In some industries, a monopolist may be able to buy or otherwise acquire the key resources needed to produce a good. For instance, an airline may be able to buy up the sole rights to fly from one airport to another. A supermarket chain may be able to buy the only plot of land available for development for a large supermarket in a small town. An electricity company may buy out all the other competing electricity companies in a country. Customers would then be faced with a sole supplier for the product.

Unfair competition Once created, a monopolist may defend itself through unfair competitive practices. For instance, an airline with a monopoly on a route may slash prices below cost if a new entrant comes into the market. When the new entrant is forced out, the monopolist then puts back up its fares. Or the monopolist may refuse to supply customers with other goods if it buys one good from a new entrant into the market.

Natural cost advantages Some firms are NATURAL MONOPOLIES. They become monopolies because not even a single firm in the industry is large enough to reduce average costs to their minimum.

Size can reduce average costs because of the existence of ECONOMIES OF SCALE. These are factors which cause average costs to fall as the scale of production is increased. There is a number of different sources of economies of scale.

● Purchasing economies. The greater the quantities

Question 1

Microsoft, the world's largest software company, is frequently accused of anti-competitive practices designed to ensure the monopoly of its Windows operating system. In 1996, Blue Mountain Arts, an independent software company, launched a greeting card service. For free, an internet user could choose a design, fill in a message and, via an e-mail, ask the recipient to collect the card from its web site. The service proved highly popular and in November 1998, Blue Mountain's internet site was the 13th busiest on the internet. But in that month, Microsoft launched its own free greetings card service. Then Blue Mountain began getting complaints. In its latest version of its web browser, Microsoft had included a new feature designed to protect users from 'spam' - unwanted e-mail, the equivalent of junk mail on the internet. Blue Mountain's cards, but not those of Microsoft, it was claimed were being put immediately into a junk mail folder in the computer. Blue Mountain immediately took Microsoft to court once it had failed to get Microsoft to sort out the problem.

Source: adapted from the *Financial Times*, 28.12.1998.

(a) In 1998, 90 per cent of the world's personal computers used Microsoft's operating systems. Why does this make it an effective monopoly?
(b) How, according to the data, did Microsoft attempt to increase its monopoly powers in late 1998?

bought of raw materials and other supplies, the lower is likely to be the average cost. Large buyers are able to negotiate larger discounts because they have more market power. It is also usually cheaper to sell large quantities. For instance, transport costs might be lower if a given quantity is delivered to one customer rather than ten as bulk orders might save on packaging.

- Marketing economies. Marketing costs, such as advertising or the cost of promotional leaflets, are often lower per unit sold the greater the volume of sales. The cost of an advertisement, for instance, is the same however many sales it generates. If a catalogue is sent out to customers, again the cost remains the same whatever the response.
- Technical economies. Larger scale machinery or plant can often be more efficient than smaller scale plant. For instance, a boat which is twice the length, breadth and depth of another boat can carry 8 times as much cargo. But it likely to cost less than four times as much to build. A large supermarket costs much less to build per square metre than a small supermarket. What's more, the larger the scale of production, the more likely it is that resources will be fully utilised. A small building firm, for instance, might own a truck which it uses only for a few hours a week to transport materials. A large firm might be able to use the truck far more intensively because it has more jobs on at any one time.
- Managerial economies. **Specialisation** (☞ unit 2) is an important source of greater efficiency. In a small firm, the owner might be part time salesperson, account, receptionists and manager. Employing specialist staff is likely to lead to greater efficiency and therefore lower costs.
- Financial economies. Small firms often find it difficult and expensive to raise finance for new investment. When loans are given, small firms are charged at relatively high rates of interest because banks know that small firms are far more at risk from liquidation than large firms. Large firms have a much greater choice of finance and it is likely to be much cheaper to raise than for small firms.

Examples of natural monopolies include transport systems, such as pipeline networks, rail tracks and electricity power grids. If these are underutilised, which they usually are, then it is possible to lower average costs by increasing throughput in the system. This would be an example of a technical economy of scale.

Prices and profits under monopoly

Monopolists, in the absence of government regulations, can set whatever price they choose to customers. They can choose, for instance, whether to charge £10 per item or £2. It should be remembered, though, that the higher the price they set, the lower will be the demand for the product, i.e. monopolists face a downward sloping demand curve.

The highest price is not necessarily the profit maximising price. If the price is set too high, they could lose profit. This is because the profit gained from sales at a high price could be less than the profit lost from even

more sales at a lower price. For instance, a firm might charge £20 for an item costing £12 for which sales are 1 million units. It then makes a profit of £8 per item or a total of £8 million (£8 x 1 million). But it might be able to sell 2 million units if it reduced its price to £17. Its profit per unit would then only be £5, but its total profit would be £10 million (£5 x 2 million).

The profit earned is likely to be **abnormal profit** (☞ unit 17). It is higher than the minimum amount needed to keep resources employed in that industry, i.e. it is higher than normal profit. The profit is therefore higher than would be earned by the industry if it were **perfectly competitive** (☞ unit 17). In a perfectly competitive industry, fierce competition between many small firms drives the price down to the point where firms are making just enough profit to stay in the industry, i.e. to the point where firms only make normal profit. If there is **imperfect competition** (☞ unit 17), firms may be able to charge higher prices than under perfect competition and earn abnormal profit. Whether the price will be as high as under monopoly, or whether the total industry profits will be as high, depends on how little price competition there is between the firms.

Monopoly, efficiency and market failure

A natural monopoly will be producing at the lowest average cost possible for the level of total demand in the

Question 2

Standard and first class tickets on Richard Branson's Virgin Trains are to rise on average by 9 per cent - compared with the present inflation rate of 1.1 per cent - making it the most expensive railway in Britain. The increases from September 26 mean that there have been cumulative increases in Virgin fares of up to 43.5 per cent over the past two years. A first class return from Wolverhampton to London will rise from £108 to £118 for instance.

Jonathan Bray, the campaign director of Save Our Railways, said that the 'great rail fares farce' was plumbing new depths with Britain's main line distance operator continuing to undermine key national fares. Fares needed stronger regulation from the government given that nearly all train companies enjoyed monopolies on their routes and passengers often had little choice but to travel by train.

Virgin Trains said the company faced a £28 million drop in its government subsidies this year and had to take account of that in its fare structures. It also said that profits were being diverted into acquiring a new fleet of tilting trains which would transform rail travel over the next ten years.

Source: adapted from *The Guardian*, 20.9.1999.

(a) Why can Virgin increase its fares by up to 43.5 per cent over two years without losing most of its passengers?
(b) How does Virgin justify its fare increases?
(c) In January 2000, the first class return fare from Wolverhampton to London was raised to £125. Explain what must happen to passenger numbers for Virgin to increase its profit from this price rise.

industry. Breaking a natural monopoly up into several smaller firms would only result in increased average costs. Hence, natural monopolies are **productively efficient**, i.e. production is at lowest cost (☞ unit 16) compared to a more competitive industry.

However, if the monopoly is not a natural monopoly, then the effect of a break up is more complex. If the industry becomes perfectly competitive, costs will be driven down to a minimum and hence productive efficiency will be achieved. By comparison, monopoly is productively inefficient. If the industry became imperfectly competitive, it is not possible to say whether prices or total profits would fall. Hence, it is impossible to make a comparison about productive efficiency.

As for **allocative efficiency** (☞ unit 16), a natural monopoly is allocatively inefficient in that the firm will have driven up prices and reduced output to earn abnormal profit. But splitting up the industry is unlikely to result in allocative efficiency because prices are likely to be even higher. This is because average costs of production will be higher with several firms in the industry than just one.

Allocative efficiency will be achieved if the firm is not a natural monopolist and it is split up into a number of perfectly competitive firms. Perfect competition will ensure that prices to customers are as low as possible and that firms are only able to earn normal profit. The reduction in price from competition will expand demand and output in the industry, again benefiting customers.

However, if a monopolist is split up but only imperfect competition results, then there may be no improvement in allocative efficiency. Prices may not fall because the new firms may still earn just as much abnormal profit, and hence output may not increase.

Productive and allocative efficiency are types of **static efficiency** (☞ unit 16). However, there is also **dynamic efficiency** to consider. This looks at whether efficiency occurs over a period of time rather than at a point in time. It can be argued that monopoly is dynamically efficient, whilst perfect competition is not. In perfect competition, there is no incentive for individual firms to spend on research and development. This is because there is perfect knowledge in a perfectly competitive industry. Any innovation will quickly become known throughout the industry and if it gives the firm a competitive advantage it will be copied.

With a monopoly, the benefits of any research and development can be exploited by the monopolist. If it develops a new drug, or a new machine, it can exploit that invention and earn abnormal profits. Hence, the ability to keep abnormal profits acts as an incentive for innovation.

What's more, it can be argued that the existence of monopolies and abnormal profits encourages those outside the industry to destroy monopolies by leapfrogging the technology used in the industry. This is called the **process of creative destruction**. For instance, the monopoly of the canals was destroyed by the invention of railways. Telephone and postal monopolies are being destroyed by e-mails and the internet.

However, it can equally be argued that a monopolist could easily become complacent and lazy, sheltering behind high barriers to entry. Lack of competition reduces the incentive to innovate. Spending on research and development is always risky and the monopolist may choose to become extremely risk adverse, preferring profits now to the possibly of higher profits in the future. What's more, the monopolist may not even attempt to profit maximise. Its management may aim to make enough profit to satisfy the shareholders (profit satisficing), and then run the firm for its own benefit. This is unlikely to involve aggressive attempts to innovate.

Question 3

Land based telephone companies have traditionally been monopolies in Europe. Usually state owned, they have had a stranglehold on voice communication. Today, those monopolies face two threats. First, their legal monopolies have been taken away as they have been privatised and their markets opened up to competition from other firms. Second, they face at the extreme the loss of most of their market to a new technology: the mobile telephone, which has only been in existence since the 1980s.

Land based phone networks are, in fact, most unlikely to disappear. They possess cost advantages for large volumes of traffic over mobile phone networks. There is no limit to the number of lines that can be laid, whereas there is a limit to the number of calls that can be made on frequencies allocated to mobile phone networks. Established land line networks also represent a 'sunk' cost - a cost that has already been paid for - and so today's cost of using the system is much lower than if the whole system had to be replaced.

Privatisation and competition have led to falling land line telephone charges in real terms. This has benefited customers as has mobile phone technology which allows customers to call from anywhere.

(a) Why might mobile phone technology represent an example of creative destruction in the telephone industry?

(b) Explain how customers have benefited from the breakdown of the monopoly of land line telephone companies.

Government intervention

Governments are able to use a number of different policies to attempt to correct the market failure caused by monopolies.

Taxes Monopolies are likely to earn abnormal profits. Governments could tax away these abnormal profits, but this is unlikely to increase efficiency. There would be no incentive for the monopolist to reduce its prices as a result. Hence, there would still be allocative inefficiency. Productive inefficiency could even increase because the monopolist would have no incentive to reduce costs. After all, any reduction in costs which led to higher profit would simply be taxed away. It would also reduce any incentive to innovate since any abnormal profits earned from innovation would be taxed. In practice, there would also be the problem of how to set the tax. It is very difficult to estimate the level of abnormal profit made by a firm in a real life situation. If the government set the tax too high, it would discourage the monopolist from even making essential routine investment and the quality and quantity of the good or service produced could deteriorate increasing rather than reducing market failure. The most important advantage of a tax on monopoly profits is that it redistributes income away from the owners of monopoly firms to the rest of the society, arguably improving **equity** in the economy.

Subsidies Monopolists are likely to be allocatively inefficient because they increase prices and reduce output compared to the situation which would occur if the industry were perfectly competitive. A way of reducing prices and increasing supply is to give subsidies to the monopolist to cut its prices and produce more. Whilst this might seem a possible solution, in practice it would be difficult to implement. It would be difficult for the government to know what would be the price and level of output which would lead to allocative efficiency. Hence, it is almost impossible to know what level of subsidy would maximise efficiency. Moreover, subsidising monopolists already earning abnormal profits would be politically unacceptable. Citizens would question why taxpayers' money was being used to increase the profits of already highly profitable firms.

Price controls If a monopolist sets its prices too high to be allocatively efficient, then the government could impose price controls, limiting the prices that the monopolist can set. This is the policy currently adopted to control UK monopoly utilities such as water, telephones and railways. It has the added advantage that there is an incentive for monopolists to increase productive efficiency. If the monopolist faces a fixed price set by the government, it can still earn higher profit if it can drive down its costs. The major drawback of price controls is that it is difficult for the government to know what price to set to maximise efficiency. The monopolist will always argue that it needs higher prices to justify investment which will lead to dynamic efficiency. For instance, the UK water industry always argues that if prices are set too low, it will have to cut back on investment to improve water quality and preserve the environment.

Nationalisation If the monopoly is a private sector company, a solution to lack of efficiency would be to NATIONALISE the firm, i.e. turn it into a state owned company. The government could then force it to set its prices to ensure allocative efficiency. Nationalisation was a very common policy throughout the world from the 1940s onwards. However, nationalised industries came to face two major problems. First, there was no incentive for these firms to reduce costs and hence, over time, they became increasingly productively inefficient. The PRIVATISATION, i.e. the transfer of ownership from the public sector back to the private sector of industries in the 1980s and 1990s has led to considerable reductions in costs and improvements in productive efficiency. Second, governments tended to starve nationalised industries of funds for investment. This damaged dynamic efficiency. Again, privatisation has usually led to considerable increases in investment, to the benefit of customers.

Privatisation and deregulation Many monopolies in the past have been nationalised industries. As already argued, the prices they set might be nearer those needed to ensure allocative efficiency than a private sector monopolist would have set. However, they tended to be productively and dynamically inefficient. So privatising them might increase overall efficiency. To prevent them exploiting the consumer by raising prices, the government could combine privatisation with price controls. Alternatively, it could attempt to bring competition into the industry. Either it could split the monopolist up at privatisation into a number of competing companies. Or it could DEREGULATE the industry by allowing competitors to set up in an industry previously protected by legal barriers to entry. Competition would then hopefully drive prices down towards the level at which allocative efficiency would be achieved.

Breaking up the monopolist The government could order the break up of a monopoly. This won't necessarily lead to any increase in efficiency if the monopoly is a natural monopoly, or if the new firms are in imperfect competition with each other. It is most likely to lead to an increase in efficiency if the new firms are in perfect competition with each other. This could be very difficult to achieve. For instance, it would be impossible if the monopolist produced branded goods.

Reducing entry barriers The government could try to reduce barriers to entry to the industry. This policy would be most easy to implement if the entry barriers were legal. For instance, a way of introducing competition in the UK postal service would be to abolish the Post Office's legal monopoly on letter delivery. However, there is no guarantee that competition would develop, especially if the monopoly is also a natural monopoly. Even if there were competition, the industry might become imperfectly competitive and there might be few efficiency gains as a result.

Question 4

The Rail Regulator, John Swift, has given the go ahead for new through services between Penzance and Manchester Piccadilly, Portsmouth and Liverpool and between London Waterloo and Manchester. The services will be operated by South Wales & West, owned by Prism Rail.

Virgin Cross Country had objected to the proposals, stating that the new services would reduce its revenues. However, John Swift stated that 'My decision is a good example of the flexible application of the new arrangements in the railway industry to improve services to passengers. It is good news for the people of the south west, the Welsh borders and the north west who will have access to better through rail services, thus making their journeys easier.'

When British Rail was being privatised the rail regulator imposed restrictions on new services which competed with existing trains until March 1999. Less onerous controls will continue for a further three years. The aim was to allow the private operators to become established and to prevent 'cherry picking' new operators, running trains at popular times while ignoring less profitable services.

The ruling indicated that the rail regulator was prepared to promote new services within the overall competition framework.

Source: adapted from the *Financial Times*, 11.5.1999.

(a) 'Virgin Cross Country had a monopoly on through trains to the West Country.' Explain what this means.
(b) How did the government, through its railway regulator, break up this monopoly?
(c) What might be the advantages and disadvantages of this break up?

key terms

Deregulation - the process of removing government controls from markets.
Economies of scale - a fall in the long run average costs of production as output rises.
Monopoly - a market structure where one firm supplies all output in the industry without facing competition because of high barriers to entry to the industry.
Nationalisation - the transfer of firms or assets from private sector ownership to state ownership.

Natural monopoly - where economies of scale are so large relative to market demand that the dominant producer in the industry will always enjoy lower costs of production than any other potential competitor.
Privatisation - the opposite of nationalisation, the transfer of organisations or assets from state ownership to private sector ownership.

Applied economics

ATMs

Over the past 20 years, banks have been encouraging their customers to switch cash withdrawals from counters inside banks to Automated Teller Machines (ATMs), often called 'holes in the wall'. For the banks, ATMs are a much cheaper way of processing cash withdrawals. Although machines are costly to install, their running costs are much lower than that of counter staff and the space in the buildings in which they work. ATMs have been one important way in which banks have maintained services to customers whilst branch bank premises have been closed.

However, they have also been a source of monopoly power. Customers, in an ideal world, would like to be able to go to any ATM and withdraw cash. Until relatively recently, they couldn't do this because they couldn't use their cards in the ATMs of many other banks and building societies. In a large town centre, this didn't matter too much. But elsewhere, there might only be one convenient ATM for a customer. The ATM had effectively a local monopoly on the supply of cash. This type of local monopoly is particularly found in rural areas where ATMs are thinly spread across the countryside. Local monopolies prove a powerful inducement for customers of the bank owning the ATM to stay with the bank, or for customers of other banks to change their accounts.

In the 1990s, banks and building societies began to forge alliances which would allow customers to withdraw cash from any ATM in the network. The Link ATM network had always been a common network between the Co-operative Bank and the building societies which founded it. However, customers were usually charged a 'disloyalty fee' by their own bank for using the ATM of another bank. Partly this covered the fee that the bank had to pay to the bank owning the ATM for the service provided. Partly, it was monopoly profit, designed to discourage use of other ATMs.

In 1999, Barclays proposed to start charging a £1 fee to non-Barclay's Bank customers with Link cards using its ATMs. This would be on top of any disloyalty fee charged by the other bank to its customers. An Abbey National customer, for instance, could withdraw £10 from a Barclay's ATM. He or she would then be charged £1 by Barclays Bank and a further £1.50 by Abbey National. The total fee would be £2.50. The actual average cost to a bank of processing an ATM transaction was around 30p.

Commentators at the time felt that Barclays Bank was attempting to retain some control of its market. In particular, it was annoyed that new telephone and internet banks, like Egg and Smile, had been so successful at winning new customers. These banks had no ATMs of their own but issued their customers with Link cards to make cash withdrawals. They often absorbed the cost of any ATM transactions. Hence, Barclays felt the need to impose an additional charge to increase the cost to non-Barclays customers and encourage them to become Barclays customers.

Did it matter from an efficiency viewpoint that Barclays Bank wanted to restrict access to its ATMs? If implemented, its effect would have been to reduce the number of withdrawals from ATMs throughout the banking system and raised their average price. Some customers would have been discouraged from withdrawing cash. They would instead have made fewer but larger withdrawals, used their branches more, or made payments by cheque or card instead of cash. Reducing output by raising price leads to allocative inefficiency in the market. So the move would have impaired efficiency.

LINK COSTS

Charges levied on customers using rival bank ATMs through the Link network at 10.7.1999

Abbey National	£1.50 from 12.7.99
(Bank Account and Business Bank Account customers can use HSBC free of charge)	
Barclays	£1 (unclear if remaining free at Lloyds)
Britannia BS	50p
Coventry BS	50p
Derbyshire BS	40p
Lloyds	£1.50
(free at Royal Bank of Scotland, Bank of Scotland. Unclear if remaining free at Barclays)	
HSBC	£1 (free at NatWest, Clydesdale and Ulster Bank)
NatWest	60p (free at HSBC, Clydesdale and TSB)
Northern Rock	60p

ATM charges are free for all Link users at Alliance & Leicester, Bank of Ireland, Bank of Scotland, Bradford and Bingley BS, Bristol & West, Chelsea BS, Clydesdale, Co-op Bank, Halifax, Nationwide, Royal Bank of Scotland, Sainsbury's and Tesco.

Figure 18.1 *ATMs charges*
Source: adapted from *The Guardian*, 10.7.1999.

There was a number of different ways in which the government could have responded. It could have judged that the welfare losses were not great enough to take any action. Alternatively, it could have imposed rules or regulations which prevented Barclays Bank and other members of the Link network from making changes to the existing pricing structure. A third option would have been for the government to impose a maximum price on ATM transactions. Banks would only be able to charge a maximum of, say, 50 pence for a withdrawal from non-customers. A more sophisticated solution to address the problem of local monopolies would be to impose maximum prices on ATMs which are located, say, more than a quarter of a mile away from the nearest ATM. The danger, though, is that banks might lose the incentive to install further ATMs or close down some existing ATMs. To prevent this from happening, the pricing structure would have to be such as to allow banks and building societies to earn at least normal profits on their ATMs.

Cloning Dolly

In 1997, the world was shocked when it was announced that scientists at Scotland's Roslin Institute had successfully cloned a sheep. It was the world's first successful cloning of an animal. The sheep, called Dolly, became instantly famous.

In 2000, a patent was granted in Britain and the US on the nuclear transfer technique used by the Institute. The patent was award to Geron-Biomed, a Californian biotechnology company that in 1999 has bought Roslin Biomed, the company spun out from the Institute.

Geron-Biomed believes that cloning had several potential medical applications. It could be used to create herds of animals with desired traits, such as one genetically modified to produce human red blood cells for transfusions. The company is also trying to clone pigs, which could be genetically altered to provide organs for human transplants. Geron's patent does not cover human reproductive cloning. In the long term, the company plans to use cloning and other techniques to grow cells, or even whole organs, from a patient's skin cells. 'This regenerative medicine would be a new segment of medicine, providing treatments for a series of degenerative diseases like Parkinson's and Alzheimer's for which current medicines are only palliative', according to a spokesperson for Geron-Biomed.

The company faces two major challenges. First, there

are many who believe that techniques that mimic fundamental biological processes should not be 'owned' by one company. They have concentrated their attack on the attempts by some companies to patent genes, the fundamental building block of life. Their argument is that such knowledge should be available to all firms and other agencies for them to develop medical and other products. It is as if, in a previous period, someone had attempted to patent the workings of the heart and thus prevented other scientists from producing heart-related drugs.

The second challenge comes from other companies also working on cloning techniques. The method used by the Roslin Institute to clone animals is only one amongst a number being worked on by bio-technology companies world-wide. It could well be that Geron-Biomed may want to defend its patent in court by arguing that another company has essentially used the same method of cloning that it has developed.

Geron-Biomed has justified taking out a patent by saying: 'Clearly there are people who don't like patents, but without them there's simply no means of financing leading-edge technology'. Patents provide the security financiers need to bankroll research projects through to market.

Source: adapted from the *Financial Times*, 21.1.2000.

1. Explain the link between a 'patent' and 'monopoly'.
2. Why do firms take out patents?

3. Discuss whether the patent on cloning taken out by Geron-Biomed is likely to lead to market efficiency or market failure.

unit 19 Externalities

Summary

1. Externalities are created when social costs and benefits differ from private costs and benefits.
2. The greater the externality, the greater the likely market failure.
3. Governments can use regulation, the extension of property rights, taxation and permits to reduce the market failure caused by externalities.

Private and social costs and benefits

A chemical plant may dump waste into a river in order to minimise its costs. Further down the river, a water company has to treat the water to remove dangerous chemicals before supplying drinking water to its customers. Its customers have to pay higher prices because of the pollution.

This is a classic example of EXTERNALITIES or SPILLOVER EFFECTS. Externalities arise when private costs and benefits are different from social costs and benefits. A PRIVATE COST is the cost of an activity to an individual economic unit, such as a consumer or a firm. For instance, a chemical company will have to pay for workers, raw materials and plant and machinery when it produces chemicals. A SOCIAL COST is the cost of an activity not just to the individual economic unit which creates the cost, but to the rest of society as well. It therefore includes all private costs, but may also include other costs. The chemical manufacturer may make little or no payment for the pollution it generates. The difference between private cost and social cost is the externality or spillover effect. If social cost is greater than private cost, then a NEGATIVE EXTERNALITY or EXTERNAL COST is said to exist.

However, not all externalities are negative. A company may put up a building which is not just functional but also beautiful. The value of the pleasure which the building gives to society over its lifetime (the SOCIAL BENEFIT) may well far exceed the benefit of the building received by the company (the PRIVATE BENEFIT). Hence, if social benefit is greater than private benefit, a POSITIVE EXTERNALITY or EXTERNAL BENEFIT is said to exist.

This is often the case with health care provision (an example of a merit good ☞ unit 20). Although one individual will benefit from inoculation against illness, the social benefit resulting from the reduced risk of other members of society contracting the illness will be even greater. Positive externalities could also result from education and training. An individual may benefit in the form of a better job and a higher salary but society may gain even more from the benefits of a better trained workforce.

Activities where social benefit exceeds private benefit are often inadequately provided by a market system. In

Question 1

(a) Why might each of the examples in the photographs give rise to positive and negative externalities?

many cases this results in either state provision or a government subsidy to encourage private provision.

Market failure

The price mechanism allocates resources. Prices and profits are the signals which determine this allocation. However, a misallocation of resources will occur if market prices and profits do not accurately reflect the costs and benefits to society of economic activities.

For instance, in the case of the chemical plant above, the price of chemicals does not accurately reflect their true cost to society. The private cost of production to the manufacturer is lower than the social cost to society as a whole. Because the price of chemicals is lower than that which reflects social cost, the quantity demanded of chemicals and therefore consumption of chemicals will be greater than if the full social cost were charged. On the other hand, if the water company is pricing water to consumers, it will have to charge higher prices to consumers than would have been the case without the chemical pollution. Demand for water and consumption of water will therefore be less than it would otherwise have been without the externality.

The greater the externality, the greater the market failure and the less market prices and profits provide accurate signals for the optimal allocation of resources.

Government policy

The government has a wide range of policies that it could use to bring about an efficient allocation of resources where externalities exist.

Regulation Regulation is a method which is widely used in the UK and throughout the world to control externalities. The government could lay down maximum pollution levels or might even ban pollution creating activities altogether. For instance, in the UK, the Environmental Protection Act 1989 laid down minimum environmental standards for emissions from over 3 500 factories involved in chemical processes, waste incineration and oil refining. There are limits on harmful emissions from car exhausts. Cars that do not meet these standards fail their MOT tests. 40 years before these MOT regulations came into force, the government banned the burning of ordinary coal in urban areas.

Regulation is easy to understand and relatively cheap to enforce. However, it is a rather crude policy. First, it is often difficult for government to fix the right level of regulation to ensure efficiency. Regulations might be too lax or too tight. The correct level would be where the economic benefit arising from a reduction in externality equalled the economic cost imposed by the regulation. For instance, if firms had to spend £30 million fitting anti-pollution devices to plant and machinery, but the fall in pollution was only worth £20 million, then the regulation would have been too tight. If the fall in pollution was worth £40 million, it implies that it would be worth industry spending even more on anti-pollution measures to further reduce pollution and thus further increase the £40 million worth of benefits.

Moreover, regulations tend not to discriminate between different costs of reducing externalities. For instance, two firms might have to reduce pollution emissions by the same amount. Firm A could reduce its emissions at a cost of £3 million whilst it might cost Firm B £10 million to do the same. However, Firm A could double the reduction in its pollution levels at a cost of £7 million. Regulations which set equal limits for all firms will mean that the cost to society of reducing pollution in this case is £13 million (£3 million for Firm A and £10 million for Firm B). But it would be cheaper for society if the reduction could be achieved by Firm A alone at a cost of £7 million.

Question 2

Jaguar, owned by The Ford Motor company, wants to expand its design centre at Coventry and build a complementary technology park alongside it, complete with hotel and conference centre. The development is estimated to create 2 500 jobs, many of which will be hi-tech well paid jobs. Failure to get planning permission to build could lead to Jaguar moving its design facilities elsewhere, including the possibility that it would go to the USA. Coventry would then face the possible loss of 5 000 jobs in the long term if Jaguar completely pulled out of the city. The problem is that the 80 acre site on which it wants to build is greenbelt land. It has been classified by English Nature as a site of importance for nature conservation. Andrew Thompson, the Trust's conservation manager, said: 'The key issue is the sustainability of wildlife. If we carry on allowing sites like these to be eroded then we won't be able to hand on such a diverse environment to our children and their children. There are 21 different kinds of grasses on this land, as well as wild flowers like hay rattle and harebell. It is one of the few places where we can see the marble-white butterfly, and the green woodpecker comes here to feed.' As for the skylarks at the site, 'it's a ground-nesting bird which can't stand high levels of disturbance. Nationally, skylarks have declined in numbers by 60 per cent over the past 25 years because of the loss of habitat.'

Source: adapted from *The Guardian*, 6.10.1999.

(a) Why would Jaguar's expansion plans create an externality?
(b) Planning permission regulations are used to balance the needs of the community and the environment with development. Suggest why they are a crude way of ensuring that social profit is maximised.

Extending property rights If a chemical company lorry destroyed your home, you would expect the chemical company to pay compensation. If the chemical company polluted the atmosphere so that the trees in your garden died, it would be unlikely that you would gain compensation, particularly if the chemical plant were in the UK and the dead trees were in Germany.

Externalities often arise because property rights are not fully allocated. Nobody owns the atmosphere or the oceans, for instance. An alternative to regulation is for government to extend property rights. It can give water companies the right to charge companies which dump waste into rivers or the sea. It can give workers the right to sue for compensation if they have suffered injury or death as a result of working for a company. It can give local residents the right to claim compensation if pollution levels are more than a certain amount.

Extending property rights is a way of **internalising the externality** - eliminating the externality by bringing it back into the framework of the market mechanism. Fifty years ago, asbestos was not seen as a dangerous material. Today, asbestos companies around the world are having to pay compensation to workers suffering from asbestosis. They have also had to tighten up considerably on safety in the workplace where asbestos is used. Workers have been given property rights which enable them to sue asbestos companies for compensation.

One advantage of extending property rights is that the government does not have to assess the cost of pollution. It is generally assumed that property owners will have a far better knowledge of the value of property than the government. There should also be a direct transfer of resources from those who create pollution to those who suffer. With regulation, in contrast, the losers are not compensated whilst polluters are free to pollute up to the limit despite the fact that the pollution is imposing costs on society.

There are problems though. One is that a government may not have the ability to extend property rights. This occurs, for instance, when the cause of the externality arises in another country. How do Western governments prevent countries like Brazil from logging huge areas of forest, leading to global warming, which imposes costs on them? One way around this is to pay the agents causing the externality to stop their economic activity. So Western countries could pay countries like Brazil not to log their forests.

Another problem is that extending property rights can be very difficult in many cases. Asbestos companies, for instance, will not pay claims to asbestos workers unless it can definitely be proved that their medical condition was caused by working with asbestos. The compensation process can take years, and many ex-workers die before their cases are settled. They receive no compensation and the asbestos company has not had to include payment in its costs. This would tend to lead to a continuing overproduction of asbestos.

A final problem is that it is often very difficult even for the owners of property rights to assess the value of those rights. For instance, one homeowner might put a far higher value on trees in his or her garden than another homeowner. If a cable company lays cable in the road, cutting the roots of trees in front gardens, should the homeowner who places a high value on trees be compensated more than the homeowner who is fairly indifferent when trees die? What happens if the homeowner wanted to get rid of the trees anyway?

Taxes Another solution, much favoured by economists, is the use of taxes. The government needs to assess the cost to society of a particular negative externality. It then sets tax rates on those externalities equal to the value of the externality. This increases costs to customers by shifting the supply curve to the left. The result is a fall in demand and output and thus fewer externalities are created.

Question 3

The European Union has issued a directive which will force motor manufacturers to recycle their cars. The measures, expected to cost the companies £6.5 billion, will apply to all cars sold in the EU whether manufactured there or not. When a car comes to the end of its useful life, owners will have the choice of either selling it for scrap to a private company or handing it back to the company which made it. Car manufacturers will have to recycle 80 per cent of the weight of the vehicle. The motor manufacturers have strongly resisted the free take back provisions of the directive. Opel, the German arm of General Motors, warned of higher car prices. 'If manufacturers have to bear the cost, customers will end up having to pay.'

Source: adapted from the *Financial Times* 23.7.1999.

(a) Why might cars, at the end of their life, create an externality?
(b) The EU scheme is an example of extending property rights. Explain why.
(c) How will the scheme reduce externalities?

For example, the government might put a tax on petrol for cars because emissions from cars contribute to global warming. The tax should be set at the level where the tax revenues equal the cost to society of the emissions. This **internalises** the externality, as explained above, making the polluter pay the cost of pollution.

Taxes, like extending property rights, have the advantage that they allow the market mechanism to decide how resources should best be allocated. Those creating the highest levels of negative externalities have a greater incentive to reduce those externalities than those creating fewer externalities.

However, it is often very difficult for government to place a monetary value on negative externalities and therefore decide what should be the optimal tax rate. With global warming, for instance, there is considerable disagreement about its likely economic impact. Some environmentalists would argue that the potential economic costs are so large that cars should be virtually priced off the roads. At the opposite extreme, some argue that global warming, if it occurs at all, will bring net economic benefits. For instance, slightly higher temperatures will increase the amount of food that can be produced and make it easier to feed the world's growing population. There is therefore no need for taxes on petrol designed to reduce emissions.

Where positive externalities occur, governments should offer subsidies. It can be argued, for instance, that parks, libraries, art galleries, concert halls and opera houses create positive externalities. Therefore they should be subsidised. As with taxes and negative externalities, the level of subsidy should equal the positive externality created.

Permits A variation on regulating negative externalities through direct controls is the idea of issuing permits. Assume that the government wishes to control emissions of sulphur into the atmosphere. It issues permits to

Question 4

In March 1999, the Chancellor of the Exchequer, Gordon Brown, announced that he would be imposing a climate change levy on energy used by industry from 2001. The tax on all forms of energy consumption by industry would be expected to raise £1.75 billion. The money would be used to lower employers' National Insurance contributions, a tax paid by industry on each worker employed. Overall, industry will be no better off or worse off. However, a small number of very high energy users could be badly affected. Companies in the aluminium industry, steel manufacturing, the chemical industry, paper manufacturing, the cement industry and glass making account for approximately half of carbon emissions per year by UK industry. These industries are highly capital intensive and employ relatively few workers.

(a) The burning of fossil fuels contributes to the global warming effect because of the release of greenhouse gases including carbon dioxide. Explain how a climate change levy might help reduce global warming.
(b) The Chancellor claims that the change in tax will overall create jobs and reduce unemployment. Explain why this might occur.
(c) (i) Explain why high energy users are most likely to suffer from the change.
    (ii) The government is proposing to levy the energy tax at a lower rate on high energy users. Discuss what factors the government should take into consideration when deciding what size of discount on the tax to offer them.

would only be £10 million, the cost that Firm A would incur, and not £25 million as with regulation. It might cost Firm B more than £10 million to buy the permits. It would be prepared to spend anything up to £25 million to acquire them. Say Firm A drove a hard bargain and sold the permits to Firm B for £22 million. Society would save £15 million (£25 million - £10 million), distributed between a paper profit of £12 million for Firm A and a fall in costs from what otherwise would have been the case for Firm B of £3 million.

Question 5

In 1997, governments met in Kyoto in Japan to discuss the environment. They agreed on targets for greenhouse gas emissions responsible for global warming. Countries signing the agreement promised to limit their emissions to 1990 levels. The United States was keen on establishing a system of internationally tradable permits to pollute. Under this system, firms are allocated permits according to their production capacity. A United States firm which finds it relatively cheap to reduce emissions might sell some of its permits to a European firm which finds it far more expensive to reduce pollution. European negotiators were concerned that the rich countries of the world would be able to continue polluting by buying permits from Eastern European and Third World countries. They felt that countries should reduce pollution levels on their own. The USA felt that imposing limits on the use of permits would dramatically increase the costs of curbing greenhouse gas emissions.

(a) Explain what is meant by a 'tradable permit'.
(b) How can a system of tradable permits reduce the cost of lowering pollution levels?

pollute, the total of which equals the maximum amount of sulphur it wishes to see emitted over a period of time like a year. The government then allocates permits to individual firms or other polluters. This could be done, for instance, on the basis of current levels of emissions by firms or on output of goods giving rise to sulphur emissions in production. The permits are then tradable for money between polluters. Firms which succeed in reducing their sulphur levels below their permit levels can sell their permits to other producers who are exceeding their limits.

The main advantage of permits over simple regulation is that costs in the industry and therefore to society should be lower than with regulation. Each firm in the industry will consider whether it is possible to reduce emissions and at what cost. Assume that Firm A, with just enough permits to meet its emissions, can reduce emissions by 500 tonnes at a cost of £10 million. Firm B is a high polluter and needs 500 tonnes worth of permits to meet regulations. It calculates that it would to spend £25 million to cut emissions by this amount.

If there was simple regulation, the anti-pollution costs to the industry, and therefore to society, would be £25 million. Firm B would have to conform to its pollution limit whilst there would be no incentive for Firm A to cut pollution.

With permits, Firm A could sell 500 tonnes of permits to Firm B. The cost to society of then reducing pollution

key terms

Externality or spillover effect - the difference between social costs and benefits and private costs and benefits. If net social cost (social cost minus social benefit) is greater than net private cost (private cost minus private benefit), then a **negative externality** or **external cost** exists. If net social benefit is greater than net private benefit, a **positive externality** or **external benefit** exists.

Private cost and benefit - the cost or benefit of an activity to an individual economic unit such as a consumer or a firm.

Social cost and benefit - the cost or benefit of an activity to society as a whole.

Applied economics

Global warming

The environmental problem

During the 1980s, there was a growing awareness that levels of greenhouse gases in the atmosphere were rising, and that this might pose a serious problem for the future of the planet. Global warming, a rise in world temperatures, comes about because greenhouse gases act as a blanket, trapping heat within the Earth's atmosphere.

Figure 19.1 shows the main sources of greenhouse gas emissions in the UK. 80 per cent of the emissions are of carbon dioxide. Industries, particularly coal fired power stations, are the main polluters. Households, in consuming gas and electricity, contribute one quarter of all CO_2 emmissions.

A rise of a few degrees in world temperatures sounds very little. However, it would be enough to cause major shifts in the desert zones of the world. Many of the major wheat producing areas, such as the American plains, would become deserts. Old deserts, such as the Sahara, would become fertile in time. However, the transition costs to the world economy would be substantial. A second problem would be that there would be some melting of the polar icecaps, with a consequent rise in sea levels. With a 3 degree centigrade rise in world temperatures, a rise at the bottom end of recent predictions, there would be an increase in sea levels of 30cm. This would be enough to flood areas such as the east coast of England, the Bangladesh delta and the Maldive Islands. Sea defences and dykes could and probably would be built, but the cost to the world economy could run to tens of billions of pounds.

Progress to date

It is easy to assume that there is a direct link between growth in the economy and pollution; the higher the income of a country, for instance, the higher its pollution levels. However, the evidence does not bear this out.

Figure 19.2 shows how certain emissions have fallen over a period when real income (GDP) increased by 70 per cent. Industry, as shown in Figure 18.3, has contributed most to this fall. The exception has been pollution due to cars, where the doubling of the number of cars on the roads since 1971 has led to an increase in pollution. Even here, though, there are some grounds for optimism. The introduction of catalytic converters and a switch to diesel cars was responsible for the fall in nitrogen oxides emissions since the late 1980s shown in Figure 19.2. New technologies, such as electric cars, are likely to reduce carbon dioxide emissions from road transport in the future.

There are two main reasons why higher growth may lead to less rather than more pollution. First, industry may, by itself, move over to less polluting forms of technology. For instance, over time, coal fired power stations have become more efficient, producing more electricity from a tonne of coal. If efficiency gains are faster than the rate of growth in the economy, economies can enjoy both higher incomes and lower pollution.

Second, governments have been implementing policies to reduce the amount of pollution. Some of these policies have come about because of agreed action on an international scale. For instance, the Montreal Protocol signed in 1987 committed 93 countries, including the major industrialised nations of the world, to phasing out the use of CFCs. The Rio Summit of 1992 led to the industrialised nations committing themselves to reducing greenhouse gas emissions by the year 2000 to their 1990 levels.

UK policies

The UK government has adopted a piecemeal approach to ensuring that it meets its greenhouse gas emission targets. Figure 19.3 shows that the single most important contributors to emissions in the UK are power stations, including power stations using deep-mined coal. Since the early 1990s, the UK government

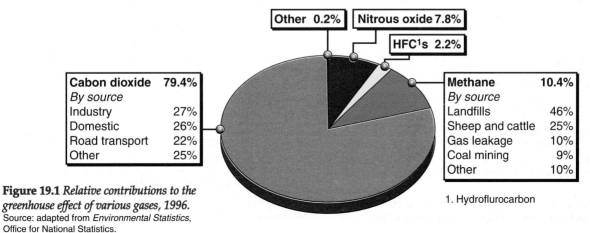

| Other 0.2% | Nitrous oxide 7.8% |
| HFC[1]s 2.2% |

Cabon dioxide	**79.4%**
By source	
Industry	27%
Domestic	26%
Road transport	22%
Other	25%

Methane	**10.4%**
By source	
Landfills	46%
Sheep and cattle	25%
Gas leakage	10%
Coal mining	9%
Other	10%

1. Hydroflurocarbon

Figure 19.1 *Relative contributions to the greenhouse effect of various gases, 1996.*
Source: adapted from *Environmental Statistics*, Office for National Statistics.

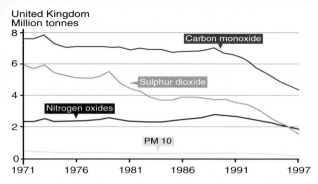

Figure 19.2 *Air pollutants: emissions of selected gases*
Source: adapted from *Social Trends*, 1999, Office for National Statistics.

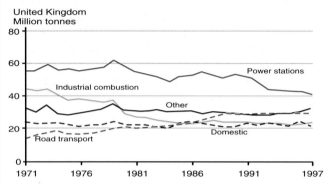

Figure 19.3 *Carbon dioxide emissions: UK, by source*
Source: adapted from *Social Trends*, 1999, Office for National Statistics.

has allowed a major shift in electricity power generation from older coal fired power stations to new, highly efficient gas-fired power stations. In the 1970s and 1980s, with the coal, gas and electricity industries owned by the state, the electricity industry was not allowed to burn gas. This was because the government needed a market for the coal being produced. In the early 1990s, government policy changed. British Coal was forced to close a large number of pits, reducing output, in order to meet government profit targets. Electricity companies embarked on a large programme of building small gas fired power stations. This has helped reduce carbon dioxide emissions from UK power stations. In the late 1990s, the government became concerned about job losses in the coal industry. It effectively put a stop to the building of new gas fired power stations. This is an illustration of how environmental goals can conflict with other policy goals.

The second most important contributor to carbon dioxide emissions is the motor car. The government is faced with the major problem of congestion on British roads. The solution of the 1960s, 1970s and 1980s was to build more roads. In the 1990s, there was a major switch in policy. The government realised that an alternative solution to congestion, which would also help the UK achieve its CO_2 target, was to stabilise or even reduce the number of cars on British roads. In his 1993 Budget, the Chancellor announced that he would increase the tax on fuel by 3 per cent more than the rate of inflation for the foreseeable future, a figure increased to 6 per cent in 1998. This increased the cost of motoring and so should have led to some reduction in car usage. This is likely to have

been small given that price elasticity of demand for petrol is relatively inelastic. More importantly, it increased the economic incentive for motorists to buy more fuel efficient cars. The limits of this policy were shown in 1999 when the government abandoned automatic real tax increases in petrol due to the political unpopularity of the policy. The government also severely cut back its road building programme, thus increasing car journey times on many routes and discouraging car use.

A third policy was the introduction of VAT on domestic fuel in 1994. The government at the time argued that it would encourage energy efficiency in the home. However, the measure became bogged down in political controversy because it was argued that the tax would fall disproportionately hard on the poor and particularly the elderly. If they became less willing to use heat in winter, it could lead to deaths. Eventually, VAT which should have been imposed at 17.5 per cent, the standard rate, was reduced to 5 per cent.

In 1999, the government announced that it would be introducing an energy tax on industry in 2001. The tax would bring in around £1.75 billion of revenue. This would be refunded to industry in the form of lower employers' National Insurance contributions. The tax was designed to encourage industry to reduce its fuel use and thus lower the UK's greenhouse emissions. Part of the problem with its implementation was that approximately 50 per cent of all energy used by industry in the UK was consumed by a handful of industries, including aluminium manufacturing, paper making and the chemicals industry. If these energy intensive industries were hit too hard, they would shift their location out of the UK. The UK would have lower emissions but the world will be no better off. What's more, the UK would have lost output and jobs. Again, this shows the conflict which often arises between environmental objectives and other objectives of government policy.

There is a variety of other policies which could be used. For instance, many economists would favour the introduction of tradable permits for industry. They have been very successful in the United States at reducing emissions at lowest cost. Unlike the energy tax, where the outcome is uncertain, emission permits allow the government to specify the maximum quantity of emissions by industry. Unlike with regulations, market forces will decide which firms cut their emissions the most.

Another alternative designed to curb growing pollution from transport is the introduction of road pricing. The problem the government faces here is that both households and firms have a low price elasticity of demand for road transport. This is because there are often no short term substitutes and even in the long term the substitutes may be poor. Road pricing may shift cars and lorries off congested roads at certain times of the day but it may have little impact on the growth of overall miles travelled. From an emissions perspectives, more appropriate policies would be those which encouraged more fuel efficient vehicles or vehicles powered by alternative fuels.

Paper recycling

Manufacturing paper is an energy intensive process. The amount of energy consumed can be significantly reduced if recycled paper is used. Recycled paper also does not involve the cutting down of trees which absorb carbon dioxide from the atmosphere, thus reducing greenhouse gas emissions.

Recycling is coming under threat from market forces. Sharp falls in the price of waste paper have meant that it is difficult to make a profit from its collection. Many paper collecting initiatives run by charities, churches and schools have been stopped while one in ten local authorities has closed its paper banks over the past 18 months. At present, local authorities are having to pay to dispose of their waste paper rather than receiving an income from it. The problem has arisen because of the Asian crisis. The economic crisis in 1997 and 1998 in high growth economies such as Indonesia and South Korea led to a sharp fall in demand for paper and prices have not recovered.

Some life-cycle studies have cast doubt on the environmental credentials of recycling waste paper. They have shown that net carbon dioxide emissions are higher for recycling than for incineration where the energy is recovered in the form of electricity or heat. However, incineration is deeply unpopular with local residents around incineration plants who complain of air pollution and who fear that airborne residues may be carcinogenic.

Environmentalists have called for the government to require newspaper publishers to use 80 per cent recycled material by 2010. At present, they use about 40 per cent. This would help lift demand for recycled paper and encourage agencies such as local authorities to increase their collections. Critics argue that the proposal would mean investment of £650 million of new plant. It could also lead to a sharp increases in imports of waste paper, which could produce the unintended side-effect of increasing the amount of waste buried in UK landfills.

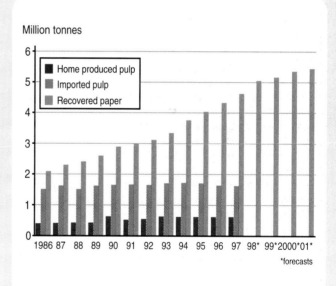

Figure 19.4 *Paper production and recycling*
Source: adapted from The Paper Federation of Great Britain.

1. **Explain what externalities might be created by the production and consumption of unrecycled paper.**
2. **Analyse what policies the government might pursue to increase the amount of recycling of paper in the UK.**
3. **Discuss whether recycling paper significantly reduces externalities.**

Summary

1. There will inevitably be market failure in a pure free market economy because it will fail to provide public goods.
2. Public goods must be provided by the state because of the free rider problem.
3. Merit goods are goods which are underprovided by the market mechanism, for instance because there are significant positive externalities in consumption.
4. Governments can intervene to ensure provision of public and merit goods through direct provision, subsidies or regulation.
5. Government failure can be caused by inadequate information, conflicting objectives, administrative costs and creation of market distortions.
6. Public choice theory suggests that governments may not always act to maximise the welfare of society because politicians may act to maximise their own welfare.

Markets and market failure

Markets may lead to an efficient allocation of resources. However, there are some goods and services which economists recognise are unlikely to be best produced in free markets. These may include defence, the judiciary and the criminal justice system, the police service, roads, the fire service and education. More controversially, some believe that the free market is poor at producing health care and housing for the less well off. There are different reasons why there might be market failure in the production of these goods.

Public goods

Nearly all goods are **private goods** (not to be confused with goods produced in the private sector of the economy). A private good is one where consumption by one person results in the good not being available for consumption by another. For instance, if you eat a bowl of muesli, then your friend can't eat it; if a firm builds a plant on a piece of land, that land is not available for use by local farmers.

A few goods, however, are PUBLIC GOODS. These are goods which possesses two characteristics:
- **non-rivalry**- consumption of the good by one person does not reduce the amount available for consumption by another person;
- **non-excludability** - once provided, no person can be excluded from benefiting (or indeed suffering in the case of a public good like pollution).

There are relatively few examples of pure public goods, although many goods contain a public good element. Clean air is a public good. If you breathe clean air, it does not diminish the ability of others to breathe clean air. Moreover, others cannot prevent you from breathing clean air. Defence is another example. An increase in the population of the UK does not lead to a reduction in the defence protection accorded to the existing population. A person in Manchester cannot be excluded from benefiting even if she were to object to current defence policy, prefer to see all defence abolished, and refuse to pay to finance defence.

Goods which can be argued to be public goods are:
- defence;
- the judiciary and prison service;
- the police service;
- street lighting.

Many other goods, such as education and health, contain a small public good element.

The free rider problem

If the provision of public goods were left to the market mechanism, there would be market failure. This is because of the FREE RIDER problem. A public good is one where it is impossible to prevent people from receiving the benefits of the good once it has been provided. So there is very little incentive for people to pay for consumption of the good. A free rider is someone who receives the benefit but allows others to pay for it. For instance, citizens receive benefits from defence expenditure. But individual citizens could increase their economic welfare by not paying for it.

Question 1

(a) Explain why lamp posts might be classed as a public good.

In a free market, national defence is unlikely to be provided. A firm attempting to provide defence services would have difficulty charging for the product since it could not be sold to benefit individual citizens. The result would be that no one would pay for defence and therefore the market would not provide it. The only way around this problem is for the state to provide defence and force everyone to contribute to its cost through taxation.

Merit and demerit goods

Even the most fervent advocates of free market economics agree that public goods are an example of market failure and that the government should provide these public goods. However, more controversial are merit and demerit goods.

A MERIT GOOD is one which is underprovided by the market mechanism (i.e. one which some people think should be provided in greater quantities). One reason for underprovision is that individuals lack perfect information and find it difficult to make rational decisions when costs occur today but the benefits received only come in, say, thirty years time. Another reason is because there are significant positive externalities (☞ unit 19) present.

Health, education and insurance are the main merit goods provided today by government in the UK. Health and insurance are two examples where consumers find it difficult to make rational choices because of time. If left totally to market forces, the evidence suggests that individuals would not give themselves sufficient health cover or cover against sickness, unemployment and old age. Young people tend to be healthy and in work. Many find it difficult to appreciate that one day they will be ill and out of work. However, the cost of health care and pensions etc. is so great that young people can only afford them if they save for the future. If they don't, they find when they are older that they do not have sufficient resources to pay for medical services, or the insurance needed to cover them against loss of earnings due to illness or retirement. Therefore it makes sense for the state to intervene and to force young people in particular to make provision against sickness, unemployment and old age.

In the case of education, the main beneficiary (the child or student) is unlikely to be the person paying for the education. Therefore there could be a conflict of interest. It could be in the interest of the parents to pay as little as possible for the child's education but in the interest of the child to receive as high quality an education as possible. Others in society also have an interest. A child who, for instance, cannot read or write is an economic liability in the UK today. He or she is more likely than not to have to receive support from others rather than contribute to the nation's welfare. There are many other examples of goods with a merit good element. Lack of industrial training, for instance, is seen as a major problem in the UK. Individual firms have an incentive not to train workers, not only because it is so costly but also because their trained workers can then be poached by competitors. Rather, they go into the market place and recruit workers who have been trained at other firms' expense. This is an example again of the free rider problem. It is partly countered by the government providing funding for organisations such as Training and Enterprise Councils (TECs) which organise training in local areas.

A DEMERIT GOOD is one which is overprovided by the market mechanism. The clearest examples of demerit goods are drugs - everything from hard drugs such as LSD to alcohol and tobacco. Consumption of these goods produces large negative **externalities**. Crime increases, health costs rise, valuable human economic resources are destroyed, and friends and relatives suffer distress. Moreover, individuals themselves suffer and are unable to stop consuming because drugs are addictive. Therefore it can be argued that consumers of drugs are not the best judges of their own interests.

Governments intervene to correct this market failure. They have three main weapons at their disposal: they can ban consumption as with hard drugs; they can use the price system to reduce demand by placing taxes on drugs; or they can try to persuade consumers to stop using drugs, for instance through advertising campaigns.

Equity

It would be extremely improbable that a free market system would lead to a distribution of resources which every individual would see as equitable. It is therefore argued by some economists that the state has a duty to reallocate resources.

In the UK today, for instance, there is some consensus that British citizens should not die for lack of food, or be

Question 2

(a) Suggest reasons why education might be considered a merit good.

refused urgent medical treatment for lack of money.

In the UK, over 30 per cent of all public spending is devoted to social security payments. Some of these payments come from the National Insurance fund and therefore could be seen as merit goods. But benefits such as family credit are an explicit attempt to redistribute income to those in need. It could also be argued that the free provision of services such as health and education leads to a more equitable distribution of resources.

Government intervention

Markets are likely to underprovide public and merit goods. This leads to **allocative inefficiency** because consumers are not able to spend their money in a way which will maximise their utility (their welfare or satisfaction). For instance, households in a city would be prepared to pay a few pounds a year to have street lighting throughout the city. But, because of the free rider problem, they are reluctant to make any contribution either because they hope everyone else will pay or because they don't want to make large payments because few others are paying. It then makes sense for government to force everyone to pay through a system of taxes.

Merit goods are more controversial, partly because they contain a private good element. The main beneficiaries of health care and education, for instance, are patients and students. Governments can attempt to increase the provision of merit goods in a variety of ways.

Direct provision Governments can supply public and merit goods directly to consumers free of charge. In the UK, primary school education, visits to the doctor and roads are provided in this way. The government may choose to produce the good or service itself, as with primary school education. Or it may buy in the services of firms in the private sector. General practitioners, for instance, work for themselves and the government buys their services.

Subsidised provision The government may pay for part of the good or service (a **subsidy**) but expect consumers to pay the rest. Prescriptions or dental care are subsidised in this way in the UK.

Regulation The government may leave provision to the private sector but force consumers to purchase a merit good or producers to provide a merit good. For instance, motorists are forced to buy car insurance by law. There is an ongoing debate in industrialised countries about whether workers should be forced to pay into private pensions. Motorway service stations are forced to provide toilet facilities free of charge to motorists whether or not they purchase anything.

There is a number of advantages and disadvantages to each of these solutions. The advantage of direct provision is that the government directly controls the supply of goods and services. It determines the number of hospital beds in the system because it provides them. It decides how many soldiers there are because it pays them directly. However, direct provision has disadvantages. It may be productively inefficient, particularly if the government

produces the good itself. Employees of the state, whether providing the good or buying it in, may have no incentive to cut costs to a minimum. It may be allocatively inefficient, especially if the goods are provided free of charge to taxpayers. The government may provide too many soldiers and too few hospital beds, for instance. Markets, in contrast, give consumers the opportunity to buy those goods which give the greatest satisfaction. In a market, if producers supplied too many soldiers, they would be left unsold. Firms would then move resources out of the production of defence and into the production of a good which consumers were prepared to buy.

Subsidies are a way of working through the market mechanism to increase the consumption of a good. So subsidising dental care, for instance, increases the amount of dental care provided, hopefully to a level which maximises economic welfare. Subsidies can also help those on low incomes to afford to buy goods. One problem with subsidies is that decisions about the level of subsidies can become 'captured' by producers. Subsidies then become too large to maximise welfare. For instance, it can be argued that farmers in Europe have to some extent 'captured' the Common Agricultural Policy. Instead of government ministers deciding what level of farm subsidy will maximise economic welfare, they bow to the pressure of the farming lobby. Farming subsidies then become far too large. The resultant welfare gains to farmers are far less than the welfare loss to consumers and taxpayers.

Regulation has the advantage that it requires little or no taxpayer's money to provide the good. Consumers are also likely to be able to shop around in the free market for

Question 3

There is a variety of ways in which the government could ensure that all households have access to dental services.
(a) It could provide the service directly, making it free to all users, and raise the required finance through taxes.
(b) It could subsidise some dental treatment considered to be essential, but not subsidise other treatment. This is the present system in the UK.
(c) It could make it a legal obligation that all households take out dental insurance to cover the cost of essential dental treatment.

Discuss the relative merits of each of these options.

a product which gives them good value, ensuring productive and allocative efficiency. However, regulations can impose heavy costs on the poor in society. How many poor families, for instance, could afford to pay for private health care insurance if it was a requirement for them to do so? Regulations can also be ignored. Not all motorists have insurance, for instance. If parents had a legal obligation to pay for their children to go to school, some parents would defy the law and not give their children an education. The more likely citizens are to evade regulations, the less efficient they are as a way of ensuring the provision of public and merit goods.

Government failure

Markets can fail, but so too can governments. GOVERNMENT FAILURE occurs when it intervenes in the market but this intervention leads to a loss of economic welfare rather than a gain. There is a number of reasons why government failure may occur.

Inadequate information Governments, like any economic agents, rarely possess complete information on which to base a decision. In some cases, the information available is positively misleading. It is not surprising, then, that governments may make the wrong policy response to a problem. For instance, governments have to make decisions about whether to fund a selective school system or a comprehensive school system. In Germany, the school system is selective. In the USA, it is comprehensive. In the UK, it is mainly comprehensive, but a significant minority of local authorities fund selective schools. The issue is important because education is a key determinant of the long term competitiveness of the UK. It also affects every individual child. However, the evidence about which is the most effective form of education is conflicting. In the 1960s and 1970s, the UK government supported the change from a mainly selective system to a mainly comprehensive system. In the 1980s and 1990s, the Conservative government favoured selective schools. It is impossible to say today who was right and selective vs comprehensive education remains an important issue.

Conflicting objectives Governments often face conflicting objectives. For instance, they may want to cut taxes but increase spending on defence. Every decision made by the government has an opportunity cost. Sometimes, a decision is made where the welfare gain from the alternative foregone would have been even higher. In the case of education, assume that those receiving a selective education in grammar schools receive a better education than if they were in a comprehensive school. In contrast, assume that those who fail to get into a selective school achieve less than if they were in a comprehensive school. There is now a conflict of objectives about which system to implement. Are the needs of those who would be selected for grammar schools more important than the rest of the school population, or vice versa? Governments may make the wrong policy decision when there are such conflicts of objective, choosing the option which gives lower economic

welfare rather than higher economic welfare. They may do this because of lack of information. Or they may deliberately choose this option because they wish to reward their supporters in the electorate who voted for them (☞ below).

Administrative costs Sometimes, the administrative cost of correcting market failure is so large that it outweighs the welfare benefit from the correction of market failure. For instance, the government may put into place a scheme to help the unemployed back into work. During a year, 100 000 pass through the scheme. Of those, 50 000 would have found jobs anyway but simply use the scheme because it is advantageous for them or their employer to do so. 10 000 find a job who would otherwise not have done so. 40 000 remain unemployed. It may cost £3 000 per person per year on the scheme, giving a total cost of £300 million. This means that the cost per worker who would otherwise not have got a job is £300 million ÷ 10 000 or £30 000 per worker. This is an enormous cost for the benefit likely to be gained by the 10 000 workers. Indeed, they almost certainly would have preferred to have been given the £30 000 rather than gain a job. Another example would be the payment of welfare benefits. If it costs £1 to pay out a £3 benefit, is this likely to improve economic welfare?

Market distortions In some cases, government intervention to correct one market failure leads to the creation of far more serious market failures. One example is government intervention in agricultural markets such as the Common Agricultural Policy. Here, governments offer farmers financial support, partly to raise farm incomes which can be low and second to even out fluctuations in income from year to year arising from changes in the size of crops. However, financial support typically leads to increases in the supply of food which may not be matched by increases in demand. The result is an over-supply of farm produce. Countries may choose to dump this over supply on world markets at low prices. This leads to lower farm incomes for world farmers outside the European Union, destroying the markets for their produce. Higher farm incomes in Europe may be gained at the expense of lower farm incomes in Egypt or New Zealand. Agricultural markets within the EU may also be distorted. For instance, the price of beef is artificially high in the EU because of CAP support but pig prices receive no subsidy. The result is that EU consumers buy less beef and more pork than they would otherwise do if there were no government intervention. Another market distortion may occur with respect to the environment. The CAP encourages over-production of food. Marginal land is brought into production when it might otherwise be left wild. Too much pesticide and fertiliser may be used to raise yields because CAP offers too high prices to farmers. Lower prices might lead to less intensive modes of production and less destruction to wildlife.

There are many examples of market distortions in the labour market. For instance, the government may want to raise income levels for the poor by setting a high minimum wage. But this may be so high that employers shed low paid workers, putting out of work large numbers of people whom the government wanted to

Question 4

In 1861, Mrs Beeton, then the authority on cookery and household management and the Victorian equivalent of Delia Smith, wrote that her readers should always make their own vinegar. This was because shop bought vinegar of the day tended to consist of diluted sulphuric acid.

Today, food manufacturers and retailers are so strictly controlled by government regulations that this could not happen. Some argue, though, that such regulations are excessive. Government red tape restricts the opening and running of new businesses. Consumers have to pay higher prices for their food because it costs firms money to conform to government regulations. For instance, in 1999, the costs of production to UK pig farmers went up because they could no longer rear pigs in stalls. Animal welfare activists would like to see battery hen production stopped and all chickens reared in free range conditions, but why shouldn't consumers have the choice about whether or not they buy cheaper battery produced eggs and chickens?

(a) Explain why markets fail according to the data.
(b) Discuss whether, in the examples given in the data, government intervention leads to government failure.

protect. Similarly, the government may raise unemployment benefit to help the unemployed. But this may discourage them from looking for work since more are now better off on the dole than working. This increases the numbers of unemployed.

Public choice theory

It is generally assumed that governments act in a way which they believe will maximise economic welfare. They may not succeed in this because of lack of information, conflicting objectives, etc. However, PUBLIC CHOICE THEORY suggests that governments may not attempt to maximise economic welfare at all.

Public choice theory analyses how and why public spending and taxation decisions are made. 'Consumers' or 'customers' are voters in the system. They vote for politicians and political parties who are the 'producers' in the system. Producers make decisions about how public money should be spent, about taxes and about laws. The decisions have to be 'sold' by politicians to voters.

The voters want to maximise the net benefits they get from the state. For instance, all other things being equal, voters would like the state to provide large quantities of goods and services but with minimal levels of taxation. Politicians want to maximise their welfare too. In the simplest models, politicians are assumed to want to maximise their votes, so that they can get into power and remain in power. In more complicated models, more sophisticated assumptions can be made, such as that politicians want to get posts in government, or use their political connections to maximise their own earnings.

If politicians want to maximise their votes, then the most obvious thing to do is to appeal to the centre ground. Consider Figure 20.1 which shows a normal distribution of votes. A right wing politician is facing a left wing

politician who has pitched his policies so that they will attract votes to the left of OA. The obvious stance to take is for the right wing politician to pitch his policies just to the right of B, as near as possible to the middle ground whilst remaining to the right of the political spectrum. On the other hand, if the left wing politician were rational, he too would move to the centre ground to try and maximise his vote.

In practice, democracies tend to throw up governments which do veer towards the centre. It is for this reason that governments like those of Margaret Thatcher's in the 1980s were so unusual. Due to Britain's first past the post voting system, a UK party can get a majority in Parliament with as little as 40 per cent of the votes cast. With a 75 per cent turnout on polling day (i.e. 25 per cent of eligible voters don't vote), this means that a British government only has to gain the vote of 30 per cent of all voters. Not surprisingly, this allows a right wing party which itself has voted in a right wing leader to gain office. The same would of course be true for a left wing party in the UK which had a left wing leader.

In much of economic theory, there is a hidden assumption that governments act so as to maximise the welfare of society as a whole. Public choice theory can help explain why governments often fail to do this.

Local interests Assume that an MP has a large textile mill in her constituency which employs 1 000 workers. The company owning the mill lobbies the MP to support the imposition of higher tariffs (taxes on imports) on textiles, arguing that the mill will have to close unless foreign competition is reduced. Economic theory would probably suggest that the mill should be allowed to close and the resources released be used to produce something which the UK is better at producing (the **theory of comparative advantage** ☞ unit 14). However, the MP may be frightened that losing 1 000 jobs could mean losing 1 000 votes. Therefore, she could well put pressure on the government to impose higher tariffs even if she knows that the nation's welfare would be lessened as a result.

Favouring minorities Assume that a political party can get elected with considerably less than 50 per cent of the

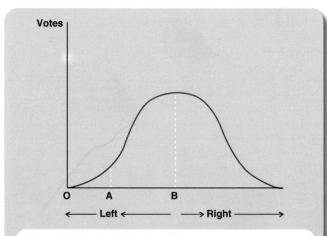

Figure 20.1 *Voting behaviour of electors.*
Politicians will tend to maximise their votes by moving to the centre ground in politics.

votes, because of the nature of the voting system and because not all voters turn out on polling day. In UK national elections, as argued above, a party could get a majority with the support of just 30 per cent of voters. In a local election, where the turnout is often only 30-50 per cent, a party can get a majority with far less. Assume that those who do vote tend to possess similar characteristics. For instance, in the UK, middle class voters are more likely to vote than working class voters. In a local election, voters from one ethnic group may be far more likely to vote than voters from another ethnic group. In these situations, it is clear that politicians wishing to maximise their share of the vote will want to appeal to a minority, not the majority, because it is the minority who cast votes. A government might, for instance, introduce government spending and tax changes which leave 30 per cent of the population better off and 70 per cent worse off. This would be rational behaviour if the 30 per cent of the population better off tended to vote for that party in a first past the post system with a 75 per cent turnout. However, it is arguable as to whether the nation's welfare would be maximised as a result.

Conflicting personal interests Politicians, parties and governments may be prone to corruption. Assume that politicians are not just interested in winning votes and retaining power, but also in gaining personal economic wealth. There may then be a conflict of interest between maximising the nation's welfare and maximising the welfare of the individual politician. Assume, for instance, that a Third World political leader can remain in power by giving massive bribes to electors at election time. Between elections, he accepts bribes from electors for granting political favours. In the process, the country fails to develop because decisions are made on the basis of maximising the wealth of the individual politician rather than that of the country. The individual politician is far better off as a rich head of a poor country than as a leader who has lost power in a fast growing country.

Short-termism In the UK, there has to be a general election at least every five years. Assume that a government wants a high growth, low inflation economy. Unfortunately, the current state of the economy at the time is one of high inflation and low growth. If the government pursues anti-inflationary policies, these will need to be long term policies if they are to be successful. But they are also likely to push up unemployment and lead to a tough tax and low government spending regime. A government coming up to re-election has two choices. It can cut taxes, increase public spending, and cut interest rates to stimulate spending and make voters 'feel good'. Or it can pursue austere policies which might keep the economy on course but leave voters feeling they are not particularly well off. Assume that the austere policies are the ones which will maximise welfare in the long term, but would mean the government losing the election. It is obvious that the government will go for the reflationary policies if that means it can win the election, even though it knows this will damage welfare.

Regulatory capture Governments are responsible for regulating many areas, such as monopolies or the environment. 'Regulatory capture' means that groups such as monopolists earning abnormal profit or polluters damaging the environment can strongly influence the way they are being regulated to their own advantage. Take, for instance, a utility which is about to be privatised. The board of the utility will want to make sure that it is as easy as possible after privatisation for it to make high profits to satisfy its shareholders and maximise the pay of members of the board. It will lobby hard to have as weak powers as possible given to the regulatory body which will supervise it after privatisation. National welfare would probably be maximised if the regulatory body were given strong powers to keep consumer prices as low as possible.

However, in the short term, the government is far more likely to be wanting to maximise its own short term electoral advantage from having a successful sale of the shares and by allowing small investors (probably its own voters) to make quick gains on the share price. This requires weak regulation. Once the company has been privatised, it will want to dominate the regulator. It will do this by supplying only the information which is favourable to its case. For instance, it will tend to underestimate revenues and overestimate costs in order to make it seem that future profits will be low. The regulator, with little evidence apart from that supplied by the utility, will constantly make decisions which are in the utility's interest.

Evidence from the UK since 1984, when the first regulator was appointed, suggests that the individual appointed to head the regulatory team can be crucial in determining whether or not the regulatory body is captured. A regulator who wants to minimise confrontation with a utility (i.e. have a quiet life) will allow him or her self to be captured.

In economic theory, it is often assumed that market failure should be corrected by government. If a monopolist is exploiting the consumer, then the government should regulate or abolish the monopoly. If a polluter is damaging the environment, then the government should act to limit the actions of those responsible. Public choice theory suggests that government may fail to act in these cases because politicians are more interested in maximising their own rewards (such as votes to stay in power) than maximising the nation's welfare. Indeed, in some cases, politicians maximising their own rewards may lead to an even greater loss of economic welfare than if market failure had been left unregulated. At one extreme, some economists argue that governments should intervene as little as possible in the economy because their interventions are likely to be more damaging than the problems they are trying to solve. On the other hand, it is argued that politicians are not all out to maximise their own self-interest. Some politicians do act in the public interest even when this does not accord with their own self-interest. A left wing MP, for instance, who votes for higher income tax rates on higher income earners is likely to pay more in tax as a result. This doesn't mean to say that he or she won't vote in favour. The more a political system can encourage its politicians to act in the public interest, the more it will accord with the traditional view that government acts as an impartial actor in the economic system, intervening to maximise national welfare.

Question 5

Table 20.1 *Shares of disposable income*

			Percentages		
	Quintile groups of individuals				
	Bottom fifth	Next fifth	Middle fifth	Next fifth	Top fifth
Year 0	10	14	18	23	35
Year 5	8	12	17	23	36
Year 10	6	11	17	23	43

A right wing political party enjoys the support mainly of above average income voters. It faces a left wing party which gains a majority of its votes from below average income supporters. The electoral system is such that a party only needs 40 per cent of the vote to secure a majority in Parliament, whilst a 45 per cent vote would give it a massive majority. On average, 75 per cent of the electorate vote, but the higher the income of the individual, the more likely they are to turn out to vote. The top 20 per cent of income earners have a turnout rate of 90 per cent.

The right wing party wins an election in year 0 committed to 'increasing incentives for individuals to earn money and create wealth for the nation'. It wins two further elections in year 5 and year 10.

(a) (i) Would Table 20.1 suggest that the nation's welfare has been maximised?
(ii) What additional information would you need to support your conclusion?
(b) Explain why the party can win elections when the relative income position of most individuals is worsening over time.

key terms

Free rider - a person or organisation which receives benefits that others have paid for without making any contribution themselves.
Government failure - occurs when government intervention leads to a net welfare loss compared to the free market solution.
Merit good - a good which is underprovided by the market mechanism. A demerit good is one which is overprovided by the market mechanism.

Public choice theory - theories about how and why public spending and taxation decisions are made.
Public good - a good where consumption by one person does not reduce the amount available for consumption by another person and where once provided, all individuals benefit or suffer whether they wish to or not.

Applied economics

Lighthouses

Public goods are goods which possess the two properties of non-excludability (once provided, it is impossible to prevent others from benefiting) and non-rivalry (benefit by one does not diminish the amount by which others can benefit). Lighthouses possess both these characteristics. Once the lighthouse is working, it is impossible to prevent any ship in the area benefiting. The fact that one ship sees the lighthouse doesn't prevent other ships from seeing it as well.

Economists from Adam Smith onwards have then argued that public goods need to be provided by the public sector because there is no economic incentive for the private sector to provide them. Non-excludability would mean that there would be large numbers of free-riders - individuals or firms which benefited but did not pay. For instance, how could ships be made to pay for lighthouses?

In the UK, government doesn't provide lighthouses.

They are provided by Trinity House, a private corporation. However, the government has given it the right to build lighthouses. In return, the government allows it to charge each ship which visits a British port a 'light charge'. This is collected by Customs and Excise, part of the government. Trinity House has to submit its budget to both the government and representatives of the shipping industry each year, where it has justify the scale of its charges. So in this case, whilst the government doesn't provide the public good, it is involved at every stage and crucially in forcing ships to pay charges for the upkeep of lighthouses.

It is in fact difficult to think of any public good for which the government doesn't provide or regulate its private provision. However, the example of lighthouses shows that a public good is not necessarily one directly provided by the government.

Housing since 1945

Housing was identified as one of the key elements of a Welfare State in the Beveridge Report of 1942. Since 1945, the government has played a key role in the housing market. In the 1950s and 1960s, government, through local authorities, built millions of houses for rent to overcome the problem of a lack of accommodation fit for human habitation at an affordable rent. It was generally felt that the private sector would not provide sufficient new housing or of the right quality to satisfy the needs of the post-war population. In the early 1960s, a series of scandals highlighted the high rents, poor quality accommodation and lack of security offered by some private landlords. As a result, the private rented sector became subject to controls through the imposition of maximum rents and the introduction of strong rights of tenure for tenants. Again, from the 1960s, a strong financial incentive to buy houses was introduced through the scrapping of a tax on the notional rent on owner occupied houses and the introduction of tax relief on mortgage payments.

1979 saw the beginnings of a marked shift in government policy. Owner occupation was given a more important priority, with government talking of the creation of a 'property owning democracy'. Council tenants were given the right to buy their rented homes at a price below the true market price of the property. Financial deregulation increased the willingness of banks and building societies to give mortgages to individuals. A severe squeeze was put on local authority spending on building of new council houses in the belief that local authorities were inefficient bureaucracies which mismanaged their housing stock and which failed to give their tenants sufficient choice and control over their dwellings. At the same time, the government channelled much larger grants to Housing Associations, charity-type bodies which had a long history of building and renting out houses at affordable rents. Central government forced local authorities to increase rents, although much of the cost of this was born by central government which then had to give larger housing benefits to individuals whose income was too low to be able to afford to pay the rent. Homelessness increased as the stock of affordable rented property declined whilst social changes, such as increased divorce rates, increased the numbers of households needing to be housed.

In the late 1980s, the government further changed its policy. House prices had rocketed in the the 1980s, but exceptionally high interest rates from 1988 onwards resulted in a collapse in house purchases and prices. The government was also concerned about the growing bill for mortgage interest relief, the subsidy to home owners buying their houses through a mortgage. The government began to cut the mortgage subsidy. At the same time, it introduced a number of measures to encourage the revitalisation of the private rented sector, allowing landlords to charge much higher rents and offer short leases. Sales of council houses to their tenants fell sharply as high interest rates and then a collapse in confidence in the housing market made tenants very wary of taking on an expensive mortgage commitment. The government continued to see Housing Associations as the main providers of new cheap rented accommodation.

By 2000, government policy was little altered. Home ownership was seen as the norm for those who could afford to buy their own houses. An active private rented sector was available for those who were fairly mobile. Those who could not afford these two options turned to local councils or Housing Associations for rented property. In the long term, the government wishes to see control of all local council housing stock pass to Housing Associations. This is because it is believed that Housing Associations are more efficient at running their housing stock than councils, and that they are better able to respond to the needs of their tenants.

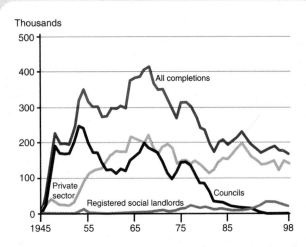

Figure 20.2 *Housebuilding completions by sector: number of new homes built*
Source: adapted from *Social Trends*, Office for National Statistics.

Table 20.2 *Age of head of household: by tenure 1998-99*

United Kingdom								Percentages
	Under 25	25-34	35-44	45-54	55-64	65-74	75 and over	All ages
Owner-occupied								
Owned outright	-	2	6	19	44	65	57	28
Owned with mortgage	20	58	68	60	32	9	4	41
Rented from social sector								
Council	31	17	12	13	15	18	25	17
Housing association	11	6	5	3	4	4	8	5
Rented privately								
Furnished	17	6	2	1	1	-	-	2
Unfurnished	20	11	7	5	4	4	6	7
All tenures	100	100	100	100	100	100	100	100

Source: adapted from *Social Trends*, Office for National Statistics.

Table 20.3 *Average weekly household expenditure on housing costs: by tenure 1998-99*

United Kingdom	£ per week
	1998-99
Owner-occupied	
Owned outright	29
Owned with mortgage	87
Rented from council	28
Rented from housing association	32
Rented privately	63
All tenures	57

Source: adapted from *Social Trends*, Office for National Statistics.

Table 20.4 *Socio-economic group of head of household: by tenure 1989-99*

United Kingdom					Percentages
	Owned outright	Owned with mortgage	Rented from social sector	Rented privately	All tenures
Economically active					
Professional	16	74	-	10	100
Employers and managers	14	75	4	6	100
Intermediate non-manual	14	66	6	13	100
Junior non-manual	14	59	17	10	100
Skilled manual	15	62	16	8	100
Semi-skilled manual	14	42	32	13	100
Unskilled manual	16	36	41	7	100
All economically active	15	63	13	9	100
Economically inactive					
Retired	62	8	26	4	100
Other	20	17	51	11	100
All economically inactive	50	11	33	6	100
All socio-economic groups	29	42	21	8	100

Source: adapted from *Social Trends*, Office for National Statistics.

1. **Outline the main changes in the housing market shown in the data.**
2. **To what extent can housing be seen as a merit good? Give examples from the data to support your arguments.**

3. **Assess whether economic welfare would be increased if government either (a) reintroduced subsidies on buying a house or (b) reduced rents for those in social housing (mainly for tenants of councils or Housing Associations).**

Summary

1. The price of a good may be too high, too low or fluctuate too greatly to bring about an efficient allocation of resources.
2. Governments may impose maximum or minimum prices to regulate a market.
3. Maximum prices can create shortages and black markets.
4. Minimum prices can lead to excess supply and tend to be maintained only at the expense of the taxpayer.
5. Prices of commodities and agricultural products tend to fluctuate more widely than the prices of manufactured goods and services.
6. Buffer stock schemes attempt to even out fluctuations in price by buying produce when prices are low and selling when prices are high.

Prices and market failure

The market mechanism establishes equilibrium prices for each good or service in the economy. However, this price or the way in which it has been set, may not lead to an efficient allocation of resources. The price may fluctuate too greatly in the short term, or it may be be too high or too low.

Large fluctuations in price In some markets, particularly agricultural and commodity markets, there can be large fluctuations in price over a short space of time. Prices act as signals and incentives to producers. Large fluctuations in price mean that these signals can give a very confusing picture to producers and result in over or under production in the short term, and over or under investment in the longer term. This is turn can lead to a less than optimal allocation of resources.

Too high a price The price of a good may be too high. It may be an essential item, such as bread, rice or housing, which poor households are unable to afford to buy sufficient amounts. The government may judge these items as **merit goods** (☞ unit 20), or it may want to reduce inequalities in society and hence want to reduce their prices. Alternatively, there could be significant positive **externalities** (☞ unit 19) in consumption. Too high a market price would lead to a less than optimal level of demand for the good.

Too low a price The free market price of goods like cigarettes may be too low because their consumption gives rise to significant negative externalities. Alternatively, the government may judge that too low a price is having a negative economic impact on producers. For instance, it may judge that farmers' incomes need to be raised because

otherwise they would leave the land and there would be rural depopulation.

Governments can intervene in markets and change prices. For instance, they can impose indirect taxes or give subsidies (☞ unit 11). They can set maximum or minimum prices or they can establish buffer stock schemes to stabilise prices. The fixing of maximum and minimum prices and buffer stock schemes will now be considered.

Maximum prices

The government can fix a maximum price for a good in a market. In Figure 21.1, the free market price is P_1 and Q_1 is bought and sold. Assume that this is the market for rented accommodation. At a price of P_1 the poorest in society are unable to afford to rent houses and there is therefore a problem of homelessness. The government intervenes by fixing a maximum price for accommodation of P_2. In the very short term, this may well seem to alleviate the problem. Landlords will continue to offer Q_1 of housing whilst the poorest in society will be more able to afford the new lower cost housing. But in the longer term, economic theory predicts that new problems will arise. At a price of P_2, demand will be higher than at P_1, whilst supply will be lower. There will in fact be an excess demand of Q_2Q_3. At the lower price, consumers will demand more housing. On the other hand, landlords will reduce their supply, for instance by selling off their properties for owner occupation, not buying new properties to rent out, or living in their own properties instead of renting them out.

Permanent rent controls will thus reduce the supply of privately rented accommodation to the market whilst

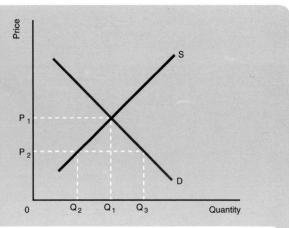

Figure 21.1 *Maximum prices*
OP₁ is the free market price. If the government sets a maximum price of OP₂ in the market, demand will increase to OQ₃ whilst supply will fall to OQ₂. The result will be excess demand in the market of Q₂Q₃.

increasing its demand. The market may react in a number of ways. In a law abiding society, queues or waiting lists may develop. It may be a matter of luck rather than money whether one is able to get rented accommodation. The state may devise systems to allocate rented accommodation on the basis of greatest need. Landlords may develop a variety of ways in which they can get round the price controls. A black market may develop, illegal and uncontrolled, where rents are fixed at, or greater than, the free market price of P_1. Economic theory therefore predicts that maximum prices may benefit some consumers - those able to obtain the goods which are

Question 1

In 1992, the Indian government partially liberalised the Indian coffee market. Prior to this, Indian coffee growers had to sell all their coffee to the Coffee Board, a state monopoly buyer of coffee. Prices paid were relatively low. Equally, however, the price of coffee sold to Indian consumers by the Coffee Board was low. The Coffee Board sold the balance of the crop for export.
From 1992, coffee growers were allowed to sell half their coffee on the free market and only had to sell half to the Coffee Board. The free market price quickly rose above the Coffee Board price with Indian consumers complaining about 'runaway' inflation in coffee prices. Coffee farmers began to invest more money in their plantations, creating new irrigation systems and planting more bushes. The 1993-94 crop was 180 000 tonnes compared to 169 000 tonnes in 1992-93 and was forecast to grow in subsequent years. Farmers want to be able to sell all their crops on the open market in order to be able to sell at world prices rather than the lower Coffee Board prices.

(a) Using a diagram and the concept of maximum price, explain why Indian coffee prices and output rose following the partial liberalisation of the Indian coffee market.

controlled in price - but will disadvantage those who are prepared to pay a higher price for the good but are unable to obtain it because of a shortage of supply.

If the maximum price were set at P_3, there would be no effect on the market. P_1, the free market price, is below the maximum price and therefore nothing will happen following the introduction of maximum price controls.

Minimum prices

Minimum prices are usually set to help producers increase their incomes. Consider Figure 21.2, which shows the market for wheat. The free market price is P_1. The government decides that this is too low a price for farmers to receive and sets a minimum price of P_2. As a result, farmers will now grow Q_1Q_3 more wheat. Consumers will react to the new higher prices by reducing their demand by Q_1Q_2. Total excess supply of Q_2Q_3 will result.

This poses a problem for the government. With maximum prices, the government did not need to intervene when excess demand appeared. The excess demand could remain in the market forever if need be. But this is not true of excess supply. If consumers only buy Q_2 of wheat then farmers can only sell Q_2 of wheat. Q_2Q_3 will remain unbought. Unless the government takes action, there will be strong pressure for farmers to sell this at below the minimum price. Average prices will fall until the market is cleared. The resulting price structure is likely to be very complex, some wheat being sold at the official minimum price of P_2 whilst the rest is sold at a variety of prices, the lowest of which is likely to be below the free market clearing price of P_1. Government action will have been frustrated.

So an effective minimum price structure must be accompanied by other measures. There are two main ways of dealing with this problem. The first is for the government to buy up the wheat that consumers refuse to buy (i.e. buy up the excess supply Q_2Q_3). This in turn creates problems because the government has to do

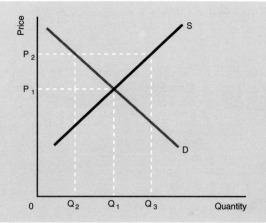

Figure 21.2 *Minimum prices*
OP₁ is the free market price. If the government sets a minimum price of OP₃ in the market, supply will increase to OQ₃ whilst demand will fall to OQ₂. The result will be excess supply in the market of Q₂Q₃.

Question 2

In 1994, the European Union (EU) spent £1.08bn buying up beef from farmers. Despite this, stocks of beef held from intervention fell from 1.1m tonnes in 1993 to 430 000 tonnes in 1994, mainly due to less beef being bought in and greater exports to countries outside the EU. The EU plans to reduce the amount of beef bought from farmers at intervention prices from 650 00 tonnes in 1994 to 350 000 in 1997.

Price support mechanisms for cereal crops such as wheat were even greater than for beef at £5.5bn in 1994. However, subsidies paid might have been even higher had it not been for the introduction of set-aside in 1992. Under this scheme, farmers are paid not to use 15 per cent of their land in a given year. The result has been a drop in annual wheat production from 185m tonnes before 1992 to an estimated 162m tonnes in 1994. With fruit and vegetables, the EU pays farmers to destroy crops which are bought at intervention prices. 600 000 tonnes of fruit and vegetables are destroyed in a typical year. The 430 000 tonnes of peaches trashed in 1992 as a result of a record harvest was headline news. Despite the lack of possibility of resale, as exists with beef or wine bought into storage, the fruit and vegetable regime is relatively cheap to run at £1.16bn spent in 1993.

Using demand and supply diagrams, explain how the EU maintains minimum prices in (a) beef, (b) wheat and (c) fruit and vegetables.

something with the wheat it buys. This has been the classic problem with the Common Agricultural Policy in the European Union. A variety of solutions, from selling wheat mountains to Third World countries at rock bottom prices, selling it back to farmers to feed to animals, or offering it at reduced prices to those in need in the EU, or simply destroying the produce, have been adopted. All have one drawback - they cost the taxpayer money because the price paid to farmers is inevitably higher than the price received from the sale of the surplus.

The second solution to the problem of excess supply is to restrict production. Governments can either force, or pay, farmers to reduce the size of their herds or leave part of their land uncultivated. At a price of P_2, the government ensures that only Q_2 is supplied to the market. If farmers are paid to set aside land, the taxpayer will have to subsidise the farmer. If farmers receive no compensation, the scheme may defeat its own purposes. As was pointed out in unit 9, whether a farmer receives a higher income by selling a smaller quantity at a higher price depends upon the price elasticity of demand. Only if the demand is price inelastic will higher prices give farmers higher revenues.

Buffer stock schemes

The free market price of **primary products** (commodities such as gold and tin, and agricultural products such as wheat and beef) tends to fluctuate much more than the price of either manufactured goods or services.

This is mainly due to supply side influences. The

demand for canned tomatoes or fresh tomatoes is likely to remain broadly constant over a twelve month period. However, the supply of these two products will differ. Canned tomatoes can be stored. Therefore the supply too will remain broadly the same over a twelve month period. But the supply of fresh tomatoes varies greatly. In the summer months, supply is plentiful and the price of tomatoes is therefore low. In winter, supply is low and prices are high.

On a year to year basis, the supply of raw agricultural commodities can vary greatly according to crop yields. A bumper crop will depress prices whilst crop failure will lead to high prices. Bumper crops can be disastrous for farmers. In Figure 21.3, if the demand for a product is price inelastic, a large fall in price is needed to sell a little extra produce. This will greatly reduce farmers' revenues.

Equally, a poor crop can be disastrous for individual farmers. Although farm income overall will be higher than average, only farmers who have crops to sell will benefit. Farmers whose crops have been mostly or completely

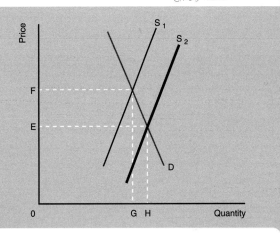

Figure 21.3 *The effect of an increase in supply on price*
If demand and supply are both relatively inelastic, then a small increase in supply from S_1 to S_2 will lead to a large fall in price of FE. Incomes will therefore be greatly reduced.

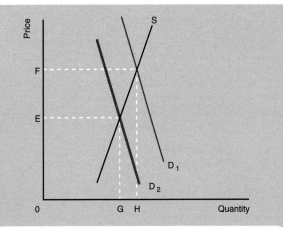

Figure 21.4 *The effect of a fall in demand on price*
If demand and supply are both relatively inelastic, then a small fall in demand from D_1 to D_2 will lead to a large fall in price of FE.

destroyed will receive little or no income.

Manufactures and services also contain greater value added than primary products. The cost of a can of tomatoes is made up not only of the cost of tomatoes themselves but also of the canning process and the can. If fresh tomatoes only account for 20 per cent of the cost of a can of tomatoes, then a doubling in the price of fresh tomatoes will only increase the price of a can by just over 7 per cent.

Demand side influences can, however, also be a source of price fluctuations for commodities. In manufacturing and services, producers devote much effort and money to stabilising demand through branding, advertising and other marketing techniques. However, Zambian copper is little different from Chilean copper. Buyers are free to buy from the cheapest source so demand fluctuates more greatly. In the short term, supply is relatively inelastic. Countries have invested in mines, oil wells and other commodity producing plant and need, often for foreign exchange purposes, to maximise output and sales. Small changes in demand, as shown in Figure 21.4, can produce large changes in price. Any slowdown in the world economy is likely to have a larger impact on commodities than on manufactured goods. Manufacturers may react to a small fall in their sales by cutting their stock levels and perhaps delaying the buying of stock by a few months. This results in a large, if temporary, fall in the price of raw materials. Whilst the slowdown persists, prices are likely to remain low. (The converse is also true - in a boom, commodity prices go up far faster than those of manufactures or services.)

Demand and supply influences combine to bring about large fluctuations in the price of commodities. Governments and other bodies have often reacted to this situation by intervening in the market place. The most appropriate way to do this is to set up a BUFFER STOCK SCHEME which combines elements of both minimum and maximum pricing. In theory it is designed to even out price fluctuations for producers. An intervention price is set. If the free market price is below this, the buffer stock agency will buy in the market until the price is at the intervention price. (It may, as the Common Agricultural Policy does, offer to buy any amount at the intervention price.) If the free market price is above the intervention price, the buffer stock will sell, forcing down the price towards the intervention price.

Buffer stock schemes are not common. One major reason for this is that a considerable amount of capital is needed to set them up. Money is required to buy produce when prices are too low. There are also the costs of administration and storage of produce purchased. But in theory, the overall running costs of the scheme should be low. Indeed, with skilful buying and selling the scheme may make an operational profit. This is because the scheme buys produce at or below the intervention price but sells at a price above the intervention price.

Buffer stock schemes also have a mixed record of success. Pressure to set up these schemes tends to come from producers who have a vested interest in setting the intervention price above the average market price. If they succeed in doing this, their revenues in the short term are likely to be larger than they would otherwise have been. But the buffer stock scheme will have been buying more produce than it sold. Eventually it will run out of money, the scheme will collapse, and prices will plummet because the accumulated stocks will be sold to pay the debts of the scheme. The glut of produce on the market will result in producers receiving below average prices for some time to come. Successful buffer stock schemes are those which correctly guess the average price and resist attempts by producers to set the intervention price above it.

key terms

Buffer stock scheme - a scheme whereby an organisation buys and sells in the open market so as to maintain a minimum price in the market for a product.

Question 3

In 1985 the International Tin Council's (ITC) price support scheme collapsed. Countries like the UK, which had agreed to support the Council's purchase of tin when tin prices fell below the intervention price, refused to provide any more money to buy tin to put into stock. Tin prices collapsed and remained weak between 1985 and 1988 as tin stocks, totalling 120 000 tonnes and equivalent to nine months of tin demand, were gradually sold. The main tin producing countries formed themselves into a cartel and agreed production quotas. By 1989, the ITC's stocks were down to 25 000 tonnes and tin prices had risen from $7 200 a lb at the end of 1988 to a peak of $10 000 a lb in 1989.

The recession in the world economy, which began in the USA and the UK in the late 1980s and which only ended in 1993, depressed tin prices despite cutbacks in output by tin producers. Tin prices surged in 1994 as the world recovery got under way.

Using diagrams, explain why:
(a) the ITC's price support scheme collapsed in 1985;
(b) the price of tin was weak between 1986 and 1988;
(c) the price of tin rose in 1989;
(d) the price of tin fell between 1989 and 1993, whilst rising in 1994.

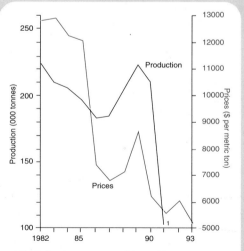

1 Excluding former communist countries.
Figure 21.5 *Prices and production of tin*

Applied economics

The Common Agricultural Policy

One of the most important steps taken by the European Union (formerly the European Community) in its early years was to create the Common Agricultural Policy in 1958. Article 39 of the Treaty of Rome cites 5 objectives of agricultural policy:

● to increase agricultural productivity;
● to ensure a fair standard of living for farmers;
● to stabilise markets;
● to guarantee availability of supplies;
● to ensure fair prices for consumers.

It was hoped that CAP would achieve this through regulation of the agricultural industry in the Union. For many products, an **intervention price** was established. Farmers could then choose to sell their produce on the open market or to the EU at this minimum fixed price. The EU guaranteed to buy up any amount at the intervention price. Farmers were protected from overseas competition through a complex system of tariffs (taxes on imported goods) and quotas (physical limits on the amount that could be imported). Tariffs and quotas effectively raised the price of imported agricultural produce to EU consumers. With high enough tariffs and quotas, agricultural produce from outside the EU could be kept out, allowing EU farmers to sell their own produce into their domestic markets at much higher prices than they would otherwise have been able to do.

CAP proved to be far more favourable to farmers than to consumers. The farming community in the EU became very good at lobbying their individual governments to vote for high intervention prices at the annual price fixing negotiations in Brussels. Consumers lost out in two ways. First, they had to pay directly for food which was much higher in price than it would otherwise have been if it had been bought on world markets. Second, as taxpayers, they had to pay for the heavy costs of running the CAP.

In theory, the CAP should have been fairly inexpensive to run. If there was a glut of produce on the market in one season, the EU would buy some of it at the intervention price and store it. The next season, when there was perhaps a shortage, the EU could take the produce out of storage and sell it. Prices would not fluctuate by as much as under a market system and the sale of produce would ensure that the major cost of the system would be administration and storage.

In practice, the cost of the CAP rose year after year. High intervention prices led to increased production, as economic theory would predict. Supply then began to outstrip demand. Instead of selling produce taken into storage to European consumers at a later date, mountains and lakes of produce developed, as shown in Figure 21.6. This produce then had to be sold, often at a fraction of the cost of production, to the former USSR, Third World countries, and to EU farmers for use as animal feed. Some was even destroyed.

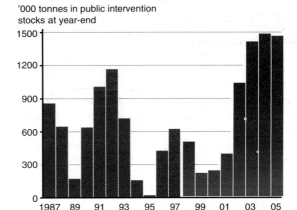

'000 tonnes in public intervention stocks at year-end

■European Commission forecasts assuming no reform of sector

Figure 21.6 *Beef mountains*
Source: adapted from European Commission.

Table 21.1 *European Union expenditure*

					Percentages
	1981	1986	1991	1996	1997
Agricultural guarantee	62	64	58	51	51
Structural funds					
Agricultural	3	2	4	4	4
Regional policy	14	7	12	14	14
Social policy	3	7	8	8	8
Other	.	.	3	6	6
All structural funds	20	16	26	32	33
Research	2	2	3	4	4
External action	4	3	4	5	5
Administration	5	4	5	5	5
Other	6	10	4	3	3
All expenditure[1] (=100%)					
(£ billion at 1997 prices)	20.6	37.5	44.3	63.8	55.0
of which spending on					
Agricultural Guarantee &					
Agricultural Guidance[1]	13.4	24.8	27.4	35.1	30.3

1. The fall in spending in £ between 1996 and 1997 was caused by a sharp rise in the value of the pound at the time. Spending measured in Ecu (or euros) actually rose slightly.
Source: adapted from European Commission.

Reform of CAP has been a long standing issue. As early as 1968, the Mansholt Plan recommended that farm size should increase to enable farmers to enjoy economies of scale and thus be better able to provide food at world market prices. By the early 1980s, political pressure was building to limit the growth of the CAP budget shown in Table 21.1. By 1985, spending on CAP was threatening to exceed the maximum amount permitted in the EU budget. At a summit meeting at Fontainebleau in that year, the first measures which would begin to tackle the CAP problem were announced.

There is a number of different ways in which the EU limits agricultural production.

Reducing guaranteed prices but giving direct aid compensation Since 1992, the EU has reduced guaranteed minimum prices for certain products, particularly cereals and beef, but made up the fall in farmers' incomes by giving them direct aid not linked to production. Guaranteed minimum prices act as an incentive for farmers to produce more. A lower guaranteed price reduces supply by removing marginal land from production. Giving direct aid in compensation for lost income to farmers gives them no incentive to produce more. They receive the aid whether they produce or not. In practice, the amount of direct aid compensation has been less than what the farmers would have received from the EU if the higher guaranteed prices had remained. In this sense, EU taxpayers benefit from what they might otherwise have had to pay out to farmers. Cutting the incentive to produce leads to lower supply and either higher market prices or less need for the EU to buy up unwanted surplus produce. Consumers are still likely to be paying higher than world market prices for the produce but farmers gain higher incomes.

Quotas Since 1985, milk production has been subject to quotas. Each member country of the EU is given a milk quota, a maximum amount of milk that can be produced. This is then divided up between farmers, originally depending on how much milk they produced before quotas were introduced. Quotas are transferable. A farmer owning a quota can sell all or part it of it to another farmer. Quotas have been seen to limit the production of milk. With supply below what it would be if there was a free market in milk, the price of milk is kept artificially high. This benefits farmers but consumers have to pay higher prices for their milk and milk-based products. The quota system is cheap to run for the EU taxpayer because dairy farmers do not receive subsidies for production of milk.

Set-aside Since 1992, cereal farmers have been subject to a set-aside scheme. They are paid for setting aside (i.e. not using) a certain proportion of their land. In the Agenda 2000 agreement, this was fixed at 10 per cent for 2000-2006. The land set aside must be rotated from year to year to prevent farmers simply setting aside their least productive land. By reducing the amount of land available for production, the supply of cereals is reduced, thus raising their price. Farmers receive a payment from the EU for each acre set-aside. Hence, not only do EU consumers pay higher prices for cereals than they would otherwise, but EU taxpayers have to pay a direct subsidy to farmers.

Many economists are highly critical of the CAP. It fixes minimum prices for certain types of agricultural produce. However, because these minimum prices are too high, it has since the 1980s established different schemes in different parts of the industry to reduce production whilst trying to maintain farmers' incomes. Minimum prices create market failure because consumers are unable to buy at the lowest price in the world market. Schemes such as milk quotas or cereal set aside further compound market failure by distorting the market even

more. For instance, with set aside, some farmers in one year will be leaving their most productive land fallow when far less productive land is being used elsewhere in the EU to produce cereals.

The most recent reform of CAP, Agenda 2000, which was agreed in 1999, has done little to remove these market distortions. Its main achievement was to limit EU spending on the CAP to between E40 920 million and E43 900 million between 2000 and 2006.

Free market economists would like to see the CAP dismantled. EU consumers would benefit through being able to buy agricultural produce at lowest world prices rather than more expensive EU producers. EU taxpayers would benefit because CAP is the single most costly item of EU expenditure. In 2000, the budget cost per capita of CAP was E110 (£68 at an exchange rate of £1 =E1.62). For a family of four, this is £272 per year. 80 per cent of all CAP spending goes to supporting the largest 20 per cent of farms in the EU. Only 20 per cent goes to supporting the 'small farmer'.

The farming lobby is very strong politically, however. It argues that farming would be devastated without high subsidies. Farmers would go bankrupt, leading to loss of jobs in the countryside. Rural areas would suffer depopulation. Some land would return to a wilderness state whilst other land would not be properly maintained. The countryside would begin to look 'untidy'. Taxpayers would lose out because they would have to pour money into the countryside in welfare benefits for the unemployed or to create new jobs. The environment would suffer because farmers were no longer maintaining the land. The traditional farming way of life would disappear, lead to a priceless loss of national heritage. EU consumers would be forced to eat food imported from outside the EU instead of buying 'British' or 'French' locally grown produce.

CAP is also supported by certain members of the EU. Countries such as France, Spain and Italy tend to resist CAP reform because they are the main beneficiaries of net CAP spending. Countries such as the UK and Sweden are more in favour of a free market because they pay more into the CAP than they receive.

In the long term, with the enlargement of the EU to take in countries in Eastern Europe, the benefits given to each farmer must fall. Otherwise, CAP would become too costly. There is also likely to be considerable pressure from countries such as the USA, Australia and New Zealand to reduce tariff barriers in the new round of world trade talks.

Rubber

The International Natural Rubber Organisation (INRO) is to break up following the withdrawal of two of the world's largest rubber producers, Thailand and Malaysia. The buffer stock scheme, set up in 1980, buys up rubber when prices fall and sells when prices rise. Members include the six leading rubber producing countries as well as the biggest consuming countries such as the US, Japan and China.

Thailand and Malaysia have become dissatisfied with the low price of rubber in world markets in recent years. They have accused INRO of failing to intervene to stop the price of rubber falling. For instance, at the start of 1998, rubber was 230 Malaysian cents a kilo. By 1999, this had fallen to 150 cents. They also accuse INRO of pursuing policies which favour member countries with low volumes of production and failing to pay sufficient attention to the interests of the three countries which account for nearly three quarter of world production. Thailand, for instance, paid around 40 per cent of the total yearly contributions which financed INRO, but was only responsible for 30 per cent of output.

Thailand and Malaysia have chosen now to work together to support prices. The bilateral agreement provides for the co-ordination of supply rationalisation, rubber trading, domestic price supports, export taxes and downstream business investment. If the two countries are to be successful in raising the world price of rubber, they must act to limit their supply of rubber onto world markets, in the same way that OPEC imposes production quotas on its members. In the long term, this means they must control the amount that their rubber farmers are producing domestically. In the short term, they face a problem with INRO's stocks of rubber being bought up to maintain prices in the past. Thailand and Malaysia want to buy the stocks to prevent them flooding onto the market when INRO is dissolved and which would prices.

Source: adapted from the Financial Times, 10.2.1999, 21.4.1999, 21.9.1999, 30.9.1999, 6.10.1999.

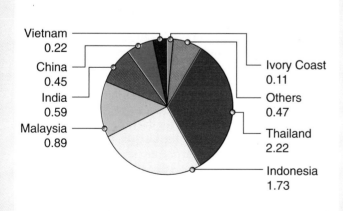

Figure 21.7 *Leading natural rubber producers, 1998, million tonnes*
Source: adapted from the Financial Times, 6.10.1999.

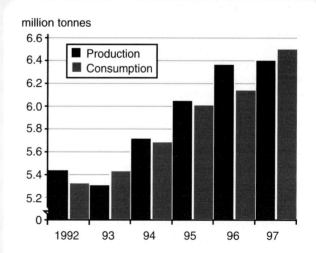

Figure 21.8 *World rubber production and consumption*
Source: adapted from International Rubber Study Group.

1. **Explain, using INRO as an example, what is meant by a buffer stock scheme.**
2. **Why had INRO built up stocks of rubber by 1999?**

3. **Evaluate whether the new bilateral agreement between Thailand and Malaysia is likely to be any more successful than INRO in preventing low prices.**

Summary

1. Cost-benefit analysis is a technique which attempts to evaluate the social costs and benefits of an economic decision.
2. Social costs and benefits may differ from private costs and benefits.
3. It is often difficult and sometimes impossible to place a price on externalities.
4. Cost-benefit analysis is often used to assess public sector investment projects.

Market failure

In a free market, decisions are based upon the calculation of **private costs and benefits**. However, there are many markets where significant **externalities** exist (☞ unit 19). This means that there are significant costs or benefits which are unlikely to be taken account of by the private economic decision maker.

COST-BENEFIT ANALYSIS is a procedure which takes into account all costs and all benefits (i.e **social costs and benefits**). Its purpose is to give guidance in economic decision making. It is used particularly by governments to evaluate important investment projects.

Costs and benefits

It is relatively easy to place a value on private costs and benefits. For instance, the government may want a toll motorway to be built round Birmingham. The company which builds and operates the motorway will be able to calculate the financial cost of constructing the road. This is the private cost to the operating company. It will also be able to calculate the revenues to be earned from tolls. These will be its private benefits. If the private benefits exceed private costs the motorway will be profitable and the operating company will be prepared to build the road.

However, there will be other costs and benefits associated with the project. These are the externalities of the road. For instance, residents near the motorway will suffer from pollution, including noise pollution. The motorway may generate more traffic on some roads joining the motorway, again increasing pollution to local residents. The motorway may go through areas of outstanding natural beauty or take away areas which have been used by local people for recreational activities such as walking. Habitats of rare species may be destroyed. Sites of historical interest may be lost. On the other hand, jobs and wealth may be created locally as industry is attracted to the area by the new motorway. Car and lorry drivers may save time using the new motorway. Traffic may be taken off some local roads, relieving congestion.

These externalities are very important costs and benefits which could be completely ignored by the operating company if it operated in a pure free market. In a cost-benefit analysis the company would attempt to place a value on these externalities in order to calculate the social cost and social benefit of the project and proceed only if social benefit exceeded social cost.

Question 1

Brighton & Hove Albion, the football club, wanted to build a new stadium. In 1997, it sold its existing stadium to property developers and has since been without a ground. Home matches have been played 75 miles away at Gillingham's ground. The proposed new site was at Falmer, a village just outside Brighton. Supporters pointed out that the stadium would be built in a field just outside the village and adjoining Sussex University. The stadium would be next to an existing railway station and park and ride schemes would be used to keep traffic away from the site. Local residents were fiercely against the proposals. They feared that the 25 000 seater stadium would lead to increased traffic congestion, noise levels and football hooliganism.

Source: adapted from *The Guardian*, 6.2.1999.

(a) What are the likely private costs and benefits to Brighton & Hove Albion football club of building and running the stadium?
(b) What might be the externalities caused by the stadium?

Problems with placing a value on externalities

The value of many externalities is difficult to estimate. For instance, assume that, as a result of the building of the motorway, 5 million travellers every year save on average 30 minutes each on their journey times around Birmingham. In a cost-benefit analysis, a value would need to be placed on the $2^1/_2$ million hours saved. However, it is unclear what value should be given to each hour since there is no obvious market in which a price is set for the time. A high cost estimate would assume that the time should be valued as if the travellers could have earned money during that time. This might give an estimate of £10 per hour at an average annual wage for the typical motorway user of £20 000. On the other hand, it could be assumed that the traveller places almost no value on the time saved. It could be just 50p per hour. Comparing these two estimates, we get a high estimate of £25 million and a low estimate of £1.25 million.

Even more difficult is how to place a value on a human life. Assume that the motorway takes traffic off other roads and as a result 5 fewer people are killed in road accidents each year. The value of a life today in a court case involving accidents is mainly determined by the expected earnings of the deceased. For instance, if a company director earning £500 000 per annum were killed in a road crash, together with her chauffeur earning £10 000 per year, then all other things being equal (age, family circumstances etc.) the family of the company director would receive far more compensation than the family of the chauffeur. These values, however, are open to much debate.

Other intangibles, such as pollution and illness, are very difficult to value in money terms. Even the values placed on private costs and benefits may be difficult to estimate. For instance, the operating company may charge £2 for a journey from one end of the motorway to the other. But that may not necessarily reflect the cost to the operating company of the journey. It may include a large element of monopoly profit, or it may be subsidised by the government to encourage people to use the motorway. It may therefore be necessary for the cost-benefit analysis to estimate a **shadow price** for the journey - a price which more accurately reflects the cost to the operating company of providing the service.

Question 2

The Department of Transport planned to build an 11-mile stretch of dual carriageway close to the existing A27 north of Lewes in East Sussex. The A27 was a travellers' nightmare. Mr Robert Caffyn, a local industrialist, said: 'Tourists enjoy Eastbourne when they arrive but complain bitterly about the last part of the journey. Large employers have left the town largely because of poor access.' The county council, which supported the scheme, wanted the extension because it would help the local tourist industry, the county's main industry, to help fill the small industrial estates in Hastings, Lewes, Newhaven and Polegate, and to boost the only port, Newhaven.

There was fierce local opposition, however. Mr Nick Davies, secretary of the A27 Action Group, said the road would cost £70m and be the biggest construction project ever in the area. He said the road 'would be polluting in terms of noise and atmospheric discharge. It would cause considerable damage to our homes, our countryside and our health. Above all, the road is unnecessary. Recent research suggests that motorways do not reduce congestion but create new traffic. This road would pull traffic through our villages.'

Source: adapted from the *Financial Times*.

(a) Explain the external costs and benefits of the proposed A27 road scheme.
(b) How might you estimate a shadow price for each of these costs and benefits?

Benefit across time

Calculations are further complicated by the fact that costs and benefits will occur at different points in time. A Channel Tunnel rail link, for instance, could still be carrying passengers in the year 2100 and beyond. Many of our major rail links today in the UK were first built over 100 years ago.

A value has to be given to future costs and benefits. Economic theory suggests that £1 of benefit in 20 years' time is worth considerably less than £1 of benefit today. This is because £1 today could be saved or invested. Each year that passes it should be worth more. For instance, if the rate of interest (or RATE OF RETURN, or RATE OF DISCOUNT) is 10 per cent per annum then £1 today is worth £1.10 in one year's time, £1.21 in two years' time, £1.33 in three years' time, £10.83 in 25 years' time and £117.39 in 50 years' time

(these figures are calculated using compound interest). It must therefore be true that a benefit of £117.39 available in 50 years' time is only worth £1 today if the rate of return is 10 per cent per annum.

So in cost-benefit analysis, all future costs and benefits need to be revalued using a rate of discount. There are two ways of doing this. Either a rate of discount is assumed and all costs and benefits are calculated as if they occurred today. This is known as calculating present values. Saying that £117.39 available in 50 years' time is worth £1 today is an example of this technique. Alternatively the internal rate of return on the project can be calculated. So if we knew that £1 had been invested today and the one and only benefit were £117.39 which would be paid in 50 years' time, then we would know that the rate of return on the project would be 10 per cent per annum.

Question 3

A rail link could be built to last either 25 years or 50 years. It has been estimated that it would cost £100 million to build it for 25 years and £200 million for 50 years. In 25 years' time the cost of upgrading it to make it last another 25 years would be £900 million.

(a) If the rate of discount (or rate of interest or rate of return) were 10 per cent, would it be cheaper to build it to last for 25 years and repair it, or build it to last for 50 years?
(b) Would your answer be different if the rate of discount were 5 per cent? Explain why.

A critique of cost-benefit analysis

Cost-benefit analysis is a procedure where:
- all costs and benefits, both private and social, are identified;
- then a value is placed on those costs and benefits, wherever possible in monetary terms.

The technique is used mainly where it is assumed that market failure is present. Calculating all costs and benefits would seem to be a more rational way of evaluating an important investment project than relying upon projections of private profit or even having no facts and figures to consider.

However, cost-benefit analysis can be a very imprecise procedure. It is difficult to place a value on certain important costs and benefits and the results depend crucially upon the rate of discount of future costs and benefits used.

So the results of cost-benefit analysis should be used with caution. The assumptions made in the analysis should be explicit. Ideally a range of results should be calculated showing what would happen to costs and benefits if different assumptions were made. Social costs and benefits which cannot be valued in monetary terms should be clearly stated.

If this is done, cost-benefit analysis can be a useful tool in the evaluation of investment projects. But it should be recognised that it is only one piece of evidence amongst many and it could well be that other considerations, such as political considerations, prove ultimately to be more important.

Cost-benefit analysis - a procedure, particularly used by governments to evaluate investment projects, which takes into account social cost and benefits.

Rate of return or rate of discount - the rate of interest or rate of profit earned on an investment project over time. The rate of discount can be used to calculate the present value of future income.

Applied economics

Vodafone's world HQ

Background

Vodafone was, in 1999, the UK's largest mobile telephone group. It had approximately 37.5 per cent market share. It had originally set up in Newbury, Berkshire, in 1982, with 50 employees. By 1999 its Newbury head office staff had grown to 3 000, working out of 57 different offices in the centre of Newbury. Working from so many different offices inevitably led to productive inefficiency. Its costs were higher than they would have been if the staff had been working under one roof. So in the second half of the 1990s it actively sought a new headquarters site. It found nothing suitable in the centre of Newbury and finally chose a site just outside the town, off the A34 by-pass, on a former showground. The site was controversial, however. It adjoined a site designated an Area of Outstanding Natural Beauty. The local plan, drawn up by West Berkshire Council, stated clearly that the land could not be built on. The application to build fulfilled environmentalists' worst fears that the A34 by-pass, which in itself had permanently damaged the local environment, would attract further building and destroy the countryside. If a cost-benefit study had been undertaken on the proposal, it would have evaluated both the private costs and benefits to Vodafone and the externalities created by the building.

Private costs and benefits

For Vodafone, the private costs and benefits were relatively simple to evaluate. The cost of the headquarters would be £120 million. To offset this, the company would save on rent for existing offices. There would also be operating efficiencies because all staff would be under one roof.

In a cost-benefit calculation, these costs and benefits would have to be taken into account. The £120 million would be paid out over the two years that it would take to complete the building. Savings would only occur in future years. The further away in time the operational savings, the less valuable they would become. For instance, assume the rate of discount was 10 per cent per annum and that the £120 million was paid in year 0. The headquarters becomes operational the first day of year 1 and each year there are operational savings of £30 million. Discounting these savings back to year zero at 10 per cent per annum, they would give:

- in year 1 savings of £27.3 million (£30 million ÷ 1.1);
- in year 2 savings of £24.8 million (£30 million ÷ 1.1^2);
- in year 3 savings of £22.5 million (£30 million ÷ 1.1^3);
- in year 4 savings of £20.5 million (£30 million ÷ 1.1^4);
and so on.

Savings in each subsequent year become smaller and smaller as they become further away from year 0.

On the other hand, if the rate of discount was 5 per cent the savings discounted back to year zero would be:

- in year 1 savings of £28.6 million (£30 million ÷ 1.05);
- in year 2 savings of £27.2 million (£30 million ÷ 1.05^2);
and so on.

Externalities

The move would have implications not just for Vodafone but also for the wider community. There would be some positive externalities. For instance, the offices that Vodafone vacated in the town centre could be put to alternative uses. The land could be used for housing, important in an area where there is a shortage of homes. Or it could be used for other businesses, creating jobs and more prosperity for the area. The move would safeguard the jobs of 3 000 workers in the area. Vodafone threatened to move to another town, such as Swindon, if planning permission were not given. If the company did move, there would an increase in local unemployment and a loss of prosperity, at least in the short term.

On the other hand, an agricultural site would be lost, with its implications for wildlife and the environment. There might be an increase in commuting if most workers found themselves further away from the new site than the centre of Newport. This would increase air and noise pollution. It would also increase traffic on the A34, built to relieve congestion in Newbury town centre. If congestion occurred on the A34, this would become an external cost. The building could also lead to a demand by other firms to use greenfield sites in the local area, further damaging the environment if granted.

Evaluating costs and benefits

It is much more difficult to place a monetary value on external costs and benefits than on private costs and benefits. For instance, what price should be put on the the loss of agricultural land? It could be valued at the market price of agricultural land in the area in 1999, but environmentalists would argue that this considerably undervalues the loss. At the other extreme, an infinite price could be put on it since it could be argued that the land is so valuable in its present state that it is priceless. Equally, what price should be put on increased commuting by workers? It is difficult to place a value on noise pollution or air pollution. As for congestion costs, it is difficult to predict how much extra congestion, if any, will be created. A range of outcomes could be included in the cost-benefit study to cover different scenarios.

Ultimately, the main problem in weighing up the costs and benefits is likely to be the different values placed on externalities. Vodafone is likely to minimise the value of negative externalities. Environmentalists would place a very high if not infinite price on the loss of the countryside.

Growing pains cause a storm

Retired Robert Sawtell had shopped in Black Country towns like Dudley, Halesowen, Tipton and West Bromwich for nearly half a century. He and his wife Phyllis went to different centres for different goods long before Merry Hill was a glimmer in a planner's eye.

News that London based Chelsfield developers wanted to expand the complex by a third prompted him to pen a warning to the *Express & Star* that it could be the final nail in their coffins.

'Money spent at Merry Hell just means profit going out of the area to be spent on millionaires' row', said 85-year-old Mr Sawtell, of Glynfarm Road, Quinton.

Destroying

'If you haven't got a car you can't get there. It's just destroying life in towns, and the majority of shops there are big multiples so the local community gets nothing out of it.'

These were familiar criticisms to those levelled at the centre since it was given planning permission in 1986.

It was doubtful whether the 2,000 people who were due to gets jobs at the larger Merry Hill would have agreed with them.

But Stourbridge Chamber of Trade, Birmingham City Council planners and Halesowen Township Council chairman Jack Deeley said that they would object to the expansion.

They feared the £100 million application to build 650,000 square feet of extra shopping space would have meant shop closures, job losses and increased traffic chaos on already swamped roads.

Dudley market traders also feared the development could tempt Beatties away from the town, leaving it without a major department store and the shoppers it attracted.

The giant complex had been dogged by such bleak warnings from the start, when building tycoons the Richardson brothers suggested it to fill the void left by the closed Round Oak steelworks.

It was supported by Dudley Council's then ruling Conservative group, but fiercely opposed by opposition Labour councillors.

The then chief executive, John Mulvehill, quit his job after issuing planning consent on instructions of the outgoing Tories the day after Labour won control of the council. After, Labour had been charged with managing the consequences of a development it never wanted.

But the success of Merry Hill - attracting 25 million shoppers a year - and Chelsfield's inclusion of £6.75 million of private money for other centres in the borough - meant expansion was unlikely to have been resisted. It would have made the centre reputedly the largest in Britain at the time and many said the prestige could only have benefited the borough.

Chairman of Dudley Retail Business Watch Stephen Schwartz, who might have been expected to oppose further expansion of Merry Hill, said he was thrilled by the idea.

'Dudley is on the way up and nothing at Merry Hill can change that. The extra people it attracts can only help us,' he said.

And Dudley Chamber of Commerce president Richard Tesh said the challenge was to bring Merry Hill shoppers to Dudley Zoo and Castle, and the Black Country Museum.

Attractions

'If we can get just a small percentage of them coming to our tourist attractions then it will help Dudley town centre.'

Dudley Labour councillor Gary Willets - the fiercest opponent of the original Merry Hill plans - was one of the few to oppose expansion.

'What happened was a planning fiasco. It was a mess and I don't believe we should have a double mess,' he said.

Councillor Willets warned that expansion would be doomed to failure unless money was pumped into road improvements in Brierley Hill, Quarry Bank and Lye.

Chelsfield had pledged £1.5 million to a scheme to improve the A4036 Pedmore Road. But Councillor Willets said the government might want a larger contribution of private cash if it was to finance a wholesale package of improvements.

Councillor Willets said Chelsfield's application was so major that the then Environment Secretary, John Gummer, would have had to 'call it in' for his consideration.

Source: adapted from the *Express & Star*.

1. **Assess the costs and benefits of the proposed Merry Hill shopping centre expansion. In your answer:**
   (a) **make a clear distinction between the private costs and benefits to the developers and the potential users of the project, and the associated external costs and benefits;**

   (b) **discuss what other information apart from that contained in the article you would need to make the assessment**

2. **Discuss whether or not, in your opinion, the expansion should have been given planning permission.**

Applied economics

The leisure industry is a significant part of the UK economy. Spending on leisure goods and services, for instance, in 1997-98, accounted for £55.10 per week per household out of total spending of £328.80. The leisure industry is highly diversified, from book publishers to travel agents to football clubs. In this unit, we will consider four markets within the leisure industry: package holidays, air travel, spectator sports and television broadcasting.

Package holidays

The package tour holiday industry in the UK is dominated by four large firms, as shown in Figure 23.1. These firms, Thomson, Airtours, First Choice and Thomas Cook, accounted for over three quarters of sales in 1998. There would therefore seem to be imperfect competition in the industry. (In fact an oligopoly may exist - competition among the few.)

In an industry dominated by a few firms, economic theory would assume that there were high barriers to entry. This would enable firms in the industry to keep out new entrants. The firms could then charge high prices and earn abnormal profit due to lack of competition. The competition between the firms would tend to be non-price competition, such as advertising or other forms of promotion. Competing on price would drive prices down, reducing profits for all firms in the industry. This would be in none of their interests, although it would benefit the customer.

The package tour industry does not fit neatly into this model. Barriers to entry are relatively low. It is easy for a firm to set up. There are thousands of small package

tour holiday companies, many offering specialist holidays such as adventure holidays in Africa, pilgrimages to Rome or bus tours of the Rhine. There are also thousands of independent travel agents. This is significant because all the four largest package tour operators own chains of travel agents. One reason for low barriers to entry is that the financial cost of entry is relatively small. A company can be run from a single room office with a telephone and a computer. A key to success is marketing, and again the four largest companies cannot control this aspect of the market. Small companies are free to advertise their brochures in newspapers and magazines, or use independent travel agents. The internet is also opening up further opportunities for small firms to communicate with potential customers.

Unable to control entry, the largest firms have been created over the past twenty years through a series of takeovers and mergers. Firms have competed on price and occasionally there have been price wars which have plunged the industry into losses. The aim of price wars has been to expand market share.

In terms of efficiency, the package tour industry can be argued to be productively efficient. The largest operators have enough size to be able to exploit economies of scale to their maximum. Smaller operators tend to cater for niche markets, where volumes are much lower. It can also be argued that the industry is allocatively efficient. Consumers have wide choice, whilst firms usually do not earn abnormal profits.

The industry has been investigated on a number of occasions by the government through what is now the Competition Commission and on the whole found not to be acting against the interests of consumers. The largest firms would, no doubt, like to extend their market power to raise profitability at the expense of consumers. The Competition Commission argued, for instance, in the late 1990s that travel agents operated by the package tour operators were offering customers discounts on holidays if they bought travel insurance at the same time. The problem was that the travel insurance was so expensive that customers would usually have been better off not having the discount on the holiday and buying the travel

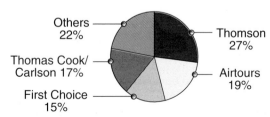

Figure 23.1 *Package tour industry by market share, 1998*
Source: adapted from CAA/ATOL, Datastream/ICV.

insurance independently. However, this type of market abuse is limited. It would be more worrying in the long term for efficiency if independent travel agents were squeezed out of the market. If the large tour operators responded by deciding only to sell their holidays in their own chains of travel agents, then consumer choice would be restricted and firms might be able to raise prices.

The market for air travel

The market for air travel is an example of what the competition authorities in the UK would call a 'complex monopoly'. Airline companies would argue that the industry is subject to fierce competition. In practice, competition is limited for two main reasons.

First, governments restrict which airlines can fly in and out of their countries. Traditionally, this was part of a deliberate attempt to stop free trade in airline services to benefit national carriers. So the United States, for instance, would allow international flights to the USA by US airlines but restrict flights by other airlines. No foreign airline is allowed to operate internal flights in the USA. Agreements about which airline can fly where are negotiated through international treaties. Many would prefer to see an 'open skies' policy where governments were not involved in decision making.

Second, airlines are restricted by which airports they can use. In the UK, most carriers would prefer to use Heathrow rather than any of the other airports in the South East. This is because Heathrow is the largest airport in the UK and acts as a 'hub'. A 'hub' is an airport where a significant number of passengers change planes to complete their journeys from one airport to another. Moreover, Heathrow has good road and rail connections. However, it operates at 100 per cent capacity during the day. Slots are allocated on a historical basis. If an airline received a slot in 1955, it will still have it today unless it has voluntarily given it up. So there are no landing or take off slots available for new entrants. This means that a carrier like British Airways has a dominant position at Heathrow because it has more slots than any other single airline. It also means that competition on routes tends to be restricted.

On the North Atlantic routes, for instance, there are only four airlines operating out of Heathrow, two UK carriers (BA and Virgin Atlantic) and two US carriers. Partly this is because of international agreements where the US, for instance, would not allow another UK carrier to fly to the US without the UK agreeing to allow another US carrier to fly into Heathrow. Partly it is because the existing four airlines would have to give up some of their slots to new competitors. They wouldn't do this voluntarily.

There are parts of the industry where there is relatively free competition. In the United States, for instance, any US airline can set up internal scheduled services. In Europe, governments have opened up routes between EU member countries. This has led to

the entry of a number of low cost budget airlines onto routes such as EasyJet and Ryanair. However, these low cost airlines tend to fly from relatively unpopular airports such as Luton or Stansted, reflecting the scarcity of landing slots at airports such as Heathrow. These low cost airlines could be said to be operating in a perfectly competitive market, with relatively low entry costs, where customers have no preference for which airline they fly and where they buy on price.

It can be argued, though, that low cost airlines have provided little competition for the more established carriers. They have created a new market with new passengers. Existing passengers tend to fall into three categories.

First, there are package tour customers who are provided with their ticket as part of the cost of the holiday. They make no decision about which airline they fly with. Bookings are made by the package tour operators, who often charter whole airlines for flights.

Second, there are individuals who wish to fly a particular route, such as Birmingham to Lyons. They are relatively price inelastic customers, prepared to pay a premium price for a particular service. Such routes are often natural monopolies - where costs per passenger are considerably lower if there is only one producer in the market. Airlines can therefore develop monopolies on these routes.

Third, there are business customers. The most important characteristic about business customers is that they are unlikely to be paying for the flight personally. It will be their employer who pays the bill. Business customers are likely to want the best service possible. Hence, advertisements for flights often talk about leg room, meals or frequent flyer incentive schemes. Demand from business flyers is perfectly price inelastic. Since they aren't paying, they don't care what price the ticket is. Demand from their employers tends to be price inelastic. Typically, they want their employees to be able to work throughout the trip and return home as soon as possible. Hence, they don't want their workers wasting time saving a few pounds flying between inconvenient airports and don't want their workers to be exhausted by travelling in uncomfortable conditions. Flying can also be seen as a perk, rewarding an employee for working long hours during a trip. Airlines exploit this market by offering business class services. These offer better facilities than standard 'tourist' services and customers can choose the time of day they wish to travel. However, the price is often several times higher. On flights to New York, for instance, the lowest return fare available might be a few hundred pounds. Business class service tickets might cost £3 000.

If a complex monopoly exists, firms should be able to earn abnormal profit. In practice, many airlines in the 1960s, 1970s and 1980s often made losses. This was mainly because lack of competition led to high levels of inefficiency. For instance, airline staff have often been paid far more than the free market wage. What's more, many airlines were national carriers owned by their governments. They failed to put sufficient pressure on their airlines to become profitable. The opening up to competition on many routes and the privatisation of many national carriers, such as British Airways, has transformed the productive efficiency of many airlines and enabled them to return to profitability.

Whether the airline industry as a whole makes abnormal profits is more debatable. On some routes where there is little competition and where there is a high volume of traffic, airlines almost certainly do make abnormal profit. On other routes where there is more competition, and where average seat capacity is low, profits are likely only to be normal. Competition, then, tends to reduce profits and prices. It also usually increases the number of services available to passengers. As such, competition in the airline industry therefore tends to lead to allocative efficiency.

Spectator sports

The market for spectator sports, like the airline market, is a complex monopoly. The main spectator sport in the UK is football. Others include rugby, cricket and boxing. The product supplied is non-homogeneous, i.e. it is different from competing products. A Manchester United game, for instance, is different from a West Bromwich Albion or Oxford United game. This is reflected in the willingness of fans to view the game. Manchester United can attract far more fans to one of its games and charge a higher price than Oxford United. Loyalty by fans to a club acts as barrier to entry to the market. Other barriers to entry include the high financial cost of running a top football club and the possible losses to be incurred of owning a lower division club. Location is also a barrier to entry. A larger proportion of the population of Newcastle is Newcastle United fans than in, say, Birmingham.

Successful football clubs exploit their monopolies in a number of different ways.

Tickets Successful football clubs tend to charge higher prices for tickets than lower division clubs. The prices of Premier League football tickets have considerably increased over the past twenty years as clubs have exploited the price inelasticity of their fans. Football clubs price discriminate, charging different prices for different types of matches, for instance. They also charge different prices to different customers. Season ticket holders are charged a lower price per match than those who buy tickets for a single game. Corporate customers who sponsor the club in return for 'free' tickets effectively pay higher prices for those tickets than individual fans.

Merchandise Clubs have exploited merchandise. In the 1990s, sales of merchandise were a major source of revenue for Premier League clubs. Their monopoly in this area is weaker than in tickets. Merchandise such as clothing is in competition with other forms of fashion accessory. At the end of the 1990s, clubs found their clothing sales falling as fans became less interested in buying yet another football strip and more interested in buying fashion clothes from the high street.

Advertising, sponsorship and broadcasting rights Clubs gain revenue from advertising, sponsorship and broadcasting rights. The last are another form of legal monopoly power. The Premier League has been able, over the past ten years, to increase considerably its revenues by negotiating deals with Sky television. Manchester United has launched its own television channel. Pay-per-view television has further potential to increase club revenues. If the most important football matches were only shown on a pay-per-view basis, fans could be charged on a one-off basis. In economic terms, football clubs are attempting to gain some of the consumer surplus (☞ unit 4) at present enjoyed by fans.

The most successful clubs, and Manchester United in particular, are international brands. In the 1999-2000 season, Manchester United decided not to play in the FA Cup but instead play in the World Club Championship to the disappointment of many UK fans. Exploiting worldwide revenues is likely to further increase the profits of the top clubs.

At the other end of the scale, second and third division clubs are likely to continue to struggle. Opportunities for non-ticket revenues are limited. Whilst a few fans may be loyal, many others in a local area will support one of the large premier division clubs.

All clubs, though, face one major problem: escalating players' wages. Football players have become increasingly able to appropriate the profit of football clubs by bargaining in a free market. The success of a football club ultimately depends on its players. The top European clubs have risen to the top by being able to afford to buy the best players. In theory, clubs are prepared to pay up to the amount of extra profit that a player will generate for the club. If there were a large supply of the best footballers, the clubs could drive wages down. In practice, there are relatively few good footballers. Supply is price inelastic, in that increasing wages will not lead to a large increase in supply. Hence, wages have been driven up. The more revenues the clubs can generate from new sources, like pay-per-view, the more they can afford to pay higher wages to attract the best players.

Television broadcasting

Television broadcasting in the UK is another example of a complex monopoly. Television in 2000 was delivered through three main vehicles.

Terrestrial television There were five terrestrial channels. Two were provided by the BBC and paid for through a tax on all television users, the licence fee. Three, ITV, Channel 4 and Channel 5, were provided by commercial television companies. Their main source of revenue was television advertising.

Cable television A number of commercial companies supplied cable television. Each company had been granted a monopoly on cable provision in a local area by the government to encourage them to make the very heavy financial investment involved in laying cable lines. Viewers had to pay a monthly fee to subscribe to cable television. Cable television also received revenue from advertising.

Satellite television OnDigital and Sky offered a satellite service. Like cable, they raised revenues from subscriptions and advertising.

The future of television broadcasting is dependent on the change to digital technology. The terrestrial channels at present are limited because there is not enough bandwidth with analogue technology to broadcast more than 5 channels. With digital technology, far more channels will be capable of being broadcast within the allocated bandwidth.

Terrestrial commercial television stations have tended to be highly profitable. This is because lack of competition has enabled them to charge high prices to their advertising customers. The growing numbers subscribing to cable and satellite companies had not led to a significant fall in their viewing numbers. Only a minority of households subscribed to satellite or cable and, even then, they continued to watch ITV and Channels 4 and 5. Television advertisers could therefore not afford to ignore them, particularly ITV.

Cable television companies have been less financially successful than Sky. They have failed to attract enough subscribers to become significantly profitable after their heavy investment in infrastructure. Lack of success has been compounded by a failure to earn sufficient advertising revenue. Advertisers, after all, are only prepared to place adverts or pay high prices for them if there are large audiences. Sky has been more successful. Its greatest success has been in attracting young male subscribers through its strategy of outbidding other television channels for exclusive television rights to the football premier league. Its children's channels have also particularly attracted subscribers.

Television companies attempt to become monopolists through the programmes they show. The clearest example of this is Sky's monopoly on live premier league football. This monopoly enables Sky both to attract and keep subscribers and raise television advertising rates. However, Sky has to pay a high price for this in terms of the contract payment it pays to the Premier League. Much of the monopoly profit therefore reverts to the owners of the successful programming. The same is true for other television programmes bought in from, say, the USA. The copyright owners of programmes such as Friends or ER are able to choose high prices for the right to transmit their shows.

Commercial television companies are arguing that television in the future will be better than in the past because digital, cable and satellite television will allow much greater choice to consumers. Instead of there being four channels as there were in the 1980s, consumers will be able to choose between hundreds if not thousands of channels.

There is an argument, though, for suggesting that greater choice will disadvantage UK viewers. Assume that the amount of money available from advertising and all other revenues is fixed. Then the amount of money that can be spent per channel on programming declines as the number of television channels increases. If the number of channels doubles, the amount available halves. The less money spent on programming, the poorer the quality of each programme. The USA is often cited as an example of this. In the USA, viewers have plenty of choice but most of what is produced is very poor quality, constrained by lack of funds. Hence, extra choice may lead to allocative inefficiency if consumers would prefer to have less choice but higher quality programming.

In practice, the amount of money available is not fixed. Television, for instance, can increase advertising revenues by competing more effectively with other advertising media such as newspapers or magazines. Cable and satellite companies can increase the number of subscribers, or increase subscription rates. The government could lower taxes and other payments made by television companies. However, revenues are unlikely to increase in proportion to the number of television channels. So extra channels are likely to be low budget, low quality channels. The danger is that money will be taken away from high cost, high quality channels to fund new channels. Quality will then suffer.

There is also pressure from commercial television for the BBC licence fee to be scrapped or at least reduced. The BBC provides considerable competition for all forms of commercial television. If the BBC had its funding reduced, it would be forced to offer lower quality programmes. Audiences would then shrink and commercial television would gain viewers. This would enable them to charge more to their advertisers or make their subscriptions more attractive to viewers. Again, this might not benefit viewers if viewers have to pay more for worse programming.

Even if programming improves, consumers could still be worse off. For instance, until the early 1990s, all viewers could watch Premier League on the BBC. Then Sky outbid the BBC for the rights to show live Premier League matches. The result was that only subscribers to Sky Sports could now watch this live football. Sky would argue that Sky Sports provides a better service than the BBC because it broadcasts more matches. On the other hand, the service is restricted. Those who do subscribe are funding the profits of Sky and a large increase in the rights paid to Premier League clubs. Is restricted access compensated by better programming?

Super league profits 'overstated'

Premier League football clubs will be told by a group of independent sports media consultants today that Media Partners, the Italian marketing company behind the proposed breakaway European super league, has overestimated the competition's likely revenues by almost 100 per cent.

A report from Oliver & Ohlbaum will reveal the super league is likely to generate just over £650 million a year in television and sponsorship revenue, and not the £1.2 billion promised by Media Partners.

The consultancy believes the Italian group is over-optimistic about how quickly pay-per-view TV will become established throughout Europe and about the revenues it would generate.

It also warns that the value of TV rights to domestic leagues in Europe will be hit badly if the super league grants a three-year exemption to elite clubs from having to qualify each season. The proposal that 18 clubs will not have to qualify for the super league every year has been one of the most controversial elements of the plan. Oliver & Ohlbaum believes that the new league would reduce the value of domestic league rights across Europe by 25 per cent, or £500 million over five years because automatic qualification for top clubs would lessen the appeal of domestic leagues, broadcasters would be more attracted to a long running super league, and domestic leagues would be reduced in size and length to accommodate it.

Source: adapted from the *Financial Times*, 18.9.1998.

1. Explain how the proposed 'super league' could (a) increase and (b) decrease the revenues of the clubs which take part.

2. To what extent might the super league increase the monopoly powers of the top European football clubs over the football market?

unit 24 National economic performance

Summary

1. Macroeconomics is concerned with the economy as a whole whilst microeconomics is the study of individual markets within the economy.

2. National economic performance can be measured in a number of different ways. Four key macroeconomic variables are the economic growth rate, unemployment, inflation and the current account balance.

Microeconomics and macroeconomics

Units 4-23 were concerned with MICROECONOMICS. This is the study of individual markets within an economy. For instance, microeconomics is concerned with individual markets for goods or the market for labour. Housing, transport, sport and leisure are all mainly microeconomic topics because they concern the study of individual markets.

In contrast, MACROECONOMICS is concerned with the study of the economy as a whole. For instance, macroeconomics considers the total quantity produced of goods and services in an economy. The price level of the whole economy is studied. Total levels of employment and unemployment are examined. Housing becomes a macroeconomic issue when, for instance, rises in house prices significantly affect the average level of all prices in the economy.

National economic performance

One of the reasons why macroeconomics is useful is because it tells us something about the performance of an economy. In particular, it allows economists to compare the economy today with the past. Is the economy doing better or worse than, say, ten years ago for instance? It also allows economists to compare different economies. Is the Japanese economy doing better than the US economy? How does the UK compare with the average in Europe?

An economy is a system which attempts to resolve the basic economy problem (☞ unit 2) of scarce resources in a world of infinite wants. An economic system is a mechanism for deciding what is to be produced, how production is to take place and who is to receive the benefit of that production. When judging the performance of an economy, one of the criteria is to consider how much is being produced. The more that is produced, the better is usually considered the economic performance. Another criterion is whether resources are being fully utilised. If there are high levels of unemployment, for instance, the economy cannot be producing at its potential level of output. Unemployment also brings poverty to those out of work and therefore affects the living standards of individuals. The rate at which prices rise is important too. High rates of price rises disrupt the workings of an economy. A national economy must also live within its means. So over a long period of time, the value of what it buys from other economies must roughly equal what it sells. In this, it is no different from a household which

cannot forever overspend and accumulate debts.

Economic growth

One of the key measures of national economic performance is the rate of change of output. This is known as economic growth (☞ unit 26). If an economy grows by 2.5 per cent per annum, output will double roughly every 30 years. If it grows by 7 per cent per annum, output will approximately double every 10 years. At growth rates of 10 per cent per annum, output will double every 7 years.

There is a standard definition of output based on a United Nations measure which is used by countries around the world to calculate their output. Using a standard definition allows output to be compared between countries and over time. This measure of output is called **gross domestic product** or **GDP** (☞ unit 25). So growth of 3 per cent in GDP in one year means that the output of the economy has increased by 3 per cent over a 12 month period.

Question 1

Table 24.1 *Economic growth rates*

	Average yearly changes, %			
	1961-73	1974-1979	1980-1989	1990-1999
United States	3.9	2.5	2.5	2.7
Japan	9.6	3.6	4.0	1.5
Germany	4.3	2.4	2.0	2.4
France	5.4	2.8	2.3	1.8
Italy	5.3	3.7	2.4	1.3
Mexico	6.6	6.1	2.0	3.0
United Kingdom	3.1	1.5	2.4	1.8

Source: adapted from OECD, *Historical Statistics, Economic Outlook*.

(a) Which country had the highest average yearly growth rate between (i) 1961 and 1973; (ii) 1974 and 1979; (iii) 1980 and 1989; (iv) 1990 and 1999?
(b) Which country enjoyed the best economic performance over the period 1961 to 1999?
(c) In 1961, the UK enjoyed one of the highest living standards in Europe. By 1999, as measured by GDP, it was one of the poorer countries. Explain how the data shows the UK's poor relative economic performance over the period.

Economic growth is generally considered to be desirable because individuals prefer to consume more rather than fewer goods and services. This is based on the assumption that wants are infinite. Higher economic growth is therefore better than lower economic growth. Periods when the economy fails to grow at all, or output shrinks as in a RECESSION or DEPRESSION, are periods when the economy is performing poorly. The depression years of the 1930s in Europe and the Americas, for instance, were years when poverty increased and unemployment brought misery to millions of households.

Unemployment

Unemployment is a major problem in society because it represents a waste of scare resources (☞ unit 29). Output could be higher if the unemployed were in work. It also leads to poverty for those who are out of work. So high unemployment is an indicator of poor national economic performance. Conversely, low unemployment is an indicator of good national economic performance.

Economic growth and unemployment tend to be linked. Fast growing economies tend to have low unemployment. This is because more workers are needed to produce more goods and services. Low levels of economic growth tend to be associated with rising levels of unemployment. Over time, technological change allows an economy to produce more with fewer workers. If there is little or no economic growth, workers are made unemployed through technological progress but fail to find new jobs in expanding industries. If growth is negative and the economy goes into recession, firms will lay off workers and unemployment will rise.

Fast economic growth, then, will tend to lead to net job creation. More jobs will be created than are lost through the changing structure of the economy. So another way of judging the performance of an economy is to consider its rate of job creation.

Inflation

Inflation is the rate of change of average prices in an economy (☞ unit 28). Low inflation is generally considered to be better than high inflation. This is because inflation has a number of adverse effects (see unit 28). For instance, rising prices mean that the value of what savings can buy falls. If a person had £50 in savings and the price of CDs went up from £10 to £25, then they would be worse off because their savings could only now buy 2 CDs compared to 5 before. Another problem with inflation is that it disrupts knowledge of prices in a market. If there is very high inflation, with prices changing by the month, consumers often don't know what is a reasonable price for an item when they come to buy it.

Today, inflation of a few per cent is considered as acceptable. When inflation starts to climb through the 5 per cent barrier, economists begin to worry that inflation is too high. Inflation was a major problem for many countries including the UK in the 1970s and 1980s. In the UK, inflation reached 24.1 per cent in 1975 for instance. However, these levels of inflation are nothing compared to the **hyperinflation** (☞ unit 28) experienced by countries such as Argentina and Brazil in the 1980s. Prices were increasing by up to 1 000 per cent per year.

The current balance

A household must pay its way in the world. If it spends more than it earns and takes on debt, then at some point in the future it must repay that debt. Failure to repay debt can lead to seizure of assets by bailiffs and the household being barred from future borrowing. The same is true of a national economy. A nation's spending on foreign goods and services is called **imports**. It earns money to pay for those imports by selling goods and services, known as **exports**, to foreigners. If imports are greater than exports then this must be financed, either through borrowing or running down savings held abroad. The economic performance of a country is sound if, over a period of time, its exports are either greater than or approximately equal to its imports. However, if its imports are significantly greater than exports, then it could face difficulties.

Where exports of goods and services are greater than imports, there is said to be a **current account surplus** (☞ unit 30). Where imports exceed exports, there is a **current account deficit**. Deficits become a problem when foreign banks and other lenders refuse to lend any more money. A 'credit crunch' like this occurred, for instance, to Mexico in 1982 and Thailand in 1998. Countries have to respond to restore confidence. This is likely to involve cutting domestic spending, which leads to less demand for imports. Cutting domestic spending, though, also leads to reduced economic growth and rising unemployment. So the current account position of a country is an important indicator of performance.

Question 2

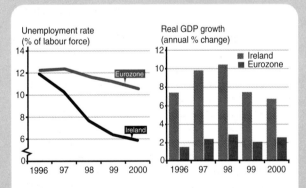

Figure 24.1 *Unemployment rate and Growth in GDP*
Source: adapted from OECD, Eurostat.

The eurozone is made up of the 11 European countries which agreed to join the European Monetary Union in 1999, leading to the creation of a single European currency.
(a) Compare the economic performance of Ireland with other countries in the eurozone.
(b) Suggest why Ireland's unemployment record in the 1990s was better than the average for the euro zone.

Question 3

In November 1997, a group of Islamic fundamentalists shot dead 58 foreign tourists visiting Luxor in Egypt. It had a devastating effect on Egyptian tourism, an industry which employs 1 in 7 Egyptian workers and is the country's biggest export revenue earner. Tourism revenues fell 19 per cent in the next 12 months from $3.64 billion in 1996-97 to $2.94 billion in 1997-98. This represented a loss to GDP, the total income of the country, of 1 per cent. By December 1998, tourist arrivals were still only 87.2 per cent of their December 1997 levels.

Source: adapted from the *Financial Times*, 11.5.1999.

(a) What effect did the Luxor massacre have on the performance of the Egyptian economy in the short term?
(b) To what extent could it have a long term impact on Egypt's economic performance?

key terms

Depression - a period when there is a particularly deep and long fall in output.
Macroeconomics - the study of the economy as a whole, including inflation, growth and unemployment.
Microeconomics - the study of the behaviour of individuals or groups with an economy, typically within a market context.
Recession - a period when growth in output falls or becomes negative. The technical definition now used by governments is that a recession occurs when growth in output is negative for two successive quarters (i.e. two periods of three months).

Applied economics

A tale of four economies

The USA, Germany, Japan and the UK are four of the largest economies in the world. They form part of the G7 group (the other three being France, Italy and Canada) which meet regularly to discuss common economic problems. For much of the post-war period, Japan and Germany were seen as highly successful. They had high economic growth, low inflation, low unemployment and a persistent current account surplus. The USA was less successful, mainly because its growth rate seemed low in comparison with Japan and much of continental Europe. As for the UK, it seemed to have a disappointing economic performance, with slow growth and persistent inflation and balance of payment problems.

The 1990s, though, have seen a reversal of fortunes as Figures 24.2 to 24.5 over the page show. Japan's growth rate at the start of the decade was not untypical of what it had achieved during the previous four decades. However, it became bogged down in a prolonged recession. In 1996, it looked as though it might emerge and begin to recover but in 1997 it began to slip back again. Inflation reflected depressed demand. In 1995, prices even fell, albeit by just 0.1 per cent. Unemployment remained low, but by the end of the decade was beginning to rise and there were fears that it would eventually climb to above 10 per cent in the next decade.

The 1990s was a difficult decade for Germany too. Part of its problems arose from the cost of reunification of East Germany with West Germany in 1990. East Germany had been a **command economy** (☞ unit 41) within the Soviet sphere of influence since 1945. By 1990, it had a relatively backward and highly inefficient economy where output per head was far below that of its highly successful western neighbour. Reunification resulted in a transfer of resources from West Germany to East Germany. Despite this, the East Germany economy remained a drag on the performance of the German economy as a whole. Growth was relatively slow after 1991. Unemployment rose to levels not seen in the previous four decades. The country began to experience persistent current account deficits on the balance of payments. The only positive economic indicator was inflation which, once the boom effects of the early years of reunification had worn off, remained low.

The 1990s saw a resurgence of confidence in the US economy. In the previous decades, the US's long term growth rate had been around $2^1/_2$ per cent per year. However, from 1992, economic growth tended to be above this. One of the consequences was that unemployment fell to very low levels for the USA and by the end of the decade was predicted to be below that of Japan. Strong growth was combined with subdued inflation. However, there was a persistent current account deficit.

The 1990s was also a good decade for the UK economy. After a deep recession in the early 1990s, the economy enjoyed above average growth rates for much of the rest of the decade. Unemployment and inflation fell and there were no serious current account problems.

Of the four economies, the USA arguably enjoyed the best economic performance during the 1990s and Japan the worst. Germany's economic performance was disappointing compared to previous decades whilst that of the UK was better. How these economies will

perform in the first decade of the new millennium is difficult to predict exactly, but the USA is unlikely to lose its status as the richest nation.

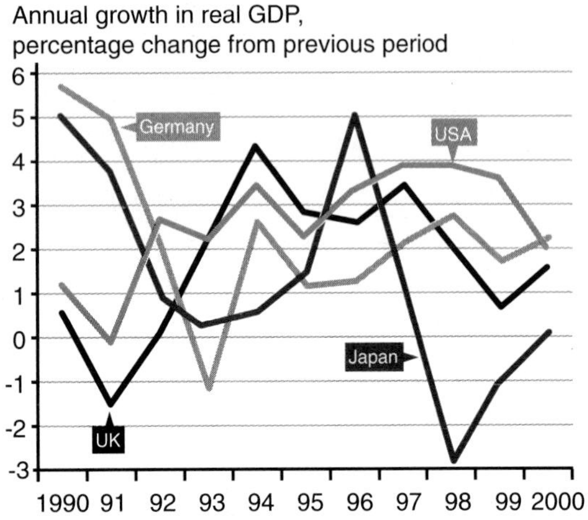

Annual growth in real GDP, percentage change from previous period

Figure 24.2 *Economic growth - USA, Germany, Japan and the UK*

Inflation, consumer prices, percentage change from previous period

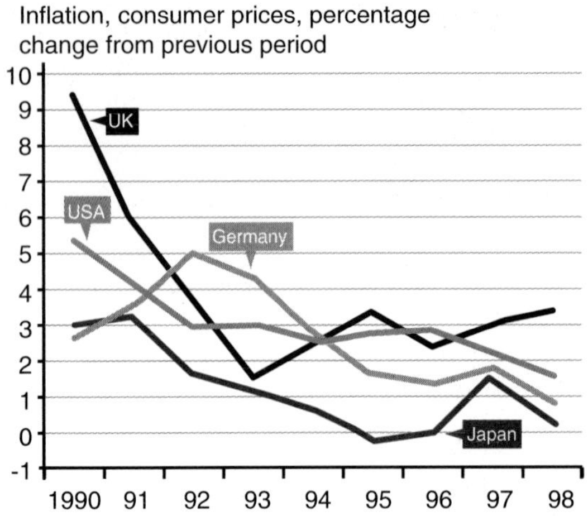

Figure 24.3 *Inflation - USA, Germany, Japan and the UK*

Standardised unemployment rate, percentage of civilian labour force

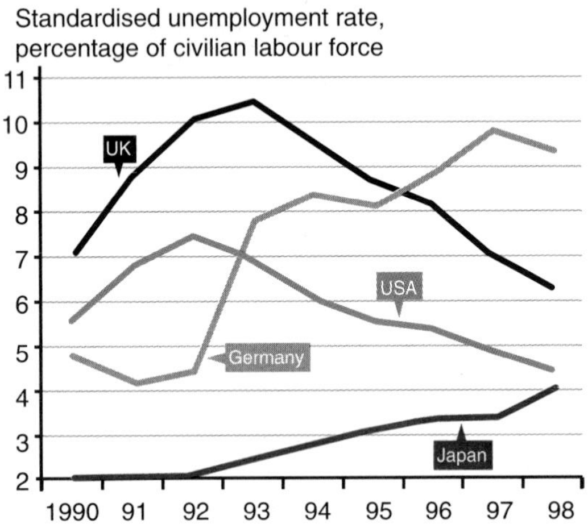

Figure 24.4 *Unemployment - USA, Germany, Japan and the UK*

Current account balances as a percentage of GDP

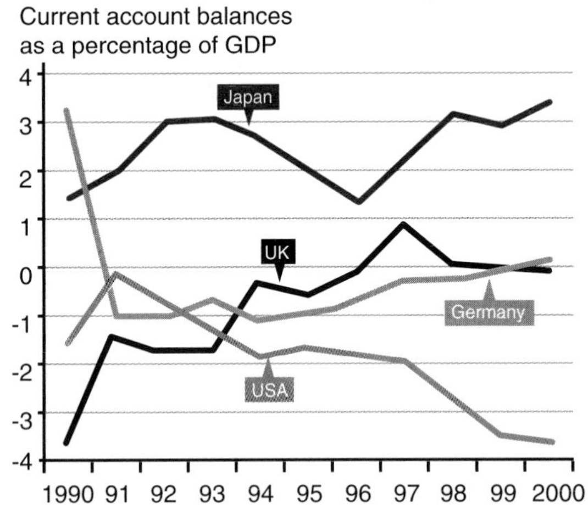

Figure 24.5 *The current balance as a percentage of GDP - USA, Germany, Japan and the UK*
Source: adapted from OECD, *Economic Outlook.*

DATA QUESTION

Spain and Italy

1. **Compare and contrast the economic performance of Spain with Italy.**
2. **What problems may these countries face in the future and how would they impact on their economic performance?**

Spain

Membership of the European Union (EU) has benefited Spain during the 1990s. High growth rates have allowed unemployment to fall, whilst living standards have risen. Even so, average income in Spain is still only 80 per cent of that of the rest of the EU and so the country has still some way to go. The goal set by the government is to increase this to 90 per cent over the next ten years. High economic growth could, though, lead to inflation problems and a return to the large current account deficits experienced at the beginning of the decade.

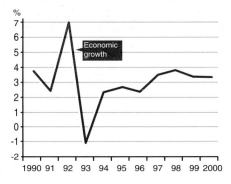

Figure 24.6 *Spain, economic growth, annual percentage change*

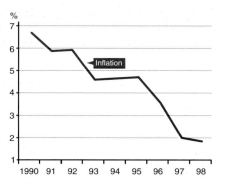

Figure 24.7 *Spain, inflation, annual percentage change*

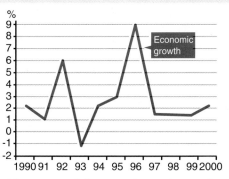

Figure 24.8 *Spain, unemployment, % of civilian labour force*

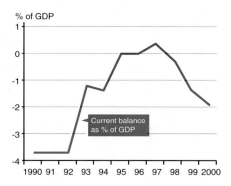

Figure 24.9 *Spain, current account as percentage of GDP*
Source: adapted from OECD, *Economic Outlook*.

Italy

Italy has had a difficult time adjusting its economy to conform to the requirements of monetary union. During the 1990s it has adopted policies to reduce its inflation rate and curb its government spending deficit. These policies have tended to have a deflationary impact. The country is still facing problems though, because of its still high projected levels of government spending. It has one of the most generous state pension schemes in Europe and, unless it cuts pensions, this will necessitate high levels of taxes over the next 40 years to pay for it. Cutting pensions, though, is highly unpopular and has already brought the Italian government in sharp conflict with trade unions.

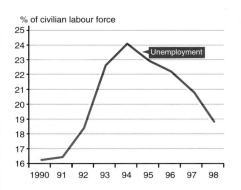

Figure 24.10 *Italy, economic growth, annual percentage change*

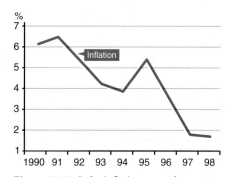

Figure 24.11 *Italy, inflation, annual percentage change*

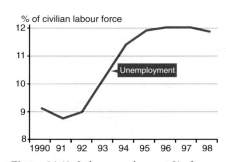

Figure 24.12 *Italy, unemployment % of civilian labour force*

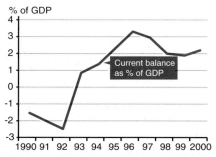

Figure 24.13 *Italy, current account as percentage of GDP*
Source: adapted from OECD, *Economic Outlook*.

Summary

1. National income can be measured in three ways: as national output, national expenditure or national income.
2. The most commonly used measure of national income is Gross Domestic Product (GDP). Other measures include Gross National Product (GNP) and Net National Product (NNP). All these measures can be at market prices or factor cost.
3. National income statistics are used by academics to formulate and test hypotheses. They are used by policy makers to formulate economic policy both on a micro-economic and macro-economic level. They are often used as a proxy measure for the standards of living and to compare living standards between countries and within a country over time.
4. National income statistics can be inaccurate because of statistical errors, the existence of the black economy, of non-traded sectors, and difficulties with valuing public sector output.
5. Problems occur when comparing national income over time because of inflation, the accuracy and presentation of statistics, changes in population, the quality of goods and services and changes in income distribution.
6. Further problems occur when comparing national income between countries. In particular, an exchange rate has to be constructed which accurately reflects different purchasing power parities.

Income, output and expenditure

Macroeconomics is concerned with the economy as a whole. A key macroeconomic variable is the level of total output in an economy, often called NATIONAL INCOME. There are three ways in which national income can be calculated. To understand why, consider a very simple model of the economy where there is no foreign trade (a CLOSED ECONOMY as opposed to an OPEN ECONOMY where there is foreign trade) and no government. In this economy, there are only households and firms which spend all their income and revenues.

• Households own the wealth of the nation. They own the land, labour and capital used to produce goods and services. They supply these factors to firms in return for rents, wages, interest and profits - the rewards to the factor of production. They then use this money to buy goods and services.
• Firms produce goods and services. They hire factors of production from households and use these to produce goods and services for sale back to households.

The flow from households to firms is shown in Figure 25.1. The flow of money around the economy is shown in red. Households receive payments for hiring their land, labour and capital. They spend all that money on the goods and services produced by firms (consumption). An alternative way of putting this is to express these money payments in **real** terms, taking into account changes in prices (unit 3 explains the distinction between real and monetary values). The real flow of products and factor services is shown in black. Households supply land, labour and capital in return for goods and services.

The CIRCULAR FLOW OF INCOME model can be used to show that there are three ways of measuring the level of economic activity.

National output (O) This is the value of the flow of goods and services from firms to households. It is the black line on the right of the diagram.

National expenditure (E) This is the value of spending by households on goods and services. It is the red line on the right of the diagram.

National income (Y) This is the value of income paid by firms to households in return for land, labour and capital. It is the red line on the left of the diagram.

So income, expenditure and output are three ways of measuring the same flow. To show that they must be identical and not just equal, we use the '=' sign.

$$O = E = Y$$

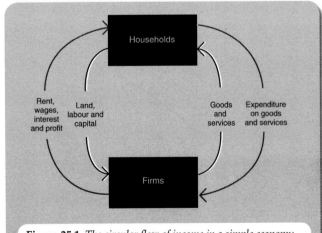

Figure 25.1 *The circular flow of income in a simple economy Households supply factors of production to firms in return for rent, wages, interest and profit. Households spend their money on goods and services supplied by firms.*

Question 1

Table 25.1

	£bn
Rent	5
Wages	75
Interest and profit	20

The figures in Table 25.1 represent the only income payments received by households. There are no savings, investment, government expenditure and taxes or foreign trade in the economy.

(a) Draw a circular flow of income diagram. Label it at the appropriate place with the value of: (i) income, (ii) output and (iii) expenditure.
(b) How would your answer be different if wages were £100 billion?

Measures of national income

Economies are not as simple as that shown in Figure 25.1. Calculating national income in practice involves a complex system of accounts. The standard used in most countries today is based on the System of National Accounts (SNA) first published in 1953 by the United Nations. This system of accounts has subsequently been developed and modified. The system currently in use in the UK is based on the European System of Accounts last modified in 1995 (ESA 1995).

The key measure of national income used in the UK is GROSS DOMESTIC PRODUCT (GDP). This is at market prices, which means it is a measure of national income that includes the value of **indirect taxes** (taxes on expenditure) like VAT. Indirect taxes are not part of the output of the economy, so this measure inflates the actual value of national income. GDP also includes the value of exports and imports and is therefore a more complex measure of national income than in the simple circular flow model described earlier. There are other measures of national income.

Gross value added (GVA) at basic cost This is GDP minus indirect taxes plus subsidies on goods. Indirect taxes minus subsidies is called the basic price adjustment.

Gross national income (GNP) at market prices GROSS NATIONAL INCOME (GNP) is GDP plus income earned abroad on investments and other assets owned overseas minus income paid to foreigners on their investments in the UK.

Net national income at market prices Each year, the existing capital stock or physical wealth of the country depreciates in value because of use. This is like depreciation on a car as it gets older. If individuals run down their savings to finance spending, their actual income must be their spending minus how much they have used from their savings. Similarly with a country, its true value of income is gross (i.e. before depreciation has been taken into account) national income minus depreciation). This is net national income.

Question 2

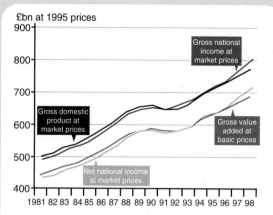

Figure 25.2 *Different measures of national income*
Source: adapted from *United Kingdom National Acccounts* (Blue Book), Office for National Statistics.

(a) Briefly explain the difference between each measure of national income shown on the graph.
(b) 'Changes in GDP at market prices broadly reflect changes in other measures of national income over time.' To what extent do the data support this?

GDP at market prices is the main headline figure used for national income because the data to calculate it is most quickly available. When comparing over time and between countries, movements in GDP at market prices are broadly similar to movements in other measures of national income. So it is a good guide to what is happening in the economy and can be used to judge the performance of the economy.

Transfer payments

Not all types of income are included in the final calculation of national income. Some incomes are received without there being any corresponding output in the economy. For instance:
- the government pays National Insurance and social security benefits to individuals, but the recipients produce nothing in return;
- students receive student grants from government, but again produce nothing which can be sold;
- children receive pocket money and allowances from their parents;
- an individual selling a second hand car receives money, but no new car is created.

These incomes, called TRANSFER PAYMENTS, are excluded from final calculations of national income. For instance, government spending in national income is **public expenditure** minus spending on benefits and grants.

Why is national income measured?

National income is a measure of the output, expenditure

and income of an economy. National income statistics provide not only figures for these totals but also a breakdown of the totals. They are used in a number of different ways.

- Academic economists use them to test hypotheses and build economic models of the economy. This increases our understanding of how an economy works.
- Government, firms and economists use the figures to forecast changes in the economy. These forecasts are then used to plan for the future. Government may attempt to direct the economy (☞ for instance unit 36 on fiscal policy), making changes in its spending or its taxes at budget time. Groups such as trade unions or the CBI will make their own recommendations about what policies they think the government should pursue.
- They are used to make comparisons over time and between countries. For instance, national income statistics can be used to compare the income of the UK in 1950 and 1995. Or they can be used to compare France's income with UK income. Of particular importance when making comparisons over time is the rate of change of national income (i.e. the rate of economic growth).
- They are used to make judgements about economic welfare. Growth in national income, for instance, is usually equated with a rise in living standards.

The accuracy of national income statistics

National income statistics are inaccurate for a number of reasons.

Statistical inaccuracies National income statistics are

calculated from millions of different returns to the government. Inevitably mistakes are made - returns are inaccurate or simply not completed. The statistics are constantly being revised in the light of fresh evidence. Although revisions tend to become smaller over time, national income statistics are still being revised ten years after first publication.

The hidden economy Taxes such as VAT, income tax and National Insurance contributions, and government regulations such as health and safety laws, impose a burden on workers and businesses. Some are tempted to evade taxes and they are then said to work in the BLACK, HIDDEN or INFORMAL ECONOMY. In the building industry, for instance, it is common for workers to be self-employed and to under-declare or not declare their income at all to the tax authorities. Transactions in the black economy are in the form of cash. Cheques, credit cards, etc. could all be traced by the tax authorities. Tax evasion is the dominant motive for working in the hidden economy but a few also claim welfare benefits to which they are not entitled. The size of the hidden economy is difficult to estimate, but in the UK estimates have varied from 7 to 15 per cent of GDP (i.e. national income statistics underestimate the true size of national income by at least 7 per cent).

Home produced services In the poorest developing countries in the world, GNP per person is valued at less

Question 3

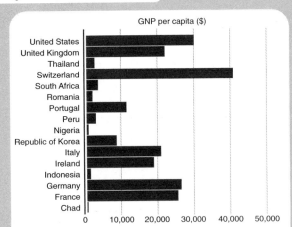

GNP per capita ($)

Figure 25.3 *Where they rank in the world (GNP per capita)*
Source: adapted from the World Bank, *World Development Report*.

(a) What statistics do governments need to collect in order to be able to calculate GNP per capita?
(b) How might (i) an economist and (ii) a government use these statistics?

Question 4

The size of the hidden economy varies enormously from country to country in Europe according to a report commissioned by the EU. It varies from 40 per cent in Greece, to 30 per cent in Italy and Belgium, 16 per cent in France, 14 per cent in Germany and 8-10 per cent in the UK. Countries like Greece and Italy are notorious for tax evasion by workers, whilst in the UK citizens are relatively law abiding, paying their taxes when needed.

In the UK, tax evasion is concentrated amongst the self-employed and in occupations such as painting, decorating, cleaning and gardening. Employees who have their tax collected through the PAYE system (Pay as you earn, a system where tax is deducted from a worker's pay packet by the employer) have less opportunity to fiddle their taxes. In 1999, there were about 3.2 million self employed workers and 24 million employees. Many of the self employed are able to conceal earnings whilst at the same time exaggerating their expenses, which they can offset against tax.

Source: adapted from *The Guardian*, 24.6.1999 and *Monthly Digest of Statistics*, Office for National Statistics.

(a) Farmers thoughout the EU tend to be self employed. How might this help account for the relatively high level of the hidden economy in a country like Greece and its relatively low level in a country like the UK?
(b) The UK government is currently aiming to create a more flexible workforce, with more part time, casual and self-employed workers as a proportion of the total workforce. What are the implications of this for the size of the hidden economy?

than £100 per year. It would be impossible to survive on this amount if this were the true value of output in the economy. However, a large part of the production of the agricultural sector is not traded and therefore does not appear in national income statistics. People are engaged in subsistence agriculture, consuming what they themselves produce. Hence the value of national output is in reality much higher. In the UK, the output of the services of housewives and househusbands is equally not recorded. Nor is the large number of DIY jobs completed each year. The more DIY activity, the greater will be the under-recording of national output by national income statistics.

The public sector Valuing the output of much of the public sector is difficult because it is not bought and sold. This problem is circumvented by valuing non-marketed output at its cost of production. For instance, the value of the output of a state school is the cost of running the school. This method of valuation can yield some surprising results. Assume that through more efficient staffing, the number of nurses on a hospital ward is reduced from 10 to 8 and the service is improved. National income accounts will still show a fall in output (measured by a drop in the two nurses' incomes). In general, increased productivity in the public sector is shown by a fall in the value of output. It looks as though less is being produced when in fact output remains unchanged.

Comparing national income over time

Comparing the national income of the UK today with national income in the past presents problems.

Prices Prices have tended to increase over time. So an increase in national income over the period does not necessarily indicate that there has been an increase in the number of goods and services produced in the economy. Only if the rate of increase of national income measured in money terms (the nominal rate of economic growth) has been greater than the increase in prices (the inflation rate) can there be said to have been an increase in output. So when comparing over time, it is essential to consider **real** and not **nominal** changes in income (☞ unit 3).

The accuracy and presentation of statistics National income statistics are inaccurate and therefore it is impossible to give a precise figure for the change in income over time. Moreover, the change in real income over time will also be affected by the inflation rate. The inevitable errors made in the calculation of the inflation rate compound the problems of inaccuracy. The method of calculating national income and the rate of inflation can also change over time. It is important to attempt to eliminate the effect of changes in definitions.

Changes in population National income statistics are often used to compare living standards over time. If they are to be used in this way, it is essential to compare national income per capita (i.e. per person). For instance, if the population doubles whilst national income quadruples, people are likely to be nearer twice as well off than four times.

Quality of goods and services The quality of goods may improve over time due to advances in technology but they may also fall in price. For instance, cars today are far better than cars 80 years ago and yet are far cheaper. National income would show this fall in price by a fall in national income, wrongly implying that living standards had fallen. On the other hand, pay in the public sector tends to increase at about 2 per cent per annum faster than the increase in inflation. This is because pay across the economy tends to increase in line with the rate of economic growth rather than the rate of inflation. Increased pay would be reflected in both higher nominal and real national income but there may well be no extra goods or services being produced.

Defence and related expenditures The GDP of the UK was higher during the Second World War than in the 1930s, but much of GDP between 1940 and 1945 was devoted to defence expenditure. It would be difficult to argue that people enjoyed a higher standard of living during the war years than in the pre-war years. So the proportion of national income devoted to defence, or for instance to the police, must be taken into account when considering the standard of living of the population.

Consumption and investment It is possible to increase standards of living today by reducing investment and increasing consumption. However, reducing investment is likely to reduce standards of living from what they might otherwise have been in the future. As with defence, the proportion of national income being devoted to investment will affect the standard of living of the population both now and in the future.

Externalities National income statistics take no account of **externalities** (☞ unit 19) produced by the economy. National income statistics may show that national income

Question 5

Table 25.2

	Nominal GDP £bn	Index of Retail Prices (1985 = 100)	Population (millions)
1948	11.8	8.4	48.7
1958	22.6	13.0	51.7
1968	43.2	17.5	55.2
1978	167.1	52.8	56.2
1988	466.5	113.0	57.1
1998	837.6	172.2	59.2

Source: adapted from *Economic Trends Annual Supplement, Monthly Digest of Statistics, Annual Abstract of Statistics,* Office for National Statistics.

(a) For each year, calculate the value of: (i) nominal GDP per head of the population; (ii) real GDP per head of the population at 1998 prices.
(b) To what extent is it possible to judge from the data whether living standards increased over the period 1948-1998?

has doubled roughly every 25 years since 1945. But if the value of externalities has more than doubled over that time period, then the rate of growth of the standard of living has less than doubled.

Income distribution When comparing national income over time, it is important to remember that an increased national income for the economy as a whole may not mean that individuals have seen their income increase. Income distribution is likely to change over time, which may or may not lead to a more desirable state of affairs.

Comparing national income between countries

Comparing national income between economies is fraught with difficulties too. Income distributions may be different. Populations will be different and therefore it is important to compare per capita income figures. National income accounts will have varying degrees of inaccuracy, caused, for instance, by different sizes of the informal economy in each country. National income accounting conventions will differ.

There is also the problem of what rate of exchange to use when comparing one country's national income with another. The day to day market exchange rate can bear little relation to relative prices in different countries. So prices in some countries, like Switzerland or West Germany, can be much higher at official exchange rates than in France or Italy. Therefore if national income statistics are to be used to compare living standards between countries it is important to use an exchange rate which compares the cost of living in each country. These exchange rates are known as PURCHASING POWER PARITIES. For instance, if a typical basket of goods costs 10 francs in France and £1 in the UK, then national income should be converted at an exchange rate of 10 francs to the £1 - even if the market exchange rate gives a very different figure.

Even this is not accurate enough. In some countries, consumers have to purchase goods which in others are free. For instance, Sweden spends a greater proportion of its national income than Italy on fuel for heating because of its colder climate. But this extra expenditure does not give the Swedes a higher standard of living. Again, countries are different geographically and one country might have higher transport costs per unit of output than another because of congestion or having to transport goods long distances. In practice, it is almost impossible to adjust national income figures for these sorts of differences.

Question 6

Table 25.3 *Output and living standards, 1998*

Country	Currency units per £		GNP	Population
	Market exchange rates	Purchasing power parities		
USA	1.6574	1.5981	$7921.3bn	270m
Japan	216.75	291.89	534865bn yen	126m
Switzerland	2.4	3.5	412.4 bn Swiss francs	7m
France	9.7681	10.5257	FF8 641 billion	59m
Italy	2876	2876	L 2 023 646 bn	58m
Germany	2.914	3.491	DM 3 732 bn	82m
Spain	247.37	209.59	82 641 bn pesetas	39m
UK	1	1.00	£762.5 bn	59m

Source: adapted from World Bank, *World Development Report*.

(a) Rank in order the countries in the table according to (i) GNP and (ii) GNP per head. Do this by converting GNP and GNP per head into pounds sterling using the purchasing power parity exchange rate.

(b) Would your rank order have been different if you had converted GNP at market exchange rates rather than purchasing power parity exchange rates? If so, explain why.

key terms

Circular flow of income - a model of the economy which shows the flow of goods, services and factors and their payments around the economy.

Closed economy - an economy where there is no foreign trade.

Gross domestic product (GDP) and gross national product (GNP) - measures of national income which exclude and include respectively net income from investments abroad, but do not include an allowance for depreciation of the nation's capital stock.

Hidden, black or informal economy - economic activity where trade and exchange take place, but which goes unreported to the tax authorities and those collecting national income statistics. Workers in the hidden economy are usually motivated by the desire to evade paying taxes.

National income - the value of the output, expenditure or income of an economy over a period of time.

Open economy - an economy where there is trade with other countries.

Purchasing power parities - an exchange rate of one currency for another which compares how much a typical basket of goods in one country costs compared to that of another country.

Transfer payments - income for which there is no corresponding output, such as unemployment benefits or pension payments.

Applied economics

France and the United Kingdom

France has a higher GNP than the UK. In 1998, French GNP was FF 8 641.2 bn compared to £762.5 bn for the UK. At an exchange rate of FF 9.7681 to the £, this meant that the French economy produced 16 per cent more than the UK economy.

Crude national income statistics like these don't say very much when making inter-country comparisons. For a start, populations may be vastly different. In this case, France and the UK have almost identical populations of approximately 59 million, with the UK having a slightly larger population than that of France. So GNP per capita gives little extra information compared to total GNP when making comparisons. Purchasing power parities (PPPs) do, however, differ substantially from market exchange rates. In the 1990s, market exchange ratese overvalued the franc in comparison with PPPs. French GNP, when converted into pounds using PPPs in 1998, was £791.6 bn. This was 8 per cent higher than the UK GNP measured at PPP rates of £735.2 bn. The conclusion must be that France had a higher GNP and GNP per head than that of the UK.

In making comparisons about living standards, national income is only one among many factors to be taken into account. One such is the distribution of income. Table 25.3 shows that income in the UK in the late 1980s was less evenly distributed than that in France. Not only does France have a higher national income, but there is less inequality in income in the country compared to the UK.

Another group of factors which are important relate to how national income is distributed between different types of expenditure. In 1998, 19 per cent of GDP in France was accounted for by general government consumption on items such as education and environmental services, compared to 21 per cent in the UK. Government spending on defence was broadly similar in both countries at 3 per cent of GNP in 1995. Spending on health was higher in France, with approximately 9 per cent of GDP being spent on public and private health care compared to 6 per cent in the UK. British households were able to spend a larger proportion of GDP than the French. Private consumption accounted for 64 per cent of GNP in the UK in 1998 compared to 61 per cent in France. This higher spending from GNP will, to some extent, have helped narrow the gap for consumers between French and UK GNP.

Quality of life is difficult to measure. The French are less urbanised than their UK counterparts. In 1998, 75 per cent of French people lived in towns and cities compared to 89 per cent in the UK. Important too is the fact that France is over twice the size of the UK and hence population density is much lower in France. Certainly, French roads are on average far less congested than in the UK and lower population densities and a more dispersed industry and population mean that air pollution is less in France than in the UK.

Many other factors need to be taken into account before concluding that the French have a higher standard of living than the British. However, on the indicators chosen above, it would seem that the British are lagging behind their French counterparts.

Table 25.4 *Income distribution*
Percentage share of income

	Lowest 20%	Next 20%	Middle 20%	Next 20%	Highest 20%
France	10.0	14.2	17.6	22.3	35.8
UK	7.1	12.8	17.2	23.1	39.8

Source: World Bank, *World Development Report*.

Living standards

Table 25.5 *National income indicators, 1998*

	GNP ($ million)	GNP per capita ($)	PPP estimates of GNP per capita ($)
Burundi	0.9	140	620
Bangladesh	44	350	1 100
Indonesia	138.5	680	2 790
Brazil	758	4 570	6 160
Russian Federation	337.9	2 300	3 950
Algeria	46.5	1 550	4 380
Greece	122.9	11 650	13 010
Australia	380.6	20 300	20 130
UK	1 263.8	21 400	20 640
USA	7 921.3	29 340	29 340

Table 25.6 *Income distribution*

	Lowest 20%	Next 20%	Middle 20%	Next 20%	Highest 20%
Burundi	na	na	na	na	na
Bangladesh (1992)	9.4	13.5	17.2	22.0	37.9
Indonesia (1996)	8.0	11.3	15.1	20.8	44.9
Brazil (1995)	2.5	5.7	9.9	17.7	64.2
Russian Federation (1996)	4.2	8.8	13.6	20.7	52.8
Algeria (1995)	7.0	11.6	16.1	22.7	42.6
Greece	na	na	na	na	na
Australia (1989)	7.0	12.2	16.6	23.3	40.9
UK (1986)	7.1	12.8	17.2	23.1	39.8
USA (1994)	4.8	10.5	16.0	23.5	45.2

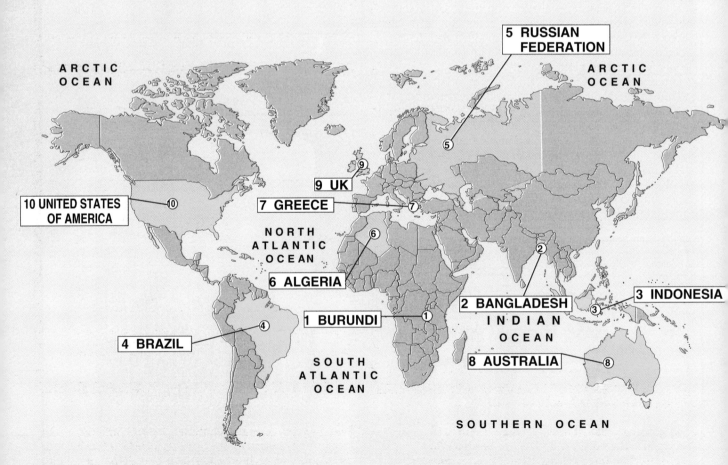

Table 25.7 *Population and infrastructure*

	Population growth, average annual growth rate % 1990-98	Urban population, % of total 1998	Telephone mainlines per 1000 people 1997	Personal computers per 1000 people 1997	Paved roads, % of total 1997
Burundi	2.7	8	3	less than 1	7
Bangladesh	1.9	20	3	less than 1	12
Indonesia	1.9	38	25	8	46
Brazil	1.6	80	107	26	9
Russian Federation	-0.1	77	183	32	na
Algeria	2.6	58	48	4	69
Greece	0.5	60	516	45	92
Australia	1.3	85	505	362	39
UK	0.4	89	540	242	100
USA	1.1	74	644	407	61

Table 25.8 *Health indicators*

	Life expectancy at birth, males, 1997	Prevalence of malnutrition (under 5s) per thousand	Under 5 mortality rate per thousand 1997	% of population with access to safe water, 1995	% of population with access to sanitation, 1995	Contraceptive prevalence rate, % of women aged 15-49, 1990-98
Burundi	41	38	200	58	48	na
Bangladesh	58	56	104	84	35	49
Indonesia	63	34	60	64	55	57
Brazil	63	6	44	69	67	77
Russian Federation	61	3	25	na	na	34
Algeria	69	35	209	na	na	51
Greece	75	na	9	na	na	na
Australia	76	0	13	99	99	na
UK	75	0	7	100	100	na
USA	73	1	15	98	98	76

Table 25.9 *Energy and the environment*

	Energy use per capita (Kg of oil equivalent), 1996	Carbon dioxide emisissions per capita, metric tonnes 1996	Average annual deforestation, %, 1990-95	Nationally protected areas as % of total land area 1996
Burundi	na	0	0.4	5.5
Bangladesh	197	0.2	0.8	0.8
Indonesia	672	1.2	1	10.6
Brazil	1 012	1.7	0.5	4.2
Russian Federation	4 169	10.7	0	3.1
Algeria	842	3.3	1.2	2.5
Greece	2 328	7.7	-2.3	2.4
Australia	5 494	16.7	0	7.3
UK	3 992	9.5	-0.5	20.9
USA	8 051	20	-0.3	13.4

Table 25.10 *Distribution of GDP by sector (%), 1998*

	Agriculture	Industry	Services
Burundi	49	19	32
Bangladesh	23	28	49
Indonesia	16	43	41
Brazil	8	36	56
Russian Federation	9	42	49
Algeria	12	47	41
Greece	-	-	-
Australia	3	26	71
UK	2	31	67
USA	2	27	71

Table 25.11 *Education*

	Adult illiteracy % of people 15 and above 1997		Net enrolment ratio, % of relevant age group, 1996		Public expenditure on education % of GNP 1996
	Male	Females	Primary	Secondary	
Burundi	46	64	na	na	3.1
Bangladesh	50	73	na	na	2.9
Indonesia	9	20	97	42	1.4
Brazil	16	16	90	20	5.5
Russian Federation	0	1	93	na	4.1
Algeria	27	52	94	56	5.1
Greece	2	5	90	87	3
Australia	na	na	95	92	5.6
UK	na	na	100	92	5.6
USA	na	na	95	90	6.7

Table 25.12 *Structure of demand, percentage of GDP[1], 1998*

	Private consumption	Government consumption	Gross domestic investment
Burundi	90	11	8
Bangladesh	80	4	21
Indonesia	63	7	31
Brazil	67	14	21
Russian Federation	67	10	20
Algeria	56	11	27
Greece	75	14	19
Australia	63	17	20
UK	64	21	16
USA	68	16	18

1. Figures do not necessarily add up to 100. This is because the balance shows net resource flows from foreign countries. For instance, Bangladesh spent 105 per cent of GDP on consumption and investment and financed this through a net 5 per cent inflow of funds from abroad.

Source: adapted from World Bank, *World Development Report.*

1. You have been asked to write an article for a magazine. The editor wants you to compare the standard of living of 11 countries using national income statistics. In your article:
(a) make such a comparison;

(b) then discuss the limitations of using national statistics to compare living standards between countries, giving examples of how different economic indicators might provide an additional or perhaps even better basis for making a comparison.

Summary

1. Economic growth is the change in potential output of the economy shown by a shift to the right of the production possibility frontier. Economic growth is usually measured by the change in real national income.
2. Economic growth is caused by increases in the quantity or quality of land, labour and capital and by technological progress.
3. It is sometimes argued that growth is unsustainable because of the law of diminishing returns. Because land in particular is fixed in supply, diminishing returns will set in. However, most natural resources are not in fixed supply and historical evidence suggests that all factors are variable over time.

Economic growth

Economies change over time. Part of this change involves changes in productive capacity - the ability to produce goods and services. Increases in productive capacity are known as ECONOMIC GROWTH. Most economies today experience positive economic growth over time. However, economic disruption caused by war as in parts of Africa, or severe economic dislocation because of changing economic systems as in Russia, can lead to negative economic growth.

It is not possible to measure the productive capacity of an economy directly because there is no way of producing a single monetary figure for the value of variables such as machinery, workers and technology. Instead, economists use changes in GDP, the value of output, as a proxy measure.

The output gap

Using GDP has its problems, particularly in the short term. This is because the economy can operate below or indeed above its productive potential over a period of time. For instance, if the economy falls into a **recession** (☞ unit 24), unemployment rises and therefore it fails to produce at its potential level of output. In a boom, the economy may operate beyond its productive potential. For instance, workers may be prepared for a short time to work excessively long hours. In the long term, they would refuse to work these hours and so the economy is operating beyond its potential output. The same could be true of an individual firm. Workers may be prepared to work large amounts of overtime to get out an important and urgent order, but they wouldn't want to work those hours every week.

Figure 26.1 shows this OUTPUT GAP. The straight line is the trend rate of growth in GDP over a long period of time. It is assumed that this shows the level of GDP

Figure 26.1 *The output gap   The trend rate of growth of GDP approximates the growth in productive potential of the economy. When actual GDP falls below this or rises above it, there is said to be an output gap.*

associated with the productive potential of the economy. The actual level of GDP may vary from this. When the economy is in recession and there is high unemployment, the actual level of GDP can be below the trend line and a negative output gap is said to exist. Sometimes, the actual level of GDP is above the trend line and a positive output gap exists. These fluctuations in the actual level of GDP around the trend rate of growth are known as the BUSINESS CYCLE or TRADE CYCLE.

The production possibility frontier

Production possibility frontiers (PPFs) can be used to discuss economic growth. The PPF shows the maximum or **potential** output of an economy (☞ unit 1). When the economy grows, the PPF will move outward as in Figure 26.2. A movement from A to C would be classified as economic growth. However, there may be unemployment in the economy. With a PPF passing through C, a movement from B (where there is unemployment) to C (full employment) would be classified as ECONOMIC RECOVERY rather than economic growth. Hence, an increase in national income does not necessarily mean that there has been economic growth. In practice it is difficult to know exactly the location of an economy's PPF and therefore economists tend to treat all increases in GNP as economic growth.

Figure 26.2 can also be used to show the conflict between investment and consumption. One major source of economic growth is investment. All other things being equal, the greater the level of investment the higher will be the rate of growth in the future. However, increased production of investment goods can only be achieved by a reduction in the production of consumption goods if the economy is at full employment. So there is a trade off to be made between consumption now and consumption in the future. The lower the level of consumption today relative to the level of investment, the higher will be the level of consumption in the future.

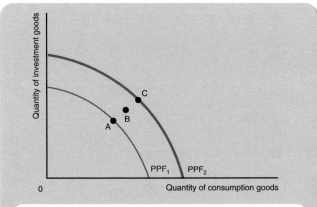

Figure 26.2 *Production possibility frontiers*
A movement from A to C would represent economic growth if there were a shift in the production possibility frontier from PPF₁ to PPF₂. A movement from B to C would represent economic recovery if the production possibility frontier was PPF₂.

The causes of economic growth

National output can be increased if there is an increase in the quantity or quality of the inputs to the production process. Output can also be increased if existing inputs are used more efficiently. This can be expressed in terms of a **production function**:

Output = f (land, labour, capital, technical progress, efficiency)

The remainder of this unit will concentrate on the ways in which the quantity and quality of the factors of production can be increased and on what determines technical progress.

Land

Different countries possess different endowments of land. Land in economics is defined as all natural resources, not

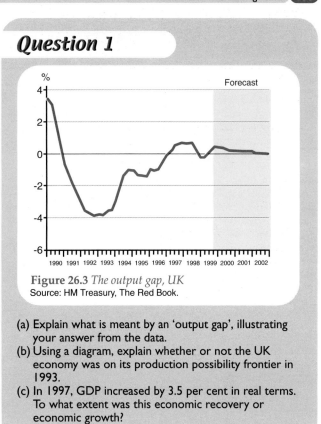

Question 1

Figure 26.3 *The output gap, UK*
Source: HM Treasury, The Red Book.

(a) Explain what is meant by an 'output gap', illustrating your answer from the data.
(b) Using a diagram, explain whether or not the UK economy was on its production possibility frontier in 1993.
(c) In 1997, GDP increased by 3.5 per cent in real terms. To what extent was this economic recovery or economic growth?

just land itself. Some countries, such as Saudi Arabia, have experienced large growth rates almost solely because they are so richly endowed. Without oil, Saudi Arabia today would almost certainly be a poor Third World country. Other countries have received windfalls. The UK, for instance, only started to exploit its oil resources in the mid 1970s. Today oil contributes about 3 per cent of GNP. However, most economists argue that the exploitation of raw materials is unlikely to be a significant source of growth in developed economies, although it can be vital in developing economies.

Labour

Increasing the number of workers in an economy should lead to economic growth. Increases in the labour force can result from three factors.

● Changes in demography. If more young people enter the workforce than leave it, then the size of the workforce will increase. In most western developed countries the population is relatively stable. Indeed, many countries will experience falls in the number of young people entering the workforce over the next ten or twenty years because of falls in the birth rate during the late 1960s and the 1970s.

● Increases in participation rates. Nearly all men who wish to work are in the labour force. However, in most Western countries there exists a considerable pool of women who could be brought into the labour force if employment opportunities were present. In the UK, for instance, almost all of the increase in the labour force in the foreseeable future will result from women returning

Question 2

Ireland is a victim of its own success. Record inward foreign investment flows and booming domestic demand in the 1990s have created high economic growth, currently around 8 per cent per annum. They have also created more jobs in the last three years than in the previous three decades. However, Ireland is already facing a labour shortage. Colin Hunt, chief economist at Goodbody's, the stockbroker, says: 'If there is a threat to the Irish growth story it is that we will run out of workers.' Eunan King, chief economist with NCB stockbrokers, estimates that to sustain a more modest economic growth rate of 5 to 6 per cent, Ireland will have to attract net inward migration of 15 000 people a year.

Source: adapted from the *Financial Times*, 10.2.2000.

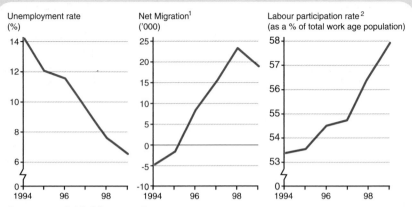

Figure 26.4 *Irish labour market*
Source: adapted from ABN Amro (Ireland).
1. Number of immigrants minus emigrants.
2. Number of workers in work and unemployed as a percentage of the total population of working age.

(a) Explain why Ireland's growth rate may fall if it 'runs out of workers'.
(b) How can (i) falling unemployment, (ii) increased participation in the labour force and (iii) increased net migration help sustain Ireland's growth rate?
(c) Explain why falling unemployment and increased participation in the labour force are only short term solutions to Ireland's problems.
(d) Discuss other ways in which Ireland could resolve its labour shortage problem.

to or starting work.

- Immigration. A relatively easy way of increasing the labour force is to employ migrant labour. Increasing the size of the labour force may increase output but will not necessarily increase economic welfare. One reason is that increased income may have to be shared out amongst more people, causing little or no change in income per person. If women come back to work, they have to give up leisure time to do so. This lessens the increase in economic welfare which they experience. Increasing the quality of labour input is likely to be far more important in the long run. Labour is not **homogeneous** (i.e. it is not all the same). Workers can be made more productive by education and training. Increases in **human capital** (☞ unit 2) are essential for a number of reasons.
- Workers need to be sufficiently educated to cope with the demands of the existing stock of capital. For instance, it is important for lorry drivers to be able to read, typists to spell and shop assistants to operate tills. These might seem very low grade skills but it requires a considerable educational input to get most of the population up to these elementary levels.
- Workers need to be flexible. On average in the UK, workers are likely to have to change job three times during their lifetime. Increasingly workers are being asked to change roles within existing jobs. Flexibility requires broad general education as well as in-depth knowledge of a particular task.
- Workers need to be able to contribute to change. It is easy to see that scientists and technologists are essential if inventions and new products are to be brought to the market. What is less obvious, but as important, is that every worker can contribute ideas to the improvement of techniques of production. An ability of all workers to

take responsibility and solve problems will be increasingly important in the future.

Capital

The stock of capital in the economy needs to increase over time if economic growth is to be sustained. This means that there must be sustained investment in the economy.

However, there is not necessarily a correlation between high investment and high growth. Some investment is not growth-related. For instance, investment in new housing or new hospitals is unlikely to create much wealth in the future. Investment can also be wasted if it takes place in industries which fail to sell products. For instance, investment in shipbuilding plants during the late 1970s and early 1980s provided a poor rate of return because the shipbuilding industry was in decline. Investment must therefore be targeted at growth industries.

Technological progress

Technological progress increases economic growth in two ways.
- It cuts the average cost of production of a product. For instance, a machine which performed the tasks of a simple scientific calculator was unavailable 100 years ago. 50 years ago, it needed a large room full of expensive equipment to do this. Today calculators are portable and available for a few pounds.
- It creates new products for the market. Without new products, consumers would be less likely to spend increases in their income. Without extra spending, there would be less or no economic growth.

Question 3

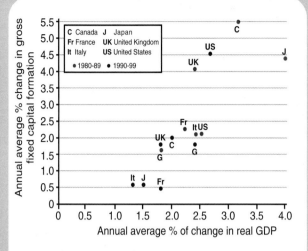

Figure 26.5 *Investment and economic growth in the G7 Group of countries*
Source: adapted from *Historical Statistics*, OECD.

(a) What relationship would economic theory suggest exists between investment and economic growth?
(b) To what extent is this relationship shown by the data?

Applied economics

Britain's growth rate

Worries about Britain's growth rate date back over a century. In Edwardian times, for instance, it was not difficult to see the economic advance of Germany and France and compare it with the poor economic performance of the UK economy. Britain's poor growth performance persisted in the 1950s, 1960s and 1970s. As Table 26.1 shows, the UK had the lowest average annual rate of growth between 1960 and 1979 of the seven largest industrial economies of the world (the **Group of Seven** or G7).

In the 1980s and 1990s, however, the UK ceased to be at the bottom of the growth league, although its average growth rate still lagged behind the average for G7 countries. Moreover, its growth rate would have been higher over the period but for two major recessions, in 1980-82 and 1990-92. It could be argued that government policy mistakes were responsible for making these recessions both longer and deeper than was necessary.

By 2000, many economists were taking the view that the UK's future growth prospects were good in

Table 26.1 *Average annual growth in GDP, G7 countries, 1960-1999*

	1960-67	1968-73	1974-79	1980-89	1990-99
United States	4.5	3.2	2.4	2.5	2.7
Japan	10.2	8.7	3.6	4.0	1.5
Germany	4.1	4.9	2.3	1.8	2.4
France	5.4	5.5	2.8	2.2	1.8
United Kingdom	3.0	3.4	1.5	2.4	1.8
Italy	5.7	4.5	3.7	2.4	1.3
Canada	5.5	5.4	4.2	3.1	2.0
Average G7	5.0	4.4	2.7	2.8	1.9

Source: adapted from OECD, *Historical Statistics, Economic Outlook*.

comparison with its major EU partners and with Japan. All economists agree that the causes of growth arecomplex and that there is no single easy answer to raising a country's trend rate of growth. What might have caused the UK to experience different growth rates from those of its major competitors?

Labour

Catching up Why can China grow by 10 per cent per annum whilst the UK barely manages a quarter of that? One suggestion is that the high economic growth rate represents the gains from transferring workers from low productivity agriculture to higher productivity manufacturing and service industries. If a worker can produce £500 per year in output as an agricultural worker but £1 000 working in a factory, then the act of transferring that worker from agriculture to industry will raise the growth rate of the economy. This theory was popular in explaining why the UK performed badly relative to the rest of the EU in the 1950s and 1960s. In 1960-67, for instance, the average proportion of agricultural workers in the total civilian working population of the then Common Market was 18.1 per cent, but was only 4.2 per cent in the UK. By the 1990s, the proportion of workers in agriculture was less than 5 per cent in France and Germany and there was little scope for major transfers of labour out of the primary sector in northern Europe. Hence, this competitive advantage viz a viz the UK has disappeared. However, this theory can still explain why countries like China or Poland, with large amounts of labour in agriculture, can grow at rates several times that of EU countries.

Class and conflict Another argument put forward is that class structures in the UK have been much more firmly entrenched than in other countries. This has led to a 'them' and 'us' attitude. Workers on the one hand see businesses and management as both exploitive and incompetent. They join together in trade unions to seek protection from their natural 'class' enemies and have to struggle to secure decent wages and working conditions. Management on the other hand see workers as lazy and greedy, unable to work effectively without proper supervision.

Whilst this may have been true for much of this century, the 1980s saw a revolution in attitudes. The power of trade unions, organisations which tended to perpetuate the rhetoric of class struggle and division, was considerably reduced by the anti-union legislation/trade union reform of the Conservative government. On the other hand, the era of the incompetent public school boss could arguably be said to have finally disappeared. The shake out in UK manufacturing industry in the early 1980s left only relatively efficient firms in business. The 1980s was the decade when MBAs (degrees in management) and reading the latest management book became fashionable. Finally, Japanese work practices, which emphasised lack of co-operation and hierarchy had a considerable influence on how firms were structured. In the 1990s, it could be argued that the UK was no more class ridden than any other European country. Trade union reforms had helped make the UK one of the least strike prone countries in the developed world. With

continued globalisation, more and more large British firms were now owned by foreign firms, particularly US companies. These foreign owners to some extent moulded their British subsidiaries into their own ways of working, further distancing the UK from its unsuccessful past.

Education and training There is widespread agreement amongst economists that education and training is one of the key factors - if not, in fact, the most important factor - in determining economic growth rates. Indeed, the Labour government won the 1997 election by putting education at the top of its list of policy priorities, so important did it see education as vital to Britain's future prosperity. The UK has an enviable record in educating the top 20 per cent of its population to the age of 21. However, there are widespread criticisms of its relative success in educating the other 80 per cent of the population and for what happens after 21. There is a considerable body of evidence which suggests that some of the UK's industrial competitors, such as Germany and Japan, educate their bottom 80 per cent of the school population to higher standards than in the UK. In the USA, where standards for all children to the age of 18 tend to be fairly low, there is a widespread acceptance that the majority of post-18 year olds will stay on and do some form of college course. The USA has the highest proportion of 18-24 year olds in full time education of any country in the world. In the workplace, countries like Germany have the reputation of spending more on training existing workers than in the UK.

In the 1980s, the UK government attempted to put in place mechanisms for improving education and training. The National Curriculum was intended to raise education achievement by setting national standards. At the end of the 1980s, there started a considerable expansion in higher education numbers which saw the number of full time students rise from 0.3 million in 1987/8 to 1.1 million in 1996/7. In the 1990s, national vocational qualifications (NVQs) were introduced, designed to provide qualifications for training in work. Their school or college based equivalent, GNVQs, were introduced to help those for whom academic A level and GCSE examinations were not suited. In the late 1990s, the government placed great emphasis on national targets, for instance for achievement in national curriculum tests. Targets were intended to raise standards in schools which performed poorly, and to give good schools an incentive to achieve even better results.

Flexible labour markets In the 1990s, the UK government saw flexible labour markets as key to its **supply side reforms** (☞ unit 38). Labour markets are flexible when it is relatively easy for firms to hire and fire labour, and for workers to move between jobs.

Inflexible labour markets create market failure, partly because they tend to lead to unemployment. There are many different aspects to creating flexible labour markets. One is education and training, discussed above. An educated workforce is more attractive to firms and helps workers to change jobs when the need arises. Another aspect is government rules and regulations about employment. Health and safety laws, maximum working hours, minimum wages, minimum holiday entitlements, redundancy regulations and maternity and paternity leave are all examples of government imposed rules which increase the cost of employment to firms and reduce the ability of firms to manage their workforces to suit their production needs.

It is argued that, in EU countries, firms have to comply with too many rules and regulations. They then become reluctant to take on workers, leading to high unemployment and lower growth. In contrast, the UK and the US have fewer regulations and this partly explains their higher growth rates in the 1990s. Other aspects of flexible labour markets include pensions and housing. If workers are to move between jobs easily, they must carry with them pension rights. If they lose their pension rights every time they change job, they will be reluctant to move. Difficulty in obtaining housing discourages workers from moving between geographical areas. Part time working is important too. In flexible labour markets, workers should be able to choose how many hours they wish to work and how many jobs they have at any time. If work structures are such that part time working is discouraged, then the skills of many workers at home bringing up children are likely to go unutilised. Equally, there may not be enough full time work in the economy, but flexible labour markets should mean that workers could choose to build up **portfolios** of jobs, making several part time jobs equal to one full time one.

Taxes Another argument put forward is that the UK has had a tax regime which has discouraged enterprise, work and investment. Before 1979, for instance, the highest marginal rate of tax on earned income was 83 per cent. Government expenditure, the main determinant of taxation levels, had been on an upward trend since the 1950s. The Conservative government elected in 1979 was committed to lowering the tax burden by lowering levels of government spending. By 1997, when it was defeated at the polls, it had succeeded in limiting government spending to around 40 per cent of GDP. In contrast, levels of government spending in other EU countries were between 45 and 50 per cent of GDP. This meant that the UK was transformed into a relatively low tax EU country. One effect of this has been to give the UK a competitive advantage in attracting inward investment from countries such as the USA, Japan and South Korea. This inward investment has played a powerful role in

regenerating UK manufacturing industry which by the 1970s was typically uncompetitive in international markets.

Another effect has been to increase employment levels in the UK. High taxes on labour in France and Germany have discouraged firms from employing labour. Instead, they have chosen to invest in physical capital, and this may be one of the reasons why France and Germany have higher investment ratios than the UK. The high unemployment that developed in Germany and France in the 1990s is likely to have proved a drag on their growth rates. The UK in contrast saw steadily falling unemployment and rising employment from 1993. This is likely to have helped economic growth. There has been a rise in the number of workers. Employers have had to place more emphasis on training as labour shortages have developed. It may also have encouraged some physical investment as demand has risen.

Capital

Table 26.2 shows that the UK has consistently devoted less of its GDP to investment than other countries. Economic theory would suggest that investment - the addition to the physical capital stock of the country - is essential for economic growth. How can an economy increase its growth rate if it does not increase the amount it is setting aside to increase the production potential of the country? There is a number of possible explanations for why the UK has such a relatively low growth rate and also one which challenges the assumption that higher investment is needed to increase growth rates.

Table 26.2 *Gross fixed capital formation as a percentage of GDP*

Per cent

	1960-67	1968-73	1974-79	1980-89	1990-99
United States	18.1	18.4	18.8	19.0	16.1
Japan	31.0	34.6	31.8	29.1	31.1
Germany	25.2	24.4	20.8	21.9	22.7
France	23.2	24.6	23.6	20.6	20.3
United Kingdom	17.7	19.1	19.4	17.5	16.9
Italy	24.9	24.0	24.0	17.5	16.9
Canada	22.6	22.1	23.5	21.3	20.3

Source: adapted from OECD, *Historical Statistics*.

Quality, not quantity Some economists have argued that it is not the quantity of investment that is important but its direction. The two classic examples used for the UK are Concorde (the supersonic plane) and the nuclear power programme. Large sums of public money were poured into the development of Concorde and the nuclear power programme in the 1960s. Both proved uncommercial. Switzerland devotes one-third more of its GDP to investment than the UK and yet has a similar growth rate. In this view, increasing investment rates without there being the investment opportunities present in the economy would have little or no effect on growth rates. The money would simply be wasted. Moreover, how could investment be increased in an economy? The simplest way would be for government to spend more on investment, either through its own programmes, by investing directly in industry, or through subsidies. Free market economists would then argue that the government is a very poor judge of industries and projects which need further investment. The money would probably be squandered on 1990s equivalents of Concorde. Only if firms increase investment of their own accord in free markets can growth increase. Even this is no guarantee of success. In the late 1980s and early 1990s, Japanese industry increased its investment because of very low interest rates on borrowed money. In 1986, Japan spent 27.3 per cent of its GDP on investment. In 1990, this peaked at 32.2 per cent. Despite this, the Japanese economy spent much of the 1990s in recession, with an average growth rate of just 1.5 per cent. In retrospect, Japanese companies had clearly overinvested. There was far too much capacity for the levels of production required.

Short-termism This view states that the USA and the UK are handicapped because of the structure of their financial institutions. In the USA and the UK, banks do not invest in companies. They lend to companies over fairly short time periods, typically up to five years, but many loans (e.g. overdrafts) are repayable on demand. Shares in companies are owned by shareholders, and these shares are traded on stock markets. Stock markets are driven by speculators who are not interested in where a company might be in five or ten years time. They are only interested in the size of the next dividend payment or the price of the share today. In contrast, in Germany and Japan banks own large proportions of industry through shareholdings. The banks are interested in the long term development of companies. Losses this year are less important if the long term future of a company is bright and secure. It is therefore argued that US and UK stock markets lead to short-termism. Firms will only invest if they can make a quick profit to satisfy shareholders who are only interested in the financial performance of the company over, say, 12 months. In Germany and Japan, firms can afford to make long term investment decisions even if these involve poorer short term performance, secure in the knowledge that their shareholders are interested in the long term future of the business.

Supporters of US style capitalism argue that long termism can mask poor investment decisions. In the 1990s, Japanese companies have often failed to take the necessary steps to restructure despite making

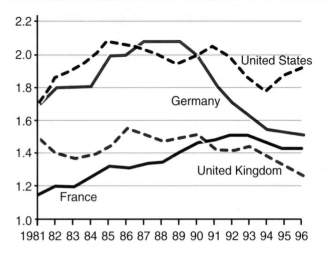

Figure 26.6 *Business R&D as a percentage of GDP*
Source: adapted from OECD.

substantial losses over a lengthy period of time. Without the pressures of shareholders wanting a fast return, they have preferred to safeguard the interests of management and workers. This has contributed to the problems of Japanese industry. In France, Germany and Italy, long termism has not prevented them suffering lower economic growth rates than the USA. Indeed, the pressures of globalisation and the single market within the EU are making their firms more short termist. They are finding that their companies are facing the threat of takeover by US or UK companies. One way of fighting this is to increase short term profitability.

Lack of savings The USA and the UK have relatively low savings ratios. Given that over the long term exports roughly equal imports for a country, and the government budget deficit tends to fluctuate around a fixed proportion of GDP, then savings must roughly equal a constant proportion of investment. Higher savings will thus allow higher investment. In the UK, firms have large tax incentives to save through not distributing all their profits to shareholders. This retained profit could be increased through even lower taxation. Or the government could increase its savings by moving to a budget surplus. Individuals could be persuaded to save more again through tax incentives.

Innovation The UK spends a relatively low proportion of its GDP on research and development (R&D). For most of the post-war period, an above average share of that R&D has been devoted to defence research. Hence, some economists argue that R&D spending in total needs to be increased for higher growth, and a larger proportion needs to be spent on civilian projects. The UK's poor R&D record is shown in Figure 26.6. Others argue that it is not so much the quantity that is important as the use to which R&D is put. It is often pointed out that the UK has a good international record in making discoveries and in inventions. However, too many of those have not been taken up by UK businesses. Instead, the ideas have gone overseas and been used by foreign firms as the bases for world-beating products. In this argument, UK firms have been very poor in the past at making a commercial success of R&D.

Catching up Catching up can apply to capital as well as to labour. For instance, a new CD factory in China is likely to increase labour productivity (output per worker) far more than a new CD factory in the UK. This is because the workers in China are more likely to have been employed in very low productivity jobs before than in Britain. So, countries like China can import foreign technologies and take huge leaps in productivity, which is then reflected in high economic growth rates. Some economists argue that, in the long run, all countries will arrive at roughly the same output per worker and grow at the same rate. This is because technology is internationally available. Countries can bring their capital stock up to the level of the most productive country in the world. Countries like the USA, however, which has grown at around 2.5 per cent per annum since the Second World War, can't take huge technological leaps like this. It has to create new technologies and new products to sustain its growth.

Privatisation and deregulation Capital may be tied up in relatively unproductive firms or industries. Releasing this capital can increase growth rates. The experience of the 1980s and 1990s in the UK has been that privatisation and deregulation are powerful ways of improving capital productivity. Nationalised industries, such as water, electricity, coal, gas and the railways were inefficient in the 1960s and 1970s. They employed too much capital and too much labour. Privatisation saw output per unit of capital and labour increase substantially as workforces were cut and assets sold off or closed down. The process was painful. In the coal industry, for instance, nearly 200 000 workers lost their jobs between 1980 and 2000. However, in a fast changing economy, failure to move resources between industries leads to inefficiency and slower growth.

Openness to international trade One way of protecting domestic jobs is to erect protectionist barriers against imports. For instance, foreign goods can be kept out by imposing high taxes on imports (called **tariffs** or **customs duties**). It can be argued, though, that protectionism is likely to lead to lower long term economic growth. This is because domestic firms can become insulated from world best practice. There is reduced incentive to invest and innovate if more competitive goods from abroad are kept out of the domestic market. The UK has tended to favour free trade in the post war period and since 1973 its policy has had to conform to EU policy. However, in the 1980s particularly, it was far more open to foreign companies wishing to set up in the UK than many other EU countries. In the car industry, for instance, France and Germany wanted to keep Japanese cars out of their markets to protect their domestic car manufacturers. They didn't at the time want a Japanese car factory in their country challenging Volkswagen or Peugeot. What they failed to realise was that competition from the Japanese could act as a powerful incentive to increase productivity and quality in the existing car industry. The UK car industry was nearly destroyed in the 1970s and early 1980s by competition from the EU and elsewhere. Japanese investment in the UK brought about a revival in the industry. Other UK based manufacturers, such as Ford and Vauxhall, transformed their manufacturing practices to meet the competition challenge. The result was a strong revival of UK car manufacturing which helped contribute to increased economic growth.

Macro-economic management

Some economists argue that recessions do not affect long term growth rates. Growth lost in a recession is made up in the boom which follows. Others argue that the fall in GDP in deep recessions may never be recouped in the subsequent upturn. This is because in a deep recession, labour can become de-skilled, leading to permanently higher unemployment. Capital can also be destroyed as firms cut costs, pulling down factories and throwing away equipment. The UK suffered deeper and longer recessions in the 1970s, 1980s and early 1990s than countries in Europe. This may help account for lower UK growth rates at the time. Equally, the higher growth rate in the UK in the 1990s may be because the UK avoided a recession in the middle 1990s which afflicted European countries. It could be that the UK could grow at 3 per cent per annum above its long term trend rate of around 2.5 per cent if it avoided the recessions which pull down the average rate of growth. This means that governments must be able to manage the economy to achieve relatively stable growth.

Growth in the first decade of the 21st century

The last half of the 20th century belonged to continental Europe and Japan. But, according to Brian Reading, international economist at analyst Lombard Street, the UK and the USA are best placed to enjoy strong growth at the start of the 21st century.

Developed economies face two major challenges. One is demographic. 'The age of ageing is about to arrive, but sooner for some than for others' he says. In the first decade of the new millennium, the working-age population in Japan, Germany and Italy will shrink at a rate of 1 per cent per year. As a result, potential growth by the end of 2010 will have slumped to 0.5 per cent or less. With fewer workers, output per worker will have to grow faster in these countries than in those with better demographics, like Britain or the USA if they are to keep up in the growth race. The alternative is to raise the proportion of the working age population in work and lower unemployment. There is plenty of scope to improve participation rates in most mainland European countries. The proportion of employees to non-workers is about 10 percentage points lower than in the USA and the UK. Halving unemployment would make a dramatic improvement in the size of the workforce: in France it would increase growth by 1 per cent. But improving participation and increasing productivity depend on the

kind of micro-economic supply side reform to which Europe and Japan have so far proved resistant. It will take a crisis, Reading believes, for Anglo-Saxon style deregulation to be adopted.

The second challenge is the information technology revolution. After years in which economists puzzled about the great productivity paradox - why companies spent so much money on new technology when the benefits in terms of increased output appeared small - the new paradigm seems to have arrived in the US at least. Reading estimates that the potential US growth rate has risen to 3 per cent a year as a result of new technology, with productivity growth approaching 2 per cent. America is the acknowledged leader in the ICT revolution with the UK not far behind. But over-regulation in European markets will inhibit these countries from adopting labour-saving technology.

The greatest threat to the USA lies in a sharp recession. The US economy is unbalanced with imports exceeding exports. If the flow of savings to the US from other countries, which finances this trade deficit, fell, then there could be a stock market crash in the USA. This would cut consumer spending and trigger a downward spiral.

Source: adapted from *The Guardian*, 24.5.1999.

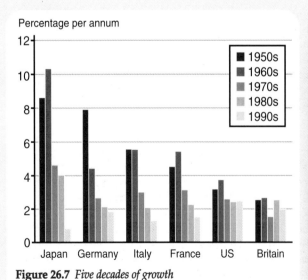

Figure 26.7 *Five decades of growth*

1. (a) Explain what is meant by economic growth.
   (b) Compare the growth performance of the six industrialised countries shown in Figure 26.7.
2. Analyse why supply side reforms in Europe and Japan are essential to counter the difficulties these economies are likely to face in the first decade of the 21st century.
3. Discuss what other strategies European countries could adopt to increase their growth rates.

Summary

1. National income is often used as the main indicator of the standard of living in an economy. A rise in GDP per head is used as an indication of economic growth and a rise in living standards.
2. However, there are many other important components of the standard of living, including political freedom, the social and cultural environment, freedom from fear of war and persecution, and the quality of the environment.
3. Economic growth over the past 100 years has transformed the living standards of people in the western world, enabling almost all to escape from absolute poverty.
4. Economic growth is likely to be the only way of removing people in the Third World from absolute poverty.
5. Economic growth has its costs in terms of unwelcome changes in the structure of society.
6. Some believe that future economic growth is unsustainable, partly because of growing pollution and partly because of the exploitation of non-renewable resources.

National income and economic welfare

National income is a measure of the income, output and expenditure of an economy. It is also often used as a measure of the **standard of living**. However, equating national income with living standards is very simplistic because there are many other factors which contribute to the economic welfare of individuals.

Political freedoms We tend to take civil liberties for granted in the UK. But other governments in the world today are totalitarian regimes which rule through fear. In some countries, membership of an opposition party or membership of a trade union can mean death or imprisonment. The freedom to visit friends, to travel and to voice an opinion are likely to be more valuable than owning an extra television or being able to buy another dress.

The social and cultural environment In the UK, we take things such as education for granted. We have some of the world's finest museums and art galleries. We possess a cultural heritage which includes Shakespeare and Constable. The BBC is seen as one of the best broadcasting organisations throughout the world. But we could all too easily live in a cultural desert where the main purpose of television programming might be to sell soap powders and make a profit. Alternatively, the arts could be used as political propaganda rather than exist in their own right.

Freedom from fear of violence If a person doesn't feel safe walking the streets or even at home, then no number of microwave ovens or videos will compensate for this loss. Equally, fears of war, arbitrary arrest, imprisonment or torture make material possessions

seem relatively unimportant.

The working environment How long and hard people have to work is vital in evaluating standards of living. One reason why the average worker is far better off today than 100 years ago is because his or her working year is likely to be about half the number of hours of his or her Victorian counterpart's. Equally, the workplace is far safer today than 100 years ago. Industrial accidents were then commonplace and workers received little or no

Question 1

Economists have long recognised that GDP is only a proxy measurement of living standards. In a book entitled *Alternative Economic Indicators* published in 1995, Victor Anderson, a British economist, argues that other measures apart from GDP should be used as measures of economic well-being.

His thesis is that, in pursuing the maximisation of the monetary value of physical production, 20th century economists have neglected the intrinsic value of human beings and their interaction, and the need to protect the natural world. 'Narrowly financial criteria have ruled economic policy-making for too long. It is time to bring human and environmental realities back into economics.' In the book he details 14 indicators which, he argues, could be considered alongside economic growth in evaluating economic outcomes. The alternative economic indicators include primary school enrolment, literacy, calorie intake, telephones per person, carbon dioxide emissions and operable nuclear reactors.

(a) What does the author mean by 'narrowly financial criteria' when discussing living standards?
(b) Why should indicators such as primary school enrolment have any impact on living standards?

compensation for serious injuries or even death.

The environment Environmental issues are currently at the forefront of people's consciousness. There is an understanding that production activities can damage the environment and that in future we may well have to stop consuming certain products if we are to safeguard the environment.

The growth debate

The rate of economic growth has accelerated historically. Even five hundred years ago, most people would have seen little change in incomes over their lifetimes. In Victorian England, the economy grew at about one per cent per annum. Over the past thirty years, the UK economy has grown at an average of just over 2 per cent.

Table 27.1 *Economic growth rate of £1 over time*

Year	Growth rates				
	1%	2%	3%	5%	10%
0	100	100	100	100	100
5	105	110	116	128	161
10	110	122	130	163	259
25	128	164	203	339	1 084
50	164	269	426	1 147	11 739
75	211	442	891	3 883	127 189
100	271	724	1 870	13 150	1 378 059

Growth at these rates over the past 50 years has led to undreamt of prosperity for the citizens of the industrialised world. Consider Table 27.1. It shows by how much £1 will grow over time at different rates. At one per cent growth, income will roughly double over the lifetime of an individual. At 2 per cent, it will quadruple over a lifetime. At 3 per cent, it is doubling every twenty five years. At 5 per cent, it only takes about 14 years to double income. At 10 per cent, it only takes about 7 years to double income.

If recent growth rates are a guide to the future, average British workers in 30 years' time will earn in real terms twice what they are earning today. When they are in their seventies, they can expect workers to earn four times as much as their parents did when they were born.

These increases in income have led to the elimination of **absolute poverty** for most citizens in industrialised countries.
- Life expectancy has doubled over the past 300 years and infant mortality rates have plummeted.
- People have enough to eat and drink. What we eat and drink is nearly always fit for human consumption.
- Housing standards have improved immeasurably.
- Nearly everyone can read and write.

Future increases in income are generally desirable. Very few people would prefer to have less income rather than more income in the future (remember economics assumes that people have **infinite wants**). So economic growth has generally been considered to be highly desirable. Moreover, two-thirds of the world's population do not live

in the affluent West. Many who live in the Third World suffer absolute poverty. The only way to eliminate malnutrition, disease, bad housing and illiteracy in these countries is for there to be real economic growth.

Arguments against growth

Despite the apparent benefits, the goal of economic growth is questioned by some economists and environmentalists.

Question 2

The photographs show a modern kitchen and a kitchen at the turn of the century. To what extent do they show that economic growth has been desirable?

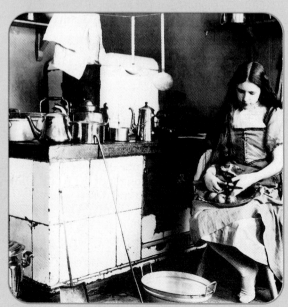

The falsity of national income statistics One argument is that the increase in national income has been largely fictitious. Three hundred years ago much of the output of the economy was not traded. Women were not on the whole engaged in paid work. Much of the supposed increase in income has come from placing monetary values on what existed already. Much of the increase in income generated by the public sector of the economy comes not from increased production but from increased wages paid to public sector workers who produce the same amount of services. Whilst there is some truth in this, it cannot be denied that material living standards have increased immeasurably over the past three hundred years. People not only consume more goods and services, they have on average far more leisure time.

Negative externalities Another argument is that modern industrialised societies have created large negative **externalities**. For instance, growth has created a large pool of migrant workers, wandering from job to job in different parts of the country. They become cut off from their roots, separated from their families. The result is alienation and loneliness, particularly of the old, and the collapse of traditional family values. Crime rates soar, divorce rates increase, stress related illnesses become commonplace and more and more has to be spent on picking up the pieces of a society which is no longer content with what it has.

Supporters of this view tend to look back to some past 'golden age', often agricultural, when people lived mainly in villages as parts of large extended families. However, historical evidence suggests that such a rural paradise never existed. Life for many was short and brutish. Drunkenness was always a problem. Family life was claustrophobic and did not allow for individuality. Most people were dead by the age when people today tend to divorce and remarry.

Growth is unsustainable Perhaps the most serious anti-growth argument is that growth is unsustainable. Consider again Table 27.1. If Western European countries continue to grow at an average 3 per cent per annum then in 25 years' time national income will be twice as large as it is today; in fifty years' time, when an 18 year old student will be retired, it will be over 4 times as large; in 75 years' time, when on current life expectancy figures that student would be dead, it will be nearly 9 times as large; and in 100 years' time it will be nearly 19 times as large. If the average wage in the UK today is £12 000 per annum, then in 100 years' time it will have risen to £355 300 per annum in real terms.

Each extra percent increase in national income uses up **non-renewable resources** such as oil, coal and copper. In the late 1970s, the Club of Rome, a forecasting institute, produced a report called 'The Limits to Growth'. The report claimed that industrialised economies as we know them would collapse. They would be caught between a growth in pollution and a decline in the availability of scarce resources such as oil, coal and timber. Oil was projected to run out in the next century and coal by the year 2 400. In the 1980s and 1990s, the world was gripped by reports that people were destroying the ozone layer

and raising the world's temperature through the greenhouse effect. The planet cannot support growth rates of even 1 or 2 per cent per year. Growth must stop and the sooner the better.

Economic theory suggests that the future may not be as bleak as this picture makes out. In a market economy, growing scarcity of a resource, such as oil, results in a rise in price. Three things then happen. First, demand and therefore consumption falls - the price mechanism results in conservation. Second, it becomes profitable to explore for new supplies of the resource. Known world oil reserves today are higher than they were in 1973 at the time of the first oil crisis! Third, consumers switch to substitute products whilst producers are encouraged to find new replacement products. After the massive rise in oil prices in 1973-74, the world car makers roughly halved the fuel consumption per mile of the average car over a period of ten years through more efficient engines. Brazil developed cars which ran on fuel made from sugar.

Governments too respond to pressures from scientists and the public. The activities of industry are far more regulated today in the western world than they were 30 years ago. Individual governments, for instance, have introduced strict controls on pollution emissions, regulated disposal of waste and sought to ration scarce resources like water or air through systems of tradable licences (☞ unit 19). Even more impressive has been the willingness of governments to sign international agreements designed to safeguard the environment. For instance, in 1987, 93 governments signed the Montreal Protocol to phase out production of CFC chemicals, a major contributor to the destruction of the ozone layer. At the earth summit in Rio de Janero in 1992, governments agreed to reduce greenhouse gas emissions by the year 2000 to below their 1990 levels.

What is worrying, however, is that the market mechanism and governments are frequently slow to act. Governments and markets are not good at responding to pressures which might take decades to build up but only manifest themselves suddenly at the end of that time period. Some scientists have predicted that global warming is now already irreversible. If this is true, the problem that we now face is how to change society to cope with this. There is no clear consensus as to how we could reverse economic growth, consume less, and cope with the coming catastrophe, without creating an economic nightmare with mass starvation.

The anti-growth lobby One point to note is that supporters of the anti-growth lobby tend to be people who are relatively well off. Cutting their consumption by 25 per cent, or producing environmentally friendly alternative technologies, might not create too much hardship for them. However, leaving the mass of people in the Third World today at their present living standards would lead to great inequality. A small minority would continue to live below the absolute poverty line, facing the continual threat of malnutrition. A majority would not have access to services such as education and health care which people in the West take for granted. Not surprisingly, the anti-growth lobby is stronger in the West than in the Third World.

Applied economics

The standard of living in the UK since 1900

GDP is often used as the major economic indicator of welfare. Table 27.2 shows that, on this basis, living standards in the UK have risen considerably this century. Between 1900 and 1931 GDP rose 23 per cent and between 1900 and 1998 it rose 597 per cent. Population has increased too, but even when this has been taken into account, the rise in income per person is impressive.

Table 27.2

	GDP (£bn at 1995 prices)[1]	Population (millions)	GDP per head (£ at 1995 prices)
1901	129.3	38.2	3 385
1911	149.0	42.1	3 539
1921	131.8	44.0	2 995
1931	159.4	46.0	3 465
1951	246.1	50.2	4 902
1961	320.6	52.7	6 083
1971	425.2	55.5	7 661
1981	498.3	55.8	8 930
1991	648.6	57.8	11 221
1998	772.3	59.2	13 046

1. At market prices.
Source: adapted from CH Feinstein, *National Income, Expenditure and Output in the United Kingdom*, 1855-1965 Cambridge University Press; *Economic Trends Annual Supplement*; *Annual Abstract of Statistics*, Office for National Statistics.

It is possible to chart a multitude of other ways in which it can be shown that the standard of living of the British family has improved. For instance, 14.2 per cent of children in 1900 died before the age of 1. In 2000, the comparable figure is less than 0.6 per cent. In 1900, the vast majority of children left school at 12. Today all children stay on till the age of 16, whilst over 60 per cent of 18 year olds are in full time education or training. In 1900, few people were able to afford proper medical treatment when they fell ill. Today, everyone in the UK has access to the National Health Service.

Table 27.3 illustrates another way in which we are far better off today than a family at the turn of the century. It shows the weekly budget of a manual worker's family in a North Yorkshire iron town, estimated by Lady Bell in her book *At The Works*. The family lived off 7½ home-made loaves of 4lb (1.8kg) each thinly scraped with butter, 4lb (1.8kg) of meat and bacon, weak tea, a quart of milk and no vegetables worth mentioning. In 1997, whilst average consumption for five people of bread was only 4.4kg a week, tea 0.2kg and sugar 0.6kg, on the other hand meat consumption was 4.7kg, potato consumption (fresh and frozen) was 4.3kg, and butter, margarine, lard and other oils consumption was 1.3kg. Moreover, today's diet is far more varied and ample with fruit and vegetables apart from potatoes playing a major part. Malnutrition, not uncommon in 1900, is virtually unknown in the UK today.

The budget in Table 27.3 also says a great deal about the very restricted lifestyle of the average family in 1908. Then, a family would consider itself lucky if it could take a day trip to the seaside. In comparison, 57 per cent of people took a holiday of 4 days or more in 1997 and of those 26 per cent took two or more holidays a year. 57 million holidays of 4 days or more in total were taken and 29.1 million of these were foreign holidays.

In 1908, houses were sparsely furnished. The main form of heating was open coal fires; central heating was virtually unknown. Very few houses were wired for electricity. Table 27.3 shows that the typical house was lighted by oil. All the electrical household gadgets we take for granted, from washing machines to vacuum cleaners to televisions, had not been invented. The 1lb (2.24kg) of soap in the 1908 budget would have been used to clean clothes, sinks and floors. Soap powders, liquid detergents and floor cleaners were not available. 'Gold Dust' was the popular name for an exceptionally caustic form of shredded yellow soap notorious for its ability to flay the user's hands. Compare that with the numerous brands of mild soaps available today.

Family budget in 1908 Income 18s 6d, family of five

	s.	d.
Rent	5	6
Coals	2	4
Insurance	0	7
Clothing	1	0
Meat	1	6
14lb of flour	1	5
3½ lb of bread meal	0	4½
1lb butter	1	1
Half lb lard	0	2½
1lb bacon	0	9
4 lb sugar	0	8
Half lb tea	0	9
Yeast	0	1
Milk	0	3
1 box Globe polish	0	1
1lb soap	0	3
1 packet Gold Dust	0	1
3 oz tobacco	0	9
7lb potatoes	0	3
Onions	0	1
Matches	0	1
Lamp oil	0	2
Debt	0	3
Total	18	6

Table 27.3

Workers worked long hours, six days a week with few holidays, whilst at home the housewife faced a life of drudgery with few labour-saving devices. Accidents were frequent and old age, unemployment and sickness were dreaded and even more so the workhouse, the final destination for those with no means to support themselves.

Ecologically, the smoke-stack industries of industrial areas such as London, the Black Country and Manchester created large scale pollution. The smogs which are found in many cities such as Mexico City and Los Angeles today were common occurrences in turn-of-the-century Britain. The urban environment was certainly not clean 90 years ago.

Socially and politically, women, who formed over half the population, were not emancipated. In 1900, they did not have the vote, their place was in the home, they were often regarded as biologically inferior to men, and they were debarred from almost all public positions of influence and authority. In many ways, the standard of living of women has improved more than that of men this century because of the repressive attitude held towards women 90 years ago.

Overall, it would be very difficult to look back on 1900 and see it as some golden age. For the vast majority of those in Britain today, the start of the new millenium is a paradise in comparison. However, whilst there might be little absolute poverty today, it could be argued that there is considerable relative poverty. It could also be argued that the poorest today are probably still worse off than the top 5 per cent of income earners in 1900.

Comparative living standards in the UK

Table 27.4 *Income, prices and population*

	1971	1998
GDP (£bn at current prices)	57.1	837.6
Retail Price Index (1985 = 100)	21.4	172.2
Population (millions)	55.5	59.2

Table 27.5 *Purchasing power*

	Hours, minutes	
	1971	1998
Length of time necessary to work to pay for:		
800g white sliced bread	0:09	0:04
1 pint milk	0:05	0:03
Dozen eggs, first quality, size 2	0:21	0:11
1kg potatoes	0:04	0:06
1kg of cod fillets	1:01	0:48
1kg rump steak	1:54	1:05
1 pint of beer (bitter)	0:14	0:13
20 cigarettes (king size filter)	0:22	0:24
Road fund tax	40:01	18:25
First class stamp	0:03	0:02
Copy of *Social Trends*	5:15	4:51

Table 27.6 *Government spending on welfare benefits*

	£bn at 1997-98 prices	
	1971-72	1997-98
Elderly	19.3	42.8
Long term sick and disabled	3.4	22.9
Short term sick	2.8	1.2
Family	3.2	18.6
Unemployed	3.2	6.3
Widows and others	2.9	2.0
Total benefit expenditure	34.8	93.8

Table 27.7 *Population*[1]

	1971	1998
Percentage of the population		
under 19	31.0	25.5
20-44	31.8	36.0
45-64	24.0	23.0
65-74	8.5	8.4
75 and over	4.7	7.3

1. Figures may not add due to rounding.

Table 27.8 *Male death rates*

	1971	1998
Death rates per 1000 males in each group		
Under 1	20.2	6.4
1-15	0.5	0.2
16-34	1.0	1.0
35-54	4.8	3.0
55-64	20.4	12.5
65-74	51.1	34.8
75 and over	131.4	110.1

Table 27.9 *Number of abortions, Great Britain*

	1971-72	1998
Abortions	63 400	190 295

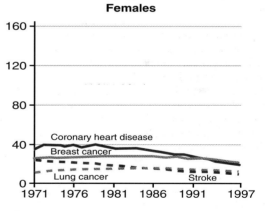

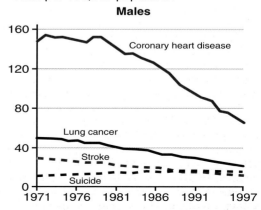

Figure 27.1 *Death rates for people aged under 65: by gender and selected cause of death, UK*

Table 27.10 *Households: by type of household and family*

	Percentages	
	1971	1998
One person		
Under pensionable age	6	14
Over pensionable age	12	14
Two or more unrelated adults	4	3
Single family households		
Couple		
No children	27	28
1-2 dependent children	26	19
3 or more dependent children	9	4
Non-dependent children only	8	7
Lone parent		
Dependent children	3	7
Non-dependent children only	4	3
Multi-family households	1	1
All households (= 100%) (millions)	18.6	23.6

Table 27.11 *Housing*

	1971	1998
% of households with no:		
bath or shower	9.1	0.0
inside toilet	11.5	0.0
Number of owner occupied properties	10.0m	16.5m
Properties taken into repossession	2 800	60 000

Table 27.12 *Percentage of households owning selected consumer durables*

	1970	1998/9
Refrigerator	66	99
Telephone	35	95
Washing machine	65	92
Video recorder	0	85
Microwave	0	79
CD player	0	68

Table 27.13 *Education*

	1970-71	1998
Ratio of pupils to teachers in state schools	22.6	18.3
Numbers in state nursery schools (millions)	0.05	0.11
Numbers in all schools (millions)	10.2	10.00
Numbers in higher education (millions)	0.62	1.94
Government spending on education as % of GDP	5.20	4.80

Table 27.14 *Health*

	1971	1997
Adult cigarette smoking % of adults		
Males	52	29
Females	41	28
Average number of patients in England per doctor	2 400	1 878

Table 27.15 *Employment, UK, millions*

	1971	1999
Males		
full time	13.1	13.7
part time	0.6	1.4
Females		
full time	5.6	6.8
part time	2.8	5.4
Unemployed[1]	0.75	1.3

1. Claimant count unemployed.

Table 27.16 *Real gross weekly earnings of selected workers, £ at April 1999 prices*

	1971	1999
Waiter/waitress	119	188
Caretaker	181	251
Bricklayer/mason	225	316
Carpenter/joiner	231	336
Nurse	161	384
Primary teacher	267	460
Solicitor	395	728
Medical practitioner	568	951

Table 27.17 *Participation in home-based leisure activities*

Great Britain			Percentages
	1977	1987	1996-97
Males			
Watching TV	97	99	99
Visiting/entertaining friends or relations	89	94	95
Listening to records/tapes/CDs	64	76	79
Reading books	52	54	58
DIY	51	58	58
Gardening	49	49	52
Dressmaking/needlework/knitting	2	3	3
Females			
Watching TV	97	99	99
Visiting/entertaining friends or relations	93	96	97
Listening to records/tapes/CDs	60	71	77
Reading books	57	65	71
DIY	22	30	30
Gardening	35	43	45
Dressmaking/needlework/knitting	51	47	37

1. Percentage of those aged 16 and over particating in each activity in the four weeks before interview.

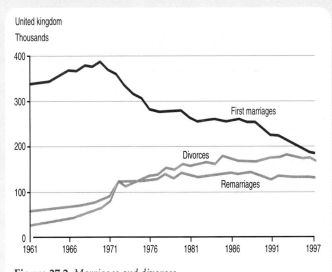

Figure 27.2 *Marriages and divorces*

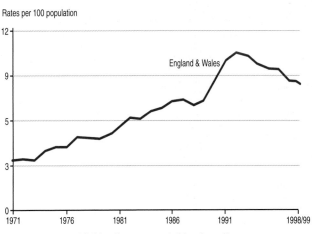

Figure 27.3 *Notifiable offences recorded by the police*

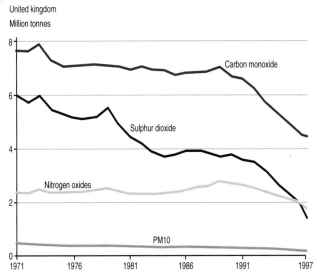

Figure 27.4 *Carbon dioxide emissions by source*

Sources for all tables and figures: adapted from *Social Trends*, *Annual Abstract of Statistics*, Office for National Statistics.

You have been asked to write a magazine article from an economic perspective comparing the early 1970s and the late 1990s. The focus of the article is a discussion of whether living standards improved in the UK over the period. Construct the article as follows.
1. In your introduction, pick out a small number of key statistics which you feel point out the differences between the two periods.
2. In the main part of the article, compare and contrast the two periods, pointing out how living standards improved and also where it could be argued that the UK was worse off in the late 1990s than in the early 1970s.
3. In the conclusion, discuss whether rising GDP will be sufficient to ensure that the UK is better off in 2020 than in the late 1990s.

Table 27.18 *Average daily flow of motor vehicles on motorways*

		Thousands
	1971	1998
Vehicles on motorways	28.52	67.1

Summary

1. Inflation is a general sustained rise in the price level.
2. Inflation is measured by calculating the change in a weighted price index over time. In the UK this index is called the Retail Price Index.
3. A price index only measures inflation for average households. It also cannot take into account changes in the quality and distribution of goods over time.
4. Inflation is generally considered to give rise to economic costs to society. These include shoe-leather and menu costs, psychological and political costs, and costs which arise from the redistribution of income in society. Some economists believe that inflation also results in higher unemployment and lower growth in the long term.
5. Unanticipated inflation tends to give rise to higher economic costs than anticipated inflation.

The meaning of inflation

INFLATION is defined as a sustained general rise in prices. The opposite of inflation - DEFLATION - is a term which can have two meanings. Strictly speaking it is defined as a fall in the PRICE LEVEL. However, it can also be used to describe a slowdown in the rate of growth of output of the economy. This slowdown or **recession** is often associated with a fall in the **rate of inflation**. Before the Second World War, recessions were also associated with falls in prices and this is the reason why deflation has come to have these two meanings.

A general rise in prices may be quite moderate. CREEPING INFLATION would describe a situation where prices rose a few per cent on average each year. HYPER-INFLATION, on the other hand, describes a situation where inflation levels are very high. There is no exact figure at which inflation becomes hyper-inflation, but inflation of 100 or 200 per cent per annum would be deemed to be hyper-inflation by most economists.

Measuring inflation

The inflation rate is the change in average prices in an economy over a given period of time. The price level is measured in the form of an **index** (☞ unit 3). So if the price index were 100 today and 110 in one year's time, then the rate of inflation would be 10 per cent.

Calculating a price index is a complicated process. Prices of a representative range of goods and services (a **basket** of goods) need to be recorded on a regular basis. In the UK, the most widely used measure of the price level is the Retail Price Index. In theory, each month, on the same day of the month, surveyors are sent out to record 150 000 prices for 600 items. Prices are recorded in different areas of the country as well as in different types of retail outlets, such as corner shops and supermarkets. These results are averaged out to find the average price of goods and this figure is converted into **index number form**.

Changes in the price of food are more important than changes in the price of tobacco. This is because a larger proportion of total household income is spent on food than on tobacco. Therefore the figures have to be **weighted** before the final index can be calculated. For instance, assume that there are only two goods in the economy, food and cars, as shown in Table 28.1. Households spend 75 per cent of their income on food and 25 per cent on cars. There is an increase in the price of

Question 1

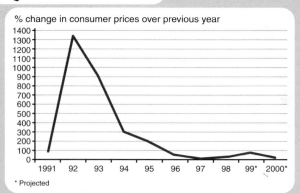

% change in consumer prices over previous year

Figure 28.1 *Inflation in Russia, 1991 to 2000*
Source: adapted from *World Economic Outlook*, IMF.

(a) Describe the changes in prices in Russia shown in the data.
(b) To what extent could Russia be said to have experienced hyper-inflation during the period shown?

food of 8 per cent and of cars of 4 per cent over one year. In a normal average calculation, the 8 per cent and the 4 per cent would be added together and the total divided by 2 to arrive at an average price increase of 6 per cent. But this provides an inaccurate figure because spending on food is more important in the household budget than spending on cars. The figures have to be weighted. Food is given a weight of $3/4$ (or 0.75 or 750 out of 1 000) and cars a weight of $1/4$ (or 0.25 or 250 out of 1 000). The average increase in prices is 8 per cent multiplied by $3/4$ added to 4 per cent multiplied by $1/4$ (i.e. 6 per cent + 1 per cent). The weighted average is therefore 7 per cent. If the RPI were 100 at the start of the year, it would be 107 at the end of the year. In order to calculate a weighting, it is necessary to find out how money is spent. In the case of the Retail Price Index, the weighting is calculated from the results of the Family Expenditure Survey. Each year, a few thousand households are asked to record their expenditure for one month. From these figures it is possible to calculate how the average household spends its money. (This average household, of course, does not exist except as a statistical entity.)

Table 28.1

Commodity	Proportion of total spending	Weight	Increase in price	Contribution to increase in RPI
Food	75%	750	8%	6%
Cars	25%	250	4%	1%
Total	100%	1 000		7%

The accuracy of price indices

It is important to realise that any price index is a weighted average. Different rates of inflation can be calculated by changing the weightings in the index. For instance, the Retail Price Index calculates the average price level for the average household in the UK. But it is possible, again using data from the Family Expenditure Survey, to calculate price indices for pensioner households or one parent households. One major difference between these households and the average household is that they spend a larger proportion of their income on food. So a 10 per cent rise in the price of food compared to a 5 per cent rise in the price of all other items will result in a higher rate of inflation for pensioners and one parent households than for the average household. In fact each individual household will have a different rate of inflation. The Retail Price Index only measures an average rate of inflation for all households across the UK.

The household spending patterns upon which the index is based also change over time. For instance, food was a far more important component of the Retail Price Index 30 years ago than it is today because spending on food was then a higher proportion of total spending. The index cannot indicate changes in the quality of goods. Cars might increase in price because their specifications improve rather than because there has been an inflationary price rise. The weights for the Retail Price Index are changed annually to take account of changes in spending patterns.

Question 2

Table 28.2

Year	Weights			% annual increase in prices	
	Food	All other items	Total	Food	All other items
1	300	700	1 000	10	10
2	250	750	1 000	5	10
3	200	800	1 000	4	6
4	150	850	1 000	3	2
5	125	875	1 000	4	4
6	120	880	1 000	6	4
7	120	880	1 000	5	7
8	110	890	1 000	8	10

Table 28.2 shows the price index weights given to food and to all other items in each of eight years. It also shows the percentage annual increase in prices of those items.
(a) Calculate the rate of inflation (i.e. the percentage increase in prices) in each year 1 to 8.
(b) What would the price index in years 2-8 be if the price index were 100 in year 1?

But this does not get round the fact that the average 'basket' or 'bundle' of goods purchased in 1950 and upon which the RPI for 1950 was calculated was very different from the average bundle of goods purchased in 1990.

Question 3

Table 28.3 *Index of Retail Prices*

	Average annual percentage change				
	1977-81	1982-86	1987-91	1992-96	1997-98
General index	13.4	5.5	6.5	2.7	3.3
Pensioner index, two person household	12.8	5.3	5.3	2.8	1.7

Source: adapted from *Economic Trends Annual Supplement*, Office for National Statistics.

(a) Explain why the change in the General Index of Retail Prices may differ from the change in the Pensioner Index.
(b) A two person pensioner household where the pensioners retired in 1976 receives pensions linked to the General Index of Retail Prices. In which years would it, on average, have seen (i) an increase and (ii) a decrease in its real purchasing power? Explain why this occurs.

The costs of inflation

Inflation is generally considered to be a problem. The higher the rate of inflation the greater the economic cost. There are a number of reasons why this is the case.

Shoe-leather costs If prices are stable, consumers and firms come to have some knowledge of what is a fair price for a product and which suppliers are likely to charge less than others. At times of rising prices, consumers and firms will be less clear about what is a reasonable price. This will lead to more 'shopping around', which in itself is a cost.

High rates of inflation are also likely to lead to households and firms holding less cash and more interest bearing deposits. Inflation erodes the value of cash, but since nominal interest rates tend to be higher than with stable prices, the opportunity cost of holding cash tends to be larger, the higher the rate of inflation. Households and firms are then forced to spend more time transferring money from one type of account to another or putting cash into an account to maximise the interest paid. This time is a cost.

Menu costs If there is inflation, restaurants have to change their menus to show increased prices. Similarly, shops have to change their price labels and firms have to calculate and issue new price lists. Even more costly are changes to fixed capital, such as vending machines and parking meters, to take account of price increases.

Psychological and political costs Price increases are deeply unpopular. People feel that they are worse off, even if their incomes rise by more than the rate of inflation. High rates of inflation, particularly if they are unexpected, disturb the distribution of income and wealth as we shall discuss below, and therefore profoundly affect the existing social order. Change and revolution in the past have often accompanied periods of high inflation.

Redistributional costs Inflation can redistribute income and wealth between households, firms and the state. This redistribution can occur in a variety of ways. For instance, anybody on a fixed income will suffer. In the UK, many pensioners have received fixed pensions from private company pension schemes which are not adjusted for inflation. If prices double over a five year period, their real income will halve. Any group of workers which fails to be able to negotiate pay increases at least in line with inflation will suffer falls in its real income too.

If **real** interest rates fall as a result of inflation, there will be a transfer of resources from borrowers to lenders. With interest rates at 10 per cent and inflation rates at 20 per cent, a saver will lose 10 per cent of the real value of saving each year whilst a borrower will see a 10 per cent real reduction in the value of debt per annum.

Taxes and government spending may not change in line with inflation. For instance, if the Chancellor fails to increase excise duties on alcohol and tobacco each year in line with inflation, real government revenue will fall whilst drinkers and smokers will be better off in real terms assuming their incomes have risen at least by as much as inflation. Similarly, if the Chancellor fails to increase personal income tax **allowances** (the amount which a worker can earn 'tax free') in line with inflation, then the burden of tax will increase, transferring resources from the taxpayer to the government.

Unemployment and growth Some economists, mainly monetarists, have claimed that inflation creates unemployment and lowers growth. Inflation increases costs of production and creates uncertainty. This lowers the profitability of investment and makes businessmen less willing to take the risk associated with any investment

project. Lower investment results in less long term employment and long term growth.

There is also a balance of payments effect. If inflation rises faster in the UK than in other countries, and the value of the pound does not change on foreign currency markets, then exports will become less competitive and imports more competitive. The result will be a loss of jobs in the domestic economy and lower growth.

Question 4

In 1997, the Index of Retail Prices rose by 3.2 per cent and in 1998 by 3.4 per cent. How might the following have been affected by the change?
(a) A pensioner on a fixed income.
(b) A bank deposit saver, given that the rate of interest on a 90 day bank deposit account was 6.0 per cent in 1997 and 6.1 per cent in 1998.
(c) A worker whose personal income tax allowance was £4 045 between April 1997 and March 1998 and £4 195 between April 1998 and March 1999.
(d) A mother with one child who received £10.80 in child benefit between April 1996 and March 1997, £11.05 between April 1997 and March 1998 and £11.45 between April 1998 and March 1999.

Anticipated and unanticipated inflation

Much inflation is **unanticipated**; households, firms and government are uncertain what the rate of inflation will be in the future. When planning, they therefore have to estimate as best they can the expected rate of inflation. It is unlikely that they will guess correctly and hence their plans will be to some extent frustrated. On the other hand, inflation may be **anticipated**. Inflation may be a constant 5 per cent per year and therefore households, firms and government are able to build in this figure to their plans.

Unanticipated inflation imposes far greater costs than anticipated inflation. If inflation is anticipated, economic agents can take steps to mitigate the effects of inflation. One way of doing this is through INDEXATION. This is where economic variables like wages or taxes are increased in line with inflation. For instance, a union might negotiate a wage agreement with an employer for staged increases over a year of 2 per cent plus the change in the Retail Price Index. The annual changes in social security benefits in the UK are linked to the Retail Price Index.

Economists are divided about whether indexation provides a solution to the problem of inflation. On the one hand, it reduces many of the costs of inflation although some costs such as shoe leather costs and menu costs remain. On the other hand, it reduces pressure on government to tackle the problem of inflation directly. Indexation eases the pain of inflation but is not a cure for it.

Moreover, indexation may hinder government attempts to reduce inflation because indexation builds in cost structures, such as wage increases, which reflect past changes in prices. If a government wants to get inflation down to 2 per cent a year, and inflation has just been 10 per cent, it will not be helped in achieving its target if workers are all awarded at least 10 per cent wage increases because of indexation agreements.

Applied economics

The Retail Price Index

Calculating the index

The Retail Price Index (RPI) is a complex index compiled from a large amount of data. Each month, 150 000 prices are collected from shops in 180 locations round the country. The 150 000 prices are gathered on 600 items, ranging from microwave ovens to grapefruit to ferry charges. The prices are then averaged out using weights. The weights are calculated from the yearly Family Expenditure Survey. This survey asks 7 000 households a year to keep diaries of what they spend over a fortnight. A spending pattern for the average family can then be worked out.

The weights are revised each year to take account of changing patterns of expenditure. For instance, rabbits were taken out of the RPI in 1956 whilst condoms were only added in 1989. In 1999, women's cardigans, brake pads and PC repairs were included whilst packet soup,

Source: adapted from Office for National Statistics.
Figure 28.2 *Changes in the basket of goods used to calculate the RPI, 1962-1998*

malt vinegar and children's coats were removed. Figure 28.2 shows how weights have changed between 1962 and 1999. The proportion spent on food in the average budget has been declining over time as incomes have risen (food has a very low positive income elasticity of demand). Travel and leisure and housing and household expenditure, on the other hand, have been rising.

Is the RPI reliable?

The RPI, as a statistical measure of inflation, has many problems. One problem, highlighted by the House of Commons Public Accounts Committee in 1990 following publication of a report earlier in the year by the National Audit Office (NAO), was that, in practice, prices were not necessarily collected each month. Of the 175 000 prices nationally collected at that time, only about 95 000 prices were recorded. Of nine offices surveyed in detail by the NAO, eight of them collected between 42 and 84 per cent of the theoretical maximum. The ninth, Camden, was on strike and therefore provided no data. There were a number of reasons why prices were not collected. In Camden, for instance, only one-third of prices were collected regularly because of lack of staff. For the remaining two-thirds, price data was copied forward from price collection forms for the previous month. In general, almost 30 per cent of specific items for which prices were collected at the beginning of the year became unavailable in the course of the year. There was a high turnover of staff collecting the statistics, and staff had no formal training in their task. Obviously, all this brings into question the reliability of the Retail Price Index.

A second, similar problem relates to the Family Expenditure Survey (FES). The Survey is nationally based on 10 000 households but 30 per cent of those asked refuse to take part. A disproportionate number of those refusing are households from ethnic minorities, manual workers and the very rich. The result is that these households are under-represented in the FES, eventually distorting the RPI. The 'average household' which emerges from the FES does not, of course, exist in reality. Hence, no inflation rate based on this 'average household' is the same as the inflation rate for a given household. The government does publish inflation rates for a few different household groups, including pensioner households. Even then, no pensioner household will be exactly the same as the average pensioner household constructed from the FES. As a result, the rate of inflation for a given household can differ significantly from that implied by the RPI.

Mortgage payments and indirect taxes

Mortgage interest rates and indirect taxes are included in the main RPI measure. However, there are arguments which would support their exclusion. The argument in favour of inclusion is a simple one. Increases in mortgage payments and prices due to indirect tax changes are genuine price changes faced by households. Therefore they should be included in a measure of changes in average prices.

The arguments against are more complex. The main argument is that changes in mortgage interest rates, the main determinant of changes in mortgage payments, and changes in indirect taxes are political decisions by government. They do not reflect underlying trends in prices in the economy. Since the 1980s, changing interest rates has been the main way in which government has attempted to influence the level of aggregate (i.e. total, ☞ unit 33) demand in the economy. When aggregate demand is rising too fast and causing inflation to rise, as in 1988, the Bank of England has responded by increasing interest rates. However, these interest rates then feed through to higher mortgage repayments and a higher RPI. A policy designed to curb inflation in the long run has the perverse effect of increasing it in the short run. Increasing short run inflation can then influence wage bargaining, with unions demanding higher wage increases to compensate for higher inflation. This magnifies the short term increase in inflation.

As for changes in indirect taxes, again a rise in indirect tax which is designed to increase overall tax revenues and therefore reduce the government borrowing (the PSNCR) is likely to be taking place at a time when there are inflationary pressures in the economy. But these increases lead to higher inflation rates measured by the RPI. Even if the indirect tax increase is not designed primarily to help combat inflationary pressures - as was the case in 1979 when VAT was increased from 8 per cent to 15 per cent to finance large cuts in income tax, or in 1990 when the poll tax was introduced in England and Wales - it can give the RPI an unwanted upward twist which is then used as a bargaining tool by unions in pay negotiations.

What is more, there are methodological arguments against including mortgage interest payments in the RPI. Only one-quarter of households have a mortgage,

and yet mortgage payments were, until 1995, the only measure of changes in the cost of owning or renting a home in the RPI. In France and Italy, mortgage costs of owner-occupation are deliberately excluded from their indices. Instead, changes in rents are measured and from that a change in the cost of owning a home is imputed (i.e. estimated). On the other hand, the proportion of houses that are rented in France and Italy is nearly twice as high as in the UK and hence rents are a more reliable statistic to include in the index than in the UK.

Since 1995, the importance of mortgage payments has been lessened by the inclusion of a measure of the cost to homeowners of keeping their houses in good condition. This has been assumed to be in proportion to the price of a house. Hence, house price changes now feed directly into the rate of inflation.

Figure 28.3 shows three different measures of inflation. The RPI includes both mortgage payments and indirect taxes. The RPIX excludes mortgage payments but includes indirect taxes. The RPIY excludes both mortgage payments and indirect taxes. The RPIX and RPIY are sometimes referred to as measures of the UNDERLYING RATE OF INFLATION, as opposed to the RPI which is called the HEADLINE RATE OF INFLATION. The RPI is the headline rate because it is the measure which tends to be quoted in newspapers and on television and radio. The RPIX and the RPIY are underlying rates because they give a more reliable measure of trends in inflation over time.

As can be seen from Figure 28.3, there are considerable differences in value of inflation depending upon which measure is used. In 1997, when the government made the Bank of England responsible for the operation of monetary policy (☞ unit 36) and the setting of interest rates, it gave the Bank of England a target rate of inflation to be achieved. This target was expressed as RPIX and not the RPI. The government therefore was acknowledging that interest rate policy could distort the true rate of inflation and that an underlying measure of inflation was perhaps a more appropriate target.

Annual % change in RPI, RPIX and RPIY

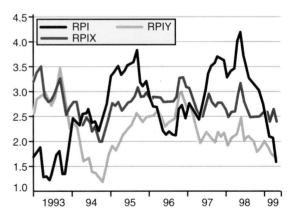

Source: adapted from Datastream/ICV; ONS; Reuters.
Figure 28.3 *Inflation rates*

Inflation

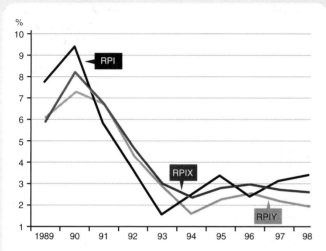

Figure 28.4 *Different measures of inflation, RPI, RPIX and RPIY; % change on previous year*
Source: adapted from *Economic Trends*, Office for National Statistics.

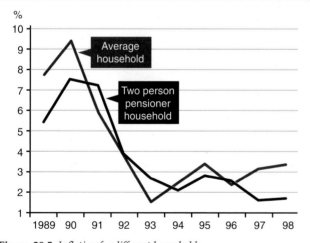

Figure 28.5 *Inflation for different households*
Source: adapted from *Economic Trends*, Office for National Statistics.

1. **What is meant by 'inflation'?**
2. **Explain different ways in which inflation might be measured.**
3. **How might each of the following have been affected by inflation in the 1990s: (a) a UK pensioner who retired in 1989 with a company pension which remained the same and a state pension which increased in line with changes in the RPI; (b) a UK 'technofreak' who loves everything from computers to hi-fi equipment to cars; (c) a homeowner in England with a £70 000 mortgage; (d) a food shopper in Brazil?**

The RPI

What exactly does the UK RPI measure? Each year, items are added to the basket of goods used in the calculation of the index and each year items are removed. You won't find corsets, rabbits or men's cardigans in the index any more, but you will find PCs, television sets and air fares. What's more, when the same item stays in the index, its specification may well change. This isn't true for potatoes, but it is true for, say, cameras. Thirty years ago, few cameras had a built in flash. Today, even the cheapest cameras come with flash as a standard feature. Forty years ago, cars didn't come with carpets as standard, but today they do. As for computers, whose specification became more powerful by the year and month in the 1990s, how can the RPI hope to reflect such changes?

Does it matter that the basket of goods is constantly changing? The simple answer is yes. By changing the composition of the index, statisticians are not measuring the change in price of a fixed and unchanging basket of goods. Instead, they are attempting to measure changes in prices of how we spend our money. Presumably, we now buy, say, trousers rather than corsets, chicken rather than rabbits or sweatshirts rather than cardigans because we prefer to do so. The amount of satisfaction to be gained from consuming some items rather than others is greater. So changes represent an increase in our living standards, the equivalent of a falling cost of living. As for increases in quality in goods, a failure to take these into account means that we overestimate the price paid for goods over time. When a company puts a flash into a new model and sells it for the same price as an old model without flash, prices have fallen, but the RPI is unlikely to pick this up.

Inflation in Brazil

Before the conquest of hyper-inflation in Brazil in 1994, both Brazilian retailers and shoppers behaved in ways which seem strange today. Workers would be paid either at the end of the week or the end of the month. With prices going up every day, consumers would rush out with their pay packets and spend as much as they could afford. So retailers became used to sharp peaks in spending at the end of each week and a very large peak at the end of the month. There was little shopping around by consumers because they found it so difficult to keep up with changing prices. They had little or no idea what was a good price and what was expensive on any single shopping expedition. As for retailers, they often made their profit not from sales but from getting free credit. They would receive goods on credit, sell them immediately, but only have to pay in 30 or 60 days time. In the meantime, they could put the money in the bank and earn interest linked to the rate of inflation. In a good month, with inflation of say, 100 per cent, they could double their money.

Summary

1. Unemployment is a stock concept, measuring the number of people out of work at a point in time.
2. Unemployment will increase if the number of workers losing jobs is greater than the number of people gaining jobs.
3. The costs of unemployment include financial costs to the unemployed, to taxpayers, and to local and national economies. They also include non-financial costs such as possible increased vandalism or increased suicides.

The measurement of unemployment

Unemployment, the number of people out of work, is measured at a point in time. It is a **stock concept** (☞ unit 45). However, the level of unemployment will change over time. Millions of people seek jobs each year in the UK. Young people leave school, college or university seeking work. Former workers who have taken time out of the workforce, for instance to bring up children, seek to return to work. Workers who have lost their jobs, either because they have resigned or because they have been made redundant, search for new jobs. Equally, millions of workers lose their jobs. They may retire, or leave work to look after children or they may resign or be made redundant from existing jobs.

Unemployment in an economy with a given labour force will fall if the number of workers gaining jobs is greater than the number of people losing jobs. In 1998, for instance, between 228 000 and 301 000 workers a month lost their jobs. However, the numbers gaining jobs were slightly higher per month than the numbers losing jobs. The result was a net fall in unemployment over the year. This flow of workers into or out of the stock of unemployed workers is summarised in Figure 29.1.

Unemployment will also increase if there is a rise in the number of people seeking work but the number of jobs in the economy remains static. During most years in the 1970s and 1980s, there was a rise in the number of school leavers entering the job market as well as more women wanting a job in the UK. It can be argued that at least some of the increase in unemployment in these two decades was a reflection of the inability of the UK economy to provided sufficient new jobs for those extra workers in the labour force.

The costs of unemployment

Long term unemployment is generally considered to be a great social evil. This is perhaps not surprising in view of the following costs of unemployment.

Costs to the unemployed and their dependants The people who are likely to lose the most from

unemployment are the unemployed themselves. One obvious cost is the loss of income that could have been earned had the person been in a job. Offset against this is the value of any benefits that the worker might receive and any value placed on the extra leisure time which an unemployed person has at his or her disposal. For most unemployed it is likely that they will be net financial losers.

The costs to the unemployed, however, do not finish there. Evidence suggests that unemployed people and

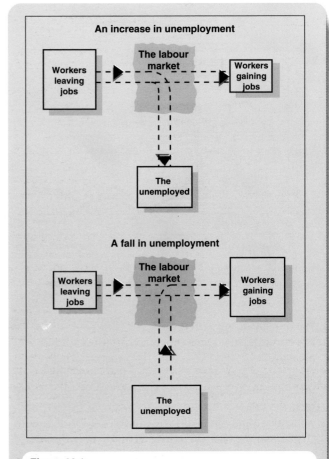

Figure 29.1

Question 1

Table 29.1 *Unemployment flows, 1999*

		Thousands
	Inflow	Outflow
January	274.0	193.5
February	279.1	287.0
March	258.4	293.7
April	249.9	278.6
May	242.2	282.8
June	240.6	274.0
July	295.8	275.3

Source: adapted from *Labour Market Trends*, Office for National Statistics.

(a) In which months did unemployment: (i) increase; and
(ii) decrease? Explain your answer.
(b) Explain whether unemployment was higher or lower
in July 1999 than in January 1999.
(c) Suggest why the numbers becoming unemployed fall
during the spring and summer, but there is a sudden
rise in inflows to unemployment in July.

their families suffer in a number of other ways. One simple but very important problem for them is the stigma of being unemployed. Unemployment is often equated with failure both by the unemployed themselves and by society in general. Many feel degraded by the whole process of signing on, receiving benefit and not being able to support themselves or their families. Studies suggest that the unemployed suffer from a wide range of social problems including above average incidence of stress, marital breakdown, suicide, physical illness and mental instability, and that they have higher death rates.

For the short term unemployed, the costs are relatively low. Many will lose some earnings, although a few who receive large redundancy payments may benefit financially from having lost their job. The social and psychological costs are likely to be limited too.

However, the long term unemployed are likely to be major losers on all counts. The long term unemployed suffer one more cost. Evidence suggests that the longer the period out of work, the less likely it is that the unemployed person will find a job. There are two reasons for this. First, being out of work reduces the human capital of workers. They lose work skills and are not being trained in the latest developments in their occupation. Second, employers use length of time out of work as a crude way of sifting through applicants for a job. For an employer, unemployment is likely to mean that the applicant is, to some extent, deskilled. There is a fear that the unemployed worker will not be capable of doing the job after a spell of unemployment. It could show that the worker has personality problems and might be a disruptive employee. It could also be an indication that other employers have turned down the applicant for previous jobs and hence it would be rational to save time and not consider the applicant for this job. The long term unemployed are then in a catch-22 situation. They can't get a job unless they have recent employment experience. But they can't get recent employment experience until

they get a job.

Costs to local communities Costs to local communities are more difficult to establish. Some have suggested that unemployment, particularly amongst the young, leads to increased crime, violence on the streets and vandalism. Areas of high unemployment tend to become run down. Shops go out of business. Households have no spare money to look after their properties and their gardens. Increased vandalism further destroys the environment.

Costs to taxpayers The cost to the taxpayer is a heavy one. On the one hand, government has to pay out increased benefits. On the other hand, government loses revenue because these workers would have paid taxes if they had been employed. For instance, they would have paid income tax and National Insurance contributions on their earnings. They would also have paid more in VAT and excise duties because they would have been able to spend more. So taxpayers not only pay more taxes to cover for increased government spending but they also have to pay more because they have to make up the taxes that the unemployed would have paid if they had been in work.

Costs to the economy as a whole Taxpayers paying money to the unemployed is not a loss for the economy as a whole. It is a **transfer payment** which redistributes existing resources within the economy. The actual loss to the whole economy is two-fold. Firstly there is the loss of output which those workers now unemployed could have produced had they been in work. The economy could have produced more goods and services which would then have been available for consumption. Secondly there are the social costs such as increased violence and depression which are borne by the unemployed and the communities in which they live.

Question 2

In a study of 6 000 employed and unemployed workers, a team of academics found that the unemployed had poor psychological health. They were more likely to be depressed, less likely to mix with people in work and had little access to social support networks or to information about jobs. One of the team, Richard Lampard of Warwick University, concluded that unemployment directly increases the risk of marriage break-up, finding that the chances of the marriage of an unemployed person ending in the following year are 70 per cent higher than those of a person who has never been out of work. The study also found that men in low-paid insecure jobs suffered almost the same level of psychological distress as those who were out of work altogether. It was found that there was a close correlation between perceived job security and psychological well-being. Women were found to be just as distressed by lack of paid work, but less affected by the prospect of an insecure low-paid job.

(a) What problems face the unemployed, according to
the article?
(b) Why might these problems give rise to costs not just
for the unemployed but also for society as a whole?

Applied economics

Measures of unemployment

In economic theory, the unemployed are defined as those without a job but who are seeking work at current wage rates. Measuring the number of unemployed in an economy, however, is more difficult than economic theory might suggest. There are two basic ways in which unemployment can be calculated.

- Government can undertake a survey of the population to identify the employed and the unemployed. This is the approach taken in countries such as the USA, Japan and Sweden. There is a measure of such unemployment based upon a standard produced by the International Labour Organisation (ILO). In the UK, monthly **ILO unemployment** figures are produced.

- The government can count all those who register as unemployed. In some countries a register of the unemployed is kept by trade unions because unemployment benefit is linked with union membership. In the UK, before 1982, the official monthly unemployment count was based on the numbers who had signed on at Jobcentres. The count was then changed to those who were claiming benefit for being unemployed from the Department of Social Security (DSS). This measure of unemployment is called the **claimant count**.

Unemployment is expressed in two ways. It can be stated as an absolute figure, as millions of workers. Or it can be stated as a relative measure, as a percentage of the workforce, the **unemployment rate**. Expressing it in millions gives a clear indication of the numbers affected by unemployment. Expressing it as percentage is better when the number of workers in the economy is changing. For instance, using absolute figures to compare US unemployment with UK unemployment may not be helpful because there are about five times as many workers in the US as in the UK. Comparing it as a percentage allows a more meaningful comparison to be made. Equally, the size of the workforce is likely to change over time. In 1950 in the UK, there were 23.7 million in the labour force of which 0.4 million were unemployed on a claimant count basis. In 1998, there were 28.8 million in the labour force of which 1.3 million were unemployed. Unemployment was much higher in 1998, but so too was the size of the workforce.

The claimant count

Until 1997, the main measure of UK unemployment was the claimant count. However, the claimant count figure had come under increasing criticism because it was felt to be open to government manipulation. In the 1980s and 1990s, the UK government introduced over

30 different changes to the way in which the claimant count was calculated, most of which served to reduce the numbers officially unemployed. For instance, the change from counting those looking for work at Jobcentres to those receiving benefits led to an estimated 200 000 fall in measured unemployment. Those lost from the unemployment count were mainly women who were looking for work, but were not entitled to claim any benefits. In 1988, 16-17 year olds were no longer able to claim benefit for being unemployed on the grounds that they were all guaranteed a place either in education or on a training scheme if they weren't in work. In 1996, unemployment benefit was cut from 12 months to 6 months, which removed many women from the unemployment register who were then not able to claim other social security payments for being out of work. Not only was the claimant count open to manipulation but it was also not an internationally recognised way of measuring unemployment. Hence, it could not be used to compare UK unemployment levels with those in other countries.

ILO unemployment

In 1998, the newly elected Labour government decided to make the ILO count the main measure of unemployment in the UK. ILO unemployment figures had been collected first on a biannual (once every two years) basis in 1973, and then annually from 1984. In 1993, it became a quarterly count and since 1997 has been monthly. The ILO count is taken from a wider survey of employment called the Labour Force Survey (LFS). 60 000 households, with over 100 000 adults, are surveyed. The questionnaire used covers household size and structure, accommodation details, basic demographic characteristics, such as age, sex, marital status and ethnic origin, and economic activity. To be counted as unemployed, an individual has to be without a paid job, be available to start a job within a fortnight and has either looked for work at some time in the previous four weeks or been waiting to start a job already obtained.

ILO unemployment compared to the claimant count

Figure 29.2 shows that ILO unemployment figures differ significantly from claimant count figures. ILO unemployment tends to be above claimant count unemployment in a recovery and boom situation, but in a recession the claimant count figure can be above the ILO measure.

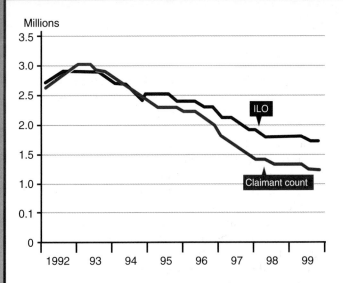

Figure 29.2 *ILO and claimant count measures of employment[1]*
Source: adapted from *Labour Market Trends*, Office for National Statistics.
1. Before 1995, ILO figures are for Great Britain, and from 1995 for the UK.

ILO unemployment is likely to be above the claimant count figure because the claimant count excludes a number of key groups of unemployed workers.

- Many female unemployed workers are actively looking for work (and are therefore included in ILO unemployment) but are not entitled to benefits for being unemployed. For instance, they might not have built up sufficient National Insurance contributions to qualify for unemployment benefit, a National Insurance benefit. They may also be living in a household where the husband or partner is earning too high a wage for them to qualify for means tested benefit.
- Older, particularly male, workers in their 50s and 60s may be collecting a pension from their previous employer or be supported financially by their spouse. They are therefore not entitled to benefits but may be actively seeking work.
- Workers are not entitled to register as unemployed with the DSS until they have been out of work for a number of weeks. However, anyone interviewed for the ILO count who is unemployed and is looking for work is counted as unemployed regardless of how long they have been unemployed.

The claimant count, however, may include some unemployed who would not be included in the ILO count. For instance, those working in the **hidden economy** (☞ unit 25) may claim benefits for being unemployed but actually be in work, usually as a self employed worker.

Both the ILO and claimant counts could be argued to underestimate overall unemployment.

- They do not include part time workers who are actively seeking full time work, for instance.

- Those on government training and work schemes who would prefer to be in proper employment are not included. This particularly affects young workers.
- There are some out of work who are not actively seeking work or receiving benefits for being unemployed but who would take a job if offered. This mainly applies to women bringing up families. Table 29.2 illustrates this point. Between 1993 and 1999, ILO unemployment fell by 1.2 million whilst the total in employment increased by 1.8 million.

However, both measures of unemployment could be argued to overestimate unemployment. Some of those out of work find it almost impossible to get a job. Those with physical and mental disabilities, some ex-criminals or some with no qualifications find the job market very difficult. Some economists would argue that these workers are unemployable and therefore should not be counted as unemployed. A minority of those working in the hidden economy may claim benefits and may declare on surveys that they are out of work and seeking work.

Table 29.2 *Employment and unemployment, UK, 1993-99, Spring each year, seasonally adjusted*

		Millions
	Total in employment	ILO unemployed
1993	25.6	3.0
1994	25.8	2.8
1995	26.0	2.5
1996	26.3	2.4
1997	26.8	2.1
1998	27.0	1.8
1999	27.4	1.8

Source: adapted from *Labour Market Trends*, Office for National Statistics.

Unemployed men and women display unemployment figures outside the House of Commons.

Unemployment in coal mining areas

The collapse of the coal industry saw a quarter of a million jobs disappear in two decades. The economic devastation was awesome: gross domestic product in the sub-region of South Yorkshire fell by almost a fifth in real terms in 20 years. Effects are concentrated. Average household income on a Barnsley estate which once lived off coal is only £5 500 a year, against a Barnsley average of £11 000. In the whole Yorkshire and Humber region the average is £18 300.

In the worst affected coal mining communities, low income is just one facet of the problems they face. Educational achievement is low. Drugs are rife. Houses are abandoned and boarded up. Crime is endemic. Younger people are moving away. Barnsley, Doncaster, Rotherham and Wakefield expect to lose 14.4 per cent, 9.2 per cent, 15.9 per cent and 15.2 per cent respectively of their 18-29 year olds by 2016.

Job regeneration is patchy. For instance, the Dean and Chapter pit in Ferryhill, County Durham, employed 1 074 miners until it shut. Today, only 50 people are employed at three firms on the site. The cost of setting up these jobs was £40 000 in land acquisition, £108 485 for the building of small factory units (part of which was financed through government grants), £4 100 in related staff costs and £1 136 for development planning. When

the Robin Hood railway line between Derby and Nottingham was reopened in 1998, many young people in depressed former coal mining areas along its path saw it as a means of escaping the unemployment and poverty which had dogged them. Many former colliery sites are still awaiting redevelopment whilst former miners remain unemployed.

Source: adapted from The *Guardian*, 22.9.1999.

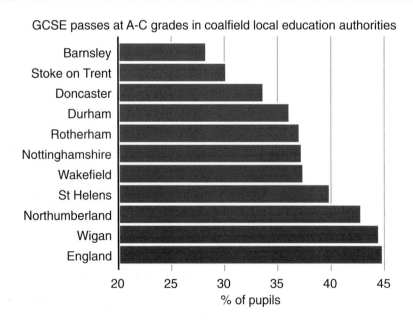

GCSE passes at A-C grades in coalfield local education authorities

- Barnsley
- Stoke on Trent
- Doncaster
- Durham
- Rotherham
- Nottinghamshire
- Wakefield
- St Helens
- Northumberland
- Wigan
- England

20   25   30   35   40   45

% of pupils

Figure 29.3 *Qualifications in coal mining areas*
Source: adapted from DFEE.

1. Suggest what has been the cost of pit closures to: (a) the miners made unemployed; (b) non-miners who live in former coal mining communities; (c) taxpayers; (d) the economy as a whole.

2. Discuss whether the government should spend money on the industrial regeneration of former coal mining areas or whether it should encourage unemployed workers in these areas to move to find new jobs. In your answer, discuss the costs and benefits of each alternative.

Summary

1. The balance of payments accounts are split into two parts. The current account records payments for the exports and imports of goods and services. The capital account records saving, investment and speculative flows of money.
2. The current account is split into two parts: trade in visibles and trade in invisibles.
3. The balance of payments accounts must always balance. However, component parts of the accounts may be positive or negative. If there is a surplus on the current account, then outflows on the capital account must be greater than inflows.
4. A current account surplus is often seen as a sign of a healthy economy, whilst a current account deficit is seen as a cause for worry. But current account deficits are not necessarily bad as they may be a sign of borrowing which could finance expansion.
5. A current account deficit is most unlikely to be financed by government. The balance of payments deficit and the government deficit are two completely different entities.

The balance of payments

The BALANCE OF PAYMENTS ACCOUNT is a record of all financial dealings over a period of time between economic agents of one country and all other countries. Balance of payments accounts can be split into two components:
- the CURRENT ACCOUNT where payments for the purchase and sale of goods and services are recorded;
- the CAPITAL ACCOUNT where flows of money associated with saving, investment, speculation and currency stabilisation are recorded.

Flows of money into the country are given a positive (+) sign on the accounts. Flows of money out of the country are given a negative (-) sign.

The current account

The current account on the balance of payments is itself split into two components.

Visibles VISIBLES are the trade in goods, from raw materials to semi-manufactured products to manufactured goods. Visible EXPORTS are goods which are sold to foreigners. Goods leave the country, whilst payment for these goods goes in the opposite direction. Hence visible exports of, say, cars result in an **inward** flow of money and are recorded with a positive sign on the balance of payments account. Visible IMPORTS are goods which are bought by domestic residents from foreigners. Goods come into the country whilst money **flows out**. Hence visible imports of, say, wheat are given a minus sign on the balance of payments. The difference between visible exports and visible imports is known as the BALANCE OF TRADE.

Invisibles INVISIBLES are made up of trade in services, investment income and other payments and receipts. A wide variety of services is traded internationally, including financial services such as banking and insurance, transport services such as shipping and air

travel, and tourism. Income results from the loan of factors of production abroad. For instance, a British teacher working in Saudi Arabia and sending back money to his family in England would create an invisible import for Saudi Arabia and an invisible export for Britain. Similarly, a Japanese company repatriating profits made from a factory based in Britain back to Japan would create an invisible import for the UK and an invisible export for Japan. Payments might be in the form of a UK contribution to EU funds and receipts may include EU subsidies to the UK.

The easiest way to distinguish between invisible exports and imports, or invisible **credits** and invisible **debits** as they are known in the official UK balance of payments account, is to consider flows of money rather than flows of services. The British teacher in Saudi Arabia is sending money back to the UK. An inflow of money means that this is classified as an export. The Japanese company repatriating profits is sending money out of the UK. An outflow of money means that this is classified as an import. The difference between invisible exports and

Question 1

A country has the following international transactions on current account:
exports of manufactured goods £20bn; imports of food £10bn; earnings from foreign tourists £5bn; interest, profits and dividends paid to foreigners £4bn; purchase of oil from abroad £8bn; earnings of nationals working overseas which are repatriated £7bn; sale of coal to foreign countries £2bn; payments by foreigners to domestic financial institutions for services rendered £1bn.

(a) Which of these items are: (i) visible exports; (ii) visible imports; (iii) invisible exports; (iv) invisible imports?
(b) Calculate: (i) the balance of trade; (ii) the balance on invisible trade; (iii) the current balance.
(c) How would your answers to (b) be different if it cost the country £3bn to transport its exports (i) in its own ships and (ii) in the ships of other countries?

invisible imports is known as the BALANCE ON
INVISIBLE TRADE or NET INVISIBLES.

The CURRENT BALANCE is the difference between
total exports (visible and invisible) and total imports. It
can also be calculated by adding the balance of trade to
the balance on invisible trade.

Current account deficits

The balance of payments account shows all the inflows of
money to and the outflows of money from a country.
Inflows must equal outflows overall and therefore the
balance of payments must always balance. This is no
different from a household. All the money going out from a
household in spending or saving over a period of time must
equal money coming in from earnings, borrowings or
running down of savings. If a household spends £60 going
out for a meal, the money must have come from somewhere.

However, there can be surpluses or deficits on particular
parts of the account. Using the example of the household
again, it can spend more than it earns if it borrows money.
The same is true of a national economy. It can spend more
on goods and services than it earns if it borrows money
from overseas. So it can have a CURRENT ACCOUNT
DEFICIT, where exports are less than imports, by running
a surplus on its capital account. Equally, it can run a
CURRENT ACCOUNT SURPLUS, exporting more than it
imports, by running a deficit on its capital account. A
deficit on the capital account for the UK means that it
invests more abroad than foreigners invest in the UK.

Often, the media talk about a 'balance of payments
deficit'. Strictly speaking, there can never be a balance of
payments deficit because the balance of payments must
always balance, i.e. it must always be zero. What the
media are, in fact, referring to is either a balance of trade
deficit or a current account deficit. Similarly, the term
'**trade gap**' is a term used in the media, usually to mean a
deficit on the balance of trade in goods.

The size of current account deficits

Current account deficits are generally seen as undesirable
and a sign of economic weakness. Conversely, current
account surpluses are usually seen as signs of the
economic strength of a country. This, though, is a very
crude way of analysing the balance of payments. One
reason why this is crude is because the size of the current
account surplus or deficit is important in deciding its
significance. Using the analogy of the household again, if
the income of a household is £100 000 per year and its
spending over the year is £100 010, it has overspent. But
overspending by £10 on an income of £100 000 in one year
is of almost no significance. On the other hand, take a
household living solely from state benefits. If income is
£60 per week, and spending is £70, then this household is
likely to be in serious trouble. Unless it has substantial
savings to draw on, overspending £10 each week on an
income of £60 will soon become unsustainable. Where
will the £10 per week come from? If it is from borrowing,
then the money must eventually be repaid, eating into a

very low income.

This is also the case for a national economy. If the
country runs a current account deficit year after year, but
this current account deficit is very small in relation to
national income over time, then it is of little significance
economically. Equally, if a country runs a large deficit
over a short period of time, but then follows this with a
large surplus over the next period, then it is relatively
unimportant. Only if the current account deficit or
surplus is large in relation to income and is sustained over
a period of time does it really matter.

Large sustained current account deficits

Large sustained current account deficits are usually
considered undesirable because they become
unsustainable. Deficits on the current account may occur
because the government of a country spends excessively on
foreign goods and services. Or it could be private firms and
individuals which are spending too much, importing far
more than they are exporting. Whether it is government or
the private sector, the current account deficit has to be
financed. Either the level of borrowings abroad is increased
or there is a net run down in savings and investments held
abroad. Governments and firms can borrow abroad so long
as foreign lenders think that they can repay the loans with
interest in the future. But if the current account deficit is
large and sustained, there usually comes a point when
lenders think that the borrowers may **default** on their loans
(i.e. not pay them). Lenders then stop lending. At this
point, the country is in serious difficulties.

Countries like Poland, Brazil and Uganda in the 1980s,
and Thailand and South Korea in the 1990s, have all faced
this **credit crunch**, the point at which foreign lenders
refuse to lend any more. They are then forced to return
their current account to equilibrium. This means cutting
down on imports, or exporting more goods which
previously might have been sold on the domestic market.
Citizens therefore have fewer goods available to them and
their consumption and standard of living falls.

If the economy is fundamentally strong, the adjustment
will be painful but relatively short, lasting just a few years
perhaps. For countries which have very weak economies,
the credit crunch can have a negative impact for decades. In
sub-Saharan Africa, the credit crunch which occurred in the
early 1980s led to Western banks and other agencies refusing
to lend significant sums for the next 20 years. This crippled
the economies of certain countries and deprived them of
foreign funds which could have helped them to grow.

However, large sustained current account deficits may
be beneficial to an economy. It depends on its rate of
economic growth (☞ unit 26). If an economy is growing
at 3 per cent per annum, but is running a large current
account deficit of 5 per cent of GDP per annum, then it
will run into problems. Its foreign debt as a percentage of
GDP will grow over time. But if the economy is growing
at 10 per cent per annum, and there is a current account
deficit of 5 per cent of GDP, accumulated foreign debt as a
percentage of GDP is likely to fall. Although foreign debt
in absolute terms will be growing, the income of the
country available to repay it will be growing even faster.
Countries like the USA in the nineteenth century, and

South Korea and Malaysia in the late part of the twentieth century, have all run significant current account deficits over a period of time, but they have tended to benefit from this because the money has been used to strengthen their growth potential. Even so, both South Korea and Malaysia were caught up in a credit crunch in the late 1990s when foreign lenders judged that too much had been lent to East Asian economies. High levels of foreign borrowing carry risks for a country even when their economies are highly successful on measures of **national economic performance** (☞ unit 24) such as economic growth, unemployment and inflation.

Question 2

Poland has been one of the few success stories of Eastern Europe in the 1990s. During the decade, it progressively transformed its economy from an inefficient command economy, where the state dominated every economic decision, to one where markets were allowed to allocate resources. In the early 1990s, Poland found it difficult to borrow money abroad, but in the late 1990s its fast economic growth gave it access to foreign capital markets.

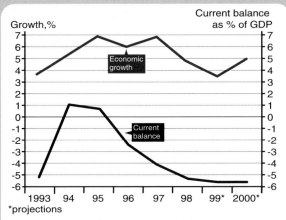

Figure 30.1 *Poland: economic growth (%) and current account balance as a percentage of GDP*
Source: adapted from *Economic Outlook*, OECD.

(a) Use the data to explain why Poland has been a success story in the 1990s.
(b) Discuss whether its large current account deficits for most of the period is a problem for Poland.

Large sustained current account surpluses

Some countries run large sustained current account surpluses. By exporting more than they import over a long period of time, these countries increase their net foreign wealth. This has the benefit that the economy then should receive ever increasing amounts of income from that wealth, which can be used to buy more foreign goods and services than would otherwise be the case. This is like a household which consistently saves money. In the long term, it can use the interest on that saving to buy more goods than it would otherwise have been able to afford.

A sustained current account surplus may also make sense if there are long term structural changes occurring.

Japan ran large current account surpluses during the last quarter of the twentieth century, consequently building up its net wealth overseas. However, in the first half of the twenty first century, the structure of the Japanese population will change dramatically. From having very few pensioners in proportion to workers, the population will age significantly and there will be a high proportion of pensioners to workers. It could well be that Japan will run down its wealth overseas to pay for the goods and services consumed by non-productive pensioners. Japan could therefore move from having sustained current account surpluses to current account deficits.

Large sustained current account surpluses have their disadvantages though. First, they reduce what is available for consumption now. If the surplus were eliminated, resources used for exports could be diverted to produce goods for domestic consumption. Or the country could increase imports, again increasing the amount available for consumption.

Second, sustained current account surpluses cause friction between countries. If Japan has a current account surplus, the rest of the world must have a deficit. If Japan is a net lender, building up wealth overseas, the rest of the world must be a net borrower, building up debts overseas. Countries which attempt to reduce their current account deficits can only be successful if other countries reduce their current account surpluses. On a microeconomic level, trade unions and firms in deficit countries often accuse firms in surplus countries of 'poaching' jobs. If Japan reduced its trade surplus by reducing exports to the United States, then firms in the United States might be able to fill the gap created by expanding their output.

In practice, the benefits to one country of another country reducing its surplus are likely to be small. If Japan's exports fall, US producers are just as likely to find that other countries like South Korea or the UK fill the market gap as them. When the USA has a large current account deficit and Japan a large surplus, a reduction in the Japanese surplus will improve the current account positions of many countries around the world, not just that of the USA. The benefit of a large reduction in the Japanese surplus to any single country, even to the USA, the largest economy in the world, will be relatively small.

Government deficits and balance of payments deficits

One very common fallacy is to equate current account deficits with government deficits (the PSNCR ☞ unit 36). Most transactions on the balance of payments are made by private individuals and firms. If the country is a net borrower, it is more than likely that this is because private individuals and firms have borrowed more from foreigners than they have lent to foreigners. There is a relationship between government borrowing and the current account deficit but the relationship is complicated, and it could well be the case that the public sector might be in surplus domestically when the current account was in deficit. So the current account deficit is **not** a government deficit in any sense.

Question 3

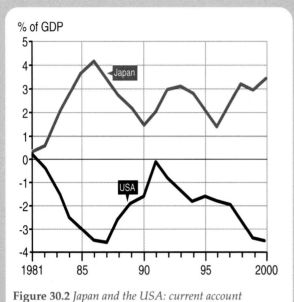

% of GDP

Figure 30.2 *Japan and the USA: current account balances as a percentage of GDP*
Source: adapted from *Economic Outlook*, OECD.

(a) Compare the current account balance of the USA with that of Japan during the 1980s and 1990s.
(b) Discuss the possible benefits and costs to Japan of running a persistent current account surplus.

key terms

Balance of payments account - a record of all financial dealings over a period of time between economic agents of one country and all other countries.
Balance of trade - visible exports minus visible imports.
Balance on invisible trade or net invisibles - invisible exports minus invisible imports.
Capital account - that part of the balance of payments account where flows of savings, investment and currency are recorded.
Current account - that part of the balance of payments account where payments for the purchase and sale of goods and services are recorded.
Current balance - the difference between total exports (visible and invisible) and total imports. It can also be calculated by adding the balance of trade to the balance on invisible trade.
Current account deficit or surplus - a deficit exists when imports are greater than exports; a surplus exists when exports are greater than imports.
Exports - goods and services produced domestically and sold to foreigners. Payments for exports come into the country.
Imports - goods and services purchased from foreign producers. Payments for imports that leave the country.
Invisibles - trade in services, transfers of income and other payments or receipts.
Visibles - trade in goods.

Applied economics

The UK current account

The parts of the current account

The Office for National Statistics divides the UK current account into four parts, shown in Table 30.1.
● Trade in goods. Exports of goods minus imports of goods is equal to the balance of trade in goods.
● Trade in services. The main services traded are transport (such as shipping or air transport), travel and tourism, insurance and other financial services, and royalties and licence fees.
● Income. Some countries, such as Pakistan or Egypt, earn substantial amounts from the repatriation of income from nationals working abroad. For the UK, such income is relatively unimportant. Nearly all income in the UK balance of payments accounts relates to UK investments abroad and to foreign investments in the UK (investment income).
● Current transfers. Most current transfers relate to the UK's membership of the European Union. The UK has to pay part of its tax revenues to the EU, but in return receives payments such as agricultural subsidies or regional grants.

Visibles in the account are the trade in goods. Invisibles are the trade in services, income and current transfers. In terms of relative size, invisibles outweigh visibles. The most important invisible is not trade in services but income. Current transfers are relatively insignificant. The UK's current balance is therefore crucially dependent not just on trade in goods and services, but also on income from foreign investments. Comparing this to a household, it is as if the financial soundness of the household is dependent not just on wage earnings and spending, but also very much on interest and dividends on savings and also on payments of interest on loans.

The current account over time

Since the Second World War, there has been a number of consistent trends on the UK current account.
● The balance of trade in goods has been negative, as can be seen from Figure 30.5. Visible exports have tended to be less than visible imports.

- The balance on invisible trade has been positive. Invisible credits (exports) have been greater than invisible debits (imports).
- Breaking down invisible trade, the balance of trade in services has always been positive - more services have been sold abroad than have been bought from abroad. The balance on income has usually been positive too. Income brought into the country by UK people living abroad and income earned from investments abroad have been greater than income leaving the country. However, the balance on income fluctuates much more from year to year than the balance of trade in services. Current transfers since the 1960s have always been negative. Since joining the EU in 1973, most of the negative balance is due to the UK paying more into EU coffers than receiving in grants.

The size of the current account balances

In the 1950s and 1960s, the current account posed a major problem for the UK. At the time, the value of the pound was fixed against other currencies. In years when the current account went into deficit, currency speculators tended to sell pounds sterling in the hope that the government would be forced to devalue the pound, i.e. make it less valuable against other currencies. So quite small current account deficits as a percentage of GDP, as in 1960 or in 1964, presented large problems for the government of the day.

From the 1970s, the value of the pound was allowed to float, changing from minute to minute on the foreign exchange markets. Figure 30.4 shows that there were two periods when the UK's current account position could have become unsustainable in the long term. In 1973-75, the UK along with most Western countries, suffered a severe economic shock from a rise in commodity prices, particularly oil prices. Following the Yom Kippur war of November 1973 between Egypt and Israel, the members of OPEC (☞ units 2 and 8) chose to restrict supply of oil to the west and as a result its price quadrupled. Import prices roses sharply and the current account approached 4 per cent of GDP in 1974. The UK government was forced to react by cutting domestic spending, which in turn reduced demand for imports. In 1986-89, there was another sharp deterioration in the current account due to the 'Lawson boom'. Fast increases in domestic spending led to sharp increases in imports. The fall in the current account deficit in the early 1990s came about because the government pushed the economy into recession. Spending fell and so imports fell too.

Over the long term, Figure 30.4 arguably shows that the UK does not have a current account problem. Years of deficit have been followed by years of surplus. There has also been no noticeable shift in the size of the individual balances which make up the current balance as can be seen from Figures 30.3. It is for this reason that UK governments since the 1980s have tended to ignore the current account position in decision making. Instead, growth, unemployment and inflation have been the key macroeconomic variables.

Table 30.1 *The current balance, 1998 (£m)*

Trade in goods		
Export of goods	163 704	
Import of goods	184 302	
Balance on trade in goods		- 20 598
Trade in services		
Export of services	61 777	
Import of services	49 099	
Balance of trade in services		12 678
Balance on trade in goods and services		- 7 920
Income		
Credits	114 145	
Debits	98 363	
Balance		15 782
Current transfers		
Credits	15 261	
Debits	21 649	
Balance		- 6 388
Current balance		1 474

Source: adapted from *Economic Trends*, Office for National Statistics.

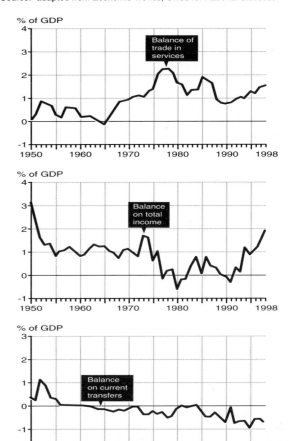

Figure 30.3 *Balances of trade in services, total income and current transfers as a percentage of GDP*

Source: adapted from *Economic Trends* and *Economic Trends Annual Supplement*, Office for National Statistics.

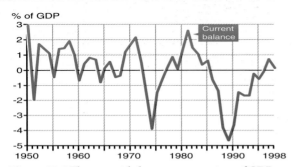

Figure 30.4 *The current balance as a percentage of GDP*
Source: adapted from *Economic Trends* and *Economic Trends Annual Supplement*, Office for National Statistics.

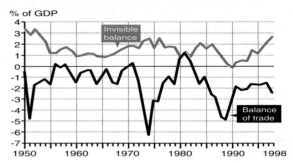

Figure 30.5 *The balance of trade in goods and the invisibles balance as a percentage of GDP*
Source: adapted from *Economic Trends* and *Economic Trends Annual Supplement*, Office for National Statistics.

DATA QUESTION

The trade gap

The trade gap at an all time high

The trade gap has reached an all time record. Never before has the UK seen such a large deficit. Britain's deteriorating external position is having severe economic consequences. With exports in deep trouble, British manufacturers are struggling for orders. There isn't a week that passes without a manufacturing firm announcing lay offs. This all helps contribute to the zero growth the UK is likely to experience this year.

Source: adapted from *The Sunday Times*, 30.5.1999.

Investment income: the mystery

The UK's investment income is growing. Why it should be doing so is a mystery because, since 1996, Britain has had growing net external liabilities. This means the value of its investment assets overseas are less than those of foreigners in the UK. Last year, the gap between the two was £58 billion, the equivalent of roughly £1 000 per person, quite a turnaround from 10 years before in 1988 when the UK had £51 billion more assets than liabilities. With net external liabilities, we ought to be paying out more in investment income than we receive. Obviously, UK investors are better at making a return on their overseas assets than foreign investors in the UK.

Source: adapted from *The Sunday Times*, 30.5.1999.

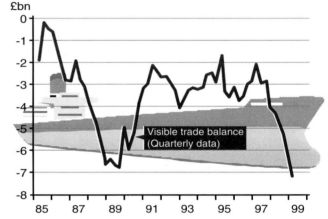

Figure 30.6 *Record deficit for the UK*
Source: adapted from Datastream.

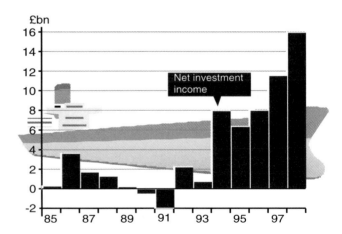

Figure 30.7 *Income balance; net investment income*
Source: adapted from Datastream.

1. Describe the changes in the balance of trade and total investment income shown in the data.
2. What might be the implications for the current account balance of the changes shown in the data?
3. Discuss the extent to which the deterioration in the 'trade gap' in the late 1990s might have been of economic significance.

unit 31 Consumption and saving

Summary

1. Consumption can be divided into spending on durable goods and non-durable goods.
2. The consumption function shows the relationship between consumption and its determinants, the main one being income.
3. Increases in wealth will lead to an increase in consumption.
4. Expected inflation tends to lead to a rise in saving and a fall in consumption. The effect of households attempting to restore the real value of their stock of savings more than outweighs the effect of households bringing forward their purchases of goods.
5. The rate of interest and the availability of credit particularly affect the consumption of durable goods.
6. A change in the structure of the population will affect both consumption and saving. The greater the proportion of adults aged 35-60 in the population, the higher is likely to be the level of saving.
7. Keynesians hypothesise that consumption is a stable function of current disposable income in the short run.
8. The life cycle hypothesis and the permanent income hypothesis both emphasise that consumption is a stable function of income only in the very long run. In the short run, other factors such as the rate of interest and wealth can have a significant impact upon consumption and savings.

Defining consumption and saving

CONSUMPTION in economics is spending on consumer goods and services over a period of time. Examples are spending on chocolate, hire of videos or buying a car. Consumption can be broken down into a number of different categories. One way of classifying consumption is to distinguish between spending on **goods** and spending on **services**. Another way is to distinguish between spending on DURABLE GOODS and NON-DURABLE GOODS. Durable goods are goods which, although bought at a point in time, continue to provide a stream of services over a period of time. A car, for instance, should last at least 6 years. A television set might last 10 years. Non-durable goods are goods and services which are used up immediately or over a short period of time, like an ice-cream or a packet of soap powder.

SAVING is what is not spent out of income. For instance, if a worker takes home £1 000 in her wage packet at the end of the month, but only spends £900, then £100 must have been saved. The saving might take the form of increasing the stock of cash, or an increase in money in a bank or building society account, or it might take the form of stocks or shares. Income in this case is DISPOSABLE INCOME, income including state benefits such as child benefit and interest on, say, building society shares, but after deductions of income tax and National Insurance contributions.

Consumption and income

There is a number of factors which determine how much a household consumes. The relationship between consumption and these factors is called the CONSUMPTION FUNCTION. The most important determinant of consumption is disposable income. Other factors, discussed in sections below, are far less important but can bring about small but significant changes in the relationship between consumption and income.

Assume that one year a household has an income of £1 000 per month. The next year, due to salary increases, this rises to £1 200 per month. Economic theory predicts that the consumption of the household will rise.

How much it will rise can be measured by the MARGINAL PROPENSITY TO CONSUME (MPC), the proportion of a change in income that is spent:

$$MPC = \frac{\text{Change in consumption}}{\text{Change in income}} = \frac{\Delta C}{\Delta Y}$$

where Y is income, C is consumption and Δ is 'change in'. If the £200 rise in income leads to a £150 rise in consumption, then the marginal propensity to consume would be 0.75 (£150 ÷ £200).

For the economy as a whole, the marginal propensity to consume is likely to be positive (i.e. greater than zero) but less than 1. Any rise in income will lead to more spending but also some saving too. For individuals, the marginal propensity to consume could be more than 1 if money was borrowed to finance spending higher than income.

The AVERAGE PROPENSITY TO CONSUME (or APC) measures the average amount spent on consumption out of total income. For instance, if total disposable income in an economy were £100 billion and consumption were £90 billion, then the average propensity to consume would be 0.9. The formula for the APC is:

$$APC = \frac{Consumption}{Income} = \frac{C}{Y}$$

In a rich industrialised economy, the APC is likely to be less than 1 because consumers will also save part of their earnings.

Question 1

Table 31.1

£bn at 1995 prices

	Consumption	Disposable income
1957	171.6	169.1
1958	176.4	172.3
1967	227.4	234.6
1968	233.8	238.9
1977	275.2	284.1
1978	290.1	305.2
1987	381.4	385.2
1988	410.4	405.5
1997	489.3	525.7
1998	502.5	525.8

Source: adapted from *Economic Trends, Economic Trends Annual Supplement*, Office for National Statistics.

(a) Using the data, explain the relationship between consumption and disposable income.
(b) (i) Calculate the MPC and the APC for 1958, 1968, 1978, 1988 and 1998.
    (ii) What happened to saving during these years?

Wealth

The wealth of a household is made up of two parts. **Physical wealth** is made up of items such as houses, cars and furniture. **Monetary wealth** comprises items such as cash, money in the bank and building societies, stocks and shares, assurance policies and pension rights.
If the wealth of a household increases, consumption will increase. This is known as the WEALTH EFFECT. There are two important ways in which the wealth of households can change over a short time period.

- A change in the price of houses. If the real price of houses increases considerably over a short period of time, as happened in the UK from 1998 to 2000, then households feel able to increase their spending. They do this mainly by borrowing more money secured against the value of their house.
- A change in the value of stocks and shares. Households react to an increase in the real value of a household's portfolio of securities by selling part of the portfolio and spending the proceeds. The value of stocks and shares is determined by many factors. One of these is the rate of interest. If the rate of interest falls, then the value of stocks will rise. So consumption should be stimulated through the wealth effect by a fall in the rate of interest.

Question 2

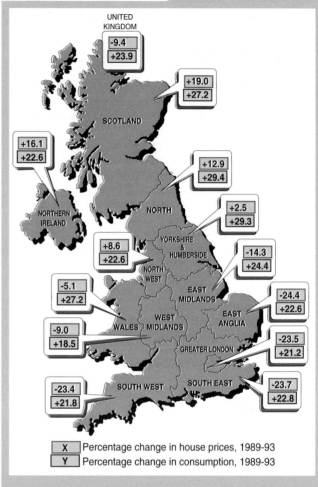

| X | Percentage change in house prices, 1989-93 |
| Y | Percentage change in consumption, 1989-93 |

Source: adapted from *Regional Trends*, Office for National Statistics.
Figure 31.1 *Percentage change in house prices and consumption, 1989-93*

(a) What happened to house prices between 1989 and 1993?
(b) To what extent do the data support the hypothesis that wealth is a determinant of consumption? In your answer you will need to compare how consumption changed in those years when house prices fell with those when they rose.

Inflation

Inflation, a rise in the general level of prices, has two effects on consumption. First, if households expect prices to be higher in the future they will be tempted to bring forward their purchases. For instance, if households know that the price of cars will go up by 10 per cent the next month, they will attempt to buy their cars now. So expectations of inflation increase consumption and reduce saving.

However, this can be outweighed by the effect of inflation on wealth. Rising inflation tends to erode the real value of money wealth. Households react to this by attempting to restore the real value of their wealth (i.e. they save more). This reduces consumption.

Overall, rising inflation in the UK tends to reduce consumption. The negative effect on consumption caused by the erosion of real wealth more than offsets the positive effect on consumption caused by the bringing forward of purchases.

The rate of interest

Households rarely finance expenditure on **non-durables** such as food or entertainment by borrowing money. However, much of the money to buy **durables** such as cars, furniture, kitchen equipment and hi-fi equipment comes from credit finance. An increase in the rate of interest increases the monthly repayments on these goods. This means that, effectively, the price of the goods has increased. Households react to this by reducing their demand for durables and thus cutting their consumption.

Many households also have borrowed money to buy their houses. Increased interest rates lead to increased mortgage repayments. Again, this will directly cut spending on other items and perhaps, more importantly, discourage households from borrowing more money to finance purchases of consumer durables.

It has already been explained above that a rise in the rate of interest reduces the value of stocks on stock markets and thus reduces the value of household wealth. This in turn leads to a fall in consumption.

The availability of credit

The rate of interest determines the price of credit. However, the price of credit is not the only determinant of how much households borrow. Governments in the past have often imposed restrictions on the availability of credit. For instance, they have imposed maximum repayment periods and minimum deposits. Before the deregulation of the mortgage market in the early 1980s in the UK, building societies rationed mortgages. They often operated queueing systems and imposed restrictive limits on the sums that could be borrowed. When these restrictions are abolished, households increase their level of debt and spend the proceeds. Making credit more widely available will increase consumption.

Expectations

Expectations of increases in prices tend to make households bring forward their purchases and thus increase consumption. Expectations of large increases in real incomes will also tend to encourage households to increase spending now by borrowing more. So when the economy is booming, autonomous consumption tends to increase. On the other hand, if households expect economic conditions to become harsher, they will reduce their consumption now. For instance, they might expect an increase in unemployment rates, a rise in taxes or a fall in real wages.

The composition of households

Young people and old people tend to spend a higher proportion of their income than those in middle age. Young people tend to spend all their income and move into debt to finance the setting up of their homes and the bringing up of children. In middle age, the cost of homemaking declines as a proportion of income. With more income available, households often choose to build up their stock of savings in preparation for retirement. When they retire, they will run down their stock of savings to supplement their pensions. So if there is a change in the age composition of households in the economy, there could well be a change in consumption and savings. The more young and old the households, the greater will tend to be the level of consumption.

The determinants of saving

Factors which affect consumption also by definition must affect saving (remember, saving is defined as that part of disposable income which is not consumed). The SAVINGS FUNCTION therefore links income, wealth, inflation, the rate of interest, expectations and the age profile of the population with the level of saving. However, because a typical AVERAGE PROPENSITY TO SAVE (the APS - the ratio of total saving to total income calculated by Saving ÷ Income) is 0.1 to 0.2 in Western European countries, income is far less important in determining saving than it

Question 3

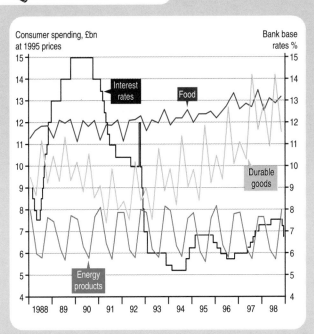

Source: adapted from *Economic Trends Annual Supplement*, Office for National Statistics.
Figure 31.2

(a) Describe the trends shown in Figure 31.2.
(b) Explain, using examples from the data, the extent to which interest rates affect consumption.

Question 4

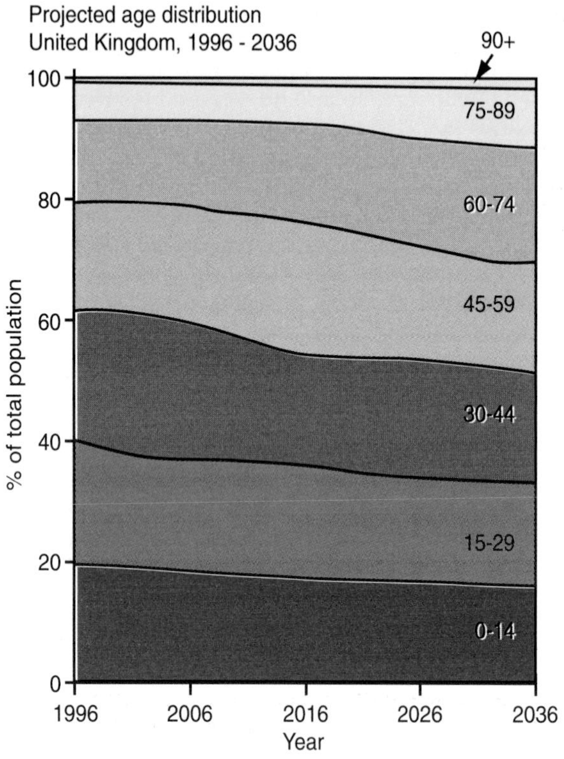

Projected age distribution
United Kingdom, 1996 - 2036

% of total population — Year (1996, 2006, 2016, 2026, 2036)

90+, 75-89, 60-74, 45-59, 30-44, 15-29, 0-14

Figure 31.3 *Projected age distribution, UK, 1996-2036*
Source: adapted from *Population Projections*, Office for National Statistics.

(a) What effects do you think that the changing structure of the population to 2036 is likely to have on consumption and saving?

is in determining consumption. Factors other than income are therefore relatively more important. This explains why, in the UK, for instance, the APS has varied from 0.03 to 0.15 in the 1980s and 1990s. The MARGINAL PROPENSITY TO SAVE (the proportion that is saved out of a change in income calculated by Change in saving ÷ Change in income) is equally unstable for these reasons.

Confusion sometimes arises between 'saving' and 'savings'. Saving is a **flow** concept which takes place over a period of time. Saving is added to a **stock** of savings fixed at a point in time. A household's stock of savings is the accumulation of past savings. For instance, you might have £100 in the bank. This is your stock of savings. You might then get a job over Christmas and save £20 from that. Your saving over Christmas is £20. Your stock of savings before Christmas was £100 but afterwards it was

£120. The savings function explains the relationship between the flow of savings and its determinants. It attempts to explain why you saved £20 over Christmas. It does not explain why you have £100 in the bank already.

The Keynesian consumption function

John Maynard Keynes was one of the greatest economists working in the first half of the twentieth century. He was the founder of modern macro-economics, the subject of much of the rest of this book. It was he who first popularised the idea that consumption was linked to income. 'Keynesian' means that an idea is linked to an idea first put forward by Keynes. Keynesian economists are economists who work within the framework first established by Keynes.

The Keynesian consumption function lays stress upon the relationship between planned current consumption and current disposable income. Other factors, particularly the availability of credit, can have an important impact upon expenditure on consumer durables. However, in the short term at least, income is the most significant factor determining the level of consumption. Changes in wealth and changes in the rate of interest (the two can be interrelated as argued above) have little impact upon short term consumption. This means that the consumption function is relatively stable. It is not subject to frequent large scale shifts.

Keynes himself was worried that increasing prosperity would lead to a stagnant economy. As households became better off, they would spend less and less of their increases in income. Eventually their demand for consumer goods would be completely satiated and without increases in spending, there could be no more increases in income.

The evidence of the past 60 years has proved Keynes wrong. There does not seem to be any indication that households are reducing their MPCs as income increases. However, this view has also led Keynesians to argue that higher income earners have a lower MPC (and therefore save a higher proportion of their income) than low income earners. Therefore, redistributing income from the poor to the rich will lower total consumption. The reverse, taking from the rich to give to the poor, will increase total consumption. But as we shall now see, this too seems to be contradicted not only by the evidence but also by alternative theories of the consumption function.

The life cycle hypothesis

Franco Modigliani and Albert Ando suggested that current consumption is not based upon current income. Rather, households form a view about their likely income over the whole of their lifetimes and base their current spending decisions upon that. For instance, professional workers at the start of their careers in their early 20s may earn as much as manual workers of the same age. But the APC of professional workers is likely to be higher. This is because professional workers expect to earn more in the future and are prepared to borrow more now to finance consumption.

A professional worker will expect, for instance, to buy rather than rent a house. The mortgage she takes out is likely to be at the top end of what banks or building societies will lend. The manual worker, on the other hand, knowing that his earnings are unlikely to increase substantially in the future, will be more cautious. He may be deterred from buying his own home and, if he does, will take out a small rather than large mortgage.

During middle age, households tend to be net savers. They are paying off loans accumulated when they were younger and saving for retirement. During retirement they spend more than they earn, running down their savings.

The permanent income hypothesis

Developed by Milton Friedman, this in many ways develops the insights of the life cycle hypothesis. Friedman argued that households base their spending decisions not on current income but on their PERMANENT INCOME. Broadly speaking, permanent income is average income over a lifetime.

Average income over a lifetime can be influenced by a number of factors.

- An increase in wealth will increase the ability of households to spend money (i.e. it will increase their permanent income). Hence a rise in wealth will increase actual consumption over a lifetime.
- An increase in interest rates tends to lower both stock and share prices. This leads to a fall in wealth, a fall in permanent income and a fall in current consumption.
- An increase in interest rates also leads to future incomes being less valuable. One way of explaining this is to remember that a sum of money available in the future is worth less than the same sum available today. Another way is to consider borrowing. If interest rates rise, households will need either to earn more money or cut back on their spending in the future to pay back their loans . Therefore, the real value of their future income (i.e. their permanent income) falls if interest rates rise.
- Unexpected rises in wages will lead to an increase in permanent income.

Friedman argued that the long run APC from permanent income was 1. Households spend all their income over their lifetimes (indeed, Friedman defined permanent income as the income a household could spend without changing its wealth over a lifetime). Hence, the long run APC and the MPC are stable.

In the short run, however, wealth and interest rates change. Measured income also changes and much of this change is unexpected. Income which households receive but did not expect to earn is called transitory income. Initially, transitory income will be saved, as households decide what to do with the money. Then it is incorporated into permanent income. The MPC of the household will depend upon the nature of the extra income. If the extra income is, for instance, a permanent pay rise, the household is likely to spend most of the money. If, however, it is a temporary rise in income, like a £10 000 win on the pools, most of it will be saved and then gradually spent over a much longer period of time. Because the proportion of transitory income to current income changes from month to month, the propensity to consume from current income will vary too. So in the short run, the APC and the MPC are not constant. This contradicts the Keynesian hypothesis that current consumption is a stable function of current income.

key terms

Average propensity to consume - the proportion of total income spent. It is calculated by $C \div Y$.
Average propensity to save - the proportion of a total income which is saved. It is calculated by $S \div Y$.
Consumption - total expenditure by households on goods and services over a period of time.
Consumption function - the relationship between the consumption of households and the factors which determine it.
Disposable income - household income over a period of time including state benefits, less direct taxes.
Durable goods - goods which are consumed over a long period of time, such as a television set or a car.
Marginal propensity to consume - the proportion of a change in income which is spent. It is calculated by $\Delta C \div \Delta Y$.
Marginal propensity to save - the proportion of a change in income which is saved. It is calculated by $\Delta S \div \Delta Y$.
Non-durable goods - goods which are consumed almost immediately like an ice-cream or a packet of washing powder.
Permanent income - the income a household could spend over its lifetime without reducing the value of its assets. This approximates to the average income of a household over its lifetime.
Savings function - the relationship between the saving of households and the factors which determine it.
Saving (personal) - the portion of households' disposable income which is not spent over a period of time.
Wealth effect - the change in consumption following a change in wealth.

Applied economics

Consumption in the UK

The composition of consumption expenditure

Total real consumption in the UK since 1955 has roughly trebled. However, as Figure 31.4 shows, there were significant differences in the rate of growth of the components of expenditure. Spending on food, for instance, only increased by approximately a half, whilst spending on durables, such as cars, furniture and carpets, increased 12 times. In general, expenditure on necessities, such as food and energy products, increased at a lower rate than expenditure on luxuries, such as durable goods and services. It is interesting to note that expenditure on alcoholic drink and tobacco fell between 1979 and 1998. Within this total, spending on drink rose slightly, but spending on tobacco fell sharply, almost certainly the result of increased awareness of the health risks associated with its consumption.

Consumption and income

Keynesian theory suggests that income is a major determinant of consumption. The evidence in Figure 31.5 would tend to support this theory. Over the period 1955 to 1998, real households' disposable income rose 3.2 times whilst real consumers' expenditure increased 3.0 times.

Keynesian theory would also suggest that the average propensity to consume declines as incomes rise over time. Figure 31.6 lends some support to this. The average APC in the 1960s was 0.95, in the 1970s was 0.93, in the 1980s was 0.92 and in the 1990s was 0.91. (Note that in Figure 31.6 income used to calculate the APC is defined as households' disposable income **plus** an adjustment for the net equity of households in pension funds. It is the accounting convention used by the Office for National Statistics [ONS]. This produces a slightly lower value of the APC than if only households' disposable income were included.) There is considerable fluctuation, however, around these long term averages. For instance, there was a sharp rise in the APC between 1986 and 1988 during the Lawson boom, (☞ unit 33) whilst the APC fell to less than 0.9 in the two major recessions of 1980-82 and 1990-92. This would suggest that other factors can be important in determining consumption apart from income.

Other determinants of consumption

Economists in the 1960s and early 1970s were fairly confident that the relationship between consumption and income was highly stable. However, from the mid-1970s a number of key variables which can affect consumption were themselves subject to large changes and this had a small but significant effect on the average propensity to consume.

Wealth A sharp appreciation in household wealth was a key feature of most of the 1980s. Figure 31.7 shows that share prices rose considerably between 1980 and 1987. This considerable increase in stock market values was a key element in persuading households to increase their spending in 1986 and 1987. In October 1987, on 'Black Monday', world stock markets crashed and 25 per cent of the value of shares on the London Stock Exchange was wiped out. This helped knock consumer confidence and the subsequent poor performance of share prices was one factor which reduced the average propensity to consume in the late 1980s and early 1990s.

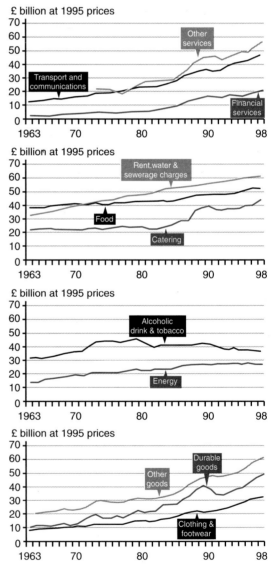

Figure 31.4 *Composition of consumer expenditure, 1950-1998*
Source: adapted from *Economic Trends Annual Supplement*, Office for National Statistics.

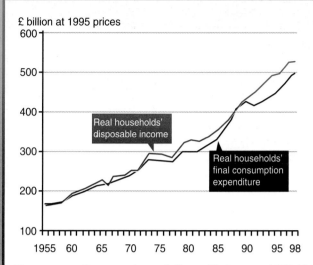

Figure 31.5 *Consumption and disposable income, 1955-1998*
Source: adapted from *Economic Trends Annual Supplement*, Office for National Statistics.

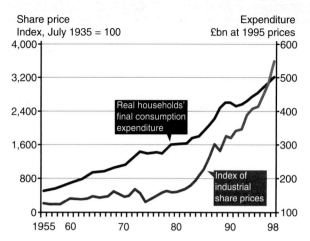

Figure 31.7 *London stock market prices (FT Ordinary share index, 1st July 1935 = 100) and real households' final consumption on expenditure*
Source: adapted from *Economic Trends Annual Supplement*, Office for National Statistics.

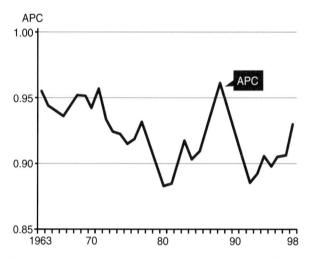

Figure 31.6 *The average propensity to consume (APC), 1963-1998*
Source: adapted from *Economic Trends Annual Supplement*, Office for National Statistics.

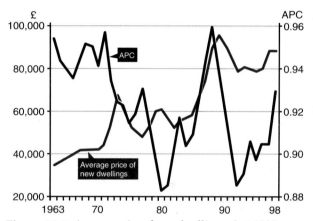

Figure 31.8 *Average price of new dwellings, £ at 1995 prices, and the average propensity to consume, 1963-1998*
Source: adapted from *Economic Trends Annual Supplement*, Office for National Statistics.

Equally, the strong performance of the Stock Market in the second half of the 1990s contributed to strong growth in spending.

Many households do not own shares but the majority own their home. Again, in the mid-1980s the boom in house prices shown in Figure 31.8 was a major determinant of increased consumer spending during the period 1986-88. Equally, the fall in house prices in the early 1990s played an important role in dampening consumption. The stagnation in house prices which followed until 1996 helped break the growth in consumer spending. Rising house prices from 1998 helped increase consumption in 1999 and 2000.

Inflation Periods of high inflation tend to be marked by a falling APC and vice versa. Following the rise in inflation during the late 1980s, consumers reacted by increasing their savings and reducing the average

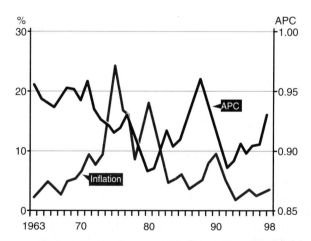

Figure 31.9 *Inflation (percentage change year on year) and the average propensity to consume, 1963-1998*
Source: adapted from *Economic Trends Annual Supplement*, Office for National Statistics.

propensity to consume. They wanted to rebuild the real value of their wealth. Equally, the low inflation of the mid and late 1990s contributed to a rise in spending out of income. The relationship between inflation and consumption is shown in Figure 31.9.

The rate of interest and the availability of credit The rate of interest and the availability of credit have a significant impact on spending on consumer durables. Figure 31.10 shows that during the Lawson boom of 1986-88, relatively low interest rates helped fuel a consumer spending boom. The raising of bank base rates to 15 per cent in 1989 and the period of high interest rates which followed were the key factors which helped reduce growth in consumer spending and push the economy into recession. The reduction of interest rates from over the period 1991-93 then helped the recovery during the rest of the 1990s.

Interest rates affect consumption in a number of ways. Higher interest rates makes borrowing more expensive and in particular hit spending on consumer durables. They also make it more expensive to buy a house using a mortgage. The rise in interest rates in the late 1980s helped bring about a crash in the housing market market, with house prices falling after 1989 in many areas of the country. This affected consumer confidence and reduced willingness to take on further debt. For most of the 1990s, consumers remained cautious about borrowing despite low interest rates. However, the late 1990s saw a sharp growth in spending as consumers became more confident that interest rates would not be driven higher.

The availability of credit was an important determinant of consumer spending. Previously there were controls on the ability of financial institutions to lend. These controls were removed in the early 1980s. For instance, before this time, building societies could not offer loans other than mortgages to their customers whilst banks could not offer mortgages. The removal of

these controls in the early 1980s led to households substantially increasing their levels of debt, which helped contribute again to the surge of spending during the period 1986-88.

Expectations Expectations have been a crucial determinant of consumption in the 1980s and 1990s. In the 1980s, the Lawson boom was fuelled by expectations that the economy would grow at fast rates for the foreseeable future. There was much talk at the time about Britain's 'economic miracle'. Unfortunately, the boom was unsustainable. In the subsequent recession, consumers became very pessimistic about the future, particularly since unemployment climbed from 1.5 million in 1989 to 3 million in 1993. In the recovery that followed consumers remained cautious about taking on large amounts of new debt , fearing that a recession would recur. It was only in the late 1990s that consumer confidence was restored and this helped increase the rate of growth of consumer spending.

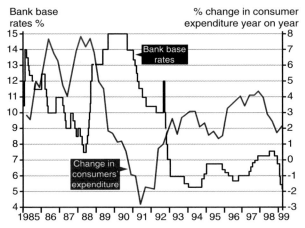

Figure 31.10 *Interest rates and the change in consumer expenditure, 1985-1999*
Source: adapted from *Economic Trends Annual Supplement*, Office for National Statistics.

The determinants of saving

You have been asked to write a report for a bank on the determinants of saving in the economy. Use the data here and in the Applied Economics section to construct your report.
- Briefly outline trends in saving and the APS since 1963.
- Briefly outline the main factors which affect saving in the economy.
- Produce a case study of the period 1989 to 1998 to illustrate your discussion.

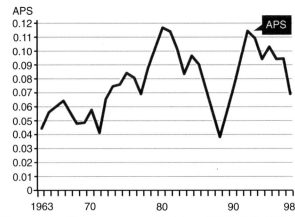

Figure 31.11 *The average propensity to save (APS), 1963-1998*
Source: adapted from *Economic Trends Annual Supplement*, Office for National Statistics.

Summary

1. Investment is the purchase of capital goods which are then used to create other goods and services. This differs from saving, which is the creation of financial obligations.
2. Marginal efficiency of capital theory suggests that investment is inversely related to the price of capital - the rate of interest.
3. Factors which shift the **MEC** or investment demand schedule include changes in the cost of capital goods, technological change, and changes in expectations or animal spirits.
4. The accelerator theory suggests that investment varies with the rate of change in income.
5. The past and current profitability of industry too may be more important than future rates of return on capital in determining current investment.

A definition of investment

Economists use the word INVESTMENT in a very precise way. Investment is the addition to the **capital stock** of the economy - factories, machines, offices and stocks of materials, used to produce other goods and services.

In everyday language, 'investment' and 'saving' are often used to mean the same thing. For instance, we talk about 'investing in the building society' or 'investing in shares'. For an economist, these two would be examples of saving. For an economist, investment only takes place if real products are created. To give two more examples:

- putting money into a bank account would be saving; the bank buying a computer to handle your account would be investment;
- buying shares in a new company would be saving; buying new machinery to set up a company would be investment.

A distinction can be made between **gross** and **net** investment. The value of the capital stock depreciates over time as it wears out and is used up. This is called **depreciation** or **capital consumption**. Gross investment measures investment before depreciation, whilst net investment is gross investment less the value of depreciation. Depreciation in recent years in the UK has accounted for about three-quarters of gross investment. So only about one-quarter of gross investment represents an addition to the capital stock of the economy.

Another distinction made is between investment in **physical capital** and in **human capital**. Investment in human capital is investment in the education and training of workers. Investment in physical capital is investment in factories etc.

Investment is made both by the public sector and the private sector. Public sector investment is constrained by complex political considerations. In the rest of this unit, we will consider the determinants of private sector investment in physical capital.

Marginal efficiency of capital theory

Firms invest in order to make a profit. The profitability of investment projects varies. Some will make a high **rate of return**, some will yield a low rate of return and others will result in losses for the company. The rate of return on an investment project is also known as the MARGINAL EFFICIENCY OF CAPITAL (MEC).

At any point in time in the economy as whole, there exists a large number of possible individual investment projects. Table 32.1 shows an economy where there are £4bn of investment projects with an MEC of 20 per cent and above, £8bn with an MEC of 15 per cent and above and so on.

How much of this investment takes

Question 1

From the photograph, give examples of: (a) past investment in physical capital; (b) past investment in human capital; (c) saving; (d) capital consumption.

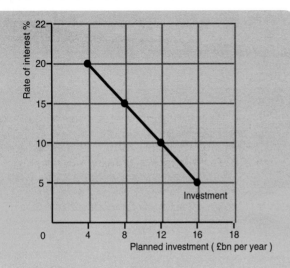

Figure 32.1 *The planned investment schedule*
A fall in the rate of interest will make more investment projects profitable. Planned investment will rise if the rate of interest falls.

Question 2

Table 32.2 *Average cost of funds (as % of sales) of top spending companies on research and development*

	Chemicals	Pharmaceuticals	Engineering	Electronics and electrical equipment
Japan	2.1%	2.8%	2.2%	1.5%
Germany	3.8%	5.1%	2.1%	2.9%
France	5.0%	n.a.	2.5%	2.8%
US	5.9%	9.5%	3.0%	4.2%
UK	5.6%	12.5%	3.1%	5.8%

Source: adapted from DTI, R&D Scoreboard 1998.

The UK's high interest rates in the 1980s and 1990s put British industry at a severe disadvantage. It means that fewer projects are worth taking on because the thresholds for returns are higher. Table 32.2 shows the cost of investment funds measured as a percentage of sales revenues for firms in different industries. In all these industries, the UK has the highest or nearly the highest cost of funds.

Source: adapted from the *Financial Times*, 9.3.1999.

(a) Explain, using a diagram, why high interest rates may have put British industry at a disadvantage in investment.
(b) During the 1990s, UK interest rates have been above those in the rest of the EU. What are the possible implications for UK investment if Britain were to join the euro?

Table 32.1 *Planned investment and the marginal efficiency of capital*

Marginal efficiency of capital (% per year)	Planned investment (£bn per year)
20	4
15	8
10	12
5	16

place will depend upon the rate of interest in the economy. If the rate of interest is 20 per cent, then firms having to borrow money will make a loss if they undertake any project with an MEC of less than 20 per cent. Hence, planned investment will be £4bn. If, on the other hand, the rate of interest is 5 per cent, then all investment projects with an MEC of 5 per cent or more will be profitable. Hence, planned investment will be £16bn. So the conclusion of marginal efficiency of capital theory is that planned investment in the economy will rise if the rate of interest falls. This relationship, using the figures from Table 32.1, is shown in Figure 32.1.

In our explanation above, the rate of interest was assumed to be the rate of interest at which firms have to borrow money. However, most investment by firms in the UK is financed from RETAINED PROFIT. This is profit which is not used to pay dividends to shareholders or taxes to the government, but is kept back by the firm for its own use. This does not alter the relationship between the rate of interest and investment. Firms which keep back profits have a choice about what to do with the money. They can either invest it or save it. The higher the rate of interest on savings, such as placing the money on loan with banks or other financial institutions, the more attractive saving the money becomes and the less attractive becomes investment. Put another way, the higher the rate of interest, the higher the **opportunity cost** of investment and hence the lower will be the amount of planned investment in the economy.

Factors which shift the planned investment schedule

Cost of capital goods If the price of capital goods rises, then the expected rate of return on investment projects will fall if firms cannot pass on the increase in higher prices. So increases in the price of capital goods, all other things being equal, will reduce planned investment. This is shown by a shift to the left in the planned investment schedule in Figure 32.2.

Technological change Technological change will make new capital equipment more productive than previous equipment. This will raise the rate of return on investment projects, all other things being equal. Hence, technological change such as the introduction of computer aided machinery will raise the level of planned investment at any given rate of interest. This is shown by a shift to the right in the planned investment schedule.

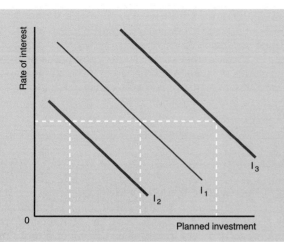

Figure 32.2 *Shifts in planned investment*
An increase in the cost of planned capital will reduce the rate of return on investment projects. Therefore at any given rate of interest, planned investment will fall. This is shown by a shift to the left in the planned investment schedule. Changes in technology which make capital more productive raise the level of planned investment, shown by a shift to the right of the schedule.

Expectations Businesses have to form views about the future. When calculating the possible rate of return on future investment, they have to make assumptions about future costs and future revenues. If managers become more pessimistic about the future, they will expect the rate of return on investment projects to fall and hence planned investment will be reduced. If, on the other hand, they become more optimistic their expectations of the rates of return on investment projects will tend to rise. Hence planned investment will rise and this will be shown by a shift to the right in the investment schedule. Keynes called the expectations of businessmen their 'animal spirits'. He believed that expectations were crucial in determining changes in investment, and that these expectations could change suddenly.

Question 3

Assume that I_1 in Figure 32.2 shows the planned investment schedule for the UK. Is it more likely to shift to I_2 or I_3 if: (a) there is a rise in the real prices of commercial property; (b) the government announces a billion pound programme to encourage the use of micro-computers in industry; (c) the economy grew much faster than expected last year and forecasts show this set to continue; (d) the price of computers and computer aided tools falls; (e) prices on the New York Stock Exchange crash?

Government policy Government can play a crucial role in stimulating private sector investment. This will be discussed in more detail in unit 38.

The accelerator theory

The ACCELERATOR THEORY of investment suggests that the level of planned investment varies with the rate of change of income or output rather than with the rate of interest.

To see why this might be the case, consider Table 32.3.

Table 32.3

Year	Annual output £m	Number of machines required	Investment in machines
1	10	10	0
2	10	10	0
3	12	12	2
4	15	15	3
5	15	15	0
6	14	14	0

A firm producing toys needs one machine to produce £1m of output per year. The machines last 20 years and for the purpose of this example we will assume that none of the firm's machines need replacing over the time period being considered (so we are considering net and not gross investment). Initially in year 1 the firm has £10m worth of orders. It already has 10 machines and therefore no investment takes place. In year 2, orders remain unchanged and so again the firm has no need to invest. However, in year 3 orders increase to £12m. The firm now needs to invest in another two machines if it is to fulfil orders. Orders increase to £15m in year 4. The firm needs to purchase another 3 machines to increase its capital stock to 15 machines. In year 5, orders remain unchanged at £15m and so investment returns to zero. In year 6, orders decline to £14m. The firm has too much capital stock and therefore does not invest.

In this example investment takes place when there is a change in real spending in the economy. If there is no change in spending, then there is no investment. What is more, the changes in spending lead to much bigger changes in investment. For instance, the increase in spending of 25 per cent in year 4 (from £12m to £15m) resulted in an increase in investment of 50 per cent (from 2 machines to 3 machines). In reality, it should be remembered that about 75 per cent of gross investment is replacement investment which is far less likely than net investment to be affected by changes in income. Even so, the accelerator theory predicts that investment spending in the economy is likely to be more volatile than spending as a whole.

The simplest form of the accelerator theory can be expressed as:

$$I_t = a (Y_t - Y_{t-1})$$

where I_t is investment in time period t, $Y_t - Y_{t-1}$ is the change in real income during year t and a is the accelerator coefficient or CAPITAL-OUTPUT RATIO. The capital-output ratio is the amount of capital needed in the economy to produce a given quantity of goods. So if £10 of capital is needed to produce £2 of goods, then the capital-output ratio is 5. The theory therefore predicts that changes in the level of investment are related to past changes in income.

This accelerator model is very simplistic. There are a number of factors which limit the predictive power of the model.

- The model assumes that the capital-output ratio is constant over time. However, it can change. In the long term, new technology can make capital more productive. In the shorter term, the capital-output ratio is likely to be higher in a recession when there is excess capacity than in a boom.
- Expectations may vary. Businesses may choose not to satisfy extra demand if they believe that the demand will be short lived. There is little point in undertaking new investment if the extra orders will have disappeared within six months. On the other hand, businesses may anticipate higher output. Despite constant income, they may believe that a boom is imminent and invest to be ahead of their rivals.
- Time lags involved are likely to be extremely complicated. Changes in investment are likely to respond to changes in income over several time periods and not just one.
- Firms may have excess capacity (i.e. they can produce more with current levels of capital than they are at present doing). If there is an increase in income, firms will respond not by investing but by bringing back into use capital which has been mothballed or by utilising fully equipment which had been underutilised.

- The capital goods industry will be unable to satisfy a surge in demand. Some investment will therefore either be cancelled or delayed.

Despite these qualifications, evidence suggests that net investment is to some extent linked to past changes in income. However, the link is relatively weak and therefore other influences must be at work to determine investment.

Profits

About 70 per cent of industrial and commercial investment in the UK is financed from retained profit. Some economists argue that many firms do not consider the opportunity cost of investment. They retain profit but rarely consider that it might be better used saved in financial assets. They automatically assume that the money will be spent on investment related to the activities of the firm. The rate of interest is then much less important in determining investment. Investment becomes crucially dependent upon two factors.

- The amount of retained profit available. So the poor investment record of companies in the UK in the 1970s, for instance, was a direct reflection of their inability to generate profits needed to plough back into their operations.
- The availability of suitable investment projects. If firms do not have suitable investment projects to hand, they will bank the cash or pay it out to shareholders in dividends. New technology or new products can act as a spur to investment on this view.

Question 4

$$I_t = 2 (Y_t - Y_{t-1})$$

(a) In year 0 income was £100m. In subsequent years, it grew by 5 per cent per annum. Calculate the level of investment in years 1 to 5.
(b) Compare what would happen to investment in each year if income grew instead by (i) 10 per cent and (ii) $2\frac{1}{2}$ per cent.

key terms

Accelerator theory - the theory that the level of planned investment is related to past changes in income.
Capital-output ratio - the ratio between the amount of capital needed to produce a given quantity of goods and the level of output.
Investment - the addition to the capital stock of the economy.
Marginal efficiency of capital - the rate of return on the last unit of capital employed.
Retained profit - profit kept back by a firm for its own use which is not distributed to shareholders or used to pay taxation.

Applied economics

Investment in the UK

The composition of investment

Gross investment is called **gross fixed capital formation** (GFCF) in UK official statistics. Figure 32.3 shows the composition of investment in 1979 and 1998. Significant changes in this composition are apparent from the data.

- There has been little change overall in the level of investment in housing. However, within this total, there has been a significant fall in public sector housing (mainly council housing), but a significant rise in the volume of private sector housing investment. This reflects changes in government policy. Between 1945 and 1979, government, through local councils, invested heavily in houses for rent. The Conservative government of 1979-1997, however, reversed the policy. It virtually halted all new building of council houses and introduced a right to buy for council tenants. Its justification was that local councils were highly inefficient in managing their stock of houses. Moreover, everyone should be encouraged to buy their own home. Buying rather than renting helped create a 'property owning democracy' where people had a stake in the economy and were responsible for making decisions about their own homes. With the stock of council houses in decline, households had to turn to the private sector for new housing and hence the increase in private sector investment.

- Investment in 'other machinery and equipment' has more than doubled. This investment ranges from milking machines to lathes to computers and desks.

- Even greater has been the increase in investment in 'other new buildings and structures', which has more than trebled.

This includes new factories and offices.

Table 32.4 shows how the composition of investment has changed by industry. 1989 was an exceptional year for investment. The Lawson boom of 1986-88 had left firms short of capacity. They had therefore sharply increased their spending on investment. Many firms came to regret this because the economy then went into a deep recession, leaving them with excess capacity. In 1993, real investment spending in the UK was nearly a third less than its peak 1989 level. Firms were reluctant to invest, fearing that the recession of 1990-92 would continue. By 1997, the economy had recovered and firms had increased their investment spending by nearly a fifth compared to 1993, but it was still less than in 1989.

The pattern of investment spending to some extent reflects trends in output between sectors of the economy. Primary industries, including agriculture and mining, have seen their share of output decline. As a consequence, investment in these industries has been

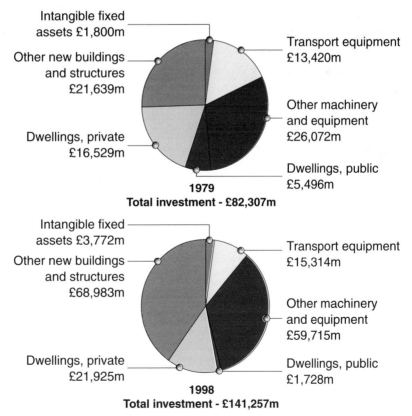

Figure 32.3 *Gross domestic fixed capital formation by type of asset, 1979 and 1998 (£ million at 1998 prices)*
Source: adapted from *Economic Trends Annual Supplement, Monthly Digest of Statistics*, Office for National Statistics.

Table 32.4 *GDP and gross fixed capital formation by industry*

	£ million, at 1995 prices			% change
	1989	1993	1996	1993 - 96
GDP at market prices	654 315	664 018	730 767	10.1
Total gross fixed capital formation	145 421	105 671	123 196	16.6
of which				
Agriculture, hunting, forestry and fishing	2 467	2 460	2 647	7.6
Mining & quarrying	6 234	6 259	5 753	-8.1
Manufacturing	19 182	11 971	18 763	56.7
Electricity, gas & water supply	4 812	6 377	4 888	-23.4
Construction	2 194	823	995	20.9
Wholesale & retail trade	14 440	11 323	13 341	17.8
Transport & communication	13 042	9 957	13 486	35.4
Financial intermediation	27 257	12 436	16 267	30.8
Public administration & defence	8 522	9 370	8 399	-10.4
Education, health & social work	5 059	4 620	5 308	14.9
Other services	7 238	5 669	6 885	21.4
Investment in dwellings etc.	34 976	24 404	26 466	8.4

Source: adapted from *United Kingdom National Accounts* (Blue Book), Office for National Statistics.

Table 32.5 *Determinants of investment*

	£ million, at 1995 prices			Per cent
	Private sector investment	Annual change in GDP	Company profits	Interest rate[1]
1979	82 307	13 862	110 142	13.68
1980	78 398	-11 312	103 846	16.32
1981	71 451	-6 437	101 816	13.27
1982	75 666	8 979	112 899	11.93
1983	79 489	18 992	126 894	9.83
1984	86 912	12 724	129 775	9.68
1985	90 421	20 516	138 098	12.25
1986	92 330	23 629	136 758	10.9
1987	100 520	25 869	144 245	9.74
1988	115 362	31 564	151 320	10.9
1989	122 158	13 728	155 421	13.85
1990	119 368	4 165	146 025	14.77
1991	109 000	-9 841	131 863	11.7
1992	108 246	336	135 138	9.56
1993	109 127	15 043	145 736	6.01
1994	113 042	29 159	164 595	5.46
1995	116 360	19 371	168 530	6.73
1996	122 042	18 219	177 046	5.96
1997	130 487	25 894	176 692	6.58
1998	141 257	15 607	172 134	7.21

1. Bank base rate.

Source: adapted from *Economic Trends Annual Supplement*; *Monthly Digest of Statistics*, Office for National Statistics.

relatively static or fallen. The tight control of public spending during the 1980s and 1990s left investment spending on public administration and defence, education, health and social work little changed. Private sector services, though, have expanded. Financial services saw a large boom in the 1980s which resulted in the industry taking nearly one fifth of total UK investment in 1989. Between 1993 and 1996, the industry increased its real investment by nearly one third. Retailing and transport and communication have also had strong investment performances. As for manufacturing, it has maintained investment spending despite the fact that manufacturing output as a share of total output has been declining over time. The trend has been for manufacturing firms to increase their ratio of capital to labour, making production more capital intensive. So manufacturing has been raising its stock of capital over time whilst shedding labour.

The determinants of investment

Economic theory suggests that there may be several determinants of private sector investment. The accelerator theory suggests that investment is a function of changes in income. Neo-classical theory argues that the rate of interest is the important determinant, whilst other theories point to the current level of profits as significant.

The evidence tends to support the idea that the level of investment is determined by a number of variables. In Table 32.5, there is some weak correlation between investment and changes in income, profits and the rate of interest. However, these variables tend to move together through the business or trade cycle and so changes in investment may in themselves affect the three variables in the data.

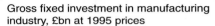

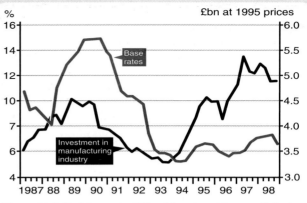

Figure 32.5 *Bank base rates (%) and investment by manufacturing industry, quarterly (£ billion at 1995 prices)*
Source: adapted from *Economic Trends Annual Supplement*, Office for National Statistics.

Gross fixed investment in manufacturing industry, £bn at 1995 prices

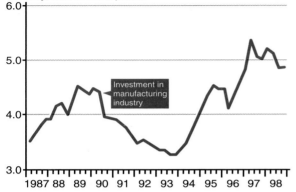

Output of manufacturing industry, £bn at 1995 prices

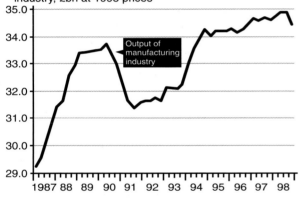

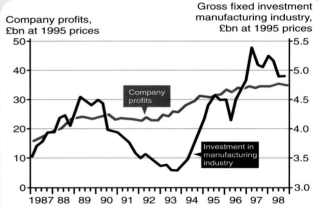

Figure 32.6 *Company profits[1] and investment by manufacturing industry, quarterly (£ billion at 1995 prices)*
1. Gross trading profit of private non-financial corporations excluding UK *continental shelf companies*, seasonally adjusted.
Source: adapted from *Economic Trends, Annual Supplement*, Office for National Statistics.

GDP, £bn at 1995 prices

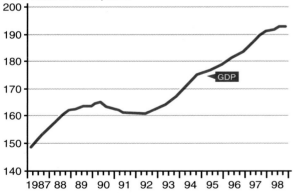

Figure 32.4 *Investment and output of manufacturing industry, and GDP, quarterly (£ billion at 1995 prices)*
Source: adapted from *Economic Trends Annual Supplement*, Office for National Statistics.

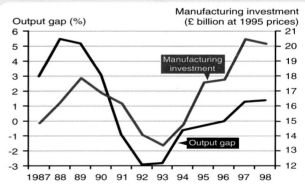

Figure 32.7 *The output gap[1] and investment by manufacturing industry[2]*
1. Deviation of actual GDP from potential GDP as a percentage of potential GDP.
2. Yearly, and so is the sum of the four quarters of investment shown in the rest of the data.
Source: adapted from *Economic Trends, Annual Supplement*, Office for National Statistics.

1. Briefly outline the trends in manufacturing investment between 1987 and 1998.
2. Taking each possible determinant of investment (a) explain why economic theory suggests there is a link between the two variables and (b) evaluate whether the evidence from 1987 to 1998 supports the theory.
3. A manufacturing company is reviewing its investment policies. Evaluate which macro-economic variable is the most important variable that it should take into consideration when making an investment decision.

Summary

1. The aggregate demand curve is downward sloping. It shows the relationship between the price level and equilibrium output in the economy.
2. A movement along the aggregate demand curve shows how equilibrium income will change if there is a change in the price level.
3. A shift in the aggregate demand curve is caused by a change in variables such as consumption and exports at any given price level.
4. Keynesian economists argue that the aggregate demand curve is steep (i.e. changes in the price level have little effect on equilibrium income). Classical economists argue that the aggregate demand curve is much shallower (i.e. increases in the prices will significantly depress the equilibrium level of income).

Aggregate demand

In unit 4, there was a discussion of what determined the demand for an individual product. Demand was defined as the quantity that would be bought at any given price. In this unit, we will consider what determines AGGREGATE demand. 'Aggregate' in economics means a 'total' or 'added up' amount. AGGREGATE DEMAND is the total of all demands or expenditures in the economy at any given price.

It was explained in unit 25 that national expenditure was one of the three ways of calculating national income, usually measured as GDP. National expenditure is made up of four components.

- **Consumption (C).** This is spending by households on goods and services (see unit 31).
- **Investment (I).** This is spending by firms on investment goods (see unit 31).
- **Government spending (G).** This includes current spending, for instance on wages and salaries. It also includes spending by government on investment goods like new roads or new schools.
- **Exports minus imports (X-M).** Foreigners spend money on goods produced in the DOMESTIC ECONOMY. Hence it is part of national expenditure. However, households, firms and governments also spend money on goods produced abroad. For instance, a UK household might buy a car produced in France. Or a British firm might use components imported from the Far East in a computer which is sold to Germany. These imported goods do not form part of national output and do not contribute to national income. So, because C, I, G and X all include spending on imported goods, imports (M) must be taken away from C + I + G + X to arrive at a figure for national expenditure.

National expenditure (E) can therefore be calculated using the formula:

$$E = C + I + G + X - M$$

The aggregate demand curve

The AGGREGATE DEMAND CURVE shows the

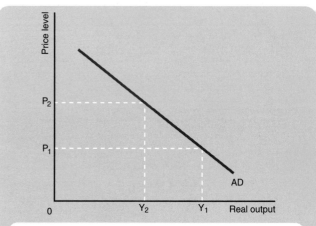

Figure 33.1 *The aggregate demand curve*
A rise in the price level will lead, via a rise in interest rates, to a fall in the equilibrium level of national income and therefore of national output. Hence the aggregate demand curve is downward sloping.

relationship between the price level and the level of real expenditure in the economy. Figure 33.1 shows an aggregate demand (AD) curve. The price level is put on the vertical axis whilst real output is put on the horizontal axis.

The **price level** is the average level of prices in the economy. Governments calculate a number of different measures of the price level. In the UK, for instance, the most widely quoted measure is the **Retail Price Index**, figures for which are published every month and are widely reported in the news. A change in the price level is **inflation** (☞ unit 28).

Real output on the horizontal axis must equal real expenditure and real income. This is because, in the circular flow model of the economy, these are three different ways of measuring the same flow. The aggregate demand curve plots the level of expenditure where the economy would be in an equilibrium position at each price level, all other things being equal.

Demand curves are nearly always downward sloping. Why is the aggregate demand curve the same shape? One simple answer is to consider what happens to a household budget if prices rise. If a household is on a fixed income, then a rise in average prices will mean that they can buy fewer goods and services than before. The higher the price level in the economy, the less they can afford to buy. So it is with the national economy. The higher the price, the less goods and services will be demanded in the whole economy.

A more sophisticated explanation considers what happens to the different components of expenditure when prices rise.

Consumption Consumption expenditure is influenced by the **rate of interest** in the economy (☞ unit 31). When prices increase, consumers (and firms) need more money to buy the same number of goods and services as before. One way of getting more money is to borrow it and so the demand for borrowed funds will rise. However, if there is a fixed supply of money available for borrowing from banks and building societies, the price of borrowed funds will rise. This price is the rate of interest. A rise in interest rates leads to a fall in consumption, particularly of durable goods such as cars which are commonly bought on credit.

Another way a rise in the price level affects consumption is through the **wealth effect** (☞ unit 31). A rise in the price level leads to the real value of an individual consumer's wealth being lower. For instance, £100 000 at today's prices will be worth less in real terms in a year's time if average prices have increased 20 per cent over the 12 months. A fall in real wealth will result in a fall in consumer spending.

Investment As has just been explained, a rise in prices, all other things being equal, leads to a rise in interest rates in the economy. Investment, according to marginal efficiency of capital theory (☞ unit 32), is affected by changes in the rate of interest. The higher the rate of interest, the less profitable new investment projects become and therefore the fewer projects will be undertaken by firms. So, the higher the rate of interest, the lower will be the level of investment.

Government spending Government spending in this model of the economy is assumed to be independent of economic variables. It is exogenously determined, fixed by variables outside the model. In this case, it is assumed to be determined by the political decisions of the government of the day. Note that government spending (G) here does not include transfer payments. These are payments by the government for which there is no corresponding output in the economy, like welfare benefits or student grants.

Exports and imports A higher price level in the UK means that foreign firms will be able to compete more successfully in the UK economy. For instance, if British shoe manufacturers put up their prices by 20 per cent, whilst foreign shoe manufacturers keep their prices the same, then British shoe manufacturers will become less competitive and more foreign shoes will be imported. Equally, British shoe manufacturers will find it more difficult to export charging higher prices. So a higher UK price level, with price levels in other economies staying the same, will lead to a fall in UK exports.

Hence, aggregate demand falls as prices rise, first, because increases in interest rates reduce consumption and investment and, second, because a loss of international comptitiveness at the new higher prices will reduce exports and increase imports.

Question 1

In 1975, inflation rose to a peak of 24.1 per cent. Real GDP fell in both 1974 and 1975. In 1980, inflation rose to a peak of 18.0 per cent and real GDP fell in 1980 and 1981. In 1990, inflation rose to a peak of 9.5 per cent. GDP fell in 1991 and 1992.

(a) How might economic theory account for this?

Shifts in the AD curve

The aggregate demand (AD) curve shows the relationship between the price level and the equilibrium level of real income and output. A change in the price level results in a **movement along** the AD curve. Higher prices lead to falls in aggregate demand.

Shifts in the aggregate demand curve will occur if there is a change in any other relevant variable apart from the price level. When the AD curve shifts, it shows that there is a change in real output at any given price level. In Figure 33.2, the shift in the AD curve from AD_1 to AD_2 shows that at a price level of P, real output increases from Y_1 to Y_2. There are a number of variables which can lead to a shift of the AD curve. Some of these variables are **real** variables, such as changes in the willingness of consumers to spend. Others are changes in **monetary** variables such as the rate of interest.

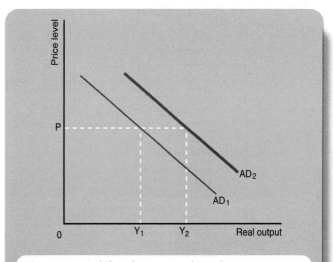

Figure 33.2 *A shift in the aggregate demand curve*
An increase in consumption, investment, government spending or net exports, given a constant price level, will lead to a shift in the aggregate demand curve from AD_1 to AD_2.

Consumption A number of factors might increase consumption spending at any given level of prices, shifting the AD curve from AD_1 to AD_2 in Figure 33.2. For instance, unemployment may fall, making consumers less afraid that they will lose their jobs and more willing to borrow money to spend on consumer durables. The government might reduce interest rates, again encouraging borrowing for durables. A substantial rise in stock market prices will increase consumer wealth which in turn may lead to an increase in spending. A reduction in the relative numbers of high saving 45-60 year olds in the population will increase the **average propensity to consume** (☞ unit 31) of the whole economy. New technology which creates new consumer products can lead to an increase in consumer spending as households want to buy these new products. A fall in income tax would increase consumers' disposable income, leading to a rise in consumption (☞ unit 31).

Question 2

Explain, using a diagram, the likely effect of the following on the aggregate demand curve for the UK.
(a) The increase in real investment expenditure between 1994 and 1999.
(b) The cuts in planned government expenditure by the Labour government between 1976 and 1978.
(c) The large cuts in taxes in the Lawson Budget of 1987.
(d) The fall in the savings ratio during the late 1990s from 10.3 in 1995 to 7.0 in 1998.
(e) The more than 20 per cent rise in the average value of the pound against other currencies between 1996 and 1998.
(f) The high inflation experienced by the UK in the mid-1970s.
(g) The pushing up of interest rates by the Thatcher government from 12 per cent in June 1979 to 17 per cent in November 1979.
(h) The 25 per cent fall in London stock market prices in October 1987.

Investment One factor which would increase investment spending at any given level of prices, pushing the AD curve from AD_1 to AD_2 in Figure 33.2, would be an increase in business confidence - an increase in 'animal spirits' as John Maynard Keynes once put it. This increase in business confidence could have come about, for instance, because the economy was going into boom. A fall in interest rates ordered by the government would lead to a rise in investment. An increase in company profitability would give firms more retained profit to use for investment. A fall in taxes on profits (corporation tax in the UK) would lead to the rate of return on investment projects rising, leading to a rise in investment.

Government spending A change of government policy might lead to a rise in government spending at any given level of prices, pushing the AD curve to the right from AD_1 to AD_2 in Figure 33.2.

Exports and imports A fall in the exchange rate of the currency will make exports more competitive and imports less competitive. So exports should rise and imports fall, pushing the AD curve to the right in Figure 33.2. An improvement in the quality of domestically-made goods would again increase domestic competitiveness and increase exports and reduce imports.

The multiplier

If there is an increase in, say, investment of £1, what will be the final increase in national income? John Maynard Keynes argued in his most famous book, *The General Theory of Employment, Interest and Money*, published in 1936, that national income would increase by more than £1 because of the MULTIPLIER EFFECT.

To understand why there might be a multiplier effect, consider what would happen if firms increased spending on new factories by £100m. Firms would pay contractors to build the factories. This £100m would be an increase in aggregate demand. The contractor would use the money

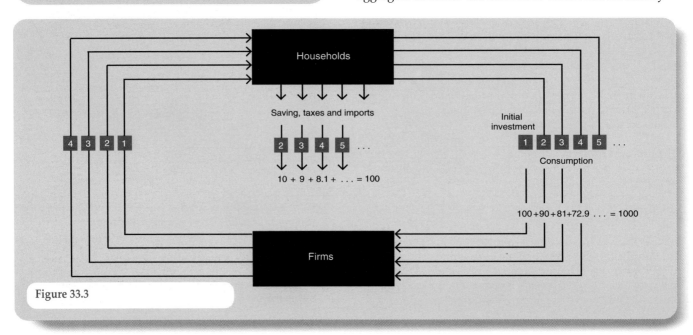

Figure 33.3

in part to pay its workers on the project. The workers would spend the money, on everything from food to holidays. This spending would be an addition to national income. Assume that £10m is spent on food. Food manufacturers would in turn pay their workers who would spend their incomes on a variety of products, increasing national income further. John Maynard Keynes argued that this multiplier effect would increase jobs in the economy. Every job directly created by firms through extra spending would indirectly create other jobs in the economy.

This process can be shown using the **circular flow of income model** (☞ unit 25). Assume that households spend $^9/_{10}$ ths of their gross income. The other $^2/_{10}$ ths are either saved or paid to the government in the form of taxes. Firms increase their spending by £100m, money which is used to build new factories. In Figure 33.3, this initial £100m is is shown in stage 1 flowing into firms. The money then flows out again as it is distributed in the form of wages and profits back to households. Households spend the money but remember that there are **withdrawals** of 0.1 of income because of savings and taxes. So only £90m flows back round the economy in stage 2 to firms. Then firms pay £90m back to households in wages and profits. In the third stage, £81m is spent by households with £19 million leaking out of the circular flow. This process carries on with smaller and smaller amounts being added to national income as the money flows round the economy. Eventually, the initial £100m extra government spending leads to a final increase in national income of £1 000m. In this case, the value of the MULTIPLIER is 10.0.

If leakages from the circular flow in Figure 33.3 had been larger, less of the increase in investment would have continued to flow round the economy. For instance, if leakages had been 0.8 of income, then only £20m (0.2 x £100m) would have flowed round the economy in the second stage. In the third stage, it would have been £4m (0.2 x £20m). The final increase in national income following the initial £100m increase in investment spending would have been £125m.

The multiplier model states that the higher the leakages from the circular flow, the smaller will be the increase in income which continues to flow round the economy at each stage following an initial increase in spending. Hence, the higher the leakages, the smaller the value of the multiplier.

The multiplier effect and increases in government spending and exports

Extra investment spending is only one possible reason why there might be a multiplier effect on aggregate demand. Any increase of the **injections** into the circular flow will lead to a multiple increase in income in the economy. So, an increase in government spending would lead to a multiple increase in income. So too would an increase in export spending.

The shape of the aggregate demand curve

Economists disagree about the shape of the AD curve. **Keynesian economists** argue that the curve is relatively

Question 3

In 1999, The Ford Motor Company announced that it was virtually to rebuild its car plant at Dagenham in Essex. From 2002, the replacement for the current Fiesta model together with a new model code-named B257 would be built at the plant. Local authorities, education institutions and private sector partners were joining forces with Ford in the project, which would cost £468 million. As well as the new Ford works, there would be new educational and training facilities, the relandscaping of an area to include a park and leisure based-access to the banks of the river Thames, and the creation of a 90 acre components supplier park. The project would create an estimated 2 000 additional jobs in the area.

Source: adapted from the *Financial Times*, 26.5.1999.

(a) Explain how there might be a multiplier effect on income from the investment at Dagenham.

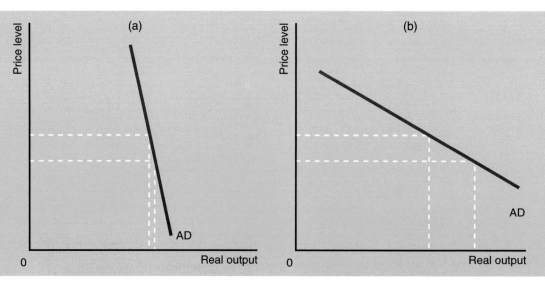

Figure 33.4 *The responsiveness of equilibrium real output to changes in the price level*
Keynesians argue that the AD curve is relatively steep because real output changes little when the price level changes. Classical economists argue that the AD curve is relatively shallow because price changes have a significant effect on real output.

steep, i.e. that changes in the price level have little impact on aggregate demand, as shown in Figure 33.4 (a) . They argue that increases in the price level have little impact on interest rates. In turn, changes in interest rates have little impact on consumption and investment expenditures. Keynesians argue that the main determinant of consumption is disposable income (☞ unit 31) whilst the main determinants of investment are past changes in income (☞ unit 32). So the link between changes in the price level and aggregate demand is very weak.

Classical economists argue that the link between the price level and aggregate demand is a strong one as shown in Figure 33.4(b). Classical economists are economists who are strongly influenced by the economic theories developed before Keynes. They look back to the nineteenth century when the basics of micro-economics were developed. In particular, they tend to argue that markets usually work efficiently and that labour market failure is relatively unimportant. In this case, they argue that increases in the price level have a strong impact on interest rates. In turn, changes in interest rates have a considerable impact on consumption and investment. Interest rates are much more important, they argue, in determining expenditure on consumer durables than Keynesian economists would suggest. Also, investment is strongly influenced by interest rates - the **marginal efficiency of capital theory** (☞ unit 32).

Important note

Aggregate demand analysis and aggregate supply analysis outlined in units 33 and 34 is more complex than demand and supply analysis in an individual market. You may already have noticed, for instance, that a change in interest rates could lead to a movement along the aggregate demand curve or lead to a shift in the curve. Similarly, an increase in consumption could lead to a

movement along or a shift in the curve. To distinguish between movements along and shifts in the curve it is important to consider what has caused the change in aggregate demand.

If the change has come about because the price level has changed, then there is a movement **along** the AD curve. For instance, a rise in the price level causes a rise in interest rates. This leads to a fall in consumption. This is shown by a movement up the curve.

If, however, interest rates or consumer spending have changed for a different reason than because prices have changed, then there will be a **shift** in the AD curve. A government putting up interest rates at a given price level would lead to a shift in the curve.

Applied economics

The Lawson boom 1986-89 and its aftermath

With the benefit of hindsight, the second half of the 1980s was disastrous for the UK economy. The government stoked up an enormous boom, known as the 'Lawson boom' after the Chancellor of the Exchequer at the time, Nigel Lawson, only to have to deflate it when it became unsustainable.

Figure 33.5 shows that for most of the period 1985 and 1988, the economy grew at over 4 per cent year. This was well above the trend rate of growth of $2^1/_2$ per cent. The high growth of 1985 and 1986 was seen as part of the recovery from the deep recession earlier in the 1980s. By 1987, the government had convinced itself that Britain was experiencing an 'economic miracle' due to its economic policies and that a 4 per cent per annum growth rate was sustainable in the long term.

There was a number of factors which led to the fast growth of aggregate demand during the period. Consumption led the boom. Consumers saw interest rates, shown in Figure 33.5, fall from a high of 14 per cent in 1985 to a low of 7.5 per cent in 1988. This helped fuel a housing boom, where house prices more than doubled in some areas of the country. Higher house prices led to higher levels of household wealth, which in itself encouraged consumption. Lower interest rates and large numbers of people moving house fuelled spending on consumer durables. Another important factor was a substantial tax cutting budget in March 1987, which saw the top rate of income tax fall from 60 per cent to 40 per cent. Lower taxes led to higher disposable income and hence higher consumption. Inflation remained low, so households did not have to increase their savings levels to rebuild the real value of their wealth. The stock market also saw share prices increasing, adding to households' wealth. Unemployment fell sharply, halving from 3 million to 1.2 million between 1986 and 1989. All these factors led to increasing levels of consumer confidence. Households were more willing than before to take out loans and were less willing to save.

As for investment, increased consumer spending which led through to high growth in GDP encouraged firms to invest. They needed more productive capacity to cope with consumer demand. Indeed, even in 1986, the economy was operating at above capacity with a positive output gap as can be seen in Figure 33.6. By 1988, the economy was operating at 5.5 per cent above its productive potential. Firms sharply increased their investment spending and planned to take advantage of the many profitable opportunities that were now available. In the meantime, importers took advantage of the UK's inability to satisfy domestic demand and a dangerously high **current account deficit** (☞ unit 30) was recorded.

Government spending was kept in tight control throughout 1986-88 and so this was not a contributory factor to high levels of aggregate demand. As for exports, there was a sharp fall in the value of oil exports in 1986 due to a sharp fall in the price of oil. The value of the pound fell sharply in consequence. However, in 1987 and 1988, the value of the pound rose, which dampened growth in exports. Hence, exports, like government spending, were not a significant contributor to the increase in aggregate demand during the Lawson boom.

The subsequent recession was the longest since the 1930s. In 1988, the government realised that the economy had overheated and that inflation would increase sharply if it did not take action. So it raised interest rates and by late 1989, as Figure 31.5 shows, they stood at 15 per cent, double their lowest 1988 value. This led to a slowdown in consumer spending. The housing market collapsed as borrowers were less willing to take out mortgages to finance new purchases. Existing mortgage borrowers found their mortgage payments increasing sharply, reducing their ability to spend. Lower house prices lowered household wealth and severely dented consumer confidence. So too did rising unemployment, which doubled between 1989 and 1993. Firms cut back their investment spending as they found themselves with too much productive capacity.

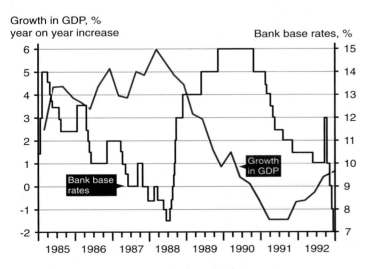

Figure 33.5 *Bank base rates and economic growth, 1985-1992*
Source: adapted from *Economic Trends Annual Supplement*, Office for National Statistics.

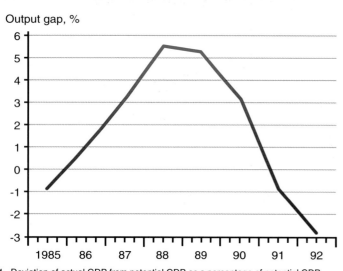

Government spending remained tight although there was some increase in government spending after John Major became Prime Minister in 1989. As for exports, their growth remained subdued because high interest rates kept the value of the pound high. The government also made the policy mistake of taking the pound into the Exchange Rate Mechanism (ERM) of the European Monetary Union (the precursor to the euro and the monetary union) at too high a level, which forced it to keep interest rates high until Britain was forced to leave the ERM by currency speculation in September 1992. By that time, falling levels of aggregate demand had kept the economy in 7 successive quarters of falling GDP.

1. Deviation of actual GDP from potential GDP as a percentage of potential GDP.
Figure 33.6 *The output gap[1], 1985-1992*
Source: adapted from *Economic Outlook*, OECD.

Aggregate demand 1992–95

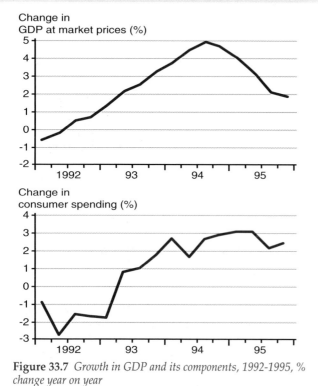

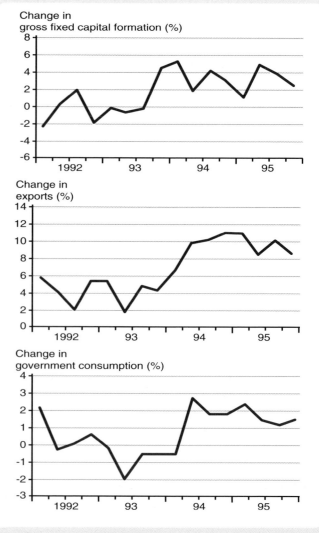

Figure 33.7 *Growth in GDP and its components, 1992-1995, % change year on year*
Source: adapted from *Economic Trends Annual Supplement*, Office for National Statistics.

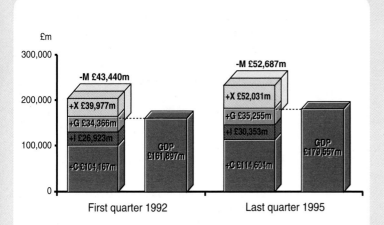

Figure 33.8 *GDP and its components, 1st quarter 1992 compared to 4th quarter 1995*
Source: adapted from *Economic Trends Annual Supplement*, Office for National Statistics.

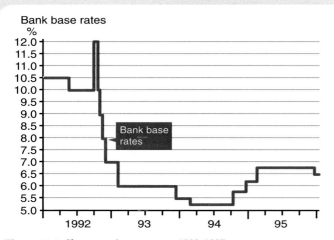

Figure 33.9 *Short term interest rates, 1992-1995*
Source: adapted from *Economic Trends Annual Supplement*, Office for National Statistics.

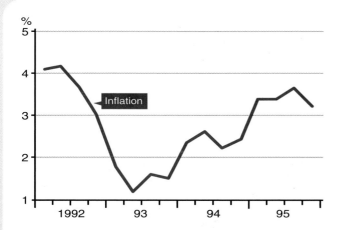

Figure 33.10 *Inflation, % change year on year*
Source: adapted from *Economic Trends Annual Supplement*, Office for National Statistics.

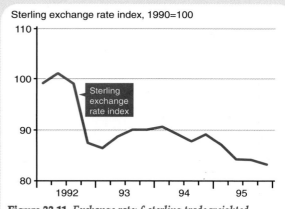

Figure 33.11 *Exchange rate: £ sterling trade weighted exchange rate, 1990=100*
Source: adapted from *Economic Trends Annual Supplement*, Office for National Statistics.

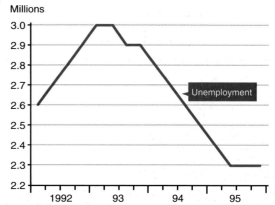

Figure 33.12 *Unemployment, claimant count, millions*
Source: adapted from *Economic Trends Annual Supplement*, Office for National Statistics.

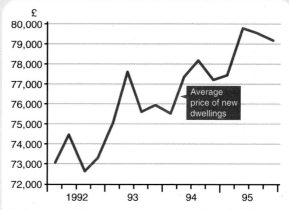

Figure 33.13 *House prices: average price of new dwellings, £*
Source: adapted from *Economic Trends Annual Supplement*, Office for National Statistics.

1. Explain what is meant by 'aggregate demand'.
2. Describe the trends in aggregate demand and its components between 1992 and 1995.
3. Analyse the factors which contributed to the change in aggregate demand over the period shown in the data.
4. Evaluate the extent to which the recovery of 1992-95 was led by a recovery in consumption.

Summary

1. The aggregate supply curve shows the level of output in the whole economy at any given level of average prices.
2. In the short run, it is assumed that money wage rates are constant. Firms will supply extra output if the prices they receive increase. Hence, in the short run, the aggregate supply curve is upward sloping.
3. An increase in firms' costs of production will shift the short run aggregate supply curve upward, whilst a fall in costs will shift it downwards.
4. In the long run, wage rates may go up or down. Classical economists argue that if wages are perfectly flexible, unemployment will be eliminated by a fall in real wage rates. With full employment in the economy, the long run aggregate supply curve must be vertical at an output level equal to the full employment level of income.
5. Keynesian economists argue that real wages may not fall far enough to eliminate unemployment even in the long run. The long run aggregate supply curve is then horizontal or upward sloping at levels of output below full employment income but becomes vertical at full employment.
6. Shifts in the long run aggregate supply curve are caused by changes in the quantity or quality of factors of production or the efficiency of their use.

The short run aggregate supply curve

In unit 5, it was argued that the supply curve for an industry was upward sloping. If the price of a product increases, firms in the industry are likely to increase their profits by producing and selling more. So the higher the price, the higher the level of output. The supply curve being talked about here is a **micro-economic** supply curve. Is the **macro-economic** supply curve (i.e. the supply curve for the whole economy) the same?

The macro-economic supply curve is called the AGGREGATE SUPPLY CURVE, because it is the sum of all the industry supply curves in the economy. It shows how much output firms wish to supply at each level of prices.

In the short run, the aggregate supply curve is upward sloping. The short run is defined here as the period when money wage rates and the prices of all other factor inputs in the economy are fixed. Assume that firms wish to increase their level of output. In the short run, they are unlikely to take on extra workers. Taking on extra staff is an expensive process. Sacking them if they are no longer needed is likely to be even more costly, not just in direct monetary terms but also in terms of industrial relations within the company. So firms tend to respond to increases in demand in the short run by working their existing labour force more intensively, for instance through overtime.

Firms will need to provide incentives for workers to work harder or longer hours. Overtime, for instance, may

be paid at one and a half times the basic rate of pay. Whilst basic pay rates remain constant, earnings will rise and this will tend to put up both the average and marginal costs per unit of output. In many sectors of the economy, where competition is imperfect and where firms have the power to increase their prices, the rise in labour costs will lead to a rise in prices. It only needs prices to rise in some sectors of the economy for the average price level in the economy to rise. So in the short term, an increase in output by firms is likely to lead to an increase in their costs which in turn will result in some firms raising prices. But the increase in prices is likely to be small because, given constant prices (e.g. wage **rates**) for factor inputs, the increases in costs (e.g. wage **earnings**) are likely to be fairly small too. Therefore the short run aggregate supply curve is relatively price elastic. This is shown in Figure 34.1. An increase in output from Q_1 to Q_2 leads to a moderate rise in the average price level of $P_1 P_2$.

If demand falls in the short run, some firms in the economy will react by cutting their prices to try and stimulate extra orders. But the opportunities to cut prices

Question 1.

During 1963, output in the UK economy boomed. GDP rose by 5.5 per cent. Using an aggregate supply curve, show the likely effect of this on prices assuming that money wage rates did not rise during the period.

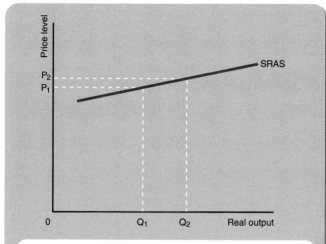

Figure 34.1 *The short run aggregate supply curve*
The slope of the SRAS line is very shallow because, whilst it is assumed that in the short run wage rates are constant, firms will face some increased costs such as overtime payments when they increase output.

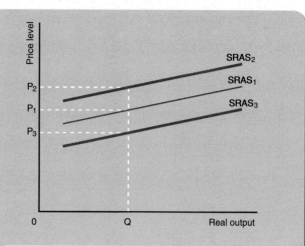

Figure 34.2 *Shifts in the short run aggregate supply curve*
The short run aggregate supply curve is drawn on the assumption that costs, in particular the wage rate, remain constant. A change in costs is shown by a shift in the curve. For instance, an increase in wage rates would push $SRAS_1$ up to $SRAS_2$ whilst a fall in wages rates would push the curve down to $SRAS_3$.

will be limited. Firms will be reluctant to sack workers and their overheads will remain the same, so their average cost and marginal cost will barely be altered. Again, the aggregate supply curve is relatively price elastic.

Shifts in the short run aggregate supply curve

The SHORT RUN AGGREGATE SUPPLY CURVE shows the relationship between aggregate output and the average price level, assuming that money wage rates in the economy are constant. But what if wage rates do change, or some other variable which affects aggregate supply changes? Then, just as in the micro-economic theory of the supply curve, the aggregate supply curve will shift. The following are three examples of SUPPLY SIDE SHOCKS, factors which cause the short run aggregate supply curve to shift.

Wage rates An increase in wage rates will result in firms facing increased costs of production. Some firms will respond by increasing prices. So at any given level of output, a rise in wage rates will lead to a rise in the average price level. This is shown in Figure 34.2 by a shift in the short run aggregate supply curve from $SRAS_1$ to $SRAS_2$.

Raw material prices A general fall in the prices of raw materials will lower industrial costs and will lead to some firms reducing the prices of their products. Hence there will be a shift in the short run aggregate supply curve downwards. This is shown in Figure 34.2 by the shift from $SRAS_1$ to $SRAS_3$.

Taxation An increase in the tax burden on industry will increase costs. Hence the short run aggregate supply schedule will be pushed upwards, for instance from $SRAS_1$ to $SRAS_2$ in Figure 34.2.

Question 2

Using diagrams, show the the likely effect of the following on the short run aggregate supply curve.
(a) Output in 1959 was 4.1 per cent higher than in 1958 but the price level was the same.
(b) Output in 1982 was the same as in 1978, yet wage rates had increased by approximately 50 per cent over the period.
(c) In 1973-4, the price of crude oil approximately quadrupled.

The long run AS curve and the labour market

In the short run, it was assumed that wage rates were fixed. Most groups of workers today in the UK economy renegotiate their wage rates annually. The short run could be seen as a period of months rather than years. What happens in the labour market in the long run?

Assume that the economy goes into recession. The demand for labour will fall because the demand for goods in the economy is falling. In Figure 34.3, this is shown by the shift to the left in the demand curve for labour. The old equilibrium real wage rate was OE. For equilibrium now to be restored, the real wage rate needs to fall to OF. If wages get stuck at OE, there will be unemployment in the economy of AC. Economists differ about how workers will respond to changed demand for labour and the consequent change in unemployment.

The classical view At one extreme are some classical, monetarist or supply side economists. They argue that the market for labour is like the market for bananas. Excess

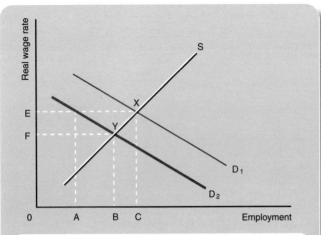

Figure 34.3 *A fall in the demand for labour*
A fall in the demand for labour from D_1 to D_2 will result in short term unemployment of AC. However, the equilibrium level of unemployment will fall from OC to OB in the longer term as a result of a fall of EF in real wage rates. This will restore the economy to full employment.

supply of bananas will bring about a rapid fall in price to clear the market. So too in the labour market. Unemployed workers will realise that they will have to accept cuts in pay if they are to get another job. Those in work will know that there is a pool of unemployed workers waiting to take their jobs if they do not show at least restraint in their wage claims. Firms know that they can pick up workers at low rates of pay. Hence in an effort to maximise profitability by minimising costs they will not be prepared to pay their existing workforce such high real wages.

Classical economists differ as to how quickly the labour market clears. Some argue that the labour market takes time to bring about a fall in wages and unemployment. This was the view taken by many during the Great Depression of the 1930s. Their view is based on a theory of ADAPTIVE EXPECTATIONS. This means that expectations of what will happen are based on what has happened in the past. In the short term, workers who are unemployed will hope that the economy will pick up and they will be able to get a job.

Firms will be reluctant to damage relations with existing workers by cutting their wages when, in fact, they could hire new workers at a lower wage rate than that being paid to existing workers. Hence, in the short term, disequilibrium can exist in the labour market. In the longer term, however, unemployed workers will realise that they will never get a job if they stick out for too high a wage. Firms will realise that the new lower level of wages is here to stay and will adopt pay cutting policies. Wages will then fall, bringing the market back to equilibrium.

New Classical economists, in contrast, believe that markets will clear instantaneously. The idea of RATIONAL EXPECTATIONS was developed in the 1970s in America by two economists, Robert Lucus and Thomas Sergeant. They argued that economic agents, such as workers and firms, base their decisions on all the

information they have, including current information and predictions of future events. Because they are using all the information they have, they are making their decisions about what to do in a rational way. In the labour market, workers know that long term unemployment can only be solved by accepting wage cuts. Equally, firms know that they can enforce wage cuts when unemployment rises. Therefore, the labour market will clear immediately. In Figure 34.3, a fall in demand for labour will lead to an immediate move from X to Y. In comparison, the adaptive expectations school would argue that it takes time to move from X to Y because workers and firms are basing their decisions on past events, without thinking clearly about where the future equilibrium will be in the market.

A traditional Keynesian view At the other extreme are some Keynesian economists who argue that unemployment will persist until there is an opposing expansion of demand for labour. They argue that real wages will never fall sufficiently to clear the labour market completely if the market goes into disequilibrium. To understand why real wage rates are unlikely to fall, it is necessary to think clearly about the nature of the labour market in a modern industrialised economy like the UK. In Victorian England, it might have been true that firms hired and fired at will, taking on unemployed workers who were prepared to work for lower wages whilst sacking those who refused to take pay cuts. It might also be true that workers were forced to submit to the iron law of the market place, taking real wage cuts when the demand for labour fell. But conditions are very different in a modern industrialised economy.

- Medium to large employers have little to gain by forcing down wages in the short term. Such action is likely to demotivate the existing workforce and lead to a loss of employee loyalty and goodwill. Employees represent valuable assets of the firm. They have received training and are familiar with working practices. Hiring new labour is a costly process if workers leave because of dissatisfaction with the firm. So such employers are likely to take a long term view of the labour market.
- Trade unions act to protect the interests of their members. Trade union members are almost all in jobs. Therefore they are not particularly concerned with the plight of the unemployed (just as firms are not in business to help alleviate unemployment). Trade unions will naturally not only resist real wage cuts but will press for higher real wages. Can a trade union be said to have achieved its objectives if the workforce of a firm shrinks through natural wastage by a few per cent and those who keep their jobs gain real wage increases?
- If there is minimum wage legislation, then employers of low paid workers will find it difficult if not legally impossible to cut wage rates.
- Benefits for the unemployed discourage workers from taking low paid jobs, preventing employers from offering very low pay when unemployment rises.
- The economy comprises a large number of different labour markets. Labour is immobile geographically in the UK, particularly low paid unskilled workers because of problems with renting low cost housing.

Labour is immobile occupationally because of the ever increasing division of labour within the economy and the failure of both firms and government to provide the level of training which would make workers mobile.

According to this view, a modern labour market is inevitably imperfect. Real wage rates may conceivably fall sufficiently in the long run to bring the economy back to full employment but then, as Keynes said, 'in the long run we are all dead'. It is little comfort to a 45 year old made redundant today to know that in 15 years' time the economy will have returned to full employment and he may then have a chance of getting a low paid job.

A moderate Keynesian view New classical economists argue that the labour market adjusts instantaneously. Moderate classical economists argue that it might take a few years. Traditional Keynesians argue that it might take decades. Moderate Keynesians argue that the process might take 5-10 years. According to this view, labour market rigidities are strong. However, in the medium term, employers in the formal sector of the economy will push down real wage rates from what they would otherwise have been. Even if this is only one per cent per year, it amounts to over 5 per cent over a five year period.

Moreover, there is a significant small business economy where wages are more flexible. Some of those made unemployed will become self-employed, accepting a lower wage in the process.

The long run aggregate supply curve

What happens in the labour market determines the shape of the LONG RUN AGGREGATE SUPPLY CURVE. Classical or supply side economists see the labour market as functioning perfectly. Unemployment represents a disequilibrium position in the market. Real wages, the price of labour, will therefore fall until demand exactly equals supply. At this equilibrium point there will be no unemployment. The classical viewpoint therefore argues that in the long run firms will always employ all workers who wish to work at the equilibrium wage. Similarly, the markets for the other factors of production, land and capital, will be in equilibrium at their full employment level. Hence in the long run firms will supply the maximum potential output of the economy. This is true whatever the level of prices. Therefore the long run aggregate supply curve is vertical and is at the full employment level of output. This is shown in Figure 34.4.

Keynesian economists argue that, even if unemployment exists, workers who have got jobs will carry on negotiating and receiving higher pay rises as the economy grows. There will be little tendency for real wages to fall, allowing the labour market to clear (they are **sticky downwards**). Traditional Keynesian economists argue that, even in the long run, the labour market may not clear. Unemployment could be a long run feature of an economy. Three possibilities then present themselves.

● If the economy is in deep recession, an increase in

Question 3

Money wage rates in an economy increase by 50 per cent in the long run but full employment output remains unchanged. Show the effect of this on the long run aggregate supply curve for the economy.

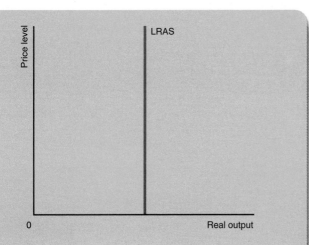

Figure 34.4 *The classical long run aggregate supply curve Classical economics assumes that in the long run wages and prices are flexible and therefore the LRAS curve is vertical. In the long run, there cannot be any unemployment because the wage rate will be in equilibrium where all workers who want a job (the supply of labour) will be offered a job (the demand for labour). So, whatever the level of prices, output will always be constant at the full employment level of income.*

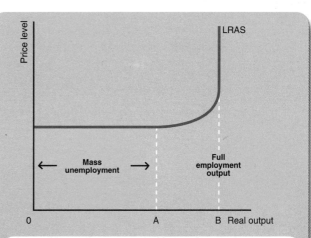

Figure 34.5 *The Keynesian long run aggregate supply curve Traditional Keynesian economists argue that, even in the long run, unemployment may persist because wages don't necessarily fall when unemployment occurs. When there is mass unemployment, output can be increased without any increases in costs and therefore prices. As the economy nears full employment, higher output leads to higher prices. At full employment, the economy cannot produce any more whatever prices firms receive.*

output is unlikely to increase prices. Workers will be too frightened of losing their jobs to negotiate pay rises even if an individual firm is expanding. Here the aggregate supply curve would be horizontal because firms could expand production without experiencing a rise in costs.

● If unemployment is relatively low, workers will be in a position to bid up wages in response to increased demand. Here the aggregate supply curve is upward sloping. The nearer full employment, the more workers will be able to obtain wages increases.

● If the economy is at full employment, firms by definition won't be able to take on any more labour, however much they offer. The economy cannot produce more than its full employment output. Hence at full employment the aggregate supply curve will be vertical.

These three possibilities are shown in Figure 34.5. At levels of output between O and A, mass unemployment exists. The aggregate supply curve is therefore horizontal. Between output levels A and B, the economy is experiencing some unemployment, so the aggregate supply curve is upward sloping. At the full employment level of output, B, the supply curve becomes vertical.

Note that both classical and Keynesian economists agree that at full employment, the long run aggregate supply curve is vertical. Whatever prices are charged, industry cannot increase its output. But Keynesian economists argue that, in the long run, the economy may operate at less than full employment, in which case the aggregate supply curve is horizontal or upward sloping.

Shifts in the long run aggregate supply curve

The long run aggregate supply curve is likely to shift over time. If we assume that it is vertical, then we are saying that the economy is always at full employment in the long run. This means that the position of the aggregate supply

curve is determined by the potential output of the economy. Economic growth occurs because the quantity or quality of the factors of production available to an economy increase or because existing resources are used more efficiently.

Figure 34.6 shows how a growth in potential output is drawn on an aggregate supply diagram. Assume that the education and skills of the workforce increase. This should lead to labour becoming more productive, in turn leading to an increase in the productive potential of the economy at full employment. The long run aggregate supply curve will then shift from LRAS$_1$ to LRAS$_2$, showing that at a given level of prices, the economy can produce more output. A fall in potential output, caused for instance by a fall in the size of the labour force, would be shown by a leftward shift in the curve, from LRAS$_1$ to LRAS$_3$.

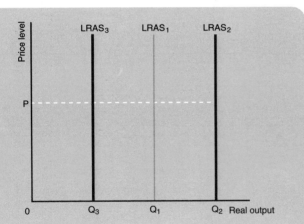

Figure 34.6 *A shift in the long run aggregate supply curve An increase in the productive potential in the economy pushes the long run aggregate supply curve to the right, for instance from LRAS$_1$ to LRAS$_2$. A fall in productive potential, on the other hand, is shown by a shift to the left of the curve, from LRAS$_1$ to LRAS$_3$ for instance.*

Applied economics

The case of oil

As Figure 34.7 shows, in 1973 a barrel of oil cost $2.83. A year later the price had risen to $10.41. This price rise was possibly the most important world economic event of the 1970s. The trigger for the rise came from a war - the Yom Kippur war - when Egypt attacked Israel and was subsequently defeated. The Arab nations, to show support for Egypt, decreed that they would cut off oil supplies from any country which openly supported Israel. Because the demand for oil in the short run is highly price inelastic, any small fall in the supply of oil is enough to bring large increases in prices. After the war finished, the oil producing nations through their organisation OPEC (the Organisation of Petroleum

Exporting Countries) realised that it was possible to maintain a high price for oil by limiting its supply (i.e. by operating a cartel). Since then OPEC has operated a policy of restricting the supply of oil to the market.

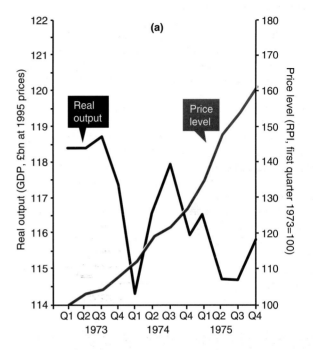

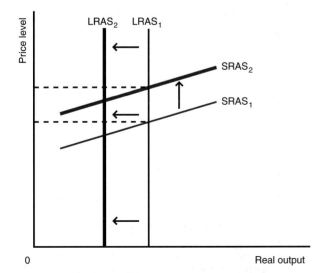

Source: adapted from *BP Statistical Review of World Energy*.
Figure 34.7 *Price of oil, Arabian Light/Dubai, $ per barrel*

Figure 34.8

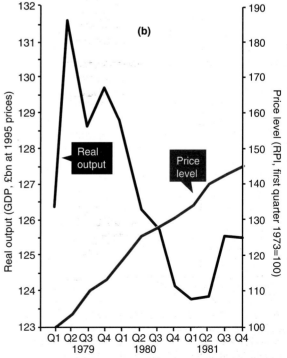

Source: adapted from *Economic Trends Annual Supplement*, Office for National Statistics.
Figure 34.9 *Real output and prices in two periods of oil price shocks*

Oil prices rose rather more slowly between 1974 and 1978. But between 1978 and 1982 the average price of a barrel of oil rose from $13.03 to $31.80. Again, a political event was a major factor in triggering the price rise. The Shah of Iran, ruler of an important oil producing country, was deposed by Muslim fundamentalists led by the Ayatollah Khomeini. The revolution plunged Iran into economic chaos and the new rulers, fiercely anti-Western, showed little interest in resuming large scale exports of oil. A small disruption in oil supplies, a situation exploited by OPEC, was again enough to send oil prices spiralling.

The rise in oil prices had an important effect on the aggregate supply curve of the UK economy. It increased the costs of firms. So at any given level of output, firms needed to charge higher prices to cover their costs. This means that the short run aggregate supply curve shifted upwards as shown in Figure 34.8. This is supported by evidence from the UK economy. There is little doubt that the rise in oil prices helped push up UK prices by 16 per cent in 1974, 25 per cent in 1975, 17 per cent in 1979 and 15 per cent in 1980, as shown in Figure 34.9.

It could also be argued that the long run aggregate curve was pushed back to the left by the oil price rises (from LRAS₁ to LRAS₂ in Figure 34.8). The rise in oil prices meant that some capital equipment which was oil intensive became uneconomic to run. This equipment was mothballed and then scrapped, leading to a once-and-for-all loss in the productive potential of the economy.

Higher prices and lost output arguably led the UK to experience the most difficult economic circumstances since the Second World War.

Aggregate supply, 1974-79

Between February 1974 and May 1979, there was a Labour government in the UK. It is often considered to have been a disastrous period for the economy. In 1975, inflation rose to a post-war peak of 24.2 per cent. Unemployment rose from half a million in 1974 to one and half million in 1977. Share prices halved in 1974. The pound fell to an all time low against the dollar in October 1976. The UK government was forced to borrow from the IMF (the International Monetary Fund in late 1976 to shore up the value of the pound. In 1978-79, during the 'winter of discontent', the economy seemed racked by strikes as workers pressed for double digit pay rises.

However, the second half of the 1970s were difficult times for all industrialised economies. Growth rates worldwide fell as economies accommodated the supply-side shock of the first oil crisis in 1973-4. Table 34.1 shows that the growth in real GDP in the UK economy was above its long run trend rate of growth of 2.4 per cent per annum in three of the six years during the period; and although the average yearly growth rate over the six years was only 1.5 per cent, if 1973, a boom year for the economy were included, the average rate of growth would be 2.3 per cent. Investment spending in the economy remained static, with investment as a percentage of GDP slightly declining. This perhaps reflected a lack of confidence in the future of the economy. Even so, this should be contrasted with the experience of the early 1980s. Investment fell in 1980 and 1981 and did not reach its 1979 levels till 1984.

The 1970s were inflationary times throughout the world. Inflation in the UK accelerated from 7.5 per cent in 1972 to 15.9 per cent in 1974 and 24.1 per cent in 1975. However, the government adopted firm anti-inflationary policies in 1975 and inflation subsequently fell to 8.3 per cent in 1978, before rising again to 13.4 per cent in 1979 as pressure from wages and import prices, including the second round of oil price rises, worsened.

Table 34.1 *Selected economic indicators, UK 1974-79*

	Real growth in GDP	Gross investment		Price level	Import prices	Wage levels
	%	£bn at 1995 prices	% of GDP	1974=100	1974=100	1974=100
1974	- 1.67	79.6	17.13	100.0	100.0	100.0
1975	- 0.69	78.1	16.92	124.1	114.1	126.5
1976	2.79	79.5	16.75	144.7	139.9	146.2
1977	2.36	78.2	16.10	167.7	161.6	161.0
1978	3.40	80.2	15.97	181.4	167.9	184.3
1979	2.77	82.3	15.95	205.8	178.7	213.1

Source: adapted from *Economic Trends Annual Supplement*, Office for National Statistics.

1. **Consider both the passage and the table carefully. Discuss, using diagrams, what happened to aggregate supply in the second half of the 1970s:**
   (a) in the short run and
   (b) in the long run.

unit 35 Equilibrium output

Summary

1. The economy is in equilibrium when aggregate demand equals aggregate supply.
2. In the classical model, where wages are completely flexible, the economy will be in long run equilibrium at full employment. In the Keynesian model, where wages are sticky downwards, the economy can be in long run equilibrium at less than full employment.
3. In the classical model, a rise in aggregate demand will in the short run lead to an increase in both output and prices, but in the long run the rise will generate only an increase in prices. In the Keynesian model, a rise in aggregate demand will be purely inflationary if the economy is at full employment, but will lead to an increase in output if the economy is below full employment.
4. A rise in long run aggregate supply in the classical model will both increase output and reduce prices. Keynesians would agree with this in general, but would argue that an increase in aggregate supply will have no effect on output or prices if the economy is in a slump.
5. Factors which affect aggregate demand may well affect aggregate supply and vice versa, although this may occur over different time periods. For instance, an increase in investment is likely to increase both aggregate demand and aggregate supply.

Equilibrium output in the short run

Units 33 and 34 outlined theories of aggregate demand and aggregate supply. Both Keynesian and classical economists agree that in the short run the aggregate demand curve is downward sloping whilst the aggregate supply curve is upward sloping. The equilibrium level of output in the short run occurs at the intersection of the aggregate demand and aggregate supply curves. In Figure 35.1, the equilibrium level of income and output is OQ. The equilibrium price level is OP.

Equilibrium output in the long run

The main disagreement amongst economists is about long run equilibrium in the economy. Classical economists argue that in the long run the aggregate supply curve is vertical, as shown in Figure 35.2. Long run equilibrium

occurs where the long run aggregate supply curve (LRAS) intersects with the aggregate demand curve. Hence equilibrium output is OQ and the equilibrium price level is OP. Associated with the long run equilibrium price level is a short run aggregate supply curve (SRAS) which passes through the point where LRAS = AD. The long run aggregate supply curve shows the supply curve for the economy at full employment (☞ unit 34). Hence there can be no unemployment in the long run according to classical economists.

Keynesian economists argue that the long run aggregate supply curve is as shown in Figure 35.3. The economy is at full employment where the LRAS curve is vertical at output OR - a point of agreement with classical economists. However, the economy can be in equilibrium at less than full employment. In Figure 35.3 the equilibrium level of output is OQ where the AD curve cuts the LRAS curve. The key point of disagreement between classical and Keynesian economists is the extent

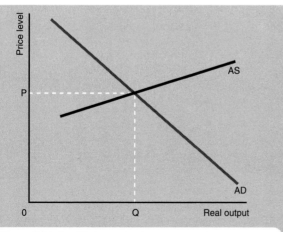

Figure 35.1 *Equilibrium output*
The equilibrium level of national output is set at the intersection of the aggregate demand and supply curves at OQ. The equilibrium price level is OP.

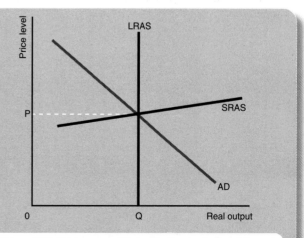

Figure 35.2 *Long run equilibrium in the classical model*
Long run equilibrium output is OQ, the full employment level of output, since wages are flexible both downwards as well as upwards.

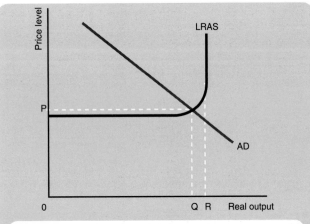

Figure 35.3 *Long run equilibrium in the Keynesian model Long run equilibrium output OQ may be below the full employment level of output OR because real wages may not fall when there is unemployment.*

to which workers react to unemployment by accepting real wage cuts.

Classical economists argue that a rise in unemployment will lead rapidly to cuts in real wages. These cuts will increase the demand for labour and reduce its supply, returning the economy to full employment quickly and automatically. Economists like Patrick Minford, of the rational expectations school of thought, argue that this short term disequilibrium is corrected so quickly that the short run can be disregarded. Keynesian economists, on the other hand, argue that money wages are sticky downwards. Workers will refuse to take money wage cuts and will fiercely resist cuts in their real wage. The labour market will therefore not clear except perhaps over a very long period of time, so long that it is possibly even not worth considering.

Having outlined a theory of equilibrium output, it is now possible to see what happens if either aggregate demand or aggregate supply change.

Question 1

What would be the effect on equilibrium income in the long run if the workers in the photograph were
(a) successful and (b) unsuccessful with their demands?

A rise in aggregate demand

Assume that there is a rise in aggregate demand in the economy with long run aggregate supply initially remaining unchanged. For instance, there may be an increase in the wages of public sector employees paid for by an increase in the money supply, or there may be a fall in the marginal propensity to save and a rise in the marginal propensity to consume. A rise in aggregate demand will push the AD curve to the right. The classical and Keynesian models give different conclusions about the effect of this.

The classical model A rise in aggregate demand, which shifts the aggregate demand curve from AD_1 to AD_2 in Figure 35.4, will move the economy from A to B. There will be a movement along the short run aggregate supply curve. Output will rise from OL to OM and this will be accompanied by a small rise in the price level from ON to OP.

But the economy is now in long run disequilibrium. The full employment level of output is OL, shown by the position of the long run aggregate supply curve. The economy is therefore operating at over-full employment. Firms will find it difficult to recruit labour, buy raw materials and find new offices or factory space. They will respond by bidding up wages and other costs. The short run aggregate supply curve is drawn on the assumption that wage rates and other costs remain constant. So a rise in wage rates will shift the short run aggregate supply curve upwards. Short run equilibrium output will now fall and prices will keep rising. The economy will only return to long run equilibrium when the short run aggregate supply curve has shifted upwards from $SRAS_1$ to $SRAS_2$ so that aggregate demand once again equals long run aggregate supply at C.

The conclusion of the classical model is that increases in aggregate demand will initially increase both prices and output (the movement from A to B in Figure 35.4). Over time prices will continue to rise but output will fall as the

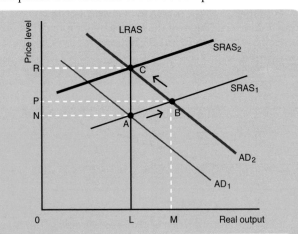

Figure 35.4 *The classical model in the short and long run A rise in aggregate demand shown by a shift to the right in the AD curve will result in a movement along the SRAS curve. Both output and prices will increase. In the long run, the SRAS curve will shift upwards with long run equilibrium being re-established at C. The rise in demand has led only to a rise in the price level.*

economy moves back towards long run equilibrium (the movement from B to C). In the long term an increase in aggregate demand will only lead to an increase in the price level (from A to C). There will be no effect on equilibrium output. So increases in aggregate demand without any change in long run aggregate supply are purely inflationary.

The Keynesian model In the Keynesian model, the long run aggregate supply curve is shaped as in Figure 35.5. Keynesians would agree with classical economists that an increase in aggregate demand from, say, AD$_4$ to AD$_5$ will be purely inflationary if the economy is already at full employment at OD.

But if the economy is in deep depression, as was the case in the UK during the early 1930s, an increase in aggregate

demand will lead to a rise in output without an increase in prices. The shift in aggregate demand from AD$_1$ to AD$_2$ will increase equilibrium output from OA to OB without raising the price level from OP as there are unused resources available.

The third possibility is that the economy is a little below full employment, for instance at OC in Figure 35.5. Then a rise in aggregate demand from AD$_3$ to AD$_4$ will increase both equilibrium output and equilibrium prices.

In the Keynesian model, increases in aggregate demand may or may not be effective in raising equilibrium output. It depends upon whether the economy is below full employment or at full employment.

A rise in long run aggregate supply

A rise in long run aggregate supply means that the potential output of the economy has increased (i.e. there has been genuine economic growth). Rises in long run aggregate supply which are unlikely to shift the aggregate demand curve might occur if, for instance, incentives to work increased or there was a change in technology.

The classical model In the classical model, an increase in long run aggregate supply will lead to both higher output and lower prices. In Figure 35.6 a shift in the aggregate supply curve from LRAS$_1$ to LRAS$_2$ will increase equilibrium output from OL to OM. Equilibrium prices will also fall from ON to OP. Contrast this conclusion with what happens when aggregate demand is increased in the classical model - a rise in prices with no increase in output. It is not surprising that classical economists are so strongly in favour of **supply side policies** (☞ unit 38 - this is why they are often referred to as 'supply side' economists).

The Keynesian model In the Keynesian model, shown in Figure 35.7, an increase in aggregate supply will both increase output and reduce prices if the economy is at full employment. With aggregate demand at AD$_1$, a shift in the aggregate supply curve from LRAS$_1$ to LRAS$_2$ increases full employment equilibrium output from Y$_E$ to Y$_F$. If the economy is at slightly less than full employment, with an

Question 2

In his Budget of 1981, with unemployment at 3 million and still rising, the Chancellor of the Exchequer, Geoffrey Howe, raised the level of taxes and significantly reduced the budget deficit in order to squeeze inflationary pressures. In a letter to The Times, 364 economists protested at what they saw as the perversity of this decision.

(a) Geoffrey Howe was influenced by classical economic thinking. Using a diagram, explain why he believed that his policy (i) would help reduce inflation and (ii) not lead to any increase in unemployment.
(b) The economists who wrote the letter to The Times could broadly be described as Keynesian. Using a diagram, explain why they believed that it was folly to increase taxes at a time when the economy was in the grip of the worst recession since the 1930s.

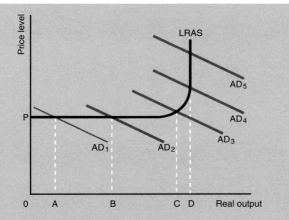

Figure 35.5 *The Keynesian model*
If the economy is already at full employment, an increase in aggregate demand in the Keynesian model creates an inflationary gap without increasing output. In a depression, an increase in aggregate demand will increase output but not prices. If the economy is slightly below full employment, an increase in aggregate demand will increase both output and prices.

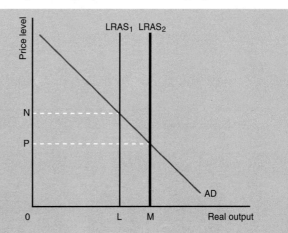

Figure 35.6 *An increase in aggregate supply in the classical model*
A shift to the right of the LRAS curve will both increase equilibrium output and reduce the price level.

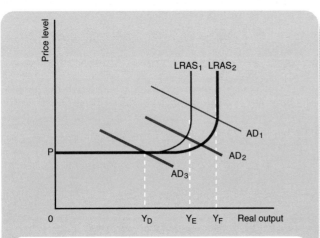

Figure 35.7 *An increase in aggregate supply in the Keynesian model*
The effect of an increase in long run aggregate supply depends upon the position of the aggregate demand curve. If the economy is at or near full employment, an increase will raise output and lower prices. However, if the economy is in depression at Y_D, an increase in LRAS will have no impact on the economy.

aggregate demand curve of AD_2, then the shift to the right in the LRAS curve will still be beneficial to the economy, increasing output and reducing prices. But Keynesians disagree with classical economists that supply side measures can be effective in a depression. If the aggregate demand curve is AD_3, an increase in aggregate supply has no effect on equilibrium output. It remains obstinately stuck at Y_D. Only an increase in aggregate demand will move the economy out of depression.

It is now possible to understand one of the most important controversies in the history of economics. During the 1930s, classical economists argued that the only way to put the millions of unemployed during the Great Depression back to work was to adopt supply side measures - such as cutting unemployment benefits, reducing trade union power and cutting marginal tax rates and government spending. John Maynard Keynes attacked this orthodoxy by suggesting that the depression was caused by a lack of demand and suggesting that it was the government's responsibility to increase the level of aggregate demand. The same debate was replayed in the UK in the early 1980s. This time it was Keynesians who represented orthodoxy. They suggested that the only quick way to get the millions officially unemployed back to work was to expand aggregate demand. In the Budget of 1981, the government did precisely the opposite - it cut its projected budget deficit, reducing aggregate demand and argued that the only way to cure unemployment was to improve the supply side of the economy.

Increasing aggregate demand and supply

In micro-economics, factors which shift the demand curve do **not** shift the supply curve as well and vice versa. For instance, an increase in the costs of production shifts the supply curve but does **not** shift the demand curve for a good (although there will of course be a **movement along**

the demand curve as a result). But in macro-economic aggregate demand and aggregate supply analysis, factors which shift one curve may well shift the other curve as well. For instance, assume that firms increase their planned investment. This will increase the level of aggregate demand. But in the long run it will also increase the level of aggregate supply. An increase in investment will increase the capital stock of the economy. The productive potential of the economy will therefore rise. We can use aggregate demand and supply analysis to show the effects of an increase in investment.

An increase in investment in the classical model will initially shift the aggregate demand curve in Figure 35.8 to the right from AD_1 to AD_2. There will then be a movement along the short run aggregate supply curve from A to B. There is now long run disequilibrium. How this will be resolved depends upon the speed with which the investment is brought on stream and starts to produce goods and services. Assume that this happens fairly quickly. The long run aggregate supply curve will then shift to the right, say, from $LRAS_1$ to $LRAS_2$. Long run equilibrium will be restored at C. Output has increased and the price level fallen slightly. There will also be a new short run aggregate supply curve, $SRAS_2$. It is below the original short run aggregate supply curve because it is assumed that investment has reduced costs of production.

Not all investment results in increased production. For instance, fitting out a new shop which goes into receivership within a few months will increase aggregate demand but not long run aggregate supply. The long run aggregate supply curve will therefore not shift and the increased investment will only be inflationary. Equally, investment might be poorly directed. The increase in aggregate demand might be greater than the increase in long run aggregate supply. Here there will be an increase in equilibrium output but there will also be an increase in prices. The extent to which investment increases output and contributes to a lessening of inflationary pressure depends upon the extent to which it gives a high rate of return in the long run.

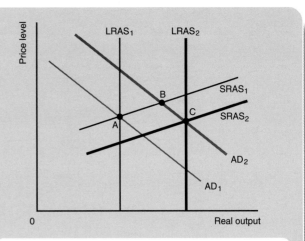

Figure 35.8 *An increase in investment expenditure*
An increase in investment will increase aggregate demand from AD_1 to AD_2, and is likely to shift the long run aggregate supply curve from $LRAS_1$ to $LRAS_2$. The result is an increase in output and a small fall in prices.

Question 3

In June 1995, a new French government unveiled a stiff budget designed to reduce high unemployment levels by 700 000 and bring down a high budget deficit from 5.7 per cent of GDP to 5.1 per cent of GDP within the fiscal year. The measures included:
- a substantial FF19bn cut in government spending affecting all ministries apart from justice and culture, with defence bearing nearly 50 per cent of the cuts;
- a rise in corporation tax from 33.3 per cent to 36.6 per cent;
- a rise in the standard rate of VAT from 18.6 per cent to 20.6 per cent;
- a 10 per cent rise in wealth tax;
- a 40 per cent cut in employment taxes paid by firms

on employment of workers at or near the minimum wage level;
- new programmes targeted particularly at youth in difficulties, offering training, apprenticeship and other policies to bring people into the workforce;
- a rise in the minimum wage by 4 per cent;
- a rise in state pensions by 0.5 per cent;
- measures to stimulate the housing market, particularly focused on lodgings for people on lower incomes.

Using diagrams, explain what effect these measures would have on aggregate supply according to:
(a) classical or supply side economists,
(b) Keynesian economists.

Question 4

Using a classical model of the economy, explain the effect of the following on: (i) aggregate demand; (ii) short run aggregate supply; (iii) output and prices in the long run.
(a) A 10 per cent rise in earnings.

(b) An increase in real spending by government on education and training.
(c) An increase in the average long term real rate of interest from 3 per cent to 5 per cent.

Applied economics

Stagflation, 1974–76 and 1979–1981

In a simple Keynesian model, rising inflation is associated with falling unemployment and vice versa. The experience of the 1950s and 1960s tended to support the hypothesis that there was this trade off between the two variables. However, in 1974-75 and 1979-1981 there was both rising inflation **and** rising unemployment: this combination of stagnation and inflation came to be called **stagflation**.

The stagflation of both these periods can be explained using an aggregate demand and supply model of the economy. The rise in oil prices in each period was an external supply side shock to the UK economy. It had the effect of raising the short run aggregate supply curve (☞ unit 34) from SRAS$_1$ to SRAS$_2$ in Figure 35.9. The economy shifted from A to B. As can be seen from the diagram, prices rose and output fell.

In the first oil crisis, inflation rose from 9.1 per cent in 1973 to 15.9 per cent in 1974 and 24.1 per cent in 1975, before falling back to 16.5 per cent in 1976. Real GDP on the other hand fell by 1.5 per cent in 1974 and 0.8 per cent in 1975, before resuming an upward path in 1976.

In the second oil crisis, inflation rose from 8.3 per cent in 1978 to 13.4 per cent in 1979 and 18.0 per cent in 1980, before falling back again in 1981. Real GDP fell by 2 per cent in 1980 and 1.2 per cent in 1981.

The classical model would suggest that, all other things being equal, the economy would fall back to A from B.

Full employment would be restored at the old price level. The above figures indicate that this did not happen. This was because the aggregate demand curve shifted to the right at the same time as the short run aggregate supply curve was shifting to the left. This led to continued inflation as output rose from 1976 and again from 1982. The rise in aggregate demand in the first period was partly due to the then Labour government increasing the budget deficit, as well as increases in the money supply (the inflation was **accommodated**). In the second period,

Figure 35.9

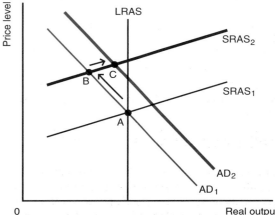

taxation rose and government spending fell during the downturn in the economy, although the money supply increased again. This difference in fiscal stance is a partial explanation of why the rise in unemployment was lower and the rise in inflation higher in the first period than in the second period. It can be argued that the shift to the right in the aggregate demand curve was greater in the mid-1970s than the early 1980s.

In Figure 35.9, the economy is now at C. In reality, the AD and AS curves are constantly shifting to the right, producing new equilibrium price levels and output levels in each time period, so the economy would not remain at C for long. But could the economy stay at C in theory? According to classical economists, the answer is no. At C, given that there is unemployment, real wages will fall, shifting the SRAS curve down and leading to a new equilibrium with lower prices and higher output. Keynesians would argue that C could well be an equilibrium position for a number of years because the labour market is not a perfect market. Extreme Keynesians would argue that the labour market does not clear in the face of unemployment and therefore the economy could remain at C even in the long run. Did the economy in practice move back to a full employment level? The second oil price shock followed quickly after the first and therefore it is difficult to answer this from the experience of the 1970s. However, unemployment did fall between 1976 and 1979, indicating perhaps a movement towards full employment. Following the second oil price shock, unemployment continued to increase until the third quarter of 1986. Then it fell rapidly, halving by late 1989. Whether the economy had moved back onto its long run aggregate supply curve is debatable. If it had, then the natural rate of unemployment must have been considerably higher in 1989 than it was, say, in the early 1970s, a somewhat surprising conclusion given the array of labour market measures implemented in the 1980s.

DATA QUESTION

Recovery and boom, 1993–98

Figure 35.10 *Changes in costs*

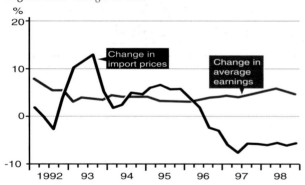

Source: adapted from *Economic Trends Annual Supplement*, Office for National Statistics.

Figure 35.12 *Inflation and unemployment, claimant count*

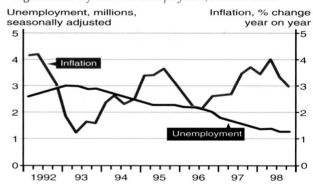

Source: adapted from *Economic Trends Annual Supplement*, Office for National Statistics.

Figure 35.11 *Short term interest rates*[1]

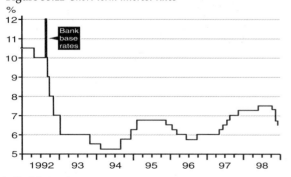

1. Bank base rates.
Source: adapted from *Economic Trends Annual Supplement*, Office for National Statistics.

Figure 35.13 *The output gap*[1]

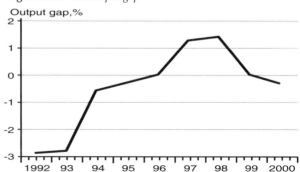

1. Deviation of actual GDP rates from potential GDP as a percentage of potential GDP.
Source: adapted from *Economic Trends Annual Supplement*, Office for National Statistics.

Figure 35.14 *Change in GDP and its components, % change year on year*

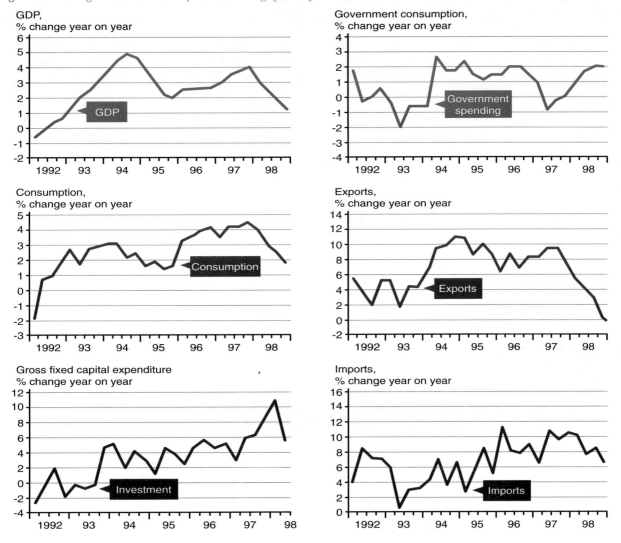

Source: adapted from *Economic Trends Annual Supplement*, Office for National Statistics.

Figure 35.15 *House prices, % change on previous year*

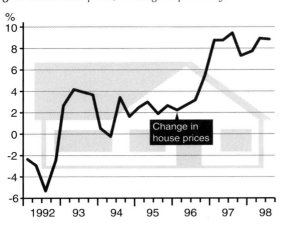

Source: adapted from *Economic Trends Annual Supplement*, Office for National Statistics.

Figure 35.16 *Exchange rate of the pound: trade weighted index, 1990=100*

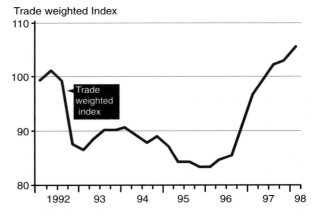

Source: adapted from *Economic Trends Annual Supplement*, Office for National Statistics.

1. Describe the changes in output between 1992 and 1998.
2. Analyse the factors which affected (a) aggregate demand and (b) aggregate supply over the period.
3. Discuss whether changes in interest rates between 1992 and 1998 more than any other factors helped maintain low inflation with high growth rates of output.

unit 36 Fiscal policy

Summary

1. Fiscal policy, the manipulation of government spending, taxation and borrowing, affects aggregate demand.
2. The effect on aggregate demand of a change in government spending or taxation is increased because of the multiplier effect.
3. Classical economists argue that fiscal policy cannot, in the long term, affect the level of output. Hence, it cannot influence unemployment, but can raise inflation.
4. Keynesian economists argue that fiscal policy can affect both output and prices. Hence, fiscal policy can be used to influence both inflation and unemployment.
5. Fiscal policy cannot, as a demand side policy, influence long term economic growth, but it can be used to help an economy out of a recession or reduce demand pressures in a boom.
6. Fiscal policy, through its effect on aggregate demand, can influence imports and the current balance.

Fiscal policy

The UK government has been responsible for between 40 and 50 per cent of national expenditure over the past 20 years. The main areas of public spending are the National Health Service, defence, education and roads. In addition, the government is responsible for transferring large sums of money round the economy through its spending on social security and National Insurance benefits. All of this is financed mainly through taxes, such as income tax and VAT.

In the post-war era, governments have rarely balanced their budgets (i.e. they have rarely planned to match their expenditure with their receipts). In most years, they have run BUDGET DEFICITS, spending more than they receive. As a result, in most years governments have had to borrow money. In the UK, the borrowing of the public sector (central government, local government and other state bodies such as nationalised industries) over a period of time is called the PUBLIC SECTOR NET CASH REQUIREMENT (PSNCR). This was formerly called the Public Sector Borrowing Requirement (PSBR). In two periods, between 1969-70 and 1988-90, the UK government received more revenue than it spent. The normal budget deficit was turned into a BUDGET SURPLUS. There is then a negative PSNCR. A budget surplus allows the government to pay off part of its accumulated debt. This debt, called the NATIONAL DEBT, dates back to the founding of the Bank of England in 1694.

The government has to make decisions about how much to spend, tax and borrow. It also has to decide on the composition of its spending and taxation. Should it spend more on education and less on defence? Should it cut income tax by raising excise duties? These decisions about spending, taxes and borrowing are called the FISCAL POLICY of the government.

The key date in the year for fiscal policy is the day of the BUDGET. Budget day in the UK occurs in March. In the Budget, the Chancellor gives a forecast of government spending and taxation in the coming financial year. Changes in taxation are also announced. However, the other side of the Budget, the government's spending plans, are announced in November in the Autumn Statement. The financial year in the UK starts on 6 April and runs until 5 April the following year.

Question 1

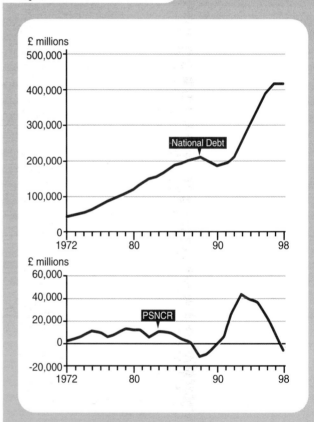

Figure 36.1 *The PSNCR and the National Debt*
Source: adapted from *Financial Statistics, Economic Trends Annual Supplement*, Office for National Statistics.

(a) (i) What is meant by the PSNCR? (ii) In which years did the government have a budget surplus?
(b) Using examples from the data, explain the link between the PSNCR and the National Debt.
(c) If a government wanted to pay off its National Debt over a number of years, how could it achieve this?

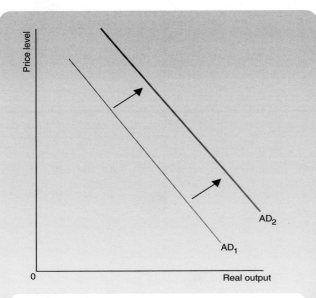

Figure 36.2 *Changes in aggregate demand*
A cut in taxes will lead to a shift to the right in the aggregate demand curve from AD$_1$ to AD$_2$.

The multiplier

A rise in government spending (G) will not just increase aggregate demand by the value of the increase in G. There will be a multiple increase in aggregate demand. This **multiplier effect** will be larger the smaller the leakages from the circular flow (☞ unit 33).

In a modern economy, where leakages from savings, taxes and imports are a relatively high proportion of national income, multiplier values tend to be small. However, Keynesian economists argue that they can still have a significant effect on output in the economy if the economy is below full employment.

Question 3

The Labour government which took office in February 1974 barely had a majority in Parliament and therefore was unwilling to increase taxes and cut public expenditure to tackle soaring inflation and a large balance of payments deficit. In November 1974, another general election took place and this time the Labour government secured a workable majority. In the 1975 Budget, it cut planned public expenditure and increased taxes, both by over £1 000 million. Further cuts in public expenditure were announced in 1976. The budget deficit fell from £10 161 million in 1975 to £8 899 million in 1976 and to £5 419 million in 1977. However, the government relaxed its fiscal stance in 1978, and the budget deficit increased to £8 340 million.

(a) What is meant by 'the multiplier'?
(b) Explain, using the concept of the multiplier, the likely effect that the change in fiscal policy between 1974 and 1976 had on national income.
(c) Using a diagram, discuss the impact that the change in the government's fiscal stance in 1978 is likely to have had on prices and output.

Question 2

Explain the probable effect the following would have on aggregate demand, all other things being equal:
(a) a rise in income tax rates;
(b) a cut in council tax rates;
(c) a cut in spending on education;
(d) a rise in VAT rates combined with an increase in spending on the NHS.

Aggregate demand

Government spending and taxation changes have an effect on aggregate demand. A rise in government spending, with the price level constant, will increase aggregate demand, pushing the AD curve to the right as in Figure 36.2.

Equally, a cut in taxes will affect aggregate demand. A cut in taxes on income, such as income tax and National Insurance contributions, will lead to a rise in the disposable income of households. This in turn will lead to a rise in consumption expenditure and hence to a rise in aggregate demand. This rise, because the price level is assumed to remain constant, will shift the AD curve to the right, as in Figure 36.2.

An increase in government spending or a fall in taxes which increases the budget deficit or reduces the budget surplus is known as EXPANSIONARY FISCAL POLICY. Fiscal policy is said to **loosen** as a result. In contrast, a higher budget surplus or lower deficit will lead to a **tightening** of the fiscal stance.

The goals of government policy

In unit 24, it was explained that the government has four major macroeconomic policy goals. These are to achieve full employment with little or no inflation in a high growth economy with an external balance (current account) equilibrium. Fiscal policy affects each of these variables through its impact on aggregate demand. Fiscal policy is therefore an example of a DEMAND SIDE POLICY or a policy of DEMAND MANAGEMENT.

Inflation An increase in government spending or a fall in taxes which leads to a higher budget deficit or lower budget surplus will have a tendency to be inflationary. A higher budget deficit or lower budget surplus leads to an increase in aggregate demand. In Figure 34.3, this is shown by a shift in the aggregate demand curve to the right. This in turn leads to an increase in the price level from P$_1$ to P$_2$. So inflation increases.

The extent to which there is an increase in inflation depends on a number of factors. One is the size of the change in government spending or taxation. If the change in the budget deficit or surplus is very small, it will have little impact on the price level. Another factor is the shape of the aggregate supply curve. The short run aggregate supply curve is likely to be relatively shallow (☞ unit 34) and so an increase in aggregate demand is likely to have a relatively small impact on prices. In the long term, however, the aggregate supply curve could vary from being horizontal to vertical. Classical economists argue that the long run aggregate supply curve (LRAS) is vertical. So, in Figure 36.4, an increase in aggregate demand has a relatively large effect on inflation. In contrast, the Keynesian view suggests that the LRAS curve is L shaped. In Figure 36.5, where the LRAS curve is horizontal, the economy has high levels of unemployment. Any increase in aggregate demand to AD_2 will have no impact on prices. If the level of output rises beyond OB, however, an increase in aggregate demand will lead to increasing inflation. The nearer the level of full employment at OD, the greater will be the rise in inflation from a given rise in government spending or fall in taxes.

Unemployment A greater budget deficit or a lower budget surplus will tend to reduce the level of unemployment, at least in the short term. A greater budget deficit will lead to an increase in aggregate demand which, as shown in Figure 36.3, will lead to a higher equilibrium level of output. The higher the level of output the lower is likely to be the level of unemployment.

As with inflation, there is a variety of factors which determines the extent to which unemployment will fall. The smaller the change in government spending and taxation, the less impact it will have on aggregate demand and the labour market. If the long run aggregate supply schedule if vertical, then increases in aggregate demand can only lead to higher inflation and they will have no impact on the level of output and unemployment. In the

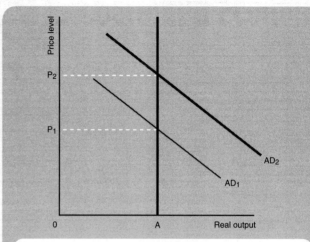

Figure 36.4 *The long run classical view*
In the long run, classical economists argue that expansionary fiscal policy has no effect on equilibrium output and therefore cannot reduce unemployment. However, it will lead to a higher level of prices.

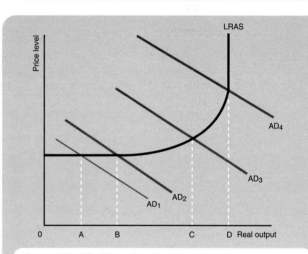

Figure 36.5 *The Keynesian view*
The effectiveness of fiscal policy depends upon how close the economy is to full employment. At output levels below OB, expansionary fiscal policy can increase output and reduce unemployment without increasing inflation. Between OB and OD, expansionary fiscal policy will increase both output and inflation. At full employment, OD, expansionary fiscal policy will result only in extra inflation.

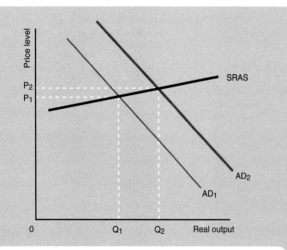

Figure 36.3 *Fiscal policy and aggregate demand*
A rise in government spending or a cut in taxes will shift the aggregate demand curve to the right from AD_1 to AD_2. In the short run this will be inflationary because the equilibrium price level will rise from P_1 to P_2, but equilibrium output will expand from Q_1 to Q_2.

classical model, shown in Figure 36.4, the economy is in equilibrium at output OA. An increase in the budget deficit might push the level of output beyond OA in the short term because the SRAS is upward sloping, but in the long term it will revert to OA. Hence, in the classical model, demand side fiscal policy cannot be used to alter unemployment levels in the long term. In a Keynesian model, this is also true if the economy is at full employment, at OD in Figure 36.5. But at output levels below this, expansionary fiscal policy will lead to higher output and lower unemployment. If output is below OB, expansionary fiscal policy can bring about a fall in unemployment without any increase in inflation.

Economic growth Expansionary fiscal policy is unlikely to affect the long term growth rate of an economy. This is because economic growth is caused by supply side factors such as investment, education and technology. However, expansionary fiscal policy is likely, in the short term, to increase GDP. As Figure 36.3 shows, in the short term an increase in aggregate demand will lead to higher output. Keynesian economists argue that expansionary fiscal policy is an appropriate policy to use if the economy is in recession below full employment. So in Figure 36.5, expansionary fiscal policy could be used to shift the aggregate demand curve from, say, AD_3 to AD_4. This would then return the economy to operating at full capacity on its production possibility frontier (see unit 1). Fiscal policy which pushes the aggregate demand curve beyond AD_4 would lead to no extra growth in output, but would be highly inflationary. In this situation, the economy would be OVER-HEATING. Classical economists argue that fiscal policy cannot be used to change real output in the long term because the long run aggregate supply curve is vertical. Shifting aggregate demand as in Figure 36.4 has no effect on output.

The balance of payments Expansionary fiscal policy leads to an increase in aggregate demand. This means that domestic consumers and firms will have more income and so will increase their spending on imports. Hence, the current account (exports minus imports ☞ unit 30) position will deteriorate. Tighter fiscal policy, on the other hand, will reduce domestic demand and hence demand for imports will fall. The current account position should then improve. There may be other less important influences on exports and imports. For instance, if domestic demand falls because of tighter fiscal policy, then domestic firms may increase their efforts to find markets for their goods by looking overseas. Equally, a fall in aggregate demand due to tighter fiscal policy should moderate the rate of inflation. British goods will be lower priced than they would otherwise have been. Hence, they will be more competitive against imports and foreigners will find British exports more keenly priced. This should lower imports and raise exports, improving the current account position.

Trade offs

Changing aggregate demand has different effects on the four key macroeconomic variables. The government may not be able to achieve improvements in one with bringing about a deterioration in the other, at least in the short term.
- Expanding the economy to bring it out of recession and reduce unemployment is likely to lead to higher inflation.
- Tightening fiscal policy to reduce inflation is likely to lead to higher unemployment and lower levels of GDP.
- Contracting the domestic economy by tightening fiscal policy to improve the current account situation will also lead to lower inflation, but will increase unemployment.

Fiscal policy therefore needs to be used in conjunction with other policies if the government is to steer the economy towards lower inflation and unemployment, higher growth and a current account equilibrium.

key terms

Budget - a statement of the spending and income plans of an individual, firm or government. The Budget is the yearly statement on government spending and taxation plans in the UK.
Budget deficit - a deficit which arises because government spending is greater than its receipts. Government therefore has to borrow money to finance the difference.
Budget surplus - a government surplus arising from government spending being less than its receipts. Government can use the difference to repay part of the National Debt.
Demand side policies or demand management - government use of fiscal and other policies to manipulate the level of aggregate demand in the economy.
Expansionary fiscal policy - fiscal policy used to increase aggregate demand.
Fiscal policy - decisions about spending, taxes and borrowing of the government.
National Debt - the accumulated borrowings of government.
Over-heating - the economy over-heats if aggregate demand is increased when the economy is already at its full productive potential. The result is increases in inflation with little or no increase in output.
Public Sector Net Cash Requirement (PSNCR) - the official name given to the difference between government spending and its receipts in the UK. It was formerly known as the Public Sector Borrowing Requirement (PSBR) and Public Sector Debt Repayment (PSDR).

Question 4

Explain, using a diagram, the likely impact of the following on unemployment, inflation, economic growth and the current balance.
(a) Large cuts in income tax in the March 1987 Budget.
(b) The virtual freezing of government spending in the early 1980s at a time when tax revenues were rising.

Applied economics

A history of fiscal policy

1950-1975

During the period 1950-75, fiscal policy was probably the most important way in which governments manipulated aggregate demand. During the 1950s, governments learnt to use the 'fiscal levers' with more and more confidence. In a recession, such as in 1958, the government would cut taxes to stimulate spending in the economy. This might also be accompanied by public spending increases, although it was recognised that these would take longer to multiply through the economy than tax cuts. In a boom, when the economy was over-heating, as in 1960, the government would increase taxes and possibly cut public spending.

Borrowing in the economy was mainly controlled through direct controls on banks and building societies, specifying who was allowed to borrow money, or through controls on hire purchase, the most common way of financing the purchase of consumer durables.

In the 1960s, governments began to recognise some of the limitations of fiscal policy. The Labour government of 1964-66 experimented briefly with a National Plan, an attempt to model the economy in terms of the inputs and outputs of each industry. This plan was then to be used to help the government identify where particular industries were failing or creating 'bottlenecks' and might need further investment. This supply side experiment was abandoned as the economy faced yet another sterling crisis, which ultimately ended in the pound being devalued in 1967. Another policy used from 1966 was an incomes policy - government limits on the pay rises that could be given to workers. This supply side measure was designed to lower inflation whilst allowing the economy to grow and enjoy low rates of unemployment.

The last bout of traditional Keynesian demand management came in 1972-73 when the government cut taxes and increased public spending to put the economy into boom. This boom, called the Barber boom (after Anthony Barker, the then Chancellor of the Exchequer), ended disastrously as inflation spun out of control, fuelled by the oil price increases of 1973-74.

1975-1995

The mid-1970s saw a wholesale disillusionment with traditional Keynesian demand management techniques. A classical model of the economy became increasingly accepted as the model for governments to work with. In 1976, the Labour Prime Minister of the day, Jim Callaghan, in addressing his party conference, stated that: 'We used to think that you could just spend your way out of a recession, and increase employment by cutting taxes and boosting government spending. I tell you in all candour that that option no longer exists, and

that in so far as it ever did exist, it worked by injecting inflation into the economy.'

The view was taken that cutting taxes produced only a temporary increase in aggregate demand. Unemployment would fall and growth would rise. However, as in the Barber boom, the medium term consequences would be a rise in the inflation rate. To reduce inflation, the government would have to tighten its fiscal stance by raising taxes. Aggregate demand would fall and the economy would return to its equilibrium position but at a higher level of prices and of inflation.

From 1979, when Margaret Thatcher won her first general election, fiscal policy was used for two separate purposes. First, it was used for micro-economic objectives as part of supply side policy for the government (☞ unit 38). For instance, income tax was cut to increase incentives to work. Second, it was used to ensure that monetary targets were met. In particular, it was felt that changes in the PSNCR (known as the PSBR at the time), such as might come about if taxes were cut, would have no effect on aggregate demand if the money for the tax cuts was genuinely borrowed from the non-bank sector. For instance, if the government cut taxes by £1 and financed this by borrowing from the non-bank sector, then there could be no increase in aggregate demand. The taxpayer would have £1 extra to spend but the lender to the government would have £1 less to spend. On this view, increases in the PSNCR completely **crowd-out** other expenditure in the economy resulting in no increase in aggregate demand. They could only work in a Keynesian manner if the increase in the PSNCR was financed through printing the money (the government has the unique power in the economy to print money) and thus increasing the money supply.

During the period of the Lawson boom (1986-89, named after Nigel Lawson, the then Chancellor) and the following recession (1990-92), the government allowed public spending and taxes to change in line with output and employment. So in the boom, the government allowed a large budget surplus to emerge. In the recession, the PSNCR was allowed to grow and by 1993 had reached over 5 per cent of GDP. In 1994-95, the government used active fiscal policy to cut this large deficit, increasing tax rates and introducing new taxes, whilst keeping a tight rein on public spending. On Keynesian assumptions, this put a brake on aggregate demand as it increased during the recovery. On classical assumptions, the tax increases have had no effect on aggregate demand because the accompanying cuts in government borrowing released resources for the private sector to borrow and spend. One of the main reasons why the government felt it was so important to reduce the PSNCR was because of concerns that otherwise the National Debt would grow out of control.

Public finances steadily improved between 1996 and 2000. The government chose repeatedly to use some of the improvement in the PSNCR to finance either spending increases or tax cuts. If it had not done so, the PSNCR would have become negative, i.e. the government would have started to repay debt rather than borrow because receipts were higher than government spending. In the first years of the millennium the PSNCR was predicted to become negative. Governments during the period 1996-2000 did not use fiscal policy to manage demand in the economy. Instead, they used it to achieve other policy objectives.

The government's stated policy at the turn of the century was that public finances should broadly balance over the trade cycle. If the economy went into recession, government spending would be allowed to

rise as more was paid out in benefits. Tax receipts would fall as there was less income in the economy. In a boom, government spending would fall as benefits fall and tax receipts rise. Since the 1980s, governments have tended to use interest rates as the main policy measure to manage demand (☞ unit 37). Allowing tax receipts and government spending to change over the trade cycle has, though, played an important, if subsidiary, part in affecting aggregate demand. Fiscal policy continues therefore to be used to achieve other policy objectives, including providing public and merit goods such as health and education (☞ unit 20), changing the distribution of income, improving the supply side performance of the economy (☞ unit 38) and meeting the potential requirements for UK membership of the Single Currency, the euro.

Preparing a budget

March 1993 Budget

The Chancellor, Norman Lamont, announced a package which included steep increases in taxes, but which would take effect mainly from April 1994. In particular, he announced that from April 1993 these would be:
- a freeze on personal allowances on income tax;
- a small widening in the 20 per cent of income tax;
- a 5 per cent rise in excise duties on beer and wine;
- a $6^{1}/_{2}$ per cent increase in tobacco duty;
- a 10 per cent rise in tax on petrol.

From April 1994:
- employees National Insurance contributions would rise by 1 per cent;
- VAT would be extended to domestic fuel and power;
- tax relief on mortgages would be cut by allowing interest to be only offset against a 20 per cent income tax rate.

Overall, the tax package was broadly neutral in 1993-94 because the small increases in tax revenues were offset by falls in tax revenues because of the weak growth in the economy in 1992-93. However, tax revenues were predicted to grow strongly in 1994-95 and subsequent years as the effects of the April 1994 Budget and growth in the economy began to take effect.

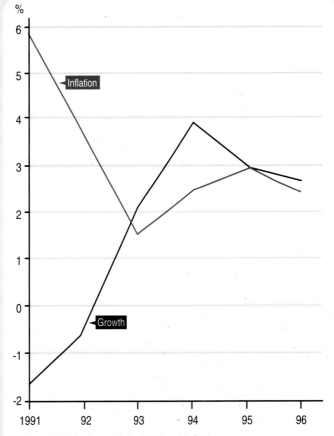

Figure 36.6 *Real growth in GDP and inflation*
Source: adapted from *Economic Trends Annual Supplement*, Office for National Statistics.

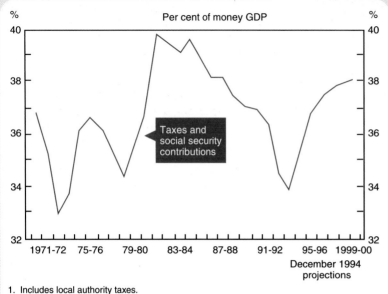

1. Includes local authority taxes.

Figure 36.7 *Taxes and social security[1] contributions as a percentage of GDP*

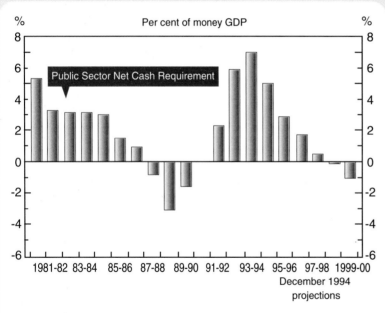

1. Known as the Public Sector Borrowning Requirement (PSBR) at the time.

Figure 36.8 *PSNCR[1]*

December 1994 Budget

The Chancellor, Kenneth Clarke, restated the plans for tax increases in 1995-96 announced in his December 1993 budget. He was defeated in his bid to further raise VAT on domestic fuel to 17.5 per cent, but made up the short-fall in revenue by further increasing taxes on petrol, drink and tobacco. Government spending remained broadly neutral.

December 1993 Budget

The Budget confirmed the April 1993 tax increases as well as adding extra tax increases. In particular:

- income tax allowances were frozen;
- the married couple's income tax allowance was limited to a 20 per cent tax rate and this was to be cut to 15 per cent in April 1995;
- the 20 per cent tax band was further widened by £500 to £3 000;
- mortgage interest tax relief was restricted to 20 per cent and a further cut to 15 per cent was announced for April 1995;
- new indirect taxes were to be imposed on from October 1995 on general insurance and airline flights out of the UK;
- increased excise duties were imposed on tobacco, wine and petrol;
- VAT at 8 per cent was imposed domestic fuel in line with the announcement in the April 1993 Budget.

Overall, taxes were predicted to rise by £8$\frac{1}{2}$bn in 1994-95, rising to £16.4bn in 1996-97. Taxes as a percentage of GDP were to increase from 36$\frac{1}{2}$ per cent in 1993-94 to 40$\frac{3}{4}$ per cent in 1998-99. Real government spending was set to fall by a very small amount in 1994-95.

1. Explain why tax revenues remained 'broadly neutral' in the financial year 1993-1994, but grew thereafter.
2. Why was it sensible not to increase tax revenues in 1993-1994 given that the main priority was to get the economy out of recession and grow by above its trend rate of 2$\frac{1}{2}$ per cent?
3. Analyse the effect of the 1994-95 tax changes on aggregate demand, output and prices from what they would otherwise have been had tax changes remained broadly neutral.
4. Evaluate whether the Chancellor might have been able to cut taxes in 1996 or 1997 if he had to maintain high growth and low inflation.

Summary

1. Governments can influence the economy through the use of monetary policy - the control of monetary variables such as the rate of interest, the money supply and the volume of credit.
2. Changing interest rates can change the level of aggregate demand through its effect on consumer durables, the housing market, household wealth, saving, investment, exports and imports.
3. A rise in interest rates is likely to reduce inflationary pressures, but lead to lower growth in output and have an adverse effect on unemployment. Exports are likely to fall, but the impact on imports is uncertain and so the overall impact on the current account is likely to vary from economy to economy.

Money and the rate of interest

Governments can, to some extent, control the rate of interest and the amount of money circulating in the economy. It can also affect the amount of borrowing or credit available from financial institutions like banks and building societies. MONETARY POLICY is the manipulation of these monetary variables to achieve its objectives.

The RATE OF INTEREST is the price of money. This is because lenders expect to receive interest if money is supplied for loans to money markets. Equally, if money is demanded for loans from money markets, borrowers expect to have to pay interest on the loans.

At various times in the past, governments have used credit controls, such as restrictions on the amount that can be borrowed on a mortgage or on hire purchase, as the main instrument of monetary policy. Equally, some governments have attempted directly to control the supply of money, the amount of money available for spending and borrowing in the economy.

In recent years, the rate of interest has been the key instrument of monetary policy. For instance, both the Bank of England and the Federal Reserve Bank, the central bank of the USA, have used interest rates to achieve their policy objectives.

Aggregate demand

The rate of interest affects the economy through its influence on aggregate demand (AD) (☞ unit 33). The higher the rate of interest, the lower the level of aggregate demand. There is a variety of ways in which interest rates affect the AD curve.

Consumer durables Many consumers buy consumer durables such as furniture, kitchen equipment and cars on credit. The higher the rate of interest, the greater the monthly repayments will have to be for any given sum borrowed. Hence, high interest rates lead to lower sales of durable goods and hence lower consumption expenditure.

The housing market Houses too are typically bought using a mortgage. The lower the rate of interest, the lower the mortgage repayments on a given sum borrowed. This makes houses more affordable. It might encourage people to buy their first house or to move house, either trading up to a more expensive house or trading down to a smaller property. There are three ways in which this increases aggregate demand. First, an increase in demand for all types of housing leads to an increase in the number of new houses being built. New housing is classified as investment in national income accounts. Increased investment leads to increased aggregate demand. Second, moving house stimulates the purchase of consumer durables such as furniture, carpets and kitchens. This increases consumption. Third, moving house may release money which can be spent. A person trading down to a cheaper house will see a release of equity tied up in their home. Those trading up may borrow more than they need for the house purchase and this may be used to buy furniture or perhaps even a new car.

Wealth effects A fall in rates of interest may increase asset prices. For instance, falling interest rates may lead to an increase in demand for housing, which in turn pushes up the price of houses. If house prices rise, all homeowners are better off because their houses have increased in value. This may encourage them to increase their spending. Equally, a fall in interest rates will raise the price of government bonds. Governments issue bonds to finance their borrowing. They are sold to individuals, assurance companies, pension funds and others who receive interest on the money they have loaned to government. Like shares, bonds can go up and down in value. Rises in the price of bonds held by individuals or businesses will increase their financial wealth, which again may have a positive impact on consumer expenditure.

Saving Higher interest rates make saving more attractive compared to spending. The higher the interest rate, the greater the reward for deferring spending to the future and reducing spending now. This may lead to a fall in aggregate demand at the present time.

Investment The lower the rate of interest, the more investment projects become profitable (the marginal efficiency of capital theory ☞ unit 32). Hence the higher the level of investment and aggregate demand. Equally, a rise in consumption which leads to a rise in income will lead, in turn, to a rise in investment (the accelerator theory ☞ unit 32). Firms will need to invest to supply the extra goods and services being demanded by consumers.

The exchange rate A fall in the interest rate is likely to lead to a fall in the value of the domestic currency (its exchange rate, ☞ units 13 and 39). A fall in the value of the pound means that foreigners can now get more pounds for each unit of their currency. However, UK residents have to pay more pounds to get the same number of US dollars or Japanese yen. This in turn means that goods priced in pounds become cheaper for foreigners to buy, whilst foreign goods become more expensive for British firms to buy. Cheaper British goods should lead to higher exports as foreigners take advantage of lower prices. In contrast, more expensive foreign goods should lead to fewer imports as British buyers find foreign goods less price competitive. Greater export levels and fewer imports will boost aggregate demand.

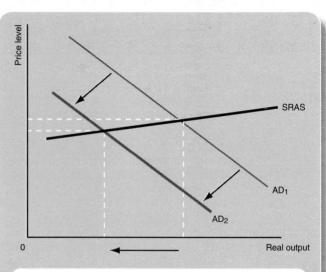

Figure 37.1 *A rise in interest rates*
A rise in interest rates shifts the aggregate demand curve left from AD₁ to AD₂. This leads to a fall in the price level.

Question 1

The British Retail Consortium called for 'an immediate and substantial cut in interest rates' in January 1999. Its survey of retail sales in December 1998 had shown no growth on a like-for-like basis compared with the same period in 1997. Moreover, retail sales shrank by 0.3 per cent during the last three months of 1998, the first time growth had turned negative in the survey's five year history. Ann Robinson, consortium director general, said that there was evidence that the consumer economy had come to a halt. 'We need the Bank of England to make a substantial cut in the interest rate immediately to show its willingness to support the economy' she said.

Source: adapted from the *Financial Times*, 12.1.1999.

(a) Why did the British Retail Consortium want a cut in interest rates?
(b) Explain how a cut in interest rates might benefit its members.

Policy objectives

The government has four key macroeconomic policy objectives - to control inflation and unemployment, to maintain a current account equilibrium and to secure high economic growth. Interest rate policy can affect all of these.

Inflation Interest rate policy today is used mainly to control inflation. Figure 37.1 shows a shift to the left in the aggregate demand curve caused by a rise in interest rates. This leads to a lower equilibrium price level.

Higher interest rates in practice rarely lead to the falling prices shown in Figure 37.1. This is because in modern economies aggregate demand tends to increase over time irrespective of government policy. For instance, most workers get pay rises each year, which increases aggregate

demand. Profits of companies tend to increase which allows higher dividends to be paid to shareholders. A shift to the right in the aggregate demand curve from AD₁ to AD₂ caused by the annual round of pay rises is shown in Figure 37.2. This leads to a rise in the price level. If the government then increases interest rates, aggregate demand shifts back to the left to AD₃. Prices are then higher than at the start of the year with AD₁ but are not as high as they would otherwise have been. Interest rates have thus moderated the increase in the price level, i.e. they have moderated the inflation rate.

A loosening of monetary policy by lowering interest rates shifts the aggregate demand curve to the right and leads to a higher equilibrium level of prices. Looser monetary policy tends therefore to be inflationary.

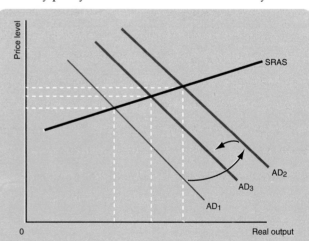

Figure 37.2 *A rise in interest rates with increasing aggregate demand*
Aggregate demand tends to increase over time. Raising interest rates moderates the increase. Instead of shifting to AD₂, the aggregate demand curve only shifts to AD₃. Inflation is thus lower than it would otherwise have been.

Question 2

The Bank of England has acknowledged that wage pressures in the economy are easing. 'The labour market remains tight but it seems to have reached a turning point' it said. 'Evidence from wage settlements and the Bank's regional agents suggests an easing of upward pressures on growth in pay.' Pay increases are slowing for several reasons. Employers are concerned about profitability in the face of an impending economic slowdown. Factory gate prices are falling, a result of weakening overseas demand due a high value of the pound. Moreover, the all items retail prices index, used to measure inflation, has come down from 4 per cent in April to 3 per cent in November. This is used as a benchmark by employers to set wage increases. The fall in wage pressures was one of the factors which persuaded the Bank of England to cut interest rates by $^1/_4$ per cent yesterday.

Source: adapted from the *Financial Times*, 8.1.1999.

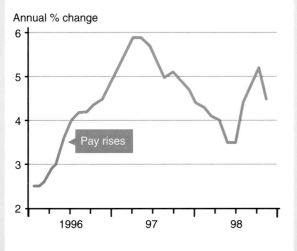

Figure 37.3 *Service sector pay rises*
Source: adapted from ONS/NTC.

(a) Explain the links between inflation and wage increases.
(b) Why does an easing of pressure on wage increases allow the Bank of England to reduce interest rates?

Unemployment Tightening monetary policy by raising interest rates will tend to lead to a fall in equilibrium output, as shown in Figure 37.1. Lower output is likely to be associated with lower levels of employment and hence unemployment is likely to rise. Loosening monetary policy by allowing interest rates to fall, on the other hand, is likely to lead to lower unemployment. Figure 37.1 shows the short run position.

The long run policy implications could be different though. According to classical economists, the long run aggregate supply curve is vertical. Changing the level of interest rates will therefore have no impact on either output or unemployment in the long run. In Figure 37.4, a

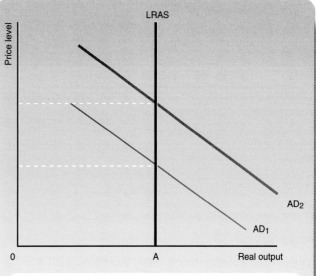

Figure 37.4 *Interest rates and the classical long run aggregate supply curve*
If the long run aggregate supply curve is vertical, changing interest rates will have no effect on either output or unemployment.

fall in interest rates pushes the aggregate demand curve to the right but real output remains at OA. However, there is an increase in the price level. For classical economists, then, any fall in unemployment in the short term caused by a loosening of monetary policy will not be sustained in the long term. Unemployment will revert to its original level.

For Keynesian economists, the impact of loosening monetary policy depends upon how near the economy is

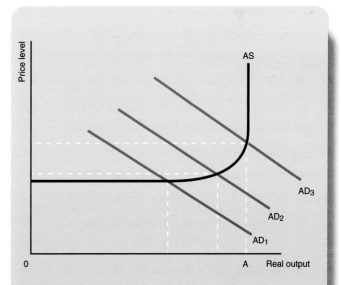

Figure 37.5 *Interest rates and the Keynesian long run aggregate supply curve*
The nearer to full employment at OA, the less impact a fall in interest rates will have on output and employment and the more on inflation.

to full employment. In Figure 37.5, the nearer the economy is to OA, the full employment level of output, the less impact falling interest rates will have on output and unemployment and the more it will have on inflation.

Economic growth Economic growth is a long run phenomenon. Shifting the aggregate demand curve is unlikely to have an impact on the position of the long run supply curve. The only possible link is if lower interest rates encourage investment which in turn increases the capital stock of the economy and its productive potential. Monetary policy can, however, be used to influence booms and recessions. In a boom, tighter monetary policy will reduce aggregate demand and thus lower the increase in short run output. In a recession, looser monetary policy may increase aggregate demand and hence increase equilibrium output.

The current balance In the 1950s and 1960s, the UK government used monetary policy to influence the current balance. Higher interest rates lead to lower aggregate demand. This reduces the amount of imports purchased and hence improves the current account position. On the other hand, higher interest rates should also raise the value of the currency (☞ unit 39). A higher value of the pound will make it more difficult for UK firms to export and easier for foreign firms to sell imports to the UK. This will lead to a worsening of the current account position. Which effect is the larger varies from economy to economy and depends upon how sensitive imports are to falls in domestic income (i.e. the value of income elasticity of demand for imports). It also depends upon how sensitive exchange rates are to changes in interest rates and the sensitivity of exports and imports to changes in exchange rates (i.e. the values of price elasticity of demand for exports and imports).

Question 3

The Bank of England yesterday cut official interest rates by $1/4$ per cent for the fourth time since September, citing a 'continuous slowdown' in the UK economy. Ciaràn Barr, senior UK economist at Deutsche Bank in London, said: 'We feel there is more to come. January's data are expected to be on the soft side, with the killer statistic being the first fall in gross domestic product since the second quarter of 1992.' Kate Barker, the Confederation of British Industry's chief economic adviser, said further rate cuts would be needed to ward off an outright recession. 'With continued weak global trends restraining prices in many sectors, inflation pressure is minimal' Ms Barker said.

Source: adapted from the *Financial Times*, 8.1.1999.

(a) Explain what was happening to the UK economy in late 1998.
(b) How might the $1/4$ per cent cut in interest rates have affected (i) output and (ii) inflation?

key terms

Bank base rate - the interest rate which a bank sets to determine its borrowing and lending rates. It offers interest rates below its base rate to customers who deposit funds with it, whilst charging interest rates above base rate to borrowers.
Central bank - the financial institution in a country or group of countries typically responsible for the printing and issuing of notes and coins, setting short term interest rates, managing the countries' gold and currency reserves and issuing government debt.
Instrument of policy - an economic variable, such as the rate of interest, income tax rates or

government spending on education, which is used to achieve a target of government policy.
Monetary policy - the attempt by government or a central bank to manipulate the money supply, the supply of credit, interest rates or any other monetary variables, to achieve the fulfilment of policy goals such as price stability.
Rate of interest - the price of money, determined by the demand and supply of funds in a money market where there are borrowers and lenders.
Target of policy - an economic goal which the government wishes to achieve, such as low unemployment or high growth.

Applied economics

The functions of the central bank in the UK

Since 1997, monetary policy in the UK has been controlled by the Bank of England. This is the CENTRAL BANK of the UK. Central banks tend to have a number of functions.

- They are responsible for the issue of notes and coins. These are sold to the banking system which in turn passes them on customers as they withdraw cash from their accounts.
- They supervise the financial system, often in conjunction with other bodies specifically set up to regulate distinct parts of the financial system.
- They manage a country's gold and currency reserves. These can be used to influence the level of the exchange rate (☞ unit 39).
- They act as bankers to the government, usually managing the National Debt of the country. They arrange for the issue of new loans to cover current borrowing by a government.
- They act as bankers to the banking system. Usually, they act as lender of last resort. If a bank gets into short term difficulties, not able to raise enough cash to meet demands from its customers, the central bank will supply cash to the banking system to relieve this liquidity shortage.

Targets and instruments

Although the Bank of England is independent of the UK government, its activities are still broadly controlled by government. With regard to monetary policy, the government sets the Bank a TARGET for inflation which it has to achieve. This target was set initially at maintaining inflation within a range of 1 to 4 per cent and subsequently modified to $2^1/_2$ per cent or less per annum. The Bank of England, therefore, has not been given any targets concerning the other three main macroeconomic policy objectives of government - unemployment, growth and the current account. These are influenced by other policies such as fiscal policy and supply side policies.

Since the mid-1980s, the Bank of England has chosen the rate of interest as its main INSTRUMENT of monetary policy. Each month, it announces whether or not it will change bank base rates. In the 1950s and 1960s, controls on credit (the borrowing of money) were significant instruments of monetary policy as well. In the 1970s and early 1980s, the emphasis shifted to the control of the money supply, the total stock of money in the economy. However, these proved unsatisfactory in an open economy like the UK, where it was increasingly easy for borrowers to gain access to funds abroad and where there was increasing competition between financial institutions.

Bank base rates

BANK BASE RATE is the rate of interest around which the main UK banks fix their lending and borrowing rates. Customers who lend money (i.e. deposit money) with a bank will get a rate of interest less than the base rate. Customers who borrow money will be charged a rate higher than base rates. The difference or **spread** between borrowing and lending rates is used by the bank to pay its operating costs and provide it with a profit. Each bank can in theory fix its own base rate. However, competitive pressure means that all banks have the same base rate. If one bank had a higher base rate, it would attract more deposits from other banks but would lose customers who wanted to borrow money. It could easily end up with far too much on deposit and too little being lent out. The reverse would be true if a bank set its base rate below that of other banks.

The Bank of England controls base rates through its day to day provision of money to the banking system. In practice, banks in the UK can't decide to have a different base rate to the one chosen by the Bank of England.

Bank base rates are short term rates of interest. They influence other interest rates in other money markets. For instance, building societies are likely to change their interest rates if bank base rates change. If they don't, they face customers moving their business to banks who might offer more competitive deposit or borrowing rates. However, many customers only use banks or only use building societies. Many would not switch their savings from one to the other if a small difference in interest rates appeared. So sometimes building societies will not change their interest rates if the Bank of England changes bank base rates by, say, one quarter of a per cent. There are many other money markets which are even less linked to bank base rates. Credit card rates, for instance, don't tend to change if bank base rates change by 1 or 2 per cent. Long term interest rates may also not be affected by changes in short term rates of interest. So the Bank of England only has very imperfect control of all the different money markets in the UK.

Factors affecting the decision to change interest rates

The decision as to whether to change interest rates in any one month is taken by the Monetary Policy Committee (MPC). This is a group of 9 people. Five are from the Bank of England, including the Chairperson of the Bank of England. The other four are independent outside experts, mainly professional economists. Inflation is the Bank of England's only target. So the Monetary Policy Committee considers evidence about whether inflationary pressure is increasing, decreasing or remaining stable at the time. If it believes that inflationary pressure is increasing, it is likely to raise interest rates to reduce aggregate demand. If inflationary pressure is weak, it can cut interest rates to boost aggregate demand and allow unemployment to be reduced and output to increase. In coming to any decision, it looks at a wide range of economic indicators·

For instance, it will consider the rate of increase in average earnings. If wages are rising at a faster rate than before, this could be an indication that labour is becoming scarcer in supply. The same could then also be true of goods and services. Equally, faster rising wages could feed through into higher costs for firms. They would then be forced to pass on these costs to customers and so this would be inflationary.

Another indicator is house prices. If house prices are rising fast, it is an indicator that households have money to spend which could spill over into higher demand for goods and services. Higher house prices also add to household wealth and could encourage them to borrow more, which would increase aggregate demand.

The exchange rate is important too. If the exchange rate is falling, it will make British exports more competitive and imports less competitive. This will increase aggregate demand. A rising exchange rate, on the other hand, will tend to reduce aggregate demand.

The output gap is another significant indicator. This measures the difference between the actual level of output and what economists estimate is the potential level of output of the economy. If all factors of production are fully utilised, any increase in aggregate demand will lead to higher inflation.

Problems facing the Monetary Policy Committee

One of the problems facing the Monetary Policy Committee is that economic data for one month is unreliable. If the statisticians say that average earnings increased 0.564 per cent last month, it is almost certain that this is not totally accurate. So the members of the MPC have to make judgments about how plausible are the statistics presented to them.

Another problem is that economists don't agree about exactly how the economy works. Some economists might attach more importance, for instance, to an increase in wage inflation than others. All economists accept that the real world is so complicated that it is often difficult to capture it and portray it in economic theories and models.

Finally, the data is often contradictory. Some indicators will suggest an increase in inflationary pressures whilst others will show a decrease. It is less common for most of the economic data to be pointing in the same direction. This is especially a problem if the Committee is being successful at controlling inflation over a period of time. Then, the output gap is likely to be around zero, with economic resources fully utilised. It is unlikely that one month's figures will show any clear trend. This is very different from a situation where there is, say, a large negative output gap, showing the economy operating at well below its productive potential and with high unemployment. Then it is likely to be clear that interest rates could be cut without fuelling inflation. Equally, if there is a large positive output gap, the situation is unsustainable in the long term and increased inflation is almost inevitable. Then it is clear that interest rates must rise to choke off demand.

Will the Bank of England cut interest rates today?

The Monetary Policy Committee, meeting today, will have to decide whether to change interest rates. Industry wants to see interest rates cut further. It is complaining that orders are being hard hit, particularly in the export sector.

On the other hand, the Monetary Policy Committee might feel that recent interest rate cuts have been sufficient and that further cuts might increase inflationary pressures. February, 1999.

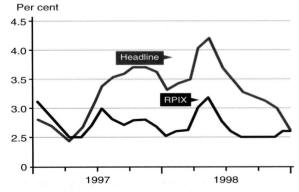

Figure 37.6 *Inflation*
Source: adapted from ONS.

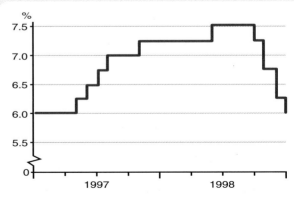

Figure 37.7 *Bank of England operational interest rate*
Source: adapted from ONS, CBI, Goldman Sachs, Datastream/ICV.

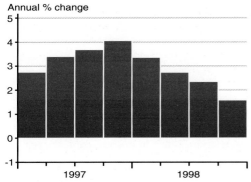

Figure 37.8 *Real GDP growth*
Source: adapted from ONS, CBI, Goldman Sachs, Datastream/ICV.

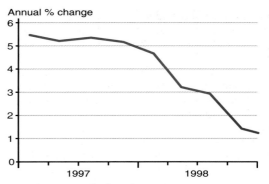

Figure 37.9 *Retail sales volume*
Source: adapted from ONS, CBI, Goldman Sachs, Datastream/ICV.

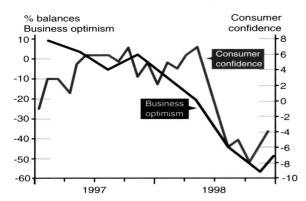

Figure 37.10 *Business optimism and consumer confidence*
Source: adapted from ONS, CBI, Goldman Sachs, Datastream/ICV.

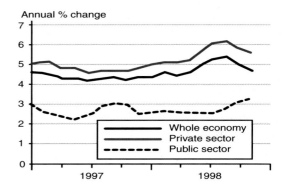

Figure 37.11 *Average earnings growth*
Source: adapted from Datastream/ICV.

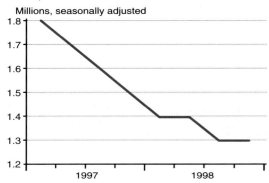

Figure 37.12 *Unemployment*
Source: adapted from ONS.

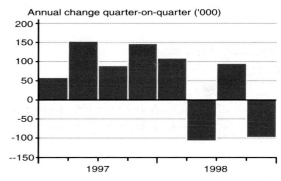

Figure 37.13 *Employment growth*
Source: adapted from ONS, CBI, Goldman Sachs, Datastream/ICV.

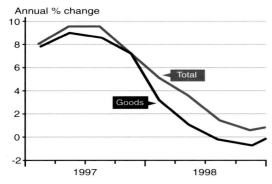

Figure 37.14 *Export volumes*
Source: adapted from ONS, CBI, Goldman Sachs, Datastream/ICV.

Figure 37.15 *Sterling*
Source: adapted from Primark Datastream.

1. Outline the trends in inflation in 1997 and 1998.
2. Explain the link between changing interest rates and inflation. Illustrate your answer by looking at the period January 1997 to July 1998 shown in the data.
3. Assess whether the Bank of England should have raised interest rates, cut them or left them the same in February 1999.
4. Why might the Monetary Policy Committee find it difficult to decide whether or not to change interest rates in any one month?

Summary

1. Supply side policies are designed to increase the average rate of growth of the economy. They may also help reduce inflation and unemployment and improve the current account position.
2. Some economists, called supply side economists, believe that governments should not intervene in the workings of the free market. The government's role, they argue, is to remove restrictions to the operations of individual markets. Keynesian economists believe that governments need to intervene on the supply side to correct market failure.
3. Aggregate supply in the economy can be increased if government intervenes to ensure that labour markets operate more efficiently and if there is an increase in human capital over time.
4. Governments need to encourage firms to invest and take risks if aggregate supply is to increase.
5. Privatisation, deregulation and increased competition can increase aggregate supply.
6. Regional policy and inner city policy can also increase aggregate supply.

Supply side policies

The long run aggregate supply curve shows the productive potential of the economy. At any point in time there is only so much that an economy can produce. Over time, the productive potential of the economy will, hopefully, grow. This can be shown by a shift outwards in the production possibility frontier (☞ unit 1) or by a shift to the right in the long run aggregate supply curve (☞ unit 34).

SUPPLY SIDE POLICIES are government policies designed to increase the rate of economic growth, the rate at which the LRAS curve is shifted to the right. In Figure 38.1, a shift to the right in the LRAS curve increases output from OA to OB. In the UK and the USA, the trend rate of growth for most of the second half of the twentieth century has been around 2.5 per cent. However, average economic growth has been higher in the late 1990s and some economists claim that better supply side policies might have lifted the trend rate of growth for both of these economies. In contrast, the Japanese economy has seen its trend rate of growth fall decade by decade since the 1960s. So long term growth rates are not necessarily a constant. They can be influenced by factors such as government policy.

Supply side policies can also affect other economic variables apart from growth. Figure 38.1 shows that a shift to right in the LRAS, all other things being equal, leads to a fall in the price level. So supply side policies which succeed in increasing the trend rate of growth of an economy can help to moderate inflation.

Supply side policies also affect unemployment. Economies are constantly changing, with new industries growing and old industries dying. Over time, new technology allows more to be produced with fewer workers. If the economy does not grow fast enough, more workers can lose their jobs in a year than new jobs are created. Unemployment therefore grows. In contrast, fast economic growth is likely to see more new jobs being created than old jobs are lost and so unemployment falls. Faster economic growth in the UK and the US in the second half of the 1990s has been associated in both countries with falling unemployment. There comes a time, as in the UK in the 1950s, when the economy is at full employment and everyone who wants a job is able to get one. Supply side policies can then play a crucial role in ensuring that inflation does not become a problem. They can help keep growth in aggregate supply equal to growth in aggregate demand.

Supply side policies affect the current account too. Increasing aggregate supply allows more goods and services to be available for export and reduces the need to import goods. In practice, effective supply side policies increase the competitiveness of domestic industry in relation to foreign industry. Domestic goods become cheaper or better quality or are of a higher specification than foreign goods. Hence exports rise compared to imports.

Different approaches

Economists agree that government can affect the supply side of the economy. However, they disagree about how

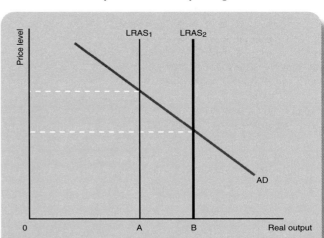

Figure 38.1 *Supply side policies*
Effective supply side policies push the long run aggregate supply curve to the right. This increases economic growth and reduces inflationary pressures. It may also bring about a reduction in unemployment and lead to higher exports and lower imports.

this should be done.

Supply side economists Supply side economists come from the same broad school of thought as neo-classical, new classical and monetarist economists. They believe that free markets promote economic efficiency and that government intervention in the economy is likely to impair economic efficiency. Government still has a vital role to play in the economy, according to these economists. Government is responsible for creating the environment in which free markets can work. This means eliminating the barriers which exist to the perfect working of markets. SUPPLY SIDE ECONOMICS therefore tends to be the study of how government can intervene using **market orientated** policies.

Keynesian and neo-Keynesian economists Keynesian and neo-Keynesian economists believe that free markets often fail to maximise economic efficiency in the economy. Governments therefore have to correct **market failure** (☞ unit 16). This means intervening in free markets to change the outcome from that which it would otherwise have been.

In the rest of this unit, we will consider these two types of supply side policy - market orientated policies and interventionist policies.

Labour market policies

The level of aggregate supply is determined in part by the quantity of labour supplied to the market and the productivity of that labour. For instance, all other things being equal, an economy with 10 million workers will produce less than an economy with 20 million workers. Equally, an economy where workers have little **human capital** (☞ unit 2) will have a lower output than one where there are high levels of human capital. Classical economists argue that there is a number of ways in which the quantity and quality of labour are restricted because markets are not allowed to work freely.

Trade unions The purpose of a trade union is to organise workers into one bargaining unit. The trade union then becomes a monopsonist, a sole seller of labour, and prevents workers from competing amongst themselves in the job market. Economic theory predicts that if trade unions raise wage rates for their members, then employment and output will be lower in otherwise competitive markets (☞ unit 2). So classical economists argue that government must intervene to curb the power of trade unions, for instance by reducing their ability to strike.

State welfare benefits Workers are unlikely to take low paid jobs if state benefits are a little below or equal to the pay being offered. Hence, state benefits reduce the level of aggregate supply because more workers remain unemployed. Classical economists argue that the solution is to cut state unemployment benefits to encourage workers to take on low paid jobs. An alternative approach is to give benefits or tax credits to those who take on low paid jobs. For there to be a positive incentive to work, the benefit plus pay must be greater than the benefits the worker would have received had he been out of work.

Minimum wages If there is a minimum wage which is set above the market clearing wage, then unemployment will be created. Minimum wages prevent some workers who would be prepared to work for lower pay from getting jobs. Hence aggregate supply is lowered. Classical economists argue that minimum wages should be abolished.

Marginal tax rates High marginal rates of tax (the rate of tax on the last £1 earned or spent) discourage economic activity. A tax on cigarettes leads to fewer cigarettes being bought. A tax on work (income tax) leads to people working less. A tax on profits (corporation tax) is a disincentive to firms to make profits. Lowering certain taxes will therefore raise the level of economic activity and increase aggregate supply.

Supply side economists believe that the supply of labour is relatively elastic. A reduction in marginal tax rates on income will lead to a significant increase in 'work'. This could mean individuals working longer hours, being more willing to accept promotion, being more geographically mobile, or simply being prepared to join the workforce. Work is, arguably, an inferior good, whilst leisure, its alternative, is a normal good. The higher an individual's income, the less willing he or she is to work. So a cut in marginal tax rates will have a negative income effect at the margin (i.e. the worker will be less willing to work). However, a cut in marginal tax rates will have a positive substitution effect because the relative price of work to

Question 1

A number of studies has been completed discussing the link between income tax cuts and incentives to work. For instance, Brown and Dawson (1969) surveyed all the studies published between 1947 and 1968 making links between tax rates and hours worked. They found that high taxation acted as a disincentive to working longer hours for between 5 and 15 per cent of the population. These workers were mainly people who could choose to vary their hours of work relatively easily - the wealthy, rural workers, the middle aged and those without families. On the other hand, a smaller group of people tended to increase their hours of work when taxes were higher. These were typically part of large families, young, less well-off urban dwellers.

In a 1988 study by C V Brown, it was found that the substantial increase in tax allowances in the 1988 Budget only increased the number of hours worked in the economy by 0.5 per cent. The cut in the basic rate of tax had no effect at all on hours worked whilst the massive cut in the top rate of tax from 60 per cent to 40 per cent only had a small effect in stimulating extra hours of work by the rich.

(a) Explain why tax rates might have an effect on incentives to work.
(b) To what extent have tax cuts increased the number of hours worked?
(c) What are the implications of the two studies described in the passage for the shape of the Laffer curve?

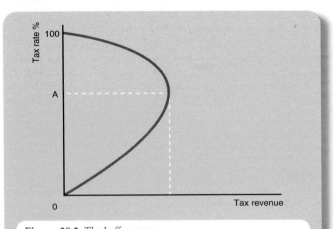

Figure 38.2 *The Laffer curve*
As tax rates increase, economic activity is discouraged and hence the rate of growth of tax revenues falls. Above OA, an increase in tax rates so discourages economic activity that tax revenues fall.

leisure has changed in favour of work (i.e. the worker will be more willing to work).

Supply side economists believe that the substitution effect of a tax cut is more important than the income effect and hence tax cuts increase incentives to work. If cutting marginal income tax rates encourages people to work harder and earn more, then in theory it could be that tax revenues will increase following a tax cut. For instance, if 10 workers, each earning £10 000 a year, pay an average 25 per cent tax, then total tax revenue is £25 000 (10 x £10 000 x 0.25). If a cut in the tax rate to 20 per cent were to make each worker work harder and increase earnings to, say, £15 000, tax revenues would increase to £30 000 (10 x £3 000). This is an example of the LAFFER CURVE effect, named after Professor Arthur Laffer who popularised the idea in the late 1970s. Figure 38.2 shows a Laffer curve, which plots tax revenues against tax rates. As tax rates increase, the rate of growth of tax revenue falls because of the disincentive effects of the tax. OA shows the maximum revenue position of the tax. At tax rates above OA, an increase in the tax rate so discourages economic activity that tax revenues fall.

Taxes on labour Firms will not take on workers if their total wage cost is too high. Part of the total cost is the wages of workers. However, many countries tax firms for employing labour, often by imposing employer contributions to state social security funds. In the UK, for instance, employers have to pay National Insurance employers' contributions. The higher the tax, the fewer workers will be employed and hence the lower will be the level of aggregate supply.

Reducing the cost of changing jobs In a modern fast-changing economy, workers are likely to be changing jobs on a relatively frequent basis. Some workers will even become **portfolio workers**, having a mix of part-time jobs at any one time rather than a single full time job. If the labour market is such that workers find it difficult to get new jobs when they are made redundant, then unemployment will rise and aggregate supply will fall. So

the government must ensure that **barriers to mobility** between jobs are as low as possible. One important barrier to mobility can be pensions. If pension rights are typically provided by individual employers, then a worker who is frequently moving from employer to employer will lose out. Hence, governments should give workers the opportunity to provide for their own pension which they can take with them them from job to job. Another problem in the UK has been a lack of geographical mobility due to rigidities in the housing market. If house prices in the South of England are much higher than in the North, then workers will be discouraged from moving from North to South. Equally, if workers are unable to rent houses at an affordable rent in an area, then low paid workers will not be able to move into that area to take up jobs.

Education and training Increasing the level of human capital of workers is vital if economies are to develop. Increased levels of education and training will raise the marginal revenue product of workers (i.e. will raise the value of output of workers). This in turn will shift the aggregate supply curve to the right. The value of human capital in the economy is one of the most important determinants of the level of aggregate supply.

Question 2

Invest in Britain Bureau (IBB), the government agency that handles inward investment for the whole of the UK, is in no doubt about its principal selling point - the labour force. The IBB boasts that the UK workforce is especially skilled in those sectors where foreign investment is most extensive - electronics, engineering, science, information technology, telecommunications and finance.

However, the UK does not always compare well with other industrialised countries. About 7 million adults have no formal qualifications, 21 million have not reached level 3 - equal to two A levels - and more than one in five have poor literacy and numeracy skills.

The problem is compounded because the needs of industry are changing. Skills shortages are almost inevitable in industries such as communication and information which are exploding worldwide.

In the long term, higher standards in schools and more going to university will help keep the UK competitive. In the short term, though, firms, in partnership with government, must take on the burden of increasing the skills of their workforce.

Source: adapted from the *Financial Times*, 16.7.1998.

(a) Using a diagram, explain why the quality of the labour force is so important for the long term growth of the UK economy.
(b) What skills problems does the economy face, according to the data?
(c) Evaluate how these skills problems can be resolved.

The capital market

Increasing the capital stock of the country, such as its factories, offices and roads, will push the aggregate supply curve to the right. According to classical economists, the government has a key role to play in this.

Profitability Firms invest in order to make a profit. The higher the rate of profit, the more investment will take place. Hence, government must create an environment in which firms can make profits for their owners. One way of doing this is by reducing taxes on company profits. Another is to reduce inheritance tax which might be paid by a small business owner when passing on his or her business to a family relative. Another is to reduce taxes on employing workers. Reducing the amount of government red tape, like planning permissions, can also help reduce costs and increase profitability.

Allocating scarce capital resources The government is in a poor position to decide how to allocate resources. It should leave this as much as possible to the private sector. Hence, state owned companies should be **privatised** wherever possible. Government should offer only limited taxpayers' money to subsidise industry. The government should stay well clear of trying to 'back winning companies'.

Increasing the range of sources of capital available to firms Firms can be constrained in their growth if they are unable to gain access to financial capital like bank loans or share capital. Government should therefore encourage the private sector to provide financial capital, particularly to small businesses. They may, for instance, offer tax incentives to individuals putting up share capital for a business.

The goods market

Inefficient production will lead to a lower level of aggregate

Question 3

The government has abandoned its review of North Sea oil taxation in the light of continuing low oil prices. It had hoped to change the tax regime so as to increase the levels of tax paid by North Sea oil operators. The industry had already responded to low oil prices and fears of increased taxation by cutting its exploration drilling. This year exploration drilling has halved whilst some development projects have been delayed.

Source: adapted from the *Financial Times*, 1998.

Table 38.1 *North Sea sensitivity to prices*

Oil price	Uncommercial projects[1]	Gas price	Uncommercial projects[1]
$18/barrel	0	14 pence/therm	0
$16/barrel	4	12 pence/therm	2
$14/barrel	9	10 pence/therm	8
$12/barrel	23	8 pence/therm	17

1. Out of a total of 45 future projects that may be developed in the short term.
Source: adapted from Wood Mackenzie, BP, HMSO, Treasury.

(a) Explain the link between company taxes and North Sea oil activity.
(b) Why might lower company taxes increase aggregate supply?

supply. For instance, if UK car workers produce 50 per cent fewer cars per worker with the same equipment as German workers, then the level of aggregate supply in the UK can obviously be increased if UK labour productivity is raised. The government has a key role to play in increasing efficiency.

Classical economists argue that the most important way of securing increased efficiency is through encouraging **competition**. If firms know that they will go out of business if they do not become efficient, then they have a powerful incentive to become efficient producers. The government can increase competition in the market in a number of ways.

Encouraging free trade (☞ unit 40) Fierce foreign competition results in a domestic industry which has to be efficient in order to survive. The government should therefore liberalise trade, removing tariffs (taxes) and other barriers to imports.

Encouraging small businesses Small businesses can operate in markets where there are no large businesses. Competition here is intense. However, small businesses can operate in markets where there are very large firms. Small businesses then force larger firms to remain cost competitive. Otherwise the larger firms will lose market share.

Privatisation (☞ unit 18) Privatising firms, and in the process creating competition between newly created firms, eliminates the distortions created by the operation of public sector monopolies.

Deregulation (☞ unit 18) Removing rules about who can compete in markets will encourage competition.

Interventionist approaches

Keynesian economists would tend to take a different approach to government policy and aggregate supply. They would tend to focus on issues of where free markets fail. For instance, they would agree with classical economists that a key aspect of government policy must be to increase education and training. However, whereas classical economists would argue that training should be left to individual companies or groups of companies in a local area, Keynesians would argue that training is best organised by government. The state should, for instance, impose levies on firms to finance state organised training placements and schemes.

With regard to investment in physical capital, classical economists would argue that profit should direct the level and pattern of investment. Keynesian economists would argue that if investment is insufficient in the economy, then the government should intervene and, for instance, use taxes to set up state owned companies or subsidise investment by private industry.

In the 1950s and 1960s in the UK, the main supply side problem was that of regional inequality with the North of England, Scotland and Northern Ireland experiencing higher unemployment rates than the South and the Midlands. The Keynesian policy response was a mixture of offering incentives to firms investing in high unemployment regions and making it difficult for firms to expand in low unemployment regions.

Question 4

The government has changed the assisted areas map. The percentage of the population living in assisted areas has fallen from 34 to 28 per cent. The criteria for inclusion has changed from unemployment in travel to work areas to neediest wards in local areas. Some areas which have lost out have been included in a new tier of areas which is able to gain new enterprise grants for small companies in the district. Firms may also be eligible to gain grants from the Single Regeneration Budget (SRB). This targets compact deprived areas and allows money to be spent not just on attracting new industry but also on education, social exclusion and crime prevention. £785 million has been allocated for regional assistance over the next three years, including £45 million for small companies, whilst the SRB has been allocated £1 billion over 7 years.

(a) How might assistance from the government increase aggregate supply?

key terms

Laffer curve - a curve which shows that at low levels of taxation, tax revenues will increase if tax rates are increased; however, if tax rates are high, then a further rise in rates will reduce total tax revenues because of the disincentive effects of the increase in tax.

Supply side economics - the study of how changes in aggregate supply will affect variables such as national income; in particular, how government micro-economic policy might change aggregate supply through individual markets.

Supply side policies - government policies designed to increase the productive potential of the economy and push the long run aggregate supply curve to the right.

Applied economics

Supply side policies in the UK

Since 1979, the government has been committed to implementing supply side policies aimed at improving the workings of free markets. A wide range of measures have been introduced which are described below.

The labour market

Trade union power Industrial relations had long been recognised as a problem for the UK. Some have argued that the solution was to increase the power of trade unions over their members and legalise their rights in the workplace in order to make trade unions more responsible decision making bodies. Others argued that trade union power needed to be drastically curtailed. In 1969, the Labour government of the time published *In Place of Strife*, a White Paper on trade union reform which floundered on trade union opposition within the government. In 1971, the Conservative government under Edward Heath passed the Industrial Relations Act which attempted to curtail trade union powers. However, the legislation was flawed and trade unions circumvented the provisions of the Act. The Labour government of 1974-79, if anything, increased the power of trade unions by repealing the Industrial Relations Act and giving unions further rights. The election of a Conservative government in 1979, however, completely transformed the industrial relations scene. A number of Acts were passed which effectively made secondary picketing illegal as firms gained the power to sue trade unions involved for damages. Industrial action called by a union now had to be approved by a secret ballot of its membership. Secret ballots were also made compulsory for elections of trade union leaders. Closed

shops, places of work where employers agreed that all workers should be trade union members, became more difficult to maintain and enforce. The government also took an extremely hard line with strikes in the public sector, refusing to give in to union demands. The breaking of strikes, such as the miners' strike of 1983-95, increased the confidence of private employers to resist trade union demands. By the mid-1990s, with the loss of over one- quarter of their members since 1979, trade unions had become marginalised in many places of work and considerably weakened in others.

The election of a Labour government in 1997 did not reverse this position. In 1999, it passed the Employee Relations Act 1999 which forced employers to recognise the negotiating rights of trade unions if a majority of workers in the workplace voted in favour. However, whilst this might increase union membership in the long term, it is unlikely in itself to greatly increase union power.

Wage bargaining Employers will only take action against employees if it is profitable for them to do so. Supply side economists view collective bargaining as an inflexible way of rewarding workers. They advocate individual pay bargaining with payment systems based on bonuses and performance related pay. By reducing the power of trade unions, the government in the 1980s and early 1990s went some way to breaking collective bargaining. It encouraged employers to move away from national pay bargaining to local pay bargaining. In the public sector, it attempted to move away from national pay agreements to local ones. Legislation passed by the new Labour government after 1997 might lead to a reversal of this trend. The 1999 Employee

Relations Act increased the ability of trade unions to force recognition by employers of their negotiating rights. At the same time, the signing of the Social Chapter influenced some larger firms to set up works councils which involve trade unions. The government is also supporting greater social partnerships between businesses and unions which may also encourage collective bargaining.

State welfare benefits Reducing benefits to those out of work increases incentives for people to take jobs. Within three years of coming to office in 1979, the government abolished earnings-related unemployment benefit and also abolished the index linking of benefits to the rise in average earnings. Benefits since that time have only been indexed to the RPI, the inflation rate.

Unemployment benefit was made subject to income tax in 1982. In 1988, in a major overhaul of the social security system, the problems of both the **poverty trap** (where an increase in wages leads to a fall in income for a worker after tax has been paid and benefits withdrawn) and the **unemployment trap** (where unemployed workers find that they can receive a higher income from remaining unemployed than by taking low paid jobs) were addressed by increasing benefits paid to those in low paid work and cutting benefit rates to those not in a job. Even so, low income families continued to face effective marginal tax rates of around 80 per cent. In another move, the government initiated the Restart programme in 1986, which forced any worker claiming benefits for being out of work to attend an interview at a Jobcentre at least once a year to review his or her position. Between 1986 and 1990, there was a dramatic fall in unemployment from 3.0 million to 1.6 million. Partly this was due to the Lawson boom in the economy. But the Restart programme was instrumental in getting many of the long term unemployed to cease claiming benefits for being unemployed, getting them onto training schemes or getting them reclassified so that they could receive invalidity benefits. From the viewpoint of increasing aggregate supply, only training leading to a subsequent job would have led to a shift to the right in the aggregate supply curve.

The Labour government elected in 1997 pursued a similar mix of policies. On the one hand, under its New Deal programme, which guarantees all young workers either a job or training, it cancelled the right to benefit for those who refuse to co-operate. Equally, older workers have been denied benefit if they refused reasonable employment. There has also been a tightening of invalidity benefit to cut the number of workers claiming that they are no longer fit for work. On the other hand, in 1999, it introduced the Working Families Tax Credit, a tax credit scheme for the low paid with children. Employers, instead of deducting tax from an employee, credited the low paid worker with extra money. Effectively, it is a benefit paid through the pay packet. The aim was to increase take-home pay of the low paid and thus increase the incentive to work rather than stay at home and live off benefits.

Social legislation Legislation was passed during the 19th and early 20th centuries which protected the rights of women and children in the workplace in the UK. For instance, workers under the age of 18 were not allowed to work more than 48 hours a week or for more than 9 hours a day. Much of this legislation was still in force in 1979, although working conditions had changed considerably. The legislation was said to restrict the ability of employers to use young workers or women flexibly in the workplace and therefore discouraged their employment. The 1989 Employment Act repealed much of this legislation, effectively removing the special protection given in law to female and young workers.

The Conservative government of the time also resisted European social legislation. In 1992, at Maastricht, it secured an opt-out clause for the Social Chapter, which gave Brussels the right to introduce regulations covering conditions of employment across the EU. This opt-out was reversed in 1997 by the incoming Labour government which argued that European regulations had little impact on employment, but provided protection for workers against unreasonable employers. For instance, the Social Chapter has led to the reintroduction of a maximum 48 hour working week for most groups of workers, although this time it applied to both male and female workers.

Training and education Education and training are recognised by the government as keystones of its supply side policies. One major concern has been the level of education attainment in schools. In 1988, the government announced the creation of a National Curriculum which would standardise educational curriculum provision across England and Wales for the first time. In the 1990s, the government increasingly set targets for schools to achieve in National Curriculum tests and at GCSE. A system of inspections by OFSTED was established to identify failing schools. At the same time, state schools were given more autonomy from Local Education Authorities (LEAs). The Conservative government in the 1980s and 1990s attempted to introduce competition amongst schools by giving them the right to opt out of LEA control. The idea was that competition between schools for pupils would raise standards. However, most schools refused to opt out and some of those which did performed poorly anyway. The Labour government from 1997 reversed this policy, relying on standard setting and changes to the curriculum to improve educational attainment. Numbers staying in post 16 education have increased considerably since 1979. For instance, the number of 17 year olds in full time education increased from 186 000 in 1979 to 206 000 in 1997 despite a fall in the number of 17 year olds in the population.

In higher education, there was a large expansion of numbers in the late 1980s and 1990s. In 1979, there were half a million students in higher education. By the late 1990s, this had doubled to a million.

Vocational training was reformed in the early 1990s with a system of National Vocational Qualifications (NVQs) being established to replace a large variety of different, sometimes little known, awards. Schools and colleges became entitled to offer non-workplace based vocational qualifications called General National Vocational Qualifications (GNVQs). The reforms have not been without their problems. There has been persistent criticism that standards set for the new qualifications were too low and that there was little consistency in awarding grades because there was little or no external national assessment of students' work. In the late 1990s, major reforms of the system were being worked on ready for implemention in the next millennium.

In the late 1980s, training provision was completely reorganised on a local basis. A local TEC (Training and Enterprise Council) was established in each area of the country. Unlike previous training programmes, which were partnerships between trade unions, employers and government at a national level, TECs were dominated by employers at a local level. Much of the finance came from national government, but EU training grants were also available and TECs secured some income by selling training packages to local businesses. The point of the reform was to make training more accountable to local employers. They would be able to decide how money should be spent in their area.

In the late 1990s, the Labour government announced that the work of TECs would be replaced after the year 2001 by a new system involving regional development agencies, learning and skills councils and the Small Business Service.

Marginal tax rates Cutting direct taxes was high on the list of government priorities after 1979. The basic rate of tax was cut from 33 per cent in 1979 to 25 per cent by 1988, whilst the highest rate of tax on earned income fell from 83 per cent to 40 per cent. In 1992, a new lower rate of income tax was established at 20 per cent on the first few thousand pounds of taxable income. By 2000, the lower rate of tax was 10 per cent whilst the standard rate had fallen to 23 per cent. Employees' National Insurance contributions had also been reformed, removing the lowest paid from the burden of paying contributions. Income tax cuts were designed in part to increase incentives to work. Incentives to accumulate wealth were given by cuts in both inheritance tax and capital gains tax rates. Employers too have gained with Employers National Insurance contributions falling. The UK has continued to have almost the lowest social security taxes on employers and employees in Europe.

Pensions With fewer workers having life time work with a single employer, it has become important to ensure that mobile workers are not penalised in their pensions by shifting jobs. Personal pensions, pension rights which could be taken from job to job, became

available from the mid-1980s. Whilst personal pensions are satisfactory for some, the evidence suggests that they have not been as successful as at first thought. First, workers have been unwilling to make the pension contributions needed to provide a satisfactory pension. It should be remembered that in ordinary pension schemes provided by employers, a typical 15 per cent of an employee's salary is put aside for pension contributions. Second, there was a gross mis-selling of personal pensions with many workers being persuaded to leave good employers' schemes to take out personal pensions which provided inferior benefits.

In 1998, the new Labour government announced that it would introduce a new system of pensions, called stakeholder pensions, aimed at those with low to medium incomes who were not paying into a company pension scheme. Personal pensions would be retained but continue to be used mainly by higher income earners. Stakeholder pensions were aimed more at increasing pension entitlement in old age than improving the supply side performance of the economy.

Housing Housing can be a major barrier to mobility. Housing policy since 1979 has, if anything, tended to discourage mobility and hence increase unemployment and reduce aggregate supply. Between 1981 and 1989, large differentials in house prices between regions in the UK opened up, making it difficult for workers to move from higher unemployment, low house price areas outside the south of England to lower unemployment, high house price areas in the south. The house price collapse between 1989 and 1992, whilst reducing house price differentials between regions, led to a stagnant housing market and negative equity. Many were unable to sell their homes. Some could not afford to sell because the mortgage on the house was greater than its value. In the rented housing market, the policy of selling council houses to tenants from 1980 reduced the stock of affordable rented council housing. On the other hand, changes in rent controls in the late 1980s meant that landlords could, under certain circumstances, charge much higher rents. This, together with an increase in demand for rented accommodation resulting from the collapse of property prices, has led to some increase in renting at the top end of the market in the 1990s. A housing boom in the late 1990s once again increased price differentials between the south of England and the rest of the country, discouraging geographical mobility.

Small businesses are important because they provide jobs and can become the big businesses of tomorrow.

Help to businesses

If aggregate supply is to increase, the private sector needs to expand. Hence, according to supply side economists, the government needs to create an environment in which business can flourish.

Deregulation of the capital and money markets For instance, Big Bang in 1986 swept away the restrictive practices found in the City of London and particularly the Stock Exchange, making money and capital markets more competitive. The Building Societies Act 1986 gave Building Societies the power to compete with banks in offering a wide range of financial services. The abolition of exchange controls in 1979 allowed free movement of financial capital in and out of the UK.

Tax privileges for saving The tax system in the UK has traditionally favoured group savings schemes, such as pensions and assurance policies. It has therefore discouraged individuals from lending money directly to industrial companies, or buying shares in businesses. The government after 1979 wished to see a far more 'level playing field', where tax privileges were evened out between different types of saving. In particular, it sought to establish a **share owning democracy**. Wider share ownership was encouraged, particularly through the privatisation programme and through Personal Equity Plans (PEPS) and their successor, Individual Savings Accounts (ISAs), savings schemes which give tax relief on savings in shares and other assets.

Help to small businesses Small businesses are important in the economy because they provide new jobs and can become the big businesses of tomorrow. Conservative governments between 1979 and 1997 placed particular importance on the development of an 'enterprise culture'. Cuts were made in taxes on small company profits. Income tax rates were reduced. Investors in small businesses were given tax breaks, whilst the unemployed were encouraged to set up in business on their own through the provision of grants. The government also attempted to reduce the administrative burden on small businesses by cutting 'red tape' although this was contrary to the ever-increasing amount of legislation that businesses have to comply with in fields such as employment, health and safety and consumer protection.

The Labour government elected in 1997 did not see small businesses as more important than other types of businesses. However, it was keen to be seen to be pro-business. In the late 1990s the development of small firms was encouraged by a number of initiatives. Business start up schemes, run by TECs, provided training, advice and short term finance for new businesses. Business links gave advice and help obtaining government funds. The government also guaranteed some loans from banks to small businesses with little track record of borrowing money. Firms locating in areas with problems were able to take advantage of funds from both the UK government (the Single Regeneration Budget) and the EU's structural funds. Proposed changes after 2000 included replacing the work of TECs by the Small Business Service and the government involving venture capitalists in an Enterprise Fund to cover small business loans.

Goods markets

It is argued that competition increases both productive and allocative efficiency. Markets should therefore be made as competitive as possible. Encouraging competition was central to government policy after 1979.

Deregulation and privatisation In the 1980s, the government introduced policies to privatise state owned companies and deregulate markets. Nearly all state owned companies were privatised by the end of the 1990s including British Telecom and the gas industry. Central government departments and local authorities were encouraged to offer such services as waste collection or cleaning to tender rather than employing staff directly to provide the service. Many controls were abolished, such as legal restrictions on pub opening hours and Sunday trading. Greater competition in postal services and the opening of the London Underground to the private sector were planned for 2000 and beyond.

Encouragement of international free trade Fierce foreign competition results in a domestic industry which has to be efficient in order to survive. Since 1979, governments have tended to advocate policies of free trade on most issues. For instance, they have been more willing than most other European governments to see greater free trade in agriculture. The UK has also been one of the most welcoming to foreign companies wanting to set up in the UK. In the 1980s and 1990s, it actively encouraged Japanese motor companies to set up in the UK, at a time when some European countries like France would have preferred not to see increased competition for their domestic producers.

Regional and industrial policy

Before 1979, the main focus of supply side policies was regional and industrial policy. Since the time when manufacturing industry began to decline, arguably from the 1920s onwards, the UK government provided a variety of incentives to encourage firms to locate themselves in high unemployment areas. A variety of incentives have been used at different times:
- grants for new investment;
- tax relief on new investment;
- subsidies on employment;
- expenditure on infrastructure, such as motorways or factory buildings then available for subsidised rent;
- a requirement for firms to obtain permission from government to set up or expand in a low unemployment area of the UK (permissions called Industrial Development Certificates).

In the 1970s and early 1980s, the main incentive used was grants for new investment. It was felt that this was not only costly to the Exchequer, but also encouraged the siting of capital intensive manufacture rather than labour intensive manufacture or service industries in high unemployment areas. It was calculated, for instance, that the average cost between 1972 and 1983 to the government of creating an extra job in the assisted regions was £70 000 (at 1998 prices), whilst a total of 500 000 jobs had been created over the period (K Hartley and N Hooper, 1990).

In 1984, government implemented a new system of more selective regional assistance. The areas eligible for assistance were substantially reduced, and were graded into two levels: development areas and intermediate areas. Firms creating new jobs in development areas were automatically eligible for a regional development grant (RDG) of 15 per cent of investment expenditure up to a ceiling of £3 000 per new job created. Regional selective assistance (RSA) was made available to firms creating jobs or safeguarding jobs in both development and intermediate areas, but was discretionary. The Department of Industry attempted to provide the minimum financial support needed to secure the creation of new jobs.

The recession of 1990-92, which particularly affected the South of England but had far less impact on the rest of the country, resulted in a levelling out of disparities between regions. This led to a major review by government of the areas which could claim assistance. There was a drastic slimming down of regional development areas and for the first time high unemployment areas in East Kent became eligible for assistance.

Whilst the amount that was being spent centrally on regional aid diminished in the 1980s and 1990s, the amount available from the European Union and through the Welsh, Scottish and Northern Ireland offices grew. For instance, in the late 1990s, firms in development areas in England were being offered an average £4 000 per job created. But the Welsh Office offered £40 000 per job created to attract South Korea's LG (Lucky Gold) to set up in South Wales.

This disparity between the regions led the Labour government in 1999 to set up Regional Development Agencies for the whole of the UK. They have the brief to promote their region and create new jobs. They have funds available to them from central government, but may also be able to use European Union funds if part of their region is designated for assistance from Brussels.

Governments have also spent money on revitalising inner cities. Certain initiatives have been launched. Nearly all have emphasised the partnership between the public sector and the private sector. Typically, government funding has been made available if private sector money has also been pledged. The targets of initiatives have ranged from attracting industry to run down areas, redeveloping abandoned industrial sites, improving housing and job training.

Regional Development Agencies

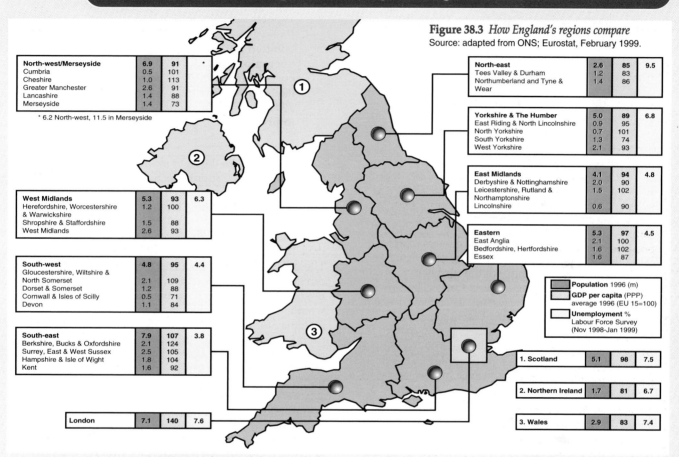

Figure 38.3 *How England's regions compare*
Source: adapted from ONS; Eurostat, February 1999.

Region / sub-area	Population 1996 (m)	GDP per capita (PPP) average 1996 (EU 15=100)	Unemployment % Labour Force Survey (Nov 1998-Jan 1999)
North-west/Merseyside	6.9	91	*
Cumbria	0.5	101	
Cheshire	1.0	113	
Greater Manchester	2.6	91	
Lancashire	1.4	88	
Merseyside	1.4	73	

* 6.2 North-west, 11.5 in Merseyside

Region / sub-area	Population 1996 (m)	GDP per capita	Unemployment %
North-east	2.6	85	9.5
Tees Valley & Durham	1.2	83	
Northumberland and Tyne & Wear	1.4	86	

Yorkshire & The Humber	5.0	89	6.8
East Riding & North Lincolnshire	0.9	95	
North Yorkshire	0.7	101	
South Yorkshire	1.3	74	
West Yorkshire	2.1	93	

West Midlands	5.3	93	6.3
Herefordshire, Worcestershire & Warwickshire	1.2	100	
Shropshire & Staffordshire	1.5	88	
West Midlands	2.6	93	

East Midlands	4.1	94	4.8
Derbyshire & Nottinghamshire	2.0	90	
Leicestershire, Rutland & Northamptonshire	1.5	102	
Lincolnshire	0.6	90	

Eastern	5.3	97	4.5
East Anglia	2.1	100	
Bedfordshire, Hertfordshire	1.6	102	
Essex	1.6	87	

South-west	4.8	95	4.4
Gloucestershire, Wiltshire & North Somerset	2.1	109	
Dorset & Somerset	1.2	88	
Cornwall & Isles of Scilly	0.5	71	
Devon	1.1	84	

South-east	7.9	107	3.8
Berkshire, Bucks & Oxfordshire	2.1	124	
Surrey, East & West Sussex	2.5	105	
Hampshire & Isle of Wight	1.8	104	
Kent	1.6	92	

London	7.1	140	7.6

	Population	GDP per capita	Unemployment %
1. Scotland	5.1	98	7.5
2. Northern Ireland	1.7	81	6.7
3. Wales	2.9	83	7.4

Regional inequalities

Britain is divided. The South East h [including London)as above average levels of income per head. Every other region is below the average. Governments for the past 70 years have attempted to narrow the gap between the regions by giving incentives for firms to set up in the poorer areas of the UK. To some extent they have been successful because regional inequalities might have been far wider today if no action had been taken. Even so, a problem remains which the government wishes to address.

1. **In what ways, according to the data, are England's regions unequal?**
2. **How can supply side policies mentioned in the data help tackle these problems?**
3. **To what extent can government funding alone increase aggregate supply in one of England's poorer regions?**

Regional Development Agencies

England's 8 Regional Development Agencies came into existence in April 1999. Their purpose is to promote economic development in the same way that the Development Agencies for Scotland, Wales and Northern Ireland have been doing for years. This includes promoting business efficiency, investment and competitiveness, skills, employment and sustainable development. However, they start at an immediate disadvantage since they have a total of £800 million-£1 billion to spend each year compared to £14 billion for Scotland and £7 billion for Wales.

What is more, their powers are highly limited. Local councils will retain powers over planning applications. The Department for Education and Employment will keep control over Training and Enterprise Councils (TECs), responsible for adult training, whilst the Department of Trade and Industry stays in charge of the business support network and regional selective assistance grants. However, the hope is that they will act as a catalyst to draw together every agency working for economic development in a region.

Their first task is to analyse their individual economies and draw up strategies for development for the next ten years. Although they control very limited budgets, the hope is that they will be able to tap into the much larger budgets of bodies such as local authorities, TECs and the EU to achieve their objectives. There is a general acceptance that the Scottish and Welsh Development Agencies have been a positive influence on economic growth in their regions. The hope is that the English Development Agencies will do the same.

Source: adapted from the *Financial Times*, 31.3.1999.

unit 39 Exchange rate policy

Summary

1. The value of a currency in a floating exchange rate system is determined by the forces of demand and supply.
2. Governments can influence the value of their currency by changing interest rates and by intervening directly on the foreign exchange markets using their gold and foreign currency reserves.
3. A rise in the value of a currency is likely to reduce exports but increase imports. A fall in the value of a currency is likely to increase exports but reduce imports.
4. Raising the exchange rate is likely to benefit inflation but will tend to reduce output, increase unemployment and lead to a deterioration in the current account. A fall in the exchange rate is likely to increase both inflation and output, reduce unemployment and lead to an improvement in the current account.

Exchange rate systems

The value of currencies like the US dollar, the Japanese yen and Britain's currency, the pound sterling, is determined by the foreign currency markets (☞ unit 13). At any point in time, there are buyers in the market for a currency and there are sellers. The forces of demand and supply then determine the price of the currency.

This system of determining exchange rates is known as a **free or floating exchange rate system**. There have been and still are other types of system. For instance, the Argentinean peso is fixed to the value of the US dollar. The Argentinean central bank guarantees to exchange pesos for US dollars at a fixed rate. This is an example of a **fixed exchange rate system**. Before 1914, the world's major currencies were fixed in value in relation to gold. In Europe, before the euro becomes the official currency of all participating states, each separate currency is fixed against each other at a specific exchange rate. The value of the French franc cannot change against the German deutschmark. The euro itself is allowed to float against other currencies and so its value is determined within a floating exchange rate system.

This unit will consider exchange rate policy within a floating exchange rate system. This is the situation that faced the government in the UK and the European Central Bank which controls the euro at the start of the new millennium.

Influencing the exchange rate

Exchange rate policy tends to be administered by the **central bank** (☞ unit 37) of a country which controls exchange rates and its gold and foreign currency reserves. There are two main ways today in which central banks influence the value of their currency.

Interest rates Increasing domestic interest rates is likely to increase the value of the currency. This is because higher interest rates in, say, the UK, makes depositing money in London more attractive. Savings are attracted into the UK from overseas, whilst UK firms and institutions are less attracted to sending their savings to New York, Tokyo or Paris. Hence the demand for pounds is likely to increase,

shown by a shift to the right in the demand curve for pounds, whilst the supply decreases, shown by a shift to the left in the supply curve. This results in a new higher equilibrium price (☞ unit 13).

Use of gold and foreign currency reserves Central banks have traditionally kept gold and foreign currency reserves. These are holdings of gold and foreign currencies which can be used to alter the value of a currency. If the Bank of England wanted to increase the value of the pound, it would sell some of its foreign currency reserves in exchange for pounds. This would increase the demand for pounds and hence raise its price. If it wanted to reduce the value of the pound, it would sell pounds for foreign currency, increasing supply and hence reducing the equilibrium price.

The ability of governments to influence the exchange rate is limited when the currency is floating. The amounts of money being traded each day on foreign exchange markets are so large that a country's foreign currency reserves could be used up within days trying to support a value of the exchange rate which the markets believed was too high. Equally, interest rate differentials between countries have to be substantial to have a significant impact on the value of the currency. Even so, governments can and do intervene to nudge exchange rates in directions which they believe desirable.

How exchange rate movements affect the economy

Exchange rate movements mainly affect the real economy through their effects on exports and imports. A rise or APPRECIATION in the exchange rate will tend to make exports more expensive to foreigners but imports cheaper to domestic customers. A fall or DEPRECIATION in the exchange rate will have the reverse effect, making exports cheaper and imports more expensive.

To understand why, consider a good priced at £100 which is being sold for export to the US by a UK firm. If the exchange rate is £1=$1, the US customer will have to pay $100. If the value of the pound rises to £1=$2, then the US customer will have to pay $200 for it. At the new

Question 1

The Japanese authorities intervened yesterday to halt the rise in the value of the yen. They spent $2 billion to $3 billion selling yen and buying up US dollars. The move was prompted by the rapid rise in the value of the yen over the past six months. The authorities did not want to see the yen rise above 1 yen = 0.91 US cents (equal to the psychologically important 110 yen = $1). There were fears that if this happened, the markets would push up the yen further to 1 yen = 1 US cents (equal to $1 = 100 yen). The authorities were responding to intense pressure from Japanese industrial firms which were finding it increasingly difficult to export as the value of the yen rose.

Source: adapted from the *Financial Times*, 13.1.1999.

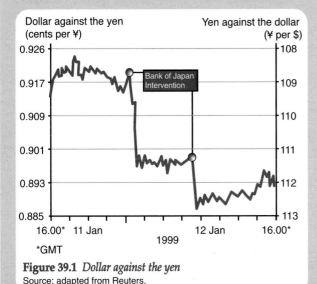

Figure 39.1 *Dollar against the yen*
Source: adapted from Reuters.

(a) (i) How did the Japanese authorities act to force down the value of the yen on January 12 1999? (ii) What effect did the intervention have on the value of the dollar against the yen?
(b) How else might the Japanese authorities have achieved their objective of reducing the value of the yen?
(c) What are the limitations of using foreign currency reserves to change the value of a currency? Illustrate your answer using the data.

higher exchange rate, the US customer has to pay more dollars to acquire the same number of pounds as before.

Similarly, consider a good priced at $100 in the US. If the exchange rate is £1=$1, then it will cost a UK customer £100. If the exchange rate rises to £1=$2, the cost to the UK customer will fall to £50.

A rise in the value of the pound will make UK firms less price competitive internationally. British exporters will find their orders falling as foreign customers switch to other, cheaper sources. In domestic markets, British firms will find that foreign imports are undercutting their prices and gaining market share. Exactly how much EXPORT and IMPORT VOLUMES, the number of goods sold, will

change depends upon their **price elasticity of demand** (☞ unit 8). If the price elasticity of demand for exports is elastic, with a value of, say, 2, then a 10 per cent rise in the price of exports to foreigners will result in a 20 per cent fall in export volumes.

Firms may, however, adopt a different response to an appreciation or depreciation of the currency. They may choose to keep prices to customers in their currency the same. For instance, with the good priced at £100 which is sold to the USA, the British firm could decide to keep the price at $100 when the exchange rate appreciates from £1=$1 to £1=$2. What this means is that the British exporter would then only receive £50 for the good. The British firm would not lose markets as a result, but it would see its profit margins fall. There are two reasons why an exporter might be prepared to accept a lower price for the product in domestic currency terms. First, it may think that the foreign currency movement is temporary. For marketing reasons, it does not want to be constantly changing its foreign currency price every time there is a small change in the exchange rate. Second, it may have been earning **abnormal profit** (☞ unit 17) previously, a higher level of profit than the minimum needed to keep the firm supplying the good.

If firms keep their prices to customers the same in their currencies, then export and import volumes will remain unchanged. However, profitability will have changed. If a currency appreciates in value, exporters will be forced to cut their prices in their own currency to maintain prices in foreign currencies. Their profitability will decline and it will become less attractive to export. Export values will fall too because, although volumes have remained the same, prices in domestic currency terms will have fallen. As for imports, foreign firms importing to the UK that choose to keep their sterling prices the same will see their profits rise. This will give them a greater incentive to sell into the UK. They might choose, for instance, to advertise more aggressively. Import volumes are therefore likely to rise, increasing import values as a result.

A third alternative is that firms may choose to change their export and import prices but not by as much as the change in the exchange rate. For instance, assume that the value of the pound rises 10 per cent against the US dollar. A UK exporting firm may choose to absorb 6 per cent of the rise by reducing the pound sterling price by 6 per cent and passing on the remaining 4 per cent by raising the dollar price. Profit margins fall and there could be some loss of market share because US customers now face higher prices. But this might be better for the firm than either cutting its sterling price by 10 per cent, eating into its profit margins, or raising US dollar prices by 10 per cent and risking losing substantial market share.

Which type of strategy a firm chooses to use to some extent depends upon the industry in which it operates. For commodity products, like steel, wheat or copper, firms are likely to have little control over their market. They will be forced to pass on price rises or falls to customers as exchange rates change. For firms which can control their markets, like car manufacturers, they tend to leave prices unaltered as exchange rates change.

Question 2

Competition from low-cost imports looks set to close another of Northern Ireland's shirt factories. The Rael Brook factory in Londonderry is another casualty of the high value of the pound. In July, the British Clothing Industry Association said that companies were being squeezed at both ends - domestic production by low-cost imports and exports by the high level of sterling. Robin Eagleson, managing director of the Shirtmakers Guild in Portadown making shirts for retailers in London's upmarket Jermyn Street, believes one way to survive is to move into higher value added production. But even here the export market has been hit badly. Mr Eagleson calculates that his German customers are paying 28 per cent more for their shirts than two years ago.

Source: adapted from the *Financial Times*, 16.9.1999.

(a) Explain the impact that the high value of the pound has had on UK exports and imports of shirts.
(b) Upmarket goods tend to carry higher profit margins. To what extent might moving upmarket have helped shirt makers in 1999?

The macroeconomic impact of changes in exchange rates

Exchange rates can be an **instrument** of government policy to achieve policy **goals** or **targets** (☞ unit 37).

Inflation Raising the exchange rate is likely to moderate inflation for two reasons. First, a higher exchange rate will tend to lead to a fall in import prices, which then feeds through to lower domestic prices. As explained above, some importers will choose to keep their foreign currency prices the same in order to increase their profit margins. But other importers will cut their foreign currency prices. The extent to which a rise in the exchange rate leads to a fall in domestic prices depends upon what proportion of importers choose to cut prices.

Second a higher exchange rate will lead to a fall in aggregate demand. Exports will fall and imports will rise as explained above. The fall in aggregate demand then leads to a fall in inflation. The extent to which aggregate demand falls depends upon the price elasticity of demand for exports and imports. The higher the price elasticities, the greater will be the change in export and import volumes to changes in prices brought about by the exchange rate movement.

The reverse occurs when there is a depreciation of the exchange rate. Import prices will tend to rise, feeding through to higher domestic inflation. Aggregate demand will rise as exports become more price competitive and imports less price competitive. As a result, inflation will tend to increase.

Economic growth Changing the exchange rate may have an impact on long term growth rates. A higher exchange rate which discourages exports and encourages imports may lead to lower domestic investment, and vice versa for a lower exchange rate. However, the main impact of a changing exchange rate will be felt on short run output. A rise in the exchange rate will dampen output in the short term because exports fall and imports rise, leading to a fall in aggregate demand. A fall in the exchange rate will lead to rising exports and falling imports, raising aggregate demand and thus equilibrium output.

Unemployment A rise in the exchange rate will tend to increase unemployment. This is because an exchange rate rise will tend to lower aggregate demand and thus equilibrium output. A fall in the exchange rate will tend to reduce unemployment. Changes in unemployment will be felt unequally in different sectors of the economy. In those industries which export a significant proportion of output, or where imports are important, there will tend to be larger changes in employment and unemployment as a result of exchange rate changes. In industries, particularly some service industries, where little is exported or imported, changes in the exchange rate will have little effect on employment and unemployment.

The current balance A rise in the exchange rate is likely to lead to a deterioration in the current balance. A rise in the exchange rate will lead to lower exports as they become less price competitive. The volume of imports is likely to rise leading to higher import values. So the current account position (exports minus imports) is likely to deteriorate. On the other hand, a fall in the exchange rate is likely to lead to an improvement in the current balance. Exports are likely to rise, but imports fall.

Question 3

The pound rose towards a six month high yesterday whilst the monthly trade deficit continued to slip. The global trade in goods deficit for January widened to £2.84 billion from £2.24 billion the previous month. The growing trade deficit has increased the calls for the government to cut interest rates. David Kernohan, the Engineering Employers' Federation senior economist, said: 'The lag effect of lost business over the last couple of years, along with the recent appreciation of the pound, is leading to accelerating job losses and falling capital investment'. Michael Saunder, UK economist for Salomon Smith Barney Citibank, added that as long as sterling remains high, Britain's growth and inflation prospects will remain sufficiently subdued to allow the Bank to lower rates.

Source: adapted from *The Times*, 25.3.1999.

(a) Suggest why engineering firms are calling for a cut in interest rates.
(b) What might have been the costs to the economy if the government had lowered exchange rates in March 1999?

key terms

Appreciation or depreciation of a currency - a rise or fall in the value currency when the currency is floating and market forces determine its value.

Export and import volumes - the number of exports and imports. In statistics, they are usually expressed in index number form. They can be calculated by dividing the value of total exports or imports by their average price.

Applied economics

UK government policy

Since September 1992, the UK government has chosen not use the exchange rate as an instrument of policy. Instead, it has allowed the pound to float freely on the foreign exchange markets. So it has not used either interest rates or its foreign currency reserves to affect the price of sterling.

This policy has been very much influenced by the experience during the period 1990-92. In 1990, the Conservative government with John Major as Chancellor of the Exchequer decided to join the Exchange Rate Mechanism (ERM) of the European Monetary Union (EMU). This was a mechanism designed to stabilise the value of European exchange rates prior to the creation of a single currency, the euro. Any single ERM currency was fixed in value against other currencies within the ERM within a band. For instance, the French franc was fixed against the German deutschmark within a $2^1/_2$ per cent band. So the French franc could appreciate or depreciate in value against the deutschmark but within very narrow limits.

The British government's main economic concern since 1988 had been combating inflation, which had risen from 4 per cent in 1987 to 10 per cent in 1990. It decided to enter the ERM at a high value for the pound. This put pressure on import prices and prevented a future fall in the exchange rate from reigniting inflation. Between 1990 and September 1992, it used its foreign currency reserves to keep the value of the pound within its band against other European currencies. More importantly, it was forced to keep interest rates high. By 1991, inflation was falling rapidly but the economy was

in a deep recession. The government wanted to ease monetary policy by cutting interest rates, but was prevented from cutting them as much as they wanted because high interest rates were needed to keep the value of the pound high. In September 1992, the pound came under fierce selling pressure. Despite using an estimated £30 billion in foreign currency reserves buying up pounds to keep its value within its band, speculation continued against the pound. On Black Wednesday, September 15, the government was forced to abandon its membership of the ERM. The pound rapidly fell 15 per cent in value.

This illustrates the problem that governments face when attempting to defend a value for the currency. Speculative flows of money are so large that it can be difficult for a government to prevent the markets from driving the currency up or down in value.

Since 1992, the UK government has chosen not to defend any particular value of the pound. However, the United Kingdom is likely to make a decision about whether to join the single European currency early in the 21st century. If it does join, it will have to peg the pound against the euro and it, together with the European Central Bank, will have to defend that value for a period of time. Under current arrangements the pound would eventually be abolished and the euro would become the UK's currency. Once the pound has disappeared, exchange rate policy will no longer be the responsibility of the UK government. It will pass to the European Central Bank.

The value of the pound

Getting worse

There are only three words used by most economists to describe the position of the UK's export sector. 'Bad' is one. 'Getting worse' are the other two. It's all due to the pound's high value. Its long ascent began in 1996 and reached a peak at the end of March 1998. Since then, analysts have declared that the pound was bound to fall,

but even five successive interest rate cuts by the Bank of England down to 5.5 per cent have done little to dent sterling. Part of the problem is that even at 5.5 per cent, UK interest rates offer a higher return than either in the euro-zone or in the USA.

Source: adapted from the *Financial Times*, 23.2.1999.

Squeeze on margins

Candford Group, based in Tyne and Wear, sells thousands of components to the broadcasting industry. European sales are priced in euros. The group reviews its prices every six month. Hugh Morgan-Williams, chairman, says the goods it is selling now were priced when the pound was worth roughly 2.75 German deutschmarks. Today, the pound is worth a little over 3 deutschmarks. So the higher the pound rises against the euro, the bigger the squeeze on margins.

Source: adapted from the *Financial Times*, 25.3.1999.

Lost orders

Philip Donnelly, managing director of Symphony, a furniture group in Leeds, says it has had to trim its European sales staff to cut costs. 'Its been hard work. We're keeping the administrative structure to maintain the existing sales business, which we're having to subsidise with discounts. The company signed several big contracts with buyers on the continents two years ago when the pound was worth 2.65 deutschmarks. 'We've been unable to support that work as the rate has gone up. We lost the work with a German mail order company. It hurts, I can tell you.' The group has abandoned plans for a new assembly plant in Rotherham, which would have created 100 jobs.

Source: adapted from the *Financial Times*, 25.3.1999.

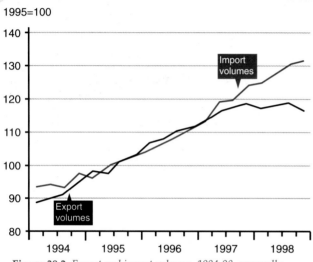

Figure 39.2 *Export and import volumes, 1994-98, seasonally adjusted, 1995=100*
Source: adapted from *Economic Trends Annual Supplement*, Office for National Statistics.

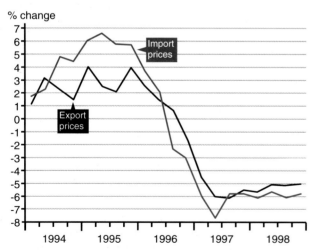

Figure 39.3 *Export and imports prices, 1994-1998, not seasonally adjusted, annual % change*
Source: adapted from *Economic Trends Annual Supplement*, Office for National Statistics.

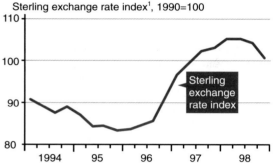

1. The sterling exchange rate index is an average of the currency values of the UK's trading partners, measured in index form.

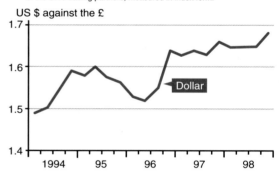

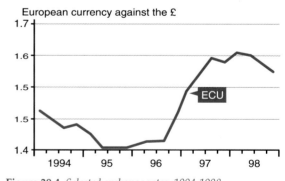

Figure 39.4 *Selected exchange rates, 1994-1998*
Source: adapted from *Economic Trends Annual Supplement*, Office for National Statistics.

1. Describe what happened to the value of the pound between 1994 and 1998.
2. Using evidence from the data and your knowledge of economic theory, analyse what effect these changes were having on exports and imports by 1998.

3. (a) Explain how the government could have reduced the value of the pound in early 1999 and
   (b) evaluate the main economic consequences of such a policy action.

unit 40 Trade policy

Summary

1. Although the gains from trade can be large, all countries choose to adopt protectionist policies to some extent.
2. Tariffs, quotas, voluntary export agreements and safety standards are some of the many ways in which countries limit free trade in goods and services.
3. The infant industry argument is one argument used to justify protectionism. It is claimed that young industries need protection if they are to survive the competition of larger more established industries in other countries. When the industry has grown sufficiently, barriers can be removed.
4. It is claimed that protectionism can save jobs. However, there is a great danger that the erection of barriers for this purpose will lead to retaliation by other trading nations, resulting in an overall welfare loss.
5. Protection against dumping will only lead to a gain in long run welfare for a nation if the dumping is predatory.
6. One valid argument in favour of protectionist policies is if the importing country is a monopsonist. The imposition of tariffs will lead to a fall in the price of imports, leading to a gain in welfare for the nation at the expense of foreign suppliers and an improvement in the terms of trade.

The benefits of free trade

Economists today tend to favour FREE TRADE between countries. Free trade occurs when there are no barriers to trade, such as taxes on imported goods or bans on imports. Free trade is beneficial for a number of reasons.

Specialisation The theory of **comparative advantage** (☞ unit 14) shows that world output can be increased if countries specialise in what they are relatively best at producing. It makes little point, for instance, for the UK to grow bananas given its climate when they can be grown much more cheaply in Latin America. Equally, it makes little sense for Barbados to manufacture motor vehicles given the size of the island, the relatively small population, the small domestic market and its geographical location.

Economies of scale Trade allows economies of scale to be maximised and thus costs reduced. Economies of scale are a source of comparative advantage. Small countries can buy in goods and services which are produced in bulk in other countries, whilst themselves specialising in producing and exporting goods where they have developed economies of scale.

Choice Trade allows consumers the choice of what to buy from the whole world, and not just from what is produced domestically. Consumer welfare is thus increased because some consumers at least will prefer to buy foreign goods

rather than domestic goods.

Innovation Free trade implies competition. A lack of free trade often leads to domestic markets being dominated by a few firms who avoid competition amongst themselves. Competition provides a powerful incentive to innovate. Not only are new goods and services being put onto the market, but firms are also competing to find production methods which cut costs and improve the quality and reliability of goods. A few firms are at the forefront of innovation in their industries. In a competitive market, however, other firms copy this innovation to remain competitive. The few countries in the world which for political reasons have chosen to isolate themselves from trade and attempt to be self-sufficient, like North Korea, have found that over time their economies have tended to stagnate. On their own, they simply do not have the resources or the incentives to keep up with the pace of innovation in the outside world.

Free trade, though, produces winners and losers. Firms which fail to innovate will go out of business. Their owners and their workers may therefore oppose free trade. Countries and firms which are particularly successful may see large rises in their incomes at the expense of less competitive nations and firms. Concerns may then be expressed about how some firms are able to charge high prices or earn high profits at the expense of consumers in other countries. Environmentalists worry that low prices in, say, the UK may be gained at the expense of the destruction of the environment in, say, Brazil. Some worry about the complexity of the world trading system, and are concerned that it is too large for any single institution like a government to control if necessary. Certainly, events like the Asian crisis of 1998, when a number of countries such as South Korea and Indonesia suffered large falls in their GDP due to a banking crisis, show that crises in one country can have a considerable impact in other countries because of the world trading system. For these, and other reasons discussed below, countries have often chosen to limit free trade by imposing barriers to trade.

Methods of protection

There is a large number of ways in which a country may choose to erect TRADE BARRIERS.

Tariffs A TARIFF is a tax on imported goods. It is sometimes called an IMPORT DUTY or a CUSTOMS DUTY. Tariffs can be used by governments to raise revenue to finance expenditure. However, they are most often used in a deliberate attempt to restrict imports. A tariff, by imposing a tax on a good, is likely to raise its final price to the consumer (although occasionally a foreign supplier will absorb all the tariff to prevent this from happening). A rise in the price of the good will lead to a fall in demand and the volume of imports will fall. A tariff should also help

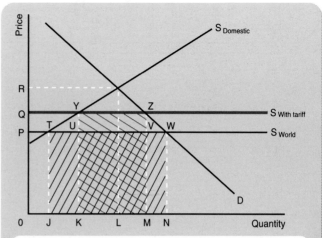

Figure 40.2 *Tariffs*
If the world price of a good is OP, a tariff of PQ will shift the supply curve upwards from S$_{World}$ to S$_{With tarrif}$. Domestic consumption will fall by MN whilst domestic production will rise by JK. Imports will fall from JN to KM.

domestic producers. Some consumers will switch consumption from imported goods to domestically produced substitutes following the imposition of a tariff. For instance, if the UK imposed a tariff on sugar cane imports, British produced sugar beet would become more competitive and demand for it would rise.

This is shown in Figure 40.2. D is the domestic demand for a good. S $_{Domestic}$ is the domestic supply curve of the product. With no foreign trade, equilibrium output would occur where domestic demand and supply were equal at OL. However, with foreign trade, world producers are assumed to be prepared to supply any amount of the product at a price of OP. Consumers will now buy imported goods because the world price OP is below the domestic price of OR. Domestic supply will fall back along the supply curve to OJ. Demand for the good will rise to ON. Imports must be JN if demand is ON and domestic supply is OJ.

Now assume that the government of the country imposes a tariff of PQ per unit. The price to domestic consumers will rise to OQ. Domestic producers will not pay the tariff. Therefore they find it profitable to expand production to OK. Higher prices cause demand to fall to OM. Hence imports will only be KM. Expenditure on imports will fall from JTWN (price JT times quantity bought JN) to KYZM. Of that area KYZM, KUVM will be the revenue gained by foreign firms. The rest, UYZV, is the tax collected on the imports and will therefore go to the government.

Quotas A QUOTA is a physical limit on the quantity of a good imported. It is an example of a **physical control**. Imposing a limit on the quantity of goods imported into a country will increase the share of the market available for domestic producers. However, it will also raise the price of the protected product.

This is shown in Figure 40.3. The world supply price of a product is £8. Domestic demand shown by the demand

Question 1

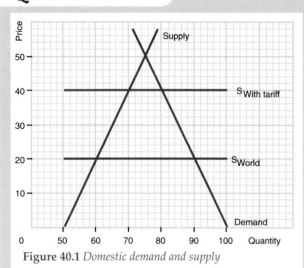

Figure 40.1 *Domestic demand and supply*

Figure 40.1 shows the domestic demand and supply curves for a good.
(a) What is the equilibrium price and quantity demanded and supplied domestically?
(b) The country starts to trade internationally. The international price for the product shown is 20. The country can import any amount at this price. What is: (i) the new level of demand; (ii) the new level of domestic supply; (iii) the quantity imported?
(c) The government, alarmed at the loss of jobs in the industry, imposes a tariff of 20 per unit. By how much will: (i) domestic demand fall; (ii) domestic supply rise; (iii) imports fall?
(d) What would happen if the government imposed a tariff of 40 per unit?

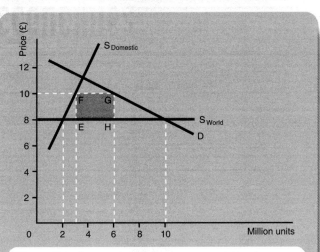

Figure 40.3 *Quotas*
If the world price of a good is £8, the introduction of a quota of 3 million units will reduce supply and raise the domestic price to £10. Domestic consumption will fall from 10 million units to 6 million units whilst domestic production will rise from 2 million units to 3 million units. Importers of the 3 million units subject to quota will make a windfall gain. Before the imposition of the quota they could only get a price of £8 per unit. After the imposition of the quota they can charge £10 per unit.

Question 2

Lamp posts The European Commission has brightened the outlook for Europe's lamp post manufacturers by forcing the Spanish government to lift a key trade restriction. The action follows a complaint from a French company, which pointed out that when it attempted to tender for the supply of lamp posts for a Spanish motorway it was rebuffed. It was informed that its product did not conform to local technical requirements.
The Commission stepped in to the dispute by invoking Article 30 of the Treaty of Rome - which guarantees the free circulation of goods - and asked the Madrid government to amend its regulations. This has since been done.

Steel US steel producers are continuing to press its government for quota protection on steel imports. The collapse of demand in Asia due to the Asian crisis of 1998 has led to severe oversupply of steel in world markets. Steel prices have come under severe pressure and led to many steel producers reporting losses. In the US, three smaller producers went bankrupt in 1998, whilst 7 000 workers were laid off and 20 000 were working reduced hours. In volume terms, imports rose by 49 per cent between July and October 1998 over the same period in 1997, while exports plunged by 20 per cent.

Source: adapted from the *Financial Times*, various.

(a) What types of protection are illustrated in the two examples?
(b) What arguments might be used by domestic producers to justify the protectionist measures?
(c) What arguments might be used in favour of greater free trade in the two cases?

curve D is 10 million units. Of that, 2 million is produced domestically. The remaining 8 million is imported. Now assume that a quota of 3 million units is imposed on imports. Because output is now 4 million units less than it would otherwise have been, price will rise to £10. Domestic production will rise to 3 million units. Domestic consumption is 6 million units. The rise in price has led to a reduction in demand of 4 million units. It should be noted that quotas, unlike tariffs, can lead to gains by importers. It is true in Figure 40.3 that foreign firms have lost orders for 4 million units. But those firms which have managed to retain orders have gained. They used to sell their units for £8. They can now get £10. This is a windfall gain for them, shown on the diagram by the rectangle EFGH.

Other restrictions There are a considerable number of other trade barriers which countries can erect against foreign imports. In the 1970s and 1980s, there was widespread use of **Voluntary Export Agreements**. These are a type of quota which is enforced by importers. For instance, the UK had an agreement with Japanese car manufacturers that they should not take more than 10 per cent of the UK car market. Another widespread barrier is non-competitive purchasing by governments. They are major buyers of goods and services and most governments round the world have a policy of buying only from domestic producers even if this means paying higher prices. Meeting different safety standards can lead to higher costs of production for importers. Simple tactics like lengthy delays at customs posts can also deter imports.

Arguments used to justify protection

The theory of comparative advantage states that there are major welfare gains to be made from free trade in international markets. However, protectionism has always been widespread. What arguments can be put forward to justify protectionist policies?

The infant industry argument This is one of the oldest arguments in favour of protection. Industries just starting up may well face much higher costs than foreign competitors. Partly this is because there may be large economies of scale in the industry. A new low volume producer will find it impossible to compete on price against an established foreign high volume producer. Once it is sufficiently large, tariff barriers can be removed and the industry exposed to the full heat of foreign competition. There may also be a learning curve. It takes some time for managers and workers in a new industry to establish efficient operational and working practices. Only by protecting the new industry can it compete until the 'learning' benefits come through.
  Some countries, such as Japan, have successfully developed infant industries behind high trade barriers. It is also true that many countries such as the UK have financial systems which tend to take a short view of investment. It is difficult, if not impossible, to find backers for projects which might only become profitable in 10 or even 5 years' time.

Question 3

Three US bicycle manufacturers are seeking protection against Chinese imports which they say severely hit their operating profits last year. The companies filed a complaint yesterday with the Federal government alleging that China is dumping bicycles in the US at 'less than fair market value'. In 1994, the US imported 7.1 million bicycles out of a market of 16.7 million. While import levels have remained steady, China's share of the overall market has risen sharply from 14.6 per cent in 1993 to 23.7 per cent last year.

'This is not a case of volume losses' said a spokesman for the US industry. 'But pricing has been a problem. The domestic industry has been forced to cut prices on every bike sold.' In 1994, China produced 40m bicycles against demand of 34m. In 1992 - the latest figures available for ownership - there were 451m bicycles in China, or 38.5 per 100 people. The US action follows the imposition of anti-dumping duties on Chinese bicycles by Canada, Mexico and the European Union.

Leading Chinese manufacturers, such as Forever and Phoenix, have been looking to exports - mostly to Asia and Africa - to provide an outlet for excess production. Forever exports about 300 000 bicycles and Phoenix 1m. Less than 5 per cent of these 'low end' products goes to the USA.

Source: adapted from the *Financial Times*, 7.4.1995.

(a) What is meant by 'dumping'?
(b) Discuss how US bicycle manufacturers might argue that Chinese bicycles are being sold in the US at 'less than fair market value'.
(c) What arguments could the Chinese use to defend themselves against accusations of dumping?

However, infant industries in general have not grown successfully behind trade barriers. One problem is that government needs to be able to identify those infant industries which will grow successfully. Governments have a poor record of picking such 'winners'. Second, industries protected by trade barriers lack the competitive pressure to become efficient. Infant industries all too often grow up to be lame duck industries. They only carry on operating because they have become skilled at lobbying government to maintain high trade barriers. Third, it is usually more efficient to use other policy weapons if a government genuinely wishes to encourage the development of a new industry. Specific subsidies, training grants, tax concessions, or even the creation of state enterprises, are likely to be better ways of creating new industries.

Job protection Another argument with a very long history is the idea that protectionism can create or at least preserve jobs. During the 1970s, the share of the UK car

market taken by domestic car manufacturers shrank drastically. It would have been possible to erect trade barriers against foreign imported cars to preserve jobs in the motor car industry. However, there are two major problems with this policy. Firstly, although the policy may benefit manufacturers and their workers, consumers are likely to have less choice and pay higher prices. Much of the gain for producers is an internal transfer of resources from domestic consumers. Moreover, foreign countries could retaliate by imposing trade restrictions on exports, leading to a loss of jobs in the domestic economy. If they do, then all countries participating in the trade war will suffer. Production will be switched from lower cost to higher cost producers, resulting in a loss of welfare for consumers. The gains from trade resulting from comparative advantage will be lost.

Dumping DUMPING can be defined in a number of ways. Broadly speaking it is the sale of goods below their cost of production, whether marginal cost, average total cost, or average variable cost. Foreign firms may sell products 'at a loss' for a variety of reasons.
- They may have produced the goods and failed to find a market for them, so they are dumped on one country in a distress sale. Knickers from China and shoes from Brazil were two examples of this during the 1980s.
- In the short run, a firm may have excess capacity. It will then sell at a price below average total cost so long as that price at least covers its variable cost. Steel and chemical manufacturers tended to sell below total cost during the second half of the 1970s and first half of the 1980s because there was so much excess capacity in those industries as a result of the two oil crises.
- Low prices could represent a more serious long term threat to domestic industry. A foreign producer may deliberately price at a loss to drive domestic producers out of business. Once it has achieved this, it can increase prices and enjoy monopoly profits. Japanese companies have been accused of doing this in, for instance, the European semi-conductor market or in the European video recorder market.

Goals of long term domination by a foreign producer might justify trade barriers, although it might be more efficient to subsidise domestic industries. It is more difficult to say whether short term distress dumping leads to a loss of domestic welfare. On the one hand, domestic producers and their workers may suffer a loss of profits and wages. The impact on employment should be limited if dumping is only a short term phenomenon. On the other hand, consumers gain by being able to buy cheap goods, even if only for a limited period.

Cheap labour Countries which have plentiful sources of cheap labour are often accused of 'unfair competition'. High labour cost countries find it difficult if not impossible to compete against products from these countries and there is pressure from threatened industries to raise trade barriers. However, cheap labour is a source of comparative advantage for an economy. There is a misallocation of resources if domestic consumers are forced to buy from high wage domestic industries rather than low wage foreign industries. Resources which are used in high cost protected industries could be used elsewhere in the

Question 4

The US government, under pressure from its trade unions, wants a social clause inserted in the WTO agreements currently under discussion at Seattle. This would cover fundamental workers' rights relating to issues such as low wages, use of child labour, union representation, and safety at work. Countries where workers are denied their fundamental rights would face imposition of tariffs and quotas on exports of their goods to countries such as the US.

Developing countries are fiercely resisting any such clause. They argue that if they are to compete in the world economy, they cannot afford to pay their workers western-style wages because productivity levels are much lower in the Third World. Higher growth will allow countries to invest in education and upgrade factories that will eventually improve productivity, but the west cannot deny developing countries the competitive advantage they gain from cheaper wages.

Source: adapted from *The Guardian*, 29.11.1999.

(a) Explain why trade unions in the USA might lobby for a social clause to be inserted in a world trade agreement when their members almost certainly already enjoy those rights.
(b) Discuss whether workers in Third World countries would benefit from such a social clause.

economy to produce products for which the country does have a comparative advantage in production.

The terms of trade One argument in favour of tariffs for which an economic case can be made is the optimal tariff argument. In Figure 40.2 it was assumed that a country could import any amount at a given price because it was a relatively small buyer on the world market. However, if a country imports a significant proportion of world production, then it is likely to face an upward sloping supply curve. The more it buys, the higher the price per unit it will have to pay. At the extreme, the country may be a **monopsonist** (i.e. the sole buyer of a product).

If the country faces an upward sloping supply curve, the marginal cost of buying an extra unit will not only be the cost of the extra unit but also the extra cost of buying all other units. For instance, a country buys 10 units at £1. If it buys an eleventh unit, the price rises to £11. The cost of the eleventh unit is therefore £11 plus 10 x £1 - a total of £21. The decision to buy the eleventh unit will be made by individual producers and consumers. The cost to them of the eleventh unit is just £11 - the other £10 extra is borne by the producers and consumers who bought the other 10 units.

Therefore the marginal cost to the economy as a whole of buying an extra unit of imports is greater than the marginal cost to the individual. But it is the individual which makes the decision about whether to buy or not. If the marginal cost of purchase is lower for the individual than for the economy as a whole, more imports will be bought than if the individual had to pay the whole cost of purchase (i.e. the cost including the increased price of previously purchased units). This would suggest that a tariff which increased prices to the point where the cost to the individual purchaser was equal to the cost borne by society as a whole

of that decision would increase economic welfare.

Imposition of a tariff will reduce demand for imported goods, and this in turn will lead to a fall in the price of imported goods (☞ unit 11 - a tariff is an indirect, ad valorem or specific tax which shifts the supply curve for imported goods to the left, resulting in a fall in equilibrium price received by suppliers). Hence the **terms of trade** (the ratio between export prices and import prices ☞ unit 14) will rise in favour of the importing country. The importing country will be able to buy goods more cheaply. But it is important to remember that this gain will be at the expense of the exporting country. If, for instance, the UK imposed a tariff on tea, the price of tea might fall. The UK will gain but only at the expense of India and Sri Lanka. Also, if the exporting country retaliates by imposing its own tariffs, both countries could be worse off than before.

Other arguments A number of other arguments are put forward in favour of trade barriers. It is sometimes argued that a country needs a particular domestic industry for defence purposes. A country may wish to preserve a particular way of life, such as preventing depopulation of remote rural areas heavily dependent upon a particular agricultural product. It may be felt that some imports are too dangerous to be sold domestically. 'Danger' could range from unsafe electrical products, to toxic waste to drugs. Alternatively, a country may decide that it is too dependent upon one industry. Some small Third World countries depend crucially upon one cash crop such as cocoa, bananas or sugar cane for their economic well being. These commodities are subject to large fluctuations in price on world markets. Falls in price can give rise to large falls in living standards in these economies. Diversifying, even if the newly established industries are uneconomic by world standards, could provide a valuable insurance policy against commodity price fluctuations. Trade barriers are one means of sheltering these industries from foreign competition.

In all of this, however, it is important to question whether trade barriers are the best means of achieving the desired objective. Economists tend to argue that other policies, such as subsidising industries, are likely to be more efficient than trade protection.

key terms

Dumping - the sale of goods at less than cost price by foreign producers in the domestic market.
Free trade - international trade conducted without the existence of barriers to trade, such as tariffs or quotas.
Tariff, import duty or customs duty - a tax on imported goods which has the effect of raising the domestic price of imports and thus restricting demand for them.
Trade barriers - any measure which artificially restricts international trade.
Quota - a physical limit on the quantity of an imported group.

Applied economics

WTO and protectionism

Economic theory suggests that free trade is likely to benefit countries. By allowing each country to specialise, production will take place in locations which enjoy a comparative advantage. World trade expanded in the 19th century. As Figure 40.4 shows, though, the first half of the twentieth century saw a fall in trade. This was partly caused by the economic disruption of two world wars. The Great Depression of the 1930s also led countries to adopt deeply protectionist policies. Governments mistakenly believed that by keeping foreign goods out, they could save domestic jobs. In practice, all countries adopted the same mix of measures. World trade collapsed, jobs were lost in export industries and consumers were left having to pay higher prices to inefficient domestic producers when before they could buy goods from overseas at cheaper prices.

After the Second World War, there was a general recognition that these protectionist policies had been self-defeating. The Bretton Woods system of exchange rates banned competitive devaluations, whilst 23 countries in 1947 signed the General Agreement on Tariffs and Trade (GATT). Under GATT rules, member countries were not allowed to increase the degree of protection given to their domestic producers. Also, under the **most-favoured nation** clause of the agreement, a country which offered a cut in tariffs to one country had to offer the same terms to all member countries.

GATT rules prevented protection increasing, but did nothing to reduce protectionism. For this reason, GATT, and its successor organisation, the WTO (World Trade Organisation), have, over the years, organised a series of negotiations (called 'rounds') aimed at reducing tariffs and quotas. By the end of the last Tokyo round of negotiations in 1979, the average tariff on industrial goods had fallen to 4.7 per cent. Between 1986 and 1994 an eighth round of negotiations, the Uruguay Round, was successfully completed.

These measures to promote free trade were a powerful influence in expanding trade in the post-war period. Figure 40.5 shows that world merchandise export volumes (manufacturing, agricultural and mining products) rose nearly three times as fast between 1950 and 1998 as world production itself.

The Uruguay Round

The Uruguay Round, so called because the first meeting took place in Uruguay in 1986, differed from previous rounds in that it did not concentrate mainly on trade in manufactured goods. The final treaty in fact covered three main areas, agriculture, textiles and services.

Agriculture tends to be highly protected throughout the world. The European Union, Japan and the United States in particular have strong protectionist regimes designed to assist their farmers. However, the cost to consumers is very high, averaging somewhere between £500 and £1 000 per household per year in the EU according to differing estimates. The Uruguay deal made a start in dismantling protectionist barriers but, even so, they remain significant. An important part of the deal was that non-tariff barriers, such as quotas, have to be converted into tariff barriers. This will make the cost of protectionism much more transparent and could make it more difficult in future for the farming lobby to argue the case for greater protection.

Textiles have traditionally been highly protected too. This is because the major industrialised countries once had important textile industries of their own which have increasingly come under competitive pressure from Third World countries. The response by many First World countries was to allow contraction of the industry but raise barriers to prevent too great a fall in employment. In 1974, this protectionism was formalised in the Multi-Fibre Agreement (MFA), an accord between Third World countries and First World countries, which allowed greater access over time for

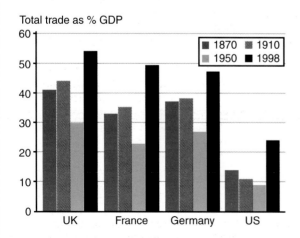

Figure 40.4 *Total trade as % of GDP, selected countries 1970-1998*

Source: adapted from Baldwin and Martin, NBER working paper, WTO.

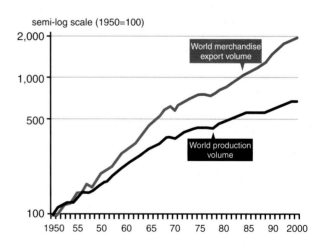

Figure 40.5 *World merchandise export volume and world production volume, 1950-1998*

Source: adapted from Baldwin and Martin, NBER working paper, WTO.

Third World textile exports to First World markets but within the framework of a highly protectionist First World regime. A World Bank study in 1995 estimated that the abolition of the MFA and the introduction of the Uruguay negotiated tariff reductions would give gains of almost $60bn per year to EU and the USA consumers alone by 2005. This is because they will be able to switch from buying high price domestic textiles to low price Third World imports.

The third part of the Uruguay deal covered services. The USA was particularly concerned that Third World countries were using 'intellectual property' - everything from pirated video games and CDs to drug formulations and manufacturing processes to trade names like Coca Cola and Microsoft - without paying copyright and royalty fees. The Uruguay Round put this firmly on the agenda even if some countries like China continue to flout international conventions. The Uruguay deal also began the process of opening up competition in highly protected national service industries such as finance and telecommunications.

Finally, it was decided to set up a new organisation to replace GATT. It would be called the World Trade Organisation (WTO). It was given greater powers and made responsible not just for promoting world trade, for instance through further rounds of negotiation on reducing protectionism, but also for policing existing agreements. It has the power to make judgments on trading disputes and, if necessary, impose financial penalties on countries which break international trading agreements to which they are signatories.

Seattle

In 1999, the WTO launched another round of talks at a meeting in Seattle in the USA. The meeting broke up without any agreement on a way forward for further trade liberalisation, but this was not surprising. Any trade deal is likely to take a decade to negotiate. The week of negotiations was notable for the street demonstrations which took place in the city. Hundreds of protest groups gathered to voice their frustration at various aspects of the world economic system. One of their targets was multinationals (firms which produce in more than one country), which they felt manipulated the economic system for their own profit at the expense of individual people. Another target was free trade itself. Some US trade unions, for instance, would like to see more protectionism in the mistaken belief that protectionism can safeguard jobs and increase prosperity. Another target was First World governments which were accused of using trade to reinforce and indeed increase inequalities in the world. The WTO stands accused of being dominated by the rich industrialised countries intent on negotiated trade agreements which would suit themselves, whatever the cost to Third World countries. Environmental issues were also raised. Increased trade is a sign of increased production and consumption which may be unsustainable, using up non-renewable resources and destroying the environment.

The talks started at Seattle will continue and agreements will eventually be signed, but at this stage it is impossible to predict the exact outcome of this next round of trade talks.

Trading blocs

Since the mid-1970s, the work of GATT and now the WTO has been made increasingly difficult by the emergence of trading blocs. A few countries have been drawing closer together and offering tariff reductions to some countries but not others in contradiction to the most-favoured nation clause. The EU, for instance, has embarked on an ambitious programme under the 1992 Single Market banner, to remove a large number of obstacles to free trade without offering the same trading opportunities to non-EU countries. The USA and Canada also signed an agreement in 1988 which effectively removed most trade barriers between the two countries. In 1994, this was extended to include Mexico under the North American Free Trade Association (NAFTA) agreement. If this were to carry on, it would be possible to see a world comprised of several large trading blocs, each with common external tariffs and free trade within the bloc. This would contradict the vision of GATT and the WTO which is to remove trade barriers between **all** countries.

Trade imbalances and dumping

In the 1980s and 1990s, there have been growing trade imbalances. Japan and Germany have consistently exported more than they have imported, resulting in trade deficits for other countries. The USA, in particular, has experienced large current account deficits on its balance of payments since the early 1980s, importing far more than it has exported. A number of traditional US industries, such as textiles, car manufacturing and steel, have been badly affected by foreign competition and there have been growing calls for measures to be taken against 'unfair' foreign competition.

It is very difficult to define 'unfair' competition. The whole basis for trade is that it is relatively cheaper to produce goods in some countries than others. It would be foolish for the UK to complain that textiles made by cheap labour in Far Eastern countries represent 'unfair' competition for domestic manufactures given that the source of Far Eastern comparative advantage in textiles lies in its cheap labour. On the other hand, it can be true that countries or companies disrupt markets through **dumping**, which the WTO defines as the sale of a product in an export market at a cheaper price than is charged in the domestic market.

Both the USA and EU have increasingly taken action against what they see as dumping. In the EU, up to 100 anti-dumping suits are investigated each year, and suits have been brought against Japanese manufacturers of photocopiers, printers and video tape recorders. But under WTO rules, the USA and EU should take the issue to the WTO and allow the WTO to judge it. Countries don't do this, partly because WTO judgments often take years, by which time the damage has been done, and partly because they are uncertain of winning the case. In many instances, anti-dumping suits have more to do with protecting inefficient domestic producers which have lobbied their governments hard, than with unfair trading practices of, say, Japanese companies which may simply be offering the best products at the cheapest prices.

Bananas

The background

Both France and the UK owned colonies until relatively recently. Some of these, particularly in the Caribbean, were highly dependent on banana exports for their income. Since independence, France and the UK have protected those banana producers through a system of tariffs and quotas. This has helped raise incomes from what they might otherwise have been. This system of protection is part of the Lome Convention, a wide ranging agreement between the EU and its former colonies giving preferential access to EU markets for some exports from those countries. The developing country members of the Lome Convention are called ACP countries - African, Caribbean and Pacific countries.

In 1999, Caribbean ACP producers accounted for just 3 per cent of world banana exports, but these formed 20 per cent of EU imports. For three ACP countries, Dominica, St Lucia and St Vincent, bananas represented about 60 per cent of total export earnings.

Caribbean ACP banana producers are high cost producers. The terrain is often hilly and farms are small. Central American producers, such as Ecuador, are much lower cost producers. Plantations in Central America tend to be much larger and are able to exploit economies of scale.

Two protectionist regimes

Before 1993 Before 1993, different EU countries operated different trade regimes. Some countries, particularly Germany, bought their bananas from the lowest cost source. In practice, this meant buying from countries in Central America such as Ecuador and Costa Rica. Other countries, notably France and the UK, had imposed tariff barriers on banana imports from most countries, including Central America, but allowed tariff free imports from its former Caribbean colonies. As a result, these former Caribbean colonies were guaranteed a market for their banana exports at prices higher than the world market price.

After 1993 On 1 January 1993, the Single Market in the EU came into existence. This prohibited different protectionist regimes between member countries. So a new agreement on banana imports was agreed with ACP countries. Banana imports were divided into three quotas. The first quota guaranteed a certain tonnage (0.85 million tonnes in 1996) to bananas grown by EU member states. The second quota (0.86 million tonnes in 1996) did the same for 'traditional' bananas grown in ACP countries. The third quota (2.25 million tonnes in 1996) was for 'dollar' bananas from Latin America and 'non-traditional' ACP bananas. Each of these quotas was further split up into quotas for individual countries. Duty of Ecu75 a tonne was imposed on all quota banana imports. Any imports above quota were exposed to a prohibitive duty of at least 150 per cent. In practice, EU and ACP 'traditional' banana producers do not have the productive capacity to exceed their quotas. So these prohibitive duties could only be paid by Latin American countries with large banana industries. In addition, 30 per cent of the rights to import under the third quota were transferred from the US companies that traditionally handled these products to EU and ACP trading organisations.

The cost of protectionism

Figure 40.6 shows the different costs and benefits of the banana regime before and after 1993. Protectionism raises the price of bananas to consumers in the EU compared with what they would pay if they could buy them at the cheapest world price. The EU price is set by the forces of demand and supply. The quota system reduces the supply to such an extent that banana prices are higher than simply the world market price plus the tariff imposed. The difference is split two ways. First, ACP growers receive a higher price than they would otherwise have done if free markets prevailed. This is the 'net benefit to subsidised growers' in Figure 40.6. However, the largest gainers are the fruit trading companies, such as Gheest, which buy bananas from individual farmers, transport them, and finally sell them to wholesalers in the EU. Because the price under the quota system is so high, they are able to sell them for a much higher price than the cost of buying and transporting them. The result is the 'monopoly profit' shown in Figure 40.6. Rights to quotas are therefore highly valuable. When 30 per cent of the rights to import under the third quota were transferred from US to EU and ACP companies, US companies lost a valuable source of profit.

Brent Borrell, who estimated the figures shown in Figure 40.6, argued that of the extra $2 billion EU consumers paid for bananas compared to a free trade price, only $150 million went to producers in the 11 ACP countries. Hence, for every $13.50 extra paid by EU consumers for bananas, just $1 went to the Third World ACP countries that were supposed to be the main beneficiaries of the regime. What's more, the new system imposed in 1993 both increased the cost to EU consumers and lowered the subsidy paid to ACP countries.

EU consumers buy fewer bananas than they would otherwise have done because of high prices. This reduces world demand for bananas and therefore reduces world prices. As a consequence, Third World banana producers such as Costa Rica receive lower prices for their bananas. The benefits received by ACP countries are therefore offset by the losses of other Third World producers.

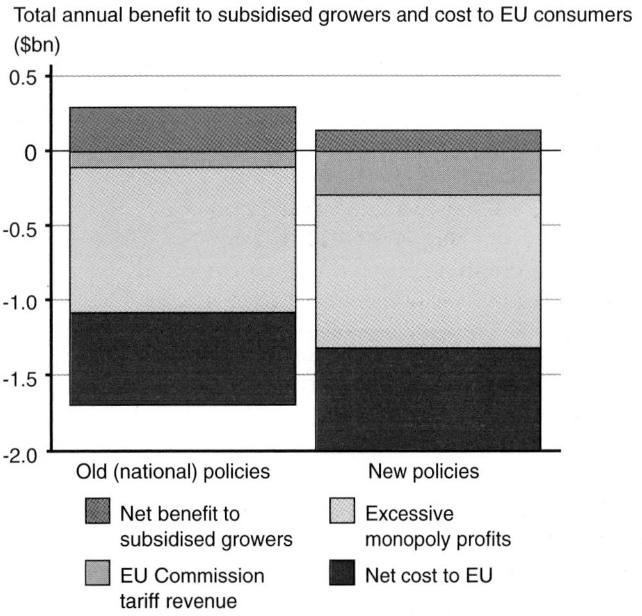

Total annual benefit to subsidised growers and cost to EU consumers ($bn)

Figure 40.6 *The cost of protectionism before and after 1993*
Source: adapted from Borrell.

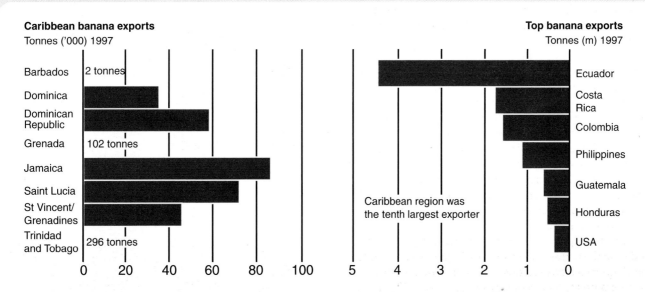

Figure 40.7 *Banana exports*
Source: adapted from UN Food and Agriculture industry.

Trade war

Latin American countries which produce bananas have lost out from the EU banana regime. So too has the United States. Its fruit companies lost out when 30 per cent of their import permits were removed in 1993. They are also unable to sell as many bananas to Europe as would be the case if there were free trade.

In 1996, the USA, Guatemala, Honduras, Mexico and Ecuador lodged a formal complaint with the World Trade Organisation about the EU banana regime. The World Trade Organisation ruled that it was against WTO rules in 1997. The EU appealed and lost. In 1998, the EU proposed some modifications to its banana regime but this failed to satisfy the USA and it

threatened to impose retaliatory tariffs on a wide range of goods imported from the EU. In April 1999, the WTO gave a ruling which stated that the US could impose $191.4 million of sanctions on EU goods to compensate for trade losses caused by the banana preferences.

The EU backed down and in June 1999 announced proposals for a new banana regime. This would give ACP countries a preferential duty free 857 000 tonne quota. Latin American countries would pay tariffs on their allocated quota. In addition, ACP countries will receive aid of about $390 million over ten years to help diversify their economies away from banana production.

'I don't know what we will do if America is successful. There's nothing here that can bring in a regular dollar like banana. There's tourism, but tourism brings in the top dollar. It stays at the top and doesn't come down to us. Banana money comes from the ground and goes up.'

Leonard Leonce, owner of 7 hectares of banana trees, St Lucia.

Removing preferential status for bananas could leave the islands 'vulnerable to annihilation. We can look forward to sudden inflationary spirals, currency instability, wage devaluations and public service restructuring.'

Jerry Scott, Agricultural Minister, St Vincent.

Views from the islands

'Who will care if, as a result of this policy, we lose our houses, our children are dying from disease or are going to be uneducated? I think we have a strong moral case; I just don't wonder who is going to listen to it.'

Rupert Gajadar, former chairman of the St Lucia Banana Growers' Association.

British consumers 'must eat more West Indian bananas. It is good if we can get them to buy more, if we could sell directly to supermarkets. The middlemen get everything now. If banana go, everything gone. Then we in trouble. When bananas stop, I die.'

Kelvin Bristol, banana grower, St Vincent.

Source: adapted from the *Financial Times*, 24.3.1999, 9.4.1999, 8.7.1999.

1. **Explain, using a diagram, how the EU banana regime implemented in 1993 raises the price of bananas to EU consumers and reduces sales.**
2. **Analyse the arguments for and against the 1993 EU banana regime from the viewpoint of: (a) ACP 'traditional' producers; (b) EU consumers; (c) Latin American banana producers; (d) EU and US fruit trading companies.**
3. **Discuss whether an EU protectionist policy is in the long term interests of Caribbean ACP banana producers.**

unit 41 Command economies

Summary

1. The function of any economic system is to resolve the basic economic problem.
2. In a command economy, the state allocates resources through a planning mechanism. Some goods and services are provided free at the point of consumption. Others are sold, although goods may be rationed if the price is below the market clearing price.
3. Command economies have mainly been associated with the former communist regimes of Eastern Europe and the Soviet Union, although Britain during the Second World War was run very much as a command economy.
4. The command economies of Eastern Europe, whilst possibly reducing inequalities in society, had relatively low economic growth rates over the past 20 years. Choice and economic freedom were limited whilst their environmental record was very poor.

Economic systems

The function of an economy is to resolve the basic **economic problem** - resources are scarce but wants are infinite (☞ unit 1). Resources therefore need to be allocated. This allocation has three dimensions:
● **what** is to be produced;
● **how** is it to be produced;
● **for whom** it is to be produced.

An ECONOMIC SYSTEM is a complex network of individuals, organisations and institutions and their social and legal interrelationships. The function of an economic system is to resolve the basic economic problem. Within an economic system there will be various 'actors'.
● Individuals. They are consumers and producers. They may own factors of production which they supply for production purposes.
● Groups. Firms, trade unions, political parties, families and charities are just some of the groups which might exist in an economic system.
● Government. Government might range from a group of elders in a village, to a local authority, to a national or international parliament. One key role of government is to exercise power. It establishes or influences the relationships between groups, for instance through the passing of laws.

Relationships between groups can be regulated by law. In many cases, however, they are regulated by custom - traditional ways of organisation which are accepted by participants within the economic system.

Command economies

In a free market economy (☞ unit 42), economic decision making is decentralised. Millions of economic agents individually make decisions about how resources are allocated. In contrast, in a COMMAND ECONOMY (or PLANNED ECONOMY) resources are allocated by government through a planning process. There are a number of key characteristics of a pure command economy.

The main actors There are three main types of actors within a planned economy- the planners (the government), consumers and workers.

Motivation Consumers, workers and government are all assumed to be selfless, co-operating together to work for the common good. This is in marked contrast with most economic agents in a market economy who are assumed to be motivated only by their own self-interest.

Public ownership All factors of production apart from labour are owned by the state (although labour services can be directed by the state). There is no private property.

Planning Resources are allocated through a planning process. At its most extreme, this means that the state will direct labour into jobs as well as directing consumers what to consume, although it is more likely that they will direct producers what to produce, thus determining the choice of goods available to consumers.

The planning process

Allocating resources through a planning mechanism is a complex operation. Planners have to decide what is to be produced. They have to decide, for instance, how many pairs of shoes, how much alcohol or how many tanks are to be manufactured. They then have to decide how it is to be made. They must decide what techniques of production are to be used and which factors of production are to be employed. Finally decisions about distribution have to be made - which consumers will receive what goods and services.

Planners tend to make use of **input-output analysis** when drawing up their plans. This is a method of charting the flows of resources in an economy. For instance, with a given technology, planners know how many workers, how much iron, how much coal etc. is needed to produce 1 tonne of steel. So they can work out what resources are needed if the economy is to produce, say, 20 million tonnes of steel. Having allocated so many tonnes of coal to steel production, planners now need to work out how many inputs are needed to produce the coal. A complex chart of the economy then arises showing how the factors of production (the inputs) are to be distributed to produce a given quantity of output. Most planned economies have used a mixture of 5, 10 or 15 year plans to outline the growth of their economies in the long term, whilst preparing yearly plans to cover short term planning.

Planning and forecasting is notoriously difficult. Accurate forecasting to produce maximum output assumes that planners know the most efficient way to produce goods and services (i.e. that they have available to them an efficient **production function** for each industry ☞ unit 1). Planners must have accurate statistics about the current state of the economy. There are also many variables which are beyond the control of forecasters. The weather is one important factor which can lead to severe misallocation in the economy.

In practice, planning is so complicated that some choices at least are left to individuals. In all command economies today, workers receive wages. They are then free to choose within limits how to spend this money. Some goods and services, such as education and health care, may be provided free of charge to citizens. Others, such as housing, may need to be paid for but there is no free market in the product. Housing is allocated by the state and it is not possible to choose which house to occupy. However, some goods are available for purchase, such as food or clothing.

Question 1

The Belarus tractor factory was a typical example of production in the former Soviet Union. It was allocated supplies of raw materials by the state, and in return manufactured approximately 100 000 tractors a year. It was the sole manufacturer of a particular class of tractor in the country and the sole supplier of these tractors to state farms. Nearly 25 per cent of the factory's output was exported to other Comecon countries. The management estimated that, at current prices, it could sell twice as many tractors as it produced if there was a free market in tractors.

(a) Why was the Belarus tractor factory a 'typical example of production' in a centrally planned economy?

Ideology and the command economy

Command economies have come to be associated with communist (or Marxist) regimes. However, there is no reason why other types of political system should not be associated with a planned economy. Many Third World countries have issued 5 year plans, although they have been to some extent 'indicative' plans because they have relied upon free market forces to deliver much of the output. During the Second World War, the British economy was run very much as a planned economy. Government directed resources and issued output targets to factories. Consumer choice was restricted through a system of rationing.

Moreover, it has been argued that underlying market economies are a complex network of command economies. A firm is a small command economy. With a given number of inputs the firm has to allocate those resources to produce a given quantity of outputs. As in a command economy, firms have to plan how to use those resources and face exactly the same questions of **what** to produce, **how** to produce and **for whom** to produce as a state. The largest firms in the world today, such as General Motors or IBM, have larger outputs than many small developing countries. So even supposedly 'free markets' have an element of planning.

Because communist regimes have tended to organise their economies under command structures, planned economies have tended to be associated with greater equality than under market systems. But again, this need not be the case. Governments could just as well plan to distribute resources in an extremely unequal fashion if they so wished, as is the case in many Third World countries.

The allocation of resources

The planning process determines the allocation of resources within a command economy. However, in practice consumers are given money to spend freely on a limited range of goods and services. There is therefore a type of market mechanism operating in the sale of these products. In a free market, resources are allocated by price. Price rises to the point where demand equals supply. Only those with money can afford to buy the goods. In a planned economy, planners may decide to limit prices so that goods are within the price range of all consumers. For instance, planners may set maximum prices for food or clothing. Experience shows, however, that low prices often result in excess demand. Everyone can afford to buy meat, for instance, but there is insufficient meat in the shops to satisfy consumer demand. There are therefore shortages and resources are usually allocated via a queueing system. When a consignment of goods arrives in a shop, a queue will develop. Those at the front of the queue will be able to buy the goods. Those at the back will be turned away empty-handed.

Question 2

In the 1980s, retail prices were determined centrally in the former Soviet Union. Essentials, such as bread and meat, were very cheap; shop prices of bakery products, sugar and vegetable oil were last changed in 1955. To travel any distance by metro, bus or trolleybus in Moscow cost only 5 kopecs (5p). Housing rent normally cost only 3 per cent of income. Low prices meant long queues and often poor quality goods. This led to large secondary and black markets. Anything more than the essentials of life, such as furniture and many articles of clothing, were very expensive and often in short supply. A typical car owner would, for instance, have saved up for seven to eight years to buy a car. However, the system threw up absurdities. For instance, in 1984 the Soviet Union, with a population of 275m, produced 740m pairs of shoes. Yet many of these were unsaleable. There were shortages of shoes in various parts of the Soviet Union and sports shoes and sandals commanded premium prices on the black market.

(a) How are resources allocated in a command economy? Illustrate your answer with examples from the data.

An evaluation of command economies

Choice In a planned economy, individuals have relatively little choice. As workers, they may be allocated jobs in particular occupations or in particular geographical areas. They may be restricted in their ability to change jobs by state requirements. As consumers, they will have little say about what is provided directly by the state, particularly in non-traded services such as education, health, public transport and housing. What is provided for purchase in shops is likely to be limited. There is no mechanism by which firms compete with each other to provide different types of the same good (what would be called **brands** in a free enterprise economy). So consumers are offered only one make of car, one make of cooker, one type of soap powder, etc.

Subsidies on many essential items such as food and clothing are likely to lead to shortages. Queueing is endemic in many planned economies. Moreover, what is available can often be of poor quality. In a planned economy, it is difficult to provide sufficient incentives for enterprises and individual workers to produce good quality products. Production targets are often set in volume terms or in value terms. A factory may be told to produce 10 000 cookers. But it is not penalised if these cookers are of poor quality. They will be delivered to state shops which in turn will receive instructions to sell them to consumers.

Income and growth Economic history suggests that, if a country has a relatively low GNP per head, both planned systems and free market systems will deliver comparable rates of economic growth. However, the experience in the 1970s and 1980s in Eastern Europe was that planned economies have consistently failed to match the growth performance of free enterprise and mixed economies. This was perhaps not surprising. As economies grow, they become more complex. The more complex the economy, the more difficult it is to plan the allocation of resources efficiently. Large firms (remember that a firm in itself is like a planned economy) in free enterprise economies have faced similar problems. They can experience **diseconomies of scale** (i.e. larger size leading to higher average costs of production) because their management structures fail to keep production efficient. Many large firms have responded by decentralising decision making. Parts of the business may become 'profit centres', responsible for attaining profit targets set by headquarters. In some firms, individual production units may even compete with each other for business.

It is not only the problems that arise from inadequate planning that can lead to low economic growth in command economies. There is also little individual incentive for enterprise and innovation. If a firm exceeds its targets for this year, its only 'reward' will be an increased target for the following year, which it might find impossible to achieve. If there are very heavy taxes on high incomes, there is little point in individuals working hard within the state sector. If there is no possibility of ownership of the means of production, there is no incentive for individuals to take risks, establishing new enterprises to do something better than existing firms in the market. There is every incentive for individuals to minimise the amount of effort they put into their official work. They are unlikely to lose their jobs, nor will they will lose income (although they may be arrested for anti-state activities - which might act as a deterrent). This contrasts with the considerable energy that the same individuals might put into their jobs in unofficial markets. There might be a thriving black market, for instance. Or the state may allow people to rent small private plots for production of food.

The distribution of income Planners may choose any particular distribution of resources within a planned economy. In practice, command economies have been

Question 3

In the early 1990s, the former Soviet Union was in the throes of an ecological crisis, compared with which most other global pollution problems paled into insignificance. For instance, the huge Aral Sea, once the world's fourth largest inland water, effectively ceased to exist. It had turned into two shrunken salt-poisoned pools in the desert, thanks to the effects of massive and thoughtless irrigation schemes. In Belarus, one-quarter of all the arable land has been destroyed by the fall-out from the Chernobyl nuclear disaster - contaminated with Caesium 137.

'The most serious problem is in fact the economic system', said academician Mr Alexei Yablokov. 'All the decision making comes from the centre - from the government, the ministries, and the Communist Party'. 'The central committee of the party decides what sort of factory is built where. All the ministries are full of people with the old thinking - more and more production, whatever the price. Their aim is not human happiness, but more production.'

(a) What ecological problems are highlighted in the passage?
(b) Why might such problems be created in a centrally planned economy?

associated with socialist or Marxist governments committed to a degree of equality of income. Hence planners have set high priorities on providing all citizens with a minimum standard of living. They have achieved this through subsidising essential goods, such as food, and providing other essential services, such as health care free of charge.

Equally, there is considerable evidence to suggest that those in power (e.g. members of the Communist Party) have used the planning system to their own advantage. For instance, special shops have been set up where a privileged few can purchase a much wider variety of goods than is generally available and without queueing. Housing allocation, or placements at university, have been biased in favour of Party members. Indeed, this is what capitalist, neo-classical economists would predict. Those in power are using that power to maximise their own utility. They are not the disinterested, selfless individuals that the model assumes.

Risk Karl Marx dreamt of creating a society in which each would receive according to their need. A family of four would have a bigger house than a family of two. A sick person would receive medical care. Those no longer able to work would still receive an income. So the risks associated with ill health, injury at work, old age and redundancy would be considerably reduced. Communist planned economies, to some extent, achieved this reduction in risk for the individual. However, it can be argued that removing risk also removes incentives to work and create wealth. If, for instance, a worker knows that he will never be made redundant, then there may be little incentive for him to do his job well. If an enterprise knows that it will always be able to sell its produce because consumers have no choice about what to buy, then it has no incentive to produce high quality goods or to be innovative.

The environment One of the problems with a market economy is that individual producers base their production decisions on **private** rather than **social** costs (☞ unit 19), thus creating negative externalities. However, the environmental record of command economies in the past is arguably worse than those of market economies. The problem is that planners have been far more interested in securing increased output than in reducing damage to the environment. If environmental objectives are not written into plans, then it is inevitable that damage will be caused to the environment by industrial production.

Political and social costs Command economies can only work if there is a centralised bureaucracy devising and implementing plans. They leave little room for individual freedom. Perhaps not surprisingly, the former command economies of Eastern Europe and the economy of China were police states, where the political rights of citizens were, to a very great extent, taken away. Whether a pure command economy could operate within a political democracy is debatable.

key terms

Command or planned economy - an economic system where government, through a planning process, allocates resources in society.
Economic system - a complex network of individuals, organisations and institutions and their social and legal interrelationships.

Applied economics

Central planning in the Soviet Union

The Soviet economy from the 1930s to the late 1980s was the country whose economic system perhaps came closest to the model of a command economy. Overall decisions about economic priorities were taken by the highest political body in the Soviet Union, the Politburo, the central committee of the Communist Party. It would decide whether more resources should be devoted to, say, defence, housing or agriculture. Its decisions would then have to be implemented by the Council of Ministers, who would decide how this could be achieved with the help of **Gosplan**, the State Planning Committee. Gosplan was the major planning body. It constructed input-output matrices for the whole of the Soviet economy and worked out production targets for each region and each industry. Over 20 000 products or groups of products needed to be structured into its plan. Yearly plans were made within the context of successive **five year plans**, the first of which was announced by Stalin in 1928. The five year plan was an attempt to plan the economy in the medium term, because a year was really too short for the achievement of longer term goals.

Production plans would then be communicated to 40 different ministries which, working with Regional Planning Commissions in each Republic of the Soviet Union, would send out orders to hundreds of thousands of production units across the country. At each stage, those lower down the hierarchy had the right to challenge the orders sent to it. Almost invariably, they would be challenged if it was felt that the orders could not be fulfilled. If the challenge was accepted, the plan would have to be modified. There

was no need for production units to communicate between themselves. If goods were poor quality, for instance, shops would complain not to the manufacturer but to the planners at the next stage in the hierarchy.

The system arguably worked reasonably well in the 1930s and 1940s. It is true that the transition from a market economy in the 1920s to a command economy in the 1930s was marked by political oppression on a scale which possibly even dwarfed the horrors of Nazi Germany, but this was more a political struggle than an economic necessity. However, by the 1960s the Soviet economy was getting far too large to manage centrally and large diseconomies of scale were emerging.

One key factor became apparent. The incentives within the system discouraged efficient production. For those with a job from which they would be unlikely to be sacked because the right to work was guaranteed, there was an incentive to devote little energy to the official job and take a job on the side to supplement earnings. For managers, the key to success was to negotiate for as many raw material and labour inputs as possible and have as low a production target as possible. Hoarding raw materials too was essential in an economy where supplies were variable. That way, production managers could easily reach and even exceed their production targets.

By the 1980s, many in the Soviet Union felt that if their economy was to be dynamic, it should not be planned centrally. Hence, economic reform to transform the economy into a market economy was begun.

The Cuban economy

The Cuban economy

Cuba has been run along socialist lines since a revolution brought Fidel Castro, the country's President, to power in 1958. In 2000, there was free, universal healthcare, education and other social services. All key industries were owned by the state with the exception of the rapidly growing tourist industry. Apart from health and education, other essential goods and services were subsidised by the state but they were rationed. For instance, food, clothes and petrol were all rationed.

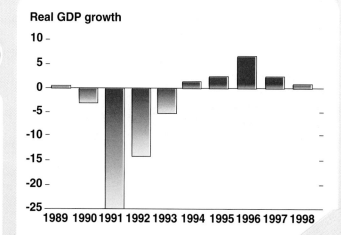

Figure 41.1 *Cuban growth*
Source: adapted from EIU.

Economic restructuring

During the 1960s and 1970s, sugar was the most important industry in Cuba. With the demise of the Soviet link in the early 1990s and low world sugar prices since then, sugar production has fallen as Figure 41.2 shows. Cuba has been forced to develop other existing industries and diversify.

Tobacco has for over a century been an important exporter earner. Havana cigars are world-renowned and, in the second half of the 1990s, tobacco growing has been extended by the state to practically every province on the island. The number of cigar factories has risen from 17 to 44 during that time.

The most important developments, though, have occurred with the help of overseas investors, first allowed to invest in Cuban industry in 1990. Figure 41.3, for instance, shows that both steel and nickel production have risen in the second half of the 1990s with considerable help from mainly Canadian companies. Crude oil and gas production have also risen, as shown in Figure 41.4. In 1999, nine foreign companies were involved in exploration and development of oil fields. Even so, Cuba was only producing about one fifth of the oil needed to make it self-sufficient.

The fastest growing industry has been tourism as shown in Figure 41.5. In 1990, there were 12 000 hotel rooms, often of poor quality. This had risen to 31 000 in 1999, with a considerable improvement in quality. The number of tourists rose from 0.5 million in 1993 to 1.7 million in 1997 and was projected to increase to 5 million in 2010.

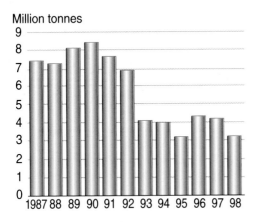

Figure 41.2 *Cuban sugar production*
Source: adapted from National Bank of Cuba; State Committee for Statistics; *Financial Times*, 24.3.1999.

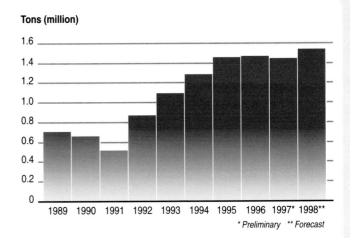

Figure 41.4 *Crude oil production*
Source: adapted from Informe Económico, 1997.

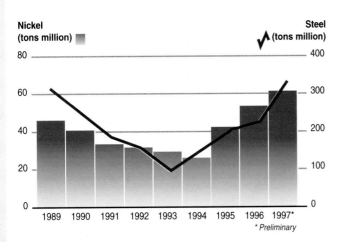

Figure 41.3 *Nickel and steel production*
Source: adapted Informe Economico, 1997.

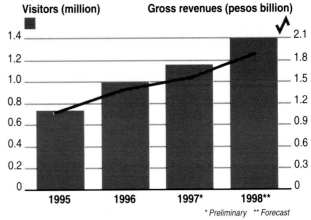

Figure 41.5 *Tourism*
Source: adapted from Informe Economico, 1997.

Black markets

Black markets are now an important feature of Cuban life since the breakdown of trade with the former Soviet Union. Most Cubans say the subsidised food and consumer goods provided by the state rationing system each month do not even come close to feeding an average family. The wide availability of US dollars in Cuba has encouraged the development of black markets in everything from meat to washing powder to repairs.

The welfare state

The Cuban government since 1958 has attempted to reduce inequalities in society and give everyone a minimum standard of living. A welfare state has been created which provides everyone with free access to education and health care. The result is that Cuba comes out very well compared to most of Latin America on certain indicators. For instance, adult literacy in 1997 was 96 per cent, whilst life expectancy was 76.

Unemployment

Cuba has a population of 11 million. Since the 1960s, the State has ensured that there has been no unemployment. However, the restructuring of the economy in the wake of the collapse of trade with the former Soviet Union in the late 1980s and early 1990s put this commitment under immense strain. Under regulations which came into effect in 1994, workers made redundant were assigned to other available jobs or to strategic social or economic tasks. If no new job was found immediately, unemployed workers had the right to receive one month's full pay and 60 per cent of their previous salary thereafter.

Self-employment was only re-legalised in 1993. In 1994 the government allowed small businesses to be set up in selected parts of the economy such as the restaurant trade. However, it was made illegal for anyone to employ another person unless they were a family member.

1. (a) What is meant by a 'command economy'?
   (b) Why might Cuba be described as command economy? Illustrate your answer with examples from the data.
2. Why does the growth of small business and foreign investment threaten the existence of the command economy in Cuba?
3. Discuss whether a lifting of the US trade embargo on Cuba would make it easier or more difficult for the Cuban government to retain a planning model for its economy.

The Soviet connection

Following the Revolution in Cuba in 1958, the former Soviet Union supported the Cuban economy financially by buying exports from it at preferential prices. In the late 1980s, 85 per cent of Cuba's exports went to the USSR. During the period, the USA imposed a trade embargo on Cuba because of its communist links. The collapse of the Soviet Union in the early 1990s brought this special relationship to an end and Cuban exports plummeted causing a major recession in the economy. Acute shortages of essential items like petrol, which previously had been sold to Cuba at subsidised prices, became common.

The dollar connection

In the 1980s, there was a growing trend for emigré families in the USA to send US dollars to their families back home in Cuba. Dollars could only be used in Cuba in the illegal black market at the time, but families which could get dollars could enjoy a much higher standard of living than those who couldn't. In the wake of the collapse of trade with the former Soviet Union, Cuba legalised the use of dollars in 1993, allowing Cubans to buy food, clothes and consumer items such as televisions at special newly opened state stores with their dollars. These dollar-only stores are not subject to any form of rationing. Any Cuban with dollars can buy as much as his or her dollars will permit. This contrasts with the peso economy where shops ration what Cubans can buy. Dollars are also widely used in black markets.

The Cuban government was forced to open dollar shops for two reasons. First, it needs dollars to finance imports of essentials which are then sold at a subsidised peso price to Cubans. Second, the alternative would have been to use the police to enforce a ban on all black market activity. The government would have received no dollar earnings from this and the GDP of the economy would have fallen, as less was being produced.

The development dilemma

Tourism shows the problems that the Cuban government has in maintaining control over the economy. Foreign companies control key assets in the economy in the form of hotels and associated leisure facilities. They also employ labour, although they are only able to do this via a Cuban intermediary company. Development of the industry is crucially dependent on foreign investment and also the state of the world economy. If tourists choose to stay at home, for instance, Cuba will suffer. Many of the 160 000 self-employed and small business owners are linked to tourism including restaurant owners and artisans. Growth of tourism will increase their numbers and provide greater opportunities for work in the private sector. Tourism also brings in US dollars, some of which filter through to the workers associated with the industry. In 1999, it was estimated that over 50 per cent of the population lived in households with access to dollars, either through tourism or from remittances from family members working abroad. Households with dollars can buy goods unavailable to other households. Inequalities are therefore widened without the state being able to prevent this.

unit 42 Market economies

Summary

1. In a free market economy, resources are allocated through the spending decisions of millions of different consumers and producers.
2. Resource allocation occurs through the market mechanism. The market determines what is to be produced, how it is to be produced and for whom production is to take place.
3. Government must exist to supply public goods, maintain a sound currency, provide a legal framework within which markets can operate, and prevent the creation of monopolies in markets.
4. Free markets necessarily involve inequalities in society because incentives are needed to make markets work.
5. Free markets provide choice and there are incentives to innovate and for economies to grow.

Characteristics of the system

A MARKET ECONOMY (also called a FREE ENTERPRISE ECONOMY or a CAPITALIST ECONOMY) is an economic system which resolves the basic economic problem mainly through the market mechanism. There are a number of key characteristics of the system.

The main actors The four main types of actors within the system are consumers, producers, owners of private property (land and capital) and government.

Motivation In a pure market economy, consumers, producers and property owners are motivated by pure self-interest. Their decisions are based upon private gain. Consumers aim to maximise their individual welfare or utility. Producers aim to maximise profit. The owners of the factors of production aim to maximise their wages, rents, interest and profits.

Government on the other hand is assumed to be motivated by considerations of the good of the community and not by self-interest. It seeks to maximise social welfare.

Private ownership Nearly all factors of production within the economy are owned mainly by private individuals and organisations. Government has a duty to uphold the rights of citizens to own property. This it does mainly through the legal system.

Free enterprise Owners of the factors of production as well as producers of goods and services have the right to buy and sell what they own through the market mechanism. Government places few limits on what can be bought and sold. Workers can work for whom they want. Homeowners can sell their houses if they so wish. People are free to set up their own businesses. Consumers are free to use their money to buy whatever is offered for sale. Producers are free to sell whatever they wish to sell.

Competition Competition will exist if economic units are free to allocate their resources as they wish. Producers will have to compete for the spending 'votes' of consumers. Workers will have to compete for the spending 'votes' of their employers. Those wishing to borrow money will have to compete with everyone else who wishes to borrow.

Decentralised decision making Because individual economic agents are free to choose how they wish to allocate resources, decision making within a market economy is decentralised. There is no single body which allocates resources within the economy. Rather, the allocation of resources is the result of countless decisions by individual economic agents. This is Adam Smith's **invisible hand** of the market. He argued that, although economic actors pursued their own self interest, the result would be an allocation of resources in the economy which would be in the interests of society as a whole.

The market mechanism

Any type of economic system must be capable of allocating resources. In particular, it must be able to provide a mechanism for deciding **what, how** and **for whom** production will take place. How are resources allocated under a market mechanism?

What is to be produced? In a pure free market, it is the consumer which determines the allocation of resources. Consumers are **sovereign**. Each consumer has a certain amount of money to spend and each £1 is like a spending vote. Consumers cast their spending votes when they purchase goods and services. Firms receive these spending votes and this in turn enables them to buy the

Question 1

In 1993, Nigel Lawson, a former Chancellor of the Exchequer, gave a speech at the British Association's annual conference. In the speech, he said: 'Throughout the western world ... capitalism has appeared to be in the ascendant and socialism in retreat.' One reason for this was that: 'the rational decisions needed to make a modern economy even halfway efficient can be taken only by a multiplicity of decision-makers armed with the knowledge provided by a myriad of market prices.' A key characteristic of the system is self interest. 'A regard for one's self-interest is a prominent feature in the make-up of almost all mankind. It is not the only feature, but it is a uniquely powerful one. The characteristic of market capitalism is not that it alone is based on the idea of channelling self-interest for the greater good - not that there is anything wrong with that. It is rather that it is a unique mechanism for doing so directly, with the least interposition of government.'

Capitalism also possesses key moral features. 'The family, which looms large in the scheme of market capitalism, is not only the foundation of a stable society, but an important bulwark against tyranny - as is of course the institution of private property, the more widely spread the better. Another key feature of market capitalism is the private sector, non-monopolistic firm. Capitalism is sometimes portrayed as an unattractive competitive jungle, where the values of co-operation are lost in a free-for-all. What this overlooks is that the private sector firm itself provides a model of effective co-operation.'

As for inequality, 'absolute equality, even in the sense in which it is theoretically attainable, must of necessity lead to misery. If there is to be no greater reward for work or saving or effort of any kind than is meted out to those who decline to work or save or make any effort, then remarkably little work, saving or effort will be undertaken. If two people are working at the same job, with equal skill, and one chooses to work overtime while the other does not, failure to pay the former more would be seen as not merely self-defeating but grossly inequitable.' Government has an important role to play here. 'Just as the sensible successful businessman who seeks to help those less fortunate will do so not by changing the way he runs his business but by applying part of his personal wealth to philanthropy, so the wise government will best help the poor not by interfering with the market but by creating a well-designed social security safety net alongside it.'

(a) Identify from the passage the main characteristics of a market economy.
(b) Why, according to Nigel Lawson, does the pursuit of self interest and the existence of inequality in society lead to greater efficiency in the economy?

factors of production needed to produce goods and services. How firms cast their spending votes on factors of production in turn will determine how much income each individual consumer has to spend. What happens if consumers want to change the composition of the bundle of goods that they are currently buying? Say, for instance, they decide they want to buy more clothes but buy fewer package holidays. The increase in demand for clothes initially will increase the price of clothes. Clothing manufacturers will consequently earn **abnormal profit** (☞ unit 17), profit over and above what is normal in the industry. They will respond to this by increasing production of clothes. New firms too will set themselves up, attracted by the high profit levels. Supply will thus expand as will the degree of competition in the industry. This will force down prices to a level where clothing manufacturers are making a high enough profit to stop some going out of business, but a low enough profit to prevent new suppliers from being attracted into the industry. In the package holiday business, the fall in demand will result in a price war. Profitability will fall. Some firms may even make losses. As a result, firms will scale back the number of holidays offered and some firms may even go bankrupt. This will continue until package holiday firms once again can earn a sufficiently high level of profit to prevent firms leaving the industry.

Changes in the goods market will then be reflected in the factor markets. Demand for workers, buildings, machines, raw materials etc. will rise in the clothing industry, but fall in the package holiday industry. There will thus be a transfer of resources from one industry to the other.

Notice the key role of profits in this mechanism. Profits act as a signal for what is to be produced. If firms are earning abnormal profits, it is a signal that consumers wish to buy more of a product. If firms are earning insufficient profits or even losses, it must be a signal that

Question 2

- A shortage of oil on world markets has led to a trebling of oil prices in a year. Countries such as the US are pressing middle east oil producers to increase their production to bring down prices.

- Bass, the brewing group, announces that it is selling its share of a joint venture which has been brewing lager in China since 1996 after if failed to make the company profitable.

- Britain is forecast to see a doubling in the number of foreign visitors to the UK over the next twenty years to more than 50 million. Eastern Europe, though, is likely to see a much faster rate of increase in tourism over the same period according to the World Tourist Organisation report.

- Chase Manhattan, the US financial organisation, announced that last year it had paid its two chief executive officers both more than $20 million in salaries and bonuses.

Source: adapted from the *Financial Times*, 27.3.2000

(a) Explain, using the data to illustrate your answer, how resources are allocated in a market economy.

consumers wish to see a fall in production in that industry.

How is it to be produced? Producers are in competition with each other. All other things being equal, consumers will buy from the producer which offers the lowest price. So producers must produce at lowest cost if they are to survive in the market place. This then determines how goods are produced. Firms will adopt the lowest cost technique of production. Hence, free markets result in **productive efficiency** (☞ unit 16).

For whom? Consumers spend money. The amount of money they can spend is determined by their wealth and by their income. In a free market economy, this is determined by ownership of the factors of production. Workers receive income from sale of their labour, owners of land receive rents, etc. Those with high incomes and wealth are therefore able to buy large amounts of goods and services. Those with low incomes and little wealth can only buy a few goods and services. In a market economy, the wealthy gain a disproportionate share of what is produced. The poor receive relatively little.

The role of government

Government has a number of key roles in a market economy.
- Some goods will not be provided by the market mechanism. Examples are defence, the judiciary and the police force. These are known as **public goods** (☞ unit 20). The government therefore has to provide these and raise taxes to pay for them.
- The government is responsible for the issue of money and for the maintenance of its value. In a market economy, the government has a duty to maintain stable prices.
- The government needs to ensure an adequate legal framework for the allocation and enforcement of property rights. It is pointless having a system based upon individual self-interest if citizens are unable to defend what they have gained. For instance, owners of private property need to be protected from the possibility of theft. There need to be laws about contracts of purchase and sale. It must be illegal willfully to destroy other people's property.
- It is equally important that property rights of any value are allocated to an economic unit in society. If they are not, they will treated as a **free good** (a good unlimited in supply) and over-consumed. The atmosphere is one example of an economic resource which in the past has been owned by no one. Producers and consumers have polluted the atmosphere. This would not be important if it weren't for the fact that we now recognise that such pollution can have an adverse impact upon economic units. At worst, it is predicted that the greenhouse effect and the destruction of the ozone layer will wipe out most life on this planet. Contrast this with the care that people show with their own private property.
- Markets may malfunction for other reasons. In

particular, firms or trade unions may seek to gain control over individual markets. Governments therefore need to have powers to break up monopolies, prevent practices which restrict free trade and control the activities of trade unions.

The role of government is vital in a market economy. Without government, there would be anarchy. But in a free market economy, the presumption is that government should intervene as little as possible. Government regulation should be the minimum necessary to secure the orderly working of the market economy. Government spending should be confined to the provision of public goods.

Question 3

Political 'democracy' that takes half of personal incomes to spend on welfare, or industrial services which give voters as taxpayers little say and less escape, can be as oppressive as communist socialism. Government cannot be depended on to redress market failure. Its electoral short-termism, its ignorance or indifference to individual preference, its vulnerability to pressure groups and its corruption create government failure that is worse than market failure because it is less corrigible. The common people are best empowered by the market. Government should concentrate on the irreducible minimum of goods and services that cannot be supplied in the market. Optimal size of government is unattainable. But it is better to risk having too little government than too much.

(a) Explain what, according to the article, should be the role of government in an economy.
(b) What arguments can be put forward to justify this position?

An evaluation of free market economies

Choice In a rich free enterprise economy, consumers will be faced with a wide range of choice. Firms will compete with each other either on price if a good is homogeneous, or on a wider range of factors such as quality if the good is non-homogeneous. However, choice is not available to all. Those with high incomes will have a great deal of choice. Those on low incomes will have little. It matters little to low income families, for instance, if there are 100 types of luxury car on the market, or if it is possible to take cruises on even more luxurious liners. In a planned economy, consumers may find it impossible to spend all their income because goods which are priced within the reach of everyone are not in the shops. In a free enterprise economy, there may be plenty of goods in the shops, but they may be out of the price range of the poorest in society.

Quality and innovation One advantage claimed of a free

market economy is that there are strong incentives built into the system to innovate and produce high quality goods. Companies which fail to do both are likely to be driven out of business by more efficient firms. However, this assumes that there is consumer sovereignty in the market. In practice, markets tend to be oligopolistic in structure, dominated by a few large producers which manipulate the market through advertising and other forms of marketing in order to exploit the consumer. So whilst choice and innovation are greater than under planned systems, the advantages of free market economies may not be as great as it might at first seem.

Economic growth In a free market economy, there may be considerable dynamism. However, some free market economies have grown at a considerably faster rate than other free market economies. Many mixed economies too have grown at comparable if not higher rates to the USA. So free markets are not necessarily the key to high economic growth.

Distribution of income and wealth In a pure free market economy, resources are allocated to those with spending power. Individuals with no source of income can pay the ultimate penalty for their economic failure - they die, perhaps from starvation or cold or disease. This fear of economic failure and its price is a major incentive within the free market system for people to take jobs, however poorly paid. One problem with this mechanism is that there are many groups in society who are likely to have little or no income through no fault of their own. The handicapped, orphaned or abandoned children and old people are examples. Free market economists point out that there is a mechanism by which such people can find support - charity. Individuals who earn money can give freely to charities which then provide for the needs of the least well off in society, or individuals can look after their aged relatives, their neighbours and their children within the local neighbourhood community. In practice, it is unlikely that individuals would give enough to charities, or that the better off would provide accommodation for tramps in their homes to fulfil this role. In a free market economy, there is no link whatsoever between need and the allocation of resources. The unemployed can starve, the sick can die for lack of medical treatment, and the homeless can freeze to death on the streets. Income is allocated to those with wealth, whether it is physical, financial or human wealth.

Risk Individuals take great care to reduce the economic risk which lies at the heart of any free market economy. They can overcome the problem of risk by insuring themselves. They take out health insurance. They buy life insurance contracts which pay out to dependants if they

should die. Unemployment and sickness can also be insured against. To cope with the problem of old age, individuals ensure that they have pension contracts.

However, only a percentage of the population have enough foresight or the income to insure themselves adequately. This then means that many in a free market economy become poor, perhaps unable to support themselves, or die through lack of medical attention.

Question 4

Socialism captured the imagination because it offered an enticing conception of social and economic progress. It promised not just a great increase in material wealth, but a world where income would not depend primarily on individuals' arbitrary endowments of financial and genetic capital. It also talked sense about freedom - which can be measured only by the choices individuals have the power to exercise. The range of choice is profoundly influenced by a person's economic means.

Capitalism, whilst offering forever increasing economic output, gives no commitment to increased equality. Quite the contrary: incentives are regarded as an essential motor of growth, and they require inequality. But the commitment to inequality means that poverty will never be eradicated. It will be institutionalised. Once a minimum standard of living is attained, people feel poor if they have less than their neighbours. If a trip to the Asteroids becomes a typical weekend jaunt in the 21st or 22nd century, those who cannot afford extra-terrestrial travel will be considered poor. And they will not be comforted by the thought that they are better off than the poor of 1989.

(a) Assess the criticisms made in the extract of a capitalist economic system.
(b) What are the causes and nature of poverty in a free market economy?

key terms

Free market economy, or free enterprise economy or capitalist economy - an economic system which resolves the basic economic problem through the market mechanism.

Applied economics

The UK – a free market economy?

In 1979, before the radical government of Margaret Thatcher took power, the UK was quite clearly a mixed economy. Many of the leading industries in the country, such as gas, electricity, telecommunications and the railways were in state control. The government was spending about 45 per cent of the country's income, a very similar proportion to other mixed economies such as France and West Germany. Education and health were both provided by the state along with a wide variety of services from libraries to parks to roads. There was widespread control of the labour market, with minimum wages in many industries and conditions of employment of workers regulated by law.

The changes implemented in the 1980s transformed the shape of the UK economy. The privatisation programme led to large amounts of state assets being sold off to the private sector. The list was long but included car companies (the Rover Group and Jaguar), steel firms (British Steel), energy companies (British Petroleum, British Gas, the electricity companies, British Coal), water companies (the water boards) and telecommunications (BT). The role of the state was cut as public spending programmes axed services. Where the government felt that it could not privatise the service, it attempted to introduce competition into the public sector. For instance, private firms were encouraged to bid for public sector contracts. In the health service, a competitive internal market was established.

Moreover, a wide range of reforms was instituted to reduce regulation and imperfections in markets. In the labour market, trade unions lost powers to act as monopoly suppliers of labour. Rules and regulations in various financial markets were removed to encourage greater competition. In the bus industry, firms were allowed to compete freely on national and local routes.

The spirit of 'Thatcherism' was to release the energies of entrepreneurs in society, to encourage people to work hard and take risks. The successful had to be rewarded and hence marginal rates of income tax were cut, particularly for high earners. On the other hand, those who avoided work should be penalised and hence benefits such as unemployment benefit were

cut. The result was an increase in inequality in society.

Some would argue that in the post-Thatcher era the UK remains a mixed economy. Health, for instance, continues to be provided by the state unlike, say, in the USA. The rest of the welfare state is also larger than in the USA. Others would argue that the gulf between the mixed economies of Europe and that of the UK shown in Figure 42.1 has become too great for the UK to be seen as a genuine mixed economy. The level of welfare spending in continental Europe is much higher than in the UK. The sick, the elderly, parents and children all receive far better care either in the form of services such as hospital treatment or in rights and benefits such as pensions.

The Labour government elected in 1997 has stated that it does not intend to raise the proportion of national income spent by the state in the long term. Higher government spending must be financed from increased tax revenues arising from economic growth and not by taking a larger slice of the national income cake. Equally, electorates in France, Germany, Italy and other European countries seem to have little willingness to embark on their own Thatcherite revolutions. They wish to retain their welfare states even if this means higher levels of taxation. If this remains the case, the UK will remain somewhere between the free market model of the United States and the mixed economies of Europe.

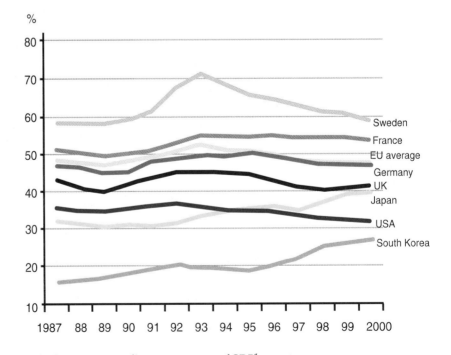

Figure 42.1 *Government spending as a percentage of GDP*[1]
Source: adapted from *Economic Outlook*, OECD.
1. Figures for 1999 and 2000 are estimates.

Table 42.1 *Income distribution and purchasing power parity estimates of GNP*

| | Date of estimate of income distribution | % share of national income | | | | | | PPP estimates of GNP per capita US$, 1998 |
		Lowest 20%	Second quintile	Third quintile	Fourth quintile	Highest 20%	Highest 10%	
United States	1994	4.8	10.5	16.0	23.5	45.2	28.5	29 340
Germany	1989	9.0	13.5	17.5	22.9	37.1	22.6	20 810
France	1989	7.2	12.7	17.1	22.8	40.1	24.9	22 320
Sweden	1992	9.6	14.5	18.1	23.2	34.5	20.1	25 620
United Kingdom	1986	7.1	12.8	17.2	23.1	39.8	24.7	20 640

Source: adapted from *World Development Report*, World Bank.

Face of America that destroys its Land of the Free myth

Until a year ago, my image of the United Stated was of a wealthy, classless, melting-pot society whose values were embodied in the tough, free-thinking rebel usually portrayed by John Wayne.

That image took a knock during seven days in Arkansas last summer and crumbled this week in Texas.

There is certainly money. In Houston, mirror-glass skyscrapers soar confidently over immaculate parks. In its fabulously wealthy River Oaks suburb, colonnaded million-dollar mansions exceed the dreams of avarice.

But look again and you see another face of America. Shacks and shanty settlements strung out along the highways. Second-hand cars at a half or even a third of British prices. Wal-Mart supermarkets where a pair of jeans costs a fiver.

At first, it strikes you as a land of bargains. Then you talk to ordinary Americans and realise that the prices match the wages and the wages, in many cases, are desperately low.

One of our coach drivers earned a wretched £4,500 a year - below the official poverty level.

The average American family of four earns barely £10,000 and to reach that level, both partners invariably work. In the Land of the Free there is no free lunch. If you can work, you do.

If that sounds fine in theory, what it means in practice is that both our coach drivers in Houston were women, one middle-aged, the other well into her 60s.

It means that a woman hotel executive I met in Brownsville returned to work two weeks after giving birth and thought her employers generous for paying her salary during her absence.

It means that employees accept two weeks' annual holiday as the norm. It means that a word like 'welfare' which has a friendly, benevolent ring to European ears, is regarded in the States as the work of the devil.

Welfare and free health care would sap the American spirit, so the story goes.

The education system is a problem too for Americans. America has recognised the appalling state of its educational system and is making much of its latest drive to improve schools and recruit better teachers.

But there is little talk of producing educated people for their own sake. The motivation, as always, is hard cash and the need to be more competitive against the better-educated Japanese

Table 42.2 *Real growth of GDP*

Annual growth in real GDP

	1960-67	1968-73	1974-79	1980-89	1990-99
United States	4.5	3.2	2.4	2.5	2.7
Japan	10.2	8.7	3.6	4.0	1.5
Germany	4.1	4.9	2.3	1.8	2.4
France	5.4	5.5	2.8	2.2	1.8
United Kingdom	3.0	3.4	1.5	2.4	1.8
Italy	5.7	4.5	3.7	2.4	1.3
Canada	5.5	5.4	4.2	3.1	2.0

Source: adapted from *Historical Statistics*; *Economic Outlook*, OECD.

and Europeans.

The campaign for better schools seems to overlook the most important point, that a good education produces thoughtful, innovative people who are prepared to break the mould and try something new.

And maybe that is deliberate. For in its present state of intellectual awareness, America is happy to swallow myths that we Europeans laughed out years ago.

They call it the Land of the Free yet small-town sheriffs and corporate bosses hold powers that feudal lords would have envied.

They boast their classlessness yet have created a society far more formal and unmixed than our own.

And they still foster the belief that any backwoods kid can make it to president, blithely ignoring the fact that every president in living memory has been very wealthy indeed.

You can still make your way to the top in America but it means climbing over rather more backs than Britons might find comfortable.

The woman hotel executive in Brownsville epitomised the thrusting, go-getting face that America likes to project. Back at work a fortnight after childbirth and every inch the liberated ambitious female. How does she do it?

Simple. She has a live-in Mexican maid on £25 a week and God knows how she looks her in the eyes on pay day.

Source: *Express and Star*, 28.4.1989.

1. **Using the USA as an example, explain how resources are allocated in a free market economy.**
2. **(a) To what extent are incomes unequal in the USA?**
   (b) Are inequalities in income desirable in a free market economy?
3. **Discuss what might be the advantages and disadvantages to an individual of migrating to work in the USA from the UK.**

unit 43 Mixed economies

Summary

1. In a mixed economy, a significant amount of resources are allocated both by government through the planning mechanism, and by the private sector through the market mechanism.
2. The degree of mixing is a controversial issue. Some economists believe that too much government spending reduces incentives and lowers economic growth, whilst others argue that governments must prevent large inequalities arising in society and that high taxation does not necessarily lead to low growth.

Mixed economies

A MIXED ECONOMY, as the name implies, is a mixture of a planned economy and a free enterprise economy. In practice, no **pure** planned economies or free enterprise economies exist in the world. They are **paradigm models** (☞ unit 45). What we call free enterprise economies are economies where most resources are allocated by the market mechanism. What are called planned economies are economies where most resources are allocated by the planning process. Mixed economies are economies where the balance between allocation by the market mechanism and allocation by the planning process is much more equal.

Characteristics

A mixed economy possesses a number of characteristics.

The main actors The four main types of actor within the system are consumers, producers, factor owners and government.

Motivation In the private sector of the economy, consumers, producers and factor owners are assumed to be motivated by pure self-interest. The public sector, however, is motivated by considerations of the 'good' of the community.

Ownership The factors of production are partly owned by private individuals and organisations, but the state also owns a significant proportion.

Competition In the private sector of the economy there is competition. In the state sector, however, resources will be allocated through the planning mechanism. This implies that consumers are offered choice of goods and services within the private sector of the economy but little or no choice within the public sector.

Government Government has a number of important functions. One is to regulate the economic activities of the private sector of the economy. It needs, for instance, to ensure that competition exists and that property laws are upheld. Another function is to provide not just public goods but also **merit goods** (☞ unit 20), like education and health care. These may be provided directly by the state, or provision may be contracted out to private firms but still paid for out of tax revenues. The state may also choose to own key sectors of the economy, such as the railways, postal services and electricity industries. Many of these will be **natural monopolies** (☞ unit 18).

The degree of mixing

There is considerable controversy about the degree of mixing that should take place in a mixed economy. In 1998, 60.8 per cent of GDP was accounted for by public spending in Sweden compared to 46.9 per cent in Germany, 40.2 per cent in the UK and 33 per cent in the free market economy of the USA.

In Sweden, there is much greater government spending per capita than, say, in the USA. This means that in Sweden compared to the USA all citizens have access to medical care free at the point of consumption, there are generous state pensions, automatic retraining for those made unemployed and free child care for all working mothers. However, there is a cost. Taxes in Sweden are much higher than in the USA. The fundamental issues concern the following.

- To what extent should the state ensure that all its citizens enjoy a minimum standard of living? For instance, should the state provide insurance for those who become unemployed? Should it in effect guarantee them a job by training longer term unemployed workers until they succeed in obtaining work? Do citizens have a right to free medical care?
- To what extent should there be inequalities in society? The degree of inequality in an economy like Sweden is far less than in the USA. Inequality in the UK increased as public expenditure during the 1980s as a proportion of GDP was cut in the 1980s.
- To what extent should citizens be free to choose how to spend their money? In Sweden, the effective tax burden is 60 per cent, leaving only 40 per cent of income for individuals and companies to choose how to spend. In Sweden, free child care for mothers is provided whether an individual wants it or not.
- To what extent are incentives needed to ensure continued high growth? Until the late 1980s, the top rate of income tax in Sweden was 72 per cent, with the ordinary worker paying between 40 and 50 per cent. Tax reforms in the late 1980s switched the burden

Question 1

From your knowledge of the UK economy, explain to what extent it possesses the characteristics of a mixed economy.

record on the environment than command economies. Indeed, the Scandinavian mixed economies are in the forefront of implementing measures to protect the environment from industrial activity.

Question 2

Since 1979, the degree of mixing between public and private sectors in the UK has changed. At its height in 1975-76, government spending accounted for 49.9 per cent of GDP before falling to 44.9 per cent in 1978-79. Ten years later it had fallen to 39.2 per cent. After a sharp rise due to the 1990-92 recession, it stabilised in the late 1990s at around 40 per cent.

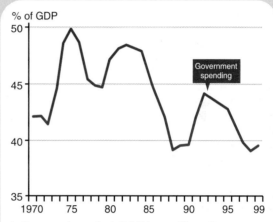

1. Government spending is Total Managed Expenditure.
2. Years are fiscal years. So, for instance, 1970 is the fiscal year 1970-71.

Figure 43.1 *Government spending as a percentage of GDP*[1][2]

Source: adapted from HM Treasury, The Red Book.

(a) Suggest the possible economic consequences of the shift in resources between the public and private sectors since 1979.

of tax from income tax, reducing it to 30 per cent for 85 per cent of workers, but extending the 30 per cent VAT rate to a much wider range of goods and services. The marginal rate of income tax is still much higher, though, than in the USA. Supply side economists would argue that higher rates of tax discourage incentives to work and take risks and that this will lead to lower economic growth (☞ unit 38).

- To what extent is government an efficient provider of goods and services compared to the private sector.

Mixed economies can be judged on the above issues. They could also be evaluated according to their environmental impact. Mixed economies have a better

key terms

Mixed economy - an economy where both the free market mechanism and the government planning process allocate significant proportions of total resources.

Applied economics

Sweden

In 1932, the Swedish Democratic Party gained power and created a model of a mixed economy which has been the envy of left wing economists ever since. The Swedish economy lies at one extreme of the mixed economy model, devoting between 60 and 70 per cent of its GDP in the 1980s and 1990s to public expenditure. Figure 43.2 shows that in 2000, general government expenditure was estimated to be 58.5 per cent of GDP, almost twice that of the USA and two thirds more than the UK.

Government spending as a percentage of GDP has changed over time, as shown in Figure 43.3. In the early 1970s, it stood at around 45 per cent. However, two factors caused it to soar. First there was continued upward pressure on public spending which the Swedish government found hard to resist. Second, the two oil shocks of 1974-5 and 1979-80 led to recessions throughout the Western World with sharp rises in unemployment. Unlike many countries, Sweden adopted Keynesian demand management policies to reduce unemployment. It increased public spending to create jobs. Large sums of money were also spent on job creation schemes and retraining for the unemployed. As Figure 43.4 shows, the Swedish government was very successful in maintaining low unemployment compared to other industrialised countries.

Increased government spending had to be financed and Sweden became one of the most highly taxed economies in the world. In 1991, a voter backlash saw the election, for the first time since the 1930s, of a right wing government. At the time, the economy was beginning to go into recession. The government refused to increase public spending to a level which would have kept unemployment relatively low. The result was a quadrupling of unemployment. Government spending as a proportion of GDP still rose to 72 per cent in 1993, partly because of rises in welfare and training expenditure on the unemployment and partly because GDP itself fell in each year between 1991 and 1993. However, the government was committed to rolling back the state, cutting spending programmes and reducing the tax burden. The rest of the 1990s saw a tight control of public spending which, combined with rising GDP, led to successive falls in government spending as a proportion of GDP.

Even so, by 2000 Sweden still had the highest proportion of government spending as a proportion of GDP amongst industrialised countries. Its welfare state is extremely generous. The old, the young and the poor receive a mix of benefits which looks lavish in comparison with spending in, say, the USA or the UK. Women, for instance, are entitled to free creche care for their children if they go out to work. This encourages Swedish women to continue with their careers full time when they have children. Equally, high taxes mean that one person working households do not have the disposable income of their English or US counterparts. To maintain a high standard of living, women have to go out to work.

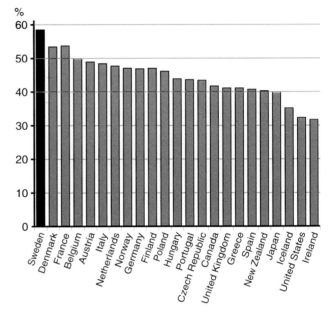

Figure 43.2 *Government spending as a percentage of GDP, 2000 estimates*
Source: adapted from OECD, *Economic Outlook*.

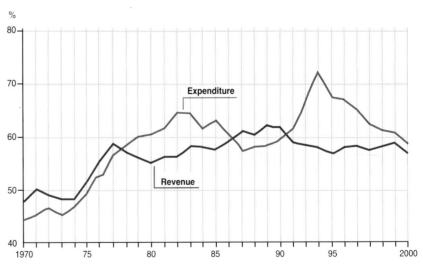

Figure 43.3 *Sweden: public expenditure and revenue as a percentage of GDP*
Source: adapted from OECD.

Critics of the Swedish model say that high taxes have reduced incentives to work and led to a flight of capital from the country. Swedish companies have been forced out of business because of high costs or have relocated outside the country. Foreign companies have been discouraged from investing in Sweden. In 1970, Sweden had the third highest GNP per capita in the world measured at purchasing power parity rates. By 1998, it had slipped to 27th. However, after coming out of recession in 1994, Sweden's growth rate was comparable to the average for industrialised countries. The Swedish government has become much more sensitive to the needs of business and has adopted policies which attempt to encourage investment in the country. At the same time, there is no desire by the majority of Swedish voters to dismantle their welfare state. Sweden is likely to remain at one extreme of the mixed economy model.

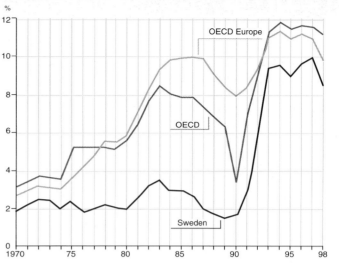

Figure 43.4 *Unemployment in Sweden, OECD countries and European OECD countries*
Source: adapted from OECD.

France

The French welfare state
France has a large welfare state. Education, from nursery provision to universities, is paid for by the state. Health care is funded through a complicated system of insurance schemes paid for mainly by employers. However, the state provides a safety net for anyone who is not in an insurance scheme, particularly the poor and the elderly. Local government is a major landlord, offering homes for rent at affordable prices. Home ownership, at less than 50 per cent, is not considered particularly desirable in France.

There is also a state pension scheme which offers pensions of 50 per cent of salary for workers who have paid 37¹/₂ years contributions. Critics say it is too generous to meet the demands of a rapidly ageing population. The scheme is a cash management system. This means that contributions by workers today into the scheme are used to pay today's pensions. There are no funds of savings stored up in the scheme to pay future pensioners. With the number of workers to pensioners rapidly declining, pension contributions will have to rise sharply from workers to fund the scheme. The French government has long recognised the problem but has failed to address it. Changing the scheme would be very unpopular amongst both pensioners and future pensioners. However, it would like to see French workers taking out more private pension schemes and saving for their retirement. If benefits in the state scheme have to be cut, this would soften the blow for at least some French workers.

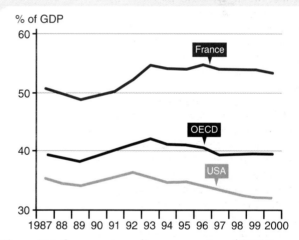

Figure 43.5 *Government spending as a percentage of GDP: France, USA and the OECD*
Source: adapted from OECD, *Economic Outlook*.

Privatisation
The French state owns an impressive list of companies, from the electricity industry to gas, water, railways and telecommunications. In the 1980s, it also owned companies such as Air France, Renault cars, the oil company Elf-Aquitaine and several major banks. The 1990s saw a slow process of privatisation, but by 2000 it was sufficiently advanced for core industries such as France Telecom to be fully or partially privatised. By 2010, the French state is likely to own little of French industry.

1. 'France is a mixed economy.' Explain what this means, illustrating your answer with examples from the data.
2. To what extent could (a) privatisation and (b) funding of pensions through private pension schemes tilt the French economy towards being a free market economy?

Applied economics

Table 44.1 *Countries in transition: change in real GDP*

Annual percentage change

	Average 1976-85	1986	1987	1988	1989	1990	1991	1992	1993	1994	1995	1996	1997	1998	1999
Albania	1.0	3.3	1.5	1.5	-0.7	-7.5	-10.8	-5.0	-0.6	4.2	6.0	4.1	2.9	2.0	5.0
Bulgaria	5.8	4.1	6.1	2.6	-1.9	-9.1	-8.4	-7.3	-1.4	1.8	3.1	-10.4	-7.0	3.0	2.0
Czech Republic	-	2.1	0.5	2.1	4.5	-1.2	-11.5	-3.2	0.5	3.3	6.4	3.9	1.0	-2.7	0.0
Georgia	-	-1.2	-2.0	7.0	-3.5	-15.1	-21.1	-44.9	-29.3	-10.3	2.6	10.8	11.3	3.0	2.0
Hungary	2.7	1.5	4.1	-0.1	0.7	-3.5	-11.9	-3.1	-0.6	3.1	1.4	1.4	4.5	5.1	4.2
Moldova	-	8.0	1.2	1.8	8.8	-2.4	-17.5	-28.9	-1.2	-31.0	-1.8	-7.8	1.7	-8.6	-5.0
Poland	1.8	4.2	1.9	4.1	0.2	-11.6	-7.0	2.7	3.8	5.1	7.1	6.0	6.9	4.8	3.0
Romania	5.2	2.3	0.9	-0.5	-5.8	-5.6	-12.9	-8.8	1.6	3.9	7.1	4.0	-6.9	-7.3	-3.0
Russian Federation	-	2.4	1.4	4.5	1.6	-3.0	-4.9	-14.5	-8.8	-12.7	-4.1	-3.5	0.9	-4.6	-5.0
Slovakia	-	4.2	2.4	2.0	1.0	-2.5	-14.6	-6.5	-3.6	4.8	7.0	6.5	6.6	4.4	1.0
Ukraine	-	1.5	3.8	1.9	5.0	-3.6	-8.7	-10.0	-14.1	-22.9	-12.2	-10.0	-3.1	-1.7	-3.5

Source: adapted from UN, *Economic Survey of Europe*.

The basic economic problem

An economic system is a way of resolving the basic economic problem - scarcity of resources in a world of infinite human wants. The Soviet Union had been a command economy since the early 1930s, following collectivisation of agriculture. Eastern European countries became command economies in the late 1940s and early 1950s following communist takeover of their governments. However, the 1990s saw these economies transforming themselves into market-orientated economies. How can an economy move from being a planned economy to, say, a mixed economy and what costs will be involved in the transition phase?

Output

The process of transformation for most Eastern Europe countries began in 1990, although Poland and the former Soviet Union began restructuring in the late 1980s. As Figure 44.1 shows, the early 1990s saw a fall in output as measured by GDP. The average fall was nearly 30 per cent. This is much larger than, say, the UK or the USA experienced during the Great Depression of the 1930s. In the prolonged UK recession of 1990-92, which saw a doubling of unemployment to 3 million, output fell 2.7 per cent between the second quarter of 1990 and the third quarter of 1992. So the fall in output in Eastern Europe was on a scale unseen in Western Europe and the USA.

This average masked very different figures for different countries. Those in Central and Eastern Europe and the Baltic on average saw economic growth return from the mid-1990s. By 2000, their output was roughly the same as in 1990. In contrast, countries in the CIS (Commonwealth of Independent States), made up of Russia and former republics of the Soviet Union,

had seen their output almost halve by 2000, with no certainty that their economies would begin to grow again. Figure 44.2 shows that the largest economy in this group, Russia, had seen its output in 1999 fall to 53 per cent of its 1989 level. Uzbekistan, a small Asian country with a relatively large oil industry, had suffered the least. Georgia had seen its output shrink to one third of its 1989 level, partly due to a disastrous civil war in the first half of the 1990s. The Ukraine and Moldova, with output levels equally at one third their 1989 levels, had suffered from gross economic mismanagement. Table 44.1 gives further data about the growth rates of individual countries under communism and in the 1990s.

It is almost inevitable that a transition from a command structure to a market structure will initially reduce output. To understand why, consider how resources are allocated in a command economy. Government planners allocate factors of production between differing production units such as factories or farms. So a food factory might be allocated so much in raw materials, say sugar beet, and a given quantity of new physical capital such as new machines. It then has to supply its output to shops in the country.

The state now attempts to introduce reforms to transform the economy into a market economy. The factory is allowed to sell its final product, sugar, to buyers, state shops or private shops. But equally, it now has to buy its inputs such as sugar beet or machinery. It decides that, in view of the economic uncertainties that it faces, it will not buy any new machines that year. This then has repercussions right through the system. The factory manufacturing machines no longer has a guaranteed market for its product. Faced with the cancellation of the order, it will have to reduce output and lay off workers. It will no longer require as much steel and other inputs from other firms in the economy. They too will lay off workers and reduce output.

On the other hand, the sugar factory may have difficulties obtaining raw materials. State farms, freed from restrictions on what to grow, may decide to grow more wheat and less sugar beet. The sugar factory may also experience problems getting its product to market.

If the sugar is being exported to other countries which are in a transition process, the disruption will be similar. Their factories and shops will be cutting down on imports, uncertain whether they will be able to pay for them. They may also decide now to buy their sugar from a cheaper source in the West, which previously they might have been forbidden to do. The sugar factory may therefore lose all its export orders to that country overnight. There may be little hope that it will ever win back the orders given that the importer now has the whole world to choose from if it wants to start importing again.

The data in Figures 44.1 and 44.2 should be treated with some caution. In the enormous upheaval that transition represents, accurate statistics for production in the official, formal sector of the economy are difficult to collect. Moreover, the countries worst affected by falls in official GDP have typically seen large growth in their informal sectors. Figure 44.3 shows, for instance, that in 1998 the informal sectors of two of the twelve CIS countries, Azerbaijan and Georgia, were estimated to be larger than the official sectors, whilst others such as Russia and the Ukraine had informal sectors approaching the size of their formal sectors.

Unemployment

The large falls in output shown in Figures 44.1 and 44.2 cannot but have led to sharp rises in unemployment. When Eastern European countries were command economies, one of their strengths was that the economies were managed to ensure almost zero unemployment. The move to a market system led to a large shake-out of labour. First, many enterprises have gone out of business. Factories and plant have been closed and their workers made unemployed. Second, enterprises have been forced to become more efficient, especially if they are now competing in sectors of the economy subject to competition from imports of

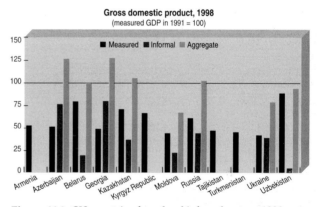

Figure 44.1 *Index of real GDP of countries in transition*
Source: adapted from World Bank, ERBD.

Figure 44.3 *CIS countries: formal and informal sectors, 1998*
Source: adapted from *Finance and Development*, June 1999, IMF.

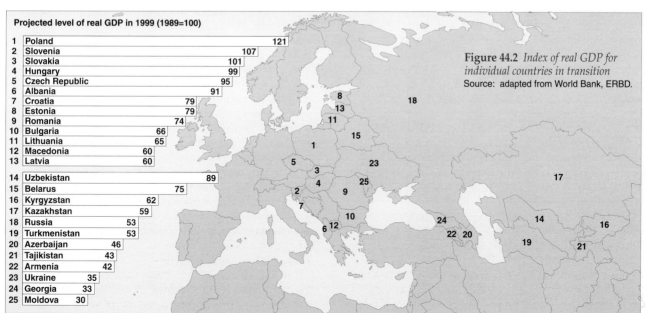

Projected level of real GDP in 1999 (1989=100)

1	Poland	121
2	Slovenia	107
3	Slovakia	101
4	Hungary	99
5	Czech Republic	95
6	Albania	91
7	Croatia	79
8	Estonia	79
9	Romania	74
10	Bulgaria	66
11	Lithuania	65
12	Macedonia	60
13	Latvia	60
14	Uzbekistan	89
15	Belarus	75
16	Kyrgyzstan	62
17	Kazakhstan	59
18	Russia	53
19	Turkmenistan	53
20	Azerbaijan	46
21	Tajikistan	43
22	Armenia	42
23	Ukraine	35
24	Georgia	33
25	Moldova	30

Figure 44.2 *Index of real GDP for individual countries in transition*
Source: adapted from World Bank, ERBD.

Western firms. Efficiency is easily gained by shedding labour and making the remaining workforce work harder and more productive.

Table 44.2 shows that some countries have achieved transition at lower costs of unemployment than others. The Czech Republic, for instance, had lower unemployment throughout the 1990s than, say, Bulgaria or Hungary. For all countries in transition, unemployment has been a heavy cost to bear of the transition process. However, it should be remembered that unemployment in Western Europe (OECD Europe in Table 44.2) was high too in the 1990s. Unemployment in Eastern Europe was not that much greater in practice.

Table 44.2 *Registered unemployment*

	Percentage of labour force, end year										
	1988	1989	1990	1991	1992	1993	1994	1995	1996	1997	1998
Albania	-	-	-	8.3	27.9	29.0	19.6	16.9	12.4	-	-
Bulgaria	0	1.6	1.6	11.1	15.3	16.4	12.8	11.1	12.5	13.7	12.0
Czech Republic	-	-	-	4.1	2.6	3.5	3.2	2.9	3.5	5.2	7.5
Georgia	0	0	0	0.2	2.3	6.6	3.6	2.6	12.0	5.0	14.0
Hungary	0.5	1.6	1.6	7.4	12.3	12.1	10.4	10.4	10.5	10.4	7.8
Moldova	0	0	0	0	0.1	0.7	1.1	1.4	1.8	1.6	-
Poland	0.3	6.1	6.1	11.8	13.6	16.4	16.0	14.9	13.2	10.5	10.4
Romania	-	-	-	3.0	8.2	10.4	10.9	9.5	6.6	8.8	10.3
Russian Federation	0	0	0	0	4.8	5.3	7.1	8.3	9.2	10.9	12.4
Slovakia	-	-	-	-	-	12.2	13.7	13.1	11.1	11.6	11.9
Ukraine	0	0	0	0	0.3	0.4	0.4	0.5	1.1	2.3	3.7
OECD[1]	9.2	8.5	8.0	8.5	9.5	10.7	11.1	10.7	10.8	10.6	9.9

Source: *Transition Report*, European Bank for Reconstruction and Development.
1. From 1993.

Inflation

Economic transformation in Eastern Europe has been associated with very high inflation. A rise in prices is almost inevitable if an economy moves towards a free market system. In a command economy, resources are rationed in a number of different ways, but not through price. In the health service, for instance, health care might be rationed according to need, with criteria decided by doctors. In housing, accommodation might be allocated according to age or length of time on a waiting list. In food, citizens might have ration books, or only a very limited range of foods might be available in shops, discouraging shoppers from making too many purchases. Consumer items such as shoes might be available on a first come, first served basis.

In a market system, resources are allocated by price. The free market price is inevitably above the old state price if consumers have been rationed in the past. So when a market system is introduced, prices rise until demand equals supply. There is no shortage because some consumers have been priced out of the market.

Figure 44.4 shows the results of a *Financial Times* survey in Moscow in March 1990. State prices for goods were on average less than one-fifth the free market price of the same goods. However, products at state prices, sold through state shops, were either unavailable or were rationed in some way. At market prices, they were freely available from private shops or stalls. But the majority of Muscovites could not have afforded a weekly shop at those market prices. Hence demand for free market produce was relatively low.

Higher prices can spark a wage price spiral. Workers in Eastern Europe have reacted to higher prices by demanding higher wages. If firms give higher wages, then employers will need to pass on those higher costs in the form of higher prices which in turn give rise to further wage demands. For the sort of inflation that was seen in Eastern Europe in the 1980s, it is necessary for the government to **accommodate** those price and wage increases by printing money. If they don't, then firms giving price increases will find that they can't find buyers for their higher priced goods. Lower orders will result in lost production and redundancies. That in turn could mean strikes, riots and civil unrest.

Table 44.3 shows the changes in prices in Eastern European countries in the 1980s and 1990s. When the countries were command economies, inflation tended to be very low, far lower than in Western market economies. The transition period has been marked by large increases in prices. In 1992, Russia saw increases of over 1 300 per cent. This was hyperinflation caused by the Russian central bank issuing huge amounts of money mainly in the form of credits (i.e. loans) to bail out loss making enterprises and prevent them from closing. A mark of how well an economy has managed its transition is its ability to control inflation. Bringing annual price increases down to single figures can be very painful because lowering inflation tends in the short term to lead to further recession, falling output and rising unemployment. Low inflation, though, is a sign that the government is resisting the temptation to bail out inefficient enterprises and that market forces are determining the allocation of resources.

	State	Market
Apples (green)	3.00	15.00
Apples (red)	3.00	8.00
Beef	2.50	12.00
Cabbage	0.16	3.00
Carrots	0.32	1.50
Cucumbers	8.50	15.00
Garlic	1.80	4.00
Grapes	4.00	15.00
Lamb	2.50	15.00
Mandarins	1.00	10.00
Onions	1.00	3.00
Pork	2.50	15.00
Potatoes	0.50	2.00
Tomatoes	3.00	15.00
Veal	2.50	15.00

(average ratio 5.6)

Figure 44.4 *Price comparisons for state and market prices in Moscow (Roubles per kilogram)*

Ownership and wealth

In a command economy, land and capital is owned by the state. In a free market economy, most land and capital is owned by the private sector. So the move from one type of economy to the other must involve the sale of state assets to private individuals or companies (what would be called 'privatisation' in a UK context). A number of ways of achieving this has been used in Eastern Europe in recent years.

- The state could give property and capital away to the individuals or companies currently employing them. For instance, tenants of state housing could be given their accommodation. Factories could be given to their workers. One problem with this is that it is a very arbitrary way of sharing out assets. A worker in a factory which produces goods for export to the West would do far better out of this than a worker whose factory was obsolete. This form of privatisation has been widespread throughout Eastern Europe, but has often been done without the official blessing of government authorities. Because the legal systems of Eastern Europe are inadequate to deal with the concept of property ownership, quick-footed factory managers have been able to get enterprises transferred into their names. At higher levels, national politicians in some countries have enriched themselves, their families and their friends by acquiring state assets. The rule of law, so important to the proper functioning of a free market economy, has been subverted to enrich a few with power.
- The state could put all assets which it proposes to sell into a fund, with each citizen receiving a share allocation in the fund. The fund would sell off assets wherever possible, replacing physical assets with cash. Either the cash would be distributed to shareholders in higher dividends or it could be used to invest in the remaining assets of the fund. Shares in the fund would be tradeable, so citizens could choose either to sell the shares and spend the proceeds now or keep them in the hope of earning dividends and making capital gains. This model of privatisation was pursued in the Czech Republic with some success. It ensured a relatively smooth transition of ownership from the public to the private sector which was seen by its citizens to be equitable.
- The state could sell assets to the highest bidder and use the proceeds to reduce past government debt, pay for increased government spending or reduce current tax levels. Assets could be sold either to

domestic individuals or producers, or to foreign companies. This model has been used in most Eastern European countries. In East Germany, for instance, an agency called the Truehand was set up into which was put all of the business assets of the former East German state. Between 1990 and 1995, the Truehand organised the sale of all these assets. Some were sold as existing enterprises to other firms or to their managers. Others were broken up and sold in part lots. Some businesses had to be closed because they were fundamentally unprofitable. In Hungary, some of the most successful enterprises, such as Tungsten lamps, were sold to foreign buyers who put in the highest bid for the companies.

The speed of privatisation in the 1990s differed enormously from country to country. In East Germany, almost all the businesses which were to be privatised had been privatised by 1995. In Hungary and the Czech Republic, the process of privatisation was broadly completed by 2000. In countries such as Turkmenistan, Belarus and the Ukraine, many enterprises were still under state ownership ten years on from the start of reforms.

The distribution of resources

The move from a command economy to a mixed economy has inevitably led to a fundamental shift in the distribution of resources. In free markets, resources are allocated to those with spending power. In turn. those with most spending power are likely to be those whose wealth, whether physical or human, is greatest. As a new wealth owning class emerges in Eastern Europe, the distribution of wealth will become less equal. It will also become less equal as wage inequalities widen. In East Germany, for instance, doctors earned less than coal miners before 1990. This was reversed as market forces reward those with higher levels of human capital.

The extent to which the distribution of income becomes less equal depends very much on the social security safety nets which are left in place after transition has been accomplished. If the former command economies retain their social security systems relatively intact, then inequalities should resemble those found in, say, West Germany. If they collapse, a distribution more akin to the USA will emerge.

Table 44.3 *Inflation in Eastern Europe*

Percentage change in consumer prices over previous year

	Average 1976-85	1986	1987	1988	1989	1990	1991	1992	1993	1994	1995	1996	1997	1998	1999
Albania	-	-	-	-	-	-	36	226	85	23	8	13	32	21	8
Bulgaria	1	3	3	3	6	26	334	82	73	96	62	123	1 082	22	7
Czech Republic	-	-	-	-	-	-	57	11	21	10	9	9	9	11	5
Georgia	-	-	-	-	-	-	71	887	3 215	15 607	163	39	7	4	20
Hungary	7	5	9	16	17	251	35	23	23	19	28	24	18	14	9
Moldova							98	1 276	789	330	30	24	12	8	25
Poland	19	18	25	60	251	585	70	43	35	32	28	20	15	12	8
Romania	3	1	1	3	19	4	161	210	256	137	32	39	155	59	45
Russian Federation	-	-	-	1	2	5	93	1 526	875	311	198	48	15	28	124
Slovakia	-	-	-	-	-	-	61	10	23	13	10	6	6	7	9
Ukraine	-	-	-	-	-	-	91	1 210	4 735	891	376	80	16	11	28
OECD average	10	6	8	8	6	7	6	5	4	5	6	5	5	4	4

Source: *Transition Report*, European Bank for Reconstruction and Development.

The speed of change

Countries have made or are making the transition at very different speeds. Poland, for instance, one of the first countries to attempt transformation, went through a crash programme in the early 1990s. The effect was severe, with a fall in GDP of over 20 per cent in two years. However, the economy quickly recovered and by 1993 was growing again at a relatively fast rate. Growth between 1994 and 2000 averaged 5.5 per cent (compared to 2.5 per cent in the European Union). By 2000, GDP was one quarter above its 1989 pre-transition level. Poland today is a recognisable mixed economy with a strong private sector, a wide tax base which finances the public sector, a stable currency and where the rule of law operates in markets.

At the other extreme, the Ukraine has failed to transform itself into a market economy. There has been privatisation, but factories and enterprises have been acquired by politicians, ex-factory bosses and criminal elements. Official GDP had fallen to one third of its 1989 level by 2000. However, the informal economy was as large as the official economy. Most large enterprises officially are loss making but they survive through a variety of means, including not paying taxes, defaulting on payments on loans and not paying their workers. The tax base is very low, partly because so much of the economy is in the informal sector. The result is that government provided services such as education and healthcare are underfunded. Anyone dependent on income from the state, from pensioners to doctors to teachers, has seen their income fall sharply in real terms since 1990 and there is no guarantee that payment will be made on time each month. The lack of rule of law in the economic sphere encourages criminal activity and discourages investment. Foreign investment in particular has been negligible. Long term growth prospects are bleak. The Ukraine is widely regarded as an example of how not to manage the process of transformation.

In general, Central and Eastern European countries and the Baltic states have managed their transitions relatively well. All have aspirations to join the European Union. To achieve this, they must satisfy certain criteria including bringing their legal systems into line with EU law, broadly balancing government budgets and having a stable currency and low inflation. The CIS, the former countries of the Soviet Union including Russia, have done far less well. In too may cases, they have failed to establish a sound legal framework within which businesses can operate. Wealth and ownership of former state enterprises have passed into the hands of unaccountable individuals who have sent large amounts of money abroad illegally. Government has been inefficient and corrupt. Their informal economies have grown in size. All these factors have distorted the workings of the market and left them in a weak position to grow.

Why was it necessary?

Table 44.1 shows that Eastern European countries were growing at rates very similar to those of their Western European competitors in the 1980s. Unemployment and inflation were low by Western standards. Nevertheless there were two main reasons why change was necessary.

First, the command systems of Eastern Europe were based on repressive political structures. The revolution in Eastern Europe was based on a desire to regain personal political freedom. Command economies can only be run at the expense of personal freedom. They rely on ordering people to take certain actions. To regain personal freedom, individuals had to regain economic freedom. This necessitated a move to a more market-orientated economy.

Second, the figures conceal much of the reality of life in Eastern Europe at the time. Inflation was certainly very low. Prices were kept stable by state enterprises on the orders of the central planning authorities. However, there were enormous inflationary pressures building up in the system in the sense that there was large excess demand in the economy. This was manifested not by rising prices but by lengthening queues. There were long waiting lists for cars and houses. Shops were all too often empty of goods. When there was a delivery of goods, word would get around and a queue would immediately form until the delivery had been completely sold.

Growth of production was satisfactory. However, too much of what was being produced was going into the defence industry, was being used inefficiently in the production process and was therefore being wasted, and was going into investment to provide goods which industry and consumers did not want. Not only production was inefficient. The goods and services that were produced were of poor quality, certainly in comparison with Western goods. The system provided few incentives for any of this to be remedied.

As for low unemployment, a growing proportion of the workforce were gaining second jobs in the black economy. They could afford to work hard at a second, usually illegal, job because they did so little in their official state job. So, in the official sector of the economy, there was huge underemployment of workers - 100 workers being employed, for instance, when 50 could have done the job.

There have been many losers from change. Inequality has widened considerably and there has been a growth in both absolute and relative poverty. However, there is a recognition that change was necessary and that the command structures of the pre-1990 era could not deliver long term growth. Some countries, such as Poland and Hungary, can look forward to catching up with Western European countries in the same way that the economies of Spain, Portugal, Greece and Ireland have been transformed by participation in European trading systems and the European Union since the 1970s. Countries of the former Soviet Union face a more uncertain future because they have failed to varying degrees to embrace the market economy. Until they reform, they cannot hope to sustain long term growth.

Poland

Shock therapy

'The objective is to set up a market system akin to the one found in the industrially developed countries. This will have to be achieved quickly, through radical actions ... We are embarking on the reshaping effort under extremely adverse conditions. The economy is in ever more tenuous disequilibrium ... The ecological disaster, the housing crisis, the foreign debt burden, the emigration by the most active part of the young generation - these have been swelling for years. In recent months, additional crisis symptoms surfaced or mounted in force: a rapid price climb linked to a wage explosion, the flight from the zloty, the growing deficit of the state budget and also a drop in output.'

Source: The Polish Government, *The Outline Economic Programme*.

Institutional restructuring

Poland has seen the creation or restructuring of many of its key economic institutions. A very successful stock exchange has been established. The central bank has been made independent of the government. Private banks have been created whilst state owned banks have shifted their lending policies to encourage new private sector enterprises. Tax reform, such as the introduction of VAT, has broadened the tax base of the government and helped it to reduce its budget deficit.

The law has been changed to bring it into line with European Union requirements as part of the process of becoming a member of the EU in the first decade of the 21st century.

Liberalisation

In 1989-90, many key prices and markets were liberalised. This meant sweeping away state controls on prices and allowing markets to decide what price should be paid for a commodity. The result was a widely predicted surge in inflation as excess demand, formerly expressed by rationing and queuing, was transformed into higher prices. Subsequent inflation has been high by EU and US standards. However, inflation did fall over the 1990s and must fall to 0-5 per cent for entry to the European Union.

Stabilisation

The Polish government achieved a mixed record on stabilisation during the period of shock therapy in the first half of the 1990s. It vacillated between controlling the money and inflation and providing enough credit in the economy to prevent enterprises from going bankrupt and workers from suffering too great a cut in real wages. In the second half of the 1990s, strong growth allowed the government to bring down the rate of inflation without inflicting too much pain in the form of lost output or higher unemployment.

Privatisation

Poland adopted a measured policy towards privatisation. It has been achieved through the sale of shares in an enterprise to individual private investors or the sale of assets to firms, mostly foreign companies. The pace of privatisation was slow, partly because the Polish government wanted to ensure the continued survival of most of its enterprises. It wanted to avoid the large scale shutdowns that became a feature of privatisation in Eastern Germany. It was also wary of selling too many enterprises to Western companies. There was a strong fear that its economy could become a satellite economy for West Europe, prone to large scale shutdowns whenever Western Europe went into recession.

It has been very liberal in allowing new firms to be set up, often in competition with state owned enterprises. Foreign investment has been considerable with companies such as Fiat and Daewoo building plants in Poland. The government has forced state companies to maintain strict financial discipline. They have not been allowed to run up substantial losses. Hence, private competition has often led to large increases in productivity in state owned companies.

By 2000, an estimated 65 per cent of GDP was being produced by the private sector and only 35 per cent by the public sector.

Source: adapted from the Financial Times 3.3.1995, 28.3.1995, 30.3.1999; World Bank, *Finance and Development*, June 1999; OECD, *Economic Outlook*, June 1999.

Table 44.4 *Poland - selected economic indicators*

	Average 1976-85	1986	1987	1988	1989	1990	1991	1992	1993	1994	1995	1996	1997	1998	1999
							Annual percentage change								
Economic growth, % change in GDP	1.8	4.2	1.9	4.1	0.2	-11.6	-7.0	2.7	3.8	5.1	7.1	6.0	6.9	4.8	3.0
Registered unemployment, % of labour force end year	-	-	-	0.3	6.1	6.1	11.8	13.6	16.4	16.0	14.9	13.2	10.5	10.4	-
Inflation, %	19	18	25	60	251	585	70	43	35	32	28	20	15	12	8

Source: *Transition Report*, European Bank for Reconstruction and Development.

1. **Poland moved from being a command economy in the 1980s to a mixed economy in the 1990s. Explain the differences between the two economic systems.**
2. **What difficulties did Poland experience in its transformation?**
3. **Discuss how it could be judged whether Poland was right (a) to make the transition and (b) to do it so quickly through 'shock therapy'.**

Summary

1. Economics is generally classified as a social science.
2. It uses the scientific method as the basis of its investigation.
3. Economics is the study of how groups of individuals make decisions about the allocation of scarce resources.
4. Economists build models and theories to explain economic interactions.
5. Positive economics deals with statements of 'fact' which can either be refuted or not refuted. Normative economics deals with value judgments, often in the context of policy recommendations.
6. Models and theories are simplifications of reality.

7. A good model is one which yields powerful conclusions, is elegant and internally consistent.
8. In addition, a good positive model is one which explains past and present events, can predict future events, is universally applicable and has realistic assumptions.
9. A good positive model must be capable of being refuted whilst a good normative model is one which sets out an ideal or paradigm state of affairs.
10. Models can be distinguished according to whether they are static or dynamic models, equilibrium or disequilibrium models, partial or general models, or micro-economic or macro-economic models.

What is a science?

There are many sciences covering a wide field of knowledge. What links them all is a particular method of work or enquiry called the SCIENTIFIC METHOD. The scientific method at its most basic is relatively easy to understand. A scientist:

- postulates a THEORY - the scientist puts forward a hypothesis which is capable of refutation (e.g. the earth travels round the sun, the earth is flat, a light body will fall at the same speed as a heavy body);

- gathers evidence to either support the theory or refute it - astronomical observation gives evidence to support the theory that the earth travels round the sun; on the other hand, data refutes the idea that the earth is flat; gathering evidence may be done through **controlled experiments**;

- accepts, modifies or refutes the theory - the earth does travel round the sun; a light body will fall at the same speed as a heavy body although it will only do so under certain conditions; the earth is not flat.

Theories which gain universal acceptance are often called LAWS. Hence we have the law of gravity, Boyle's law, and in economics the laws of demand and supply.

Economics – the science

Some sciences, such as physics or chemistry, are sometimes called 'hard sciences'. This term doesn't refer to the fact that physics is more difficult than a science such as biology! It refers to the fact that it is relatively easy to apply the scientific method to the study of these subjects. In physics much of the work can take place in laboratories. Observations can be made with some degree of certainty. Control groups can be established. It then becomes relatively easy to accept or refute a particular hypothesis.

This is all much more difficult in social sciences such as economics, sociology, politics and anthropology. In economics it is usually not possible to set up experiments to test hypotheses. It is not possible to establish control groups or to conduct experiments in environments which enable one factor to be varied whilst other factors are kept constant. The economist has to gather data in the ordinary everyday world where many variables are changing over any given time period. It then becomes difficult to decide whether the evidence supports or refutes particular hypotheses. Economists sometimes come to very different conclusions when considering a particular set of data as their interpretations may vary. For example, an

Question 1

Table 45.1

Year	Change in households' final consumption expenditure, £bn at 1995 prices	Change in households' disposable income, £bn at 1995 prices	Bank base rate (%)	Change in house prices (%)
1991	-7.4	6.7	11.7	-2
1992	1.8	16.4	9.56	-3
1993	12.5	13.9	6.01	3.7
1994	12.7	16	5.46	1.2
1995	7.6	2.7	6.73	2.5
1996	16.4	10.8	5.96	3.5
1997	18.7	20.3	6.58	14
1998	13.2	0.1	7.21	4

Source: adapted from *Economic Trends; Financial Statistics; Social Trends,* Office for National Statistics.

(a) Economists suggest that changes in consumer spending vary with changes in the incomes of consumers (their personal disposable income), interest rates (such as banks' interest rates) and changes in the personal wealth of consumers. Does the evidence in Table 45.1 support or refute this hypothesis?

unemployment rate of 12 per cent in the North region compared to a national average of 8 per cent may indicate a failure of government policy to help this area. Others may conclude that policy had been a success as unemployment may have been far greater without the use of policy.

It is sometimes argued that economics cannot be a science because it studies human behaviour and human behaviour cannot be reduced to scientific laws. There is an element of truth in this. It is very difficult to understand and predict the behaviour of individuals. However, nearly all economics is based on the study of the behaviour of groups of individuals. The behaviour of groups is often far more predictable than that of individuals. Moreover, we tend to judge a science on its ability to establish laws which are certain and unequivocal. But even in a hard science such as physics, it has become established that some laws can only be stated in terms of probabilities. In economics, much analysis is couched in terms of 'it is likely that' or 'this may possibly happen'. Economists use this type of language because they know they have insufficient data to make firm predictions. In part it is because other variables may change at the same time, altering the course of events. But it is also used because economists know that human behaviour, whilst broadly predictable, is not predictable to the last £1 spent or to the nearest 1 penny of income.

Theories and models

The terms 'theory' and MODEL are often used interchangeably. There is no exact distinction to be made between the two. However, an economic theory is generally expressed in looser terms than a model. For instance, 'consumption is dependent upon income' might be an economic theory. '$C_t = 567 + 0.852Y_t$' where 567 is a constant, C_t is current consumption and Y_t current income would be an economic model. Theories can often be expressed in words. But economic models, because they require greater precision in their specification, are often expressed in mathematical terms.

The purpose of modelling

Why are theories and models so useful in a science? The universe is a complex place. There is an infinite number of interactions happening at any moment in time. Somehow we all have to make sense of what is going on. For instance, we assume that if we put our hand into a flame, we will get burnt. If we see a large hole in the ground in front of us we assume that we will fall into it if we carry on going in that direction.

One of the reasons why we construct theories or models is because we want to know why something is as it is. Some people are fascinated by questions such as 'Why do we fall downwards and not upwards?' or 'Why can birds fly?'. But more importantly we use theories and models all the time in deciding how to act. We keep away from fires to prevent getting burnt. We avoid holes in the ground because we don't want to take a tumble.

Positive and normative models

These two uses of models - to investigate the world as it is and to use the model as a basis for decision making - lead us to distinguish between two types of economic model.

POSITIVE MODELS and positive economics deal with objective or scientific explanations of the economy. For instance, the model of price determination which states that a rise in price will lead to a fall in the quantity demanded is a positive model. It is capable of refutation. It is argued by some economists that positive models are value free.

NORMATIVE MODELS and normative economics attempt to describe what ought to be. A normative statement is one which contains a value judgement. A normative model sets a standard by which reality can be judged. For instance, 'The government has a duty to protect the incomes of everybody in society, not just the well-off' would be a normative statement. It contains a value judgement about the role of government.

For some, the study of economics is fascinating in itself. Studying and constructing positive models is reward enough. But most who study economics are principally interested in the subject because of its normative aspects. They want to know how society can be changed - 'Should society help the poor and disadvantaged?', 'How best might pollution be dealt with?'.

Academic economics has a long tradition of the study of positive economics. But 'political economy', the normative study of economics, has an equally long

Question 2

From the Countess of Sandwich.
Sir, I welcome John Major's statement of belief in 'the cascade of wealth between generations' and his desire to abolish inheritance tax for 'the majority of citizenry'. (The FT Interview: 'Ready to fight for his political life', July 1/2). For many people now this statement is both irrelevant and insensitive. This 'majority' is spending its savings on its own old-age care, and the 'cascade of wealth' to which he refers is being dissipated in nursing home fees and means-tested health and social services support.

The cost and efficiency of old-age care is a problem for governments across Europe, not just in the UK. But Major's new manifesto contains no solutions, and his upbeat comments are no sop to those who have - now vainly - worked to pass something on to their children. More importantly, his comments do nothing to advance the discussion on the long-term costs of caring for Europe's ageing population. Instead they ring with the same tired comments on the virtues of 'the enterprise economy' and seem to ignore the distress of many of 'the citizenry' and its professional helpers.
Caroline Sandwich.
Mapperton,
Beaminster, Dorset DT8 3NR

(a) Which are the positive statements and which are the normative statements in this letter?

tradition going back to Adam Smith. In fact it is difficult to separate the two. To know how best to help raise the living standards of the poor (normative economics) we need to know how the economy operates and why people are poor.

Some economists argue that positive economics cannot be distinguished from normative economics because positive economics is subtly value laden. Why, for instance, did economists become so much more interested in the role of the entrepreneur (the risk-taking small businessman) during the 1980s? Much of the answer must be because Margaret Thatcher and Ronald Reagan made such important claims about the benefits of entrepreneurial activity for an economy.

In practice, all economists make value judgements. But many economists argue that 'good' economics distinguishes between positive and normative aspects. Value judgements are exposed so that we can see whether the analysis can lead to different conclusions if different value judgements are made.

Simplification

One criticism made of economics is that economic theories and models are 'unrealistic'. This is true, but it is equally true of Newton's law of gravity, Einstein's Theory of Relativity or any theory or model. This is because any theory or model has to be a simplification of reality if it is to be useful. Imagine, for instance, using a map which described an area perfectly. To do this it would need to be a full scale reproduction of the entire area which would give no practical advantage. Alternatively, drop a feather and a cannon ball from the top of the leaning tower of Pisa. You will find that both don't descend at the same speed, as one law in physics would predict, because that law assumes that factors such as air resistance and friction don't exist.

If a model is to be useful it has to be simple. The extent of simplification depends upon its use. If you wanted to go from London to Tokyo by air, it wouldn't be very helpful to have maps which were on the scale of your local A to Z. On the other hand, if you wanted to visit a friend in a nearby town it wouldn't be very helpful to have a map of the world with you. The local A to Z is very much more detailed (i.e. closer to reality) than a world map but this does not necessarily make it more useful or make it a 'better' model.

Simplification implies that some factors have been included in the model and some have been omitted. It could even be the case that some factors have been distorted to emphasise particular points in a model. For instance, on a road map of the UK, the cartographer will almost certainly not have attempted to name every small hamlet or to show the geological formation of the area. On the other hand, he or she will have marked in roads and motorways which will appear several miles wide according to the scale of the map. There are a number of reasons why this occurs.

- Models are constructed in an attempt to present a clear and simple explanation of reality. Trying to include weather and geological information on a large scale road map would make it much more difficult for the motorist to see how to get from A to B. On the other hand, distorting reality by making roads very wide is

extremely helpful to a motorist studying a map because it is much easier to read thick lines than thin lines.
- Models must assume that explanations for much of what is contained in the model lie elsewhere. For instance, a model which explains that consumption varies with income doesn't explain what determines income itself.
- The creator of a model may not be interested in a particular aspect of reality (which is an example of how normative values can be superimposed on supposedly positive models). The cartographer, for instance, preparing an ordinary road map is not interested in the geology of an area.
- The model may be constructed deliberately to distort and mislead. For instance, employers might choose to use a model which predicts that minimum wages always increase unemployment, whilst trade unions might construct a different model which showed that minimum wages increased employment.

Models may also omit variables because the author does not believe them to be of importance. This may be a correct premise. On the other hand, it may be false, leading to the model being poorer than it might otherwise be. For instance, few would criticise a weather model which omits the UK rate of inflation from among its variables. On the other hand, a weather model of the UK which omits wind speed is unlikely to perform well.

In conclusion, all subject disciplines simplify and select from a mass of data. This process seems to cause little concern in sciences such as physics and chemistry. However, it is unfortunate for economists that many critics of the subject seem to think that simplification in economics shows that economists have little or no understanding of economic matters. Nothing could be further from the truth!

'Good' models

Many of the units in this book are devoted to one economic model or another. Which of these models are 'good' models? A number of criteria can be used to judge a model.

One important criterion by which a positive economic model may be judged is the extent to which it accurately **explains reality**. Reality exists in three different time periods: **the past, the present and the future**. A very powerful model, such as the model of price determination, is able to explain what happened in the past, explain what is happening today and predict what will happen in the future. Price theory provided an explanation of why the rise in oil prices during the 1970s led to a fall in world wide demand for oil. Today it helps us understand why a restriction in the supply of oil by OPEC leads to a price rise. We can predict with confidence that as world oil reserves, all other things being equal, diminish over the next 300 years, the price of oil will rise.

The simple Keynesian theory of income determination, however, is not such a good theory. It explains relatively well the workings of the UK economy in the 1950s and 1960s but only gives a partial insight into how the economy performed in the 1970s and 1980s. This is because the simple Keynesian model ignores both changes in the money supply and supply side shocks - reasonable simplifying assumptions in the 1950s and 1960s but very misleading in the context of economic events in the 1970s and 1980s. It may be that the 1970s and 1980s were an exceptional time period and perhaps in the future the simple Keynesian model will once again prove to be a good one.

Macro-economic computer models of the economy, such as the Treasury model, the London Business School (LBS) model or the National Institute of Economic Research (NIESR) model, are judged mainly on their ability to predict the future. They are specifically called **'forecasting models'**. It could be that the best predictor of next year's rate of inflation is this year's rainfall in the Sahara desert. A model which incorporated this would be a good model if we were solely interested in its ability to forecast but it would be a poor model if we wished to understand the causes of inflation in the UK.

There are a number of economic models which are claimed to be good predictors but are not based on **realistic assumptions**. An example is the neo-classical theory of the firm. In the real world there are virtually no industries which conform to the assumptions of either perfect competition or pure monopoly yet these theories are widely taught and discussed. One justification is that although the assumptions are unrealistic the models provide very powerful and clear predictions about the extremes of behaviour of firms. If we know how firms behave at either end of the spectrum of competition then we can predict how firms will behave between these two extremes. Unfortunately these justifications have no logical or empirical validity. It could be argued that the models of perfect competition and monopoly give us little help in understanding the behaviour of firms in the real world, which is why there are so many alternative theories of the firm.

Positive models must be capable of refutation. A good model will be one where it is possible to gather data and perhaps perform controlled experiments to refute or support the model.

Normative models need to be judged on different criteria. A normative model does not claim to mirror reality. It attempts to provide a guide as to what is desirable or to be recommended. The neo-classical theory of the firm provides such a **paradigm**. By making a number of assumptions, it is possible to show that efficiency will be maximised in an economy where all firms are perfectly competitive. Increasing the degree of competition in industry then becomes an ideal or a goal to be aimed for. Monopoly, on the other hand, is shown to diminish welfare. Therefore the policy goal should be to break up monopolies.

Ultimately it is impossible to judge between competing normative theories. It is impossible to prove or disprove a statement such as 'Citizens should not be economically dependent upon the state'. However, it is possible to expose false reasoning within a normative model. In the 1950s, Lipsey and Lancaster, for instance, proved that greater competition might lead to a loss of welfare in the economy if at least one industry in the economy was not perfectly competitive. This 'theory of the second best' rebutted the general assumption prevalent at the time (and indeed still prevalent amongst certain economists and politicians) that greater competition was always good

Question 3

Table 45.2

	Investment[1] (£billion at 1995 prices)	Rate of interest[2] (%)	Change in national income[3] (£billion at 1995 prices)
1991	109.0	11.70	-9.9
1992	108.2	9.56	0.4
1993	109.1	6.01	15.0
1994	113.0	5.46	29.2
1995	116.4	6.73	19.3
1996	122.0	5.96	18.3
1997	130.5	6.58	25.6
1998	141.3	7.21	16.6

1. Gross private sector investment.
2. Bank base rate.
3. Gross domestic product at market prices.

Source: adapted from *Economic Trends Annual Supplement*, Office for National Statistics.

To what extent does the data show that (a) the accelerator model (investment in one year is determined by the change in national income in the previous year) and (b) the marginal efficiency of investment model (that investment is determined by the rate of interest) are 'good' models of investment behaviour?

whilst greater monopoly was always bad.

All models need to be judged on the grounds of internal consistency, and elegance. **Internal consistency** simply means that the logic in the argument is correct and that no mistakes have been made with any mathematics used. An **elegant** model is one which is as simple and as lucid as possible.

Finally, models need to be judged on their power. Price theory is a very **powerful** model. With few assumptions and a minimum of logic, it can be used to explain important events across time and between countries. Aggregate demand and aggregate supply analysis similarly is a powerful model which can show the effects of a variety of demand side and supply side shocks on the price level and output.

Realism and models

It is often said that some economic models are poor because they are not 'realistic'. However, before coming to this conclusion about any particular theory, it is important to consider what is the purpose of the theory.

- The model may be used to predict **future** events. In this case, it is unimportant if the assumptions or workings of the model are realistic. The value of the model should only be judged in terms of its predictive power.
- The model may be used to analyse the workings of a **group** of individuals. The fact that some individuals behave in a different way to that predicted by the model which attempts to say how groups work on the whole does not make the model unrealistic.
- The model may be used to explain the **workings** of a market or an economy. The detail may be realistic even if the overall predictive power of the model is relatively weak. In this case, the fact that the predictions of the

model are unrealistic is not particularly important.
- The model may be **normative**, used to describe what ought to be rather than what is. In this case, realism is obviously not an important criterion.
- The model may be very **simple**. With a few assumptions, the model may come to powerful but simplified conclusions. The fact that predictions are not accurate to the nearest 0.1 per cent does not mean that the model is unrealistic.

Forms of expression

There is a variety of ways in which models can be expressed.

Verbally A model can be expressed in words. 'Consumption increases when disposable income increases' would be an example. The advantage of using words is that models can be made accessible to a wide variety of readers. On the other hand, the use of jargon, such as 'disposable income', can be a barrier to the non-economist. Words can also be imprecise. In the above statement, we don't know the extent to which the increase is proportional.

Algebraically Over the past thirty years there has been an explosion in the use of algebra in academic economics. It

enables relationships to be set down very precisely but is often totally incomprehensible to the non-specialist. It also presumes that economic relationships are precise. Many economists argue the contrary - that economic relationships, whilst consistent, cannot be expressed so accurately.

Graphically The use of graphs has a long history in economics. It provides a convenient shorthand, encapsulating what would otherwise take many words to explain. Graphs, however, have their limitations. For instance, the fact that they can only be used in two dimensions with any ease limits the number of variables that can be used in a model.

Statistically Statistics are essential for economists if they are to verify hypotheses. They encourage precision, but as with algebra, they can be difficult for the non-specialist to understand and can give a misleading impression of accuracy in economics. **Econometrics**, the empirical testing of economic theories using statistical data, is an important branch of economics.

Exogenous and endogenous variables

Economic models are built with two types of variables. EXOGENOUS VARIABLES are variables whose value is determined outside the model. For instance, in the simple Keynesian model of income determination, investment, government expenditure and exports are exogenous variables. Their values are constant whatever the change in other variables in the model unless it is assumed otherwise. The value of exogenous variables therefore cannot be calculated within the model.

ENDOGENOUS VARIABLES are variables whose value is determined within the model. For instance, in the simple Keynesian model of income determination both consumption and income are endogenous variables. Their value is determined by variables such as income within the consumption function equation. The value of endogenous variables will change if other variables within the model change too.

Static and dynamic

A DYNAMIC model is one which contains time as one of its variables. A STATIC model is one which contains no time element within the model. Nearly all the models explained in this book are static models. For instance, neither the theory of perfect competition nor the Keynesian theory of income determination contain a time variable. Static models can be used to compare two different situations, a technique called **comparative static analysis**. In the theory of perfect competition, it is common to compare one equilibrium situation with another equilibrium situation. For instance, a short run equilibrium position may be compared to the long run equilibrium position. A time element may even be implicitly assumed within the model - it is assumed that the movement from one equilibrium position to another in perfect competition will take place over a period of time rather than instantly at a point in time. However, the model does not explain the path which the industry or the

---

Question 4

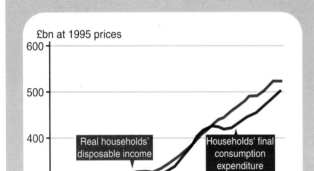

£bn at 1995 prices

Real households' disposable income

Households' final consumption expenditure

Figure 45.1 *Real consumers' expenditure and real personal disposable income at 1995 prices*
Source: adapted from *Economic Trends Annual Supplement*, Office for National Statistics.

Look at the diagram.
(a) To what extent does it show that there is a positive correlation between consumers' expenditure and their income?
(b) How might you express the relationship between consumers' expenditure and income (i) verbally and (ii) algebraically?

firm will take in the move from one equilibrium position to another. It merely assumes a 'before' and 'after' situation.

The cobweb theorem and the accelerator theory are the only two dynamic models explained in this book. The cobweb theorem, for instance, explicitly charts the movement over time of a market in a disequilibrium state.

Dynamic models are in one sense more 'realistic' than static models. Time is a very important variable in the real world. However, as we have already argued, greater realism is not always a desirable characteristic in a model. Dynamic models in economics are more complex and difficult to work with than static models and their predictions are not necessarily more powerful. For instance, if we wish to know how much revenue a government will raise by increasing taxes on beer, all we need is a static price model comparing the equilibrium situation before and after the imposition of the tax. There is no need to know the exact path that the market takes to get from one equilibrium position to another. Dynamic models are not therefore 'better' or 'worse' than static models - that judgement depends upon the use to which a model is to be put.

Equilibrium and disequilibrium models

Equilibrium is a central feature of all the models studied in this book. In economics, EQUILIBRIUM can be described as a point where expectations are being realised and where no plans are being frustrated. For instance, in the Keynesian model of national income determination, equilibrium national income is the point where planned expenditure equals actual income. In neo-classical price theory the cobweb theory is a disequilibrium model because it charts the behaviour of the market as planned demand and supply differ from actual demand and supply. All static models are equilibrium models because they deal with equilibrium positions.

An equilibrium position may be stable. If there is a movement away from equilibrium for some reason, there will be an in-built tendency for equilibrium to be restored. If the equilibrium point is unstable, there will be no tendency to move towards an equilibrium point once disequilibrium has been established.

It is easy to make the incorrect assumption that the market (or whatever is being studied) will always return to an equilibrium position; or that the equilibrium point is somehow the optimal or most desirable position. Neither is necessarily true even if economists tend to believe that knowing where is the equilibrium point is helpful in explaining economic events and in making policy recommendations.

Partial and general models

Just as there is no clear distinction between theories and models, so too there is no clear dividing line between a partial and a general model. A GENERAL MODEL can be said to be one which contains a large number of variables.

For instance, a model which includes all markets in the economy is a general model. A PARTIAL MODEL is one which contains relatively few variables. A model of the oil market or the demand for money would be partial models.

A partial model will be one in which most variables are assumed to be in the category of CETERIS PARIBUS. Ceteris paribus is Latin for 'all other things being equal' or 'all other things remaining the same'. It is a very powerful simplifying device which enables economists to explain clearly how an economy works. For instance, in neo-classical price theory ceteris paribus is used constantly. When the effect of a change in price on demand is analysed we assume that incomes, the prices of all other goods, and tastes remain the same. In the Keynesian multiplier model, it is assumed that government spending, exports, the marginal propensity to consume etc. do not change when analysing the effect of a change in investment on national income.

A general model may be realistic because it contains more variables. But again it is not necessarily better than a partial model. If we wish to study the effects of a rise in indirect taxes on the car industry, it is much simpler and easier to use a partial model of price determination than to use a general model. The general model may provide marginally more information but the extra information is unlikely to be worth the time and effort needed to generate it.

Macro-economics and micro-economics

A macro-economic model is one which models the economy as a whole. It deals with economic relationships at the level of all participants in the economy. A micro-economic model, on the other hand, deals with the economic behaviour of individuals or groups within society. For instance, the study of the spending decisions of individual consumers or consumers within a particular market such as the market for cars (demand theory) would be micro-economics. The study of consumption patterns for the whole economy (the consumption function) would be an example of macro-economics. The study of the determination of wage rates (wage theory) would be micro-economics. The study of the overall level of wages in the economy (part of national income accounting) would be macro-economics.

Question 5

Consider the following economic models and explain whether they are static or dynamic, equilibrium or disequilibrium, partial or general, and macro-economic or micro-economic models: (a) the model of demand, supply and price determination in the goods market; (b) the cobweb theorem; (c) the model of perfect competition; (d) the aggregate demand and supply model of income determination; (e) the accelerator model of investment.

key terms

Ceteris paribus - the assumption that all other variables within the model remain constant whilst one change is being considered.

Endogenous variables - variables whose value is determined within the model being used.

Equilibrium - the point where what is expected or planned is equal to what is realised or actually happens.

Exogenous variables - variables whose value is determined outside the model under consideration.

Law - a theory or model which has been verified by empirical evidence.

Normative economics - the study and presentation of policy prescriptions involving value judgements about the way in which scarce resources are allocated.

Partial and general models - a partial model is one with few variables whilst a general model has many.

Positive economics - the scientific or objective study of the allocation of resources.

Static and dynamic models - a static model is one where time is not a variable. In a dynamic model, time is a variable explicit in the model.

The scientific method - a method which subjects theories or hypotheses to falsification by empirical evidence.

Theory or model - a hypothesis which is capable of refutation by empirical evidence.

Applied economics

Positive and normative economics

The *Financial Times* devoted its lead editorial to the subject of 'Paying for Healthcare' on 22 January 2000. The NHS had at the time been in the news because of a flu epidemic which had filled hospital beds, leading to cancelled operations. Tony Blair, the Prime Minister, had subsequently suggested that government spending on health care in the UK should rise to the European average, measured as spending as a percentage of GDP.

The leader writer introduced the article by making a number of positive statements about healthcare worldwide. For instance, statistics are quoted: 'In the US ... health care absorbs a huge 14 per cent of gross domestic product, but fails effectively to cover 44 million Americans.' Again: '...a French government think-tank complains about widespread waste and concludes that France does not get noticeably better health care for its 9.6 per cent of GDP than the UK at 6.8 per cent.'

The leader writer goes on to make another positive statement: 'Health care systems each have their strengths and weaknesses.' But then a normative statement is made. 'This makes it especially difficult to judge what might be the "right" level of health spending'. This is normative because some would argue that it is not difficult to make judgments about the 'right' level of health spending. In France, for instance, most look to the USA and see waste or poor coverage, but look at the UK and see a system which is so underfunded that it cannot provide basic services such as immediate access to operations.

Later on in the article, the leader writer discusses some of the possible solutions to lack of funding in the UK. A number of normative statements are made about the role of the private sector for instance. '... contracts should be signed with the private sector for non-emergency surgery where they offer good value. The private sector's spare capacity should also be used to ease winter pressures. Some NHS hospitals might also be run by private contractors on a trial basis.' These are normative statements because they represent the value judgments of the writer.

The leader writer continues with another normative statement. 'But however successful such reforms maybe, more money must be found.' Again, this is a value judgment because some would argue that money is not the solution to the problems of the NHS. Instead, higher quality health care could be provided if the NHS were run more efficiently. Alternatively, it could be argued, as the Conservatives do according to the leader writer, that more people should be encouraged to provide for themselves under the private system, relieving pressure for resources in the NHS.

The leader writer concludes that 'general taxation remains the fairest and most efficient way of funding the great bulk of health care.' This is a value judgment based on arguments presented in the article for and against using taxes to fund health care. He goes on to say that the UK general public support this because 'whichever way the (opinion) polls are cut, they show the public is willing to pay, and pay more if necessary'.

The GM Debate

In February 2000 Professor Ingo Potrykus, a Swiss scientist, announced that he had developed a new strain of rice called 'golden rice'. Named after its colour, it contains Vitamin A. Lack of Vitamin A in the diet kills an estimated 2 million children each year in the Third World and blinds many more. The development was funded by a charity, the Rockefeller Foundation, which will make it available free of charge to national research centres. Golden rice is a genetically modified (GM) grain. GM crops have been the subject of fierce controversy in recent years.

Following the announcement, two letters appeared in the *Financial Times* giving contrary views of the development.

'Golden' rice a desperate - and unnecessary - genetic fix

From Mr Hugh Warwick

Sir, Vitamin A deficiency is a very serious problem in the developing world. It is a consequence of poverty and unsustainable agricultural policies. However, the solution advocated by Michela Wrong in "Field of dreams" (February 25), to engineer rice genetically to contain Vitamin A, is an absurd concoction of biotech corporations' PR departments.

Already solutions to vitamin A deficiency have been tried and tested. These include simple measures to encourage people to grow vitamin A-rich plants alongside their paddy fields. But it is purely a lack of political will that fails to see them implemented adequately. And while these ideas fail to be utilised, $100m has been spent in the laboratories getting to the point where there is a slight possibility that in 10 years' time there might be "golden" rice in the fields.

This genetic fix is a desperate attempt by a sorely battered industry to gain some credibility. And while Tony Blair joins the ranks of the sceptics, the real issue at stake is far more serious. Yet again we are looking to an "end of pipe" solution to poverty and unsustainable agricultural practices.

Rather than sit back and hope that in 10 years the rice will turn golden, the time and money would be better spent alleviating the causes of such misery with a systematic restructuring of the global food market.

Hugh Warwick,
Acting Director,
The Genetics Forum,
94 White Lion Street,
London N1 9PF

Scientists worldwide convinced of biotechnology's potential

From Ms Barbara Rippel.

Sir, Michela Wrong's article "Field of dreams" points to some of the important research being carried out into biotechnology products that could have significant benefits for developing countries. It is because of those benefits that many scientists are strong supporters of this technology - not out of the naive belief that modern biotechnology is a "magic bullet" that will solve all the world's ills, but from the conviction that it can be an important tool in improving food security and living conditions around the world.

A recent declaration in support of biotechnology has now been signed by more than a thousand scientists worldwide - among them the Nobel Prize winners Norman Borlaug and James Watson.

It states that "recombinant DNA techniques constitute powerful and safe means for the modification of organisms and can contribute substantially in enhancing quality of life by improving agriculture, healthcare and the environment".

To realise the full potential of this technology, a critical public debate is needed that looks at the potential risks of the new, as well as the risks of technological stagnation, when faced with current and future problems in producing safe and sustainable food supplies.

Barbara Rippel,
Policy Analyst,
Consumer Alert
1001 Connecticut Avenue NW,
#1128, Washington, DC 20036, US

1. **Explain the difference between positive and normative statements. Give at least six examples from the letters to illustrate your answer.**

2. **Evaluate the case for and against the introduction of 'golden rice' into the Third World.**

Summary

1. A production function shows the relationship between output and different levels and combinations of factor inputs.
2. The short run is defined as that period of time when at least one factor of production cannot be varied. In the long run, all factors can be varied, but the state of technology remains constant. In the very long run, the state of technology may change.
3. If a firm increases its variable inputs in the short run, diminishing marginal returns and diminishing average returns will eventually set in.
4. Constant returns to scale, or economies and diseconomies of scale, may occur in the long run when all factors are changed in the same proportion.

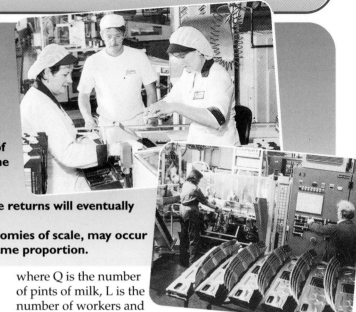

The production function

A farmer decides to grow wheat. In economic terms, wheat is then an output of the production process. To grow wheat, the farmer will have to use different factors of production (☞ unit 2).

- She will grow the wheat on land.
- It will be planted and harvested using labour.
- She will also use capital. If she is a Third World farmer, the capital may be some simple spades, hoes, irrigation ditches and sacks. If she is a First World farmer, she may use tractors, combine harvesters, fertilizers and pesticides.

The land, labour and capital used to produce wheat are the factor inputs to the production process.

A PRODUCTION FUNCTION shows the relationship between output and different levels and combinations of factor inputs. For example, if it needs 50 cows and 1 worker to produce 50 pints of milk a day, then the production function could be expressed as:

$$50Q = L + 50\,C$$

where Q is the number of pints of milk, L is the number of workers and C is the capital input, the number of cows.

A production function assumes that the state of technology is fixed or given. A change in the state of technology will change the production function. For instance, the microchip revolution has enabled goods (the outputs) to be produced with fewer workers and less capital (the inputs).

The short run and long run

Economists make a distinction between the short run and the long run. In the SHORT RUN, producers are faced with the problem that some of their factor inputs are fixed in supply. For instance, a factory might want to expand production. It can get its workers to work longer hours through overtime or shift work, and can also buy in more raw materials. Labour and raw materials are then variable inputs. But it only has a fixed amount of space on the factory floor and a fixed number of machines with which to work. This fixed capital places a constraint on how much more can be produced by the firm.

In the LONG RUN, all factor inputs are variable. A producer can vary the amount of land, labour and capital if it so chooses. In the long run, the firm in the above example could move into a larger factory and buy more machines, as well as employ more labour and use more raw materials.

In the long run, existing technologies do not change. In the VERY LONG RUN, the state of technology can change. For instance, a bank would be able to move from a paper-based system with cheques, bank statements and paper memos to a completely electronic paperless system with cards, computer terminal statements and memos.

The way that the short run and the long run are defined in the theory of production means that there is no standard length of time for the short run. In the chemical industry, a plant may last 20 years before it needs

Question 1

C W Cobb and P H Douglas, two American economists estimated, in an article published in 1938, that the production function for US manufacturing industry between 1900 and 1922 was:
$$x = 1.10\ L^{0.75}\ C^{0.25}$$
where x is an index of total production per year, L is an index of labour input and C an index of capital input.

Using a calculator with a power function, calculate the increase in the index of production if:
(a) the quantity of labour inputs were increased by
(i) 10% and (ii) 20%;
(b) the quantity of capital inputs were increased by
(i) 20% and (ii) 30%;
(c) the quantity of both labour and capital inputs were increased by (i) 30% and (ii) 50%.

replacing and so the short run might last 20 years. In an industry with little or no permanent physical capital, the short run may be measured in months or even weeks. The short run for a market trader, who hires everything from the stall to a van and keeps no stock, may be as short as one day, the day of the market when she is committed to hiring equipment and selling stock.

Question 2

In late December 1994, Pentos, the company which owned Dillons, the bookstore, and Ryman, the office stationery group, forced another of its subsidiary companies, Athena, into receivership. Athena sold prints, posters and cards. In the first half of 1994, it had made a loss of £5m on sales of £16.2m. Pentos argued that it would take between £9 million and £12 million to get Athena back into profit. It was simply unwilling to invest this amount of money into the business. Critics of Pentos argued that this was another example of the company making the wrong decision. The former owner of Dillons, Mr Terry Maher, who was removed from the Board in 1993, criticised the new management for understocking and understaffing the bookshops.

Explain carefully what would be the time scale (short run, long run or very long run) for:
(a) Athena ordering new stock;
(b) Dillons reducing staff and stock levels in their bookshops;
(c) Pentos closing down Athena;
(d) At some future date, Pentos possibly being forced to close Dillons because of competition from on-line booksellers.

The short run: diminishing returns

In the short run at least one factor is fixed. Assume for example that a firm uses only two factors of production - capital, in the form of buildings and machines, which is fixed and labour which can be varied. What will happen to output as more and more labour is used?

Initially, output per worker is likely to rise. A factory designed for 500 workers, for instance, is unlikely to be very productive if only one worker is employed. But there will come a point when output per worker will start to fall. There is an optimum level of production which is most productively efficient (☞ unit 16). Eventually, if enough workers are employed, total output will fall. Imagine 10 000 workers trying to work in a factory designed for 500. The workers will get in each other's way and result in less output than with a smaller number of workers. This general pattern is known as the LAW OF DIMINISHING RETURNS or the LAW OF VARIABLE PROPORTIONS.

Question 3

You wish to employ cleaners to clean your house. They will use your own cleaning equipment (brooms, mops, dusters, polish etc.). Using the law of diminishing returns, explain what would happen if you employed 1 cleaner, 5 cleaners, 20 cleaners or 1 000 cleaners to clean at one time.

Total, average and marginal products

The law of diminishing returns can be explained more formally using the concepts of total, average and marginal products.
- TOTAL PRODUCT is the quantity of output produced by a given number of inputs over a period of time. It is expressed in physical terms and not money terms. (Indeed, economists often refer to total physical product, average physical product and marginal physical product to emphasise this point.) The total product of 1 000 workers in the car industry over a year might be 30 000 cars.
- AVERAGE PRODUCT is the quantity of output per unit of input. In the above example, output per worker would be 30 cars per year (the total product divided by the quantity of inputs).
- MARGINAL PRODUCT is the addition to output produced by an extra unit of input. If the addition of an extra car worker raised output to 30 004 cars in our example, then the marginal product would be 4 cars.

Now consider Table 46.1. In this example capital is fixed at 10 units whilst labour is a variable input.
- If no workers are employed, total output will be zero.
- The first worker produces 20 units of output. So the marginal product of the first worker is 20 units.
- The second worker produces an extra 34 units of output. So the marginal product of the second worker is 34 units. Total output with two workers is 54 units (20 units plus 34 units). Average output is 54 ÷ 2 or 27 units per worker.
- The third worker produces an extra 46 units of output. So total output with three workers is 100 units (20 plus 34 plus 46). Average output is 100÷3 or approximately 33 units per worker.

Table 46.1 *Total, average and marginal products*

Units

Capital	Labour	Physical product as labour is varied		
		Marginal	Total	Average[1]
10	0		0	0
		20		
10	1		20	20
		34		
10	2		54	27
		46		
10	3		100	33
		51		
10	4		151	38
		46		
10	5		197	39
		33		
10	6		230	38
		20		
10	7		251	36
		-17		
10	8		234	29

1. Rounded to the nearest whole number.

Initially, marginal product rises, but the fifth worker produces less than the fourth. **Diminishing marginal returns** therefore set in between the fourth and fifth worker. Average product rises too at first and then falls, but the turning point is later than for marginal product. **Diminishing average returns** set in between 5 and 6 workers.

The law of diminishing returns states that if increasing quantities of a variable input are combined with a fixed input, eventually the marginal product and then the average product of that variable input will decline.

It is possible to draw total, average and marginal product curves. The curves in Figure 46.1 are derived from the data in Table 46.1. All three curves first rise and then fall. Marginal product falls first, then average product and finally total product.

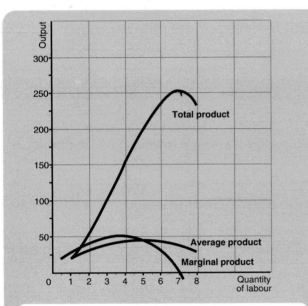

Figure 46.1 *Total, average and marginal product*
The curves are derived from the data in Table 38.1. Note that diminishing marginal returns set in before diminishing average returns. Note too that the marginal product curve cuts the average product curve at its highest point, whilst the total product curve falls when the marginal product curve cuts the horizontal axis.

The long run: returns to scale

The law of diminishing returns assumes that firms operate in the short run. In the long run, firms can vary all their factor inputs. What would happen to the output of a firm if, for instance, it were to increase all its inputs by the same proportion? There are only three possibilities.

- INCREASING RETURNS TO SCALE occur if an equal percentage increase in inputs to production leads to a more than proportional increase in output. If a firm doubles its land, labour and capital inputs, but as a consequence trebles its output, then increasing returns to scale have occurred. For instance, if as in Table 46.3, 1 unit of capital and 1 unit of all other factors of production are used, then 20 units of output are produced. Doubling the inputs to 2 units of capital and 2 units of all other factors more than doubles output to 50 units. An increase in inputs by 50 per cent from 2 to 3 units of all factors increases output by more than 50 per cent from 50 units to 80 units. Therefore the firm is operating under conditions of increasing returns to scale.

Question 4

Table 46.2

		Units
Capital	Labour	Total product
10	1	8
10	2	24
10	3	42
10	4	60
10	5	70
10	6	72

Table 46.2 shows the change in total product as the quantity of labour increases and all other factor inputs remain constant.
(a) Calculate the average and marginal product at each level of labour input.
(b) Draw the total, average and marginal product curves on a graph.
(c) At what level of output do (i) diminishing marginal returns and (ii) diminishing average returns set in?

- CONSTANT RETURNS TO SCALE occur if an equal percentage increase in inputs to production leads to the same percentage increase in output. For example, if a firm doubles its inputs and this leads to a doubling of output, then constant returns to scale occur.
- DECREASING RETURNS TO SCALE occur if an equal percentage increase in inputs to production leads to a less than proportional increase in output. So decreasing returns to scale occur if a firm trebles its inputs but only doubles its output.

Table 46.3 *Increasing returns to scale*

		Units of capital		
		1	2	3
Units of all other factors of production	1	**20**	35	45
	2	30	**50**	65
	3	35	63	**80**

Question 5

Table 46.4

		Units of labour				
		1	2	3	4	5
Units of all other factors of production	1	1	2	4	5	6
	2	2	3	6	8	10
	3	3	5	9	11	12
	4	5	7	10	12	13
	5	7	9	11	13	14

The table shows the output of a firm given different levels of factor inputs over the long run. Over what range does the firm experience:
(a) increasing returns;
(b) constant returns;
(c) decreasing returns to scale?

key terms

Average product - the quantity of output per unit of factor input. It is the total product divided by the level of output.

Law of diminishing returns or variable proportions - if increasing quantities of a variable input are combined with a fixed input, eventually the marginal product and then the average product of that variable input will decline. Diminishing returns are said to exist when this decline occurs.

Long run - the period of time when all factor inputs can be varied, but the state of technology remains constant.

Marginal product - the addition to output produced by an extra unit of input. It is the change in total output divided by the change in the level of inputs.

Production function - the relationship between output and different levels and combinations of inputs.

Returns to scale - the change in percentage output resulting from a percentage change in all the factors of production. There are increasing returns to scale if the percentage increase in output is greater than the percentage increase in factors employed, constant returns to scale if it is the same and decreasing returns to scale if it is less.

Short run - the period of time when at least one factor input to the production process can be varied.

Total product - the quantity of output measured in physical units produced by a given number of inputs over a period of time.

Very long run - the period of time when the state of technology may change.

Applied economics

Increasing returns at petrol stations

The production function

Petrol stations provide a service to their customers. They buy in fuel and other merchandise in large quantities, store it and then sell it in smaller quantities to customers when they want to make their purchases. Other inputs apart from stock to this production process include the land on which the petrol station is built, capital in the form of buildings and equipment, and labour.

Changing product mix

Petrol stations tended originally to be attached to garages which repaired and perhaps also sold cars. Garages aimed to provide a complete service to the motorist. Increasingly, however, petrol stations were built without the provision of other garage services. This enabled them to benefit from specialisation.

By the 1970s, petrol stations started to undergo another change. New petrol stations began to be built by the supermarket chains. They were able to undercut existing petrol station prices by selling large volumes of petrol and by buying at lowest prices on the world oil markets. While there were few supermarket petrol stations in a region, this posed little threat to traditional suppliers. By the late 1980s, however, supermarket petrol stations could be found in most localities. Traditional petrol stations started to close under the fierce price competition.

In 1996, Esso decided to stem the tide of falling sales at its petrol stations by committing itself to matching the cheapest petrol price in a local area. This usually meant matching the local supermarket price. Other major petrol companies followed suit. Profit margins at traditional petrol stations fell as a result. Many independent petrol retailers closed down. Companies like Esso could only make a profit at the new prices by increasing throughputs at their stations.

Increasing returns

Petrol stations rarely operate at maximum capacity. Most could supply petrol to more customers without having to increase the size of their site or install new pumps. So more petrol sales could be achieved by combining existing capital with more petrol.

Petrol companies have also realised for many years that other goods could be sold from petrol stations. Typically, this started off with confectionery and a few motor products like oil. However, they have increasingly turned petrol station kiosks into mini convenience stores. By combining groceries, snack foods, motor products and newspapers, they have again been able to achieve increasing returns to scale, selling more products without increasing their stock of fixed capital.

DATA QUESTION

Overfishing

In the early 1950s, the world fish catch was a little over 20 million tonnes. By 1989 it had risen to 100 million tonnes. But already there were warning signals coming from different fisheries around the world that overfishing was destroying the industry. From Newfoundland to the Mediterranean to the North Sea, fish stocks were reaching critical levels. Fishing stocks were declining. Off Newfoundland, the fishing industry destroyed the fish stock in the 1980s. In Europe, the EU and member governments were forced to introduce a quota scheme to restrict fish catches, much to the anger of the fishing industry which had been expanding dramatically. The problem is that fish stocks are not infinite. If the fish population is not kept at a critical level, fish stocks will decline over time and eventually will completely collapse.

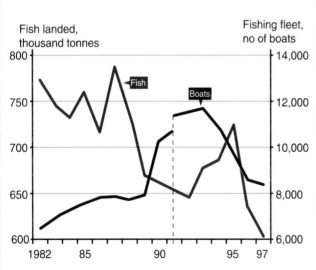

Figure 46.2 *British fishing (fish landed and number of boats[1])*
1. England, Wales and Scotland before 1991, UK after 1991.

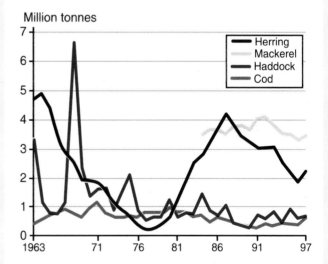

Figure 46.3 *North Sea fishing stocks*
Source: adapted from *Social Trends*, Office for National Statistics.

1. Outline the problem of overfishing.
2. Giving examples from the data, explain why fishing was subject to diminishing returns in the 1980s and 1990s.
3. Three possible solutions to the problem of overfishing include tightening existing quotas on fish catches, reducing the number of boats licensed to fish and increasing taxes on fish sales. Discuss these solutions, evaluating whether they would help solve the problem and who might benefit and lose out from their implementation.

Summary

1. Economists use the word 'cost' of production in a way different to its general usage. Economic cost is the opportunity cost of production.
2. Many costs are imputed - that is they form part of the cost of production but the producer does not directly pay for them.
3. Fixed costs (or indirect or overhead costs) are costs of production which do not vary directly with the level of output. Variable costs (or direct costs) are costs which increase as the level of output increases.
4. Economists distinguish between the total, average and marginal costs of production.
5. Total, average and marginal revenues can be distinguished too.
6. Economic or abnormal profit is the difference between total revenue and total cost. Normal profit is an economic (i.e. opportunity) cost of production.

The economic definition of cost

Economists use the word 'cost' in a very specific sense. The ECONOMIC COST of production for a firm is the opportunity cost of production. It is the value that could have been generated had the resources been employed in their next best use.

For instance, a market trader has some very obvious costs, such as the cost of buying stock to sell, the rent for her pitch in the market and the petrol to get her to and from the market. Money will be paid for these and this will be an accurate reflection of opportunity cost. But there are a number of costs which are hidden. Resources which have an opportunity cost but for which no payment is made must have an IMPUTED COST. There are a number of examples that can be used to illustrate imputed cost.

Labour A market trader working on her own account may calculate that she has made £50 'profit' on a day's trading. But this may not include the value of her own time. If she could have earned £40 working in another job for the day, then her economic profit is only £10. Hence, the opportunity cost of her labour must be included as an economic cost of production.

Financial capital A small businessman may start a company with his own money investing, say, £50 000. The economic cost of production must include the opportunity cost of that start-up capital. If he could have earned 10 per cent per annum in an alternative investment, then the economic cost (the opportunity cost) is £5 000 per year.

Depreciation The **physical capital** of a company will deteriorate over time. Machines wear out, buildings need repairs, etc. Moreover, some capital will become obsolete before the end of its physical life. The economic cost of depreciation is the difference between the purchase price and the second hand value of a good. A car, for instance, which lasts for 8 years does not depreciate at $12\frac{1}{2}$ per cent each year. In the first year, cars depreciate on average by 40 per cent. So a company paying £10 000 for a new car which depreciates by 40 per cent over its first year only has an asset worth £6 000 at the end of the year. £6 000 is the monetary value of the opportunity cost of keeping the car rather than selling it at the end of that year.

Goodwill A firm trading over a number of years may acquire a good reputation. It may produce branded goods which become household names. The goodwill of these brands has an opportunity cost. They could be sold to a rival company. Therefore the interest foregone on the potential sale value of these must be included as an economic cost. For instance, Nestlé bought Rowntree Mackintosh in 1988 for £2.3 billion. It paid £1.9 billion over and above the value of buildings, machinery, etc. This was effectively a payment for the brand names of Rowntree Mackintosh products such as KitKat, Smarties, Polo and After Eight as well as the relationships which the company had with its suppliers and customers. The opportunity cost of this sum (e.g. the interest that could have been received had the money been lent) should have been included as an economic cost for Rowntree Mackintosh.

It can be seen from this discussion that economists differ in their use of the word 'cost' from accountants, tax inspectors, businesses and others. Accountants have developed specific conventions about what is and what is not a cost and what should and should not be included on a balance sheet and an accountant's balance sheet may be very different from that of an economist.

Question 1

A business person runs her own business. Over the past twelve months, she has paid £12 000 for materials and £6 000 in wages to a worker whom she employs. She runs the business from premises which her parents own. These premises could be rented out for £4 000 a year if she were not occupying them. She has £20 000 worth of her own capital tied up in the business. She is a trained teacher and at present works exactly half of her time in a school earning £10 000. She could work full time as a teacher (earning £20 000) if she didn't run the business. The current rate of interest is 10 per cent. The total revenue of her business over the past 12 months was £36 000.

(a) On the basis of these figures, what were her accounting costs and what were her economic costs? Did she make a profit last year?

Fixed and variable costs

Economists distinguish between two types of cost: fixed and variable cost.

A FIXED COST (also called an INDIRECT or OVERHEAD COST) is a cost which does not vary directly with output. As production levels change, the value of a fixed cost will remain constant. For instance, a company may rent premises. The rent on the premises will remain the same whether the company produces nothing or produces at full capacity. If a firm pays for an advertising campaign, the cost will be the same whether sales remain constant or increase. Costs commonly given as examples of fixed costs are capital goods (e.g. factories, offices, plant and machinery), rent and rates, office staff and advertising and promotion.

A VARIABLE (or DIRECT or PRIME) COST is a cost which varies directly with output. As production increases, so does variable cost. For instance, a steel maker will use iron ore. The more steel produced, the more iron ore will be needed, so the cost of iron ore is a variable cost. Raw materials for production are the clearest example of variable costs for most firms. It is not always easy to categorise a cost as either fixed or variable. Many costs are SEMI-VARIABLE COSTS. Labour is a good example. Some firms employ a permanent staff, which could be classified as a fixed cost. They might ask the permanent staff to do overtime when necessary, or employ temporary labour. These costs would be classified as variable. But permanent staff could be seen as a variable cost if a firm were willing to hire and fire staff as its output changed. In practice, firms do adjust staff numbers with output, but the adjustment is sluggish and therefore the cost of labour is neither variable nor fixed - it is semi-variable.

In the **short run** (☞ unit 46), at least one factor input of production cannot be changed. So in the short run, some costs are fixed costs whilst others will be variable. In the long run, all factor inputs can vary. So in the long run, all costs will be variable costs.

Question 2

Rachel Hughes owns a whole food vegetarian restaurant. Explain which of the following costs would be most likely to be fixed costs, variable costs or semi-variable costs for her business: rice; rent; wages of casual staff; interest payments on a loan; electricity; cooking oil; pots and pans; her own wage; VAT.

Total, average and marginal cost

It is important to distinguish between the total, average and marginal costs of production. The TOTAL COST (TC) of production is the cost of producing a given level of output. For instance, if a manufacturer produces 100 units a week and its weekly costs come to £1 million, then £1 million is the total cost of production. Increased production will almost certainly lead to a rise in total costs. If the manufacturer increased output to 200 units a week, it would need to buy more raw materials, increase the number of workers, and generally increase its factor inputs.

Table 47.1 *Total costs of production*

(1) Output (per week)	(2) Total variable cost (£)	(3) Total fixed cost (£)	(4) Total cost (columns 2+3) (£)
0	0	200	200
1	200	200	400
2	300	200	500
3	600	200	800
4	1200	200	1400
5	2000	200	2200

This is illustrated in Table 47.1. At an output level of 1 unit per week, the total cost of production is £400. If output were 2 units per week, total costs would rise to £500.

The total cost of production is made up of two components:

- TOTAL VARIABLE COST (TVC) which varies with output;
- TOTAL FIXED COST (TFC) which remains constant whatever the level of output.

So in Table 47.1, total variable cost increases from zero to £2 000 as output increases from zero to 5 units per week, whilst total fixed costs remain constant at £200 whatever the level of output. Total variable costs when added to total fixed costs are equal to total cost. Mathematically:

$$TVC + TFC = TC$$

The AVERAGE COST OF PRODUCTION is the total cost divided by the level of output. For instance, if a firm makes 100 items at a total cost of £1 000, then the average cost per item would be £10. If a firm made 15 items at a cost of £30, then the average cost of production would be £2. Mathematically:

$$AC = \frac{TC}{Q}$$

where AC is average cost, TC is total cost and Q is quantity or the level of output.

Average cost, like total cost, is made up of two components.

- AVERAGE VARIABLE COST (AVC) is total variable cost divided by the level of output.
- AVERAGE FIXED COST (AFC) is total fixed cost divided by the level of output.

The average costs of production for the example given in Table 47.1 are given in Table 47.2.

MARGINAL COST is the cost of producing an extra unit of output. For instance, if it costs £100 to produce 10 items and £105 to produce 11 items, then the marginal cost of the eleventh item is £5. If it costs £4 to produce 2 items but £10 to produce 3 items, then the marginal cost of the third unit is £6. Mathematically, marginal cost (MC) is calculated by dividing the change in total cost (ΔTC) by the change in total output (ΔQ).

$$MC = \frac{\Delta TC}{\Delta Q}$$

The marginal costs of production for the figures in Tables 47.1 and 47.2 are given in Table 47.3.

Table 47.2 *Average costs of production[1]*

(1)	(2)	(3)	(4)
Output (per week)	Average variable cost (£)	Average fixed cost (£)	Average total cost (columns 2+3) (£)
1	200	200	400
2	150	100	250
3	200	67	267
4	300	50	350
5	400	40	440

1. Rounded to the nearest pound.

Table 47.3 *Marginal costs of production*

(1)	(2)	(3)
Output (per week)	Total cost (£)	Marginal cost per unit of output (£)
1	400	400
2	500	100
3	800	300
4	1400	600
5	2200	800

Question 3

Table 47.4

£

Output	Total fixed cost	Total variable cost	Total cost	Average fixed cost	Average variable cost	Average cost	Marginal cost
0	40						
1		6					
2		11					
3		15					
4			60				
5			66				

(a) Complete Table 47.4, calculating the missing figures.

Total, average and marginal revenues

A firm's revenues are its receipts of money from the sale of goods and services over a time period such as a week or a year. The relationships between total, average and marginal revenue are the same as between total, average and marginal cost.

- TOTAL REVENUE (TR) is the total amount of money received from the sale of any given level of output. It is the total quantity sold times the average price received.
- AVERAGE REVENUE (AR) is the average receipt per unit sold. It can be calculated by dividing total revenue by the quantity sold. If all output is sold at the same price, then average revenue must equal the price of the product sold.
- MARGINAL REVENUE (MR) is the receipts from selling an extra unit of output. It is the difference between total revenue at different levels of output. Mathematically:

$$MR = TR_n - TR_{n-1}$$

where n and n-1 are the last and last but one goods sold respectively. For instance, if a firm sold 9 units for a total of £200 and 10 units for £220, then the marginal revenue from the tenth unit sold would be £20.

Question 4

Table 47.5

Sales (million units)	Average revenue (£)	Marginal revenue (£)
1	20	
2	18	
3	16	
4	14	
5	12	
6	10	
7	8	
8	6	
9	4	
10	2	

Calculate (a) total revenue and (b) marginal revenue at each level of sales from 1 million to 10 million.

Profit

The **profit** of a company can be calculated by taking away its total cost from its total revenue:

$$\text{Profit} = TR - TC$$

It can also be calculated by finding the average profit per unit, which is average revenue minus average cost, and multiplying that by the quantity sold.

It should be remembered that cost for an economist is different from that for an accountant or business person. As explained above, the economic cost of production is its **opportunity cost**. It is measured by the benefit that could have been gained if the resources employed in the production process had been used in their next most profitable use. If a firm could have made £1 million profit by using its resources in the next best manner, then the £1 million profit is an opportunity cost for the firm. In economics this profit, which is counted as an economic cost, is called **normal profit** (☞ unit 17).

If the firm failed to earn normal profit, it would cease to produce in the long run. The firm's resources would be put to better use producing other goods and services where a normal profit could be earned. Hence, normal profit must be earned if factors of production are to be kept in their present use.

Economic profit (also called **pure profit**, or **abnormal profit** or **supernormal profit**) is the profit over and above normal profit (i.e. the profit over and above the opportunity cost of the resources used in production by the firm). It is important to remember that the firm earns normal profit when total revenue equals total cost. But total revenue must be greater than total cost if it is to earn abnormal profit.

Question 5

A business person leaves her £70 000 a year job to set up a company from which she draws a salary of £30 000 in its first year, £50 000 in its second year and £70 000 in its third year. She puts £50 000 of her own savings into the company as start up capital which previously had been invested and could earn a rate of return of 10 per cent per annum. Accountants declare that the costs of the firm over the first twelve months were £250 000, £280 000 in the next twelve months and £350 000 in the third year. Revenues were £270 000 in the first year, £310 000 in the second year and £450 000 in the third year.

For each year, calculate the firm's:
(a) accounting profit;
(b) economic profit;
(c) normal profit.

Applied economics

Nissan

During the 1990s, Nissan, the Japanese car manufacturer, found itself increasingly in financial difficulties. As Figures 47.1 and 47.2 show, it made a loss in six out of ten years of operation whilst its global market share fell. Part of its troubles lay with the state of the Japanese economy. Japan experienced a prolonged recession for most of the 1990s which led to stagnant and even falling demand for consumer goods, including cars. Problems in Asia in the late 1990s which saw severe downturns in some of Nissan's overseas markets also didn't help sales revenues.

In 1998, Renault, the French car group, entered an alliance with Nissan, buying 36.8 per cent of Nissan shares. It dispatched Carlos Ghosn, a Brazilian who had transformed Renault's finances, to become chief operating officer at Nissan. In October 1999, he announced a £6 billion package to reduce costs, spread over three years as shown in Figure 47.3. Most of the cost cutting was to come from Japan, rather than Nissan's relatively more efficient overseas operations.

Fixed costs were to be cut. Five factories in Japan were to be closed between 2001 and 2002. Existing factories would be worked more intensively by increasing the number of hours worked per year from 3 600 hours to 4 400 hours. Introducing extra shifts at factories was part of a strategy of increasing the use of capacity at Nissan's plants from 53 per cent to 82 per cent over three years. This would reduce average fixed costs. The number of workers at Nissan was to be cut too in every department from manufacturing to sales. 21 000 workers out of a workforce of 148 000 would go. In Japan, it is difficult to shed labour because of strict labour laws and powerful

trade unions and hence labour is arguably a fixed cost rather than a semi-variable or variable cost.

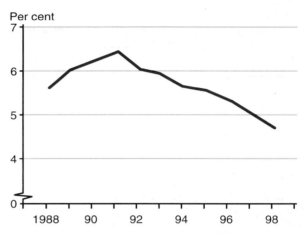

Figure 47.1 *Nissan, global market share*
Source: adapted from company information, Primark Datastream.

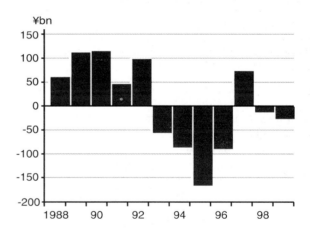

Figure 47.2 *Nissan, net profit/loss*
Source: adapted from company information, Primark Datastream.

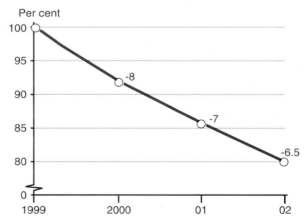

Figure 47.3 *Nissan, proposed cost reduction*
Source: adapted from company information, Primark Datastream.

Variable costs would be cut too. Suppliers would be expected to cut their prices for components by 20 per cent over three years. Many suppliers would be unable to achieve this, leaving only the most efficient in Nissan's supply chain. As a result, the number of suppliers was expected to halve from 1 145 to 600, in itself reducing overhead costs because Nissan would have to deal with fewer suppliers.

Components would be streamlined. For instance, its current 24 platform car portfolio would be reduced to 15 platforms within three years. A car platform is basically the chassis on which the car is built. Reducing the number of platforms means that more cars are built on the remaining chassis models. Their production

therefore goes up, allowing the company to exert greater buying pressure and reduce the complexity of production. The move into profit would reduce Nissan's borrowing and interest payments on its debts.

Cost cutting was essential for Nissan to survive, but its future remained uncertain. Whilst it aimed to cut costs between 1999 and 2002, so too did other major car manufacturers, putting competitive pressure on Nissan. The company also needed to consider its revenues. However much it cut costs, profits would only be made if Nissan had attractive models for sale.

Source: adapted from the *Financial Times*, 19.10.1999.

A music business

David and Clare Howells run the Belsize Music Rooms. Opened in 1996, it is a set of three rooms in North London available for rent by the hour. David Howells has long been a professional pianist who was earning about £20 000 a year when the rooms opened from a mixture of teaching and performing. The teaching was done in his North London flat, but he felt that this was unsatisfactory.

The solution to the problem came when his wife spotted a 19th century town house nearby for rent. It had been used by a firm of music publishers. The Howells immediately saw the potential to create three large music practice rooms, with a flat for themselves on the top floor. The building was ideal because of its thick walls which gave good sound proofing and excellent acoustics, as well as large windows which gave plenty of light.

The landlords agreed to a 15 year lease with an option to purchase at a fixed price at five-year intervals. It cost £70 000 to convert the building and they spent a further £60 000 on equipment, the largest items being pianos.

Advertising was essential. Initially, they assumed that local people would be the principle users of the rooms, but they were sorely disappointed. In the first week, their

takings were £8. So they devised a marketing campaign which included advertising in the national Classical Music magazine. They wrote to 1 200 musicians and 110 concert agents and more than 200 music associations, ensembles, orchestras, choirs and opera groups. They set up a web site too. This all paid quick dividends and soon the rooms were being hired by a variety of professional groups including Opera North, the European Union Youth Orchestra and the London Philharmonic. At the end of the first year of operation, David Howells thought that Belsize Music Rooms had become London's leading audition rooms. Weekly income now ranged from £300 a week to £1 300.

By the end of the second year, income had doubled and the business was breaking even with accounting costs equalling revenues. David was still teaching and performing, but the publicity associated with the rooms had increased the number of his pupils, so his teaching income had increased. He hoped that in his third year of operation, the business would generate enough income to pay him a salary.

Source: adapted from the *Financial Times*, 20.9.1998.

1. **Explain, giving examples, the different types of costs faced by the business.**
2. **(a) Using a diagram, explain what has happened to total revenue in the first two years of operation.**
   (b) How could David and Clare Howells increase
   average revenue in the future?
3. **Discuss whether David and Clare Howells were making an economic profit or loss at the end of the second year of operation.**

Summary

1. The short run average cost is U-shaped because of the law of diminishing marginal returns.
2. Diminishing average returns set in when average variable cost begins to increase.
3. Diminishing marginal returns set in when marginal cost begins to increase.
4. If factor input prices are constant, the average and marginal product curves are the mirror image of short run average and marginal cost curves.
5. The marginal cost curve cuts the average variable cost and average cost curves at their lowest point.

Diminishing returns

It was explained in unit 46 that in the short run a firm was faced with employing at least one factor input which could not be varied. For instance, it might have a given number of machines or a fixed quantity of office space. If it were to increase output by using more of the variable factor inputs, diminishing marginal returns and then diminishing average returns would set in eventually.

Diminishing returns are a technical concept. Therefore, they were expressed in terms of physical inputs and physical product (the output of the firm). But it is possible to express physical inputs in terms of costs. For example, a firm which employed 5 workers at a wage of £200 per week, and had no other costs, would have total weekly costs of £1 000. If each worker produced 200 units of output, then the average cost per unit of output would be £1 [£1 000 ÷ (5 x 200)]. The marginal cost of the 200 units produced by the fifth worker would be her wage (£200), and so the marginal cost per unit of output would be £1 (£200 ÷ 200).

Short run cost schedules

Having looked at inputs, it is now possible to see how the law of diminishing returns affects short run costs. Table 48.1 is an example of how this can be done. It is assumed that the firm can employ up to 8 workers at identical wage rates (i.e. the supply of workers over the range 1 to 8 is **perfectly elastic**). The price of capital per unit is £100 and the price of labour is £200 per unit.

Capital is the fixed factor of production. Therefore whatever the level of production, total fixed cost will be £1 000 (10 units x £100). Total variable cost will increase as more and more labour is added. So the total variable cost of producing 20 units is £200 (1 unit of labour x £200), of 54 units it is £400 (2 units of labour x £200), and so on.

Total cost is total fixed cost plus total variable cost. Once the three measures of total cost have been worked out, it is possible to calculate average and marginal costs (☞ unit 47). Alternatively, it is possible to calculate marginal cost per unit by finding the cost of the additional

Table 48.1

| | | Units | | | | | | | £ |
| Capital | Labour | Total physical product (output) | Total cost[1] | | | Average cost[2] | | | Marginal cost |
			TVC	TFC	TC	AVC	AFC	ATC	MC
10	0	0	0	1000	1000	0	-	-	
									10.0
10	1	20	200	1000	1200	10	50	60	
									5.9
10	2	54	400	1000	1400	7.4	18.5	25.9	
									4.3
10	3	100	600	1000	1600	6.0	10.0	16.0	
									3.9
10	4	151	800	1000	1800	5.3	6.6	11.9	
									4.3
10	5	197	1000	1000	2000	5.1	5.1	10.2	
									6.1
10	6	230	1200	1000	2200	5.2	4.3	9.6	
									9.5
10	7	251	1400	1000	2400	5.6	4.0	9.6	
									22.2
10	8	260	1600	1000	2600	6.8	3.8	10.0	

1. Assuming that capital costs £100 per unit and labour costs £200 per unit.
2. The three measures of average cost have been calculated to the nearest decimal from total figures. ATC therefore does not always equal AVC+AFC because of rounding.

labour and dividing it by the marginal physical product. In our example, the cost of hiring an extra worker is a constant £200. So the marginal cost of producing, say, an extra 34 units once 20 have been made is £200 (the cost of the second worker). The marginal cost per unit is then £200 ÷ 34. Average variable cost can be calculated in a similar manner.

Question 1

Table 48.2

	Units
Labour	Total physical product
1	20
2	45
3	60
4	70

Table 48.2 shows how total physical product changes as the number of units of labour changes with a fixed quantity of capital. The cost of the capital employed is £200. The firm can employ any number of workers at a constant wage rate per unit of labour of £50. What is the value of the following if: (a) 1 unit of labour (b) 2 units of labour; (c) 3 units of labour; (d) 4 units of labour are employed?
(i) Total fixed costs (ii) Total variable costs (iii) Total costs (iv) Average fixed costs (v) Average variable costs (vi) Total average cost (vii) Marginal cost.

Short run cost curves

The cost schedules in Table 48.1 can be plotted on a graph (Figure 48.1) to produce cost curves.

Total cost curves The total fixed cost (TFC) curve is a horizontal straight line, showing that TFC is constant whatever the level of output. The total cost (TC) and total variable cost (TVC) curves are parallel because the vertical distance between the two (the difference between TC and TVC) is the constant total fixed cost. The inflections in the TC and TVC curves are caused by the change from increasing returns to diminishing returns.

Average cost curves The average fixed cost (AFC) curve falls as output increases because fixed costs represent an ever decreasing proportion of total cost as output increases. The average cost (AC) curve and average variable cost (AVC) curve fall at first and then rise. They rise because diminishing average returns set in. The vertical distance between the AC and AVC curves is the value of average fixed cost. This must be true because average cost minus average variable cost is equal to average fixed cost.

Marginal cost curve The marginal cost (MC) curve at first falls and then rises as diminishing marginal returns set in.

Points to note

U-shaped AC and MC curves The MC and AC curves in Figure 48.1 are 'U-shaped'. This is a characteristic not just of the sample figures in Table 48.1, but of all short run MC and AC curves. They are U-shaped because of the law of diminishing returns. The lowest point on the MC and the AVC curves shows the point where diminishing marginal returns and diminishing average returns set in respectively.

Product and cost curves The marginal and average cost curves shown in Figure 48.1 are mirror images of the marginal and average product curves that could be drawn from the same data in Table 48.1. Marginal and average physical product rise when marginal and average cost fall, and vice versa. This is what should be expected. If marginal physical product is rising, then the extra cost of producing a unit of output must fall, and similarly with average physical product and average variable cost. For instance, when the second worker produces 34 units, the third worker 46 units and the fourth worker 51 units, the marginal cost of production must be falling because the increase in output is rising faster than the increase in cost. When marginal physical product is falling, the extra cost of producing a unit output must rise for the same reason. However, the cost and product curves will only be mirror images of each other if there are constant factor costs per unit. If, for instance, we assumed that the unit cost of labour rose as more workers were employed, so that the average wage of three workers was higher than the average wage of two, then the product and cost curves would not be mirror images.

MC curve cuts AC curve at its lowest point In Figure 48.1, the marginal cost curve cuts the average cost curve and average variable cost curve at their lowest points. To understand why this must be so, consider the example of a group of students whose average height is 6 feet. A new student (the marginal student) arrives in the group. If the student is above 6 feet then the average height of the group will now rise. If the student is less than 6 feet, the average height of the group will fall. If the student is exactly 6 feet herself, then the average height of the group will stay the same. Now apply this to average and marginal cost. If the average cost curve is falling, then the cost of an extra unit of output (the marginal cost) must be less than the average cost. If average cost is rising, it must be true that the cost of an extra unit of output is even higher than the average cost. When average cost is neither rising or falling, marginal cost must be the same as average cost. Hence we know that:
- the average cost curve is above the marginal cost curve when average cost is falling;
- the average cost curve is below the marginal cost curve when average cost is rising;
- average cost and marginal cost are equal for all levels of output when average cost is constant; if the average cost curve is U-shaped, this means that marginal cost will be equal to and will cut the average cost curve at its lowest point.

The same chain of reasoning applies to the relationship between the average variable cost curve and the marginal cost curve.

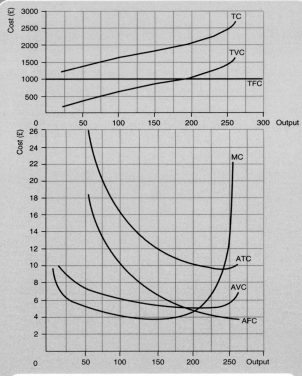

Figure 48.1 *The shape of short run cost curves*
The shape of the average and marginal cost curves is determined by the law of diminishing returns. The curves are drawn from the data in Table 48.1. Assuming constant factor prices, diminishing marginal returns set in at an output level of 145 when the marginal cost curve is at its lowest point. Diminishing average returns set in at the lowest point of the average variable cost curve at an output of 210 units.

Question 2

Table 48.3

		Units
Capital	Labour	Total product
10	0	0
10	1	8
10	2	24
10	3	42
10	4	60
10	5	70
10	6	72

Table 48.3 shows the change in total product as more labour is added to production and all other factor products remain constant. The price of capital is £1 per unit whilst labour is £2 per unit.

(a) Calculate the following over the range of output from zero to 72 units: (i) total fixed cost; (ii) total variable cost; (iii) total cost; (iv) average fixed cost; (v) average variable cost; (vi) average total cost; (vii) marginal cost.
(b) Plot each of these cost schedules on graph paper, putting the total cost curves on one graph and the average and marginal cost curves on another.
(c) Mark on the graph the point where (i) diminishing marginal returns and (ii) diminishing average returns set in.

Applied economics

Diminishing returns in agriculture

In agriculture, farmers combine land, labour and capital to produce their crops. Land could be said to be a fixed factor of production. Labour and capital, however, are variable. Therefore, in theory, farmers could face diminishing returns. Is there any evidence to suggest that this is the case?

Table 48.4 shows growth rates of total food production across the world by area during the period 1961 to 1992. The annual rate of growth of food production fell from 3.1 per cent in the 1960s to 1.9 per cent in the 1980s and early 1990s. This might suggest the existence of diminishing returns, but any such conclusion would, in fact, be very debatable for a number of reasons.
● Whilst regions have seen a fall in the annual rate of growth of production, some increased their rate of growth between decades. The socialist countries of

Asia, which includes China, had a higher growth rate of output in the 1980s and early 1990s than they did in the 1970s. The 1980s were also difficult times for agriculture in certain parts of the world due to drought. Sub-Saharan Africa was badly affected throughout the decade, whilst, for instance, the US drought of 1988 saw an overall 7 per cent fall in US food production in that year.
● The figures say nothing about factor inputs. The proportion of the world's labour force working in agriculture fell from 71 per cent in 1960 to 59 per cent in 1980 in the developing world, whilst in the developed world it fell from 28 per cent in 1960 to 12 per cent in 1980. This meant that the agricultural labour force increased in the Third World but decreased in the First World. In the First World, where diminishing returns should have been found

Table 48.4 *Annual average growth rate of food production*

	Total food production		
	1961-70	1970-80	1980-92
World	3.1	2.4	1.9
Developed market economies	2.3	2.0	0.6
of which			
US	2.2	2.3	0.8
Canada	2.4	2.4	0.9
UK	1.5	1.6	0.5
Developing countries	2.9	2.9	2.8
Eastern European countries	3.6	1.4	0.4
Socialist countries of Asia	5.4	3.3	4.2

Source: adapted from UNCTAD, *Handbook of International Trade and Development Statistics.*

to be greatest because land is being used most intensively, increases in output per worker throughout the period 1961-92 averaged 3 per cent per annum. Fewer workers produced more food.
● Both in the USA and in the EU, the 1980s and 1990s saw an attempt by government to restrict the growth of food output. Supply was far outstripping demand in domestic markets where farmers were receiving large subsidies. So the fall in the growth of output in these regions probably had far more to do with government policy than with the law of diminishing returns.

Why is there little clear evidence of diminishing returns in agriculture? Part of the reason must be that land itself is in one sense not a fixed factor of production. Although the total quantity of land is in fixed supply, its productive potential has a great deal to do with the quality of land. The productivity of land can be greatly improved, for instance through drainage, irrigation and the use of fertilizers. Many economists in the past, including Malthus, an early 19th century British economist, have predicted that agricultural production could not keep up with the growth in population. However, so far they have been proved wrong. The average world increase in food production per capita was 0.54 per cent per annum between 1961 and 1992, and in the developed world, the main problem in agriculture is not under-production but over-production.

Holiday cottages

1. **Identify the fixed and variable costs involved in running the Edwards' estate of 10 holiday cottages.**
2. **To what extent would the Edwardses suffer increasing or diminishing returns if: (a) they increased their advertising; (b) their occupancy rates went up from 65 per cent to 75 per cent?**
3. **(a) What might happen to costs if the Edwardses bought another 5 cottages, but didn't increase advertising, their own time spent working for the business or their drawings (their income taken) from the business?**
   (b) Suggest what the Edwardses should consider in making a decision about whether or not to buy an extra 5 cottages.

Jim and Mavis Edwards run a holiday accommodation business in the Lake District. Jim retired in 1985, earning a large golden handshake. He used the money to buy his first four cottages. Having found them immediately profitable, he bought up another six in quick succession, using all the cottages as collateral for mortgages on the new properties.

Jim and Mavis didn't take anything out of the business in its first four years. With hindsight, this was possibly the wisest decision they made. They were able to make large inroads into their mortgages in the first few years. By the time mortgage interest rates had climbed to astronomical levels in 1989, much of their debt was repaid and they were able to survive the recession of the early 1990s despite falls in occupancy rates.

Jim and Mavis aimed up market. They refurbished the properties to create the atmosphere and quality they themselves would want out of a holiday cottage. Fees were pitched slightly higher than others in local villages. 'You must charge a decent rental or you can't pay to keep it up. Then the place goes downhill and visitors don't return.' Today, they have a repeat booking rate of 65 per cent.

Initially, they hired all the help they needed locally, but changed that policy in 1989 because the standard was variable. Now they sub-contract the cleaning to a company in Barrow-in-Furness. 'It's worked very well. We now spend £6 500 per year on cleaning.'

All other labour continues to be local. The Edwards have built up a reliable army of builders and plumbers, who will come out at short notice at inconvenient times. This reliability matters in a remote rural area. 'If the plumbing fails in one cottage, it's important that clients see us dealing with a problem straight away.'

They advertise in a range of publications. However, they found that increasing their advertising budget substantially brought in few extra bookings. On the other hand, the year they cut back their advertising by 25 per cent saw a near disastrous 25 per cent fall in bookings. The most effective advertising they do is simply placing a stand outside their home with free leaflets which are taken by passing tourists. 'The cheapest publicity brings in the most enquiries.'

Summary

1. Economic theory suggests that the long run average cost curve is U-shaped.
2. Production is at an optimal level when average cost is lowest.
3. Sources of economies of scale are technical, managerial, purchasing, marketing and financial.
4. Diseconomies of scale may arise due to the inability of management to control large organisations.
5. External economies will shift the average cost curve downwards.
6. The long run average cost curve of a firm is an envelope for the firm's short run average cost curves.

Economies of scale and average cost

In the long run, all factors of production are variable. This has an effect on costs as output changes. To start with, long run costs fall as output increases. **Economies of scale** are then said to exist. For instance, a firm doubles its output from 10 million units to 40 million units. However, total costs of production only increase from £10 million to £20 million. The average cost of production consequently falls from £1 per unit (£10m ÷ 10m) to 50p per unit (£20m ÷ 40m).

Empirically (i.e. from studying real examples of the costs of firms), economists have found that firms do experience economies of scale. As firms expand in size and output, their long run average costs tend to fall. At some point, which varies from industry to industry, long run average costs become constant. However, some firms become too large and their average costs begin to rise. They are then said to experience DISECONOMIES OF SCALE. For instance, if a firm doubled its output, but as a result its costs were four times as high, then the average cost of production would double.

This pattern of falling and the rising long run average costs is shown in Figure 49.1. At output levels up to OA, the firm will enjoy falling long run average costs and therefore experience economies of scale. Between output levels of OA and OB, long run average costs are constant. To the right of OB, long run average costs rise and the firm faces diseconomies of scale.

LRAC in Figure 49.1 is drawn given a set of input prices for costs. If the cost of all raw materials in the economy rose by 20 per cent, then there would be a shift upward in the LRAC curve. Similarly, a fall in the wage rates in the industry would lead to a downward shift in the LRAC curve.

The optimum level of production

Productive efficiency is said to exist when production takes place at lowest cost. If the long run average cost curve is U-shaped, then this will occur at the bottom of the curve when constant returns to scale exist. The output range over which average costs are at a minimum is said to be the OPTIMAL LEVEL OF PRODUCTION. In Figure 49.1 the optimal level of production occurs over the range AB.

The output level at which lowest cost production starts

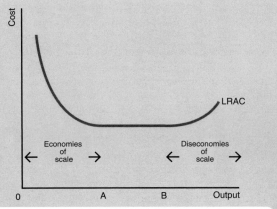

Figure 49.1 *Economies of scale.*
The long run average cost curve is U-shaped because long run average costs:
- *at first fall over the output range OA showing economies of scale;*
- *then are constant over the output range AB;*
- *then rise when output exceeds OB showing diseconomies of scale.*
Over the output range AB, the minimum cost level of production, the firm is said to be at its optimum level of production.

Question 1

Table 49.1

| Output (million units) | Long run average cost (£) | | | | |
	Firm A	Firm B	Firm C	Firm D	Firm E
1	10	20	16	19	20
2	8	18	14	18	17
3	5	16	15	17	15
4	5	11	17	16	14
5	5	10	20	15	14
6	5	10	24	14	14
7	6	11	30	13	14

For each firm, A to E, give:

(a) the range of output over which there are:
  (i) economies of scale; (ii) diseconomies of scale;
(b) the optimum level or range of output;
(c) the minimum efficient scale of production.

is called the MINIMUM EFFICIENT SCALE (MES) of production. In Figure 49.1, the MES is at point A. If a firm is producing to the left of the MES, then long run average costs will be higher. To the right, they will either be the same (if there are constant returns) or will be increasing (if there are diseconomies of scale).

Sources of economies of scale

Economies of scale occur for a number of reasons.

Technical economies Economies and diseconomies of scale can exist because of **increasing** and **decreasing** returns returns to scale (☞ unit 46). These economies and diseconomies are known as **technical economies**. They arise from what happens in the production process. For instance, many firms find that they need equipment but are unable to make maximum use of it. A small builder may use a cement mixer on average only 3 days a week. If he were able to take on more work he might be able to use it 5 days a week. The total cost of the cement mixer is the same whether used for 3 days or 5 days a week (apart from possible depreciation) but the average cost per job done will be lower the more it is used. This is an example of an **indivisibility**. The larger the level of output, the less likely that indivisibilities will occur.

Technical economies arise too because larger plant size is often more productively efficient. For instance, because an oil tanker is essentially a cylinder, doubling the surface area of the tanker (and therefore doubling the approximate cost of construction) of an oil tanker leads to an approximate three-fold increase in its carrying capacity. It is generally cheaper to generate electricity in large power stations than in small ones. The average cost of production of a car plant making 50 000 cars a year will be less than one making 5 000 cars a year.

So far, it has been assumed that unit costs are constant. However, unit costs may change as a firm changes in size. Other factors, apart from technical economies, can then lead to economies and diseconomies of scale.

Managerial economies Specialisation (☞ unit 2), is an important source of greater efficiency. In a small firm, the owner might be part time salesman, accountant, receptionist and manager. Employing specialist staff is likely to lead to greater efficiency and therefore lower costs. The reason why small firms don't employ specialist staff is because staff often represent an indivisibility.

Purchasing and marketing economies The larger the firm the more likely it is to be able to buy raw materials in bulk. Bulk buying often enables these firms to secure lower prices for their factor inputs. Large firms are also able to enjoy lower average costs from their marketing operations. The cost of a sales force selling 40 different lines of merchandise is very much the same as one selling 35 lines. A 30 second TV commercial for a product which has sales of £10 million per annum costs the same as a 30 second TV commercial for one which has sales of only £5 million per annum.

Financial economies Small firms often find it difficult and expensive to raise finance for new investment. When loans are given, small firms are charged at relatively high rates of interest because banks know that small firms are far more at risk from bankruptcy than large firms. Large firms have a much greater choice of finance and it is likely to be much cheaper than for small firms.

Question 2

Two pharmaceutical companies, Zeneca and Astra, announced in December 1998 that they would merge. Part of the justification for the merger was that the new company would enjoy lower average costs. The new management promised to cut costs by $1.1 billion, roughly 12 per cent of operating costs. Two thirds would be derived from overlaps in general administration including marketing, with some savings in basic technology and in the longer term from production costs.

Source: adapted from the *Financial Times*, 10.12.1998.

(a) Discuss what increased economies of scale the combined company might enjoy as a result of the merger of Zeneca and Astra.

Diseconomies of scale

Diseconomies of scale arise mainly due to management problems. As a firm grows in size it becomes more and more difficult for management to keep control of the activities of the organisation. There are a variety of ways of dealing with this problem. Some companies choose to centralise operations with a small, tightly-knit team controlling all activities. Sometimes a single charismatic figure, often the founder of the company, will keep tight control of all major decisions. In other companies, management is decentralised with many small subsidiary companies making decisions about their part of the business and head office only making those decisions which affect the whole group. However, controlling an organisation which might employ hundreds of thousands of workers is not easy and there may come a point where no management team could prevent average costs from rising.

Geography too may lead to higher average costs. If a firm has to transport goods (whether finished goods or raw materials) over long distances because it is so large, then average costs may rise. Head office may also find it far more difficult to control costs in an organisation 1 000 miles away than in one on its door step.

Movements along and shifts in the long run average cost curve

The long run average cost curve is a boundary. It represents the minimum level of average costs attainable at any given level of output. In Figure 49.2, points below the LRAC curve are unattainable. A firm could produce above the LRAC boundary, but if it were to do this it would not use the most efficient method to produce any given level of output. So a firm could, for instance, produce at the point A, but it would be less efficient than a firm producing the same quantity at the point B.

An increase in output which leads to a fall in costs would be shown by a **movement along** the LRAC curve. However, there are a variety of reasons why the LRAC might **shift**.

External economies of scale The economies of scale discussed so far in this unit have been INTERNAL ECONOMIES OF SCALE. Internal economies arise because of the growth in output of the firm. EXTERNAL ECONOMIES OF SCALE arise when there is a growth in the size of the industry in which the firm operates. For instance, the growth of a particular industry in an area might lead to the construction of a better local road network, which in turn reduces costs to individual firms. Or a firm might experience lower training costs because other firms are training workers which it can then poach. The local authority might provide training facilities free of charge geared to the needs of a particular industry. The government might assist with export contracts for a large industry but not a small industry. External economies of scale will shift the LRAC curve of an individual firm downwards. At any given level of output, its costs will be lower because the industry as a whole has grown.

Taxation If the government imposes a tax upon industry, costs will rise, shifting the LRAC curve of each firm upwards. For instance, if the government increased employers' National Insurance contributions, a tax upon the wage bill of a company, the total cost of labour would rise, pushing up average costs.

Technology The LRAC curve is drawn on the assumption that the state of technology remains constant. The

introduction of new technology which is more efficient than the old will reduce average costs and push the LRAC curve downwards.

External diseconomies of scale These will shift the long run average cost curve of individual firms in the industry upwards. They occur when an industry expands quickly. Individual firms are then forced to compete with each other and bid up the prices of factor inputs like wages and raw materials.

Question 3

Most locks manufactured in the UK are made by one of about 25 lockmakers grouped in Willenhall in the West Midlands. This manufacturing cluster goes back three centuries at least. One of the oldest companies still trading, Henry Squire & Son, was started in 1780. By 1855 there were roughly 500 lockmakers in the Willenhall area. 'One reason for the concentration of companies here is the large number of specialist component makers which are still in the region' according to John Squire, sales director of Henry Squire's. 'It's much more convenient to deal with people close by, rather than import the components from further away.' A huge number of different lock types are made in Willenhall. One local maker of lock keys produces up to 2 000 different key 'blanks' to suit this diversity. The diversity creates pressure on suppliers to be flexible and work to short production runs - factors in which proximity to the customer is important. Making lock components on this basis is a 'black art' where the skills are often passed between succeeding generations of the same family. Williams, whose other lock brands include Yale and Union, employs 1 200 making locks and related products in Willenhall. It says that all but a small proportion of its employees live close to the town, highlighting the importance of lock making in the local community.

Source: adapted from the *Financial Times*, 30.12.1998.

(a) Explain the possible sources of external economies of scale for the Willenhall lock manufacturing cluster.

The relationship between the short run average cost curve and the long run average cost curve

In the short run, at least one factor is fixed. Short run average costs at first fall, and then begin to rise because of diminishing returns. In the long run, all factors are variable. Long run average costs change because of economies and diseconomies of scale.

In the long run, a company is able to choose a scale of production which will maximise its profits. Assume in Figure 49.3 that it decides to produce in the long run at point A. It buys factors of production such as plant and machinery to operate at this level. Later it wishes to expand production by PQ but in the short run it has fixed factors of production. Expanding production may well lead to lower average costs as it does in Figure 49.3.

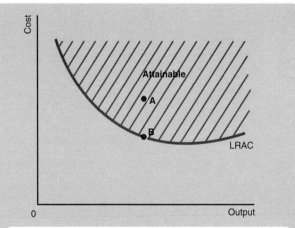

Figure 49.2 *The LRAC as a boundary*
The LRAC curve is a boundary between levels of costs which are attainable and those which are unattainable. If a firm is producing on the LRAC curve, then it is producing at long run minimum cost for any given level of output, such as at point B. If long run production is inefficient, cost will be within the LRAC boundary such as at point A.

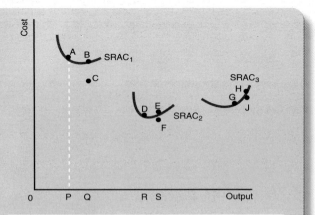

Figure 49.3 *The long run average cost curve*
In the long run, all factors are variable. Points A, D and G show long run cost levels at different levels of production. If the firm in the short run then expands production, average costs may fall or rise to B, E or H respectively. But they will be above the long run costs, C, F and J, for those levels of output because the cost of production with at least one fixed factor is likely to be higher than the cost if all factors were variable.

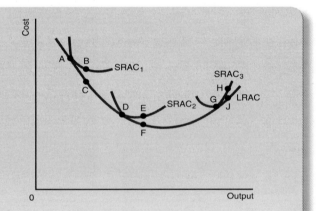

Figure 49.4 *The long run average cost curve envelope*
The long run average cost curve is an envelope for all the associated short run average cost curves because long run average cost is either equal to or below the relevant short run average cost.

Diminishing average returns have not set in at point A. But production must be less cost efficient at B compared to the long run situation where the firm could have varied all its factors of production and produced at C. At B the firm is working with plant and machinery designed to work at optimum efficiency at a lower output level OP. At C, the firm is working with plant and machinery designed to produce at C.

Similarly, if D and F are long run cost positions, a firm producing at E with plant and machinery designed to produce at D must be less cost effective than a firm operating at F with a factory designed to produce OS of output.

A, C, D, F, G and J are least cost points in the long run.

Combining these, as in Figure 49.4, we get a long run average cost curve. For each point on this curve there is an associated short run average cost curve, such as AB. If the firm operates in the short run at the point where the short run cost curve just touches (is tangential to) the long run cost curve, then it is operating where the company thought it would operate when it was able to vary all its factor inputs. If short run output is different from this position, then its short run costs will be higher than if it could have varied all its factors of production. But it could be higher or lower than the tangency point depending upon whether diminishing returns have or have not set in.

The long run average cost curve is said to be the envelope for the short run average cost curves because it contains them all.

Question 4

In 1989, Ford announced that it was to transfer part of the production of its (now discontinued) Sierra model from Dagenham in the UK to Genk in Belgium. Dagenham in future would only make the Fiesta model. It blamed the move on high costs of production at Dagenham. Part of the problem lay in the inefficient physical layout of the 50 year old Dagenham plant. At the same time, Toyota was announcing the building of a green field motor manufacturing plant near Derby.

(a) Using a diagram, explain why you might expect Toyota to enjoy lower average costs of production at its Derby plant than Ford at its Dagenham plant.

key terms

Diseconomies of scale - a rise in the long run average costs of production as output rises.
External economies of scale - falling average costs of production, shown by a downward shift in the average cost curve, which result from a growth in the size of the industry within which a firm operates.
Internal economies of scale - economies of scale which arise because of the growth in the scale of production within a firm.
Minimum efficient scale of production - the lowest level of output at which long run average cost is minimised.
Optimal level of production - the range of output over which long run average cost is lowest.

Applied economics

Economies of scale

Economic theory suggests that, in the long run, a firm will experience first economies of scale, but eventually diseconomies of scale will set in. The long run average cost curve is therefore U-shaped. However, research in this area tends to support the view that long run average cost curves in practice are not U-shaped but L-shaped. Firms experience economies of scale, but when output reaches the minimum efficient scale of production, average costs do not start to climb but remain constant. For instance, CF Pratten (1971) studied 25 industries, including newspapers, soap, oil, bread and steel and found L-shaped rather than U-shaped long run average cost curves.

Figure 49.5 shows an estimate of economies of scale in three areas of vehicle production:- diesel engine production, commercial vehicles and cars. For instance, there was an approximate 34 per cent fall in costs if car production increased from 100 000 to 2 million. The minimum efficient scale of production for cars had not been reached by the 2 million level although the largest falls in costs occurred at production levels between 0 and 500 000. The market for commercial vehicles and diesel engines was much smaller than for cars and manufacturers had not reached their minimum scale of production according to the study. Larger production volumes would further reduce costs to those shown in Figure 49.5.

The sources of economies of scale in car manufacturing are shown in Table 49.2. For instance, the minimum efficient scale of production for the casting of an engine block was 1 million units a year whilst in final assembly it was 250 000 units. Economies of scale were greatest in research and development at 5 million units a year.

The car industry has steadily moved to exploit economies of scale in recent years. Many car manufacturers have merged or been taken over, including Rover by BMW, General Motors and Daimler Benz, Renault and Nissan, Peugeot and Citroen, Volkswagen and Seat and Skoda, and Ford and Mazda. Motor manufacturers have cut component costs by reducing the number of their suppliers. Each supplier then tends to supply greater volumes enabling them to exploit economies of scale. Research and development and production costs have been cut by reducing the number of platforms on which cars are built. A platform is basically the chassis. Building, say, five different models on one basic platform means that there are economies of scale in the production of the platforms, only one set of development costs is incurred in the design of the platform and expensive time between design and production is reduced.

At the same time, car manufacturers have been increasing the number of models offered for marketing reasons. Customers want greater choice. The challenge has therefore been how to reduce the minimum efficient scale of production for any one model. Sharing components between as many different models of car as possible has been one key way of achieving this. Another has been the ever increasing automation of the production line which allows different variants of car to be produced on the same line.

Table 49.2 *Economies of scale in car production*

	Minimum efficient scale of production volume output per year (millions)
Technical economies	
Casting of engine block	1
Casting of various other parts	0.1-0.75
Power train (engine, transmission, etc.) machining and assembly	0.6
Pressing of various panels	1-2
Paint shop	0.25
Final assembly	0.25
Non-technical economies	
Advertising	1.0
Sales	2.0
Risks	1.8
Finance	2.5
Research and development	5.0

Source: G.Rhys, 'The motor industry: an overview, '*Developments in Economics*, Vol 15, 1999, edited by G.B.J. Atkinson, Causeway Press.

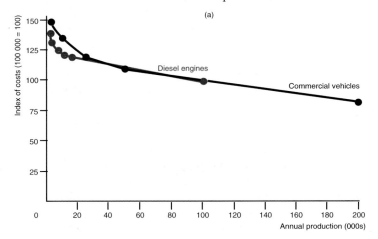

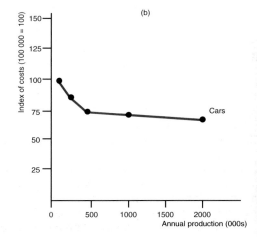

Figure 49.5 *Economies of scale in vehicle manufacture*
Source: G.Rhys, 'The motor industry: an overview, '*Developments in Economics*, Vol 15, 1999, edited by G.B.J. Atkinson, Causeway Press.

Wal-Mart takes over Asda

Wal-Mart's entry into the UK market

Wal-Mart, the world's largest retailer, has offered £6.72 billion for Asda. Wal-Mart is continuing to expand worldwide and Asda will provide an ideal entry for the US giant into the UK industry. Shares in UK supermarkets like Sainsbury's and Tesco have fallen on the news. Wal-Mart has a ferocious reputation for offering the lowest prices in the market and existing UK supermarket chains are likely to lose market share if Wal-Mart's success is repeated at Asda.

Table 49.3 *Distribution of Wal-Mart sales: USA vs rest of the world*

	Sales ($bn)		
	1997	1998	1999
Domestic US	99.9	110.4	125.4
International	5.0	7.5	12.2
Asda			5.0

Source: adapted from Primark Datastream.

Europe's top food retailers
By worldwide sales 1998 (€bn)

Wal-Mart	US	117.2
Metro	Germany	38.0
Intermarché	France	30.8
Carrefour	France	30.8
Rewe	Germany	29.2
Edeka	Germany	27.6
Promodès	France	27.6
Ahold	Netherlands	26.5
Tesco	UK	25.0
Tengelmann	Germany	24.7
Auchan	France	24.0
J.Sainsbury	UK	22.1
Aldi	Germany	21.7
Leclerc	France	19.4
Casino	France	14.2
Delhaize	Belgium	12.7
Lidl	Germany	11.6
Safeway	UK	10.7
Asda	UK	10.5
Migros	Switzerland	9.6

Figure 49.6 *Europe's top food retailers*
Source: adapted from Morgan Stanley Dean Witter.

The Wal-Mart menace

Wal-Mart has become the world's largest retailer through offering lower prices than its rivals. The chain was founded by the legendary Sam Walton in Bentonville in Arkansas where it still has its headquarters. He cut costs to a minimum and offered his customers a wide range of goods from groceries to clothes to electrical equipment. Today, Wal-Mart can boast two main competitive advantages over its rivals. First, it has enormous buying power. For instance, it is Procter & Gamble's, the maker of products like Bold and Ariel, largest customer. It buys 20 per cent of the world's production of Pampers disposable nappies. It uses that buying power to negotiate the keenest prices from suppliers. Second, it has the world's most sophisticated computer retailing system. It is IBM's largest EPOS (electronic point of sale) customer and its computer database is said to come close to that of the Pentagon in capacity. Immediately an item is bought at the till, it is registered on the computer system and may trigger a reorder for the store. The sophistication of the system means that it carries less stock at any store than its rivals, cutting costs and freeing up space for sales. The system tailors stock to each locality. It means that Wal-Mart is able to optimise the profitability of what is on the shelves at each store. It also prevents the store from buying stock which customers don't want to buy.

The Wal-Mart store formula

Wal-Mart runs a range of different sized stores. The largest are Sam's Clubs which are like cash and carry stores in the UK. Customers get very low prices but cheaper items are only sold in bulk. Discount stores are Wal-Mart's original formula, selling general merchandise, but this does not include food. Supercentres, the first only opened in 1991, are like European hypermarkets, selling both general merchandise and food. However, the mix of general merchandise to food is much larger than in Europe at 60-40. At Asda, which has the largest general merchandise to food mix of the UK supermarket chains, the mix is 40-60. Wal-Mart has also started to roll out smaller Neighbourhood Market Stores, more akin to European supermarkets in their product range with a greater emphasis on groceries, health and beauty products and impulse buys.

Asda's 229 UK stores are on average 50 per cent larger than those of its UK competitors. They include 29 hypermarkets occupying about 60 000 sq ft each. However, they are small compared to Wal-Mart's US Supercentres which range from 109 000-220 000 sq ft. The size of stores in the UK is limited by the difficulty of getting planning permission. Some analysts feel that, in the UK, Wal-Mart will not be able to achieve the prices it sells for in the USA because of the higher costs of operating smaller sites.

Source: adapted from the *Financial Times*, 19.6.1999, 23.6.1999, 21.9.1991; *The Sunday Times*, 25.7.1999; *The Times*, 15.6.1999, 19.6.1999.

1. What economies of scale does Wal-Mart enjoy?
2. To what extent might Asda be able to reduce its costs because of its takeover by Wal-Mart?
3. The government is increasingly concerned about the environmental impact of transport but also would like to increase the degree of competition amongst supermarkets to reduce prices to consumers. Using diagrams, assess the impact on the environment and on supermarket prices of: (a) increases in taxes on petrol and diesel, road pricing and taxes on companies per car parking space that they offer to employees and customers; (b) a relaxation of planning restrictions which allows supermarket chains to buy up sites on industrial parks which are currently used by other types of business.

Summary

1. Shareholders, managers, workers, government, consumers and others influence decision making in a firm.
2. Neo-classical theory assumes that firms are short run profit maximisers. In the short run, such firms will operate so long as their revenue is greater than their variable cost.
3. The neo-Keynesian theory of the firm assumes that firms are long run profit maximisers.
4. Managerial theories assume that managers maximise their own utility subject to a profit satisficing constraint.
5. Behavioural theories assume that decision making within a firm is not controlled by any one group, such as shareholders, but by all parties involved with the firm.

Control

The question of what motivates a firm in its actions can only be answered if there is a clear understanding of who controls the decision making process. This control is likely to lie with one or more of the firm's **stakeholders** (☞ unit 2). In a UK context these are as follows.

The owners or shareholders It might seem obvious to state that it is the owners or shareholders of a company who control it. This is perhaps true for small businesses where the owner is also the director or manager of the business. The owner of a small local corner shop, for instance, who also runs the shop will make the decisions about the business. However, it is less obvious that owners control the business they own when there is a very large number of shareholders.

Directors and managers Shareholders in a public limited company elect directors to look after their interests. Directors in turn appoint managers who are responsible for the day to day running of the business. Therefore there may be a divorce between ownership and control. The only way in which owners can influence decision making directly is by sacking directors at the Annual General Meeting (AGM) of the company. In practice the company needs to be going bankrupt to stir sufficient shareholders for this to happen. Shareholders can also sell their shares, forcing the share price down and making the company more vulnerable to a takeover bid. If there is a takeover the directors and managers may well lose their jobs and hence there is pressure on managers to perform well.

The workers The workers, particularly through their trade unions, may be able to exert strong pressure on a company. They do not have the power to run the company in the way that shareholders or managers might be able to do. However, they can have an important influence on matters such as wages (and therefore costs), health and safety at work and location or relocation of premises.

The state The state provides an underlying framework for the operation of the company. Legislation on taxation, the environment, consumer protection, health and safety at work, employment practices, solvency and many other issues forces companies to behave in a way in which they might otherwise not do in an unregulated environment.

The consumer The consumer, through organisations such as the Consumers' Association or various trade organisations, can bring pressure to bear on companies in an attempt to make them change their policies. This form of influence is often rather weak; **consumer sovereignty** (☞ unit 66) is more important. In a free market, consumers cast their spending votes amongst companies. Companies which do not provide the products that consumers wish to buy will go out of business whilst companies which are responsive to consumers' needs may make large profits. According to this argument, it is the consumer who ultimately controls the company. This assumes that consumer sovereignty exists. In practice, firms attempt to manipulate consumer preferences by marketing devices such as advertising. Firms are therefore not the powerless servants which theory implies.

Short run profit maximisation

In neo-classical economics it is assumed that the interests of owners or shareholders are the most important. Just as consumers attempt to maximise utility and workers attempt to maximise their rewards from working, so shareholders will be motivated solely by maximising their gain from the company. Therefore it is argued that the goal of firms is to maximise profits.

Firms are not always able to operate at a profit. They may be faced with operating at a loss. Neo-classical economics predicts that firms will continue in production in the short run so long as they cover their variable costs.

Consider Table 50.1. The company would lose £20 million in any period in which it shut down its plant and produced nothing. This is because it still has to pay its fixed costs of £20 million even if output is zero. Total fixed costs represent the maximum loss per period the company need face.

Question 1

In 1999, Vodafone, the UK mobile telephone company, offered to buy Mannesmann, the German telecommunications company, for £77 billion. The offer provoked strong opposition in Germany. The Board of Directors of Mannesmann rejected the bid on financial grounds, saying that Vodafone's offer grossly undervalued the company. Unions at Mannesmann were vocal in their opposition to the merger too, fearing job losses and large scale restructuring. Klaus Zwickle, head of the IG Metal union, called for a European law to ban aggressive bids. Gerhard Schroder, the German chancellor, attacked the hostile bid. He said such bids destroyed the culture of the company targeted and damaged it economically, as well as eventually damaging the predator company. 'Those who launch such actions in Germany underestimate the virtues of partnership management, which is at the heart of German capitalism. Jürgen Rüttgers, a German opposition politician, said: 'It can't be that a functioning firm like Mannesmann can be beaten down, and that thousands of jobs are destroyed just because international investors want to make a short-term profit.' Another politician, Wolfgang Clement, the Social Democrat Prime Minister of North Rhine Westphalia where the headquarters of Mannesmann was located, said: 'We should hold on to our culture - and that applies to our business culture as well.' German newspapers were relatively balanced about the takeover. For instance, the Frankfurter Allgemeine Zeitung said: 'The world of shares and finance is shaped predominantly in an Anglo-Saxon way. The measure of all things is profit. Particularly in Germany, a republic of consensus, this can run into a lack of understanding'. However, one newspaper, *Bild*, the German equivalent of the *Sun*, said: 'Mannesmann - is financial greed winning the day? In just three weeks, the profit margin for shareholders has risen to more than DM200 a share. As for Germany's industrial tradition and 130 000 jobs, how much do they count for against so much profit?' Interestingly, Mannesmann had earlier in 1999 bought Orange, the UK mobile telephone company.

Source: adapted from *The Guardian*, 22.11.1999, the *Financial Times*, 20.11.1999, *The Sunday Times*, 21.11.1999, the *Financial Times*, 22.11.1999.

(a) Explain who were the stakeholders in Mannesmann at the time of the Vodafone bid in 1999.
(b) Suggest what might have been their objectives at the time.

Table 50.1

£ million

Period	Total variable cost	Total fixed cost	Total cost	Total revenue	Profit or loss	
					If production takes place	If plant is shut down
1	30	20	50	60	+10	-20
2	30	20	50	50	0	-20
3	30	20	50	40	-10	-20
4	30	20	50	30	-20	-20
5	30	20	50	20	-30	-20

The table shows that the firm is facing a steadily worsening trading situation. Its costs remain the same throughout, but each period its revenue declines. In period 1, total revenue exceeds total costs. The firm makes a profit of £10 million if production takes place. In period 2, it makes no profit by operating its plant (although it should be remembered that cost includes an allowance for normal profit ☞ unit 47).

However, this is better than the alternative of shutting down and making a £20 million loss. So too is producing in period 3. Although the company makes a loss of £10 million, it will continue to produce because the alternative to not producing is a loss of £20 million. In period 4 the company is on the dividing line between whether to produce or not. In period 5, the company will clearly not produce. Its operating losses would be greater than if the plant were shut down.

So short run profit maximisation implies that a firm will continue to produce even if it is not fully covering its total costs. It will only shut down production when its total revenue fails to cover its total variable cost.

Question 2

A company has fixed costs of £10 million. Its variable costs increase at a constant rate with output. The variable cost of production of each unit is £1 million. Explain whether it will produce:
(a) 10 units if total revenue is £30 million;
(b) 15 units if total revenue is £25 million;
(c) 20 units if total revenue is £22 million;
(d) 25 units if total revenue is £20 million.

Long run profit maximisation

Neo-Keynesian economists believe that firms maximise their long run rather than their short run profit. This is based upon the belief that firms use COST PLUS PRICING techniques. The price of a product is worked out by calculating the average total cost of operating at full capacity and adding a profit mark-up. The price set and therefore the profit aimed for is based upon the long run costs of the firm.

Short run profit maximisation implies that firms will adjust both price and output in response to changes in market conditions. However, according to neo-Keynesians, rapid price adjustments may well damage the firm's position in a market. Consumers dislike frequent price changes. Price cuts may be seen as a sign of distress selling and large buyers may respond by trying to negotiate even larger price reductions. Price increases may be interpreted as a sign of profiteering, with consumers switching to other brands or makes in the belief that they will get better value for money. Price changes also involve costs to the company because price lists need to be changed, sales staff informed, advertising material changed, etc. Therefore it is argued that firms attempt to maintain stable prices whilst adjusting output to changes in market conditions.

This may mean that a firm will produce in the short run even if it fails to cover its variable cost. If it takes the view that in the long run it may make a profit on production of a particular good, it may prefer to produce at a loss rather

Question 3

A firm has total fixed costs of £900 and variable costs of £1 per unit.
(a) What will be the price per unit if it sets out to manufacture 300 units a week and make a 25 per cent profit over costs?
(b) Demand is not as great as the company hoped. If it maintains its price, what is the minimum number of units that must be sold per week if the company is to break-even?
(c) Demand is 150 units per week. The company is offered an order for an extra 350 units a week if it drops its price on all units sold to £3 per unit. But it believes that demand will slowly increase in the future to the planned 300 units a week if the original price is maintained. Should the firm accept the order?

than disrupt supplies to the market. Equally, it may cease production in the short run even if it can cover its variable costs. It may prefer to keep prices above the market price in the short run and sell nothing if it believes that price cutting in the short run would lead to a permanent effect on prices and therefore profits in the long run.

Managerial theories

Managerial theories of the firm start from the assumption that there is some divorce between ownership and control of companies. The shareholders are assumed to be a different group of people from the managers of the company. Shareholders will wish to see profits maximised. However, it is far from obvious that managers will share this goal. As workers they will attempt to maximise their own rewards. These may include their own pay and fringe benefits, their working conditions, their power within the organisation, their ability to appropriate resources, and the amount of effort they have to make. For instance, a manager may be more interested in which company car he or she will get, whether there is time to play golf on a Wednesday afternoon, or whether there is an extra £1 million available for the budget, than whether the company has maximised its profits at the end of the financial year.

This does not mean to say that making a profit is not important. Managers have to be seen to be efficient enough to justify their salaries. A shareholders' revolt is always a possibility. Some directors may take it upon themselves to promote actively the interests of the owners of the company. There is always the threat of takeover or bankruptcy leading to a loss of jobs, so managers have to make enough profit to satisfy the demands of their shareholders. This is known as PROFIT SATISFICING. But once a satisfactory level of

Question 4

From Mr Edward Leigh MP.

Sir, The problems surrounding shareholder control of executive salaries were accurately and extensively reflected in your leader ('Can pay, will pay', December 6).
I am glad to hear that the government intends to act, as this was an issue which I addressed in a policy pamphlet which I published on November 28. I said there that the way forward was to empower shareholders. Two days later the prime minister told the House of Commons that he was prepared to consider a similar solution.
In my pamphlet, Responsible Individualism, I wrote that the public is justifiably suspicious when executives raise each other's salaries in a round of mutual pocket-lining. Especially since many of them perform roles more akin to ministers presiding over large bureaucracies than to genuine entrepreneurs who innovate and create wealth and jobs.
It is indisputable that capitalism and the market are the most effective systems to generate wealth and improve the material well-being of the nation. But man cannot live by those alone; a sense of right and justice must also be part of the equation. Politicians should give a lead.
The issue cannot be dismissed by the simple argument that British companies must be free to offer world-class salaries. There has been a real public outrage and that is something companies and government ignore at their peril. There is an important moral dimension and it is this which has been missing on recent economic policy. A sense of duty and service on the part of executives and a sensitivity to the feeling of those on low wages would

not go amiss.
I do not advocate the Labour remedies of intervention and state regulation. We should empower shareholders - who, after all, own the companies and employ the managers - to enable checks to be placed on what the public suspects are unnecessarily large pay packages.
This can be achieved, first by fiscal measures to encourage direct share ownership - something lacking at present; and, second, by legislation to ensure that City institutions take due note of the views of the beneficial owners of the shares they nominally hold.
I recognise there are difficulties in devising a mechanism by which the latter could be achieved, but it should be possible to introduce a legal system, however rough and ready, which would make fund managers respond to the opinions of the millions of investors whom they represent.
We should trust the people in this respect. The public is bright enough to know when they need adequately to reward an entrepreneur who boosts their dividends, asset values and pensions, but jaundiced enough to recognise blind greed.
Edward Leigh
House of Commons,
London SW1A 0AA

Source: Edward Leigh, MP.

(a) Explain what evidence the writer of the letter, Edward Leigh, puts forward to argue that managers and not shareholders control large companies in the UK.
(b) Discuss the benefits and problems to businesses of implementing his suggested solutions.

profits has been made, the managers are free to maximise their own rewards from the company.

One theory put forward in the 1950s by William Baumol was that firms would attempt to maximise sales rather than profits. Increased sales and increased salaries for top managers and directors tend to go hand in hand. Another more complicated theory put forward by O. Williamson postulates that managers have a utility function consisting of factors such as salary, size of the workforce directed by the manager, the amount of money under his or her control and the number of perks, such as company cars, that the manager receives (☞ unit 59).

Behavioural theories

Behavioural theories of the firm, pioneered by the American economist Herbert Simon, argue that decision making within a company is made not by any one group but by all groups involved in the firm. It is only by studying the relative power of each group and the power structures within the organisation that the way in which a firm behaves can be understood.

For instance, it could be argued that in the 1960s and the 1970s trade unions were very powerful in large companies. They were influential in increasing the share of revenues allocated to wages and reducing the share that went to shareholders. During the 1980s and 1990s, government legislation and mass unemployment seriously weakened the power of unions in the UK. At the same time, shareholders became more conscious of their right to make profits. The result was a large increase in the returns to shareholders, which could be seen as being financed by a reduction in the returns to the workers of the firm. Shareholders are more important today in company board rooms and workers less important than they were 20 years ago.

Behavioural theories assume that each group has a minimum level of demands. Shareholders demand that the firm makes a satisfactory level of profits. The government demands that laws be obeyed and taxes paid. Workers will require a minimum level of pay and work satisfaction if they are to stay with the company. Consumers demand a minimum level of quality for the price they pay for goods purchased. Local environmentalists may be able to exert enough moral pressure on the company to prevent gross over-pollution.

Other goals

Some firms have clearly distinct aims apart from those mentioned above. Consumer co-operatives aim to help consumers (although there is considerable debate in the UK as to whether they do not, in practice, serve the interests of their workers and management more). Worker co-operatives are often motivated by a desire either to maintain jobs or to produce a particular product, such as health foods. There have been examples of philanthropic owners in the past, such as Rowntree or Cadbury, who have placed great priority on improving the living conditions of their workers. Nationalised industries in the UK prior to 1979 had a whole range of goals from avoiding a loss to maintaining employment to providing a high quality service.

So it is simplistic to argue that all firms aim to maximise profit. However, there is much evidence to suggest that large firms whose shares are freely traded on stock exchanges, and which are vulnerable to takeover, place the making of profit very high on their list of priorities. Therefore it is not unreasonable to make an assumption that, in general, firms are profit maximisers.

Question 5

During the 1960s and 1970s, it was difficult to see who controlled the Fleet Street newspaper industry. Owners of the newspapers were often rich entrepreneurial-type figures who allowed their titles to make little or no profit in return for the prestige and influence over the UK public that ownership gave them. Trade unions had a virtual veto on changes in working practices. Trade unions, not management, controlled shop floor appointments. The ability to call wildcat strikes which would lose a paper its entire production run for a day ensured that shop floor workers earned wages which bore no resemblance to the wages of workers in other comparable occupations.

Consumers rewarded with more sales those newspapers which included more page 3 pin-ups and less serious political news. Governments, meanwhile, made public noises about deteriorating press standards whilst in private attempting to get the press to toe the current party line. Management were caught in the middle, attempting to balance all the conflicting demands made of them.

New technology and soaring property prices put paid to all this. In the 1980s it became apparent that newspapers could make large profits for their owners. The key to success was to sack as many shop floor workers as possible and replace them with machines.

Those kept on would be paid reduced rates. Fleet Street offices could be sold off at vast profit on a soaring property market, the proceeds more than paying for a move to new technology premises elsewhere. The unions resisted but not even continual mass pickets and what came to be called the 'Wapping riots' in 1986 could prevent change.

Today, union power is much reduced and, in some newspaper jobs, unions are not recognised by management for negotiating purposes. Newspapers are more profit orientated although most of the British press arguably can still be relied upon to support the Conservative Party.

(a) To what extent can behavioural theories of the firm explain the history of the Fleet Street newspaper industry?

Applied economics

The role of the shareholder

Shareholder power

In both the UK and the USA, large companies tend to claim that shareholders are powerful. Company chairs make referrals to 'serving the interest of shareholders' or 'maximising shareholder value'. However, the power of the shareholders tends to be an indirect one. Annual general meetings (AGMs) of quoted companies are poorly attended, annual shareholder reports are not understood (even when read) by many shareholders, and directors rely on getting blocks of proxy votes before AGMs from key investors to push through any resolutions they recommend, including their own election to the board.

On the whole, shareholders' power lies not in being able to influence decisions directly, but in their ability to sell their shares freely. If enough shareholders are disappointed with a company's performance and sell their shares, then the share price will fall and make the company an attractive takeover target. The directors and management of a company taken over could, at worst, face immediate redundancy. So in the UK and the USA, shareholder power is vitally dependent upon free and open stock markets.

There has been some revival of direct shareholder power in the USA. Individual speculators wanting to make money have bought blocks of shares in companies which they consider are performing poorly. They have then used their voting rights to agitate for reform. Sometimes they have secured a seat on the board of directors. Once changes of policy have been implemented and monetary benefits have accrued to shareholders, perhaps in the form of higher dividends, a much higher share price or the issue of free shares in companies which have been split off from the main company, the speculator sells out and turns his or her attention to another company. Despite a trend towards more aggressive individual shareholders in the USA, most US companies and UK companies can still ride out shareholder dissatisfaction without necessarily

implementing change.

In continental Europe and Japan, shareholder power is exercised in a different way. It is far more difficult for companies to be taken over. In Italy, for instance, hardly any of the approximately 200 companies listed on the stock market are open to a British-style takeover bid. This is because hardly any have more than half their shares in public hands, the rest being held by families or other companies.

In Spain, shareholdings are not even disclosed but bank, family and corporate cross shareholdings tie up control of most companies. In France, it is estimated that more than half of the 200 largest quoted or unquoted companies are family controlled and many of the rest have key blocks of shares held either by the government or by single private shareholders. In Germany, three large banks, which for more than a century have financed German industry, have huge stakes. In Japan, companies prevent individual shareholders from becoming too powerful by buying them out or diluting their shareholding by the issue of more shares. There is also a strong tradition of corporate cross holdings.

Short-termism

For many years now, there has been a debate in the UK about whether or not the system of shareholding has a major influence on the behaviour of firms. There are those who argue that the UK system leads to 'short-termism'. Companies are forced to pursue the goal of maximising short term profit for fear that they will otherwise be taken over. This makes it difficult for them to pursue other objectives, particularly investment both in capital equipment and in their workers which have long pay-back periods.

In contrast, on the Continent and in Japan, companies can afford to take a long term view. Ultimately the company will only survive if it makes a profit. But profit should increase if the company grows over time. Hence it is the interests of the company which are paramount. The company is not just the shareholders, but also the workers, the management, the customers, the local citizens etc. Because shareholders do not expect their companies to maximise short term profits, management is free to invest in a way which will maximise the long term growth of the company.

In the 1970s and 1980s, it seemed that taking the long term view produced superior results over a longer period. Companies in Europe and in Japan prospered and their economies grew at higher rates than those of the UK and the USA. However, in the 1990s, the Anglo-Saxon short term shareholder model seemed to gain superiority. Many Japanese companies overinvested at the end of the 1980s. When the Japanese economy went into recession in the early 1990s, they were left with far too much capacity and many struggled to make a profit throughout the decade. By the turn of the millennium, many Japanese companies were sacking workers and restructuring to survive. The consensus based model was breaking down. In South Korea, where Japanese long termism had seen the growth of industrial giants, the Asian crisis of 1997-1998 revealed these companies to be debt ridden and over extended. They were forced to retrench, and some subsidiaries were sold off to US companies. In Europe, UK and US firms were taking over key firms which were available for sale. In some sectors, continental firms were found to be inefficient in comparison with their UK and US counterparts.

Short termism, then, whilst it clearly has its inadequacies, also has strengths. It prevents complacency and inertia in firms which a long term perspective can allow to gain hold.

Stakeholder power

Social reporting

There is a small but growing trend by the world's largest companies towards environmental, ethical and social reporting. This means publishing information not normally released to the general public about a wide range of issues relating to the behaviour of the company.

BT (British Telecommunications) this week produced its first social report. Not all of it is favourable to the company. A survey of employee satisfaction shows, for example, that only 39 per cent were happy with leadership at BT, a figure that compares unfavourably against a benchmark of comparable companies. The report is a serious, if tentative, attempt to provide quantitative, independently compiled data on BT's relationships with shareholders, customers, employees and the community. Independent verification is provided by the Ashridge Centre for Business and Society, which provides a broadly favourable verdict while suggesting areas for improvement.

Source: adapted from the *Financial Times*, 15.7.1999.

British Telecom: mission and aims

Our vision
To be the most successful worldwide communications group.

Our mission
To generate shareholder value by seizing opportunities in the communications market world-wide, building on our current business and focusing on high growth segments, while playing our part in the community and achieving the highest standards of integrity, customer satisfaction, and employee motivation.

Legal framework
We operate in the UK under a regulatory framework set in a licence issued by the Government and monitored by the Office of Telecommunications (Oftel).

There are a number of conditions in our operating licence which govern the way in which we provide services to customers and behave towards our competitors.

Outside the UK we are committed to trading fairly in all the countries in which we operate. We are governed by the regulatory regimes within those countries and any overarching legislation, for example European Union competition law.

Source: BT, *An Issue of Responsibility*.

BT: social responsibility

...we believe that we have a responsibility to all the constituencies that have an interest in BT - our shareholders, customers, employees, suppliers and the communities in which we operate.

We simply cannot ignore the fact that the things we do can have a significant impact on the individuals and organisations we do business with, and on the world around. And we have a duty to manage that impact and report on it.

There is a view that environmental, health and safety programmes are a luxury in business, but this is proving to be increasingly unsustainable. Certainly, at BT, we have found that they are an asset to us as a business, as well as to society more generally.

Source: BT, *A Matter of Fact; Environmental, Health and Safety Performance Report 1999*.

By 1999, over 50 per cent of BT usage came from data traffic rather than voice calls. BT's profits in the second half of the 1990s grew strongly, partly on the back of a large year on year increase in data traffic including use of the Internet. In 1999, the UK government voiced concerns that BT's tariff structures were discouraging internet use. BT was charging at least 1p a minute for internet calls whereas in some other countries, such as the US, internet calls were free because all local telephone calls were free. This led to UK users spending far less time on the Internet than, say, their US counterparts. BT responded by offering new price packages. For instance, it offered to supply unlimited internet access to a customer via an Internet Service Provider, at a cost which would work out at around £120 per year. It could be argued that BT has little incentive to lower the price of internet calls because they are highly profitable. Once a connection has been made, the cost to BT of keeping a customer online is virtually zero.

1. Explain who might be the stakeholders in BT.
2. Discuss the extent to which their interests
   (a) conflict and (b) coincide.

Summary

1. Market structures are the characteristics of a market which determine firms' behaviour within the market.
2. The number of firms within a market may vary from one (as in monopoly), to several (as in oligopoly), to a large number (as in monopolistic competition or perfect competition).
3. Barriers to entry prevent potential competitors from entering a market.
4. Industries may produce homogeneous or differentiated (branded) goods.
5. Perfect knowledge or imperfect knowledge may exist in an industry.
6. Firms may be independent or interdependent.

Market structure

Market structures are the characteristics of a market which determine firms' behaviour. Economists single out a small number of key characteristics:
- the number of firms in the market and their relative size;
- the number of firms which might enter the market;
- the ease or difficulty with which these new entrants might come in;
- the extent to which goods in the market are similar;
- the extent to which all firms in the market share the same knowledge;
- the extent to which the actions of one firm will affect another firm.

The number of firms in an industry

The number of firms in an industry may vary from one to many. In the UK market for letter deliveries, the Post Office is essentially the sole supplier. In agriculture, on the other hand, there are tens of thousands of farms supplying potatoes and carrots to the market in the UK.
- A **monopoly** is said to exist where there is only one supplier in the market.
- In a market dominated by a few large producers, the market structure is **oligopolistic**. In an oligopolistic market there may be a large number of firms, but the key characteristic is that most are small and relatively unimportant, whilst a small number of large firms produces most of the output of the industry.
- In **perfect competition** or in **monopolistic** competition there is a large number of small suppliers, none of which is large enough to dominate the market.

Barriers to entry

Market structures are not only affected by the number of firms in an industry and their relative output, but also by

Question 1

(a) How many firms are there in each of the industries in which these particular firms operate?
(b) In which of these industries do a few large firms dominate output?

the potential number of new entrants to the market. Firms in an industry where there are unlikely to be any new entrants may behave differently from firms in an industry where there are many strong potential competitors.

There is a number of **barriers to entry** (☞ unit 17) which prevent potential competitors from entering an industry.

Capital costs Buying a local corner shop is relatively cheap and therefore the entry cost to most forms of retailing is low. Buying a car plant or an aluminium smelter, on the other hand, is extremely expensive. Entry costs to these industries are very high and only large companies on the whole can pay them. Capital costs therefore represent a very important barrier to entry and vary from industry to industry.

Sunk costs SUNK COSTS are costs which are not recoverable. For instance, a woman may set up a gardening business, buying a lawnmower, a van, garden tools and paying for advertising. If the business folds, she will be able to get some money back by selling the van, the tools, and mower, but she won't be able to get any of the money back from the advertising. The cost of advertising and the difference between the purchase price and resale price of the capital equipment would be her sunk costs. High sunk costs will act as a barrier to entry because the cost of failure for firms entering the industry will be high. Low sunk costs, on the other hand, will encourage firms to enter an industry because they have little to lose from failure (☞ unit 58, the theory of contestable markets).

Scale economies In some industries, economies of scale are very large. A few firms operating at lowest average cost (the **optimum level of production** ☞ unit 49) can satisfy all the demand of buyers. This will act as a barrier to entry because any new firm entering the market is likely to produce less and therefore have much higher average costs than the few established producers. In some industries, it could be that a few firms supplying the whole industry are still unable to exploit fully the potential economies of scale. A **natural monopoly** is then likely to result, with just one firm surviving in the industry, able to beat off any new entrants because it can produce at lowest costs.

Natural cost advantages Some producers possess advantages because they own factors which are superior to others and which are unique (i.e. have no close substitutes). For instance, a petrol station site on a busy main road is likely to be superior to one in a sleepy country village. A stretch of desert in Saudi Arabia with oil underneath may be superior for oil production to the most beautiful of the Derbyshire Dales. The Victoria and Albert Museum should be able to attract more visitors because of its wide collection than a small provincial town museum. As a result, they will either be able to produce at lower cost or be able to generate higher revenues than their potential competitors.

Legal barriers The law may give firms particular privileges. Patent laws can prevent competitor firms from making a product for a given number of years after its invention. The government may give a firm exclusive rights to production. For instance, it may give broadcast licences to commercial television companies or it may make nationalised industries into monopolies by legally forbidding private firms to set up in the industry, as is the case with the Post Office in the UK.

Marketing barriers Existing firms in an industry may be able to erect very high barriers through high spending on advertising and marketing. The purpose of these is to make consumers associate a particular type of good with the firm's product, creating a powerful brand image. One

example of this from 50 years ago was the success of the Hoover company with its vacuum cleaner. Even today, many people still refer to vacuum cleaners as 'hoovers'. Similarly, a personal stereo is often called a 'Walkman', the brand name of Sony which first put it on the market. In the UK detergent industry, a national launch of a new brand of soap or washing powder will cost in excess of £10 million. Soap and washing powders are low technology products whose costs of production are relatively low. Marketing barriers, however, make the industry almost impossible to enter.

Restrictive practices Firms may deliberately restrict competition through restrictive practices. For instance, a manufacturer may refuse to sell goods to a retailer which stocks the products of a competitor firm. A manufacturer may refuse to sell a good, when it has a monopoly in production, unless the buyer purchases its whole range of goods. Firms may be prepared to lower prices for long enough to drive out a new entrant to the business.

These barriers to entry may be divided into two groups. Some occur inevitably. These are known as **innocent entry barriers**. Most cost advantages fall into this category. However, other barriers are created by firms in the industry **deliberately** to keep out potential competitors. Marketing barriers and restrictive practices are examples of these.

The extent to which there is freedom of entry to a

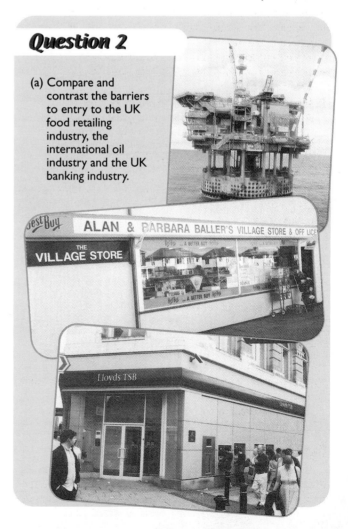

Question 2

(a) Compare and contrast the barriers to entry to the UK food retailing industry, the international oil industry and the UK banking industry.

market varies enormously. Manufacturing industries, with high capital costs and with extensive marketing power, tend to have higher barriers than service industries. But many service industries have high barriers too. Banking, for instance, has a high capital cost of entry, legal permission is required, and marketing barriers are high. In the professions, like law, architecture and accountancy, new entrants are kept out by enforcement of minimum qualification levels, qualifications which are impossible to obtain except through working in the profession itself.

Product homogeneity and branding

In some industries products are essentially identical whichever firm produces them. Coal, steel and potatoes are examples. This does not mean to say that there are not different grades of coal or types of steel, but no producer has a monopoly on the production of any such grade or type. Goods which are identical are called **homogeneous goods**.

Firms find it much easier to control their markets if they

can produce goods which are non-homogeneous. Differentiating their product from their competitors, and creating **brands** (☞ unit 17) allows them to build up brand loyalty. This in turn leads to a reduction in the elasticity of demand for their product. A branded good may be physically no different from its competitors, or it may be slightly different. But branding has value for the firm because consumers think that the product is very different, so different that rival products are a very poor substitute for it. This perception is built up through advertising and marketing and enables firms to charge higher prices without losing very much custom (i.e. demand is relatively inelastic).

Knowledge

Buyers and sellers are said to have **perfect information** or **perfect knowledge** if they are fully informed of prices and output in the industry. So if one firm were to put up its prices, it would lose all its customers because they would go and buy from elsewhere in the industry. Hence, there can only be one price in the market.

Perfect knowledge also implies that a firm has access to all information which is available to other firms in its industry. In UK agriculture, for instance, knowledge is widely available. Farmers can obtain information about different strains of seeds, the most effective combinations of fertilizers and pesticides and when it is best to plant and reap crops.

Perfect knowledge does not imply that all firms in an industry **will** possess all information. An inefficient farmer might not bother to gather relevant information which is readily available. In the short term, the farmer might survive, although in the longer term the farm will be driven out of business by more efficient competitors. Equally, perfect information does not imply that all firms know everything about their industry and its future. Farmers do not know if in 6 months' time a drought will destroy their crops. They have to work on the basis of probability. Perfect knowledge only means that all firms have the same access to information.

Firms have imperfect knowledge where, for instance, there are industrial secrets. Individual firms may not know the market share of their competitors or they may be unaware of new technology or new products to be launched by rival companies. Information could then act as a barrier to entry, preventing or discouraging new firms from entering the industry.

Interrelationships within markets

There are two possible relationships between firms in an industry. Firms may be **independent** of each other. This means that the actions of any one firm will have no significant impact on any other single firm in the industry. In agriculture, for instance, the decision of one farmer to grow more wheat this season will have no direct impact on any other farmer. It will not affect his next door neighbour. This independence is one reason why perfect knowledge exists to some degree in agriculture. There is

Question 3

Nothing demonstrates the value of brands more clearly than the frequency which which they are copied and counterfeited around the world by fly-by-night operators in search of a quick profit. International Distillers and Vintners (IDV), the drinks subsidiary of Grand Metropolitan, has taken action against about 50 pirate brands during the past year.

'A brand is costly to create and establish, but can be very easy and profitable to copy', says Michael Leathes, legal director of IDV. 'Brands are our most important assets. Through them we communicate the quality of our products to consumers. They represent a huge investment of time, effort and money, that can be diluted, weakened, even destroyed by those who copy them. Counterfeits or imitations can be sold cheaply. Their producers do not have to spend on advertising and marketing. Nor do they have to bother about the quality of the drink or the packaging. We have to be rigorous in the protection of our brands against the damage that copies can do to them.'

Brand counterfeiting is a criminal offence in most countries in which the drinks groups operate, and, once the counterfeiters are identified, it is relatively easy to stop. The main problems arise from imitations which deliberately seek to deceive consumers by suggesting an affinity with a leading brand: using a similar name, or similar designs and colours in their bottles and labels. IDV's Bailey's Irish Cream liqueur, for instance, has encouraged the illegal production of a host of copies, including Bailes, Teleys and Raylas, all in squat brown bottles with pastoral scenes incorporated into the labels.

(a) What are the costs and benefits to a firm of developing a brand?
(b) To what extent do consumers benefit from being offered branded rather than non-branded goods to purchase?

no point in keeping secrets if your actions will not benefit you at the expense of your competitors.

If firms are **interdependent** then the actions of one firm will have an impact on other firms. An advertising campaign for one brand of soap bar, for instance, is designed mainly to attract customers away from other brands. Firms are more likely to be interdependent if there are few firms in the industry.

Competition and market structure

The neo-classical theory of the firm recognises a number of market structures derived from the characteristics above. In units 53 to 59 these market structures will be considered in greater detail. Here, however, the key features are summarised. In neo-classical theory, there are three main types of market structure.

- **Perfect competition**. A large number of firms, each producing a homogeneous good, compete in the industry. None of the firms is large enough to have a direct impact on any other firm or on the market price of the good. There is freedom of exit and entry to the industry.
- **Monopoly**. There is only one firm in the industry. Barriers to entry make it impossible for new firms to enter.
- **Imperfect competition**. This exists where there are at least two firms in the industry, and the industry is not perfectly competitive. For instance, non-homogeneous goods may be produced, there may be imperfect knowledge or firms may be interdependent, or some combination of these.

Firms in imperfectly competitive industries can compete in a number of ways. For instance, they can compete on:

- **price** - offering a lower price should attract more orders;
- **quality** - consumers are likely to prefer a better quality good;
- **after-sales service**;
- **delivery date** - a buyer may look elsewhere if a firm cannot deliver quickly and on time;
- **image** - building a strong brand image through advertising and other forms of marketing is likely to be a major factor in determining demand for the product.

In perfect competition, firms are not in direct competition with each other. One firm can expand output without affecting either the price received by or the sales of another firm. Each firm is a price taker, facing a perfectly elastic demand curve. However, competition is 'perfect' because any firm which charges a higher price than its competitors, or sells an inferior product, will lose

all its sales as perfectly informed consumers buy elsewhere in the market. The discipline of the market is so strong in a perfectly competitive industry that, in the long run, productive inefficiency (production at above minimum cost) cannot exist.

Question 4

In 1998, Dixons launched Freeserve, a subscription-free internet provider service. It proved a phenomenal success given that its main competitors at the time were typically charging £10 a month for internet access. By the time Dixons had signed up 1 million subscribers in a matter of months and become the UK's largest internet provider, it became obvious that it had the only business model worth copying. Not surprisingly, a large number of firms too began offering free internet access services, from banks to insurance companies to newspapers to supermarkets. They were able to advertise their service to their existing customer base and used the service to advertise their own products. They were also forced to buy in content pages from internet content providers and provide services such as chat rooms. At the same time, subscription services began to fight back. Some started to bundle free internet telephone access with a subscription. This was attractive because any user of a 'free' service was still having to pay telephone charges to British Telecom or another telephone company.

(a) How did internet service providers compete according to the data?
(b) To what extent was the competition mainly based on price?

key terms

Concentration ratio - the market share of the largest firms in an industry. For instance, a five firm concentration ratio of 60 per cent shows that the five largest firms in the industry have a combined market share of 60 per cent.
Sunk costs - costs of production which are not recoverable if a firm leaves the industry.

Applied economics

Market structures in the UK

What is an industry or market?

How many firms are there in an industry or market (here we will assume that the two terms can be used interchangeably)? The answer to this question will depend on how we define the market or industry. For instance, the economy could be split up into three very broad market classifications, - the market for primary goods, the market for secondary goods and the market for tertiary goods. There are a large number of firms operating in each of these markets. At the other extreme, one could ask how many UK firms produce balls for use in professional cricket. This is an extremely narrow market in which there are only two producers.

It should be obvious that the more narrowly a market is defined, the more likely it is that there will be relatively few producers. In the transport market, there are bus companies, rail companies, airlines, etc. In the air transport market, there will be fewer companies. In the market for air travel to the Isle of Skye there is only one company.

The Standard Industrial Classification

The Office for National Statistics (ONS) conducts regular censuses of production in the UK. The statistics record production levels in different industries using the Standard Industrial Classification 1992. This is a classification system which subdivides industry into broad divisions. For instance, Section C comprises mining and quarrying. Section D is manufacturing, whilst Section E is electricity, gas and water. Each section is then divided into sub-sections. Sub-section DA, for instance, is food, drink and tobacco. DB is textiles and textile products. The ONS classification is one way of grouping firms into individual industries, each sub-section representing an industry or group of industries.

Concentration ratios

Having classified firms into industries, it is possible to see how many producers there are in the industry. The number of producers is likely to be less important in studying the behaviour of the industry than the economic power of individual producers within the industry. One way of measuring this potential power is to calculate how important are the top few companies in the market. It can be done by looking at their importance in terms of market share in the industry, how many workers they employ or some other measure. This measure is then called a

CONCENTRATION RATIO.

A three-firm concentration ratio would be the total share of the market (by output, employment or some other measure) held by the three largest producers in the industry; a four-firm concentration ratio would be the total share of the market held by the four largest producers; etc.

Market concentration in the UK

Table 51.1 shows the five-firm concentration ratios for UK manufacturing industry in 1992. On average the largest five firms in an industry accounted for approximately 40 per cent of net output. However, an industry can be widely defined. For instance, one of the 103 industries included in Table 51.1 is passenger car production (Class 351 under the 1980 Standard Industrial Classification). A revised 1992 Standard Industrial Classification is currently being used for figures later than those shown in Table 51.1. Within that industry, it could be argued that there are a number of different markets, for instance the small car market, the family-size saloon car market and the luxury car market. The concentration ratio is likely to be higher in each of these markets than in the market for passenger car production as a whole because there will be fewer producers in each market segment. In general, the narrower the definition of the market, the higher the concentration ratio is likely to be.

Table 51.1 *Five-firm concentration ratios[1]: manufacturing industries, 1992*

Percentage of net output of the five largest firms in the industry	Number of industries
0-9	4
10-19	17
20-29	12
30-39	13
40-49	19
50-59	11
60-69	11
70-79	5
80-89	2
90-99	5

1. Percentage of total sales and work done by the five largest enterprises.
Source: adapted from Census of Production, Summary Tables, *Business Monitor*, PA 1002.

Figure 51.1 shows concentration ratios for selected industries in the UK. This ranges from 6.8 per cent in the metal working machine tool industry to 99.5 per cent in the tobacco industry.

In manufacturing, there has been increasing concentration this century. A slight fall in concentration during the 1970s can be partially explained by the decline in manufacturing industry at the time due to severe international competitive pressure. Many large manufacturers cut back production or left the market altogether, reducing their power within the market place. However, the take-over boom in the 1980s and continued European economic integration post-1992 saw a renewed upward trend in industrial concentration once again.

Figure 51.1 *Five-firm concentration ratios[1] for selected UK industries, 1992*

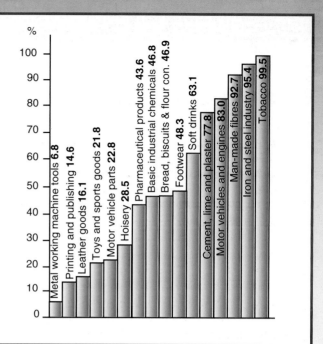

The DIY market

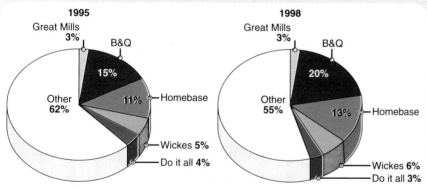

Figure 51.2 *The DIY market*
Source: adapted from Salmon, Smith, Barney.

B&Q announces expansion

B&Q, the do-it-yourself company owned by the Kingfisher group, announced aggressive expansion plans yesterday. Over the next five years, it will open almost 100 B&Q Warehouse stores at a cost of £750 million. This will take the chain to 125 stores. This is in addition to its existing standard Supercentre stores which are only one third of the size of a Warehouse store. It aims to double existing sales of £2 billion and double its 20 000 staff.

Source: adapted from *The Guardian*, 27.10.1999.

B&Q Warehouses are 'category killers'. Competitors, such as Homebase and Wickes, have found it difficult to compete with them because of their large scale, range of stock, service and low prices. The past ten years have already seen much consolidation. Many local independent hardware shops have disappeared. Chains have merged. For instance, Texas Homecare was taken over by Sainsbury's Homebase, whilst Boots sold Do It All to the Focus chain. Each chain has attempted to differentiate itself by appealing to a slightly different sector of the market. Wickes, for instance, is geared towards the serious DIY and small professional builder, whilst Homebase appeals more to the amateur DIY enthusiast interested in home furnishing. The problem they face is that a B&Q Warehouse, three times the size of a conventional outlet, can appeal to most customers in the market.

Source: adapted from *The Guardian*, 27.10.1999.

1. Briefly outline what is meant by 'market structure'.
2. Analyse the market structure of the DIY industry in the UK.
3. B&Q hopes that its market share will rise to at least 35 per cent. Discuss what factors might prevent it gaining a monopoly of the DIY market in the UK.

Summary

1. Profit is maximised at a level of output where the difference between total revenue and total cost is greatest.
2. At this profit maximising level of output, marginal cost = marginal revenue.
3. An increase in costs will lower the profit maximising level of output.
4. An increase in revenues will raise the profit maximising level of output.

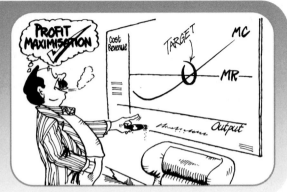

Total cost and total revenue

Profit is the difference between **revenue** (the receipts of the firm) and **costs** (the monies paid out by the firm). A firm will make the most profit (or **maximum** profit) when the difference between total revenue and total cost is greatest.

This is shown in Table 52.1. Total revenue is shown in the second column whilst total cost is in the third column. Profit is the difference between the two. At low levels of production, the firm will make a loss. The BREAK-EVEN point, where total revenue equals total cost, is reached at an output level of 3 units. Thereafter profit increases as output increases.

There are two levels of output where profit is highest at £27. But it should be remembered that the difference between revenue and cost here is **abnormal** or **economic profit**. Normal profit is included as a cost of production (☞ unit 47). So profit, both normal and abnormal, is at a maximum at an output level of 7 units rather than 6 units because the cost of the seventh unit includes an allowance for normal profit.

Table 52.1

Output	Total revenue (£)	Total cost (£)	Profit (£)
1	25	35	-10
2	50	61	-11
3	75	75	0
4	100	90	10
5	125	106	19
6	150	123	27
7	175	148	27
8	200	182	18
9	225	229	-4

Marginal cost and marginal revenue

Marginal cost and marginal revenue can also be used to find the profit maximising level of output. Marginal cost is the addition to total cost of one extra unit of output. Marginal revenue is the increase in total revenue resulting

Table 52.2

Output	Marginal revenue (£)	Marginal cost (£)	Addition to total profit (£)
1	25	35	-10
2	25	26	-1
3	25	14	11
4	25	15	10
5	25	16	9
6	25	18	8
7	25	25	0
8	25	34	-9
9	25	47	-22

from an extra unit of sales.

Table 52.2 shows the marginal cost and marginal revenue figures derived from Table 52.1. Marginal revenue minus marginal cost gives the extra profit to be made from producing one more unit of output. The firm makes a loss of £10 on the first unit, and £1 on the second. But the third unit of output yields a profit of £11, the fourth £10 and so on. So long as the firm can make

Question 1

Table 52.3

Output (million units)	Total revenue (£ million)	Total cost (£ million)
1	10	8
2	20	14
3	30	20
4	40	30
5	50	50
6	60	80

(a) Calculate the total profit at each level of output.
(b) What is the profit maximising level of output?
(c) Calculate the marginal revenue and marginal cost of production at each level of output.
(d) Explain, using the data, why MC = MR at the profit maximising level of output.

additional profit by producing an extra unit of output, it will carry on expanding production. But it will cease extra production when the extra unit yields a loss (i.e. where marginal profit moves from positive to negative). In Table 52.2, this happens at an output level of 7 units. The seventh unit contributes nothing to abnormal profit.

However, as explained above, cost includes an allowance for normal profit and therefore the firm will actually produce the seventh unit. The eighth unit yields a loss of profit of £9. The firm will therefore not produce the eighth unit if it wishes to maximise its profit.

Economic theory thus predicts that profits will be maximised at the output level where marginal cost equals marginal revenue.

Cost and revenue curves

These same points can be made using cost and revenue curves. The revenue curves in Figure 52.1 are drawn on the assumption that the firm receives the same price for its product however much it sells (i.e. demand is perfectly price elastic) So the total revenue curve increases at a constant rate.The marginal revenue curve is horizontal, showing that the price received for the last unit of output is exactly the same as the price received for all the other units sold before (☞ unit 54 for a discussion of the alternative assumption that a firm has to lower its price if it wishes to increase sales). The shape of the cost curves are as described in units 48 and 49.

The total revenue and total cost curves show that the firm will make a loss if it produces between O and B. Total cost is higher than total revenue. B is the break-even point. Between B and D the firm is in profit because total revenue is greater than total cost. However, profit is maximised at the output level C where the difference between total revenue and total cost is at a maximum. If the firm produces more than D, it will start making a loss again. D, the second break-even point on the diagram, is the maximum level of output which a firm can produce without making a loss. So D is the sales maximisation point subject to the constraint that the firm should not make a loss.

Now consider the marginal cost and marginal revenue curves. It can be seen that the profit maximising level of output, OC, is the point where marginal cost equals marginal revenue. If the firm produces an extra unit of output above OC, then the marginal cost of production is above the marginal revenue received from selling the extra unit. The firm will make a loss on that extra unit and total profit will fall. On the other hand, if the firm is producing to the left of OC the cost of an extra unit of output is less than its marginal revenue. Therefore the firm will make a profit on the extra unit if it is produced. Generalising this, we can say that the firm will expand production if marginal revenue is above marginal cost. The firm will reduce output if marginal revenue is below marginal cost.

It should be noted that there is another point in Figure 52.1 where MC = MR. This is at the point A. It isn't always the case that the marginal cost curve will start above the marginal revenue curve at the lowest level of

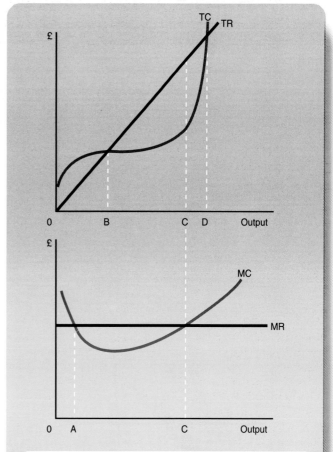

Figure 52.1 *The profit maximising level of output*
Profit is maximised at the level of output where the difference between total revenue and total cost is at its greatest, at OC. This is the point where marginal cost equals marginal revenue. OB and OD are break-even points.

output. However, if it does, then the first intersection point of the two curves, when marginal cost is falling, is not the profit maximising point. The MC = MR rule is therefore a **necessary** but not **sufficient** condition for profit maximisation. A second condition has to be attached, namely that marginal cost must be rising as well.

Question 2

(a) From the data in Table 52.3, draw two graphs showing (i) total revenue and total cost curves and (ii) marginal revenue and marginal cost curves. Draw the graphs one underneath the other using the same scale on the output axis.

(b) Mark on each of the graphs (i) the break-even levels of output and (ii) the profit maximising level of output.

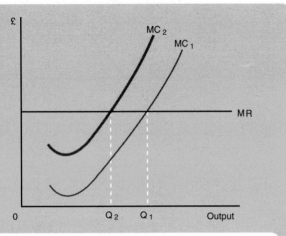

Figure 52.2 *An increase in costs*
An increase in costs of production which pushes up the marginal cost curve from MC_1 to MC_2 will lead to a fall in the profit maximising level of output from OQ_1 to OQ_2.

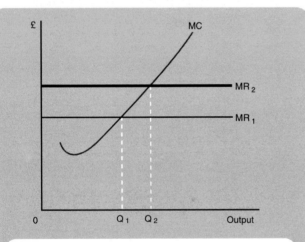

Figure 52.3 *An increase in revenue*
An increase in revenue at any given level of output will push the marginal revenue curve upwards from MR_1 to MR_2. This will lead to a rise in the profit maximising level of output from OQ_1 to OQ_2.

Question 3

Consider the data in Table 52.3. What is the new profit maximising level of output if:
(a) marginal revenue falls to £6 million at each level of output;
(b) marginal revenue increases to £20 million at each level of output;
(c) marginal cost increases by £4 million at each level of output;
(d) total cost increases by £5 million at each level of output;
(e) total revenue doubles at each level of output?

Shifts in cost and revenue curves

It is now possible to analyse in greater depth the effects of changes in costs or revenues on output. Assume that costs, such as the price of raw materials, increase. This will mean that the marginal cost of production at every level of output will be higher. The marginal cost curve will shift upwards as shown in Figure 52.2. The profit maximising level of output will fall from OQ_1 to OQ_2.
Hence a rise in costs will lead to a fall in output.

On the other hand a rise in revenue will lead to an increase in output. Assume that revenue increases at every given level of output. Perhaps consumers are prepared to pay higher prices because their incomes have increased, or the good has become more fashionable to purchase. This will push the marginal revenue curve upwards as shown in Figure 52.3. The profit maximising level of output will then rise from OQ_1 to OQ_2.

Good models

The MC = MR condition is one which is very important in the neo-classical theory of the firm. However, economists know from studies made that most businessmen are not familiar with the economic concepts of marginal cost and marginal revenue, and even fewer could state their current marginal cost of production.

In one sense this is very damning for the neo-classical theory of the firm. It will be explained in unit 45 that one criterion for judging a good model or theory is whether the model is realistic.

However, neo-classical economists would not claim that businessmen decide on their output levels by equating marginal cost and marginal revenue. They would start from the premise that firms attempt to maximise profits. If they don't, then in the real world they tend either to be forced out of business by more efficient firms which are maximising profit or they are taken over and made more efficient. So there are strong pressures forcing businesses towards their profit maximising levels of output. Economists then find it helpful to analyse the profit maximising level of output in terms of marginal cost and marginal revenue.

The MC = MR rule then is not an attempt by economists to explain how businesses arrive at their level of output. Rather, it is a rule which says that if businesses have maximised profit, it must logically be true that marginal cost equals marginal revenue. Parallels can be found in the physical sciences. A cricketer throwing a ball to another player will not analyse the throw in terms of velocity, friction, wind speed etc. But a physicist, using these concepts, could work out the optimum trajectory for the ball. The theory is not worthless because it fails to describe accurately how the player thinks and acts about the throw. Rather the theory helps us to understand the science behind everyday reality.

key terms

Break-even point - the levels of output where total revenue equals total cost.

Applied economics

Halifax profits

Halifax has traditionally been the UK's largest mortgage lender. However, during the 1990s, it came under increasing pressure from existing firms in the market and new entrants who wanted to increase or gain market share. Inevitably, that could only come partially at the expense of the Halifax. As Figure 52.4 shows, Halifax's share of outstanding mortgages fell from 20 per cent in 1996 to 18 per cent in 1998 and the increase in 1995-96 only occurred because Halifax took over the Leeds Permanent, another large building society.

Halifax could have chosen to maintain market share by cutting its interest rates. It chose not to do this because this was not the profit maximising option. It could still sell mortgages at higher rates of interest because there is not perfect knowledge in the market. In 1999, there was an estimated 2 000 different mortgage packages on offer by mortgage lenders to the UK homebuyer, all slightly different. Halifax used its large branch network, mailing to existing customers who might, for instance, only have a savings account with it, and national advertising to sell mortgages. It also relied on the inertia of its existing customers with mortgages not to transfer their mortgages to another cheaper lender.

In terms of marginal cost and marginal revenue, it took the decision that the marginal cost of selling more mortgages would be greater than the marginal revenue gained from so doing. The marginal cost would include the administrative cost of gaining and running the mortgage. It would also include the interest cost of borrowing the money, either from small savers through their branch network, or larger lenders on the money markets in London. The marginal revenue would include the interest charged on the mortgage. However, if Halifax wanted to increase its market share significantly, it might have to lower interest rates to some or all of its existing customers in order to attract new customers. For instance, it might gain £500 million extra a year in interest from new customers. But if it had to drop interest rates to existing customers and in so doing lost £300 million, then the marginal revenue would only be £200 million.

This illustrates the point that selling more could well lead to lower profits rather than higher profits. Charging a higher price and selling less can be more profitable than selling more at a lower price. For Halifax, it took the decision in the late 1990s that marginal cost equalled marginal revenue at a lower level of sales than it had traditionally experienced.

Hence, it would have to lose market share in order to maximise profit.

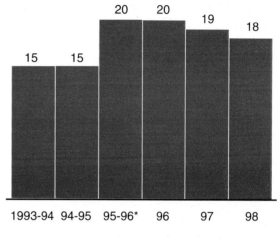

Figure 52.4 *Halifax: estimated market share of UK mortgages outstanding (%)*
Source: adapted from company information, Datastream/ICV.

Diversification and the Halifax

Halifax to sell 224 estate agencies

Halifax, the UK's largest mortgage lender, announced yesterday that it would sell one-third of its estate agencies with a loss of 1 500 jobs. The outlets were mainly in East Anglia, the Southwest and Wales where Halifax believes that it has too few agencies to create a critical mass that is necessary for profitability.

The move is part of a large scheme to reorganise the Halifax. At present Halifax divides the country into 123 banking and estate agency areas for customer marketing and this is to be reduced to 50. Halifax estimates that this will cut costs by £50 million a year, although sales are initially expected to fall by as much as £30 million.

In the second half of the 1980s, it became fashionable for building societies to establish chains of estate agents. Usually, the building society would go on a spending spree, buying up independent estate agents to create their chains. The synergies were simple to see. Estate agents sold houses to buyers who would usually want a mortgage. The estate agent could then be a 'one stop shop' for the home buyer. In 1998, for instance, 10 per cent of Halifax's mortgage business came through its chain of estate agents, with £1 billion loaned as a consequence.

Unfortunately, the housing market crashed at the end of the 1980s and estate agents saw their sales collapse. The building societies lost large sums of money and gradually began disposing of their recent acquisitions. Nationwide,

for instance, sold off its loss making 300 branch network in 1994 for £1 having lost a total of £200 million on the venture over the years. The Woolwich sold its 167 branch chain for £23 million in 1998, part of which had been brought from Prudential, the insurance company, for £20 million in 1990.

The problem for the banks and building societies that owned estate agents was twofold. First, running an estate agent's business at a profit is a business skill which financial institutions usually didn't have even when the housing market had recovered. Second, estate agents often failed to draw in enough business on the mortgage side to compensate for the low profits or losses that the estate agent business was making.

The way ahead

Many City observers believe that Halifax needs to make a substantial acquisition in the near future to reduce its core savings and mortgage activities. These account for 71 per cent of profits. However, mortgages are a mature business with weak growth prospects. In 1998, profits on

its core activities rose just 1.2 per cent whilst profits among its diversified businesses rose 33 per cent. These included life assurance and consumer credit, such as credit cards and personal loans.

Source: adapted from the *Financial Times*, 19.2.1999 and 15.4.1999; *The Times*, 15.4.1999.

1. Explain the possible (a) costs and (b) revenues of Halifax in its estate agents business.
2. Using the concepts of marginal cost and marginal revenue, suggest why Halifax sold off 224 estate
agency outlets in 1999.
3. Discuss what factors Halifax should take into consideration in deciding whether to diversify further from its core mortgage and savings activities.

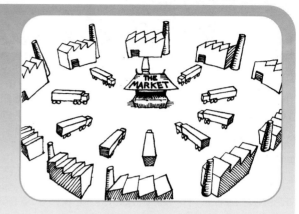

Summary

1. In a perfectly competitive market it is assumed that there is a large number of small firms that produce a homogeneous product. Firms are price-takers. There are no barriers to entry or exit and there is perfect knowledge.
2. The demand curve facing an individual firm is perfectly elastic because the firm is a price taker. This means that price = AR = MR.
3. The short run supply curve of the firm is its marginal cost curve above its average variable cost curve.
4. If firms in the short run are making abnormal profits, new firms will enter the industry, increasing market supply and thus reducing price. This will continue until only normal profits are being made.
5. If production is unprofitable, firms will leave the industry, reducing market supply and increasing price. This will continue until only normal profits are being made.
6. In long run equilibrium, AR = AC because no abnormal profits are made.

Assumptions

The model of perfect competition (☞ unit 17) describes a market where there is a high degree of competition. The word 'perfect' does not mean that this form of competition produces ideal results or maximises economic welfare; in other words, the word 'perfect' should not have any **normative** overtones (☞ unit 45).

A perfectly competitive market must possess four characteristics.

- There must be **many buyers and sellers** in the market, none of whom is large enough to influence price. Buyers and sellers are said to be **price takers**. This type of market has many relatively small firms that supply goods to a large number of small buyers.
- There is **freedom of entry to and exit** from the industry. Firms must be able to establish themselves in the industry easily and quickly. Barriers to entry must therefore be low. If a firm wishes to cease production and leave the market, it must be free to do so.
- Buyers and sellers possess **perfect knowledge** of prices. If one firm charges a higher price than the market price, the demand for its product will be zero as buyers buy elsewhere in the market. Hence the firm has to accept the market price if it wishes to sell into the market (i.e. it must be a price taker).
- All firms produce a **homogeneous** product. There is no branding of products and products are identical.

There are relatively few industries in the world which approximate to this type of market structure. One which might is agriculture. In agriculture there is a large number of farmers supplying the market, none of whom is large enough to influence price. It is easy to buy a farm and set up in business. Equally it is easy to sell a farm and leave the industry. Farmers on the whole possess perfect knowledge. They know what prices prevail in the market, for instance from the farming press. Finally, farmers produce a range of homogeneous products. King Edwards potatoes from one farm are indistinguishable from King Edwards potatoes from another. In Europe and in many countries round the world, farming is in certain instances

Question 1

Thousands of farmers around the world depend upon sugar for their livelihood. However, the late 1990s saw sugar prices fall to a ten year low as demand declined in Asia. This was due to the Asian crisis which saw countries like Indonesia and South Korea fall into a deep recession with a consequent cut in consumer demand. Farmers were powerless to prevent prices falling in what was already a weak market. Continued low prices will inevitably lead to a shake out in the industry, with farmers diversifying into other crops.

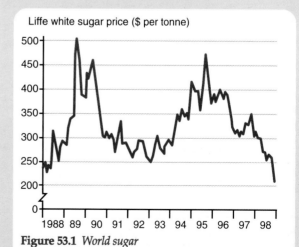

Figure 53.1 *World sugar*
Source: adapted from Datastream/ICV, ED&F Man.

(a) Discuss why farmers in the sugar market might be said to operate in a perfectly competitive market.

not a perfectly competitive market. This is because governments may interfere in the market, buying and selling to fix a price (☞ unit 21).

Demand and revenue

It is an assumption of the model of perfect competition that there is a large number of sellers in the market. Assume that one of these firms decides to double output. Industry supply will increase, pushing the supply curve to the right. However, the increase in supply is necessarily very small because the firm is small. In fact it will be so small that the resulting movement along the demand curve will be impossible to distinguish and the price will not change.

This can be seen in Figure 53.2. The area around the existing equilibrium point has been enlarged. An increase in supply by one firm has shifted the supply curve from S_1 to S_2, reducing equilibrium price by AC and increasing equilibrium quantity demanded and supplied by CB. However, AC is so small that it has no effect on the overall equilibrium price of OE and it is impossible to draw two supply curves thinly enough to show this shift in supply.

In agriculture, for instance, it would be surprising if the decision of one farmer to double wheat output were to have any perceptible influence on equilibrium price. His or her extra output is so insignificant that it cannot affect the market price for wheat. Of course, if all farmers were to double their wheat output, the price of wheat would collapse. But here we are interested only in the effect on price of the production decisions of a single farm.

A firm in perfect competition can therefore expand output or reduce output without influencing the price. Put another way, the firm cannot choose to raise price and expect to sell more of its product. It can lower its price but

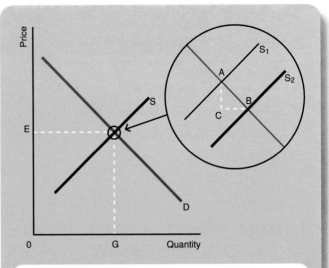

Figure 53.2 *The effect of an increase in supply by one firm in a perfectly competitive industry*
An increase in supply by one firm from S_1 to S_2 will have such a small effect on total supply that equilibrium price will remain at OE.

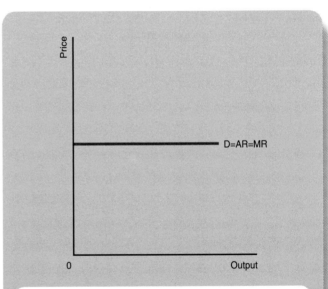

Figure 53.3 *The demand curve facing a firm in perfect competition*
A change in output by the firm will have no effect on the market price of the product. Therefore the firm faces a perfectly elastic demand curve. This is also the firm's average and marginal revenue curve.

Question 2

Table 53.1 *Market demand and supply*

Quantity demanded (million units)	Quantity supplied (million units)	Price (£)
1000	6000	10
3000	4000	8
5000	2000	6

(a) Draw the market demand and supply curves on graph paper.
(b) There are 1000 firms in the industry each producing the same quantity. One firm now doubles its output.
 (i) Show the effect of this on market demand and supply.
 (ii) On a separate graph draw the demand curve facing the firm.
(c) All firms in the industry now double their output.
 (i) Show the effect of this on market demand and supply.
 (ii) What will be the effect on the demand curve for the individual firm?

there is no advantage in this since it can sell its entire output at the higher market price. The demand curve for an individual firm is therefore horizontal (i.e. **perfectly elastic** ☞ unit 8) as in Figure 53.3. (Note that if a firm expanded output sufficiently its demand curve would become downward sloping. But then the industry would be made up of one large firm and many small firms and would no longer be perfectly competitive.)

This demand curve is also the firm's average and marginal revenue curve. If a firm sells all its output at one price, then this price must be the average price or average revenue received. If a firm sells an extra or marginal unit, it will receive the same price as on preceding units and therefore the marginal price or revenue will be the same as the average price or revenue.

Cost and supply curves

In a perfectly competitive market, the supply curve of the firm will be its marginal cost curve.

- The marginal cost of production is the lowest price at which a firm would be prepared to supply an extra unit of output. For instance, if the marginal cost were £3 when price received was £5, then the firm would be able to make £2 **abnormal profit** (profit over and above the **normal profit** included in cost on that unit). The firm would definitely produce this marginal unit. If marginal cost were £3 when price were £3 it would still produce this marginal unit because it would earn normal profit on it. However, if marginal cost were £3 when price was £2 it would not produce the extra unit because it would make a £1 loss on it.
- In the short run, a firm will not necessarily shut down production if it makes a loss (☞ unit 50). A firm has fixed costs which it has to pay whether it closes down and produces nothing or whether it continues to operate. Any revenue over and above variable cost will make some contribution towards paying its fixed costs. Therefore it will only close down (i.e. cease to supply) if average revenue or price is below average variable cost.

The firm's short run supply curve will therefore be that part of the marginal cost curve above its average variable cost curve - the thick portion of the marginal cost curve in Figure 53.4 (a).

In the long run there are no fixed costs and the average total cost and average variable cost curves are one and the same. The firm will not produce unless it can cover all its costs. Therefore in the long run, the firm's supply curve is the marginal cost curve above its average cost curve as shown in Figure 53.4 (b).

The supply curve for the industry can be constructed by horizontally summing the individual supply curves of each firm.

Short run equilibrium

In perfect competition it is assumed that firms are short run profit maximisers. So the firm will produce at that level of output where marginal cost equals marginal revenue (the MC= MR rule ☞ unit 50). The price it charges is fixed by the market because the individual firm is a price-taker.

Figure 53.5 shows one possible short run equilibrium situation. The demand curve is perfectly elastic at a price of OE. The marginal cost curve cuts the marginal revenue curve at H and hence the equilibrium, profit maximising level of output for the firm is OQ. At this level of output, average revenue (QH) is higher than average cost (QG)

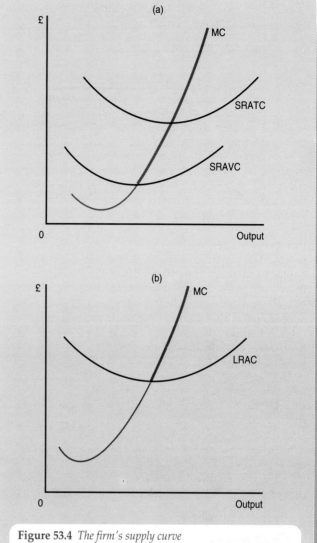

Figure 53.4 *The firm's supply curve*
The marginal cost of production is the lowest price at which a profit maximising firm will sell a marginal unit of production. Therefore the marginal cost curve is the supply curve for the firm. However, in the short run the firm may stay in production providing it can cover its average variable costs. Hence the short run supply curve is the marginal cost curve above average variable cost as in Figure 53.4(a). In the long run a firm will leave the industry if it makes a loss. Hence, the supply curve in the long run is the marginal cost curve above the average cost curve as in Figure 53.4 (b).

and so the firm will make an abnormal profit. This is given by the shaded area EFGH and is average profit (EF) multiplied by the quantity produced (FG).

Figure 53.6 gives another possible situation. Here the firm is making a loss at its equilibrium, profit maximising (or in this case loss minimising) level of output OQ where MC = MR. Price OF is lower than average cost and hence the firm makes a total loss of EFGH. The firm will stay in production if this loss is smaller than the loss it would make if it shut down (i.e. so long as average revenue is above average variable cost).

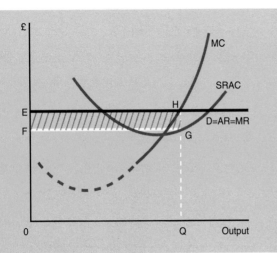

Figure 53.5 *Short run profit maximisation*
The firm produces at its profit maximising equilibrium level of output OQ where MC = MR. Because AR is greater than AC, it makes an abnormal profit of EFGH.

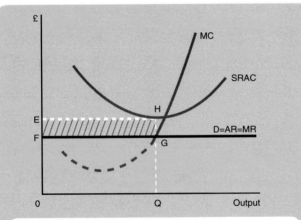

Figure 53.6 *Short run operation at a loss*
The firm produces at its profit maximising equilibrium level of output OQ where MC = MR. In this case, because AR is less than AC, it will make a loss shown by the shaded area EFGH. This is the minimum loss it will make if AR is greater than AVC.

Long run equilibrium

In the long run, a perfectly competitive firm will neither make losses nor abnormal profits.

Consider a situation where firms were making losses. In the long term, some firms would leave the industry. It is pointless carrying on production in the long term at a loss. If firms leave the industry, total supply will fall. The more firms that leave the industry, the greater will be the fall in supply and the greater will be the rise in price of the product. Firms will continue to leave the industry until the industry as a whole returns to profitability. This is shown in Figure 53.7. When the supply curve is S_1 the firm is making a loss. Firms leave the industry, pushing the

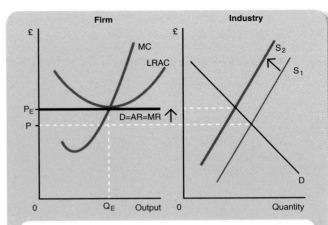

Figure 53.7 *Long run equilibrium following short run losses*
If losses are being made in the short run firms will leave the industry, pushing the supply curve from S_1 to S_2. At S_2 there will no longer be any pressure for firms to leave because they will be able to make normal profits on their operations.

supply curve to the left. With S_2, the price is just high enough for firms to make **normal profit**. If on the other hand a firm were making abnormal profit in the short run, other firms would enter the industry eager to gain high profits. This is shown in Figure 53.8. At a price of P, firms are making abnormal profit. This encourages new entrants to the industry, increasing supply from S_1 until with S_2 the price is just low enough for firms to make a normal profit.

In the long run, then, competitive pressures ensure

Question 3

Table 53.2

£

Output	Marginal cost (£)	Total fixed cost	Total variable cost	Total cost	Average variable cost	Average total cost
2		100	100			
	40					
3						
	30					
4						
	40					
5						
	60					
6						
	100					
7						

Table 53.2 shows the costs of production of a firm.

(a) Calculate for levels of output from 2 to 7 units:
(i) total fixed cost (ii) total variable cost; (iii) total cost; (iv) average variable cost; (v) average total cost.
(b) Plot the firm's short run supply curve on a graph.
(c) Would a firm cease production (1) in the short run and (2) in the long run if the sales price per unit were: (i) £80; (ii) £70; (iii) £60; (iv) £50; (v) £40; (vi) £30?

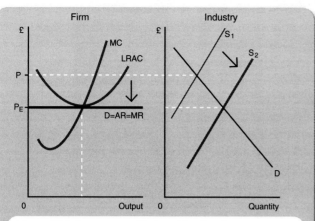

Figure 53.8 *Long run equilibrium following short run abnormal profit*
If abnormal profits are being made in the short run, firms will enter the industry, pushing the supply curve from S_1 to S_2. At S_2 firms will no longer be attracted into the industry because they will only be able to make normal profits on their operations.

equilibrium is established where the firm neither makes abnormal profits or losses. This means that in equilibrium, average revenue equals average cost (AR = AC). It should also be remembered that MC = MR because the firm is profit maximising and that AR = MR because the demand curve is horizontal. Putting these three conditions together, it must be true that for a firm in long run equilibrium in a perfectly competitive market:

$$AC = AR = MR = MC$$

Long run cost curves

One interesting point to note is that the model of perfect competition predicts that all perfectly competitive firms will have identical costs in the long run. Assume a firm discovers some new technique of production which enables it to reduce costs and increase profits in the short run. Other firms will respond by copying this technique. They can do this because there is perfect knowledge in the industry and therefore there can be no industrial secrets. Firms will then start to cut prices, hoping to be able to expand their sales. If a firm fails to adopt the new techniques, it will start to make a loss when other firms expand supply and undercut its price. Eventually it will be forced either to leave the industry because it is uncompetitive, or adopt the latest production techniques.

Alternatively, a firm may possess some unique factor of production. It may have an exceptional manager, or find that it is far better sited than other firms. In a perfectly competitive world the manager will be able to demand increases in salary which match the extra profit that she is generating for the firm. If the firm fails to pay this, she will be headhunted by another firm which realises the potential of the manager to create profits. As for the better site, the firm could sell it to another firm in the industry for a much higher price than those sites owned by competitors. Therefore the opportunity cost of the site is much higher

than other sites and it is the opportunity cost, not the accounting cost, that is shown in economists' cost curves.

Question 4

Wood pulp is the raw ingredient for paper and cardboard. In 1998, the price of long fibre or NBSK pulp fell below the $500 a tonne barrier. At this level, many producers find it difficult to even cover their costs. The result has been that companies have been cutting back on investment plans. They have also reduced the throughput of their plants and in some cases have mothballed or dismantled existing plant. The fall to $500 a tonne has been mainly the result of the Asian crisis. Countries like South Korea and Indonesia were caught in a financial meltdown which led to a sharp and sudden recession in their economies. Demand for pulp consequently fell. Not only did producers in Europe and North America lose markets, but they suddenly found Asian producers diverting supplies into European and North American domestic markets.

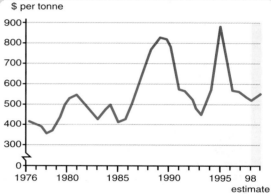

Figure 53.9 *Price of Northern Bleached Softwood Kraft (NBSK) pulp*
Source: adapted from Panmure Gordon.

(a) How can the model of perfect competition explain the output and investment decisions of firms in the pulp industry in 1998?
(b) Using a diagram, explain why higher prices would lead to increased output in the pulp industry.

Question 5

In 1988, it was reported that Pompes Funébres Générales (PFG), the largest firm of French undertakers, had bought a 29 per cent stake in Kenyon Securities, the third largest quoted undertaking business in Britain. In France a declining mortality rate had hit undertakers hard and PFG was looking for new markets. One reason why the UK was attractive was because there were more cremations in the UK than in France. 70 per cent of the UK market was accounted for by cremations whereas in France the figure was only 4 per cent. Profit margins on cremations are much higher than on burials.

(a) Why might PFG have been prepared to pay more for its stake in Kenyon Securities than it would have had to pay if it attempted to set up a rival undertaking business from scratch in the UK?

Applied economics

The UK coal industry

Today, there is only a handful of major mining companies in the British coal industry. During the 1990s, coal faced difficult times. The privatisation of the electricity and gas industries introduced fierce competition into the energy market. For the first time, the UK electricity industry, the major customer of the British coal industry, was able to choose whether to buy British coal or foreign coal, or whether to use coal or another fuel, particularly gas, to generate electricity. British coal mines were exposed to the harsh reality of a perfectly competitive market.

The market for coal is a worldwide market. As Figure 45.10 shows, large and increasing volumes of coal are shipped around the world from coal mine to customer. Transport is a significant cost and so less efficient coal mines can survive if they are near to their customers. Coal itself is a homogeneous product, although it comes in many different grades and qualities. There is perfect knowledge in the coal mining industry, with easy access for firms to coal mining technology and to information about prices. There is no buyer or seller in the market large enough to be able to influence price.

In the UK, the coal producers had signed a relatively generous five year contract with electricity producers in 1993. This could not prevent the decline in coal sales shown in Figure 45.11, but it ensured the survival of some of the industry. In December 1998, the contracts were renegotiated and this time the electricity power generating firms forced the price down to world price levels. Before, coal producers were getting around 140p a gigajoule; after it was about 120p, almost the same as the 119p cost of production at the time.

UK coal mining companies have responded to the downward pressure on both sales and prices by closing mines and increasing productivity at those that remain. The question is whether they have any long term future. If world coal prices fall, UK customers may choose to buy even more imported coal rather than domestically produced coal. Equally, if the economics of gas fired electricity power stations improve even further, the future of British coal mines will be bleak.

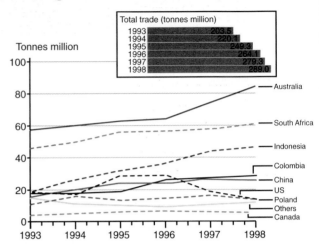

Figure 53.10 *Seaborne steam coal trade*
Source: adapted from *South African Coal Statistics and Marketing Annual*, 1999.

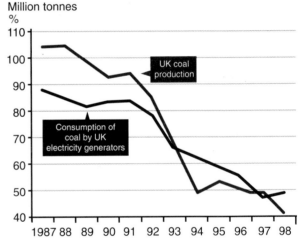

Figure 53.11 *UK coal production by mining firms and consumption by electricity generators, million tonnes*
Source: adapted from *Annual Abstract of Statistics, Monthly Digest of Statistics*, Office for National Statistics.

Pig production

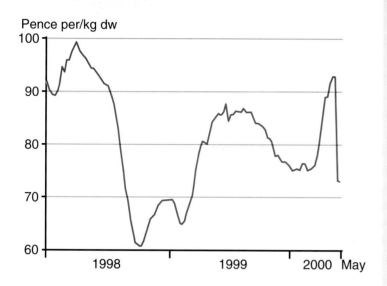

Figure 53.12 *Pig prices (pence per kilogram deadweight)*
Source: adapted from *Farmers Weekly*.

Pig farmers face bankruptcy

A crisis has hit British pig farming. Pig production is down 10 per cent this year. One in ten of Britain's 4 000 pig farmers face going out of business with many more slimming down their pig herds. Prices are 40 per cent down on what they were two years ago.

The industry has been hit from all sides. The high value of the pound has meant that cheap imports have flooded into the British market, whilst UK pig farmers have seen their export price competitiveness eroded. The BSE crisis has added to the cost of British pork because of the extra safety precautions now required. On top of that, pig farmers have had to invest in new facilities as the use of narrow stalls and tethers was banned in January on animal welfare grounds. British pig farmers are complaining bitterly that continental pig producers do not have to meet such strict safety and animal welfare standards.

Source: adapted from *The Guardian*, 6.10.1999.

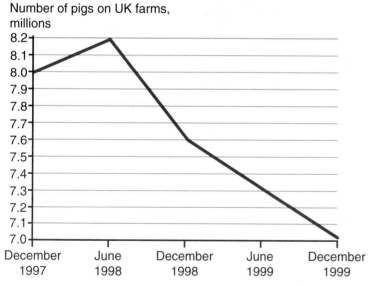

Figure 53.13 *Pigs on UK farms*
Source: adapted from *Monthly Digest of Statistics*, Office for National Statistics.

1. Why is pig farming a perfectly competitive industry?
2. Explain, using diagrams, why: (a) there was a fall in the number of pigs on UK farms in 1999; (b) pig farmers continued to produce in 1999 despite making losses.
3. Discuss what might happen to the number of pig farmers in 2000-2001.

Summary

1. A monopolist is the sole producer in an industry.
2. The demand curve faced by the monopolist is the market demand curve.
3. The monopolist's demand curve is also its average revenue curve.
4. The marginal revenue falls twice as steeply as the average revenue curve.

5. The profit maximising monopolist will produce where MC = MR and price on its demand curve.
6. The monopolist is likely to be able to earn abnormal profit because average revenue will be above average cost at the equilibrium level of output.
7. A monopolist may be able to price discriminate and further increase abnormal profit.

Assumptions

The neo-classical theory of monopoly assumes that a **monopoly** (☞ unit 18) market structure has the following characteristics:
- there is only one firm in the industry - the monopolist;
- barriers to entry prevent new firms from entering the market;
- the monopolist is a short run profit maximiser.

There are many industries in the world economy which possess most or all of these characteristics. In the UK, for instance, gas, electricity, telecommunications, rail transport and water supply are monopolies. Some of these monopolies are state owned whilst others were state monopolies which have since been privatised without the creation of genuine new competition (☞ unit 18).

Some monopolies, such as the UK water companies,

possess considerable market power because there are no good substitutes for their products. The Post Office too is a monopolist, but its monopoly position is weaker because it faces competition from other forms of communication service. In fact the existence of monopoly depends upon how an industry is defined. For instance, the Post Office is a monopolist in letter delivery, but not in communication services. Shell is not a monopoly supplier of petrol to the UK market, but it may have a monopoly in a rural area if it owns the only garage for miles around.

Monopolies can only remain as monopolies if there are high barriers to entry to the industry (☞ unit 51). In the case of a natural monopoly (☞ unit 18), economies of scale are so large that any new entrant would find it impossible to match the costs and prices of the established firm in the industry. Other barriers to entry include legal barriers such as patents, natural cost advantages such as ownership of all key sites in an industry, marketing barriers such as advertising, and restrictive practices designed to force any competitor to leave the market.

Revenue curves

A monopoly firm is itself the industry. Because the industry faces a downward sloping demand curve, so too must the monopolist. It can therefore only increase sales by reducing price, or increase price by reducing sales. It can set either price or output but not both.

The demand curve shows the quantity bought at any given price. For instance, a water company might sell 2 billion gallons of water at 1p per gallon. This price is the same as its average revenue; on average it will receive 1p per gallon. So the downward sloping demand curve facing the firm is also the average revenue curve of the firm.

If average revenue is falling, marginal revenue must be falling too and at a faster rate. For example, assume a firm sells 10 units at £20 each. To sell an eleventh unit, it needs to lower its price, say to £19. Not only will it have to lower its price on the eleventh unit, but it will also have to lower its price on the other 10 units. This is because it cannot charge a higher price to some consumers than others (although we will see later on in this unit that it is possible in limited cases). There is a loss of revenue not just of £1 on the sale of the eleventh unit but of a further £10 on the

---

Question 1

British Gas was created by the Labour government of 1945-1951 from a network of local gas companies, some owned by local authorities. As a nationalised industry, it was the sole supplier of piped gas in the UK. In 1986, the industry was privatised as one company retaining the legal power to be the sole supplier of gas. Then the government decided that there would considerable efficiency gains if the gas market were to become competitive. In 1988, the company was forced to allow other gas companies to supply gas to industrial customers using British Gas pipelines. In 1996, British Gas was split into two parts. Transco owned the gas pipeline network and would earn revenues from charging other gas companies to transport gas into homes and business premises. British Gas retained the gas supply business. However, in 1997-98, the gas market to domestic users was opened up to other companies. Now, both homes and businesses could choose which supplier to use, although all the gas was transported through Transco pipelines.

(a) To what extent was British Gas a monopoly supplier of gas in the UK in: (a) 1986; (b) 1990; (c) 2000?
(b) To what extent was the gas industry a monopoly in 2000?

first 10 units. Total revenue increases from £200 (£20 x 10 units) to £209 (£19 x 11 units). So marginal revenue on the eleventh unit is £9 (£209 - £200) whilst the average revenue on selling 11 units is £19 (£209 ÷ 11 which is, of course, the price).

Table 54.1 gives a further example of falling marginal and average revenues. Note that the fall in marginal revenue is twice as large over any given change in quantity as the fall in average revenue. This is true of all straight line average revenue curves. Plotting these figures

Table 54.1

Quantity	Average revenue or price £	Total revenue £	Marginal revenue £
0			
			8
1	8	8	
			4
2	6	12	
			0
3	4	12	
			-4
4	2	8	
			-8
5	0	0	

on a diagram, we arrive at Figure 54.1. The marginal revenue figures, as with all marginal figures, are plotted half way between 'whole' output figures. So the marginal revenue of the second unit is plotted half way between 1 and 2 units. It can be seen that at any given level of output, average revenue is twice marginal revenue. Total revenue is maximised when marginal revenue is zero. If marginal revenue (the addition to total revenue) becomes negative then total revenue will automatically fall. Total

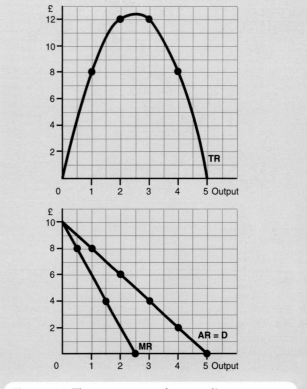

Figure 54.1 *The revenue curves of a monopolist*
A monopolist, being the sole supplier in the industry, faces a downward sloping demand or average revenue curve. Marginal revenue falls at twice the rate of average revenue and becomes zero when total revenue is maximised.

revenue is zero if average revenue, the price received per unit of output, is zero too.

Equilibrium output

The neo-classical theory of the firm assumes that a monopolist will be a short run profit maximiser. This means that it will produce where MC = MR.

Figure 54.2 adds the traditional U-shaped average and marginal cost curves (☞ units 48 and 49) to the average and marginal revenue curves outlined above.

- **The equilibrium profit maximising level of output** is OA where MC = MR.
- **The price** will be OE. Buyers are prepared to pay OE for this output. We know this because the average revenue curve is also the demand curve and the demand curve shows the maximum price buyers will pay for any given level of ouput.
- **Abnormal profit** of EFGC will be made. The abnormal profit per unit (GF) is the difference between the average revenue received (AF) and the average cost incurred (AG). OA units are sold. Therefore total abnormal profit is OA x FG, or the area EFGC. Note that this is abnormal profit because economic cost includes an allowance for normal profit.

Note also that price is not equal to the intersection of the MC and MR curves (i.e. price is not AB). This is because

Question 2

Table 54.2

Output (units per week)	Marginal revenue (£)
0	
	10
1	
	7
2	
	4
3	
	1
4	
	-2
5	

(a) Calculate (i) total revenue and (ii) average revenue at output levels 0 to 5 units.
(b) (i) Draw the axes of a graph with revenue from £0 to £10 and output from 0 to 10. (ii) Plot the marginal and average revenue curves. (iii) Extend the average revenue curve to the output axis assuming that average revenue continues to fall at the same rate as in the table.
(c) What is the value of marginal revenue when total revenue is at a maximum?

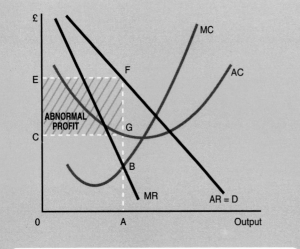

Figure 54.2 *Profit maximising output*
The monopolist will maximise profits by producing where
MC = MR at OA. It will base its prices on its average revenue
curve, charging OE. It will be able to earn abnormal profit of
EFGC because average revenue is greater than average cost at
this level of output.

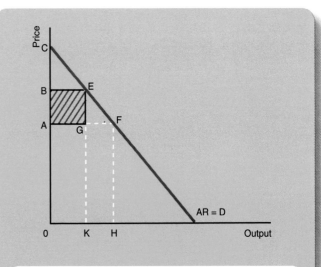

Figure 54.3 *The appropriation of consumer surplus*
A monopolist can appropriate ABEG of consumer surplus by
price discriminating:- selling OK output to those consumers
prepared to pay a minimum OB, and selling KH to other
consumers only prepared to pay a minimum OA.

the firm, although deciding on the level of output by the MC = MR condition, fixes its price on the average revenue or demand curve. Also abnormal profit is not the area EF x FB (i.e. it is not the area between the average revenue curve and the marginal revenue and cost curves). Profit per unit is the difference between average revenue and average cost.

Discriminating monopoly

Some buyers in the market will almost certainly be prepared to pay a higher price for a product than other buyers. In Figure 54.3, the profit maximising output for a monopolist is assumed to be OH and the profit maximising price is therefore OA. OA represents the maximum price that the marginal consumer is prepared to pay. Other consumers are prepared to pay a higher price. If output were only OK, the marginal consumer would be prepared to pay OB. The area ACF represents the area of consumer surplus (☞ unit 4), the difference between what consumers are prepared to pay in total for a good and what they actually pay. For instance, a rail commuter is likely to be prepared to pay more for a journey at 8 o'clock in the morning to take her to work than would a shopper. A millionaire faced with the need for heart surgery will pay more than a poor person with the same complaint.

A monopolist may be able to split the market and PRICE DISCRIMINATE between different buyers. In Figure 54.3, the monopolist may be able to charge OB for OK of output, and then charge a lower price of OA for KH of output. In this way, the monopolist appropriates ABEG of consumer surplus in the form of higher profit (i.e. higher producer surplus).

There is a number of different ways in which a

monopolist may choose to discriminate.

- Time. It may charge a different price at different times of the day or week, as do the electricity distribution companies or rail companies.
- Place. It may vary price according to the location of the buyer. The same car can be bought at different prices in different countries of the EU, for instance.
- Income. It may be able to split up consumers into income groups, charging a high price to those with high incomes, and a low price to those with lower incomes. Examples of this can be found in medical practice and amongst lawyers. Hairdressers (who may be local monopolists) offering reduced rates to pensioners are likely to be price discriminating according to income too.

Three conditions must hold if a monopolist is to be able to price discriminate effectively.

- The monopolist must face different demand curves from separate groups of buyers (i.e. the elasticity of demand of buyers must differ). If all buyers had the same demand curve, then the monopolist could not charge different prices to buyers.
- The monopolist must be able to split the market into distinct groups of buyers, otherwise it will be unable to distinguish between those consumers prepared to pay a higher price and those prepared to a pay a lower price.
- The monopolist must be able to keep the markets separate at relatively low cost. For instance, it must be able to prevent buyers in the high priced market from buying in the low price market. If a German car company sells its cars at 25 per cent less in Belgium than in the UK, then it must be able to prevent UK motorists and UK retailers from taking a day trip to Belgium to buy those cars. Equally, it must be able to

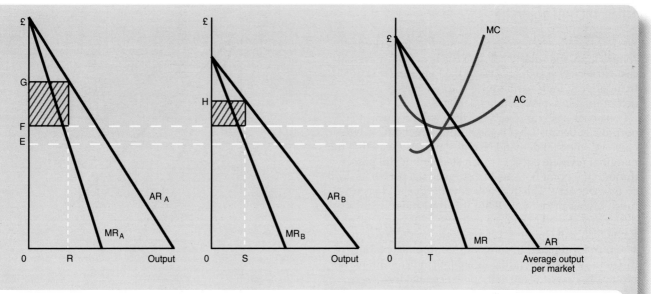

Figure 54.4 *Price discrimination*
By charging a different price in two markets, a monopolist is able to earn higher profits than it would if it charged the same price.

prevent traders from buying in the low price market and selling into the high price market at a price which undercuts that of the monopolist.

Price discrimination can be analysed using the concepts of marginal cost and marginal revenue. Assume that the

Question 3

Table 54.3 *Business calls, 1999, pence per minute*

	Daytime Mon to Fri 8am-6pm	Eve. & night-time Mon to Fri before 8am & after 6pm	Weekend Midnight Fri to midnight Sun
To fixed phone lines			
Local	3.36	1.30	0.85
National	6.73	3.36	1.702
To mobile phones			
SunCellnet			
Number Ranges	16.9	16.3	1.7
Vodafone			
Number Ranges	17.5	12.8	6.3
One2one and Dolphin			
Number Ranges	21.5	15.2	6.9
Orange			
Number Ranges	21.1	15.2	6.7
International calls			
Australia	41.70	35.67	33.28
China	92.00	87.40	81.60
France	24.19	22.68	19.67
North Korea	115.08	109.98	102.00
USA	20.10	19.10	17.75

Note: subject to a minimum fee of 4.2p
Source: adapted from BT website.

(a) Using diagrams, explain why BT has such a complicated tariff structure for business users.

monopolist is able to divide its market into two and that the costs of production are identical for both markets.

The firm needs to allocate production between the two markets so that the marginal revenue is identical for each market if it is to maximise profit. To understand why, take a situation where marginal revenue in one market, A, is higher than in another market, B. The firm could increase its total revenue from a given output by switching goods from B to A. Marginal revenue in market B will now rise because it can charge a higher price if it sells less. Marginal revenue in market A will fall because it has to lower price to sell more. For instance, if marginal revenue in market A were £10 when it was £6 in market B, then the firm could gain an extra £4 of revenue by switching the marginal unit of production from market B to market A. It will carry on switching from market B to A until there is no more advantage in doing so, which occurs when the marginal revenues are the same.

In Figure 54.4, the demand curves in markets A and B are drawn first. From these demand or average revenue curves, the marginal revenue curves in each market can then be calculated. The average and marginal revenue curves for the total market can be calculated by summing horizontally the average and marginal revenue curves in each market. The profit maximising monopolist will produce where MC = MR across the whole market, at output level OT. This output (OT) is then split between the two markets (OR and OS) so that the marginal revenue is equal in both individual markets (OE). In each market, a firm's price will be based on the average revenue curve. A price of OG can be charged in market A, and a price of OH can be charged in market B. Average cost of production is OF and the abnormal profit earned in each market is shown by the shaded areas on the diagram. This will be higher than the abnormal profit the firm would have made if it had not discriminated.

Three technical points

Absence of a supply curve in monopoly In perfect competition, the supply curve of the firm is its marginal cost curve above average cost in the long run (☞ unit 53). In monopoly, there is no supply curve which is determined independently of demand.

Look back at Figure 54.2. The firm will produce at output OA because that is the output where MC = MR. Now assume that demand changes in such a way that the marginal revenue curve is much steeper but still passes through the point B. If the MR curve is steeper, so too will be the AR curve. The firm will now be able to charge a much higher price than OE for its product. For each differently sloped MR curve that passes through the point B, the firm will charge a different price to the consumer. The firm is prepared to supply OA output at a variety of different prices, depending upon demand conditions. So no supply curve for the monopolist can be drawn. (Contrast this with the firm in perfect competition. Falls in demand which reduce prices received by the firm will result in a fall in quantity supplied as the firm moves down its supply curve.)

A monopolist will produce only where demand is elastic Look back to Figure 54.1. It should be obvious that the firm will not produce more than 2½ units of output. If it produces 3 units, it will almost certainly have higher costs than if it produces 2½ units but total revenue will fall. Profit therefore is bound to fall. 2½ units is the output where marginal revenue is zero. It is also the point where price elasticity of demand is unity because we are now half way along the demand or average revenue curve (☞ unit 8). To the left, elasticity is greater than 1, to the right less than 1. Since the firm will only produce to the left of 2½ units, it must produce where demand is elastic. An alternative explanation is to remember that a fall in price (needed to increase quantity sold) will only increase revenue if demand is elastic. Therefore a monopolist would not increase sales to the point where demand became inelastic.

Short run and long run operation So far no distinction has been made between the short run and the long run. A firm will produce in the short run if total revenue is greater than total variable cost (☞ unit 50). In the short run, a monopolist may therefore operate at a loss but it will close down if it cannot cover its variable costs. In the long run, a monopolist will not operate if it cannot cover all costs of production. Such a situation is shown in Figure 54.5. To maximise profits or minimise losses, it will produce where MC = MR, but at this level of output average cost is greater than average revenue. Because the monopolist is the sole supplier in the industry, long term losses will mean that no firm will supply and hence the industry will cease to exist.

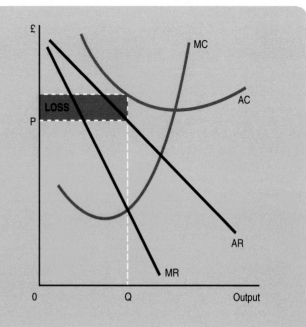

Figure 54.5 *An industry where no firm will produce The figure shows an industry in the long run. Because AC is greater than AR, no firm will be prepared to operate and therefore no goods will be produced.*

Question 4

Draw two diagrams showing the change in equilibrium output of a profit maximising monopolist if: (a) its marginal revenue increases; (b) its marginal cost increases.

key terms

Price discrimination - charging a different price for the same good or service in different markets.

Applied economics

Virgin Wolverhampton to London

When British Rail was broken up in 1996, Virgin won the franchise to operate trains on the West Coast line. This included taking over the Wolverhampton to London line. In one respect, this is a monopoly service. No other train operator has the legal right to run express services from Wolverhampton through Birmingham New Street Station and Milton Keynes down to London Euston. The terms of the franchise issued by the government therefore constitute a legal barrier to entry to this market.

However, travellers have alternatives. There are three train operators running from Birmingham to London: Virgin, Silverlink and Chiltern Railways. Wolverhampton passengers can therefore travel to Birmingham and change to either Silverlink or Chiltern. However, Silverlink only runs stopping trains to London Euston with a typical journey time 1 hour longer than Virgin. The rolling stock itself is suburban carriages designed for short journeys rather than the intercity rolling stock of Virgin. The journey is therefore far less comfortable. As for Chiltern, it runs from different stations to Virgin. At Birmingham, it runs out of Snow Hill Station. Most trains into Birmingham, including Virgin trains, go to Birmingham New Street. Making a connection between New Street and Snow Hill requires a long walk or a journey on public transport. In London, Chiltern Railways goes to Marylebone Station and not Euston Station. Both Silverlink and Chiltern Railways offer cheaper tickets from Birmingham to London than Virgin, particularly at peak times. However, their services have proved poor substitutes for those travelling from Birmingham to London and even more so from Wolverhampton to London.

Virgin, therefore, has a strong monopoly on rail journeys from Wolverhampton to London and is in a dominant position on the Birmingham to London route.

Price discrimination

As a monopolist, Virgin is able to price discriminate. The range of prices on the Wolverhampton to London route is shown in Table 54.4. It splits up the market in many ways. First, it price discriminates by the time of day and

Table 54.4 *Virgin fares Wolverhampton-London and London-Wolverhampton, November 1999*

		£
	Wolverhampton-London return	London-Wolverhampton return
First class	118.00	118.00
Standard open	79.50	79.50
Saver	30.80	37.00
Cheap day	24.50	31.50
1 day Virgin Value	23.00	23.00
7 day Virgin Value	17.00	17.00

weekday/weekend when the journey is taken. Those who need to get to London from Wolverhampton by 9 a.m. on a weekday tend to have a low price elasticity of demand. They tend to be business travellers, many of whom have their journey paid for them by their employer. Virgin can charge very high prices without losing too many passengers amongst this group.

Second, it price discriminates on advance booking. Virgin, along with a number of other rail companies, has decided that it is in its interests to encourage as much advance booking as possible. It improves cash flow because tickets are paid in advance. It locks passengers into travelling when, on the day, they might otherwise have chosen not to travel by Virgin or travel at all. It also spreads passenger loads. Passengers unable to book a ticket to travel at the most popular times may switch to a less popular time. Advance booking allows passengers to book a seat, important if there is likely to be overcrowding on the train. But also the cheapest tickets on the Wolverhampton to London route are only available by booking in advance for a specific timed journey. They are likely to be bought by passengers with the highest price elasticity of demand: those who would otherwise not travel if the price were much higher. Only a very small proportion of seats on a train are available at the cheapest price. So Virgin can advertise very low prices without losing too much revenue. They can also offer the bargain hunter travel at a less crowded and popular time, allowing Virgin to spread travel numbers during the day.

Virgin has a large number of other ways in which it price discriminates. It encourages children and families to travel by offering reductions for children and Family Rail Cards. Students can get reductions by buying a Student Rail Card. Old Age Pensioners are offered a similar card. Travellers starting out from London tend to get charged more than those starting from Wolverhampton, presumably because Londoners have a lower price elasticity of demand than residents of Wolverhampton.

Virgin's pricing policy over time would suggest that it

has a keen understanding of price elasticity of demand. Its lowest cost fares have changed little over time as Table 54.5 shows. However, the cost of travelling to London first class for a business traveller has increased by 44 per cent. By charging higher prices, it has been able to appropriate the consumer surplus of business customers and turn this into profit or producer surplus for itself. At the bottom end of the market, it has encouraged larger numbers of private customers to travel at less popular times of the day. Every extra passenger that would otherwise not have travelled on these services is 100 per cent profit for Virgin because the marginal cost of taking them is zero.

Table 54.5 *Virgin Trains Wolverhampton-London return fares[1]*

	1995 £	1999 £	Percentage increase 1995-1999
First class open	82.00	118.00	44
Standard class open	57.00	79.50	39
Cheap day return	19.50	24.50	26
Cheapest pre-booked fare	15.00	17.00	13

1. 1995 prices are British Rail fares prior to the takeover of the route by Virgin.

Football clubs

Manchester United to raise prices by 14 per cent

Manchester United is to charge an extra £2 a ticket next season, a rise of 14 per cent on this season's tickets. It said that it needed the funds to pay its growing wage bill. David Gill, Manchester United's finance director, pointed out that his club's tickets were only the ninth most expensive in the Premier League.

Source: adapted from *The Times*, 1.4.1999.

Leeds United continues to diversify

Premier League football clubs are in grave danger of losing fans if they keep trying to recoup soaring players' wages through higher ticket prices, Peter Ridsdale, the Chairman of Leeds Sporting said yesterday. He was announcing an interim pre-tax profit of £1.9 million, up from £11 000 previously. The huge leap in profit was made on the back of a 30 per cent increase in sales turnover. Leeds Sporting, the company which owns Leeds United, is continuing to diversify. It had started three new businesses - a travel agency, a financial services group and a publishing company - and was considering several other initiatives.

Source: adapted from *The Times*, 1.4.1999.

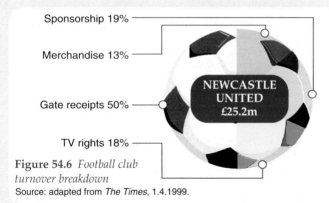

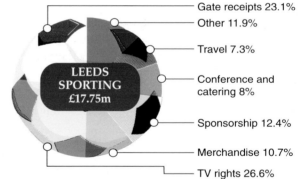

NEWCASTLE UNITED £25.2m
- Sponsorship 19%
- Merchandise 13%
- Gate receipts 50%
- TV rights 18%

LEEDS SPORTING £17.75m
- Gate receipts 23.1%
- Other 11.9%
- Travel 7.3%
- Conference and catering 8%
- Sponsorship 12.4%
- Merchandise 10.7%
- TV rights 26.6%

Figure 54.6 *Football club turnover breakdown*
Source: adapted from *The Times*, 1.4.1999.

The demise of the replica shirt

In 1998, the media published the story of how Newcastle United directors Douglas Hall and Freddy Shepherd boasted that they fleeced their club's fans by selling them £40 replica shirts which cost only £5 to produce. A month later, Manchester United unveiled its 13th new jersey in only 5 years.

British clubs have certainly cashed in on fans' desire to sport their club's colours. Only last week, Fulham announced it had decided to change its away kit every year. Fans will have to buy three new strips every two years at £67.97 for the full shirt, shorts and socks.

However, the clubs may find themselves caught in a change of fashion. Sales of branded football clothing have been collapsing. At Newcastle, sales have collapsed to £3.3 million over the past 6 months compared with £5.5 million in the same period last year. Manchester United announced a 20 per cent fall in shirt sales over the past 12 months. High prices may have something to do with it. But it is part of a larger shift away from sports clothing for casual wear which has also seen falling sales at companies like Adidas and Nike.

Source: adapted from the *Guardian*, 1999.

1. **What are the sources of monopoly power? Illustrate your answer with examples from the data.**
2. **What pricing and output decisions might a football club make if it wants to maximise profits? Use a diagram to illustrate your answer.**
3. **'Football clubs compete fiercely with each other.' 'The least successful football clubs are still examples of local monopolies. The most successful are international monopolies.' Discuss which of these two statements is likely to be most accurate.**

Summary

1. Most industries operate in imperfectly competitive markets.
2. The monopolistic competition model makes the same assumptions as that of perfect competition except it is assumed that each firm produces a differentiated product and is therefore a price-maker.
3. In long run equilibrium, each firm will only earn normal profit and therefore AC = AR. Each firm will produce at its profit maximising output where MC = MR.

Imperfect competition

Perfect competition and monopoly are at either end of a spectrum of market structures. There are relatively few industries which conform to the strict characteristics of these two models. Most industries fall somewhere in between. In most industries:

- competition exists because there are at least two firms in the industry;
- competition is imperfect because firms sell products which are not identical to the products of rival firms.

The neo-classical theories of perfect competition and monopoly were first developed during the latter half of the 19th century. At the time, it was not unreasonable to suggest that many industries were made up of a large number of small firms producing identical or homogeneous products. In the 20th century fewer and fewer industries can be said to be perfectly competitive. So a number of theories of **imperfect competition** have been advanced to explain the behaviour of firms. One important model, the model of MONOPOLISTIC COMPETITION, was developed by Edward Chamberlain, an American economist, in the 1930s, and his work was mirrored by an English economist, Joan Robinson, at the same time.

Assumptions

The theory of monopolistic competition makes almost the same assumptions as that of perfect competition, namely:

- there is a large number of buyers and sellers in the market, each of which is relatively small and acts independently;
- there are no barriers to entry or exit;
- firms are short run profit maximisers;
- there is perfect knowledge in the market.

However, one assumption is different:

- firms produce differentiated or non-homogeneous goods.

It can be argued that relatively few industries possess these characteristics. One possible example would be retailing in the UK. It has traditionally been fragmented. Even in areas where there are large national chains such as groceries (Sainsbury's, Tesco, Waitrose, Co-op) or DIY (Do-it-all, B&Q, Texas Homecare), **concentration ratios** (☞ unit 51) are relatively low. Firms possess a certain amount of market power because of the location of stores or brand images, but this power is relatively weak in most cases.

Question 1

In the 1990s, the large assurance and pension fund companies increasingly advertised their products, either through television and other media or through direct mail shots. By the late 1990s, the internet too was providing a source of sales. Previously, they had very much relied on their sales forces to deliver new business from millions of potential customers. The industry is fragmented with hundreds of different firms offering products in the market for long term savings. Although firms need a licence to operate, to ensure their financial credit-worthiness, it is relatively easy for other financial institutions to enter the industry. Some banks and building societies have entered the market with their own products, whilst others have chosen to form partnerships with or buy up existing assurance companies to sell their products along with their savings and mortgage services.

(a) To what extent could the life assurance and pension fund market be said to be monopolistically competitive?

The downward sloping demand curve

If a firm produces a product which is slightly different from that of its competitors, then it has a certain amount of market power. It will be able to raise price, for instance, without losing all its customers to firms which have kept their prices stable. So it is not a **price-taker** like a perfectly competitive firm. However, because there are a large number of firms in the industry producing relatively close substitutes, its market power is likely to be relatively weak. Small changes in price are likely to result in relatively large changes in quantity demanded as consumers switch to close substitutes (i.e. demand is likely to be relatively elastic).

The demand curve facing the firm is therefore downward sloping but elastic (i.e. it will operate on the upper portion of its demand curve). The firm's marginal revenue curve will fall twice as steeply as the average revenue curve (or demand curve), as shown in Figure 55.1.

Long run equilibrium

The firm will produce where MC = MR because it is a profit

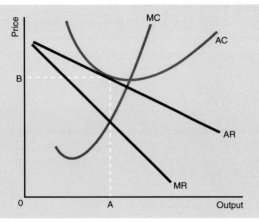

Figure 55.1 *Long run equilibrium for a monopolistically competitive firm*
A firm will produce where MC=MR. Because there are no barriers to entry, the firm will be unable to earn abnormal profits in the long run. Therefore it must also be true that AC=AR at the equilibrium level of output. This occurs when the AC curve is tangential to the AR curve.

Question 2

Table 55.1

Sales	Average revenue (£)
100	10
200	9
300	8
400	7
500	6

The table shows the average revenue curve for a firm operating under conditions of monopolistic competition.
(a) On graph paper, draw
     (i) the demand curve facing the firm and (ii) the firm's marginal revenue curve.
(b) How do these curves differ to those of a monopolist and a firm operating in a perfectly competitive industry?

maximiser. In Figure 55.1, this means that it will produce at an output level of OA. It will charge a price based on its demand or average revenue curve, in this case OB.

The firm in the long run will not be able to earn abnormal profit. This is because there is freedom of entry to the market. If the firm is making abnormal profit in the short run (which would be shown on the diagram by average cost falling below average revenue at output OA), then firms will come into the industry attracted by the high level of profits. This will increase supply, shifting the average revenue curve downwards to the point where average revenue is just equal to average cost. If firms in the industry are making losses in the short run, then firms will leave the industry, reducing supply and shifting the average revenue curve upwards to the point where average revenue is just equal to average cost.

Question 3

Next, the fashion retailer, had grown rapidly in the 1980s, first expanding its chain of women's and men's clothing shops, and then diversifying into mail order, jewellery, childrenswear and household furnishings, as well as buying a chain of newsagents. In late 1988, the bottom began to fall out of the clothing market. Next's young customers had been hard hit by the large rises in mortgage interest rates since June 1988. Sales revenues fell, whilst rising interest rates added to Next's costs since it had borrowed heavily to finance expansion. The company moved from being highly profitable to showing large losses.

Slowly the economy moved into recession, adding to Next's problems. The company responded by contracting in size. It sold most of its non-core businesses like its newsagent chain, a carpet wholesaling business called Mercado and Grattan, the mail order catalogue. It closed down over 60 of its Next stores. By 1993, it was back in profit but in a very much slimmed down form.

(a) (i) What evidence is there that Next earned abnormal profits before 1988? (ii) Draw a diagram showing the short run equilibrium of Next during this period.
(b) (i) Use the theory of monopolistic competition to explain why Next contracted in size after 1988.
    (ii) Using a diagram, analyse the long run equilibrium position of the company.

So in monopolistic competition two conditions must hold in long run equilibrium:
● MC = MR because the firm is a profit maximiser;
● AC = AR because competitive pressures mean that a firm cannot either make a loss or earn abnormal profit.
This means that at the profit maximising output, the average cost curve is tangential to the average revenue curve.

key terms

Monopolistic competition - a market structure where a large number of small firms produces non-homogeneous products and where there are no barriers to entry or exit.

Applied economics

The hotel trade

The hotel trade in the UK is arguably monopolistically competitive. There is a large number of firms in the industry. Figure 55.2 shows that in the mid-1990s, there were approximately 12 000 hotel businesses, nearly all of which ran just one hotel. In 1997, for instance, there were 11 382 hotel and motel firms running 13 317 hotels and motels. Figure 55.3 shows the top 20 hotel groups with the number of properties they owned in May 1999. They accounted for approximately 10 per cent of the total number of hotel properties in the UK.

The industry has a large number of customers. For most of the year, business customers dominate weekday bookings, whilst tourists dominate weekend bookings and high season stays.

There are low barriers to entry to the industry. Small hotels can be bought at relatively low prices. They can be run successfully by new entrants with little knowledge of the hotel trade. It is not untypical to find hotels owned and managed by people who have retired from a salaried job and who want a business where they can be their own boss. For new entrants which want to start on a larger scale, it is, again, relatively easy to find chains of hotels up for sale. In 1999, for instance, the Stakis chain of hotels was bought by Hilton Group for £1.46 billion. In 1998, at a more moderate cost of £66 million, Thistle sold 30 of its smaller hotels to Pamco. So it could be argued that there is freedom of entry to the market. Equally, there is freedom of exit. There is a good market for hotels for those wanting to sell.

Most hotel firms are owned by those who run them. They are typically small family businesses. So it could be argued that they are profit maximisers. The

minority of hotels are part of larger chains owned by publicly quoted companies listed on a stock exchange. Today, in an era where large companies would say that at least one of their goals was to 'maximise shareholder value', it could be argued that they too are profit maximisers.

There is a degree of perfect knowledge in the market. Certainly, there are no industrial secrets amongst firms. Some hotels are better run than others, but this depends on the skill, talent and motivation of the workforce. As for customers, many have little knowledge of the range of choice available in a local area. They rely for information on sources such as hotel guides, *Yellow Pages* and the internet. They prefer to pick a hotel using a fairly crude search method because the cost of acquiring more information is not worth the likely benefit from so doing. However, this does not mean to say that they could not get the information. They could, for instance, visit every hotel in an area to make a choice. So customers have access to perfect information in the market if they so choose.

Hotels do not produce a homogeneous product. Every hotel is different. Most hotels do not even produce a standard product within their premises because each hotel room tends to be slightly different. Customers satisfied with a stay in one room can be dissatisfied with a stay in another room in the same hotel. This lack of homogeneity is picked up by some motel companies which build their premises in such a way that every room is identical, with standard room sizes and standard fittings. Hotels do attempt to brand themselves in order to attract repeat customers. But the branding is typically weak.

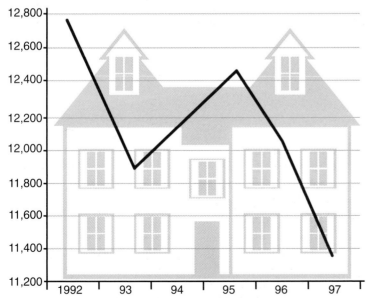

Figure 55.2 *Number of hotel firms, UK*

Source: adapted from *Annual Abstract of Statistics*, Office for National Statistics.

Part of the problem is that hotels are situated in a particular geographical location. So a customer who particularly liked a hotel in Cornwall will not be able to use it to visit Scotland. Hotel chains have an advantage here because they are able to replicate a formula across a geographical area. Their coverage, though, may be patchy and the nature of the buildings they use and the quality of staff may produce very different products between hotels.

Hotels, then, can choose at what price to set their services. They face a downward sloping demand curve, though. If their prices are too high in comparison with competing hotels of a similar standard in an area, they will lose customers. Equally, if they set their prices above those of a hotel offering a better quality service, they are unlikely to have a very high bed occupancy rate.

Hotels are unlikely to earn abnormal profit even in the short run. Many family hotels operate on very low margins because they place a positive value on independence. As for chains, companies have often found it difficult to make sufficient profit on their operations to justify their retention with other activities. There have been some spectacular failures. Queens Moat recorded the largest single corporate loss for one year's operation in the history of British business in the early 1990s. Takeover and merger activity is relatively high in the industry, suggesting that existing owners are often unsatisfied with the performance of their hotel assets. So competition is likely to be keeping profits down to a level equal to normal profit over the long term.

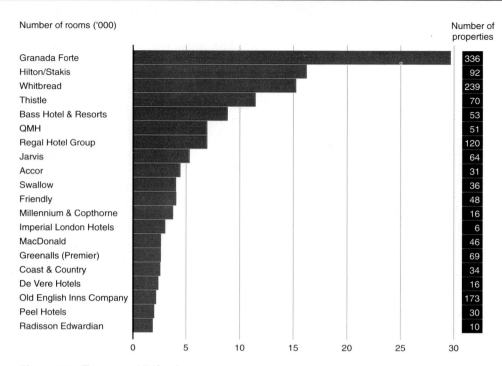

Figure 55.3 *Top twenty UK hotel groups*
Source: adapted from Primark Datastreasm, Huddersfield University/Frank Knight Research, May 1999.

Furniture retailing

There are some large chains in the furniture retailing market - DFS, MFI, UNO and Courts are the four largest quoted companies - operating from out of town parks. However, the industry also has many independent firms, typically sited in town centres.

Furniture retailers have had a terrible time recently. Sales in 1997 and the first quarter of 1998 were relatively buoyant because many households received windfall payments from the demutualisation of building societies like the Halifax. But sales during the rest of 1998 were down on 1997, not helped by rising interest rates and a slowing economy. Furniture sales are closely linked both to the state of the economy and the housing market. When households begin to fear that unemployment will go up or that their employers will cut pay rises, they tend to cut back on spending on large items like furniture. Equally, when interest rates rise, the cost of borrowing rises, fewer people move and this depresses furniture sales.

Even the most pessimistic forecasters within the sector believe there will be an upturn in 1999 and 2000. The question is, which furniture retailers will be able to take advantage of it? 'We would not be surprised to see fall-out among the furniture retailers' said Louise von Blixen, a retail analyst at SG Securities. 'Some rationalisation is needed given the low barriers to entry.'

Furniture retailers in the past have generally competed too heavily on price through mechanisms such as interest-free credit, and are relatively unsophisticated compared with other retailers in terms of creating brands and loyalty. Richard Hyman, chairman of Verdict, the retail consultants, said: 'There has not been much development of the format, service or aftercare. If you took the names off the doors to a showroom and put typical customers inside, they would generally not know where they were.'

Source: adapted from the *Financial Times*, 7.4.1999.

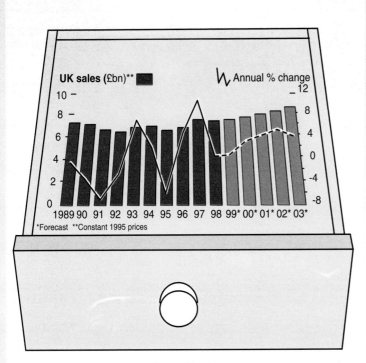

Figure 55.4 *Furniture retailers: UK sales*
Source: adapted from Verdict Research, Datastream/ICV.

1. **Discuss the market characteristics of the furniture retailing industry.**
2. **(a) Explain what is likely to have happened to profits amongst furniture retailers between April 1998 and March 1999.**
   (b) Use the model of monopolistic competition and a diagram to analyse the possible effect of this on the industry (i) in the short term and (ii) in the long term.

Summary

1. Most markets are oligopolistic.
2. An oligopolistic market is one where a small number of interdependent firms compete with each other.
3. Non-price competition is an important feature of oligopolistic markets.
4. The neo-classical kinked demand curve model assumes that a firm will reduce its price if a competitor starts a price war, but will leave price unchanged if a competitor raises its price.

The importance of oligopoly

Most industries could be said to be imperfectly competitive. A few are monopolistically competitive but the majority are **oligopolistic**. Most industries in the UK, the EU and the USA are dominated by a few suppliers. Therefore the theory of OLIGOPOLY is arguably the most important of the theories of the firm. Yet there is no single dominant model of oligopoly within economics. Rather there is a number of competing models which make different assumptions and draw different conclusions. Some of these models will be outlined in this and the next three units, but first the characteristics of an oligopolistic market will be described.

Characteristics of oligopoly

For a market to be called 'oligopolistic', it must possess two characteristics.

- Supply in the industry must be concentrated in the hands of relatively few firms. For instance, an industry where the three largest firms produce 80 per cent of output would be oligopolistic. Note that alongside a few very large producers there may also be a much larger number of very small firms. So an industry with 100 firms, where the three largest firms produced 80 per cent of the output, would still be classed as oligopolistic.
- Firms must be interdependent. The actions of one large firm will directly affect another large firm. In perfect competition, firms are independent. If one farmer decides, for instance, to grow more wheat, that will have no impact on price or sales of other farmers in the industry. In oligopoly, if one large firm decides to pursue policies to increase sales, this is likely to be at the expense of other firms in the industry. One firm is likely to sell more only by taking away sales from other firms.

In addition, the neo-classical theory of oligopoly assumes that:

- there are barriers to entry to the industry. If there were no barriers, firms would enter the industry to take advantage of the abnormal profits characteristic of oligopolies and would reduce the market share of the few large producers in the industry.

Question 1

The mobile phone market in the UK started off as a duopoly, with Vodafone and Cellnet being granted licences to establish networks. By 1995, there were four players in the market, the original two companies and Mercury One-2-One and Orange. The government recognised that the mobile operators faced heavy capital costs creating nationwide networks and therefore, unlike with British Telecom, they chose not to regulate prices in the industry. Over the years, prices have slowly dropped as capacity has expanded and firms have recouped their heavy initial investment outlay. Competition between companies has tended to be non-price competition. Advertising and the quality of the networks have been important; so too have the pricing packages put to different groups of customers. As capacity has grown, the mobile companies have wanted to sign up more and more customers. But they can only do this by dropping their prices, to make their services more affordable. To maximise revenues, they have segmented their markets, offering different prices to different groups of customers. They have been careful not to start price wars with their rivals which would not be in the interests of any company in the industry.

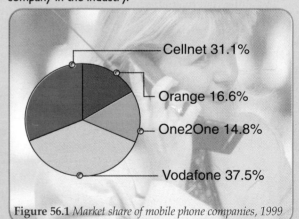

Cellnet 31.1%

Orange 16.6%

One2One 14.8%

Vodafone 37.5%

Figure 56.1 *Market share of mobile phone companies, 1999*

Source: adapted from Orange, *Annual Report and Accounts*.

(a) Using information from the passage, explain why the market for mobile phone calls could be said to be oligopolistic.

In unit 58, it will be argued that some oligopolistic markets have low barriers to entry. A different theory, the theory of **contestable markets**, can then be used to explain the behaviour of firms in this type of market.

Features of oligopolistic markets

Studies of oligopolistic markets have shown that individual firms can exhibit a wide number of different behaviour patterns. However, there are some features which are common to most oligopolistic markets. It is these features which an economic model of oligopoly must be able to incorporate or explain.

Non-price competition In a perfectly competitive market, firms producing homogeneous goods compete solely on price. In the short run, factors such as delivery dates might assume some importance, but in the long term price is all that matters. In an imperfectly competitive market, price is often not the most important factor in the competitive process. Firms decide upon a MARKETING MIX - a mixture of elements which form a coherent strategy designed to sell their products to their market. The marketing mix is often summarised in the '4 Ps'. Firms produce a **product** which appeals to their customers. The product may or may not be differentiated from rivals' products. A **price** needs to be set but this could be above or below the price of competing products depending upon the pricing strategy to be used. For instance, a high price will be set if the product is sold in a quality market. A low price will be set if the firm wishes to sell large quantities of a standard product. **Promotion** (advertising and sales promotion) is essential to inform buyers in the market that the good is on sale and to change their perceptions of a product in a favourable manner. A good distribution system is essential to get the product to the right **place** at the right time for the customer.

Many markets are dominated by **brands**. A branded good is one which is produced by a particular firm and which appears to possess unique characteristics. These may be real characteristics, such as a unique formulation or a unique design. A Mars Bar or a Rolls Royce car, for instance, are unique products. But often more important than the real characteristics are the imagined characteristics of the product in the mind of the buyer. This image is likely to have been created by advertising and promotion. So it is possible for the same baked beans or the same breakfast cereal to be packaged differently and sold on the same supermarket shelves at different prices. Often the higher priced branded product will sell far better than the lower priced unbranded product despite the fact that the product itself is the same.

Price rigidity Prices in oligopolistic markets seem to change far less than in perfectly competitive markets. Despite changes in underlying costs of production, firms are often observed to maintain prices at a constant level.

L-shaped average cost curves Economic studies (☞ unit 49) have established that in the real world average variable cost curves are often more L-shaped than U-shaped. Over a wide range of output, large firms face the same average variable costs whether they increase or decrease output, as shown in Figure 56.2.

Collusion Oligopolistic firms will often benefit if they collude. This means that they make agreements amongst themselves so as to restrict competition and maximise their own benefits. Before such **anti-competitive practices** (☞ unit 65) were made illegal in the UK by the 1956 Restrictive Trade Practices Act, most large UK manufacturing companies had entered into agreements with other firms.

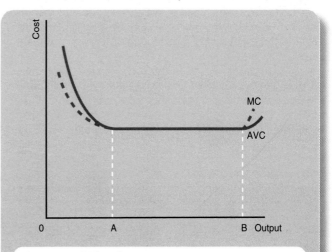

Figure 56.2 *L-shaped average cost curve*
Many firms in practice seem to face an L-shaped average cost curve. The minimum efficient scale of production extends over a wide range of output, from OA to OB in this diagram.

Question 2

The National Lottery was launched in 1995. It was an instant success, exceeding the forecasts made by Camelot, the company which runs the lottery. The gambling market is dominated by a few large players. The most obvious rivals to the Lottery were the pools companies, Vernon and Littlewoods. However, it was also in competition with bingo clubs such as those owned by Rank, and betting shops such as Ladbrokes. Smaller competitors included casinos and amusement arcades.

Following the introduction of the Lottery, there was little change in either the products or the prices of competitors. Inevitably, some lost market share. The largest losers were the pools companies which had to scale down the size of their operations, although neither was driven out of the market as some predicted. Other firms made greater efforts to differentiate their product. The bingo companies, for instance, emphasised that the gambling experience they offered was a night out as much as a chance to win prizes. Betting shops won the legal right to stay open longer hours to attract more customers. The total gambling market has grown, easing the pain on those which lost market share to the Lottery.

(a) Explain, using examples from the gambling industry, how firms in an oligopolistic market compete.

The neo-classical kinked demand curve model

One model of oligopoly was developed in the late 1930s by Paul Sweezy in the USA and R Hall and C Hitch in the UK. Any theory of oligopoly must make an assumption about how one firm will react to the actions of another firm. The kinked demand curve model assumes that there will be an asymmetrical reaction to a change in price by one firm. If the firm increases its price, other firms will not react. The firm which has increased its price will then lose market share. On the other hand, if it reduces its price its competitors will reduce price too in order to prevent an erosion of their market share. The firm will gain little extra demand as a result. The demand curve therefore facing a firm is more elastic for a price rise than for a price fall.

This is shown in Figure 56.3. Price is initially at OP. If the firm increases price to OR it will lose far more sales than it would gain if it reduced price by an equal amount. This occurs because of the different reactions to price increases and decreases by competitors. Therefore the demand curve is kinked around the original price. If the demand curve (i.e. the average revenue curve) is kinked, then this produces a discontinuous marginal revenue curve. At output level OQ, there will be a jump in marginal revenue between a small increase in price and a small decrease in price (an example of this is given in Question 3).

The firm is assumed to be a short run profit maximiser. Therefore if the price is OP and the firm is producing OQ, the marginal cost curve must cut the marginal revenue at output OQ, somewhere between price OV and OW. This means that there are a number of possible marginal cost curves which would produce a price of OP. It could, for instance, be MC_1 or MC_2. Assume that it is MC_1 then a rise in costs to MC_2 would result in no change in price. The oligopolist would absorb the whole of the cost increase by reducing its profit.

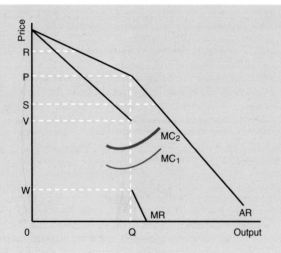

Figure 56.3 *The kinked demand curve model*
With a demand curve kinked round the prevailing price OP, a rise or fall in marginal cost will not affect the profit maximising level of output or price. Hence this model can be used to explain relative price stability in oligopolistic markets.

This theory provides one explanation of why prices in oligopoly are relatively stable. Changes in costs which shift the marginal cost curve will not change either the profit maximising level of output or the profit maximising price.

However, there is a number of weaknesses in the theory. First there is no explanation of how the original price, P, was arrived at. Second, the theory only deals with price competition and ignores the effects of non-price competition. Third, the model assumes a particular reaction by other firms to a change in price of a firm's product. It is unlikely that firms will react in exactly this way all the time. A much wider range of possible reactions needs to be explored.

Question 3

Table 56.1

			£
Output	Average revenue	Total revenue	Marginal revenue
1	49	49	
			45
2	47		
3	45		
3	45		
			25
4	40		
5	35		
6	30		

(a) Complete Table 56.1, filling in the missing figures.
(b) Plot the average and marginal revenue curves on a graph. Remember that marginal revenue for the second unit of output should be plotted at output level $1\frac{1}{2}$, the third at $2\frac{1}{2}$, etc. Also mark on the graph a vertical line at output level 3 and draw the marginal revenue curves up to the line on either side of it as in Figure 56.2.
(c) Why is the marginal revenue curve discontinuous?
(d) Table 56.2

Output	Marginal cost (£)
	40
2	
	32
3	
	36
4	

Draw the marginal cost curve in Table 56.2 onto your graph.

(e) Why is the firm in equilibrium at an output of 3 units?
(f) Explain what would happen to equilibrium output and price if marginal cost (i) rose by £4 and (ii) fell by £2 at every level of output.

key

terms

Marketing mix - different elements within a strategy designed to create demand for a product.

Oligopoly - a market structure where there is a small number of firms in the industry and where each firm is interdependent with other firms. Barriers to entry are likely to exist.

Applied economics

The UK detergent market

Two firms dominate the UK detergent industry: the US giant, Procter and Gamble (P&G), and the Anglo-Dutch company, Unilever. They have been in competition with each other since the 1920s, battling for supremacy of the market. In the mid-1980s, each had a market share of approximately 43 per cent, making the industry a virtual duopoly. By 1999, P&G had overtaken Unilever, securing over 50 per cent market share against Unilever's 34 per cent.

Detergents are not a particularly high technology product. There are plenty of small manufacturers supplying supermarket own brand products and commercial buyers such as laundries. Whilst P&G and Unilever tend to lead the field in product development, small manufacturers are easily able to imitate the products and supply acceptable quality goods to customers who are buying on price. Neither product nor the cost of purchase of equipment is a barrier to entry.

The major barrier to entry is the promotion costs of a brand. P&G and Unilever are the two highest spenders on advertising in the UK. Combined advertising budgets exceeded £100 million in 1999. Typically, one-quarter of the shop price of a packet of P&G or Unilever detergent is accounted for by promotion costs, the equivalent of 5p per wash. No small entrant to the market can in any way match these expenditures. Even large potential entrants are deterred. Advertising by itself cannot establish a new brand in the market place. To gain a significant foothold in the market, a new entrant would probably have to sell a product which was superior to existing P&G or Unilever products and spend large amounts on advertising.

The two detergent giants do not compete on price. On the supermarket shelves, own brands or unadvertised brands can sell for less than half the price of a P&G or Unilever product and yet still fail to capture more than a few per cent of the market. This indicates that the two firms have had considerable success in making demand for their products relatively price inelastic. Instead of competing on price, they fight it out through the establishment and maintenance of strong brands. Each company sells a range of brands. In the UK, the main Unilever brand is Persil. Its Tablets variant alone had taken more than 20 per cent of the market in 1999. The

other main Unilever brand is Surf with 6 per cent of the market in 1999. P&G's brands proved more successful in the 1980s, mainly because they were quicker into the market to produce concentrate powders and liquids than Unilever. Ariel is P&Gs main brand, and it produces other brands such as Daz.

In the early 1990s, Unilever successfully launched a new brand onto the market called Radion. With very heavy advertising, it quickly managed to take over 6 per cent of the UK market before falling back. Launching new brands is a high risk exercise. If they fail, it will have cost the company millions of pounds in product development, market research and promotion. One estimate put the spending on developing, manufacturing and market the unsuccessful Power products launched by Unilever in 1994 at £200 million. On the other hand, establishing a successful new brand, or a variant on an existing brand, will take market share away from existing brands. Radion, for instance, helped halt the growing market share of P&G in the early 1990s. The launch of Persil Tablets in the late 1990s helped Unilever gain market share from P&G which only put a rival tablet form of Ariel onto the market after the success of Persil Tablets became apparent. These examples show how the two companies are interdependent. Marketing campaigns and the launch of new products by one company can have significant effects on the market share of the other. Without marketing and product development, brands fall away. In 1999, Unilever announced that it would be phasing out production of Radion because it could no longer support a product with what was now less than 2 per cent of the market. It preferred to concentrate its resources on its two largest brands, Persil and Surf.

It is difficult to find direct evidence as to whether a change in marginal cost would have any effect on price or output. However, it is interesting to note that soap powders tend to be 'positioned' in the market in pricing terms. The marginal cost of producing a packet of Ariel is almost certainly little different for P&G than the marginal cost of Daz. Yet Daz is sold at a slightly cheaper price to appeal to cost conscious customers. This would tend to indicate that small falls and rises in marginal cost are unlikely to affect the pricing strategies of P&G and Unilever.

The soft drinks market

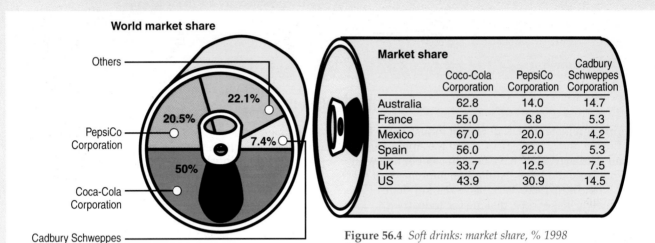

World market share

- Others — 22.1%
- PepsiCo Corporation — 20.5%
- Coca-Cola Corporation — 50%
- Cadbury Schweppes Corporation — 7.4%

Market share	Coco-Cola Corporation	PepsiCo Corporation	Cadbury Schweppes Corporation
Australia	62.8	14.0	14.7
France	55.0	6.8	5.3
Mexico	67.0	20.0	4.2
Spain	56.0	22.0	5.3
UK	33.7	12.5	7.5
US	43.9	30.9	14.5

Figure 56.4 *Soft drinks: market share, % 1998*
Source: adapted from *Beverage Digest*.

'Always Coca-Cola'

Coca-Cola has, over the years, developed a formidable reputation for its marketing. It is one of the world's best known brands and much of this over the past few decades has been due to its commitment to have Coca-Cola within 'arm's reach of desire' for its customers. This is defined as being within five minutes of most consumers, preferably in chilled storage for immediate consumption. This could only be achieved by having a global distribution system where Coca-Cola is available in corner stores, newsagents and garages as well as supermarkets. Also key to the strategy is the distribution of vending machines in places of work and leisure. Coca-Cola down the years has invested billions of pounds in this distribution system.

Source: adapted from the *Financial Times*, 30.4.1999.

The competition

Coca-Cola's main rival is the PepsiCo Corporation. In most markets, it comes second to Coca-Cola but is strongest in its home market, the USA. Cadbury Schweppes Corporation was the world's third largest soft drinks manufacturer but in 1998 it agreed to sell its non-US soft drinks business to Coca-Cola. Cadbury Schweppes didn't have the critical mass outside the US to make distribution cost-effective. In contrast, Coca-Cola can push new brands through its distribution system at little extra cost. Just think of the vending machine. Coca-Cola can add a new brand to many of its vending machines at little or no extra cost. Cadbury Schweppes might have to install a new vending machine to get distribution at the same site. However, competition authorities in many countries have refused to allow through the deal because it would further increase Coca-Cola's dominance in the market.

Source: adapted from the *Financial Times*, 30.4.1999.

Pricing

Coca-Cola is sold in different countries by licensed local bottling companies. Coca-Cola will typically own half the shares in the enterprise. Pricing policies, though, are similar throughout the world. A set price is fixed in a local market which takes into account ability to pay and costs of production and distribution . Then the price may be varied where necessary through special offers. For instance, there may be an offer on buying a multi-pack, or the size of the bottle may be slightly larger for a limited period. However, price is used as part of a much wider marketing package to draw the attention of the customer to the product. When Coca-Cola comes under threat from new entrants, as for instance with Virgin Cola or Sainsbury's Classic Cola in the mid-1990s, it does not reduce its prices.

Source: adapted from the *Financial Times*, 30.4.1999.

1. Discuss the market characteristics of the soft drinks market worldwide.
2. Explain using a diagram why it is not in the interests of Coca-Cola to permanently reduce its prices in a market.
3. In the 1990s, Coca-Cola has expanded rapidly in developing countries. Discuss whether, in the long-term, local soft drinks suppliers in the Third World are likely to survive the entry of Coca-Cola into their markets.

Summary

1. Game theory explores the reactions of one player to changes in strategy by another player.
2. Oligopoly is characterised by price stability. One explanation of this is that changing price is a very risky strategy for one firm because it will provoke a reaction by other firms.
3. Non-price competition is common in oligopolistic markets. It is a less risky strategy than price competition.
4. Successful branding enables producers to charge a premium price and earn abnormal profit on a product.
5. Collusion enables oligopolistic firms to move to their most profitable output level.
6. The large number of different market strategies available to oligopolistic firms may result in permanent disequilibrium in the market.

Game theory

Central to any understanding of oligopoly is interdependence. The actions of one large firm in the industry will directly affect all other firms in the industry. It is therefore essential, in any theory of oligopoly, to understand the nature and consequences of those reactions.

One very powerful tool for analysing oligopolistic behaviour is GAME THEORY. It has a wide variety of applications, from playing cards through to nuclear deterrence. In a game the players are interdependent. The best move for a player depends upon how the other players will react.

Price stability

One commonly observed feature of oligopoly is price stability. Firms maintain stable prices over a pricing season which may last from 6 months to several years. Price stability may be a rational strategy for oligopolists.

If an oligopolistic firm raises price, it risks losing market share if its competitors do not follow suit. Lower market share could lead to lower profits and, if investment and research and development budgets are cut, a reduced ability to compete in the long run.

If it lowers its price, it risks starting a price war. It could be that the size of the market will expand as consumers buy more of the industry's products. But the benefits in the form of larger sales could well be more than offset by losses in revenue due to lower prices. All firms in the industry could see sharp falls in profits as they battle it out. Eventually, prices will have to rise again to restore profitability and the firm which started the price war could have lost market share.

So changing prices is a risky strategy. When prices do change, all firms tend to change their prices by the same percentage. For instance, a rise in the interest rate by one large building society tends to lead to a rise in all building society interest rates. A rise in petrol prices by one company is usually matched by the other petrol suppliers.

Game theory can be used to explain this. Consider Table 57.1. There are just two firms in the industry (it is a DUOPOLY). Each firm has two strategies. It can either raise the price of its product or leave it unchanged. The figures in the box represent the change in profits for firm A which would result from each strategy. We will assume that each firm has the same expectations of what would happen to profits as a result of each strategy. We will further assume that the game is a ZERO SUM GAME. This means that any gain by one player is exactly offset by a loss by the other player. For instance, if firm A raises its price and firm B reacts to this by raising price too, then firm A will be the winner. Its profits will increase by £10 million whilst firm B's profits will fall by £10 million. If on the other hand firm B were to react by keeping its price unchanged, firm A would see its profits fall by £2 million whilst firm B would see its profits rise by £2 million.

The game in Table 57.1 has an equilibrium solution. Firm A will decide to leave its price unchanged. This is because if it raises its price, it could gain an extra £10 million in profits if firm B also raised its price. But it knows that firm B would be most unlikely to react in this way because firm B would stand to lose £10 million by adopting that strategy. So firm B would adopt the strategy of leaving its price unchanged. This would result in losses

Table 57.1

		Firm B	
		Raise price	Leave price unchanged
Firm A	Raise price	£10 million	-£2 million
	Leave price unchanged	-£1 million	0

of £2 million for firm A if it raised price. If, on the other hand, firm A kept its price unchanged, the most it would stand to lose is £1 million.

As for firm B, raising price would be a very dangerous strategy because it would lose £10 million in profit if firm A raised its price too. Leaving price unchanged would either result in no change in profits or a gain in profits of £2 million.

So both firms will choose to leave their prices unchanged. This is the safest strategy for both firms. The alternative for each firm would lead to losses because of the rival firm's reactions.

Now consider Table 57.2 which shows a game where firms cut prices. The game here is not a zero sum game. The change in profits of firm A of a particular combination of strategies is shown in black, whilst the change in profits for firm B is shown in red. For instance, if both firms cut prices, firm A will lose £10 million in profits whilst firm B will lose £20 million.

Table 57.2

		Firm B	
		Lower price	Leave price unchanged
Firm A	Lower price	-£10m/-£20m	+£5m/-£27m
	Leave price unchanged	-£13m/+£5m	0

It is clear from the table that it is in both firms' interests to leave prices unchanged. If one firm decides to lower its price in order to gain market share, the other firm would suffer a large drop in profits. For instance, firm A would lose £13 million in profits if it left its price unchanged when firm B lowered its price. It would prefer to lower its price too and limit the loss in profits to £10 million. The same is true for firm B. If it dropped its price and firm A

did not react, it would increase its profit. But if firm A reacted by dropping its price too, the resulting price war would have disastrous consequences for both sides.

Many economists have argued that firms avoid risk (they are said to be 'risk averse'). Competition is always risky and strategies which aim to reduce market share and profits of competitors especially so. 'The best of all monopoly profits is a quiet life', argued J R Hicks (1935).

Non-price competition

A characteristic of oligopoly is the lack of price competition. Price wars can be very damaging for firms in an oligopolistic industry. So firms choose to compete in other ways apart from price. An advertising campaign, for instance, by firm A is likely to be limited in cost and may increase market share. Other firms in the industry may react by launching their own advertising campaign, but there is a reasonable chance that the advertising campaign of the competitors may not be as good, plus the fact that advertising may expand the market as a whole. The reward for firm A will be a small increase in market share and, presumably, profits. Other firms, however, will not be hit too hard and so will not take drastic measures which might affect the profitability of all firms in the industry. On the other hand, firm A's campaign may back-fire if another firm launches a more successful advertising campaign. But the potential loss is unlikely to be very great.

This suggests that, in oligopoly, firms might not attempt to drive their main rivals out of the market. This would be an extremely risky strategy which might lead to themselves being the victim of such a move. Rather, oligopolists limit competition in order to limit the risks to their own market shares and profits.

Non-price competition is also a very powerful means of deterring potential competitors - firms which might enter the industry. This is discussed further below.

Branding

Interdependence limits the ability of oligopolistic firms to exploit markets to their own benefit. Ideally oligopolistic firms would like to turn themselves into monopolists with full control of their markets. One way of doing this is by the creation of strong brands. A strong brand has two major advantages for a producer.

- A strong brand has few good substitutes so far as the buyer is concerned. The firm is therefore able to charge a premium price (a relatively high price for the good) and earn monopoly profit on the good without seeing too great a fall in demand for it.
- It is very difficult for competitors to challenge the supremacy of the brand. For instance, Kellogg's Corn Flakes, Mars Bars, and Jaguar cars all have stable demands at premium prices in the short run. In the long run, tastes may change or new strong brands may appear. But even then old brands, such as Ovaltine, Horlicks or Ambrosia rice pudding may continue to be highly profitable to their owners, still commanding

Question 1

The major building societies tend to move their saving and mortgage interest rates at the same time, usually following a change in bank base rates, the rate of interest around which banks structure their saving and borrowing rates. Occasionally, building societies have responded to government concern and not raised interest rates to mortgage borrowers when banks have increased their rates. The result has been a flow of funds from building societies to banks as savers have switched their money to take advantage of higher interest rates. Equally, at such times, building societies have tended to increase their share of the mortgage market at the expense of the banks. Before too long, the building societies have been forced to raise their interest rates in order to attract back the savings to meet the demand for mortgage loans.

(a) Use game theory to explain why building societies tend to move their interest rates in line with each other and with those of the banks.

Question 2

American comic books represent a small niche market in the much larger market for magazines in the UK. In 1994, three companies dominated the niche market. Marvel Comics, which publishes Spider-man, The Fantastic Four and The X-Men, held 40 per cent of the market. DC comics, which publishes comics featuring Superman and Batman, held 30 per cent of the market. Finally, Image Comics, publishers of Spawn and Youngblood, held 24 per cent of the market.

There is no real price competition. Prices of comics are fixed in comparison with prices of rival comics. Instead, comics compete on the strength of their story lines and characters. Free gifts, special editions and graphic novels help keep existing customers loyal or attract new customers.

Until 1992, the market had been essentially a duopoly, with DC Comics and Marvel Comics carving up sales between them. Many others had tried to establish themselves, but lacked knowledge and money to create a range of comics which could compete with the two large companies. However, in 1992 a group of artists left Marvel Comics to set up the successful Image Comics. They were able to establish themselves for two reasons. The Image artists had gained considerable reputations through their work at Marvel. This 'core group' of artists attracted a large number of consumers to purchase the new Image comics and were able to create new characters which instantly appealed to consumers. Heavy promotion of the products by the company was also an

important factor in generating sales.

By 2000 the picture was much the same as in 1994. Marvel Comics and DC Comics between them held 77 per cent of the market. Image Comics had a 13 per cent market share.

(a) How do American comic book publishers establish a brand image?
(b) Use game theory to suggest why Marvel Comics and DC did not engage in a price war to drive Image Comics out of the market in 1992 and 1993.
(c) Why might game theory suggest that it is worthwhile to a company to pay key employees more than the going rate for the job?

premium prices at lower sales volumes but with little or no development costs.

Strong brands are difficult to create, which is why many firms prefer to take over other companies and their brands at very high prices rather than attempt to establish new brands. For instance, Nestlé paid £1.9 billion for the brands of Rowntree Mackintosh, a recognition of how much it would possibly cost to establish rival brands from scratch. To establish a new brand, a company usually has to produce an innovative product (innovative could mean anything from changing the colour or smell of a product to a radically new technological breakthrough) and then market it effectively. The failure rate of new brands in some markets such as food and confectionery can be as high as nearly 100 per cent. With this in mind, it is hardly surprising that a firm would be prepared to pay millions of pounds for an established brand rather than employ research workers to devise new products.

Collusion

Another way in which an oligopolist can turn itself into a monopoly is by colluding with other firms. In markets which are unregulated by government, there is a strong tendency for firms to collude (i.e. to join together and act as if they were one firm). Cartels and restrictive trade practices (☞ unit 65) were the norm in British manufacturing industry before such practices were made

illegal in the 1950s.

Game theory can help us understand why this is the case. Consider Table 57.3. The figures show the profits to be gained by two firms, A and B, depending upon whether they adopt a high or low price strategy. Firm A, whose profit figures are in black, would like to adopt a low price strategy in opposition to a high price strategy by its rival. That would result in profits of £25 million. But it can see that firm B would not allow such a situation because its profits would only be £5 million. However, a high price strategy for firm A would be worse because it would face making the lowest possible profit, £10 million, should firm B choose to adopt a low price strategy. So firm A will choose a low price strategy, hoping that firm B will

Table 57.3

		Firm B	
		Low price	High price
Firm A	Low price	£15m/**£10m**	£25m/**£5m**
	High price	£10m/**£20m**	£20m/**£25m**

adopt a high price strategy, but more realistically knowing that it too will adopt a low price strategy. Firm A will then make a profit of £15 million - the highest minimum profit it can make.

Firm B will adopt a low price strategy too. Although it stands to gain £25 million in profit by a high price strategy if firm A too goes for a high price stategy, it risks only making £5 million if firm A were to go for a low price. So it will maximise its minimum profit of £10 million and go for a low price strategy.

The result is that both firms adopt low price strategies because they fear the reactions of their competitor. They would have been considerably better off if they had both adopted high price strategies. The only way to get into the high price 'box' is for the two firms to come to some form of understanding that they will not adopt low price strategies (i.e. they must collude).

The figures shown in Table 57.3 are an example of what is often called the 'Prisoner's Dilemma'. Substitute profits for prison sentences and prices for pleading guilty or not guilty. If both prisoners kept apart in different cells plead not guilty, then they will be released through lack of evidence. But if one prisoner pleads guilty, then he will get a reduced sentence and the other will get a heavier sentence. If both plead guilty they will get heavy sentences. If they could get together (i.e. collude) they would choose to plead not guilty. But in isolation they cannot trust the other prisoner. So each chooses to plead guilty and they both suffer!

Disequilibrium

So far the games considered have had a definite solution. An equilibrium set of strategies has been arrived at which leads to stability within the market. However, there are many games which lead to disequilibrium, where the players are unable to pursue stable strategies. A move by one firm will lead to a change in strategy of the other firm and so on.

Moreover, only two-firm, two-option situations have been discussed. In reality there are likely to be more than two firms in the industry, each with more than two policy options. For instance, a six policy zero-sum game for two firms is shown in Table 57.4. There are 36 (6x6) different possible solutions to this game. If there were 3 firms in the industry, the number of possible solutions would rise to 216 (6x6x6).

Game theory predicts, then, that there is a large number of different possible outcomes in an oligopolistic setting. Given this very large number, it is perhaps not surprising that economic theory has found it difficult to provide one unified model which would explain price and output decisions in the industry.

Table 57.4

			Firm B					
			Price			Advertising expenditure		
			Raise	Lower	Leave unchanged	Raise	Lower	Leave unchanged
Firm A	Price	Raise	£10m	-£5m	-£10m	£2m	-£1m	-£2m
		Lower	£2m	-£1m	-£4m	-£1m	£2m	£1m
		Leave unchanged	£3m	-£5m	0	£2m	-£4m	0
	Adv. exp.	Raise	-£1m	£7m	£5m	£3m	-£5m	-£1m
		Lower	£2m	-£3m	-£5m	£4m	-£2m	-£1m
		Leave unchanged	£2m	-£2m	0	£3m	-£1m	0

Question 3

In 1998, 13 bus operators in the Kingston upon Hull area were accused of anti-competitive practices. Kingston-upon-Hull City Council had put its home-to-school bus services out to tender, but suspected local bus companies of collusion. The Office of Fair Trading, investigating the allegation, said that it had found evidence that the bus operators had met secretly in a hotel and agreed on minimum prices at which they would tender for the business and which routes each operator would bid for. Under the 1998 Competition Act, anti-competitive agreements could lead to fines of up to 10 per cent of turnover for each company. Previously, firms engaged in a cartel would most likely have received no financial penalty but simply be told to desist from their practices.

Source: adapted from *The Times*, 20.11.1998.

(a) Use game theory to suggest why the bus companies might have found it in their interests to collude before the 1998 Competition Act came into force.
(b) Discuss, using game theory, whether their decision would have been any different after the Act came into force.

key terms

Duopoly - an industry where there are only two firms.
Game theory - the analysis of situations in which players are interdependent.
Zero sum game - a game in which the gain of one player is exactly offset by the loss by other players.

Applied economics

Apple vs Microsoft

Apple has had a chequered history. Founded in 1976 by two students, Steve Jobs andSteve Wozniak, it produced the world's first real personal computer (PC). In 1984 it launched a revolutionary operating system named Macintosh for its PCs. Apple introduced the 'desktop' screen with the now familiar icons. These could be accessed through another first, the mouse.

In contrast, Bill Gates at Microsoft was struggling with an operating system, MS Dos, which had been bought second hand from another company. It was complicated to use and prone to crashing. However, the operating system had one key advantage. Bill Gates had developed it for use on IBM machines. IBM in the 1970s was the world's dominant computer business, often accused by competitors of being and acting as a monopolist. However, IBM was worried that the traditional computer market, based around large mainframe computers, was changing irrevocably with the advent of the PC. In game theory terms, if it did nothing, it could see the new PC upstarts take all the computer market. If it produced its own PCs, it might at best gain a dominant position in this market as it had in the mainframe market. At worst, it could survive as one of many competing firms in the PC market with hopefully some mainframe business remaining. So it decided to manufacture a PC but needed an operating system immediately. That was what Bill Gates provided.

IBM was such a powerful company that other computer manufacturers decided to produce clones - similar

machines - to the PCs of IBM. This meant using the same operating system, which would allow their PCs to run the same software packages as IBM machines. IBM's agreement with Microsoft did not prevent Microsoft from licensing MS Dos to other computer manufacturers. Bill Gates was only too willing to allow MS Dos to be used on non-IBM machines. In contrast, Apple decided that its Macintosh operating system would only be used on Apple manufactured machines. In game theory terms, it judged that the profits it could make by selling both the machine and the operating system were greater than if it licensed the operating system to other PC manufacturers, but as a consequence sold fewer machines because of the increased competition.

That judgment was, with hindsight, flawed. What Apple failed to realise at the time was that PC consumers wanted a universal operating system on which all software would work and which would allow machines to talk to each other. MS Dos came to provide that, even if technically it was a poorer system than Apple's Macintosh system. In the 1990s, Microsoft went on to develop MS Dos into Windows and incorporated many of the revolutionary features of the Macintosh system, such as the use of the mouse and icons. By 2000, Windows had 90 per cent of the world's market for operating systems. But dedicated Macintosh users claim that, even in 2000, it is still technically inferior to Apple's system. Financially, Microsoft won its game convincingly even if there were doubts about the technology.

The UK launch of digital television

In 1998, two companies launched digital television services, BSkyB and On Digital. At the time, British homes were equipped with televisions that could only receive analogue signals. To get digital, they needed a set top box which would process the signal and allow it to be seen on a traditional television. The two companies used incompatible systems, so a BSkyB set top could not receive On Digital services and vice versa.

The set top boxes were subsidised by the the two firms but were launched at a retail price of around £200. Consumers then had to buy a subscription to the services which cost a minimum of £7.99 a month. The more channels the subscriber wanted, the higher the subscription.

By April 1999, BSkyB had acquired 551 000 subscribers, although 100 000 of these were existing BSkyB subscribers who had switched from satellite to digital. On Digital

had signed up 110 000 subscribers.

In May 1999, BSkyB announced that it would be giving away its boxes free. It would also convert all its existing three and a half million satellite customers to digital by 2002 and then switch off its analogue satellite transmissions. Included in the subscription would now be a 40 per cent discount on all standard BT (British Telecommunications) telephone calls. This matched similar deals being offered by cable television companies which bundled television services with cheap telephone calls. Within two weeks, On Digital decided that it too would provide its set-top boxes for free. It had also signed up with a telephone company to offer its subscribers cheap telephone calls.

Source: adapted from the *Financial Times*, 6.5.1999, 25.5.1999; *The Guardian*, 6.5.1999, 25.5.1999.

1. Use game theory to explain why: (a) both BSkyB and On Digital launched their set top boxes at the same price of around £200; (b) BSkyB decided to offer free set top boxes in April 1999; (c) On Digital offered the same package of free set top boxes and cheap telephone calls as BSkyB two weeks later.

2. BSkyB is in competition not just with On Digital but also with cable television companies and the five mainstream channels including the BBC. Using game theory, suggest why two key components of its competitive strategy have been (a) to buy up sporting rights even though this has been very expensive and (b) to offer as many channels as possible.

Summary

1. In a contestable market, there are one or a number of firms which profit maximise. The key assumption is that barriers to entry to the industry are relatively low, as is the cost of exit from the industry.
2. Firms in a contestable market will only earn normal profit in the long run. If they earn abnormal profit in the short run, then new firms will enter the industry and drive prices and profits down.
3. The existence of potential entrants to the industry will tend to keep profits to their normal level even in the short run because existing firms will want to deter new entrants from coming into the market.
4. Contestable markets are both productively and allocatively efficient in the long run and are likely to be efficient in the short run as well.
5. It is not necessarily possible to predict the exact output of an individual firm in a contestable market if average cost curves are L shaped.

Contestable market theory vs neo-classical theory

Many, if not most, markets in the UK and in other industrialised economies are dominated by a few producers. The **neo-classical theory of oligopoly** (☞ unit 56) assumes that oligopolistic markets feature high **barriers to entry** (☞ unit 51). However, there is also evidence to suggest that many oligopolistic markets have low barriers to entry. Therefore, firms in the industry are likely to behave in a different way to that predicted by neo-classical theory. The theory of contestable markets explores the implications of low barrier to entry markets.

Assumptions

The theory of contestable markets makes a number of assumptions.
- The number of firms in the industry may vary from one (a monopolist) having complete control of the market, to many, with no single firm having a significant share of the market.
- In a CONTESTABLE MARKET, there is both freedom of entry to and exit from the market. This is a key assumption of the model. Its implications are discussed below.
- Firms compete with each other and do not collude to fix prices.
- Firms are short run profit maximisers, producing where MC = MR.
- Firms may produce homogeneous goods or they may produce branded goods.
- There is perfect knowledge in the industry.

Normal and abnormal profit

The theory of contestable markets shows that in a contestable market:
- abnormal profits can be earned in the short run;
- only normal profit can be earned in the long run.

Question 1.

To what extent do (a) clothing manufacturers and (b) clothing retailers operate in contestable markets?

Assume that firms in a contestable market were making abnormal profit in the short run. Then new firms would be attracted into the industry by the abnormal profit. Supply would increase and prices would be driven down to the point where only normal profit was being made. This is the same argument that is used in the theory of perfect competition (☞ unit 53). Equally, if a firm is making losses, it will eventually leave the industry because in the long run it cannot operate as a loss making concern.

Entry to and exit from the industry

The ability of firms to enter and leave the industry is crucial in a contestable market and is not necessarily linked to the number of firms in the industry as in neo-classical theories of the firm. In neo-classical theory, low barriers to entry are linked with a large number of firms in an industry (perfect competition and monopolistic competition ☞ units 53 and 55) whilst high barriers are linked with few firms in the industry (oligopoly or monopoly ☞ units 54 and 56). Perfectly competitive and monopolistically competitive industries are contestable because an assumption of both these models is that there are low barriers to industry. But what of oligopolies and monopolies?

Some barriers to entry are natural (sometimes called **innocent entry barriers**). For instance, the industry may be a natural monopoly (☞ unit 18) as in Railtrack. Alternatively, there may be very high capital entry costs to the industry, as in car manufacturing. Neo-classical theory would predict that firms in these industries would earn abnormal profits. Contestable market theory suggests that this depends to a large extent on the costs of **exit** from the industry.

For instance, assume that the natural monopolist is charging high prices and earning abnormal profit. A competitor then enters the industry and takes market share by charging lower prices. The natural monopolist reacts by cutting prices and the competitor leaves the industry, unable to compete on these new lower prices because its costs are too high. So long as the cost of leaving the industry is small, it still makes sense for the competitor to have earned profit in the short run by entering the industry. The costs of exit are the **sunk costs** of operating in the industry (i.e. the fixed costs of production which cannot be recovered if the firm leaves the industry). Money spent on advertising would be an example of a sunk cost. So too would capital equipment which had no alternative use. If the sunk costs are low - the firm has done little advertising and capital equipment has been leased on a short term basis, for instance - then the firm has lost little by entering and then leaving the industry. But in the meantime, it has earned profit at the expense of the existing firm in the industry.

Some barriers to entry, however, are erected by existing firms in the industry. In the soap powder market, soap powder producers spend large amounts of money advertising and branding their products. It may still be worth a firm entering this industry if the new entrant can charge a high enough price to cover the cost of entering

and then possibly being forced to leave the industry. For instance, a firm might seek to earn £10m profit over 12 months. It is then forced to leave the industry because existing firms drive down prices or increase their advertising budget. If it earned £15m operating profit but lost £5m in leaving the industry, it would still be worthwhile for the firm to have entered and operated for a year.

Question 2

Explain whether the following would make it more likely or less likely that there would be potential entrants to an industry.
(a) The inability of firms in the industry to lease capital equipment for short periods of time.
(b) Very high second hand prices for capital equipment.
(c) Heavy advertising by existing firms in the industry.
(d) The existence of a natural monopolist which was highly inefficient and had high costs of production.
(e) Patents held by an existing firm in the industry which were crucial to the manufacture of the product.
(f) Government legislation which gave monopoly rights to a single producer in the industry.

Potential competition

In a contestable market, firms are able to enter and leave the industry at relatively little cost. So far, we have implied that, in the short run, existing firms in a contestable market may well be earning abnormal profit. However, contestable market theory suggests that, in practice, established firms in a contestable market earn only normal profit even in the short run (i.e. they behave as if they operated in a perfectly competitive market).

Assume that a monopolist is the established firm in an industry. If it charges prices which would lead to it earning abnormal profit, then another firm may enter the industry charging lower prices. The new entrant will remain so long as the existing firm is earning abnormal profit, taking market share away from it and reducing its overall profits. To force the new entrant out, the monopolist would have to lower its prices. If it did this, and the new entrant left, and then the monopolist put up its prices again, all that will happen is that another firm will enter the industry. The only way to prevent new entrants constantly coming into the industry is for the existing firm to price at a level where it only earns normal profit.

Hence, the ability of firms to earn abnormal profit is dependent on the barriers to entry and exit to the industry, not on the number of firms in the industry as neo-classical theory would imply. With low barriers, existing firms will price such that AR = AC (i.e. no abnormal profits are being earned) because they are afraid that otherwise hit-and-run entrants to the industry will come in and damage the market for them. They are also afraid that new entrants may stay on a permanent basis, reducing the market share of existing firms in the industry.

Question 3

The Encyclopaedia Britannica is 200 years old. For nearly all its existence, it has been sold in book form. But the arrival of the home computer changed all that. Sales of the hard backed 13 volume set costing over £1 000 peaked in 1991. In 1994, the Encyclopaedia Britannica became available on a CD-Rom priced at more than £400. The price fell quickly and is currently around £90.

In 1999, there was a further shift. The Encyclopaedia Britannica became available free over the internet. Surfers could access the Encyclopaedia Britannica free on line. Encyclopaedia Britannica would in future earn its revenues not from the sale of the product but from sponsorship, advertising and cuts in the spending from e-commerce transactions related to the use of the web site.

The Encyclopaedia Britannica is the most well known brand name in the encyclopaedia market. 'There are two centuries of trust out there. We have to keep building on that authority' said James Strachan, managing director of the company. Encyclopaedia Britannica had been rapidly losing market share in terms of use to Encarta, the encyclopaedia produced by Microsoft and often supplied free to home users on CD-Rom when computers are purchased.

Source: adapted from the *Financial Times*, 20.10.1999.

(a) What do you think are the barriers to entry to the encyclopaedia market: (i) in book form; (ii) as a CD-Rom; (iii) supplied over the internet?
(b) Explain, using the theory of contestable markets and the concept of potential competition, why Encyclopaedia Britannica decided to supply its product free over the internet.

Efficiency

In the long run, firms (apart from those which are natural monopolies) in a contestable market will operate at the bottom of their average cost curve (i.e. at the **optimal level of output** where MC = AC ☞ unit 49). To understand why, assume that they didn't operate at this level. Then a new entrant would be able to establish itself, producing at the bottom of its average cost curve and charging at this level

too, undercutting other firms' prices. Existing firms would then be forced to cut costs if they wanted to stay in the industry. Hence, firms in the long run in a contestable market must be **productively efficient** (☞ unit 16).

They must also be **allocatively efficient** (☞ units 16 and 61). It has already been argued that firms in a contestable market can only earn normal profits in the long run (i.e. AR = AC). It has just been argued that firms will be productively efficient, producing where MC = AC. Hence, since AR = AC and MC = AC, firms must produce where AR = MC. This is the condition for allocative efficiency.

Stability of contestable markets

It is not always possible to predict the level of output of a firm in a contestable market. To understand why, assume that total market demand is 300 units at a price of £10 whilst lowest average cost for a single producer is £10 at an output of 100 units. Three firms will therefore find it profitable to produce in the industry, but each firm will only earn normal profits because AC=AR. With only normal profits being earned, the industry is in long run equilibrium because there is no incentive for other firms to enter.

However, a problem arises if market demand is, for instance, 300 units but the optimal level of production for each firm is 120 units. If there were only two firms in the industry, each firm would be producing under conditions of diseconomies of scale if each produced 150 units. There would be an incentive for a new firm to enter the industry and produce the optimum lowest cost level of output of 120 units. It would be difficult to believe that the two existing firms would not react by reducing output, moving towards the optimal level. But if there were three firms each producing the same output of 100 units, then one firm could expand output and experience greater economies of scale. The other firms in the industry would then be likely to react by expanding their own output. Market price would fall below the minimum average cost of production and firms would make losses, sending back signals that firms should cut their production. There is in fact no level of output which would produce an equilibrium situation.

This is likely to be less of a problem if average cost curves are L-shaped rather than U-shaped. If demand is 300 units, and the minimum efficient scale of production is 120 units, then two firms could produce 150 units each at lowest cost. The theory does not, however, predict whether one firm will produce 120 units and the other 180, or both produce 150 units, or some other combination, subject to a minimum of 120 units.

key terms

Contestable market - a market where there is freedom of entry to the industry and where costs of exit are low.

Applied economics

The bus industry

The bus industry in the UK is competitive. Four large companies have come to dominate the local transport market through a series of aggressive takeovers in the 1980s and 1990s. These are Arriva, Stagecoach, Go-Ahead and Firstbus. Being a large company gives certain competitive advantages. Access to finance for expansion and cheaper finance is one. Another is common operating systems devised to minimise cost.

However, there are large numbers of small bus companies too that provide competition in a local area. They can gain access to the market because barriers to entry are relatively low. Anyone is free to buy a bus and start running a service along a particular route. Small companies typically run old buses which are cheap to purchase, although they can prove expensive to maintain. They can cut running costs by paying cheaper wages to drivers than those paid in larger companies. Owners may also be prepared to accept lower profit margins than would be acceptable to a large company quoted on a stock exchange. The entry of these small competitors into the market since deregulation of the bus industry in the early 1980s explains why, as Figures 58.1 and 58.2 show, there has been an expansion in the number of bus miles travelled despite a fall in the number of passengers.

If viewed nationally, the local bus transport market could be viewed as oligopolistic in nature and therefore it might be presumed that the large firms in the industry would earn abnormal profit. In practice, the contestability of the market by small companies tends to lead to companies only earning normal profit.

Bus companies over the past 15 years have attempted

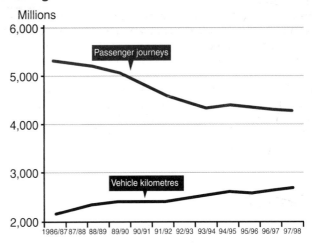

Figure 58.1 *Local bus services, number of passenger journeys and vehicle kilometres travelled, GB, millions*
Source: adapted from *Transport Statistics*, Office for National Statistics.

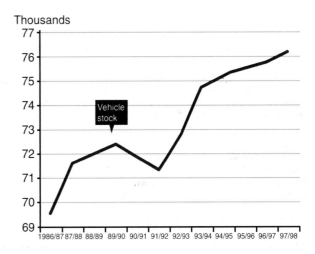

Figure 58.2 *Bus and coach services, vehicle stock, GB, thousands*
Source: adapted from *Transport Statistics*, Office for National Statistics.

to reduce this contestability through anti-competitive practices. They have been accused of forming cartels to bid for contracts from local authorities. They have also been investigated for adopting tactics to drive smaller competitors out of local markets, such as reducing fares on routes where there is competition. If the market were not contestable, they would have no need to resort to such tactics. They could simply charge high prices and rely on barriers to entry to keep competition out.

The package tour holiday industry

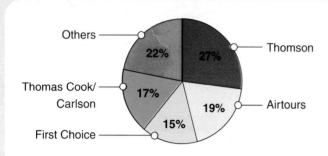

Figure 58.3 *UK package holiday market share (%), 1998*
Source: adapted from CAA/ATOL, Datastream/ICV.

Vertical integration

The package tour industry has a complex structure. Most companies use either travel agents or the media to market their product. However, the largest companies own their own chains of travel agents. Thomson owns Lunn Poly. Airtours owns Going Places and Travelworld. First Choice owns Intratravel, whilst Thomas Cook owns Thomas Cook travel agents. These travel agents offer a wide range of holidays from different companies and not just from the companies which own them. Travel agents which sell a holiday from a rival company receive a commission. Independent travel agents rely solely on these commissions for revenues. During the 1990s, the industry was investigated twice by the government through the Monopolies and Mergers Commission (renamed the Competition Commission in 1999) because there were fears that the large companies were exploiting their dominant position. For instance, travel agents of large companies were accused of putting pressure on customers to buy a holiday from their company and not from a rival company. The MMC found little evidence of such basic abuse of market power. They did find, though, evidence of unfair cross selling of products. In particular, customers were being offered discounts on holidays but only if they bought travel insurance from the company. The travel insurance was far more expensive than was available if holiday makers shopped around.

Source: adapted from *The Guardian*, 30.4.1999, 21.5.1999, 11.9.1999, 11.6.1999 and the Financial Times, 22.4.1999, 8.11.1999

1. **What is meant by a 'contestable market'?**
2. **Suggest why the package tour market is a contestable market.**
3. **In 1999, Airtours tried but failed to buy First Choice. To what extent would the market have become less contestable if it had succeeded?**

Source: *The Mail on Sunday*, 4.5.2000

The UK package tour industry is dominated by four companies - Thomson, Airtours, First Choice and Thomas Cook. These companies have been created during the 1980s and 1990s through a process of amalgamation and takeover. Profit, though, has not always been very high. Indeed, tour operators have been prone to make substantial losses. Part of the problem for the tour operators is that they have tended to compete on price. They have found it difficult to establish substantial brand loyalty. Customers typically shop around, getting brochures from a number of different companies, choosing on location, facilities and price rather than which company is offering the holiday.

Demand and supply

Tour operators work by booking facilities in advance. If they plan for 1 million holidays, but only sell 950 000, they still have to pay for much of the cost of the 50 000 unsold holidays. In practice, tour operators will attempt to sell the 50 000 holidays at knock down prices because any revenue is better than none. This, however, encourages consumers to be price sensitive.

In the past, tour operators have attempted to win market share by aggressively expanding the number of holidays on offer. However, the tactic can easily misfire because the company can be left with large numbers of unsold holidays, disposed of cheaply at the last minute at far below cost. The company then plunges into loss and is forced to retrench, offering fewer holidays the following season and losing market share.

Summary

1. The neo-Keynesian theory of the firm assumes that firms are long run profit maximisers which determine prices according to cost-plus pricing principles. Price stability is a feature of this model.
2. Baumol's sales maximisation model assumes that firms aim to maximise sales subject to a profit satisficing constraint.
3. Managerial theories predict that costs and output are likely to be higher than neo-classical theory would suggest.
4. Both managerial and behavioural theories predict that organisational slack is likely to be present.
5. Limit pricing occurs when firms don't attempt to maximise short run profits for fear that this will attract competitors into the market, resulting in overall smaller long run profits. Instead, they set prices which are low enough to deter new entrants from entering the market, and which result in maximum long run profits given the potential competition in the market.

The neo-Keynesian model

R Hall and C Hitch in the 1930s outlined a radically different model of the firm from existing neo-classical models. Their research indicated that firms did not equate marginal cost and marginal revenue in an attempt to maximise short run profits. Rather, firms maximised profits in the long run (☞ unit 50). Firms then determined prices by calculating costs and adding a profit mark-up (hence the term **cost-plus pricing**). Prices are stable because firms take a long term view of the market.

In the model, it is argued that firms respond to changes in demand and cost not by changing price but by changing output. A large inflow of orders will not lead to a rise in price but to an increase in production. If a manufacturer is already producing at normal full capacity, it may attempt to produce at over-full capacity by encouraging its employees to work overtime or extra shifts. In the service sector, a booming supermarket will not increase prices if it proves far more popular than expected. Rather it will allow overcrowding in the short term and in the longer term may open longer hours, open an extension or build a new supermarket close by. Alternatively, a firm may allow waiting lists to develop. (A waiting list may be helpful in some cases to the image of a product because it is a sign that there are customers who think the product is so good that they are prepared to wait to buy it.)

If demand falls or costs rise, a firm will not necessarily respond by reducing price. Rather it will reduce output. If losses threaten to become too high, it will close down production rather than reduce price which may be seen to be damaging to the longer term prospects for the product.

Prices may not change on a daily basis (as for instance for carrots or tomatoes in the agricultural market) but, equally, firms' prices are not permanently fixed. The frequency of price changes will vary from industry to industry, but a yearly review of prices is not uncommon in British manufacturing industry.

The size of the profit mark-up will vary too. However, the mark-up will tend to be higher where:

- firms in the industry are able to collude, acting as if they were a monopolist;
- there are only a few large firms in the industry, which results in less price competition;
- barriers to entry are high, limiting the possibility of new firms entering the industry;
- there is a large number of small buyers in the market, rather than a few significant buyers who are able to use their buying power to exert downward pressure on prices.

The neo-Keynesian theory of the firm is able to explain relative price stability in the market. However, it is pointed out by neo-classical economists that traditional cost curves should include an allowance for the cost of changing price - in other words, the insight that price changes can be costly can be incorporated within a neo-classical model.

Question 1

Richard and Margaret Nelson are traditional cheesemakers. From their farm in Devon, they have built up a small business selling cheeses made from the milk of ewes. Their customers are mainly small retailers scattered across the country which sell speciality cheeses. The cheese is sold wholesale at roughly £6 a kilo. This price is based on the cost of production. Richard and Margaret buy in their sheep's milk and they have costed their time and other costs. Profit margins are wafer thin because of competition from France. When the value of the pound went up in 1996, the Nelsons lost half their market to imports. They were not prepared to drop their prices to match the new lower prices of French competitors. The result is that they only make cheese one day a week now compared to two in 1995.

(a) What is meant by cost-plus pricing? Illustrate your answer from the data.
(b) If demand suddenly rose for the Nelsons' cheeses, do you think they would increase their prices? Explain your answer carefully.

Revenue maximisation model

Neo-classical theory assumes that firms are short run profit maximisers. In the early 1950s an American economist, W Baumol, put forward an alternative model suggesting that firms might maximise sales revenue rather than profits. He recognised that firms cannot make a loss if they are to survive in the long term, so at least some profit must be made. Managers also need to make enough profit to satisfy their shareholders (☞ unit 50).

In Figure 59.1, total cost and total revenue curves are drawn. The difference between the two is profit, shown by the curve at the bottom of the graph. The firm can operate anywhere between output levels OA and OD without making a loss. It will maximise profit at OB. If shareholders are content to earn just normal profit and managers wish to maximise sales, then the firm will operate at OD. On the other hand, if the minimum acceptable level of profit for shareholders is OE, then output will be at OC. As can be seen from the diagram, the higher the profit satisficing level of output, the lower will be the level of output and the nearer it will be to the profit maximising level of output.

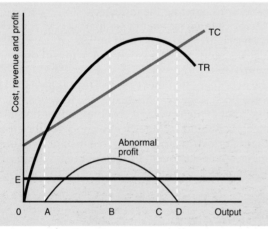

Figure 59.1 *Sales maximisation*
A firm maximising sales will earn normal profit at an output level of OD. If shareholders demand a minimum level of profit of OE, then it will maximise sales by producing at OC. Both output levels will be above the profit maximising level of output OB.

Question 2

(a) A monopolist is a sales maximiser subject to the constraint that it needs to make normal profits to satisfy its shareholders. Draw a standard neo-classical monopoly diagram (☞ unit 54). Mark on it:
   (i) the sales maximising level of output;
   (ii) the firm's sales maximising level of output subject to its profit constraint.
(b) Compare the effect on output and price if a monopolist moves from being a profit maximiser to being a sales maximiser.

Managerial and behavioural theories of the firm

In both managerial and behavioural theories of the firm (☞ unit 50), it is argued that there is a divorce of ownership and control. In managerial theories, it is assumed that managers control the firm subject to a profit satisficing constraint.

Managerial models tend to make three clear predictions.
● Costs will be higher than neo-classical theory would predict. Higher salaries, expensive company cars and unnecessary levels of staffing have to be paid for.
● Firms will produce at higher levels of output than neo-classical theory would predict. This is because higher output and higher sales will lead to more staff being employed, which is beneficial to the utility of managers. Moreover, higher output levels may be more important in determining salary levels than increased profitability.
● In a recession, management may suffer disproportionately. In the attempt to prevent the company from sliding into loss and possible take over or bankruptcy, managers may be sacked as administration is streamlined and their salaries and perks reduced. In an economic boom, managers may benefit more than most as they are able to increase their own salaries and perks whilst increasing profits too. Shareholders find it difficult to prevent this because they are unable to gauge how much more profit the company could have made if managers had not increased costs unnecessarily.

In behavioural theories, it is argued that it is not just shareholders and managers who determine the behaviour of firms. Other interested parties, such as government, trade unions and other pressure groups like environmentalists, can have an important say too. The eventual outcome will depend upon the relative strength of the various competing parties. In the UK newspaper industry in the 1970s, for instance, it could be argued that trade unions played an unusually dominant role in decision making, which led to exceptionally high wages being paid to their members. In the 1980s, shareholder power became more fashionable. In the 1990s environmentalists increased their power over corporate decision making. The main supermarket chains in the UK, for instance, now carry a wide range of 'environmentally friendly' products which were not on the shelves ten years ago. A profit maximising assumption is then seen to be simplistic and will necessarily lead to misunderstanding about how firms behave.

Both managerial and behavioural theories predict that ORGANISATIONAL SLACK is likely to be present. Organisational slack or X-INEFFICIENCY were terms used by Professor Harvey Leibenstein to describe the tendency of firms in non-competitive markets to produce at higher than minimum cost. So when a manager receives a Jaguar when he would have been content with a Mondeo, or when a trade union member receives £500 a week when he would have worked for £300, or when a chargehand chooses to organise production in a traditional way when a far more efficient modern method is available, then organisational slack is present.

Organisational slack exists partly because of a lack of knowledge. Decision makers don't know the exact minimum amount for which a worker might be prepared to work, for instance. Perhaps more importantly, organisations are often very conservative. They might order components from a firm they have always dealt with even if they know that the components could be purchased more cheaply elsewhere. Or they might be reluctant to invest in new machinery because all investment is a risk, despite the fact that potentially there are considerable cost savings to be made.

Different interest groups in the firm might be able to exploit their potential power to their advantage, thus increasing organisational slack. Environmental groups, for instance, might force a firm to adopt stricter environmental standards than cost-minimisation would dictate by threatening a media campaign against the firm. Trade unions might threaten to strike, causing short term chaos, unless their demands are met.

In a recession, organisational slack tends to decline. Firms are forced to concentrate on safeguarding profits and, as a result, unnecessary costs tend to be pruned first. Everything, from the size of the company director's car to working practices on the shop floor to the provision of food in the company canteen, is likely to be affected.

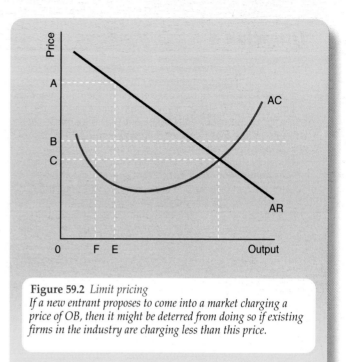

Figure 59.2 *Limit pricing*
If a new entrant proposes to come into a market charging a price of OB, then it might be deterred from doing so if existing firms in the industry are charging less than this price.

Question 3

According to a letter by K P McCann in the *Financial Times*, 'the maximisation of shareholders' wealth (is not) necessarily regarded as an overriding objective in many countries outside the UK. This is especially true in Germany where ... the relative lack of importance attached to the stock markets, social and employment legislation, tax regulations and the approach to financing industry all point to an economic culture which believes that a business is important in many different ways to a country, its economy and its society. The idea that shareholders' interests alone should prevail is not widely accepted.'

(a) Explain why this letter supports a behavioural view of the firm.

Limit pricing

LIMIT PRICING is when firms in an oligopolistic industry set a low enough price (the 'limit price') to deter new entrants from coming into the market. Limit pricing theories assume that firms look beyond maximising short run profits. For instance, assume that firms in an industry can earn £50 million in abnormal profit this year by charging an average price of £10 for each product sold. However, at £10, new firms would be prepared to enter the market, driving down both price and market share of existing firms in the future. It might pay existing firms to charge a lower price than £10 now and lessen the risk of new entrants coming into the market.

Consider Figure 59.2. Assume that existing firms in the

industry all have identical cost and revenue curves. Company X, shown in the figure, produces at a short run profit maximising level of output of OE where MC = MR. A new entrant is considering coming into the market. Initially, it proposes to produce OF. Because it is a new entrant, it will not be able to price on the same demand curve as Company X. It will have to sell at a discount. However, so long as it receives a price equal to OB, it will at least make normal profit. How might Company X and other firms in the industry react to the new entrant? Assuming that the new entrant could potentially take away large parts of the market, they should lower their price to below OB. If they do this, they will force the new entrant to make a loss. So long as their price is above OC, revenues will exceed costs and they will continue to earn some abnormal profit.

This assumes that all existing firms in the industry will lower their prices below the short run profit maximising price. This would be easier to achieve if firms openly **colluded** - getting together to fix prices and output to maximise profit. However, firms may achieve the same result through custom and practice, prices settling down at a level where there is some stability in the market and where no firm believes that it is in its long term interests to change price.

The limit price will be greater, the higher the barriers to entry to the industry. This is because the higher the barriers to entry, the less likely it is that a new entrant will come into the industry. For instance, if there were large financial barriers to entry because setting up would be highly costly, then new entrants would be worried that they would lose large amounts of money if the venture proved unprofitable and they had to withdraw. A relatively small reduction from the short run profit maximising price might therefore be enough to completely deter a potential new entrant.

Question 4

Barclays announced yesterday that it would cut 6 000 jobs as part of an ongoing three year cost cutting programme. The 6 000 jobs will in the long term save the company £200 million a year. However, many analysts are disappointed by the scale of the cuts. They point out that the cost savings amount to just 5 per cent of the combined £3.74 billion of annual operating expenses in the corporate and retail banking divisions. Other banks have managed closer to 10 per cent savings this year. What's more, the short term cost of the redundancies is high. Barclays has set aside £400 million to cover staff and property costs arising from the programme. The rule of thumb for the relationship between restructuring charges and cost savings in the banking industry tends to be one for one. The reason why is that the redundancy package being offered to staff is very generous by industry standards. For instance, staff over 50 can take early retirement on full pension. Unifi, the banking union, has supported the package and described it as a deal which should become a model for the industry.

Source: adapted from the *Financial Times*, 21.5.1999.

(a) What evidence is there from the data that Barclays in 1999 was not a short run profit maximiser but instead was behaving in a way best explained by behavioural theories of the firm?

key terms

Organisational slack or X-inefficiency - inefficiency arising because a firm or other productive organisation fails to minimise its costs of production.

Limit pricing - when a firm, rather than short run profit maximising, sets a low enough price to deter new entrants from coming into its market.

Applied economics

Japanese companies

The behaviour of large Japanese companies arguably differs from that of large US and UK companies. In the Anglo-Saxon world, shareholders are supposed to be the most important economic agents in a company. They are the owners and the company should be run for their benefit. This means maximising shareholder value. This comes in two main forms. First, companies should aim to maximise their dividend payments, which means maximising short term profits. Second, companies should aim to maximise their share price and the growth in the share price so that shareholders can make capital gains. A number of fashionable business concepts, such as Total Quality Management (TQM) emphasise the important of providing high quality products or services to customers. Government initiatives, such as Investors In People, stress the importance of training the workforce. However, building up a happy, loyal and productive workforce and ensuring that customers are satisfied with what they are buying are not ends in themselves. A hard working staff is only important ultimately because that staff is likely to make higher profits for the company than if it is demotivated and unhappy. Happy customers are only important because if they were unhappy they might take their custom to another company.

In continental Europe and Japan, attitudes differ. Shareholders are important, but they are only one group amongst many which influence decision making in the company. Partly this is because shareholders are unable to exert as much power. In Anglo-Saxon countries, direct shareholder involvement in the running of large companies is rare. Shareholders exert power through the buying and selling of shares on stock exchanges. A poorly performing company tends to see its share price slide as shareholders sell their stock in the face of poor dividend and share price growth. The company then becomes easy prey to a take-over bid from another company. In continental Europe and Japan, few companies are open to be taken over in this way because the majority of their voting shares are not tradeable on the stock exchange - they are owned by family members or by other large companies.

Shareholders in continental Europe and Japan are also far less likely to be short run maximisers than in Anglo-Saxon countries because of who owns shares. In the UK and the USA, banks are not allowed to hold company shares as part of their reserves. In Germany and Japan, in contrast, banks have always been encouraged to invest capital in company shares. As a consequence, bankers sit on the boards of companies in these countries. Banks are not particularly interested in short term profits. They wish to see the companies in which they own shares prosper over a long period of time. A company which produces shoddy goods might make a fast profit initially, but is unlikely to grow and prosper in the long term. Equally, shareholders in family controlled businesses are likely to be in business to secure the long term growth and prosperity of the company rather than pursuing the highest profit in the next month.

The importance of workers in a company is emphasised in the European Union through the Social Charter. Under the Charter, all large companies must have works councils, comprising representatives of workers and management, which have some power to influence long term decision making in a company. In the UK, the Conservative government in the early 1990s opted out of the Social Charter and declared that it would not encourage UK firms to organise works councils. The new Labour government elected in 1997 took a different view and signed the Social Charter.

In Japan, workers are seen as one of the key stake holders in a company. Large companies have a policy of providing jobs for life whilst trade unions see it as their role to safeguard the prosperity of the company to ensure that jobs can be for life.

European and Japanese governments have a history of being more interventionist than in the UK or the USA. In Japan, for instance, the government heavily influenced the development of individual industries in the post-war period. In France, national plans in the 1950s, 1960s and 1970s directed the growth of different sectors in the economy. Whilst direct government

intervention in industry has diminished in the 1980s and 1990s, no European or Japanese government has gone down the road pursued by Margaret Thatcher and Ronald Reagan in the 1980s of minimising the role of government in the economy as much as possible.

Anglo-Saxon firms, then, can be seen broadly as short term profit maximisers. Continental European and Japanese firms, in contrast, tend to pursue long term profit objectives. The way they work is perhaps best described by behavioural theories of the firm, where a number of competing interest groups in a business come to a consensus about the direction the firm should pursue. However, it can be argued that the world's largest businesses are moving more to an Anglo-Saxon model. In continental Europe, increasingly firms have been bought out and become subsidiaries of Anglo-Saxon firms. This changes their corporate behaviour. Equally, in Japan the very difficult economic conditions of the 1990s, where there has been prolonged recession, has left many large companies in a state of financial collapse. They have been forced to restructure to return to profitability and repay some of their large debts. This has meant cutting staff and closing factories. Short run profit has become more important as a company goal than in the past.

DATA QUESTION

A traditional pub

Phil Sawyer owns and runs a traditional pub. Over the past fifteen years he has actively changed the product mix. Originally almost all the sales revenue came from drinks. Today half comes from sale of food. The menu offers a few traditional English dishes along with more adventurous French inspired dishes.

Phil operates a simple rule of thumb on food pricing. The cost of the food should be around one third of the price charged to customers. The remaining two thirds, the gross profit margin, pays for fixed overhead costs and the net profit earned. For instance, the food cost of a fish dish with vegetables is around £2.50. So he charges £7.49 on the menu. Part of the success of the pub is that much of the menu is changed regularly. This appeals to his regular clientele who enjoy eating out. Any new dish which fails to sell well within two weeks is withdrawn from sale. The chef sometimes objects and tells Phil to 'give it a chance'. The chef has suggested that

customers might see it as overpriced and that cutting its price could increase sales. Phil, though, is ruthless. 'If I can't sell it at a profit, then it has no place on my menu.'

Last year, the pub in the next village was bought and turned into a Mexican themed pub. It proved very popular, particularly with younger customers in their twenties. Phil was a little nervous when he saw its business take off and he noticed that fewer young customers were now visiting his pub to eat. He vaguely discussed with his chef whether changing price would have any effect on custom, but decided that price was not an issue in this situation. The key was providing value for money for his customer base. Sales the following year still grew by 6 per cent over the year, a little down on previous years but still a very satisfactory result.

1. **Explain what type of pricing technique Phil Sawyer is using. Illustrate your answer from the passage.**
2. **Discuss how Phil Sawyer is likely to react if: (a) there are violent storms in the North Sea and the wholesale price of the fish used at Phil Sawyer's pub doubles that week; (b) there is a downturn in the local** economy and unemployment rises; (c) some Saturday nights he has to turn food customers away because the eating area is full; (d) overcrowding in the restaurant becomes a regular occurrence.
3. **Discuss whether there is likely to be organisational slack in the running of the pub.**

Applied economics

Transport

Transport is a service. The transport industry is responsible for the movement of passengers and freight from one geographical point to another. Examples include an individual flying on holiday from Manchester to Paris, a container load of television sets being sent by lorry from the UK to Spain and a business executive travelling by rail from Durham to London for a meeting.

Transport is almost always a **derived demand** (☞ unit 7). A firm needs transport because it wishes to supply goods to a customer. An individual has to use transport to travel to a holiday destination. A business executive uses air transport to fly to a meeting as part of the activity of producing goods for customers. Very occasionally, individuals make a journey the sole object of their demand. A man taking a 'spin' in his sports car, or a railway enthusiast spending a Saturday travelling on an unfamiliar line would be examples.

Like any service, it is produced using factors of production.

Land The land along which roads and railways are built is included here. So too are all the facilities associated with transport, such as the land on which lorry parking lots exist, or on which warehouses and ports are built. The sea through which ships pass and the air through which aeroplanes fly are also examples of land as a factor of production.

Labour 978 000 workers were classified as working in the transport and storage industry in the UK in 1999. The Standard Industrial Classification breakdown of this employment is shown in Table 60.1. A wide variety of skills is required in the transport industry from workers. Jobs range from managers to clerical staff to drivers to unskilled labourers. In common with all industries, the levels of human capital required are increasing over time. Fifty years ago, for instance, large numbers of unskilled workers were employed at Britain's ports to load and unload ships. Today, only a fraction of this number is needed because the process of loading and unloading has become highly mechanised, including the use of containers for small shipments. In contrast, there is an increasing demand for workers

with ICT skills or with marketing experience.

Capital A wide range of capital is employed in the transport industry. Partly it represents part of the **infrastructure** of an economy - roads, railways, ports, pipelines and airports. Transport also requires capital such as cars, lorries, locomotives, ships and aircraft.

Entrepreneurship Entrepreneurs are those who bring together the factors of production to organise output. These therefore include managers. In the traditional definition of the term, however, they must also be risk takers. Classic entrepreneurs are people like Brian Souter who founded Stagecoach, the bus and rail group, and Richard Branson who founded Virgin Atlantic, the airline.

Table 60.1 *Employee jobs in transport and storage, June 1999*

Land transport, transport via pipelines	498 000
Water transport	23 000
Air transport	83 000
Supporting and auxiliary transport activities, activities of travel agents	374 000
Total	978 000

Source: adapted from *Annual Abstract of Statistics*, Office for National Statistics.

Modes of transport

The main modes of transport today are roads, railways, pipelines, aircraft and ships. In the 18th and 19th century, inland barge traffic was very important but has been mostly replaced by road transport. When deciding which mode of transport to use, buyers use a number of different criteria.

Availability For many journeys, there is little or no choice in the market. For instance, if a commuter wishes to travel door to door by one mode of transport, the car is almost certainly the only available option. Equally, few businesses are connected directly with their suppliers or customers by rail, leaving lorry transport as the sole choice. If a UK firm wishes to send goods overseas, it must use sea or air transport, unless it sends the goods through the Channel Tunnel.

Cost Transport users will seek to minimise cost, all other things being equal. The relevant cost they consider is marginal cost. In the short run, when capital costs are fixed, this is a variable cost (☞ unit 47). For instance, when deciding on cost grounds whether to travel by train or car to work, a car owning commuter will compare the price of a train ticket with the petrol cost of the journey (☞ unit 61). Similarly, a firm which owns a lorry will compare the variable cost of using the lorry to transport goods with the total cost of alternative modes of transport. In the long run, all factors are variable. Therefore transport users will consider all costs when making decisions at the margin.

In freight transport, there is a considerable cost involved if goods have to be changed from one mode of transport to another during a journey. There is the loading and unloading cost, as well as likely time delays which in itself is a cost. This has made rail transport increasingly uneconomic compared to road transport over the past 50 years. Rail transport is particularly cost effective when there is a dedicated rail link to a production site and where large volumes of product can be loaded directly onto a train. For instance, a rail link between a coal mine and an electricity power station can provide a more cost effective form of transport than lorries.

Equally, rail transport becomes more economical compared to road transport the longer the distance travelled. It is often argued that rail transport begins to become particularly competitive for journeys over 400 miles. Within the UK, very little freight is carried this sort of distance, and therefore rail freight companies find it difficult to bring prices down to a level which would make their customers switch from road to rail.

Sea transport per tonne is relatively cheap because of technical economies of scale. Ships can carry large amounts of freight compared to, say, a lorry or an aeroplane, and this reduces the cost per tonne carried. At the other extreme, air freight is particularly expensive because the operating costs per mile of an aeroplane are very high but the cargo capacity of an aeroplane is very limited.

Pipelines are a highly cost effective way of carrying liquids and gases between two points. The marginal operating cost is almost zero. Virtually all the cost of a pipeline is the fixed cost of laying it.

Speed Speed is a key determinant of many transport decisions. For passenger transport, time taken travelling has an opportunity cost. So if it takes two hours to complete a journey by train but three hours by car, travelling by car has an opportunity cost of one hour. This opportunity cost must be included in the financial cost of the journey to calculate a total cost. For firms, speed too is likely to represent an opportunity cost. For instance, a parcel with replacement parts for a damaged machine might be sent air freight rather than overland. If the extra cost is £500 but the parts arrive two days earlier, the £500 must be compared with the losses that will be incurred during the extra two days the machine is out of action. In general, air and road transport take less time than sea and rail transport respectively. The current poor performance of rail on speed is a major cause for concern for those wishing to move more freight onto the railways and off the roads.

Reliability Reliability is another key factor in determining modes of transport. Commuters, for instance, may choose the car over public transport because they find car journey times more predictable than the bus or the train. Many firms now are dependent on reliable transport for their business. Supermarkets must have fresh deliveries every day. Car manufacturers keep very low levels of stock and expect just in time deliveries from suppliers. Reliable transport can minimise stock levels and thus keep production costs to a minimum. It is also vital in marketing products to consumers.

Safety Some modes of transport are chosen over others for safety reasons. Nuclear waste, for instance, is unlikely to be transported by aeroplane. Pipelines are a particularly safe way of transporting gas and oil. Safety is, in one sense, a cost issue. Today, accidents are likely to incur heavy costs, especially if they involve dangerous or polluting substances. Firms may choose to adopt a more costly mode of transport rather than run the risk of accidents with a cheaper mode of transport.

Public vs private sector provision

Thirty years ago, much of the transport industry was in

public ownership. Today, most has been privatised.

Road transport Roads in the UK are almost always provided by the state and funded through taxes. The first toll motorway operated by a private company, the Birmingham Relief Road, is due to be completed this decade. However, the government remains committed to state provision of the road network. In some other countries, key road links, mainly motorways, are run by private companies, although they often receive substantial subsidies from government. The vehicles which use the road system are owned within the private sector. Passenger cars are owned by private sector households. Lorry freight companies are all private sector firms. Long distance buses were privatised and deregulated in the 1980s, shortly followed by local bus services.

Rail transport British Rail was privatised in 1995, when it was split up into a large number of separate companies. The industry is now made up of five separate parts.
- Railtrack was privatised as the monopoly owner of the existing rail infrastructure. It is responsible for maintaining and upgrading everything from rail lines to railway stations and bridges. It earns revenues from the rail companies which run trains across its tracks.
- A number of train operating companies run services along the railway network. These include SouthWest Trains, owned by Stagecoach, Virgin West Coast and ScotRail. They have won a franchise from the government to run a given level of service for a fixed number of years. They receive revenues by charging passengers and often receive subsidies from government. Most train operating companies are monopolies along their routes. Where there is competition, this is often limited because one company provides a superior service to another.
- There are two rail freight companies, English, Welsh & Scottish (EWS) and Freightliner. These compete for business in the freight market.
- Train sets (locomotives and carriages) are leased from one of three train leasing companies. These are responsible for maintaining existing stock and buying new stock. They receive their revenues from the train operating companies.
- There is a number of companies which compete for work repairing and maintaining railway infrastructure, as well as upgrading the system. They earn their revenues from Railtrack, which puts such work out to tender.

Sea transport Shipping companies are mainly private sector companies throughout the world. They compete for traffic amongst themselves.

Air transport There has been a long history of airlines being owned by the state. For instance, until the 1980s, British Airways was owned by the UK government. KLM, Air France and Al Italia were also state owned

carriers. Most airlines have now been privatised or will soon be privatised. Airlines fly in and out of airports. These may be owned by the private sector or they may be owned by the state. Some airports, such as Birmingham airport, for instance are owned by local authorities.

The demand for and supply of transport

This is discussed in detail in the Applied Economics sections of unit 6 (passenger transport) and unit 7 (commercial transport).

Transport forecasts

Transport forecasts are predictions of transport volumes. They are prepared using a variety of data. At their simplest, they are extrapolations of previous trends. For instance, if road transport volumes in the UK have been growing at 2 per cent per annum on average for the past 20 years, then a crude forecast would be that they will continue to grow at this level for the next 20 years.

There is a variety of factors which economists could take into account to make this forecast more sophisticated. For instance, growth in transport is linked to growth in GDP. If GDP growth is expected to rise in the future, then transport growth is likely to rise too, and vice versa. The number of passenger cars is also linked to growth in population, the age distribution of the population (because those under 17 and above 75 tend not to own cars) the numbers in work and the number of households. Transport growth is affected by government policy. For instance, a raising of the maximum tonnage which can be carried by a single freight vehicle will reduce the number of lorries on the road. Road pricing could cut transport volumes. Investment in rail infrastructure, encouraged by government, could shift passengers and freight off the roads and onto the railways.

Sometimes forecasts need to be made for new infrastructure where there are no past trends to form the basis of the prediction. An example would be vehicle use of a new bypass. Transport economists in this case would estimate current traffic passing through the town or village affected and extrapolate how much of this traffic would use the bypass. They would then make an estimate of how much additional traffic would be generated (known as **induced traffic**). For instance, some motorists will now make journeys which they would previously not have made. Others will switch routes to use the bypass. Economists should have available data from previous bypass schemes to help them predict what will happen in this specific case. However, every bypass scheme is different. Transport economists, for example, considerably underestimated traffic use of London's motorway bypass, the M25.

Transport forecasts are used in a variety of ways. They can be used to plan for growth in transport infrastructure. Until the late 1980s, for instance, the UK government had a '**predict and build**' policy for roads. Predictions were prepared about road transport volumes and roads were built to accommodate this. Any private sector company involved in the transport industry is keenly interested in transport forecasts. Motor manufacturers, for instance, use transport forecasts in deciding whether or not to invest in new manufacturing plant.

Transport forecasts are used to make financial decisions. Railway operating companies can only decide how much to bid for a franchise by predicting how the market will grow (or shrink) over the lifetime of the franchise. A shipping company must make a forecast of future trade before it orders a new ship. An airline company will prepare forecasts of passenger numbers before it opens a new route.

Government uses transport forecasts when deciding upon policy. For instance, the government today wants to curb the growth of road traffic from what is predicted for environmental and congestion reasons. It wishes to boost rail traffic from current forecasts to relieve pressure on the roads. Once policies have been decided, governments can then produce new forecasts showing what they predict will happen after government intervention compared to before.

Public transport markets

The public transport market is a complex mix of different markets, some of whose services are close substitutes, whilst others have little in common with each other. In terms of traditional theories of the firm, they can relatively easily be categorised.

Rail travel The railway network in the UK consists, for the most part, of monopolies. Railtrack, which owns the infrastructure, is a natural monopoly. The train operating companies, which run services across the infrastructure, have mostly been given monopoly rights by the government which granted them their franchises. However, they have limited ability to exploit that monopoly because they are subject to regulation and also because their franchises are limited in time. The train operating companies, not surprisingly, would like to see the regulatory price regime loosened and the length of franchises extended.

Bus travel The bus industry is more complex. Nationally, there are four main groups of bus companies which dominate local bus services: Stagecoach, Arriva, Go-Ahead and First Bus. This could therefore be considered an oligopolistic industry. However, in many areas, only one of these bus companies offers services. It may or may not be in competition with smaller bus companies. On many routes, there is only one bus service and therefore the bus company offering it has a monopoly. The ability of bus companies to exploit this monopoly depends to

some extent on agreements entered into with local authorities, which often subsidise what would otherwise be loss making routes. Where a subsidy is given, the local authority is likely to fix a price for fares in the operating contract.

Air travel There is a large number of airlines operating on routes within and out of the UK. However, the market is not perfectly competitive for a number of reasons. First, airlines offered a branded service and business travellers typically have a preference for which airline they use. Second, there is limited choice on any particular route. London to New York is quite competitive. But London to Shanghai or Birmingham to Nice have only one airline flying directly between these destinations. It is, of course, possible to change at another airport, but this is a significant deterrent to passengers who want the shortest journey time. Third, popular airports like Heathrow tend to be full during the day. In the UK, there is no tradable market in airport landing slots. So airlines setting up a new service at, say, Heathrow either have to close down another of their services or use another less popular airport (☞ the Data Question in unit 8 and Question 3 in unit 61).

Lastly, air routes have traditionally been highly regulated by governments to benefit their national carriers. For instance, airlines wishing to fly from the UK to the USA have to gain permission from both the UK and US authorities (again ☞ units 8 and 61). Such permissions tend to be traded - the US authorities will only give permission for a UK airline to fly to the USA if a US airline is given new rights to fly a route to the UK. Many would like to see all governments adopt 'open skies' policies where any carrier could fly to any destination in the world. There is now an open skies policy within the EU for EU airlines, and similarly US carriers have the freedom to fly anywhere internally within the USA. Even open skies policies, though, do not necessarily make markets competitive. Some airports, such as London Heathrow, are already operating at 100 per cent capacity during the day and this limits new competition in the market. Moreover, there is some evidence from the USA (☞ Question 3 in unit 65) that airline companies engage in anti-competitive practices to preserve monopolies on routes. In the UK, budget no-frills airlines were dismayed when British Airways decided to set up Go in 1999 to compete directly in this market. They feared that British Airways would drive them out of the market using predatory pricing techniques and then close down Go to force passengers back onto the much more expensive traditional airlines, including of course British Airways.

Shipping Freight shipping tends to be a perfectly competitive market. There is a large number of shipping companies offering services between different destinations. Passenger shipping tends to be either oligopolistic or a monopoly. For instance, there are only a few companies offering cross-Channel services, whilst there is only one company offering a service between the mainland and the Isle of Wight.

Contestability and public transport markets

Neo-classical theories of perfect competition, monopolistic competition, oligopoly and monopoly (☞ units 52-55) may provide poor explanations of the behaviour of transport industries if different assumptions are made about the contestability of a market (☞ unit 58).

The rail industry Railtrack is an example of a natural monopoly. Along the routes that Railtrack owns, no other competitor would want to or legally be allowed to enter the market. Even on proposed new routes, Railtrack has a considerable competitive advantage. For example, the Channel Tunnel high speed rail link from London to the Tunnel was put out to tender, but eventually it was Railtrack that was chosen to complete the route. Again, a company has been trying to secure legal permission and financial backing to build a new railway and use existing Railtrack from the Midlands to the Channel Tunnel. However, it has failed so far to gain either sufficient financing or legal permission to complete this project. The capital costs of these ventures are so large that they have had difficulty getting off the ground.

The passenger transport rail market is equally uncontestable in the short term. The rail operators have bought monopoly franchises from the government. However, the market becomes contestable when the franchises come up for renewal. The existing operators have sought to make the market less contestable by applying pressure on the government to extend existing franchises in return for improvements in the service they currently offer. Typically, they try to link investment in new rolling stock with franchise extension. The government, so far, has resisted this pressure. As franchises near their end, though, it becomes increasingly difficult for a train operator to justify any long term investment. This could lead to underinvestment in the railways, leading to dynamic inefficiency. When franchises do come up for renewal, there are likely to be only a few firms interested in bidding for the renewal. These are likely to be the largest of the existing rail operators. To gain the franchise, they will have to offer to invest in the service whilst taking either the lowest subsidy or paying the government the highest price for the franchise. The bidders will also have to consider how they can exit the franchise if they fail to win the renewal bid next time round.

Bus and coach transport This was discussed in the Applied Economics section of unit 58.

Air transport The air transport market is frequently not contestable for the reasons outlined above.

Shipping Shipping tends to be a contestable market because ship owners can move their ships round from route to route depending upon demand. In the passenger transport market, for instance, the opening of the Channel Tunnel led to a reduction in the number of ships on cross-Channel routes. These ships were put to work on other routes in Northern Europe.

Price, output and profit

Different market structures lead to different allocations of resources. Multi-plant monopolists, for instance, will tend to reduce output in order to raise prices and profits compared to a perfectly competitive structure for the industry (☞ unit 54). Transport markets provide a wide range of examples of different price and output practices.

Because so many transport markets are monopolies, **price discrimination** (☞ unit 54) is widespread. For instance, airlines charge a wide variety of different tariffs for essentially the same journey. They can do this because different passengers have different **price elasticities of demand** (☞ unit 8 for a discussion of pricing on the North Atlantic route). The purpose of price discrimination is to maximise revenues for the airlines and increase **producer surplus** (☞ unit 5). Railways also price discriminate (☞ unit 54 for the example of Virgin West Coast).

Where firms in the transport market are forced to compete, they may attempt to limit that competition. For example, transport firms often press governments to **regulate** markets for the benefit of existing firms in the market. Typically this means giving firms exclusive rights to operate on a route, preventing new entrants from gaining a share of the market. Equally, they may be tempted to **collude**, joining together to create a monopoly (☞ unit Question 3 in unit 57 for an example).

Where there is fierce competition, short run prices can be driven below average total cost. New entrants to a local bus route or an airline route often use old and cheap vehicles or aircraft. Partly this is because it cuts down their cost of entry and reduces potential losses to a minimum if they have to exit the market. Partly it is because it enables them to undercut the prices of existing firms on the routes which are likely to be using more expensive newer equipment. Existing firms can react in a number of different ways. They could attempt to force the new entrant out of the market by **predatory pricing** - slashing their prices below that of the new entrant and hoping that it will consequently make such losses that it will exit the market (☞ unit 65). They could allow the new entrant to gain a share of the market and accept lower revenues and profits. They could attempt to move up market by providing a better service for fewer customers at a higher price. BA adopted this strategy in 1999-2000 when it announced that it would be increasing the proportion of business class passengers and reducing that of economy class passengers on some of its routes.

Expansion of port operators

There is currently a surge in port construction as world trade expands. Much of this activity is driven by a handful of new international players which are transforming a sector that has traditionally been in fragmented, public ownership. More than 100 ports have been privatised, although many of the world's largest, including Rotterdam and Long Beach California remain in public hands.

One example of private sector investment has been the opening of Aden Container Terminal in Yemen by PSA Corporation, originally the operator of the port of Singapore but now with a string of terminals around the world. Another example is a $200 million contract won by the ports division of P&O jointly with a local construction group to build and operate a container terminal at Derince in Turkey. This will replace a cramped facility in Istanbul, 50 miles away. It takes P&O's terminal portfolio to 21 in 14 countries.

There are now five main international private sector port groups including PSA and P&O. The creation of these global groups is a response to the growing power of international shipping lines - the result of mergers and alliances - which has allowed the lines to exert pressure on the fees the ports charge their customers. 'In some ports, one shipping line can be responsible for 20-30 per cent of the business, which restricts the port operator's ability to adjust his prices' according to consultant AT Kearney.

The growth of global port groups also reflects the profits that can be made in the industry since two of the seven main port groups - P&O and Maersk, the Danish group - are primarily shipping companies. The shipping lines are drawn into port ownership for strategic reasons. It gives them direct control of the terminals where their ships berth and allows them to plan their sailing schedules with greater certainty. Chronic overcapacity and tough competition in the container trade means the shipping lines are also attracted to port operations for purely financial reasons. 'Ports can be more profitable than the shipping business' says Alistair Baillie of P&O.

Port operators are now looking for a portfolio of locations to achieve economies of scale and balance the power of shipping lines. A geographical spread of ports also allows an operator to match a downturn in one region's trade with activities elsewhere. This makes it easier to finance the investment needed to keep a port competitive.

Source: adapted from the *Financial Times*, 9.11.1999.

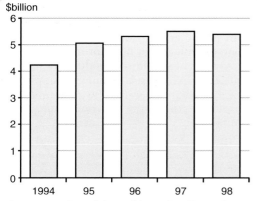

Figure 60.1 *Growth in world merchandise trade*
Source: adapted from WTO, Containerisation International.

Table 60.2 *Port traffic league*

Port traffic league

Ranking 1997 96		Port	20 feet containers (m) 1997	96	Country/ region
1	1	Hong Kong	**14.57**	13.46	**China**
2	2	Singapore	**14.14**	12.94	**Singapore**
3	3	Kaohsiung	**5.69**	5.06	**Taiwan**
4	4	Rotterdam	**5.49**	4.97	**Netherlands**
5	5	Busan	**5.23**	4.73	**South Korea**
6	6	New York/New Jersey	**4.13**	3.52	**US**
7	8	Long Beach	**3.50**	3.01	**US**
8	7	Hamburg	**3.34**	3.05	**Germany**
9	10	Antwerp	**2.97**	2.65	**Belgium**
10	9	Los Angeles	**2.96**	2.68	**US**

Source: adapted from WTO, Containerisation International.

1. Explain in the context of the worldwide port industry what is meant by (a) 'privatised' and (b) 'economies of scale'.
2. Suggest why companies like P&O invest in ports such as Derince in Turkey.
3. A port is arguably a local monopoly. (a) What pricing strategies might a port use to achieve its objectives? (b) Why can large shipping lines 'restrict the port operator's ability to adjust his prices'?
4. Discuss whether further investment in port facilities worldwide is likely to weaken the monopoly powers of ports.

Summary

1. Efficiency can be both static and dynamic. Productive efficiency and allocative efficiency are static measures of efficiency.
2. Allocative efficiency is present if the marginal cost of production equals price in all markets in an economy.
3. To judge whether there is an optimal allocation of resources in an economy, it is necessary to make value judgments about the allocation of resources.
4. In the absence of market failure, a free market will achieve an optimal allocation of resources.
5. There are many examples of market failure, including imperfect competition and monopoly, externalities and missing markets.
6. The General Theory of the Second Best shows that in an imperfect market economy, a move towards marginal cost pricing in one industry may not lead to a Pareto improvement.

Efficiency

Efficiency is concerned with how well resources are used to resolve the three fundamental questions in economics of how, what and for whom production should take place. There are two types of **static efficiency**:

● **Productive efficiency** which occurs when production takes place at least cost;
● **Allocative efficiency** which is concerned with whether resources are used to produce the goods and services that consumers wish to buy.

Static efficiency is concerned with efficiency at a point in time. **Dynamic efficiency**, in contrast, is concerned with whether resources are used efficiently over a period of time.

Allocative efficiency

Allocative or **economic** efficiency measures whether resources are allocated to those goods and services demanded by consumers. For instance, assume that consumers place equal value on the marginal consumption of shoes and jumpers. However, the last 1 million pairs of shoes produced in the economy cost 10 times as much to manufacture as an extra 1 million jumpers would have done (i.e. the economy could have produced either 1 million pairs of shoes or 10 million jumpers). It would have been more allocatively efficient if 1 million jumpers had been produced rather than the 1 million pairs of shoes because:

● consumers value the jumpers as much as the shoes;
● either an extra 9 million jumpers or 900 000 pairs of shoes or some combination of the two could have been produced **as well as** the 1 million jumpers (assuming constant costs of production).

This argument can be developed using demand and cost curves. Demand and marginal cost have a particular significance in WELFARE ECONOMICS, the study of how an economy can best allocate resources to maximise the utility or economic welfare of its citizens.

● The demand curve shows the value that consumers place on the last unit bought of a product. For instance, if a utility maximising consumer bought a pair of tights

at £2, then the pair of tights must have given at least £2 worth of value (or **satisfaction** or **utility**). If total demand for a product is 100 units at a price of £10, then the value placed by consumers on the hundredth unit must have been £10. The value placed on each of the other 99 units bought is likely to be above £10 because the demand curve slopes back upwards from that point. The marginal (or extra) value of a good to the consumer (i.e. the marginal utility) is given by the price shown on the demand curve at that level of output.

● The marginal cost curve shows the cost to firms of producing an extra unit of the good. 'Cost', we will assume here, is the cost of production to society as well as to firms. In practice the **private cost** of production of the firm may differ from the **social cost** because of **externalities**, and that this has important implications for allocative efficiency (☞ unit 19).

In Figure 61.1, two markets are shown. In the wheat market, current output is OB. The market price is £1 per unit, but farmers receive £3 per unit, for instance because the government subsidises production. In the gas market, output is OE. Price is £6 but gas suppliers receive only £4, for instance because the government

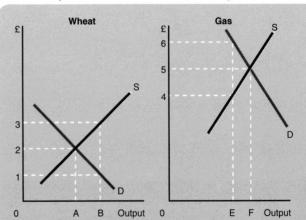

Figure 61.1 *Allocative efficiency*
Transferring resources from the wheat market where price is below marginal cost to the gas market where price is above marginal cost will lead to allocative efficiency.

imposes a £2 tax per unit.

In the wheat industry, price is below marginal cost (P < MC). This means that the value that consumers place on the product is less than the cost to society of producing the product. Consumers value the last unit produced at OB at £1 (shown on the demand curve). The cost to society of producing the last unit is £3 (shown on the marginal cost curve). Therefore consumers value the last unit of wheat purchased at £2 less than it cost to produce.

In the gas market, price is above marginal cost (P > MC). This means that the value consumers place on the last unit produced is more than the cost to society of its production. Consumers value the last unit produced at OE at £6 whilst its cost to society is only £4. Hence consumers value the last unit of gas purchased at £2 more than it cost to produce.

This suggests that scarce resources would be more efficiently allocated if less wheat and more gas were produced in the economy, but how much wheat and gas should be produced? If price is equal to marginal cost in both markets (P = MC), then consumers value the last unit

consumed of both wheat and gas as much as it costs to produce those commodities. If the price of wheat in Figure 52.1 were £2 and gas £5, then it would be impossible to reallocate resources between the two industries to the advantage of consumers.

Hence allocative efficiency will exist if price is equal to marginal cost in each industry in the economy. This is a very important conclusion but we shall see below that this conclusion needs to be very heavily qualified.

If P=MC in all industries (such as wheat and gas in the above example), it is impossible to make any one better off without making someone else worse off. The allocation of resources is then said to be PARETO EFFICIENT (after Vilfredo Pareto, an Italian economist, who first put forward this condition in 1909 in a book entitled *Manuel D'Economie Politique*). If an allocation of resources is said to be Pareto inefficient, then it must be possible to make some or all people better off without making anybody worse off.

Efficiency and the production possibility frontier

The various concepts of efficiency can be illustrated using a **production possibility frontier - PPF** (☞ unit 1). A production possibility frontier shows combinations of goods which could be produced if all resources were fully used (i.e. the economy were at full employment). If there were productive inefficiency in the economy, production would take place within the boundary, for instance at points A, B or C in Figure 61.2. With all resources fully employed, it would be possible to move, for instance, from A to D if costs were minimised.

A, B and C are also Pareto inefficient. This is because it is possible to increase output for both John and all other people without making anyone worse off by moving to a point north east of these combinations. So production at D

Question 1

Table 61.1

Millions	£ per unit			
	Goods		Services	
Quantity	Price	Marginal cost	Price	Marginal cost
1	10	2	10	4
2	8	4	9	5
3	6	6	8	6
4	4	8	7	7
5	2	10	6	8

The table shows the relationship between quantity demanded and price and between output and marginal cost for the only two commodities produced in an economy. Producing 1 million units of goods and 5 million units of services would not be allocatively efficient. This is because, at this level of output, the price of goods (£10 per unit) is above marginal cost (£2 per unit) whilst the price of services is below the marginal cost of production (£6 compared to £8). Consumers would be better off if resources were transferred from the production of services, where the marginal cost of production is greater than the marginal, value placed on them by consumers, to the production of goods where the opposite is the case.

(a) The economy produces 3 million units of goods and 4 million units of services. Why is this an allocatively efficient level of production?

(b) Explain, using a diagram, why there would be a loss of economic efficiency if the allocation of resources changed such that: (i) only 2 million units of goods were produced and the resources released were switched to the production of services;
(ii) only 2 million units of services were produced and the resources released were switched to the production of goods.

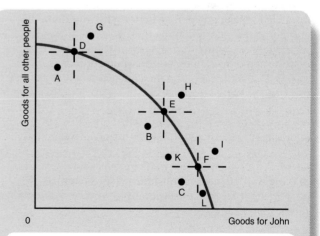

Figure 61.2 *Pareto efficient points of production*
Points on the production possibility frontier, such as D, E and F are Pareto efficient because it is not possible to produce more goods for John without reducing the production of goods for other people. Points G, H and I are unattainable whilst points A, B and C are Pareto inefficient because it is possible to increase production and produce more goods for both John and all others.

is more efficient than at A, production at E is more efficient than at B etc.

On the other hand, D, E and F are Pareto efficient. At any of these points it is not possible to produce more for John without reducing production for all other people. This is true for all points on the production possibility frontier. Hence, all points on the PPF are Pareto efficient.

All points on the PPF also satisfy the P=MC condition. So points on the frontier are both productively and allocatively efficient.

Note that it is only possible to make Pareto efficiency statements about points which are north east and south west of each other. For instance, F is Pareto efficient whilst C is not. But K cannot be compared with F because at K all other people are better off than at F but John is worse off.

Question 2

Many scientists have predicted that the destruction of the Brazilian rain forests will add to the 'greenhouse effect', in turn leading to a rise in world temperatures and a rise in sea levels. Much of the destruction is being carried out by ranchers who wish to clear land to rear cattle. They can then earn a profit by selling the beef to First World countries such as the USA and the UK.

(a) Using a production possibility frontier (putting 'beef' on one axis and 'rain forest' on the other), discuss whether a ban on the felling of trees in the Brazilian rain forests would lead to Pareto efficiency.

The optimal allocation of resources

All points on the production possibility frontier are productively and allocatively (i.e. Pareto) efficient. Therefore in one sense all points on the frontier represent an OPTIMAL ALLOCATION OF RESOURCES. It is not possible to make one person better off without making another worse off. In making this judgement, we are implicitly assuming that it is not possible to say that one distribution of resources is better than another.

This gives little help to policy makers who believe that one distribution of resources is superior to another. For instance, in Figure 61.2, points E and F are both Pareto efficient and therefore in one sense represent an optimal allocation of resources. However, the government may believe that society would be better off if there were fewer goods for John and more goods for everybody else. It is making a value judgement about what constitutes economic welfare. So the economy would be better off at E rather than F.

The market and economic efficiency

It is possible to shows that if all markets are **perfectly competitive** (☞ unit 53), resources in the economy will be efficiently allocated.

- In long run equilibrium in a perfectly competitive market, firms will produce at the bottom of their average cost curves. Therefore there will be productive efficiency.

- For there to be allocative efficiency, the cost to society of producing an extra unit of output must equal the value placed on consumption of that good by the individual (the price = marginal cost condition outlined in unit 52). In a perfectly competitive market, firms maximise profits by producing where marginal cost = marginal revenue. Marginal revenue is equal to price because the perfectly competitive firm is a price taker. Therefore marginal cost = price. On the other hand consumers maximise their utility by equating the marginal utility of each good consumed per £1 spent. Hence price is an accurate reflection of the value of the good (the marginal utility) to the individual.

It is also true that allocative efficiency in the sense of Pareto efficiency will exist in an economy where all markets are perfectly competitive. Because firms are producing at least cost, the economy must be on its production possibility frontier and therefore the allocation of resources must be Pareto efficient.

Market failure

If all markets in an economy are perfectly competitive, then two conditions must hold.

- There must be perfect competition in all goods markets. Consumers must be able to allocate their resources in a way which will maximise their utility. They must possess perfect knowledge, for instance. There must be enough consumers in any market to prevent undue

Question 3

There's not much on the menu when it comes to flying the Atlantic. On 90 per cent of the capacity between Heathrow and New York the choice is between just two British and two American airlines. Whereas travellers using other European cities, Amsterdam and Frankfurt for example, already have the distinctive alternative of Singapore Airlines. You've been promised more choice - but when will it arrive? The British Government say they want to 'see the liberalisation of transatlantic services ... on the basis of fair competition.' After negotiating patiently for 10 years we're hoping that our next meeting with the UK officials results in a happy outcome. Not more of the same but more of a difference. Particularly for discriminating passengers who have handed Singapore Airlines 11 UK awards, including two for best airline in the world, two for long haul and one for the best in-flight service, during this year alone. We already have permission from the US. Just a nod from the Government stands between you and the real choice of Singapore Airlines over the Atlantic. The minute they open the skies for us we'll be opening champagne for you.

Source: adapted from advert placed by Singapore Airlines in the *Financial Times*, 4.11.1999.

(a) Why is the British Government's refusal to allow Singapore Airlines to fly from New York to Heathrow an example of market failure?
(b) What efficiency gains might there be if permission was given?

pressure being exerted on producers to their advantage. Production too must be organised under conditions of perfect competition. Each industry must comprise a large number of small producers, all of whom are price takers. There must be freedom of entry and exit to every industry and all firms must possess perfect knowledge.

- All factor markets must be perfectly competitive. There must be perfect mobility of labour, for instance. There must be no trade unions which act as monopoly suppliers of labour. Neither must there be any

monopoly employers, such as the UK government with teachers and nurses. Capital must flow freely between industries and regions according to the levels of profit being made.

No real economy is like this. Imperfections exist in all sectors of modern industrialised economies, just as they do in developing economies, which **prevent** the efficient allocation of resources through the market mechanism. This is **market failure**. The three main types of market failure occur because of imperfect competition or monopoly (☞ unit 63), externalities (☞ units 19 and 62) and missing markets (☞ unit 20).

Efficiency vs equity

Even if a market were efficient, it would not necessarily lead to a socially desirable distribution of resources between individuals. Both efficiency and **equity** (☞ unit 68) contribute to the level of economic welfare. For instance, Pareto efficiency exists when an economy operates on its production possibility frontier. But there are an infinite number of points on the frontier. Which is the one which is most desirable? That question cannot be answered without some view about the distribution of resources within an economy. Most would agree that an economy where one person enjoyed 99 per cent of the resources whilst the other 100 million people were left with 1 per cent would be unlikely to provide a higher level of welfare than one where the distribution of resources was more equal. Most (but not all) would agree that it is unacceptable in today's Britain to allow people to die of hunger on our streets. The question of what distribution is desirable or is judged to maximise total welfare is a value judgement.

The theory of the second best

An economy will be economically efficient if all markets are perfectly competitive. Therefore it might seem like common sense to argue that economic efficiency will be increased in an economy where there are many instances of market failure if at least some markets can be made perfectly competitive and market distortions removed.

In the late 1950s, Richard Lipsey and Kelvin Lancaster (1956-7) published an article entitled 'On the General Theory of the Second Best'. They assumed an economy where some firms were not pricing at marginal cost. They then showed that a move towards marginal cost pricing by one firm might lead to an an increase in efficiency, but equally it could lead to a decrease in efficiency. The radical conclusion was that introducing marginal cost pricing could lead to efficiency losses rather than efficiency gains.

For instance, consider Figure 61.3. It shows two industries. The food industry is assumed to be monopolistic. Output is set at OA where MC = MR (the profit maximising condition) and price is then set at OP on the average revenue or demand curve. The entertainment industry is perfectly competitive. Output is at OF where marginal cost equals price. Assume that resources were transferred from the entertainment industry to the food industry such that output in the food industry rose to OB whilst output in the entertainment industry fell to OE. The

Question 4

It is difficult to imagine that many East Germans have a yearning to go back to the old days of the Communist regime before 1990. They lived in a police state where the economy was in a terrible shape. Shortages were chronic and goods sold were shoddy. The noisy and uncomfortable Trabant car was a fitting symbol of the system. Yet today, East Germans are voting in increasing numbers for the PDS, the reformed Communist party. These voters, according to opinion polls, believe that the Communist regime was better at providing healthcare, education, industrial training, law and order, gender equality, social security and housing. These are precisely the goods which tend not to be provided by the market mechanism on which Western economies are based. As for those goods which are provided by markets, like cars or foreign holidays, these are only available to those with high enough incomes. East Germany has gone from having no unemployment under the Communist regime to an official 20 per cent today. So large sections of the East German population can't afford the goods which more efficient markets provide.

Source: adapted from the *Financial Times*, 4.11.1999.

(a) Explain why an efficient market system which provides a high average income might lead to some consumers being worse off than if they lived in an inefficient state planned economy where average incomes were much lower. Illustrate your answer with examples from the data.

welfare gain in the food industry, shown by the difference between demand and marginal cost, is the shaded area on the graph. This is larger than the welfare loss in the entertainment industry, shown by the shaded triangle. Hence in this case there is a net welfare gain if there is a move away from perfect competition in the entertainment industry.

It can be shown that, in general, efficiency can be increased by transferring resources to industries where price is far in excess of marginal cost from industries where it is less so or where demand is less than marginal cost. Efficiency is likely to be achieved where the difference between price and marginal cost is the same throughout an economy.

This is a very important conclusion. Every economy suffers from market failure. It will never be the case that marginal cost can equal price across all sectors of the economy. Therefore simple rules or slogans such as 'competition good, monopoly bad' are unlikely to lead to good economic policy making. What the theory of the second best suggests is that distortions within an economy need to be evened out as far as possible. Eliminating them in some markets but allowing them to remain high in others could well lead to less efficiency overall than decreasing them in markets where they are high but actually increasing them in markets where distortions are low.

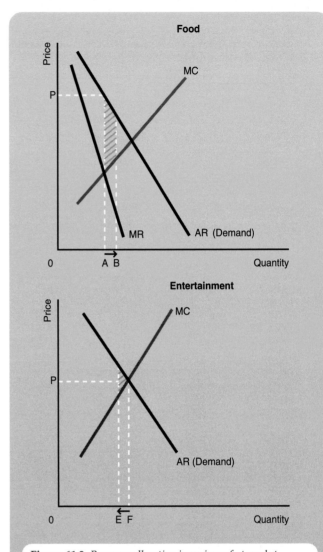

Figure 61.3 *Resource allocation in an imperfect market*
If some markets are imperfectly competitive or a monopoly, there could be efficiency gains if resources are transferred from a perfectly competitive market to the imperfectly competitive market or the monopoly. The loss of efficiency in the entertainment market, shown by the shaded area, is less than the gain in welfare in the food market in this example.

key terms

Optimal allocation of resources - occurs when resources are efficiently used in such a way as to maximise the welfare or utility of consumers.

Pareto efficiency - occurs when no one can be made better off by transferring resources from one industry to another without making someone else worse off. Pareto efficiency is also called allocative efficiency. It exists in an economy if price = marginal cost in all industries.

Welfare economics - the study of how an economy can best allocate resources to maximise the utility or economic welfare of its citizens.

Applied economics

The misallocation of resources in transport

It is widely argued that public transport is underutilised, whilst private modes of transport, mainly the car, are overused. Partly, this view is held because cars create externalities (☞ unit 62). However, it is also true that the pricing structure of private and public transport leads directly to a misallocation of resources.

When travellers consider what mode of transport to use, they will look at a number of factors.

● Feasibility. Many journeys are impossible to make using certain modes of transport. For instance, most people find it impossible to use the train to go from door to door on a journey. If they do use the train, they often have to use another mode of transport at either end of the journey. Public transport is often not available at night.

● Time. The length of the journey is important. Travellers from London to New York almost invariably today take the plane rather than the boat because of this factor. Eurostar has competed successfully with airlines on the London to Paris route because journey times door to door are often comparable.

● Comfort. Travellers often prefer cars because it is a very comfortable mode of transport. Car drivers can create their own environment within the car. Train and bus commuters, on the other hand, often dislike the journeys they make because of overcrowding and poor facilities.

Another important factor, though, is cost. Decisions are made at the margin. How much will it cost to undertake this extra journey? For the motorist, the marginal cost is the variable cost of motoring. This is petrol plus any car parking fees. The fixed costs of motoring, which include purchase, insurance and road tax, do not enter into the decision making process for a single journey. These costs have already been paid and do not change if an extra journey is made.

In contrast, the price of public transport includes both fixed and variable cost. For instance, when the train passenger buys a ticket, it includes the fixed cost of the payment to Railtrack for the use of the infrastructure and the cost of the train. On top of that is the variable cost of the train driver and the fuel. How much of the fixed cost the passenger pays depends on the pricing policy of the rail company. The tendency is for the train companies to load most of the fixed cost onto passengers travelling at peak times.

So the price that travellers pay excludes fixed costs in private motoring but, particularly for peak time travellers, includes it on public transport. Not surprisingly, this tends to make private motoring seem cheap for any single journey compared to public transport. This is particularly true if there is more than one passenger travelling in the car because the marginal cost of carrying an extra passenger is zero.

The result is that there is a misallocation of resources. In public transport, price tends to be set above the marginal cost of a single journey, whereas in private motoring, it is equal to marginal cost. The result is that too many car journeys are made and too little use is made of public transport.

It could be argued that taxes and subsidies go some way towards reducing this misallocation. Nearly all the cost of petrol today is tax, whilst public transport is not subject to VAT. Equally, many public transport services are subsidised. Even so, taxes on petrol and subsidies on public transport are probably not high enough to eliminate this misallocation. A solution might be to introduce road pricing, where motorists are charged for use of a particular road at a certain time of day and use the proceeds to subsidise public transport on the same route.

To what extent is there a misallocation of resources in transport?

Grey goods

The market in grey goods had been expanding rapidly in the UK in the 1990s. Grey goods, or parallel import goods, are branded products bought outside of normal distribution channels. The market came to a halt in 1998, however, following a judgment of the European Court. Silhouette, an upmarket Austrian sunglasses manufacturer, had sold 21 000 pairs of out of date stock to a Bulgarian company at a knock down price in 1995. The contract stipulated that they would be sold either in Bulgaria or the Soviet Union. Within months, however, they were back in Austria, being sold by the discount chain Hartlauer at cut prices. Silhouette took Hartlauer to court and eventually the European Court of Justice ruled in Silhouette's favour.

The judgment had far reaching consequences. It was standard practice for many manufacturers of branded goods to charge different prices in different markets. For instance, manufacturers' prices to US customers were on average 12 per cent lower than those for UK customers. Prices to Middle East customers, or to Eastern Europe were often much lower than European prices.

Manufacturers were, in economic terms, segmenting their market and selling at the highest price possible into each market. The growth of grey imports threatened completely to disrupt this trading pattern. Retailers, like Asda and Tesco, were increasingly able to bypass the manufacturer's official distribution channels and buy at knock down prices from merchants abroad. The judgment killed this trade at a stroke.

Brand owners argue that they have a right to choose their distributors. Adidas, for instance, stated that restricting the distribution network was an advantage to customers. 'We make an important commitment to our customers that our products will be consistently of high quality' it said. Many brand owners have been dismayed to find their products being sold cheaply in supermarkets. It devalues the exclusiveness of the brand and negates the image they have tried to build up through advertising and other promotion of a high class product.

Source: adapted from the *Financial Times*, 17.7.1998.

Prices of branded products are often lower in Eastern Europe than in the West.

1. Explain how, before 1998, a supermarket like Tesco could sell designer label products at a very large discount to the official manufacturer's price.
2. Analyse whether the Silhouette judgment will lead to allocative inefficiency in markets.
3. Brand owners, like Adidas, Honda or Givenchy, would argue that grey imports threaten dynamic efficiency in the EU. To what extent do you think this is likely to be the case?

Summary

1. Externalities can lead to economic inefficiency if the marginal social cost of production is not equal to price.
2. Externalities can also redistribute real income within the economy.
3. One method for the government to control externalities is to impose regulations.
4. Another method is to internalise the externality by extending property rights.
5. A third method is to impose taxes on externalities.
6. Tradable permits are another solution to limiting the impact of externalities.

Externalities

Externalities (☞ unit 19) exist when there is a difference between private costs and benefits and social costs and benefits. For instance, a factory may run at a private profit because its revenues exceed its private costs. However, it may be polluting the atmosphere as a result of its production at no private cost to itself. It would then create an externality. If this were large enough, the social profit would be negative because social costs (private costs plus the externality) would exceed social benefits (in this case just the private benefits or revenues).

The efficient allocation of resources

Externalities imply that there is an inefficient or sub-optimal allocation of resources. Consider Figure 62.1. Assume that all other markets in the economy are producing at a point where marginal social cost equals marginal social benefit. Marginal cost and benefit curves are drawn on the diagram.

● Marginal cost curves are U-shaped (☞ units 48 and 49). The cost of producing an extra unit of output is assumed to fall at first, and then to rise. This is because of diminishing marginal returns in the short run or economies and diseconomies of scale in the long run.
● Marginal benefit curves are downward sloping. This is because the benefit from consuming an extra unit of output is assumed to decline the more is consumed. The marginal benefit curve is also the demand curve for the product since the demand curve shows the value that consumers place on consuming an extra unit of the good.

Figure 62.1 shows that the marginal social cost of production is above the marginal private cost. Therefore, there are external costs of production in this market. The vertical distance between the two lines shows the external cost at any given level of output. The equilibrium quantity demanded and supplied in a free market would be where

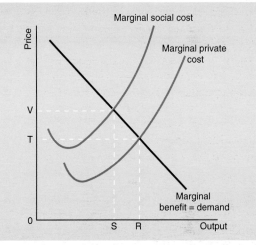

Figure 62.1 *Allocation of resources with external costs*
If marginal private cost is below marginal social cost, then the free market equilibrium production level of OR will be above the socially optimal level of output of OS, assuming all other markets in the economy produce where price equals marginal social cost.

marginal private cost equalled marginal benefit. Market signals are such that OR will be produced and sold at a price of OT. However, resources could be allocated more efficiently if marginal benefit were equated with the full cost of production shown by the marginal social cost line. If all costs were taken into consideration, equilibrium quantity produced and consumed would fall to OS whilst price would have to rise to OV. This is what one would expect. Society needs, for instance, to consume less chemicals and pay a higher price for them if their production leads to pollution of the environment.

The same analysis can be applied to external benefits. Figure 62.2 shows a situation where marginal private benefits are lower than marginal social benefits. The free market would lead to an underconsumption of the

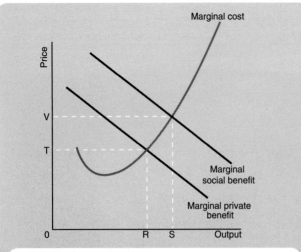

Figure 62.2 *Allocation of resources with external benefits*
If marginal private benefit is below marginal social benefit, then the free market equilibrium production level of OR will be below the socially optimal level of output of OS, assuming all other markets in the economy produce where price equals marginal social cost.

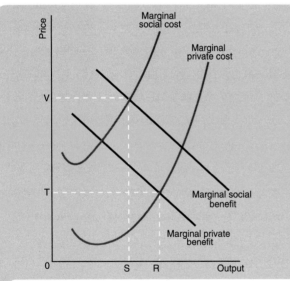

Figure 62.3 *Allocation of resources with both external costs and benefits*
If marginal private costs and benefits are below marginal social costs and benefits, then the free market equilibrium production level of OR will be above the socially optimal level of output of OS, assuming all other markets in the economy produce where price equals marginal social cost.

product. Production and consumption of OS should lead to a more efficient allocation of resources than the free market equilibrium point of OR.

Combining these two, Figure 62.3 shows a market where there are both external costs and external benefits. The free market equilibrium output point is OR. The socially optimal point is OS.

Welfare losses

If it is assumed that all other markets are producing where price = marginal cost (the demand or marginal benefit equalling marginal cost condition just discussed), then **allocative efficiency** (☞ unit 61) will exist in a market if it too produces where price = marginal cost. On the other hand, there will be allocative inefficiency if private cost or benefit differs from social cost or benefit and markets are free. The size of this allocative inefficiency can be seen in Figure 62.4. Production should only be at OA if price is set equal to marginal social costs. Overproduction of AB leads to allocative inefficiency. The efficiency loss to society is given by the difference between the cost to society of production of AB (shown by the marginal social cost curve) and the value placed by society on consumption of AB (shown by the demand curve). The difference is the shaded triangle HJK. The greater the difference between marginal social cost and marginal private cost, the greater will be the net social cost shown by the area of the triangle.

It is interesting to note that the welfare loss arising from an external cost is likely to be less under conditions of imperfect competition than under perfect competition. If the market shown in Figure 62.4 were perfectly competitive, then the supply curve of the industry would be the marginal private cost curve and production would take place where demand equalled supply, at the point K as has already been argued above. There would be a net welfare loss of HJK.

If, on the other hand, the market were supplied by a monopolist, then production would be lower than under perfect competition (☞ unit 63). Monopolists charge a higher price than an industry with competition. Therefore, in Figure 62.4, the free market price under a monopolist would be higher than OE and production would have to

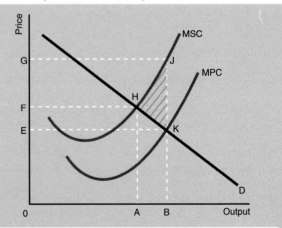

Figure 62.4 *Social cost arising from an externality*
If an industry is perfectly competitive, long run production will take place where price = marginal private cost (MPC) at output OB. This, assuming that all other markets produce where P=MC and that private and social costs and benefits are the same, is also the allocatively efficient level of production. But if there is a negative externality leading to marginal social cost being higher than MPC in this one market, then output should be lower to maximise efficiency. The externality causes overproduction of AB.

be lower than OB. Hence, the welfare loss will be less than HJK. It could be the case that the monopolist will so reduce output that production is to the left of OA. Then, there will be a welfare loss not due to overproduction but to underproduction by the monopolist. Given that there is no supply curve under monopoly (☞ unit 54), it is impossible to say whether the free market equilibrium point will result in overproduction or underproduction.

Question 1

According to Professor James Cooper, director of the Cranfield Centre for Logistics and Transportation, manufacturers in Europe are now transporting goods twice as far as they did 30 years ago. Partly this is because of changes in production techniques. Factories and companies have become increasingly specialised. Moreover, the development of just-in-time production techniques leads to more frequent deliveries of smaller consignments, keeping stock levels to a minimum but leading to more journeys.

Greater distances have also come about because of a demand for greater variety of goods by customers. British consumers are no longer satisfied with just being able to buy UK made goods. They want to be able to choose from European, American or Asian products as well. This growth in transport has led to a large increase in environmental pollution.

(a) Using a demand curve diagram, explain why there has been a growth in transport in recent years.
(b) Using the same diagram, but now including marginal private and social cost curves, analyse why this growth has probably led to an increase in allocative inefficiency in the economy.

Distributional effects

Externalities don't just create potential inefficiencies. There are also distributional implications. For instance, in the example under Market Failure above, there is a redistribution of income from consumers of water, who pay too high a price for water, to consumers of chemicals who pay less than the social cost of production.

Assume that the price of chemicals is raised by a tax on output to reflect the marginal social cost of production. This should correct the market failure present in the market for chemicals. However, the water company downstream is still having to pay to clean up the pollution created by the chemical company. Only if the chemical company pays the water company will there also be efficiency in the market for water. In this case it would seem to be relatively simple for an arrangement to be made for the water company to charge the chemical company for the latter's dumping of chemical waste in the river.

But there is likely to be no such simple remedy for local residents and local anglers. Their welfare may be diminished by the polluted river. How do you decide who to compensate in the local community and how much compensation should you give? One answer which

economists have suggested involves local residents and local anglers and the chemical company paying the other party an amount which is equal to the welfare loss. If citizen A is willing to pay £5 a year, and citizen B £10 a year and all other citizens £9 985, then the value of a clean river to the local community is £10 000. That is how much:
● either the chemical company should give in compensation to the local community;
● or the local community should pay to the chemical company to stop them polluting the river.

In this example, it might **seem** clear that the chemical company should pay the local community. However, to show that it is not quite as obvious as it first seems, take another example. Assume that the chemical company is making an anti-malaria drug for use in Third World countries. These drugs are cheap to produce and are widely used. If the chemical company compensates local residents for polluting the river, its costs will double and so too will the price of the drug. This will make the drug too expensive for many in the Third World and an extra 50 000 people a year will die. In this case, if might **seem** clear that local residents should pay the chemical company to reduce its pollution.

This shows that there is no simple answer to the question of 'who should compensate whom'. Should it be the customer of the polluting company paying through higher prices for its product, or should it be the individual, group or firm which bribes the company to stop polluting? What is more, it is often impossible to find out who exactly loses how much as a result of an externality. Therefore, taxes or other methods of reducing externalities may lead to over-compensation or under-compensation. These are issues about the distribution of income and resources more than the efficient allocation of resources.

Question 2

In 1994, 30 000 households in the Worcester area were affected by a pollution alert. People complained that their tap water smelled and tasted of paraffin. Severn Trent, the local water company, immediately advised the 100 000 people in the area to stop drinking the water. As it turned out, there was no serious risk from the organic industrial solvent that contaminated the water. However, the alert, during which households were advised not to drink the water, lasted several days. Severn Trent paid compensation of £10 a day to each household for the period of the alert. The final cost would be over £1m. The source of the pollution was traced to a firm on an industrial estate in Wem in Shropshire.

(a) How did the Shropshire firm create a negative externality?
(b) What distributional impact did the spillage have?

Regulation

Regulation is a method which is widely used in the UK and throughout the world to control externalities. The government could lay down maximum pollution levels or might even ban the pollution-creating activities altogether.

For instance, in the UK, the Environmental Protection Act 1989 laid down minimum environmental standards for emissions from over 3 500 factories involved in chemical processes, waste incineration and oil refining. The system is policed by HM Inspectorate of Pollution. There are limits on harmful emissions from car exhausts. Cars can be failed on their MOT if exhausts do not meet the standard. 40 years before the MOT regulations came into force, the government banned the burning of ordinary coal in urban areas.

Regulation will only result in an efficient allocation of resources in the economy if the government equates the pollution cost to society of producing an extra unit with the benefit to society of consuming that good after all non-pollution costs have been taken into account. This can be expressed using a diagram, as in Figure 62.5.

- The marginal pollution cost (MPC) line shows the damage done to the environment when output is increased by an extra unit. Cost here is defined as external cost. It is the cost which producers don't pay in the production process but impose on society. The MPC line is drawn upward sloping on the assumption that the extra damage to the environment caused by the activity increases the more is produced. For instance, at output level OA, there is production but pollution levels are so low that an extra unit can be produced at no pollution cost. At output OB, on the other hand, the pollution cost of the last unit produced is OD. It could be that marginal pollution costs are constant. For instance, if the pollution cost of producing an extra barrel of oil from the North Sea were exactly the same whether 1 billion were being produced per year or 100bn barrels of oil were being produced per year, then the MPC line would be horizontal.
- The marginal net private benefit line (MNPB) shows the value to society of producing an extra unit of output. It is defined as the difference between the marginal revenue of a firm and its marginal private

cost of production (i.e. the profit it makes on the last unit). The firm will want to produce at OC because at this point its profit is maximised. If it produces less than OC, it could expand output and gain extra profit. If it produced more than OC, it would make a loss on its last unit of output.

For society, the optimal level of output and pollution is OB. The government should then set limits of OB on the amount of pollution that a firm can create. A ban on pollution would only be economically justifiable if the marginal pollution cost were greater than marginal net private benefit at all levels of output. This situation is

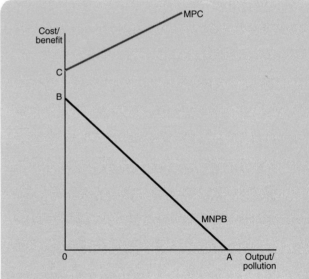

Figure 62.6 *Production bans*
If the marginal pollution cost MPC is higher at all levels of output than any benefit to be gained from production, shown by MNPB, then the government should impose a ban on the pollutant.

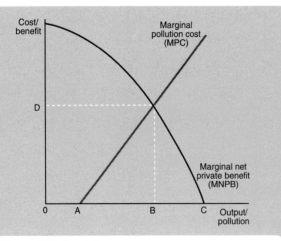

Figure 62.5 *Regulation*
Governments should impose regulations to reduce pollution to OB because this is where the marginal pollution cost (MPC) is equal to the marginal net private benefit (MNPB) for the firm and therefore society.

Question 3

In 1993, checks on carbon monoxide and other emissions became a compulsory part of the MOT test. Cars failing to meet the standard would fail their MOT. It also became illegal to drive cars exceeding the emission limit. In February 1995, the Minister for Transport, Mr Brian Mawhinney, announced that there would now be regular curbside checks on cars and lorries which were suspected of grossly polluting the environment, particularly in city centres. The checks would be nationwide and would include fines for drivers. Vehicle inspectors would be able to issue a prohibition notice requiring drivers to take their vehicles off the road, or give drivers a specified time to repair the vehicle.

(a) How, according to the article, is the government intending to tighten up on fuel emissions?
(b) With the help of a diagram, discuss how you might decide whether or not the emission levels for motor vehicles set by the Department of Transport are too lax or too tight.

shown in Figure 62.6. The marginal pollution cost of producing even one unit of output is OC whereas the benefit to the firm of production is lower at OB. There is no level of output where the MNPB is greater than the MPC.

If physical regulations are to be used to achieve an optimal allocation of resources, the government must be able to assess accurately costs and benefits and act accordingly. If pollution controls are too lax, permitting production above OB in Figure 62.5, then there will be a misallocation of resources. Firms will produce above OB and will have no incentive to reduce pollution levels below the minimum legal requirement. On the other hand, pollution controls might be too strict. If pollution levels were fixed below OB in Figure 62.5, society would make a net gain by an increase in output and the associated increase in pollution.

Extending property rights

If a chemical company lorry destroyed your home, you would expect the chemical company to pay compensation. If the chemical company polluted the atmosphere so that the trees in your garden died, it would be unlikely that you would gain compensation, particularly if the chemical plant were in the UK and the dead trees were in Germany.

Externalities often arise because property rights are not fully allocated. Nobody owns the atmosphere or the oceans, for instance. An alternative to regulation is for government to extend property rights. They can give water companies the right to charge companies which dump waste into rivers or the sea. They can give workers the right to sue for compensation if they have suffered injury or death as a result of working for a company. They can give local residents the right to claim compensation if pollution levels are more than a certain level.

Extending property rights is a way of **internalising the externality** - eliminating the externality by bringing it back into the framework of the market mechanism. Fifty years ago, asbestos was not seen as a dangerous material. Today, asbestos companies around the world are having to pay compensation to workers suffering from asbestosis. They have also had to tighten up considerably on safety in the workplace where asbestos is used. Workers have been given property rights, which enable them to sue asbestos companies for compensation. This has resulted in a fall in the production of asbestos. The marginal net private benefit to the firm of producing asbestos has fallen from $MNPB_1$ to $MNPB_2$ in Figure 62.7 because it has had to pay compensation to victims. The new marginal pollution cost line MPC_2 is horizontal, running along the horizontal axis. This shows that the industry is no longer imposing any external costs on society. The result is that the industry reduces its free market production from OA to OB. An optimal allocation of resources has been achieved.

In some cases, the owner of property rights may have no other option than to pay a polluter to stop polluting rather than the other way round. As explained in unit 19, it would be rational for property owners in a local community to offer to pay a chemical company to stop polluting the local environment if the government was failing to do anything about it. There have been

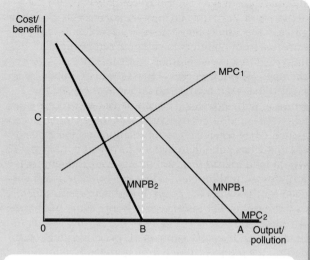

Figure 62.7 *Extending property rights*
If property rights are fully extended, the polluter will have to pay what was before an external cost. The new external cost is therefore zero at all levels of output, shown by the horizontal MPC_2 line running along the bottom axis.

suggestions, for instance, that First World countries should pay Third World countries to stop chopping down tropical rainforests, or to reduce emissions of greenhouse gases.

One advantage of extending property rights is that the government does not have to assess the cost of pollution. It is generally assumed that property owners will have a far better knowledge of the value of property than the government. There should also be a direct transfer of resources from those who create pollution to those who suffer. With regulation, on the other hand, the losers are not compensated whilst polluters are free to pollute up to the limit despite the fact that the pollution is imposing costs on society. One problem is that it is very difficult to extend property rights in many cases. Who, for instance,

Question 4

Texaco, the oil company, was being sued over damages caused in Ecuador. The plaintiffs charged that Texaco deliberately dumped oil and toxic waste water into the Amazonian rain forest, resulting in the destruction of food and water supplies. Texaco operated in Ecuador as a minority partner with the state oil company between 1964 and 1990. Texaco said the allegations were baseless and that it used standard industry practices to dispose of waste. The case became high profile because the Ecuadorean environmental group suing Texaco took out adverts in the USA showing a Texaco fuel truck pulling up to a leafy, white suburban neighbourhood and spraying a family with black oil.

Source: adapted from the *Financial Times*, 25.9.1999.

(a) With the help of a diagram, explain how the legal system is being used in this story to internalise an externality.

should pay and who should be compensated for the depletion of the ozone layer or the increase in greenhouse gases in the atmosphere? A second problem is that transfers from polluters to sufferers can be highly imperfect. Asbestos companies, for instance, will not pay claims to asbestos workers unless it can definitely be proved that their medical condition was caused by working with asbestos. The compensation process can take years, and many ex-workers die before their cases are settled. They receive no compensation and the asbestos company has not had to include payment in its costs. This would tend to lead to a continuing overproduction of asbestos. A final problem is that it is often very difficult even for the owners of property rights to assess the value of those rights. For instance, one homeowner might put a far higher value on trees in his or her garden than another homeowner. If a cable company lays cable in the road, cutting the roots of trees in front gardens, should the homeowner who places a high value on trees be compensated more than the homeowner who is fairly indifferent when trees die?

Environmental taxes

Another solution, much favoured by economists, is the use of environmental taxes. Government needs to assess the cost to society of pollution. It then sets tax rates on polluters so that the tax is equal to the value of the externality. Because costs of production then increase, firms reduce their output and thus reduce their pollution emissions.

In Figure 62.7, the marginal tax rate would be set equal to the marginal pollution cost, MPC_1. The optimal point of production for the firm would be OB. At OB, the firm would have to pay a marginal tax of OC. This would mean

that all of the profit from the last unit produced would be paid in pollution tax. The firm would have no incentive to produce a higher output because the extra pollution tax would then outweigh any extra profit made. Firms which were polluting above OB before the imposition of a pollution tax would now have an economic incentive to reduce their pollution levels.

Environmental taxes, like extending property rights, have the advantage that they allow the market mechanism to decide how resources should best be allocated given that pollution is included as a cost of production. Heavy polluters have an incentive to reduce pollution emissions, whilst light polluters, who might have had to cut production under a system of government pollution regulations, can now expand production and pollution but to the benefit of society as a whole.

However, it is difficult for government to place a monetary value on pollution and therefore decide what should be the optimal tax rate. Production of some goods might still have to be banned because their environmental costs were so high that no level of taxes could adequately compensate society for their production.

Pollution permits

A variation on regulating pollution through direct controls is the idea of pollution permits. Here, the government sets a limit on the amount of pollution permitted. In Figure 62.7, this would be at OB. The government then allocates permits to individual firms or other polluters. These permits can then be traded for money between polluters. For instance, one electricity generating company might have relatively modern power plants which in total let out fewer emissions than its permits allows. It could then sell surplus permits to another electricity company which had older plants which, if allowed to run, would exceed its permits given by the government.

The main advantage of permits over simple regulation is that costs in the industry and therefore to society should be lower than with regulation. Each firm in the industry will consider whether it is possible to reduce emissions and at what cost. Assume that Firm A, with just enough permits to meet its emissions, can reduce emissions by 500 tonnes at a cost of £10m. Firm B is a high polluter and needs 500 tonnes worth of permits to meet regulations. It calculates that it would need to spend £25m to cut emissions by this amount.

- If there was simple regulation, the anti-pollution costs to the industry, and therefore to society, would be £25m. Firm B would have to conform to its pollution limit whilst there would be no incentive for Firm A to cut pollution.
- With permits, Firm A could sell 500 tonnes of permits to Firm B. The cost to society of then reducing pollution would only be £10m, the cost that Firm A would incur. It might cost Firm B more than £10m to buy the permits. It would be prepared to spend anything up to £25m to acquire them. Say Firm A drove a hard bargain and sold the permits to Firm B for £22m. Society would save £15m, distributed between a paper profit of £12m for Firm A and a fall in costs from what otherwise would have been the case for Firm B of £3m.

Question 5

The government published a Transport White Paper in 1998 in which it outlined a series of proposals to help solve the growing problem of road congestion and transport pollution. One proposal was the taxing of car parking spaces in city centres. In 1999, local councils in the West Midlands were reported to be considering imposing levies of £250 a year per parking space maintained by businesses excluding supermarkets. The monies raised would be used to improve public transport in the area.

Source: adapted from the *Financial Times*, 21.7.1998 and 20.5.1999.

(a) Explain, using a diagram, why a car parking tax might lead to greater efficiency.
(b) Businesses in the West Midlands are strongly opposed to the car parking tax. What arguments might they put forward against it?
(c) Discuss whether the money raised from a car parking tax might be better spent on building new roads rather than improving public transport.

Question 6

The United Nations Conference on Trade and Development (UNCTAD) has backed the idea of a worldwide market in carbon dioxide emission permits as the most cost-effective way of tackling global warming and transferring resources to poorer nations. UNCTAD has called for a start to be made by the USA, Japan and the EU, the three largest world emitters of greenhouse gases. Between them, they account for almost 40 per cent of global carbon dioxide emissions. Under the proposal, an overall emissions target would be set. Tradeable carbon dioxide permits would then be issued to these three countries and to developing countries. The three industrialised countries would be issued with fewer permits than they would be expected to hold whilst developing countries would be issued with a surplus of permits. Heavy polluters in the rich countries would then have to buy permits in the open market, expected to be worth more than $8bn per year.

Because of the initial issue of permits, some of those permits would have to bought from developing countries holding a surplus of permits. Thus, in addition to an efficient fall in emissions, there would also be a net transfer of resources from the rich to the poor countries of the world. US experience of sulphur dioxide emission permits, traded since 1992 shows that the system would let global warming targets be reached more cheaply than through legal regulation or emission charges such as carbon taxes, UNCTAD argues.

(a) What is a 'pollution permit'?
(b) Using a diagram, explain why pollution permits might 'let global warming targets be reached more cheaply than through legal regulation or emission charges'.
(c) What distributional effects would the UNCTAD proposal have?

Applied economics

Road transport

Britain's roads are becoming increasingly congested. Figure 62.8 shows the explosion of car ownership in the UK since 1951. The motor car has revolutionised the way we live. It has brought immense benefits. At the same time, there have been significant costs.

The private benefits have been so significant that households have been prepared to spend an increasing proportion of household income on motoring (☞ unit 6). Cars are used for work. Some mileage is accounted for by people who use the car as a work tool, such as electricians or sales representatives. Others use it as a quick, convenient and relatively comfortable way to travel to and from work. Public transport is a second best solution for most, involving longer journey times and uncomfortable walks to and waits at bus stops or train stations, followed by a journey on a crowded bus or train. Cars are also in derived demand from other expenditures of the household. The car is used to get the weekly shopping, get the family to a leisure centre or take a relative to catch a train. The car's advantages over public transport include door to door travel, privacy during a journey and, on most journeys made, faster journey times.

The private costs of a motor car differ significantly from those of public transport for the user. As Table 62.1 shows, the single largest cost for most motorists is the purchase of the car, a fixed cost. Road tax, insurance and maintenance, fixed or semi-variable costs, are large too. Petrol, a variable cost, accounts for only approximately one-quarter of the total cost of running a car. When considering whether to make an individual journey, a motorist only considers his or her marginal cost, the cost of the petrol. On public transport, however, the user will almost certainly have to pay part

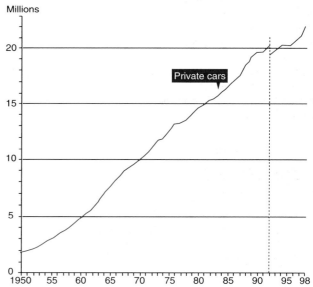

* Discontinuity at 1992 due to the way in which statistics were calculated.

Figure 62.8 *Number of private cars licenced: 1950-98*
Source: adapted from *Transport Statistics*, Office for National Statistics.

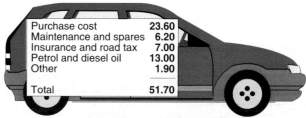

Purchase cost	23.60
Maintenance and spares	6.20
Insurance and road tax	7.00
Petrol and diesel oil	13.00
Other	1.90
Total	51.70

Table 62.1 *Average household weekly expenditure on motoring (£), 1998-99*
Source: adapted from *Family Expenditure Survey*, Office for National Statistics.

or all of the average fixed cost of the journey. Hence, a single journey by public transport is usually more expensive than a single journey by car.

Cars give rise to significant externalities. First, they cause noise pollution. When new roads are built, such as motorways, houses near the new road are sometimes offered double glazing to cut down the noise pollution they now have to suffer. Second, cars emit harmful gases and particles. Carbon monoxide, for instance, is a greenhouse gas. Lead in leaded petrol can damage the brain, particularly in children. Petrol fumes are blamed by many doctors for a significant rise in asthma in recent years in the UK. Third, cars kill and injure people. It could be argued that this cost is accounted for in the cost of compulsory insurance. However, insurance companies have an incentive to undercompensate victims of road accidents. Lastly, one car can lead to longer journey times for other cars. On a congested road, the marginal car slows down the speed of other cars. At its most extreme, you get 'gridlock' - a situation where there are so many cars on the road that nothing moves. On an uncongested road, one extra car will not give rise to lower speeds for other cars and there is no externality.

It could be argued that motorists already pay others for the externalities they create. Motoring is heavily taxed. Nearly one-third of the annual cost of running a car to the motorist is accounted for by tax, including the tax on petrol. These tax revenues, however, are not used to compensate systematically those who lose out from the negative externalities caused by the motor car. For instance, those who suffer from noise pollution are not

compensated by regular payments. No compensation is given to asthma sufferers who might suffer as a result of car fumes. Some individuals are therefore major losers.

It could also be argued that, whilst motorists pay taxes, these payments are only a fraction of the external costs which arise from car use. On this argument, motorists would have to be far more heavily taxed if their contribution to, say, global warming were to be quantified in money terms. Organisations like Friends of the Earth would say that the private motor car is a luxury which society cannot afford. Only public transport can allow travellers to travel at a cost which includes both private and external costs.

The problem of the motor car

Road pricing

The introduction of road pricing has been part of government policy since 1994. However, to date, there have only been small scale trials. The technology varies from the simple to the complex. At its simplest, motorists could be asked to purchase a licence to enter a zone at certain times. The licence, like a car parking ticket, would be prominently displayed and traffic wardens would police the system. At its most complex, all cars would be fitted with electronic devices which would be activated by beacons. Tolls would vary depending upon levels of congestion, time of day or day of the year. Meters could be read electronically by devices in the beacons and bills sent monthly. Or they could be read manually at the time of the MOT test. Or

drivers could have to buy cards to put into their meters, rather like telephone cards.

Many are worried that the technology will not work and that it will be costly to install and run. On a more fundamental level, there is considerable resistance to tolls amongst motorists. They overwhelmingly believe that roads should be free at the point of use. To relieve severe congestion, many motorists would have to be priced off roads. Achieving this would require very high tolls given the price inelasticity of car journeys. Both those who are priced off the roads and who would have to find alternative ways of travelling, and those who were forced to pay the high tolls would suffer.

Toll motorways

In countries such as France and Italy, toll motorways are part of the overall transport network. Tolls help to finance the building and maintenance of the motorway system. They can also be used to relieve congestion. For instance, tolls into Paris on some motorways are higher at peak times than others.

Critics argue that the motorway tolls discourage people from using the motorways and encourage them to continue using the existing untolled road network. New roads also create extra traffic across the whole of the road network. So non-motorway roads in areas surrounding a motorway become more congested.

Building new roads

The UK government has had a long term programme of improving existing roads and building new roads. Up to the 1990s, policy was based on the principle of 'predict and build'. Estimates were made of future use and roads were built to accommodate this. In 1989, the government, for instance, launched a £23 billion 'Roads for Prosperity' programme with 500 road schemes planned. The 1990s, saw a reversal of this policy after strong lobbying from environmental groups. In successive reviews, most of the 500 road schemes were axed. By 2000, very few new road schemes were left on the planners' books.

The transport lobby in the UK, including motoring organisations such as the AA and the RAC, as well as commercial organisations like the British Road Federation, believe this policy is a disaster. They wish to see a return to new road building. Bypass schemes and motorways take traffic away from urban areas, reducing pollution. Better roads also lead to shorter journey times, resulting in a massive saving for the economy as transport costs fall.

The environmental lobby, such as Transport 2000, argues that building new roads simply helps to create problems. It argues that shorter journey times encourage businesses and people to make more journeys. Some switch from other forms of transport, such as from rail to car. Others increase the number or length of journeys made. For instance, workers have tended to move away from their place of work over the past 40 years. A 1994 report, *Trunk Roads and the Generation of Traffic*, by the Standing Advisory Committee on Trunk Road Assessment, a government committee made up of independent transport experts, concluded that additional or 'induced traffic can and does occur, probably quite extensively, though its size and significance is likely to vary widely in different circumstances' when new roads were built.

Increasing fuel duties

In 1993, the government announced that it would increase duties on petrol and other fuels by 3 per cent per year in real terms for the foreseeable future. This was later raised to 5 per cent and then 6 per cent in 1998.

One advantage of increasing duties is that there would be no extra cost of collecting the taxes since duties are already being paid, unlike the introduction of road tolls. It would encourage the development and purchase of more fuel efficient cars, helping the UK meet its greenhouse gas emission targets.

Their main disadvantage is that fuel taxes fail to distinguish between use of cars on congested roads and on empty roads. They work by discouraging all travel. Increases have also proved politically unpopular. The freight transport industry in particular launched nationwide protests following the April 1999 increase in duties. In November 1999, the Chancellor announced the abandonment of the fuel duty escalator. In future, increases in fuel duty would be decided on a year by year basis.

Such insight could re-write history

From Mr Colin S Jones
Sir, The standing advisory committee on trunk road assessment (Sactra) offers us a valuable insight in suggesting that new roads generate new traffic. It is a pity that the railway builders a century and a half ago did not refrain from laying down new railway lines for fear that they might generate new economic activity. Or indeed, the canal builders in the 18th century.

Come to think of it, it is a pity that the same insight was not shared by electronic engineers, chemists, pharmaceutical scientists, steel makers, oil prospectors, or indeed the explorers of the 15th, 16th and 17th centuries.

Source: the *Financial Times*.

Taxing car parking spaces

In its 1998 White Paper on transport, the government proposed taxing car parking spaces in city centres provided for employees or customers by firms. This would discourage firms providing car parking and thus make it more difficult for motorists to achieve the objectives of their journey. Revenue from the taxes would go to local authorities, which could use it to subsidise public transport. Firms strongly opposed the proposals, suggesting that they would have little effect on the number of car parking spaces but would be yet more tax on business. They could encourage firms to move out of city centres and put increased pressure on development in the countryside.

Improving public transport

In its 1998 White Paper on transport, the government committed itself to improving public transport. It has put pressure on rail companies to increase their investment. Revenues from measures such as car parking taxes could provide extra cash for local authorities to subsidise bus or rail networks in their area. The government would also like to see far more use made of bus lanes. For instance, a bus lane was introduced on the M4 into London.

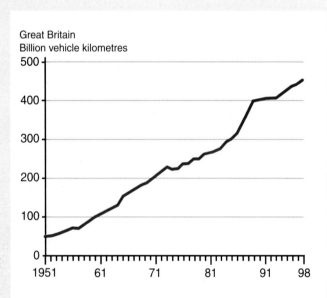

Figure 62.9 *Road traffic growth*
Source: adapted from *Social Trends*, Office for National Statistics.

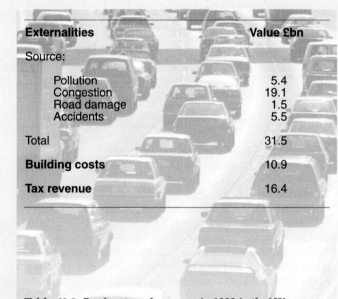

Externalities	Value £bn
Source:	
Pollution	5.4
Congestion	19.1
Road damage	1.5
Accidents	5.5
Total	31.5
Building costs	10.9
Tax revenue	16.4

Table 62.2 *Road costs and revenues in 1993 in the UK*
Source: Royal Commission on Environmental Pollution, 1994.

A new government has just been elected and has commissioned a report on the problem of congestion on UK roads. The government wants to maintain freedom of movement in the UK. It wishes to reduce congestion rather than limiting the number of journeys being made by motorists. At the same time, it is committed to reduce emissions of the 'basket' of six greenhouse gases by 12.5 per cent relative to the 1990 level over the period 2008-2012, and cut carbon dioxide emissions by 20 per cent below 1990 levels by 2010. The government is also interested in finding ways of funding its expenditure. Write a report outlining possible solutions to the problem.
1. (a) Outline briefly the nature of the problem. You may want to use material in units 6 and 7 as well as the information in this unit to help you do this.
   (b) What might be the optimal level of road traffic?
2. Summarise the main possible solutions, explaining briefly in one or two sentences how each would achieve its objectives.
3. Which solution or combination of solutions would you recommend? In your answer, you need to consider:
   (a) how far each solution would enable an optimal level of road traffic to be achieved;
   (b) the economic cost of implementing differing solution(s);
   (c) the distributional effects of differing solution(s), e.g. the different impact it would have on high and low income households.

Summary

1. Neo-classical theory suggests that monopoly has higher prices and lower output than perfect competition.
2. This is only likely to be true for a multi-plant monopolist. A natural monopolist may have far lower costs than if the industry were split up into competing units.
3. A monopolist might have higher costs because it needs to maintain barriers to entry. It may also suffer from X-inefficiency.
4. On the other hand, monopolies may be far more innovative than perfectly competitive firms.
5. Government may attempt to correct market failure caused by monopoly. It could tax abnormal profit away, subsidise production, set maximum prices, nationalise the industry, break it up or reduce entry barriers.

Perfect competition vs monopoly

Traditional neo-classical economic analysis has tended to support the view that competition increases efficiency. One argument used is that allocative efficiency will be reduced if a perfectly competitive industry becomes a monopoly.

Multi-plant monopolists In a perfectly competitive industry there is a large number of small producers each operating at the bottom of the average cost curve. Each firm has therefore exploited all potential economies of scale. If new firms enter the industry because of price increases, their cost curves will be identical to the cost curves of existing firms. Equally, firms leaving the industry will have the same cost curves as those firms remaining.

If the industry became a monopoly, the new firm would be made up of a large number of small factories or plants. The monopolist would not attempt to merge these plants because they were already at their most efficient size under perfect competition. Hence the monopolist will become a MULTI-PLANT MONOPOLIST.

If, in the long run, the multi-plant monopolist wished to expand output, it would do so not by expanding an existing plant but by building a new one. It would operate the plant at its most efficient scale, at the bottom of the plant's average cost curve. If it wanted to contract output in the long run it would close down a plant rather than maintain the same number of plants each producing at less than the most efficient scale of production. Hence, the long run average cost curve for a multi-plant monopolist is horizontal. It can increase or reduce output in the long run at the same minimum average cost.

Allocative efficiency The demand curve for the monopolist is downward sloping (☞ unit 54). The marginal cost curve will be the same as the average cost curve if the AC curve is horizontal (for the same reasons that AR = MR if average revenue is constant ☞ unit 27). Hence, the cost and revenue curves facing the multi-plant monopolist are as shown in Figure 63.1.

If the industry were perfectly competitive, it would produce where demand equals supply (i.e. where price is equal to marginal cost). If it is a monopoly, the firm will produce at its profit maximising position where MC = MR, and price on its demand or average revenue curve. Hence, under perfect competition output will be at OB whilst price will be at OE. If the industry were a monopoly, long run output would fall to OA and price would rise to OF. This leads to the conclusion that output will be lower and price

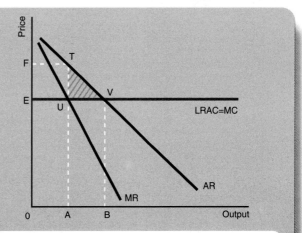

Figure 63.1 *Net social cost if a perfectly competitive industry becomes a monopoly*
If the industry were producing under conditions of perfect competition, price and output would occur where price = MC, at output OB and price OE. If the industry were a monopoly, output would be where MC = MR at OA whilst price would be on the demand curve at OF. Price is higher and output lower in the monopoly industry. The welfare loss is the shaded triangle.

will be higher in monopoly than under perfect competition. The multi-plant monopolist is **allocatively inefficient.**

The net social cost (or welfare cost) can be shown on the diagram. It is assumed that there are no externalities. The demand curve shows the marginal social benefit received by consumers of the product (☞ unit 61). The marginal cost curve is the marginal social cost curve, the cost to

society of producing an extra unit of output. Consumers were prepared to pay OF for the extra unit at OA whilst it would only have cost OE to produce. Therefore the net social cost (the difference between social benefit and social cost) on the last unit of output is EF. Similarly the vertical distance between the demand curve and the average cost curve shows the net social cost of each unit not produced between OA, the monopoly output, and OB, the output under perfect competition. Hence the net social cost to society of multi-plant monopoly production compared to production under conditions of perfect competition is the shaded triangle TUV.

The net social cost might be even greater than this triangle for two reasons.
● The monopolist might have to create and maintain barriers to entry to keep potential competitors out of the industry. For instance, it might have to spend large sums of money on advertising or other promotions. This will increase its average and marginal cost in the long run. Output will then be even lower and price even higher than if it operated under the same cost conditions as perfect competition.
● The firm may be able to shelter behind barriers to entry and as a consequence inefficiency may result. **X-inefficiency** is the term used to describe inefficiencies which occur in large organisations which are not under pressure to minimise cost. Average costs will therefore be higher than under perfect competition, resulting in even lower output and even higher prices.

Natural monopoly

So far it has been assumed that the monopolist is a multi-plant monopolist. However, many monopolies are **natural monopolies** (☞ unit 18). Natural monopolies occur in industries where not even a single producer is able to exploit fully the potential economies of scale. Hence, the

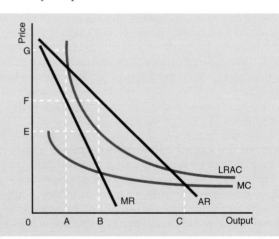

Figure 63.2 *Natural monopoly*
In a natural monopoly, economies of scale are so large that not even a single producer could fully exploit them. Competition would be highly inefficient, raising the average cost of production. The profit maximising level of output for the monopolist is OB, but output would be greater at OC where price = MC.

Question 2

Transco is the monopoly operator of Britain's national gas pipeline network. In 1999 it was accused by Ofgas, the industry regulator at the time, of anti-competitive practices. The issue was the prices charged for new connections to the network. There is no monopoly on laying pipes from new housing estates or industrial premises to the national network. Transco is just one amongst many companies which provide this service. However, if a rival firm to Transco wins a contract to lay pipes, it still has to employ Transco to complete part of the work for safety reasons. Transco was condemned by the gas regulator for overcharging rival gas connection companies for this work. For instance, Exoteric Gas Solutions, a Wembley-based gas connections company, said that in one instance Transco had quoted £17 500 for a connection when 'it should not have charged any more than £4 000 had it complied with its statutory duty'. Transco also allegedly issued a memo to staff, subsequently withdrawn, not to deal with Exoteric. In other instances, Transco deliberately delayed giving quotations for work in order to disrupt the businesses of rival companies. These practices all helped Transco win more contracts to lay pipes at the expense of its rivals.

Source: adapted from the *Financial Times*, 9.1.1999.

(a) Explain why Transco is a natural monopolist.
(b) (i) How, according to the regulator, might it have engaged in unfair competition with rivals in the gas connection market?
    (ii) Suggest why it might have engaged in these practices.

However, there are also important **dynamic** considerations. The Austrian economist, Joseph Schumpeter (1883-1950), argued that monopoly might be far more efficient over time than perfect competition.

In perfect competition, there is a large number of small firms operating in the market. No one firm will have large enough funds available for research and development. Small firms in general find it more difficult to raise finance for growth and expansion than large firms, and banks are likely to be unsympathetic if borrowed money is to be used on risky research projects. Moreover, perfect knowledge is assumed to exist in the market. The invention of one firm will quickly be adopted by other firms, so there is little or no incentive to undertake research and development.

Patent laws and copyright laws can protect the inventions of small firms, providing some encouragement to innovate. However, it is noticeable that in the few perfectly competitive industries which might be argued to exist, innovation is often provided not by individual firms but by government funded or government organised research institutions. In agriculture, for instance, major advances in crop strains in the Third World have been developed by state-funded universities and research institutes. This is an example of government correcting **market failure**.

A monopolist, safe behind high entry barriers, can react in two ways. It may choose to take the easy life. Sleepy and inefficient, it exploits the market and earns enough profits to satisfy shareholders. Research and development, which imply potential change, are unlikely to be a high priority for this type of firm.

Schumpeter, however, argued that the reverse was likely. The monopolist would have the resources from its abnormal profits to spend on research and development. In the UK, for instance, about 70 per cent of all investment is funded from retained profit. The monopolist would also have the incentive so to spend. It would be able to exploit any new products or new techniques of production to its own advantage, safe from competitors behind its high entry barriers. Productive efficiency would increase because costs would fall. Allocative efficiency would increase because the monopolist would bring new products to the market.

Moreover, a monopolist is never safe from competition. In the 18th century, the canal seemed unassailable as a form of industrial transport. Yet during the 19th century, the monopoly of canals, and the monopoly profits of canal owners, were destroyed by the coming of railways. In the 20th century, the same process turned railways into loss making concerns as railway monopolists saw their markets taken away by the motor car and lorry. Schumpeter called this 'the process of creative destruction'. High barriers mean that potential competitors have to produce a substitute product which is radically better than the old. It is not good enough to add some fancy packaging or change the colour of the product or add a few gadgets. Therefore monopoly encourages fundamental rather than superficial progress. So Schumpeter argued that a system of monopoly markets was far more likely to produce efficiency over a period of time than perfect competition.

dominant firm in the industry, the firm with the largest output and the lowest cost, is always able to undercut competitors in price and force them out of the industry if it so chooses.

This is shown in Figure 63.2. The monopolist will produce where MC = MR at output OB and earn abnormal profit by pricing at OF. However, it would be a nonsense to talk about making the industry more competitive. Splitting the industry into two, for instance, with each firm producing OA (half of OB), would increase the average cost of production from OE to OG. More competition in the industry would result in a loss of welfare, not a gain. It should also be noted that producing at the Pareto-efficient level of output where price = MC would result in a loss for the firm. At output OC, average revenue is less than average cost.

Natural monopolies tend to occur in industries where fixed costs are very large. For instance, it would be inefficient to have two railway companies with two sets of tracks in the same area running between two towns. In gas, electricity, water and telephones, it would be inefficient to have two or more sets of lines or pipes to every household so that they had the choice of which company to buy from. The Channel Tunnel is a natural monopoly too. It would make no economic sense to build a second tunnel until the first is being used to full capacity.

Innovation

So far, the analysis has been **static**. Perfect competition and monopoly have been compared at a point in time.

Question 3

The history of the consumer electronics market is littered with failures. Companies like Sony, Phillips and Matsushita have launched new products only to see them fail. The prize, though, for the technologies which succeed can be enormous. They can earn royalties for the companies owning the patent on the technology, and they can lead to increased sales as consumers replace their old technology, as for instance, happened with colour television and black and white television.

Over the past ten years, successive companies have attempted to find a replacement for the audio cassette and the CD. Between them, these two technologies account for nearly all the $50 billion worth of audio equipment and $38 billion worth of recorded music sold each year. Sony, for instance, has invested heavily in its MiniDisk system. MiniDisks are small enough to be played on a Walkman size player and so are highly portable. The format has established itself in a niche market, but has failed to replace the CD as the standard audio format. Other formats like DAT (Digital Audio Tape) have flopped.

In 1999, Sony and Phillips launched a new format, SACD (Superior Audio CD). Another group of companies, led by Matsushita, Pioneer and Toshiba, later launched a direct rival product, DVD-Audio. Both formats give improved sound quality compared to the CD format. However, whether the improvement will be large enough to persuade consumers to throw away their existing CD players remains to be seen. If past evidence is anything to go by, the new formats will fail to take off. The shift in technology has got to be much larger than the one they offer.

Source: adapted from the *Financial Times*, 19.5.1999.

(a) Suggest why consumer electronics companies want to replace existing formats in audio products.
(b) Using the data, explain why consumers benefit from the process of creative destruction.

Imperfect competition

So far, monopoly has been contrasted with perfect competition. The same arguments can be used to consider the social costs or benefits of imperfect competition. In imperfect competition output is likely to be lower and price higher than in perfect competition and hence there is a net social cost. Abnormal profits are likely to be made, again imposing net social costs.

In perfect competition and in many cases of monopoly, the consumer is offered only a homogeneous product. On the other hand, imperfect competition is characterised by the selling of a large number of different branded goods. Welfare is likely to be increased if consumers can choose between many, if fairly similar, products rather than being faced with no choice at all.

Schumpeter's arguments about innovation apply to imperfect competition too. Oligopolists, for instance, are more likely to innovate than perfectly competitive firms.

The verdict?

It can now be seen that it is not possible to come to any simple conclusions about the desirability of competition in the market. Competition is by no means always 'best'. On the one hand, multi-plant monopolists and many imperfectly competitive firms may exploit the market, earning abnormal profits at the expense of consumers, reducing output and increasing price. This leads to a welfare loss. On the other hand, natural monopolies are far more efficient than any alternative competitive market structures. There may or may not be a link between monopoly and innovation.

Government policy

Governments have a range of possible COMPETITION POLICIES which can be used to improve economic efficiency.

Taxes and subsidies Abnormal profit can simply be taxed away. This may improve equity within the economic system, transferring the resources which the monopolist has expropriated from consumers back to taxpayers. Unfortunately, this will not improve allocative efficiency. A tax on profits will not affect either marginal cost or marginal revenue. Therefore the monopolist will continue to produce at less than the efficient level of output.

However, it is possible to shift the marginal cost curve downwards by providing a **subsidy**. At any given level of output, the government could subsidise production, reducing marginal cost. If the government wishes the monopolist to produce where MC = price, it will need to find out the level of output where the marginal cost curve cuts the average revenue curve before a subsidy is given.

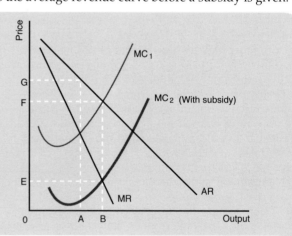

Figure 63.3 *Subsidising a monopolist to improve efficiency*
A profit maximising monopolist will produce at OA where MC = MR and price is OG. Output under perfect competition would be at OB, where price = MC. A subsidy of EF on the last unit of output would shift the marginal cost curve downwards from MC_1 to MC_2. The monopolist would now produce at the perfect competition level of output. The government could recoup the subsidy by a tax on profits.

In Figure 63.3, this occurs at output level OB where $MC_1 = AR$. The size of the subsidy required on the last unit of output is EF. This shifts the marginal cost curve to MC_2. The monopolist produces OB because this is now the level of production where MC = MR, and society benefits because production is at a level where the true cost to society, MC_1, is equal to price. The government can recoup that subsidy by taxing away the profits made by the monopolist.

This seems an ideal solution. Unfortunately there is a number of practical problems. First, giving subsidies to private sector monopolists is likely to be politically impossible for any government. It is difficult enough for governments to subsidise nationalised industries. Second, the policy requires an accurate knowledge of cost and revenue curves. When the policy is first imposed there is some chance that a reasonable guess can be made. However, taxes and subsidies distort the market so that in the long term it becomes very difficult to guess where hypothetical points on the curves might be. Third, it has already been discussed in detail whether allocative efficiency would increase by moving to a price = MC level of output in one industry (☞ unit 61). Imposing taxes and subsidies assumes that there is clear understanding of what the efficiency maximising level of output and price might be.

Price controls An obvious method of controlling monopolists would be to impose price controls on their goods. The maximum price that a monopolist could charge would be set equal to the marginal social cost; in Figure 63.4 where MC = price. To the left of output OA, the average revenue curve is horizontal because the government has imposed a maximum price of OB. To the right, the free market average revenue curve reappears. If the monopolist wishes to sell more than OA, it has to lower its price. Marginal revenue is equal to average revenue if average revenue is constant (☞ unit 53). There is then a discontinuity at OA for the marginal revenue curve. The monopolist will produce at OA because that is now the level of output where MC = MR. The policy works because the government has effectively turned the marginal revenue curve from being downward sloping to being horizontal up to the efficiency maximising level of output.

This type of policy is being used to control privatised industries in the UK (☞ unit 67). However, it suffers from the same defects as subsidies. It is difficult to know where the cost and revenue curves lie and what is the allocatively efficient level of output.

Nationalisation The private monopolist is assumed to maximise profit. This leads to an inefficient level of output. Another way of controlling monopoly is to change the goals of the firm. This could be achieved by nationalising the industry. The industry is then charged with maximising social welfare and not private profit.

Privatisation and deregulation Many monopolists in the past have been government owned monopolies such as gas or telephones. Their monopolies have been protected by laws preventing private firms setting up in the industry. It is difficult for state owned companies to compete on the same terms as private sector firms. Governments judge investment in a different way from a private firm. They can also always pay any debts if the firm runs up large losses. So to create a 'level playing field' where all firms are competing on the same terms, it is argued that state monopolies should be privatised. At the point of privatisation, they can either be split up into competing firms or barriers to entry can be lowered so that competitors can come into the market (an example of **deregulation** ☞ unit 67), both of which are discussed below.

Breaking up the monopolist The monopolist can be broken up into competing units by government. This might be an effective solution for a multi-plant monopolist with a large number of plants where the **minimum efficient scale of production** (☞ unit 49) is very low. But most monopolists or oligopolists have relatively high minimum efficient scales. The welfare gain from splitting a monopolist into a duopoly, for instance, might be negligible. In the case of natural monopolies, breaking up a monopolist would almost certainly lead to welfare losses. Breaking up cartels is more likely to increase welfare.

Reducing entry barriers It is impossible for governments to reduce entry barriers to industries which are natural monopolies. However, many multi-plant monopolists and oligopolists earn abnormal profit because they artificially maintain high entry barriers and keep potential competitors out. Governments can reduce entry barriers by a variety of means (☞ unit 65).

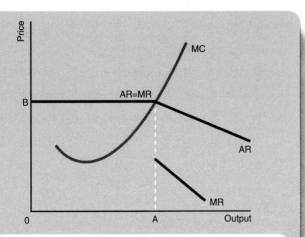

Figure 63.4 *Price controls in a monopoly industry*
Price controls change the shape of the average and marginal revenue curves. A maximum price of OB will produce a kinked average revenue or demand curve. To the left of OA, the average revenue curve is horizontal, showing the maximum price of OB that the firm is allowed to charge. To the right the average revenue falls because the free market price is below the maximum price. The monopolist will now produce at OA, the output level of a perfectly competitive industry where MC = price. This is because OA is now the profit maximising level of output (i.e. where MC = MR for the monopolist).

Question 4

In September 1998, Ladbroke was told by the government to sell off the Coral chain of betting shops that it had acquired ten months earlier. Ladbroke was the largest betting shop chain in the UK, whilst Coral was the third largest after William Hill. The judgment stated that the merger 'would lead to a weakening of price competition at national level to the detriment of punters, have a dampening effect on innovation and reduce punters' choice of major chains of betting shops, as well as reducing their local choice of betting shops in many areas'. Ladbroke acknowledged that in some local areas, competition would have been affected. For this reason, it had agreed to sell 133 Coral shops to the Tote, the state-owned betting business. However, it felt that local competition would not have been diminished by retaining the rest of the 833 shop Coral chain. As for competition at the national level, the government felt that there was a growing trend for telephone betting, although horse and greyhound betting still accounted for 90 per cent of turnover. Greater concentration amongst suppliers could have limited competition in this growing market.

Source: adapted from the *Financial Times*, 24.9.1998

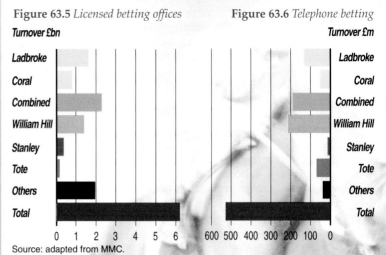

Figure 63.5 *Licensed betting offices*   **Figure 63.6** *Telephone betting*

Source: adapted from MMC.

(a) Explain why the government thought that the takeover of Coral by Ladbroke would impair efficiency in the market.
(b) (i) How has the the government chosen to improve efficiency in the market?
    (ii) Suggest ONE alternative policy that it could have used in this case and compare its effectiveness with its chosen policy.

key terms

Competition policy - government policy to influence the degree of competition in individual markets within the economy.

Multi-plant monopolist - a monopoly producer working with a number of factories, offices or plants.

Applied economics

Competition policy

The legislative framework

It was widely recognised during the inter-war years that there was a lack of competition in British industry which could have operated against the interests of the consumer. In 1948, the government passed the Monopolies and Restrictive Practices (Inquiry and Control) Act designed to curb anti-competitive practices. It set up what is now the Competition Commission (formerly known as the Monopolies and Mergers Commission). Current competition policy is set out in the Competition Act, 1998.

- A Director General of Fair Trading is appointed by the government. He or she is responsible for co-ordinating competition and consumer protection policy and advising the Secretary of State for Trade and Industry. Either the Director General or the Secretary of State has the power to refer monopolies for investigation to the Competition Commission.
- The Competition Commission is an administrative tribunal which investigates potential monopoly situations. A firm, or group of firms acting together, is defined as having a **dominant position** if it has a market share of 40 per cent. It has a monopoly if it has a market share of at least 25 per cent. These figures could apply either to a national market or a

local market. The result of an inquiry by the Commission is given in a Report. This explains the Commission's findings and lists its policy recommendations.

- The Secretary of State for Trade and Industry is the minister responsible for competition policy. He or she receives reports of the Competition Commission. The Secretary of State may decide not to act, effectively rejecting the Commission's recommendations. Until the passing of the Competition Act 1998, the most likely outcome of a negative report was that the Secretary of State would ask the Director General of Fair Trading to negotiate a voluntary agreement with the firms concerned. This would be designed to curb the malpractices found by the Commission. The Competition Act 1998, however, gives the Office of Fair Trading the power to fine firms up to 10 per cent of their turnover for anti-competitive practices.

The Competition Act was designed to make UK practice conform to EU law. Under Article 86 of the Treaty of Rome, the European Commission has the power to investigate monopolies. To date, the Commission has been more concerned with mergers and restrictive trade practices than with monopolies.

The effectiveness of policy

In the USA, monopolies are illegal because it is presumed that monopoly will always act against the public interest. The basis of UK and EU law is different. Monopoly is permissible so long as the firm or group of firms does not engage in anti-competitive practices which, for instance, raise prices to customers, restrict supply, discourage innovation or damage competitors. Such anti-competitive practices are discussed in unit 65.

The 1998 Competition Act gives greater powers to the competition authorities to curb monopolies. In the past, competition policy has often been accused of being too weak and its application inconsistent.

- The Competition Commission has been criticised for adopting different standards from investigation to investigation. This in part arises from the fact that the Competition Commission is made up of part time members who vary from investigation to investigation. No two reports are written by the same group of people.
- The government has been accused of manipulating competition policy to serve its own political ends. For instance, throughout an investigation, it is likely to be lobbied hard by the industries concerned. The government may decide to ignore recommendations from the Competition Commission because of their impact on jobs or exports. During the 1980s, the Competition Commission conducted a number of investigations into nationalised industries, firms which were owned by the government itself. This was widely seen as part of the government's attack at the time on the public sector and was part of the public relations strategy for the eventual privatisation of these industries. The 1980s also saw fewer investigations into private sector firms, which again could be interpreted as reflecting the pro-capitalist stance of the government at the time.
- Firms have tended to lose little if found to be engaged in anti-competitive practices. Typically they have been required to modify their behaviour, but there has been no penalty applied for past behaviour even though this might have been highly profitable at the expense of customers and competitors.

It is hoped that the 1998 Competition Act will considerably tighten competition policy. In particular, firms face fines of up to 10 per cent of turnover if found guilty. Both in the USA and the EU, large companies have been fined millions of pounds for engaging in anti-competitive behaviour. They have also risked being sued for compensation by injured parties. These financial penalties should act as a substantial deterrent for firms.

Microsoft

The operating system

A computer operating system is a standard, like that for CDs or VHS cassettes. Standards bring enormous advantages. I can borrow your CD or rent a video or DVD and play it on my machine. With computers, a common operating standard means that the same software will run on many different machines and that one computer can talk to another. A computer operating system is, in fact, an example of a natural monopoly. Having a number of different standards increases the worldwide cost of operating systems. This is one of the key reasons why Microsoft's Windows operating system has come to have a 90 per cent market share.

Microsoft enjoys so much power in the market for Intel-compatible PC operating systems that if it wished to exercise this power solely in terms of price, it could charge a price for Windows substantially above that which could be charged in a competitive market ... In other words, Microsoft enjoys monopoly power in the relevant market.

Furthermore, Microsoft expends a significant portion of its monopoly power, which could otherwise be spent maximising price, on imposing burdensome restrictions on customers and in inducing them to behave in ways that augment and prolong that monopoly power.

Microsoft's monopoly power is also evidenced by the fact that, over the years, Microsoft took actions that could only have been advantageous if they operated to reinforce monopoly power ...

Microsoft's actions have inflicted collateral harm on consumers who have no interest in using a Web browser at all. Microsoft has forced Windows 98 users uninterested in browsing to carry software which ... brings all the costs associated with carrying additional software. Corporate consumers ... are further burdened in that they are denied a simple and effective means of preventing employees from attempting to browse the web.

Most harmful of all is the message Microsoft's actions have conveyed to every enterprise with potential to innovate in the computer industry. Through its conduct toward Netscape, IBM, Compaq, Intel and others, Microsoft has demonstrated it will use its prodigious market power and core products.

Microsoft's past success in hurting such companies and stifling innovation deters investment in technologies and businesses that exhibit the potential to threaten Microsoft. The ultimate result is that some innovations that would try benefit consumers never occur for the sole reason that they do not coincide with Microsoft's self-interest.

Source: extracts from findings of Judge Thomas Penfield Jackson.

Browser wars

When you start up your computer, you load the operating system. 90 per cent of the world's PCs (personal computers) use a version of Windows from Microsoft. Then you load up applications like a word processing package which can only be used on one operating system. But what if you could load up a web browser which would allow you to use any software available on the internet whatever your operating system? The operating system ceases to be important as a standard. This was the threat that Microsoft woke up to in the first half of the 1990s. At that time, internet use began to explode and there was a web browser available from a company called Netscape. Microsoft rapidly developed its own browser called Microsoft Explorer to protect its dominance in the PC software market. First put on the market in August 1995, it quickly became the overwhelming market leader. Microsoft's strategy for this was to bundle Microsoft Explorer with its operating system. It basically refused to sell Windows to computer manufacturers like Compaq and Hewlett-Packard unless they also loaded Microsoft Explorer. Windows 98 went one step further, integrating the operating system with the web browser in one piece of software. The result was that Netscape could no longer sell its browser for loading before delivery to manufacturers of computers designed to use Windows.

Market power

Microsoft is renowned in the computer industry for its aggressive tactics. The browser war was just one example. Critics of Microsoft accuse it of destroying innovation in the industry. If a rival company, like Netscape, comes up with a successful product, Microsoft, it is said, either buys it up or attempts to marginalise it. For instance, Intel, the computer chip manufacturer, claims that it was forced to drop the development of some of its own software because Microsoft saw it as a potential rival. Microsoft persuaded Intel to do this by threatening to cease co-operation in future development of software for Intel chips. Another example is that of Java, a programming language that can be used to develop software which will run on several operating systems. Sun Microsystems, the developer of Java, accused Microsoft of subtly changing the language in such a way that software applications would only run on the Windows operating system. Microsoft claimed it was 'improving' Sun's technology.

Source: adapted from the *Financial Times*, 25.6.1999 and 8.11.1999.

1. **Explain why Microsoft could be seen as a monopolist.**
2. **Analyse how, according to Judge Jackson, Microsoft could be said to have abused its market power, which may have led to a loss of economic efficiency.**
3. **In 2000, a number of different ways of dealing with Microsoft's alleged monopoly were outlined. One was to split the company up into several companies. One company would produce the Windows operating system. Other companies would be given the rights to all the software produced by Microsoft, such as Internet Explorer and Office for Windows. Another solution would be to regulate Microsoft, preventing it from engaging in anti-competitive practices. Discuss which of these might be most likely to lead to greater economic efficiency.**

Summary

1. Small firms in an industry exist because economies of scale may be limited, barriers to entry low and the size of the market may be very small.
2. A healthy small firm sector in the economy may lead to increased economic efficiency if it increases competition, reduces prices and increases future efficiency.
3. Firms may grow internally or through mergers, amalgamation or takeover.
4. Mergers may be horizontal, vertical or conglomerate.
5. Firms grow in order to exploit potential economies of scale, control their markets or reduce risk through diversification.
6. Firms may choose to grow by amalgamation, for instance, because it is cheaper to buy a firm than grow internally.
7. Evidence suggests that many mergers fail to increase economic efficiency.

The size of firms

Although production in the UK is dominated by large firms, there are many industries where small and medium sized enterprises play a significant role.

Large firms exist for two main reasons. First, economies of scale in the industry may be significant. Only a small number of firms, producing at the minimum efficient scale of production, may be needed to satisfy total demand. The industry may be a natural monopoly where not even one firm can fully exploit potential economies of scale. Second, barriers to entry may exist which protect large firms from potential competitors. Conversely, small firms survive for the opposite reasons.

Economies of scale may be very small relative to the market size A large number of firms in an industry may be able to operate at the minimum efficient scale of production. Small firms may also be able to take advantage of the higher costs of larger firms in the industry caused by diseconomies of scale.

The costs of production for a large scale producer may be higher than for a small company In part, this may be due to productive inefficiency - a large firm operating within its average cost curve boundary. For instance, larger firms may be poorly organised in what they see as small unimportant segments of the market (called **market niches**). Or X-inefficiency may be present (☞ unit 61). Equally, the average cost curve of a large producer may be higher in certain markets than for a small producer. For instance, a large firm may be forced to pay its workers high wages because it operates in formal labour markets (☞ unit 75). A small firm may be able to pay relatively low wages in

informal labour markets. Indeed, owners of small companies can work exceptionally long hours at effective rates of pay which they would find totally unacceptable if in a normal job. Or a small producer, like a corner shop sole proprietorship, may be prepared to accept a much lower rate of return on its capital employed than a large company.

Barriers to entry may be low The cost of setting up in an industry, such as the grocery industry or the newsagents' market, may be small. Products may be simple to produce or sell. Finance to set up in the industry may be readily available. The product sold may be relatively homogeneous. It may be easy for a small firm to produce a new product and establish itself in the market.

Small firms can be monopolists A monopolist offers a product for sale which is available from no other company. Many small firms survive because they offer a local, flexible and personal service. For instance, a newsagent may have a monopoly on the sale of newspapers, magazines, greetings cards, toys and stationery in a local area. Consumers may be unwilling to walk half a mile extra to buy greetings cards at a 10 per cent discount or travel 10 miles by car to a local superstore to buy a £2 toy at a 25 per cent reduction. Or the newsagent may double up as a grocery store and off-licence, opening till 10 o'clock at night and all day Sunday, again offering a service which is not offered anywhere else in the locality. A small shop could be the only place locally where informal credit is offered, or where it is possible to buy a single item instead of a pack of six. Equally in the case of some products, such as cricket balls or croquet mallets, the size of the market is so small that one or two very small firms can satisfy total demand.

Question 1

(a) Why can small firms survive successfully in the hotel industry?
(b) What economic forces might favour hotel chains in the future?

Efficiency and size

There is no direct correlation between the size of a firm and economic efficiency. Some economists argue that small firms are a major source of economic efficiency in the economy.

- The small firms of today are the large firms of tomorrow. Historically in the UK and the USA, today's top largest 100 firms bear little relation to the list of the largest 100 firms 50 years ago. It is important to have as large a number of small firms as possible so that a few can become the large firms of tomorrow.
- Small firms provide the necessary competition to prevent large firms from exploiting their markets. Large firms would be less efficient and their prices higher if they were not aware that small firms could enter the market and take away parts of their market.

In some markets, economies of scale are small relative to market size. The alternative to a large number of small firms would be multi-plant oligopolists or monopolists which would erect barriers to entry to the industry and then make abnormal profit. Prices would then be higher and output lower, leading to a loss of efficiency.

There are, however, a number of arguments which suggest that large firms can be more efficient. Large firms may be necessary to exploit economies of scale. They are more likely to be in a position to undertake research and development. Moreover, the size of firms and the number of firms in an industry is not necessarily an indication of competition or the lack of it. As the **theory of contestable markets** (☞ unit 58) shows, what is important is not size or number of firms operating in the industry but the degree of potential competition. Barriers to entry are the key indicator of likely inefficiency, not size of the firm.

Question 2

Anita Roddick's Body Shop was one of the success stories of the 1980s and 1990s. Providing a range of environmentally sound products, it grew steadily in the face of competition from established multiples such as Boots and from the large scale advertising and promotion of giants such as Revlon and Unilever.

(a) In what sense might it be said that Body Shop contributed to greater economic efficiency in the UK economy in recent years?

The growth of firms

Firms may grow in size in two ways:
- by **internal growth**;
- through MERGER, AMALGAMATION or TAKEOVER.

Internal growth simply refers to firms increasing their output, for instance through increased investment or an increased labour force. A merger or amalgamation is the joining together of two or more firms under common ownership. The boards of directors of the two companies, with the agreement of shareholders, agree to merge their two companies together. A takeover implies that one company wishes to buy another company. The takeover may be amicable. Company X makes a bid for company Y. The board of directors considers the bid and finds that the price offered is a good price for the shareholders of the company. It then recommends the shareholders to accept the offer terms. However, the takeover may be contested. In a hostile takeover the board of directors of company Y recommends to its shareholders to reject the terms of the bid. A takeover battle is then likely to ensue. Company X needs to get promises to sell at the offer price of just over 50 per cent of the shares to win and take control.

Types of merger

Economists distinguish between three types of merger.
- A HORIZONTAL MERGER is a merger between two firms in the same industry at the same stage of production, for instance, the merger of two building societies, or two car manufacturers or two bakeries.
- A VERTICAL MERGER is a merger between two firms at different production stages in the same industry. **Forward integration** involves a supplier merging with one of its buyers, such as a car manufacturer buying a car dealership, or a newspaper buying newsagents. **Backward integration** involves a purchaser buying one of its suppliers, such as a drinks manufacturer buying a bottling manufacturer, or a car manufacturer buying a tyre company.

Question 3

Explain whether each of the following is a horizontal, vertical or conglomerate merger.
(a) Asda with Wal-Mart (a US retailer) (1999).
(b) W H Smith with Hodder Headline (a publisher) (1999).
(c) McDonald's with Aroma (a UK chain of coffee bars) (1999).
(d) British Steel with Hoogovens (A Dutch steel manufacturer) (1999).
(e) Kwik-Fit with Ford (1999).
(f) British American Tobacco with Farmers Group (a US insurance group) (1988).
(g) Lloyds TSB with the Scottish Widows assurance company (1999).

- A CONGLOMERATE MERGER is the merging of two firms with no common interest. A tobacco company buying an insurance company, or a food company buying a clothing chain would be conglomerate mergers.

The reasons for growth

It is suggested that profit maximising companies are motivated to grow in size for three main reasons.
- A larger company may be able to exploit economies of scale more fully. The merger of two medium sized car manufacturers, for instance, is likely to result in potential economies in all fields, from production to marketing to finance. Vertical and conglomerate mergers are less likely to yield scale economies because there are unlikely to be any technical economies. There may be some marketing economies and more likely there may be some financial economies.
- A larger company may be more able to control its markets. It may therefore reduce competition in the market place in order to be better able to exploit the market.
- A larger company may be able to reduce risk. Many conglomerate companies have grown for this reason. Some markets are fragile. They are subject to large changes in demand when economies go into boom or recession. A steel manufacturer, for instance, will do exceptionally well in a boom, but will be hard hit in a recession. So it might decide to **diversify** by buying a company with a product which does not have a cyclical demand pattern, like a supermarket chain. Other industries face a very uncertain future. It became fashionable in the 1970s and early 1980s for tobacco companies to buy anything which seemed to have a secure future, from grocery stores to insurance companies.

Reasons for amalgamation

Why do profit maximising companies choose to grow through amalgamation rather than through internal growth?

Cost One answer is that it is often cheaper to merge than to grow internally. For instance, a company may wish to expand and calculates that it will cost £50 million if it does so internally. It then looks to the stock markets and sees that a firm which already has the capabilities required is valued at £25 million. Even after paying the likely premium on the share price involved in takeover bids, it would be cheaper to buy the existing firm than undertake new investment. The ratio between the value of assets of a firm and its stock market price is called the **valuation ratio**. In theory, the larger the difference between asset values and stock market prices, the greater the incentive for firms to grow through takeovers rather than grow internally.

The position is often complicated because it is very difficult to place a value on the assets of a firm. In particular, it has become clear in recent years that intangible assets, particularly brands, can be more valuable than all the factories, offices, stock and other physical assets put together. A strong brand represents a guaranteed income for the foreseeable future. It is also a block on which to build. However large the company, it cannot guarantee to establish a new brand in the market place. Companies can invest money for years in the attempt to build a brand, and fail.

Asset stripping Not all companies in the merger market are necessarily interested in growing in size. Some companies specialise in asset stripping. The predator company will look for companies which have high asset values but low stock market prices. Companies being stalked may well have inefficient management who are unable to manage the company to earn the profit expected by shareholders and the stock market in general. Once a company is taken over, it will be broken up in the most profitable manner to the asset stripper. For instance, parts of the company may be sold as going concerns to other companies. Parts may be closed down. A factory site may be far more profitable sold off as building land than as a working factory. The predator company will then keep the rest to add to its portfolio of companies. A successful asset stripper will often aim to sell off some of the parts of the company for more than it paid for the whole. The part of the company which the predator might keep is then a useful addition to the profit made on the whole deal.

Rewards to management So far, it has been assumed that companies are motivated to grow because of profit. But there is much evidence to suggest that profits of merged companies are often no more and sometimes less than the combined profits of the two individual firms would have been. **Managerial and behavioural theories** of the firm (☞ units 50 and 59) can explain this by pointing out that the goal of a firm is not necessarily to maximise profit. The managers of the firm have a vested interest in seeing a firm grow because their rewards (their pay, bonuses, company cars, prestige and influence) tend to increase with the size of the firm. The managing director of a company which doubles its size overnight is likely to receive a substantial pay rise in the not-too-distant future.

Moreover, the financial markets have a strong incentive to encourage takeovers and mergers. Banks, merchant banks and other financial institutions can make very large profits from organising takeovers.

Mergers and efficiency

There is much controversy as to whether mergers increase economic efficiency. Productive efficiency will increase if average costs of production after the merger fall because of economies of scale. Allocative efficiency will increase if the merged company provides a wider range of goods, better quality products, etc.

On the other hand, mergers tend to reduce competition in the market. The loss of efficiency which might arise was discussed in detail in unit 63.

Moreover, asset stripping is very controversial. Its supporters argue that the asset stripper performs a useful economic function. The value to society of a company can be calculated by the sum of its component parts. If greater profit can be made by demolishing a factory, sacking the workforce and selling the land for shops, houses or offices than by keeping the factory operational, then the asset stripper is performing a useful social role by doing so. The asset stripper is reallocating resources according to the signals of the market. The problem is that market prices may not be an accurate reflection of true social value. Short run profit maximisation by one company may well not lead to an economically efficient outcome for society.

Question 4

In 1994, Service Corporation International, the biggest funeral company in the USA, offered to buy two of the largest funeral companies in the UK. The first, Great Southern Group, ran 150 funeral homes, 12 crematoria and two cemeteries, mainly in the south of England. Its taxable profits in 1993 were £6.2m. The second, Plantsbrook, buries one in ten people in the UK, mainly in the north of England. Its profits in 1993 were £12m. Service Corporation International will have paid £306m to buy the two UK companies. It is a highly acquisitive group. In the USA, it spent $250m in 1994 financing acquisitions and expansion. It operates Australia's largest funeral business and has a substantial presence in Canada. Bill Heiligbrodt, president and chief operating officer of Service Corporation International said, when it made a bid for Great Southern Group, that the UK was 'a large mature market in terms of population'.

(a) Suggest why Service Corporation International wanted to buy the two UK companies.

key terms

Conglomerate merger - a merger between two firms producing unrelated products.
Horizontal merger or integration - a merger between two firms in the same industry at the same stage of production.
Merger, amalgamation, integration or takeover - the joining together of two or more firms under common ownership.
Vertical merger or integration - a merger between two firms at different production stages in the same industry.

Applied economics

Mergers and efficiency

Merger activity

This century, there has been a significant growth in the importance of large firms in the UK economy. For instance, in 1949 the share of the 100 largest private enterprises in manufacturing net output was 22 per cent. By 1975, this had risen to 42 per cent. Since then it has fallen back as manufacturing industry has shrunk under competitive pressures. Most of this increase in concentration (☞ unit 51) has come about through mergers, particularly horizontal mergers. There has been a similar trend in both primary and tertiary industry.

Merger activity has tended to be relatively uneven over time and tends to happen in waves. The mergers in the 1960s were often motivated by a desire to increase in size in order to gain market power or to cut costs. The abolition of restrictive trade practices by the 1956 Act (☞ unit 74) in particular increased mergers. Unable to collude to rig the market in their favour, firms resorted to taking over other firms to gain sufficient control of the market to gain monopoly profits. The mergers of the 1980s were often more concerned with buying market share in what could be difficult to enter oligopolistic markets. By the late 1980s, there was also a growing realisation that only large firms would survive in many markets when a Single Market was created in the European Union in 1993 (☞ unit 98).

The recession of the early 1990s led to a fall in merger activity. There were even some de-mergers, such as the split of ICI into two companies, ICI and Zeneca. This reflected a new business awareness that two smaller companies might be more efficient than a single larger company.

Better economic conditions by the second half of the 1990s led to a resurgence of merger activity. The large deals tended to be done on an international basis. For instance, French and US companies bought up English water companies. BT expanded overseas. Asda was bought by the world's largest retailer, Wal-Mart, a US company. This reflects the steady movement towards both European integration and globalisation of business.

The legislative background

Merger policy is governed by the Competition Act 1998. This lays down that mergers are initially considered by the Director General of Fair Trading (DGFT). The vast majority of mergers are too small to be of concern to the regulatory authorities. Very large mergers which involve European or other foreign firms with a UK firm may be considered by the EU competition authorities, rather than the UK authorities. However, the Director General will consider it if:

- the merger involves a takeover of a firm with more than £70 million of assets worldwide;

- or the merger will create a firm with 25 per cent or more of a market;
- or it involves a firm with an existing 25 per cent or more market share;
- or the firms are in the newspaper or water industry.

The DGFT makes a recommendation to the Secretary of State for Industry about whether a merger which falls into one of these categories might be against the public interest and what action should be taken.

- The merger may be judged to have no adverse effect on competition and be allowed to proceed.
- It may be deemed to be against the public interest but, after talks with the firms, a compromise may be reached. For instance, the firms may agree to sell off part of the new firm to reduce market dominance.
- It may be deemed against the public interest and a referral to the Competition Commission should be made.

The Secretary of State must then decide whether to accept or reject the DGFT's recommendations. If a referral is made to the Competition Commission, it will investigate the merger and produce a report with a recommendation about whether the merger should be allowed to go ahead, and if so under what conditions. The Secretary of State can accept the findings or reject them.

Mergers and economic efficiency

Evidence suggests [see, for instance, G Meekes (1977) or K G Cowling (1980)] that most mergers do not lead to any efficiency gains. Many in fact lead to losses of economic efficiency. There is a number of ways in which this could be measured.

- Profits of the combined company decline from what they might otherwise have been. This is often anticipated in the stock market where the share price of a company taking over another falls when the takeover is announced.
- Turnover falls. Mergers may well lead to 'rationalisation' of plant and other facilities. In the process the capacity of the firm falls, leading to a loss of turnover. This reduction of capacity may not be compensated for by an increase in capacity elsewhere in the economy, pushing the production possibility frontier backwards towards the origin.
- Employment falls. Rationalisation often involves reducing the workforce. These workers may then be added to a pool of long term unemployed people.

If mergers fail to improve efficiency, why do mergers take place? Is there any significance in that merger activity increased during the high growth years of the 1980s and 1990s, but fell back sharply when the economy went into recession from 1990 to 1992? One factor which has fuelled merger activity has been availability of finance. In the recession of 1990-1992, interest rates were very high. Hence the cost of borrowing to acquire companies was very high. Also, stock market prices were relatively low, which made it expensive for companies to issue new shares to finance acquisitions. In the boom years of the 1980s and 1990s, in contrast, interest rates were lower and stock market values were booming. It was cheaper and easier, therefore, to raise the finance for a takeover.

Another factor which fuels merger activity is the gains to be made by the economic actors in the business community. City financial institutions which help companies with takeovers and mergers have a vested self interest in promoting them. The higher the level of merger activity, the higher the fees they can collect. Equally, top managers and directors can benefit. The larger the company, the higher the total remuneration package likely to be offered to a top manager or director. Sometimes planned mergers fail to go ahead because the top executives of the two companies fail to agree on who is to get what post in the new company. This would tend to support managerial theories of the firm.

In a recession, managers and directors are often too busy fire-fighting to make long term strategic decisions such as whether to take over or merge with another company. With sales and profits falling, they are too busy trying to stabilise and reinvigorate existing business activities.

The effectiveness of mergers control

Merger policy has done little to prevent the increased concentration of UK industry. Some have argued that:
- too few cases have been referred to the Competition Commission (formerly known as the Monopolies and Mergers Commission);
- there is little rationale behind the choice of which potential mergers are referred;
- this lottery is made worse by the inconsistency of the stance taken by a Competition Commission staffed by different people at different times.

It can then be argued that a much tougher line needs to be taken. In particular, companies should need to prove more than just that a merger would not be against the public interest. Merging companies should be forced to prove that the merger is likely to be in the public interest.

Free marketeers take an opposite viewpoint. They would say that governments are ill placed to decide what would be in the public interest and what would not. This is because governments cannot predict what will happen after a merger with any certainty. More government intervention would be likely to lead to a series of mistakes with beneficial mergers being stopped because of government interference. Even if it were true that most mergers lead to no increase in economic efficiency, letting the market decide is unlikely to lead to wrong decisions being made. Whatever happens, free market forces lead to better decision making than anything government could achieve.

Ford buys Kwik-Fit

Ford buys Kwik-Fit for £1 billion

Ford yesterday launched a £1 billion agreed cash takeover bid for Kwik-Fit, the tyres and and exhaust business. Kwik-Fit is Europe's largest fast-fit repair chain, over half of whose outlets are in the UK. In Europe, Kwik-Fit trades under the Speedy International brand name, a chain which it acquired last year.

Source: adapted from the *Financial Times*, 18.9.1999 and 13.4.1999.

Kwik-Fit

Kwik-Fit has grown because of its commitment to price and service. In an industry renowned for shoddy, poor value service, Kwik-Fit promised while-you-wait repairs at a keen price. If there was any problem with the work, Kwik-Fit fixed it with no fuss. In 1995, the group expanded into selling motor insurance. Then in 1998, it expanded into Europe by paying £105 million for Speedy, the French chain. However, the group needed far more cash to expand rapidly to take advantage of opportunities in Europe and, in the long term, in the rest of the world. For instance, in Germany, the number of its outlets could easily increase from 160 to 450. In Spain and Portugal, where there are hardly any outlets, there is a potential for 250. Ford can give the group the financial backing to undertake this expansion.

Source: adapted from the *Financial Times*, 18.9.1999 and 13.4.1999.

Ford to become a consumer business

Ford wants to become a leading consumer services business. At present, it manufacturers cars, but often has little control of downstream services such as repairs and motor insurance. The purchase of Kwik-Fit is the first step in Ford's new vision. It plans to roll the Kwik-Fit format out throughout Europe, building on existing outlets, and then develop the concept in emerging markets around the world, from central and Eastern Europe to Latin America.

In theory, the motor manufacturers should have a strong hold on the after sales market. In Europe, they have dedicated dealer networks which both sell and repair cars. However, these dealers are seen as being expensive and giving poor value for money by most motorists. Once the warranty period on a new car has run out, motorists typically use other outlets to service and maintain their cars. Kwik-Fit has been able to exploit this market by offering low prices and good service.

Ford had already attempted to enter the market in the UK by developing its Rapid-Fit chain. The chain had some success with cars up to five years old increasingly using the outlets. It became obvious, though, that it would never challenge Kwik-Fit for market leadership.

Ford is also buying up traditional dealerships. It has set itself a target of making a 5 per cent return on sales. Volume vehicle manufacturers typically manage 2 per cent but further down the chain, returns are much higher. Kwik-Fit, for instance, achieves a profit margin on sales of 12.5 per cent in 1998.

Ford's strategy is contrary to industry trends, where motor manufacturers have been outsourcing component supply and selling off parts and other related businesses to concentrate on their core business of vehicle development and production.

Source: adapted from the *Financial Times*, 18.9.1999 and 13.4.1999.

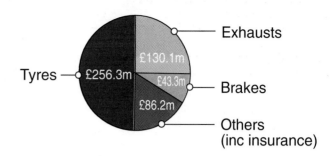

Figure 64.1 *Kwik-Fit: turnover by product (year end Feb 28, 1999)*
Source: adapted from Datastream/ICV, company.

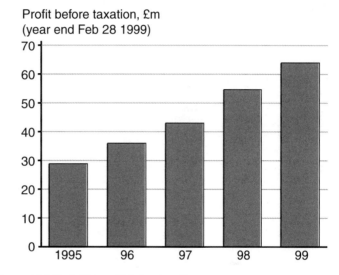

Figure 64.2 *Kwik-Fit: profit before taxation*
Source: adapted from Datastream/ICV, company.

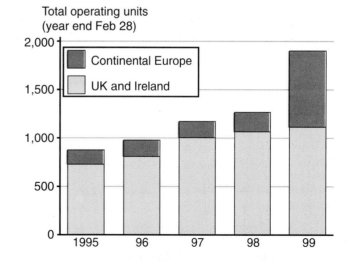

Figure 64.3 *Kwik-Fit: total operating units*
Source: adapted from Datastream/ICV, company.

1. **Discuss whether Ford buying Kwik-Fit is an example of a horizontal or vertical merger.**
2. **Analyse why Ford decided to buy Kwik-Fit.**
3. **Discuss whether the merger will lead to greater economic efficiency.**

unit 65 Price fixing and collusion

Summary

1. Collusion enables individual producers to share monopoly profits with other producers.
2. Cartels may collapse. Individual members have an incentive to cheat on the agreement. Non-cartel members may increase their market share at the expense of cartel members.
3. Restrictive trade practices are likely to lead to a loss of economic efficiency.

Collusion

During the 19th century and for most of the 20th century, British industry was dominated by collective agreements. Firms COLLUDED to restrict competition. By colluding, firms could gain some monopoly power over their markets. As a result, they became price-makers rather than price-takers.

Consider Table 65.1. It shows the cost and revenues for an industry. If the market were perfectly competitive, then long run output would be 6 million units. This is because no firm in the industry could earn abnormal profit. If it did, competitor firms would be attracted into the industry, increasing supply and driving down prices and profits until abnormal profit was eliminated.

Table 65.1

Million units			£ millions
Output	Average revenue	Average cost (including normal profit)	Total abnormal profit
(a)	(b)	(c)	(b - c) x a
1	10	5	5
2	9	5	8
3	8	5	9
4	7	5	8
5	6	5	5
6	5	5	0

Question 1

A firm operates in a perfectly competitive market with another 9999 firms in the market. A cartel is now formed in the industry, with all firms agreeing to join the cartel. The cartel is successful in erecting barriers to entry to the industry. The new cartel price is double the old free market price but all members of the cartel have had to reduce their output by 20 per cent.

(a) Draw a diagram for an individual firm in perfect competition marking on it the long run equilibrium output of the firm.
(b) Show what happens to the firm's equilibrium output and price after it has joined the cartel.
(c) Explain why the firm benefits from the cartel.

However, individual firms could earn abnormal profit if they combined together to force up price, restrict output and keep potential competitors out of the industry. The profit maximising level of output for the industry as a whole is 3 million units. If each firm in the industry agreed to halve its current output, £9 million of abnormal profit could be shared between the colluding firms.

The problems facing cartels

A CARTEL is a group of producers which has agreed to restrict competition in the market. Possibly the most famous cartel today is OPEC, the Organisation of Petroleum Exporting Countries. Restricting competition is not necessarily easy.

● An agreement has to be reached. This is likely to be easiest in oligopolistic industries where only a few firms dominate the market; the larger the number of firms, the greater the possibility that at least one key participant will refuse to collude. It is also likely to be easiest in stable mature industries where no single firm has recently been able to gain advantage by pursuing aggressive competitive strategies. For instance, collusion is far more likely in a mature industry like steel manufacturing or cement making than in a rapidly changing industry like the computer industry.
● Cheating has to be prevented. Once an agreement is made and profitability in the industry is raised, it would pay an individual firm to cheat so long as no other firms do the same. For instance, it would pay a small cartel producer with 10 per cent of the market to expand production to 12 per cent by slightly undercutting the cartel price. The profit it would lose by the small cut in price on the 10 per cent is more than offset by the gain in profit on the sale of the extra 2 per cent. However, if every producer does this, the market price will quickly fall to the free market level and all firms will lose the privilege of earning abnormal profit.
● Potential competition must be restricted. Abnormal profits will encourage not only existing firms in the industry to expand output but also new firms to enter the industry. Firms already in the industry which don't join the cartel may be happy to follow the policies of the cartel in order to earn abnormal profits themselves. To prevent this, cartel firms could agree to drive other firms which compete too aggressively out of the market. Cartel firms could also agree to increase barriers to entry to the industry.

Question 2

The De Beers diamond cartel is one of the oldest cartels operating in the world. De Beers is a South African company which owns diamond mines in the country. It runs the Central Selling Organisation (CSO). This buys up approximately 70 per cent of world diamond production. All the world's major diamond mining companies have agreements to sell their diamond production to the CSO. The advantage to other producers is that the CSO is able to maintain a higher long term price for diamonds than would otherwise be the case. For instance, in 1998 demand for diamonds fell sharply due to the economic crisis in Asia. To prevent prices falling, the CSO withdrew diamonds for sale and added unsold production to its stockpile of gems. In good years, the CSO sells diamonds from the stockpile as demand outstrips production.

The CSO is constantly having to fight to control production. For much of the 1980s and 1990s, for instance, there was a large flow of diamonds onto the market from Angola. This African country was torn apart by civil war at the time and its diamond production was unregulated. Equally, in the mid-1990s Russian producers began to flood the market with gems. De Beers had to negotiate hard with them to show that it was to their advantage to join the cartel.

Source: adapted from the *Financial Times*, 15.12.1998.

Explain (a) how a cartel can raise prices in a market and (b) why it is vulnerable to changes in production from producers outside the cartel. Illustrate your answer from the data.

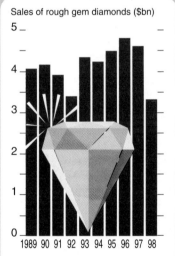

Figure 65.1 *Sales of rough gem diamonds by the De Beers' Central Selling Organisation*
Source: adapted from De Beers.

Anti-competitive practices and efficiency

ANTI-COMPETITIVE PRACTICES or RESTRICTIVE TRADE PRACTICES are strategies used by producers to restrict competition in the market. Cartels use them to enforce their collective agreements and to deter competitors. Individual firms use them to establish or reinforce dominance in a market. A wide variety of practices has been used and continues to be used, including the following.

Resale price maintenance A firm may wish to fix a price at which its goods are sold on by a buyer. This is RESALE PRICE MAINTENANCE (RPM). This most commonly occurs with manufacturers and retailers. A manufacturer wishes to prevent competition in the market and so it will only sell to a retailer if it charges a minimum price to consumers. This RPM price is above what would otherwise be the market price for the product if there were price competition between retailers. Although the manufacturer is likely to sell less, it will be at a higher price. The manufacturer should set the price so that its profit is maximised.

Refusal to supply a competitor or customer A firm may have a variety of reasons for refusing to supply a competitor or customer. For instance, a manufacturer may enforce a policy of resale price maintenance by refusing to supply a retailer which does not does sell at the RPM price. Alternatively, a manufacturer may wish to force a discount retailer out of the market for fear that it will become its largest customer and be able to erode its profit margins because of its buying power.

Predatory pricing PREDATORY PRICING occurs when a dominant firm in a market is threatened by a new entrant. The dominant firm cuts its price to such a low level that the new entrant is unable to make a profit, forcing it out of the market. Once it has left, the dominant firm puts its price back up again. Predatory pricing can also be used by a dominant firm against an established firm in the market. If the dominant firm feels, for instance, that a smaller firm is gaining too much market share, or is likely to threaten its dominant position, it may wish to take defensive action by forcing it out of the market.

Discriminatory pricing policies A firm may price discriminate (☞ unit 54). For instance, a firm may offer discounts to a buyer if it also buys other products from the firm. It may charge lower prices for bulk orders. Many forms of price discrimination are not anti-competitive, so firms need to be careful when using price discrimination to find out from the competition authorities whether their pricing policies are legal.

The tie in of non-related goods or services A firm may refuse to sell a good unless the buyer also purchases other goods from the firm. For instance, a firm may enjoy a dominant position in sales of one good because of genuine product superiority. It may then boost sales of another of its products which suffers much more severe competition in the market place by refusing to supply the first good unless the second is bought. This raises overall sales and is also likely to boost the price at which goods facing competition can be sold.

Refusing to allow a competitor to use essential facilities To illustrate this, consider an airport which owns its own railway station. It may refuse a train company the right to use the railway station if it threatens to compete with existing highly profitable bus or airline services. Alternatively, an ice cream manufacturer may tell its independent distributors that it will refuse to supply them if they also act as the distribution agents for a rival brand of ice cream.

Refusing to licence intellectual property rights A firm may discriminate between other firms which supply related products. For instance, a firm producing an operating system for a computer may licence use of the operating system to computer manufacturers which also install other software produced by the firm. But it may refuse to licence the operating system to other manufacturing firms which want to install software products from rival companies.

Anti-competitive practices are designed to benefit the firm or group of firms which carry them out. In particular, they typically:
- raise prices from what they would otherwise be in a competitive market place;
- restrict output;
- restrict choice of product to the customer;
- raise barriers to entry, thus reducing potential competition and the incentive to produce at minimum cost;
- defend existing technologies or allow firms to earn high levels of abnormal profit on new technologies.

As such, they are designed to reduce levels of consumer surplus and raise levels of producer surplus. They lead to both productive and allocative inefficiency (☞ unit 16) and are likely to lead to dynamic inefficiency. The last would not be the case if dominant firms used their abnormal profits to invest in new products and technologies.

key terms

Anti-competitive practices or restrictive trade practices - tactics used by producers to restrict competition in the market.
Cartel - an organisation of producers which exists to further the interests of its members, often by restricting output through the imposition of quotas leading to a rise in prices.
Collusion - collective agreements between producers which restrict competition.
Predatory pricing - a firm driving its prices down to force a competitor out of a market and then putting them back up again once this objective has been achieved.
Resale price maintenance - fixing a price at which a customer may sell on a good or service.

Question 3

In 1999, the Justice Department in the United States accused American Airlines of seeking to protect its monopoly at Dallas/Fort Worth airport with predatory pricing. American Airlines uses this airport as its main hub, flying passengers into the airport to be taken on to other destinations when no direct flight is available. The Justice Department claims that the airline drove three competitors - Vanguard, Sun Jet and Dallas - out of the market. When these airlines set up services from Dallas/Fort Worth, American Airlines swamped their routes with new flights at reduced fares. When the three airlines withdrew their services, American Airlines cut back on their services and raised its fares back to their previous level or even higher.

Source: adapted from the *Financial Times*, 24.5.1999.

(a) Explain what is meant by predatory pricing, using the data to illustrate your answer.
(b) To what extent was there a loss of economic efficiency because of the actions of American Airlines?

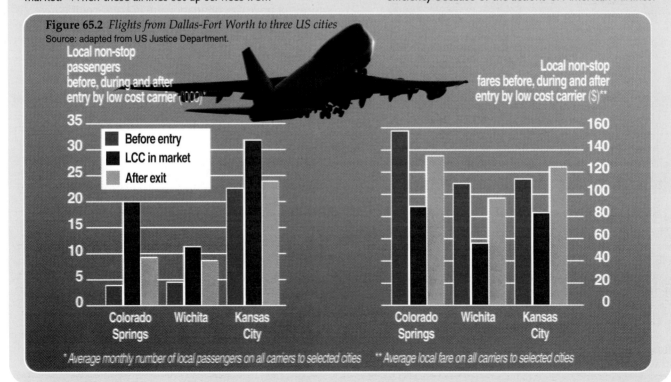

Figure 65.2 *Flights from Dallas-Fort Worth to three US cities*
Source: adapted from US Justice Department.

Local non-stop passengers before, during and after entry by low cost carrier ('000)*

Local non-stop fares before, during and after entry by low cost carrier ($)**

- Before entry
- LCC in market
- After exit

Colorado Springs   Wichita   Kansas City

* Average monthly number of local passengers on all carriers to selected cities   ** Average local fare on all carriers to selected cities

Applied economics

The UK ice cream market

The UK ice cream market has been regularly investigated by what is now the Competition Commission (formerly the Monopolies and Mergers Commission). Birds Eye Wall's, part of Unilever, has over 50 per cent of the UK ice cream market. Competitors claim that it has consistently used anti-competitive practices to retain a stranglehold on the market. Distribution practices lie at the centre of the problem.

Freezer exclusivity

Prior to 1979, Wall's refused to supply its ice cream products to retailers other than large supermarkets which stocked products from rival companies. It was forced to abandon this after a Monopolies and Mergers Commission investigation. But it found a way around this through freezer exclusivity agreements. Wall's supplied freezer cabinets free of charge to retailers if they agreed only to stock Wall's products in the cabinet. They were at liberty to stock rivals' products, but only if they were stored in another freezer cabinet. Figure 65.3 shows that 59 per cent of all exclusive freezer cabinets in the UK were supplied by Wall's. In the impulse buy market, typically newsagents, premises were so small that ice cream sales did not justify the presence of two freezer cabinets. So small shops tended to stock just one brand, usually Wall's, the market leader.

Freezer exclusivity was strongly challenged by Mars, the US food company. It entered the European ice cream market in 1989, but quickly found its sales limited by freezer exclusivity despite the popularity of its products with consumers. In the UK, a Competition Commission report into the ice cream industry recommended in 1999 the ending of freezer exclusivity. In future, firms supplying free freezer cabinets would have to allow up to 40 per cent of the space to be stocked by products of rivals.

Dedicated distribution channels

Traditionally, Wall's has used independent distributors to get its products from factory to retailer. Some of these independent distributors were dedicated distributors, selling only Wall's products. Others were wholesalers, distributing products from a number of manufacturers. Dedicated distributors were charged lower prices by Wall's than wholesalers. In 1998, what is now the Competition Commission declared that this was an anti-competitive practice because it gave an unfair price advantage to distributors which only sold Wall's products.

In response, Wall's decided to set up its own distribution system and terminated contracts with 19 out of 27 of its dedicated distributors. They, like other wholesalers, were still able to buy from Wall's.

However, they claimed that Wall's discriminated against them on price, effectively charging higher prices to them compared to Wall's Direct. They also claimed that Wall's used heavy handed tactics to persuade their customers, mainly newsagents, to switch to Wall's Direct.

In 1999, the Competition Commission declared that this was anti-competitive and that Wall's must give independent distributors the same terms as Wall's Direct. If it failed to do this, it might be forced to closed down Wall's Direct and be banned from the distribution market.

Buying selling space

A third practice adopted by Wall's has been to pay outlets such as theme parks and motorway service stations only to stock its products. This therefore

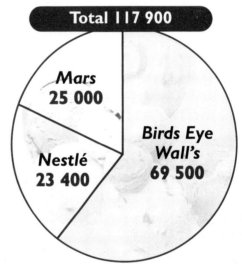

Figure 65.3 *Number of exclusive freezer cabinets provided to retailers, 1997*
Source: adapted from MMC, Birds Eye Wall's.

Estimated UK ice cream market share

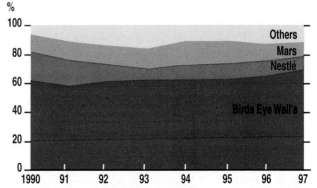

Figure 65.4 *Ice cream: UK market share*
Source: adapted from MMC based on Birds Eye Wall's data, Euromonitor, Datastream/ICV.

excludes rival products from these high profile, high volume outlets.

The future

Wall's has been highly successful in the UK, increasing its market share from 61 per cent in 1990 to 69 per cent in 1997 as Figure 65.4 shows. Ice cream has become a very important business worldwide for Unilever, the parent company. In 1997, it was the world's largest ice cream manufacturer with 20 per cent of the world market. Its brands, such as Magnum, Cornetto and Sollero, are heavily supported by advertising and other promotion, which in itself constitutes a formidable

barrier to entry to the market. Independent distributors found in 1999 that most of their customers did not want to devote large amounts of freezer space to non-Wall's products. However, they did want to stock a few items from companies such as Mars and Nestle. The anti-competitive practices of Wall's were essentially designed to squeeze even this little amount of choice from the market. Economic efficiency was thus impaired. The lack of competition also prevented any price competition in the market. One reason why ice cream is important for Unilever is that it tends to earn high profit margins on sales. Consumers are therefore not necessarily getting the lowest possible price for the product.

OPEC

The strengths of OPEC

There are a number of reasons why OPEC has been one of the few international cartels which has survived over a long period of time.

- There is no need for any buffer stocks or large amounts of financial capital. If OPEC wishes to reduce supply, member countries simply produce less and leave their oil in the ground.
- There are a relatively small number of members of OPEC. Member countries are able to exert a high degree of control over the volume of oil lifted within their countries. This contrasts, for instance, with coffee, where governments wishing to limit production have to control tens of thousands of small farmers.
- Oil production is not particularly affected by the vagaries of weather. Hence supply need not fluctuate wildly and randomly from year to year as it does in many agricultural markets.
- OPEC countries supply a significant proportion of total world output and control an even larger proportion of known oil reserves. Because non-OPEC producers tend to produce at maximum capacity, countries such as the USA and the UK are unable to exert downward pressure on oil prices even if they wanted to.

The cartel

OPEC, the Organisation of Petroleum Exporting Countries, was founded in 1960. For the first 13 years of its existence, it remained an obscure and relatively unimportant organisation, but in 1973, with the Arab-Israeli Yom Kippur War, it leapt to world prominence. The members of the organisation realised that they could form an effective cartel if they agreed production quotas amongst themselves. By slightly reducing supply in 1974, they were able to quadruple the world price of oil.

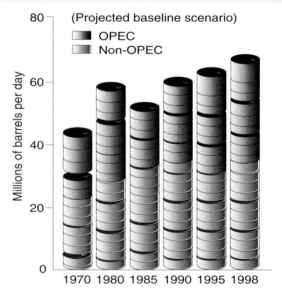

Source: adapted from UN/DESIPA.
Figure 65.5 *World crude oil production*

Weaknesses

In real terms, oil prices today are little different from those at the start of 1973. OPEC countries increased their revenues substantially in the mid-1970s and again in 1979-80 but these were short lived gains. OPEC suffers from three fundamental weaknesses.

● The large increases in oil prices in the 1970s led to stagnant demand for oil until the mid-1980s. Consumers substituted other types of energy for oil and there was a shift towards much greater energy conservation.

● Large increases in oil prices also led to a large increase in supply from non-OPEC countries. Known oil reserves are higher today than they were at the time of the 'energy crisis' in the 1970s. The operation of market forces led to a substantial increase in exploration and subsequent output from non-OPEC countries. This increase in supply has depressed world prices since the start of the 1980s.

● The increase in non-OPEC supply has led to strains amongst OPEC members. In any cartel, there is an incentive to cheat. If one country can increase its production above its allocated quota, it can sell this extra output at a price almost equal to that of the cartel price. However, if countries cheat, then the price will fall rapidly.

1998-99

In late 1997, OPEC leaders decided that the world oil market was relatively buoyant. Demand was forecast to increase in 1998 and so they decided to increase total OPEC production. They miscalculated. Almost immediately, the Asian crisis of 1998 hit demand. Countries like South Korea and Thailand, heavy importers of oil, experienced a severe downturn due to a collapse in their financial systems. Countries affected experienced a fall in GDP of up to 20 per cent in one year. With this sharp fall in demand for oil, its price fell from around $20 a barrel to below $10. In late 1998, OPEC was forced to respond. It cut back production quotas. Moreover, much to the surprise of many in the industry, countries which previously had tended to overproduce, like Venezuela, stuck to their quotas. The result was that by 1999, oil prices had risen back to over $20 a barrel.

Write a report outlining possible future trends in the world oil market for the government of a small OPEC producer. Your report needs to cover the following.

1. **A summary of past trends in oil production, prices and proven reserves since 1970.**
2. **An economic analysis using demand and supply diagrams of (a) why oil prices have changed and (b) why the market share of OPEC countries has shifted since 1970.**
3. **Future trends in the world oil market. In your analysis, use the evidence of what has happened over the past 20 years to predict the future. Consider too the implications of oil being a non-renewable energy source.**
4. **Suggestions of the best course of action over the next ten years for a small OPEC producer given your predictions in 3. Assume the producer wishes to maximise revenues from its oil exports.**

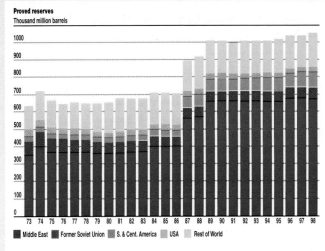

Source: adapted from *BP Statistical Review of World Energy*.
Figure 65.6 *World proven oil reserves, 1969-98*

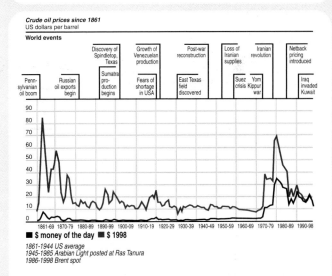

Source: adapted from *BP Statistical Review of World Energy*.
Figure 65.7 *Crude oil prices since 1861*

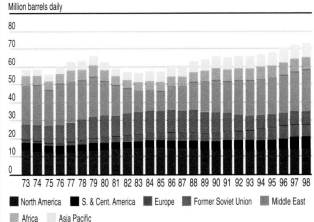

Source: adapted from *BP Statistical Review of World Energy*.
Figure 65.8 *Supply of oil, production by area*

Summary

1. Consumer sovereignty exists when consumer choices determine the allocation of resources in the economy.
2. Consumer sovereignty can only fully exist if there is perfect information in the market.
3. Consumers are less likely to possess perfect information if they make infrequent purchases, if goods are technically complex, if time and risk are elements of the purchase and if the product is heavily advertised.
4. Advertising can be informative or persuasive. The former increases knowledge in the market. The latter is intended to manipulate consumer preferences.
5. Governments can increase consumer sovereignty by passing laws and increasing the availability of information in the market.

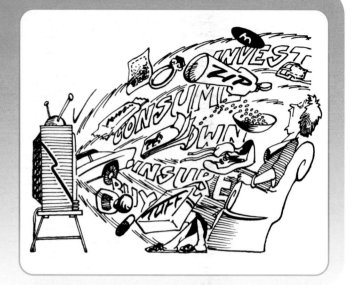

Consumer sovereignty

CONSUMER SOVEREIGNTY exists when resources are allocated according to the wishes of consumers. This will occur in a perfectly free market. Consumer spending is comparable to votes in an election. The companies which receive the most votes will be able to purchase the factors of production needed to produce the goods demanded by consumers. Firms which receive no votes will go out of business.

Perfect information

Total consumer sovereignty only exists if there is perfect knowledge or perfect information in the market place (☞ unit 53). If consumers are to allocate their resources in a way which will maximise their utility, they need to know about the products they are buying. In many cases, consumers are well placed to make consumption decisions. For instance, a consumer is likely to be the best judge of whether to buy bananas or apples. However, there are markets where consumers have less than perfect knowledge.

In many markets, like those for cars, television sets or solicitors, consumers make infrequent purchases. If they buy, and find for whatever reason that they don't like the product, then it is very expensive to make a fresh choice. When they come to replace an item the product range may have changed completely. This is different from markets like food where consumers are making frequent purchases. In the food market, consumers can experiment at little cost and find the products they prefer. So in general, the less frequent the purchase, the less likely it is that consumers will have built up sufficient knowledge of the product to make a optimal choice.

Consumers may not be capable of making rational choices because of the technical nature of the product. For instance, consumers for the most part are unable to tell which make of freezer has the best insulation, which television set has the most durable components, or which solicitor might do the best conveyancing job on a house purchase.

Time and risk too pose problems. Consumers often find it difficult to project forward. Healthy 25 year olds may see little point in providing for health care or paying into a pension scheme. Yet when they have a serious accident or come to retire they may think that their utility would have been greater over time if they had made different spending decisions.

There are other reasons why consumers are sometimes not the best judge of what they should buy. Some goods, such as drugs (including alcohol and tobacco), are addictive, so the consumer is unable to make a rational choice about present and future consumption. Often these same goods also create externalities, such as increased crime or road accidents, not to mention the cost of medical treatment. Society, through government, may choose to limit or ban the sale of these goods because it does not wish to pay the cost of the externality.

Finally, consumer choices are deliberately manipulated by producers through advertising and other forms of marketing.

Informative and persuasive advertising

Between 1 and 2 per cent of UK national income is spent each year on advertising. On some products, such as some brands of soap powder, 25 per cent of the cost to the consumer is advertising cost. Advertising is a cost to the producer (a cost which of course will ultimately be borne by the consumer). Therefore producers must be convinced that advertising increases demand for their products if such large sums are spent on advertising each year.

Neo-classical economic theory predicts that advertising

Question 1

(a) Why might consumers find it difficult to make rational choices about each of these products?

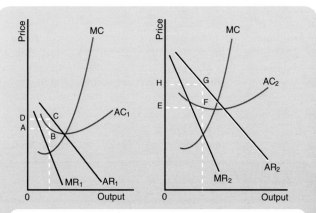

curve of AR_1 and average and marginal cost curves of AC_1 and MC. A successful advertising campaign will push the firm's demand curve to the right to AR_2. The advertising campaign will cost money. It is debatable as to whether advertising is a fixed or variable cost, but here we will assume that it is a fixed cost. Hence the marginal cost curve will stay the same but average total cost will rise to AC_2. (The analysis is fundamentally no different if advertising is treated as a variable cost which consequently raises marginal cost too.) It can be seen that monopoly profits rise from ABCD to EFGH. The extra revenue generated as a result of the advertising campaign has been greater than the cost of the advertising campaign and the extra costs of production.

Two types of advertising can be distinguished. INFORMATIVE ADVERTISING is advertising which increases consumer knowledge about a product. Small ads in local newspapers, for instance, inform potential buyers that a product is for sale. Consumers may need to be made aware that a new product has come onto the market through a national advertising campaign. Firms may wish to inform consumers in local telephone directories that they supply services. In general, economists would argue that this type of advertising increases consumer sovereignty because it enables consumers to make a more rational choice of what to buy. It gives them more information about what is available in the market place.

PERSUASIVE ADVERTISING is advertising intended to manipulate consumer preferences. Most television advertisements or large advertisements in magazines and

Question 2

(a) To what extent do these advertisements increase consumer sovereignty?

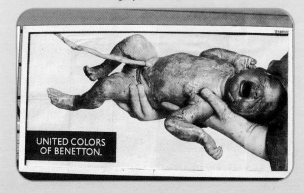

Figure 66.1 *The gains from advertising for a monopolist*
An advertising campaign which increases demand will increase abnormal profit from ABCD to EFGH despite an increase in average costs.

could be beneficial for a firm. Figure 66.1 shows the cost and revenue curves for a profit maximising monopolist. Before advertising, it faces a demand or average revenue newspapers are persuasive. These advertisements may contain some information, but the main aim is to persuade consumers that a particular product is more desirable than competitors' products. At best, persuasive advertising may tip the balance for a consumer who is undecided between alternative products. At worst, persuasive advertising makes consumers buy products they would otherwise not have bought.

Government policy

It is difficult to assess the extent to which consumer sovereignty exists in a modern industrialised economy. J K Galbraith, in his book *The New Industrial State*, argued that consumer sovereignty was largely lacking in markets dominated by oligopolistic and monopoly industries (i.e. most of manufacturing industry and much of the service industry). Producers were able through advertising and promotion to channel consumer spending. Of course consumers won't buy just any product because it is advertised. But they will buy product X rather than product Y if the producer can find the right combination of jingle, story, sex symbol or other image to associate with the product.

On the other hand free market economists argue that even if consumer knowledge is imperfect, the alternatives which involve the state deciding what is desirable or undesirable leads to a far less efficient allocation of resources.

Governments have a wide range of choice of policies to correct possible market failure arising from imperfect consumer knowledge.

Governments can try to prevent sellers from misinforming the consumer. Much of consumer protection legislation is designed to protect the consumer from unfair practices on the part of sellers. For instance, the Trade Descriptions Act 1968 made it illegal for retailers to sell goods with misleading descriptions. Government can also encourage or force sellers to provide information which they might otherwise prefer not to give. Contents of manufactured food, or 'best before' dates, are two such examples.

The government can help consumers fight more effectively for redress against often better financed sellers. Making it cheaper to take a firm to court, for instance through a Small Claims Court system, makes consumers far more powerful.

The government can also provide information itself to the consumer, or encourage independent bodies to do so. Bodies such as the British Standards Institution and local Trading Standards Departments help in this area.

More controversial are bans on advertising. Alcohol and tobacco advertising is already limited in the UK. It would be possible to introduce much wider controls on advertising, particularly to control persuasive advertising. However, governments have chosen not to, partly because of a scepticism (not shared by industry) about the effectiveness of such advertising. Moreover, advertising creates tax revenue and pays for commodities such as television services which otherwise might have to be paid for by government or by consumers. The consumer lobby is also far weaker than industrial lobbies because consumers are fragmented whilst large firms may spend considerable sums of money persuading government of their case. As Galbraith pointed out, governments can be 'captured' by industry and manipulated to serve the interests of business against the interests of the consumer.

Ultimately it may be felt that consumers are not in the best position to decide how resources should be allocated and that collective provision is necessary. Health care, education and pension provision are some of the markets where governments have decided that free markets can lead to market failure.

Question 3

Teach her a lesson. Cut out the coupon.

Teaching children about smoking isn't easy. You don't need us to tell you that.

However, our free 'Smoking and Pollution' pack should make for interesting lessons.

It's aimed at eleven to twelve year old children. It looks into the harmful effects of smoking, not just to individuals but to the environment as well.

And it comes in the form of three booklets. One for teachers, one for pupils, and one for parents.

How many 'Smoking and Pollution' packs would you like?

(a) To what extent do this advertisement extend or limit consumer sovereignty?

Applied economics

Advertising in the UK

Advertising is big business in the UK. As Figures 66.2 shows, advertising expenditure has risen broadly over time, with spending averaging 2 per cent of national income (measured by GVA) in the 1990s. In 1998, it represented a spending of approximately £240 per head, or £960 for a family of four per year. If advertising were banned, consumers would have to pay for commercial television, for instance through decoder systems as with satellite and cable television. They would also have to pay much higher prices for newspapers and many magazines. Even so, the advertising industry uses up a significant proportion of resources in the economy, resources which have an opportunity cost.

Producers use advertising because they know that it influences consumer preferences and therefore, arguably, reduces consumer sovereignty and increases producer sovereignty. For instance, Unilever, a global consumer products manufacturer, has developed the Dove brand for soap and other toiletries. In Australia, sales were stagnant and the brand was going nowhere. It launched an advertising campaign but kept all other aspects of the product the same including price, formulation and packaging. For every $100 it spent on advertising in the following two years, it found that revenues increased by $146.

Another example of successful advertising is Baileys. Launched in 1974, it is a sweet cream liqueur which initially appealed to older women. The product was highly successful, gaining 50 per cent of the market for cream liqueurs worldwide. Advertising was essential in this success. To raise sales, the product's maker, now part of the international drinks group Diageo, decided to appeal to new areas of the market. First it targeted younger women by showing advertisements of a man delivering a bag of ice to a single woman living on the top floor of an apartment block. This was backed up by a marketing campaign to the pub trade to serve Bailey's in larger measures in a larger glass with ice. Then, later in the 1990s, it targeted younger male drinkers. This advertising campaign showed a girl in a pool hall, who identifies the person who stole her drink by kissing each of her male colleagues.

Not all advertising is successful, of course. However, firms only advertise because they know that advertising has the potential to change consumer preferences. Consumers do buy products which are advertised in preference to ones which are not advertised.

Because advertising is widely recognised to change consumer behaviour, governments have been forced to regulate advertising. In the UK, the advertising industry regulates itself through the Advertising Standards Authority (ASA). This is an 'independent' body paid for by the advertising industry. It has the powers to request but not order a company to halt a particular advertising campaign if it is not legal, decent, honest and truthful. Consumers or other interested

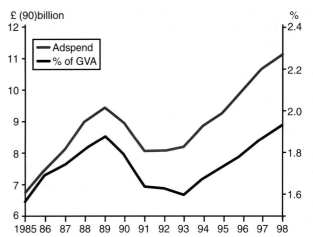

Figure 66.2 *Advertising expenditure at constant (1990 prices) and as a % of Gross Value Added (GVA) at basic prices*
Source: adapted from *Advertising Statistics Yearbook*, 1999, The Advertising Association.

parties are free to complain to the ASA which will then look at the complaint and either uphold it or reject it. If the complaint is upheld, the company will be asked to withdraw the advertisement. If they refuse, the ASA will bring pressure to bear on the company to change its mind. It will make it known in the media that the company is being awkward. It will ask newspapers, magazines, television companies, etc. to refuse to carry any further advertisements. It will also ask the Post Office to refuse to carry any advertising literature through the post from the company.

Self-regulation is cheap for the industry and for anyone wishing to make a complaint. However, there are many situations where a much tougher line is needed. For instance, withdrawing an advert does not help dissatisfied customers see firms prosecuted and get their money back. In this case, there are consumer laws, such as the Trade Descriptions Act or the Sales of Goods Act, which deter firms from making misleading claims and which allow consumers to claim compensation.

In other cases, the government has regulated advertising directly. For instance, tobacco manufacturers have long been restricted in their advertising in the UK. In 1998 the EU announced that it would ban tobacco advertising in all media in 2001. The tobacco manufacturers argue that this is a restriction on liberty and free speech. It reduces consumer sovereignty because consumers are denied access to information about what brands are available on the market. They further argue that advertising cannot increase demand for a particular type of product, such as cars or cigarettes. Instead, advertising merely increases demand for a particular brand of product. Hence, bans on tobacco advertising have no effect on overall smoking levels but do affect which brand of cigarette is being smoked. Taking another example, a ban on advertising of alcoholic drink would not reduce sales of alcohol but it would affect what type of alcohol was being consumed.

Economists would argue that economic efficiency would be increased if informative advertising were encouraged whilst persuasive advertising were discouraged. However, because it is almost impossible to draw a dividing line between the two types of advertising, it is difficult to lay down practical policy guidelines. What's more, heavy advertisers tend to be precisely the firms which maintain close links with those in power, such as MPs and government departments. 'Capture' by firms of government maintains economic inefficiency.

Tobacco

From Mr A.D.C. Turner.
Sir, Lucy Kellaway, in her article ('Fighting to the last gasp', February 8) about tobacco advertising ban proposals emanating from Brussels, asks why, if there is no link between advertising and consumption of tobacco, would the tobacco industry wish to advertise?

The answer remains as it has been over many years of a declining UK market; namely that the 300 brands of cigarettes currently on sale must advertise to retain, or gain, market share. A total ban would simply see an immediate freezing of the brand share picture with total consumption not necessarily being related.

European Commission officials appear to have little or no understanding of the role of advertising as it pertains to a mature product category.

A.D.C. Turner,
Deputy Chief Executive,
Tobacco Advisory Council,
Glen House, Stag Place, SW1.

Source: *Financial Times.*

Conservatives urge freeze on tobacco duty

The Conservatives will today set out to win the support of Britain's smokers with a surprise decision to fight the government's planned rise in tobacco duty. They will argue that rises in duty encourage smuggling from countries such as Belgium where a packet of 20 cigarettes costs about £3 compared with £3.80 in the UK. 'Small shopkeepers are losing tens of thousands of pounds of revenue, and people are losing their jobs', said Whittingdale, Tory Treasury spokesman. 'But the most absurd effects of Labour's policy are that more people are smoking and the Treasury is actually losing revenue to the tune of £1.5 billion a year.'

Source: adapted from the *Financial Times*, 4.5.1999.

World Bank debunks tobacco industry claims

Higher cigarette taxes, advertising bans and health warnings could bring unprecedented health benefits without harming economies, according to a World Bank study. By 2030, tobacco is expected to be the world's biggest killer, accounting for about one third of all adult deaths. This will be 10 million deaths a year, up from 4 million today. Of these, 70 per cent will be in developing countries.

The World Bank says that many consumers, especially in the developing world, do not fully appreciate the risks of smoking. Since most smokers start young, they may not be in a position to evaluate the risks, including lifetime addiction.

The most effective way to reduce consumption is to raise taxes on tobacco to a recommended level of between two-thirds and four-fifths of the retail cost of a packet of cigarettes. Despite a consequent fall in demand, high taxes bring in higher revenues, with a 10 per cent increase in taxation raising revenues by 7 per cent on average. Other highly cost-effective measures, such as advertising bans, health warnings and smoking restrictions in public places, as well as help for smokers to quit, could save millions of lives.

Source: adapted from the *Financial Times*, 18.5.1999.

Tobacco is dangerous

The world's tobacco manufacturers knew that smoking was both addictive and a major health risk as early as the 1950s. However, they consistently denied both, attempting to discredit scientific studies which showed the opposite. Following leaks of confidential papers from the tobacco manufacturers, they were finally forced to admit the damaging effects of smoking. Philip Morris, the world's largest tobacco company, for instance, admitted that smoking was 'addictive as that term is most commonly used today' and accepted that there was an 'overwhelming medical and scientific consensus' that smoking can lead to lung cancer, emphysema and heart disease.

Source: adapted from *The Guardian*, 14.10.1999.

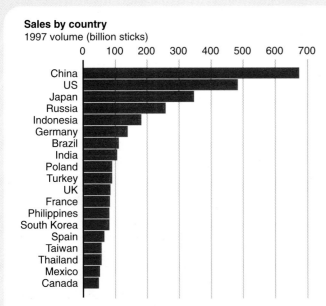

Sales by country
1997 volume (billion sticks)

Figure 66.3 *Cigarettes: sales by country*
Source: adapted from Euromonitor.

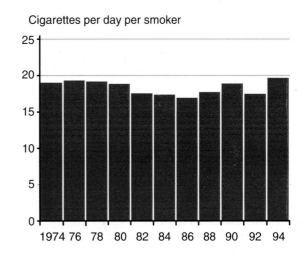

Cigarettes per day per smoker

Figure 66.4 *Cigarettes per day per smoker: UK*
Source: adapted from the *Financial Times*, 23.9.1998.

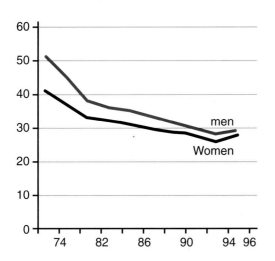

UK smokers
Percentage of adult population

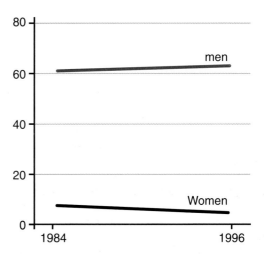

Chinese smokers
Percentage of adult population

Figure 66.5 *Smoking: UK compared to China*
Source: adapted from ASH, World Health Organisation.

Government aims to ban smoking promotion

In a White Paper published in 1998, the government announced that it intended to ban billboard advertisements for cigarettes from 1999. It was also proposed that tobacco sponsorship for sport would be banned by 2003 and a ban on advertising in the print media was being considered.

Tobacco companies spend a considerable proportion of their revenues each year on promotion. Relatively little goes on direct advertising. Far more goes on other forms of promotion. For instance, in the United States, tobacco companies hold sophisticated databases of smokers. They use these to target potential clients for new brands by sending them free samples. They reinforce existing brand loyalty by offering free gifts or special price promotions. Children and teenagers are targeted through branding by association. Joe Camel, a highly successful international brand, is also a cartoon character on television. It is also a brand of clothes. Sports sponsorship has been a highly successful strategy, associating cigarette smoking with health, fitness and machismo. In the United States, Philip Morris ran a highly successful advertising campaign in 1999 informing viewers that the company supported charities financially. Having stated that it gave away $75 million a year, the advertisement ends with the slogan: 'Working to make a difference. The people of Philip Morris.'

Source: adapted from the *Financial Times*, 11.12.1998; *The Guardian*, 14.10.1999.

Costs of smoking

Smoking is a cost to society in a number of ways. First, it leads to the premature deaths of many smokers. Second, illness and death impose health care costs, which will be met by non-smokers if tax revenues on tobacco are less than medical costs. Third, illness is a cost for industry because employees report sick for work. Lastly, smoking causes other costs for non-smokers apart from health care costs. Many non-smokers find cigarette smoke unpleasant. More seriously, repeated exposure to the cigarette smoke of others, 'passive smoking', is itself a health risk and can lead to illness and death. Those who live with a heavy smoker, or who work in a place where smoking is common, are most at risk.

1. Outline patterns of cigarette consumption in the UK and the rest of the world.
2. Explain how cigarette manufacturers promote their products.
3. Discuss to what extent (a) advertising and other forms of promotion of cigarettes and (b) cigarettes themselves reduce consumer sovereignty in the market.
4. Evaluate from an economic perspective whether there should be: (a) a rise in taxes on tobacco; (b) a complete ban on all forms of promotion of cigarettes; (c) a ban on the sale of cigarettes.

Summary

1. State ownership of key industries in the economy was the norm in western Europe for most of the post-war era. Industries were taken into state ownership for a number of reasons including the desire to achieve economies of scale, improve management and run these industries for the benefit of the whole nation.
2. Privatisation is the sale of state owned assets to the private sector.
3. A number of arguments have been used to justify privatisation including lower costs of production, increased choice, quality and innovation, wider share ownership and a reduction in state borrowing and debt.
4. Arguments used against the privatisation process include concerns about monopoly pricing, increasing inequalities in society and increasing externalities.
5. Allocative efficiency can be increased in the privatised utilities if they are either subject to greater competition or if they are regulated.
6. Deregulation can improve economic efficiency through increasing competition.
7. Competitive tendering may lead to lower costs and thus increase productive efficiency.

State ownership

As western economies developed in the late nineteenth and twentieth centuries, the role of the state grew. Governments came to intervene more actively in the management of the economy. Also, they gradually acquired ownership of many industries and became producers and providers of a wide variety of goods and services. These included:
● public goods, such as defence, police and the judiciary;
● merit goods, such as education and health;
● other goods and services, such as telephones, gas, electricity and railways - key basic industries in the economy.

By the late 1970s, state or NATIONALISED INDUSTRIES (if organised as a separate firm, called PUBLIC CORPORATIONS in the UK) played a significant role in production in all western European countries. A number of arguments were put forward as to why the state should own and run firms.

Lower costs Nationalised industries could be more **productively efficient** than equivalent firms in the private sector. Most of the post-war nationalisation programme involved the purchase of a number of private firms in an industry. For instance, before 1947 there were a number of private railway companies operating throughout the UK. It was argued that **economies of scale** could be achieved by merging the competing firms into one, dispensing with duplication of production resources. Moreover, competition with expenditure on advertising and promotion was seen as wasteful. The elimination of such marketing costs would result in even lower total costs of production. To a great extent, these arguments rely upon the fact that industries which were nationalised were

natural monopolies (☞ unit 18).

Better management Supporters of nationalisation often held a very poor view of private sector management. They argued that private firms were often run in a very amateurish way by managers or owners more interested either in enjoying a quiet life or short run profit than in the welfare of the company and the economy. Nationalisation was seen as a chance to appoint efficient modern management which would run the industries to maximise net social benefit. In some of the industries, particularly coal, there was an poor record of industrial disputes. It was hoped that nationalisation would make labour relations more harmonious because workers would see the industry as 'their' industry and management would no longer see workers as enemies.

Control of monopolies Many of the nationalised firms, such as railway companies and gas suppliers, were local monopolists. Nationalisation was seen as the easiest and most effective way of controlling these monopolies and preventing them from reducing social benefit by raising prices and lowering output.

Maximisation of net social benefit and not private profit Significant **externalities** were seen to be present in the industries which were nationalised. For instance, in the coal industry it was felt that private companies had too little regard for the welfare of their workers. The safety and lives of coalminers were sacrificed for the sake of private profit. Nationalised industries were given the task of maximising net social benefit even if this meant sacrificing private profit.

Greater control of the economy State ownership of some of the most important industries in the economy (sometimes called control of the **commanding heights** of the economy) was seen as essential if the government was to manage an unstable market economy. The 1930s, for instance, were seen as an example of the inability of free market forces to bring stability and prosperity to an economy. Nationalisation was effectively a move towards a more centrally planned type of economy. In the 1970s, a number of key UK companies, such as Rolls Royce and British Leyland (now the Rover Group), were taken into public ownership because they went bankrupt under private management. It was felt that the state had to intervene to prevent free market forces from destroying companies which played a key role in assuring the long term prosperity of the country.

A fairer distribution of resources Private firms are in business to make private profit for their owners. Before 1945 most firms were owned by the people who ran them. The family firm was the most typical business organisation. It was therefore easy for workers to see the difference in income of owners and workers. Coal miners, for instance, could compare the standard of living of their children, with barely enough to eat, badly clothed, perhaps not having a pair of shoes and sleeping several to a room, with the comparatively luxurious life-style of the mine owner's children. Capitalist profit was seen as expropriation of money which had been earned by the workers. Nationalisation was an opportunity to seize those profits and use them for the benefit of everybody in society, both workers and consumers, not just a few capitalists.

There is a number of assumptions made in these arguments which are of direct relevance to the current privatisation debate.
- The public sector is seen as more efficient than the private sector. In particular, public sector management is seen as better at allocating the economy's resources than private sector management.
- The private sector is seen as exploitative of workers and consumers. State control is needed to neutralise monopoly power and the pursuit of private profit at the expense of the public interest.
- Profit is seen more as an indication of monopoly power than as a signal which allocates resources efficiently within the economy.

Overall, there was a presumption that state allocation of resources was as good as if not better than private sector

allocation - or to mimic George Orwell (in '*Animal Farm*'), 'public sector good, private sector bad'.

Privatisation

Privatisation has come to be associated with the sale of large nationalised industries to the private sector. British Steel, British Gas and British Telecom are examples of public corporations which have been sold off. Such sales are just one part of a wider programme aimed at transferring resources from the public sector to the private sector. Other aspects of privatisation include the following.
- Sales of parts of nationalised industries to the private sector. For instance, Jaguar cars (part of the Ford Motor Company) was part of British Leyland before it too was sold off to British Airways.
- Sales of individual assets of government bodies. For instance, local authorities are now forced to allow council house tenants to buy their own homes if they wish. Government departments have been encouraged to sell surplus land and buildings.
- The creation of private sector competition to state monopolies. Regulations, often created at the time of nationalisation, prevented effective competition in industries such as telecommunications, coal and gas. Abolishing these regulations has enabled competitors, such as Mercury and cable companies, to enter markets previously supplied exclusively by public sector concerns.
- Compulsory competitive tendering. Many services, often local authority services, have been provided by public sector employees in the past. Dustbins have been emptied by council refuse collectors, schools cleaned by council cleaners and hospital sheets washed by health service employees. The government has now forced its own departments, local authorities, and other government bodies to put these services out to tender. Workers who previously provided the services have been sacked, although most have regained their jobs working for the private sector companies which gained the contracts.

Arguments in favour of privatisation

A number of arguments have been put forward in favour of privatisation.

Cost Publicly owned industries have no incentive to cut costs. The result is that there is likely to be X-inefficiency (☞ unit 61) in the industry. There is no incentive because there is little or no mechanism by which government can bear down on costs. There is also often little comparison with what costs might be if reduced to a minimum since the state owned firm is often a monopoly. State owned industries also tend to behave like bureaucracies, where the interests of the workers are as important as the interests of the owners (the state) and consumers. **Behavioural theories of the firm** (☞ unit 50) are more appropriate to understanding their decision making than traditional neo-classical profit maximising theories. A privatised profit maximising company does have an

Question 1

Amalgamation under public ownership will bring great economies in operation and make it possible to modernize production methods ... Public ownership ... will lower charges, prevent competitive waste, open the way for co-ordinated research and development... Only if public ownership replaces private monopoly can industry become efficient.'

Source: *Labour Party Manifesto*, 1945.

(a) Explain the economic arguments which lie behind the views expressed in the Labour Party Manifesto of 1945.

incentive to reduce cost because reduced cost is translated into higher profit. This is true whether the privatised company faces competition in the market place or whether it enjoys a monopoly. Hence privatisation leads to greater **productive efficiency** (☞ unit 16).

Choice and quality Public sector organisations have little incentive to produce goods which consumers want to buy. They tend to be 'product led' organisations, mass producing a limited range of goods and services which state employees feel is what consumers ought to be provided with. This is particularly true where the public sector organisations are monopoly or near-monopoly providers. In contrast, private sector firms have an incentive to provide both choice and quality. If they are in competitive markets, then a failure to provide choice and quality will result in consumers buying from other firms which do provide these. Even if they are monopolists, privatised firms can often raise prices and expand their market by providing quality services with choice. Higher prices and greater sales can then feed through to higher profits, the ultimate goal of private sector firms. Choice and quality are aspects of **allocative efficiency** (☞ unit 16).

Innovation As with choice and quality, state organisations have little incentive to innovate. Private sector organisations, however, can earn higher profit if they innovate and persuade consumers to buy more of their product. This increases **dynamic efficiency** in the economy.

The invisible hand of the market Market forces allocate resources so that they are used in the most efficient manner. Consumer spending decisions in a free market act like votes in a democratic election, indicating consumer preferences. Monopoly state organisations, on the other hand, lack the knowledge of consumer preferences to make efficient allocative decisions on their behalf. Moreover, governments interfere in the market place and misallocate resources for short term political objectives. Governments are the enemy of economic freedom because they have such overwhelming political power. Therefore, governments should have as little control over the economy as possible. Only the operation of free market forces will ensure the optimal allocation of resources.

Other considerations in favour of privatisation

The process of privatisation can also be used to achieve other goals.

Wider share ownership It has been argued that wider share ownership is desirable. In the past, share ownership has been too narrow. Only a few relatively rich people have chosen to invest their savings in shares. The result has been a divide between workers and capitalists, with some workers seeing share owners as parasites who skim off the profits which arise from the efforts of workers. In a wide share owning democracy, the distinction between worker and capitalist is not present because workers are also capitalists. Workers will be better able to appreciate the risks that capitalists take with their assets and will be able to see, for instance, that wage increases are not necessarily economically desirable. The wealth of the country will be more evenly spread and this too can be seen as desirable.

Reduction in public borrowing and state spending In the short term, the sale of state owned assets raises money for the government which can be used to reduce public borrowing for the year or even pay off part of the National Debt. There will also be an improvement in state finances in the long term if, as if often the case, state owned enterprises make losses and need to be subsidised. Less borrowing leads to lower interest repayments and hence less need for taxes, as do reduced subsidies to state industries.

Question 2

'In privatising British Telecom, we stimulated competition by licencing Mercury as a competing network. We have also liberalised other aspects of telecommunications - permitting anyone to provide value added and data services and to run their own branch system; introducing competition in paging, cellular, other mobile radio and satellite services; allowing 'telepoint' services and personal communications networks to develop; and giving choice to the public over the telephone apparatus they buy. The result is a dramatic improvement in the variety and quality of services available to the public and of course a growing and flourishing telecommunications service sector able to compete in the international market place.'

Source: Nicholas Ridley, then Secretary of State for Trade and Industry.

(a) How, according to Nicholas Ridley, did privatisation increase economic efficiency?

Question 3

Privatisation share issues in the UK, typically many times oversubscribed, have tended to favour the small investor. For instance, applicants for the minimum number of shares (often 100 shares) were often allocated all the shares they applied for. Shareholders applying for more than the minimum had their applications scaled down - the larger the number of shares applied for, the larger the scaling down.

(a) Why did the government allocate shares in privatisation issues in this way?

Potential problems with privatisation

There is a number of potential problems with privatisation.

Monopoly Some state owned industries operate in a competitive market place already. Before privatisation, British Steel, for instance, although a monopoly producer in the UK, faced fierce competition from overseas steel producers. However, some were privatised as monopolies and remain monopolies. Traditional neo-classical theory would suggest that they would then exploit that position, charging high prices and restricting output, leading to a loss of allocative efficiency (☞ unit 63). Two ways around this problem are discussed below - breaking up the monopoly and regulating the monopoly.

Equity Nationalised industries do not necessarily price in the same way that a privatised company would do. The process of privatisation is likely to lead to a change in the pricing structure. This will result in there being gainers and losers amongst consumers. There will be also be a change in equity arising from ownership of shares and payouts of dividends to private shareholders.

Externalities Nationalised industries may have given greater weighting to factors such as the impact of their operations on the environment than a privatised industry. Privatisation may then lead to greater negative externalities (☞ unit 19). On the other hand, nationalised industries may not have to conform to environmental or other legislation because the state has given them exemption. In this case, privatisation will lead to fewer negative externalities.

The control of privatised companies

As explained above, some companies or industries which were privatised already operated within a competitive environment. However, others, such as electricity, gas and water in the UK, were monopolies before privatisation. If left as monopolies, they could exploit their monopoly position, leading to allocative inefficiency. There are two main ways in which this can be prevented.

The creation of competition There are two ways of creating competition. The first is to privatise the company or industry as a whole, but encourage other private sector companies to set up in the industry. For instance, the UK government gave a licence to Mercury to set up in competition with British Telecom. In the gas industry, the government forced British Gas to allow other gas companies to supply to the industrial gas market. The second way of creating competition is to split the industry up into competing companies at the point of privatisation. For instance, electricity generation was split up into three parts at privatisation - PowerGen, National Power and Nuclear Electric.

Regulation of the industry A second route is to allow the monopoly to remain after privatisation but create a regulatory framework which prevents it from earning abnormal profit and creating allocative inefficiency. All the privatised utilities in the UK have regulators which act by limiting prices.

There are two main issues which arise from regulation. The first relates to the objective of regulation. The ultimate goal is to prevent the monopoly earning abnormal profit and to encourage it to be productively efficient (i.e. produce at lowest cost). In the USA, regulators have tended to focus on profits, limiting the amount of profit a regulated company can earn. This, it is argued, neither encourages the firm to reduce its costs nor be innovative by creating new products and new markets. In the UK, regulation has centred on prices. Privatised utilities have been set price limits but allowed to earn as much profit as they can within those limits. This, it is argued, leads to greater efficiency. If the firm cuts costs and thus becomes more productively efficient, it can retain part of or all of the gains in the form of higher profits. Equally, if the company is successful in gaining new sales and expanding its market, then it can share in this success by keeping the resulting higher profits.

A second issue arising from regulation is that of **regulatory capture** (☞ unit 20). It is argued that regulators of privatised companies can be 'captured' by the industries they are supposed to be regulating. The decisions of the regulator are often based on information which is given to them by the industry. The privatised company will obviously only want to pass on to the

Question 4

In February 1994, National Power and PowerGen agreed with the industry regulator, Offer, that they would sell off some of their power stations. National Power agreed to dispose of between 3 000 and 4 000 MW of its generating plant within two years. PowerGen agreed to dispose of 2 000 MW of capacity. This is the equivalent to six large power stations or 10 to 15 per cent of the two companies' generating capacity. The agreement was part of a larger package of measures which also included a reduction in prices in the wholesale electricity pool of 7 per cent. The pool is a market for electricity where prices are set on a day-to-day basis, depending on the supply of electricity offered by the power generators and the demand for electricity from large industrial users and the regional electricity distribution companies.

The regulator, Professor Littlechild, wants to increase the amount of competition in the electricity generation market. At present, there are only three major suppliers of electricity, National Power, PowerGen and Nuclear Electric. By forcing two of the companies to sell off some of their power stations, he hopes that new companies will enter the market.

(a) Explain what is meant by 'competition'. Illustrate your answer with examples from the electricity industry.
(b) What effect might the agreement described in the passage have on electricity prices?
(c) Why would a higher degree of competition in the electricity industry reduce the need for a regulator in the industry?

regulator information which supports the need to keep prices high. If the regulator assumes that the company is giving it full and impartial information, then the regulator can be said to have been 'captured' by the company because it is effectively acting in the best interests of the company, rather than the best interests of consumers. More worrying would be situations where a regulator benefited in some way from allowing weak regulation of the industry. Bribery would be one obvious way for the company to achieve this. However, an intimate association between regulator and the regulated company, where the company was paying the regulator large amounts of expenses, could well lead to the regulator failing to take an impartial approach to regulation.

Deregulation

Deregulation is the process of removing government controls from markets.

- The government may allow private firms to compete in a market which is currently being supplied by a state monopoly. An example of this would be if the government allowed private firms to compete with letter delivery against a state owned postal service.
- The government may lift regulations which prevent competition between private firms. For instance, the government may limit the number of premises in a local area which can be used for the sale of pharmaceutical drugs. Deregulation could then lead to the abolition of this licensing system, with any retailer free to sell drugs from its premises.
- The government may lift regulations when an industry is privatised. For instance, when coal was privatised in the UK, the regulation that no private coal mine could employ more than 10 workers was abolished.

Deregulation attempts to improve economic efficiency through the promotion of competition. This, it is argued, will lower costs (leading to greater productive efficiency) whilst reducing prices and increasing output (increasing allocative efficiency). The major problem with deregulation to date is that it has encouraged 'creaming' of markets (firms only providing services in the most profitable areas of the market). For instance, in the bus industry, deregulated in the 1980s, bus firms have concentrated on providing bus services on profitable urban routes into town centres, arguably to the detriment of country passengers. It has been suggested that one of the reasons why the government backed down on privatisation of the Post Office in 1994 was that it was feared that privatisation would be accompanied by deregulation, with the Post Office losing its letter monopoly. New private firms would enter the industry, but they would concentrate on urban services. These would go down in price, but the privatised Post Office would be forced to put up the price for rural deliveries because it could no longer afford to cross-subsidise these services.

Contracting out

The government has to provide certain goods and services because they are public or merit goods, or because state provision is more efficient or more equitable than private

sector provision (☞ unit 20). However, this does not imply that the state has to be the producer of all or part of these goods and services. For instance, in the UK the state has never made the sheets that are in NHS hospitals, or the tanks that are used in the British army. These are produced by private sector firms and sold to the public sector.

In theory, a government could CONTRACT OUT provision of all goods and services provided. It could employ private firms to operate everything from roads to hospitals to the army. This process is likely to be accompanied by COMPETITIVE TENDERING. The government draws up a specification for the good or service. It then invites private sector firms to bid for the contract to deliver it. The firm offering the lowest price, subject to quality guarantees, wins the contract.

The main advantage claimed for contracting out services is that the government saves money. It is argued that public sector provision is bureaucratic and inefficient. There is no incentive for public sector providers to reduce costs or be innovative. Competition, on the other hand, whether the contract goes to a private sector firm or a government body, forces down prices, leading to greater productive efficiency. The buyer of the service, the government, is also able to concentrate on deciding the exact specification of what is to be bought, rather than having to worry about how the service will be provided.

On the other hand, there is concern that private sector providers might fail to meet the specifications of the contract. Whilst this might not be too important in the area of, say, ground maintenance, it is obviously a very serious issue if a private firm is contracted to run an old people's home or if it is refitting a warship. There is also concern that only a relatively small number of firms will bid for any contract. If only two firms bid for a contract, there must be some doubt about whether either is bidding at the lowest price possible. There is also the danger of collusion (☞ unit 65), with private firms choosing to divide the market amongst themselves rather than compete. Finally, lower costs may only be achieved because private firms pay their workers less and work them harder than if those workers were public sector employees. The apparent increase in productive efficiency arising from the lower costs of the contract may have only been achieved at the expense of redistribution in society, with taxpayers gaining and the workers involved losing.

key terms

Contracted out - getting private sector firms to produce the goods and services which are then provided by the state for its citizens.
Competitive tendering - introducing competition amongst private sector firms which put in bids for work which is contracted out by the public sector.
Nationalised industries and public corporations - state owned industries or companies.

Question 5

Management at the Post Office throughout the 1990s campaigned for the corporation to be privatised. It nearly achieved this in 1994, but the government was forced to back down by opposition from rural MPs. Instead, the government has chosen to deregulate aspects of the postal industry. In proposals announced in 1999, the government announced that the Post Office would be able to keep a greater proportion of its profits and borrow up to £75 million without government permission. This would give it extra financial capital for investment. At the same time, the legal monopoly on letter delivery would be relaxed by allowing private sector firms to carry letters at a minimum charge to the customer of 50p instead of the £1 minimum previously. This would increase competition in the letter market.

(a) Explain what is meant by 'deregulation', illustrating your answer from the passage.
(b) Discuss TWO ways in which efficiency might be increased by the measures described in the data.

Applied economics

Nationalisation and privatisation in the UK

History

The state is responsible for organising the production of many goods and services. Some, such as defence and education, have traditionally been financed through taxes and have been provided free at the point of sale. However, there has also been a long tradition of the state selling goods and services in the same way that a private company might. For instance, a public postal service was established in 1840 which has grown to be today's Post Office. In 1912, the Post Office first provided a national telephone service. During the 1920s and 1930s, successive UK governments established the British Broadcasting Corporation, the London Passenger Transport Board (now London Transport), the British Overseas Airways Corporation (now part of British Airways) and the Central Electricity Generating Board. Local authorities also provided many goods and services such as public baths, bus transport and gas.

Up to the Second World War, government enterprises were set up on an ad hoc basis where it was felt that state provision would be better than private provision in that particular case. However, the Labour government elected to office in 1945 believed strongly that nationalisation in general was likely to be beneficial. Clement Attlee's government nationalised coal, rail, steel, the Bank of England and road transport. It created the gas boards and electricity boards that existed for the next 40 years. The Labour Party after 1951 remained committed to further nationalisation but it was not a high priority. The two remaining firms which passed into public ownership were both firms which went bankrupt and were taken over in the national interest - Rolls Royce in 1971 by the Conservative government of Edward Heath and British Leyland cars in 1975 by Harold Wilson's Labour government.

Privatisation was not even specifically mentioned in the 1979 Conservative Party manifesto. Yet within 10 years, many public sector companies had been sold off to the private sector. Table 67.1 shows the timetable for the sale of state owned assets to the private sector from 1979.

Table 67.1 *Sale of state owned companies to the private sector*

Date begun			
1979	*British Petroleum	1986	British Gas
	*ICL	1987	British Airways
	*Ferranti		Rolls Royce
	Fairey		Leyland Bus
1981	British Aerospace		Leyland Truck
	*British Sugar		Royal Ordnance
	Cable and Wireless		British Airport Authority
	Amersham International	1988	British Steel
1982	National Freight Corporation		British Leyland
	Britoil	1989	Water Boards
1983	*Associated British Ports	1990	Electricity Area Boards
	British Rail Hotels	1991	Electricity Generation
1984	British Gas Onshore Oil	1994	British Coal
	Enterprise Oil	1995	British Rail
	Sealink Ferries	1996	British Energy
	Jaguar Cars	2000+	British Nuclear Fuels
	British Telecom		
	British Technology Group		

*Partly owned by government at the time of sale.

Initially, relatively small companies with healthy profits were put up for sale. These were in markets where there was already competition. The first public monopoly to be privatised was British Telecom in 1984.

By 2000, the only substantial companies left in public hands were the Post Office, British Nuclear Fuels, the London Underground and the British Broadcasting Corporation (BBC). Of these, British Nuclear Fuels was likely to be privatised, whilst the London Underground was left in state ownership but its operation would be contracted out to private companies.

Utilities - the regulatory regime

Each of the utilities privatised in the 1980s and 1990s - British Telecom, the gas and electricity industries, the water industry and British Rail - has a regulatory body.
- Telecommunications is regulated by Oftel.
- Gas and electricity are regulated by Ofgem. This

body replaced Ofgas and Offer in 1999.
- Water is regulated by Ofwat.
- Rail is regulated by ORR.

Their task is to ensure that no firm is able to abuse what monopoly powers it has to exploit its customers. They can achieve this in four main ways - by limiting prices, prohibiting anti-competitive practices, increasing competition and setting minimum investment levels.

Price limits In the UK, price limits have been set on privatised utilities using a formula linked to the inflation rate - an RPI plus X or RPI minus X formula. Price limits are fixed for a set of period of time. In industries where the regulator expects to see efficiency gains with no substantial change in long term investment, the regulator is likely to set an RPI minus X limit. This means that prices must fall by inflation minus a fixed percentage each year. Gas, electricity and telecommunications firms have been forced to cut their prices since privatisation because of this regulatory formula. In the water industry, firms have been forced to undertake an expensive investment programme to bring the UK's water and disposal standards up to those set by the EU. Water companies were therefore allowed to increase their prices. However, in the 1999 price review which fixed prices to 2005, the water companies were judged to be able to finance new investment from existing revenue levels. Given that there should be efficiency gains over the five years, the regulator imposed cuts in prices on the water companies to 2005.

Prohibiting anti-competitive practices The privatised utilities are prone to using anti-competitive practices to protect their monopolies. For instance, the electricity generators have been repeatedly accused by industrial customers of artificially manipulating prices in the electricity 'pool' - a market for electricity which fixes prices on an hour by hour basis outside of long term contracts. By restricting supply at times of shortages, they can sharply increase electricity prices for a few hours because buyers have inelastic demand. Regulators have the power to force utilities to change their behaviour and, in some cases, to impose fines.

Increasing competition Regulators, working with the government, can increase competition in an industry by abolishing legal barriers to entry. For instance, at privatisation, British Gas was given a legal monopoly on

gas supply, but gradually it has been forced by the regulator to allow competitors to supply gas to customers. The regulator can also increase competition by banning anti-competitive practices by dominant firms.

In some cases, competition is not possible because part of an industry is a natural monopoly. Examples include the rail network, gas pipelines, the electricity grid and telephone lines. In these cases, regulators and governments have split the supply of a good or service from its transmission. Supply can be competitive, but transmission remains a natural monopoly.

For instance, in the gas industry, British Gas responded to pressure from the regulator by splitting itself into two separate companies. Transco became the owner of the pipe network and is a natural monopoly. It charges gas suppliers, including British Gas, for the transmission of gas from supplier to customer. British Gas has become one of many gas suppliers. In the industrial market, which was opened up to competition from the late 1980s, it has lost most of the market. But it was more successful in retaining domestic customers when the market was opened up to competition between 1996 and 1998. One of the reasons for this is that domestic customers are less likely to switch from their original supplier, British Gas, unless there is a substantial saving in price. There is customer loyalty. Moreover, the benefits to be gained in lower gas bills are often outweighed by the perceived nuisance value of having to change supplier.

In the gas and rail industries, the natural monopolists, Transco and Railtrack, are independent companies from product providers like British Gas or Virgin Trains. In

In the rail industry Railtrack, a natural monopolist, is independent from train operators such as Virgin.

telecommunications, electricity and water, the natural monopolists are also product providers. So, BT for instance both owns most of the land line telephone infrastructure in the UK and offers telecommunications services. Competitors, like Mercury, have to pay BT to use its infrastructure. This is a potential source of anti-competitive practices. Competitors to BT have persistently complained that it has charged higher prices than it should and has made it difficult to establish new services. These problems have had to be sorted out by the regulator.

Setting minimum investment levels In the water and rail industries, the regulator has specified minimum levels of investment. This is because it has judged that there has been underinvestment in the past. In the water industry, investment is needed to bring water standards up to EU regulation levels. In the rail industry, the government wants to see a better public transport system. Investment is an essential part of persuading more people to travel by rail.

Advantages and disadvantages of privatisation

Privatisation, although fiercely opposed by many in the 1980s, is now generally considered to have been a success. Few would argue that companies such as ICL, British Steel or British Aerospace would have performed better if they had remained in state ownership.

In the gas, electricity, telecommunications, water and rail industries, privatisation, together with the regulatory regime, has led to large falls in costs. The old nationalised industries can now be seen to have been highly X-inefficient, with overmanning a particular problem. Privatisation, with large scale falls in the number of workers in these industries and the sale of many surplus assets, has led to greater productive efficiency. In the cases of gas, electricity and telecommunications, the fall in costs has been far greater than the profits that now have to be paid to shareholders. The result is that consumers have benefited through substantial price reductions in real terms. In water and rail, increases in productive efficiency have been used to pay for investment, which increases dynamic efficiency. Quality of service has, if anything, improved. Consumers tend to have greater choice and firms are more responsive to customer needs and complaints.

However, there is a number of concerns about the privatisation process.

- The movement of share prices in most of the privatised companies would indicate that the government sold off the companies at too low a price. This has benefited new shareholders at the expense of the taxpayer.
- There were considerable productivity improvements in most privatised companies in the years before privatisation as companies were told to adopt a more commercial approach before being sold off. If

these gains could be achieved when the companies were still state-owned, why did they need to be privatised?

- The profits of the privatised utilities have sometimes been substantial, and far in excess of rates of return on capital in other comparable industries. This has been reflected in the high share prices of the companies. It must then be questioned whether the regulators have not been too lenient with the utilities and whether they have been **captured**. Critics would argue that shareholders have received far too much of the efficiency gains made by the utilities and that consumers have received too little. If dividends had been lower, prices could have been lower. The evidence would suggest that no regulator has as yet deliberately set out to collude with its industry to keep prices as high as possible. However, there is considerable evidence that companies have deliberately set out to be as 'economical with the truth' as possible, usually by providing highly pessimistic forecasts of future trends and by withholding as much data as possible. Sir James McKinnon, the first gas regulator, enjoyed a notoriously bad relationship with British Gas, as British Gas attempted to marginalise him in decision making processes. Professor Littlechild, the first regulator of the electricity industry, undertook his first five year review of electricity prices in 1994 and announced that the electricity companies would have to cut prices by the RPI minus 2 per cent per year. Then Northern Electric, one of the regional electricity companies, was subject to a takeover bid. In its defence, it predicted much larger future profits than it had previously forecast. Professor Littlechild then announced a review of his review, and imposed an RPI minus 3 per cent cut on prices in March 1995. He was criticised at the time for having listened too much to the industry which naturally wanted to present a very pessimistic forecast of future profits to him.
- Whilst services have been maintained and in some cases improved, there have also been casualties of the new commercial approach of the utilities. There has been a dramatic increase in the number of households disconnected by the water companies for failure to pay bills, for instance. Disconnecting telephones is arguably fair practice in the case of BT, but water is an essential service. Households with no water face serious health risks. Equally, the number of disconnections for gas and electricity has increased, again giving cause for concern especially where there are children in the household. Fears that services would be cut in rural areas was arguably a major reason why the government was forced to abandon its plans to privatise the Post Office.

The water industry

Region-by-region: The cost of water[1]

	1979/80	1984/85	1989/90	1994/95	1999/00	2004/05
South West	£54.57	£93.48	£145.87	£304.87	£356.00	£320.00
Welsh	£49.08	£92.77	£147.20	£256.02	£302.00	£264.00
Wessex	£57.22	£85.59	£138.30	£224.68	£272.00	£251.00
Anglian	£48.83	£93.96	£156.07	£263.16	£277.00	£247.00
Southern	£43.80	£83.84	£124.62	£198.13	£278.00	£239.00
North West	£37.90	£68.25	£110.53	£181.95	£247.00	£238.00
Yorkshire	£39.36	£72.64	£122.74	£192.51	£241.00	£210.00
Northumbrian	£48.91[2]	£74.32	£107.99	£188.28	£244.00	£197.00
Severn Trent	£40.51	£67.88	£106.30	£179.73	£231.00	£193.00
Thames	£39.05	£76.75	£101.32	£162.72	£206.00	£180.00
Retail Price Index (RPI)	100	157.4	203.0	254.0	291.8	na

1. Prices are averages
2. This is 1981/82 cost, the earliest available for the Northumbrian area.
Table 67.2
Source: adapted from the *Daily Mail*, 26.11.1999.

The regulator has announced the first cuts in water bills for households since privatisation in 1989. There will be a one off cut in 2000, followed by price rises to 2005. Households should pay less for their water in 2005 than in 1999. The industry has fought hard against the cuts, arguing that it will damage investment and lead to dividend cuts for shareholders.

Investment targets

The regulator has set investment targets for the water industry to 2005. These include:
- replacing Victorian sewerage systems and raising the proportion of UK bathing waters meeting mandatory European Union standards to 97 per cent;
- accelerating programmes to upgrade sewage outflows and extend secondary treatment (treating water as well as removing solids) to all coastal sewage discharges for populations of 2 000 or more;
- increasing replacement of lead piping to meet new EU drinking water standards.

The regulator estimates that the cost of these works will be £8 billion. The water companies have put a price of £10 billion on achieving the targets.

Source: adapted from the *Financial Times*, 26.3.1999.

Leaks

Water companies have been ordered by Ofwat to cut leaks by an average 16 per cent by March 2000. Thames Water will have to make the biggest reduction at 30 per cent. It said: 'We beat Ofwat targets for 1997-98 and are well on the way to achieving the target set for 1998-99. I am confident that we will continue to drive leakages down despite the particular problems we face in London.' It plans to finance the leakage reduction from its existing £300 million five year budget for leakage reduction.

Leakage reduction is an important part of the government's strategy for meeting increased demand from customers. It wishes to avoid politically damaging increases in supply from sources such as new reservoirs.

Source: adapted from the *Financial Times*, 15.10.1998.

Competition

Ofwat has decided to apply the conditions of the Competition Act 1998 to the water industry. Since March 2000, water companies have had to open their infrastructure to competitors. For instance, a competing water company could sign a contract to deliver water to a customer in the Thames area. Thames Water would charge the competitor carriage costs for the water. These costs would have to be the same that it charged itself for the carriage of its own water to its own customers.

1. **Explain the role of the regulator in the water industry.**
2. **Analyse the ways in which economic efficiency in the water industry has been increased through (a) privatisation and the consequent creation of firms whose aim is to make a profit for their shareholders** and (b) regulation of profit maximising private sector firms. **Illustrate your answer from the data.**
3. **Discuss whether regulation could ever be abolished in the UK water industry without damaging economic efficiency.**

unit 68 Equality and equity

Summary

1. In a market economy, there is a variety of reasons why the incomes of individuals and households differ, including differences in wage rates, economic activity and financial wealth.
2. A Lorenz curve can be used to show the degree of inequality in income in society.
3. Two types of equity or fairness can be distinguished - horizontal equity and vertical equity.
4. There can be a conflict between efficiency and equity, although redistributive government policies need not necessarily result in greater inefficiency.

Resource allocation, equality and equity

The chairperson of a large company may earn hundreds of thousands of pounds per year. A pensioner might exist on a few thousand pounds per year. This distribution of income in the economy is the result of the complex interaction between the workings of the market and government intervention in the market. Markets are impersonal. They produce a particular allocation of resources which may or may not be efficient but is almost certainly not equal. In this unit, we will consider how the market allocates resources and then consider how the market may be judged on grounds of equality and EQUITY (or fairness).

The distribution of resources in a market economy

Individuals receive different incomes in a market economy. This is because it is based on the ownership of property. Individuals, for instance, are not slaves. They are able to hire themselves out to producers and earn income. They might own shares in a company and receive dividends, a share of the profits. They might own a house from which they receive rent. How much they receive depends upon the forces of demand and supply.

Workers with scarce skills in high demand, such as chairpersons of companies, can receive large salaries. Workers with few skills and in competition with a large number of other unskilled workers are likely to receive low wages. Workers who fail to find a job will receive no wage income through the market mechanism. These workers might be highly capable and choose not to take a job. On the other hand, they might be disabled or live in a very high unemployment region. Similarly, the market decides upon the value of physical assets and the income that can be earned from them through the market mechanism. If an individual inherits a house, all other things being equal, the house will be worth more if it is in Central London than if it is in Doncaster. The rent on the house will be higher in Central London. Shares in one company will be differently priced to shares in another company, and the dividends will be different.

The owners of assets which have a high value are likely to earn a high income. The **human capital** (☞ unit 2) of the chairperson of Barclays Bank is likely to be very high and therefore he or she will be able to command a high salary. The Duke of Westminster, the largest individual landowner in London, owns large amounts of physical capital. This too generates large incomes. Some individuals own large amounts of financial capital, such as stocks and shares. Again, they will receive a far larger income than the majority of the population, who own little or no financial capital.

In a pure free market economy, where the government plays only a small role in providing services, such as defence, those with no wealth would die unless they could persuade other individuals to help them. Usually, non-workers are supported by others in the family. In many societies, the family network provides the social security net. Charities too may play a small role.

In the UK, the government has made some provision for the poor since medieval times. In Victorian England, the destitute were sent to workhouses where conditions were made so unpleasant that it was meant to encourage people to work to stay out of these institutions. Since 1945, a welfare state has been created which goes some way towards altering the distribution of income to ensure greater equality (☞ unit 69). In other words, government has decided that the market mechanism produces an allocation of resources which is sub-optimal from an equality viewpoint and attempts to correct this situation.

Causes of inequality in income

There is a number of reasons why the PERSONAL DISTRIBUTION OF INCOME is unequal in a market economy.

Earned income Some workers earn more than others. The reasons for this are explored in units 71-75.

Unemployment and retirement Not all people work. Non-workers are likely to receive lower incomes than those in work. The increase in the number of pensioners in recent years in the UK, for instance, is likely to have been a cause of increases in poverty.

Physical and financial wealth Those in society who own a great deal of physical or financial wealth will be able to generate a higher income from their assets than those who own little or nothing. Wealth is accumulated in two main ways. First, a significant proportion of wealthy individuals has inherited that wealth. Second, wealthy individuals may have built up their wealth over their life time from working or from multiplying their existing assets, for instance through playing the Stock Exchange or simply holding onto an asset which grows in value at a particularly fast rate.

Household composition How income is measured can be important in determining inequalities. An individual may earn a high salary. However, if he or she has to support a large family, then the income per person in the household may be quite low. On the other hand, a household where there are two parent wage earners and four child wage earners may have a high income despite the fact that all six adults are individually 'low paid'. So inequalities differ according to whether they are being measured per individual or per household.

Government policy The extent to which government redistributes income through taxes and benefits will affect the distribution of income. This is explored in unit 69.

The degree of competition in product markets
Imperfectly competitive markets will result in a different distribution of income and wealth than perfectly competitive markets. Consider Figure 68.1. It shows the cost and revenue curves for an industry (☞ unit 63). If the industry were perfectly competitive, production would take place where price = MC at output level OB. If the industry now became a multi-plant monopolist, output would be at OA where MC = MR. EFG is the allocative loss to society. It is sometimes called a **deadweight loss** because the loss is not recoverable. However, there is also a transfer of income from consumers to the monopoly producer represented by the rectangle CDEF. Under perfect competition, the consumer would only have paid OCFA for the output OA. Under monopoly, consumers are forced to pay ODEA.

In a free market system, monopolies are owned by private shareholders. In the nineteenth century, these private shareholders would, for the most part, have been private individuals. Undoubtedly some, such as the Rockefellers and the Vanderbilts, grew extremely rich from monopoly profits. Today, monopolies are more likely to be owned by pension funds, assurance companies and a host of other financial institutions which channel savings through the money and capital markets on behalf of wealthy and not so wealthy individuals. In the nineteenth century, elections, particularly in the USA, could be won or lost on this monopoly profit issue. Today, it is a less important issue because monopoly profits are distributed more widely through the economic system. However, it should still be remembered that monopolies effectively impose a 'tax' on consumers, the revenue being received by shareholders.

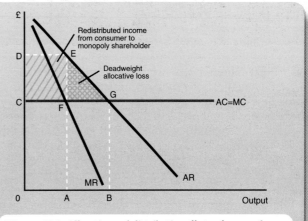

Figure 68.1 *Allocative and distributive effects of monopoly If the industry is perfectly competitive, it will produce at OB where price = MC. If it were a multi-plant monopolist, it would produce at OA where MC = MR. EFG is the deadweight allocative loss to society. CDEF is the total 'tax' of the monopolist on the consumer. It results in a redistribution of income from consumer to shareholder*

Question 1

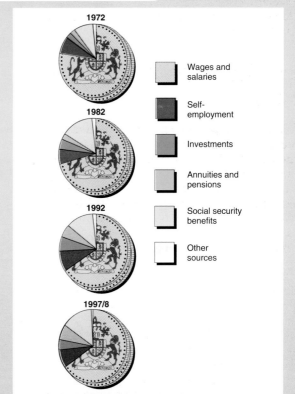

Source: adapted from Family Expenditure Surveys.
Figure 68.2 *How sources of income have changed*

(a) How have the sources of income for UK households changed between 1972 and 1997/8?
(b) Inequalities have increased over the twenty year period. Using the data, suggest why this has occurred.

Measuring inequality

One common way to measure inequalities in income is to use a LORENZ CURVE. On the horizontal axis in Figure 68.3, the cumulative number of households is plotted, whilst the vertical axis shows cumulative income. The straight 45° line shows a position of total equality. For instance, the line shows that the bottom 20 per cent of households receive 20 per cent of total income whilst the bottom 80 per cent of households receive 80 per cent of income. Hence, each 1 per cent of households receives 1 per cent of income and there is complete equality of income.

Line 1 shows an income distribution which is relatively equal. The bottom 20 per cent of households receive 10 per cent of income. This means that they receive half the average income. The top 10 per cent of households (between 90 and 100 on the horizontal axis) receive 20 per cent of income (from 80 to 100 on the vertical axis). So they receive twice the average income.

Line 2 shows a very unequal society. The bottom 50 per cent of the population receive only 10 per cent of income. Therefore half of all households receive one-fifth (10 ÷ 50) of average income. The top 10 per cent of income earners, on the other hand, earn 60 per cent of all income (from 40 to 100 on the vertical axis). That means the top 10 per cent earn 6 times the average income.

These two examples taken together show that the farther the Lorenz curve is from the 45° line, the greater the income inequality in society.

Inequality is sometimes discussed in terms of ABSOLUTE and RELATIVE POVERTY. Absolute poverty occurs when human beings are not able to consume sufficient **necessities** to maintain life. Human beings who are homeless or malnourished suffer from absolute poverty. Absolute poverty can be eradicated from society. In the UK today there are some suffering from absolute poverty, such as homeless young people, but the vast majority of the population have a sufficiently high income not to be poor in this sense. The largest concentrations of absolute poverty today are to be found in the Third World.

Relative poverty is always present in society. The poor in this sense are those at the bottom end of the income scale. There is no exact measure of this, like the poorest 10 per cent or 20 per cent of society. But Adam Smith gave one measuring rod of relative poverty when he wrote that necessities were 'whatever the custom of the country renders it indecent for creditable people, even of the lower order, to be without.'

Question 2

Table 68.1 *Distribution of disposable household income*[1]

	Quintile groups of households				
	Bottom fifth	Next fifth	Middle fifth	Next fifth	Top fifth
1979	10	14	18	23	35
1997-98	7	11	17	24	41

1. After direct taxes and benefits.
2. Figures may not add up due to rounding.
Source: adapted from *Social Trends*, Office for National Statistics.

(a) Construct two Lorenz curves from the data above.
(b) Has the distribution of income become more or less equal between 1979 and 1997-98?

Horizontal and vertical equity

Inequalities are not necessarily unfair. For instance, assume one worker worked 60 hours per week and another in an identical job worked 30 hours per week. It would seem fair that the 60 hour per week worker should receive roughly twice the pay even though this would then lead to inequality in pay between the two workers. Similarly, many poor pensioners today are poor because they failed to make adequate pension provision for themselves whilst they were working. It seems only fair that a worker who has saved hard all her life through a pension scheme should enjoy a higher pension than one who has decided to spend all her money as she earned it. Nevertheless, there is an inequality in this situation. In economics, EQUITY or fairness is defined in a very precise way in order to distinguish it from inequality.

Horizontal equity HORIZONTAL EQUITY is the identical treatment of identical individuals in identical situations. Inequitable treatment can occur in a number of different situations in our society today. An Asian applicant for a job may be turned down in preference to a white applicant even though they are the same in all other respects. A woman may apply to a bank for a business loan and be refused when a male applicant for exactly the same project may have been successful. A 55 year old may be refused a job in preference to a 25 year old despite identical employment characteristics. An 18 year old may

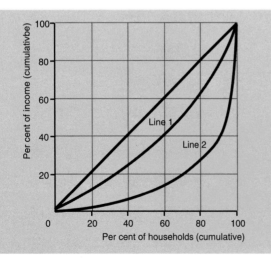

Figure 68.3 *Lorenz curves*
A Lorenz curve shows the degree of inequality of income in a society. The farther from the 45° line is the curve, the greater the degree of inequality.

gain a place at university in preference to another solely because her father is much richer.

Vertical equity Everybody is different, from the colour of their hair to the size of their toes and from their intellectual capacities to their social background. VERTICAL EQUITY is the different treatment of people with different characteristics in order to promote greater equity. For instance, if equity were defined in terms of equality, vertical equity would imply that everybody should have the opportunity to receive the same standard of education and the same standard of health care whatever their job, race, income or social background.

likely that large housing subsidies combined with no subsidies to any other goods would lead to less economic efficiency than small subsidies spread across all goods in the economy. Equally, low levels of unemployment benefit available to all unemployed workers in the economy are likely to lead to greater economic efficiency than high levels of unemployment benefit available only to male manual employees.

Question 3

Table 68.2 *Gross weekly earnings, gross hourly earnings and hours worked per week, male and female UK[1]*

	Average gross weekly earnings (£)		Hours worked per week		Average gross hourly earnings (£)		Retail Price Index (1985=100)
	Males	Females	Males	Females	Males	Females	
1971	32.9	18.3	42.9	37.4	0.74	0.47	21.4
1981	140.5	91.4	41.7	37.2	3.32	2.42	79.1
1991	318.9	222.4	41.5	37.4	7.55	5.91	141.1
1999	438.3	324.4	41.4	37.5	10.64	8.64	174.8

1. Full time employees on adult rates whose pay was not affected by absence.
Source: adapted from *Employment Gazette*, Office for National Statistics.

(a) To what extent has horizontal equity between males and females increased over time in the UK?
(b) Suggest reasons why there has been this change.

Equity vs efficiency

Governments intervene in the market to redistribute income because it is widely accepted that the distribution of income thrown up by the workings of free market forces is unacceptable. In a pure free market, efficiency is maximised because all production takes place where price = MC (☞ unit 61). If a government then intervenes in the market, say by subsidising food for the poor, imposing taxes of any kind to pay for government expenditure, subsidising housing or providing welfare benefits, it introduces a distortion in the market. Hence, government intervention leads to allocative inefficiency.

In practice there are no pure free market economies. Economies are riddled with market imperfections, such as oligopolistic and monopoly industries, monopoly unions and externalities. The theory of the second best shows that introducing another distortion, such as welfare payments to the poor, may in fact lead to greater economic efficiency. The theory suggests that efficiency will be greatest if the distortion is spread thinly across many markets rather than concentrated on a few markets. For instance, it is

Question 4

In 1976, the government replaced a scheme whereby a few per cent of handicapped people received specially adapted small cars, by Mobility Allowance, a benefit which all handicapped people with mobility problems would receive. Those who used to receive a car complained bitterly because the new Mobility Allowance was only a fraction of what a car cost to buy and run.

To what extent did the change described lead to (a) greater equity and (b) greater efficiency?

key terms

Absolute poverty - absolute poverty exists when individuals do not have the resources to be able to consume sufficient necessities to survive.
Equity - fairness.
Horizontal equity - the identical treatment of identical individuals or groups in society in identical situations.
Lorenz curve - shows the extent of inequality of income in society.
Personal distribution of income - the distribution of the total income of all individuals.
Relative poverty - poverty which is defined relative to existing living standards for the average individual.
Vertical equity - the different treatment of individuals or groups which are dissimilar in characteristics.

Applied economics

The distribution of income and wealth in the UK

The distribution of income

Income is distributed unevenly in the UK. Table 68.3 gives three measures of distribution of income between households. Original income is the gross income of households from sources such as wages and salaries, private pensions and investment income. Disposable income is gross income after income tax and National Insurance contributions have been paid but including state welfare benefits such as unemployment benefit, family credit and the state old age pension. Final income is disposable income minus indirect taxes such as VAT, but including the value of state services such as education and the National Health Service.

Table 68.3 *Distribution of income*[1]

	Percentage of total					
	Bottom fifth	Next fifth	Middle fifth	Next fifth	Top fifth	Total
Original income						
1976	4	10	18	26	43	100
1997/98	2	7	15	25	51	100
Disposable income						
1976	10	14	18	23	36	100
1997/98	8	12	16	23	42	100
Final income						
1976	10	14	18	23	36	100
1997/98	10	12	17	23	38	100

1. Figures may not add up to 100 due to rounding.
Source: adapted from *Social Trends*, Office for National Statistics.

The statistics give an indication of the extent of inequality in income. For instance, in 1997/98, the bottom 20 per cent of households (mostly pensioner households and those with unemployed adults) received only 2 per cent of total original income generated in the UK. That means that each household received just 0.1 (2 ÷ 20) of average income in the UK. In comparison, the top 20 per cent of households received 51 per cent of total UK original income. On average each of these households received 2.55 times (51 ÷ 20) the average income.

In a welfare state, it should be expected that the distribution of disposable income and final income would show less inequality than original income. Taxes should fall most heavily on the better off whilst benefits should be received mainly by the poorer sections of society. Table 68.3 shows that to some extent this is true in the UK. The share of disposable income of the bottom 20 per cent of households was 8 per cent in 1997/98 (compared to 2 per cent of original income). That means that the average household in the bottom 20 per cent

received 0.4 (8 ÷ 20) of the average income. The share of the top 20 per cent of households was 42 per cent giving the average household 2.1 times the average income in the UK. Figures for final income (disposable income minus indirect taxes such as VAT plus the value of benefits in kind such as education and the NHS) differ little compared to disposable income although the bottom 20 per cent of households show some increase in their share of income under this measure.

It should be remembered that there will be considerable variation in income within each of the quintile groups (groups of 20 per cent). For instance, in the bottom quintile there will be some households whose final income will be markedly less than the average for the group. On the other hand in the top quintile there will be a few who will earn hundreds of times the national average income. Equally, the statistics say nothing about how many people live in a household. A one person household in the bottom quintile may have a higher income per person than a six person household in the middle quartile.

Trends in the distribution of income

For most of this century, the long term trend has been for income differentials to narrow. Since 1979, this trend has been reversed. Figure 68.4 shows that in the 1980s the poorest 10 per cent of households saw only a six per cent increase in their real household disposable income. In contrast, average incomes for the top 10 per cent of households rose 46 per cent. In the 1990s, increases in income have been spread more evenly between income groupings. Even so, household disposable income was less equally spread by the end of the century than it was

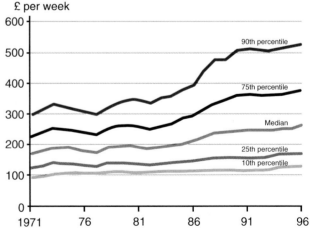

Figure 68.4 *Real household disposable income*
Source: adapted from *Social Trends*, Office for National Statistics.

in 1980.

There is a number of reasons why this occurred. First, wage inequalities have widened. In 1999, the real hourly wage rate for men in the bottom tenth of the earnings league was 61 per cent higher than the 1979 level. In contrast, the wages of the top 10 per cent had increased by over 97 per cent of the same period. Why wage inequalities have increased is debatable. However, it is likely to have something to do with the fall in demand for unskilled labour in an economy which is becoming more and more capital intensive, the decrease in trade union power which previously had helped lift the wages of the low paid, and the increased internationalisation of the UK economy which puts unskilled labour in direct competition with unskilled labour in the third world.

Second, there has been a growth in occupational pension income. These are incomes paid by pension schemes to former employers. High income earners tend to be part of occupational pension schemes. When they retire, they tend to be relatively well off. Low income earners, on the other hand, are often not offered membership of such schemes. When they retire, they have to rely almost entirely on the state pension scheme. Since 1981, this has only grown in line with inflation. Hence, there is a growing inequality between pensioners who rely on the flat rate state pension which is not growing at all in real terms, and those who retire on occupational schemes which are linked to rises in earnings.

Third, since 1979, the government has limited increases in state benefits, the most important source of income to the bottom 20 per cent of income earners. Broadly, benefits have not been increased in real terms at all, whilst some benefit rates have been cut or even abolished. In contrast, income tax rates have fallen. The largest falls, particularly for high income earners, occurred during the Thatcher years of the 1980s when the top rate of tax was cut from 83 per cent to 60 per cent in 1979 and then to 40 per cent in 1987. The benefits of income tax cuts during the 1990s have been more evenly spread. However, cuts in any form of direct taxation tend to disproportionately favour the better off.

The distribution of wealth

The distribution of wealth in the UK is far less equitable than the distribution of income. Table 68.4 shows that in 1996 the top 1 per cent owned 19 per cent of marketable wealth in the UK. That meant that the richest 1 per cent of the population owned 19 times the national average. Perhaps even more surprising is that half the population owned just 7 per cent of the nation's wealth. Each person on average in the bottom 50 per cent owned a mere 0.14 of the average wealth per person in the UK. The single most important divide today between 'rich' and 'poor' is home ownership. Approximately one-third of marketable wealth, according to *Social Trends,* is now made up of the value of owner occupied houses.

Table 68.4 *Distribution of wealth*

Percentage of marketable wealth owned by:	1911	1954	1971	1981	1991	1996
Most wealthy 1%	69	43	31	21	17	19
Most wealthy 5%	-	-	52	40	35	39
Most wealthy 10%	92	79	65	54	47	52
Most wealthy 25%	-	-	86	77	71	74
Most wealthy 50%	-	-	97	94	92	93
Least wealthy 50%	-	-	3	6	8	7

Source: adapted from *Social Trends*, Office for National Statistics.

Horizontal equity

Horizontal inequity exists in the UK in a number of different ways. One measure is the relative earnings of males and females. As Table 68.2 showed, there is a wide disparity between the relative earnings of males and females. Part of this can be explained by factors such as different education and training experiences, different age compositions of the male and female workforce and the loss of work experience by women during the crucial years when they might leave the workforce to raise children. However, despite equal pay legislation, it is unlikely that all of the difference in pay between males and females can be explained in this way and therefore horizontal inequity can be said to exist between males and females.

Table 68.5 *Distribution of household income by region, 1995-1998*

	Average gross weekly household income (£)
London	491
South East	474
UK	408
East	419
South West	405
East Midlands	401
North West	384
West Midlands	381
Scotland	371
Wales	360
Yorkshire and Humber	360
Northern Ireland	336
North East	333

Source: adapted from *Regional Trends*, Office for National Statistics.

Another measure of horizontal inequity is the North-South divide in the UK. Table 68.5 shows average annual income per week per household in the UK between 1995-1998. The South East had the highest income whilst the North East of England had the lowest. The difference in real income is likely to be less than that implied by Table 68.5 because of lower prices, for instance for houses in areas outside the South.

Table 68.6 points to another aspect of horizontal

inequity. Children are disproportionally represented in low income households. Nearly one third of children in 1996-97 were being brought up in households in the bottom fifth of income groupings. Women are also less likely to be in a high income grouping than males. Partly this occurs because women are less likely to work than males, particularly when there are young children in the family.

Table 68.6 *People in households: by gender and income grouping, 1996-97*

United Kingdom				Percentages
	Men	Women	Children	All
Income grouping				
Bottom fifth	16	19	29	20
Next fifth	17	20	21	19
Middle fifth	21	21	20	21
Next fifth	23	21	18	21
Top fifth	23	19	13	19
All	100	100	100	100

Source: adapted from *Social Trends*, Office for National Statistics.

Absolute and relative poverty

Absolute poverty is rare in the UK. The main indicator of absolute poverty in the UK is homelessness which has grown over the past 20 years. If there is little absolute poverty in the UK, there is, by the definition of the term, relative poverty. The extent of relative poverty is difficult to gauge. One common measure is to see how many people are living at or below the minimum income set by government for the receipt of means tested benefits. Table 68.7 shows numbers claiming a

variety of different benefits. Income support is paid to those out of work (including retired people). Family credit is paid to those in low paid jobs. Housing benefit is paid to any household on a low income. Each claimant of benefit is likely to have dependants, so the total number of people in poverty is much higher than the number receiving benefit. Many benefits also have low take-up rates. On the government's own estimates produced by the DSS, there were 6 million people in relative poverty in 1979, 8.8 million in 1983 and over 11 million today.

There are those who point out that using benefit levels to define poverty has the perverse effect of increasing poverty when benefits are raised whilst reducing poverty when benefits are lowered. It is also pointed out that relative to our Victorian ancestors, nearly all in society today enjoy a very high standard of living. However, relative poverty is most commonly defined in terms of poverty relative to the average in the society of the day. The evidence shows that there has been an increase in relative poverty since 1979.

Table 68.7 *Number of people in receipt of selected social security benefits*

			Millions
	1979-80	1988-89	1997
Supplementary pensions and supplementary benefit/income support[1]	2.92	4.22	4.33
Family income supplement/ family credit[1]	0.08	0.29	0.81
Housing benefit	1.43	4.03	4.64

1. Major reforms of the benefit system in April 1988 saw supplementary pensions and supplementary benefits replaced by income support whilst family income supplement was replaced by family credit.

Source: adapted from *Social Trends*, Office for National Statistics.

The distribution of income

Life changes

Change can have an important effect on your income. For instance, the Institute for Social and Economic Research (ISER) has produced evidence (see Table 68.9) that more than half of females who separate from their partner see a significant fall in their income. They fall down the income league by at least one quintile. Splitting up is likely to be less harmful to income if you

are a male. Only one quarter of males move into a lower quintile grouping after a break up. The other single most important factor which is likely to lead to a loss of income is moving away from home. Over half of children who leave the parental home fall down the income league by at least one quintile.

Table 68.8 *Distribution of equivalised disposable income: by family type, 1996-97*

Great Britain   Percentages

	Bottom fifth	Next fifth	Middle fifth	Next fifth	Top fifth	All (=100%) (millions)
Pensioner couple	23	29	21	15	12	5.1
Single pensioner	25	33	21	13	7	4.1
Couple with children	19	17	24	22	17	17.2
Couple without children	10	11	16	26	38	10.5
One adult with children	42	35	14	6	3	4.6
One adult without children	18	17	19	22	24	8.2
All individuals	20	20	20	20	20	49.7

Source: adapted from *Social Trends* , Office for National Statistics.

Table 68.9 *Adults moving within the income distribution between consecutive years: by type of household change, 1991-1996*

Great Britain   Percentages

	Income fell 1 or more quintiles	Income stable	Income rose 1 or more quintiles
No change	19	61	21
Birth only	32	54	14
Adult child departs only	26	47	27
Death of partner only	21	35	44
Child leaving parental home[1]	53	25	22
Join with partner			
Males	32	43	25
Females	21	37	42
Seperate from partner[2]			
Males	25	41	34
Females	52	29	19
Other changes	25	44	31
All adults	21	58	22

1. Change in income group experienced by the departing child. Excludes those who join with a partner in the same year.
2. Excluding those who separate and join with another partner in the same year.
Source: adapted from *Social Trends 1999*, Office for National Statistics.

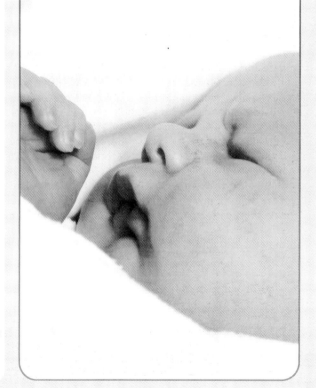

1. What type of individuals according to the data experience: (a) low incomes and (b) high incomes?
2. Analyse whether the data suggests that there is:
   (a) horizontal equity and (b) vertical equity in the UK.
3. Since the mid-1980s, UK governments have encouraged working individuals to make private provision for their pensions. Discuss whether this is likely to reduce poverty in the UK in the next 50 years.

Summary

1. Governments redistribute income and wealth because they believe that this will increase economic welfare.
2. They can do this through fiscal means, raising taxes from the relatively well off to spend on services and benefits for the relatively less well off.
3. Governments can also legislate to promote greater equality, for instance through passing equal pay legislation or imposing minimum wages.
4. Some economists argue that redistribution gives rise to large welfare losses. These include lower economic growth and higher unemployment.

They conclude that the poor would be better off in the long term without any redistribution of income and wealth by government.

5. Other economists argue that there is little or no evidence to suggest that economies where government redistributes a considerable proportion of income and wealth perform any differently from more free market economies.
6. Critics of the market approach reply that many groups in society, such as the handicapped and the elderly, can only enjoy rising living standards if government deliberately intervenes in their favour.

The distribution of income and wealth

Free market forces give rise to a particular distribution of income and wealth in society. This distribution is unlikely to be either **efficient** or **equitable**. In units 15-21 and 61-67, the causes of inefficiency in a market economy, were outlined as were the government policies which might correct this **market failure**. This unit outlines how government might intervene to make the distribution of income and wealth in society more equitable.

The current distribution of income and wealth can be seen by government as undesirable for various reasons.

- **Absolute poverty** (☞ unit 68 for a definition of this and other terms used in this section). Absolute poverty may exist in society. At the extreme, people may be dying on the streets for want of food, shelter or simple medicines.
- **Relative poverty** may be considered too great. The government may consider the gap between rich and poor in society to be too wide.
- **Horizontal equity may not exist**. For instance, men may be paid more for doing the same jobs as women. Workers from ethnic minority groups may be discriminated against in employment and housing.
- The current distribution may be seen to conflict with considerations of **economic efficiency**. For instance, it might be argued that income and wealth differentials need to be increased in order to provide incentives for people to work harder.

The first three of the above arguments suggest that income and wealth differentials should be narrowed. In recent years, however, **supply side economists** (☞ unit 38) have argued strongly that income differentials need to be widened if economic growth is to be increased.

How can governments change the distribution of income and wealth in society?

Government expenditure

Government expenditure can be used to alter the distribution of income. One obvious way is for

Question 1

The government is proposing to move towards a system of road pricing in the UK in an attempt to solve problems of congestion on British roads. There is a variety of technologies available which might be used, one of which is a meter installed in a car which would read signals from road side beacons or gantries across the road. There is also a variety of possible metering tariffs. One is that road users will be charged for the use of roads only when roads are congested or likely to be congested. For instance, motorists might be charged to use main roads into town and city centres at peak rush hour times or cities might charge motorists to use roads in the centre at any time of the day. Congested motorways, such as the M25, might be tolled for much of the day.

(a) To what extent is access to a road system which is free at the point of use an issue of equality of opportunity?
(b) How would the distribution of income change if the government imposed congestion metering whilst at the same time: (i) cutting the basic rate of income tax by the amount raised in the new road taxes; (ii) using the money raised from the new road taxes to subsidise public transport?

government to provide monetary benefits to those requiring financial support. Social security and National Insurance benefits now account for over 30 per cent of UK government expenditure.

However, governments may wish to target help more precisely. For instance, an increase in the old age pension will not necessarily relieve absolute poverty amongst some old people. They may live in houses which are damp and cold and be unable or unwilling to pay considerable sums of money to remedy the situation. So the government may choose to spend money on housing for the elderly, for instance providing low rent housing or offering renovation grants for owner-occupied property. Similarly, governments may choose to help children in need not by increasing child benefit but by offering free clothes or food coupons.

Another important area of government activity is the provision of goods and services which give citizens equality of opportunity in society. The Beveridge Report of 1942 argued that citizens should have access to a minimum standard of health care, housing and education as well as minimum incomes and employment. Some argue that education, housing and health care are no different from cars or holidays. If people have a high income, they should be able to buy better education for their children and better health care for themselves, just as they can buy better cars or more expensive holidays. Others argue that all people should have equal access to the **same** education and health care because these are basic to any standard of living in a modern industrialised economy. Private education and private health care should not be available to those who are capable of affording them.

Taxation

The taxation system plays a crucial role in determining the distribution of income in society. Taxes can be classified according to their incidence (☞ unit 11) as a proportion of income.

A PROGRESSIVE TAX is a tax where the proportion of income paid in tax rises as the income of the taxpayer rises. For instance, income tax would be progressive if a worker earning £4 000 a year were to pay 5 per cent of income in tax, but 25 per cent on income of £40 000.

A REGRESSIVE TAX is a tax where the proportion of income paid in tax falls as the income of the taxpayer rises. An extreme example of a regressive tax was the poll tax in the UK between 1990 and 1992. The amount paid in poll tax was identical for most poll tax payers. A person earning £8 000 per year and paying £400 a year in poll tax paid exactly the same amount as a person earning £40 000. So the proportion of tax paid was different - 5 per cent of income for the person earning £8 000 a year (£400 ÷ £8 000), but only 1 per cent for the person earning £40 000 a year (£400 ÷ £40 000).

A PROPORTIONAL TAX is one where the proportion paid in tax remains the same as the income of the taxpayer changes (although the actual amount paid increases as income increases). VAT is an example of a broadly proportional tax. Whilst lower income earners spend a higher proportion of their income on zero-rated goods and services, higher income earners tend to save more of their income. Hence, the average rate of VAT paid by individuals tends to be a little less than 17.5 per cent.

The distinction between progressive, regressive and proportional taxes is made because it is important in the study of the distribution of income and wealth. The more progressive the tax, the greater the link with ability to pay the tax and the more likely it is to result in a redistribution of resources from the better off in society to the less well off.

Question 2

Between 1979 and 2000, the government introduced a number of tax changes. These included:
- in 1979, a reduction in the highest rate of income tax from 83 per cent to 60 per cent and a 2p cut in the standard rate of income tax, accompanied by an increase in the standard rate of VAT from 8 to 15 per cent;
- in 1987, a reduction in the highest rate of income tax from 60 per cent to 40 per cent and a further 2p cut in the standard rate of income tax;
- between 1990 and 1993, the replacement of the domestic rating system, a tax on property, by the council tax, another tax on property but which effectively reduced the tax on high priced properties and increased it for low priced properties. At the same time, VAT was raised by $2\frac{1}{2}$ per cent to reduce average tax bills;
- between 1994 and 1999, the imposition of a yearly 5-6 per cent real increase in tax on petrol;
- between 1994 and 2000, the gradual abolition of income tax relief given to those who had taken out a mortgage to buy a home;

(a) Explain the likely effect of these tax changes on the distribution of income in the UK.

Question 3

National Insurance contribution rates: contracted-in employees, 2001-02.

Earnings slices:
- Up to £58 a week - 0%
- £58 - £535 a week - 10%
- £536 and over per week - 0%

(a) A worker earning £40 a week would pay no National Insurance contributions, whilst one earning £600 a week would pay £47.80. Show how these figures would be calculated.
(b) Calcualte the total amount of National Insurance contributions a worker would pay if her weekly earnings were: (i) £158; (ii) £358; (iii) £536.
(c) Are National Insurance contributions progressive, regressive or proportional over the weekly income range: (i) £40 to £158; (ii) £158 to £358; (iii) £358 to £536; (iv) £536 to £600?

Legislation

The government may alter the distribution of income directly through its spending and taxation decisions. However, it can also influence the behaviour of private economic agents through legislation. For instance, governments may choose to introduce minimum wage legislation (☞ unit 75), forcing employers to increase rates of pay for the lowest paid workers. They may also choose to make discrimination illegal through measures such as equal pay legislation, or they may force employers to provide benefits such as sickness benefit, pensions and medical care for their employees, or redundancy payments. They may attempt to raise the incomes of the low paid and the unemployed through effective retraining or helping workers to be more mobile geographically.

The costs of redistribution

Intervention in the economy may well lead to higher economic welfare for some, but it may also lead to lower economic welfare for others.

There is an obvious cost to those in society who lose directly from increased taxation. Some economists argue that any taxation results in a loss of freedom. The taxpayer loses the ability to choose how to allocate those scarce resources which are now being expropriated by the state. Therefore in a free society taxation should be kept to an absolute minimum. On the other hand, THE LAW OF DIMINISHING MARGINAL UTILITY would suggest that taking resources away from an affluent individual to give to a poor person will lead to an increase in the combined utility of the two individuals. This law states that the higher the spending of individuals, the less utility or satisfaction they get by spending an extra pound. For instance, an extra £10 a week to a poor family would give them more utility than getting an extra £10 a week having suddenly won £1 million on the lottery. The law implies, for instance, that £1 spent on a coffee by a high income earner in the UK gives less utility than £1 spent on food by a poor individual in Bangladesh. So the implication is that redistributing income from the rich to the poor increases total utility because the loss of utility by the rich person will be less than the gain in utility by the poor person. One of the problems with this approach is that the law of marginal utility refers specifically to spending changes by a single individual. One pound is worth less to an individual earning £1 million a year than if she were only earning £5 000 a year. The law in its strictest sense cannot be used to compare income changes between individuals because it is not possible to make direct utility comparisons between individuals.

Classical or supply side economists would suggest that redistribution involves heavy costs in terms of economic growth and employment. Raising income tax rates lowers the incentives of those in employment to work (☞ unit 38) thus reducing the rate at which the aggregate supply curve shifts to the right. Classical economists would also argue that redistribution reduces the incentive of those out of work to find jobs. High unemployment benefits can make it more worthwhile to remain unemployed than to gain employment. This raises the natural rate of

unemployment and depresses the level of output in the economy. Minimum wage legislation and equal pay legislation may lead to a loss of employment. Economic theory suggests that if firms are forced to pay higher wages, they will employ fewer staff. High tax rates can lead to a flight of capital and labour from an economy. Individual entrepreneurs may choose to leave the country, taking their money and skills with them. Firms may choose to locate abroad to take advantage of lower tax rates, leading to a loss of domestic jobs and income.

There is also a host of other distortions which become endemic in the system. For instance, some have argued that subsidies to home owners through mortgage income tax relief have led to too great an investment in the housing stock of the country at the expense of investment in wealth-creating industry. Provision of free children's school clothing can lead to some parents selling the

Question 4

Table 69.1 *Shares of total income tax liability*

United Kingdom					Percentages
	1976-77	1981-82	1986-87	1992-93	1997-98
Top 1 per cent	11	11	14	16	20
Top 5 per cent	25	25	29	33	37
Top 10 per cent	35	35	39	44	48
Next 40 per cent	45	46	43	43	40
Lowest 50 per cent	20	19	16	13	12

Source: adapted from *Social Trends*, Office for National Statistics.

During the 1980s, rates of income tax were lowered. The highest rate of tax effective in 1976-77 was 83 per cent. This was lowered to 60 per cent in 1979 and then 40 per cent in 1987. The basic rate of tax fell during the same period from 33 per cent to 25 per cent. In the 1990s, the basic rate fell to 23 per cent whilst a reduced starting rate of tax of 10 per cent was introduced. However, several tax allowances, amounts of income on which no tax was paid, were abolished. In particular, the allowance given to married people was phased out, as were income tax subsidies on the purchase of homes.

(a) (i) Explain why large cuts in income tax rates on the better off might lead to falls in the proportion of income tax paid by high earners.
　　(ii) What actually happened to the proportion of income tax paid by high earners in the 1980s?
　　(iii) Suggest TWO reasons why this might have happened and briefly discuss whether it led to an increase in economic welfare.
(b) (i) Why might the abolition of tax allowances on the purchase of homes help explain the trends in income tax paid in the 1990s?
　　(ii) Discuss briefly whether this might have led to an increase in economic welfare.

clothing immediately and using the money for other purposes. High taxes lead to the growth of tax avoidance and evasion where a considerable amount of resources is devoted to circumventing tax legislation.

The role of government

Free market economists argue that the costs of government intervention are extremely large. They are so large in fact that any possible welfare benefits resulting from the redistribution of income from the rich to the poor are far outweighed by the welfare losses which result. They argue that economic growth will increase if taxation is low, if government regulation of the economic activities of the private sector is minimal and if state production of goods and services is kept to the barest minimum. The poor may lose out because there will be little in the way of state benefits. But they will be more than compensated for this through increased economic growth. The wealth generated by the better off in society will **trickle down** to the less fortunate. For instance, the poor would be better off receiving 10 per cent of a 'national cake' of £20 bn than 15 per cent of a cake of only £10 bn.

The argument that the poor would be better off if income differentials were wider rather than narrower is dependent upon a number of propositions:
- that being better off is a matter of absolute quantities rather than relative quantities;
- it must be true that high marginal income tax rates are a disincentive to work and to enterprise;
- a generous benefit system must act as a disincentive to work;
- there must be a mechanism through which increased wealth in society will benefit not just the rich but also the poor, particularly those who for whatever reason are unable to work.

This could be the case for many employed people but there is no mechanism apart from charity in a free market economy for groups such as the handicapped, the sick and the elderly to benefit from increased prosperity enjoyed by the rest of society.

key terms

The law of diminishing marginal utility - for an individual, the satisfaction derived from consuming an extra unit of a good falls the greater the consumption of the good.

Progressive, regressive and proportional taxes - taxes where the proportion of income paid in tax rises, falls or remains the same respectively as income rises.

Question 5

In 1989, the Methodist Conference, the governing body of the Methodist church, attacked the government's 'divisive' social and economic policies which victimised the poor. In reply, the then Prime Minister, Margaret Thatcher, stated: 'Over the past decade living standards have increased at all points of the income distribution - that includes the poorest.'

'After allowing for inflation, a married man with two children who is in the lowest tenth of earnings has seen his take-home pay go up by 12.5 per cent'.

'Of course some have, through their own endeavours and initiative, raised their living standards further. They are also paying more in taxes, and those who earn most are contributing a higher proportion of the total that government receives from income tax'.

'You equate wealth with selfishness. But it is only through the creation of wealth that poverty can be assisted.'

'Our task is to enlarge opportunity so that more and more people may prosper.'

(a) Over the 1980s, the distribution of income became more unequal. Explain how Margaret Thatcher defended this in her reply to the Methodist Conference.

Applied economics

Redistributive policies in the UK

Taxation and spending

The Welfare State, whose foundations were laid down by Clement Attlee's Labour administration of 1945-51, should ensure that every citizen of the UK enjoys a minimum standard of living. To achieve this, higher income earners are taxed more than lower income earners and the money is used to provide a variety of benefits in kind and in cash.

Table 69.2 is an ONS (Office for National Statistics) estimate of how this redistribution affects incomes. It is based on figures from the Family Expenditure Survey, a yearly sample of approximately 7 000 households in the UK. The households have been split into quintile groups (i.e. fifths) according to original incomes of households. For instance, the bottom fifth of

Table 69.2 *Redistribution of income through taxes and benefits, 1997-98*

£ per year and percentages

	Quintile groups of households[1]					
	Bottom fifth	Next fifth	Middle fifth	Next fifth	Top fifth	All households
Average per household						
Wages and salaries	1 510	4 680	12 090	20 780	35 110	14 830
Imputed income from benefits in kind	10	30	90	320	1 010	290
Self-employment income	320	570	1 070	1 700	5 580	1 850
Occupational pensions, annuities	300	940	1 500	2 060	2 770	1 520
Investment income	220	340	610	920	2 980	1 020
Other income	160	210	170	180	160	170
Total original income	2 520	6 780	15 530	25 960	47 610	19 680
plus Benefits in cash						
Contributory	2 010	2 510	1 910	1 150	760	1 670
Non-contributory	2 770	2 490	1 680	900	360	1 640
Gross income	7 300	11 780	19 120	28 000	48 720	22 980
less Income tax[2] and NIC[3]	320	960	2 710	5 090	10 530	3 920
less Local taxes[4] (net)	430	540	660	770	910	660
Disposable income	6 550	10 280	15 760	22 140	37 280	18 400
less Indirect taxes	2 010	2 550	3 570	4 680	5 770	3 720
Post-tax income	4 540	7 730	12 180	17 460	31 520	14 690
plus Benefits in kind						
Education	1 750	1 280	1 190	1 040	640	1 180
National Health Service	1 910	1 870	1 850	1 530	1 320	1 700
Housing subsidy	90	80	40	20	10	50
Travel subsidies	50	60	60	70	110	70
School meals and welfare milk	80	20	10	-	-	20
Final income	8 430	11 030	15 330	20 120	33 590	17 700
Household type (percentages)						
Retired	38	41	27	14	9	26
Non-retired						
1 adult	14	12	11	16	22	15
2 adults	9	12	18	26	35	20
1 adult with children	15	8	4	1	1	6
2 adults with children	18	16	25	24	20	20
3 or more adults	6	11	16	19	14	13
All household types	100	100	100	100	100	100

1. Equivalised disposable income has been used for ranking the households.
2. After tax relief at source on mortgage interest and life assurance premiums.
3. Employees' National Insurance contributions.
4. Council tax net of council tax benefits, rates and water charges. Rates net of rebates in Northern Ireland.

Source: adapted from *Social Trends*, Office for National Statistics.

Table 69.3 *Taxes as a percentage of gross income for non-retired households by quintile group, 1997-98*

	Quintile groups of non-retired households[1]					All non-retired house-holds
	Bottom	2nd	3rd	4th	Top	
Percentages						
Direct taxes						
Income tax[2]	3.7	7.9	11.4	13.8	17.9	13.7
Employees' NIC	2.3	4.4	5.5	5.8	4.3	4.8
Local taxes[3]	4.8	3.6	3.0	2.4	1.7	2.5
All direct taxes	10.7	15.9	19.9	22.0	23.9	21.0
All indirect taxes	28.5	21.7	17.8	16.2	11.3	16.0
All taxes	39.2	37.7	37.7	38.2	35.2	36.9

1. Households are ranked by equivalised disposable income.
2. After tax relief at source on mortgage interest and life assurance premiums.
3. Council tax, domestic rates and water charges after deducting discounts, council tax benefit and rate rebates.

Source: adapted from Inland Revenue.

households ranked by original income had an original income of just £2 520 per year. The top fifth of households had an original income of £47 610, earning on average 18.9 times as much.

These sharp inequalities are reduced through the effects of the tax and benefit system. Benefits in cash, contributory (i.e. National Insurance benefits) and non-contributory benefits increase the incomes of the bottom quintile of income earners from £2 520 to £7 300 a year. Whilst many benefits are targeted on low income households, some benefits are universal benefits, available to all whatever their income. The most important universal benefit is child benefit.

Benefits have to be paid for by taxes and National Insurance contributions (NICs). The tax system is often considered to be **progressive**. However, as Table 69.2 and 69.3 show, it is in practice arguably regressive. The indirect tax system is clearly regressive. For instance, the bottom fifth of households paid 28.5 per cent of their gross income in regressive taxes whilst the top fifth paid only 16.0 per cent. In contrast, direct taxes are progressive. The bottom fifth of households paid 10.7 per cent of their gross income in direct taxes, whilst the top fifth paid 23.9 per cent. Overall, the tax system is regressive over the bottom 40 per cent of the income range, with the bottom fifth of households paying a slightly larger proportion of the income in tax than the next fifth. Over the 40-80 per cent of income range it is progressive, before becoming regressive again at the top of the income range. The top fifth of income earners pay less in tax as a proportion of their income than the bottom fifth.

Government policy over time

Tables 69.2 and 69.3 illustrate the position in 1997-98. However, income inequalities change over time. As Figure 69.1 (in the data question) shows, during the 1960s and 1970s, the percentage of individuals below half average income fluctuated between 7 and 11 per cent. The 1980s saw a radical change, with levels of inequality rising sharply. Partly this was due to changing patterns of pay in the labour market, where higher income earners saw substantial pay increases over the decade whilst those in unskilled and semi-skilled jobs saw little if any change in their real pay. Partly, though, it was due to government policy.

- In the labour market, government policies which reduced trade union power and saw the eventual abolition of minimum wages left lower paid workers more exposed to downward pressures on pay.
- The rise in unemployment, from one and half million in 1979 to three and half million by 1986, impoverished those made unemployed and put further downward pressure on the wages of the least skilled. Throughout the 1980s, the government allowed unemployment to rise to whatever level it thought was necessary to contain inflation. Unemployment and the poverty that it brought with it were seen as a price to pay for low inflation.
- In the early 1980s, government cut the link between rises in state benefits, including pensions, and rises in wages established in the 1970s. Instead, rises in benefits were fixed to rises in prices. Given that real wages rise on average by $2\frac{1}{2}$ per cent per year, this has led to an ever widening gap between those on benefits and those in work.
- Tax changes such as the reduction of income tax paid for by an increase in VAT in 1979, the fall in the top rate of tax to 40 per cent in 1987 and the introduction of the poll tax in the late 1980s all helped to widen post tax income differentials from what they would otherwise have been.

Since 1997 and the election of the first Labour government in 18 years, there has been a commitment to reducing poverty and inequality. In the short term, the main thrust of government policy was to encourage those out of work to get a job. More was spent on government training schemes for the unemployment. Tax credits were introduced for the low paid to increase their after tax income. A minimum wage was introduced.

In the longer term, the government wanted to increase the employability and skills of the workforce in the future through increased spending on education and training today. Education has a long payback period and the benefits of improved education will only begin to appear over the next 10 or 20 year period. The government also reformed pension provision. Its long term aim here is to ensure that all pensioners have an income which is at least 20 per cent of average income.

For those who are poor during their working life, this will be achieved through two state pensions, the existing state pension plus a second state pension. For those who are better off, the government is encouraging them to make their own pension provision through saving schemes. Either they will be part of an occupational pension scheme set up by their employer or they will save individually through a personal pension plan or a stakeholder pension plan.

The government also remains committed to targeting state benefits more carefully. This means either narrowing the number of people who are entitled to a state benefit, or means testing it (i.e. making it payable only to those below a certain level of income).

Overall, these measures are designed to remove certain key groups from poverty, in particular pensioners, one parent families, the out of work and children. At best though, such policies can only eliminate absolute poverty and reduce relative poverty. In a free market economy, too little income inequality reduces incentives to work to such an extent that the economy ceases to function efficiently. In former command economies such as the Soviet union, for instance, workers subverted the official system by getting second jobs in the illegal informal sector. Inequality is therefore desirable within limits.

Poverty in the UK

Members of a private think tank have come up with a number of different ways to reduce poverty in the UK.
- Raise the minimum wage to £6.00 an hour.
- Raise the state old age pension and the limits below which pensioners can claim means tested benefits by £30 per week per pensioner on average.
- Raise child benefit by £10 per child per week.
- Raise the jobseekers' allowance by an average of £30 per week per worker.
- Cut the standard rate of income tax by 2p in the pound.
- Cut the higher rate of income tax from 40p in the pound to 30p in the pound.
- Provide free 24 hour nursery care and creche facilities for workers.
- Abolish National Insurance contributions (both employer and employee) for part-time workers employed for less than 15 hours per week.
- Cut all benefits to workers able to work but not in work.
- Increase government spending on education and training by 10 per cent.
- Reintroduce the link cut in the early 1980s between yearly rises in state benefits, including the state old age pension, and rises in average earnings.

Key characteristics of people with low incomes

By 1994/5, some key characteristics of people with low incomes were:
- nearly 80 per cent of the population below half average income were non-pensioners (compared to just over half in the late 1960s);
- but pensioners were still disproportionately in the poorest half of all incomes; one quarter of all pensioners were in the bottom fifth of income whilst one third were in the next fifth; only 3 per cent of pensioners were in the top fifth of income earners;
- 29 per cent of children lived in households in the bottom fifth of income, whilst another 21 per cent lived in the next fifth by income;
- three quarters of lone parents and their children were in the poorest 40 per cent;
- one third of the poorest fifth had earnings; two-thirds did not;
- three quarters of those in social housing were in the poorest 40 per cent (compared to under half in 1979);
- the positions of different ethnic minority groups vary widely: two thirds of the Pakistani and Bangladeshi population were in the poorest fifth, but this was true for only 25 per cent of the Indian population.

Source: adapted from Joseph Rowntree Foundation, *Income and Wealth: the latest evidence; Social Trends*, Office for National Statistics.

Percentage of total population

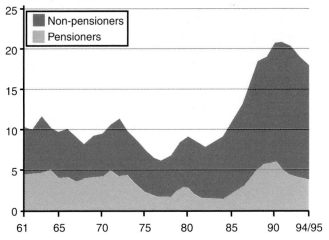

Figure 69.1 *Number of individuals below half average income*
Source: adapted from Joseph Rowntree Foundation, *Income and Wealth: the latest evidence.*

Income mobility

Those who are in the poorest tenth by income one year may well see an increase in their incomes the next and move up the income scale. According to the British Household Panel Survey, this is true for four fifths of those in the bottom tenth. However, the poor tend to remain poor. 36 per cent of the poorest tenth in Year 1 were in the poorest tenth in Year 5, according to the survey, even if in between they had moved up. Two thirds of those who move up from the poorest tenth in a year move into the next decile or tenth and thus remain in the poorest fifth of income earners. Two thirds of those in the poorest fifth remain there over long periods of time. So whilst some escape from poverty, the majority stay in poverty. The same is true for higher income earners. Less than 5 per cent of the top 10th of income earners move down the income scale in any one year. If you can get to the top, you are likely to stay there over time.

Source: adapted from Joseph Rowntree Foundation, *Income and Wealth: the latest evidence.*

The widening income gap, 1979-1995

Income differentials increased substantially in the 1980s. This was due to a variety of factors.
- The gap between high and low pay grew rapidly, partly linked to increasing premiums for skills and qualifications, in turn linked to technological change.
- There was a decline in importance of unions and minimum wage protection.
- The number of workless households rose faster than the overall official unemployment rates, with more households with only one adult and polarisation between no-earner and two-earner couples.
- After the early 1980s, price-linking of benefits rather than raising them in line with increases in average earnings meant that those remaining on benefits automatically fell further behind the rest of the population when overall incomes rose.
- Taxation had a fairly neutral impact; government introduced tax changes which widened inequality, but this roughly offset the effects of the tax system which tends to narrow income inequalities over time with rising income.

Between 1992/3 and 1994/5, there was a lessening of income inequalities.
- Earnings differentials did not widen much between 1993 and 1995, whilst incomes grew more slowly in the 1990s than in the 1980s.
- Unemployment fell and the number of income support recipients stopped growing.
- Real earnings grew little, so price-linking of benefits did not increase inequality as it had in the late 1980s.
- The proportion of new pensioners fully dependent on state benefits was smaller than amongst the older pensioners they were replacing.

Source: adapted from Joseph Rowntree Foundation, *Income and Wealth :the latest evidence.*

You have been asked to evaluate the various proposals for reducing poverty put forward by the private think tank. In your report:
1. Outline the characteristics of poverty in the UK;
2. Take each proposal and explain why it might have an impact on poverty. Assess its advantages and disadvantages as a policy measure;
3. Put forward ONE other proposal of your own for the relief of poverty and assess its costs and benefits;
4. Assess which of the proposals, or combination of proposals, is most likely to reduce poverty without imposing too great a cost on the economy.

Applied economics

Resource allocation

Resources in the UK transport market are mostly allocated by the market mechanism but they are also partly allocated by the state (☞ unit 60). For example, nearly all roads along which vehicles travel are provided free at the point of use to vehicle users by the state. The state decides what roads are to be built and which are to be upgraded. The rest of the road transport system tends to be provided within markets. Freight journeys are bought and sold between customers and transport companies. Buses charge their customers. Individual car owners buy their cars, petrol and servicing within markets. Until the 1980s in the UK, the state was heavily involved in providing goods and services to be sold in transport markets. Most bus companies were owned either by central government or local authorities. Vehicle manufacturers British Leyland, which became the Rover group, were nationalised in the the 1970s. The government owned half of the oil company BP. This state involvement has now disappeared through privatisation in the 1980s and 1990s.

In markets, economic actors allocate their resources to maximise their own rewards. For instance, households spend money on transport to the point where the marginal cost of an extra journey is just equal to the satisfaction or utility gained from that journey (☞ unit 61). Firms which profit maximise will produce at the level of output where marginal cost equals marginal revenue (☞ unit 50). When marginal cost and marginal gain differ, there will be an incentive for resources to be allocated differently. Households and firms are not able to do this, however, when the state provides a good or service free of charge at the point of use. A household can decide whether to spend money on petrol to make an extra car journey. It cannot decide whether the road the car travels along is a dual carriage-way or a motorway. Decision making in the short term at the margin can be affected by the extent to which total cost is made up variable rather than fixed cost. For instance, one reason why private motorists tend to use their car rather than the train is because the marginal cost of a car journey to them is just the petrol cost, whereas a train ticket includes an allowance for fixed cost as well as variable cost. This distorts the market as discussed in the Applied Economics section of unit 61.

In transport markets, resources will be allocated differently depending upon the degree of competition in the market (☞ units 60 and 63). Where there are monopolies, firms will tend to raise prices and reduce output compared to a situation where the industry was more competitive. There will be therefore be allocative inefficiency. It can be argued, though, that monopolies lead to greater dynamic efficiency because monopolies have an incentive and the resources to invest (☞ units 18 and 63). In the rail industry, for instance, companies are arguing strongly when bidding for franchises that they must be given monopoly rights over routes and long franchises if they are to justify spending large amounts on new rolling stock.

Objectives of transport policy

Because transport is a major item of public sector spending, governments tend to draw up transport policies. These policies are likely to set out a variety of objectives.

Efficiency Transport is typically a derived demand. Freight transport, for example, is a cost of production for a good whilst commuters use cars to get to work. Therefore a key objective of transport policy must be that transport resources are allocated to maximise efficiency in the markets which transport serves. **Productive efficiency** exists if costs are at a minimum. Journey times are a key cost in any journey. So minimising journey times is likely to increase productive efficiency. Congested road or rail links will impair productive efficiency. So too will poor infrastructure. Too many bends on a railway line or on a road will slow down traffic and increase journey times. Airports which are sited in the wrong place equally will impair productive efficiency. So on efficiency grounds, the issues of congestion and quality of transport infrastructure must be addressed in any transport policy.

The environment Transport has a considerable impact on the environment. This is because transport creates **negative externalities** (☞ units 19 and 62). In particular, transport vehicles create noise and air pollution whilst transport infrastructure is built upon land which has alternative uses. A key objective of transport policy must therefore be to minimise negative externalities. The concept of **sustainable development** (☞ unit 101) can be applied in this context. Sustainable development can be defined as the ability to meet the needs of the present generation without compromising the needs of future generations. Building a road through an area which contains the only breeding ground in the UK for a particular species of animal or plant, for instance, is an example of unsustainable development. For the benefit of present road users, future generations will not have available this particular species.

Accessibility It can be argued that travel is a **basic human need** (☞ unit 1). Everyone should have the opportunity to be able to live away from their workplace, visit friends and relations, go on holiday and be able to buy goods from all over the world. Just as everyone should have access to education, health care, housing and food, so too should they be able to travel. This means making travel available and affordable to all. For instance, poor pensioners in a rural village should not just have access to a bus or rail service but the fares should be affordable. One of the key issues about road pricing is that most motorists, according to surveys, believe that roads should be accessible to all whatever their income. Road pricing could restrict the use of certain roads only to the better off. Transport therefore raises issues about **equity** (☞ unit 68).

Public finances Most transport expenditure takes place within markets. Customers are therefore able to choose how much they wish to spend on transport and so can allocate their resources to maximise their welfare. They cannot do this when the state provides a transport good or service free of charge, such as roads. Governments decide upon how to allocate resources in a number of different ways (☞ units 20 and 80). Extra spending on roads has an opportunity cost. It could be financed through reducing spending on, say, education or health; the government could raise taxes, reducing the amount available to be spent by the private sector; or it could borrow the money, which again in the short term would reduce resources available to the private sector. Governments, therefore, have to decide upon their fiscal priorities when drawing up transport policies.

Ideally, government will have an **integrated transport policy**. This is when policy from different transport areas is coordinated to form a single coherent policy. For instance, decisions about whether or not to expand an airport will have an impact on road policy in the local area. Expanding an airport, but not upgrading the local road system, is unlikely to lead to an optimal allocation of resources. Equally, in London, decisions about the London Underground should be taken in the context of decisions about buses, taxis, private cars, road freight and Heathrow Airport. All too frequently, policies in different transport areas are prepared which conflict with each other.

One of the problems of drawing up an integrated transport policy is that policy objectives are likely to conflict. For instance, the freight industry argues that Britain's road transport network is far too congested, which raises transport costs considerably. These costs ultimately have to be borne by the consumer. The industry advocates a resumption of road building in the UK. Environmentalists, on the other hand, argue that roads cause

considerable negative externalities. So far as new road building is concerned, externalities arising from new infrastructure are almost inevitably so great that no amount of cost savings to individual motorists or to the freight industry could outweigh them. In drawing up an integrated transport policy, government has to reconcile these conflicting viewpoints and accept that there will be costs as well benefits from any decisions made. In terms of Pareto efficiency (☞ unit 61), any change will lead to Pareto inefficiency in that there will always be losers as well as winners.

Market failure and government policy

Externalities (☞ units 19 and 62) in transport lead to market failure. Road transport and externalities are discussed in detail in the Applied Economics section of unit 62. The private sector ignores the externalities it creates when making decisions. It only takes into account its private costs and benefits. Government, however, should take into account all social costs and benefits, which include externalities. It will be better placed to make rational decisions if it has conducted **cost-benefit analysis** (☞ unit 22).

Governments can play a crucial role in **correcting market failure**. Different types of policy available to governments are discussed in units 19 and 62. They include regulation, taxes and subsidies and permits. The Data Question in unit 62 provides information about government policy and road pricing, whilst Question 5 in the same unit discusses taxing car parking spaces.

Lack of competition can also lead to market failure. Monopolies, discussed in unit 63, or anti-competitive practices, discussed in units 63 and 65, distort transport markets. Governments therefore need to apply competition policies, discussed in unit 63, to these problems. In the rail industry, the government has imposed a **regulatory regime** to improve efficiency which is discussed in unit 67.

Rail freight

Rail freight operator unlikely to meet target

Britain's main rail freight operation has admitted it will not meet government targets to treble volumes by 2007, amid criticisms of policies to cut road congestion. English Welsh & Scottish (EWS) said in 1997 that it wanted to double volumes in five years and treble them in 10, figures endorsed in the government's 1998 Transport White Paper. Instead, EWS, which carries about 90 per cent of British rail freight traffic, saw volumes rise by 34 per cent between 1996 and 1999, and is forecasting that it will grow 8 per cent per year in the medium term. This would double business over the next decade.

EWS's announcement will be a blow to ministers, who hoped to take up to 20 000 lorries off the road, cutting congestion and pollution. Last night a Department of Transport official said ministers were 'disappointed' but were helping rail freight with a doubling of grants for the industry and through the Strategic Rail Authority. The government has been criticised in the industry for recent policies, including allowing heavier 44-tonne trucks on the roads and soft-pedaling on congestion charges. Railtrack estimates rail freight could grow by as little as 3 per cent a year or more than 20 per cent depending on government policy. Critics also blame poor reliability by EWS and lack of investment, inflexible scheduling and high charges by Railtrack. Traditional industrial demand has also fallen. However, it should be remembered that growth in rail freight from 5.7 per cent in 1996 to 7.1 per cent of the total freight market was the first sustained rise since 1950.

Source: adapted from the *Financial Times* , 5.4.2000.

Railtrack seeks 25 per cent increase in freight fees

Railtrack, the network operator, wants to put up rail freight charges by 25 per cent, threatening a further blow to the government's policy of reducing the number of lorries. Railtrack proposes to double the average user charge, which makes up about a quarter of the total cost to operators, from £2 to £4 a tonne/km. It also wants to add another average £3 a tonne/km to charges on routes where it agrees to expand capacity. Railtrack is also reviewing fixed charges.

Nick Ford, Railtrack's head of freight, said that previous costs were set too low and rising volumes increased the cost of maintaining and renewing track without enough extra income. Meanwhile unit changes, including the fixed element, had fallen by more than one-third since 1994 as volumes had grown. 'We have at least to cover our total costs which are attributable to freight and we have to recover at least the additional cost of running greater volumes and capacity for that to be a rational business proposition' he said.

The news is a blow for freight operators, who have already criticised Railtrack for investing too little in making new freight paths. They argue access charges must fall to win more business and tackle growing road congestion, especially as marginal new business often demands lower prices. Railtrack admits the higher £4 change could reduce the market by a fifth, and the £3 enhancement surplus could have twice that impact. However, Railtrack hopes higher motoring taxes, rising road congestion and operating efficiency would offset the fall.

Source: adapted from the *Financial Times* , 8.4.2000.

Land Rover plans £40 million investment in rail link

Land Rover plans to invest £40 million in a new rail line linking Land Rover's manufacturing plant at Solihull near Birmingham with the country's main rail network. The scheme, which the company claims would save over 100 000 heavy truck movements and 5 million road freight miles per year, would allow Land Rover to rail freight more than 100 000 vehicles a year for export directly to continental European markets via the Channel Tunnel to Southampton for shipment to the US and other overseas markets.

The projected link, which would represent one of the biggest single corporate investments in new rail infrastructure in recent years, could lead to big transport cost savings for Land Rover, which exports more than 70 per cent of its production. Ian Robertson, Land Rover's managing director, said there would be extensive consultation on the project involving local residents, councils and community organisations. The link will almost certainly involve a public inquiry.

Source: adapted from the *Financial Times*, 20.4.1999.

Brussels aims to put freight back on track

The European Commission yesterday produced a blueprint to force European Union rail freight companies to compete and to reinvigorate a sector where average speeds have fallen to 16 km per hour. Its proposals, which include measures to harmonise a profusion of ill-matched operating systems, are aimed at arresting an alarming decline in rail's share of the freight market, from 32 per cent in 1970 to less than 13 per cent today. The proposals are the first in a series planned to bring about a single market in transport. Airlines and shipping would follow.

In tackling railways first, the Commission is trying to fend off the growing likelihood of gridlock on EU roads and protect the environment from vehicle pollution. Trains are more environmentally friendly and safer than cars and lorries. The blueprint builds on an agreement between EU transport ministers in October to open up a large chunk of the rail freight market to competition in spite of concerns of countries, including France, about the effects on state monopoly finances. The Commission yesterday defined a trans-European rail freight network, including 'all important rail corridors, ports and terminals' to which railway companies would be given access. Competition would be encouraged by ensuring a 'clear division' between the operation of railway services and the management of railway infrastructure. Existing companies will be allowed to remain intact but the infrastructure and

operation arms will have to file separate accounts. Another proposed law sets rules for allocating infrastructure capacity and charging 'non-discriminatory' fees for using it. A regulatory body would be set up to ensure fair treatment between companies which wanted to run trains over the track and the companies which owned the track itself, who in most cases would also offer passenger and freight services.

Source: adapted from the *Financial Times*, 26.11.1999.

The Transport White Paper, 1998

The Transport White Paper 1998 made a number of recommendations concerning rail freight. At present 6 per cent of total UK freight is carried by train - down from more than 40 per cent in the 1950s. This compares with 15 per cent in France and 21 per cent in Germany. Under the government's proposal, the rail traffic grant scheme's annual budget is to be increased from £30 million to £40 million. This is a subsidy payable to attract marginal users onto the railways. The government will prevent the British Railways Board from selling further land until its potential for use as freight depots had been investigated. £100 million will be provided for an infrastructure investment fund to invest in key bottlenecks on the rail network. A new regulatory body, the Strategic Rail Authority, will be set up which will be responsible for both passenger and freight services. It will be given the remit to increase the share of freight carried by rail.

Source: adapted from the *Financial Times*, 21.7.1998.

1. (a) **Outline recent trends in freight transport.**
   (b) **Using a diagram, explain who might be affected if Railtrack succeeds in putting up charges to EWS.**
2. **Explain how, according to economic theory, the following resource allocations are likely to be made. Illustrate your answer from the data.**
   (a) **A company deciding whether or not to send a consignment by rail or road.**
   (b) **A company deciding whether to build a rail link to its factory.**
   (c) **Railtrack deciding whether to encourage an increase or decrease in the volume of freight traffic using its lines.**
3. **Why might switching freight from road to rail reduce market failure?**
4. (a) **Outline briefly the government and EU policies mentioned in the data designed to increase rail freight volumes.**
   (b) **Evaluate the effectiveness of TWO of these policies in bringing about a more efficient use of resources.**

Summary

1. In the long run, the demand curve for labour is downward sloping because capital can be substituted for labour.
2. In the short run, the downward sloping demand curve for labour can be explained by the law of diminishing returns.
3. The marginal revenue product curve of labour is the demand curve for labour. This is true whether the firm operates in a perfectly competitive or imperfectly competitive market.
4. The elasticity of demand for labour is determined by time, the availability of substitutes, the elasticity of demand for the product and the proportion of labour costs to total costs.

The downward sloping demand curve

Firms need workers to produce goods and services. The demand curve for labour shows how many workers will be hired at any given wage rate over a particular time period. A firm, for instance, might want to hire 100 workers if the wage rate were £2 per hour but only 50 workers if it were £200 per hour.

Economic theory suggests that the higher the price of labour, the less labour firms will hire.

- In the long run, other things remaining equal, firms can vary all factors of production. The higher the wage rate, the more likely it is that firms will substitute machines for workers and hence the lower the demand for labour.
- In the short run, firms are likely to have an existing stock of capital. They will have to produce with a given amount of factory or office space and with a fixed amount of plant, machinery and equipment. The more workers that are added to this fixed stock of capital, the less likely it is that the last worker employed will be as productive as existing employees. Hence the wage rate would have to fall to encourage the employer to take on an extra worker.

So the demand curve for labour is likely to be downward sloping both in the long run and the short run. Why do the long run and short run demand curves slope downward and what determines the elasticity of demand for labour?

The long run demand for labour

In the long run, all factors of production are variable. A firm has complete freedom to choose its production techniques. In the Third World, where labour is cheap relative to capital, firms tend to choose labour intensive methods of production. In the First World, labour is relatively expensive and hence more capital intensive techniques of production are chosen. So in the First World, far more use is made of tractors and other machinery, whilst in the Third World, far more workers per acre are employed.

Question 1

Table 71.1 *Real gross capital per employee in the UK* (£ at 1990 prices)   £

| | Real gross capital per employee | |
	1979	1996
Agriculture, forestry and fishing	101 000	117 000
Energy and water supply	299 000	746 000
Manufacturing	45 000	95 000
Construction	16 000	23 000
Distribution, hotels and catering, repairs	21 000	37 000
Transport and communication	107 000	138 000
Banking, finance, insurance etc.	57 000	67 000

Source: adapted from *National Income Accounts; Annual Abstract of Statistics*, Office for National Statistics.

(a) How has real capital per employee changed over the period 1979 to 1996?
(b) Real average earnings rose 36 per cent between 1979 and 1996. There was little difference in this rise between industries. Assuming that the real cost of capital did not increase over this period, would a firm setting up in 1996 be likely to have used a more or less capital intensive technique of production than if it had set up in 1979? Give reasons for your answer.

The short run demand for labour

In the short run, at least one of the factors of production is fixed. Assume that all factors are fixed except labour. The **law of diminishing returns** states that marginal output will start to decline if more and more units of one variable factor of production are combined with a given quantity of fixed factors. One common example is to imagine a plot of land with a fixed number of tools where extra workers are employed to cultivate the land. Diminishing returns will quickly set in and the eleventh worker, for instance, on a one acre plot of land will contribute less to total output than the tenth worker.

This is shown in Table 71.2. Labour is assumed to be a variable factor of production whilst all other factors are fixed. As extra workers are employed, total output, or TOTAL PHYSICAL PRODUCT increases. However, MARGINAL PHYSICAL PRODUCT, the number of extra units of output a worker produces, starts to decline after the employment of the second worker. So diminishing marginal returns set in with the third worker. Assume that the firm is in a perfectly competitive industry and therefore faces a horizontal, perfectly elastic demand curve. This means that the firm can sell any quantity of its product at the same price per unit. In Table 71.2, it is assumed that the price of the product is £10. MARGINAL REVENUE PRODUCT can then be calculated because it is the addition to revenue from the employment of an extra worker. For instance, the first worker produces 8 units and so, at a price per product unit of £10, her marginal revenue product is £80 (£10 x 8). The marginal revenue product of the second worker is £90 (£10 x the marginal physical product).

Table 71.2

						Per week
1	2	3	4	5	6	7
Labour input	Total output	Marginal physical product	Price of product	Marginal revenue product (3 x 4)	Wage rate per worker	Contribution (5 - 6)
(workers)	(units)	(units)	£	£	£	£
1	8	8	10	80	70	10
2	17	9	10	90	70	20
3	25	8	10	80	70	10
4	32	7	10	70	70	0
5	38	6	10	60	70	-10
6	43	5	10	50	70	-20

It is now possible to calculate how many workers a firm will employ. The contribution to the payment of fixed costs and the earning of profit of each worker is the difference between the marginal revenue product of the firm and the cost to the firm of the worker. Assume that the firm is able to employ any number of workers at a wage rate of £70. The contribution of the first worker is £10, her marginal revenue product minus her wage (£80 - £70). The contribution of the second worker is £20 (£90 - £70). It can be seen from Table 71.2 that the first three workers each make a positive contribution. The fourth worker neither increases nor decreases total profit for the firm. The firm would definitely not employ a fifth worker because her employment would result in a loss of £10 to the firm. Her wage of £70 would exceed her marginal revenue product of £60. So marginal revenue product theory suggests that the firm will employ a maximum of 4 workers because this number maximises total profit (or minimises the loss) for the firm.

If the wage rate were to fall to £50, the firm would employ more workers. The fourth worker would now definitely be employed because her contribution would be £20. The fifth worker too would contribute a positive £10. The firm might also employ a sixth worker although her contribution is zero. Marginal revenue product theory

therefore suggests that the lower the wage, the more workers will be employed.

Question 2

Table 71.3

Number of workers employed	Total physical product per week	Total revenue product	Marginal revenue product
1	10		
2	24		
3	36		
4	44		
5	50		
6	53		

Table 71.3 shows the total physical product per week for a small firm as the number of workers employed varies. The price of the product sold is £10 per unit.
(a) Calculate total revenue product at each level of employment.
(b) Calculate marginal revenue product as employment increases.
(c) Explain how many workers the firm should employ if the weekly wage per worker were: (i) £60; (ii) £30; (iii) £120; (iv) £100.

The demand curve for labour

Figure 71.1 shows a firm's marginal revenue product curve for labour. It is downward sloping because marginal revenue product declines as output increases (as shown in Table 71.2). If the wage rate is OF, the firm will employ OB units of labour. If the wage rate rises, the firm will cut back employment to OA. If, on the other hand, wage rates fall to OE, then the firm will take on extra workers and increase the labour force to OC. The marginal revenue product curve therefore shows the number of workers the firm will employ at any given wage rate. But this is the definition of the firm's demand curve for labour. Therefore

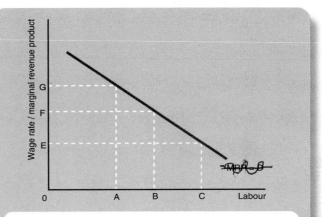

Figure 71.1 *The MRP curve is the demand curve for a factor*
The MRP curve shows the maximum price a firm would be prepared to pay for an extra unit of a factor of production and therefore it is the demand curve for that factor.

the marginal revenue product curve is also the firm's demand curve for labour.

This is true for all factors of production. Figure 71.1 shows the familiar price/quantity diagram. The price of labour is the wage rate. Quantity is the quantity of labour employed. The downward sloping marginal revenue product curve gives us the familiar downward sloping demand curve.

Perfect and imperfect competition

So far it has been assumed that the employer is supplying goods in a perfectly competitive market. This is because it has been assumed that the firm can supply any quantity of goods to the market at the same price per unit (i.e. the firm faces a horizontal demand curve). The marginal revenue product curve falls because of diminishing returns.

However, if the employer supplies goods in an imperfectly competitive market, then it faces a downward sloping demand curve for its product. If it expands output, price per unit sold will fall. Consider Table 71.2 again. The fall in marginal revenue product would be even greater than that shown if the price of the product did not remain at £10 per unit, but fell as output expanded. So the marginal revenue product curve for an imperfectly competitive firm falls not only because of diminishing returns but also because the price or average revenue of the product sold falls too as output expands.

Whether the firm is perfectly or imperfectly competitive, it is still true that the demand curve for labour is the marginal revenue product curve of labour.

Question 3

The firm in Table 71.4 produces in an imperfectly competitive market. As output increases, the price falls.
Table 71.4

Number of workers employed	Number of units produced and sold per week	Price per unit £
1	10	£15
2	24	£14
3	36	£12
4	44	£11
5	50	£10
6	53	£9

(a) Calculate (i) the total revenue product and (ii) the marginal revenue product of labour as employment increases.
(b) How many workers would the firm employ if the weekly wage were: (i) £20; (ii) £40; (iii) £60; (iv) £80; (v) £100; (vi) £120?

Determinants of the elasticity of demand for labour

The elasticity of demand for labour is a measure of the responsiveness of the quantity demanded of labour to changes in the price of labour (i.e. the wage rate; ☞ units 8 and 9 for a full discussion of elasticity). For instance, if

elasticity of demand for labour were 2 and wage rates increased 10 per cent then, all other things being equal, the demand for labour would fall by 20 per cent. If demand for labour fell by 1 per cent when wage rates rose by 100 per cent, all other things being equal, then elasticity of demand for labour would be 0.01 (i.e. highly inelastic).

Time The longer the time period for adjustment, the easier it is to substitute labour for other factors of production or vice versa. In the short term, a firm may have little choice but to employ the same number of workers even if wage rates increase rapidly. Workers will have contracts of employment. There may be severe financial penalties in the form of redundancy payments if workers are sacked. Or a firm may not wish to lose skilled staff because they would be difficult to replace. In the longer term, the firm can buy new labour saving machinery and carry out changes in its methods of work which will reduce the labour employed. Hence the longer the time period, the higher will tend to be the elasticity of demand for labour.

Availability of substitutes The easier it is to substitute other factors for labour, the greater will be the response by firms to a change in real wage rates. So the better the substitutes, the higher will tend to be the elasticity of demand for labour.

Elasticity of demand for the product Labour is a **derived demand**. It is only demanded because the goods that it produces are demanded. For instance, if there is a collapse in demand for coal, then there will also be a collapse in the demand for coal miners. This means that the elasticity of demand for labour in an industry is directly correlated with the elasticity of demand for the product made in the industry. If the elasticity of demand for the product is low, as for instance for gas or electricity, then a sudden rise in wages which pushes up gas or electricity prices will have little effect on demand for gas or electricity. There will be little effect on employment in the industry and hence the demand for labour will be low. If, on the other hand, elasticity of demand for the product is high, elasticity of demand for labour will be high. Corus Group (formerly British Steel), for instance, faces highly elastic demand for many of its products. A rise in wages not matched elsewhere in the industry is likely to increase its prices and lead to a loss of orders and therefore jobs.

The proportion of labour cost to total cost A rise in costs will reduce the supply of a product, shifting the supply curve upwards and to the left. This will lead to a reduction in quantity demanded. The bigger the shift, the larger the reduction in demand. If a group of workers gains a 50 per cent pay rise but these workers only account for one per cent of the total cost of production, then the supply curve of the product will hardly shift. There will be little fall in demand and hence little loss of employment in the firm. If, however, this group of workers accounted for 50 per cent of the costs of the firm, then a 50 per cent pay rise would have a dramatic effect on the supply curve and lead to a large decrease in quantity demanded of the product. This in turn would lead to a large fall in employment. Hence, the larger the proportion of labour cost to total cost, the higher the elasticity of demand for labour.

Question 4

(a) Explain whether you would expect the elasticity of demand for labour on North Sea oil rigs to be relatively high or low.

key terms

Marginal physical product - the physical addition to output of an extra unit of a variable factor of production.
Marginal revenue product - the value of the physical addition to output of an extra unit of a variable factor of production. In a perfectly competitive product market where marginal revenue equals price, it is equal to marginal physical product times the price of the good produced.
Total physical product – the total output of a given quantity of factors of production.

Applied economics

Performance-related pay

Performance-related pay began to be a significant way of rewarding managers in the 1980s. Performance-related payment systems link the performance or output of an individual worker to his or her wages. It had been quite common on the shop floor for a long time. Many manual workers were on a piece-rate system. The more they produced, the higher their wages were at the end of the week. Equally, many sales people have been rewarded mainly on sales commission rather than basic pay.

Such systems can be seen as an attempt by employers to pay workers according to their revenue product. For instance, if one worker produces twice as many steel bars as another per week, it might seem logical to pay one worker more than the other. If one foreign exchange dealer generates a £300 000 surplus on foreign exchange dealings over the year for his bank, whilst another only generates £30 000, then the £300 000 dealer should be paid more than the other.

It also enables companies to decide whether or not to retain staff. For instance, if a foreign exchange dealer is paid £35 000 a year, but only generates £15 000 a year surplus for his bank, then he should be sacked. Equally, if a company has five workers, all equally productive, but the output of one worker is sold at a loss, then one worker should be sacked.

Piece rates became less common in the 1980s. It was felt that they encouraged individualism. The emphasis in manufacturing in the 1980s was on team work. Japanese production techniques, copied by many UK manufacturing companies, stressed the importance of co-operation. Just-in-time manufacturing techniques, for instance, demanded that workers act in the best interests of the group, not themselves.

At the same time, there was a move away from collectivism at management level. The **entrepreneur** became a role model for many. Companies tried to identify the contribution of an individual manager or director to the business. This could then be used to set targets for future performance. It could also be used to set remuneration levels.

The 'performance' of the individual manager or director could be linked to a number of variables. At chief executive level, it could be linked to profit, share price or dividends paid. These variables are chosen because of the view that shareholders are the most important group in a company and they seek to maximise their returns on their shareholding. At a managerial level, it might be linked to factors such as costs, sales, labour productivity or customer satisfaction. All these variables ultimately affect profit, share price and dividends.

The 'pay' which is related to performance is varied. Managers and directors almost invariably are paid a basic salary. On top of this, though, they may receive cash bonuses in years when they achieve targets. Alternatively, the company may attempt to retain staff by offering rewards which can only be realised for cash in the longer term. A director may be offered shares if he or she is still with the company in three years time. Alternatively, they may be offered share options. These are opportunities given to buy shares at some point in the future at a price fixed now - usually the current share price. For instance, an executive might be given an option for 100 000 shares at a price of £3, which can be exercised in three years' time if the executive is still with the company. If the share price has risen to £5 over that period, the executive can buy the shares in three years' time and immediately sell them on the open market, making a profit of £2 per share or £200 000 overall. The justification for this is that a higher share price presumably indicates that the company has performed well over the period, in part because of the work of the executive.

Firms are willing to pay large salaries and bonuses to top staff because the demand for their labour is relatively inelastic. Whether a chief executive is paid £500 000 or £1 million is almost irrelevant to a company with a turnover of £1 000 million or £5 000 million. A new chief executive who increases profits from, say, £750 million per year to £1 000 million is well worth a few extra hundred thousand pounds in salary. There are also few good substitutes. A machine can replace a machine operator or a bank clerk but can't replace a chief executive.

There are two major problems with performance related pay. First, there seems to be little overall link between the performance of companies and bonuses paid to senior executives. Whilst it is clear why some executives receive large bonuses, outsiders are often baffled as to why an executive should be given a large bonus in a year when profits have fallen. Second, it is not clear that the revenue product of a senior executive can be clearly separated from the performance of the staff under him or her. Effective leadership is important, but so too is the reaction of staff willing to make the effort to change and adapt.

Firms may be willing to pay high salaries to managers because demand for their labour is relatively inelastic.

DATA QUESTION

Banking

How the banks have pruned their branches

	End-December			
	1985	**1990**	**1995**	**1998**
Abbey National	674	681	678	791 *
Bank of Scotland	551	515	411	359
Barclays	2,874	2,566	2,050	1,950
Lloyds	2,229	2,111	1,776	1,793 **
TSB Group	1 591	1,489	1,082	1,008 ***
HSBC	2,311	1,957	1,701	1,663
NatWest	3,172	2,805	2,215	1,727
Royal Bank of Scotland	884	841	687	652
Total	14,286	12,965	10,600	9,943

* Include former National & Provincial Building Society branches
** Include branches of Cheltenham and Gloucester
*** TSB and TSB Bank Scotland

Table 71.5 *Number of bank branches*
Source: adapted from British Bankers' Association.

A changing climate

Banking used to be seen as a safe, stable if somewhat unexciting career. In the 1950s and 1960s, banks essentially provided a place for individuals and businesses to deposit their money. In return, they either got the use of a cheque book but no interest, or they received interest but no cheque book. Banks lent money, of course. However, there was little effective competition. Other financial institutions offered different services. The major banks offered roughly the same terms and the same rates of interest. There was little point in competing because the government, through the Bank of England, controlled lending. There were restrictions on the total amount banks could lend, and for what they could lend. There were restrictions, for instance, on the amount a bank could lend to an individual if the person wanted to use the loan to buy a car.

In the 1970s, banking began to change, with many of the restrictions on lending being removed. This process was completed by the early 1980s. This decade saw a radical transformation in banking. Banks increased their market share in a number of markets. They built on experience in the 1970s to become major mortgage lenders to individuals, competing with building societies. They embraced government policies, encouraging wider share ownership by promoting their share dealing services and unit trust plans. They became significant providers of personal pensions and, to a lesser extent, insurance. The result was that, by the end of the 1980s, the banks liked to think of themselves as providers of a wide range of financial services, rather than just deposit takers and loan givers. With a booming economy, employment in the industry rose. Wages rose too, and many were attracted into the industry by the high wages and job security that seemed on offer.

The first half of the 1990s was more difficult for the banks. The recession of 1990-92 led to losses for some banks as some of their borrowers defaulted on loans. Competition from building societies intensified, as they expanded into sectors of the financial market which previously banks had monopolised. A number of building societies, such as the Abbey National and the Halifax, even changed their status to become banks. The second half of the 1990s saw a more favourable macroeconomic climate and the most efficient banks became highly profitable again.

But many workers did not share in this prosperity. Throughout the 1980s and 1990s, banks invested heavily in computers and automated equipment. Increasingly, bank branches lost their traditional function of the payment and receipt of monies and came to be seen as spaces in which banks could sell services to customers. Most dealings with personal customers could be dealt with through 'hole in the wall' machines. Much of the back room operations of processing cheques, previously done at branch level, was transferred to larger separate automated processing centres. In the late 1990s the development of telephone banking meant that customers could use banking services without visiting their branches. Consequently, the number of branches fell, as Table 71.5 shows, and there was a considerable fall in the need for workers involved in money transmission services, offset by some increase in the number of employees in sales. The result was recurring rounds of redundancies, with older workers being offered generous packages to take early retirement.

Basic wage rises tended to be limited, with some banks giving virtually no increases in some years. But there was an increase in performance related pay. Staff were increasingly awarded bonuses for the volume of financial products sold. Some staff were put on individual bonuses. Others were grouped, such as all the staff in a branch, and set targets for which, if reached, they shared a bonus. Banks increasingly had to fight to sell financial products. The most successful and profitable banks, like Lloyds TSB, were those which succeeded in selling portfolios of products to customers and achieved substantial cuts in their cost base.

In the 1990s a number of building societies changed their status to become banks.

1. **Outline three factors which affected the demand for workers in banking in the post-war period.**
2. **To what extent is the demand for workers in banking inelastic?**
3. **Using economic theory, suggest why banks have increasingly changed over to paying bonuses to their workers.**

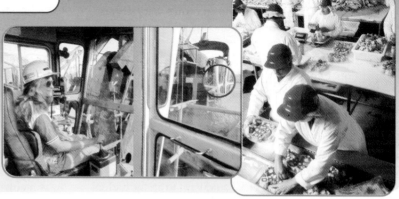

Summary

1. The supply curve for an individual worker is backward sloping at high levels of income.
2. Backward sloping supply curves result because the negative income effect of a wage increase outweighs the positive substitution effect.
3. The supply curve of labour to a firm, to an industry and to the economy as a whole is likely to be upward sloping.

The supply curve for an individual worker

A supply curve shows the quantity that will be supplied to the market at any given price. For an individual worker, the quantity supplied is the number of hours worked over a time period, such as a year. Neo-classical theory starts by assuming that a worker can decide how many hours to work per week and how many weeks' holiday to take per year. The price of labour is the wage per time period (i.e. the wage rate). The wage rate that determines supply is the **real wage rate** (the money or nominal wage rate divided by the price level). This is because the worker decides how many hours to work by relating it to what the wage will buy. For instance, a worker might take a job if a week's wages of £300 were to buy a television set, but she would be likely to turn it down if £300 were to only buy a newspaper.

Figure 72.1 shows a backward bending supply curve for labour. Between wages rates O and B a rise in real wage rates will lead to an increase in working hours supplied. For instance, the worker will offer to work DF extra hours if real wage rates increase from A to B . However, a rise in real wage rates above OB, for instance from B to C, will

lead to a desire for shorter working hours.

To understand why this might be the case, consider a part time factory worker. Initially she is low paid, as are nearly all part time workers. The firm she works for then doubles her real wage rate. She is likely to respond to this by wanting to work longer hours and perhaps become a full time worker. Further increases in real wage rates might persuade her to work overtime. However, there are only 24 hours in a day and 365 days in a year. Eventually it is likely that increases in wage rates will make her want to reduce her working week or increase her holidays. She will value increased leisure time more than extra money to spend. Put another way, she is choosing to buy leisure

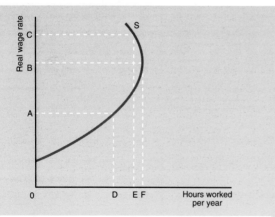

Figure 72.1 *The backward bending supply curve*
The supply curve for an individual worker is assumed to be this shape because at high levels of income the worker will prefer to work shorter hours rather than receive the extra income he or she could have earned.

Question 1

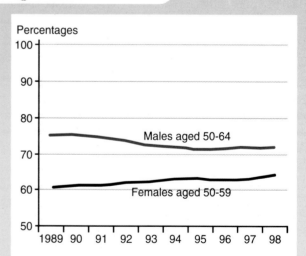

Source: adapted from *Annual Abstract of Statistics*, Office for National Statistics.

Figure 72.2 *Activity rates: totally economically active as % of all persons in relevant age group*

(a) Real wage rates in the UK increased between 1989 and 1998. Does the data support the idea that the supply curve of labour for an individual worker is backward sloping?

time by forgoing the wages she could otherwise have earned and the goods she could otherwise have bought. This is an example of the concept of opportunity cost.

This process can be seen at work over the past 100 years in the UK. Real wage rates have risen considerably but hours worked have fallen. The typical Victorian working week was 60 to 70 hours with few or no holidays. Today, average hours worked per week for full time workers are down to about 42 hours with a typical holiday entitlement of 4 weeks per year. Workers have responded to increases in wage rates by supplying less labour.

Note that when wage rates increase, workers are likely to be able to both increase earnings **and** reduce hours worked. For instance, if real wage rates increase by 20 per cent from £10 per hour to £12 per hour, then workers can cut their hours worked by 10 per cent from 40 hours to 36 hours per week and still see an increase in earnings from £400 per week (40 x £10) to £432 per week (36 x £12). Real wage rate increases in the neo-classical model give workers a choice between increased earnings or increased leisure time or some combination of the two.

Income and substitution effects

The backward bending supply curve occurs because of the interaction of **income and substitution** effects. An increase in real wage rates means that the reward for working, rather than not working and taking more leisure hours, increases. For instance, a worker receiving a pay rise of 10 per cent after tax and deductions can now buy 10 per cent more goods and services. The opportunity cost of not working therefore rises. Workers will therefore **substitute** work for leisure if the rate of pay increases.

However, work is arguably an **inferior good** (☞ unit 10). The higher the income, the fewer hours individuals will wish to work. For instance, it is pointless being able to buy tennis or squash equipment if you don't have the time to play. Earning more money has little use if you can't take the time off to have a holiday, go to the pub or go shopping. So the **income effect** of work tends to be negative for most individuals. The higher the income, the less work and the more leisure time is demanded.

At low levels of income, the positive substitution effect outweighs the negative income effect of a wage rise. Hence, a rise in pay for these workers leads to an increase in the number of hours worked. At higher levels of income, the positive substitution effect is likely to be equally matched by the negative income effect. Wage increases then have neither an incentive nor a disincentive effect on working hours. But at high levels of income, the positive substitution effect of a wage increase is more than offset by the negative income effect. Hence the worker will choose to work fewer hours.

This can be shown in Figure 72.3. At wage rates up to OA, higher wage rates will lead to increased hours of work. Between A and B the supply curve is vertical, showing that increased wages have no effect on hours worked. Between A and B the negative income effect cancels out the positive substitution effect as wages rise. Above OB the supply curve slopes backward showing that the negative income effect of a wage rise more than offsets its positive substitution effect.

In the real world, many workers have little choice about

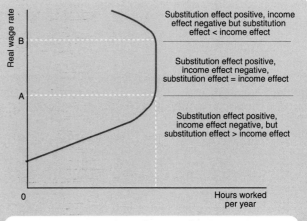

Figure 72.3 *Substitution and income effects*
Up to real wage rate OA, an increase in wages leads to an increase in the number of hours worked because the positive substitution effect of the wage rise outweighs its negative income effect. At real wage rate rises above OB, an increase in wages leads to a fall in hours worked, because the negative income effect outweighs the positive substitution effect.

how many hours they work. However, rising incomes have been associated with longer holidays and also a shorter working life. Those on higher incomes often want to retire as early as possible given that they have been able to save up enough over their working life to finance a reasonable pension. Many other workers do have the opportunity to work longer hours during the week by taking overtime. There is a limit, though, to the amount of overtime employees are prepared to work, showing the negative income effect in operation.

Question 2

In 1986, the results of a government commissioned report on the incentive effects of cuts in income tax were published. The report, by Professor C V Brown of Stirling University, found no evidence that tax cuts encourage people in employment either to work harder or to work longer. Lower taxes did encourage women, particularly in part time jobs, to work longer because they would keep more of their earnings. But for males on average earnings, the boost to existing income provided by lower taxes tended to be more important than the incentive (i.e. substitution) effect of the tax cut.

Using the concepts of income and substitution effects, explain the typical effects found by Professor Brown of income tax cuts on:
(a) a male worker on average earnings and
(b) a female part time worker.

Supply of labour to a firm

In a perfectly competitive market there are many buyers and sellers (☞ unit 53). In a perfectly competitive factor market, there are many firms hiring many individual workers. This means that an individual firm will be able to hire an extra worker at the existing wage rate.

Figure 72.4 (a) shows the supply curve of labour facing the firm. The firm is small and wants to expand its workforce from 20 workers to 21 workers. Figure 72.4 (b) shows the supply curve of labour for the industry to be upward sloping, as will be argued below. 100 000 workers are currently employed in the industry. The movement up the industry supply curve from 100 000 workers to 100 001 workers is so small that the firm can employ the extra worker at the ruling industrial wage rate. Therefore the supply curve facing the firm is horizontal (i.e. perfectly elastic).

Many industries, however, are either oligopolies or monopolies. Firms in these industries are therefore likely to be significant employers of particular types of labour. For instance, the government employs over 90 per cent of all UK teachers. If a firm is a monopsonist (i.e. is the sole buyer) in its labour market, then the supply curve of labour to the firm will also be the supply curve of labour to the industry. It will be upward sloping, showing that the firm has to offer increased wages if it wishes to increase its labour force.

Table 72.1

Units of labour supplied	Cost per unit (£)	Total cost (£)	Marginal cost (£)
0	-	0	
			10
1	10	10	
			30
2	20	40	
			50
3	30	90	
			70
4	40	160	

The cost of employing an extra worker (the marginal cost) will be higher than the wage rate the firm has to pay the extra worker. This is because it not only has to pay a higher wage rate to the worker but it must also pay the higher wage rate to all its other workers. In Table 72.1, for instance, the firm has to increase the wage rate as extra workers are employed. The wage rate needed to attract 3 workers to the industry is £30 per worker. However, the marginal cost of

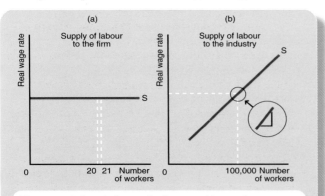

Figure 72.4 *Supply in a perfectly competitive market*
The supply curve of labour facing a firm in a perfectly competitive factor market is perfectly elastic. The firm can hire new workers at the existing wage rate because their employment has an insignificant impact on the total supply of labour in the market.

the third worker is £50; £30 for the third worker plus an extra £10 paid to each of the first two workers.

The supply curve of labour to the firm and the firm's marginal cost of labour derived from the data in Table 72.1 are shown in Figure 72.5. The marginal cost curve for labour for the monopsonist employer is higher than the supply curve of labour.

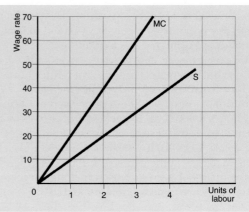

Figure 72.5 *Supply curve and marginal cost curve of labour facing a monopsonist employer*
The supply curve for labour facing a monopsonist employer is upward sloping. The marginal cost of hiring extra workers is more than the wage rate because the higher wage rate paid to the marginal worker needs to be paid to all existing workers.

Question 3

Table 72.2

Number of workers employed	Wage per week per worker (£)
100	200
200	220
300	240
400	260

The table shows the wage rates per week a firm has to offer to recruit workers.
(a) Draw (i) the supply curve of labour and (ii) the marginal cost curve of labour facing the firm. (Remember that the marginal cost of, for instance, the 100 workers employed between 300 and 400 is drawn at the 350 point.)
(b) How would the supply curve and marginal cost curve differ if the firm could recruit any number of workers at a wage rate of £200 per week?

The supply curve of labour for an industry

An industry can increase the number of hours worked by its labour force in two ways:
● it can increase the number of hours worked by its existing labour force;
● it can recruit new workers.

As explained above, a rise in real wage rates, all other things being equal, may or may not increase the supply of labour by individual workers in the industry. However, it is likely to attract new workers into the industry. These new workers may be from other industries or they may be workers who previously did not hold a job, such as housepersons or the unemployed. Therefore the supply curve of labour for an industry is likely to be upward sloping, the ability of firms to recruit new workers outweighing any possible disincentive effect on existing workers. The higher the industry real wage rate, the more workers will want to enter that particular industry.

The **elasticity of supply of labour** to an industry will depend upon a number of factors.

The availability of suitable labour in other industries
An engineering company wanting to recruit unskilled workers will be able to 'poach' workers relatively easily from other industries because there is a large pool of unskilled workers spread throughout industry. The National Health Service will have more difficulty recruiting brain surgeons because nearly all brain surgeons in the UK are already employed by the NHS. So the elasticity of supply of a pool of workers spread across many industries is likely to be higher than that of a group of workers concentrated in the recruiting industry.

Time Elasticity of supply is likely to be lower in the short run than in the long run. For instance, the NHS might not be able to recruit large numbers of brain surgeons tomorrow. But it could expand supply considerably over a 20 year period by training more of them.

The extent of under-employment and unemployment
The higher the level of unemployment, the higher is likely to be the elasticity of supply. With high unemployment, firms are more likely to be able to recruit workers at the existing real wage rate from the pool of the unemployed.

It could be that there is a **cobweb** effect (☞ unit 12) in a market. For instance, the large increase in numbers in the 5-16 age group in the 1960s and first half of the 1970s due to high birth rates led to a considerable increase in the number of workers entering the teaching profession. Pupil numbers then began to decline as the birth rate fell. The demand for teachers fell. It so happened that governments between 1975 and 1985 also wanted to cut public spending. An easy way of doing this was to cut public sector pay relative to the private sector. This cut recruitment onto teacher education courses. It also led to an increase in the number of students completing teacher training courses taking up non-teaching jobs. By the late 1980s, there was a crisis in teaching, with considerable shortages of suitable teachers. In other words, a move away from the equilibrium of the mid-1970s led to a fall in teachers' relative pay. This in turn led to a fall in supply of teachers after a period of time. Government reacted in the late 1980s by putting up teachers' relative pay. The result was an increase in the numbers of people wanting to become teachers by entering teacher training courses and taking first jobs in teaching. By the mid-1990s, it could be argued that there was over-supply. This may have encouraged government to cut relative pay for teachers again, leading at a later date, to excess demand for teachers.

This cobweb effect is the result of there being a delayed response in the market to current market conditions. In occupations where there are long training periods and

where it is difficult for existing workers to change to another job, decisions about whether to supply labour today are based on decisions about whether to enter the occupation a year ago, five years ago or perhaps even thirty years ago.

Question 4

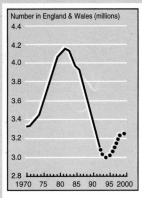

Source: adapted from Population Estimates Unit, OPCS.

Figure 72.6 *15 to 19 year-olds: number in England and Wales (millions)*

In the mid to late 1980s, it was widely predicted that there would be a severe shortage of young people in the labour force. The National Economic and Development Council published a report, *Defusing the Demographic Time Bomb*, which urged employers to diversify their recruitment patterns to meet the coming crisis. The report in particular suggested that employers take on more mature workers, people with disabilities and the unemployed.

(a) Using the concept of elasticity of supply, suggest why a supermarket is more likely to be able to fill jobs like shelf stackers or checkout assistants than managerial posts from people aged 50+.

(b) The predicted shortage failed to occur in the first half of the 1990s. This was mainly because the economy went through a deep recession in 1990-1992 which lead to a fall in the demand for labour by industry. Why should a recession, like that of 1990-92, lead to a rise in the elasticity of supply of labour to an industry?

Supply of labour to the economy

The supply of labour to the economy as a whole might seem to be fixed (i.e. perfectly inelastic). However, this is unlikely to be the case.

● In the UK, only about three-quarters of people aged 16-64 are in employment. The rest tend to be in education, at home looking after children, unemployed or have taken early retirement. This pool of people are potential workers and some would enter the workforce if real wages rose.

● Some of the retired could be brought back to work if there were sufficient incentives for them.

● Immigration too could expand the domestic supply of labour. Immigration was used by the UK to solve labour supply problems in the 1950s.

So the supply of labour to the economy as a whole is likely to be upward sloping too. There is some evidence to suggest that it might also be backward sloping. Over the past ten years there has been an increase in early retirement. This has been due to many factors, but one is that males particularly have been able to earn sufficiently high wages during their working life to make early retirement with a reduced pension attractive. Workers are choosing to reduce the number of hours worked over their lifetime.

Question 5

Table 72.3 *Women: pay and number in the labour force, UK*

	1971	1981	1991	1998
Real average earnings of full time females (at 1998 prices)	£149.99	£200.19	£271.42	£309.60
Total number of women in the labour force (millions)	9.3	10.4	12.2	13.6

Source: adapted from *Annual Abstract of Statistics*, Office for National Statistics.

(a) Do the data support the theory that the supply curve for labour in an economy is upward sloping?
(b) What other factors apart from earnings might affect the supply of female labour in an economy?

key terms

Activity or participation rates - the percentage or proportion of any given population in the labour force.
Economically active - the number of workers in the workforce who are in a job or are unemployed.
Net migration - immigration minus emigration.
Population of working age - defined in the UK as men aged 16 to 64 and women aged 16-59.
Workforce or labour force - those economically active and therefore in work or seeking work.
Workforce jobs - the number of workers in employment. It excludes the unemployed.

Applied economics

The supply of labour in the UK

The UK labour force

In 1999, the population of the UK was approximately 59.3 million people. Not all were available for work. Those below the age of 16 were in full time education whilst women over 60 and men over 65 were officially counted as retired. The rest, those aged 16-60/65, are known as the POPULATION OF WORKING AGE. Figure 72.7 shows that the numbers in this age group have increased in recent decades from 31.7 million in 1971 to 35.9 million in 1999.

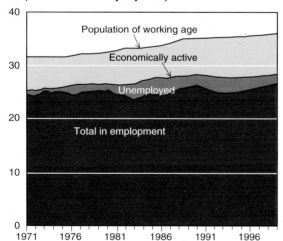

UK (millions seasonally adjusted)

Source: adapted from *Labour Market Trends*, Office for National Statistics.
1. Before 1987 claimant count, 1988 onwards ILO unemployed.
2. All figures relate to males aged 16-64 and females aged 16-59.
Figure 72.7 *Population of working age, economically active, total in employment and unemployed*[12]

Not all those of working age are ECONOMICALLY ACTIVE and part of the WORKFORCE or LABOUR FORCE or WORKING POPULATION. Many women choose to leave employment to bring up children. Young people too may stay on in education after the age of 16. There is also a growing trend for the over-50s to take early retirement. So the workforce is smaller than the population of working age.

The workforce, made up of those who are economically active, is made up of two groups - those in work and those seeking work and who are therefore unemployed. Figure 72.8 gives a breakdown of those in work with WORKFORCE JOBS. Most are **employees**, who work for someone else, their **employer**. A minority work for themselves and are known as **self-employed**. The rest are in the armed forces or are on government training schemes. Note that the numbers in the armed forces has declined as a proportion of total workforce jobs over time, partly due to smaller armed forces and partly due to the increase in the size of the workforce. Self employment grew particularly in the 1980s whilst government training schemes were only introduced in the late 1970s. The rest of the workforce is made up of the unemployed.

Figure 72.7 shows that the workforce has tended to increase over time, from 25.3 million in 1971 to 28.3 million in 1999. The growth in workforce jobs has been less smooth than that of the workforce itself. Three major recessions, 1975-1977, 1980-1982 and 1990-1992, resulted in large increases in unemployment and falls in the number of workforce jobs. The recessions of 1980-1982 and 1990-1992 were so deep that there was even a fall in the numbers of those economically active. In the early 1980s, the workforce fell from 26.7 million in 1980 to 26.5 million in 1982, whilst in the early 1990s, the workforce fell from 28.2 million in 1990 to 27.2 million in 1993. Workers, particularly women, became discouraged from looking for work and disappeared from official counts of the unemployed.

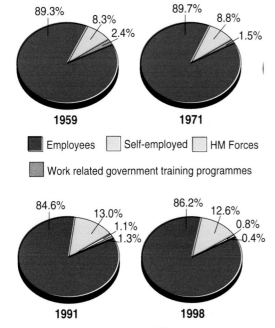

Figure 72.8 *Workforce jobs: United Kingdom*
Source: adapted from *Annual Abstract of Statistics*, Office for National Statistics.

Male and female employment

The workforce has grown at a faster rate than the population of working age in recent times. Table 72.4 shows that whilst the total population of working age grew by 13.2 per cent over the period 1971 to 1999, the workforce has grown by 16.4 per cent. The totals, however, mask a much larger change in the composition by sex of the labour force. There has been little change in the male force over the period. The growth has come from an increase in the number of women working, from 9.3 million in 1971 to 12.9 million in 1999.

Within the female total, there has been a substantial growth in employment of women aged 20-54 as indicated in Figure 72.9. This figure shows ACTIVITY or PARTICIPATION RATES. These are the percentages of any given population in the labour force (i.e. the percentages of an age group either in work or officially counted as unemployed). There is a number of reasons why a larger proportion of females have gone out to work.

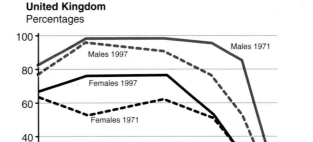

Figure 72.9 *Economic activity rates by gender and age, 1971 and 1997*
Source: adapted from *Social Trends*, Office for National Statistics.

- Real wages have increased over the period. Economic theory would predict that an increase in real wages will increase the supply of labour into the market.
- Through changes in social attitudes and legislation, women now have much greater opportunities in employment than in 1971 and far more than say in 1931 or 1901. Again, this means that more women are getting higher paid jobs, attracting them to make careers for themselves.
- The opportunity cost of going out to work has fallen. A hundred years ago, women created a large number of household services, from cleaning the house to baking bread to making clothes. They had to spend large amounts of time each week doing this. Today, cheap and efficient machines do much of this work. What's more, the real price of washing machines, microwaves etc. has tended to go down over time. Households have been able to afford to buy more and more of these gadgets. The result is that women have increasingly been able to combine a career with running a home. Moreover, changes in social

Table 72.4 *Labour force[1] and population of working age*

Great Britain				Millions
	Civilian labour force			Population of working age
	Males	Females	Total	
Estimates				
1971	15.6	9.3	24.9	31.7
1976	15.6	10.1	25.7	31.9
1981	15.6	10.6	26.2	32.9
1986	15.6	11.3	26.9	33.9
1991	16.4	12.4	28.8	35.1
1996	16.0	12.6	28.6	35.5
1999	16.1	12.9	29.0	35.9

1. 1986 and before claimant count, 1991 onwards ILO unemployed.

Source: adapted from *Social Trends*, *Labour Market Trends*, Office for National Statistics.

attitudes over the past 20 years have meant that men have increasingly begun to share in domestic chores, again helping to create time for women to work in paid employment.

● Falls in the number of children in a family help explain why there was an increase in the number of women working over the period 1900 to 1970. However, family size has remained roughly constant since 1970. What has changed is an increase in nursery education and in pre-school and child-minding facilities. Women have found it easier to get their children looked after at an affordable cost since 1970.

Male activity rates, in contrast, have fallen. In 1971, virtually all males aged 25-59 were in the labour force. This is still broadly true for men aged 25-50. The small decline in activity rates for this group has come about mainly because more men now have the opportunity to retire through ill health or disability than in 1971. The sharp fall in activity rates for the over-50s comes from the trend towards early retirement. Increased staying on rates in education account for the fall in activity rates for the 16-25 age group.

The distribution of men and women between different occupations is very different as Figure 72.10 shows. For instance, there are almost no women in skilled construction trades. In contrast, there are almost no men employed in secretarial occupations. There is in fact no occupation where there are roughly equal numbers of male and female workers. There is a number of possible

reasons which might explain this. Traditionally, males have taken jobs which require heavy manual labour. Women, in contrast, have been associated with the caring professions, such as nursing. Secretarial and clerical work is another area which has traditionally been female over the past 100 years. The greater willingness of males to study science at school and university and therefore build up human capital in this area is reflected in the large number of males amongst science and engineering professionals. Women are also disproportionately represented amongst occupations where there are large numbers of part-time workers. Due to child care commitments, many women prefer to work part-time rather than full-time and therefore occupations which offer opportunities for part-time work are likely to attract more female workers. Sexual equality is a relatively recent phenomenon and males are still disproportionately represented in higher paid jobs, such as corporate managers and administrators. This could be due to discrimination against women. However, it might also reflect that women in the past were more likely than men to take a career break to bring up children. Even a few years out of the labour force has a considerable impact on promotion prospects. Finally, the differences in Figure 62.10 may simply reflect occupational preferences between males and females. Males may prefer to mix concrete rather than act as a receptionist. This would suggest that the supply curve for any occupation is different between men and women.

Figure 72.10 *Occupations of women and men in employment: UK, spring 1998*
Source: adapted from *Labour Market Trends*, March 1999, Office for National Statistics.

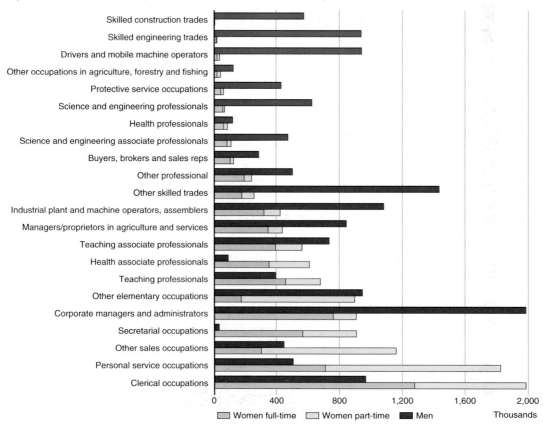

Table 72.5 *Civilian labour force: by age*

Great Britain				Millions[1]
	16-24	25-44	45 and over	All aged 16 and over
Estimates				
1971	5.1	9.7	10.1	24.9
1976	5.1	10.8	9.8	25.7
1981	5.8	11.4	9.1	26.2
1986	6.2	12.5	8.3	26.9
1991	5.5	13.9	8.7	28.1
1997	4.4	14.5	9.8	28.7
Projections				
2001	4.5	14.6	10.3	29.4
2011	5.1	13.5	12.0	30.6

Source: adapted from *Social Trends*, Office for National Statistics.

1. Figures may not add up due to rounding.

Employment by age

Not only has the balance of the labour force changed between the sexes, it has also changed by age as Table 72.5 shows. Since 1971, there has been a significant increase in the proportion of 25-44 year olds in the labour force. The numbers and percentages of workers over 45 declined between 1971 and 1986 because of increased early retirement. The numbers in this age group have only increased again since then because of a growth in numbers coming through from higher birth rates in the post-war period.

The numbers of 16-24 year old workers have fluctuated. Between 1971 and 1986, the numbers in this age group increased, again because of increasing birth rates in the post-war period. Some economists believe that this was a prime cause of the increase in unemployment over that period, and particularly the increase in youth unemployment. The economy was unable to provide jobs for a growing number of young workers entering the labour market for the first time. However, a fall in the birth rate from the mid-1960s led to falls in the 16-24 age group in the labour force from the mid-1980s. At the height of the Lawson boom, in 1986-88, many commentators predicted that there would be a crisis in recruitment of young people in the 1990s. Demand for young workers would be increasing at a time when their supply was falling. The crisis failed to materialise, partly because the demand for labour fell sharply during the recession of 1990-92. However, growth in the number of women willing to work has also helped cover the shortage of young workers. Some employers, particularly in the retail industry, have deliberately targeted workers over the age of 50 when before they would have been looking for school leavers for posts. So employers have become more flexible in their recruitment patterns and have found good substitutes for young workers.

Employment by ethnic group

Detailed statistics for the employment of different ethnic groups in the population can be found in the data question. In general, the employment patterns of those of non-white origin seem less favourable than those of the white population.

Employment by industry and by region

The supply of workers to different industries and different regions has changed considerably over the past 30 years. Broadly, there has been a major shift of workers from the primary and secondary sectors of the economy to the tertiary sector. Consequently, regions heavily dependent upon coal mining and heavy manufacturing have seen losses of jobs and population to regions which have traditionally specialised in light manufacturing and service industries. These trends are discussed in more detail in unit 97.

Other factors affecting the labour force

There are factors other than the increased participation of women and the growth of early retirement amongst men which affect the labour force.

Migration If immigration is larger than emigration, then the workforce is likely to increase. During the 1950s, the UK encouraged immigration from new Commonwealth countries to fill an acute labour shortage. In the 1960s and 1970s, following the 1961 Immigration Act, NET MIGRATION (immigration minus emigration) tended to be negative. More people left the country than entered. In the 1980s and 1990s, the trend has been reversed. However, net migration tends to account for only 25 per cent of the total population change in the UK. What is happening to the birth rate and to activity rates is a far more important determinant of the size of the labour force in the longer term.

Part-time work The numbers and proportion of part-time workers in the workforce have been growing over the past 50 years. In 1971, for instance, 15 per cent of all employees were part-time. By 1999, this had grown to 28 per cent. Most part-time workers are female as

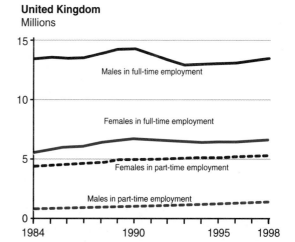

United Kingdom
Millions

Figure 72.11 *Full and part-time employment: by gender*
Source: adapted from *Social Trends*, Office for National Statistics.

Figure 62.11 shows. 44 per cent of women employees were part-timers in 1999 compared to just 8 per cent for males. Part-time working is growing amongst both males and females.

Figure 62.10 shows that part time working is particularly concentrated in service industries. Workers in primary and secondary industry, such as construction and engineering, tend to be full time male workers. The most likely explanation for this is that, historically, service industries have tended to be female dominated. They have therefore been forced to offer opportunities for part-time work because so many females prefer to work part-time rather than full-time. This preference for part-time work is shown in Table 72.6. 80.0 per cent of women, when asked why they had taken part time work stated that they didn't want a full-time job compared to only 42.1 for men.

Table 72.6 *Reasons why people take part-time work: United Kingdom, Spring 1999*

| | | | Per cent |
Reason	All	Men	Women
Student	14.9	33.0	10.5
Ill/disabled	1.7	3.0	1.4
Couldn't find full-time job	10.4	21.4	7.7
Didn't want full-time job	72.6	42.1	80.0

Source: adapted from *Labour Market Trends*, Office for National Statistics.
Note: figures may not add to 100 due to rounding.

The main reason why women want to work part-time is because they want or are forced to take the main responsibility for bringing up children and looking after the household. Part-time jobs enable them to fulfil these roles and hold a job. As society changes and men increasingly share in domestic responsibilities, it is likely that there will be a much greater proportion of males amongst part-time workers. Male part-time working is also likely to increase as more men take early retirement and combine their retirement with part-time employment. The increasing proportion of young people staying on in education aged 16-21 has increased part-time working too as they have been forced to seek work to supplement pocket money and grants given by parents.

Self employment As Figure 72.12 shows, there was a considerable increase in self-employment during the 1980s. In the 1990s, self-employment has slightly declined. The growth of self-employment in the 1980s was probably due to two main factors.

● The Conservative government under Margaret Thatcher attempted to create an **enterprise culture**. It believed that small firms should be encouraged because they created jobs, increased competition, innovation and efficiency in markets, and increased wealth in society. Government policy was directed towards helping small businesses and the self-employed. For instance, income tax, capital gains tax and inheritance tax were all changed to allow successful entrepreneurs to keep more of the money they earned. Various schemes lowered the cost and increased the accessibility of finance for business start ups. The unemployed were encouraged to become self-employed through grants. Training was directed at those becoming self-employed and setting up their own business.

● The economy went into a severe recession between 1980 and 1982, with unemployment rising from 1.5 million to over 3 million. Unemployment did not begin to decline until 1987. So there were six years of high unemployment. The difficulty of getting a job encouraged some workers to become self-employed and set up their own businesses. Equally, during these years there was a constant flow of workers being made redundant, some of whom were eligible for sizable redundancy payments. This created a pool of financial capital available for these unemployed workers to set up on their own.

During the 1990s, there was less emphasis by government on encouraging self-employment, although small businesses continued to be a focus for government policy. Average unemployment was lower during the decade than in the 1980s and therefore there was less need for workers to become self-employed. The 1990-92 recession also led to many business failures and workers became far more aware of the risks involved in being self-employed. Hence, in the 1990s self-employment has become slightly less attractive an option.

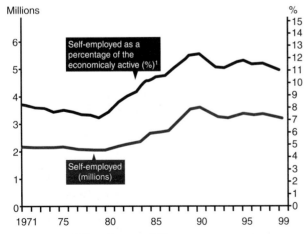

Figure 72.12 *Self-employment, UK*
1. Discontinuity in 1988. Prior to 1988, the unemployment figure used to calculate the number economically active is the claimant count. 1998 and after, it is the ILO count.
Source: adapted from *Annual Abstract of Statistics, Labour Market Trends*, Office for National statistics.

Temporary work Figure 72.13 shows that there has been a growth of temporary employment in the 1990s. As can be seen from Table 72.7, this is not because workers particularly seek temporary work. Only

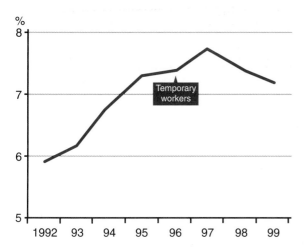

Figure 72.13 *Temporary workers: percentage of all employees*
Source: adapted from *Labour Market Trends*, Office for National Statistics.

approximately one third of temporary workers did not want a permanent job. Rather, it reflects the wishes of firms to employ a more flexible labour force. Taking workers on permanently means that labour becomes a fixed cost. Temporary workers are a variable cost because they can be sent away at short notice. Any firm with seasonal demand for its product is therefore likely to find it attractive to employ temporary workers to cover work above that of its slackest period. Temporary workers are also used by firms which are uncertain of whether an increase in output is likely to be permanent. Sacking workers is costly and therefore to be avoided. Finally, when firms are operating efficiently, there is no slack to be taken up when workers fall ill, are away on holiday or gone on maternity leave. Temporary workers can be used to cover these situations.

The employment of temporary workers can, however, impose costs on firms. Temporary workers can be unfamiliar with an individual's work environment and therefore not be as productive as a permanent member of staff. Motivation amongst temporary workers can also be less than with permanent staff. This is particularly true if an employee works for a long period of time for a firm but is never given a permanent contract.

Table 72.7 *Reasons for temporary working: UK, spring 1999*

			Per cent
Reason	All	Men	Women
Couldn't find a permanent job	34.9	40.3	29.8
Did not want a permanent job	31.6	26.6	36.4
Had a contract with period of training	6.7	8.1	5.3
Some other reason	26.5	25.0	27.9

Source: adapted from *Labour Market Trends*, Office for National Statistics.

Hours of work and holidays Hours of work have changed little since the early 1970s. On average, full time workers have worked 41 hours per week in the 1970s, 1980s and 1990s. However, whilst weekly hours of work have remained broadly constant, yearly hours of work have decreased because holiday entitlements have significantly increased. In 1961, workers were typically entitled to just two weeks paid holiday per year. By 2000, workers were entitled by law to four weeks paid holiday a year plus bank holidays. Many workers received even longer holiday entitlements. Longer holidays and shorter working lives due to early retirement would tend to indicate that either workers prefer increases in leisure time to be in blocks of time rather than a few hours extra per week, or that employers see the 40 hour week as optimal for completing work efficiently and prefer to concede the desire for shorter hours in longer holidays or shorter working lives.

The quality of the labour force

Greater production can be achieved by using more labour. However, the size of the UK labour force is likely to change only slowly over the next 50 years. Of more significance are likely to be changes in the quality of the labour force. Rising educational standards, as shown for instance by greater numbers gaining high grades at GCSE, 'A' levels, GNVQs and degrees, would suggest that the labour force is becoming potentially more productive over time. Figure 72.14 illustrates one aspect of this. A larger proportion of 17/18 year olds are gaining A levels or their equivalent. It should be noted that females have improved their performance relative to males. Male underachievement in the education system is now a target for government policy. Despite these improvements, many argue that the UK has been left behind in international terms in the quality of its labour force. This explains why governments in the 1990s and today have placed such stress on education and training to improve the supply side performance of the economy.

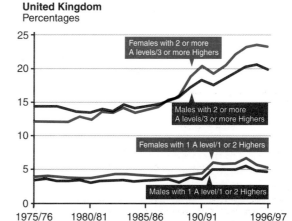

Figure 72.14 *Achievement at GCE A level or equivalent: by gender*
Source: adapted from *Social Trends*, Office for National Statistics.

Ethnic groups in the labour force

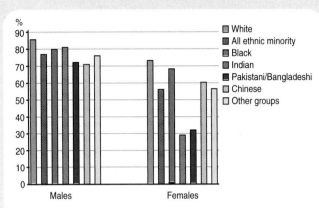

Figure 72.15 *Employment rates[1]: by ethnic group and gender, Great Britain, average, 1997*

1. Percentage of those of working age in employment or self-employment.

Source: adapted from *Labour Market Trends*, Office for National Statistics, December 1998.

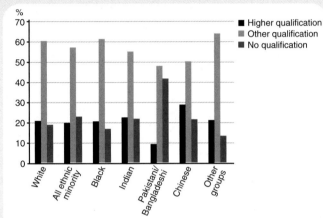

Figure 72.16 *Highest qualification of people of working age by ethnic group, average 1996-98*

Source: adapted from *Labour Market Trends*, Office for National Statistics, December 1998.

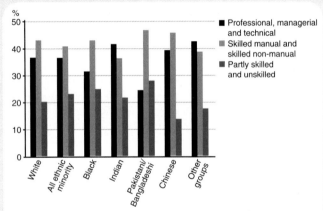

Figure 72.17 *Employees and self-employed by level of employment, average 1996-98*

Source: adapted from *Labour Market Trends*, Office for National Statistics, December 1998.

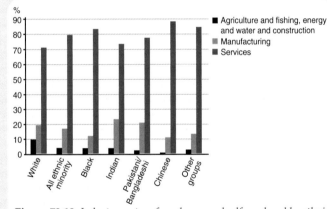

Figure 72.18 *Industry sector of employees and self-employed by ethnic origin, Great Britain, average 1996-98*

Source: adapted from *Labour Market Trends*, Office for National Statistics, December 1998.

1. **Describe the position of workers from ethnic minorities in the labour force as shown in the data.**
2. **Suggest why workers from ethnic minority groups are on average less likely to (a) supply themselves to the labour market and (b) achieve higher levels of employment than white workers.**
3. **Evaluate what economic measures could be taken to improve the position of workers from ethnic minorities relative to that of whites.**

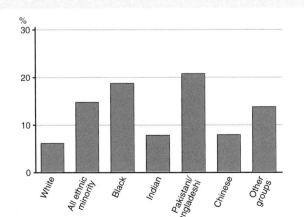

Figure 72.19 *ILO unemployment rate (%), Great Britain, average 1997*

Source: adapted from *Labour Market Trends*, Office for National Statistics, December 1998.

Summary

1. The wage rate of labour is determined by the demand for labour and the supply of labour.
2. In an economy where labour is homogeneous and all markets are perfect, wage rates would be identical for all workers.
3. Wage differentials are caused partly by market imperfections and partly by differences in individual labour characteristics.
4. In a perfectly competitive market, individual firms face a horizontal supply curve and will hire labour up to the point where the wage rate is equal to the marginal revenue product of labour.
5. In an imperfectly competitive market, either the firm is a monopsonist or there is a monopoly supplier of labour, such as a trade union, or both. A monopsonist drives down wage rates and employment levels, whilst a monopoly supplier increases wage rates.

How wage rates are determined

Prices are determined by demand and supply. So the price of labour, the real wage rate, is determined by the demand for and the supply of labour.

The demand curve for labour in an industry is the marginal revenue product curve of labour (☞ unit 71). This is downward sloping, indicating that more labour will be demanded the lower the real wage rate. The supply curve of labour to an industry is upward sloping (☞ unit 72), indicating that more labour will be supplied if real wage rates increase. This gives an equilibrium real wage rate of OA in Figure 73.1. OB units of labour are demanded and supplied.

The demand and supply curves for labour can shift for a variety of reasons, giving new equilibrium real wage rates and levels of employment in the industry. The demand curve for labour will move to the right showing an increase in the demand for labour if the marginal revenue product of labour increases. This might occur if:

- productivity improves, perhaps due to changing technology or more flexible working practices, increasing output per worker;
- there is a rise in the selling price of the product, increasing the value of the output of each worker;
- the price of capital increases, leading to a substitution of labour for capital.

The supply curve might move to the right, showing an increase in supply, if:

- there is an increase in the number of workers in the population as a whole, perhaps because of changing demographic trends, or because government alters tax and benefit levels increasing incentives to work;
- wages or conditions of work deteriorate in other industries, making conditions relatively more attractive in this industry.

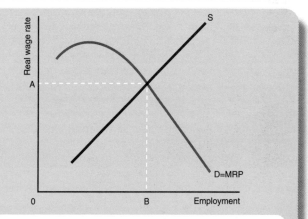

Figure 73.1 *Equilibrium wage rate in an industry*
The equilibrium real wage rate is OA whilst the level of employment in equilibrium is OB.

Question 1

(a) On a diagram, draw a demand and supply curve for labour in the CD production industry.
(b) Mark on the diagram the equilibrium wage rate and the equilibrium level of employment.
(c) Show how the demand curve or the supply curve might shift if there is:
  (i) a fall in labour productivity;
  (ii) an increase in wage rates in all other labour markets in the economy;
  (iii) a fall in demand for CDs;
  (iv) an introduction of new labour saving technology;
  (v) a fall in the number of 16-25 year olds in the population as a whole.

A labour market where all workers are paid the same

Consider an economy which has the following labour market characteristics.

- Labour is homogeneous (i.e. all workers are identical, for instance in age, skill and sex).
- There is perfect knowledge in the labour market. A worker in Scotland is as aware of job opportunities in London as a Londoner.
- There is perfect mobility of labour. Workers can move at no cost between jobs in the same industry, between different industries and between geographical areas. Equally, there are no costs to firms in hiring and firing workers.
- All workers and employers are price takers. There are no trade unions or monopsonist employers.
- There are no barriers which prevent wages rising and falling to accommodate changes in the demand for and supply of labour.
- Firms aim to maximise profit and minimise costs of production, whilst workers aim to maximise their wages.

In this perfect labour market, all workers would be paid the same wage rate. To show that this must be true, consider two markets where wage rates are different. In the Welsh steel industry, wages are higher than in the catering market in London. London catering workers would know this because there is perfect knowledge in the market. They would apply for jobs in Welsh steel firms. They would be prepared to work for less than existing Welsh steel workers so long as the wage rate was higher than their existing wage rate as caterers. Welsh steel makers, seeking to minimise cost, would then either sack their existing workers and replace them with cheaper London catering workers, or offer to continue employing their existing workforce but at a lower wage. Meanwhile, London catering firms would be threatened with a loss of their workers. To retain them they would need to put up their wage rates. Only when the two wage rates are equal would there be no incentive for London catering workers to become Welsh steel workers.

Why wage rates differ

In the real world, wage rates differ. One important reason is because labour is not homogeneous. Each worker is a unique factor of production, possessing a unique set of employment characteristics such as:

- age - whether young, middle aged or old;
- sex - whether male or female;
- ethnic background;
- education, training and work experience;
- ability to perform tasks - including how hard they are prepared to work, their strength and their manual or

Question 2

The second half of the 1980s saw a construction boom in commercial property. Developers refurbished or built millions of square feet of office space in, for instance, the City of London and its surrounding areas. Canary Wharf came to be the symbol of what turned out to be a massive over expansion of property. There were insufficient construction workers at the time in London and the South East, so large numbers of workers from other areas of the country came to work in the capital. Friday early evening trains from London to Liverpool, for instance, were packed with construction workers returning home for the weekend. On Sunday nights, the workers would return to London, sleeping through the week in bed and breakfast accommodation or in vans or cars. Liverpool, even at the height of the Lawson boom, still faced high unemployment and relatively low wages,

(a) Using diagrams, show how this flow of workers might have helped to equalise wage rates between Liverpool and London.

Question 3

Name	Judith Ashton
Age	29
Occupation	Personnel assistant
Location	Chester
Earnings	£13,500 per year

Name	Errol Grant
Age	49
Occupation	Finance director
Location	London
Earnings	£70,000

Name	Mike Jones
Age	17
Occupation	Receptionist
Location	Tenby, West Wales
Earnings	£6,825 per year

Name	Geoff Pennington
Age	44
Occupation	Civil engineer
Location	Preston
Earnings	£28,500 per year

(a) Why do the earnings of these workers differ?

mental dexterity.

For instance, a manager of a company is likely to be paid more than a cleaner working for the same company. On the one hand, the marginal revenue product of the manager is likely to be higher. Her education, skills and work experience are likely to provide greater value to the company than the cleaner's. On the other hand, the supply of managers is lower than the supply of cleaners. Most workers in the workforce could be a cleaner, but only a few have sufficient qualities to be managers. Greater demand and less supply lead to higher wage rates for managers than cleaners.

Wage rates also differ because workers do not necessarily seek to maximise wages. Wages are only part of the net benefit workers gain from employment. Workers whose jobs are dangerous, unpleasant, tedious, where there is little chance of promotion, where earnings fluctuate and where there are few or no fringe benefits, may seek higher wages than workers whose jobs possess the opposite characteristics. Market forces will tend to lead not to equality of wage rates but to equality of net benefits to workers.

Labour is not perfectly mobile. Hence there can be unemployment and low wages in Scotland whilst employers offering much higher wages are crying out for labour in London. Part of the reason why there is a lack of mobility is the absence of perfect knowledge within the labour market. Workers in Scotland may be unaware of job opportunities in the South of England. There are also many other imperfections in the market which prevent wage rates rising or falling in response to market pressures (☞ unit 75).

Perfectly competitive labour markets

In a perfectly competitive factor market, there is a large number of small firms hiring a large number of individual workers. For the individual firm operating in such a market:
- the demand curve for labour, the marginal revenue product curve of labour, is downward sloping (☞ unit 71);
- the supply curve of labour is perfectly elastic and therefore horizontal (☞ unit 72); the firm can hire any number of workers at the existing industry wage rate.

How many workers should this type of firm employ? If a worker costs £200 per week, but increases revenue net of all other costs by only £150, then he should not be employed.

Putting this theoretically, the firm will hire workers up to the point where the marginal cost of labour is equal to the marginal revenue product of labour. If the marginal cost were higher than marginal revenue product, for instance at OC in Figure 73.2, the firm would make a loss on the output produced by the marginal worker and hence it would cut back on employment of labour. If the marginal revenue product of labour were higher than the marginal cost of labour, for instance at OA, then it would hire more workers because these workers would generate a profit for the firm.

Hence, in Figure 73.2 the equilibrium level of

employment by the firm is OB. This is the point where the marginal cost of labour (the supply curve) is equal to the marginal revenue product of labour (the demand curve). The equilibrium real wage rate is OW. This is the ruling equilibrium wage rate in the industry as a whole.

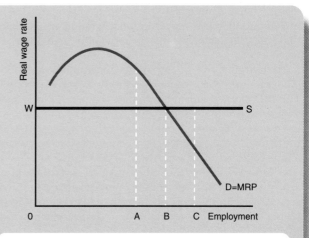

Figure 73.2 *Equilibrium employment and wage rates for a firm in a perfectly competitive factor market*
In a perfectly competitive factor market, the supply curve for labour facing the firm is horizontal. The equilibrium real wage rate, OW, is set by the industry as a whole. The firm will then employ OB workers in equilibrium.

Question 4

Table 73.1

Number of workers employed	Total revenue product (£ month)
1	700
2	1300
3	1800
4	2200

The data show the monthly total revenue product of a profit maximising manufacturing company in a perfectly competitive industry.
(a) Plot the marginal revenue product curve on graph paper (remembering to plot the MRP half way between whole numbers on the employment axis).
(b) What would be the maximum number of workers the firm would employ if the monthly wage per worker were:
(i) £600; (ii) £400; (iii) £425; (iv) £800; (v) £525?

Imperfectly competitive labour markets

An imperfectly competitive labour market is one where:
- either the firm is a dominant or monopoly buyer of

labour;

● or the firm is faced by a monopoly supplier of labour, which is most likely to be a trade union.

If the firm is the sole buyer of labour, it is called a **monopsonist**. The state, for instance, employs over 90 per cent of teachers in the UK and therefore is essentially a monopsonist. A monopsonist is able to exploit market power and therefore common sense would suggest that the monopsonist would use this power to force down wage levels.

The marginal cost of employing an extra unit of labour is higher for the monopsonist than the average cost or wage. This is because the firm has to raise wage rates to attract extra labour into the industry. So the cost of employing an extra unit of labour is not just the higher wage paid to that unit but also the extra wages that now need to be paid to all the other workers in the industry (☞ unit 72).

In Figure 73.3, the demand and supply curves for labour are drawn. The firm will employ workers up to the point where the marginal cost of an extra worker is equal to the worker's marginal revenue product. Therefore the monopsonist will employ OA workers, the intersection of the marginal cost curve and the marginal revenue product or demand curve. The firm does not then need to pay a real wage rate of OG to each worker. It only needs to pay a real wage rate of OE to attract OA workers to the industry.

If the market were perfectly competitive, employment would be OB and the equilibrium wage rate would be OF. So economic theory suggests that a monopsonist drives down wages and reduces employment levels compared to a perfectly competitive factor market. Note that this is similar to the perfect competition/monopoly analysis in a goods market where it is argued that a monopolist reduces output and raises prices compared to a perfectly competitive market.

The effect of a monopoly supplier of labour will be considered in the next unit on trade unions.

Question 5

Teachers' pay in the UK is currently determined by the findings of a pay review board. This takes evidence from the government, which generally wishes to keep wage increases to a minimum, and from trade unions, which want to see high increases in wages. The government can choose either to accept the recommendations of the pay review board or to impose its own, invariably lower, pay deal. The government is effectively a monopsonist employer for teachers because only **9** per cent of teachers work in private sector schools.

(a) Draw a diagram to show the situation of the government facing trade unions in the market for teachers.

The government would like to see work place bargaining in teaching, with individual teachers negotiating with each school in which they are employed.

(b) Using a diagram, compare the wages and level of employment this system might create to the current system of national bargaining.

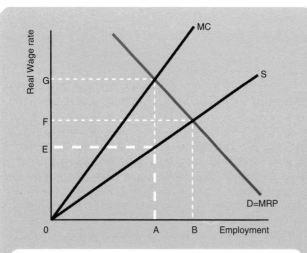

Figure 73.3 *Monopsony in the labour market*
A monopsonist will hire labour to the point where MC = MRP (i.e. up to the point OA). It will then pay labour the lowest wage rate possible which is OE. If the industry had been perfectly competitive then both the equilibrium wage rate OF and the equilibrium level of employment OB would be higher than under monopsony.

Applied economics

Wage determination

Wage structure by occupation

Economic theory would suggest that wage rates would be the same if all labour was homogeneous and all jobs possessed the same characteristics. In the real world workers are not identical. They differ, for instance, in where they are prepared to work, their hours of work and their levels of **human capital** (☞ unit 2). Jobs differ too. In particular, the marginal revenue product curve for each type of job is different.

For example, the average weekly earnings of managers and administrators in 1998 were £571. This compares with plant and machine operatives who earned on average £315 a week (Table 73.2). Neo-classical economic theory suggests that such differences are due to differences in the demand for and supply of different types of labour.

Table 73.2 *Average gross weekly earnings by occupational major groups, Great Britain, April 1998*

Full-time employees on adult rates whose pay for the survey period was unaffected by absence	Average gross weekly pay (£)	Average hourly pay excluding overtime (£)	Average total weekly hours	Average weekly overtime hours
Occupational group (SOC)				
Managers and administrators	571	14.65	39.0	0.5
Professional occupations	525	14.77	35.7	0.6
Associate professional & technical	457	11.78	38.2	1.0
Clerical & secretarial occupations	269	6.94	38.4	1.3
Craft & related occupations	349	7.70	43.8	4.7
Personal & protective service occupations	286	6.93	40.9	1.9
Sales occupations	291	7.38	39.2	1.0
Plant & machine operatives	315	6.81	45.1	5.5
Other occupations	263	5.82	44.0	4.9
All occupations	**384**	**9.54**	**40.2**	**2.3**

Source: adapted from *Labour Market Trends*, Office for National Statistics.

On the supply side, there are potentially far more workers with the ability and training to become manual workers than non-manual workers. The general administrator in Table 73.3 earning £1 116.90 a week could become the kitchen porter earning £166.80 a week, but the kitchen porter could not necessarily become a successful general administrator. Not all workers are prepared to take on any particular job. Occupations which are unpleasant or dangerous, or where earnings can fluctuate greatly, are likely to attract fewer workers than others where the non-pecuniary

Table 73.3 *Highest and lowest paid occupations, Great Britain, April 1998*

Full-time employees on adult rates whose pay for the survey period was unaffected by absence	£ per week
Highest paid	
1 General administrators; national government	1,116.9
2 Treasurers and company financial managers	976.5
3 Medical practitioners	901.2
4 Underwriters, claims assessors, brokers, investment	794.3
5 Organisation and methods and work study managers	743.4
6 Police officers (inspector and above)	720.1
7 Advertising and public relations managers	716.6
8 Marketing and sales managers	686.9
9 Education officers, school inspectors	685.6
10 Computer systems and data processing managers	683.2
Lowest paid	
1 Kitchen porters, hands	166.8
2 Bar staff	175.7
3 Hairdressers, barbers	175.9
4 Retail cash desk and check-out operators	176.2
5 Petrol pump forecourt attendants	178.9
6 Waitors, waitresses	182.0
7 Counterhands, catering assistants	185.0
8 Launderers, dry cleaners, pressers	187.1
9 Other childcare and related occupations n.e.c.	190.9
10 Sewing machinists, menders, darners and embroiderers	195.2

Source: adapted from *Labour Market Trends*, Office for National Statistics.

(i.e. non-monetary) advantages are much greater. Hence, earnings in construction and mining are likely to be higher than average, all other things being equal, because of the danger of the job. In general, the larger the potential supply of labour to an occupation, the lower is likely to be the level of earnings.

On the demand side, non-manual jobs are likely to carry a higher marginal revenue product than manual jobs. Without an effective manager, a company may lose thousands and perhaps millions of pounds of potential revenue or suffer high costs of production. But the company could get by without an effective office cleaner. Hence professional workers in management and administration are paid more highly than workers in catering, cleaning and hairdressing because their revenue product is greater.

So far we have assumed that labour markets are perfectly competitive and that they are in equilibrium. In practice, many of the differences in wages between occupations may be accounted for by trade unions or monopsony employers. For instance, print workers in the 1980s saw their trade union power decline as employers, such as Times Newspapers, won a number of key industrial disputes.

Alternatively, the market may be in disequilibrium. In

the 1980s, for instance, earnings in the shipbuilding industry were depressed as the industry declined. On the other hand, earnings in occupations related to computers have been buoyant over the past 15 years as the industry has expanded.

Changes in wage structure by occupation

The last thirty years of the twentieth century saw considerable changes in relative pay between different occupations. Figure 73.4, for instance, shows how waiters and waitresses saw almost no increase in their real pay per week between 1981 and 1998. In contrast, nurses saw their pay almost double, whilst solicitors increased their pay by approximately two thirds.

On average, as Figure 73.5 shows, non-manual workers have enjoyed higher wage increases than manual workers. In 1979, both groups earned approximately £100 per week. By 1998, non-manual workers earned approximately 40 per cent more than manual workers. What's more, in 1998, the average working week of manual employees at 44.1 hours was six hours longer than for non-manual workers. So manual workers were working longer hours for considerably less weekly pay.

Wage inequality increased particularly in the 1980s, but as Figure 73.6 shows, it carried on increasing in the 1990s. Figure 73.6 shows that in only three years out of the 13 years between 1986 and 1998 did the bottom tenth of wage earners receive a higher average pay increase than the top tenth.

There is a number of reasons for these trends. One has been the relative decline of primary and secondary industries in the UK and the growth of the service sector. Well paid manual jobs were concentrated in manufacturing industry and primary industries such as mining and tended to be occupied by men. The number of manual jobs in service industries has grown, but traditionally these have been low paid jobs done by women.

Another factor has been the decline of trade unionism. Union membership before 1980 was heavily concentrated amongst males in primary and secondary industries and public sector workers. Trade unions were able to secure higher wages than the free market rate in many cases. Anti-union legislation (☞ unit 74) in the 1980s weakened the power of trade unions at a time when there was considerable shrinkage in the number of jobs in primary and secondary industries. This dealt a double blow to relatively well paid male manual workers.

The government also weakened minimum wage legislation present in certain industries during the 1980s before finally abolishing minimum wages in 1993.

Globalisation has put added pressures on poorly skilled low paid workers. There has been an ever increasing trend for work requiring high labour low skill inputs to go to the developing world where wages are a fraction of what even low paid workers earn in the UK. In contrast, the long term trend for UK manufacturing and services in areas which are

internationally traded is for the UK to specialise in producing ever more sophisticated technological products. This requires highly skilled labour inputs and therefore increases the demand for workers who are already better educated, better trained and better paid.

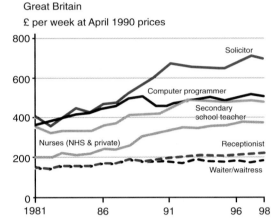

Figure 73.4 *Real gross weekly earnings by selected occupation*
Source: adapted from *Social Trends*, Office for National Statistics.

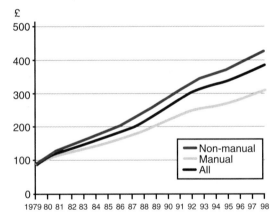

Figure 73.5 *Average gross weekly earnings, full-time employees on adult rates: Great Britain*
Source: adapted from *Labour Market Trends*, Office for National Statistics.

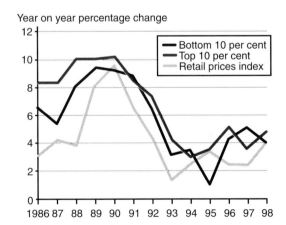

Figure 73.6 *Earnings growth of top and bottom deciles, GB, 1986-98*
Source: adapted from *Labour Market Trends*, Office for National Statistics.

The outlook for the lowest paid is better today than at the start of the 1990s. The reinstatement of the minimum wage, this time across all industries, in 1998, helped set a floor for wages. The government set itself targets for achievement in education and training which should reduce the number of unskilled workers with no qualifications over the next 40 years. The numbers unemployed have also fallen considerably since the peaks of 3 - 3.5 million seen in the first half of the 1980s and in 1991-93. This increases the scarcity of labour and helps push up wage rates.

However, the pace of introduction of labour saving new technology is not slowing down. It is often the least skilled jobs which are easiest to automate. There are still plenty of Third World countries with large pools of very low paid workers which can take jobs away from the UK. Moreover, some Third World countries are also developing increasingly skilled workforces which can compete with UK workers at lower cost. This is likely to put downward pressure on many wages across the pay spectrum in the UK.

As for the highest paid, it could be argued that their wages are likely to continue to outperform the average. This is because the potential marginal revenue product of a top worker is considerable. In football, for instance, fans will pay high prices to see the best players perform on the pitch, but few want to go and see second rate footballers. The result is that the most successful clubs over the past ten years have been prepared to pay ever larger sums to their players to secure them for the club. The same is true at the top of business organisations. One person can have an enormous effect on earnings and profits for a firm, but there are only a relatively few people who can have the abilities required. The result was an explosion in the pay of directors and top managers in firms in the 1980s and 1990s.

Wage structure by gender

Females have traditionally earned considerably less than men. Economic reasons can be put forward for this. In the past, women were denied the same educational opportunities as men and were thus unable to acquire the same level of human capital. Equally, they were denied access to all but a narrow range of jobs.

Today, possibly the most important factor causing inequality in earnings between the sexes in the UK is the unequal burden of child care. It is still almost universal for women to take primary responsibility for bringing up children. Many women still choose to abandon their careers to return home and look after their children. When they do return to work, many take up low paid, part time work which fits in to their primary role as child-carers.

Taking a break in a career is enormously costly in terms of human capital. Those who continue in employment will not only receive formal training, but will build up informal knowledge and understanding of new work methods, new technology, new products, etc. On average, earnings of both men and women rise by about 3 per cent a year when in work. The skills of

Table 73.4 *Wage relativities by gender: ratio of female to male gross weekly earnings, full time employees*

	1971	1976	1981	1986	1991	1996	1998
Manual employees	.53	.62	.62	.62	.63	.65	.64
Non-manual employees	.52	.61	.61	.60	.63	.65	.65
All employees	.57	.66	.67	.67	.70	.72	.73

Source: adapted from *Social Trends*, Office for National Statistics.

the woman who left work 10 years ago in comparison will be outdated. A woman's earning potential drops by 3 per cent a year for every year a woman is out of the labour force (M J Artis, 1989). The time when women choose to leave their careers is also important. It is traditional for workers to make their most important career progressions between the ages of 20 and 40, precisely the time when many women are out of the workforce. Employers respond to the less stable work patterns of women by offering less training to female employees. There is also evidence to suggest that, despite legislation, women are passed over in promotion.

Table 73.4 shows the relative weekly earnings of men and women. During the 1970s, the gap between male and female earnings narrowed. This was mainly the result of the Equal Pay Act 1970 and the Sex Discrimination Act 1975. The 1970 Act made it illegal to pay women less than men if they were doing the same job. The 1975 Act guaranteed women equality of opportunity. Table 73.4 would suggest that this was a once and for all gain. Relative earnings then hardly changed for a decade. From the mid-1980s, however, there has been another substantial gain by women. It could be that the relatively tight labour market created by the Lawson boom of 1986-88 forced employers to increase the relative pay they offered to their female employees. This gain was then not lost when unemployment rose back to 3 million in the recession of 1990-92.

A number of other factors affect the pay of women. Earnings of women are lower than those of men simply because women work shorter hours. In 1998, full-time women worked on average 37.6 hours per week compared to 41.7 hours for men. Even so, in 1998, hourly rates of pay averaged only 80.1 per cent those of men. Many occupations, such as secretarial work, are dominated by females, and it could be that the marginal revenue product of occupations traditionally filled by women is lower than that of occupations which are traditionally male dominated. Women are slightly less likely to be members of trade unions, and this could affect their relative pay. However, discrimination is still likely to play a part in the determination of female rates of pay.

Wage structure by age

Age is an important determinant of pay as Figure 73.7 shows. Economic theory would suggest that older workers would receive higher rates of pay because of higher levels of human capital due to education, training and experience. To offset this, older workers in their 40s, 50s and 60s may be less physically strong and agile, important for manual work, or less adaptable, important for any job. Figure 73.7 provides some support for this. Male hourly earnings peak in the 40-49 age group, whilst female earnings peak even earlier in the 30-39 age group. Earnings of full-time females aged 40 and over are likely to be depressed by the earnings of those women who return to full time work having spent time looking after their children either without a job or in part-time work.

Figure 73.7 shows that the earnings gap between females and males increases with age. For all females, the male/female earnings gap up to the age of 29 is no more than 8 per cent. This difference might be due to discrimination or other factors. From the age of 30, however, the gap begins to widen and for those over 40 is approximately 25 per cent. This is almost certainly due to the effects of women taking time off work to look after children, which damages their human capital in the job market. This particularly affects non-manual female workers. Up to the age of 29, female non-manual workers are better paid relative to men than

female manual workers. But after 40, the reverse is true. This is likely to be because non-manual female workers lose relatively more human capital than manual female workers when they take time off work to bring up children. So, a female manager is likely to lose more training and experience by taking 5 years off work than a female shop assistant.

Part-time and full-time working

Part-time workers in the UK are likely to hold less responsible jobs within an organisation. For this reason, as Figure 73.8 shows, they earn less on average than full-time workers per hour. It is also true that most part-time workers are females. In Spring 1998, for instance, 5.4 million out of a total of 12.0 million female workers were part-time. This compared to 1.3 million out of a total 14.9 million for males. The differential between female and male workers applies to part-time workers as well as full-time workers as Figure 73.9 shows.

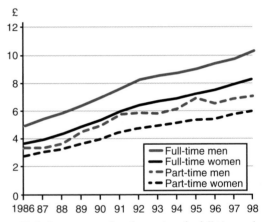

Figure 73.8 *Average gross hourly earnings for full-time and part-time employees by sex, Great Britain*
Source: adapted from *Labour Market Trends*, Office for National Statistics.

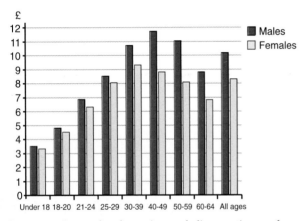

Figure 73.7 *Average hourly earnings excluding overtime pay for male and female workers by age, Great Britain, April 1998*
Source: adapted from *Annual Abstract of Statistics*, Office for National Statistics.

Wages by ethnic group

Workers from ethnic minorities tend to earn less than white workers. Table 73.5 shows that the hourly rate of pay of ethnic workers is only 92 per cent that of white workers' pay. This figure, however, conceals large differentials. The average hourly rate of pay of black women workers, for instance, is 6 per cent more than that of white women workers, whilst males of mixed origin are paid 3 per cent more than white males per hour on average. On the other hand, the hourly rate of pay of workers of Pakistani or Bangladeshi origin is considerably less than that of white workers. Overall, women workers from ethnic minority groups earn almost the same hourly rates as those of white women workers. The difference in overall hourly earnings between white and ethnic minority groups comes almost entirely from differences in male earnings.

There is a number of factors which cause male workers from ethnic minority groups to earn less on average than white workers. First, workers from ethnic minorities, on average, tend to be less well qualified than white workers. This means workers from ethnic minorities are more likely to be in manual jobs than white workers, and also less likely to be in managerial posts. Second, workers from ethnic minorities are more likely to work in distribution (including shops), hotels, catering and repairs, and in the health services than white workers. In 1993, for instance, 29 per cent of all ethnic minority workers worked in the distribution, hotel, catering and repair industries compared to only 17 per cent of white workers. Some jobs in these industries are well paid, such as being a doctor, but there is an above average proportion of low paid jobs. So the choice of which sector to work in may account for some of the difference in earnings. Third, where workers live may affect their wage rates. A disproportionate number of workers from ethnic minorities compared to white workers live in the South East, particularly Greater London. Given that wages in the South East are higher than the average for the UK, this should reduce the differential between ethnic minority workers and white workers. However, to counter-balance this, a disproportionate number of jobs in distribution, hotels, catering and repairs are found in the South East. So workers from ethnic minorities are more likely to work in low paid jobs in this high pay region than white workers, helping to account for the wage differentials. Finally, there is evidence that pay discrimination against workers from ethnic minorities takes place, despite Equal Pay legislation. There is also discrimination against ethnic minority workers when it comes to recruitment, selection, promotion and training.

Table 73.5 *Average hourly pay rates of full time employees by ethnic groups and sex; Great Britain, average of Winter 1993-94 to Autumn 1994 (not seasonally adjusted)*

(£)

Ethnic origin	All	Men	Women
Average hourly pay			
All origins	7.42	7.97	6.39
White	7.44	8.00	6.40
Ethnic minority groups	6.82	7.15	6.31
Black	6.92	7.03	6.77
Indian	6.70	7.29	5.77
Pakistani/Bangladeshi	5.39	5.47	5.15
Mixed/Other origins	7.70	8.45	6.77
Average hourly pay of ethnic minority groups as a percentage of that of the white population			
Ethnic minority groups	92	89	99
Black	93	88	106
Indian	90	91	90
Pakistani/Bangladeshi	72	68	81
Mixed/Other origins	103	106	106

Source: Department of Employment, *Employment Gazette*, June 1995.

Regional earnings and employment

Table 73.6 *Average weekly earnings, April 1998*

£

	Males	Females
United Kingdom	425.60	308.70
London	565.60	402.80
South East	453.90	323.50
East	416.70	307.70
North West	404.40	287.10
West Midlands	399.10	282.30
Scotland	394.60	276.70
South West	392.40	286.20
East Midlands	387.80	271.50
Yorkshire and the Humber	378.70	281.00
North East	377.50	273.60
Wales	376.40	282.80
Northern Ireland	367.70	277.60

Source: adapted from *Regional Trends*, Office for National Statistics.

Table 73.7 *Net migration between regions*[1,2,3]

Thousands

	1981	1986	1991	1996	1997
South West	20	46	22	29	36
South East	36	39	13	29	26
East	17	17	9	18	20
East Midlands	5	17	9	8	11
Wales	3	5	5	2	5
Scotland	-1	-12	9	-7	2
Northern Ireland	-3	-6	4	-1	-3
North East	-8	-10	-1	-6	-6
Yorkshire and the Humber	-5	-12	0	-7	-7
North West	-20	-26	-9	-9	-10
West Midlands	-12	-8	-5	-10	-11
London	-32	-49	-53	-45	-55

Source: adapted from *Regional Trends*, Office for National Statistics.

1. Net migration: immigration minus emigration. Positive figures in black show an increase in the population of a region whilst negative figures in red show a reduction in population of a region due to migration.
2. Only migration flows between British regions are given. International migration is not included.
3. Regions ranked by size of net migration in 1997.

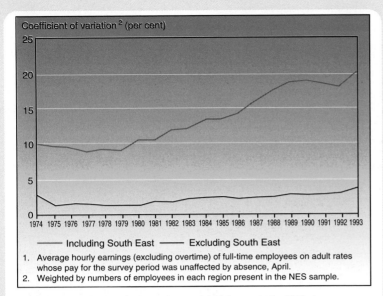

1. Average hourly earnings (excluding overtime) of full-time employees on adult rates whose pay for the survey period was unaffected by absence, April.
2. Weighted by numbers of employees in each region present in the NES sample.

Figure 73.9 *Regional dispersion of average hourly earnings of full-time employees[1]; Great Britain, 1974-1993*

Table 73.8 *Cost of living comparison between regions 1995-98; average weekly spending on housing and fuel, light and power*

	Housing	Fuel, light and power
£ per week		
United Kingdom	49.70	12.90
London	64.10	12.10
South East	60.70	12.40
East	51.90	12.50
South West	50.30	12.50
East Midlands	46.70	12.70
North West	45.50	13.10
West Midlands	45.00	13.00
Wales	43.00	14.20
Yorkshire and the Humber	42.90	12.70
Scotland	42.20	13.80
North East	40.60	12.70
Northern Ireland	29.40	15.80

Source: adapted from *Regional Trends*, Office for National Statistics.

Table 73.9 *Employee jobs: by industry[1], September 1997*

Per cent of employees

	Primary industry and construction[2]	Manufacturing	Financial & business services	Other services[3]
United Kingdom	5.7	18.0	18.3	58.0
London	3.6	8.2	30.8	57.4
South East	5.6	14.0	21.7	58.7
East	5.8	17.7	19.0	57.5
North West	5.6	20.7	15.5	58.2
West Midlands	5.6	26.5	15.1	52.8
Scotland	8.3	16.4	14.8	60.5
South West	5.7	17.3	16.4	60.6
East Midlands	5.9	25.8	14.2	54.1
Yorkshire and the Humber	5.9	21.9	14.9	57.3
North East	7.1	21.2	12.4	59.3
Wales	6.0	22.2	11.3	60.5
Northern Ireland	8.4	18.0	8.4	65.2

Source: adapted from *Regional Trends*, Office for National Statistics.

1. Regions are ranked according to average weekly earnings.
2. Agriculture, hunting, forestry and fishing, mining and quarrying including oil and gas extraction, electricity, gas and water, and construction.
3. Distribution, hotels and catering, repairs, transport, storage and communication, public administration and defence and education, social work and health services.

Table 73.10 *Examination achievements, 1996-97*

	Percentage achieving	
	5 or more grades A* to C at GCSE[1]	2 or more A levels 3 or more SCE Highers[2]
United Kingdom	46.2	29.7
Scotland	54.8	30.1
Northern Ireland	53.5	36.9
South East	51.1	35.7
South West	50.1	32.5
East	48.5	32.3
London	44.0	28.8
North West	43.7	27.3
Wales	43.7	26.6
East Midlands	43.4	28.1
West Midlands	42.2	27.6
Yorkshire and the Humber	39.7	25.2
North East	38.1	22.4

Source: adapted from *Regional Trends*, Office for National Statistics.

1. Percentage of pupils in their last year of compulsory education.
2. Those aged 17-19 achieving 2 or more A levels or 3 or more SCE Highers as a percentage of the 18 year old population.

Table 73.11 *Table Regional unemployment rates*

Per cent

	1981	1986	1991	1996	1999
South East	na	7.2	4.1	5.5	2.4
East	na	8.5	4.8	6.4	3.0
South West	5.7	9.2	5.3	6.5	3.2
North West	na	11.9	6.8	7.0	5.0
East Midlands	6.4	9.9	5.8	7.2	3.9
West Midlands	8.3	12.7	6.6	7.6	4.7
UK	6.9	11.0	6.6	7.7	4.4
Scotland	8.8	13.2	8.0	7.8	5.4
Yorkshire and the Humber	7.6	12.3	7.4	8.3	5.2
Wales	9.2	13.9	7.6	8.3	5.3
London	4.4	9.0	6.2	9.1	4.8
North East	na	16.7	10.2	11.1	7.3
Northern Ireland	11.7	16.1	12.5	11.2	6.7

Source: adapted from *Regional Trends*, Office for National Statistics.

1. **Outline the main differences in wages and employment between the regions in the UK.**
2. **What economic factors might account for differences in average earnings between regions?**
3. **Evaluate what government policies could be pursued to reduce the earnings gap between regions.**

Summary

1. Trade unions exist to further the interests of their own members.
2. Neo-classical economic theory predicts that trade unions increase wages but create unemployment in perfectly competitive industries.
3. Theory also predicts that a monopsonist buyer of labour will employ more workers and pay them a higher wage rate when bargaining with a union than in a situation where it is bargaining with a large number of individual employees.
4. Trade unions will be more powerful the larger the trade union membership, the less elastic the demand for labour and the greater the profitability of the employer.
5. Trade unions will reduce efficiency in a perfectly competitive economy, but they may increase efficiency if the economy is imperfectly competitive.
6. Trade unions may reduce costs of production for firms if they facilitate change and perform some of the tasks, such as personnel management, which management would otherwise have to undertake.

Collective bargaining

A trade union is an organisation of workers who combine together to further their own interests. Within a company organisation, an individual worker is likely to be in a relatively weak bargaining position compared to his or her employer. The employer possesses far greater knowledge about everything from safety standards to the profitability of the firm than an individual worker. Moreover, the loss of an individual worker to a firm is likely to be far less significant than the loss of his or her job to the employee.

So workers have organised themselves in unions to bargain collectively. Instead of each individual worker bargaining with the firm on a wide range of wage and employment issues, workers elect or appoint representatives to bargain on their behalf. From an economic viewpoint, trade unions act as monopoly suppliers of labour.

Trade unions play a very controversial role in the economy. Critics argue that trade unions, by forcing up wages and resisting changes in working practices, create unemployment. Neo-classical economic theory supports this view, assuming that factor markets are perfectly competitive. However, as will be argued below, it also suggests that trade unions increase employment if a trade union represents workers in a firm which is the sole buyer of labour.

Competitive industries

Trade unions act to further the interests of their members.

One of the key ways in which they do this is to press for higher wages. In economic terms, they attempt to fix a minimum price for the supply of labour. This produces a kinked supply curve.

In Figure 74.1 the non-union demand and supply curves for labour in an industry are D and S_1 respectively. A union agreement to raise wages from the free market wage of OA to the unionised wage rate of OB means that

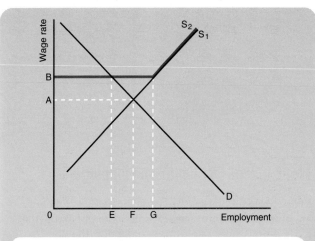

Figure 74.1 *Trade unions in a competitive market*
The entry of a trade union to a competitive factor market is likely to 'kink' the supply curve of labour. OB is the union negotiated wage rate in an industry. Employment will fall from OF to OE whilst wage rates will rise from OA to OB.

employers in the industry cannot hire workers below a wage rate of OB. The supply curve therefore is perfectly elastic (i.e. horizontal) over the employment range OG. The union agreement does not prevent employers paying higher wages than the negotiated wage. Employers would need to pay higher wage rates if they wished to hire more workers than OG. Above OG the new supply curve S_2 is the same as the old supply curve S_1. The new equilibrium wage rate is OB, the wage rate that the union negotiated. However, employment in the industry falls from OF (the equilibrium in a non-unionised market) to OE.

Neo-classical micro-economic theory therefore suggests that trade unions increase wages for their members, but also cause unemployment in the industry. Wages would be lower and employment higher if the industry were non-unionised.

Question 1

In early 1993, Timex, whose core business is the manufacture of watches, decided that it had to stem the losses being made at its Dundee plant which manufactured circuit boards for computers. It cut staff, imposed a wage freeze and cut fringe benefits substantially. The workers came out on strike. The company responded by employing new workers, 'scab labour', who had to cross union picket lines. Several attempts at mediation between unions and management failed because the striking workers refused to accept the compromises negotiated on their behalf.

In June 1993, Timex announced that it was closing the plant. Although it had a full order book, and indeed had won new business since early 1993 which would have required almost doubling the workforce, the company said that it had been left 'financially exhausted' by the strike. Its employment of non-union labour with the old workers manning picket lines outside the factory had attracted worldwide negative publicity for Timex. With a pay freeze and reduced fringe benefits, estimated to amount to a 27 per cent pay cut by the unions, the factory was economically viable. But Timex was not prepared to run it on this basis if strikers were to continue to get publicity coverage. Neither was it prepared to give in to the strikers and allow the plant to be unprofitable.

(a) 'Trade unions raise wage levels in an industry but cause a loss of jobs.' Explain, using a diagram and the example of Timex, why this might be the case.

Trade unions vs monopsony employers

Many trade unions operate in factor markets where there are monopsony employers. A sole seller of labour (the trade union) faces a sole buyer of labour (the monopsonist).

Economic theory suggests that a trade union will increase both wages and employment compared to a factor market where a monopsony employer negotiates with a large number of individual employees. Figure 74.2 (a) shows the wage and employment levels in an industry

with a monopsonist and many individual employees (☞ unit 73 for a full explanation of the graph). Employment is OA and the equilibrium wage rate is OE. Figure 74.2 (b) shows the entry of a trade union to the industry. Assume that the trade union forces the wage rate up to OF. This produces a kinked supply curve. The monopsonist cannot pay a wage rate lower than OF because of its union agreement. However, it is free to pay higher wage rates if it wishes to employ more than OB workers. This produces a kink in the marginal cost of labour to the firm. Up to OB, the marginal cost of labour is the same as the union negotiated wage rate. The employer can hire an extra unit of labour at that wage rate. If it employs more than OB workers, the wage rate will rise, resulting in a jump in marginal cost at OB. The monopsonist has a profit incentive to hire extra workers so

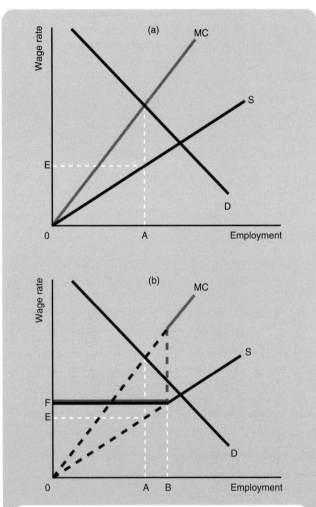

Figure 74.2 *A trade union vs a monopsonist employer A monopsonist facing a large number of employees in an industry will force wage rates down to OE and restrict employment to OA. The entry of a trade union to the industry which sets a minimum wage of OF will 'kink' the supply curve of labour and produce a discontinuity in the marginal cost curve for labour. The monopsonist has a profit incentive to hire extra workers so long as the marginal revenue product of labour, shown by the demand curve, is greater than the marginal cost of labour. Hence it will employ OB workers.*

long as the marginal revenue product of labour, shown by the demand curve, is greater than the marginal cost of labour. Hence it will employ OB workers.

Why should a monopsonist buy more labour at a higher wage rate from a union than it would otherwise? It should be remembered that a firm bases its decision on how much labour to hire not on the wage rate (the average cost of labour) but on the marginal cost of labour. It can be seen from Figure 74.2 that the marginal cost of unionised labour is lower between employment levels A and B than it would have been if labour had been non-unionised. In the former case it is flat at OF, whilst in the latter it is rising steeply above OF.

Question 2

Table 74.1

					£
Units of labour employed	Wage rate per worker		Marginal cost of employing 1 extra worker		Marginal revenue product of labour
	With no trade union	With a trade union	With no trade union	With a trade union	
2	4	8	4	8	16
3	5	8	6	8	14
4	6	8	8	8	12
5	7	8	10	8	10
6	8	8	12	8	8
7	9	9	14	14	6
8	10	10	16	16	4

The table shows wage rates, marginal employment costs and MRPs facing a monopsonist employer of labour.
(a) (i) What is the maximum number of workers the firm would employ if the labour force were non-unionised?
    (ii) What would be the equilibrium wage rate?
(b) What is the maximum number of workers the firm would employ if workers belonged to a trade union and it had negotiated a minimum wage rate of £8?
(c) Explain why trade unions might increase rather than decrease the level of employment in an industry.

The power of trade unions

There is a variety of factors which make trade unions more or less powerful.

Trade union membership and militancy A union which has 100 per cent membership in an industry is likely to be stronger than a union which only represents 10 per cent of potential members. It could be argued that the RMT is far more powerful in the railway industry than the Transport and General Workers Union is in the hairdressing industry. Equally, unions are more likely to call for industrial action if union members are militant. The more militant the union membership, the more costly a dispute is likely to be for an employer.

The demand curve for labour is relatively inelastic A rise in wage rates will have far less impact upon employment in the industry if the demand for labour is relatively inelastic than if it is elastic. Hence, there will be far less cost to the union of a wage rate increase in terms of lost membership and to its members in terms of lost employment (☞ unit 71 for a discussion of why the demand for labour might be inelastic).

Profitability of the employer A trade union is unlikely to be able to negotiate large wage increases with an employer on the verge of bankruptcy. It is likely to be in a stronger position with a highly profitable firm. This implies that trade unions will be stronger in monopolistic and oligopolistic industries, where firms are able to earn abnormal profit, than in perfectly competitive industries where only normal profit can be earned in the long run.

Question 3

(a) How would economic theory account for the strength and weakness of union power in these industries?

Efficiency

Neo-classical economic theory suggests that trade unions operating in competitive industries reduce employment levels and raise wage rates. If all industries but one were perfectly competitive then a trade union in that one industry would mean that the economy as a whole was not Pareto efficient (☞ unit 61).

However, most industries in the UK are imperfectly competitive. A trade union facing a monopsonist will redress the balance of power in the industry and lead to a level of employment and a wage rate which will be nearer to the free market price of labour. It could well be that the presence of a trade union increases economic efficiency in an imperfectly competitive market. Hence the effect of trade unions on economic efficiency depends on the structure of markets in an economy.

A further important argument needs to be considered. Some economists have suggested that trade unions raise economic efficiency because they lower costs of production to the firm. The trade union performs many of the functions of a personnel department within a firm. It deals with workers' problems and obviates the need for the firm to negotiate pay with each and every worker. More importantly, it can be a good vehicle for negotiating changes in working practices. A firm may wish to implement changes which will lead to less pleasant working conditions for its workers. Perhaps it wishes to increase the speed of the assembly line, or force workers to undertake a variety of tasks rather than just one. It may find it difficult to implement these changes on a non-unionised workforce because some workers may take unorganised industrial action or do their best to disrupt any changes being introduced. A union may help the firm to persuade workers that changes in working practices are in their own interest. The union will usually demand a price for this co-operation - higher wage rates for its members. But it still leads to an increase in economic efficiency because the firm is able to make higher profits whilst workers receive higher wage rates. According to this view, trade unions increase productivity in the economy.

Question 4

In December 1998, Rover, then part of BMW, struck a deal with Rover unions over flexible working and shorter basic hours. Manual workers at Rover were represented by five unions - engineering union AEEU, general unions GMB and the T&G, manufacturing science and finance union MSF, and building workers' union UCATT. Workers agreed to adopt collective working time arrangements. This meant that they agreed to allow management to shorten working hours when demand for cars was slack and transfer the hours not worked to other periods when demand was higher and production needed to be increased. The overall limit per year for this was plus or minus 200 hours. Workers could also be asked to have flexible lunch breaks and start half an hour earlier than usual. Unions also agreed other measures designed to cut costs. These included 2 500 jobs losses, but no enforced redundancies, loss of the 1999 holiday bonus, a six month pension fund holiday, and union involvement in quality and attendance initiatives. In return, Rover agreed to phasing in a 35 hour working week. In addition, BMW made commitments to over £2 billion worth of investment, subject to government grant aid and the development of new models.

Tony Woodley, national automotive secretary for the T&G and chief negotiator for the Rover unions, said that he saw the deal as a 'win win' situation for both the company and workforce alike. He said that it 'dispels the myth that you can't have shorter hours with efficiencies'.

Source: adapted from *Labour Research*, February 1999.

(a) How might the changes described in the data increase efficiency?
(b) Suggest what were the advantages to Rover management of being able to negotiate with unions over the proposed changes rather than dealing directly with individual workers.

key terms

Closed shop - a place of work where workers must belong to a recognised trade union.

Trade union mark-up - the difference between wage rates in a unionised place of work and the wage rate which would otherwise prevail in the absence of trade unions.

Applied economics

Trade unions

Trade unions in the UK have existed for over 200 years. In the early 19th century, trade unions were outlawed for being anti-competitive. By the early 20th century there were 2 million trade union members and, as Figure 74.3 shows, this rose to a peak of over 13 million in 1979.

Since 1979, there has been a sharp fall in the number of trade union members. By 1998 membership had fallen to 7.8 million. There is a number of possible explanations for this radical change in union membership.

● The recessions of 1980-82 and 1990-92 both created over one and half million unemployed. The unemployed tend to allow their union membership to lapse. So it is not surprising that the drop in union membership was highest in both of these periods. The lowest fall in membership over the period 1979-1992 occurred in the boom year of 1987.

● The 1980s and 1990s saw a radical restructuring of British industry. Employment in primary industries and manufacturing, both sectors which were very highly unionised, fell significantly. The new jobs that were created tended to be in the service sector of the economy, traditionally far less unionised than manufacturing. Moreover, most of the lost jobs were full-time whilst many of the new jobs were part-time. In 1998, 33 per cent of all full-time workers were union members compared to only 20 per cent of part-time workers. Important too was that many jobs lost were traditionally male jobs and the new jobs created were traditionally female jobs. In 1998, 31 per cent of male workers were union members compared to 28 per cent for female workers.

● Between 1979 and 1997 government showed a marked hostility to trade unions. This has affected the willingness of workers to join unions and increased the confidence of those employers attempting to reduce or eliminate trade union activity in their workplaces.

● A perceived loss of power of trade unions has made workers less willing to join.

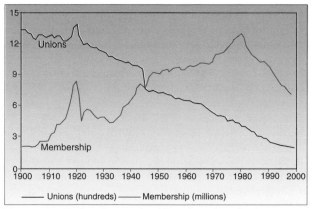

Figure 74.3 *Trade union membership and number of unions*
Source: adapted from *Employment Gazette*, Office for National Statistics.

The trade union mark-up

Economic theory suggests that trade unions will increase wage rates for their members by shifting the supply curve of labour upwards. Studies of the UK economy tend to confirm that such a MARK-UP, the difference between actual wage rates in unionised labour markets and the wage rate which would otherwise prevail in the absence of trade unions, is indeed present. Figure 74.4 shows an estimate of the union mark-up in the 1960s, 1970s and 1980s. It suggests that the size of the mark-up tends to be **cyclical** (☞ unit 78). When the economy is in boom and unemployment is falling, non-union wages tend to rise faster than union wages. Hence the mark-up falls. When the economy is in recession and unemployment is rising, non-union wages tend to rise more slowly than union wages. Hence the mark-up tends to rise.

The union mark-up varies from industry to industry. M Stewart (1983) found that the mark-up ranged from 18 per cent in shipbuilding to 2 per cent in electrical engineering. The results are shown in Table 74.2.

Table 74.2 *Estimate of the trade union mark-up by industry 1975*

Industry	Mark-up (%)
Shipbuilding and marine engineering	18.2
Paper, printing and publishing	11.4
Other manufacturing industries	10.9
Metal goods not elsewhere specified	10.7
Clothing and footwear	10.1
Chemicals and allied industries	9.6
Vehicles	9.6
Timber and furniture	9.1
Instrument engineering	8.6
Food, drink and tobacco	6.6
Metal manufacture	5.4
Mechanical engineering	4.1
Bricks, pottery, glass and cement	2.4
Electrical engineering	2.0

Source: M. Stewart (1983).

In another study, Blanchflower (1984) found that the mark-up for skilled workers was only 1 per cent but was 10 per cent for semi-skilled manual workers. Given that trade union power has declined since the study was made, and that fewer semi-skilled workers are now union members, this mark up for semi-skilled manual workers may well be less today. This might then be one cause of the relative decline in the earnings of low paid workers (☞ unit 73).

Sources of trade union power

It can be seen from Figure 74.4 that the mark-up rose from about 3.5 to 4 per cent in the early 1950s to between 5 and 9 per cent in the 1970s. The union mark-up then broadly fell in the 1980s. What factors might determine the size of this union mark-up and why does the union mark-up vary from industry to industry?

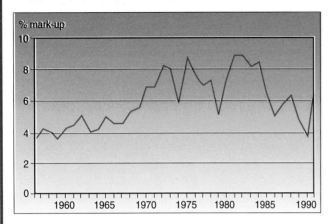

Figure 74.4 *Estimated mark-up of union over non-union wages, 1956-91*
Source: adapted from Layard and Nickell (1986) and G Jones and G Taylor, *The UK Economy*, Weidenfeld and Nicolson, 1992.

Union density Union density refers to the proportion of the workforce which belongs to a trade union. Figures 74.3 and 74.4 show that over the 1950s, 1960s and 1970s trade union membership rose at the same time as the union mark-up. So the size of the mark-up may be linked to the percentage of workers belonging to a trade union. Indeed, the industries with a high union mark-up shown in Table 74.2, such as shipbuilding and printing, have traditionally been highly unionised. Many firms within these industries were CLOSED SHOPS. In a closed shop, all workers have to belong to a recognised trade union. Closed shops are commonly assumed to increase trade union power at the expense of the employer.

The decline of union membership in the 1980s may help to account for a decline in the union mark-up in the 1980s. The power of closed shops was also weakened in the 1980s. Legislation between 1980 and 1990 limited the power of trade unions to enforce closed shop agreements. Moreover, the decline in union membership directly led to a decline in the number of informal closed shops. Millward found that the number of manual workers covered by closed shop agreements fell from 3.7 million in 1984 to 0.5 million in 1990, for instance.

Union density is likely to increase as a result of the Employee Relations Act, 1999. This was the first piece of union legislation passed by the new Labour government elected in 1997. The Act gives workers the right to union representation in a workplace if a majority of them vote in favour. Unions hoped that it could add over a million members to trade union organisations. However, it could be argued that by 1999, unions were in a relatively weak position to recruit new members. Only 19 per cent of workers in the private sector belonged to a trade union, compared to 61 per cent for the public sector. Moreover, trade unionism is much weaker in the South of England,

which has the faster growth in the workforce. Only about one quarter of workers in London and the South are union members compared to 30 per cent for the whole country. It could be argued that most private sector workers perceive trade unions as being only at best of marginal relevance to their work and therefore they are unlikely to join a trade union in future. The contrary argument is that trade unions now have considerable opportunities to recruit new members.

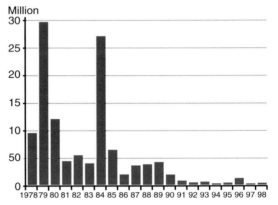

Figure 74.5 *Working days lost: United Kingdom, 1978-98*
Source: adapted from *Labour Market Trends*, June 1999, Office for National Statistics.

Union militancy The willingness of trade unions to take industrial action may be another factor influencing the size of the union mark-up. Industrial action may take a variety of forms, including strikes, work-to-rules, and overtime bans. The greater the willingness of unions to strike, the more costly industrial action will be to employers and therefore the more likely it is that they will concede high pay rises. In practice, it is difficult to measure the degree of union militancy and therefore it is difficult to gauge the degree of correlation between such militancy and the change in the union mark-up.

However, Figure 74.5 shows that there has been a broad fall in the number of working days lost in industrial disputes since the 1970s. Workers in the 1980s and 1990s have been less willing to take industrial action than in the 1970s. Again, this may help explain a fall in the union mark-up in the 1980s.

Collective bargaining Collective bargaining involves trade unions negotiating with employers. In the 1970s, large numbers of workers were covered by national agreements. Trade unions would negotiate with groups of employers representing a whole industry. In some cases, this would then be followed up by local bargaining at plant level where workers in an individual place of work would negotiate a deal based on the national agreement. Conservative governments between 1979 and 1997 put pressure on employers to cease national collective bargaining. Trade union legislation passed during the period led to firms de-recognising trade unions, i.e. ceasing to recognise their right to negotiate on behalf of their members. The government, instead, encouraged firms to adopt individual bargaining with workers, linking this

Table 74.3 *Union recognition and collective bargaining: Great Britain, 1993-98*

Year	Number of employees in workplaces with recognition (000s)	Percentage change in number since previous year	Percentage of employees in workplaces with recognition	Number of employees whose pay is determined by collective agreement (000s)	Percentage of employees whose pay is determined by collective agreement
1993	10 420		48.9		
1994	10 374	-0.4	48.2		
1995	10 226	-1.4	46.8		
1996	10 141	-0.8	45.8	8 091	36.5
1997	10 032	-1.1	44.3	8 058	35.5
1998	10 081	0.5	43.5	7 984	34.5
Change since 1993	-339	-3.7	-4.6		

Note: Includes all employees, except for members of the armed forces. Those who did not report their union recognition status, or who were not contactable in the autumn quarter, have been allocated on pro-rata basis.
Source: adapted from *Labour Market Trends*, Office for National Statistics.

perhaps to performance. The ability to bargain collectively is at the heart of the power of a trade union to gain a mark-up for its members. With individual bargaining, the rate of pay should be set at the market clearing level, i.e. the mark up should be zero. Where individual pay bargaining was impossible, the government encouraged firms to negotiate on a local basis, plant by plant or region by region for instance, again weakening the power of trade unions. Table 74.3, for instance, shows that between 1993 and 1998, the percentage of employees working in places where trade unions were recognised fell from 48.9 per cent to 43.5 per cent. Moreover, over the short three year period between 1996 and 1998 the percentage of employees whose pay was determined by collective agreements fell from 36.5 per cent to 34.5 per cent. The 1999 Employee Relations Act attempted to reverse these trends by giving workers the right to trade union recognition in the workplace where a majority voted in favour. Whether this will lead to more collective bargaining remains to be seen.

The legislative background Unions have to work within a legal framework. Unions in the UK gained the right to organise in 1824 with the repeal of the Combination Acts. Their right to strike without being sued for damages by an employer was enshrined in the Industrial Disputes Act of 1906. During the 1960s, however, there was a growing feeling that trade unions and their members were using their power in a way which was damaging to the economy as a whole. The Labour government of 1964-1970 shelved plans to introduce trade union reforms in the face of trade union opposition, but Edward Heath's Conservative government of 1970-1974 did take action. The Industrial Relations Act (1971) was highly controversial, met substantial opposition from the trade union movement and failed to reduce their power effectively. It was repealed in 1974 when a new Labour government came into office and trade union rights were extended by various pieces of legislation in the following two years. The 1980s, arguably, saw a transformation in the climate

of industrial relations in the UK. The Conservative government, instead of introducing large scale legislative reform, passed a number of acts each of which restricted union power at the margin. By the mid-1990s:

- secondary picketing (picketing by workers not involved in a dispute, e.g. miners picketing a school where the teachers are on strike in 'solidarity' with the teachers) had been made illegal;
- trade unions had to hold a secret ballot and gain a majority of the votes cast to call an official strike;
- social security benefits were withdrawn from the dependants of striking workers;
- union officers had to be elected by secret ballots;
- closed shop agreements were restricted and greater opportunities were given for employees to opt out of closed shops.

Power within the union movement shifted. Before 1979, small groups of workers who were willing to take unofficial strike action and certain militant trade union leaders tended to dominate at least the newspaper headlines. The reforms of the 1980s and 1990s made it more costly and more difficult for workers to take widespread unofficial action. The power of trade union leaders to call strikes was curbed because workers now had to be balloted on strike action. Moreover, the democratisation of union voting procedures made it much more difficult for militant trade union leaders to get elected to key posts within trade unions.

The government also shrewdly distanced itself from the prosecution of trade unions. Previous legislation had concentrated on criminal law, where offenders were prosecuted by the state and could be fined or imprisoned. Government always risked creating trade union 'martyrs'. Much of the union legislation of the 1980s and 1990s concentrated on civil law. Employers were given powers to sue trade unions for breaches of the law. For instance, if a trade union calls a strike without holding a secret ballot, it is the employer affected which sues the trade union for damages. The government has no power to prosecute the union. This means that trade unions risk losing considerable sums of money if they do not comply with the law, but individual trade union members cannot gain public sympathy by being sent to prison as they could in theory under the 1971 Industrial Relations Act.

Not only has the government considerably reduced the ability of trade unions and their members to take industrial action, it also, during the 1980s and 1990s, took a strong stance with public sector trade unions. The most important trade union defeat in the public sector was the breaking of the miners' strike in 1984-5.

Furthermore, the government completely cut off the trade union movement from decision making at a national level. This contrasted with the 1960s and 1970s when governments, both Labour and Conservative, would often consult trade union leaders before making important decisions.

It is perhaps not surprising, then, that the trade union mark-up declined in the 1980s. Some groups of workers, such as miners and print workers, saw substantial cuts in their mark-up as a result of employers winning bitter strikes in the mid-1980s. In the 1990s, the government continued to implement policies designed to produce a **flexible market** (☞ unit 75). In the view of the Conservative government to 1997, trade unions would have little or no place in this market. The Labour government elected in 1997 was more pro-union but it did not want to see a return to the industrial relations strife of the 1960s and 1970s when Labour were last in power. Instead, it wanted to see a partnership between unions and employers where unions were able to add value to the running of a firm as well as protecting their members interests. Certainly, it had no intention of repealing most of the anti-union legislation of the 1980s and it could be argued that the 1999 Employee Relations Act did little to redress the balance of power in favour of trade unions.

The role of unions

Firm sacks workers in wages row

Around 30 workers have been sacked from a Wolverhampton factory in a dispute about overtime and a cut in wages, a union chief claimed today. Welders at Thompson Chassis United Pressings & Fabrications Ltd, which provides chassis for Rover, were dismissed after they complained about impossible work targets and a cut in bonuses, it was alleged. The workers refused to work overtime on a weekend after £15 had been docked from their wages during the week for failing to meet production targets. Their union, the AEEU, accused the firm of refusing to negotiate on the issue. It threatened to take the firm to an industrial tribunal for unfair dismissal.

Source: adapted from the *Express & Star*, 31.10.1998.

In 1998, Wales had the highest union density (the proportion of all workers belonging to a union) in the UK. It also had one of the lowest levels of strike activity. Union leaders claimed that this shows the benefits of trade unionism to an employer. The trade union is able to help the employee manage industrial relations in a less confrontational way. It is able to secure the pay and conditions for its members which motivates a workforce and reduces the dissatisfaction which leads to strike action.

However, there are other explanations for the Welsh phenomenon. One is that there is no clear correlation between union density and strike activity across time or between regions and countries. In recent years, falling membership in France has been accompanied by falling strike rates, but the reverse has been true in Sweden. Another possible explanation is that low levels of disputes are linked to job insecurity. Wales is a high unemployment, low wage economy in comparison with the rest of the UK. Many Welsh workers are afraid of the losses they would face if they lost their jobs because of union action. Another factor is that many Welsh workers are relatively young, since older workers have found it difficult to get new jobs once they become out of work. Younger workers are less likely to vote for industrial action. They are more likely to search for another job if they are dissatisfied with their pay and conditions. Finally, many Welsh employers have signed 'partnership deals' with unions, giving a union exclusive rights to represent workers in a place of work in return for flexible labour practices. These deals tend to lay down exhaustive negotiating procedures which make it difficult for industrial action to take place. Some critics of these deals, though, claim that trade unions are then 'captured' by management and cease to represent their members' interests effectively.

Source: adapted from the *Financial Times*, 14.9.1999.

In November 1998, LSG Sky Chefs, a firm providing in-flight catering for 14 airlines operating out of Heathrow, dismissed 273 workers on the first day of a strike. The company had decided to introduce flexible working practices with different shift patterns to cut costs. The workers had refused the package despite the company offering higher pay and went on strike when the company attempted to implement the package. Having dismissed the workers, the company employed new workers. A year later, with the backing of their union, the TGWU (Transport and General Workers Union), the workers were still on strike with no end in sight to the dispute.

Source: adapted from the *Financial Times*, 20.11.1999.

New unionism needs to be a partnership of equals. You won't agree all the time, but if there's open and honest dialogue between the parties, differences can be worked through more easily than by going down the historical route of conflict.

Partnerships have to be carefully negotiated - otherwise they could end being sweetheart deals, where employers promise the earth tomorrow to get them through a difficult period today.

Genuine partnership is based on mutual understanding of the business and an acceptance by employers than the workforce has a right to be included in decisions.

Ed Sweeney, General Secretary of the finance union Unifi, quoted in *The Guardian*, 14.9.1999.

Land Rover stoppage

Workers stopped production at the Solihull Rover plant three times this week over the new flexible working agreement. The problem has been caused by rising sales of Discovery and Freelander models. The management has asked the workforce to work an extra 15 minutes per day Monday to Thursday and an extra 6 hour shift on Friday to increase production. Under a recently signed agreement, management can ask workers to work up to seven hours a week extra for no more pay in return for paid time off in the past or in the future. Union leaders have stated that management are within their rights to ask the workers to work the extra seven hours. But they want to negotiate on when the hours are worked 'to try to satisfy that in a way that's more socially acceptable'. The management at Rover said the company was 'relaxed' about settling the dispute.

Source: adapted from the *Financial Times*, 12.6.1999.

1. What is the role of a trade union? Give examples from the data to illustrate your answer.
2. Analyse the effect of trade unions on wages and employment in the UK.
3. Discuss whether economic efficiency would be improved if further restrictions were placed on trade union activity.

Summary

1. In a perfectly competitive labour market, there is no unemployment, no discrimination and market forces allocate workers to their highest paid occupations.
2. In practice, there are many examples of market failure in labour markets.
3. One major cause of labour market failure in the UK is the lack of mobility of labour, in turn caused principally by failure in the housing market and by a lack of skills amongst workers.
4. In segmented labour markets, the formal sector is unlikely to make short term adjustments to unemployment and hence labour markets may be prevented from clearing.
5. Trade unions and monopsonist employers, such as government, may reduce employment in the market. So too might government policy.
6. Governments attempt to correct labour market failure in a variety of ways, including minimum wage legislation and equal pay legislation. These may lead to an increase in wages for some workers but may also lead to unemployment for others.

Efficiency, equity and market failure

An economy where all markets are perfectly competitive is Pareto efficient (☞ unit 61). All labour markets will clear. Everyone who wants a job at the going wage rate is able to obtain one and therefore there is no unemployment. There is perfect factor mobility and therefore there can be no regional or sectoral unemployment. The market mechanism will allocate workers to their highest value occupations, ensuring that total output in the economy is maximised.

In a real modern industrialised economy, few markets are perfectly competitive. There are many instances of market failure and this is true not just in the goods market (☞ unit 16) but also in labour markets. Market failure can be judged against a number of criteria of efficiency including:
- full employment - the extent to which the market mechanism provides jobs for those who wish to work;
- maximum labour productivity - the extent to which the potential, the talents and the skills of workers in jobs are fully utilised in an economy.

Market failure can also be judged against different criteria of equity:
- equal opportunities - the extent to which all groups in society including women, the young, the elderly and those from ethnic minorities are not discriminated against in the labour market;
- wage differentials - the extent to which individual workers receive a 'fair' wage for the work they do.

Causes of labour market failure

There is a considerable number of ways in which labour markets are imperfect.

Mobility of labour In a perfect labour market, there is complete mobility of labour. Workers are free, at no cost to themselves, to move jobs between industries and between regions. In practice, there are major obstacles to mobility.
- Many workers have job-specific skills. For instance, a teacher could not easily become a manager. A manager could not easily become a concert pianist. A concert pianist could not easily become a chef. When industries, such as the steel industry or the shipbuilding industry, shrink as they did in the 1970s and 1980s in the UK, redundant skilled workers in these industries find it difficult to find any employment except unskilled, low paid jobs. Industrial training by firms and by government favours young workers. So older workers find it difficult to move from industry to industry, even if they so wish.
- Knowledge is imperfect in the labour market, particularly in occupations where there is a long tradition of labour immobility. There are high SEARCH COSTS for workers and employers in finding out about employment opportunities. These search costs include time spent looking for jobs, or job applicants, and money costs such as travel, postage and advertisements. The higher the search costs, the less likely a search will take place and the less labour mobility there will be.
- Workers are not just workers. They belong to families and local communities. They take a pride in their area or in the skills they have acquired over a long period of time. Many people prefer not to move round the country in pursuit of a job or a career. They prefer to remain unemployed or stay in a job which is not particularly rewarding rather than move.
- The housing market can also be a major barrier to mobility. In the UK, the rented sector declined in importance in the post-war period. Today, most rented property is owned by local authorities or housing associations and is available mainly to low income families. Long waiting lists mean that workers in higher unemployment areas such as Scotland cannot move to lower unemployment areas such as the South East and secure family accommodation at a low rent. Young single workers are better catered for because there is a relatively plentiful supply of cheap low quality bed-sit/flat accommodation available nationally. Private good quality family accommodation is available in small quantities but at such high rents that it is only affordable by workers on above average incomes. Most homes, however, are now owner occupied. This in itself can cause labour immobility. When the housing market is depressed, workers can find it difficult to sell their

houses in order to move to another area. When the housing market is in boom, a large gap tends to emerge between house prices in London and the South of England and the rest of the UK. A worker in the North of England may then be discouraged from taking up a job in the South of England because of the high price differential in houses.

Question 1

A survey published in 1993 by the CBI and Black Horse Relocation Services suggested that employee resistance to job relocation at the time was growing. Nearly 40 per cent of the 251 companies surveyed said a working spouse 'represented a key inhibitor to relocation'. Ms Sue Shortland, head of the Confederation of British Industry's relocation group, said: 'The issue of the working partner will increase with more women working and more dual-income families.' She pointed out that it was not only the temporary loss of income that caused problems but also the damage to the partner's career, promotion and income potential.

A third mentioned concern was children's education and just more than a quarter of the survey sample quoted family ties and roots as reasons for reluctance to move with the company.

The property price slump in the early 1990s was the most serious barrier to relocation. As many as 44 per cent of the sample said inability to sell their home inhibited them from being moved to another part of the country by their employer.

Source: adapted from the *Financial Times*.

(a) What barriers to labour mobility were highlighted by the 1993 survey?
(b) Explain why labour immobility can lead to inefficiency in the economy.

Trade unions and monopsony employers It is argued that trade unions and monopsony employers create unemployment in the market. A full explanation of this was given in units 74 and 75.

Segmented labour markets Some economists have argued that labour markets are segmented so that there is little movement of labour from one market to another. One version of this argument is the DUAL LABOUR MARKET HYPOTHESIS. In the formal, primary or planning sector of the economy, workers, often unionised, are employed by large employers such as oligopolistic or monopoly firms or by government. Workers in the formal sector tend to be better qualified and better paid. In the informal, secondary or market sector, workers, mainly non-unionised, are employed by small firms or are self-employed. These workers tend to be low-skilled or unskilled workers on low pay.

In the formal sector, workers are seen as important assets by their employers. They are trained and are expected to pursue a life-long career in their occupation. They are seen as reliable, dependable and loyal. In return for these qualities, firms are prepared to give a complete remuneration package, including not just pay, but also benefits such as pension schemes, sickness benefit and paid holidays. At times, this package may be far in excess of the equilibrium wage rate (i.e. the firm could employ workers at far lower wages). However, reducing wages to take advantage of short term weaknesses in the labour market would be counter-productive in the long run. It might lead to lower morale, greater uncertainty and lower productivity amongst existing staff. If workers are brought in from outside the company, it may take time for new staff to become familiar with often complex work routines and there may be friction between these outsiders and existing company staff. Reducing wages in the short term may also deter young people, who see that wages can be volatile, from entering the industry.

In the informal sector, workers are expected to be mobile. Job security is low. Training is minimal. Workers are not expected to stay with their employers and hence little is provided in the form of extra benefits, such as sickness benefits or pension schemes.

If the economy is in fact divided into these two sectors, there are important implications for unemployment and discrimination. Market economists argue that unemployment in an industry can only be a short term phenomenon because wages will fall to clear the market. However, employers do not react to unemployment by

Question 2

Table 75.1 *Average earnings, inflation and unemployment, 1990-1993*

	1990	1993
Average earnings 1990 = 100		
Electricity, gas, other energy and water supply	100	122.2
Food, drink and tobacco (manufacture)	100	125.0
Education and health services	100	120.2
Motor vehicles and parts (manufacture)	100	119.5
Whole economy	100	118.5
Hotels and catering	100	118.0
Leather, footwear and clothing (manufacture)	100	117.2
Construction	100	116.5
Distribution and repairs	100	113.3
Retail price index (1990=100)	100	114.3
Unemployment (millions)	1.66	2.92

Source: adapted from Department of Employment, *Employment Gazette*.

Electricity, gas, other energy and water supply, food, drink and tobacco, education and health services and motor vehicles and parts are industries which are characterised by an above average proportion of full time permanent jobs. Hotels and catering, leather, footwear and clothing, construction and distribution and repairs are industries which have above average proportions of part-time workers and casual workers.

(a) The UK economy suffered a severe and prolonged recession between 1990 and 1992. How might the theory of segmented labour markets help to explain the difference in the earnings increase between the sectors at the time?

cutting wages in the formal sector of the economy. On the contrary, workers may continue to receive pay rises in line with their career expectations. In the informal sector, there will be wage cuts which will expand employment. Overall it will take much longer for the economy to return to full employment because only the informal sector behaves in the way economic theory suggests. What is more, the process of adjustment will lead to widening income differentials. Whilst workers in the formal sector will be receiving pay rises, those in the informal sector will receive wage cuts. So the burden of adjustment falls disproportionately hard on those most likely to receive low wages.

For a variety of reasons discussed below, women and those from ethnic minorities tend to form a much larger percentage of the workforce in the informal sector of the economy than in the formal sector. Hence, this dual economy reinforces discrimination against these groups.

Government policy Government policies, ranging from taxation on cigarettes to interest rate policy to health and safety legislation, affect the labour market in a variety of ways. Each individual policy lessens market failure or leads to an increase in market failure. Many aspects of the debate on this issue are discussed in units on supply-side economics, but it is important to realise that government policies designed specifically to deal with labour market failure may well themselves create further labour market failure.

Correcting market failure

Governments have adopted a variety of policies in an attempt to improve both efficiency and equity in the labour market. However, some economists believe that the problems created by these policies are worse than the problems they were originally designed to counter.

Minimum wage legislation One way of tackling low pay is for the government to enforce minimum wage rates on employers.

This would seem to be an ideal solution to the problem

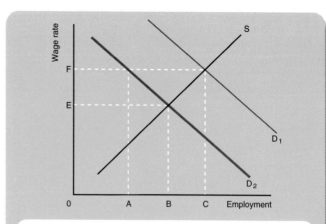

Figure 75.2 *Minimum wages can cause unemployment*
A fall in demand for labour from D_1 to D_2 should lead to a fall in wage rates from OF to OE. However, a minimum wage of OF will prevent this and will cause unemployment of AC to arise.

of poverty amongst workers. However, economic theory predicts that the policy will have undesirable secondary effects. Figure 75.1 shows the demand and supply curves for labour in an industry. The equilibrium wage rate is OE whilst the equilibrium level of employment is OB. The government now imposes a minimum wage of OF, forcing industry wage rates to rise to OF. Firms demand AB less labour whilst BC more workers wish to gain jobs in the industry. The result is AC unemployment.

Existing workers have not necessarily benefited. OA workers have gained higher wages. But AB workers have lost their jobs as a result of the legislation. What is more, the workers who have lost their jobs are likely to be the least employable. Firms will have fired their least productive employees.

Minimum wage legislation can also prevent the market from clearing when there is an increase in unemployment. In Figure 75.2, D_1 and S are the original demand and supply curves respectively. Assume that the minimum wage is set at OF. Then the equilibrium market wage rate is equal to the minimum wage rate and there is no unemployment. Now assume that the economy goes into recession. Demand for the industry's product falls and so the demand for labour in the industry falls (remember, labour is a derived demand). The new demand curve is D_2. If the market had been free, wage rates would have fallen to OE and any transitional unemployment in the market would have disappeared. But with a minimum wage of OF, unemployment of AC is created. So it is argued that minimum wage legislation can cause unemployment.

Equal pay legislation Equal pay legislation is designed to raise the wage rates of groups of workers who perform work of equal value to other workers doing the same job who are at present paid higher wages. In the UK, equal pay legislation has been applied particularly to women and to workers from ethnic minorities.

Economic theory suggests that equal pay legislation will have the same effect as the imposition of a minimum wage. Equal pay legislation is designed to raise the wages of workers who are discriminated against. In the UK, there

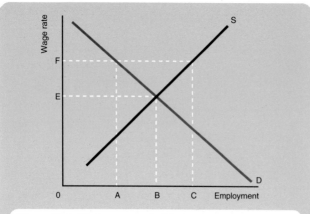

Figure 75.1 *Minimum wage legislation*
A minimum wage of OF will result in higher wage rates in the industry. However, AB workers will lose their existing jobs whilst a total of AC unemployment will be created.

is evidence to suggest that it has been partially successful in achieving this. However, raising wages will reduce the demand for and increase the supply of labour. If the market was in equilibrium to start with, then the introduction of legislation would cause unemployment amongst those groups whom it is designed to benefit. There is a direct trade-off between higher pay and fewer jobs.

Health and safety legislation and other employment protection measures Government has passed many acts designed to improve the living standards of workers. For instance, health and safety legislation is designed to protect workers against accidents at work. These measures have the effect of raising the cost to firms of employing labour. Not only do firms have to pay workers a wage, but the legislation also forces a rise in labour-related costs. For instance, machines have to be made safe and minimum and maximum work temperatures have to be maintained. This shifts the supply curve upwards and to the left. At any given level of employment, workers will only work for a given wage rate plus the cost of protection measures, in turn leading to a fall in employment. Hence it is argued by free market economists that measures designed to protect the employee usually lead to a fall in employment.

The extent to which government legislation giving workers extra rights leads to a rise in unemployment depends crucially upon three factors.
- The first relates to the difference between the new rights and existing free market rights. For instance, if the market wage rate is £4 per hour and a minimum wage is set at £3 per hour, the minimum wage will have no effect. It won't raise wages in the market or create unemployment. If the minimum wage is set at £3 when market clearing rates are £2.75 per hour, there will be a small increase in average wages but equally it is unlikely that much unemployment will be created. A minimum wage of £6 with market clearing rates of £2 per hour, on the other hand, will give substantial

benefits to workers employed but is likely to create substantial unemployment.
- Second, the amount of unemployment created depends on the relative elasticities of demand and supply for labour. Consider Figure 75.3 and compare it to Figure 75.1. Both diagrams relate to the introduction of a minimum wage. The market clearing wage is OE and the minimum wage set is OF. Unemployment of AC is created by the introduction of the minimum wage. In Figure 75.1, the demand and supply curves are relatively elastic between OE and OF. The unemployment created is large. In Figure 65.3, the demand and supply curves are relatively inelastic between OE and OF. The unemployment created is relatively small.
Indeed if the demand for labour is perfectly inelastic, a rise in wages will have no effect on the demand for labour. One conclusion that could be drawn from the argument above is that the demand for labour is relatively less elastic in the formal sector of the economy than in the informal sector. So minimum wage legislation or equal pay legislation will have a much greater impact on jobs in the informal sector than in the formal sector. This would correspond with evidence which suggests that semi-skilled and unskilled workers have suffered disproportionately from unemployment in the 1970s and the 1980s in the UK.
- Third, what might be true for a single industry might not be true for the economy as a whole. For instance, minimum wage legislation in the hairdressing industry might result in unemployment amongst hairdressers. But minimum wage legislation across all industries might have little or no effect on unemployment. In economics, it is not possible to conclude that the economy as a whole will behave in the same way as an individual market.

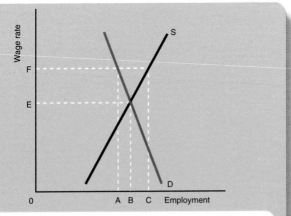

Figure 75.3 *Inelastic demand and supply curves for labour. The more inelastic the demand and supply curves for labour, the less unemployment is created when minimum wages are introduced.*

Question 3

The Disability Discrimination Act, 1995 created more rights for disabled people in the workplace. The measures would require employers to make a 'reasonable adjustment' to working conditions to overcome the practical difficulties of a disability. For example, a reasonable adjustment might include lowering a light switch to place it within easier reach for a disabled person or redecorating part of the premises to provide better contrast for someone with visual impairment. The minister for the disabled estimated at the time that the changes to physical access required by the legislation would impose an overall cost to industry of no more than £1.1bn, with an 'average cost to the average business' of between £500 and £1 500.

Employers' organisations found it hard to oppose the principles behind the measures. However, they were worried that they were too vague. Mr Ian Smedley, the Institute of Directors' small business executive, said: 'The government has in effect issued a blank cheque which business will have to pay.'

(a) Using diagrams, discuss the possible impact of the government measures described in the data on employment.

Applied economics

The minimum wage

In April 1999, the government introduced a national minimum wage (NMW) of £3.60 per hour for adults aged 22 and over. The rate for 18-21 year olds was set at £3, whilst employers were allowed to offer whatever they wanted for workers aged 17 and below.

In total, it was estimated that nearly 2 million workers would see an increase in their wages as Table 75.2 shows. The single largest gainers were estimated to be 1.12 million female part-time workers. They were concentrated in three industries shown in Figure 75.4 - retailing, hospitality (including hotels and catering) and market services. In terms of how much different groups would gain, homeworkers, shown in Figure 75.5, would gain the most, seeing their pay rise by over 30 per cent. Part time workers previously on pay below the minimum wage would, on average, gain 22 per cent it was estimated.

Arguments in favour of minimum wages

The main argument in favour of a national minimum wage is one of **horizontal equity** (☞ unit 68). Every worker should receive the same rate of pay for working an hour. In a market economy, this is not possible. The market produces wage differentials in order to create an efficient economy where wages act as signals, creating

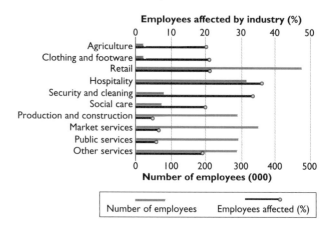

Figure 75.4 *Employees affected by minimum wage (by industry)*
Source: adapted from New Earnings Survey, Labour Force Survey.

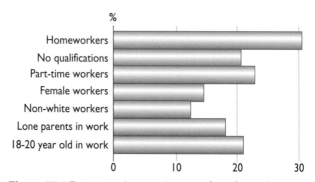

Figure 75.5 *Percentage increase in rates of pay for workers earning below the minimum wage*
Source: adapted from New Earnings Survey, Labour Force Survey.

incentives for workers with higher skills to take on jobs with higher marginal revenue products. However, a minimum wage sets a floor below which market forces cannot drive wages. It gives a minimum reward to labour which can be seen as a 'fair' reward. It prevents workers in the UK from receiving Third World wage rates and creating a society which is highly unequal.

Minimum wages could also be argued to promote dynamic efficiency in a rich industrialised country. Firms will employ workers if their wage is equal to or less than their marginal revenue product (MRP). The MRP of labour can be raised if workers receive training and become more skilled. Equally, the MRP of labour

	Numbers affected (000s)	Proportion of group affected (000s)	Increase in wage bill (%)	Average increase for those affected (%)
All 18+	1 960	9	0.6	30
18-21	225	15	2.4	*30
22+	1 735	8	0.6	30
Male full-time	295	3	0.3	-
Male part-time	230	25	3.0	-
Female full-time	320	5	0.7	-
Female part-time	1 120	21	2.7	-

*Approximate but unlikely to be much different.

Table 75.2 *Estimated coverage and cost of the national minimum wage*
Source: adapted from Low Pay Commission, OECD.

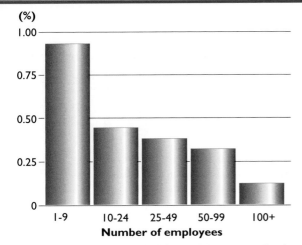

Figure 75.6 *Increase in wage bill from minimum wage by size of enterprise (%)*
Source: adapted from Labour Force Survey.

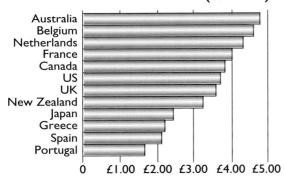

Figure 75.7 *Minimum wages at parity with sterling (end 1997)*
Source: adapted from OECD.

can rise if firms invest in capital equipment. A minimum wage encourages firms to invest in both human and physical capital which can lead to higher economic growth in the long term. This will be true if low wages before the introduction of a minimum wage had led to underinvestment and an inefficient use of scarce labour.

Similarly, it can be argued that minimum wages encourage rich countries like the UK to move away from the production of low value added products to higher value added products. In the long term, if countries are to grow, they will produce ever more sophisticated products. The introduction of a minimum wage encourages this trend because it encourages investment.

In terms of world poverty, minimum wages in developed countries can help Third World countries become more competitive. Some low value, unskilled jobs will disappear in rich countries which introduce a minimum wage. Third World countries will then be able to fill the gap left by exporting those products to the rich country. This is mutually beneficial. The foreign exchange earned by the Third World country will be spent on goods and services from other

countries, including exports from rich countries. They are likely to be higher value goods, those goods which rich countries have a competitive advantage in producing.

Economic theory suggests that where there is a monopsonist employer in the market, there will be allocative inefficiency. This is because a monopsonist will employ fewer workers at a lower rate of pay than if there is a number of employers in a market (☞ unit 75). The introduction of a minimum wage to a market where a monopsonist is paying low wages will both raise wages and raise employment. Allocative inefficiency is likely to be reduced. What's more, the taxpayer should also gain with fewer workers entitled to benefits for being on low incomes, and tax income increased as wages are higher and there are more in work.

Arguments against minimum wages

The main argument against minimum wages is that it creates unemployment. Evidence on this is contradictory. In the UK, the effect on unemployment of the 1999 minimum wages levels was probably negligible. This was because the minimum wage was set at such a low level that it had little impact on costs for employers. Figure 75.6, for instance, shows that the average increase in the wage bill for employers was estimated to be only 0.9 per cent for small firms and 0.1 per cent for large employers with over 100 workers.

The extent to which unemployment is created depends in part on whether low paid jobs are in the internationally traded goods and services sector, and the rates of pay of the UK's international competitors. Figure 75.7 shows that the UK's minimum wage was set below that of richer countries like the USA but above that of poorer countries like Portugal and Spain. So jobs might be lost to poorer members of the European Union, to Eastern Europe and Third World countries. However, most workers affected by the minimum wage are in the non-traded sector anyway as can be seen from Figure 75.4. So relatively few jobs are at risk.

Evidence from abroad where national minimum wages are relatively common gives contradictory evidence. For instance, a study of the extension of the US minimum wage to Puerto Rico, a Third World economy in the Caribbean, in 1974 showed that there was a consequent fall in employment. By 1980, the Federal minimum wage was 75 per cent of the average wage in Puerto Rico's manufacturing compared to 43 per cent in mainland USA. Unemployment rose from 11.3 per cent to 23.4 per cent between 1974 and 1983, of which one-third was attributed to the rise in the minimum wage. In contrast, a 1992 study by L Katz and A Krueger of 314 fast food restaurants in Texas found that, following a 45 per cent rise in the US minimum wage in 1991, employment rose. Moreover, the restaurants which had had to raise their wages the most also tended to have the largest increase in employment. The study found that for every 10 per cent rise in wages, there was a 25 per cent increase in full-time employment.

Another argument against minimum wage legislation is that it imposes compliance costs on individual firms. They have to ensure that they are meeting the requirements of the law and are able to prove to inspectors that they are so doing. This is just another example of 'red tape' which imposes particularly high costs on small firms.

1. The graphs show what percentage of workers received hourly earnings between £0.60 and £1.80. For instance, in 1999 approximately 0.2 per cent of workers received £3.50, approximately 1.9 per cent of workers received exactly the minimum wage of £3.60 and approximately 0.8 per cent of workers received £7.80 per hour.

Figure 75.8 *Workers' hourly pay before and after the introduction of the minimum wage, UK, % of employees*

Source: adapted from New Earnings Survey, ONS.

Perhaps the most important argument against the 1999 introduction of the minimum wage in the UK is that it did little to reduce poverty. Figure 75.8 shows that the numbers of workers earning less than £3.60 an hour was far smaller in 1999 after the introduction of the minimum wage than in 1998. However, as Table 75.2 shows, the main beneficiaries were female part-time workers. A majority of these lived in households where there was another adult working and therefore the household was not poor. The Institute of Fiscal Studies estimated that only 4 per cent of households in the bottom half of the income distribution in the UK gained from a £3.60 minimum wage. In contrast, 7 per cent of households in the upper half of the income distribution were better off. The introduction of a minimum wage therefore did little to increase equity in the UK.

The Social Charter

The Maastricht Treaty

In December 1991, European governments gathered together at a Dutch town called Maastricht to hammer out a treaty which would take the European Union through into the next century. The main item on the agenda was a timetable for monetary union. However, the Maastricht Treaty also contained a chapter on social issues (the Social Chapter) which laid out a Social Charter for the European Union.

The Social Charter was felt to be a vital part of economic integration which had been taking place since the foundation of the European Union in 1956. Countries at the time agreed to dismantle tariff and quota barriers between themselves. In 1987, under the Single European Act, they agreed to dismantle all non-tariff barriers to trade from 1 January 1993. Monetary union was a further step along the road to an integrated Europe.

However, there was a fear that firms would respond to integration by moving production to the lowest cost country in the EU, enabling them to exploit local workers. The Social Charter was an attempt to harmonise policies on labour between countries to prevent large shifts of capital in this way.

Opt-out and opt-in

In 1991, the Conservative government under John Major negotiated an opt-out for Britain from the Social Charter. It believed that the Social Charter would raise employment costs in the UK and make the economy less competitive. It also prevented the UK from setting laws which might be to its own benefit. The decision was bitterly attacked at the time by other European countries signing up to the Charter. They were worried that firms would shift production facilities from the rest of Europe to the UK. Jacques Delors, president of the European Union at the time, said that 'Britain will become a paradise for investment'.

In 1997, the new Labour government under Tony Blair, decided to opt into the Social Charter. Its view was that the Social Charter was beneficial to the interests of UK workers. It also did not believe that the UK had increased its competitiveness significantly since 1991 because of its opt out. Tony Blair said that the UK would still have 'the most lightly regulated labour market of any leading economy in the world'.

Implementation of the Social Charter

Examples of Social Charter directives implemented in the UK include the following.
- The EU working time directive came into force in October 1998. Employers had to limit the working time to a maximum of 48 hours a week. Certain exemptions were permitted. Three weeks paid holiday, which rose to 4 weeks from November 1999, had to be given. Workers became entitled to designated rest breaks, whilst night work became more tightly regulated.
- The EU parental leave directive was implemented in December 1999. Paid maternity leave was extended from 14 to 18 weeks, whilst three months' unpaid parental leave after the birth of a child became a legal right.
- The European works council directive became part of UK law in October 1998. All UK-based companies employing 1 000 people, 150 of whom are in more than two EU countries, have to set up consultation committees covering transnational issues.

The Social Charter

The Social Charter, or the European Community Charter of Workers' Fundamental Social Rights, was put forward in the 1980s, approved by the European Commission in 1989 and ratified by the Maastricht Treaty in 1991. It is not a body of law. Instead, it is a mechanism for enacting directives as and when the European Union feels that workers' rights need to be protected. Directives first have to be approved by the Council of Ministers. Once approved, they must be passed into national law by individual parliaments. Individual directives can be and sometimes are rejected by the Council of Ministers. However, once approved there, they become legally enforceable in all member countries whether or not national parliaments have passed the necessary legislation, because individuals can always go to the European Court to have European law upheld.

Source: adapted from the *Financial Times*, 28.2.1992 and 18.6.1998.

You are an economist working for a trade union. You have been asked to prepare a report on the implications of the Social Charter.
1. Write an introduction outlining the history of the Social Charter and giving examples of its provisions.
2. Outline ways in which workers are likely to benefit from it.

3. Using diagrams, analyse how workers in the UK might lose out from the decision to opt into the Social Charter in the late 1990s.
4. Evaluate whether the trade union should push for further regulation of the labour market in the EU in the future.

Applied economics

Population change in the UK

The population of the UK has increased this century from 38 million in 1901 to a current figure of nearly 60 million. There are three ways in which a country's population can increase.

The numbers being born can rise As Figure 76.1 shows, there has been a considerable fluctuation in the number of births this century. The two World Wars saw sharp falls in the number of births. Other periods of economic uncertainty or recession - the 1920s and 1930s, and the late 1960s and early 1970s - were also associated with falls in births. The period of sustained economic growth from 1950 to the mid-1960s saw an increase in births - the so-called post-war baby boom. Subsequently the number of births did not begin to increase again until the late 1970s.

The BIRTH RATE, the numbers of live births as a proportion of the total population, is determined by two factors. First, the larger the number of women of child bearing age, the higher the birth rate is likely to be. For instance, the bulge in births in the 1950s and mid-1960s produced an increase in the numbers of women of child-bearing age from the late 1970s onwards. Hence this provides a partial explanation for the increase in the birth rate from the late 1970s. Second, the birth rate is determined by the FERTILITY RATE, the numbers of live births as a proportion of women of child-bearing age.

What determines the fertility rate is difficult to say. One reason why fertility rates were much higher in the pre-First World War era was the high infant mortality rate. Because so many children died, women needed to have a large number of children if some of these were to survive into adulthood. Today few children die and therefore parents are fairly confident that if they have two children, then those two will survive into adulthood.

Increased use of contraception and abortion too are likely to have affected the fertility rate. However, it should be remembered that contraception and abortion only became widely practised in the 1960s with the introduction of the pill and the legalisation of abortion. So they are unlikely to be major determinants of the changes in the birth rate seen in the first half of this century.

The economics of child rearing is likely to provide a more significant explanation of the trend in all developed countries to lower fertility rates. The opportunity cost of rearing children has steadily increased. In many Third World countries, children are economic assets for the parents. They can be put to work at an early age and custom often demands that children have a duty to look after parents in their old age - having children is the equivalent of investing in a pension scheme. In developed countries, the average leaving age for children from full time education is slowly increasing. More and more children need to be supported through to the age of 21. Children are

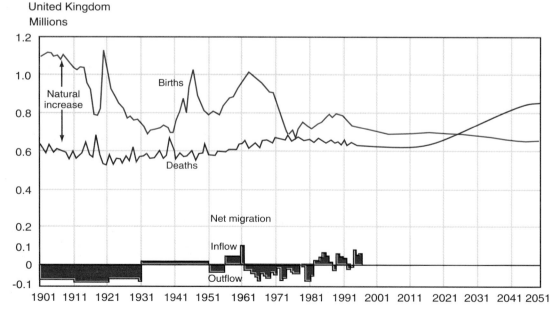

Figure 76.1 *Population changes and projections*
Source: adapted from *Social Trends*, Office for National Statistics.

expensive to keep. There is little tradition in the UK of financial support of parents in old age. What's more, the opportunity cost for women of staying at home to rear children has increased. Women have been able to obtain higher and higher wages and leaving employment for any length of time has a devastating effect on a woman's long term earnings potential (☞ unit 73). In countries such as Germany, the birth rate today is so low that the population is actually falling.

The number of deaths can fall Figure 76.1 shows that the number of deaths has increased since the Second World War. This is due to increased numbers in the population. However, the DEATH RATE, the proportion of deaths to the total population, has been falling as life expectancy has increased. Better food, improved housing, safer working conditions as well as medical advances have been the cause of this trend towards greater longevity.

Net migration can be positive Net migration is the difference between immigration and emigration. If it is positive, it means that more people enter the country than leave to settle abroad. Figure 76.1 shows that the UK has tended to suffer a loss of population through migration over time. However, the numbers involved are relatively small. In the 1980s and 1990s, net migration tended to be positive. In 1996, approximately 40 per cent of all immigrants were British citizens returning home. One-fifth of the total were citizens of other European Union countries. Nearly another tenth were citizens of Australia, New Zealand and Canada. Only approximately 15 per cent were from new Commonwealth countries such as Pakistan and Caribbean countries. The change in total population resulting from migration was a mere 0.01 per cent.
  Some predict that, with the Single European Market and the Social Charter, migration to and from other

European Union countries will increase over the next 10-20 years. They point to the considerable migration flows experienced between states in the USA over time. However, language and cultural barriers are much greater in the EU than in the USA. The main flows are likely to be of three types. One is of managerial workers, transferring from country to country employed by pan-European companies. Another is of young skilled workers wanting to gain language skills before returning home. The third is of migrants from outside the EU who initially settle in one country but then choose to go to live in another European country.

The changing age structure of the population

The death rate has changed only slowly over time, and has tended to fall. However, the birth rate in the UK this century has fluctuated significantly and it is this fluctuation which has caused major changes in the age structure of the population. Table 76.1 summarises the most important changes which have occurred since 1971 and are projected to occur by the year 2025. Four major changes can be singled out.

Children The number of pupils in schools, shown by the population aged 5-15, declined during the 1970s and 1980s. This resulted in widespread closure of schools. However, the increase in the birth rate from 1978 led to an increased demand for school places in the 1990s although it will fall again in the next century. This means that there was an increase in demand for goods such as school buildings, children's books and clothing, and teachers in the 1990s.

Young workers The number of school leavers and young workers aged 16-19 grew substantially in the 1970s. This is likely to have been a significant factor in the growth of youth unemployment in that decade.

Table 76.1 *Selected social and economic needs of population groups by age*

UK								Indices 1991 = 100
	1971	1981	1986	1991	2001	2011	2025	Social and economic needs of different age groups of the population
People aged								
Under 1	110	89	92	100	93	87	93	Maternity services, Health visiting, Preventive medicine.
1-4	118	87	93	100	102	91	97	Day care, Nursery education.
5-15	125	116	103	100	113	107	104	Compulsory education.
16-19	101	125	119	100	95	110	93	Further and higher education, Training, Employment.
15-44 (females)	86	95	100	100	95	91	89	Maternity services.
20-49	86	90	95	100	96	94	90	Employment, Housing, Transport.
50-59/64[1]	111	106	102	100	117	126	133	Pre-retirement training, Early retirement.
60/65[2]-74	99	103	101	100	95	108	123	Retirement, Pensions.
75-84	70	86	95	100	104	101	126	Retirement pension, Health care, Home
85 and over	55	68	81	100	132	150	154	helps, Sheltered housing, Retirement homes.

Notes: 1. 59 for females, 64 for males.
   2. 60 for females, 65 for males

Source: adapted from *Social Trends*, Office for National Statisitcs.

However, in the 1990s, the number of young workers fell significantly. This was referred to as the 'demographic timebomb'. It was widely predicted in the late 1980s that employers would be faced with a severe shortage of youngsters on the job market. However, the deep and prolonged recession of 1990-92 led to a sharp fall in demand for young workers which in the first half of the 1990s was probably greater than the fall in supply. The result was increased youth unemployment. In the second half of the 1990s, an expanding supply of female labour, together with the take up of one and a half million unemployed workers into jobs, helped prevent any excess demand for labour appearing across the economy.

The 'baby-boomers' The generation of workers born in the post-war baby boom is now moving through the age structure of the population. This can be seen in Figure 76.2, an age-gender pyramid which reveals key points in the history of the 20th century. The number of births broadly increased each year between 1900 and the mid-1960s. The two World Wars briefly interrupted this trend. The fall in the number of males and females females born between 1914-18, the period of the First World War, can be seen on the diagram by looking at the numbers of 79-83 year olds on the diagram. Then in 1919, there was a large increase in the number of births and hence a bulge in the number of 78 year olds in the population in 1997. Similarly, for the Second World War, there is a fall in the number of those aged around 55 in 1997 in the population. The large number of 50 year olds alive in 1997 represents the sharp increase in the number of births immediately after the Second World War. The baby boomers, born in the 1950s and 1960s, are the bulge on the diagram centered round those who were 32 in 1997. Over time, this bulge will move itself up the age-gender pyramid, with significant economic implications. In the 1970s and early 1980s, as they first entered the workforce, they suffered unemployment because the economy was not able to absorb them. The 1970s and 1980s were difficult times for the UK with high levels of inflation, oil price shocks and the restructuring of manufacturing industry. In the 1990s and the first decade of the 21st century, this group have come to occupy key positions in their places of work. But 2015 is likely to be a turning point. At this point, the peak number of baby boomers will turn 50. Some will already be taking early retirement. By 2025, the vast majority of those born in 1965 will have left the labour force and be pensioners. By 2035, the children born in the 1970s will have retired too. The workforce will then be made up of those aged 20 or less shown on the age-sex pyramid for 1997. So the baby boomers will dominate the workplace for the first 20 years of the 21st century. They will constitute a disproportionately large share of the workforce and hold the key positions. They will have considerable spending power. Then in retirement, they will still be an important force. Their sheer numbers are likely to give them an important political voice which they are likely to use to direct spending towards the elderly. In the market place, they will be a significant group of consumers.

The elderly A growing proportion of the population is now retired. In 1971, there were 7.4 million aged 65 and over, 13.3 per cent of the total population. This grew to 8.5 million in 1981 and to 9.1 million in 1991. This is projected to rise to 9.3 million in 2001, 12.0 million in 2021 and 14.0 million in 2031 as the baby-boomers retire. As Table 76.1 shows, these overall numbers mask significant changes in the composition of the elderly population. In the 1990s, there was little change in the total figure. But the number of 75 year olds and over (born before or immediately after the First World War) increased whilst the numbers of 65-74 year olds (the generation born in the 1920s and 1930s) decreased.

This has major implications for the state. Those aged 75 and over tend to be on very low incomes and therefore need income support. Many are unable to look after themselves and therefore need care in the community or in institutions such as old people's homes. They are particularly expensive for the National Health Service (NHS). Therefore NHS, social security and social services budgets will have to increase in real terms if the standard of living of the elderly is to be maintained or there will have to be much more private provision by individuals. However, the balance of population amongst the elderly will start to change as the baby-boomers begin to retire. In the 2020s and 2030s, the baby-boomer 65-75 year olds, retiring on good pensions and having been brought up accustomed to post-war affluence, are likely to be a powerful

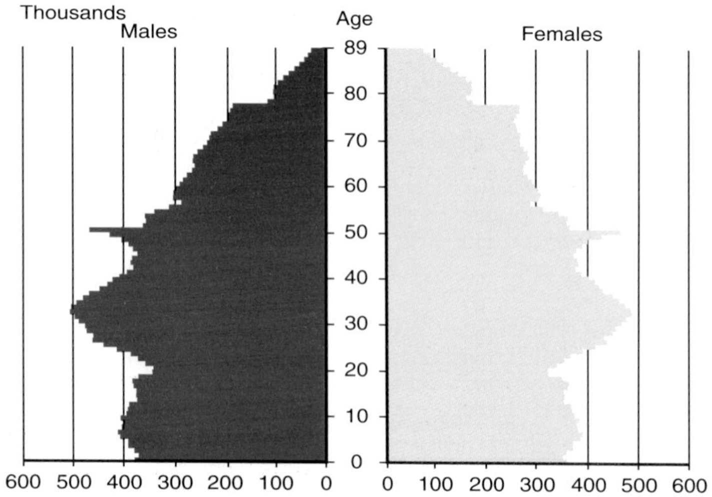

Figure 76.2 *Population by gender and age, 1997, UK*
Source: adapted from *Social Trends*, Office for National Statistics.

force in society and in the market place.

An international comparison

In the developing world, most countries have a relatively young population compared to the UK. Their problems are those of paying for the education of their children and the provision of jobs as these children move into the workforce. In the developed world, the major problem that countries now face is the ageing of the population. Figure 76.3 shows the change in the percentage of the population aged 65 and over in selected OECD countries. Of the countries shown, the UK will be least affected by the 'greying' of its population. Over the period from 1960 to 2020, the percentage of the population over retirement age is projected only to increase by 50 per cent. In Japan, it

will nearly quadruple and in Germany it will double.

As argued above, this has considerable implications for government spending and the economy. For instance, currently health spending is more than four times as high per capita on the over-65s as on the under-65s in OECD countries. For the over-75s, the proportion rises to nearly 6 times.

However, it also has implications for the standard of living of workers in the population. The higher the DEPENDENCY RATIO, the proportion of dependants (i.e. non-workers) to workers in the population, the lower will be the after-tax incomes of workers if dependants are to receive a given income. For instance, workers will see their share of national income fall over the next 70 years in France and Germany if pensioners are to increase their incomes at the same rate as workers. The worsening ratio of people aged 15-64 to pensioners in OECD countries is shown in Figure 76.4.

One response to this is for the government to cut expenditure on state pensions. In the UK, successive measures since 1981 have reduced state pension entitlements (see below in Data Question) whilst workers have been encouraged to make their own private provision. In Europe, where state pension entitlements are far more generous, state pension systems face becoming unaffordable over the next 50 years. Inter-generational transfers of income from workers to pensioners are likely to become a source of political conflict as pensioners attempt to protect their incomes whilst workers balk at paying the high taxes this is likely to entail.

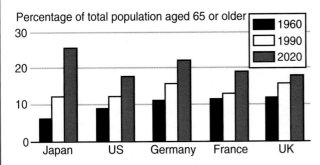

Figure 76.3 *Percentage of total population aged 65 or older*
Source: adapted from OECD.

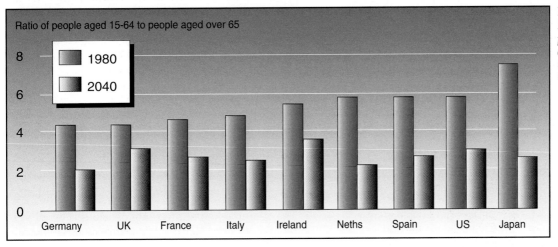

Figure 76.4
Percentage of total population aged 65 or older
Source: adapted from Hills (1993).

key terms

Birth rate - the numbers of live births as a proportion of the total population.
Death rate - the number of deaths as a proportion of the total population.
Dependency ratio - the proportion of

dependants (i.e. non-workers) to workers in the population.
Fertility rate - the numbers of live births as a proportion of women of child-bearing age.

The pensions time bomb

The pensions problem

The population of most of the world's richest countries is ageing. Over the next 50 years, most countries will see a rise in their dependency ratios, the number of non-workers as a proportion of workers. In particular, the number of pensioners to workers is likely to rise substantially. This poses a major problem. The goods and services that pensioners consume are made by the workers in the population. The more pensioners consume, the less is available to workers. Getting the balance right between these inter-generational transfers is proving to be a crucial economic and political focus for government policy.

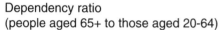

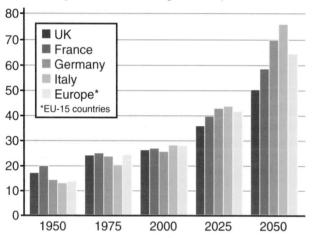

Figure 76.5 *The ageing of Western Europe*
Source: adapted from US Census Bureau.

Paying for pensions

There are two main ways in which pensions are financed. Pay as you go schemes rely on today's workers paying for today's pensions. For instance, the UK state old age pension is financed in this way. The government collects taxes and pays out pensions from that revenue. Similarly, the UK teachers' pension scheme is a pay as you go scheme. The scheme collects pension contributions from today's teachers and their employers and uses the money to pay pensions to today's retired teachers. Pay as you go schemes are relatively cheap to run and easy to understand. But they face major problems if, as will be the case over the next 50 years, the number of pensioners to workers rises. The only way to finance this, assuming that pensions retain their value relative to earnings, is to increase the taxes or contributions of workers. In Japan, for instance, which has a particularly acute problem, the cost of state pensions is forecast to quadruple by 2030. This implies large rises in taxes.

The other method of financing pensions is to adopt a funded approach. Here, today's workers put money aside which is invested. When they come to retire, their pensions are paid out of the pot of money which has been built up over the years. This pot may be individual, a personal pension for example, or it may be collective. A group of workers working for the same employer may contribute into a fund, with the employer usually paying in amounts too. The fund then pays out a pension to retired members of the scheme.

Financing: does it matter?

It could be argued that it doesn't matter how pensions are financed. Pay as you go and funded schemes both mean that today's workers produce the goods and services that pensioners consume today. A pensioner can't store up hair cuts, bus rides or even computer equipment from when they were working at age 30 to consume at age 80. Funded schemes simply give an illusion that pensioners have real resources at their disposal. Economic changes or governments can strip that illusion bare. For instance, high rates of inflation can quickly erode the real value of pensions. Equally, a government could simply pass a law cancelling all pension contracts.

However, it can also be argued that funded schemes are superior to pay as you go schemes. The argument is that funded schemes invest at least part of their funds in businesses, for instance through buying new share issues on stock markets. This money is then used to finance investment which would otherwise not have been undertaken. So workers contribute to increasing the capital stock of a country through their pension contributions. When they come to retire, the output of the economy is larger than it would otherwise have been. They are then able to consume goods and services which, if they hadn't paid pension contributions, would not have been produced. In contrast, there is no build up of physical capital associated with pay as you go schemes because today's pension contributions become today's pensions.

The UK state old age pension

Governments have been aware of the pension problem for a long time now. In 1979, the incoming Conservative government under Margaret Thatcher was committed to cutting state spending. State benefits were the single most important item of government spending even then and, with growing numbers of old age pensioners, was forecast to carry on rising. The government decided that one way to reduce the long term tax burden of state benefits was to change the rules about the state old age pension. Since the Second World War, governments had been raising it roughly in line with increases in average earnings. In 1981, the government announced that in future it would only be raised in line with average prices. As Figure 76.6 shows, this will have a dramatic impact on its cost. From being over 20 per cent of average earnings in 1981, it will fall to only 8 per cent by 2044 and eventually will fall to zero. Over the same period, the ratio of people aged 65 and over to those aged 20-64 in the UK is forecast to double. With the state pension falling to 40 per cent of its value compared to real earnings, taxpayers in 2044 will pay lower taxes to fund the state pension than they did in 1981.

Figure 76.6 also shows what is planned to happen to SERPS, the State Earnings Related Pension Scheme. This was introduced in 1975 to provide pensions linked to an individual worker's earnings and was aimed at mainly lower paid workers not in employers' occupational pension schemes. In the 1980s and 1990s, the government gradually scaled back the value of the pensions that workers in the scheme would eventually get to reduce its cost. It was a pay as you go scheme and so any deficits in the fund in a year (the difference between contributions from workers and pensions paid) would have to come out of taxes. In 1998, the government announced its eventual abolition, partly because it was not helping the very low paid and those not in work. It is to be replaced by a state second pension scheme. This will provide a fixed rate pension, not linked to the earnings of the worker. Those on low incomes will get a higher pension than under SERPS. Those on higher incomes will get a lower pension. It is designed to provide a minimum pension for all who have not contributed to a non-state pension scheme.

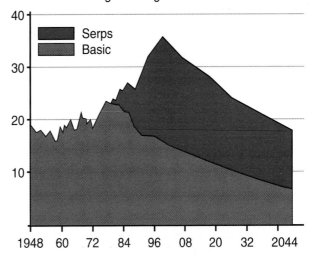

Figure 76.6 *The value of state pensions*
Source: adapted from Government Actuary's Department, Association of British Insurers, NPI.

Occupational pension schemes

An occupational pension scheme is one linked to an individual's job. Typically, the employer sets up the scheme and pays into it as well as the employees in the scheme. The employers' contributions are effectively a fringe benefit for the employee because they typically increase the final pension that is paid. Pensions can sometimes be based solely on the contributions made by an individual worker and the investment performance of the money saved. Sometimes, however, pensions are based on final salary and the number of years of contributions made. Final salary schemes are easy to understand for workers and take much of the risk out of the investment performance of the money in the fund for the employee. But workers who leave the employer before retirement are often penalised with much lower pensions. So they discourage workers from moving jobs. As Figure 76.7 shows, they are also becoming less common mainly because fewer employers are prepared to set up funds or continue with them. In a typical fund, the employer pays in more than the employee, and so not having a fund cuts the cost of employment for firms.

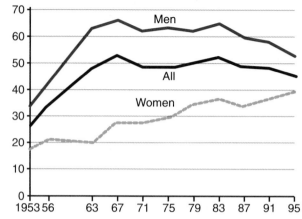

Figure 76.7 *Proportion of workers covered by occupational pension funds*
Source: adapted from Government Actuary's Department, Association of British Insurers, NPI.

Personal pensions, AVCs and stakeholder pensions

Governments in the 1980s pursued policies which encouraged people to take responsibility for their own affairs. State pensions and even occupational pension schemes were seen as discouraging personal initiative. So, in the 1980s, the government established personal pensions. Workers could pay into a personal pension which was effectively a personal saving scheme. They could get the same generous income tax rebates for saving in this way as they could for paying into an employer's occupational scheme. At retirement, whatever was in their individual pot of savings could be used to buy a pension (an 'annuity') for the rest of their life. Personal pensions were attractive to workers whose employer did not offer an occupational pension scheme. They were also better for workers who expected to change employers several times in their working life because occupational pension schemes penalised this type of worker. In practice, though, only higher income earners used personal pensions in the way they were intended because only they could afford the high levels of savings needed to create any significant pension fund.

To encourage more people to save, the government created AVCs (Additional Voluntary Contributions). This allowed a worker paying into an occupational pension scheme to save for a second pension and get income tax rebates as an incentive. Although these have proved popular, the amount of pension that the typical worker will get at retirement will be relatively small. They have also been sold mainly to above average income earners.

To attract workers below average income to save for their retirement, the government announced in 1998 that

it would created a new scheme, stakeholder pensions. Like personal pensions, these would be individual pots of saving built up over a lifetime and used to buy a pension at retirement. However, any financial company offering stakeholder pensions would have to cut commission fees and administration fees to a minimum on any stakeholder scheme they sold. Like personal pensions, there will be tax incentives for making contributions and they will be particularly suitable for those who move jobs frequently. Many question, however, whether those on lower incomes will be able to afford to save anything. If they can't, stakeholder pensions will be as unattractive as personal pensions to this group.

Personal pension benefits

How does a personal pension operate? The worker saves up over a period of time. The pot of savings increases as more is put in and through growth of the fund, for instance with interest. At retirement, the worker uses the fund to buy an annuity, a promise to pay a pension for the rest of the worker's life. In 2000, a male aged 65 could get a pension of £9 000 a year at a cost of £100 000. To retire earlier at 60, make the pension payable to his wife if he dies and to have the pension increase in line with inflation, £100 000 would only buy a £4 000 a year pension. The sums of money are no different for occupational pension schemes.

Pensions are therefore very expensive. It is hardly surprising that lower income earners are unable to build up savings to provide them with a reasonable pension. In practice, only higher income earners who save large amounts of money during their working life, or those who work for a long time for an employer with an occupational pension scheme, tend to retire on a decent pension. Figure 76.8 shows that the average pensioner today receives only £31 a week from their non-state pension - £ 1 612 a year.

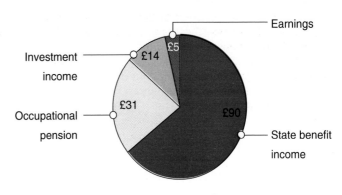

Figure 76.8 *Single pensioner income, 1996-97*
Source: adapted from The Pension Provision Group, Association of British Insurers.

The international problem

Most workers in the UK face a bleak future as pensioners. Governments over the past 20 years have cut back on their commitment to paying what, by international standards, has always been a relatively ungenerous amount. More people have built up larger amounts of money in occupational and personal pension funds, but many have not saved enough to give them a decent pension. The most vulnerable tend to be low paid workers and those prone to unemployment.

In Europe, there is a different problem. Non-state pension schemes for workers tend to be more generous. For instance, many workers who have worked 40 years are entitled to retire on two thirds final salary, whilst in the UK the maximum is typically half. What's more, governments have become involved in providing generous pension entitlements. Low paid workers, the self-employed, the unemployed and women can all look forward to much higher state

pensions than they would if they were in the UK. These pensions are financed from social security taxes (the equivalent of National Insurance contributions). These social security taxes tend to be high today because they need to finance today's pensioners. But with an increasing dependency ratio, they will have to be much higher in twenty or thirty years time. Many analysts predict that these systems will become unaffordable because workers will not be prepared to pay the high taxes needed to finance them. The most commonly advocated solution is to cut state pension benefits, as has been achieved in the UK, and to encourage workers to save for private pensions. Already in Italy, at the end of the 1990s, there was political controversy when the government wanted to cut state pension entitlements because it said that they were unaffordable. This is unlikely to be the only attempt to cut pensions in the future.

1. Briefly outline the pensions problems that face:
   (a) governments; (b) workers; (c) pensioners in Europe over the next 50 years.
2. (a) Briefly explain the differences between 'pay as you go' pension schemes and funded pension schemes.
   (b) What implications do these two types of funding

   have for (i) occupational mobility and (ii) economic growth?
3. Why might pensions be classified as a merit good?
4. Discuss whether governments should force all citizens to save for a pension.

Summary

1. The functional distribution of income is the share of national income received by each factor of production.
2. A factor receives economic rent if its earnings are above its transfer earnings. Quasi rent is rent earned only in the short run.
3. Economic rent will be greater, the more inelastic the supply curve.
4. A change in economic rent will not affect the allocation of resources.

The functional distribution of income

The factors of production are classified into **land**, **labour**, **capital** and **entrepreneurship** (☞ unit 2). The owners of factors of production receive a reward for renting out their factors. Landowners receive rent, labour receives wages, the providers of capital receive interest and entrepreneurs earn profits.

The FUNCTIONAL DISTRIBUTION OF INCOME shows the share of national income received by each factor of production. This is different from the **personal distribution of income** described in unit 68. An individual or household may receive income from several factors of production. For instance, a pensioner may have a part time job, receive rent from a property which she owns and receive dividends from shares.

The functional distribution of income depends in part upon the price that each factor of production is paid. Neo-classical economic theory suggests that the price of a product is determined by the forces of demand and supply. For instance, the wage rate of labour will be determined by the demand for labour and the supply of labour (☞ unit 73). Rent on land will be determined by the demand for land and the supply of land. The laws of demand and supply are as applicable in factor markets as they are in the goods markets.

The exact shapes of the demand and supply curves for land, labour and capital vary. However, they are broadly the same shape as in a goods market (i.e. the demand curve is downward sloping whilst the supply curve is upward sloping).

Demand and supply analysis can be used to show the functional distribution of income. In Figure 77.1 OC is, the equilibrium wage rate in the labour market. OA workers are employed and therefore the total wage bill is OA x OC (the number of workers employed x the wage rate per worker). The value to the employer of OA workers is given by the area OEBA, the sum of the marginal revenue product of each worker employed up to OA workers (the marginal revenue product of each worker is the vertical distance between the MRP curve and the horizontal axis).

Total revenue received by the employer is OEBA. OCBA is paid in wages. Therefore BCE is the amount left, after wages have been paid, to reward the other factors of production employed by the firm. Out of BCE it has to pay rent, interest and profits to the owners of land and capital and to entrepreneurs.

Figure 77.1 shows the market for labour. The same analysis would apply if the market for land or capital were shown.

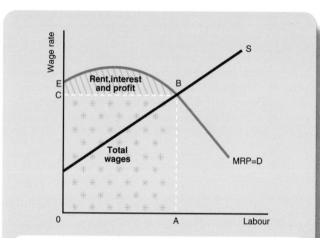

Figure 77.1 *The functional distribution of income*
Total revenue for the firm is the sum of the marginal revenue product of each worker (i.e. OEBA). The total wage bill for the firm is OCBA. Therefore BCE is left to distribute in the form of rent, interest and profit.

Economic rent

David Ricardo, writing in the early part of the 19th century, developed a theory of economic rent which today can be applied to all factors of production. During the Napoleonic Wars, land rents rose steeply at the same time as the price of corn. Many argued that the rise in the price of corn was due to landowners increasing rents on agricultural land. Ricardo, however, argued that it was the rise in the price of corn that resulted in farmers demanding more land for corn production and thus bidding up the price of land. Rent, he argued, was price determined and not price determining.

In Figure 77.3, the supply of land is shown to be perfectly inelastic. There is only a fixed amount of land available for corn production. An increase in the derived demand for land to rent, due to an increase in the price of corn, will push the demand curve for land from D_1 to D_2 and the price or rent of land will increase from OA to OB.

Question 1

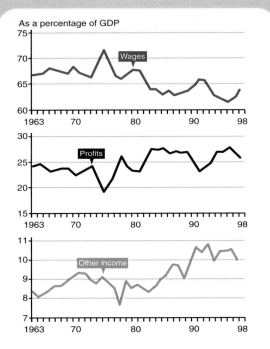

Figure 77.2 *The functional distribution of income, UK 1963-98*

Wages are compensation of employees. Profits are the gross operating surplus of corporations. Other income includes income from self employment. National income is gross value added at factor cost.

(a) Describe the trends in the functional distribution of income shown in the data.

(b) Using diagrams, explain the following arguments which might account for the data in Figure 77.2:
 (i) trade union reform in the 1980s resulted in workers being prepared to work for lower wages;
 (ii) in recessions, such as 1974-76, 1980-81 and 1990-92, firms find it hard to cut their wage bills in line with the fall in the marginal revenue product of labour and so their profitability falls.

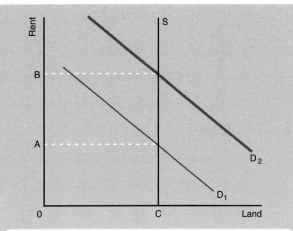

Figure 77.3 *Land in fixed supply*
If the supply of land is perfectly inelastic, any increase in its demand will raise rents but will have no effect on allocation of land as a resource in the economy.

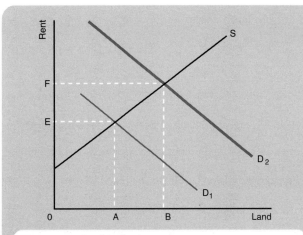

Figure 77.4 *Land in elastic supply*
If the supply of land is not perfectly inelastic, then an increase in its demand will affect not only its price but also the allocation of land within the economy.

A change in the rent on land in Figure 77.3 caused by a change in demand would have no effect on the allocation of resources in the economy. Because the supply is perfectly inelastic, land would be used to grow corn whether the price was almost zero or much higher than OB.

However, supply is not perfectly inelastic for most factors of production. For instance, the land used for growing corn in our example above could have alternative uses, such as growing vegetables or grazing animals. A change in the price of the factor will then have an allocative effect. In Figure 77.4, an increase in demand from D_1 to D_2 will lead to an increase of AB units of the factor being used.

The theory of economic rent distinguishes between two elements in the payment made to a factor of production.
● The TRANSFER EARNINGS of the factor. This is the **minimum** payment needed to keep the factor in its present use. If a worker is paid £200 a week, but could

only earn £150 a week in her next best paid occupation, then her transfer earnings would be £150 per week. Transfer earnings are the **opportunity cost** of employing the factor. A change in transfer earnings will affect the allocation of resources. If the worker could now earn £250 a week in her next best paid occupation, economic theory would predict that all other things being equal she would leave her present £200 a week job and take the more highly paid job.
● The ECONOMIC RENT of the factor. Economic rent is the payment over and above the minimum needed to keep the factor in its present use (i.e. it is the difference between its current payment and its transfer earnings). Economic rent will not affect the allocation of resources. If the transfer earnings of a worker were £150, she would remain in her present job whether she earned £200 a week or £250 a week.

The theory of economic rent can be explained using a

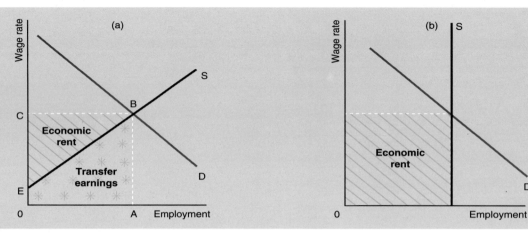

Figure 77.5 *Economic rent*
In Figure 67.5 (a), the total transfer earnings of OA labour is the area OABE. Total wages paid are OABC. So the economic rent paid to the factor is EBC. The less elastic supply of a factor, the greater the element of economic rent. If the supply is perfectly inelastic, as in Figure 67.5 (b), all the payment to the factor is economic rent.

demand and supply diagram. In Figure 67.5 (a), the equilibrium wage rate of labour is OC. However, only the last worker employed has transfer earnings of OC. The first worker would be prepared to work for a wage rate of OE. We know this because the supply curve shows the minimum wage rate for which workers would be prepared to work. As successive workers are employed, so the transfer earnings of the marginal worker (the last worker employed) increase. The transfer earnings of the first worker are OE whilst those of the last worker are AB (i.e. it is the vertical distance between the horizontal axis and the supply curve). So the total transfer earnings of all the workers employed, OA, is the area OABE.

The total earnings of OA workers is the area OABC (total number of workers OA times the wage rate per worker OC). The difference between the total payment to a factor and its transfer earnings is its economic rent. Hence the economic rent of labour in Figure 77.5 (a) is the area EBC.

Economic rent will be greater the more inelastic the supply curve. If, as in Figure 77.5 (b), supply is perfectly inelastic, then all the factor payment is economic rent and the transfer earnings of the factor are zero. Transfer earnings are zero because the factor will be supplied whether the payment received is zero or infinity (as shown by the vertical supply curve). Similarly, if demand is perfectly elastic (i.e. the demand curve is horizontal), all the factor payment is transfer earnings and economic rent is zero. Whatever quantity bought, a higher price would result in demand for the factor falling to zero. The factor cannot earn any more than the minimum needed to keep it in its present use.

Quasi-rent

Sometimes, economic rent can be earned in the short run, but not in the long run. Economic rent which can only be earned in the short run is called QUASI-RENT. For instance, a firm may buy a piece of machinery which is so specialised that it has no alternative uses. Then its transfer

earnings are zero and hence all the payments received from the use of the machine are quasi-economic rents. In the long run, the machinery must be replaced completely or not at all, and hence part or all of the earnings of this piece of capital will be transfer earnings. In the long run the machine will need at least to cover its economic cost or it will not be replaced.

Government policy

The amount of economic rent earned by a factor of production will not affect the allocation of resources within the economy. Hence, it is theoretically possible for the government to tax economic rent from a factor without altering economic efficiency in the economy (it will be argued in unit 79 that taxes might have an adverse effect on economic efficiency). For instance, the UK government places heavy taxes upon North Sea oil production, but attempts to levy them in such a way as not to discourage the development of marginal fields (i.e. oil fields which are only just profitable and which would not be developed if costs, including taxes, were higher).

Those who argue in favour of taxing economic rents usually want to see a redistribution of income from rich to poor. They argue that it offends against principles of equity that owners of some factors of production should receive high payments whilst others should receive little or nothing. Why should footballers or popstars earn hundreds of thousands of pounds a year when many workers earn a wage which is less than one per cent of that figure? Why should a farmer suddenly acquire a windfall gain of £1 million because his land has been given residential planning permission by the local council?

The problem with a tax on economic rents is that it is very difficult to tax just economic rent and not tax transfer earnings. As soon as transfer earnings are taxed, there will be allocative effects and there may be a loss of efficiency in the economy.

Question 2

With oil prices at a 12 year low, Britain's offshore oil industry is facing an uncertain future. Current production is relatively safe. Industry estimates suggest that 93 per cent output from the UK continental shelf is profitable at prices as low as $7 a barrel compared to today's price of $10-$12. However, it is exploration, appraisal and development that are most hit by low oil prices. Prices need to be at $12 a barrel to justify the life cycle costs of the average field. The $12 covers not just the $7 operational cost but also the exploration and development costs. With prices below $12, firms will not make on average a high enough rate of return to justify their investment.

Source: adapted from the *Financial Times*, 16.2.1999.

(a) '93 per cent of oil fields were profitable at prices at or below $7 a barrel'. If the price of oil was $12 a barrel, explain, using a diagram, how much economic rent was being earned (i) on these 93 per cent of fields and (ii) on the remaining 7 per cent if they were profitable at prices between $7 and $12.

(b) Explain, using another diagram, why firms would stop exploration in the North Sea if the average life cycle cost of a new field was $12 a barrel when the market price of oil was $8.

Question 3

(a) Explain why this field in Lancashire might be worth around £2 500 an acre as farming land but £250 000 an acre as building land.

(b) Should farmers be allowed to keep any capital gain on land following the decision by a local authority to grant planning permission for building on the land?

Economic rent - the payment made to a factor over and above its transfer earnings in the long run.

Functional distribution of income - shows the share of national income received by each factor of production.

Quasi-rent - economic rent earned only in the short run.

Transfer earnings - the minimum payment needed to keep a factor of production in its present use. It is the opportunity cost of the factor.

Applied economics

Crossing the Channel

In 1994, the Channel Tunnel finally opened for business. Twelve months late, and having cost nearly twice as much to build as originally forecast, the project was on the knife edge of financial survival. It was forced to renegotiate on its mountain of debt because the revenues from passengers could not cover both the day to day operating costs and the interest payments. By 1999, approximately half of its revenue was being used to pay operating costs and the other half to pay interest on loans.

The Channel Tunnel is a formidable competitor to the ferry companies on the route. By 1999, it had taken approximately half of the traffic on the Dover-Calais run. The ferry companies have responded by cutting their costs and by reducing the number of ships in the Channel. By 1999, there were only 7 ships on the

Dover-Calais route compared to 13 in 1996. The ferry companies can be flexible in this way. If a ship is failing to make a profit, its owner can simply transfer it to another route. However, the Channel Tunnel has no alternative use.

The concepts of economic rent and transfer earnings can be used to explain and analyse this situation. In the case of Eurotunnel, the Tunnel has no alternative use. Its transfer earnings are therefore zero and all its earnings are economic rent. In terms of Figure 77.6, the supply curve is perfectly inelastic. The Tunnel will continue in operation whether demand is D_1 or D_2. For the ferry companies, however, their supply curve is very elastic as shown in Figure 77.7. Almost all of their earnings are transfer earnings and very little are economic rent. If the rates of return of their Dover-

Calais routes fall to any significant extent, they will stop offering services and transfer the ships to other routes.

A fall in demand from D_1 to D_2 would be enough to leave Eurotunnel with a monopoly on the route.

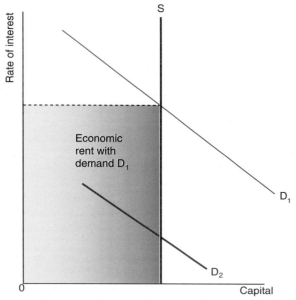

Figure 77.6 *The market faced by Eurotunnel*

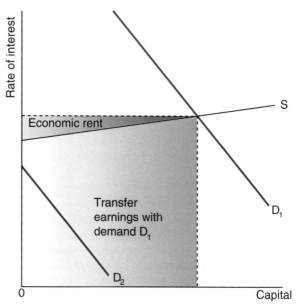

Figure 77.7 *The market faced by the Channel ferry companies*

Economic rent

A report from Deloitte & Touche, the accountancy firm, shows up a major problem for England's Premier League clubs. In 1998, wages for players rose by more than 40 per cent on average but sales turnover only increased by 23 per cent. At some stage, wage increases would have to slow or clubs would go bankrupt. The temptation to pay more, though, is high. The four top clubs in the 1997/98 season had four of the five highest wage bills. The bottom three clubs had three of the four lowest wage bills.

Source: adapted from the *Financial Times*, 30.4.1999.

An earnings survey by *Labour Research* in 1998 showed the pay and percentage changes in earnings of selected celebrities earning over £1 million a year. Top of the list was Phil Collins, who earned over £11 million, a 34.5 per cent increase from the previous year. Second was Sting, who earned nearly 10 million. All three former Beatles, Paul McCartney, George Harrison and Ringo Starr appeared in the top ten, as well as John Lennon's widow Yoko Ono. Each earned over £5 million.

Source: adapted from *Labour Research*, 1998.

Top pay for Britain's directors continues to grow at much faster rates than average earnings. In 1998, directors gave themselves pay rises of more than 26 per cent, five times the growth in average earnings. The number of chief executives earning more than £1 million a year also continues to grow. For instance, Pearson, the publishing group which owns the *Financial Times*, paid its chief executive £1.04 million in 1998/99. This included a bonus of £545 000. Niall Fitzgerald, co-chairman of Unilever, saw his salary rise from £600 000 to £680 000 whilst his total pay after benefits of £104 333 and a rise in performance related bonus from 240 000 to £332 000 came to £1.16 million, 19.4 per cent up on the year before.

Source: adapted from the *Financial Times*, 1.4.1999 and *The Guardian*, 19.7.1999.

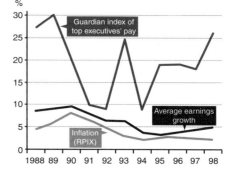

Figure 77.8 *Increases in pay*
Source: adapted from *The Guardian*, 19.1.1999.

1. Account for the size of the economic rent of the workers/individuals above.
2. Should high income earners have a large part of their

income taxed away? In your answer, include a discussion of both efficiency and equity considerations.

Summary

1. Business cycles have been a feature of capitalist economies in the 19th and 20th centuries.
2. The business cycle has four phases - boom, recession, slump and recovery.
3. The business cycle can be explained using the AD/AS model of the economy.
4. The multiplier-accelerator theory states that cycles are caused by the interaction of the Keynesian multiplier and the accelerator theory of investment.
5. The inventory cycle theory argues that cycles are caused by regular fluctuations in the levels of stocks in the economy.
6. Long wave cycles have been explained by changes in construction levels and by changes in technology.
7. Monetarists believe that trade cycles are caused by changes in the money supply.

Characteristics of cycles

It has long been observed in economics that income and employment tend to fluctuate regularly over time. These regular fluctuations are known as **business cycles** or **trade cycles**.

Figure 78.1 shows the various stages of a traditional cycle, such as occurred during the 19th century, during the 1930s or during the 1970s and 1980s in the UK.

- **Peak or boom**. When the economy is at a peak or is in a boom, national income is high. It is likely that the economy will be working at beyond full employment. **Overheating** is therefore present (although the economy could be at less than full employment, according to Keynesians, if there are bottlenecks in certain industries in the economy). Consumption and investment expenditure will be high. Tax revenues will be high. Wages will be rising and profits increasing. The country will be sucking in imports demanded by consumers with high incomes and businesses with full order books. There will also be inflationary pressures in the economy.
- **Recession**. When the economy moves into recession, output and income fall, leading to a fall in consumption and investment. Tax revenues begin to fall and

government expenditure on benefits begins to rise. Wage demands moderate as unemployment rises. Imports decline and inflationary pressures ease.
- **Trough or slump**. At the bottom of the cycle, the economy is said to be in a trough or slump. Economic activity is at a low in comparison with surrounding years. Mass unemployment exists, so consumption, investment and imports will be low. There will be few inflationary pressures in the economy and prices may be falling (there will be **deflation** in the strict sense of the term).
- **Recovery or expansion**. As the economy moves into a recovery or expansion phase, national income and output begin to increase. Unemployment falls. Consumption, investment and imports begin to rise. Workers feel more confident about demanding wage increases and inflationary pressures begin to mount.

During the 1950s and 1960s, the UK saw much milder trade cycles, as shown in Figure 78.2. National income did not fall but there were regular fluctuations in the rate of economic growth. A recession occurred when the rate of economic growth fell. Recovery or expansion was present when the growth rate picked up again. The economy was in a boom when economic growth was at its highest compared to surrounding years. There were troughs too

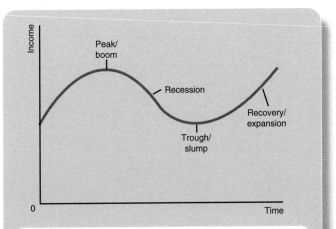

Figure 78.1 *The traditional business cycle*
The economy moves regularly from boom through recession to slump before recovering again.

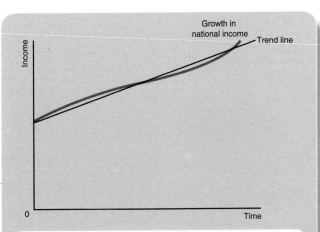

Figure 78.2 *The UK trade cycle of the 1950s and 1960s*
Peaks and troughs occurred when economic growth is high or low respectively.

when growth was particularly low but they were not really 'slumps' in the traditional sense. In the post-war period in the UK, the business cycle has tended to last four or five years from peak to peak. This contrasts with longer seven to nine year cycles in the 19th century. Some economists have claimed that there are longer 50 year KONDRATIEV CYCLES, so named after the Russian economist who first put forward the idea.

Question 1

Table 78.1

	Growth of GDP	Investment	Balance of payments current balance	Unemployment
	%	(£ billion at 1985 prices)		(millions)
1978	2.9	54.9	1.7	1.4
1979	2.8	56.5	- 0.9	1.3
1980	- 2.0	53.4	3.9	1.6
1981	- 1.2	48.3	8.4	2.5
1982	1.7	50.9	5.4	2.9

(a) Identify the four phases of the business cycle from the data.

Output gaps

Business cycles are movements around the long term trend rate of growth of an economy. At the height of a boom output is likely to be above what its long term growth rate would predict. In a recession it will be below it. The **output gap** measures the difference between the actual level of output and its trend level. In Figure 68.3 there is a negative output gap at OA in a recession because actual output is below the trend level. There is a positive output gap at OA, when the economy is in boom, because actual output is above its trend level.

Hysteresis

Figure 78.3 might suggest that there is little cost associated with fluctuations in the level of activity. Output lost in a recession is regained during a boom, leaving the economy no better or worse off in the long term. However, there are possible other costs.

- Those made unemployed during a recession, however mild, suffer a loss in their income even if the majority of workers are unaffected.
- Those on fixed incomes suffer in a boom if inflation rises. Their spending power is eroded because of higher prices.
- Some economists argue that in a deep recession, economies do not bounce back to their previous trend level of growth. This is an example of HYSTERESIS. Instead, the economy remains at a lower level of output, albeit still growing at its previous trend rate. In Figure 78.4, the economy starts off on a trend growth path of AA. However, a deep recession with its trough at OR means that the economy only booms at a level consistent with a lower growth path of BB. The economy then suffers another deep recession with a trough at OS. The trend line of growth shifts down to CC. After this, the business cycle is much shallower and actual output fluctuates around the trend line of CC. One reason why an economy may fail to recover fully from a deep recession is that there is a permanent loss of human capital. In a recession, millions can lose their jobs. Some take early retirement, with a consequent loss of output for the economy. Others suffer long periods of unemployment and become deskilled. They are therefore less productive than before. Another reason is that there can be a permanent loss of physical capital. In a recession, firms cut back on their investment. If they

Figure 78.3 *Output gaps*
At OA there is a negative output gap because the actual level of output is below the trend level of output. At OB, it is positive because output is above its trend level.

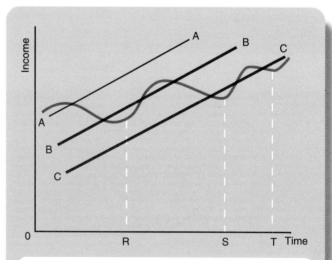

Figure 78.4 *Hysteresis*
The trend rate of growth of an economy can shift downwards if there is a deep recession because of permanent losses of human and physical capital.

fail to make this up in the next boom, there is less physical capital in the economy than would otherwise have been the case. Potential output must then fall.

Business cycle models

Business cycle models can be divided into two types.

Exogenous models argue that business cycles are started by a shock to the economic system, such as wars, revolutions, gold discoveries or large movements of population. It could be argued that the four-fold increase in the price of oil in 1973-74 gave a significant supply side shock to world economies. These effects rippled through time until economies returned to equilibrium.

Endogenous theories argue that trade cycles are caused by factors which lie within the economic system. Even if there were no supply side shocks, the economy would fluctuate regularly over time, although the fluctuations might be quite mild.

Question 2

Explain how a major world recession, an exogenous shock to the UK economy, could trigger a business cycle.

Aggregate demand and aggregate supply analysis

The business cycle can be explained using aggregate demand and aggregate supply analysis. Consider Figure 78.5. The economy is in both short run and long run equilibrium at A.

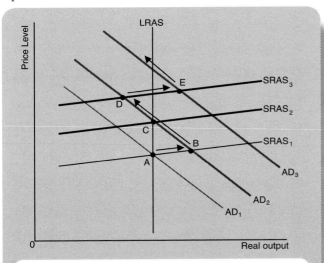

Figure 78.5 *The business cycle*
The economy is initially disturbed, moving to B. It then moves from C through to E and beyond as it returns to equilibrium on the LRAS line.

Boom An exogenous shock to the economy now shifts the aggregate demand curve from AD_1 to AD_2. For instance,

the government might reduce income tax in the run up to a general election, or the stock market might suddenly boom, increasing the real wealth of households and encouraging them to spend more. The economy now moves from A to B. This is a long run disequilibrium point. The economy has overheated, with aggregate demand being greater than long run aggregate supply. The result will be over-full employment. Wage rates and other factor prices will rise. This rise in factor prices shifts the short run aggregate supply curve upwards, eventually reaching $SRAS_2$, with the economy at C. This ought to be the new long run equilibrium point.

Recession However, why should the SRAS curve stop rising at $SRAS_2$? It is possible that it will overshoot, eventually stopping at, say, $SRAS_3$ with the economy in recession. It will be the recession which eventually brings wage inflation to a halt, not a possible long run equilibrium position. With the economy in recession, equilibrium output will have fallen, shown on the diagram by D being left of C.

Recovery Eventually, though, there will be an increase in aggregate demand at the given price level. In the move from B to D, consumers and producers have cut their real spending. Consumers will have particularly cut spending on consumer durables whilst firms will have cut investment spending. There comes a point when expenditure on these items has to start rising. Consumers, for instance, having delayed buying new cars, eventually have to replace their old cars. Firms, having deferred new investment spending, have to replace worn out machinery or stop producing. So the AD curve shifts again to the right, producing the upturn in the cycle.

Boom As consumer and business confidence returns, spending further increases to AD_3. But this produces a new short run equilibrium point where the economy is again at over-full employment, a long run disequilibrium position. Wages start to rise, pushing the SRAS curve upwards to produce the downturn in the economy.

Figure 78.5 shows an economy where the initial demand shock produces smaller and smaller cycles over time. Eventually, the economy will converge to a long run equilibrium position on the long run aggregate supply curve. It is likely that, before this happens, another exogenous shock will have occurred which yet again increases the amplitude of the cycle.

Different schools of economists emphasise different aspects of this basic explanation. Keynesian economists tend to emphasise the change in real variables, such as investment, which then produce fluctuations in output which characterise the business cycle. Monetarist economists tend to emphasise the role of money in the process which lead to fluctuations in prices as well as output. These individual explanations will now be discussed.

The multiplier-accelerator model

One Keynesian explanation of the business cycle is the MULTIPLIER-ACCELERATOR MODEL. The **accelerator theory** of investment says that investment is a function of past changes in income (☞ unit 32). If national income is growing, so too will investment. This increase in investment will lead to a multiple increase in national income via the **multiplier effect** (☞ unit 33). This leads to a further increase in investment. Hence the economy keeps on growing. On the other hand, if income falls, so too will investment, feeding through via the multiplier process to a further fall in income. Investment then falls again. The economy is on a downward path.

So far we have a possible explanation of why an economy might grow or contract over time but there is as yet no explanation of the trade cycle in it. There are two ways of using the multiplier-accelerator model to construct a business cycle model. The first is to construct a far more complicated accelerator model than, for instance, the $I_t = k (Y_t - Y_{t-1})$ theory developed in unit 32. Some formulations of the accelerator model will produce regular cycles. Whether these formulations are realistic can only be gauged when they are tested against real data.

The other way is to postulate the existence of **ceilings** and **floors** in the cycle. An annual growth rate of 5 to 6 per cent has proved unsustainable for the post-war UK economy. The economy moves to full employment and then beyond full employment. There simply isn't any more labour to be hired to sustain the boom. This puts a brake on the economy. As the rate of increase in output slows down, so the rate of growth of investment falls, producing the downturn in the economy. Similarly, national income will not keep falling to zero. At some point firms have to increase investment to replace worn-out machinery. Consumers will increasingly resist falls in their consumption and will be prepared to call on savings or borrow money to prevent their living standards falling even further. This is the turning point for the economy.

Output will begin to rise, pulling up consumption expenditure and encouraging investment expenditure.

The inventory cycle

Another Keynesian explanation of the business cycle is the INVENTORY CYCLE hypothesis. **Inventories** is another name for stocks of raw materials and finished products held by producers. For instance, a car manufacturer will hold stocks of steel, car components and finished cars.

Some economists argue that there is an inventory cycle of business activity in the economy. Changes in inventories cause regular fluctuations in the level of national income. For instance, assume that the government increases its expenditure in real terms. Firms will initially meet part of the extra demand by supplying goods from existing stocks. So they will need to increase their production levels, firstly to replace those stocks and secondly to meet the continued extra demand from government. This leads to an increase in national income via the multiplier process. Eventually firms will have replenished their stocks to their desired levels. They will then reduce their orders from other firms to the level needed to satisfy long term demand. But this reduction in orders will produce a downturn in the economy via the multiplier process. The economy will only pick up once firms have so run down their stocks that they are forced to increase their orders again.

Question 3

Table 78.2 *Investment and natural income, UK, 1986-98*

£ million at 1995 prices

	Gross fixed capital formation	Change in gross fixed capital formation	Change in gross domestic product at market prices
1986	92 330		
1987	100 520	8 190	25 869
1988	115 362	14 842	31 564
1989	122 158	6 796	13 728
1990	119 368	-2 790	4 165
1991	109 000	-10 368	-9 841
1992	108 246	-754	336
1993	109 127	881	15 043
1994	113 042	3 915	29 159
1995	116 360	3 318	19 371
1996	122 042	5 682	18 219
1997	130 487	8 445	25 894
1998	141 257	10 770	15 607

(a) According to Keynesian economic theory, a rise in investment will cause a rise in national income (GDP). The multiplier is the number of times that national income will rise from a given increase in income. Changes in other economic variables such as government spending and exports can also have a multiplier effect on income. Would the data support the view that there is a multiplier effect between investment and income?

(b) The accelerator theory suggests that investment is determined by changes in income over previous time periods. Would the data support this theory?

(c) Would the data support the multiplier-accelerator model?

Question 4

Table 78.3 *Change in stocks and GDP, 1979-1983*

	£ billion at 1985 prices	
	Increase in stocks and work in progress[1]	GDP[2]
1979	3.3	283.4
1980	- 3.4	277.4
1981	- 3.2	274.3
1982	- 1.3	279.2
1983	1.4	289.2

1. At market prices.
2. At factor cost.
Source: adapted from CSO, *Economic Trends Annual Supplement*.

(a) Explain how the changes in stocks and work in progress might have contributed to the change in GDP over the period 1979-1983.

Long wave cycles

A number of economists have argued that long wave cycles exist. Like the multiplier-accelerator theory and the inventory cycle theory, these theories emphasise that cycles are caused by changes in real variables.

In the inter-war period, Kuznets claimed that there was a 15-20 year building cycle. Economic fluctuations were caused by regular long cycles in building and construction.

Again in the inter-war period, a Russian economist named Kondratiev suggested that 50 year cycles existed. These were caused by lumpiness in the pace of technological change. The idea was further developed by the Austrian economist, Schumpeter, who identified waves of technological progress. For instance, in the mid-nineteenth century the development of the railways was a major boost to world demand. In the early part of this century, it was the motor car and electricity that provided the stimulus to technological advance. In the post-war period up to 1970, it was the development of chemicals, plastics, nuclear power and a wide range of electrical consumer goods. Today, the world economy is making a start on exploiting biotechnology and the microchip.

These waves of innovation produce characteristic cycles. Take the micro-chip revolution. In the 1970s and early 1980s, microchips began to make an impact on products and output. Initially, some new products came onto the market (like calculators). But the biggest impact was on existing products. Costs were cut by incorporating micro-chips into existing machines. This led to a shake out of employment because the new machines could produce more output with less labour.

The world economy moved to slump both in the mid-1970s following an oil price shock, and again in the early 1980s. On both occasions, unemployment rose substantially and remained at very high levels historically. By the mid-1990s, however, the USA was beginning to grow at historically high rates with falling unemployment. The 1980s and the 1990s have been decades of high unemployment. The long wave cycle hypothesis would suggest that the new products appearing on the market - ranging from integrated home entertainment equipment providing digital television, internet capability with CD and games facilities, to new biotechnological drugs to cars running on non-oil based fuels - will lead to an upturn in the world economy early in the 21st century. The USA, the world's technological leader, had already begun to enjoy the benefits of the long term upswing in the second half of the 1990s, with other countries following later. By 2010 to 2020, the boom will begin to falter as exciting new products will be more difficult to invent. So economic growth rates will begin to fall. The economy will then be in its recession phase. By 2020-30, the economy will be again approaching a slump which should occur in the 2030s. Once again new technologies will emerge, but they will only help lift the world economy from recession by the 2040s.

A monetarist explanation

Milton Friedman has suggested that trade cycles are essentially monetary phenomena, caused by changes in the **money supply** (☞ unit 82). In their important book *A Monetary History of the United States, 1867-1960*, Milton Friedman and Anna Schwartz argued that US business cycles were preceded by changes in the money supply.

The argument put forward is that changes in the money supply lead to changes in real variables, such as unemployment and national income, before finally leading to an increase in prices. The path to an increased price level is not a smooth one but is cyclical. The oscillations in the cycle become more and more damped as time goes on. Of course they can become more amplified again if there is another excessive increase in the money supply.

The link between changes in the money supply and changes in income is known as the **transmission mechanism**. Assume that there is a once and for all increase in the money supply when the economy is in long run equilibrium. The money supply is now greater than the **demand for money.** Economic agents, such as banks, firms and consumers, will adjust their portfolio of assets. Some of the excess supply will be used to buy physical assets - goods and services. The rest will be saved, reducing interest rates and thus encouraging the borrowing of money again to buy physical assets. The increase in consumption and investment will result in an increase in income. The economy is now in boom. Prices will begin to rise. This, together with increased real spending, will increase the demand for money. It is most unlikely that the economy will return to equilibrium with the demand and supply for money being equal. What will happen is that the demand for money will carry on increasing so that the demand for money exceeds the supply of money. Once this happens, economic agents will start to adjust their portfolios in the opposite direction. They will cut back on purchases of physical and financial assets. Interest rates will rise. Investment and consumption will begin to fall. The economy is now in recession with falling income. This reduces the demand for money, bringing it back past the equilibrium point to the bottom of the cycle where once again supply is greater than demand for money. There will be a further bout of portfolio adjustment and aggregate demand will start to rise, bringing the economy into the recovery phase of the cycle. This will carry on, although Friedman argues that without further shocks the oscillations will become smaller and smaller over time.

Question 5

Monetarists argue that the business cycle can be explained by changes in the money supply. For instance, Friedman and Schwartz (1963) argue that the Great Depression of the 1930s in the USA was caused by a drastic fall in the supply of money. They write: 'An initial mild decline in the money stock from 1929 to 1930, accompanying a decline in Federal Reserve credit outstanding, was converted into a sharp decline by a wave of bank failures beginning in late 1930.' Those failures produced (a) widespread attempts by the public to convert deposits into currency and hence a decline in the deposit-currency ratio, and (b) a scramble for liquidity by the banks and hence a decline in the deposit-reserve ratio.

(a) How and why, according to Friedman and Schwartz, did the US money supply contract from 1929?
(b) Suggest how this contraction in the money supply then led to depression.

key terms

Hysteresis - the process whereby a variable does not return to its former value when changed. In terms of the business cycle, it is used to describe the phenomenon of an economy failing to return to its former long term trend rate of growth after a severe recession.
Inventory cycle - fluctuations in national income caused by changes in the level of inventories or stocks in the economy.
Kondratiev cycles - long 50 year trade cycles caused by the 'lumpiness' of technological change.
Multiplier-accelerator model - a model which describes how the workings of the multiplier theory and the accelerator theory lead to changes in national income.

Applied economics

The UK business cycle in the post-war period

Duration and amplitude

The duration of the business cycle in the UK in the post-war era has averaged 4 to 5 years from peak to peak. As Figure 78.6 shows, during the 1950s and 1960s, booms and recessions were very mild. Recessions meant declines in the rate of growth of output rather than falls in output. However, the 1970s and 1980s saw much greater swings, and the recession of 1980-82 was the severest since the Great Depression of the 1930s, whilst the recession of 1990-92 was the longest.

The 1950s, 1960s and early 1970s

In the 1950s, 1960s and early 1970s, booms in the

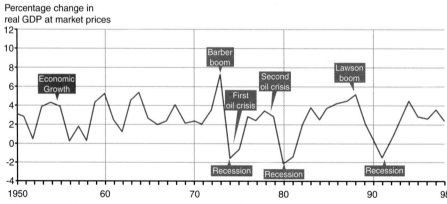

Figure 78.6 *Economic growth*
Source: adapted from *Economic Trends Annual Supplement, Monthly Digest of Statistics*, Office for National Statistics.

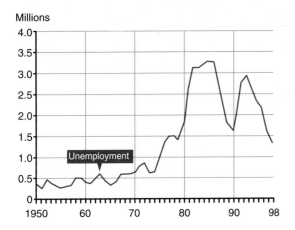

Figure 78.7 *Unemployment, claimant count*
Source: adapted from *Economic Trends Annual Supplement, Monthly Digest of Statistics*, Office for National Statistics.

economy (1954-5, 1959-60, 1964, 1968 and 1973) were associated with low unemployment, high inflation and a current account deficit on the balance of payments. It is noticeable from Figure 78.7 that unemployment shifted upwards in the late 1960s. The fall in unemployment that could have been expected in the boom of 1968 did not take place. This represented an upward shift in the **natural rate** of unemployment in the economy (☞ unit 86). It is an example of **hysteresis**, where an economic variable changes but does not bounce back to its original position when economic circumstances change.

1974-1979

The recession of 1974-75 was unusual in that it coincided with a severe supply side shock to the economy. The quadrupling of oil prices pushed the current account on the balance of payments into record deficit, whilst it led to an increase in the inflation rate. This produced the phenomenon of **stagflation** in 1974. There was rising inflation, a worsening balance of payments, rising unemployment and a fall in output. Within a couple of years, however, more traditional patterns reasserted themselves. The boom of 1978-79 saw faster growth, falling unemployment coupled with rising inflation and a deteriorating current account.

The recession of 1980-81

The recession of 1980-81 was even more severe than that of 1974-75 and again there was stagflation. Unemployment more than doubled and output fell by 4.2 per cent. Manufacturing industry was very badly affected, experiencing a 14.6 per cent fall in output from peak to trough. At the same time, inflation increased from 13.4 per cent in 1979 to 18.0 per cent in 1980 before falling back to 11.9 per cent in 1981. The balance of payments current account moved strongly into surplus. The recession of 1980-81 was untypical when compared

to recessions of the 1950s and 1960s in many ways. The second oil crisis of 1978-79 fuelled inflation and created a downturn in the international economy which fed through to lower demand for UK exports. At the same time, North Sea oil was beginning to have a major impact on the balance of payments and led to a rise in the exchange rate, again dampening demand for UK non-oil exports. The government also, for the first time in the post-war era, reduced aggregate demand as the economy went into recession, first by increasing domestic interest rates and second by cutting public spending and raising taxes.

The 1980s and the Lawson boom

Perhaps not surprisingly, the economy took some time to recover. There was a faltering in the economy in 1984, but no major recession as the experience of the previous 30 years would have suggested. However, there was a boom in the economy in 1987-89, approximately ten years after the last major boom of 1977-79. The boom had many of the characteristics of two previous booms, in 1963-64 and 1972-74. All, in different ways, were fuelled by government policy changes. The Barber boom of 1972-74 was fuelled by a disastrous loosening of monetary policy combined with a large fiscal expansion driven by tax cuts and increases in government spending. The Lawson boom of 1987-89 too saw a failure to control growth in the money supply at an early enough point in the boom. Whilst overall fiscal policy remained broadly neutral, major income tax cuts in 1987 further boosted already strong consumer confidence which fed through into higher consumption, spending and borrowing.

Increasing house prices at the time were both a symptom of inflation and a cause of rising demand and rising prices. Fast increases in house prices increase the wealth of households and encourage them to borrow and spend more. Over the three year period 1963-65, house prices rose by 20 per cent, higher than the average for the 1950s and 1960s. Over the three year period 1972-74, house prices rose 90 per cent, whilst over the four years of 1986-89 they increased 72 per cent. Certainly, the house price boom of the mid-late 1980s was encouraged by the government through generous tax concessions on mortgages and a political climate which equated home ownership with success.

In all three booms, the current account on the balance of payments went into substantial deficit - 1.2 per cent of GDP in 1964, 4.2 per cent of GDP in 1974 (although this was partly caused by the oil supply side shock) and a record 5.1 per cent of GDP in 1989. This was because these booms sucked in imports as British industry failed to meet domestic demand.

The recession of 1990-92

The Lawson boom was followed by a prolonged

recession. It was caused by a considerable tightening of monetary policy. Interest rates were doubled in 1988-89 from $7\frac{1}{2}$ per cent to 15 per cent in a bid by the government to stem a small rise in inflation. In 1990, the UK joined the ERM at too high a rate of the pound against other European currencies. The result was that the government was forced to maintain high interest rates to defend a weak pound throughout 1991 and 1992, long after the inflationary threat had passed. As a consequence, the recession was the longest since the 1930s. It was only when the UK was forced to leave the ERM, and the government quickly cut interest rates, so that the economy came out of recession.

The 1990s

The rest of the 1990s saw year on year growth. As in the mid-1980s, there was a slight faltering in growth in the mid-1990s corresponding to the point where a five year trade cycle would predict a downturn. However, the end of the 1990s did not lead to a boom and bust situation as happened at the end of the 1970s and the 1980s. There was a mild downturn in 1998-99 but it was comparable in its severity to the downturns of the 1950s and 1960s, rather than the severe recessions of the 1970s and 1980s. One reason why the boom of the 1990s did not end in a severe

recession was that there were no significant external shocks such as the oil crises of the 1970s. The Asian crisis of 1997-98, when a number of fast growing Far Eastern countries suffered a severe financial crisis and saw their GDPs fall by as much as 20 per cent in one year, could have sparked a worldwide recession, but strong growth in the USA limited its impact. Another reason for the mildness of the downturn in the late 1990s was that government policy arguably played a positive role in managing the economy. The Lawson boom had been fuelled by both tax cuts and low interest rates. In the late 1990s, the government kept a tight control of fiscal policy, whilst the newly independent Bank of England raised interest rates in 1998-99 to counter what it feared might be rising inflation caused by overheating at the top of a boom. Higher interest rates helped dampen demand sufficiently to reduce growth but they were not large enough to push the economy into a full blown recession on the scale of the early 1990s.

In the United States, the economy had grown for nine consecutive years from 1991. Some economists were predicting that it might be possible for the UK to enjoy sustained growth over long periods in the 21st century without there being large recessions. In the absence of external shocks, the economy might settle down to the very mild cyclical pattern last seen in the 1950s.

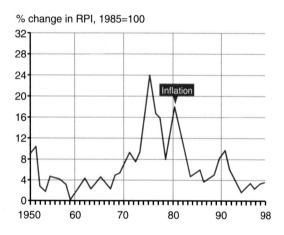

Figure 78.8 *Inflation*
Source: adapted from *Economic Trends Annual Supplement, Monthly Digest of Statistics*, Office for National Statistics.

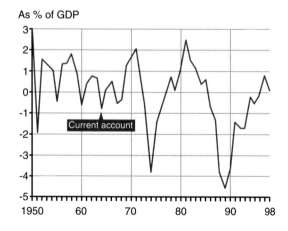

Figure 78.9 *Current account*
Source: adapted from *Economic Trends Annual Supplement, Monthly Digest of Statistics*, Office for National Statistics.

'Output gap' leads to inflation alert

The strong growth in the US has now eroded all of the spare capacity in the US economy, suggesting that inflationary pressures may soon intensify, the OECD outlook said yesterday.

Germany also has a relatively low level of spare capacity in its economy, even though recovery has started only recently there. However, the UK has more spare capacity than any other of the six largest industrialised economies, closely followed by France.

These findings are likely to fuel the debate about the timing of interest rate rises in OECD countries and the significance of the so-called 'output gap', not least because the OECD yesterday announced reforms in its calculations of this gap.

In recent years, western governments have attached growing significance to the concept of an output gap, since it has been assumed that an erosion of the spare capacity will lead to higher inflation. The output gap is usually defined as the difference between the actual growth rate in an economy and its theoretical potential growth rate if all capacity were used.

However, economists and governments have remained sharply divided over the correct way to measure the output gap. Although the Bank of England, for example, uses its own calculations of the UK output gap to help determine the timing of interest rate rises, it refuses to publish figures on this.

In the past, the OECD's own calculations of the output gap have relied on a mixture of historical statistical analysis, and judgements about broader trends in the economy, such as changes in labour market flexibility.

However, the OECD is now relying on a more complicated modelling technique that seeks to estimate the total productive capacity in an economy, compared with its actual growth.

The OECD admits that the concept remains extremely slippery. Nevertheless, its finding that the US economy has now eroded all of its spare capacity may add to pressure for a further rise in US interest rates.

'There is widespread agreement that full employment has been reached (in the US),' the OECD said. It forecasts that inflation in the US will rise to more than 3 per cent in the next 18 months. Conversely, the surprising conclusion that the UK now has more spare capacity than most other European countries not only highlights the depth of the recent UK recession - but may also fuel complaints from some economists that further rises in the UK interest rates are unnecessary.

France is also estimated to have a relatively large output gap, which again may indicate the depth of its recent recession.

Meanwhile the output gap in Japan, which is only now emerging from recession, is predicted to remain little changed over the next two years, highlighting the fact that inflationary pressures are likely to remain subdued, creating little need for interest rate rises.

The OECD warned that Italy, in particular, was one country that needed to address the problem of the budget deficit, although the Italian government had introduced some reforms.

Source: the *Financial Times*, 21.12.1994.

Table 78.4 *Output gaps*

Deviations of actual GDP from potential GDP as percentage of potential GDP

	US	Japan	Germany	France	Italy	UK	Canada
1986	-0.4	-3.8	-1.3	-2.2	0.1	0.5	1.0
1987	0.2	-3.8	-1.8	-2.3	1.5	2.8	2.6
1988	1.7	-1.2	-0.5	-0.5	2.9	5.0	4.6
1989	2.2	0.1	0.2	1.1	4.0	4.6	4.0
1990	1.4	1.8	2.3	1.2	3.7	2.2	0.8
1991	-1.4	3.1	3.8	-0.2	2.6	-2.5	-3.5
1992	-1.3	2.0	2.5	-1.0	0.8	-5.1	-4.8
1993	-0.4	-0.2	-1.2	-3.7	-2.1	-5.2	-4.4
1994	1.0	-2.3	-1.2	-3.5	-2.0	-3.9	-2.9
1995	1.5	-2.8	-1.1	-2.6	-1.4	-2.9	-1.7
1996	1.0	-2.5	-0.5	-1.6	-0.7	-2.3	-0.8

Source: adapted from OECD, *Economic Outlook.*

1. What does it mean when the article states that 'Japan ... is ... now emerging from a recession'?
2. Explain the link between a recession in the economy and an 'output gap'.
3. Using Table 78.4, discuss in which years different countries were (a) in a recession and (b) in a boom.
4. Discuss, using diagrams, why governments might have wanted to raise interest rates in 1995.

Summary

1. Governments need to raise taxes to pay for public spending. Taxes are also used to correct market failure, to redistribute income and wealth and to manage the economy.

2. The canons of taxation are a set of principles by which taxes can be evaluated.

The reasons for taxation

Governments use taxation for a number of purposes.

To pay for government expenditure Governments need to raise finance for their expenditure programmes (☞ unit 80). They can borrow a limited amount of money for this, but most of the finance must come from taxation if inflation is to be avoided.

To correct market failure such as externalities Governments can intervene in individual markets by changing taxes and thus changing demand. For instance, tobacco consumption can be reduced by raising taxes on cigarettes, pollution can be controlled by imposing pollution taxes, or sales of books can be increased by exempting them from VAT. Used in this way, taxation becomes a way of increasing economic efficiency.

To manage the economy as a whole Taxation can have an important influence on the **macro-economic** performance of the economy (☞ units 36 and 81). Governments may change tax rates in order to influence variables such as inflation, unemployment and the balance of payments.
To redistribute income A government may judge that the distribution of resources is inequitable. To redistribute income, it may impose taxes which reduce the income and wealth of some groups in society and use the money collected to increase the income and wealth of other groups (☞ unit 69).

Question 1

Each year in the Budget, the Chancellor of the Exchequer announces whether or not he will change the level of excise duties on tobacco. In most years, this is increased at least in line with inflation, although in some years, particularly election years, it is not increased at all. Why might the government change the level of excise duty on tobacco each year?

Direct and indirect taxes

Taxes are classified into two types. A DIRECT TAX is a tax levied directly on an individual or organisation. For instance, income tax is a direct tax because individual income earners are responsible for paying it. Corporation tax, a tax on company profits, is a direct tax too because companies have to pay it directly to the Inland Revenue.
An INDIRECT TAX is a tax on a good or service. For instance, value added tax is an indirect tax because it is a 17.5 per cent tax on most goods and services. Local Authority rates were an indirect tax on the notional rent of a property as is the Uniform Business Rate for businesses.

Question 2

Explain which of the following taxes are direct taxes and which are indirect:

(a) income tax; (b) National Insurance contributions; (c) inheritance tax; (d) corporation tax; (e) capital gains tax; (f) council tax; (g) VAT; (h) excise duties.

The canons of taxation

Taxation has been a source of much controversy since the first tax was introduced. Adam Smith wrote at length on the subject of taxation in his book *An Enquiry into the Nature and Causes of the Wealth of Nations*, published in 1776. He argued that a good tax was one which had four characteristics:
- the cost of collection should be low relative to the yield of the tax;
- the timing of collection and the amount to be paid should be clear and certain;
- the means of payment and the timing of the payment should be convenient to the taxpayer;
- taxes should be levied according to the ability to pay of the individual taxpayer.
These canons relate to efficiency and equity. For instance, the cost of collection is about productive efficiency. Ability to pay is about equity.
There have been examples in history where taxes did not possess these canons. For instance, at certain periods in Roman history tax collecting was privatised. The Roman government sold the right to collect taxes in a province to the highest bidder. This individual would buy the right, hoping to charge more in taxes than he paid to the Roman authorities. With luck he might make 100 per cent profit on the contract - in this case the cost of collection would hardly be low. He would terrorise the province, forcing anyone and everyone to pay as much tax as he could exact from citizens. No attempt was made to

make means of payment or timing suitable to the taxpayer. It was not clear on what basis citizens were being taxed, and there was no attempt to link taxes to ability to pay, since it was the poor who were the most easily terrorised whilst better off citizens were left alone for fear that they might complain to Rome!

Economists today have argued that in addition to Adam Smith's canons, a 'good' tax should be one which:
- leads to the least loss of economic efficiency, or even increases economic efficiency;
- is compatible with foreign tax systems, and in the case of the UK, particularly with EU tax regimes;
- automatically adjusts to changes in the price level - this is particularly important in a high inflation economy.

These three criteria relate to economic efficiency.

Sometimes it is argued that taxes should be linked to the benefits that taxpayers receive from the tax. For instance, road groups in the UK often point out that revenues from taxes on motorists far exceed government expenditure on roads. They then conclude that either taxes on motorists are too high or that spending on roads is too low. A tax whose revenue is specifically linked to an area of government spending is called a **hypothecated tax**. In the UK, National Insurance contributions could be argued to be a hypothecated tax because they are used solely to pay for spending on National Insurance benefits and make a small contribution towards the cost of the National Health Service. The benefit principle is one of equity. It is an argument which states that linking payment and benefit is 'fairer' than a tax which fails to do this.

Taxation, inefficiency and inequality

A tax is likely to lead to a fall in supply and a consequent reduction in the quantity demanded of the product or service being taxed. For instance:
- VAT and excise duties on a product push the supply curve to the left which in turn leads to a fall in the quantity demanded of the product (☞ unit 11);
- Income tax is likely to lead to a fall in the supply of labour to the market (☞ unit 38);
- Corporation tax is likely to lead to a fall in the supply of entrepreneurs to the market.

Taxes therefore distort markets. This may be beneficial in some markets, particularly if there are important negative externalities present and the tax brings private costs and benefits into line with social costs and benefits (☞ unit 19).

In other markets, taxes may lead to a loss of efficiency. For instance, if all markets were perfectly competitive, then the economy would be Pareto efficient (☞ unit 61). The introduction of a tax on one commodity, such as petrol, would then lead to a loss of efficiency in the economy because marginal cost would no longer equal price in that market. In practice, there are so many examples of market failure that it is impossible to come to any simple conclusions about whether a tax does or does not lead to efficiency losses. However, the **theory of the second best** (☞ unit 61) suggests that taxes which are broadly based are less likely to lead to efficiency losses than narrow taxes. Low rates of tax spread as widely as possible are likely to be less damaging to economic welfare than high rates of tax on a small number of goods or individuals. For instance, a single rate VAT is likely to result in greater efficiency than a tax solely on petrol which raises the same revenue. Or an income tax which all earners pay is likely to lead to lower efficiency losses than an income tax paid solely by manufacturing workers.

It should be remembered that taxes are raised mainly to pay for government expenditure. Even if the imposition of taxes does lead to a loss of efficiency, this loss should be outweighed by the gain in economic efficiency resulting from the provision of **public** and **merit** goods (☞ unit 20) by the government.

Taxes are also raised to ensure a redistribution of resources within the economy. There will be an increase in economic welfare if the welfare gains from a more desirable distribution of resources outweigh the welfare losses from the greater inefficiency arising from taxation.

Question 3

Table 79.1 *Revenue and cost of collection for selected taxes*

	Revenue	Administration costs		Compliance costs	
	£ bn	£m	%	£m	%
Income tax, capital gains tax & National Insurance contributions	65.1	997	1.53	2 212	3.4
VAT	21.4	220	1.03	791	3.69
Excise duties	16.5	42	0.25	33	0.20
Average central government	122.3	1 369	1.12	3 409	2.33

Revenue is defined as the total revenue received by the government from the tax. Administrative costs are the costs to the government of collecting the tax (in £m and as a percentage of the revenue raised in tax). Compliance costs are an estimate of the cost of collection which is borne by private firms and individuals (again in £m and as a percentage of the revenue raised in tax). For instance, businesses have to spend time and therefore money accounting for the VAT they charge customers.

(a) To what extent is VAT a 'good tax'?

Question 4

In 1994, the Conservative Chancellor of the Exchequer imposed VAT on domestic fuel at 8 per cent. Previously, gas, electricity and coal used by households had been exempt from the standard rate of VAT of 17.5 per cent. The government wanted to increase the VAT rate on domestic fuel to 17.5 per cent from April 1995, but was prevented from doing this by a back bench revolt in Parliament. In 1997, the incoming Labour government cut the rate to 5 per cent in line with an election promise.

(a) Discuss the effect of the imposition of 8 per cent VAT on domestic fuel in terms of: (i) efficiency and (ii) equity.
(b) Was efficiency increased by the cut in the rate to 5 per cent?

key terms

Direct tax - a tax levied directly on an individual or organisation, such as income tax.

Indirect tax - a tax levied on goods or services, such as value added tax or excise duties.

Applied economics

Taxation in the UK

The main taxes in the UK

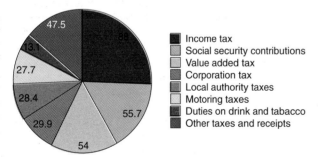

Income tax
Social security contributions
Value added tax
Corporation tax
Local authority taxes
Motoring taxes
Duties on drink and tabacco
Other taxes and receipts

Figure 79.1 *Government revenue, 1999-2000, £billion*
Source: adapted from HM Treasury, Red Book.

Figure 79.1 gives a broad breakdown of government revenue for 1999-2000. The largest tax by revenue is income tax, which raises one quarter of all government receipts. The three largest taxes (income tax, social security contributions and value added tax) raise approximately 60 per cent. If corporation tax, local authority taxes (business rates and the council tax), motoring taxes (duty on fuel and vehicle excise duty) and duties on drink and tobacco are added to these, then these taxes contribute nearly 90 per cent of government revenues. Table 79.2 gives a more detailed breakdown of tax and other revenues.

Income tax This is the single most important source of revenue for government. It is a tax on the income of individuals. Each person is allowed to earn a certain amount before paying income tax each year. This amount is called a **tax allowance**. One tax allowance to which everyone is entitled is the **personal allowance**. In 2000-01, this was worth £4 385. So every individual could earn £4 385 between 6th April 2000 and 5th April 2001 free of income tax. Payments into pension funds are tax free, whilst additional allowances are available for the over 65s.

Income earned over the value of allowances (the tax **threshold**) is liable to tax and is called **taxable income**. In 2000-01, the first £1 520 of taxable income was taxed at the **starting rate** of 10 per cent. The next £26 880 was taxed at the **basic rate** of 23 per cent. The **higher rate** of 40 per cent was paid on all taxable income over £28 400. Table 79.3 gives an example of how the income tax of an individual is calculated.

For very low income earners, such as part-time workers, the **marginal rate** of income tax is 0 per cent. This is because they can earn an extra £1 and still be within their personal tax allowance. For instance, a worker earning £3 000 a year could work an extra shift and pay no income tax on the earnings. Slightly better paid workers will have a marginal rate of 10 per cent. The majority of workers, though, earn enough to have

Table 79.2 *Government revenues 1999-2000[1] (£ billion)*

Inland Revenue

Income tax	88.0
Corporation tax	29.9
Stamp duties	5.7
Capital gains tax	3.2
Inheritance tax	2.0
Petroleum revenue tax	0.1
Total Inland Revenue	**128.9**

Customs and Excise

Value added tax	54.0
Fuel duties	23.1
Tobacco duties	7.0
Beer and cider duties	2.9
Spirits duties	1.6
Wine duties	1.6
Customs duties and levies	1.8
Betting and game duties	1.5
Insurance premium tax	1.4
Air passenger duty	0.8
Landfill tax	0.4
Total Customs and Excise	**96.2**

Other taxes and royalties

Social security contributions	55.7
Business rates	15.6
Council tax	12.8
Vehicle excise duties	4.6
Oil royalties	0.2
Other taxes and royalties	7.9
Total other taxes and royalties	**98.8**

Other receipts

Interest and dividends	3.7
Gross operating surpluses and rent	18.4
Other receipts and accounting adjustments	1.0
Total other receipts	**23.1**
Total government revenues	**344.3**

1. Forecast March 1999.

Table 79.3 *Income tax payable: an illustration*

	£	£
Income before tax		60 000.00
Allowances		
Personal allowance	4 385.00	
Pension payments	3 615.00	
Total	8 000.00	
Taxable income		52 000.00
Tax		
1 520 at 10%	152.00	
26 880 at 23%	6 182.40	
23 600 at 40%	9 440.00	
Total tax paid	15 774.40	15 774.40
Income after tax		44 225.60

to pay the basic rate of income tax. For high income earners, the marginal rate is 40 per cent. However, there is a difference between marginal rates of tax and average rates of tax.

Consider Table 79.3. This individual is earning £60 000 before tax. In 2000-01, she would have paid £15 774.40 in tax. Therefore her average rate of tax was 26.3 per cent (£15 774.40 ÷ £60 000). But her marginal rate is 40 per cent because she pays 40p in tax on the last £1 earned. **The average rate of tax is always less than the marginal rate for income taxpayers**. This is because all income earners can earn a portion of their income 'tax free'. Moreover, basic and higher rate taxpayers pay lower rates of tax on part of their taxable earnings. So basic rate taxpayers in 2000-01 paid no tax on their income covered by allowances, 10 per cent on the next £1 520 and only then did their income begin to be taxed at 23 per cent.

Income tax from employed workers is collected by employers through the PAYE (pay as you earn) system. Employers are then responsible for paying the deductions to the Inland Revenue.

National Insurance contributions (NICs) All taxes apart from NICs and local authority taxes are paid into one central fund (called the **Consolidated Fund**) and are used to pay for government spending. However, there is a separate National Insurance Fund out of which is paid National Insurance benefits, such as state pensions and Jobseekers Allowance. The National Insurance Fund also pays for a small part of the cost of the National Health Service. Strictly speaking, contributions are not taxes because they are a form of insurance premium. However, increasingly they have come to be seen, and used by, government as a form of tax. The link between payments made into the Fund and benefits taken out by individuals has been eroded over time. In 2000-01, contracted-in employed workers paid contributions of 10 per cent on earnings between £76 and £535. Unlike income tax, which is calculated on yearly income, National Insurance contributions are based on weekly income. A 17 year old student who earns £100 one week, £50 the next and nothing for the rest of the year will pay no income tax because she is within her personal allowance figure. But she will have to pay NICs in the week she earned £100 because she was above the £76 threshold. The next week, she will pay no NICs because she is below £76. In addition, employers have to pay employers' National Insurance contributions at 12.2 per cent on employees' earnings that exceed £84 a week. There are different rates of National insurance contributions for contracted-out workers and the self-employed.

Corporation tax Corporation tax is a tax on company profits. The top rate of tax in 2000-01 was 30 per cent for companies earning more than £1.5 million in profits a year. For the smallest companies earning less than £10 000 a year in profits, their rate of tax was 10 per cent, with a 20 per cent tax rate for companies with profits between £50 000 and £300 000 a year. Companies can claim numerous allowances, including investment allowances which can be **set against** their profits. This reduces their taxable profits in one year.

Capital gains tax This is a tax on capital gains - the difference between the buying price and selling price of an asset. Most goods and services are exempt, including the buying and selling of a person's main home. It is paid mainly on stocks and shares. Individuals in 2000-01 could make capital gains of up to £7 200 a year tax free. Thereafter, capital gains were included with income and taxed at the appropriate marginal rate of income tax.

Inheritance tax This is a tax on the value of assets left on death by an individual. In 2000-01, the first £234 000 of any inheritance was tax free. Thereafter, it was taxed at 40 per cent. There are numerous exemptions. For instance, any money left by one spouse to another is completely tax free. Also, there is no tax on gifts made during the lifetime of an individual provided that they are made 7 years before death.

Excise duties These are not to be confused with customs duties - taxes on imported goods. Excise duties are taxes levied on a narrow range of goods: fuel, alcohol, tobacco and betting. They are calculated not on value (as with VAT) but on the volume sold. For instance, excise duty is paid per litre of petrol sold. If the price of petrol rises, the amount paid in VAT rises, but the excise duty remains the same.

Value added tax This is a tax on expenditure. There are different rates of tax. Essential commodities - food, water, children's clothing, books, newspaper, magazines and public transport - are tax exempt (i.e. they are **zero rated**). Domestic fuel (gas, electricity, heating oil and coal) is taxed at a reduced rate of 5 per cent. All other goods and services are taxed at 17.5 per cent. VAT is collected by each business and is imposed on the value added to a product by that business.

Petroleum revenue tax and oil royalties These are taxes on the output of North Sea oil.

Council tax Council tax is a tax imposed on domestic property by local authorities. Each dwelling has been assessed for sale value in April 1992. The property has then been put into one of 7 bands, from band A for properties up to £40 000 to band H for properties over £320 000. For instance, a £130 000 property would be put in Band F, which covers properties between £120 000 and £160 000. The local authority then fixes a charge each year to each band. The differences in charges between bands are fixed by law. For instance, properties in Band H, the highest band, pay three times the Council tax of properties in Band A, the lowest band in a local area.

Business rates Business rates are a local authority tax on business property. Each business property has been given a rateable value based on an estimate of the yearly rent at which that property might reasonably have been let. The amount paid by the business is the rateable value multiplied by a 'factor'. This factor is called the 'Uniform Business Rate'. It is fixed by the government each year and is the same for all areas of the country.

Progressive, proportional and regressive taxes

Some taxes in the UK are progressive, i.e. the higher the income, the higher the proportion of income paid in tax. Income tax is progressive because there are personal allowances and because there are three rates of tax depending upon how much is earned. For instance, in Table 79.3 the £60 000 income earner paid an average rate of tax of 26.3 per cent. If the same individual had a gross income of £40 000, with the same allowances and pension payments, the amount of tax paid would have been £6 595 (i.e. £8 000 less). The average rate of tax paid would have been 16.5 per cent [(£6 595 ÷ £40 000) x 100%].

National Insurance contributions are mildly progressive up to the upper earnings limit. This is because employees can earn up to £76 a week (in 2000-01) without paying contributions. However, they become regressive for individuals earning over the upper earnings limit. For instance, a worker earning £100 a week paid a lower average rate of contributions than one earning £500 a week even though both pay exactly the same marginal rate in 2000-01. However, a worker earning £1 000 a week paid no contributions on earnings over £535. Hence, the average rate of employees' National Insurance contributions began to fall once the £535 limit had been passed.

Council tax is highly regressive. The highest council tax payer only pays a maximum three times that of the lowest council tax payer, but may earn considerably more than them. The poorest receive rebates on their council tax, but this makes little difference to its regressivity.

Corporation tax could be argued to be progressive. Corporation tax leaves less profit to be distributed to shareholders. Given that shareholders tend to be higher income individuals, this means that higher income individuals tend to be more affected by corporation tax.

Capital gains tax is certainly progressive. It is paid only by those with enough (mainly) financial assets to make capital gains over £7 200 a year (in 2000-01). Similarly, inheritance tax is in general progressive over much of the income range. Wealth and income tend to be correlated. So the larger the amount left, the larger tends to be the income of the deceased and indeed of those who inherit. Very high income earners, though, who are also very wealthy are likely to pay very little inheritance tax. This is because inheritance tax can be avoided, for instance by giving wealth away before death. The greater the wealth, the more incentive there is to avoid the tax and hence at the top of the income scale, inheritance tax might become regressive.

Indirect taxes tend to be regressive. A much larger proportion of low income households' budget is spent on alcohol, tobacco and betting than that of high income households and hence excise duties are regressive. It could be argued that VAT is progressive because items which form a disproportionate part of low income budgets, such as food and public transport, are zero rated. On the other hand, higher income earners tend to save a larger proportion of their income than low income earners, and hence the proportion of income paid in VAT declines as income rises - a regressive effect.

Table 79.4 *Taxes as a proportion of income, 1997-98*

	Bottom fifth	Next fifth	Middle fifth	Next fifth	Top fifth	All households
Original income (£)	2 520	6 780	15 530	29 960	47 610	19 680
State cash benefits (£)	4 780	4 990	3 590	2 050	1 120	3 300
Income after state cash benefits (£)	7 300	11 770	19 120	32 010	48 730	22 980
Direct taxes[1] (£)	750	1 500	3 360	5 860	11 440	4 580
Indirect taxes (£)	2 010	2 550	3 570	4 680	5 770	3 720
Total taxes (£)	2 760	4 050	6 930	10 540	17 210	8 300
Proportion of income paid in tax						
Direct taxes						
% of original income	29.8	22.1	21.6	19.6	24.0	23.2
% of income after benefits	10.3	12.7	17.6	18.3	23.5	19.9
Indirect taxes						
% of original income	79.8	37.6	23.0	15.6	12.1	18.9
% of income after benefits	27.5	21.7	18.7	14.6	11.8	16.2
Total taxes						
% of original income	109.5	59.7	44.6	35.2	36.1	42.2
% of income after benefits	37.8	34.4	36.2	32.9	35.3	36.1

1. Income tax, employees' National Insurance contributions and council tax net of rebates.
Source: adapted from *Economics Trends*, Office for National Statistics.

Table 79.4 gives a broader view of the tax system. If state benefits are not included, both direct and indirect taxes are regressive. In the case of direct taxes, the highly regressive nature of the council tax outweighs the progressive nature of income tax and National Insurance contributions for most of the income scale. This leads to the whole tax system being regressive overall. If state benefits are included in income, then direct taxes as a whole become progressive whilst indirect taxes remain regressive. Overall, the tax system is broadly proportional over the income range with the bottom fifth of households paying a slightly higher percentage of income in tax than the top fifth.

International comparisons

Figure 79.2 gives an international comparison of taxes.

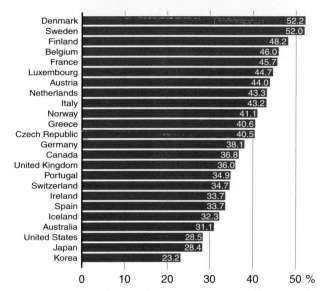

Figure 79.2 *Total taxes and social security contributions as a percentage of GDP, 1996*
Source: adapted from *Economic Trends*, March 1999, Office for National Statistics.

In the 1970s, it was argued that Britain was highly taxed and that this had contributed to low economic growth rates. In fact, Britain has tended to tax less than continental Europe whilst taxing more highly than countries such as the USA and Japan. Figure 79.2 shows that in 1996, the UK was towards the bottom of the taxation league for the rich developed OECD countries. The UK also tends to collect a lower proportion of taxes in direct taxes than most developed countries. Conversely, indirect taxes tend to be relatively high. Compared to continental Europe, for instance, social security taxes are far lower in the UK.

Changes in tax

Since 1979, there have been significant changes in the burden of tax. Table 79.5 shows three years. 1979 and 1999 were both boom years for the economy, whilst in 1993, the UK was only just coming out of recession.

Income tax In the 1979 Budget, the government cut the top rate of income tax from 83 per cent on earned

Table 79.5 *Central government income*

	1979	1993	1999
Taxes on income			
Paid by person	32.5	27.1	32.9
Paid by corporations	7.5	8.1	10.5
Taxes on expenditure	33.1	42.6	30.2
Social security contributions	17.4	18.0	17.0
Rent, interest, dividends, royalties and other income	7.4	4.4	9.4

Source: adapted from *National Income and Accounts* (Blue Book), *Financial Statistics*, Office for national Statistics.

income and 98 per cent on unearned income to 60 per cent. Throughout the 1980s, it made it a priority to cut income tax rates. The basic rate of income tax fell from 33 per cent in 1979 to 25 per cent in 1987. The 1987 Budget also saw a fall in the top rate of tax to 40 per cent. Since then, the standard rate has fallen to 23 per cent and a lower starting rate of tax has been introduced. Despite these falls in the rate of tax, the revenues from income have tended to rise for three reasons. First, although rates of income tax have been falling, governments since the late 1980s have been cutting tax allowances. In the 1990s, for instance, income tax relief on mortgage interest rate payments was gradually abolished. The married man's allowance has been reduced. Child allowances were abolished. Second, economic growth has raised the taxable income of the nation. Third, high income earners have increased their tax payments. Reductions in the top rate of tax have considerably reduced the incentive to avoid tax. For instance, there is far less incentive for millionaires to move to the Bahamas or Jersey today than there was in 1979. Moreover, widening income differentials mean that the top 10 per cent of income earners receive a larger share of total income than in 1979. More income is therefore subject to the top rate of tax. In contrast, the bottom 10 per cent receive a smaller share. The amount of untaxed income has therefore tended to fall.

VAT VAT rates have risen and its scope has been widened. In the 1979 Budget, the rate of VAT was raised from 8 per cent to 15 per cent to pay for income tax cuts. In 1991, the rate was increased to 17.5 per cent to pay for a cut in local authority poll tax. 1995 saw the introduction of VAT on domestic fuel, previously zero rated.

A reduction in the incidence of taxes on capital In the 1980s, the Conservative government considerably reduced capital gains tax and inheritance tax. These taxes bring in relatively little revenue but tended to be highly progressive. Today, with careful tax planning, taxpayers can avoid paying either tax.

Rises in excise duties In the 1990s, there was a considerable increase in excise duties on cigarettes and petrol. The former was justified on health grounds, whilst the latter was argued to be for the benefit of the environment. The increase in excise duties on cigarettes has led to the UK having much higher after tax prices on cigarettes than France and Belgium. By 2000, this was causing a major smuggling problem. It was estimated that three quarters of all hand rolled tobacco consumed in the UK had been smuggled in from the Continent whilst up to a third of all cigarettes sold were now contraband. As for petrol, the rises seem to have had little impact on the number of miles driven, showing that petrol is highly price inelastic in demand. The tax rises, therefore, whilst bringing in large amounts of extra revenue for the government, have not succeeded in either reducing transport congestion or limiting car exhaust emissions.

Local authority taxes The changes in local authority taxes are described in the Data Question.

Has the tax system become more regressive?

The tax changes introduced in the 1980s served to shift the burden of taxation from the better off to those worse off. Cuts in income tax, particularly for higher rate tax payers, helped increase post-tax incomes of the better off which was partly paid for by increases in VAT paid for by lower income households. The introduction of the poll tax in 1989-1990 hit low income earners particularly hard whilst giving substantial tax gains to the better off. In the 1990s, this trend was to some extent reversed. The Poll Tax was replaced by the council tax. Income tax cuts, particularly after the election of a Labour government in 1997, tended to favour the less well off. The removal of income tax allowances, such as mortgage relief, hit the better off. Overall, however, the system remains only mildly progressive.

Local authority finance

Local authority rates

Local authority rates were a long standing tax on the rental value of property in an area. Rates were relatively cheap to collect. A Price Waterhouse study, for instance, estimated that the average collection cost per authority was £560 000 in 1989-90. It was cheap because there were a limited number of properties in an area. There was little risk of default on payment because local authorities could secure a charge against any property if its owner failed to pay. Households on low income received rate rebates, and some as a result paid no rates at all. Rates were unpopular though. It was pointed out that a poor pensioner living on her own in a house would pay the same rates as an identical house next door where there were two parents and four children all working. It discouraged people from putting up extensions because the rateable value would be increased. It also meant that a property with a notional rent of £2 000 per year would pay 20 times as much in rates as a property with a notional rent of £200 per year.

Rates were also unpopular with businesses. They complained that some local authorities imposed high rates on businesses in order to reduce the bills faced by domestic rate payers.

Four taxes in four years

Traditionally, local authorities have raised taxes through local authority rates. These were a tax on the notional rental value of both domestic property and commercial and industrial property. In theory, the notional rental values should have been reviewed every few years. However, because any rate review brings losers whose notional rents are increased, as well as gainers, and because governments didn't want to lose votes, rate reviews kept on being put off after 1973, the date of the last review. By the time of the general election in 1987, the government had decided that rates for domestic property should be abolished and replaced by a poll tax system.

Business rates would continue, but in a modified form. The poll tax, a tax per head of the population, was introduced in Scotland in April 1989 and in England and Wales in April 1990. Within 8 months of its introduction into England and Wales, the government announced a fundamental review of local authority finance. In its March 1991 Budget, the government reduced poll tax bills by £140 per person and financed this by increasing VAT from 15 per cent to 17.5 per cent. A month later, it announced that the poll tax would be scrapped and replaced by a new council tax from April 1993. The council tax would be a tax on property values.

The community charge or poll tax

The poll tax was a tax on each adult (over 18) living in a local authority. Low income adults paid 20 per cent of the full poll tax; otherwise, there was no linkage of the tax to income. This was justified on the grounds that local authority services should be paid for like cornflakes or soap. Just as everyone, whatever their income, pays the same for a packet of cornflakes, so it was only fair that everyone, whatever their income, should pay a fixed price for local authority services. Unlike the previous rating system, households were taxed according to the number of adults in the house. So a poor pensioner living on her own would only have paid one-sixth of the poll tax compared to a household with two parents and four adult children working.

The introduction of the poll tax brought substantial gainers and losers. On the whole, the gainers were households which before had above average rates. The losers, on the whole, were households which paid below average rates or the very large number of people who had never paid rates because they didn't own or rent their own home. The cost of administering the poll tax was substantially greater than the rates - an estimated average £1 271 000 per local authority. The cost of collection was higher because there was approximately twice the number of taxpayers as under the old rating system. Costs also proved higher because there was widespread evasion. Many initially refused to pay the tax and had to be taken to court at considerable expense. For instance, 2.3 million court summonses were issued at the end of 1992 to non-payers. Others simply disappeared. Electoral registers shrank at the time. Local authorities are still owed millions of pounds today in unpaid poll tax.

The council tax

The council tax is a tax on the value of domestic property. Each property was valued at April 1992. Properties are then put into one of eight bands shown in Table 79.6. The local authority then fixes a rate. The amount paid by each homeowner is then determined by a fixed ratio shown in Table 79.6. Houses where there is only one adult occupant receive a 25 per cent rebate. Like the old rating system, there is also a sliding scale of council tax rebates for low income families. The council tax should be no more expensive to collect than the old rates since the tax base is identical. The transition to the council tax created winners and losers. On the whole, the winners were those living in rented accommodation and low income families who owned their own homes. The losers tended to be higher income home-owning families. Any extensions to the property are not assessed for tax.

Table 79.6 *Council tax valuation bands (England)*

Band	Range of values	Proportion payable*
A	Up to £40 000	100
B	£40 000 - £52 000	117
C	£52 001 - £68 000	133
D	£68 001 - £88 000	150
E	£88 001 - £120 000	183
F	£120 001 - £160 000	217
G	£160 001 - £320 000	250
H	Above £320 000	300

*As a percentage of the tax payable in A

Local authority finances

Since 1979, central government had attempted to control local authority spending and borrowing. It felt that local authorities spent too much, providing unnecessary services inefficiently. The main way in which central government controlled local authority spending was through a system called **rate capping**. Central government placed a ceiling on the amount local authorities could spend. This was only partially successful. Local authorities which normally spent below their ceiling could increase their spending in any one year. One feature of the system was that only a minority of individuals felt the impact of any rate rise because only a minority of the population owned property. Local authorities which were at the ceiling found ways round the restrictions, for instance through selling assets and then leasing them back again.

The government hoped that the poll tax system would curb local authority spending. When the poll tax was introduced, the government deliberately cut grants to local authorities in real terms whilst leaving business rate revenue unchanged. This meant that local authorities either had to cut their real spending or increase their poll tax demands. What's more, because only approximately 25 per cent of local authority revenue came from the poll tax, a 1 per cent fall in other revenues would have to be made up by a 3 per cent rise in the poll tax. Alternatively, assume a local authority was told by central government that it should be spending £100 million. £50 million would come in central government grants, £25 million in business rates and £25 million in poll tax. If the local authority wanted to spend £110m, the extra £10 million would have to come from the poll tax. Local poll tax payers would have to pay £35 million in poll tax rather than just £25 million. A 10 per cent increase in spending would result in a 40 per cent extra poll tax bill.

The government assumed that local authorities would reduce spending. It was argued that large poll tax bills would be very unpopular and local voters would vote out councils which imposed these charges. Instead, local authorities didn't cut spending and set very high poll tax bills. The voters blamed central government for the bills and many refused to pay the tax.

When the poll tax was replaced, the government was forced to reintroduce a form of rate capping. This was removed by the newly elected Labour government in 1997. It was felt that local authorities were now responsible enough not to spend wastefully and that they ought to be given the right to change their spending if they so wished.

Uniform business rates

In 1990, local authorities in England and Wales lost the power to fix their own business rates. Under the new system, all businesses were assessed for rates in 1989. The government then imposed a single uniform rate across the whole country. Hence, a firm owning premises with a rateable value of £20 000 in London would pay exactly the same amount of rates as a firm owning £20 000 premises in Manchester. Business rates are not allowed by law to increase by more than the rate of inflation year on year. The new system meant that high spending local authorities could no longer charge much higher rates on similar property to a low spending authority next door.

A unique tax

All industrialised countries have some form of tax on property. No industrialised country has a poll tax. In fact, poll taxes are a rarity even in the developing world. They are associated with the introduction of a taxation system into a market economy when it is difficult to identify either levels of spending or income.

1. **What were the main differences between the systems of local authority taxation described in the data?**
2. **To what extent was each system (a) efficient and (b) equitable?**
3. **Two alternative systems of local authority taxation that have been suggested are (a) a local income tax and (b) a local sales tax (similar to VAT). Discuss whether these would be better taxes than a property tax.**

unit 80 Government spending

Summary

1. The size of the state grew during the 20th century.
2. Factors which determine the optimal level of public spending include efficiency of public vs private sector provision, equity, the effects on taxation and government borrowing, and the need to intervene over the trade cycle.
3. The size of the state can be reduced through privatisation, outsourcing, internal markets, public/private sector partnerships, or the abandonment of provision.
4. Whether the state or the private sector should produce an individual good or service depends upon the criteria of productive and allocative efficiency and equity.

The size of the state

Government spending, as a proportion of national income, tended to rise worldwide during the 20th century. Two World Wars led to a significant upward shift in state spending. Then, in Europe at least, the creation of welfare states further increased spending. There is a number of factors which determine what might be the optimal level of public spending in an economy.

Efficiency Free markets can be less efficient in the production of some goods and services than the state. The free market, for instance, will produce too few **public goods** and **merit goods** (☞ unit 20). The state therefore has to organise production of services such as defence, law, order and protective services and education. Production of too few goods and services is an aspect of allocative inefficiency. Free markets, though, can also be productively inefficient. It can be argued, for instance, that health care should be provided by the state because costs, for the same level of services, are higher when it is provided by the private sector. This is to do with economies of scale and the ability of a sole buyer (a monopsonist) to drive down prices of suppliers to the market such as doctors, hospitals and drugs companies. The state should therefore produce those goods and services which it can provide more efficiently than the private sector.

Equity Free markets can produce an inequitable distribution of resources. In health care, for instance, those likely to face the largest bills are the elderly, typically in the lower income brackets of income distribution. Unless the state provides assistance, many elderly people would not be able to afford health care. Similarly, if education had to be paid for, children from poor families would suffer most. Governments therefore can be argued to have an obligation to spend in such a way as to reduce inequity.

The burden of taxation Government spending has to be paid for, typically through taxation. A country like the UK, where government spending is around 40 per cent of its GDP, has a lower tax burden than, say, Sweden, where it is nearer 60 per cent. The level of taxation can be important to both efficiency and economic growth. Taxes can act as a disincentive. For instance, high marginal rates of income tax can reduce incentives to work. High marginal rates of tax on employment reduce the willingness of employers to take on workers and can lead to higher unemployment. High tax levels can discourage overseas investors from investing in a country, whilst encouraging domestic firms to relocate abroad. This leads to a drain of capital from a country, perhaps resulting in lower economic growth. Hence, the optimal level of government spending cannot be considered without taking into account the welfare implications of different tax levels.

Government borrowing High levels of government spending are often associated with high levels of government borrowing. This is because governments face political pressures to spend more but tax less. They can

Question 1

Pfizer, one of the most successful inward investors in South East England, is warning that it will not be able to continue growing at its present rate unless improvements are made to south-east Kent's infrastructure. The US owned healthcare group, makers of the drug Viagra, says that it needs better road, rail and bus links, hotels, executive housing and schools near its site at Sandwich, where 4 500 staff are employed. The company has hired almost 2 000 staff in the past three years and is building a research facility with space for 1 000 more, two thirds recruited from other parts of the UK and Europe. Sandwich is in the poorer eastern side of south-east England, near areas of high unemployment. Pfizer claims that every job at its site indirectly supports another five in the region. The company is building a UK headquarters for up to 900 staff at Reigate in Surrey in order to hire managers in the Greater London markets and relieve pressure on Sandwich.

Source: adapted from the *Financial Times*, 19.6.1999.

(a) Explain the arguments in favour of the state providing improved infrastructure, such as schools and roads, around Sandwich.
(b) To what extent should the state be involved in providing increased housing in the area?

do this if they borrow more. However, ever increasing levels of government borrowing are unsustainable (☞ unit 81). Government spending levels must therefore be low enough to be financed adequately in the long run.

The trade cycle Governments may want to use their spending to smooth out the trade cycle. John Maynard Keynes advocated that governments should spend more if the economy were in a depression to increase aggregate demand. If governments finance this through increased borrowing, they must ensure that government spending falls again when the economy recovers. Otherwise, there are dangers that both government spending and levels of national debt will forever increase, which is unsustainable in the long term.

State provision of goods and services

There is a number of different models of state provision of goods and services, shown in Figure 80.1.
- The public sector may both physically produce and provide (i.e. pay for out of tax revenues) goods and services. For instance, in the UK this is the case for health care, defence, education and libraries.
- The public sector may provide a good or service but not produce it. Instead it buys it in from the private sector. For instance, in the UK the government pays for the building of new roads, but it employs private sector contractors to do the work. Most places in old people's homes are paid for by local authorities, but the homes are in the private sector. The government buys in food for the army, textbooks for schools or electricity for hospitals from the private sector.
- The government may produce a good or service but sell it to the private sector. Before privatisation, government owned the gas, electricity, water and telecommunications industries, but sold these to private sector customers.
- The fourth alternative shown in Figure 80.1 is that the state is involved in neither the provision nor funding of services. These are goods and services produced and sold in the private sector, from cars to baked beans to package holidays.

In the 1950s, 1960s and 1970s, the state in the UK was much larger than it is today. In particular, the state owned the 'commanding heights of the economy', key industries such as coal, gas, electricity, railways and telecommunications. In the 1980s and 1990s, the size of the state was considerably reduced in a number of ways.

Privatisation This saw the sale of state owned companies and other assets to the private sector. In Figure 80.1, privatisation represented a move mainly from Box B to Box C.

Outsourcing Outsourcing is the process of asking another producer to provide a good or service rather than producing it in-house. In this case, government would ask private sector firms to bid for the provision of services to the state. For instance, construction companies might be asked to tender for a road contract, or catering firms might tender for the provision of food to a school. If the good or service had previously been produced by the state, this would then be a move from Box A to Box D in Figure 80.1.

Internal markets In some cases, the government might decide that only it can both pay for and produce a good or service. However, it may decide to introduce competition by creating an internal market where different public sector providers compete amongst themselves. For instance, schools in a local area may compete for pupils. Internal markets leave a good or service in Box A in Figure 80.1.

Public/private sector partnerships The government can try and persuade the private sector to enter into a partnership with it. For instance, rather than pay completely for the

Paid for by		
	Public sector	Private sector
Public sector (Produced by)	A Schools, National Health Service	B The Post Office
Private sector	D Cleaning services in schools, old people's homes	C Motor vehicles, Ice creams

Figure 80.1 *State provision in year 2000, UK*

Public services should increasingly be delivered by voluntary organisations in the place of the state, said William Hague, the leader of the Conservative Party, yesterday. He said he wanted to 'build on our experience of paying for public services out of taxes but having them delivered by voluntary organisations'. His main examples of how churches and charities could take over from social services related to 'the plight of children in local authority care and of young people leaving care' which was a 'silent scandal'. He said the state was 'failing these young people' because most of them failed to find jobs and made up 'nearly 40 per cent of young prisoners'. Consideration should therefore be given to transferring from social services departments all or part of their responsibility under the Children Act to 'advise, assist and befriend' youngsters leaving care. Mr Hague also suggested giving the voluntary sector, including the churches, a 'greater role in running this country's childrens' homes'.

Source: adapted from the *Financial Times*, 17.11.1998.

(a) Identify how, according to Mr Hague, the state was failing to provide an efficient service for those in local authority care.
(b) Explain how services in this area are organised at the moment and how they would be organised under Mr Hague's proposals.

redevelopment of a run down area, the government may invite private companies to pay part of the cost in return for a share of future revenues. The Private Finance Initiative (PFI) is another example. In this case, a private company builds and operates a building, road, bridge or other piece of infrastructure instead of government. The state then pays a 'rent' over a period of years for the use of the infrastructure before it reverts to state ownership. PFI would put provision of a good into Box D.

Abandonment of provision The government may attempt to abandon paying for a service which it also produces. For instance, new toll motorways will be paid for by the motorists that use them rather than the taxpayer (a move from Box A to Box C). The government could make patients pay for the services of their GP (a move from Box D to Box C).

Choosing between public sector and private sector provision

Whether state provision or private provision is more desirable depends on a number of factors.

Productive efficiency There can be large **economies of scale** available if a service is provided for the total population by one producer. For instance, it will almost certainly be more costly for two competing refuse collection companies to collect refuse from a housing estate than just one. Therefore, it may be more efficient for the state to organise household refuse collection rather than allow each household to employ different firms. The same might apply to the National Health Service (NHS). The amount spent on the NHS is about two-thirds of that in France and Germany and half that of the USA as a percentage of national income. It could be argued that this is because the NHS provides lower quality health care than in other countries. But there is evidence to suggest that there are significant economies of scale in the NHS which are not found in the private health care systems of continental Europe and the USA. For instance, bed utilisation in NHS hospitals is considerably higher than in Europe or the USA because the NHS has much greater control of when patients are to be treated. Equally, drug costs are lower because doctors in the NHS are encouraged to prescribe the minimum doses necessary of the cheapest drug available.

On the other hand, it is sometimes claimed that **diseconomies of scale** are present in organisations like the NHS. They are such large bureaucracies that management is unable to control costs and utilise resources efficiently. **X-inefficiency** (☞ unit 61) raises costs as workers within the organisation manipulate the system for their own advantage. Only the break-up of the organisation and the creation of strong competition in the market place can lower costs and eliminate inefficiency. This provides a strong argument for either breaking up a public sector monopoly and then selling the competing parts to the private sector, as for instance happened to the electricity generating industry in 1991, or the creation of strong

internal markets, where, say, schools or hospitals have to compete with each other for pupils or patients.

Allocative efficiency State production or tendering systems are unlikely to create much consumer choice. Households, for instance, are unlikely to have any choice about who collects their refuse or who polices their neighbourhood. Moreover, they are unable to influence the amount spent on services except perhaps indirectly through the ballot box.

Choice is much greater in the private sector. UK consumers now, for instance, have a choice about which telephone company or gas supplier to use. By the late 1990s, households will be able to choose which company supplies them with gas. Already they can shop around for gas appliances or gas repair services. State provision, however, can involve an element of choice. Parents in the UK have the right to choose which school they wish to send their child to. Patients can choose their doctor. Choice may be not as great as it might seem though. Consumers of education or health care are likely to want to buy from their nearest supplier. Therefore, weak local monopolies are likely to emerge, particularly in rural areas. The 'best' schools in an area might be oversubscribed and turn applicants away. Hospitals are likely to be full and so patients are unlikely to be able to exercise much choice about when to have an operation.

Choice also implies that consumers are able to make rational choices. But there may be little **consumer sovereignty** (☞ unit 66) in the market. Producers may use their market power to distort information supplied to customers. Consumers may also have extremely limited understanding of the services they are asked to buy themselves.

Distribution of resources The transfer of resources from the public sector to the private sector can have important implications for the distribution of income. For instance, when the state ceases to pay for certain activities through the tax system, individuals have to pay the full cost themselves. A student wanting to study at a drama school might before have been financed by collecting a fraction of a penny per year from local taxpayers. If the local authority ceases to pay a grant, then the student or the student's family has to pay the full cost of thousands of pounds.

Question 3

It has been suggested that local authorities should no longer provide public libraries. Instead, they could either contract out, getting a private company to run the service in return for a fee from the local authority, or the local authority could stop offering a service at all and leave the market mechanism to decide whether library services should be offered to consumers and in what form. Libraries are used by all age and income groups but are disproportionately used by females and older people.

(a) Discuss the impact of both contracting out and completely privatising the library service on efficiency and equity.

Applied economics

Public expenditure in the UK

Public expenditure totals

The public sector in the UK comprises central government, local government and government enterprises such as public corporations. Central government is responsible for approximately three-quarters of total public spending. Compared to other countries, the size of Britain's public sector is unexceptional. As shown in Table 80.1, it is greater as a proportion of GDP than the free market economies of the United States or Japan, at the bottom end of the range of our EU partners, but much lower than a country like Sweden which has a long tradition of high public spending.

Public expenditure totals can be divided by function, as illustrated in Figure 80.2.

- The largest single item of public expenditure is social protection. This covers **transfer payments** such as child benefit and Jobseekers allowance. The most costly benefit is the state retirement pension, received by around 10 million pensioners.
- Spending on **health** is the second largest category of expenditure. Most of this is accounted for by the cost of the National Health Service.
- **Education** covers local government spending on primary and secondary schools, and colleges of further education. Central government pays for higher education and research grants.
- **Defence spending** is expenditure on the army, navy and airforce.
- **Public order and safety** covers spending on the police, the judiciary, prisons and the fire service.
- **Housing** is mainly grants to Housing Associations to build new homes and to local councils for the repairs and maintenance of their existing stock.
- **General public services** includes services such as refuse collection, public transport, roads, street lighting and parks.
- **Gross debt interest** is the interest that the government has to pay on the money it has borrowed in the past - the National Debt.
- **Other expenditure** includes expenditure on overseas aid, agriculture, forestry and fishing, the arts, libraries, and embassies abroad.

Table 80.1 *Government expenditure as a percentage of GDP*

	1960-67	1968-73	1974-79	1980-89	1990-89
Sweden	34.8	44.3	54.4	62.9	64.0
France	37.4	38.9	43.3	50.2	53.4
Italy	31.9	36.0	42.9	44.9	52.8
Germany	35.7	39.8	47.5	47.8	48.1
UK	34.7	39.5	44.6	44.9	43.0
Canada	29.3	34.7	39.2	39.7	46.3
US	28.3	31.0	32.6	35.8	34.6
Japan	18.7	20.5	28.4	32.8	34.5

Source: adapted from OECD, *Historical Statistics* and *Economic Outlook*.

Trends in public expenditure

Total UK government spending in real terms has tended to rise over time as Table 80.2 shows. Increased income from economic growth has partly been spent on improving public services. Trends in government spending as a percentage of GDP are more complex. Figure 80.3 shows that the two World Wars caused large spikes in public spending as defence expenditure soared. The two World Wars also led to new levels of public spending being established. Before the First World War, public expenditure was around 12 per cent of GDP. In the inter-war period, it rose to around 25 per cent, whilst after the Second World War it rose to around 35 per cent. The 1960s and first half of the 1970s saw an upward trend in public spending as a percentage of GDP as the welfare state expanded. This trend came to a halt in 1975 when the then Labour government declared that the country could no longer afford to keep on spending more and more on public services. This was reinforced by the election of a Conservative government under Margaret Thatcher in 1979 which was committed to reducing public spending. Within ten years, it had succeeded in stabilising public spending at around 40 per cent of GDP. In a recession, as in 1990-92, this rises because of increased spending on welfare benefits. In a boom, it is likely to fall below this. The Labour government elected in 1997 was broadly committed to maintaining this level of spending.

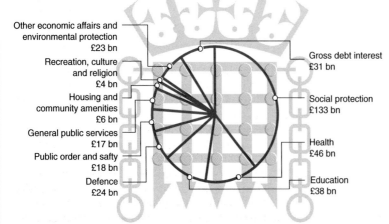

Other economic affairs and environmental protection £23 bn

Recreation, culture and religion £4 bn

Housing and community amenities £6 bn

General public services £17 bn

Public order and safty £18 bn

Defence £24 bn

Gross debt interest £31 bn

Social protection £133 bn

Health £46 bn

Education £38 bn

Figure 80.2 *General government expenditure, 1998-99*
Source: adapted from The Treasury, *Financial Statement and Budget Report*.

Changes in the components of public spending in recent years are shown in Figure 80.4. There were large falls in real spending on defence and housing between 1987 and 1998. Defence was cut as a result of the collapse of the Soviet Union in 1990 and the ending of the cold war. This represented a 'peace dividend' for the UK and other NATO countries. Housing expenditure was cut as part of the Conservative government's policy to reduce subsidies to local authority housing departments and council house tenants. It felt that the private sector, both rented and owner occupied, should play a large role in the provision of housing. Education increased at the same rate as the overall increase in public spending. The Labour government elected in 1997 made education one of its top priorities and therefore spending on this area may increase at a faster rate in the future. Health, social security and public order and safety have all increased at a faster rate than the total. A 50 per cent increase in spending on public order and safety reflected fears about increased crime. Health spending has risen for four reasons: longer life expectancy has increased the number of old people in the population who are the major consumers of health care; improvements in knowledge have allowed more illnesses to respond to medical treatment; there are rising expectations about what level of health care should be delivered; and the labour intensive nature of medical care has made it difficult to contain costs at the same rate of inflation as the rest of the economy. Social security spending has risen too despite the fact that increases in benefits have been linked to the rate of inflation since 1981. The rise in social security spending is mostly accounted for by the increase in the number of people claiming benefits. For instance, between 1987 and 1997 the number of people claiming sickness and invalidity benefit/incapacity benefit rose from 1.2 million to 1.8 million. For attendance allowance (paid to those looking after the disabled), the increase was from 0.7 million to 1.2 million. Mobility allowance/disability living allowance claimants rose from 0.5 million to 2.0 million. The largest group of benefit recipients, old age pensioners, rose from 9.9 million to 10.9 million.

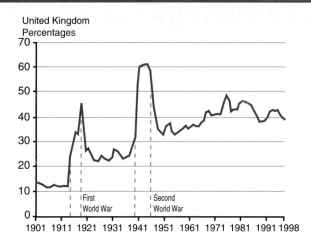

Figure 80.3 *General government expenditure as a percentage of GDP*
Source: adapted from *Social Trends*, Office for National Statistics.

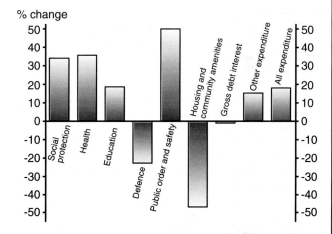

Figure 80.4 *% change in real government expenditure, 1987-1998*
Source: adapted from *Social Trends*, Office for National Statistics.

Table 80.2 *General government expenditure at 1997-98 prices*

	£ billion	Index 1970-71=100
1970-71	183.2	100.0
1975-76	238.1	130.0
1980-81	245.3	133.9
1985-86	261.8	142.9
1990-91	277.5	151.5
1995-96	326.7	178.3
1999-2000	332.0	181.2

Source: adapted from The Treasury, *Financial Statement and Budget Report*.

Are public services improving?

There are major problems in assessing whether there has been a growth in public services in recent years. Taking the National Health Service as an example, there are four key factors which need to be considered.

Efficiency gains Each year, the NHS claims an improvement in efficiency. It measures this, for instance, through improvements in the number of patients being treated per doctor, reductions in waiting lists and occupancy rates of beds. Efficiency improvements come from two sources. First, there is the adoption of best practice throughout the service, eliminating **X-inefficiency** (☞ unit 61). This is a one-off effect in that once best practice has been adopted, it is impossible to make further efficiency gains. Second, advances in medical knowledge, new equipment and better trained staff can increase efficiency. This, in theory, is a dynamic process and it should be possible to generate efficiency gains from this source for the foreseeable future.

The cost of the service Data are often presented 'at constant prices'. This means that figures are adjusted for the general rate of inflation in the economy (measured by the GDP deflator rather than the Retail Price Index). However, increases in real expenditure on services do not necessarily mean that the volume of services has increased. This is because inflation in the public sector is likely to be higher than inflation in the economy as a whole. The public sector is far more labour intensive than the private sector. There is also far less scope for increases in productivity. Earnings on average increase about 2 per cent more than the increase in inflation each year. Hence the NHS has to pay more in real terms each year to buy the same number of doctors, nurses, etc.

The needs of the patients The population structure is slowly changing. In particular, there is a growth in the number of over 75 year olds. This age group is a particularly heavy user of NHS facilities. If public spending on the NHS is kept constant, the level of service to the average patient will inevitably decline.

Expectations and technology Each year, consumers expect to be able to buy better products. They expect to see more advanced cars, eat a wider range of foods and go to more exotic places for their holidays. They also expect to receive better health care. Advances in medicine mean that more and more illnesses are capable of treatment. But if these illnesses are to be treated, then extra money must be found to pay for treatment. Consumers also expect better facilities - everything from potted plants in waiting rooms, to private hospital rooms, to being able to choose the timing of medical treatment. These cost money.

Our expectations are for spending on the NHS to rise each year well above the rate of inflation. But this is not happening. The result is growing

dissatisfaction with the National Health Service. Overall, it is probably right to claim that the quality of care in the National Health Service has improved over the past 50 years. The problem is that consumers are dissatisfied with the pace of change. J K Galbraith, in his book *The Affluent Society*, talked about 'private affluence and public squalor'. Opinion polls consistently show that consumers and taxpayers wish to spend more of their income on a better National Health Service. Government policy which curbs public spending frustrates those desires. In this argument, there is market failure. Some argue that the same applies in areas such as education and road building. On the other hand, the electorate voted three times in general elections between 1979 and 1993 for a party which was perceived to be the party of low public spending. Consumers want more public spending, but they want others to pay for it - the free-rider problem. Political pressure to reduce public spending remains today. Assuming that the health service is run efficiently, the issue is one of opportunity cost. Do we want better health care or more spending on all other goods?

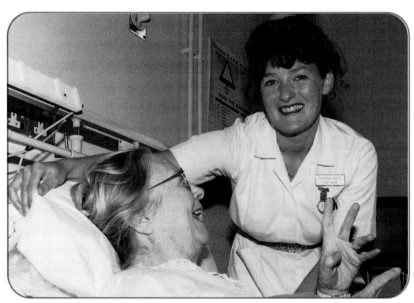

The Welfare State

The cost of the Welfare State is not exploding out of control, but neither has there been a significant 'rolling back' of its boundaries, says a book published today[1]. While spending has risen in real terms, the Welfare State has consistently absorbed about a quarter of GDP since the 1970s. This is despite the pressure from increased expectations, an ageing population and higher costs.

However, the pressures have changed what the welfare state provides and the proportion of welfare costs now met by the private sector. Spending on private education, for example, has risen as the share of GDP going on state education has fallen. Private pension provision has increased as the value of the state retirement pension relative to earnings has fallen. The scale of state-provided housing has been heavily cut back, whilst spending by the elderly on domestic help at home has replaced state services.

In contrast, private health cover amounts to only 3 per cent of NHS spending, and the state's share of total expenditure on welfare services, which include health, education, social security, housing and social services, has remained stable.

The Welfare State's performance has improved in many areas over the past 25 years. The NHS is more efficient, housing standards have risen and many more people are gaining better educational qualifications.

Dissatisfaction with the system has risen, however, because performance and quality standards are rising even faster in the rest of the economy. Whilst Welfare State spending rose by a half in real terms, expenditure doubled on cars and quadrupled on recreation, insurance and foreign holidays.

Policy options for the future include:
● spending more, possibly through ear marked taxes;
● improving efficiency;
● creating more public/private sector partnerships;
● restricting the scope of the welfare to core services.

For instance, the last option could be achieved through requiring students to a pay a greater share of their higher education costs, and compelling companies and individuals to make more private provision while leaving individuals with choices about how the money is spent. Rates were also unpopular with businesses. They complained that some local authorities imposed high rates on businesses in order to reduce the bills faced by domestic rate payers.

1. *The State of Welfare*, ed H Glennerster and J Hills, OUP.

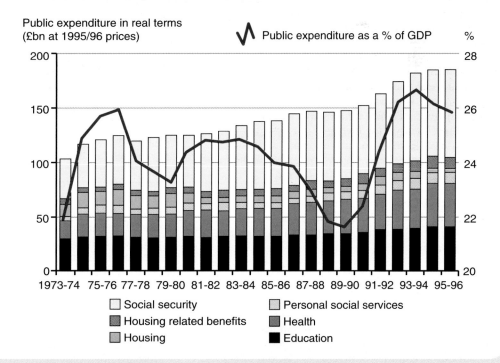

Figure 80.5 *The cost of the welfare state*
Source: adapted from *The State of Welfare*, ed H Glennerster and J Hills, OUP.

1. **Describe the trends in public spending on the Welfare State since the 1970s.**
2. **(a) Explain why there has been upward pressure on Welfare State spending.**

(b) Analyse how governments have constrained such pressures.
3. **Evaluate THREE ways in which a future government could increase the performance of secondary schools.**

Summary

1. Fiscal policy, through changes in the size of the budget deficit, can have an impact on aggregate demand.
2. Government expenditure and tax revenues which change automatically as income changes are called automatic stabilisers. They break the fall of national income when the economy moves towards a depression and limit the rise of income when the economy is in boom.
3. Active fiscal policy is the deliberate manipulation of government expenditure and taxes to influence the economy.
4. Demand management through the use of fiscal policy has its limitations. There are time lags involved in the implementation of policy, economic data on which to base decisions are inadequate, economic theory itself is not sufficiently well developed for governments to be able to fine tune the economy to meet precise targets, and continued deficits can lead to national debt problems. Countries belonging to the European Monetary Union also have restrictions placed upon their use of fiscal policy.
5. Because of these limitations, governments today tend to use monetary policy to manipulate aggregate demand.
6. Fiscal policy can be used to influence the supply side of the economy.

Fiscal policy and macro-economic management

Fiscal policy concerns the decisions of government about its spending, taxation and borrowing. In unit 36, it was explained that fiscal policy can have an impact on aggregate demand. **Expansionary fiscal policy**, where government spending is increased relative to taxation and hence government borrowing increases or a budget surplus is reduced, leads to an increase in aggregate demand. This in turn is likely to lead to a rise in GDP and falling unemployment, but rising inflation and a deterioration in the current account on the balance of payments. **Deflationary fiscal policy**, where the budget deficit falls or surplus rises, is likely to lead to the opposite, with falling economic growth but also falling inflationary pressures.

Automatic stabilisers

In the 1930s, large falls in export earnings and investment spending led to the Great Depression. Today, any reduction in export earnings or investment would have less impact on the economy because AUTOMATIC or BUILT-IN STABILISERS are greater. Automatic stabilisers are expenditures which automatically increase when the economy is going into a recession. Conversely, they automatically fall when national income begins to rise.

Government spending and taxation are both automatic stabilisers. When the economy goes into recession and unemployment rises, the government automatically increases its social security spending, paying out more in unemployment benefits and other related benefits. The fall in aggregate demand is therefore less than it would otherwise have been. Tax revenues fall too at a faster rate than the fall in income. This is because tax rates tend to be higher on marginal income than on average income. For instance, a worker paid on commission may sell less in a recession. Her tax rate might then fall from the higher rate of 40 per cent to the basic rate of 23 per cent. If household spending has to be cut, then it is likely that consumption items such as consumer durables taxed at $17^{1}/_{2}$ per cent VAT will see falls rather than zero rated food. With the government collecting less tax, disposable incomes are higher than they would otherwise be and therefore consumption can be at a higher level than would be the case without this automatic stabiliser.

When the economy goes into boom, government spending falls as the benefit budget falls automatically. Tax revenue increases at a faster rate than the increase in income. An unemployed person will pay very little tax. Once the unemployed get jobs, they start to pay substantial amounts of direct and indirect tax. So aggregate demand is lower than it would otherwise be with these automatic stabilisers.

Active or discretionary fiscal policy

ACTIVE or DISCRETIONARY FISCAL POLICY does not rely on the economy automatically changing the amount the government spends or collects in taxes. It is the deliberate manipulation of government expenditure and taxes to influence the economy. The deliberate decision by government to cut tax rates, leading to a fall in tax revenues, would be an example of active fiscal policy. Another would be a decision to increase spending on education.

There is a large number of reasons why governments use discretionary fiscal policy. They might be influenced by non-economic arguments. For instance, the Conservative government between 1979 and 1983 deliberately increased spending on defence in the belief that the UK spent too little on defence in the 1970s. The government may also alter government spending and taxation to win votes. It may wish to influence the **supply side** of the economy. It may also wish to influence aggregate demand. This is known as **demand management**.

Question 1

Explain whether the following are likely to be examples of automatic stabilisers or active fiscal policy:
(a) the rise in VAT rates from 8 to 15 per cent in 1979;
(b) the cut in the highest rate of income tax on earned income from 83 per cent to 60 per cent in 1979;
(c) the rise in payments of unemployment benefit from £680 million in 1979-80 to £1 328 million in 1980-81;
(d) the one per cent fall in the real value of taxes on income during 1980;
(e) the abolition of earnings related unemployment benefit in January 1982.

Demand management

Keynes developed his ideas about changing demand through the use of fiscal policy in the 1930s against the backdrop of the Great Depression. During the depression of the 1930s, millions of workers all over the world lost their jobs. In both the USA and Germany, unemployment levels reached 25 per cent. The economic orthodoxy of the time advocated **balanced budgets**, where government spending equalled taxation, and argued that the government could do little directly to influence the level of income and employment. Keynes argued that an increase in demand would cut unemployment. If firms wouldn't increase demand by increasing investment, and consumers wouldn't increase their demand by increasing their average propensities to consume, then the government would have to step in and, through creating a budget deficit, increase demand in the economy.

This view became the economic orthodoxy of the 1950s and 1960s. After the terrible unemployment of the 1930s, the goal became to create FULL EMPLOYMENT. In the 1944 White Paper *Employment Policy* (Cmnd 6527), it was stated that: 'The government accepts as one of their

primary aims and responsibilities the maintenance of a high and stable level of employment after the war.' Full employment is the level of output at which all the factors of production in the economy are fully utilised at given factor prices. For instance, it is where every worker who wants a job at the current wage rate is in employment.

So, when the economy was suffering from a rise in unemployment, government would increase the budget deficit. When the economy was at full employment, aggregate demand was threatening to rise even further and inflation was increasing (a situation known as **overheating** (☞ unit 36)), government would reduce the budget deficit to reduce aggregate demand.

In fact, unemployment levels in the 1950s and 1960s tended to fluctuate between 1 and 2 per cent. As time went on, economists and politicians felt more and more that the economy could be FINE-TUNED to a very precise level of unemployment through the use of fiscal levers. This was called DEMAND MANAGEMENT of the economy - the use of government policy to manage the level of aggregate demand in the economy. But even in the 1950s and 1960s, it was recognised that there were limitations to fine tuning.

The limitations of fiscal policy to manipulate aggregate demand

Conflicting policy objectives Governments in the 1950s and 1960s found it impossible to maintain a **stable** level of low unemployment. The economy tended to move from boom to mild recession - what came to be known as the STOP-GO CYCLE. When unemployment was low, economic growth tended to be high. However, inflation tended to rise and the balance of payments slipped into deficit. It was

Question 2

Michael Portillo, Shadow Chancellor, has urged Gordon Brown, the Chancellor, to cut taxes in his Budget despite the danger of higher interest rates and an overheating economy. Mr Portillo claimed the Chancellor would have to cut taxes by £15 billion to return the tax burden to the level it was when Labour came into power. He said 'I am not proposing that the Chancellor should cut taxes by £15 billion. I think in the present circumstances that would not be a responsible thing to advocate. My prediction would be that he's going to have some scope to have a fiscal loosening. That means he can either reduce taxes or he can increase public spending. I would recommend he use that money to reduce the stealth taxes he has imposed.'

Source: adapted from the *Financial Times*, 13.3.2000.

(a) Explain the likely effect on aggregate demand if the Chancellor adopted Mr Portillo's proposal.
(b) Given the government's commitment to maintaining low inflation, suggest why there would be a 'danger of higher interest rates' if there were substantial tax cuts.

particularly the balance of payments which worried governments at the time. So when the balance of payments moved into deficit, the government would reduce the budget deficit and the economy would fall into mild recession. Then the balance of payments would move into surplus, the government would apply the fiscal levers again, expanding the economy and the cycle would start all over again.

Time lags Assume that the government announces a £500 million increase in civil servant salaries and a £500 million increase in road building. If the multiplier were 2, this would lead to a £2 000 million increase in equilibrium income in the Keynesian model. However, it may take some years for the full increase to work through the economy. The increase in civil servant salaries will work through relatively quickly. Civil servants will increase their spending within a few months of receiving the pay increase. The road building programme may take years even to start. So a government needs to be careful to take account of lags in spending when using fiscal policy to fill or remove deflationary or inflationary gaps. If a government wishes to reflate or deflate the economy quickly, it needs to change those taxes and those items of expenditure which will have an immediate impact on aggregate demand. Changing income tax rates, social security payments and public sector wages will all act quickly to change demand. Long term capital projects, such as road building or hospital building, are inappropriate for short term changes although they may be ideal in a serious longer term depression such as that which occurred during the 1930s and early 1980s.

In the past, governments have been accused of even destabilising the economy through the use of active fiscal policy. Government would reflate the economy just at a time when the economy was moving into boom of its own accord, just as it arguably was in 1972 when the Chancellor reflated the economy. The combination of extra private sector spending and extra public sector spending would then create an inflationary gap. The more inherently stable the economy, the more potential damage there would be from wrong timing in active fiscal policy. Hence some economists argue that the inability to predict time lags accurately makes it impossible to use fiscal policy to fine tune the economy.

Inadequacy of economic data Active fiscal policy assumes that the Chancellor knows the current state of the British economy. But statistics are notoriously unreliable. Unemployment statistics and inflation statistics are not revised after publication, but national income statistics and the balance of payments statistics are frequently revised. Moreover, there are often 'black holes' in these statistics where two or more sets of figures which should match fail to do so. In official statistics these are varyingly described as 'balancing items', 'residual errors' or 'statistical discrepancies'. If the current account on the balance of payments is in deficit, the Chancellor will not know how much of this is due to a genuine deficit and how much is due to inaccurate recording of statistics. Fine-tuning then becomes very difficult. The Chancellor could well reflate the economy even though it was at full employment because he had been misled by statistics showing a recession.

Inadequate economic knowledge Active fiscal policy assumes that we know how the economy behaves. However, there is scepticism that economics will ever be able to predict changes in variables to the last few per cent. This is important because so many of the variables which governments wish to control have very small values. For instance, the government may wish to reduce economic growth from 3 per cent to 1½ per cent. But active fiscal policy is unlikely ever to be sufficiently sensitive to achieve exactly that 1½ per cent fall.

The inadequacy of the model The computer-based macro-economic forecasting models used today by decision makers are highly complex. Even so, they provide at best an approximation of possible outcomes.

Question 3

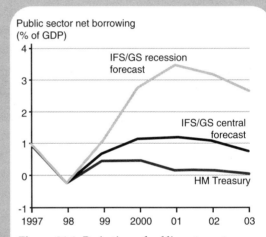

Figure 81.1 *Projections of public sector net borrowing, January 1999*
Source: adapted from Institute of Fiscal Studies, Goldman Sachs.

At first glance, the outlook for the UK budget is pretty satisfactory. The economy is expected to come out of its mild downturn this year or next. Public sector borrowing as a percentage of GDP has risen during the downturn but is set to fall once growth is back to its trend rate. However, the Institute for Fiscal Studies and Goldman Sachs in their 'Green Budget' also present a less likely but still possible scenario - that the downturn becomes a recession. Then the budget deficit would rise to over 3 per cent of GDP by 2001. How should the Chancellor react? Not by raising taxes or cutting public spending now. First, forecasts can easily be wrong and anyway the IFS/GS recession forecast is not their central forecast. Second, even if the scenario did occur, the Chancellor should allow the budget deficit to grow to enable the automatic stabilisers to work to reduce the impact of the recession.

Source: adapted from the *Financial Times*, 4.2.1999.

(a) Explain the forecasts shown in Figure 81.1.
(b) Why should a Chancellor not necessarily actively change the government's fiscal policy on the basis of economic forecasts?

Partly this is because the data that is fed into the models is not accurate, particularly the most recent data. Partly it is because models cannot capture the exact behaviour of an economy. They cannot, for instance, forecast sudden economic shocks such as the Asian crisis of 1998. Partly it also reflects the changing nature of economies. Until the 1980s, UK forecasting models failed to take into account the importance of large changes in house prices for aggregate demand, simply because large changes had not been experienced until that point. Today, there is controversy amongst model builders about the significance of the information technology revolution. Some economists argue that it has increased productivity in a way which is not being shown up by traditional models. This would enable the economy to grow at a faster rate without sparking off a rise in inflation. Other economists remain sceptical and remember the mid to late 1980s when the Conservative government of Margaret Thatcher claimed that a new 'miracle' economy had been created through its supply side reforms which would allow the economy to grow at a faster non-inflationary rate. This belief led to an overheated economy which then went into the longest recession since the 1930s.

Fiscal policy and monetary policy Governments in Europe and the United States have, since the 1980s, tended to manage demand through **monetary policy** rather than active fiscal policy. One reason for this is that fiscal policy cannot be independent of monetary policy.

For instance, if the government increases its borrowing, this must be financed in some way. Governments, unlike households and firms, have the ability to print money to finance extra borrowing. In a modern economy, this is achieved through governments borrowing money from the banking system rather than by increasing notes and coins in circulation. Printing money, though, increases the money supply and is potentially inflationary. Printing money and increasing the money supply is a monetary policy decision. Hence fiscal policy and monetary policy are interlinked.

Governments can avoid printing money by genuinely borrowing the money for an increased budget deficit from the private sector. But this increases the demand for borrowed funds and interest rates are likely to rise. Higher interest rates will reduce the willingness of the private sector to borrow and therefore spend. So the increase in aggregate demand from a higher budget deficit will to some extent be offset by reduced aggregate demand from less private sector borrowing. This reduces the impact of fiscal policy. Allowing interest rates to rise is part of monetary policy and again this shows how monetary and fiscal policy are linked.

Higher government borrowing may not lead to higher interest rates if the economy is in a deep depression. This is called a LIQUIDITY TRAP situation. When there is a liquidity trap, borrowing can increase without changing interest rates. This occurs because interest rates are so low that they cannot fall any further. Lenders, though, are prepared to increase the supply of money without seeing a rise in interest rates. Monetary policy cannot be used to get the economy out of depression because the government cannot push interest rates down any further. So expansionary fiscal policy is the only policy option left.

This is the insight which made Keynes famous in the 1930s.

The national debt Since the Second World War, many governments have abandoned attempts to balance their budgets. They find it politically easier to spend more than they tax and borrow the difference. Demand management policies then become a question of increasing budget deficits when the economy has high unemployment and reducing them when the economy is at full employment. In the long term, this can present a major problem for governments.

Governments are no different from individuals. If they continually borrow money, then eventually a national debt is built up which is increasingly difficult to **service** (i.e. pay interest on the debt). For instance, assume that a government is taking 40 per cent of national income in taxes. It has a national debt equivalent to 100 per cent of national income. Interest on the debt averages 10 per cent per annum. Then, the government has to pay 10 per cent of national income in interest, which amounts to one-quarter of its tax revenues (10% ÷ 40%). If it is continuing to run a budget deficit, then the proportion of taxation going on servicing the debt will increase further over time.

Eventually, lenders will begin to be scared that the government will default on its debt (i.e. it will not pay the interest and will not pay back loans as they mature). Governments in this position have to offer higher rates of interest on new loans in order to persuade lenders to take the risk of lending to them. This makes the situation worse, because the government is now having to pay even more interest on its debt. In the worst case, lenders will refuse to lend or the government will become overwhelmed by its debt and begin to default on its loans. Either way, the government will have gone bankrupt.

There is a way around this in the short term. The government, unlike an individual, can pay its debt by simply printing money. More money in the economy is likely to lead to inflation (☞ unit 84). Inflation reduces the real value of the debt. For instance, in the example above, if the government creates a doubling of prices, then the real value of the national debt will fall from 100 per cent to 50 per cent because national income at current prices will double but the national debt at current prices will stay the same. However, this is not a long term solution. Lenders will demand much higher rates of interest if there is high inflation in a country. Budget deficits will continue to increase the size of the national debt. The government will have to be creating large amounts of inflation simply to stand still in terms of national debt.

European Monetary Union When plans were made to create the European Monetary Union (☞ unit 95), it was recognised that large budget deficits and a sizable national debt could destabilise the economies of individual member countries and therefore the whole monetary union. It was made a condition of membership, therefore, that fiscal deficits could not be more than 3 per cent of GDP whilst the national debt of a country could not be more than 60 per cent of GDP. This further limits the ability of governments of member countries to use fiscal policy to steer the economy. It equally limits the policy of future applicant countries. If the UK wants to join the single currency, it must show that government finances have conformed to these criteria for a number of years before joining.

Fiscal policy and supply side economics

Fiscal policy can also be used to affect aggregate supply. For instance, cutting income tax might increase incentives to work. Reducing business rates in an area might encourage firms to locate there. Subsidising workers might encourage firms to take them off the unemployment registers. These are examples of **supply side** measures, discussed in more detail in unit 38. Fiscal policy today in the UK arguably plays a far more important role in influencing the supply side of the economy than the demand side.

The same problems, though, face governments wishing to use fiscal policy to manipulate aggregate supply as when manipulating aggregate demand. There may be conflicting objectives of policy. For instance, a government wishing to reduce government borrowing cannot also cut income tax, all other things being equal. Supply side measures such as increased spending on education can take decades to have a significant effect on economic growth and so there are time lags from implementation to effect. Governments often have to base their decisions on inadequate economic data. For instance, unemployment is difficult to estimate and therefore inappropriate supply side policy responses may be applied to the problem. Equally, the precise effects of supply side policies are often unknown. In the 1980s, there was fierce controversy about the extent to which cuts in income tax would increase incentives to work.

Other uses of fiscal policy

Fiscal policy is also used to achieve a number of other objectives. For instance, it is used to redistribute income and wealth (☞ unit 69). It is also used to achieve environmental objectives (☞ units 19 and 62).

Question 4

The government's £4.9 billion five-year welfare-to-work programme will continue to focus on the needs of the under-24 long-term unemployed, although the Chancellor announced a new scheme is being introduced this year to help over-50s back into work. Under the new voluntary scheme, over 50s who have not worked for more than six months and those in the same age group who are not economically active will be provided with tailor-made personal advice from the employment service on how to find a job. They will also be eligible to receive in-work training grants of up to £750 to help them gain accredited training to take and keep a job. In addition, the Chancellor is introducing a new employment credit for the over-50s. This is designed to tackle the problem of the low levels of in-work income that older workers receive on average as they move off welfare and back into work. The wages they earn are usually a quarter less than they received in their previous job, which is a far bigger drop in income than for young workers.

Source: adapted from the *Financial Times*, 10.3.1999.

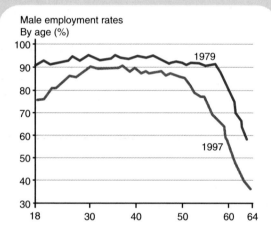

Figure 81.2 *Male employment rates*
Source: adapted from Economic and Social Research Council.

(a) Explain how the measures outlined in the data might help improve the supply side performance of the economy.

key terms

Active or discretionary fiscal policy - the deliberate manipulation of government expenditure and taxes to influence the economy.
Automatic or built-in stabilisers - mechanisms which reduce the impact of changes in the economy on national income.
Demand management - government use of fiscal or other policies to manipulate the level of aggregate demand in the economy.
Fine-tuning - the attempt by government to move the economy to a very precise level of unemployment, inflation, etc. It is usually associated with fiscal policy and demand management.

Full employment - the level of output in an economy where all factors of production are fully utilised at given factor prices.
Stop/go cycle - the movement from boom to recession in the trade cycle.
The liquidity trap - where the economy is in such a deep depression that interest rates have fallen as far as they will ever go. This means that governments cannot use monetary policy through reducing interest rates to stimulate aggregate demand. Only fiscal policy can help revive demand.

Applied economics

Japan in the 1990s

Japan for much of the post-war period was a miracle economy. It consistently grew faster than Europe and the United States. From being a Third World country in 1945, it surpassed GDP per capita for countries such as the UK or France in the 1980s. Yet the 1990s were disastrous for Japan's economy.

Its problems lay in a huge asset bubble created in the second half of the 1980s. Japan had developed large trading surpluses with the rest of the world which caused trade frictions, particularly with the United States, which accused Japan of destroying its domestic industry. To make Japan less competitive, an informal agreement in 1985 (the Plazza accord) led to countries pushing up the value of the yen on foreign currency markets. This made Japanese exports more expensive and hence less competitive. The plan worked sufficiently for the Japanese authorities to fear that the economy would go into recession. So interest rates were pushed down from 5 to 2.5 per cent, the lowest in the world. These low interest rates encouraged an investment boom in industry. The

investment-GDP ratio rose to 32.2 per cent in 1990 from 27.3 per cent in 1986. Low interest rates also created an asset bubble. Share prices trebled between 1985 and 1989. Land and property prices soared.

The bubble burst in 1990. Stock market values began to fall and were soon back to their pre-bubble prices. Land prices plummeted. This led to a downturn in the economy as Figure 81.3 shows. Consumer spending fell as household wealth fell. Firms cut back on their investment, finding they had over-invested in the second half of the 1980s and many now had spare capacity. Problems then developed with the Japanese

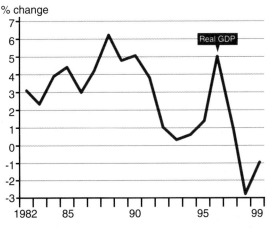

Figure 81.3 *Growth in real GDP, Annual percentage change*
Source: adapted from OECD, *Economic Outlook*.

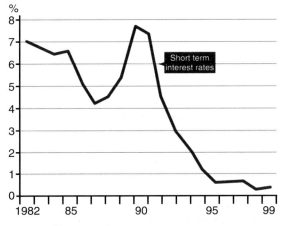

Figure 81.4 *Short term interest rates*
Source: adapted from OECD, *Economic Outlook*.

banking system. It had lent large sums for property purchases. With falling property prices and an economy going into recession, borrowers began to default, leaving the banks with mounting levels of bad debts. The banking system for the first half of the 1990s concealed these problems, but in the second half of the 1990s it became obvious that there would have to be a restructuring of the banking system, with banks that had particularly large levels of bad debts closing.

The Bank of Japan, the Japanese central bank, found it difficult to respond. It had raised interest rates in 1989 and 1990, as Figure 81.4 shows, in an attempt to curb the strong economy. It then progressively cut short term interest rates down to 0.6 per cent by 1996, attempting to use monetary policy to revive the economy. However, it broadly failed. Low interest rates did not kick-start the economy back to long term growth. In the second half of the 1990s, Japan was arguably suffering from a liquidity trap. Interest rates were already so low that they could not fall any further. Some argued that the Bank of Japan should flood the markets with new money in the hope that some of it would be spent. Others, however, felt that this would simply be saved rather than spent. Firms were reluctant to increase investment because the economy was stagnant, whilst households were reluctant to increase borrowing as unemployment rose and insecurity was rife.

Monetary policy, then, proved ineffective. Instead, the government increasingly used traditional Keynesian fiscal techniques to stimulate the economy. Figure 81.5 shows how government spending as a percentage of GDP rose during the 1990s. Increases in spending were

mostly financed through borrowing, which led to the rapidly rising levels of national debt shown in Figure 81.6. By 2000, these levels of debt were beginning to seem unsustainable. It should be remembered that the maximum level of debt allowed amongst members of the European Monetary Union is 60 per cent. So the Japanese government must begin to rebalance its finances during the first decade of the 21st century. The economy will have to get used to lower budget deficits or even budget surpluses.

Expansionary fiscal policy could be argued to have been a failure. Fiscal pump priming has failed to get the Japanese economy back to consistent long term growth of the $2^1/_2$ to 3 per cent of which the European and US economies seem capable. On the other hand, without large injections of extra government spending, it could be argued that Japan would have suffered a prolonged slump for much of the 1990s. In reality, both arguments are probably correct. This is because expansionary fiscal policy has not helped solve Japan's underlying problems. Without a solution to the bad debts of the banking system, banks cannot play their proper part in the efficient functioning of a market economy. Many firms also need to restructure to make themselves fundamentally profitable again. In the 1990s, many put off this restructuring in the hope that good times would return and painful decisions about closing down plant and laying off workers could be avoided. Expansionary fiscal policy, therefore, has worked in that it has staved off a deep depression. But it cannot by itself make the Japanese economy competitive again.

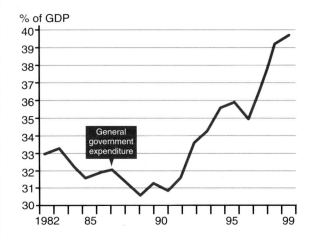

Figure 81.5 *General government expenditure as a percentage of GDP*
Source: adapted from OECD, *Economic Outlook*.

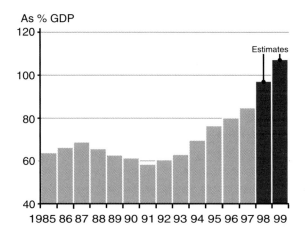

Figure 81.6 *General government gross debt as a percentage of GDP*
Source: adapted from OECD, *Economic Outlook*.

Budget speech by the Chancellor of the Exchequer, March 1999

In the past, Britain has suffered greater volatility in output and inflation than most other major industrial countries. Such volatility imposed both social and economic costs. On coming into office, the government therefore introduced a new framework for monetary and fiscal policy to promote economic stability, while ensuring that macroeconomic policy responded sensibly to economic shocks. This included:

- a new monetary framework to deliver low and stable inflation: the Bank of England's monetary policy committee has been given operational independence to set interest rates to deliver the government's inflation target;
- a new fiscal framework, including two strict fiscal rules - the golden rule[1] and the sustainable investment rule[2] - to get the public finances under control. Borrowing has been reduced by a cumulative £29 billion over the last two years and tight control has been maintained over public expenditure;
- and a new public expenditure regime which, together with new three year spending plans, will provide greater certainty and encourage longer-term planning.

The rewards of the new framework are already evident. Inflation is close to target. Interest rates peaked at $7^1/_2$ per cent last year, half their peak level in the last cycle. Debt interest payments are falling. And employment is up by more than 400 000 since May 1997; long term and youth unemployment have fallen by 50 per cent.

The Budget 99 forecast confirms that:

- RPIX inflation is forecast to remain at the target level of $2^1/_2$ per cent;
- and growth will be lower this year than last, following the global slowdown.

However, the economy is well place for stronger growth into 2000, in line with independent forecasters. This means that this cycle is set to be much more moderate than those in recent decades.

Budget 99 locks in the economic stability that the new framework has delivered. As a result of the strengthening underlying fiscal position, the fiscal rules are still met while the new Budget measures provide an extra £6 billion support over the next three years to boost the economy during the period when output is below its trend level. The public finances forecast shows that:

- the surplus on current budget is projected to average 0-4 per cent of GDP over the current economic cycle;
- and net public debt is projected to decline significantly as a proportion of GDP to below 35 per cent by 2003-4.

Meeting these rules will allow the UK to:

- maintain high quality public services and deliver the spending commitments - including £40 billion additional investment in education and health over the next three years - announced in the Comprehensive Spending Review (CSR);
- and ensure the overall position of the public finances remains sound. As both rules are set over the economic cycle, they will also allow the automatic stabilisers to play their part so that fiscal policy continues to support monetary policy in the next phase of the cycle.

In addition, illustrative baseline projects for the next 30 years indicate a sustainable fiscal position, capable of delivering equitable outcomes for future generations.

Source: adapted from HM Treasury in the *Financial Times*, 10.3.1999.

1. The golden rule - on average over the trade cycle, government borrowing for current spending will be zero. The government may choose, though, to borrow to finance investment spending which will yield benefits beyond the time scale of a typical cycle.
2. The sustainable investment rule - public sector net debt (the National Debt) as a proportion of GDP will be held over the economic cycle at a stable and prudent level. This level has been set by the government at 40 per cent of GDP or less.

1. Describe the state of the economy in March 1999.
2. Analyse the use by government in 1999 of (a) public spending and (b) automatic stabilisers to achieve its policy objectives.
3. Discuss why the sustainable investment rule is important for the long term management of the economy.

Summary

1. Money has four functions: as a medium of exchange; a unit of account; a store of value; and a standard for deferred payment.
2. Characteristics of good money include acceptability, portability, durability, divisibility and limited supply.
3. In a modern economy, cash and sight deposits are the assets which best fulfil the function of a medium of exchange. These are known as narrow monies.
4. Near monies, assets which are good units of account and stores of value and can easily be converted into assets which are a medium of exchange, include time deposits in banks and building societies. Broad money is narrow money plus near money.
5. Money substitutes, such as credit cards, are items which act as a medium of exchange but are not stores of value.
6. The money supply is the total amount of money circulating in the economy.
7. Households and firms hold their wealth in money, in non-money financial assets or in physical assets. The opportunity cost of holding money is the benefits foregone from holding other financial or physical assets.
8. The demand for money varies with income and with the rate of interest.

The functions of money

Most people today in Britain, if asked 'what is money?', would reply 'notes and coins'. What is it about notes and coins that make them money, and is there anything else which possesses these same properties? If something is to be money, it must fulfil four FUNCTIONS (i.e. it must do four things).

A medium of exchange This is the most important function of money. Money is used to buy and sell goods and services. A worker accepts payment in money because she knows that she will be able to use that money to buy products in the shops.

There is no money in a BARTER economy. Exchange is conducted directly by swopping one good with another. For instance, a farmer might pay a dozen eggs to have his horse shod or a woman might trade a carpet for a cow. This requires a **double coincidence of wants**. If the blacksmith didn't want eggs, then he might refuse to shoe the farmer's horse. If the woman with a carpet was offered a horse instead of a cow, again she might refuse to trade. Barter requires that each party to the transaction wants what the other has to trade. This is costly and difficult, if not impossible, and therefore trade is discouraged. Without trade there can be no specialisation. Without specialisation, there can be little or no increase in living standards. So barter is associated with types of economy where individuals or small groups are self-reliant, and so the need for trade is small.

Money separates the two sides of a barter transaction. The farmer can sell his eggs for money. The blacksmith will accept money for shoeing the farmer's horse because he knows that he will be able buy the goods that he wants with the money.

A unit of account Money acts as a measure of value. If a dress costs £30 and a skirt costs £15, we know that the value of one dress equals the value of two skirts. At times of very high inflation, such as in Germany in 1923, money ceases to act as a unit of account. Prices may change by the hour. A dress costing £30 in the morning might only buy one skirt in the evening. High inflation therefore destroys the ability of money to perform this function. It is very difficult under a barter sytem to establish an agreed unit of account as people's opinions of the value of certain items differ greatly.

A store of value A worker who receives wages is unlikely to spend the money immediately. She may defer spending because it is more convenient to spend the money later. She will do this only if what she can buy in the future is approximately equal to what she can buy today. So money links the present and the future. It acts as a store of value. High inflation destroys this link because money in the future is worth far less than money today. In the German hyperinflation of 1923, people started to refuse payment in German money because it would lose so much value by the time they had spent it.

A standard for deferred payment If a person lends

money today, she will only do so if she thinks that she will be able to buy roughly the same amount of goods when it is paid back. In trade, a company which accepts an order at a fixed price today for delivery and payment in a year's time will only do so if it is confident that the money it receives will have a value which can be assessed today. So again money must link different time periods when it comes to borrowed as well as saved money.

When money ceases to have this function, credit and borrowing collapse and this is very damaging to investment and economic growth in an economy.

Question 1

(a) Explain which of these items might be considered 'money' and which would not.

The characteristics of money

Pigs, silver, gold, teeth, and even wives have been used as money in the past. Some cultures today still use animals as currency. However most, if not all, of these have been unsatisfactory because of their characteristics. Ideally, money should be:

- acceptable to all - it is inconvenient if a type of money is only accepted in some shops but not others for instance;
- portable - pigs, for instance, are not easy to carry around and this limits the trade which is conducted using pigs as a medium of exchange;
- durable - pigs die and teeth deteriorate; ideally money should be durable over time;
- divisible - whole live pigs can't be used to buy the small things in life because they are too valuable; money must be capable of being split into small denominations;
- limited - if ordinary stones are used as money, prices of goods are likely to be very high in terms of stones because they are so easy to obtain;
- difficult to forge - forgeries make money worth less and can lead to its becoming unacceptable in exchange.

Question 2

(a) To what extent do each of the items in the previous question possess the characteristics of a good money?

Forms of money in a modern economy

In a modern economy there is a number of assets which can be classified as money.

Cash Cash means notes and coins. Cash is a **token money**. It has little or no intrinsic value (unlike gold which would be classified along with items such as pigs and cigarettes as **commodity money**). It is issued either by government or with the permission of government. Government reinforces the acceptability of cash by making it **legal tender**. This means that it must be accepted by law as a means of payment.

During much of the 19th century, bank notes were **convertible**. This meant that it was possible to go into a bank and convert the notes into something of real value: in this case, gold. However, more notes were issued than their value in gold. The value of notes and coins printed over and above the value of gold in bank vaults was called the **fiduciary issue**. Today UK bank notes are not convertible into gold and therefore all notes are **fiat** money, money made legal tender by government decree.

Cash is not perfect money. In the UK it is an almost perfect medium of exchange. But inflation affects three of the functions of money - those of a unit of account, a store of value and a standard of deferred payment. In 1975 for instance, UK inflation was nearly 25 per cent. Anyone holding £1 at the beginning of the year could only buy 75 pence worth of goods with it at the end of the year. The higher the rate of inflation, the less it can be said that cash is a 'good' money.

Money in current accounts Banks and building societies in the UK offer customers current account facilities.

Current accounts (called SIGHT DEPOSIT ACCOUNTS in economic theory) have two distinguishing features. First, cash can be withdrawn on demand from the account if it is in credit. So deposits can be immediately converted into money if the account holder so wishes. Second, account holders are provided with a cheque book. Cheques can be used to purchase goods and services. Cheque book money therefore is a medium of exchange. It is not perfect because people and firms can refuse to accept cheques in a transaction. Moreover, little or no interest is offered on accounts and so current account deposits lose value over time with inflation, damaging their store of value function. But deposits in current accounts are nearly as good a form of money as cash.

Near monies NEAR MONIES are assets which fulfil some but not all of the functions of money. In particular, they act as units of account and stores of value but cannot be used as mediums of exchange. However, they are convertible into a medium of exchange quickly and at little cost. (The ease with which an asset can be converted into money without loss of value is termed LIQUIDITY. The more liquid an asset, the more easily it is convertible into money.) In the UK, the most obvious type of near monies is TIME DEPOSITS with banks and building societies. They pay higher rates of interest than current accounts. They are therefore used more for saving and less for making transactions than current accounts. Depositors need to give notice if they wish to withdraw from the account (hence the term 'time' deposit). Alternatively, many accounts offer instant access if an interest rate penalty is paid (i.e. the saver loses money for the privilege of instant withdrawal).

Non-money financial assets All financial assets can be converted into money. However, for most assets the potential penalties for doing this are great. There can be a long waiting time for withdrawal and there can be considerable loss of money from conversion. This impairs their functions as units of account and stores of value. Economists do not classify these assets as money. Shares, for instance, are easily sold, but it can take up to a month to receive the money from the sale. Shares can also change value rapidly and are therefore not a good store of value (when share prices fall) or a standard for deferred payment (when share prices rise).

Money substitutes

Money is not the only means of payment for goods and services. Charge cards and credit cards have become increasingly important over the past 30 years as a medium of exchange. But they are not stores of value. This is because possession of a card does not show that the cardholder has money in the credit card account. The card only represents an ability to borrow money instantly. So credit cards are not money but they are MONEY SUBSTITUTES (i.e. they are used instead of money).

Question 3

Emma Higgins has £250 in a building society share account. She owns a £100 000 house but owes £50 000 in the form of a mortgage loan. Her current account at her bank is in credit by £200 and she has an overdraft facility of £300. In her purse she has £20 in cash. She has recently purchased £50 worth of goods using her credit card. Her credit card limit is £1 000.

(a) Explain how much money Emma Higgins possesses.

The money supply

The MONEY SUPPLY is the total amount of money circulating in the economy. It has been argued above that there is no financial asset which perfectly possesses all the functions of money. So financial assets can be placed on a spectrum as in Figure 82.1. At the left of the spectrum is the asset which comes closest to fulfilling most of the functions of money today - cash. At the other end are assets which are extremely illiquid, such as shares in companies not traded on a stock exchange. In between there is a range of assets. As we move right assets possess fewer and fewer of the functions of money.

It is now clear that the cut off point between those assets which are money and those which are not is to some extent arbitrary. In the UK, there is a number of official

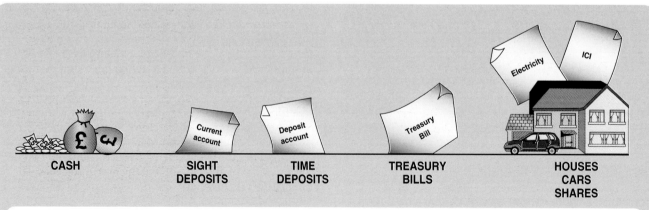

| CASH | SIGHT DEPOSITS | TIME DEPOSITS | TREASURY BILLS | HOUSES CARS SHARES |

Figure 82.1 *A spectrum of liquidity*

definitions of the money supply. There are two broad types of money supply definition.

- NARROW MONEY - money which can be used as a medium of exchange.
- BROAD MONEY - narrow money plus near monies.

Current money supply definitions used in the UK are described below in the applied economics section.

The demand for money

Households and firms hold their wealth in a variety of different assets. Two main types of assets can be distinguished:

- **financial assets**, either monetary assets, such as cash and deposits in current accounts at banks, or non-money assets such as stocks and shares;
- **physical assets**, such as houses, buildings, cars, furniture, machinery, computers and inventories.

When economists talk about the DEMAND FOR MONEY, they do not refer to how much money people would like to have in a world where they were infinitely rich. What they mean is how much households and firms choose to hold in the form of money as opposed to holding either non-money financial assets or physical assets.

There is therefore an **opportunity cost** to a household if it holds £300 in cash. It could instead buy shares, and receive dividends and possibly capital gains. It could put money into a pension plan and increase the value of pension payments at some time in the future, or it could buy a new television and enjoy the services which it provides. Hence the price of holding money is the benefits foregone from holding another type of asset.

The demand for money is determined by two main factors.

Income The higher the level of income in the economy, the greater the demand for money. This is because the higher the level of income, the greater will be spending in the economy. The more households spend, the more money they need to use to complete transactions.

The rate of interest One of the alternative uses for money is to buy financial assets which yield interest. A household could, for instance, hold bonds which are issued by the government and on which interest is payable. The higher the rate of interest, the greater the opportunity cost of holding money. If interest rates on government bonds are 5 per cent, then the opportunity cost of holding £100 for one year in money is £5 in lost interest. If the rate of interest is 20 per cent, the opportunity cost is £20.

Figure 82.2 shows this relationship between the demand for money and interest rates and income. The higher the rate of interest, the lower will be the demand for money. A rise in income would shift the demand for money curve to the right, from MD_1 to MD_2. This is because a rise in income raises the demand for money at any given rate of interest. Conversely, a fall in income would lead to a shift in the demand for money curve to the left.

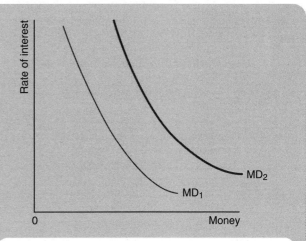

Figure 82.2 *The demand for money*
The demand for money curve is downward sloping because a rise in the rate of interest increases the attractiveness of exchanging money for an interest bearing non-money asset. A rise in income will shift the demand for money curve to the right from MD_1 to MD_2 because spending and therefore the need to have money to spend will rise.

Question 4

Kim Yip has £250 in cash, £500 in a building society account earning 5 per cent per annum interest, £400 worth of government bonds with a market rate of interest of 7 per cent, £900 worth of British Telecom shares earning a 3 per cent dividend, a house valued at £70 000 on which there is a mortgage of £40 000, furniture and personal possessions insured for £30 000, and a car worth £2 500 secondhand.

(a) What might be the opportunity cost for Kim of holding: (i) the £250 in cash; (ii) the £900 in British Telecom shares; (iii) the £70 000 house?

(b) Long term interest rates on government bonds rise by 3 per cent, all other things being equal. How might this affect Kim's holding of money?

key terms

Barter - swopping one good for another without the use of money.

Broad money - narrow money plus near monies.

Functions of money - money must be a medium of exchange, a store of value, a unit of account and a standard for deferred payment.

Liquidity - the degree to which an asset can be converted into money without capital loss.

Money substitutes - those which can be used as a medium of exchange but which are not stores of value. Examples are charge cards or credit cards.

Money supply - the total amount of money in circulation in the economy.

Narrow money - money which is primarily used as a medium of exchange.

Near money - an asset which cannot be used as medium of exchange in itself but is readily convertible into money and is both a unit of account and a store of value.

Sight deposit accounts - Accounts with financial institutions where deposits are repayable on demand and where a cheque book is issued. In the UK, they are more commonly called current or cheque accounts.

The demand for money - the total amount of money which households and firms wish to hold at a point in time.

Time deposit accounts - accounts where interest is paid but savers are not able to withdraw without either giving notice or paying an interest rate penalty.

Applied economics

The money supply in the UK

There is no single definition of money because no financial asset possesses all the characteristics or fulfils or the functions of money perfectly. A variety of different financial assets possess some of the functions to some degree, and hence it is possible to provide a large number of definitions of the money supply. In the United Kingdom, there are only two main measures which form the basis for policy, called M0 and M4. Figure 82.3 shows the relationship between these two different measures.

M0 is equal to the notes and coins in circulation together with cash in the tills of banks and the balances held by banks with the Bank of England for operational reasons. It is **narrow money**. This means that the assets measured are used mainly as a medium of exchange. Households and firms hold this money to buy goods and services.

M4 is made up of three main types of asset. Notes and coins are the smallest part. The largest part is deposits by households and firms with banks and building societies. Some of the deposits are held mainly to be spent. Typically, these accounts come with a cheque book and debit card. Other deposits are held mainly as a form of saving and tend to pay higher rates of interest than cheque book accounts. Lastly, there are wholesale deposits with banks and building societies. These are very large deposits which typically are made in millions of pounds. They are made by firms and financial institutions. M4 is **broad money**, money which is used not just for spending but also for saving.

The Bank of England also calculated a measure called M2 which is M4 minus wholesale deposits, i.e. notes and coins plus retail deposits.

Figure 82.4 shows the relative size of the value of notes and coins in circulation with M0, M2 and M4.

In the past, the Bank of England published figures for six main measures of the money supply, M0 to M5. In the 1980s, the two measures which were most closely monitored were M1 and M3. Their abandonment gives a very good example of how the definition of what constitutes money in a real economy can change very rapidly.

In the 1960s and 1970s, there was a clear division between cheque book accounts (called current accounts) operated by banks and savings accounts operated by both banks and building societies. Cheque book accounts were used for day to day spending. Savings accounts were used for longer term saving. Banks used the deposits from all types of accounts to lend out to customers. This lending helped finance everything from cars to holidays to new factories. Building societies lent out money only for mortgages on houses, an area of business which the banks traditionally did not conduct. It was judged that money lent out for mortgages would not have any significant effect on spending on anything outside the housing market.

M1 measured notes and coins in circulation together with money in cheque book accounts. It was a narrow measure of the money supply. M3 was made up of M1 plus savings accounts at banks. M4 was M3 plus savings at building societies. In the 1980s, however, the government encouraged banks and building societies to compete. Banks began to lend substantial sums in house mortgages. From 1986, building societies were allowed to lend money out for any purpose and not just to buy a house. Building societies also began to offer cheque book accounts. Many used building society accounts not as a form of saving but as a place to deposit the month's wages and withdraw it as and when needed. So the distinction between deposits at banks and deposits at

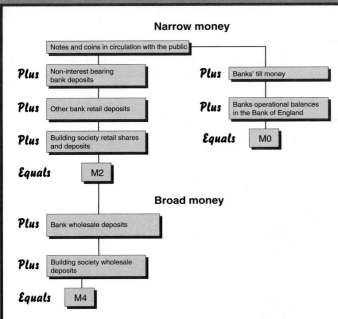

Figure 82.3 *Relationships between measures of the money supply*

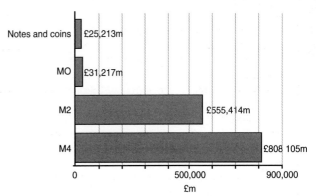

Figure 82.4 *The relative size of different measures of the money supply, amount outstanding at end 1999, seasonally adjusted*
Source: adapted from *Financial Statistics*, Office for National Statistics.

building societies disappeared. It was no longer possible clearly to distinguish between money that would quickly be spent and money that would be saved. It was also no longer possible to separate out how banks and building societies would use their deposits when lent out. The distinction between M1 and M3 ceased to be very useful. Then in 1989 the Abbey National building society changed its legal status to become a bank. This created a

large one-off jump in the value of M3. With further building society conversions expected, it was clear that M3 would cease to be very meaningful and that M4 should be used as the main monetary measure instead.

Today, the Bank of England uses its money supply data with caution precisely because what constitutes money is not entirely clear and may change very rapidly. Small changes in the rate of growth of the money supply are not considered to be significant. Only relatively large changes would be taken account of when deciding upon monetary policy.

DATA QUESTION — Money in the UK

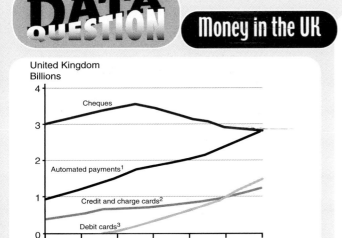

Figure 82.5 *Non-cash transactions by method of payment*
Source: adapted from *Social Trends*, Office for National Statistics.

1 Includes direct debits, standing orders, direct credits, inter-branch automated items and CHAPS transactions.
2 Visa, Mastercards, travel/entertainment cards and store cards.
3 Visa Delta and Switch cards in all years; includes Electron cards from 1996 and Solo cards in 1997.

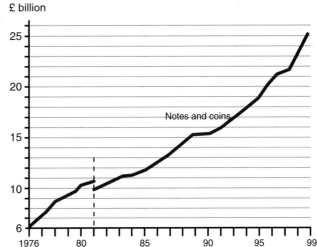

Note. Discontinuity in 1981.

Figure 82.6 *Notes and coins in circulation*
Source: adapted from *Financial Statistics*, Office for National Statistics.

A manufacturer of bank notes and plastic cards has commissioned a report on prospects in the UK market for money. Write the report:
1. distinguishing between money and money substitutes;
2. explaining how the market for (a) money and

(b) money substitutes has changed over the period;
3. discussing how means of payment are likely to change in the future and the implications this will have for the money supply in the UK.

Summary

1. The price of money is the rate of interest.
2. The rate of interest is determined by the demand for and supply of money.
3. An increase in the demand for money or a fall in the supply of money will increase the rate of interest. A fall in the demand for money or an increase in the supply of money will lead to a fall in the rate of interest.
4. Different interest rates exist in different money markets. Interest rates tend to move together in the same direction over long periods of time.
5. Factors which cause interest rates to differ in the same market include time, risk and administrative cost.
6. The loanable funds theory states that the rate of interest is determined by the demand for and supply of loanable funds for investment and saving.
7. The real rate of interest is the nominal rate adjusted for inflation.

Determination of the rate of interest

Economic theory suggests that, just as the price of a good is determined by the forces of demand and supply (☞ unit 6), so too is the price of money. So what is the price of money? It is how much needs to be paid if money is borrowed - it is the **rate of interest**.

Figure 83.1 shows the demand and supply curves of money. The demand curve for money (☞ unit 82) is sometimes called the **liquidity preference schedule**. It is downward sloping because the higher the rate of interest, the more households and firms will wish to hold non-money assets such as bonds or shares. The money supply is drawn as a vertical line, showing that the supply of money remains constant whatever the rate of interest. This assumes that the central bank can and does control

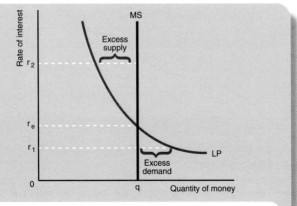

Figure 83.1 *The equilibrium rate of interest*
r_e *is the equilibrium rate of interest - the rate of interest where the demand for and supply of money are equal.*

the supply of money in the economy independently of its price (☞ unit 85). The money supply is then said to be **exogenous** (i.e. is not linked with any variable in the economic model but is determined outside the model). It would make no difference to our conclusions here if the money supply were assumed to be upward sloping and therefore **endogenous** (i.e linked with a variable in the model, in this case the price of money, the rate of interest), with the money supply determined by the rate of interest rather than by the decisions of the central bank. The equilibrium rate of interest r_e occurs where the demand for money equals the supply of money.

Economic theory suggests that if the rate of interest is above or below this level then it will tend towards its equilibrium value.

● Assume that the rate of interest is r_1 (i.e. there is an excess demand for money). Households and firms want to hold more money than they are currently holding. They will react by selling some of their non-money assets and converting them into money. If money is defined in narrow terms such as M0, then households could increase their holdings of money by withdrawing some from building society accounts. Building societies will now have a shortfall of deposits and will react by putting up their interest rates to attract more savings. If money is defined in broad terms, households might react by selling savings such as government bonds (also known as government stock or gilts). Extra buyers for such bonds, a form of long term borrowing, will only be found if they pay out a higher financial reward through an increase in the effective interest rate paid out on them. So long term interest rates will rise. Excess demand for money will push up interest rates, leading to a movement back along the liquidity preference schedule. This will continue until households and firms are in equilibrium where the demand for money equals the supply of money.

● Now assume the converse: that there is excess supply of money such as would exist at a rate of interest of r_2. Households and firms hold more money than they wish, so they will attempt to put it into a building society, or buy bonds, shares or other types of assets. This will lead to a fall in interest rates back towards the equilibrium interest rate r_e.

Shifts in the money demand and supply curves

What happens if the demand or supply of money changes (i.e. there is a **shift** in either the money demand or supply curves)?

Assume that the liquidity preference schedule shifts to the right as in Figure 83.2. This means that more money is demanded at any given rate of interest. This could be caused by an increase in income, an increase in the price level (we are assuming that the LP curve shows the demand for nominal balances) or an increase in the perceived risk of holding non-monetary assets such as bonds or shares. The rate of interest will consequently

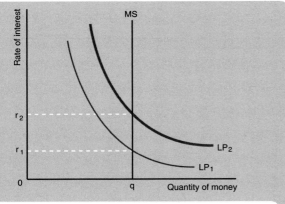

Figure 83.2 *An increase in the demand for money*
An increase in the demand for money, shown by a shift in the liquidity preference schedule to the right, will increase the rate of interest from r_1 to r_2.

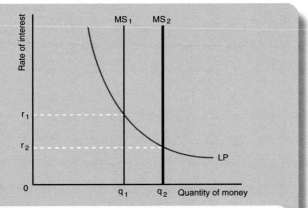

Figure 83.3 *An increase in the money supply*
An increase in the money supply, shown by a shift in the money supply curve to the right, will lead to a fall in the rate of interest from r_1 to r_2.

increase from r_1 to r_2. So an increase in liquidity preference shown by a shift to the right in the LP curve will increase interest rates, but not change the supply of money which is fixed by the authorities. Conversely, a fall in the demand for money will lead to a fall in interest rates.

Now assume that the government increases the supply of money. This is shown by a shift to the right in the supply curve in Figure 83.3. The result will be a fall in the rate of interest from r_1 to r_2. Conversely a fall in the money supply will lead to an increase in interest rates.

Question 1

Draw a diagram showing the liquidity preference schedule and the money supply curve. Show the likely effect on the equilibrium rate of interest if there is:
(a) a fall in the money supply;
(b) an increase in the price level;
(c) increased use of credit cards in payment for goods and services;
(d) a fall in national income at current prices;
(e) an increase in notes and coins in circulation in the economy.

Different markets, different rates of interest

So far, it has been implicitly assumed that there is one market for money and one equilibrium rate of interest in the economy. This is a very useful simplification in macro-economic theory. However, in reality there are many markets for money and many rates of interest in an economy. For instance, in the Treasury Bill market, the government borrows short term from banks and other large financial institutions. In the credit card market, households borrow money on credit cards from banks and other financial institutions which provide a credit card service. In the mortgage market, building societies and banks lend money to households purchasing property. If all these markets were perfect, and all loans and borrowing were identical, then the rate of interest in all markets would be the same. But there are many barriers between markets and loans are not identical. Hence interest rates differ. For instance, when banks offer higher rates of interest on their accounts than building societies, the building societies will not suffer major drains of funds. This is partly because customers find it inconvenient to change money from one account to another. But also many customers are unaware of differences in interest rates. Equally, in some markets borrowers and lenders are locked into fixed term contracts. These are likely to be short - anything up to, say, 6 months. This means that money cannot flow into another market to take advantage of higher interest rates.

Barriers to the flow of money between markets exist but on the whole they are not high enough to insulate markets completely. When interest rates increase in the City of London, the major banks will almost certainly increase their interest rates too. The effect will ripple out into the rest of the economy. Building societies may not respond initially but they will suffer a drain of funds in the medium term if they do not increase their interest rates. So interest rates tend to move in the same direction over a period of time.

There is a number of factors which can cause interest rates to differ in the same market.

Time The longer the period of the loan, the higher tends to be the rate of interest. If money is lent out for just 24 hours, the lender has complete flexibility either to stop lending the money or to switch money to another market. If it is lent out for 25 years, there is no such flexibility. So higher interest is necessary to compensate lenders as the length of the term of a loan increases.

Expectations If the market expects interest rates to fall in the near future, then longer term loans could attract a lower rate of interest than shorter term loans. For instance, if current interest rates are 12 per cent for overnight loans, but you expect them to fall to 10 per cent in a month's time, then you might be prepared to lend money for three months at somewhere between 10 and 12 per cent.

Risk Lending money to an unemployed worker is likely to be far more risky than lending it to the HSBC. So the greater the risk of default on the loan, the higher will be the rate of interest.

Administrative cost Lending out £100 million in lots of £100 at a time is likely to be far more administratively costly than lending out £100 million to one customer. So the higher the administration cost, the higher will tend to

be the rate of interest. Equally, lenders of money may find it more costly to move their money around to gain the highest rate of interest available at a point in time than leaving their money in an existing account earning a lower rate of interest.

Imperfect knowledge Borrowers and lenders may have imperfect knowledge. For instance, credit card holders may be unaware that they could cut their interest payments by changing their credit card provider. A saver with a building society may be unaware that another building society is offering higher rates of interest on a savings account which is otherwise identical to an existing account.

Loanable funds theory

Another theory which explains how the rate of interest is determined is the LOANABLE FUNDS THEORY. Assume that the only demand for borrowed funds comes from firms or government wishing to invest. The investment schedule is downward sloping as in Figure 83.4 (☞ unit 32). The higher the rate of interest, the lower the

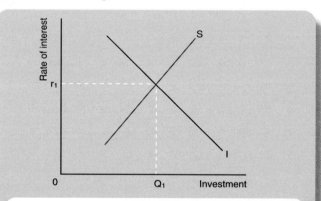

Figure 83.4 *Loanable funds theory*
According to loanable funds theory, the rate of interest is determined by investment and saving in an economy. The equilibrium rate of interest is fixed where the level of savings equals the level of investment at r_1.

Question 2

Table 83.1 *Selected interest rates and yields, 6 January 2000*

Source	Period of loan	%
Interbank money markets	overnight	$5\frac{1}{2}$ to 3
	one month	$5\frac{3}{4}$ to $5\frac{9}{16}$
	one year	$6\frac{7}{8}$ to $6\frac{25}{32}$
Treasury Bills	one month	$5\frac{19}{32}$ to $5\frac{17}{32}$
	three months	$5\frac{7}{8}$ to $5\frac{13}{16}$
Gilt edged stock (high yield)	five years	6.35
Bank base rate		5.50
Mortgage rate (Scarborough Building Society)		5.80
Personal loan unsecured (Abbey National)		10.90
Authorised overdraft (Abbey National)		13.4
Alliance and Leicester credit card		17.4
Marks and Spencer store card		25.7

Source: adapted from the *Financial Times*, 1.1.2000 and 7.1.2000.

In the interbank money market in London, banks lend to each other for short periods of time from just overnight to one year. Treasury Bills are short term loans to the UK government mainly from financial institutions such as banks or assurance companies. Gilt edged stock is a form of long term loan to the UK government. It is bought mainly by assurance companies and pension funds. The bank base rate is the rate of interest around which banks in the UK set their interest rates. Borrowers have to pay above base rate whilst those lending to UK banks get less than base rate.

(a) Suggest reasons why the interest rates in Table 83.1 differ from each other.

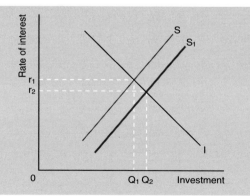

Figure 83.5 *An increase in the level of saving*
If at any given rate of interest households decide to save more, this will push the savings curve to the right from S to S_1. The equilibrium rate of interest in the economy will then fall from r_1 to r_2.

amount of investment. One reason for this is that the higher the rate of interest, the higher the cost to firms of borrowing money to finance investment. The higher the cost, the less profitable an investment project becomes. An investment project which might have been highly profitable if funds could be borrowed at 5 per cent might only earn normal profit at 8 per cent and be unprofitable at 15 per cent. The higher the rate of interest, the fewer investment projects are profitable and hence the lower the amount of investment.

In contrast, the savings schedule is upward sloping as shown in Figure 83.4. The higher the rate of interest, the more attractive it becomes for households and firms to save. They can earn more money in interest, the higher the rate of interest.

The equilibrium rate of interest is where the investment schedule cuts the saving schedule at r_1. If, as in Figure 83.5, households decide to save more at any given rate of interest, perhaps because there is an increased fear of unemployment, the savings schedule shifts to the right. This will lead to a fall in the equilibrium rate of interest to r_2. A rise in investment at any given level of interest rates, would shift the investment schedule to the right and lead to a rise in the equilibrium rate of interest.

Loanable funds theory can explain how the rate of interest is determined in a simple economy where the main demand for money comes from investment and the main supply of money comes from savings. However, in a modern economy, money markets are far more complex. In an open economy like the UK, for instance, interest rates are affected by flows of money between countries. Modern economic theory, therefore, tends to use models based on the demand and supply of money to explain how interest rates are determined.

Nominal and real interest rates

When a building society offers a rate of interest of 10 per cent, it is offering a NOMINAL RATE OF INTEREST. The interest is unadjusted for inflation. But each year, prices in the economy are likely to rise. £100 placed in the building society today will, excluding any interest payments, buy fewer goods and services in a year's time.

The REAL RATE OF INTEREST is the rate of interest adjusted for inflation. For instance, the real rate of interest would be 5 per cent if the nominal rate of interest were 10 per cent and the rate of inflation were 5 per cent. With a nominal rate of interest of 12 per cent and a rate of inflation of 8 per cent, the real rate of interest would be 4 per cent.

Real interest rates can be negative as well as positive. In 1975, with the UK inflation rate at 25 per cent and nominal

interest rates about 7 per cent, the real rate of interest was **minus** 18 per cent. Anyone saving at 7 per cent would have lost 18 per cent of the purchasing power of their money during 1975. Why do people save when real interest rates are negative? One reason is that much saving is highly illiquid. People can't liquidate assurance or pension fund contracts easily or without cost for instance. Another reason is that people need to save if only because they do not wish to spend all their income when they receive it on pay day. What's more, savers might have lost 18 per cent. But people who kept their money in cash lost 25 per cent!

Nominal interest rates and inflation

Economic theory predicts that higher inflation will push up nominal interest rates. Assume that there is zero inflation and the nominal rate of interest is 3 per cent (i.e. the real rate of interest is 3 per cent). Then, £100 today would grow into £103 in a year's time. That £100, if saved rather than spent today, would enable the saver to buy 3 per cent more goods and services in 12 months time. Now assume that inflation rises to 5 per cent. If nominal interest rates are still 3 per cent, then £100 today would only buy £98 worth of goods in a year's time because the real rate of interest is - 2 per cent. Savers would therefore save less. Borrowers, on the other hand, would borrow more because they are effectively being paid to borrow money. The market for loanable funds would therefore fall into disequilibrium. It can only return to equilibrium when nominal rates of interest have risen sufficiently to approximately the original real rate of interest of 3 per cent.

Irving Fisher, an American economist in the early part of this century, argued that a 1 per cent increase in inflation would be associated with a 1 per cent increase in nominal interest rates. So, if the real rate of interest is 3 per cent, then nominal interest rates would be 13 per cent if the inflation rate were 10 per cent, 23 per cent if the inflation rate were 20 per cent and so on.

This can be seen in Figure 83.2. The demand for money is a demand for real balances. So when prices rise, the demand for money increases, shown by the shift to the right in the liquidity preference curve in Figure 83.2. But this rise in demand raises interest rates. The analysis is more complex than this, though. Large increases in prices are associated with large increases in the money supply (☞ unit 84). So high inflation are associated with shifts to the right in the money supply curve too. What the Fisher hypothesis implies is that the shift to the right in the demand for money curve would be greater than the shift to the right in the money supply curve, and this would produce rising nominal interest rates.

key terms

Loanable funds theory - the loanable funds theory of interest rate determination argues that the rate of interest is determined by the demand for and supply of loanable funds, in particular for the purchase of capital.

Nominal interest rates - interest rates unadjusted for inflation.
Real interest rates - nominal interest rates adjusted for inflation.

Question 3

Figure 83.6 *Nominal interest rates[1] and inflation[2] in OECD countries*
1. Short term rates, annual average.
2. Average annual percentage change in consumer prices.

(a) Explain the possible link between nominal interest rates and inflation rates.
(b) To what extent does the data in Figure 83.6 support economic theory?

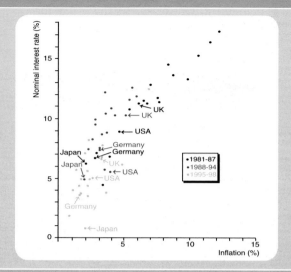

Applied economics

The rate of interest in five money markets

The rate of interest in each money market in the UK is determined by the demand for and supply of money in that market. It is possible to identify the main borrowers and lenders in most money markets. For instance, in the UK domestic mortgage market, banks and building societies are the two most important suppliers of money. People wanting to borrow money to buy a house demand money. The rate of interest on a mortgage loan is low compared to, say, an ordinary overdraft or bank loan. This is mainly because a mortgage loan is secured on a property. If a borrower defaults on the loan, the bank or building society can force the borrower to sell the property and pay back the loan with the money raised. So a mortgage loan is regarded as being relatively free of risk by lenders.

Banks have traditionally been the main source of loans and overdrafts, although secondary banks and building societies have recently entered the market too. The demand for money comes from individuals and companies who want to borrow to finance everything from repairs to a car, to a new kitchen or a new factory. Interest rates tend to be set according to risk of default. Large companies can usually get lower rates of interest on loans than small companies, whilst individuals are charged much higher rates than on a mortgage loan. It could be argued that loans through credit cards form part of this market too. Interest rates on credit cards tend to be above overdraft and personal loan rates for individuals. Not only is the risk of default higher on a credit card than on a personal loan but there are much greater administrative costs in handling credit card loans than in handling personal loans and overdrafts.

In a City money market, such as the interbank market, discount market or local authority market, individual transactions tend to be for far greater sums of money. In the interbank market, banks borrow and lend between themselves. This can be just for 24 hours when one bank has a very short term surplus of funds,

whilst another bank might need to borrow money over night. Borrowing and lending can be for longer periods up to a year also. In the discount market, the government demands money by issuing Treasury Bills and money is supplied for their purchase mainly by financial institutions such as banks or assurance companies. In the local authority market, local authorities demand money whilst banks and other financial institutions supply funds. Table 83.2 shows interest rates in these three markets at a point in time. Treasury Bills carried a lower rate of interest than local authority deposits or interbank loans because central government was considered a marginally better risk than banks or local authorities.

Table 83.2 *Selected interest rates, 6.1.2000*

Per cent

	Overnight	7 days notice	1 month	3 months
Treasury Bills	-	-	$5^{19}/_{32}$ - $5^{17}/_{32}$	$5^{7}/_{8}$ - $5^{13}/_{16}$
Local authority deposits	$5^{1}/_{4}$ - 5	$5^{1}/_{16}$ - 5	$5^{3}/_{4}$ - $5^{9}/_{16}$	$6^{3}/_{16}$ - $6^{1}/_{16}$
Interbank money markets	$5^{1}/_{2}$ to 3	5 - $4^{5}/_{8}$	$5^{3}/_{4}$ - $5^{9}/_{16}$	$6^{1}/_{8}$ - 6

Source: adapted from the *Financial Times*, 7.1.2000.

The rate of interest on Treasury Bills with three months to maturity was slightly higher than with one month to maturity. This is what economic theory would predict. In the local authority market and the interbank market interest rates tended to rise, the longer to maturity of the deposit. Interestingly, the 7 day notice deposit in both the interbank and local authority markets carried a lower rate of interest than the overnight rate. This probably reflects an excess supply of 7 day deposit money rather than a response to interest rate fundaments such as risk or time.

DATA QUESTION

Interest rates and inflation

Table 83.3 *Inflation and selected interest rates*

Percentages

	Inflation rate	Banks base rate	British government securities, long dated 20 years.	Treasury Bill yield
1980	18.0	16.32	13.78	13.45
1981	11.9	13.27	14.74	15.35
1982	8.6	11.93	12.88	9.96
1983	4.6	9.83	10.80	9.04
1984	5.0	9.68	10.69	9.33
1985	6.0	12.25	10.62	11.49
1986	3.4	10.90	9.87	10.94
1987	4.2	9.74	9.47	8.38
1988	4.9	10.90	9.36	12.91
1989	7.8	13.85	9.58	15.02
1990	9.4	14.77	11.08	13.50
1991	5.9	11.70	9.92	10.45
1992	3.8	9.56	9.13	6.44
1993	1.6	6.01	7.87	4.95
1994	2.5	5.46	8.05	6.00
1995	3.4	6.73	8.26	6.31
1996	2.4	5.96	8.10	3.26
1997	3.2	6.58	7.09	7.13
1998	3.4	7.21	5.45	5.63
1999	1.5	5.33	4.70	5.70

Source: adapted from *Economic Trends Annual Supplement*, Office for National Statistics.

1. (a) What is meant by a 'real rate of interest'?
   (b) During which years shown in the data were real interest rates positive in the UK?
2. Why are some interest rates higher than others? Illustrate your answer from the data.
3. Discuss whether changes in interest rates reflect changes in the rate of inflation.

Summary

1. Money is neutral if changes in the supply of money only affect the price level of the economy.
2. The Fisher equation of exchange states that $MV \equiv PT$.
3. The quantity theory of money states that changes in M, the money supply, are the sole determinants of changes in P, the price level.
4. Monetarists argue that V is constant in the short term and changes only slowly in the long run.
5. They also argue that the money supply must grow over time to match any increase in T, the level of real income; if the growth in T were greater than the growth in M, there would be a fall in prices.
6. Keynesian economists dispute whether V is constant in the short run. They also suggest that increases in prices may well lead to increases in the money supply.

The neutrality of money

In 1960 the President of France, General Charles de Gaulle, cut the value of all French money by a factor of 100. He passed a law which decreed that on the 1 January 1960, 100 Francs would be called 1 Franc. So a 1 000 Franc note was reduced in value to 10 Francs. 10 000 Francs in a French bank account was only worth 100 Francs. A company which had borrowed 100 million Francs would only have to repay 1 million Francs. This change in the value of the Franc had little or no effect on the **real economy**. Because all monetary values were changed on the same day, relative values remained unchanged. Prices were only 1 per cent of their former level, but so too were wages. The company which had its loan cut by a factor of 100 still had to earn 100 times more in Francs to pay off the loan. The owner of a 1 000 Franc note saw its value reduced 100 fold, but then prices were reduced by the same factor. The note bought exactly the same quantity of goods and services as before.

This is an example of the neutrality of money. Money is said to be NEUTRAL if changes in the money supply only affect the level of prices in the economy. But economists disagree about the extent to which money is neutral. Some economists argue that changes in the money supply can have important effects on the real economy, in particular on variables such as national income and unemployment, whilst others argue that it is neutral.

The equation of exchange

The EQUATION OF EXCHANGE distinguishes between the real and the money side of the economy. The most famous formulation of the equation was made by Irving Fisher, an American economist who worked during the first half of this century. The FISHER EQUATION is:

$$MV \equiv PT$$

M is the total amount of money in the economy (i.e. the money supply). V is the VELOCITY OF CIRCULATION of money (sometimes also called the INCOME VELOCITY). V is the number of times the money supply changes hands over a period of time, such as a year. P is the average price of each transaction made in the economy. T is the total number of transactions made over a period of time.

The equation of exchange is an identity (i.e. it is true by definition ☞ unit 45). Assume that there is £100 of money (M) in circulation in the economy. On average, each £1 changed hands 4 times (V) during the year. So we know that £400 must have been spent during the year (M x V). If the average price of each transaction was £2 (P), there must have been 200 separate transactions (T) over the period. Similarly, if 100 transactions (T) take place over a year and each transaction was for an average of £5 (P), then the total amount spent was £500. If there was only £50 of money in circulation (M), that money **must** have changed hands on average 10 times during the year. So the velocity of circulation of money (V) must have been 10.

Different formulations

There are a number of other ways of expressing the equation of exchange.

- T, the number of transactions in the economy over a period of time, can be equated with real national income, the physical volume of output in the economy. Hence:

$$MV \equiv PY$$

  where Y is real national income.
- P times Y, the average price of each transaction times the level of real national income, is equal to y, the level of nominal national income, or national income at current prices. So:

$$MV \equiv y$$

- If $MV \equiv PY$ and we divide both sides of the identity by V, then:

$$M \equiv \frac{PY}{V}$$

- If $1 \div V$ is called k, we then have:

$$M \equiv k\,PY$$

- Alternatively, if $Y \div V$ is called a, we have:

$$M = aP$$

We will now use these different formulations to explain the quantity theory of money.

Question 1

The money supply M is £200, V is 10 and T is 100.
(a) What is the value of P?
(b) The money supply now doubles. If V and T remain constant, what is the new value of P?
(c) At the new money supply level, T now increases from 100 to 150. What will happen to the price level if there is no change in the money supply and V remains constant?
(d) At the new money supply level, what is the level of (i) national income at constant prices and (ii) national income at current prices?
(e) If M = aP, what is the value of a at the new money supply level?

The quantity theory of money

The QUANTITY THEORY OF MONEY is one of the oldest economic theories, dating back at least 500 years if not more. The theory states that increases in prices are caused solely by increases in the money supply. As Milton Friedman put it in his 1968 book *Dollars and Deficits*, 'inflation is always and everywhere a monetary phenomenon'.

It is necessary to make a number of key assumptions if we are to make the transition from the equation of exchange, which is an identity and therefore always true, to the quantity theory of money. The simplest way of doing this is to assume that k, the inverse of the velocity of circulation of money, and Y, the real level of national income, are both constant. Then:

$$M = aP$$

where a is the constant kY (or $Y \div V$). If M increases, then so must P. In the crudest form of monetarism, M and P will change by the same percentage. So a 10 per cent increase in the money supply will increase prices by 10 per cent. Money is therefore neutral.

Advocates of the quantity theory of money are called MONETARISTS and the belief that inflation is caused solely by increases in the money supply is called MONETARISM. Why do monetarists argue that V and Y can be assumed to be constant?

The velocity of circulation The velocity of circulation of money is the average number of times a unit of money changes hands over a period of time. For instance, a £10 note may change hands 50 times a year.

One factor which determines the velocity of circulation is the way in which households receive money and make purchases.

- The velocity of circulation of broad money will tend to fall if there is a change from paying workers once a week to once a month. Households will now hold money for longer periods of time to cover expenditure later in the month.
- The increased use of **money substitutes**, such as credit cards, will also reduce the velocity of circulation of money itself. Instead of making many separate money transactions, the card holder will make one transaction at the end of the month to the credit card company.

On the other hand, increased use of cheques and debit and credit cards will tend to lead to an increase in the velocity of circulation of notes and coins (M0). Households and firms increasingly do not keep cash as savings at home, but use it for transactions purposes. Cash card machines mean that households keep less and less cash as a proportion of income and spend it very quickly.

Another factor which is important in determining the value of V is the extent to which money is used for speculation in financial assets such as stocks and shares. If there is a large **speculative demand for money**, then V can vary as asset portfolios are switched in and out of money. Keynesians argue that when the rate of interest rises, households and firms desire to hold less money because the opportunity cost of holding money will have risen. The opportunity cost is the interest or return they could have obtained if they had placed their money in, say, a building society account or in stocks or shares. When the rate of interest rises, less money will be held to make the same number of transactions. Households and firms will make their smaller stock of money work harder (i.e. the velocity of circulation will rise).

So the debate about the value of the velocity of circulation of money is the same debate as the one about the determinants of the demand for money. Monetarists argue that the speculative demand for money is relatively unimportant because money is held mainly for transactions purposes. In the long run V can change as institutional factors change, but the change will be slow. In the short run, V is broadly constant because the demand for money is a stable function of income. Keynesians, on the other hand, argue that changes in the rate of interest lead to significant changes in **liquidity preference** (i.e. the demand for money) and therefore the velocity of circulation is volatile in the short run.

National income Real national income tends to rise slowly over time. The annual growth rate of the UK economy over the past 40 years has averaged about 2½ per cent. If M = kPY, and k is constant, then the money supply can grow by the rate of growth of real income without generating a rise in prices. Monetarists indeed argue that the money supply should be expanded in line with real growth, otherwise prices will fall. Falling prices can be just as undesirable as inflation. But any expansion of the money supply over and above the rate of growth of real income will be inflationary, according to monetarists.

Question 2

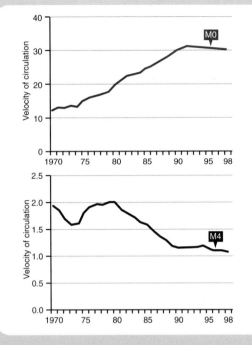

Figure 84.1 *Velocity of circulation*

Figure 84.1 shows two different measures of the velocity of circulation of money: that of M0, narrow money and of M4, broad money.
(a) To what extent is the velocity of circulation of money constant over time?
(b) Suggest reasons why the velocity of circulation may have changed over the period shown.

The money supply and inflation

The quantity theory of money, according to monetarists, shows that price increases are the result of increases in the money supply. This conclusion is dependent upon the assumptions that the velocity of circulation of money is constant, and that income (and therefore transactions and output) changes only slowly over time. Keynesians, on the other hand, argue that the demand for money is unstable and therefore the velocity of circulation of money is unstable too. A rise in M could be offset by a decrease in V rather than leading to a change in the price level. Keynesians also point out that monetarists assume that causality runs from M to P. But logically it could equally be true that price increases could lead to an increase in the money supply. There are two ways in which this might occur.
● Assume that the money supply is **endogenous** (i.e. it cannot be controlled by the central bank but instead is created by the banking system). A rise in wages will lead to increased demand for money from the banks. Firms will need more money to pay their workers, whilst workers will increase their demand for money because their incomes have gone up. An increased demand for money will push up interest rates and banks will find it more profitable to create money. Therefore the money supply will expand.

● If the money supply is **exogenous**, (i.e. its size is controlled by the central bank), it is not necessarily true that the central bank will choose to restrict the growth of the money supply. It may well allow the money supply to expand rather than accept the consequences of restricting its growth. This policy is known as **accommodating** the factors, causing the increase in demand and therefore supply of money.

The quantity theory of money equation also suggests that an increase in the money supply **could** lead to an increase in real income. If M = kPY, and k and P are assumed to be constant, then an increase in M will lead to an increase in Y. Some monetarists (such as Patrick Minford and others from the Rational Expectations school of thought) argue that an increase in M will feed through so quickly to an increase in P that Y will not be affected at all (i.e. there will no time lag between an increase in M and an increase in P). Other monetarists, such as Milton Friedman, argue that, in the short term, much of the increase in the money supply will indeed initially lead to an increase in real income. This link between increases in M and increases in Y is known as the monetary **transmission mechanism** (☞ unit 89). But, they argue, in the longer term, real income will revert to its previous level whilst all of the increase in the money supply will have fed through to an increase in prices (i.e. there is a time lag between increases in the money supply and increases in the price level).

Economists are agreed that very large increases in the money supply will inevitably lead to high inflation. If the money supply increases by 200 per cent over a year, it would be impossible for either V or Y to change sufficiently for P to be unaffected. The monetarist-Keynesian debate centres round the effects of relatively small increases in the money supply. Are money supply increases of 5 or 10 or even 20 per cent necessarily inflationary?

Question 3

The broad measure of money supply expanded faster for the first time in seven months, reinforcing suggestions that the economy's recovery is advancing. M4 showed a seasonally adjusted monthly growth of 1.2 per cent in April. This took the annual rate of expansion to 7.4 per cent.
 The figures suggest the private sector has responded to the cuts in interest rates by the Bank of England. Growth in lending by the banks was particularly strong, which fed through into higher deposits.
 The Bank of England's monetary policy committee has given little weight to monetary aggregates in making decisions on interest rates since it was set up in 1997. The Bank of England's latest Inflation Report said the Bank expected money supply growth to slow in line with the monetary policy committee's projections for a slowdown in the economy and in inflation.

Source: adapted from the *Financial Times*, 25.5.1999.

(a) Using the data, explain the possible links between the money supply, the level of economic activity and inflation in 1999.

Equation of exchange (the Fisher equation) - the identity $MV \equiv PT$ where M is the money supply, V is the velocity of circulation of money over time, P is the price level and T is the number of transactions over time.

Monetarists - economists who believe that the quantity theory of money shows that inflation is always and everywhere caused by excessive increases in the money supply.

Neutrality of money - the theory that a change in the quantity of money in the economy will affect only the level of prices and not real variables such as unemployment.

The quantity theory of money - the theory, based on the equation of exchange, that increase in the money supply, M, will lead to increases in the price level P.

The velocity of circulation of money/income velocity - the number of times the stock of money in the economy changes hands over a period of time.

Applied economics

Inflation and the money supply

The quantity theory of money suggests that inflation is caused by increases in the money supply over and above the rate of real growth in the economy. If this were true, it would be possible to see a strong correlation between money supply growth and the rate of change of prices across a number of countries.

Figure 84.2 is a scatter diagram, giving data for OECD countries. On the horizontal axis is the average annual percentage growth of broad money. On the vertical axis is the average annual percentage change in prices. There does seem to be some general correlation between the two variables: the higher the percentage increase in the money supply, the higher the rate of inflation.

Figure 84.3 shows the relationship between the four variables in the Fisher equation for the UK from 1970. The 1970s and the 1990s would tend to support the view that changes in the money supply lead to a change in the rate of inflation.

- The growth in M4 between 1970 and 1972 led first to a fall in the velocity of circulation of money and then to an increase in growth in GDP. This was shortly followed by a rise in the inflation rate in 1974 and 1975. It was this experience which was particularly influential in converting many economists and politicians to monetarism.
- The fall in the rate of growth of

M4 in 1973-7 led to initial rises in the velocity of circulation of money and falls in the growth of GDP, followed by falling inflation rates between 1975 and 1978.

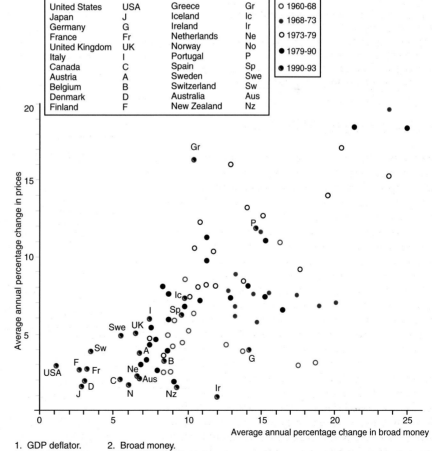

1. GDP deflator. 2. Broad money.
Source: adapted from OECD, *Historical Statistics*.
Figure 84.2 *Inflation[1] and the percentage change in the money supply[2] for OECD countries*

- The fall in the rate of growth of M4 from 1989 led to falls in the rate of inflation from 1991 onwards. However, there is little correlation between growth of M4 and inflation in the late 1970s and most of the 1980s and 1990s. During the late 1970s and the first half of the 1980s, there was an increasing disillusionment amongst economists and politicians with what was sometimes called 'crude' monetarism (Denis Healey, Chancellor of the Exchequer from 1976 to 1979 called it 'punk' monetarism!). The targeted measures of the money supply (M1 and M3, now no longer calculated) grew at a much faster rate than inflation. In the middle 1980s, for instance, with inflation at around 5 per cent, M4 was growing in the 12-16 per cent range.

Monetarists today would argue that this arose mainly because of financial deregulation. For instance:

- exchange controls (restrictions on the ability of UK citizens to exchange pounds for others currencies) were abolished in 1979;
- controls on bank lending were removed in 1980;
- competition in the banking sector was increased, by allowing building societies to offer banking services under the Building Society Act 1986;
- the London Stock Market was deregulated in 1986.

This led to individuals and companies increasing their demand for money (i.e. controls had rationed the amount of money available to them). Increases in money holdings relative to all other variables led to falls in the velocity of circulation of money, previously thought by monetarists to be broadly constant over time. However, by the end of the 1980s, these one-off effects had fed their way throught the economy.

There then followed a sharp fall in the growth of the money supply from 19.0 per cent for M4 in 1989 to 2.7 per cent in 1992. This was accompanied by a sharp fall in both prices and economic growth. Inflation fell from 9.4 per cent in 1990 to 1.6 per cent in 1993, whilst the economy went into a prolonged recession between 1990 and 1992. Monetarists would argue that it was the sharp fall in the rate of growth of the money supply which led

to first a recession and then the fall in inflation. In the second half of the 1990s low inflation was accompanied by economic growth above the trend rate. This, with a slow fall in the velocity of circulation of money, allowed M4 to grow between 5 and 10 per cent per annum.

For monetarists, the evidence of the past 30 years shows clearly that inflation is a monetary phenomenon. They also have an explanation for the unusual relationship between the money supply and prices in the 1980s. For Keynesians, the whole period shows that there is no predictable relationship between the money supply and prices and changes in V often absorb changes in M. Moreover, it may be that the causality is running from increases in prices to increases in the money supply, rather than the other way around as monetarists would suggest. In short, the evidence could be used to support a wide variety of conflicting opinions about the causes of inflation.

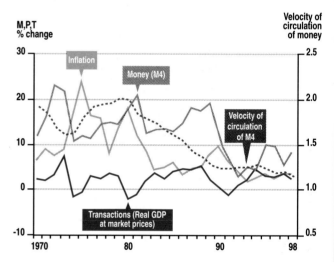

Source: adapted from *Economic Trends Annual Supplement*, Office for National Statistics.

Figure 84.3 *Annual percentage change in prices, real GDP, the money supply (M4) and the velocity of circulation of M4*

Housing and the money supply

Housing boom continues

The housing boom is continuing with house prices up 1 per cent in December, and 13 per cent in the year. The average house price is now £75 219 according to the Nationwide Building Society. The boom is linked to rapid growth in mortgage lending, up 4 per cent in December, with the average loan value for house purchases now being £72 400.

This growth in mortgage lending is one factor fuelling growth in the money supply. What the banks and the building societies lend out, they mostly get back in new deposits from people selling houses but not buying, and from those trading down.

Source: adapted from *The Times*, 30.12.1999.

The property scare

The Bank of England is concerned that the property boom could fuel a rise in inflation. In the Lawson boom of the 1980s, the property boom was a key factor in pushing up inflation rates. At the time, the confidence of homeowners increased as they saw the prices of their properties rise. They became more willing to borrow money because they judged they were now wealthier. It also became common for those buying a house to borrow more than they needed to finance the purchase. The balance was used particularly to buy furniture, new kitchens, new bathrooms or other purchases for the house. Equally, though, some used it to buy everything from cars to holidays. The fear is that the increase in property prices in the late 1990s could spark off a similar rise in spending at the start of this millennium.

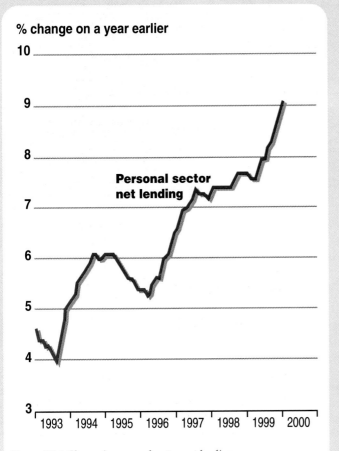

% change on a year earlier

Figure 84.4 *Change in personal sector net lending*
Source: adapted from the *Sunday Times*, 9.1.2000.

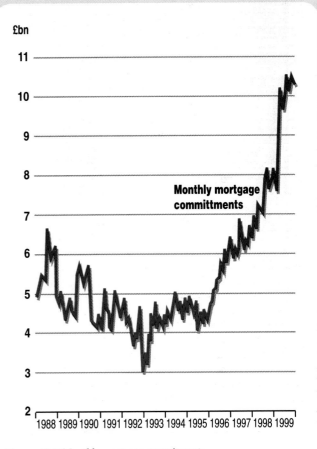

£bn

Figure 84.5 *Monthly mortgage commitments*
Source: adapted from the *Sunday Times*, 9.1.2000.

The recession that wasn't

In 1998 and 1999, the UK economy slowed down. It should have come to a halt if the Bank of England had had its way in order to stop a predicted rise in inflation. In fact, the downturn was very mild and inflation failed to take off. The problem at the start of 2000 is that consumers seem very optimistic. With the job market tightening further, they are less worried about unemployment. Their houses are going up in value. The last major recession was now eight years ago. So they are spending by saving less and borrowing more. Banks and building societies are only too happy to supply them with the money. But the Bank of England may intervene to stop the party by raising interest rates. The greater the danger of inflation, as it sees it, the more likelihood interest rates will have to rise.

Using the data to illustrate your answers:
1. explain the link between increases in house prices and increases in the money supply;
2. analyse how increases in the money supply can feed through to increased inflation;
3. discuss the extent to which a rise in the money supply might be offset by a fall in the velocity of circulation of money.

Summary

1. The main instrument of monetary policy in the UK in recent years has been the control of interest rates.
2. Interest rates are inversely related to aggregate demand, which in turn influences inflation.
3. The rate of interest is determined by the demand and supply of money.
4. Central banks can attempt to control the money supply directly rather than using interest rate policy. For instance, they can use open market operations, monetary base control or impose rules and regulations on banks.
5. Central banks may also attempt to control other monetary variables such as hire purchase credit, or lending for export contracts.
6. The higher the level of genuine government borrowing, the higher the interest rate in the market. Sometimes, though, the government chooses to finance its budget deficit by printing money and therefore increasing the money supply and not necessarily affecting interest rates.
7. Higher interest rates will lead to higher levels of the exchange rate.
8. The credit multiplier measures the number of times an increase in high powered money increases the total volume of bank deposits.
9. Monetary policy only works imperfectly, partly because the exact relationship between changes in variables is unknown, partly because the economy is constantly changing and there is therefore uncertainty, partly because data is imperfect, and partly because policy implementation can itself distort the variables that it is attempting to control.

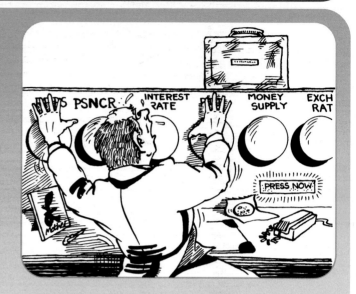

Monetary policy

The operation of monetary policy was outlined in unit 37. Monetary policy is the attempt by the government or its agent, the central bank, to manipulate monetary variables such as the rate of interest or the money supply to achieve policy goals. The four main macro-economic policy goals are price stability, low unemployment, high economic growth and balance of payments equilibrium.

Interest rate policy

Today, the main instrument of monetary policy in Europe and the USA is the control of interest rates. Raising interest rates reduces aggregate demand because consumers spend less whilst firms reduce their investment. This occurs directly, for instance because higher interest rates increase the cost of borrowing to buy consumer durables or investment goods. It also occurs indirectly. For instance, a rise in interest rates is likely to raise the exchange rate, which in turn is likely to make exports less price competitive and imports more price competitive. Exports thus fall whilst importers can increase their sales at the expense of domestic producers. Changes in interest rates can also affect wealth, for instance changing the prices of stocks and shares, or the

Question 1

At its meeting in September, the Monetary Policy Committee had plenty to think about. Consumer spending in the second quarter was up 1.4 per cent, giving a year on year increase of 4 per cent. Investment was growing at a 6.7 per cent annual rate. Economic growth for the year, forecast to rise by 0.5 per cent in the spring, was now on course to rise by 1.5 per cent. Import growth was strong too, being sucked in by higher than expected spending. The housing market was causing concern. With house prices rising at over 10 per cent per annum, there were growing signs that homeowners were beginning to use their increased wealth to increase spending. Equity withdrawal, borrowing money using a house as security, or trading down from a more expensive to a cheaper house and spending the proceeds, seemed to be on the increase. Finally, with unemployment still falling despite low growth, households seem no longer particularly worried about losing their jobs. This must be encouraging spending.

Source: adapted from *The Guardian*, 9.9.1999.

(a) In September 1999, the Monetary Policy Committee decided to raise interest rates. Explain why a rise in interest rates might have helped them maintain inflation at its target rate of 2.5 per cent.

price of houses. These changes affect the consumption of households.

A rise in interest rates, then, reduces the level of aggregate demand. On an aggregate demand and supply curve diagram, the aggregate demand curve is shifted to the left, bringing about a lower equilibrium price level in the economy (☞ unit 35).

The money supply and the rate of interest

Central banks can only fix interest rates because they control at least part of the **money supply** (☞ unit 82). In fact, the money supply and the rate of interest are completely interlinked. Consider Figure 85.1 which shows a downward sloping demand curve for money in a money market (☞ unit 82 for what is meant by the demand for money and why the demand curve is downward sloping). The rate of interest is the price of money. The equilibrium rate of interest is determined by the demand for and supply of money. So, if the equilibrium rate of interest is r_1, then the money supply in equilibrium must be M_1. The money supply curve must therefore pass through the point A. If interest rates rise to r_2, the money supply at that equilibrium must be M_2. The money supply has therefore fallen from M_1 to M_2. The new money supply curve must have shifted backwards and passed through the point B.

In practice, when central banks announce a new rate of interest for the economy, they only fix a new rate of interest for one money market which they control. In the UK, this rate of interest is the **repo rate**. However, the repo rate then fixes the base rates of commercial banks. This is turn influences most short term interest rates, such as building society mortgage rates. It is also likely to affect longer term interest rates, although the link is weaker (☞ unit 83). So a central bank can influence the structure of interest rates throughout the whole economy by fixing just one interest rate in one money market.

The interest rate that the central bank fixes is likely to be

linked to the market in which banks borrow and lend money at very short notice. On any one day, banks may have a surplus of money which is not committed to longer term loans to customers. They may, for instance, have received £50 million more in cheques than they paid out to other financial institutions. Some banks may be short of immediate funds, owing money, say, to other banks because their customers have paid out more in cheques than they have paid in. To cover this, banks will borrow short term, overnight (i.e. for 24 hours) typically from banks with a surplus of funds. The central bank has the unique power to print or create money. If it wants interest rates to fall, it can increase the supply of money to this market by buying back bills (short term loans it has issued) or other financial assets it owns in exchange for money. If it wants to increase interest rates, it can sell financial assets like bills to the banks for money. Hence, governments can only control interest rates if they can control at least part of the money supply.

Question 2

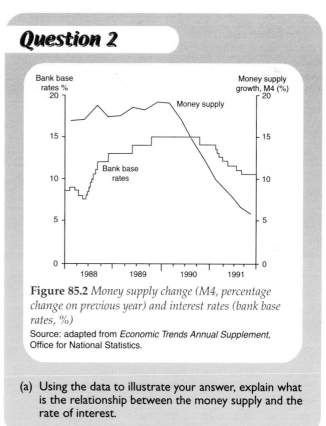

Figure 85.2 *Money supply change (M4, percentage change on previous year) and interest rates (bank base rates, %)*
Source: adapted from *Economic Trends Annual Supplement*, Office for National Statistics.

(a) Using the data to illustrate your answer, explain what is the relationship between the money supply and the rate of interest.

Controlling the money supply

Controlling short term interest rates gives only indirect control over the whole money supply. In theory, there is a number of ways in which more direct control can be exercised.

Open market operations The central bank can issue government bonds and other forms of government debt. If these are bought by the non-financial sector, then money passes from the non-financial sector to the central bank. The amount of money, the money supply, is therefore

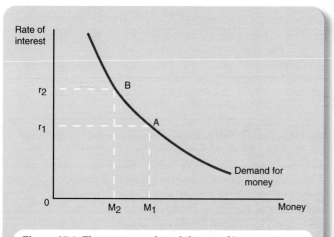

Figure 85.1 *The money supply and the rate of interest*
If the rate of interest rises from r_1 to r_2 without any shift in the demand for money curve, then the equilibrium level of the money supply must have fallen from M_1 to M_2.

reduced because, typically, money at the central bank is not counted in the money supply. This is known as OPEN MARKET OPERATIONS. The reverse is also true. The central bank can increase the supply of money by buying back part of its debt. It can do this because the central bank is the only institution with the legal power to 'print' or create money.

Monetary base control Another way of controlling the money supply is for the central bank to designate certain types of financial assets as RESERVE ASSETS for banks. Reserve assets are also sometimes called HIGH POWERED MONEY or the MONETARY BASE. Reserve assets are aware which a bank must hold if it is to lend out money. In the past, central banks tried to prevent commercial banks from failing by insisting they keep a fixed percentage of their assets in **liquid assets**, i.e. either cash itself or assets which could be sold easily and quickly and converted into cash if their customers wanted to withdraw their money. But central bankers realised that these assets could be used to control total bank lending if they could manipulate their supply.

For instance, assume that banks had to keep 1 per cent of all the deposits made by their customers in a special account at the central bank. At one point in time, banks had £100 billion in deposits and therefore kept £1 billion at the central bank. It then decides that it wants to see a reduction in the money supply. So it returns £0.1 billion to the banks, leaving them with only £0.9 billion at the central bank. With only £0.9 billion, they can only have deposits of £90 billion with their customers (1 per cent of £90 billion is £0.9 billion). So the banks contract their activities, lending less and accepting fewer deposits until the £90 billion figure is reached. The money supply has now gone down by £10 billion because bank deposits are included in broad measures of the money supply (☞ unit 82). The reserve assets which the central bank forces commercial banks to keep are the **monetary base** of the economy. They are a base because, without them, banks can't borrow and lend. If the central bank wants to increase the money supply, it allows commercial banks to increase their deposits with it. For instance, in the above example, a £2 billion increase in reserve assets would allow the banks to increase the volume of deposits from customers by £200 billion (because £200 billion x 1 per cent = £2 billion). Reserve assets are **high powered money** because its possession enables the banks to create extra money.

Rules and regulations The central bank may impose rules and regulations on banks whose deposits make up most of broad money. For instance, a central bank may impose financial penalties on banks which increase their deposits (and therefore their lending) by more than a certain percentage over a period.

Controlling other monetary variables

Central banks may choose to control other monetary variables. For instance, in the 1950s and 1960s, the Bank of England placed restrictions on hire purchase borrowing. It limited the amount that could be borrowed, stipulated the size of the deposit that had to be made and restricted the

number of months within which the loan had to be paid. This made sense at the time because the commonest form of financing the purchase of consumer durables then was hire purchase. The central bank could restrict bank or building society lending for the purchase of houses if it felt that house price inflation was a serious problem. The Bank of England in the 1940s and 1950s also ordered banks to give priority for loans to firms needing the finance for exports. Central banks can force commercial banks to charge different rates of interest for different types of loan. For instance, firms wanting to invest might be given a much lower rate of interest than a personal customer wanting to buy a car.

The money supply and the PSNCR

Since the Second World War, governments have traditionally spent more money than they have raised in taxes. The result is that they have had to borrow money. In the UK, this borrowing is known as the **public sector net cash requirement**, the PSNCR (☞ unit 36). Governments have two ways of raising this money, assuming that they are not going to borrow it from foreigners. The first is to borrow the money from the general public (known as the **non-bank sector**). This has no effect on the money supply but it does affect the rate of interest. If the government wishes to increase the amount, it will have to compete for funds with consumers and firms. This extra demand for borrowed funds will increase their price (i.e. the rate of interest will rise). Conversely, a fall in the PSNCR will reduce total demand for borrowed funds and thus the rate of interest will fall. So the government cannot choose both the level of the PSNCR and the rate of interest if genuine borrowing takes place.

The government has a second option when financing the PSNCR. It could choose to print the money. In a modern economy, it does this by selling government debt to the **banking sector**. To understand why, consider a situation where the central bank sells £100 million of government debt to the banks. They pay for this and the government uses it to finance its spending. For instance, it might use it to pay the wages of civil servants. The government makes the wage payment into its bank accounts. The banks therefore receive an inflow of deposits which will roughly match the loan they have made to the government by buying its debt. But the extra deposits made by customers of the banks are an increase in the money supply. Therefore a central bank selling debt to the banking sector increases the money supply and is effectively a way of printing money. This is different to the situation where the central bank sells debt to the non-bank sector. Here the non-bank sector withdraws money from its bank accounts to pay for the purchase of the debt. When the government spends the money, the money comes back to the banks in the form of new deposits. The withdrawals and the new deposits cancel each other out, leaving no increase in the money supply.

There is a long history of governments resorting to the printing presses to finance spending. This method has the advantage that the government does not need to raise taxes. It also means that interest rates do not need to rise because increasing the money supply should lead to a fall in interest rates.

The money supply, the rate of interest and the exchange rate

The **exchange rate** is the rate at which one currency can be exchanged for another (☞ units 13 and 93). It is a market price, and therefore the exchange rate is determined by the forces of demand and supply. Governments can intervene to try and fix the exchange rate at a particular level by either buying or selling currency. For instance, if the Bank of England wanted to make the value of the pound fall against other currencies, then it could sell pounds for currencies such as dollars and deutschmarks. But the pounds it sells must come from somewhere. If the Bank prints the money, it will raise the money supply. If it borrows the money from the public, it will raise the demand for loans and hence raise the rate of interest.

Alternatively the value of the pound can be changed by changing interest rates. A rise in interest rates in the UK will attract an inflow of funds to the country, increasing the demand for the currency and hence raising its price. The rise in interest rates can only be engineered through a fall in the money supply. So the Bank of England again faces a trade-off in its policy objectives.

The money supply, the rate of interest, the PSNCR and the exchange rate are all interlinked. If the government fixes a value for one, it cannot fix a value for others. Hence a government may choose not to control the money supply in order to control other variables such as the rate of interest.

Question 3

In 1987 and early 1988, the value of the pound rose against other currencies. The Chancellor of the Exchequer, Nigel Lawson, believed that this would prove damaging to the economy and he attempted to limit this rise by cutting interest rates. Bank base rates fell from 11 per cent at the start of 1987 to a low of $7^1/_2$ per cent in mid-1988. However, there were worrying signs that inflation was beginning to increase. The government sharply increased interest rates to 15 per cent by the end of 1988 to brake the rise in the money supply. At the same time, the foreign exchange markets lost confidence in the pound, the value of the pound fell and the Chancellor had to raise interest rates again in 1989 to prevent the pound from falling further.

(a) Using illustrations from the passage, explain the policy conflict between control of the money supply, control of interest rates and exchange rate control.

The credit multiplier

If banks have to keep a proportion of their assets as reserve assets, then a CREDIT MULTIPLIER can be calculated. For instance, assume that a bank has to keep 10 per cent of the deposits of its customers as cash (i.e notes and coins). If it has £100 in deposits, it must therefore keep £10 in cash. The rest it can loan out to customers and charge interest which contributes to its profit. If it has an extra £1 in cash, it could increase its customer deposits by £10. With £11 (£10 + £1) of cash, customer deposits can now be £110 (£100 + £10) because 10 per cent of £110 is £11. With £1 more of notes and coins, the bank can create £10 of customer deposits.

There is a formula for calculating a credit multiplier. It is:

$$\text{Credit multiplier} = \frac{1}{\text{reserve ratio}}$$

In the example above, reserve assets are notes and coins. The reserve ratio is 10 per cent. So the credit multiplier is $1 \div 10$ per cent which is 10. For every £1 of notes and coins kept by the bank, it can hold £10 of customer deposits. Table 85.1 shows other examples of the calculation of the credit multiplier. Notice that the smaller the reserve ratio, the larger the credit multiplier.

Credit multipliers are important if a central bank is attempting to control the money supply through some form of monetary base control. Assume that the money supply is currently £100 and that the central bank wishes to increase this to £110. Furthermore, the reserve asset ratio is 10 per cent, which gives a value for the credit multiplier of 10 ($1 \div 10$ per cent). Then the central bank knows that the banks must obtain an extra £1 in reserve assets for the final £10 in extra deposits at the banks to be achieved. The extra £10 in deposits form the £10 increase in the money supply. If the central bank wants to reduce the money supply by £10, then it must remove £1 of reserve assets from the banks.

Table 85.1

Reserve asset ratio	Credit multiplier	
1%	$\dfrac{1}{1\%}$	= 100
5%	$\dfrac{1}{5\%}$	= 20
20%	$\dfrac{1}{20\%}$	= 5
25%	$\dfrac{1}{25\%}$	= 4
50%	$\dfrac{1}{50\%}$	= 2

The limitations of monetary policy

Monetary policy is used ultimately to control real variables such as inflation, economic growth and unemployment. Achieving, for instance, low inflation or low unemployment are **objectives** of monetary policy. A government may give the central bank specific **targets** to achieve, such as 2 per cent inflation. The central bank then

Question 4

The money supply is £110 billion. Of this, £10 billion is cash held by the general public and £100 billion is bank deposits. The central bank has decreed that banks must keep 10 per cent of their total liabilities in the form of cash. So the banking system has £10 billion worth of cash in bank vaults and £90 billion worth of loans on its books.

(a) Which asset is high powered money?
(b) What is the reserve ratio?
(c) What is the value of the credit multiplier?
(d) The central bank increases the reserve ratio to 25 per cent. Assuming that there is no change in the amount of cash held by the general public, what will be (i) the new level of bank assets and liabilities and (ii) the new level of the money supply?
(e) What would the answers be in (d) if the reserve ratio were 5 per cent?

uses **instruments** to achieve these objectives and targets. For instance, it might use interest rates or the money supply. In practice, the operation of monetary policy poses a number of difficulties for the central bank.

The link between different monetary variables, and monetary variables and the real economy One problem is that the links between different monetary variables, such as interest rates and the money supply, are uncertain. Some economists argue that concepts such as the credit multiplier are of little use to policy makers because the value of the credit multiplier changes from month to month depending on how easy banks are finding it to borrow and lend money. Certainly the credit multiplier is of little interest to policy makers if they don't attempt to control the volume of high powered money in the banking system. The link between monetary and real variables can also be uncertain. For instance, if the central bank raises interest rates by 2 per cent, what will be the exact effect on inflation and economic growth? There is a substantial difference if a 2 per cent rise in interest leads to a 1 per cent fall in GDP compared to one where it is 3 per cent. Moreover, changes to do not occur instantaneously. The effects of any change in monetary variables take place over a period of time. Responses are therefore **lagged**. A 2 per cent rise in interest rates may lead to a 0.5 per cent fall in GDP in the first six months, 1 per cent after one year and 2 per cent after 2 years. The quicker the response, the easier it is for policy makers to steer the economy. If it takes two years to achieve a significant effect, it becomes more difficult to prevent sudden rises in inflation, or sudden falls in GDP due to unplanned economic shocks.

Uncertainty Any type of policy, whether fiscal, monetary or other, is limited in its effectiveness by uncertainty. For instance, the oil price shocks of 1973-74 and 1978-79, the stock market crash of 1987 and the Asian crisis of 1997-98 all had significant effects on western economies. But these events could not have been predicted by policy makers. So an economy can be blown off course by an external event outside of the control of policy makers. The policy response may then be inadequate or inappropriate if policy makers fails to assess accurately the importance of the economic shock. The economic shock may also lead to a situation where existing economic models fail to explain the new situation. In the 1970s, for instance, Keynesian and monetarist economists presented radically different views of why the oil crises had left to stagflation, the combination of high inflation with the economy being in a slump. In the 1980s, UK policy makers failed to appreciate the importance of rising house prices and rising mortgage lending on aggregate demand and inflation.

Lack of reliable data Economic data is imperfect. Data collected today are often revised as further data are accumulated. For instance, GDP figures can undergo substantial revisions over time, partly because the service sector is difficult to monitor. Policy makers have to make judgments based on the data available at the time. If GDP is growing at 2 per cent rather than 1 per cent, it can make a substantial difference to the decisions of policy makers. At 2 per cent, they might decide to raise interest rates; at 1 per cent they might decide to leave them unchanged. Yet between the two figures, there is only a 1 per cent margin of error, which is very small.

Defining monetary variables Another problem with monetary policy is that instruments of monetary policy, such as the money supply, can change their characteristics because they are being controlled. This is known as GOODHART'S LAW. Professor Charles Goodhart argued that if policy makers attempted to manipulate one variable which had a stable relationship with another variable, then that relationship would change or break down as behaviour adapts to manipulation. He was specifically referring to the relationship between bank lending and the money supply. In the late 1970s and early 1980s, the Bank of England attempted to control the growth of the money supply because it believed that inflation was caused by increases in the money supply. The chosen measures of the money supply to be controlled were M1 and M3. The most important components of these were deposits with commercial banks. Controls, however, led to **disintermediation**. Banks artificially reduced their recorded deposits from customers by encouraging very large customers, such as firms, to lend directly to other bank customers. The deposits and loans failed to appear on the bank's books but effectively the bank was still acting as an agent for a deposits and loans. This artificially reduced the money supply. When restrictions on growth in bank deposits were abolished in 1980 by the Bank of England, there was a sudden large jump in the money supply as the money which had gone outside the official controlled system was brought back in.

Question 5

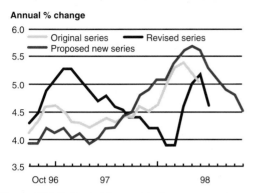

Annual % change

Legend: Original series, Revised series, Proposed new series

Figure 85.3 *Estimates in growth of average earnings*
Source: adapted from Office for National Statistics.

In November 1998, the Office for National Statistics (ONS) suspended publication of one of the most important economic series it compiles. The average earnings index was found to be giving inaccurate information. The average earnings index is a measure of how much earnings in the whole of the UK are rising. It is calculated monthly by taking data from thousands of returns from businesses.

They report on whether or not they have given any pay rises during the previous month and if so, by how much.

Problems arose because of different ways of calculating the average. In October 1998, the ONS launched a new series for average earnings which used a different way of calculating the average than before. But as Figure 85.3 shows, this revised series gave very different figures than the original series. It also didn't fit in very well with what other economic indicators were showing at the time.

A government enquiry found that the revised series was based on inadequate statistical methods which gave too much importance to large changes in earnings by small businesses. In March 1999, a new series was published which followed more closely the old series.

(a) (i) According to the revised series, what was happening to changes in average earnings in 1997?
(ii) Why should the Bank of England have cut interest rates on the basis of this evidence?
(b) (i) How did the evidence from the revised series conflict with that of the proposed new series?
(ii) Why might the Bank of England's monetary policy response have been different if it had used the data from the new series?

key terms

Credit multiplier - the number of times a change in reserves assets will change the assets of the banking system and thus the money supply.
Goodhart's Law - if the authorities attempt to manipulate one variable which had a stable relationship with another variable before, then the relationship will change or break down.
Open market operations - the buying and selling of financial securities in exchange for money in order to increase or decrease the size of the money supply.
Reserve assets, high powered money or the monetary base - those assets which banks have to keep either because they are needed to satisfy customers' requirements (like cash) or because the government forces banks to keep them to operate its monetary policy.

Applied economics

UK monetary policy

Controlling interest rates

As explained in unit 37, UK monetary policy today centres around interest rate policy. The Bank of England controls short term interest rates in the City of London money markets. These control bank base rates, the rate of interest set by banks round which they set borrowing lending rates. In turn, these heavily influence the rate of interest set by building societies. The link between short term interest rates and other interest rates in the economy, like the rate of interest on credit cards or longer term

interest rates, is more tenuous. However, over longer periods of time all interest rates in the economy tend to move together (☞ unit 83).

The Bank of England controls short term interest rates by controlling the demand for or supply of money in the short term money markets in the City of London. Take a situation when the supply of money in these markets exceeds demand. For instance, in the late 1990s, a number of building societies and assurance companies demutualised, i.e. they ceased to be owned by their members and became public companies or part of public companies owned by shareholders. At the point of demutualisation, the members of the building society or assurance company received a payment, which might have been cash if it was being taken over, or shares in a new public limited company which would be quoted on the stock exchange. These 'windfall' gains made by society members might have ended up as new bank or building society deposits. This increases the amount of money that banks own as assets. They will initially lend this out short term on the London money markets in order to get some return on the money. This increase in supply of funds will drive down short term interest rates. The Bank of England prevents this by selling mainly Treasury Bills to the markets. Treasury Bills are 91 day loans to the government. These sales of Treasury Bills mop up the excess liquidity in the market by increasing the demand for money. The Bank of England has increased demand to match supply, and thus is able to fix the price of money, in this case the short term rate of interest.

If the supply of money in the short term markets is less than demand, the Bank of England does the opposite. This could occur, for instance, because there is a large withdrawal of funds from banks by the self employed to pay their taxes on 31 January and 31 July. The banks are then short of money and need to borrow in order to restore their liquidity. This borrowing would push up short term interest rates. Instead, the Bank of England buys 'eligible securities' from the banking system. Eligible securities are securities like repos (a form of government borrowing) , Treasury Bills or Commercial Bills (91 day loans made by firms). Buying bills increases the supply of money into the markets, stabilising interest rates.

The Bank of England raises interest rates whenever it thinks that the economy is likely to be operating above its productive potential, i.e. when the output gap is positive. If actual output is above the trend rate of output, there is likely to be demand-pull inflationary pressure. If, however, the economy is operating below capacity and inflation is stable or is falling, then the Bank of England lowers interest rates to allow the economy to grow at a faster rate.

Central bank independence

Since 1997, the Bank of England has been independent of the government and in particular the Treasury, the government department led by the Chancellor of the Exchequer responsible for the overall economic management of the economy. The government sets the Bank of England a target for inflation which it has to achieve. Decision making about interest rates at the Bank of England is the responsibility of the Monetary Policy Committee (MPC), made up of four independent experts, usually professional economists, four members from the Bank of England staff and the Governor of the Bank of England. They meet every month and consider a wide range of economic statistics which help them to decide whether inflation is likely to increase, decrease or remain stable in the future. The data are often contradictory. For

instance, wage rises may be increasing (a sign of possible future inflation increases), but exports might be falling (a sign of deflation and therefore falling inflationary pressures). A vote is taken and the committee is rarely unanimous.

The process has been criticised. It can be argued that the Bank of England should not be independent and the government should have retained control over such a key macro-economic weapon. It is also argued that setting interest rates should not just be about reaching an inflation target, but that other targets, such as the rate of unemployment, should be taken into consideration. Some have argued that there is an inbuilt deflationary bias to the decision making because the committee will tend to want to undershoot the inflation target (which would be seen as a 'success') rather than overshoot it (seen as 'failure'). Others argue that the Bank of England is too unaccountable and that responsibility should lie with an elected government.

However, having an independent central bank makes it far more difficult for the political party in power to manipulate the economy in its favour at election times. In the past, governments have been accused of stoking up a boom at election time in order to generate the 'feel-good' factor which will ensure them re-election only for the country to have to pay the price in terms of higher inflation and then a recession afterwards. An independent central bank is also not insensitive to other policy objectives such as growth and unemployment. The Bank of England has certainly not attempted to achieve its inflation target by having a persistent recession. Indeed, such tactics would be likely to lead to a continual undershooting of the target which in itself would be seen as a failure by the Bank of England. Both the US central bank, the Federal Reserve Bank, and the euro-zone central bank, the European Central Bank, are independent. So the UK would be out of line if its central bank were not independent. Most importantly, the Bank of England has been successful in containing inflation without causing a major recession since 1997. Its track record is therefore sound.

What follows below is a history of monetary policy in the UK which shows how different types of monetary policy have been used in the past and the reasons why they have been abandoned.

1950 - 1971

Before 1971, the two main intermediate targets of UK monetary policy were the rate of interest and the growth in credit. The rate of interest was considered significant because it could affect the level of investment in the economy and, more importantly, influence the value of the pound on foreign exchange markets. The amount of credit offered by banks and finance houses affected the total demand for goods and services in the UK, including the demand for imports.

The Bank of England exercised control over interest rates through operations in the discount market, setting a bank rate (the discount rate explained above) which then influenced all other money market interest rates.

The volume of credit was in part controlled through the imposition of **lending ceilings**. These were an example of **quantitative** controls. The Bank of England set limits on the growth of bank lending. There was a **qualitative** element in that restrictions on lending were made far tighter for personal customers than for businesses. A company wanting to borrow money for a factory to produce exports, for instance, would be far more likely to be granted a loan than an individual wanting to borrow to buy a car. There were also controls on **hire purchase**. Credit cards were only introduced in the late 1960s, and hire purchase was a very important way in which ordinary people borrowed money. The Bank of England set maximum repayment periods and minimum deposits in an attempt to regulate the demand for hire purchase.

In theory, the Bank of England had the power to use monetary base control. Banks had to keep 8 per cent of their liabilities in cash and 28 per cent in other liquid assets such as Treasury Bills and commercial bills. By limiting the amount of cash held by the banks or by reducing the supply of liquid assets, the Bank of England could have induced a multiple contraction in the money supply. Indeed, in 1960, the Bank moved one step towards this when it introduced the **special deposits** scheme. This allowed the Bank of England to force the banks to deposit with it a proportion of their assets. Special deposits were, therefore, forced loans by the banks to the Bank of England and in theory reduced their ability to make loans to consumers and industries. However, except possibly in 1969, the banks were not, in practice, constrained in their lending by the scheme.

1971-1976

In the 1960s, as the number of banks and other financial institutions in the UK grew, it became increasingly apparent that a significant number of borrowers were avoiding the lending ceilings imposed on the main clearing banks by borrowing money from financial institutions not subject to Bank of England controls (this is known as **disintermediation**). The Bank responded by changing its approach to monetary policy. In 1971, in a document entitled *Competition and Credit Control*, it declared that it would control credit in future not through lending ceilings (a form of rationing) but via the price mechanism. The rate of interest would be used to restrict credit and control the growth of the money supply. Lending ceilings and hire purchase restrictions were abolished, although the special deposits scheme was retained. The 8 per cent cash ratio and 28 per cent liquid assets ratio were replaced by a $12^1/_2$ per cent reserve asset ratio (reserve assets were a variety of liquid assets such as Treasury Bills, but not cash) with banks agreeing to keep $1^1/_2$ per cent of their assets as balances with the Bank of England. Bank rate was renamed minimum lending rate (MLR), although its function remained the same as before.

Competition and Credit Control proved to be a failure.

Its introduction was followed by an explosive increase in the money supply. M4 increased by 70 per cent between 1971 and the end of 1973. Part of the failure was due to the fact that borrowers who had been limited in their borrowing before 1971 increased their borrowings. Perhaps more importantly, it was introduced at a time when the Conservative government of Edward Heath and his Chancellor Anthony Barber was preparing to spend its way out of a recession. Interest rates needed to be kept low if investment and consumer spending were to be encouraged. But low interest rates encouraged record borrowing. In December 1973, the Bank of England was forced to reintroduce hire purchase controls. It also introduced the **supplementary special deposits scheme**, the 'corset', which penalised banks exceeding lending limits by forcing them to deposit money with the Bank of England at a zero rate of interest.

Essentially, *Competition and Credit Control* failed because the government was unwilling to impose sufficiently high interest rates to curb the credit boom. Instead it reverted to the quantitative controls of the 1950s and 1960s.

1976-1979

Before 1976, the intermediate targets of monetary policy had been the rate of interest and the volume of credit. In 1976, the Labour Chancellor of the Exchequer, Denis Healey, introduced a new intermediate target, growth of the money supply M3 (notes and coins plus bank deposits, a definition of the money supply now no longer calculated). In the first half of the 1970s, many economists had become convinced that changes in the money supply caused changes in inflation (the belief known as **monetarism** ☞ unit 84). Therefore, control of the money supply was essential if governments were to reduce inflation.

It was not intended that monetary policy should actively be used to achieve the target set. Rather, the target was to be used as an indicator when planning the level of government borrowing or setting interest rates. In practice, since 1976 the money supply has always tended to grow at a faster rate than the target set by the government.

The Labour government of 1974-9 used a range of monetary policy instruments to constrain credit and the growth of the money supply. Quantitative controls in the form of the corset were in use, as were restrictions on hire purchase. There was also much greater awareness that the way in which the public sector net cash requirement (PSNCR, formerly the public sector borrowing requirement) was financed and its size could have an important impact on the growth of the money supply and on interest rates. The Bank of England was no longer allowed to print the money needed by government to cover the PSNCR (printing money would otherwise have led to an increase in the money supply). This was achieved by ensuring that new government debt was sold only to the non-bank sector.

It was also recognised that the size of the PSNCR would have an impact on interest rates. The lower the PSNCR, the lower could be the rate of interest.

1979-1985

The Conservative administration that came into office in June 1979 was, to start with at least, monetarist in its views. Its most important policy goal was the reduction of inflation and it believed that inflation was caused by excessive increases in the money supply. It therefore attached far more importance to money supply targets than the previous Labour administration. Money supply targets (the **intermediate target** of monetary policy, along with the PSNCR) were written by the Chancellor of the Exchequer Geoffrey Howe into the **Medium Term Financial Strategy**, first published with the 1980 Budget. A reduction in the money supply was to be achieved by:
● setting interest rates high enough to lower the demand for money;
● financing the PSNCR without printing money by selling government debt to the non-bank sector;
● allowing the exchange rate to float, to prevent the buying and selling of foreign currencies from affecting the money supply.
Interest rates, the PSNCR and the exchange rate therefore became the **monetary instruments** of government policy.

High interest rates were achieved through increasing Minimum Lending Rate in the discount market. Within five months of coming into office, the government increased MLR from 12 per cent to 17 per cent.

The government attempted to cut the PSNCR by reducing government expenditure and raising taxes. Cuts in the PSNCR were seen as essential, partly because it was feared that the PSNCR would in practice be financed through printing money (despite the sale of new debt to the non-bank sector), and partly because cuts in the PSNCR were essential if interest rates were to be reduced from their record levels.

The absence of government intervention in the foreign exchange market resulted in an increase in the value of the pound. The effective exchange rate index increased from 107 in the second quarter of 1979 to 127 in the first quarter of 1981, an appreciation of 19 per cent in less than two years.

Unfortunately for the government, its policy instruments proved neither adequate nor suitable to the task of constraining the money supply within pre-set targets. In the early 1980s, the money supply grew at approximately twice the rate set by the government. In part, this can be explained by the government's desire to deregulate financial markets. In 1979, the government abolished **exchange controls**, controls on the amount of sterling that could be taken abroad for investment purposes. The corset was abolished in June 1980, leading to a sudden jump in the money supply as hidden money returned to the official banking system.

There were therefore no quantitative controls on bank lending left. This led to an increase in bank borrowing, and therefore the money supply, as individuals and companies increased their borrowings to their 'free market' level. Increases in debt as a proportion of income rose throughout most of the 1980s fuelled by further measures such as the deregulation of building societies in 1985.

1985-1992

By the mid-1980s, the government realised that there was no simple connection between the rate of interest, increases in the money supply (however measured) and the rate of inflation. One explanation of this is that controlling the money supply through interest rates assumes that the demand for money is a stable function of income - which it cannot have been in the early to mid-1980s. Indeed, the demand for money must have considerably increased, indicating that the controls of the 1960s and 1970s had artificially depressed the demand for money.

By the mid-1980s, the government had effectively abandoned attempts to control the growth of the money supply, and in November 1985 abandoned M3 as an intermediate target.

The government was divided about whether or not the exchange rate should be used as a new intermediate target. The Chancellor of the Exchequer, Nigel Lawson, believed that fixing the value of the pound against the deutschmark would prevent increases in inflation resulting from devaluations of the pound. He also believed that a fixed value of the pound would impose a discipline on government and industry. To prevent devaluation, the UK inflation rate would have to fall to the level of the German inflation rate. Governments therefore would be forced to set sufficiently high interest rates to reduce growth of the money supply and therefore the level of inflation. Industry could not expect government to finance inflationary pay awards by increasing the money supply and then devaluing the pound to restore UK industrial competitiveness on world markets. Others, led by the Prime Minister Margaret Thatcher, believed that the UK should use interest rates as the main policy weapon to reduce the money supply and bring down inflation, and allow the exchange rate to find its own level.

In 1987, the Chancellor indicated that the pound would 'shadow' the deutschmark. For a variety of reasons, the pound almost immediately began to rise against the deutschmark, and the Chancellor reacted by bringing down interest rates. By mid-1988, it became clear that inflationary pressures were building up again in the UK economy. The government decided to combat inflation by raising interest rates. But raising interest rates would also lead to a rise in the value of the pound against the deutschmark. The Chancellor lost the argument about pegging the exchange rate and bank base rates were increased from 7.5 per cent in May 1988 to 15 per cent by October 1989 whilst the value of the pound increased from 3.00 deutschmarks in the second half of 1987 to nearly 3.25 deutschmarks in the first quarter of 1989. But by October 1990, the government, due to pressure from its EU partners, reversed its policy of allowing the pound to float and joined the European Exchange Rate Mechanism, thus putting stability of the exchange rate as an intermediate target once again.

Britain's entry to the ERM was, in retrospect, a disastrous move. It forced the Bank of England to keep interest rates at too high a level. Bank base rates were cut in October 1990 to 14 per cent and then slowly came down to 10 per cent by May 1992. However, real interest rates increased over the period, from 3.6 per cent in the third quarter of 1990 to 5.8 per cent in the second quarter of 1992. The result was that the economy remained stuck in a what became the longest recession since the 1930s. Critics of ERM membership said that inflation had been defeated in 1990-91 and there should have been a substantial relaxation in monetary policy then aimed at getting the economy moving again. Many proponents of Britain's membership of the ERM felt that the UK had entered at too high an exchange rate. The decision to go in at a very high exchange rate was based on previous thinking which had led to the shadowing of the deutschmark in 1987. A high pound would force firms to cut costs and keep them low. If they didn't, they would lose business and could go bankrupt because they were in direct competition with low inflation German and French firms.

1992-2000

On 16th September 1992, 'Black Wednesday', the government's economic policies were shattered when the foreign exchange markets forced the pound out of the ERM. This, arguably, proved a turning point for the success of government policy. It enabled the government to bring down interest rates rapidly, from their 10 per cent level before Black Wednesday to 6 per cent in January 1993 and to a low of 5.25 per cent in February 1994. The economy quickly got moving again with much lower interest rates and a pound which had been devalued by approximately 13 per cent. The government was even prepared in 1993-94 to underfund the PSNCR by £5 billion by selling government stock to the bank sector, thus directly increasing the money supply.

Money supply growth during 1992-95 remained very subdued. This was despite a pick up in the economy and a huge £46 billion PSNCR in 1993-94. In fact, the government and the Bank of England increasingly discounted the evidence from money supply figures about what was going on in the economy at the time and what the future rate of inflation might be. M0 growth was erratic, with speculation that a growth in the **hidden economy** (☞ unit 25) at a time of high unemployment was fuelling demand for high denomination notes. M4 growth was dampened because of subdued bank and building society lending. Investment till 1995 was low, and hence firms were not borrowing to expand. Consumers only began to increase their net consumer debt in 1995. High real interest rates, previous indebtedness, high unemployment and a lack of confidence all made consumers cautious about borrowing. More importantly, mortgage lending was stagnant with the housing market stuck in a deep rut. On the other hand, by 1994 the economy was growing at above long term average growth rates and there were signs that bottlenecks were already appearing in a few industries. International commodity prices were increasing along with many raw material prices. Consequently, the government began to put interest rates up again in September 1994, reaching 6.75 per cent in March 1995.

This rise in interest rates was enough to slow the economy a little and stem the rise in the underlying rate of inflation. From late 1995, the Bank of England felt confident enough to cut interest rates and successive cuts reduced it to 5.75 per cent by June 1996. This helped raise the growth rate again and by late 1996, the Bank of England felt that growth was too strong and might reignite inflationary pressures. In October 1996, it raised interest rates to 6 per cent and then gradually further increased them to 7.5 per cent by June 1998.

The rise in interest rates in 1997 and 1998 was accompanied by a substantial strengthening of the value of the pound, as economic theory would predict. However, the size of the increase in the value of sterling took most economists by surprise. In 1992-93, it lost around 15 per cent of its value against the average of other major currencies. In 1997-98, it regained all of this and for a time in 1998 stood 5 per cent higher than its pre-September 1992 value. This large rise hit manufacturing hard. Manufacturers account for the majority of exports and imports of goods and services, and so service industries are less affected by changes in the value of the pound. Manufacturers had to cope with either cutting their prices by upwards of 15 per cent to remain competitive or they had to accept losing orders and markets because they were not longer price competitive against imports. Growth in exports faltered whilst imports rose fast, helping to deflate the economy. By mid-1998, growth was slowing and inflation began to fall. In October 1998, the Bank of England began to cut interest rates again, down to 5 per cent by Summer 1999. However, through 1999, it became apparent that the downturn, widely expected to bring zero or even negative growth, would be very mild. Consequently, the Bank of England began raising interest rates again from September 1999 because it feared that the economy was operating at full capacity with a zero output gap.

The Bank of England

The Bank of England has its own economic model of the economy. This is a set of equations which describes the relationships between key variables. The model used by the Bank of England is at best only an approximation of what might happen in the economy. 'The bank's use of economic models is pragmatic and pluralist. In an ever-changing economy, no single model can possibly assimilate in a comprehensive way all the factors that matter for policy. Forming judgments about those factors, and their implications for policy, is the job of the committee, not something that can be abdicated to models or even to modellers. But economic models are indispensable tools in that process.' (Eddie George, Governor of the Bank of England).

The Bank of England model makes a number of predictions about how changes in interest rates affect the economy. Overall, a one per cent rise in base rates cuts gross domestic product by 0.2 to 0.35 per cent. Inflation is reduced by between 0.2 to 0.4 per cent. However, these overall effects only take place over a period of time. The path taken, the monetary transmission mechanism, is complex. There are four key links.

- Official interest rate decisions affect other interest rates in the economy, such as mortgage rates and bank deposit rates, either directly or because of expectations about future interest rate changes.
- Changes in interest rates affect the spending, saving and investment decisions of households and firms.
- Changes in interest rates also affect the value of the pound, which in turn leads to changes in demand for goods and services produced in the UK.
- Changes in the value of the pound also have a direct impact on inflation

The effects of any interest rate change are lagged. A one per cent rise in base rates will fairly quickly over a period of around 5 quarters lead to the maximum fall of 0.2-0.35 per cent in GDP. After that GDP will begin to rise again back to its long run trend value. The effect on inflation is lagged behind the change in GDP. Inflation changes little in the first year after a rise in interest rates. In the second year, however, inflation falls sharply, reaching its maximum fall of between 0.2 to 0.4 per cent for every 1 per cent rise in interest rates after 9 quarters.

Source: adapted from *The Guardian*, 29.4.1999.

1. Explain how a rise in interest rates is likely to lead to a fall in GDP followed by a fall in inflation.
2. Analyse what might be the correct policy response for the Bank of England if inflation is rising beyond its target rate of growth but the US economy has just entered a deep recession.
3. What problems does the Bank of England face in implementing monetary policy?

Summary

1. There is equilibrium in the labour market when the demand for and supply of labour are equal.
2. If supply exceeds demand in the labour market and it is therefore in disequilibrium, then unemployment is either cyclical or classical.
3. Unemployment can still exist even if the labour market is in equilibrium. Unemployment would then be frictional, seasonal or structural.
4. Voluntary unemployment occurs when workers choose not to take jobs offered at existing wage rates. Frictional, seasonal, structural and classical unemployment are all examples of voluntary unemployment.
5. The rate of unemployment in the economy given voluntary unemployment is called the natural rate of unemployment.
6. Involuntary unemployment occurs when workers are willing to work for existing wage rates but jobs are not offered to them. Cyclical unemployment is an example of involuntary unemployment.

Labour market equilibrium

Equilibrium in the labour market is achieved when the demand for labour is equal to the supply of labour (☞ unit 73). The demand for labour in an economy is determined by the **marginal revenue product** of labour. As more and more workers are combined with a fixed stock of land and capital, the marginal revenue product of labour (the addition to output of the extra worker) declines (an example of the **law of diminishing returns**). Hence the demand curve for labour is downward sloping.

The supply curve for labour in an economy is likely to be upward sloping. As real wage rates increase, more adults, particularly women, are attracted into the workforce. In the very short term, employers can also

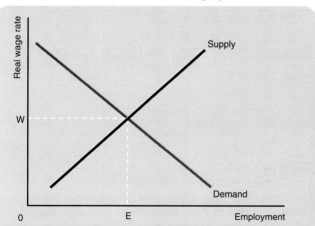

Figure 86.1 *Labour market equilibrium*
The labour market is in equilibrium when the demand for labour is equal to the supply of labour.

persuade existing workers to work overtime if they offer higher rates of pay.

Figure 86.1 shows the equilibrium level of employment in the economy. Employment is OE whilst the equilibrium wage rate is OW. Unemployment in the economy then occurs for two reasons. Either the labour market moves away from its equilibrium position, with actual wages being above OW, or there is still some measured unemployment even when the labour market is in equilibrium. These two possibilities are explored in this unit.

Unemployment when the labour market is in disequilibrium

Sometimes the labour market moves away from its equilibrium position. Figure 86.2 shows such a situation. The actual wage rate, OV, is above the market clearing wage rate of OW. Compared to the equilibrium position:
● FE fewer workers are demanded by employers because the wage rate is too high;
● EG more workers want a job because the wage rate is so high.
The result is that there is FG unemployment in the economy.

If wage rates were to fall to OW, unemployment would fall as firms demanded more workers and some workers dropped out of the labour market, not willing to work at the lower wage rates. There is a number of reasons why the labour market can be in disequilibrium and each gives rise to a particular type of unemployment.

Cyclical or demand-deficient unemployment When an economy goes into recession, unemployment rises because there is insufficient demand within the economy. It is not just labour which becomes unemployed, factories,

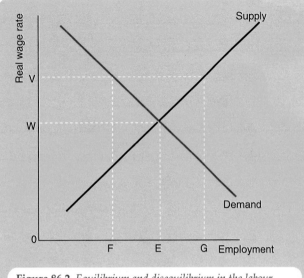

Figure 86.2 *Equilibrium and disequilibrium in the labour market*
At a wage rate of OW, there will be equilibrium in the labour market. At a wage rate of OV, however, there will be disequilibrium with unemployment of FG.

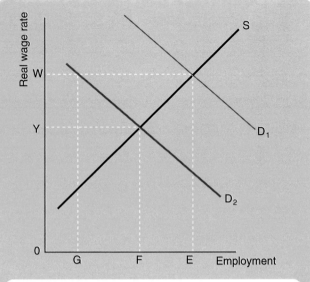

Figure 86.3 *Cyclical unemployment*
When the economy goes into recession, there is a fall in demand for labour, shown by the shift from D_1 to D_2. With wages remaining at OW, cyclical unemployment of GE will be created.

machines, mines, offices and farms (i.e. land and capital) become unemployed too. Figure 86.3 shows what happens in the labour market in a recession. The demand for labour falls, shown by a shift to the left in the demand curve. Employment used to be at OE. Now it is at OG with the old wage rate of OW. This is because OE workers want a job but only OG workers are demanded by firms.

This unemployment of GE is CYCLICAL or DEMAND-DEFICIENT UNEMPLOYMENT. It is also sometimes called KEYNESIAN UNEMPLOYMENT because it was Keynes who argued in the 1930s that the Great Depression was caused by a lack of demand within the economy. In a recession, the economy is in disequilibrium. Macro-economic forces will work to restore the economy to its long run equilibrium position. The extra demand for goods will then generate extra demand for labour. Therefore, in the long run the demand curve for labour will shift back to the right in Figure 86.3. In the short run, however, there is unemployment.

Classical unemployment CLASSICAL UNEMPLOYMENT or REAL WAGE UNEMPLOYMENT exists when the real wage rate is above that needed to clear the labour market even when the economy is booming. Jobs exist but workers choose not take them because they are not prepared to accept the wages being offered, or they are unable to take them because of trade union power or government legislation. In Figure 86.2, the actual wage rate of OV is too high to clear the market. What's more, wages are 'sticky downwards'. This means that there are factors preventing wages from falling to clear the market.

One reason why unemployed people refuse to take jobs is because unemployment benefit levels are too near the level of pay being offered. If benefit levels are above OW in Figure 86.2, there is no point in workers accepting a job at a wage rate of OW. The ratio between the benefit

actually received and the wage a worker could receive is known as the REPLACEMENT RATIO. If the ratio were 1.0, then the unemployed would receive exactly the same from working as from being unemployed. If the ratio were 2, the unemployed would be twice as well off on the dole as working. One way of reducing the replacement ratio and giving the unemployed a greater incentive to take a job is to cut unemployment benefits.

Another reason why the labour market may fail to clear is because of minimum wage legislation. If the minimum wage is OV in Figure 86.2, then there will inevitably be unemployment (☞ unit 75).

Another factor could be trade unions forcing up wages above their equilibrium level. Trade unions serve the interests of their members, nearly all of whom are in employment. Pushing up wage levels, even if this means long term job losses, is likely to be seen as advantageous by the trade union (☞ unit 74).

Unemployment when the labour market is in equilibrium

Even when the labour market is in equilibrium, there might still be unemployment for a variety of reasons.

Frictional and search unemployment Most workers who lose their jobs move quickly into new ones. This short-term unemployment is called FRICTIONAL UNEMPLOYMENT. There will always be frictional unemployment in a free market economy and it is not regarded by most economists as a serious problem. The amount of time spent unemployed varies. The higher the level of unemployment benefits or redundancy pay, the longer workers will be able to afford to search for a good job without being forced into total poverty. Equally, the better the job information available to unemployed workers through newspapers, Jobcentres, etc. the shorter the time workers should need to spend searching for jobs. Hence SEARCH UNEMPLOYMENT will be lower.

Seasonal unemployment Some workers, such as construction workers or workers in the tourist industry, tend to work on a seasonal basis. SEASONAL UNEMPLOYMENT tends to rise in winter when some of these workers will be laid off, whilst unemployment falls in summer when they are taken on again. There is little that can be done to prevent this pattern occurring in a market economy where the demand for labour varies through the year.

Structural unemployment Far more serious is the problem of STRUCTURAL UNEMPLOYMENT. This occurs when the demand for labour is less than its supply in an individual labour market in the economy. One example of structural unemployment is **regional unemployment**. Throughout the post-war period, the South of England has tended to be at full employment while regions such as Northern Ireland have consistently suffered unemployment. This has occurred because of a

lack of mobility of factors of production between the regions (☞ unit 75). Another example is **sectoral unemployment**. The steel and shipbuilding industries in the UK declined sharply in the late 1970s and early 1980s leaving a considerable number of skilled workers unemployed. Unfortunately their skills were no longer needed in the economy and without retraining and possible relocation, they were unable to adapt to the changing demand. **Technological unemployment** is another example of structural unemployment. Groups of workers across industries may be put out of work by new technology. Again, without retraining and geographical mobility these workers may remain unemployed.

The natural rate of unemployment

In a boom period, there is no cyclical unemployment. When the economy goes into recession, workers lose their jobs and they have difficulty getting another job because there are too few jobs in the economy at existing wage rates. Cyclical unemployment is therefore INVOLUNTARY UNEMPLOYMENT. It is involuntary because unemployed workers can't choose to go back to work, because there are no jobs available.

However, all other types of unemployment are examples of VOLUNTARY UNEMPLOYMENT. This occurs when workers refuse opportunities of work at existing wage rates. For instance, a worker who is frictionally unemployed could choose to spend less time searching for work and take a job which is less well paid than he or she might have wanted. Seasonal workers could find odd jobs, such as working in pubs or cleaning, to fill in the months when they are out of work from their main occupation. Those suffering from structural unemployment could get a job if they were prepared to accept a lower rate of pay or worse conditions of work. For instance, unemployed workers in Northern Ireland could come to the South of England to find jobs. Redundant steel workers could become bar attendants or security guards. Classical unemployment is voluntary because individual workers, trade unions or governments choose to allow unemployment to exist by maintaining too high wages. The NATURAL RATE OF UNEMPLOYMENT is the percentage of workers who are voluntarily unemployed. The economy is said to be at **full employment** when there is no involuntary unemployment in the economy. The distinction between voluntary and involuntary unemployment can be shown on diagrams. In Figure 86.4, the long run aggregate supply curve for the economy is drawn with an equilibrium output level of OE. At this output level, the economy, including the labour market, is in long run equilibrium. However, some workers choose not to work at the equilibrium wage level in the economy. In Figure 86.4, the equilibrium wage rate is OW. Two supply curves for labour are drawn. $S_{workers}$ shows the number of workers who are prepared to accept a job at any given wage rate. $S_{Labour\ force}$ is $S_{workers}$ plus those who claim they wish to work, but are not prepared to work at the given wage rate. Official statistics therefore show that there is EF unemployment in the economy. This unemployment is voluntary and OE is the **natural level of employment** in the economy. EF is the **natural level of unemployment**. The **natural rate of unemployment** is the

Question 1

Unemployment has fallen from 3.5 million to 1.5 million over the past four years. However, the economy is going into recession and unemployment is now beginning to rise. The following workers in London find themselves unemployed. Explain how you would classify the type of unemployment faced by each of these workers.
(a) Mr Robert Quinn, 24, has been unemployed for two months after being laid off from his labouring job. 'I think the firm was short of money', he said. He could not find any jobs and his marriage had broken up.
(b) Mr David Kimber, 26, originally from Liverpool, became unemployed three weeks ago when his contract as a tower crane driver expired. 'I have been promised contracts but jobs are being put back.'
(c) Mr Kirpal Singh, 24 and single, quit two months ago after two years as a computer operator for Harrods, the department store, 10 miles away. 'It was just too far to travel every day', he said. He was optimistic about getting another job and said he was being called for second interviews.
(d) Ms Susan Morrison, 19, was pessimistic about getting another job in word processing. She left one job in January after a month when she was told she was 'not the right person' for the job. She previously resigned from British Telecom because she believed she was the lowest paid person in her office.
(e) Ms Patricia Jones, 24, a former deputy catering officer at a large London further education establishment, said: 'There was no career development being offered. I have got all the qualifications to progress in catering so I want a good job with a salary in five figures.'
(f) Mr Peter Vass, 24, a former merchandiser with Maples, the furniture group, resigned because: 'I was paid about £8 000 a year and it just was not enough.' Unemployed for 13 weeks, he was optimistic about getting a new job.

natural level of unemployment divided by the labour force, EF ÷ OF.

What if the economy is at output level OD in Figure 86.4? Here, the economy is in a recession with output below the full employment level of OE. There will therefore be cyclical unemployment, which is involuntary unemployment. The market will return to equilibrium at OE and in the process will reduce the level of cyclical unemployment to zero.

The extent to which unemployment is voluntary or involuntary has been a major controversy in economics. Keynesian economists have argued that most of the unemployment in the Great Depression of the 1930s and the major recessions of 1980-82 and 1990-92 was demand-deficient in nature. At the other extreme, classical economists of the rational expectations school of thought have argued that labour markets will adjust almost instantaneously to large rises in unemployment. Wage rates will fall and the labour market will clear. According to this view, there were plenty of jobs around in the 1930s and 1980s but workers refused to take them. Hence there was no involuntary unemployment.

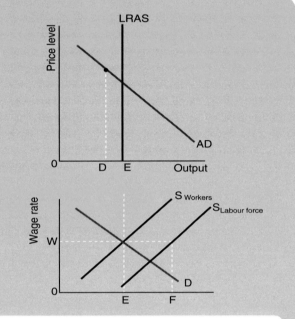

Figure 86.4 *Voluntary employment*
Voluntary unemployment exists when a part of the labour force refuses to work at the going wage rate. Equilibrium full employment exists at OE. At OW, the equilibrium wage rate, EF workers choose not to work. The natural rate of unemployment is therefore EF÷OF. Cyclical unemployment occurs if the economy is below the equilibrium output and employment level of OE, such as OD.

Question 2

In a study of 6 000 employed and unemployed workers, a team of academics found that, contrary to popular opinion, the jobless were more committed to employment than those already in work. 77 per cent were willing to take a job even if there were no financial necessity, compared with 66 per cent of those with jobs who said they would continue to work. There was no evidence that the unemployed were difficult to please in the job market. Only 12 per cent of the unemployed said they expected pay above that of the average of their employed counterparts. 45 per cent of all those out of work said they had seriously considered re-training in order to find work, with 40 per cent prepared to move area.

The study also considered whether the unemployed were intrinsically less 'employable'. Two methods were used to compare the unemployed and those in work. First, an examination of the work histories of the unemployed showed that people out of work had previously held almost exactly the same number of jobs as the employed - by far the biggest factors determining work experience were age, sex and industry. Second, the fact that the average duration of the longest jobs of the unemployed was 74 months, and for the employed 76 months which, the study says, 'suggests employability rather than behavioural instability.'

(a) To what extent does the study outlined in the article suggest that unemployment is mainly voluntary?

key terms

Classical or real-wage unemployment - when real wages are kept at such a high level that the demand for labour is greater than the supply of labour.
Cyclical, demand-deficient or Keynesian unemployment - when there is insufficient demand in the economy for all workers who wish to work at current wage rates to obtain a job.
Frictional unemployment - when workers are unemployed for short lengths of time between jobs.
Involuntary unemployment - unemployment which exists when workers are unable to find jobs despite being prepared to accept work at the existing wage rate.
Replacement ratio - unemployment benefits divided by the wage an unemployed worker could receive if in work.

Search unemployment - when workers spend time searching for the best job available.
Seasonal unemployment - when workers are unemployed at certain times of the year, such as building workers or agricultural workers in winter.
Structural unemployment - when the pattern of demand and production changes leaving workers unemployed in labour markets where demand has shrunk. Examples of structural unemployment are regional unemployment, sectoral unemployment or technological unemployment.
The natural rate of unemployment - the proportion of the workforce which chooses voluntarily to remain unemployed when the labour market is in equilibrium.
Voluntary unemployment - workers who choose not to accept employment at the existing wage rate.

Applied economics

The causes of unemployment in the UK

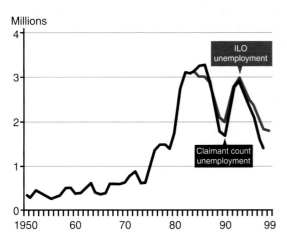

Figure 86.5 *Unemployment, claimant count and ILO unemployed[1], UK millions*
1. ILO unemployed Spring of each year, 1984-87 figures are for GB.

Unemployment in the post-war period

Figure 86.5 shows that unemployment in the 1980s and 1990s was much higher than in the 1950s and 1960s. In the first two decades, unemployment tended to be less than 0.5 million workers. But in the 1970s, unemployment peaked at 0.9 million in 1972, 1.5 million in 1977, 3.3 million in 1986 and 2.9 million in 1993. This was not just a UK phenomenon. Unemployment rates in both Europe and the US were higher too. Unemployment rates in the UK and the US fell substantially in the second half of the 1990s whilst those in Europe remained stubbornly high. Why was this the case?

Cyclical unemployment

Unemployment patterns correspond closely to movements in the trade cycle. In a recession, unemployment rises whilst in a boom it falls. So the peaks of unemployment in the post-war period were followed by troughs. For instance, unemployment fell from 3.3 million in 1986 to 1.7 million in 1990 on a claimant count basis.

The exact amount of cyclical unemployment can be gauged from the movement from peak to trough. For instance, the fall of 1.6 million in the numbers unemployed between 1986 and 1990 would suggest that cyclical unemployment in 1986 was approximately one and half million. It might have been even more if it could be argued that the economy in 1990 was operating at below its productive potential. However, it is likely that there were other types of unemployment apart from cyclical unemployment throughout this period.

In the UK, unemployment has tended to lag behind other trade cycle indicators. At the start of recession, firms are reluctant to shed labour because they hope that the downturn in trading conditions will be temporary. At the end of a recession, firms wait to take on extra labour fearing that the recession will continue. Increases in output tend to be met by an increase in overtime work. The major recessions of 1971-72, 1974-75, 1980-82 and 1990-92 have this lagged response, although the lag at the end of the 1992 recession was very short.

Certain economists argue that some cyclical unemployment is not reversible. When unemployment rises in a recession, it does not fall back to its previous trough level when the economy is in boom. Figure 86.5 shows clearly the upward trend in unemployment in the 1970s and 1980s. The argument is that workers lose skills when made unemployed in a recession. For instance, assume that a worker is made unemployed and because of the depth of the recession fails to find a job within a year. After a year, employers become reluctant to take on that worker. They fear that the worker has lost job specific skills and begin to doubt whether he or she has retained general work skills such as the ability to turn up to work on time. After several years of unemployment, workers can find themselves almost unemployable.

The pace of technological change today makes this more of a problem than, say, 50 years ago. Some workers will become discouraged from looking for work, and as a result miss opportunities for employment when vacancies begin to increase again. The major recessions of 1974-76 and 1980-82 were also particularly damaging to manufacturing industry, with a substantial proportion of the capital stock of manufacturing being dismantled. With it went forever the jobs of the people who were employed in those factories. Cyclical unemployment causing structural unemployment is an example of **hysteresis** - the current value of a variable (in this case unemployment) being directly affected by its previous value (in this case, previous levels of unemployment).

Frictional and search unemployment

Frictional and search unemployment rose in the 1960s and 1970s because of a significant rise in the late 1960s of the replacement ratio, the ratio of unemployment benefits relative to wages. Workers could now afford to remain unemployed longer, searching for the right job. For instance, in the 1960s approximately half of those unemployed were unemployed for less than 8 weeks. By the early 1980s, approximately 85 per cent of the unemployed were out of work for more than 8 weeks. Part of this represented other difficulties in finding work, but part was because workers chose to spend longer looking for the right job.

Structural unemployment

Structural unemployment in the 1970s and 1980s rose for a number of reasons. First, there was a devastating run down of most manufacturing industries and some primary industries such as coal mining. This process of de-industrialisation (☞ unit 97) left many workers with unwanted skills in the job market. At the same time, there were often shortages of other types of skilled worker leading to the paradoxical situation of high unemployment and excess demand for certain types of worker.

North Sea oil made matters worse by raising the exchange rate of the pound, particularly between 1979 and 1981. This made imports cheaper to British consumers but UK exports more expensive to foreigners. For many key periods in the 1970s, 1980s and 1990s, it could be argued that the pound was overvalued with a consequent effect on unemployment.

Labour was also poorly distributed between regions. The primary and secondary jobs that disappeared were spread fairly evenly over the country as a proportion of the labour force. However, the South experienced much faster growth in service industries than the rest of the country over the period. This enabled the South to transfer workers from manufacturing into service jobs relatively easily. But it took much longer elsewhere. Inappropriate housing policies, which encouraged expensive home ownership and discouraged affordable renting, then prevented lower paid workers from moving out of high unemployment regions to the South. The 1990-92 recession hit service industries particularly hard and the unemployment gap between the regions narrowed considerably. But in the upturn during the rest of the decade, it began to open up again, as the service sector boomed in the South but manufacturing jobs continued to fall in the rest of the country.

This run down in primary and secondary industry employment compounded other trends in the economy. The 1970s and early 1980s saw a substantial increase in the numbers of 16 years olds in the population who needed to find jobs. This put considerable pressure on youth unemployment. This trend was reversed in the mid-1980s which helped ease the problem. There was also a substantial decrease in the number of well paid semi-skilled and unskilled jobs traditionally taken by males. These were jobs in primary and manufacturing industry, such as coal mining or working on a production line in a car factory. There was a boom in other types of unskilled work, but these jobs were in service industries. They were low paid and typically taken by women. The result was rising unemployment rates for unskilled male workers but a large increase in employment for female workers.

Classical unemployment

Many semi-skilled and unskilled male workers were caught in the **poverty trap** in the 1970s and 1980s.

Taking on a low paid job would lead them to lose as much or even more in state benefits than they would gain in wages after tax. Although successive reforms of the tax and benefit system in the 1980s and 1990s led to some improvement in this situation, effective marginal rates of tax and withdrawals in benefits remained high at low incomes.

Some economists argue that trade unions were a major cause of unemployment because of their power in the 1960s and 1970s. They were able to raise wages for their members above the market clearing rate for the labour market, but only by reducing the supply of labour and thus reducing the number of jobs on offer.

Another possible source of classical unemployment were wages councils. These were bodies which set minimum wages in a number of industries traditionally associated with low pay. These were abolished in 1994.

Some economists also believe that other forms of legislation which raise the cost of labour to employers helped create higher unemployment. In the 1970s and 1980s, examples such as equal pay legislation and health and safety at work regulations increased costs for firms despite the fact that the Conservative governments of 1979-1997 repealed some legislation which protected the rights of workers.

Unemployment today

During the 1990s, unemployment fell steadily from its peak of 2.9 million in 1993. There is a number of reasons for this.
- Cyclical unemployment fell and was arguably zero by the end of the 1990s.
- Structural unemployment also fell. Although there continued to be a fall in manufacturing employment, this was at a much lower rate and involved fewer jobs than in the 1970s and 1980s. What's more, the service economies of the regions outside the South of England were much stronger and able to create more jobs than previously. The incoming Labour government in 1997 launched the 'New Deal' programme specifically aimed at getting young people and other groups which found difficulty finding employment into a job. There was a recognition that only increased education and training would reduce unemployment further.
- Classical unemployment fell too. Reforms of the tax and benefit system helped many out of the poverty trap.

Some economists, however, felt that the introduction of the minimum wage in 1999 and acceptance of European Union labour legislation would increase classical unemployment. They also felt that new trade union legislation, passed in 1999 and which gave trade unions rights to force their negotiating rights in the workplace, would increase trade union power and thus raise unemployment.

Classical economists argue that the high unemployment seen in most of Europe in the 1990s was the result of too high a level of union power, excessive employment taxes on firms, too generous unemployment benefits for workers and labour legislation which gave workers too many rights in the workplace. These factors raised the cost of workers to employers and made them less flexible. The natural rate of unemployment has therefore been high in Europe. In contrast, they would argue that the prolonged fall in unemployment in the USA and to some extent in the UK has been the result of flexible labour markets. Trade unions are weak, employment taxes are low and the state has a light hand in regulating the labour market. This has resulted in a falling natural rate of unemployment.

The falls in unemployment in the UK in the 1990s have led some to believe that unemployment could fall to levels last seen in the 1960s, with less than 1 million unemployed. This would require further supply side changes in the economy and continued high growth to maintain aggregate demand.

The causes of unemployment

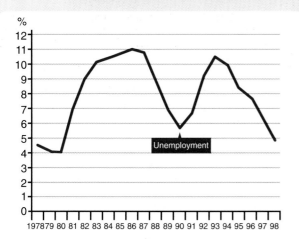

Figure 86.6 *Unemployment, UK, %*
Source: adapted from *Economic Trends Annual Supplement*, Office for National Statistics.

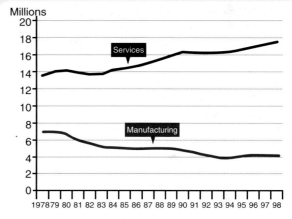

Figure 86.7 *Employee jobs[1] in manufacturing and service industries, millions*
1. 2nd quarter of each year
Source: adapted from *Economic Trends Annual Supplement*, Office for National Statistics.

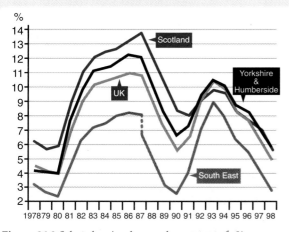

Figure 86.8 *Selected regional unemployment rates[1], %*
1. Discontinuity in the data for the South East in 1987 due to a redrawing of the regional boundary.
Source: adapted from *Economic Trends Annual Supplement*, Office for National Statistics.

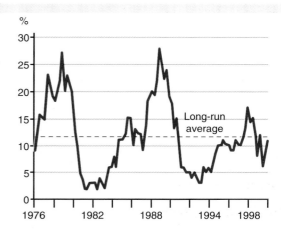

Figure 86.9 *CBI survey of skilled labour shortages[1]*
1. Percentage of firms surveyed which stated that they were unable to recruit sufficient skilled labour.
Source: adapted from HM Treasury, Red Book.

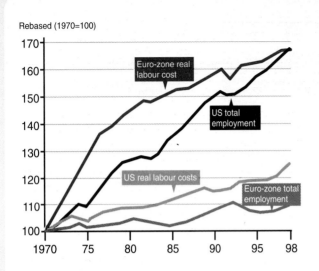

Rebased (1970=100)

Figure 86.10 *Labour costs and employment: euro-zone compared to US*
Source: adapted from OECD, IMF.

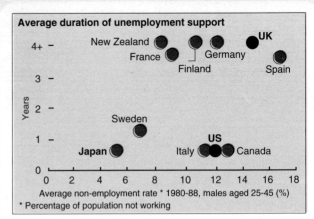

Average duration of unemployment support

1. The vertical axis shows the average length of time an unemployed worker can expect to receive unemployment benefits from the state. The horizontal axis shows the percentage of the male workforce aged 25-54 who are not in a job. This includes both the officially unemployed and 'discouraged workers' - workers who would like a job but have become discouraged from looking and therefore no longer appear on the unemployment statistics.
Source: adapted from Layard and Jackman; OECD.
Figure 86.11 *Average duration of unemployment support*
Source: adapted from OECD, IMF.

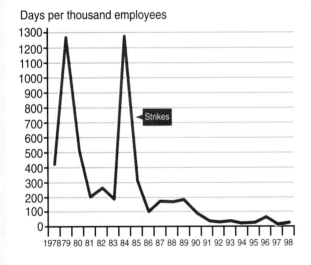

Days per thousand employees

Figure 86.12 *Strikes - working days lost per thousand employees*
Source: adapted from *Labour Market Trends*, Office for National Statistics.

A magazine has asked you to write an article on the causes of UK unemployment in the 1990s. In your article:
(a) outline the main trends in unemployment during the period shown in the data;

(b) discuss the possible causes of unemployment, distinguishing between the main types of unemployment identified by economists;
(c) evaluate which factors have been most important in determining unemployment levels.

Summary

1. The Phillips curve shows the relationship between the rate of change of money wages and unemployment. High unemployment is associated with a low rate of change of money wages, whilst low unemployment is associated with a high rate of change of money wages.
2. Following publication of Phillips's findings in 1958, a view developed that there was a trade-off between unemployment and inflation.
3. From the mid-1960s, the Phillips curve relationship broke down in the UK. The most widely accepted explanation of this is that the original Phillips curve shows the short run adjustment process of the economy, assuming money illusion on the part of workers. From the mid-1960s onwards, workers ceased to have money illusion.
4. Classical economists argue that the long run Phillips curve is vertical. Unemployment will always return to its natural rate. The Phillips curve trade off exists only in the short run.
5. A government which increases demand in the economy will succeed in reducing unemployment at the cost of high inflation in the short run, but in the long term unemployment will return to its natural rate at a higher rate of inflation.
6. Policies which succeed in reducing inflation will create unemployment in the short run. Keynesians tend to argue that the unemployment cost will be severe and prolonged. At the other extreme, new classical economists argue that the unemployment cost will be negligible and that the short run adjustment process is rapid.

The original Phillips curve

In 1958, Professor A W Phillips at the London School of Economics published *The Relation between Unemployment and the Rate of Change of Money Wage Rates, 1861-1957*. He showed that there was a remarkably stable relationship between the rate of change of money wages and the level of unemployment. As can be seen from Figure 87.1, high rates of unemployment were associated with low (and even negative) rates of change of money wage rates whilst low rates of unemployment were associated with high rates of change of money wage rates. The line of best fit came to be called the PHILLIPS CURVE.

This relationship provides a useful insight into the causes of inflation. Changes in money wage rates are a key component in changes in prices. Assume money wage rates rise by 10 per cent whilst all other factors remain constant. If 70 per cent of a firm's costs are wages,

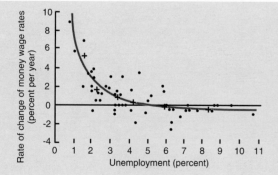

Figure 87.1 *The Phillips curve*
The original Phillips curve was derived from data from the period 1861 to 1913. Phillips then showed that the curve predicted the relationship between the rate of change of money wage rates and unemployment in the period 1913 to 1957.

Question 1

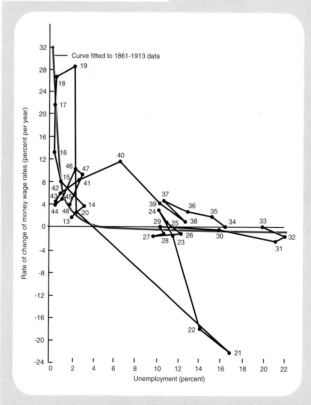

Figure 87.2 *Phillips curve data, 1913-1948*

(a) To what extent do the data shown in Figure 87.2 support the view that there is a stable relationship between unemployment and the rate of change of money wage rates?

then its costs will rise by 7 per cent. It is likely to pass these costs on in the form of higher prices. These higher prices will feed through to higher costs for other firms or directly into the inflation rate (for instance, the Retail Price Index in the UK). The higher the rate of change of money wages, the higher the likely rate of inflation. Hence the Phillips curve hypothesis can be altered slightly to state that there is an inverse relationship between inflation and unemployment. When unemployment is low, inflation will be high. When unemployment is high, inflation will be low or even negative (i.e. prices will be falling).

The initial importance of the Phillips curve

The article was important initially for two reasons. First, it helped Keynesians to develop a more sophisticated theory of inflation. In the simplest Keynesian model, the aggregate supply curve is shaped as in Figure 87.3.

Up to the full employment level of income, the supply curve is horizontal. Any increase in aggregate demand will increase output without causing inflation. At full employment, the supply curve is vertical. Any increase in aggregate demand will increase prices without increasing output. But the evidence of the 1950s suggested that the aggregate supply curve was upward sloping near the full employment level of output. Changes in aggregate demand affected both output and inflation.

Second, policy makers (and particularly governments) changed their views about how the economy might be managed. Many became convinced that there was a trade-off between unemployment and inflation. Zero inflation (i.e. price stability) could be achieved but only by keeping unemployment at what for the time seemed a relatively high level. On the other hand lower unemployment could be achieved by accepting higher levels of inflation. But it was impossible to set both the rate of unemployment and the rate of inflation.

The breakdown of the simple Phillips curve relationship

Following publication of Phillips' article, a great deal of work was done in the UK and abroad to test the relationship between unemployment and inflation. In general, the relationship seemed to occur in other countries too. In the early 1960s the relationship continued to hold true in the UK. Then from 1966 onwards, it broke down completely. Year after year, points to the right of the original Phillips curve were recorded as shown in Figure 87.7. Even more serious was the fact that no new pattern seemed to emerge. Some economists argued that the original Phillips curve never existed anyway. The accepted theory today is that the Phillips curve as originally plotted was a special case and can be understood only in the wider context of aggregate demand and aggregate supply analysis.

The short run Phillips curve

Assume that prices are stable and that there is an increase in aggregate demand. Perhaps planned investment has increased, or the government wishes to increase its expenditure. This will shift the aggregate demand curve to the right in Figure 87.4. The economy moves along its short run aggregate supply curve from A to B. Note that the movement involves an increase in output and an increase in the price level. An increase in output is usually associated with a fall in unemployment. The increase in the price level is of course inflation. Hence the move from A to B shows the Phillips curve trade-off - higher inflation for lower unemployment. The relationship would be no different if aggregate demand fell, shifting the aggregate demand curve to the left except that lower inflation would be traded off for higher unemployment. So the Phillips curve as originally plotted by Phillips shows what

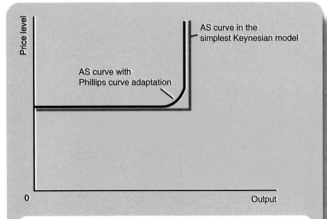

Figure 87.3 *The Keynesian aggregate supply curve*
The simplest Keynesian model assumes that the aggregate supply curve is horizontal at less than full employment levels of output and then vertical at full employment. With a Phillips curve relationship introduced into the model, the aggregate supply curve becomes upward sloping before reaching full employment output.

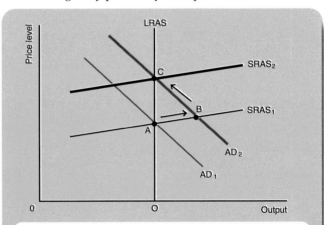

Figure 87.4 *Aggregate demand and aggregate supply*
An increase in aggregate demand from AD_1 to AD_2 will increase prices. It will also increase output and therefore reduce unemployment. This movement from A to B shows the short run Phillips curve relationship. In the long run the economy moves back to C. There is no trade off in the long run between unemployment and inflation.

happens when the economy adjusts in the short run to a **demand-side shock**.

The long run Phillips curve with zero inflation

On classical assumptions, point B in Figure 87.4 is not a long run equilibrium point (☞ unit 86). Given that the economy is at full employment at the point A, the economy has moved to a position of over-full employment at B. In the labour market, workers will be able to bid up wage rates, shifting the short run aggregate supply curve upwards. The economy will only return to equilibrium at the point C where aggregate demand once again equals long run aggregate supply. The movement from B to C involves a rise in measured unemployment whilst inflation falls back to zero again when the economy reaches the point C (remember we assumed that the economy had no inflation at A and once the economy reaches C there are no forces which will increase prices any more). In the long run, therefore, there is no trade-off between inflation and unemployment.

The vertical long run Phillips curve

When inflation is zero or very low, as for instance in the UK in the 1950s or the late 1990s, economic agents are likely to suffer from MONEY ILLUSION. This is the belief that prices are stable when in fact they might not be. For instance, if workers receive a money wage increase of 2 per cent, they may believe they are 2 per cent better off. However, if inflation is also running at 2 per cent then they are in fact no better off at all because their real wages would be unchanged. They would then be said to be suffering from money illusion.

When economic agents become aware that inflation is eroding the value of income and wealth, they change their behaviour. Workers, for instance, may negotiate on a real terms basis. Instead of negotiating for, say, a 2 per cent wage increase, they might negotiate for 2 per cent plus the expected rate of inflation. Such behaviour affects the position of the short run Phillips curve.

In Figure 87.5, the original Phillips curve is PC_1. Workers and firms assume that there will be no price changes and the economy is in equilibrium at the point A. The government now increases aggregate demand, pushing the economy to the point Z on the short run Phillips curve PC_1, reducing unemployment and increasing inflation to 5 per cent. If workers suffer from money illusion, the economy will eventually return to the point A as explained above. But assume that they are more sophisticated and expect inflation to continue at 5 per cent per annum. Workers will bargain for even higher money wages which further push up prices. Hence real wages fall and workers drop out of the labour market. Unemployment will return to a level of OA but a 5 per cent inflation rate will become permanent. The short run Phillips curve will have shifted to PC_2 and the economy will be at B. If the government attempts again to reduce unemployment, inflation will rise, say to 10 per cent on PC_2. In the long run the economy will return to unemployment OA but on a higher Phillips curve PC_3.

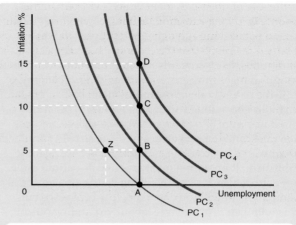

Figure 87.5 *The long run Phillips curve*
In the long run, the Phillips curve is vertical. Attempts by government to reduce unemployment below the natural rate of unemployment OA will be successful in the short run, for instance moving the economy from A to Z. But in the long run the only result will be higher inflation.

The natural rate of unemployment

In Figure 87.5, why does the economy keep tending back towards the same level of unemployment, OA? OA is known as the **natural rate of unemployment** (☞ unit 86).

Question 2

In January 2000, the year on year head line inflation rate, the change in the RPI, was 1.5 per cent. A number of pay deals were concluded around this time including the following.
- Around 5 000 workers at Nissan Motor Manufacturing received a basic pay increase of 1.7 per cent from 1 January 2000 in the second stage of a two-year deal. The award was based on the October 1999 headline RPI plus 0.5 per cent. Last January, employees received a 4 per cent rise in the first stage of the deal.
- Basic pay for 4 500 staff at the Department of Health rose by an average of 4.2 per cent from August 1999, following agreement with civil service unions FDA, IPMS and PCS.
- Following a pay freeze last year, employees at BorgWarner's manufacturing plant in Margam, South Wales, received a 5 per cent rise in basic rates effective from 1 January 2000. Around 273 employees, represented by the AEEU engineering union, were covered by the deal.
- Around 1 000 scientific staff, represented by the IPMS union, have accepted a two-stage pay deal with an annualised value of 2 per cent. In addition, staff will receive performance related pay awards funded from a merit pot worth 2.5 per cent of the paybill for grades 6 and 7.

Explain whether these workers' decisions to accept their pay offers would have been different if inflation had been running at: (a) 0 per cent and (b) 15 per cent.

It is the rate of unemployment which exists when the economy is in long run equilibrium (i.e. where aggregate demand equals long run aggregate supply). It was explained in unit 35 that the economy, based on classical assumptions, tends towards its long run equilibrium level through changes in wages and prices. If the economy is below the natural rate of unemployment, then aggregate demand is above long run aggregate supply, as at the point B in Figure 87.4. Workers will be able to bid up wage rates, and the short run aggregate supply curve will shift upwards till long run equilibrium is once again re-established. If unemployment is above its natural rate, aggregate demand is less than long run aggregate supply. Unemployment will force workers to accept wage cuts. Firms will then take on more labour, expanding output and lowering unemployment to its natural level.

If the economy is in long run equilibrium, the labour market will also be in equilibrium. So another definition of the natural rate of unemployment is that it is the rate of unemployment which occurs when the demand for labour equals the supply of labour.

In the long run, the economy will always tend towards its natural rate of unemployment. Hence the long run Phillips curve is vertical. It is the line ABCD in Figure 87.5. There is no long run trade-off between unemployment and inflation. A government can reduce unemployment below its natural rate in the short run but, in the long run, unemployment will climb back up again and inflation will be higher.

Reducing inflation

Yet another way of defining the natural rate of unemployment is that it is the rate of unemployment which can be sustained without a change in the inflation rate. Sometimes it is called the NAIRU - THE NON-ACCELERATING INFLATION RATE OF UNEMPLOYMENT. To understand why, consider what happens if the government attempts to reduce inflation. In Figure 87.6, the government wishes to reduce the inflation rate from 10 per cent to 5 per cent. It can only do this by travelling down the short run Phillips curve from the point A to the point B, increasing unemployment in the short term from 1½ million to 3 million. The economy will now slowly return to its natural rate of unemployment of 1½ million at the point C. So to reduce inflation, the government must accept higher unemployment in the short run. If it is not prepared to pay this price, inflation will remain constant at 10 per cent with 1½ million unemployed.

An increase in the inflation rate above 10 per cent can only come about through an increase in aggregate demand over and above what it would otherwise have been. This increase will again move the economy off the point A, this time up the short run Phillips curve to D.

So the labour market can be in equilibrium at the natural rate of unemployment (at the NAIRU) with any inflation rate. Hence, once again the long run Phillips curve is vertical.

The only way to reduce the NAIRU (i.e. push the vertical long run Phillips curve to the left), according to classical economists, is to adopt supply side policies (☞ unit 38).

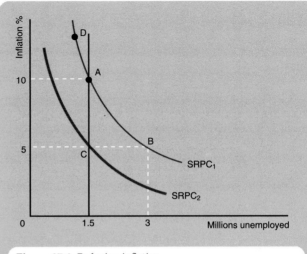

Figure 87.6 *Reducing inflation*
A government can only reduce inflation by moving down the short run Phillips curve, for instance from A to B. In the long run the economy will settle at C, but a heavy price will have been paid in the form of high transitional unemployment.

Keynesians, monetarists and classical economists

The theory that the Phillips curve was vertical in the long run was put forward by the founder of modern monetarism, Milton Friedman. It was he too who suggested that workers might not suffer from money illusion. Hence his theory is sometimes called the **expectations-augmented Phillips curve hypothesis** or **adaptive-expectations hypothesis**.

Keynesians have tended to doubt the existence of a natural rate of unemployment. This is because they believe that it takes a very long time for labour markets to clear if there is mass unemployment. In Figure 87.6, a government which creates unemployment of CB in order to reduce inflation may well find that the economy gets stuck with an unemployment level of 3 million. Unless it is prepared to wait perhaps a decade or more, it can only reduce unemployment by expanding demand again and accepting higher inflation.

On the other hand, New Classical economists have suggested that the short run Phillips curve does not exist. In their theory of **rational expectations** they argue that economic agents, such as workers, trade unions and employers, are able to see whether inflation and unemployment are likely to rise or fall in the future. If the government states that it is prepared to accept a rise in unemployment in order to reduce inflation, workers will immediately moderate their wage demands in order to avoid unemployment. Inflation therefore falls immediately. So the conclusion is that the economy will always be on the vertical long run curve because economic agents perfectly adapt their expectations in the light of economic news.

key terms

Money illusion - when economic agents such as workers believe that changes in money values are the same as changes in real values despite inflation (or deflation) occurring at the time.

NAIRU, the non-accelerating inflation rate of unemployment - the natural rate of unemployment, the level of unemployment which can be sustained with a change in the inflation rate.

The Phillips curve - the line which shows that higher rates of unemployment are associated with lower rates of change of money wage rates and therefore inflation and vice versa.

Question 3

Table 87.1 *Unemployment and inflation*

	Unemployment, claimant count, millions	Inflation %
1988	2.4	4.9
1989	1.8	7.8
1990	1.7	9.4
1991	2.3	5.9
1992	2.8	3.8
1993	2.9	1.6
1994	2.6	2.5
1995	2.3	3.4
1996	2.1	2.4
1997	1.6	3.2
1998	1.4	3.4

Source: adapted from *Economic Trends Annual Supplement*, Office for National Statistics.

(a) Explain between what years shown in the data a normal short run Phillips curve relationship would seem to hold.

(b) (i) What is meant by the NAIRU?
(ii) Explain between what years the NAIRU might have fallen.

Applied economics

The Phillips curve from 1963

Between 1957, the date of publication of Phillips' original article, and 1965 the UK economy behaved in a way that the original Phillips curve would have predicted. In Figure 87.7, the points for 1963, 1964 and 1965 lie on the original Phillips curve. However, from 1967 combinations of unemployment and inflation rates moved to the right of the original curve. Indeed, rising inflation became associated with rising unemployment, contrary to the predictions of the Phillips curve which suggests a negative correlation between the two variables.

The expectations-augmented Phillips curve hypothesis would suggest that the downward sloping short run Phillips curve had shifted to the right because workers had increased their expectations of future inflation rates. They no longer suffered from money illusion and hence they took into account future price rises when bargaining for wage increases. Is there any evidence to suggest that workers ceased to suffer from money illusion from the mid-1960s onwards?

One factor must be that inflation from 1964 onwards was much higher than it had been over the previous 40 years. Apart from a brief period during the Korean War in the early 1950s, inflation had at worst been 1 or 2 per cent per annum. Therefore it was a reasonable assumption on the part of workers that money wage increases would roughly equal real wage increases. However, from 1964 onwards, inflation increased substantially, and by 1975 had peaked at 24.1 per cent. It

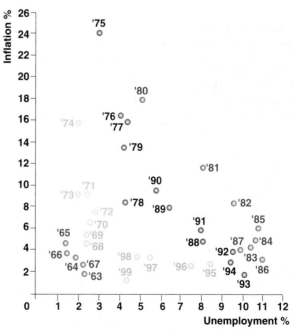

Source: adapted from *Economic Trends Annual Supplement*, Office for National Statistics

Figure 87.7 *Phillips curve data, 1963-1999*

would be surprising if workers had not lost their money illusion after 1964 given these trends.

Another factor must be that 1965 saw the

implementation of the first statutory prices and incomes policy (☞ unit 90). The Labour government of Harold Wilson announced that no wage increases could be awarded for a period of six months in order to curb rising inflation. This ensured that inflation and its control became a central issue in British politics. Workers could not help but become aware that inflation was important for the purchasing power of their wage packets.

The Edward Heath government of 1970-1974 positively encouraged trade unions in 1972-3 to settle for index-linked pay deals with employers as part of its prices and incomes policy. It believed that inflation would fall in the short term and that therefore such deals would produce lower pay rises than if unions had bargained on the basis of the current rate of inflation. In fact, rising world commodity prices, particularly of oil, made these deals inflationary.

During the 1970s and 1980s, it could be argued that trade unions bargained on the basis of 'RPI+' (the RPI, the Retail Price Index, is the most commonly used measure of inflation in the UK ☞ unit 28). If inflation was running at 10 per cent, then trade unions negotiated on the basis of securing 10 per cent plus a real pay increase.

This pattern of bargaining could lead to perverse effects. Assume the government attempted to reduce inflation by increasing interest rates (monetary policy) or increasing indirect taxes (to reduce aggregate demand through fiscal policy). Both of these in the short term have the effect of increasing the inflation rate

because both the mortgage interest rate and indirect tax rates are included in the RPI measure of inflation. Unions would then negotiate higher wage rises based on the higher RPI, which had in part been caused by government policy attempting to reduce inflation.

The **supply side reforms** (☞ unit 38) of the 1980s and 1990s helped break the link between wage increases and inflation. The move away from national collective bargaining, for instance, reduced the power of trade unions which had become skilled at using the expected rate of inflation as a bargaining tool in any negotiations. The prolonged recession of 1990-92 also helped psychologically to reduce the importance of inflation in wage negotiations. During this time, unemployment rose from 1.5 million to 3 million whilst inflation fell from 10 to 2 per cent.

To what extent is there a link between rising prices and unemployment in the UK?

Keeping a job became more important to many workers than securing a pay increase. During the 1990s, low inflation in the 2-4 per cent range further helped to reduce the importance of the inflation rate to wage bargaining. By 2000, it could be argued that money illusion had once again become the norm amongst workers and consumers.

These changes can be used to help explain the data shown in Figure 87.7. It could be argued that between 1988 and 1994, the economy was on a single short run Phillips curve. Between 1995 and 1999, however, the short run Phillips curve shifted backwards. With little change in inflation, unemployment as measured by the claimant count fell from 3 million to 1.5 million. This would imply that the long run vertical Phillips curve has been shifting backwards too as the natural rate of

unemployment, or NAIRU, has fallen. Some economists have argued that this was one of the benefits of the supply side reforms of the 1980s and 1990s. It could also be argued that the low inflation of the 1990s led to the reappearance of money illusion and that the economy is moving back to the pre-1965 Phillips curve position. Other economists argue that the data in Figure 87.7 shows that the natural rate of unemployment doesn't exist. A natural rate which falls from 3 million to 1.5 million in five years is scarcely believable. On this view, the high unemployment of the first half of the 1980s and 1990s was not an inevitable price which had to be paid to secure low inflation. If the government had pursued less deflationary policies, unemployment could have been lower with the same rate of inflation.

Unemployment and inflation in OECD countries

Table 87.2 *Inflation (percentage change on previous year)*

	United Kingdom	Germany	France	Italy	EU	United States	Japan	Major 7 OECD countries[1]	All OECD countries[2]
1990	9.5	2.7	3.6	6.1	5.4	5.4	3.1	5.0	7.0
1991	5.9	3.6	3.2	6.5	4.9	4.2	3.3	4.3	6.3
1992	3.7	5.1	2.4	5.3	4.3	3.0	1.7	3.1	5
1993	1.6	4.4	2.1	4.2	3.4	3.0	1.2	2.7	4.3
1994	2.5	2.8	1.7	3.9	2.9	2.6	0.7	2.3	5.0
1995	3.4	1.7	1.8	5.4	3.0	2.8	-0.1	2.4	5.6
1996	2.4	1.4	2.0	3.8	2.4	2.9	0.1	2.3	5.2
1997	3.1	1.9	1.2	1.8	1.9	2.3	1.7	2.1	4.5
1998	3.4	0.9	0.8	1.7	1.6	1.6	6.0	1.4	3.8

Table 87.3 *Unemployment rates (percentage of total labour force)*

	United Kingdom	Germany	France	Italy	EU	United States	Japan	Major 7 OECD countries[1]	All OECD countries[2]
1990	7.1	4.8	9.0	9.1	8.4	5.6	2.1	5.6	6.1
1991	8.8	4.2	9.5	8.8	8.7	6.8	2.1	6.3	6.8
1992	10.1	4.5	10.4	9.0	9.5	7.5	2.2	6.8	7.5
1993	10.5	7.9	11.7	10.3	10.7	6.9	2.5	7.3	8.2
1994	9.6	8.4	12.3	11.4	11.1	6.1	2.9	7.1	8.1
1995	8.7	8.2	11.7	11.9	10.7	5.6	3.2	6.8	7.7
1996	8.2	8.9	12.4	12.0	10.8	5.4	3.4	6.8	7.7
1997	7.0	9.9	12.3	12.0	10.6	4.9	3.4	6.6	7.4
1998	6.3	9.4	11.7	11.9	9.9	4.5	4.1	6.4	7.1

1. UK, Germany, France, Italy, USA, Japan and Canada.　　2. 29 countries.
Source: adapted from *Economic Outlook*, OECD.

1. **Distinguish between short run and long run Phillips curves.**
2. **Do the data suggest that Phillips curves exist in OECD countries?**

3. **To what extent can governments use demand management policies to reduce unemployment without affecting inflation?**

Unemployment and government policy

Summary

1. Demand management techniques can be used to reduce cyclical unemployment in the economy.
2. Voluntary unemployment is best tackled by a variety of supply side policies. Supply side economists would advocate measures such as improving job search information, reducing the benefit to wage ratio, training, abolishing minimum wages and increasing the mobility of workers.
3. The natural rate of unemployment can be reduced if long run aggregate supply in the economy grows.

Demand management

Unemployment can be classified into five types (☞ unit 86). If unemployment is Keynesian, or demand-deficient in nature (i.e. caused by too little spending in the economy), then it may be appropriate for government to use policies which lead to an increase in aggregate demand.

During the 1950s and 1960s, successive British governments used **demand management** techniques (☞ unit 81) to keep unemployment at extremely low levels by historical standards. If the economy was below full employment, the government intervened to raise aggregate demand and eliminate the output gap. The government could most easily change its own spending. It could also change consumption spending by changes in tax. Either of these measures would lead to an increase in the PSNCR and constitute a loosening of fiscal policy. The government could also loosen monetary policy, mainly by relaxing controls on the availability of credit in the economy (☞ unit 85). Similarly, if there was excess demand in the economy and inflationary pressures built up, the government would reduce aggregate demand by reducing the PSNCR and tightening credit controls.

The change in the budget deficit or surplus did not need to be of the same magnitude as the size of the output gap. This was because of the **multiplier** effect (☞ unit 33). For instance, if aggregate demand needed to be raised by £10 000 million and the multiplier were 2, then the government would only need to increase its spending by £5 000 million to return the economy to full employment.

Aggregate demand could be manipulated even if the government's budget deficit remained unchanged. If the government increased both government spending and taxation by the same amount, then aggregate demand would rise because of the **balanced budget multiplier effect**. This effect occurred because £100 of government spending would raise aggregate demand by £100. However, a £100 rise in taxes would not reduce aggregate demand by £100. This was because households would finance part of the £100 by saving less. So consumption might only fall by £90. A £100 rise in government spending, but a £90 fall in consumption because of higher taxes, would increase aggregate demand by £10 - the balanced budget multiplier effect.

The effects of demand management policies can be seen in Figure 88.1. A Keynesian aggregate supply curve is assumed (☞ unit 34). The economy is initially at A, below

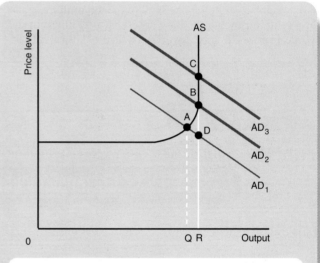

Figure 88.1 *Demand management*
According to Keynesians, expansionary fiscal or monetary policy can shift the AD curve to the right. If the economy is at A, at less than full employment, then an increased budget deficit could move the economy to B. If the economy is already at B, fiscal expansion will be purely inflationary.

the full employment level of output of OR. An increase in aggregate demand from AD_1 to AD_2 will restore the economy to full employment, albeit at some cost in terms of higher prices. However, a further increase in aggregate demand, from AD_2 to AD_3, will be purely inflationary, since the economy is already at full employment.

Keynesians today recognise that the demand management policies undertaken in the 1950s and 1960s were too simplistic and failed to take account of both inflation and the natural rate of unemployment. Despite this, modern Keynesians argue that **cyclical unemployment** can be tackled by fiscal policy. For instance, in a recession, it would be wrong for a government deliberately to set out to keep its budget balanced as happened in the 1930s. It should allow the **automatic stabilisers** (☞ unit 81) of reduced tax revenues and increased spending on unemployment benefit to break the fall in output. It could also use **active fiscal policy**, deliberately increasing public spending and cutting taxes, to speed up the recovery. Governments, though, need to be very careful not to overstimulate the economy given the inflation and balance of payments constraints (☞ unit 92). With high natural rates of unemployment as well, demand management policies can only be part of the solution to reducing unemployment rates.

Classical economists argue that the long run aggregate supply curve is vertical (☞ unit 34). The economy will always revert to its full employment level. Demand management policies are therefore at best unnecessary and at worst seriously damaging to the economy. If nothing else, expansionary policy will always lead to higher inflation than would otherwise be the case. In Figure 88.1, with an aggregate demand curve of AD_1 and the economy initially at A, there would be a movement back to full employment at D if there were no government intervention. Active demand management, which shifts the aggregate demand curve to AD_2, results in the same output level but higher prices at B.

Question 1

In his 1959 Budget, the Chancellor of the Exchequer, Heathcoat Amory, substantially reduced taxes. He justified this in the following words:
'The prospect for home production as I have set it out does not represent a full enough use of the capital resources which have been created in recent years. Nor can we be content with the possibility that unemployment might continue at around the present levels ... (However) we must at all costs make it our business not to return to an overload on the economy, which would make a resumption of inflation inevitable. At the present time, however, this is clearly not an immediate danger.'

(a) Using an aggregate demand and supply diagram, explain why the Chancellor cut taxes.
(b) Would his policy have been any different if inflation had been rising at the time?
(c) The economy grew very strongly in the second half of 1959 and in 1960. Over the next three years the government was to restrict the growth of demand both through fiscal and monetary policies. Using a diagram, suggest why the government adopted deflationary policies.

Supply side policies

Economists are divided about the best way to tackle cyclical unemployment. However, they agree that demand management policies cannot be used to tackle other types of unemployment. These need to be reduced by **supply side policies**.

Frictional unemployment If unemployment is short term, then there is a variety of measures which the government could employ to reduce this type of unemployment. One is to increase the flow of information to unemployed workers by providing better employment services. In the UK, for instance, this would mean more spending on Jobcentres. If unemployed workers can be matched to vacancies more quickly, they will spend less time on the dole and frictional unemployment will fall.

Another measure would be to reduce or withdraw benefits to the short term unemployed. For instance, if all benefits were cut after three months, rather than, say, six months or a year, there would be a greater incentive for unemployed workers to find work quickly. Increased benefit rights and increased redundancy payments can only act as incentives for the short term unemployed to spend longer searching for jobs.

Measures to combat structural unemployment, such as increasing the mobility of labour between regions or industries might also help reduce frictional unemployment.

Question 2

In 1995, the government passed legislation which would replace unemployment benefit, a non-means tested benefit, by a new Jobseeker's allowance. Unemployment benefit was payable for up to 12 months to workers. Those receiving the benefit could continue receiving it even if they turned down jobs which they considered were unsuitable for them.

The Jobseeker's allowance, in contrast, would last only 6 months before being means tested. Jobseekers must take any job offered, regardless of the level of pay. If they didn't, then they would lose their entitlement to the allowance. Anyone failing to look for work under a jobseeker's agreement, a contract which the unemployed person must sign, or refusing to be directed into a job on offer, could have benefit entitlement withdrawn for up to 26 weeks, with only discretionary payments available where a claimant could prove hardship. Any person judged to be 'voluntarily' unemployed would have their entitlement to the allowance withdrawn. They would then be forced to rely on hardship payments for a possible 26 weeks.

It was estimated that the government would save £400 million a year through the change as fewer workers became entitled to receive the jobseeker's allowance compared to the old unemployment benefit.

(a) How might the introduction of the jobseeker's allowance have helped to reduce frictional unemployment?
(b) Discuss whether it would have had an impact on any other type of unemployment.

Structural unemployment Longer term structural unemployment is difficult to deal with. If the unemployment is regional, with some regions having much higher unemployment rates than other regions, then Keynesian economists would argue that the government should give financial incentives for firms to move to those areas. All countries in the EU, for instance, have regional funds which they use to lure large companies to set up in high unemployment regions. Spending on infrastructure, such as motorways, or on human capital such as retraining, can also lure firms into a region. Classical economists would tend to rely more on free market forces. They argue that high unemployment regions are likely to be characterised by low land and labour costs. This, in itself, should attract inward investment. They also argue that regional funds tend to pay out money to firms which would have moved into the region anyway . They are therefore largely a waste of taxpayers' money.

If the unemployment is industrial, caused for instance by the decline of a traditional industry, then Keynesian economists would argue that governments should spend money on retraining workers from those industries. Declining industries also tend to create local unemployment blackspots and therefore an injection of regional funds can be helpful too. Classical economists would again tend to rely more on free market forces. In particular, they would suggest that large redundancy benefits and high unemployment benefits will prolong any search for work. They would therefore suggest lower benefits and cutting benefits to workers who refuse to take lower paid jobs.

Some unemployed workers remain unemployed because of their length of time out of work. The longer the time spent out of the workforce, the lower will be a worker's human capital. On the other hand, employment creates human capital if only because of the addition made through experience of work. There is also considerable evidence that employers sift through applications on the basis of length of unemployment. The long term unemployed are unlikely even to be invited for interview. In one sense, this discrimination represents rational behaviour on the part of employers because unemployment destroys human capital. Some economists have argued that employers who take on the long term unemployed should receive a subsidy, such as a proportion of the benefits that the unemployed worker would have received if he or she had remained unemployed.

Classical or real wage unemployment As has already been mentioned, cutting real wage unemployment can be accomplished by cutting unemployment benefits. This gives a greater incentive for workers to take on low paid work. Paying employers to take on unemployed workers would also cut real wage unemployment. This is because at given wage rates, the demand for the long term unemployed is less than its supply. Equally, the government giving benefits to low paid workers cuts real wage unemployment because those employed workers might otherwise not be willing to take on that low paid work.

Classical economists would also argue that reducing trade union power and abolishing minimum wages are solutions to real wage unemployment. Trade unions act to increase the real wages of workers. Without unions, wages would be lower and therefore employers would be willing to take on more workers. Equally, minimum wage legislation prevents employers from creating jobs below the minimum wage and hence unemployment is increased.

The natural rate of unemployment

The supply side measures outlined so far are only some of the measures which can be taken to reduce the **natural rate of unemployment** (☞ unit 86). They tend to be measures which make existing labour markets function more efficiently. However, another way of reducing the natural rate of unemployment is to increase the growth rate of the whole economy. This assumes that increased economic activity will increase the number of jobs in the economy and therefore reduce the rate of unemployment.

Classical economists believe that tax rates are crucial to economic decision making. Hence, cuts in the marginal rate of income, social security or profit taxes will lead to significant increases in incentives to work, take risks and increase wealth. Policies such as **privatisation, increased competition** and **deregulation** will also increase the productive potential of the economy according to classical economists. Keynesian economists tend to emphasise more the role of investment in both physical and human capital and policies which governments can adopt to increase investment in the economy.

Question 3

Ray Brown is 20 years old with no qualifications. He has been out of work for more than six months and has been turned down for eight jobs. He wants to be a television scriptwriter. He is attending his first interview with a personal adviser at the Brixton Hill Jobcentre in South London. This interview is the first part of the 'gateway' to the New Deal, the government's welfare to work programme for the long term unemployed.

The gateway period, which lasts four months, is designed to make him more employable through interviews and job-seeking training. At the end of the four months, he will be offered one of four options for a further six months: a private sector job, a place on an environmental taskforce, work in the voluntary sector or more education and training.

For the time being, his personal adviser is keen to get him into work. She offers him warehouse jobs at slightly above the minimum wage.

More than 40 per cent of New Dealers find a permanent unsubsidised job while they are in the gateway. However, critics argue that this does little for the longer term employment prospects of these individuals. 'The gateway is failing to prepare people in gaining the skills and confidence that they need to enter the world of work' according to one report.

In Lambeth, another deprived area of London, more than one third of men and just under one quarter of women aged between 18 and 24 have no formal educational qualifications. As many as one quarter live alone without any domestic support network. More than 30 per cent of a sample survey said they had experienced arrest, although only 4.5 per cent had been to prison.

Source: adapted from the *Financial Times*, 15.6.1999.

(a) To what extent can government employment agencies and training schemes for the unemployed, such as the New Deal, reduce structural unemployment? Use evidence from the passage in your answer.

Applied economics

Unemployment policy in the UK, 1950-2000

The experience of the 1930s and 1940s

During the period of the Great Depression in the 1930s, unemployment in the UK rose to 13 per cent of the labour force. Some regions were worse affected than others, and many industrial towns had unemployment rates exceeding 25 per cent. The poverty that unemployment caused scarred this generation of workers. Therefore, when the ideas of John Maynard Keynes, put forward throughout the 1930s, most famously in his *General Theory of Employment, Interest and Money*, held out the promise that the problem of unemployment could be solved by increasing government spending, they were eagerly taken up in the post-war period. In 1944, a White Paper stated that it would become a government policy objective to secure a 'high and stable level of employment' after the war was over. The experience of the war itself, when unemployment fell to almost zero, was confirmation for many that government could achieve this aim of low unemployment.

1950-65, the era of demand management

The 1950s and early 1960s saw governments using Keynesian demand management policies with increasing confidence. Unemployment throughout the period remained low by historical standards, averaging only 1.7 per cent. When unemployment rose in a recession, the government would increase its spending, reduce taxes and loosen credit controls. When the economy overheated, with low unemployment but rising inflation and a worsening current account balance, the government would reduce aggregate demand by raising taxes, reducing government spending and tightening credit controls.

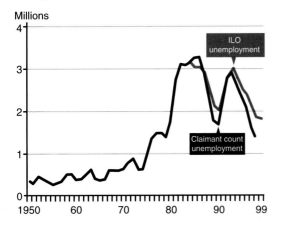

Figure 88.2 *Unemployment, claimant count and ILO unemployed, UK millions*

For instance, in 1963, with unemployment rising to nearly half a million, a post-war peak, and growth faltering, the Conservative government of the day put forward a highly reflationary Budget. Unemployment fell sharply to 300 000 by 1965 but the current account went into deficit, giving rise to exchange rate crises for the pound.

Structural unemployment was a problem throughout the period. It was caused mainly by the decline of traditional primary industries such as coal mining, heavy manufacturing such as shipbuilding, and certain other manufacturing industries such as textiles. These industries were concentrated in the North of England, Scotland, Wales and Northern Ireland. Hence, structural unemployment manifested itself primarily as regional unemployment. The government tackled this through a range of regional incentives to firms setting up in high unemployment regions (☞ unit 38).

1966-1979, the growing disenchantment with demand management

By the mid-1960s, governments were finding it increasingly frustrating that they could not achieve both low unemployment and low inflation combined with a current account surplus. It was recognised that demand management techniques had their limitations. In 1966, the Labour government under Harold Wilson imposed a **prices and incomes policy** (☞ unit 90). The aim of the policy was to reduce inflation without having to deflate the economy through higher taxes or reduced government spending. Nevertheless, deflationary fiscal unemployment designed to combat the current account deficit, and a rising **natural rate of unemployment**, led to a near doubling of unemployment between 1966 and 1967 and it remained at a post-war high of half a million till 1970.

The incoming Conservative government under Edward Heath was quickly faced by a recession in the economy. In the winter of 1971-72, unemployment gradually increased to nearly 1 million. The government felt forced to do a U-turn in its free market policies and in 1972, the Chancellor, Anthony Barber, gave a large fiscal boost to the economy in his March Budget - his 'dash for growth' as it was called at the time. This was to be the last time that any government put the control of unemployment as its main economic priority. In the resulting boom, growth accelerated to near record levels, unemployment fell back towards the half a million level, but inflation went out of control and the current account went into a large deficit. A vicious twist to the Barber boom was then given by the quadrupling of oil prices in 1973-74 (☞ unit 8). The government lost an election in February 1974 and the incoming Labour government, still committed to the 1944 objective of low unemployment, failed to provide any coherent policy response to the huge problems imposed by the **stagflation** of the time.

The following year, however, the government made the control of inflation its main economic priority, with the recognition that the current account had to be returned to balance in the medium term.

Deflationary fiscal and monetary policies were combined with a prices and incomes policy to reduce aggregate demand and force down inflation rates. The commitment to full employment was abandoned, at least in the short term, although the Labour Party continued to see this as a long term objective. This enormous change in thinking, which was led by a revival of interest in monetarist ideas, is perhaps best summarised in a speech given by the Labour Prime Minister of the day, Jim Callaghan, to his Party Conference in 1976. He said: 'We used to think that you could just spend your way out of a recession, and increase employment, by cutting taxes and boosting government spending. I tell you in all candour that that option no longer exists, and that in so far as it ever did exist, it worked by injecting inflation into the economy.'

Unemployment rose quickly from 600 000 in 1974 to nearly 1.5 million in 1978. The government had little coherent response to this rise in unemployment. Youth unemployment was tackled by introducing government work and training schemes, similar to what is now the New Deal. A variety of make-work schemes were offered to adult unemployed workers, which eventually became the adult training schemes of today. However, the rise in unemployment was considered a necessary price to pay for the fall in inflation, which fell from 24 per cent in 1975 to 8 per cent in 1978. Nevertheless, the government was unwilling to see unemployment rise further. In 1978-79, against a backdrop of a reflationary fiscal and monetary policy, it attempted to bring inflation down further by tightening the pay ceiling in its incomes policy. Workers rejected this, and in the 'winter of discontent' of 1978-79 a series of major damaging strikes which secured large pay rises for the workers concerned ripped the incomes policy apart. The government was left with no credible anti-inflationary policy.

1979-2000, the abandonment of the objective of full employment

Labour lost the election of June 1979 and the Conservative Party came into power under Margaret Thatcher committed to a complete abandonment of many of the policies which had characterised the post-war period. The government believed that its main objective should be to control inflation through the pursuit of sound monetary policy. It should also reduce state involvement in the economy in order to allow private sector markets to work more efficiently. Sound money and less government intervention would provide higher economic growth and greater prosperity. In the short term, a price that might have to be paid to achieve this was a further rise in unemployment. The government abandoned any commitment to keeping unemployment low or stable. Unemployment would settle down at the NAIRU, the non-accelerating inflation rate of unemployment (☞ unit 87). This was the natural rate of unemployment at which stable prices could be maintained.

The government abandoned any attempt to manipulate aggregate demand through fiscal or monetary policy. Demand management was seen to be counter-productive given that the long run aggregate supply curve in the economy was vertical. Short run falls in unemployment could be secured by moving down the Phillips curve and up the short run aggregate supply curve. However, the consequent boom could only lead to a following recession in which all the gains in unemployment would be lost again. The only way to reduce unemployment was through supply side policies designed to reduce the natural rate of unemployment.

The incoming government in 1979 immediately began to tackle rising inflation by sharply increasing interest rates. With a rising pound as well, caused by high interest rates and North Sea oil, the economy quickly went into a recession. The recession of 1980-82 was the worst recession since the Great Depression. Unemployment rose to over 3 million, almost matching the unemployment rate of the 1930s. A traditional Keynesian response would have been to reduce taxes and increase public spending in 1981 to get the economy out of recession. The Chancellor at the time, Geoffrey Howe, actually increased taxes in his 1981 budget in order to reduce the PSNCR, thus putting less pressure on interest rates, which are affected by the size of government borrowing.

Unemployment remained stubbornly high between 1982 and 1986, hardly changing at all from the 3 million figure. The government then made a fundamental policy mistake, pursuing too lax a fiscal and monetary policy in the mistaken belief that their supply side reforms could now enable the economy to grow above its trend rate for the post-war period. In the ensuing Lawson boom, unemployment fell rapidly, from 3.3 million in 1986 to 1.6 million in 1990. However, the expansion of aggregate demand which caused this fall in unemployment also led to a small build up of inflationary pressures. In 1988, the government reacted savagely by doubling interest rates. The economy slowly went into recession. Deflationary pressures were increased when the government deliberately entered the Exchange Rate Mechanism (ERM), the precursor to European Monetary Union and the creation of the euro, at a very high rate of exchange in 1990. Its policy was to use a high value of the pound to put further downward pressure on inflation. It certainly was deflationary because exports were hit whilst imports rose. This added to the rise in unemployment already happening because of high interest rates. This exchange rate policy turned out to be counter-productive. By 1991, it was clear that inflation had returned to an acceptably low level. The government wanted to relax monetary policy but it was unable to reduce interest rates by as much as it wanted because by this stage the pound was relatively weak.

Larger cuts in interest rates would have led to substantial selling of the pound. This would have pushed its value below the minimum set for the ERM. Failure to reduce interest rates sufficiently through 1991 and most of 1992 prolonged the recession and helped increase unemployment further. In September 1992, the foreign exchange markets drove the value of the pound below its minimum ERM value and the UK was forced out of the ERM. With no exchange rate value to protect, the government quickly cut interest rates from 10 per cent in September 1992 to 5.25 per cent in February 1994.

The recession would have been made even worse if the government had attempted to balance its budget. In the early 1990s, as recession hit its tax revenues and increased its spending on welfare benefits, the PSNCR grew rapidly in size. The government used its increased budget deficit as an automatic stabiliser.

The subsequent recovery was relatively fast. Unemployment peaked at 2.9 million in 1993, but then fell rapidly. With above-trend economic growth, unemployment on a claimant count basis fell steadily. By 1998, it had fallen to 1.3 million, lower than its previous trough of 1.5 million in 1990. What's more it continued to fall very slowly.

During this period, the government tightened its fiscal stance, increasing taxes from 1995 in an attempt to balance its budget. It then used interest rates to maintain low inflation. However, it could be argued that, unlike in the first half of the 1980s, aggregate demand was allowed to expand at a fast enough rate to bring down cyclical unemployment. Unemployment also fell because of the long term effects of the supply side reforms of the 1980s and 1990s.

The Conservative governments from 1979 were convinced that supply side reforms were essential if the UK was to regain international competitiveness and perform as well as the European and Japanese economies. Supply side reforms were designed to increase efficiency at all levels in the economy. In the long term, this should lead to an increase in employment. However, in the short term, many supply side policies led to job losses. For instance, the privatisation process led to a shake-out of jobs in the privatised industries, the result of increased **productive efficiency**. To reduce unemployment, these needed to be more than matched by new jobs created in the economy. The government attempted to create an 'enterprise culture' (☞ unit 38), particularly encouraging the growth of small firms in the economy. It had a positive attitude to inward investment, for instance from Japanese companies. This was in marked contrast to the attitude of some European governments which saw inward investment as being harmful to their domestic industries. From the late 1980s, there was considerable emphasis put on education and training in order to increase levels of human capital in the economy.

Creating a climate where businesses could set up, expand and earn high profits was seen as essential for higher economic growth and therefore lower unemployment. But equally, the government believed that high unemployment could only be tackled through reform of the labour market. Trade unions were seen as driving up wages and creating uncertainty through constant industrial action, thus destroying jobs. So the government introducing sweeping trade union reforms which broke the power of the union movement. Government legislation which gave protection to women and children in the workplace was repealed in order to 'free' markets. Wages councils, which set minimum wages in low pay industries, and which were claimed to create unemployment, were finally abolished in 1994. Encouragement was also given to employers to reduce employment costs by making it easier to cut staff when necessary. There was a marked increase in the numbers of workers working part-time or on fixed term contracts. These moves to create a **'flexible' labour market** were driven by a belief that jobs could be created and prosperity increased if the UK could become a lower wage, less regulated economy than her main trading partners, particularly in Europe. The rapid fall in unemployment in 1993 and 1994 as the economy came out of recession was claimed by some economists to be the direct result of this new flexibility in the labour market. Firms which fired labour as the economy went into recession were confident enough to hire again as the economy came out of recession.

The Labour government elected in 1997 did not change the direction of unemployment policy. Macro-economic policy was still directed at maintaining low inflation and unemployment was allowed to find its own level consistent with this objective. For instance, when the value of the pound rose in 1997 and stayed high, manufacturing industry was hit and unemployment rose in areas still highly dependent on manufacturing jobs. The government, through the Bank of England, did not cut interest rates to bring down the value of the pound in order to help manufacturing industry.

However, micro-economic policy initiatives were launched which reinforced previous policies. In particular, the New Deal was launched. This was an extension of training and work-experience programmes which had been going on since 1978. What made the New Deal different was that it was funded more generously than previous programmes. It also explicitly recognised that many of the long term unemployed lacked the skills to gain and hold onto permanent jobs. Hence, a heavy emphasis was placed on gaining skills. The New Deal was set against part of a wider programme to improve educational standards for all young people. The government also instituted a series of reforms of the tax and benefit system to reduce marginal rates of tax and withdrawal of benefit for the low paid. This increased work incentives for groups particularly vulnerable to unemployment.

Some economists argued that other Labour initiatives helped increase unemployment. In particular, new rights for trade unions to gain recognition in the workplace in 1998, acceptance of the EU Social Charter which increased workers rights and the introduction of a minimum wage in 1999 all increased costs of employment to firms. The extent to which these measures increased unemployment remains to be seen.

Unemployment policy

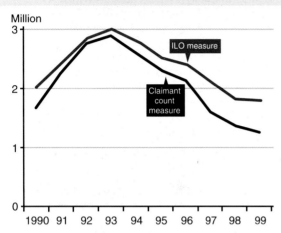

Figure 88.3 *Unemployment, claimant count[1] and ILO unemployed[2]*
1. Annual average. 2. Spring each year.
Source: adapted from *Economic Trends Annual Supplement*, Office for National Statistics.

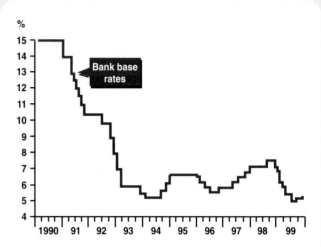

Figure 88.4 *Bank base rates*
Source: adapted from *Economic Trends Annual Supplement*, Office for National Statistics.

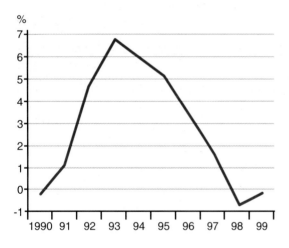

Figure 88.5 *PSNCR as a percentage of GDP*
Source: adapted from *Economic Trends Annual Supplement*, Office for National Statistics.

The Budget, 1999

From October 1999:
• there will be a minimum income guarantee of £200 per week for full-time working families;
• no family will pay net income tax until they earn more than £235;
• National Insurance contributions will be eliminated for about 900 000 people earning too little even to pay income tax;
• there will be a cut in National Insurance contributions for low earning self-employed people from April 2000;
• there will be a new 10p rate of income tax from April 1999 which halves the tax bill for 1.8 million taxpayers;
• there will be a cut in the basic rate of income tax to 22p from April 2000 to reward work and ensure working families are better off.
Source: adapted from HM Treasury, The Red Book.

Claimant compulsion

All new benefit claimants, except the bereaved and severely disabled, will be legally compelled to accept an obligation to find work or face losing their entitlement to benefit, the government announced yesterday. Under the plan, new benefit claimants would be interviewed by a personal adviser to establish their individual needs. They would be given guidance on employment, training or rehabilitation needs as well as being made aware of their responsibilities to look for work if they wish to claim benefit.

Source: adapted from the *Financial Times*, 14.1.1999.

New Deal figures show uneven success rate

The government's welfare-to-work programme is having an uneven impact across the country according to figures published by government. The figures indicate the New Deal has had more success in Scotland, Wales and the west of England than in London, the South-East and the Midlands. Part of the difference seems to be that areas where private sector organisations are taking the lead role in providing the programme have done less well than those administered by public employment service partnerships. The Unemployment Unit & Youthaid are concerned about the long period young people spend in the 'gateway', the assessment and initial training part of the programme, before being offered one of the four 6 month options - a private sector job placement, training and education, or a position in the voluntary sector or the environmental taskforce.

Source: adapted from the *Financial Times*, 15.12.1998.

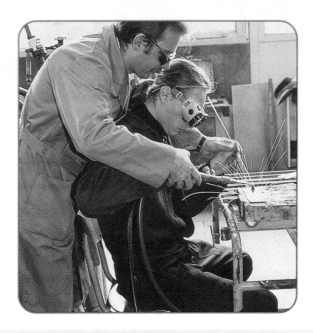

Inward investment

By any standards, the UK's performance in the global battle for foreign direct investment is outstanding. With just one per cent of the world's population, Britain gets nearly 8 per cent of the world's cross-border direct investment. One key reason for this is Britain's membership of the European Union. Many of the companies that locate here from North America and Asia do so because they gain easy access to EU markets. But why not France or Germany then? Some argue that the UK has a high reputation for innovation and technological and financial expertise. Others point to the generally business-friendly tax system, culture and regulatory system. The liberalised telecommunications market, the availability of relatively cheap skilled labour and the English language also help to make the UK an attractive destination for capital.

Source: adapted from the *Financial Times*, 14.10.1999.

1. **Briefly outline the different policies described in the data which have been used by government to reduce unemployment.**

2. **Compare the effectiveness of these different policies in reducing (a) structural unemployment and (b) cyclical unemployment.**

Summary

1. Some Keynesians believe that excess demand in the economy is the principal cause of inflation - the demand-pull theory of inflation.
2. Other Keynesians argue that inflation is primarily cost-push in nature.
3. Monetarists argue that inflation is caused by excessive increases in the money supply.
4. If inflation is caused by shifts in the aggregate demand or aggregate supply curves, it can only persist if it is either validated or accommodated by an increase in the money supply.

Demand-pull inflation

Keynesians have traditionally argued that inflation occurs because of changes in **real** variables in the economy. One important Keynesian theory is that inflation is caused by excess demand in the economy. The DEMAND-PULL THEORY of inflation says that inflation will result if there is too much spending in relation to output. In an individual market, like the market for bananas, excess demand will lead to a rise in price. The same is true for a whole economy. If aggregate demand exceeds aggregate supply, the price level will rise and therefore there will be inflation.

Figure 89.1 shows an aggregate demand curve with a Keynesian aggregate supply curve (☞ unit 34). The economy is at full employment at income Y_F. Assume that there is a rise in aggregate demand from AD_1 to AD_2. This could be the result of an increase in consumer confidence which raises autonomous consumer spending. Investment might rise because the rate of return on capital increases. The government might increase its spending. Alternatively, there might be a rise in exports because of strong economic growth in other countries. The result of these increases in real expenditure is a rise in both output and inflation. Output rises from OA to OB whilst the price level rises from OE to OF. Rising output will lead to a fall in unemployment. Falling unemployment accompanied by rising inflation is the **Phillips curve** relationship (☞ unit 87).

If the economy is already at full employment, with the aggregate demand curve at AD_3, then a rise in real expenditure which shifts the aggregate demand curve to AD_4 will lead only to a rise in inflation with no rise in output or decrease in unemployment. The Phillips curve then becomes vertical.

Policy makers today attempt to measure excess demand through output gaps (☞ unit 26). The output gap is the difference between the actual level of national income and a prediction of what it ought to be given its trend rate of growth in recent years. There is excess demand when the output gap is positive, i.e. actual national income is above its trend level. However, there can be demand-pull inflation even when the output gap is negative. As Figure 89.1 suggests, demand-pull inflationary pressures increase the nearer the output gap approaches zero, corresponding to the full employment level of income. For instance, the output gap may be negative overall, but certain industries or certain regions may be experiencing excess demand. So the South East of England and the service sector may be overheating when there is still excess capacity in the North East of England and in manufacturing industries. The

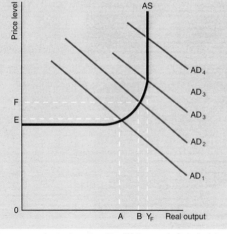

Figure 89.1 *Demand-pull inflation*
A rise in aggregate demand when the economy is at less than full employment will result in an increase in both prices and output. If the economy is at full employment, increases in aggregate demand simply lead to increases in inflation.

Question 1

Table 89.1 *Excess demand and inflation, UK*

	Real GDP % change	Unemployment %	Inflation %
1970	2.3	2.6	6.5
1971	1.4	2.6	9.2
1972	3.5	2.9	7.5
1973	5.9	2.0	9.1
1974	-0.6	2.1	15.9
1975	-2.1	3.1	24.1
1976	4.0	4.2	16.5
1977	2.2	4.4	15.8
1978	3.5	4.4	8.3

Source: adapted from *Economic Trends Annual Supplement*, Office for National Statistics.

(a) Outline a demand-pull theory of inflation.
(b) To what extent do the data support a demand-pull theory of inflation?

excess demand in the South East and in services will
generate inflation throughout the economy even if other
regions or industries are depressed.

Cost-push inflation

A second Keynesian theory of inflation is the COST-PUSH
theory of inflation. This argues that inflation is caused by
changes in the supply-side of the economy, which increase
costs of production. There are four major sources of
increased costs.
- Wages and salaries. They account for about 70 per cent
  of national income and hence increases in wages are
  normally the single most important cause of increases in
  costs of production.
- Imported goods. An increase in the price of finished
  manufactured imports, such as television sets or cars,
  will lead directly to an increase in the price level. An
  increase in the price of imported semi-manufactured
  goods and raw materials, used as component parts of
  domestically produced manufactured goods, will feed
  through indirectly via an increase in the price of
  domestically produced goods.
- Profits. Firms can raise their prices to increase their
  profit margins. The more price inelastic the demand for
  their goods, the less will such behaviour result in a fall in
  demand for their products.
- Taxes. Government can raise indirect tax rates or reduce
  subsidies, thus increasing prices.

  There has been a number of occasions in the past when
there was a significant rise in prices due to an increase in one
of these costs. For instance, all Western economies suffered
sharp rises in prices after the four-fold increase in the price of
oil in 1973-4.

However, Keynesian economists have argued that a cost-
push spiral can develop which leads to a long term cycle of
inflation. Consider a developed economy with zero inflation
and few natural resources. International commodity prices
of products such as oil, gas and coal increase by 50 per cent in
one year. Domestic prices rise by 10 per cent as a result.
Workers will now be 10 per cent worse off in real terms. So
they will press for higher wages. If in the past they have
become accustomed to receive a 2 per cent increase in real
wages per year, they will be prepared to settle for 12 per cent.
Firms pay the 12 per cent and pass on the increase in their
costs in the form of higher prices. This fuels inflation. The
following year, trade unions will once again fight for pay

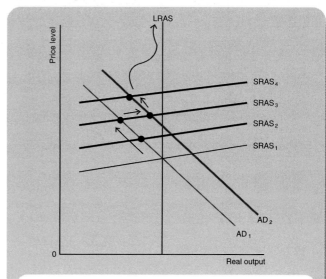

Figure 89.3 *Cost-push inflation*
*An initial rise in costs leads to a chain of wage increases and
increases in demand which feed back to increases in costs. Hence,
the short run equilibrium level of prices in the economy is
constantly moving upwards.*

increases of 2 per cent plus the rate of inflation. In the
meantime, the profits of firms will have been declining in
real terms. So firms are likely to attempt to increase their
profit margins in money terms, again fuelling inflation. This
process, shown in Figure 89.2, is called a WAGE-PRICE
SPIRAL or sometimes a COST-PUSH SPIRAL.

This wage-price spiral can also be seen in Figure 89.3. An
initial price shock, say from a large increase in oil prices,
shifts the short run aggregate supply curve up from $SRAS_1$ to
$SRAS_2$. With higher prices, workers demand higher wages
which employers concede. This pushes the short run

Question 2

Table 89.2 *Costs and prices, UK*

			Percentage change
	Average weekly earnings	Import prices	Retail Price Index
1970	12	4	6.5
1971	11	5	9.2
1972	13	5	7.5
1973	14	28	9.1
1974	18	46	15.9
1975	27	14	24.1
1976	16	22	16.5
1977	9	16	15.8
1978	13	4	8.3

Source: adapted from *Economic Trends Annual Supplement*, Office for
National Statistics.

(a) Outline a theory of cost-push inflation.
(b) To what extent do the data support the view that
    inflation is mainly cost-push in origin?

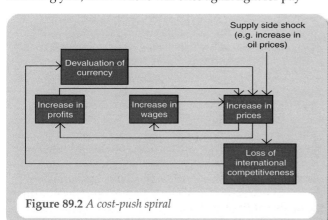

Figure 89.2 *A cost-push spiral*

aggregate supply curve up even further to SRAS₃. The increase in wages leads to an increase in aggregate demand which shifts the aggregate demand curve to the right from AD₁ to AD₂. This further raises the price level. So workers again demand higher wage increases which employers concede. So the short run aggregate supply curve shifts up again to SRAS₄. And so it goes on, with wage rises fuelling both increases in costs to firms, hence shifting the SRAS curve upwards, and fuelling increases in aggregate demand.

Keynesian economists differ in their views of whether the spiral is explosive, with inflation increasing over time, as is the case in Figure 89.3. They also differ as to the causes of the cost-push inflation. Some point out that, for the UK for instance, all the major bouts of inflation since 1918 have been started by large increases in the price of imports. Others say that increases in trade union militancy can cause the initial supply side shock which starts the inflationary spiral. Others argue that cost-push inflation is inevitable in a modern economy because of the struggle between workers and capitalists. Both wish to increase their share of national income. Workers force firms to give inflationary pay increases whilst firms increase prices so as to increase their profit margins. There is no solution to this struggle and therefore inflation is bound to be endemic in a modern industrialised society.

The monetarist explanation

Monetarists believe that inflation is demand-pull in nature. However, they argue that changes in the real economy cannot lead to sustained inflation. Only increases in the money supply will fuel demand-pull inflation. As Milton Friedman put it, 'inflation is always and everywhere a monetary phenomenon'.

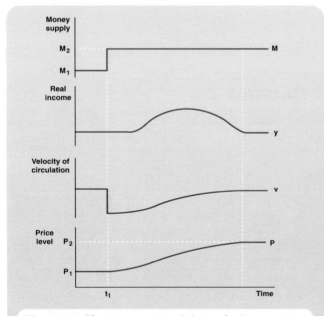

Figure 89.4 *The monetary transmission mechanism*
An initial increase in the money supply from M₁ to M₂ leads to an immediate fall in V, the velocity of circulation of money. Then money begins to be spent, raising y and V. The rise in spending also leads to demand-pull inflation. With P rising, real income will eventually begin to fall. At the final equilibrium, V and y return to their initial levels, but P is now higher.

This view can be explained using the Fisher formulation of the **quantity theory of money**:

$$MV \equiv PT$$

where M is the money supply, V is the velocity of circulation of money, P is the price level and T the number of transactions over a period of time. In the short run, increases in M will feed through to higher levels of transactions (i.e. national income will rise and unemployment is likely to fall), and a fall in V. This is known as the MONETARY TRANSMISSION MECHANISM. But in the long run, with V constant, increases in M over and above the rate of real growth in the economy (the change in T) will feed through to changes in P (☞ unit 84).

This transmission mechanism is illustrated in Figure 89.4. At a point in time t_1, there is an increase in the money supply from M_1 to M_2. The immediate effect is a fall in the velocity of circulation, but as time goes on, this money begins to be spent, leading to a rise in real output and income, y. This in turn leads to demand-pull inflation and prices begin to rise. Rising prices lead to less real spending as consumers can now afford to buy less with their money. y begins to fall and equilibrium is restored when y and V are back to their original levels. In the meantime, prices have risen from P_1 to P_2.

The monetary transmission mechanism can be analysed in more depth using the concepts of the demand for and supply of money. Assume that the money market starts off in equilibrium with the demand for money equal to the supply of money (☞ unit 82). Then assume that, for some reason such as the government wanting to reduce interest rates in order to reduce unemployment, there is an increase in the money supply. Disequilibrium in the money market will now be present. The money supply will be greater than the demand for money. For instance, banks are likely to be holding excess supplies of money. They will respond by increasing their lending to households and firms. Two things will now happen.

- Households and firms, having borrowed more money, will spend it on physical assets. They will buy cars, holidays, kitchens, new equipment and new premises.
- Households and firms will also buy non-monetary financial assets. For instance, they will buy stocks and shares. Greater demand will increase the price of financial assets and this in turn will push down yields and interest rates. After all, if there is more money being saved, borrowers don't need to offer such attractive returns, such as interest rates, to attract funds. A fall in the rate of interest will in itself lead to an increase in the level of consumption and investment.

So an increase in the money supply will result both directly and indirectly in a rise in the level of aggregate demand in the economy. This is known as the monetary transmission mechanism - the mechanism through which a change in the money supply affects the real economy. Some monetarist economists even calculate **money multipliers** (not to be confused with credit multipliers used in creation of credit theory). The money multiplier is the number of times an increase in the money supply is multiplied to give the final increase in national income. Many monetarists argue that the money multiplier is large. Hence, small

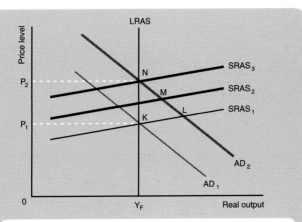

Figure 89.5 *An increase in the money supply*
An increase in the money supply will shift the aggregate demand curve from AD₁ to AD₂. After an initial rise in output, shown by the movement from K to L, the economy will return to long run equilibrium at N. Prices have risen but output remains unchanged.

Consider Figure 89.5. Monetarist or classical economists would argue that the long run aggregate supply curve is vertical. The equilibrium level of output is the full employment level Y_F and the initial price level is P_1. An increase in the money supply shifts the aggregate demand curve to the right from AD_1 to AD_2. Initially the economy moves up the short run aggregate supply curve $SRAS_1$ from K to L. But in the longer run, with increased prices and over-full employment, workers will demand and gain wage rate increases which will push the short run aggregate supply curve up to $SRAS_2$ and then to $SRAS_3$. N is the new long run equilibrium point where aggregate demand is once again equal to long run aggregate supply. Output, having initially risen, has returned to its long run full employment level. But prices have risen from P_1 to P_2.

Keynesian analysis suggests that the initial shift in the aggregate demand curve from an increase in the money supply is relatively small. Hence, the final increase in prices is relatively low. Monetarists would argue that changes in monetary values, such as the money supply

changes in the money supply produce large shifts in aggregate demand. Keynesians on the other hand argue that the money multiplier is very small. They argue that physical assets are a poor substitute for financial assets such as money. Therefore an increase in the money supply will mainly affect holdings of financial assets such as stocks and shares and have little effect on holdings of physical assets. Secondly, they argue that consumption and investment are relatively insensitive to the rate of interest (☞ units 31 and 32). Hence quite large changes in the rate of interest will have little impact upon planned aggregate expenditure.

The monetarist viewpoint can also be illustrated using aggregate demand and aggregate supply curves. An increase in the money supply will lead to an increase in aggregate demand through the transmission mechanism.

Question 3

Table 89.3 *The money supply and inflation, UK*

| | | Percentage change | |
	Money supply (M4)	Real GDP	Prices
1970	8.6	2.3	6.5
1971	13.8	1.4	9.2
1972	22.8	3.5	7.5
1973	20.6	5.9	9.1
1974	15.7	- 0.6	15.9
1975	12.8	- 2.1	24.1
1976	11.8	4.0	16.5
1977	10.9	2.2	15.8
1978	17.2	3.5	8.3

Source: adapted from *Economic Trends Annual Supplement*, Office for National Statistics.

(a) How do monetarists account for the causes of inflation?
(b) To what extent do the data support this view?

Question 4

Table 89.4 *Inflation, money and economic growth, UK*

| | | | Per cent |
	Change in M4	Inflation	Economic growth
1983	14.0	4.6	3.7
1984	12.5	5.0	2.0
1985	13.1	6.1	4.0
1986	15.9	3.4	4.0
1987	14.7	4.2	4.6
1988	17.2	4.9	5.0
1989	18.2	7.8	2.2
1990	17.6	9.5	0.4
1991	8.0	5.9	-1.7
1992	4.4	3.7	-0.5

Source: adapted from *Economic Trends Annual Supplement*, Office for National Statistics.

Between 1983 and 1987, broad money growth averaged 14.0 per cent whilst inflation averaged 4.7 per cent. Broad money growth then jumped to an average of 17.7 per cent between 1988 and 1990 whilst inflation rose to a peak of 9.5 per cent in 1990 from 4.9 per cent in 1988.
(a) How would monetarists account for this?
The average real growth rate of GDP over the period 1983-1987 was 3.7 per cent. At the time, there was a substantial deregulation of financial markets which led to an explosion of borrowing both by households and companies.
(b) How would a monetarist explain why, despite 14 per cent per annum increases in the money supply, there was only 4.7 per cent per annum average increase in inflation over the period?
The annual rate of growth of the money supply fell from 18.2 per cent in 1989 to 2.6 per cent in 1993. At the same time, the rate of growth of the economy collapsed from a peak of 5.0 per cent in 1988 to - 1.7 per cent in 1991.
(c) Why might this be an example of how the monetary transmission mechanism operates?

and the rate of interest, have a large impact on aggregate demand. Hence the shift in the aggregate demand curve will be great with a correspondingly large impact on inflation. There is also disagreement about the shape of the long run aggregate supply curve. If it is upward sloping, as argued by Keynesians in Figure 89.1, and the economy is at less than full employment, then a rise in the money supply which increases aggregate demand could lead to a permanent increase in real income. The further away from full employment is the economy, the larger will be the permanent impact on y, real income, and the less on P, the price level. If there is mass unemployment with a serious depression as in the 1930s, then a rise in the money supply might have no effect on inflation but lead only to an increase in real output because the aggregate demand supply curve is horizontal.

Monetary accommodation

Keynesians tend to argue that whilst hyper-inflations are caused by excessive increases in the money supply, the creeping inflation experienced in recent decades in the industrialised world has been caused mainly by changes in real variables. Either there has been excessive spending (demand-pull inflation) or there have been supply side shocks which have increased costs of production. Monetarists would not deny that a supply side shock like the four-fold increase in oil prices in 1973-74 increased prices. But they would argue that this was a once-and-for-all increase, rather like a seasonal increase in the price of tomatoes. It was an increase in prices but it was not inflationary (i.e. it did not in itself cause a general and sustained increase in prices).

Consider Figure 89.6. An increase in oil prices has shifted the short run aggregate supply curve from SRAS$_1$ to SRAS$_2$. The economy has moved from full employment at A to below full employment at B and prices have risen. The economy is now in a position of STAGFLATION or SLUMPFLATION with both price increases and unemployment. Keynesian theory would suggest that workers will now demand higher wage increases to compensate them for increases in prices. But monetarists would question where the money to pay these inflationary wage increases is going to come from. If the money supply is fixed, the aggregate demand curve cannot shift. Wage increases for some workers must be compensated for by wage losses for others. Some workers will 'price themselves out of jobs' as the short run aggregate supply curve rises to SRAS$_3$.

Unemployment therefore increases. Eventually workers will start to accept cuts in their wages and this will start to shift the short run aggregate supply curve downwards. Eventually the economy will return to full employment at A at the original price level. So a supply side shock will only be inflationary in the long run if the government allows the money supply to rise to ACCOMMODATE the inflationary pressures within the economy.

Accommodation is a very attractive political solution in the short run. Faced with unemployment and inflation, a government can at least reduce unemployment by increasing the money supply and thus increasing aggregate demand. But in the long run such a policy is simply

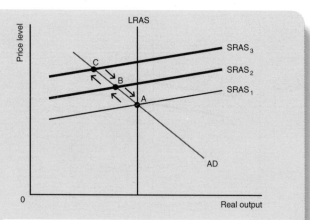

Figure 89.6 *Monetary accommodation*
A supply side shock which shifts the short run aggregate supply curve from SRAS$_1$ to SRAS$_2$ may lead workers to demand inflation-compensating wage increases, shifting the short run aggregate supply curve even farther upward and to the left. But the economy will return to the original point A so long as the government does not accommodate the price rise (i.e. does not increase the money supply which would have the effect of shifting the aggregate demand schedule to the right).

inflationary. What is more, monetarist economists argue that the economy would have returned to full employment anyway through the process of real wage cuts.

The same argument applies to increases in aggregate demand. Assume that government increases its spending when the economy is already at full employment, thus increasing aggregate demand. Prices rise slightly. The increase in spending will almost certainly result in an increase in the demand for borrowed funds. This will increase interest rates. Consumption will fall, whilst on the foreign exchanges there will be an inflow of money from abroad which will finance an increase in imports. Hence domestic aggregate demand will fall to its original level. The expansion in demand is said not to have been VALIDATED if the money supply is not increased. If the money supply had been expanded, firms would have reacted by bidding up the price of labour, shifting the short run aggregate supply curve upwards, producing a potential inflationary spiral.

So monetarists argue that demand and supply side shocks cannot cause inflation. It is only if the money supply is allowed to increase that inflation will ensue.

Question 5

(a) Distinguish between monetary accommodation and monetary validation.
(b) Consider the data in Tables 89.1, 89.3 and 89.4. Is there any evidence to suggest that monetary accommodation or validation occurred in the period 1970 to 1978?

Cost-push inflation - inflation caused by increases in the costs of production in the economy.
Demand-pull inflation - inflation which is caused by excess demand in the economy.
Monetary policy accommodation - a change in the nominal money supply which the government permits following a supply side shock in order to keep the real money supply constant.
Monetary policy validation - a change in the nominal money supply which the government permits following a change in aggregate demand

in order to keep the real money supply constant.
Monetary transmission mechanism - the mechanism through which a change in the money supply leads to a change in national income and other real variables such as unemployment.
Stagflation or slumpflation - a situation where an economy faces both rising inflation and rising unemployment.
Wage-price or cost-push spiral - the process whereby increases in costs, such as wages, lead to increases in prices and this in turn leads to increases in costs to firms.

Applied economics

Inflation in the Lawson boom, 1986-1989

In the first half of the 1980s, the inflation rate fell from 18.0 per cent in 1980 to 4.6 per cent in 1983. Inflation then hovered in the 5 per cent range for the next five years but in mid-1988 it began to increase again. By the end of 1990, the annual growth of the Retail Price Index was over 10 per cent. Why was there this doubling of the inflation rate?

From a monetarist view, the increase in inflation in 1988 can be linked to the jump in the rate of growth of the money supply from 1986. In the early part of the 1980s, the money supply, whether measured as M1, M2, M3 or M4, had grown considerably faster than the level of nominal GDP (i.e. faster than PT in the Fisher equation). As Table 89.5 shows, the annual rate of growth of M4 increased from below 15 per cent per annum to over 15 per cent in 1986 and by 1988 was averaging over 17 per cent. This increase was sufficient to produce the increase in inflation from the middle of 1988. It would suggest that there was a one to two year time lag between initial increases in the rate of growth of the money supply and subsequent increases in the inflation rate at the time.

Keynesians too can provide an explanation of the increase in inflation. As can be seen from Table 89.5, the rate of growth of real GDP increased from a rate of about 3 per cent per annum between 1983 and 1986 to over 4 per cent from the last quarter of 1986. By the first quarter of 1988, annual growth was an unsustainable 5.6 per cent. This very fast growth quickly reduced unemployment from over 3 million in the first half of the 1980s to 1.6 million by the last quarter of 1989, with areas such as the South East of England suffering severe shortages of many types of labour.

Another way of viewing excess demand is consider the output gap at the time. Figure 89.7 shows that the economy was in deep recession at the start of the 1980s with actual output nearly 5 per cent below its trend rate of output. By 1986, this negative output gap had been

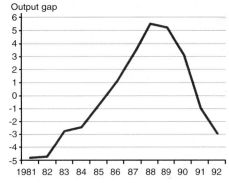

Figure 89.7 *The output gap[1], 1981-1992*
1. Deviations of actual GDP from potential GDP as a percentage of potential GDP.

eliminated and the economy was operating slightly above its potential level. At the height of the Lawson boom in 1988 and 1989, the economy was operating at over 5 per cent above its trend rate. This was unsustainable and inevitably led to rising inflation.

Table 89.5 also shows cost-push inflationary pressures. Wages are the most significant cost for employers on average. From 1984, there was a gradual increase in the rate of growth of earnings. In the first quarter of 1984, it was 6.1 per cent per annum, but by 1989 it was nearly 10 per cent. This could provide evidence for a cost-push explanation of the rise in inflation.

In fact, it is likely that the increased inflation from 1988 onwards was due to a combination of the above factors.

Most economists would accept that aggregate demand increased from 1986 relative to aggregate supply. The increase in the money supply came about, partly because of lower interest rates, but also because of deregulation in the financial markets. In particular, the second half of the 1980s saw the aggressive selling of mortgages as building societies, freed from many of their previous constraints, encouraged customers to borrow money. Banks too entered the mortgage market in an aggressive manner. People moving houses tended to borrow more than they needed to cover the cost of the house purchase and used the cash to buy everything from carpets and curtains to new cars. Increased lending also led to rapid increases in house prices. This encouraged home owners to borrow money secured against the increase in value of their houses.

The consequent increase in consumption then led to increased investment by industry at a time when export sales were growing fast too. Extra spending which led to increased output meant that unemployment fell. With increased tightness in the labour market, workers were able to secure higher wage increases, which led to pressures on costs and prices.

Between 1986 and the middle of 1988, the government **accommodated** the increase in demand by allowing the money supply to rise. However, between 1988 and 1989, in a bid to curb inflation, it doubled interest rates. It takes time for policy to work. The economy began to slow down in 1989 and by 1991 was in recession. Paradoxically, the increases in interest rates, designed to curb inflation, led in the short term to increases in the Retail Price Index, which may well have led to increased wage demands by workers attempting to prevent the erosion of their real wage levels. However, by 1991, inflation was beginning to fall.

Table 89.5 *Inflation and its possible determinants*

		Percentage change over previous 12 months				Millions
		Inflation	Money supply	Real GDP	Average earnings	Unempl- oyment
1983	Q1	4.9	14.7	3.2	8.8	3.2
1984	Q1	5.2	11.7	3.4	6.1	3.2
1985	Q1	5.4	14.0	2.3	7.5	3.3
1986	Q1	5.0	13.7	3.3	8.4	3.4
	Q2	2.8	15.3	2.9	8.1	3.3
	Q3	2.7	15.6	4.0	7.4	3.3
	Q4	3.5	15.9	4.8	8.0	3.2
1987	Q1	3.9	14.6	4.3	7.2	3.2
	Q2	4.2	14.1	4.0	7.5	3.1
	Q3	4.3	15.4	4.7	7.9	2.9
	Q4	4.1	16.2	4.2	8.4	2.8
1988	Q1	3.3	16.8	5.6	8.8	2.7
	Q2	4.3	16.9	4.7	8.3	2.5
	Q3	5.5	18.6	4.4	8.4	2.3
	Q4	6.5	17.6	4.1	9.6	2.1
1989	Q1	7.8	18.0	3.0	9.3	2.1
	Q2	8.2	18.6	2.6	9.3	1.9
	Q3	7.7	17.6	1.4	9.9	1.8
	Q4	7.6	18.3	0.9	8.7	1.6

Source: adapted from *Economic Trends Annual Supplement, Monthly Digest of Statistics*, Office for National Statistics.

Inflation, 1990–98

Table 89.6 *Inflation*

	Percentage change over previous 12 months	
	RPI	RPIX
1990	9.4	6.9
1991	5.9	7.6
1992	3.8	4.7
1993	1.6	3.1
1994	2.5	2.3
1995	3.4	2.7
1996	2.4	2.7
1997	3.2	2.4
1998	3.4	2.2

Table 89.7 *Demand: the output gap and change in GDP*

	GDP Percentage change over previous 12 months	Output gap
1990	0.64	3.1
1991	-1.50	-0.9
1992	0.60	-2.9
1993	2.31	-2.8
1994	4.40	-0.6
1995	2.78	-0.3
1996	2.57	0
1997	3.50	1.3
1998	2.30	1.4

Source: adapted from *Economic Trends* , Office for National Statistics.

Table 89.8 *Cost change: average earnings, import prices and profits*

	Percentage change over previous 12 months		
	Average earnings	Import prices	Profits[1]
1990	9.6	2.4	1.4
1991	7.8	1.2	-3.4
1992	6.0	0.9	-1.4
1993	3.1	10.0	9.0
1994	3.6	0.4	15.0
1995	3.1	6.0	7.7
1996	3.6	0.1	6.7
1997	4.2	-6.3	6.2
1998	5.1	-5.9	2.2

1. Profit at current prices: gross trading profit of private non-financial corporations excluding UK continental shelf companies.

Table 89.9 *Monetary variables: the money supply M4 and bank base rates*

	M4 Percentage change over previous 12 months	Bank base rates average for the year %
1990	11.97	14.77
1991	5.69	11.70
1992	2.73	9.56
1993	4.91	6.01
1994	4.18	5.46
1995	9.93	6.73
1996	9.67	5.96
1997	5.59	6.58
1998	8.22	7.21

The Bank of England has asked you, as one of their economists, to prepare a report on the main causes of inflation during the period 1990-1998.

1. Briefly describe the main trends in the economy during the period.

2. Outline each main theory of inflation which you know, and discuss the extent to which the evidence from the period supports the explanation.

3. Write a conclusion in which you evaluate which theory best explains the pattern of inflation during the period.

Summary

1. The main instrument of counter-inflationary policy today in Europe and the USA is the rate of interest. Rises in the rate of interest are used to deflate the economy to reduce inflation. When inflation is low, interest rates are lowered to allow the economy to grow at a faster rate.
2. Fiscal policy can be used to manipulate aggregate demand. A smaller budget deficit or larger surplus will reduce aggregate demand, deflate the economy and reduce demand-pull inflation. Changing indirect taxes and subsidies or controlling the prices charges by nationalised industries can affect cost-push inflation.
3. Maintaining a stable exchange rate or pegging the exchange rate against a low inflation currency is another appropriate policy which can be used to control inflation.
4. Keynesians advocate prices and incomes policies as a possible way of reducing the inflationary impact of supply side shocks. However, it is inappropriate to use them to control inflation caused by excess demand in the economy.

Monetary policy

Both in Europe and the USA, the main instrument of counter-inflationary policy today is monetary policy and in particular the control of short term interest rates. Monetary policy is used to adjust the level of aggregate demand.

A rise in interest rates will lead to a fall in aggregate demand because:

● consumers spend less on consumer durables, often financed through loans, when interest rates rise;
● firms spend less on investment as fewer investment projects remain profitable at higher interest rates;
● the wealth of households tends to decline with higher interest rates because higher interest rates tend to have a negative impact on stocks and shares; they can also adversely affect house prices as mortgages become more expensive;
● the exchange rate tends to rise, making it more difficult for exporters to sell abroad and making imports more competitive against domestic producers;
● higher interest rates encourage saving.

Falling aggregate demand leads to a fall in price, all other things being equal.

Deflationary monetary policy is often not politically popular. A rise in interest rates can only curb inflation if economic growth slows or even becomes negative. A sharp deflation is likely to lead to rising unemployment as well. Hence, governments may be reluctant to raise interest rates, particularly if there is an important election coming up. For this reason, some economists in recent years have argued that monetary policy should be administered by a central bank which is independent of government and therefore independent of short term political pressures.

Independent central banks typically are given the objective of maintaining low inflation, but do not have to take into account the consequences of their actions on economic growth and unemployment. Some economists argue that this distorts government policy because it places too high a value on low inflation at the expense of other variables. For instance, it is not necessarily obvious that an economy with 2 per cent inflation and 3 million unemployed is more desirable than an economy with 6 per cent inflation and 1 million unemployed. Keynesian economists would argue that such trade-offs can persist over decades. Monetarists, on the other hand, argue that there is no trade off between inflation and unemployment in the long run. The long run Phillips curve is vertical. A central bank which reduces inflation through deflationary monetary policy in the short term may cause unemployment. But unemployment will quickly fall back to its natural rate, leaving no unemployment cost.

Another problem with using interest rates to reduce inflation is that in the short term such monetary policy can lead to a perverse increase in inflation. In the UK, mortgage interest payments are included as part of the headline inflation rate measure, the RPI. A rise in interest rates leads to a rise in mortgage interest payments. At

Question 1

In the UK it has long been taken for granted that the government has the right to use public resources to purchase election victories... Since the Second World War, growth in the UK has tended to peak at around the time of an election, with inflation duly following a year or two thereafter... A government that wishes to increase public expenditure or lower taxes will find it politically more effective to do so by increasing its borrowing than by raising taxes or cutting spending. In time, a larger deficit will usually result in monetary expansion and so inflation... The solution is to tie the government's hands... The Prime Minister should sacrifice political control and choose an independent Bank of England that would be as good as the German Bundesbank.

Source: adapted from an article by Martin Wolf in the *Financial Times*.

(a) Explain why there might be a link between elections and inflation.
(b) Why might giving independence to the Bank of England have helped break this link?

relatively low rates of interest, rises in mortgage interest payments can have a significant impact on the RPI. The problem is worsened if workers are pressing for pay rises based on the RPI inflation measure. This makes the adjustment to a lower rate of inflation a more difficult and prolonged process.

Fiscal policy

In the 1950s and 1960s, governments in the Western world tended to use fiscal policy as a prime means of controlling inflation.

Demand-pull inflation If inflation is demand-pull in nature, then reducing the level of aggregate demand in the economy will reduce inflationary pressures. Assume in Figure 90.1 that the aggregate demand curve over the next 12 months will shift from AD_1 to AD_3. Prices would therefore rise from OA to OC. By cutting the rise in aggregate demand to AD_2, the government can reduce the rate of inflation with prices rising only to OB.

Keynesians tend to argue that fiscal policy can play a crucial role in cutting aggregate demand. The key variable which the government can manipulate is the PSNCR, government borrowing. If it reduces the level of borrowing it will cut aggregate demand. It can cut borrowing either by reducing the level of government spending or by increasing taxes. If it reduces government spending, there will be a **multiplier effect** on national income with aggregate demand falling by more than the initial cut in government spending (☞ unit 33).

Cost-push inflation Governments can also influence cost-push spirals by artificially manipulating indirect tax rates. In a cost-push spiral, workers press for wage increases which are equal to a real increase plus the rate of inflation. For instance, if workers want a 2 per cent real increase and the expected inflation rate is 8 per cent, then

they will press for a 10 per cent pay rise. But if the inflation rate is 18 per cent they will press for a wage rise of 20 per cent. Governments can reduce the expected rate of inflation by not raising indirect taxes in money terms. For instance, in the UK excise duties tend to be raised each Budget in order to maintain the real value of the tax. Fully indexing all excise duties tends to add about 1 per cent to the Retail Price Index each year. If the Chancellor chooses not to raise duties, the expected rate of inflation will fall, thus moderating pay claims.

If the government owns key industries, like the railways or the Post Office, it can again reduce expected inflation by not raising prices in line with inflation. The result is that these industries make lower profits or even losses, but this may be a small price to pay for lower inflation.

Lower taxes paid by industry will reduce industry's costs. Reducing corporation tax or employers' National Insurance contributions may therefore help break a cost-push spiral. It would be foolish for a government to lower taxes and leave government spending unchanged if the aim were to reduce inflation. It would replace an element of cost-push inflation with more demand-pull inflation. So real public expenditure must be reduced too. One way of reducing real public expenditure is to keep public sector pay below the rate of inflation. This has the added counter-inflationary bonus that government can set an example to private sector workers of what might be the 'going-rate' of pay increase. If the government sets a ceiling of 4 per cent instead of 8 per cent on public sector pay increases when the rate of inflation is 8 per cent, then private sector workers may be prepared to accept 9 per cent wage increases instead of 10 per cent.

Governments became increasingly disillusioned with using fiscal policy in the 1970s and 1980s to combat inflation for a number of reasons.
- They became less convinced that fiscal policy could be used to change economic variables such as inflation with any accuracy.
- The **stagflation** (☞ unit 35) seen in the 1970s, caused by sharp rises in world oil prices, led monetarists to say that the foundations of Keynesian economics were false. Using taxes and government spending to reflate and deflate economies only worked because in fact governments were changing the money supply to achieve this. Therefore governments should use monetary policy to steer the economy.
- Active use of fiscal policy became associated with budget deficits and a growing National Debt.

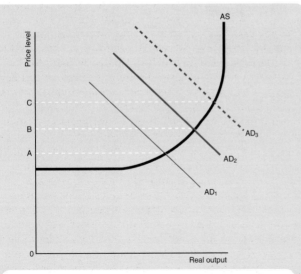

Figure 90.1 *Using fiscal policy to control demand-pull inflation Reducing the PSBR so that an increase in aggregate demand is moderated from AD_3 to AD_2 will reduce the rate of inflation.*

Question 2

Each year, the Chancellor in his Budget is faced with choices about whether or not to change tax rates. Explain, using diagrams, why the following might lead to a fall in the inflation rate:
(a) raising income tax rates;
(b) on cost-push grounds, reducing duties on alcohol, tobacco and petrol;
(c) increasing a budget surplus (i.e. a negative PSNCR);
(d) increasing public sector pay by less than the rate of inflation.

Following plans to create a single currency in the EU in the late 1980s and 1990s, achieving a low budget deficit and a low level of National Debt became part of the criteria by which countries were judged to be ready to take part in monetary union.

Exchange rate policy

The value of the currency is an important variable in determining inflation. If the currency is falling in value, the price of imports will rise, thus increasing cost-push inflation. It will also make exports cheaper to foreigners. Demand for exports will therefore rise, leading to demand-pull inflation.

Controlling the exchange rate can therefore be part of an anti-inflationary strategy. One way in which to do this is through interest rates. The higher the level of interest rates, the higher the level of the currency. Interest rate policy and exchange rate policy can therefore be seen as two parts of a single overall strategy.

Some economists argue that it is sometimes appropriate for governments to peg their currency to a low inflation currency. For instance, Argentina has pegged its currency to the US dollar. The UK pegged the pound to the German deutschmark for a short time in 1986 and 1987. If a high inflation economy were to peg its currency to a low inflation economy with which it traded, higher rates of inflation would begin to erode its competitiveness. Exports would be going up in price compared to the other country, leading to fewer exports. Imports would be going down in price relative to domestically produced goods, increasing imports and reducing domestic production. This would be deflationary. Unemployment would rise and firms would be unable to offer inflationary pay rises to their workers without going out of business. Pay settlements would moderate, firms would be forced to reduce price increases or even cut their prices and the rate of inflation would fall. In practice, pegging the exchange rate is difficult to achieve without making exchange rate policy the most important priority. In Europe, some countries have solved the problems of pegging exchange rates by creating a monetary union and a single currency. A weaker commitment, such as that of the UK in 1986 and 1987, can easily be derailed by an economic crisis which forces the country to abandon its exchange rate target.

Question 3

'The exchange rate is the link between one country's price level and another's. If sterling is linked to a non-inflationary currency such as the D-Mark, there is no way in which the movement of prices in traded goods and services in Britain can diverge from that of Germany's in the long run; and a link with the D-Mark becomes a partial substitute for the Gold Standard anchor.'

Source: Samuel Brittan, *Financial Times*.

(a) Explain why Samuel Brittan argues that UK inflation can be reduced if it is linked to the deutschmark.

Prices and incomes policies

PRICES AND INCOMES POLICY is a policy designed to limit the growth of prices and incomes directly. For instance, a government could impose a price freeze and/or an incomes freeze. This means that prices and incomes are not allowed to rise. The government, however, could just control incomes, limiting their growth to 2 per cent, for instance, or allowing them to rise only in line with inflation.

Incomes policies became fashionable in the 1960s when it was hoped that their introduction could push the short run Phillips curve to the left. This would enable a government to run the economy with a given level of unemployment at a lower rate of inflation than would otherwise be the case. Unfortunately this displayed a lack of understanding of the economics behind the Phillips curve.

Incomes policies can help reduce inflation caused by supply side factors. Assume that there is a sharp rise in the price of imports which in turn leads to a sharp rise in the Retail Price Index. Workers increase their wage demands, threatening to set off a wage-price spiral. The government could react by tightening monetary policy, allowing the economy to fall into recession and purging the economy of inflation through increased unemployment. An incomes policy offers a less harsh solution. By imposing maximum pay increases, the government breaks inflationary expectations and hence the cost-push spiral and helps the economy return to price stability at much lower cost in terms of unemployment.

However, prices and incomes policies cannot be used to repress inflation caused by demand side factors indefinitely. If government continues to allow aggregate demand to exceed aggregate supply, for instance through its own excessive spending or through excessive money supply expansion, then prices will rise sharply following the ending of an incomes policy compared to what they would have been without the policy. Indeed the excess demand will tend to contribute to the breakdown of the incomes policy. This is because firms and workers will expect prices to rise given demand conditions in the economy. Firms will know that they could charge higher prices for their products because there is excess demand. Therefore they will be more prepared to award higher wage rises to workers than if there were no excess demand. Workers will realise that firms are prepared to pay higher wages and will be prepared to fight, for instance by taking industrial action. The incomes policy collapses leading to a surge of inflationary wage increases.

An incomes policy may help curb inflation in the short run if inflation is caused by supply side factors by breaking inflationary expectations. But there is considerable debate about whether an incomes policy has any place in the long run management of an economy. Any guidelines or maximum levels of pay imposed by a policy tend to become norms - every worker receives the government set pay increase. Pay differentials between workers therefore do not change. But pay differentials would change over time if all markets were free. This creates grave problems. In expanding industries, for instance, employers would probably like to pay their workers more in order to recruit labour, whilst in declining industries employers might want to pay their workers less, unworried that they might then lose workers. Firms and workers therefore become increasingly resentful of the operation of the incomes policy and have an ever increasing incentive to break it.

Question 4

Table 90.1

	1974	1975	1976	1977	1978
Change in money supply[1] %	11	6	8	9	15
Change in prices %	16	24	17	16	8

1. £M3.
Source: adapted from *Economic Trends Annual Supplement*, Office for National Statistics.

In 1973-74, the UK economy suffered a severe supply side shock arising from large increases in the price of imported commodities, particularly oil. Import prices rose 46 per cent in 1974. In 1975, the Labour government negotiated an incomes policy with the trade unions which was to last till 1979. However, by 1978, workers were becoming increasingly frustrated with low pay increases. In the winter of 1978-79, the 'winter of discontent', key groups of workers succeeded in breaking the pay guidelines.

(a) Why might the incomes policy described in the passage have helped reduce inflationary pressures?
(b) Why might the changes in the money supply shown in Table 90.1 help explain why workers found it possible to break the incomes policy in 1978-79?

key terms

Prices and incomes policy - a policy designed to limit the growth of prices and incomes directly.

Applied economics

The control of inflation in the UK

The 1950s and 1960s

In the 1950s and first half of the 1960s, governments used a mixture of fiscal and monetary policies to control rising prices. Apart from the period of the Korean war in the early 1950s, inflation at the time was invariably associated with booms in the economy. Hence, measures to reduce the growth rate of the economy also helped reduce this demand-pull inflation. Favoured weapons included increases in taxes and tighter controls on bank lending and hire purchase lending. It was felt that these, compared to, say, decreases in government spending, would have a rapid impact on aggregate demand.

In 1966, a new policy was implemented to control inflation. Inflation had risen from 2.1 per cent in 1963 to 4.7 per cent in 1965 as the economy expanded. The new Labour government, under Harold Wilson, decided that a prices and incomes policy might enable the economy to enjoy both a cut in inflation and maintain the relatively low unemployment at the time (i.e. it hoped to shift the short run Phillips curve back to the left). In August 1966 a **statutory** (i.e. legally enforceable) policy was imposed. It became illegal for firms to raise prices or award pay increases. Inflation during the rest of the year and in 1967 moderated. However, as the policy was relaxed inflation began to creep up again, despite a highly deflationary Budget in 1968 which was designed to tackle the balance of payments problem at the time. By 1969, annual inflation had risen to 5.1 per cent, higher than when the prices and incomes policy was first imposed.

The 1970s

In the 1970 election incomes policy was a key issue. The opposition Conservatives promised to scrap the policy whilst the Labour government remained committed to its use, despite rising inflation. The Conservatives won the election and duly scrapped the policy. However, for the following two years they failed to have any coherent policy response to the ever rising inflation rate. Indeed, in his 1972 Budget, the Chancellor, Anthony Barber, gave a fiscal boost to the economy by making a sizeable cut in taxes which in Keynesian terms could only have fuelled inflation. The boost given to the money supply by the printing of money to pay for the increased budget deficit was compounded by the 1971 reform, called 'Competition and Credit Control', of the way in which monetary policy was operated. It led to an unplanned explosion in the money supply which, on monetarist grounds, could only have led to higher inflation. Another factor adding to inflationary pressures was the abandonment of the UK's fixed exchange rate in 1972 and the consequent fall in the value of the pound which pushed up import prices. Finally, there was an explosion of commodity prices in 1972-73 which culminated in a quadrupling of the price of oil in 1973-74. This led to severe cost-push inflation.

To tackle the growing problem, the government announced in November 1972 the reintroduction of a statutory prices and incomes policy. Like the previous policy, it started with a wage and price freeze, and was followed by a gradual relaxation of policy. For a short time, inflation fell, but the inflationary pressures on the economy were so strong that price increases soon resumed their upward march. Interest rates were slowly raised from 6 per cent in July 1972 to 13 per cent by November 1973. Competition and Credit Control was abandoned in December 1973 and replaced by tighter controls on bank lending. However, the government lost a snap election held in February 1974 on the issue of whether miners could receive a pay increase above the limit allowed in the incomes policy.

The incoming Labour government, without a majority in Parliament, did little to curb inflation. It held a second election later in 1974 when it won a majority but continued to seem to have little policy response to the enormous economic problems - growing inflation, growing unemployment, a recession and a large balance of payments deficit - facing the economy. It had hoped that its 'Social Contract', negotiated with the unions during 1974, which promised to increase pensions, repeal anti-union laws and take other measures which would favour trade union members in return for moderation in pay bargaining, would reduce cost-push inflation. However, the unions only paid lip-service to the contract. In 1975, the government then negotiated another more binding, but still voluntary, contract with the unions. The trade unions agreed to accept a maximum £6 a week pay increase, with nothing for those earning over £8 500 a year, for one year from August 1975. This, together with falls in worldwide commodity prices, led, according to cost-push proponents, to the rapid fall in inflation from 24.1 per cent in 1975 to 16.5 per cent in 1976 and to a low of 8.3 per cent in 1978.

However, there were also demand side factors at work in the fall in inflation between 1975 and 1978. There were considerable cuts in planned government spending in 1975 and 1976, as well as tax rises. As a consequence government borrowing, the PSNCR, fell from £10.2bn in 1975 to £5.4bn in 1977. This deflationary fiscal policy was accompanied by a tightening of monetary policy. On the money side, the first official money supply targets were announced in July 1975 and a tight rein was kept on money supply growth. M4, which had grown by 56 per cent in 1972 alone following the introduction of Competition and Credit Control, grew by only 10 per cent in 1975. Bank base rates were kept very high, in the 10-14 per cent range, for nearly all of 1975 and 1976.

Success in reducing inflation led the government to relax its fiscal and monetary policy from 1977 onwards. The economy began to grow strongly again, with aggregate demand increasing because of increases in spending from the private sector. Inflation, even at 8 per cent, was still higher than our major industrial competitors and still high in historical terms. So the government attempted to enforce a tightening of its incomes policy from August 1978. It demanded a reduction in the target rate of wage increases from the 10 per cent of 1977-78 to 5 per cent in 1978-79. The unions refused to endorse this and in the autumn and winter of 1978-79 (the **winter of discontent**) there was a series of crippling strikes. The government had no legal power to force private sector employers to keep to the 5 per cent guideline because the incomes policy was voluntary. Strikes in the public sector were eventually ended by a promise to set up a commission to consider pay comparability. These pay awards came to be called 'Clegg awards' after the Chairman of the Commission set up to judge the claims. However, the incomes policy had effectively been pushed aside by the unions and the winter of discontent was an important factor in causing the Labour Party to lose the June 1979 election to the Conservatives.

The 1980s and 1990s

The incoming Conservative government of Margaret Thatcher was firmly monetarist. It argued that incomes policies were completely irrelevant to the control of inflation. An incomes policy could paper over the cracks for a short time, but if the economy was continually being fuelled by increases in the money supply, then the inevitable longer term consequence was inflation.

The incoming government faced a difficult challenge. Commodity prices, particularly oil, had once again risen sharply in the world boom of 1978-79, causing a considerable jump in import prices. Wage increases were into double figures with large salary increases promised to public sector workers through the Clegg Commission. On the demand side, 1978-79 were boom years for the economy. The government made matters worse by increasing VAT from 8 per cent to 15 per cent in their first Budget in July 1979. This move paid for a substantial cut in income tax rates. The overall tax impact was neutral, but the 7 per cent increase in VAT fed immediately through to an estimated 5 per cent increase in the RPI, the inflation index. Workers then attempted to regain that 5 per cent by pressing for higher wage increases in 1979-80.

As a monetarist government would, it chose to tighten monetary policy. Interest rates were raised from 12 per cent before the election to 17 per cent in November 1979. In its 1980 Budget, it announced a Medium Term Financial Strategy (MTFS). Money supply growth was to be curbed. This would be achieved by high interest rates and by a commitment to fully fund the PSNCR (i.e. not to allow any printing of money to fund government borrowing). The PSNCR itself was to be reduced in order to allow interest rates to come down, since the government believed that higher government borrowing increased interest rates in the economy (because higher borrowing led to a higher demand for funds in the loans markets). The publication of the MTFS was also meant to lead to a lowering of inflationary expectations in the economy (based on a **rational expectations model** ☞ unit 34). The argument was that workers based their wage demands on inflation. If workers could be made to believe that future inflation would very low, then wage demands would be low and this would help reduce inflationary pressures in the economy in itself.

Between 1980 and 1981, the economy went into a deep recession. High interest rates caused massive destocking by British industry, which in turn led to lay offs and rapidly rising unemployment. At the same time, the exchange rate of the pound rose considerably due to increased exports of North Sea oil. This helped reduce import prices and hence inflation, but it led to a large contraction of manufacturing industry which found itself unable to compete against cheap foreign imports. So a tight monetary policy, combined with an exchange rate policy which allowed the pound to go up in value, helped reduce inflation from 18.0 per cent in 1980 to 11.9 per cent in 1981. In his 1981 Budget, the Chancellor, Sir Geoffrey Howe, further tightened the squeeze by substantially increasing taxes, producing a fiscal deflationary impact. By 1982, inflation had fallen to 8.6 per cent and in 1983 it was 4.6 per cent.

Throughout the 1980s and early 1990s, fiscal policy was used only to achieve micro-economic objectives, such as cutting income tax rates to increase incentives to work, or as a means of achieving monetary or exchange rate targets. Monetary policy became the chief weapon in the fight against inflation, helped by exchange rate policy.

The government rapidly became disillusioned with targeting the money supply directly. The first half of the 1980s saw double digit annual growth of the money supply despite rapidly falling inflation. It became clear that a simple link between money supply growth and inflation did not exist. In consequence, in 1982, the government stopped targeting just one money supply measure, sterling M3, and set targets for another two money supply measures and, by 1985, the government had downgraded sterling M3 from a targeted variable to just one of many variables which it monitored.

By the mid-1980s, the focus of anti-inflationary policy had moved to the exchange rate. Falls in the value of the pound would feed through to higher import prices and therefore higher inflation. If the pound could be pegged against a low inflation currency, in practice the deutschmark, then UK inflation rates would have to remain at the levels of that country. From 1987, the government operated an exchange rate policy where the pound shadowed the deutschmark. Interest rates were raised or lowered according to whether the pound was falling or rising against the deutschmark. This policy proved misguided.

The problem was that economic growth moved from an annual average of 2.5 per cent in 1982-84 to 4.0 per cent in 1985-86 to 4.8 per cent in 1987-88. This growth in demand was unsustainable and began to show through in a deteriorating balance of payments situation and

eventually in 1987-88 in rising inflation. The government in the meantime had decided that it had transformed the economy through its supply-side measures and that non-inflationary growth of 4 to 5 per cent was now feasible. It was only in Summer 1988 that the government became convinced that the economy was over-heating and that action would have to be taken to control inflation. It broke the link with the deutschmark and raised interest rates, from 7.5 per cent in May 1988 at the height of the Lawson boom, to 13 per cent by November 1988 and 15 per cent by October 1989. The government hoped for a rapid fall in inflation and a 'soft-landing' for the economy where growth might fall back a little without the economy going into recession. Inflation, however, continued to climb. The government's interest rate policy contributed to its short-term problems. The unprecedented 7.5 per cent increase in interest rates fed through to rises in mortgage interest rates and then into the retail price index. The result was that the headline RPI figure increased at a faster rate than most other measures of inflation in the economy and workers pressed for wage increases based on the higher RPI rates.

However, throughout this period, the then Chancellor of the Exchequer, Nigel Lawson, remained convinced that pegging the pound to the deutschmark was the only credible anti-inflationary policy. The Prime Minister, Margaret Thatcher, a fierce anti-European, believed that monitoring the domestic money supply was still the key to inflation policy, and that the problems of rising inflation in 1988 were directly linked to the lax monetary policy which the government had been forced to maintain with low interest rates as a result of the shadowing of the deutschmark in 1987 and early 1988. That disagreement was one of the key factors in the political events that led to the ousting of Margaret Thatcher as Prime Minister and her replacement by John Major. It was under his leadership that a decision was finally made in 1990 to join the ERM (☞ unit 95), pegging the pound against the deutschmark at the very high central level of £1 = DM2.95. The level was deliberately chosen to provide a further counter-inflationary twist to the higher interest rate policy of the time. Firms competing against foreign companies found it almost impossible to pass on any price increases to customers at this rate of exchange and consequently were forced to give very low wage increases, if any, to their workers. The high exchange rate was also deflationary because exporters found it hard to increase exports at that rate whilst importers found it easier to compete against UK firms in the UK.

The headline rate of inflation reached a peak of 9.5 per cent in 1990 before falling eventually to a low of 1.6 per cent in 1993. Very high interest rates and then a high exchange rate proved successful in reducing inflation. Fiscal policy remained neutral, with the government allowing its budget to move from substantial surplus in 1988 to a very large deficit by 1993. However, between 1993 and 1996, the government increased taxes to reduce the PSNCR and this in itself led to a fiscal squeeze on the economy, which contributed to continuing low rates of inflation. Monetary policy began to ease from 1990 with interest rate cuts. The exchange rate policy of the government collapsed in September 1992 when it was forced to leave the ERM. The subsequent 15 per cent fall in the value of the pound undoubtedly helped raise inflation from 1.6 per cent in 1993 to 2.5 per cent in 1994. However, the long recession of 1990-92, with unemployment nearly doubling from 1.6 million in 1990 to 2.9 million in 1993, kept a tight lid on inflationary pressures in the economy.

Even so, the economy was growing at a relatively fast rate in this recovery phase of the trade cycle and in September 1994 the Bank of England chose to raise interest rates. It feared that the cost-push pressures resulting from the 15 per cent fall in the value of the pound since September 1992, and the demand-pull pressures arising from strong economic growth could lead to unacceptably high levels of inflation in 1995. Interest rates rose from 5.25 per cent at the start of September 1994 to 6.75 per cent for nearly all of 1995. By the end of 1995, inflation was beginning to fall as Figure 90.2 shows, and the Bank of England began to cut interest rates, down to 5.75 per cent between June and October 1996. Then inflation began to increase again and the Bank of England raised interest rates to a peak of 7.5 per cent in June 1998. It then cut interest rates, partly because the Asian crisis of 1998 was assumed to have hit exports to Far Eastern countries and thus would reduce aggregate demand. Official statistics also showed that GDP growth had slowed to produce a very mild recession. In fact, growth in 1998 and 1999 was much stronger than was thought at the time and in November 1999 the Bank of England began increasing interest rates again to counter perceived inflationary pressures.

From the time that the UK was forced out of the Exchange Rate Mechanism in September 1992 and was forced to abandon an exchange rate target, interest rate policy has been the principle instrument used to control inflation. Whenever inflationary pressures have been assumed to have risen, the Bank of England has raised interest rates. In 1997, the Bank of England was made independent by the incoming Labour government. Instead of the government deciding when to raise or lower interest rates, it now became the Bank of England's responsibility to decide. The Bank of England was also given only one target, to maintain inflation (measured by RPIX) at 2.5 per cent or less. The intention was to remove inflation policy from day to day political decision making and prevent governments trading off higher inflation for, say, higher growth or lower unemployment.

An evaluation of policy

In retrospect, it can be argued that anti-inflation policy in the UK has often been misguided. Prices and incomes

policies (a policy aimed at the supply-side of the economy) failed to work when the government was allowing the economy to grow rapidly (i.e. there were demand pressures building up). Governments have reacted too late in the inflationary cycle to stem inflationary pressures (e.g. in 1973) and have sometimes then over-reacted, producing too deep a recession (e.g. in 1989 and 1990). Warning signs have been ignored (e.g. the excessive monetary growth in 1972) whilst some measures designed to reduce inflation have, at least in the short term, increased inflation (e.g. the increases in interest rates in 1988-89). The reaction to inflation has often been ambivalent because of conflicting policy objectives (e.g. in 1994 when the government relaxed policy to encourage recovery in the economy). However, the commitment to full employment, which many economists now believe was a major contributor to rising inflation in the 1960s and 1970s, was abandoned in the late 1970s.

Today, politics should have been removed from policy making because the Bank of England is independent. Critics of the present system argue that the Bank of England changes interest rates too frequently and causes too much uncertainty in the economy as a result. They point out that the European Central Bank changes its interest rate far less and yet there is low inflation in the euro zone. On the other hand, inflation has remained relatively low since 1992. This, it could be argued, shows that relying on frequent changes of interest rates to keep inflation low has been highly successful. What this one instrument policy has failed to cope with yet, however, is a severe supply side shock like that of the oil price rises of the 1970s, or a demand side shock like the stock market crash of 1929. It could be that the present system is only working because the economic climate for much of the 1990s was very favourable to maintaining low inflation. If oil prices quadrupled, or shares lost most of their value, would relying solely on changes in interest rates be enough to keep prices roughly constant?

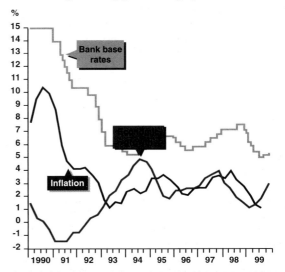

Figure 90.2 *Inflation (change in RPI), bank base rates, and economic growth in the 1990s*
Source: adapted from *Economics Trends* and *Economic Trends Annual Supplement*, Office for National Statistics.

Inflation, 1986–88

Table 90.2 *Changes in GDP and its components at 1990 prices, seasonally adjusted*

	Percentage change over previous 12 months					% of GDP[1]
	GDP	Consumers' expenditure	Investment	Exports	Imports	PSNCR[2]
1986						
Q1	3.3	6.1	-4.7	4.4	1.2	- 2.4
Q2	2.9	7.8	1.4	1.7	7.6	+ 3.1
Q3	4.0	6.9	6.5	4.8	10.4	+ 4.3
Q4	4.8	6.4	7.6	7.0	8.5	- 2.0
1987						
Q1	4.3	4.7	4.2	6.8	4.4	- 0.9
Q2	4.0	4.1	10.4	4.4	5.9	+ 1.6
Q3	4.7	5.4	11.5	7.4	10.0	+ 0.5
Q4	4.2	6.8	14.9	4.1	10.6	- 2.6
1988						
Q1	5.6	8.1	19.4	0.0	13.2	- 2.9
Q2	4.7	7.3	19.5	3.1	12.4	- 1.7

1. Not seasonally adjusted.   2. + indicates budget deficit, − indicates budget surplus.

Table 90.3 *Prices and earnings*

	Percentage change over previous 12 months				
	RPI	House prices[1]	Import prices	Output of manu-factured goods[2]	Average earnings
1986					
Q1	5.0	13.5	- 8.5	- 16.1	8.1
Q2	2.8	18.8	- 8.2	- 16.5	7.4
Q3	2.7	19.8	- 3.7	- 16.6	8.0
Q4	3.5	15.9	+ 2.6	- 16.7	7.2
1987					
Q1	3.9	17.3	+ 4.4	+ 3.7	7.5
Q2	4.2	14.2	+ 4.1	+ 3.8	7.9
Q3	4.3	16.3	+ 4.3	+ 3.6	8.4
Q4	4.1	21.3	- 0.5	+ 3.8	8.8
1988					
Q1	3.3	27.3	- 2.7	+ 3.9	8.3
Q2	4.3	27.8	- 1.3	+ 4.1	8.4

1 Average price of new dwellings purchased with a mortgage.
2 Producer price index. Output of all manufactured products, home sales.

Table 90.4 *Unemployment, the exchange rate and interest rates*

	Unemployment (millions)	Exchange rate (sterling against the deutschmark)	Bank base rate
1986			
Q1	3.4	3.38	12.30
Q2	3.3	3.39	10.45
Q3	3.3	3.10	10.00
Q4	3.2	2.87	10.85
1987			
Q1	3.2	2.84	10.80
Q2	3.1	2.96	9.35
Q3	2.9	2.97	9.58
Q4	2.8	2.99	9.20
1988			
Q1	2.7	3.01	8.75
Q2	2.5	3.14	8.17

Source: adapted from *Economic Trends*; *Economic Trends Annual Supplement*, Office for National Statistics.

An economics magazine has asked you to write an article about the Lawson boom and what might have been an alternative policy response to the one chosen at the time by the government to combat rising inflation.

1. Outline the economic conditions prevailing between the first quarter of 1986 and the second quarter of 1988.
2. Explain, using diagrams, how the chosen policy of the government - to raise interest rates from 7.5 per cent in May 1988 to a peak of 15 per cent in November 1989 - should, in theory, reduce inflation.
3. Evaluate, using diagrams, what alternative policies the government could have pursued at the time.
4. The chosen policy response - to raise interest rates in 1989 and 1990 and then to join the ERM in 1990 - led to the longest recession since the 1930s. Discuss whether it might not have been better simply to have done nothing in 1988, 1989 and 1990.

unit 91 Economic growth and government policy

Summary

1. Government policy to increase economic growth over the long term should be directed towards increasing labour productivity, either by raising the skills of the labour force or by increasing the quantity or quality of the capital stock.
2. Some economists argue that governments should intervene in the market place if high economic growth is to be achieved. They advocate such policies as increased expenditure on education and training, subsidies for investment, direct government investment in the economy and grants or subsidies for Research and Development.
3. Other economists argue that government is poorly placed to judge how resources should be allocated within an economy. They argue that it is the role of government to liberate markets of restrictions. They advocate the use of supply side policies to increase the rate of economic growth.

The causes of economic growth

Economic growth occurs when there is an increase in the quantity or quality of the factors of production or when they are used more efficiently. A government wishing to increase growth in the economy fundamentally must pursue policies which will increase **labour productivity** (i.e. output per worker). There are three main ways to achieve this:

- the quality of the labour force can increase, meaning that each worker on average can produce more output with an existing stock of capital and an existing state of technology;
- the quantity of the capital stock can increase, meaning that workers are able to use more capital, thus raising average output;
- the state of technology can change, meaning that a given capital stock can be more productive with a given labour force.

Government policies to promote growth therefore need to be directed at both the labour and capital markets.

An interventionist approach

Some economists believe that the market mechanism is unlikely to lead to optimal rates of economic growth. There are so many forms of **market failure** (☞ unit 16), that the government must intervene in the market place. For instance, it can be argued that the economic prosperity of countries such as France, Germany and Japan are based upon **interventionist** policies of their governments. There are many ways in which government can act to increase the growth rate of the economy.

Increased public expenditure on education and training
The quality of the workforce can be increased if educational standards are raised. This could be achieved if, for instance, more children stay on at school or college after the age of 16, or more people go to university or polytechnic. But a significant increase in the numbers in full time education is likely to require significant increases in the education budgets of government.

Alternatively, employers could provide more training for their staff. But in a free market, firms are under strong cost pressures to spend as little as possible on training. Many firms may find it far cheaper, rather than to train staff directly, to 'poach' trained staff from other firms. The result is market failure - the inability of the free market to provide sufficient training for the country's workforce. Here again there is a crucial role to be played by government. The government could force the private sector to undertake more training, for instance by passing laws which state that firms must pay for at least one day's training a week for all 16 to 18 year olds employed. Or it could encourage training at work by providing generous subsidies to employers with strong training programmes.

Subsidising investment Economic theory suggests that firms will invest more if the cost of capital declines (☞ unit 32). So the government could subsidise investment if it wished to increase investment spending in the economy.

Question 1

The abolition of industry training bodies in the early 1980s was a grave mistake according to some economists. Firms in industries with a training council paid a levy per employee to the council. They were then able to send workers on courses provided by the council. Firms which chose not to train workers, but instead hired trained workers from other firms when needed, still had to make a financial contribution to training. Today's situation encourages free riding. Firms which train workers may get some financial support from their local TEC (Training and Enterprise Council). However, the bulk of the training cost has to be paid for by the firm. Not surprisingly, small firms spend little or nothing on training and rely on being able to recruit staff trained by other firms when vacancies occur. The result is that the UK's workforce is poorly trained in comparison with those of industrialised competitors such as Germany and Japan.

(a) (i) What is meant by 'free riding'? (ii) Why might the present UK training system encourage free riding whilst the previous system might not?
(b) Explain why firms have an incentive to over-consume training and thus waste training resources if they are provided free or at little cost by government.
(c) What is the possible link between training and economic growth?

It has a variety of ways to do this. It could, for instance, provide direct subsidies for new investment, giving a grant for a proportion of any new investment undertaken by a firm, or it could offer tax incentives. Investment could be offset against corporation tax liability. Governments could offer selective assistance to particular industries which it believed would be important in the future. This is known as a policy of 'picking winners'.

Alternatively, the government could reduce the cost of capital by lowering interest rates, leading to a move along the **marginal efficiency of capital schedule**. One way of possibly reducing interest rates is to increase the personal savings ratio. The argument here is that investment tends to be financed from domestic savings. Hence an increase in S, total savings, will lead to an increase in I, the level of investment. This occurs through the interest rate mechanism. Thus measures which encourage saving, such as tax allowances, may increase the level of investment.

Direct government investment Free market forces, even when working in their most efficient way, may still result in a less than socially desirable level of investment in the economy. The government may then be forced to intervene directly, rather than attempting to influence the private sector indirectly. For instance, the government may choose to nationalise firms or industries (i.e. take them into public ownership). It may do this following disappointing performance in the private sector. In some cases, the industry or firm may otherwise go out of business and the government has to step in to rescue it for the nation.

The government may also choose to co-operate with the private sector in developing an industry. The government could set up in partnership with an existing private sector company to develop a new product. In the small business sphere, the government may fund a government owned company to take equity stakes in growing businesses.

Encouraging Research and Development Government can encourage technological progress in a variety of ways. For instance, it can fund universities and polytechnics to engage in fundamental research. It can establish research institutions. It can give grants or tax subsidies to private firms undertaking research and development. It can encourage the widespread dissemination of new inventions and new technologies by subsidising their price, or offering free assistance to firms wanting to know how new technologies might be of benefit to them.

Another way is to encourage the growth of large monopolies and to discourage the existence of small and medium size companies in the market. In the Austrian view(☞ unit 63), large monopolies are the firms which are the most likely to have the money and the incentive to engage in Research and Development. They have the money because they are able to earn abnormal profit. They have the incentive because their monopoly power depends upon their hold over the market with existing technology. In the process of **creative destruction**, monopolies can be destroyed by new competitor firms offering new products to satisfy the same wants. For instance, the monopoly power of the railways of the 19th century was destroyed by the coming of the motor car. On the other hand, firms in perfect competition have no incentive to undertake Research and Development because there is perfect knowledge in the market. Any invention will quickly become common knowledge and will be copied by all firms in the industry.

Protectionism The government may feel that domestic industry is failing to invest because of foreign competition. For instance, the **infant industry argument** (☞ unit 40) says that industries which are just starting up may need initial protection because they do not have the economies of scale available to established large foreign competitors. It could be that the whole economy of a country is inefficient compared to international rivals and that a period behind high protectionist barriers, where domestic industries can earn high profits and afford to make large investments, is needed to prevent a complete collapse of industry.

The limits to interventionism

Countries are finding it more difficult to adopt interventionist policies as time goes on. This is because international agreements are limiting the scope for interventionism. For instance, the UK government is

---

Question 2

Raising the rate of business investment was one of Labour's pre-election objectives. Today, the trade and industry department publishes an international study showing that capital spending has slowed, and Britain shows few signs of closing an accumulated investment gap of at least 30 per cent with comparable countries.

The accumulated investment gap reflects a long history of relatively low investment. The reasons are well known; a history of economic volatility has made businesses reluctant to invest for fear of being caught out by gyrating exchange rates or panicky u-turns in monetary and fiscal policy, and low wage costs make capital investment less attractive than in many other countries.

The best way of tackling volatility is to divorce monetary policy from politics, budget for the long term and give business protection from many of its currency problems by entering the European single currency. Labour is doing, or showing signs of wanting to do, all these things.

Low wages present a more complex problem. If capital investment replaces workers, the productivity of the remaining employees will rise, and so will their incomes. But the country will not be better off unless the displaced workers find equally well-paid jobs. Britain has a lower rate of unemployment than many comparable countries in part because low wages often make workers more attractive than machines.

However, ministers are right to want to help businesses invest. The danger is that a constant stream of policy initiatives will cause confusion and distort the tax system, rather than encouraging investment. The government should instead give its macroeconomic policies the chance to work. If it promotes stability and steady growth, rational companies will make sensible investments.

Source: adapted from the *Financial Times*, 6.12.1999.

(a) Explain why, according to the article, Britain has a low investment rate.
(b) Discuss whether the author of the article would support government moves to invest in what it saw as key industries for the future.

severely limited in its domestic policies by its membership of the EU. It cannot increase subsidies to individual industries without running the risk of being forced to stop by the European Commission. Monopolies are subject to EU law too. The UK obviously cannot put up tariff barriers against goods coming from other Common Market countries. It is also limited in its ability to protect domestic industries against foreign competition by being a signatory to international treaties which limit protectionism, which are now policed by the World Trade Organisation (WTO).

Not only the legal and institutional constraints on interventionism have increased over the past 30 years. The intellectual climate in favour of interventionism has waned, whilst that of the free market alternative has strengthened. Nationalisation, monopolisation and protectionism are policies which many governments around the world have abandoned. The move towards privatisation was, for instance, first started by the UK government in 1980. At the same time, countries like South Korea and Singapore, both of which have had very high growth rates in recent decades, are interventionist in the sense that government has promoted education and training and deliberately worked with the private sector in choosing which sectors of industry should be promoted.

A free market approach

The alternative approach has a long tradition in economics. Free market economists argue that the market is the most efficient way of allocating resources. Government intervention is at best ineffectual and at worst seriously damaging to the long run economic growth of the economy.

For instance, governments are not best placed to judge what type of training is needed by companies. If companies don't train their workers, it is because the economic rate of return on such training is too small. Companies must be using their scarce resources in more profitable ways (i.e. ways which increase national income more than expenditure on training). Subsidising investment too is economically damaging. It alters the balance between present and future consumption, making future consumption seem more valuable than it is. It encourages capital intensive industry and discriminates against labour intensive industry (because capital intensive industry will receive a large subsidy) without there being any economic justification for this distortion.

As for 'picking winners', government has a long history of throwing money at loss making ventures. Concorde, the shipbuilding industry, and nuclear power are examples of 'winners' that successive UK governments have picked. Nor has the quality of research in British universities given us a competitive advantage over the Japanese and the Germans.

Education and training Whilst recognising that the state has an important role to play in providing or organising education and training, free market economists would emphasise the importance of choice and private sector involvement in provision. Free market economists would stress that individuals and businesses are often better at determining their own needs than governments. Hence, governments should allow choice, for instance by providing individuals with education vouchers which they can use to

buy the education of their choice. When it comes to higher education, governments should be mindful of the need to avoid high levels of taxation. Higher education is very expensive and the main beneficiaries of higher education are those receiving education themselves. This is reflected in the higher wages of graduates.

Therefore, the best way to maximise the numbers of those going into higher education is to avoid government funding which can only be limited, but to embrace schemes where students themselves pay for their own education. Students will also work harder at university and be keen to use the skills they have learnt if they have to pay for that education.

In training, businesses are better placed than government to decide the training needs of their workers. Hence schemes such as the system of TECs in the UK, which place training under the control of businesses and encourage joint funding of training between the public sectors and private sectors, are more likely to yield a high rate of return than government directed schemes.

Investment Investment is best left to private industry. Profit maximising firms have the incentive to direct investment towards the highest yielding projects. If government intervenes, it often has other goals such as reducing unemployment or increasing prosperity in a particular area of the country. Yet for high growth, investment should be directed towards investment projects with high yields.

The size of the state The size of the state should be as small as possible, according to free market economists. The state needs to exist to provide a legal and monetary framework in which the free market can operate. It also needs to provide **public goods** (☞ unit 20). However, state spending crowds out free market spending. £1 spent on a council house is £1 that could have been spent in the private sector. In a free market consumers can choose what they want to buy. Their spending patterns are dictated by their aim to maximise their own utilities. But in the public sector the government forces consumers to accept the bundle of goods and services that the state has decided consumers ought to have. This bundle may be very different from the bundle that consumers would buy if they had a choice in a free market. So the conclusion is that welfare will be greater, the more resources are allocated in private free markets. Moreover, the private sector creates wealth through ongoing investment. Although the state does invest, a much greater proportion of its spending goes on consumption goods and services.

Free trade Free trade and competition are vital for growth. Free trade and competition mean that only those firms which are most efficient will survive. Protectionism and monopoly allows firms to remain in business which are likely to be far from efficient, exploiting the consumer through high prices and selling poor quality products. Free market economists point to the economic success of countries such as Hong Kong and South Korea which have been export orientated, succeeding in selling products at the right price and the right quality throughout the world.

Free market ideas are at the heart of **supply side economics** (☞ unit 38). They are also at the heart of free trade and the gains to be made from the exploitation of **comparative advantage** (☞ unit 14).

Question 3

Companies' successes in introducing new products have no connection with the overall climate for innovation in the countries in which they are based, according to a study published today. The report by Agamus, a German consulting group, raises doubts about the benefits of broad-based government schemes to boost innovation, such as research and development grants, educational programmes or tax breaks. It says the companies that perform best in innovation are the ones that devote most management resources to planning new products, sometimes in collaboration with other businesses with which they compete.

For instance, Germany is considered in the report to have the worst overall climate for business innovation as measured by social factors and the economic environment, even though the country appears to be among the leaders in innovation performance. The study suggests that while broadly based government measures to alter the economic and social climate for innovation may not work, there is a place for more targeted schemes to encourage companies at a 'micro' level in areas linked to the innovation process. It finds for instance that successful innovative companies are likely to have projects to reduce the number of defects in their products or to increase their technological content and to reduce costs. Agamus says only 5 per cent of production innovation funding by companies comes from public subsidies, whilst venture capital contributes just 0.4 per cent.

Source: adapted from the Financial Times, 19.7.1999.

(a) Explain the possible link between success in innovation and government schemes to boost such innovation.
(b) Agamus found no such link. To what extent might this be because 'only 5 per cent of production innovation funding' comes from public subsidies?

Applied economics

Industrial policy

In the 1980s and 1990s, various governments, notably in the UK and the USA, have pursued vigorous free market supply side policies in the belief that economic growth can best be stimulated by reducing government intervention in the market and liberating the energy and dynamism of market forces. This non-interventionist approach has already been discussed at length in unit 38. Here we will consider the alternative strategy of interventionist industrial policy.

It has been argued by some economists that countries such as Japan, Germany and France have experienced higher growth rates than the UK as a direct result of interventionist policies pursued by the governments of these countries. In Japan, for instance, the Ministry of International Trade and Industry (MITI) has used a wide range of policies in the post-war period aimed at transforming Japan into a world industrial super-power. Following Japan's defeat after the Second World War, US economists advised Japan to rebuild industries in which it had a comparative advantage, such as textiles and agriculture. This advice was rejected because it was felt that such a development strategy would create a Japan which would always lag behind the USA and Europe in economic development. Instead, through MITI, a number of key industries were identified which would be the industries of the future. Initially these included ships and steel, and later cars, electrical and electronic goods and computers. MITI then used a battery of policies to stimulate growth in these industries. These included:

- indicative plans for the whole economy, showing how output was set to grow industry by industry in the future;

- tax incentives, precisely targeted and withdrawn once a particular goal had been achieved;
- the creation of state owned companies to undertake research and production in high-risk areas of investment;
- large scale public funding of research and development programmes;
- encouraging co-operation between producers where this would enable Japanese companies to compete more successfully in international markets, even if this discouraged domestic competition;
- encouraging the free exchange of views and ideas between companies, particularly with regard to the fulfilling of state plans for the economy;
- subsidising investment in key industries;
- selective use of import controls, particularly to protect emerging industries.

The relationship between MITI and private industry was an informal one. Firms did not need to follow MITI plans. However, the deference to authority within Japanese society meant that Japanese companies on the whole conformed to the plans laid down by the ministry. MITI seemed to have been successful at 'spotting winners' - selecting those industries which were likely to have high growth rates in the future.

In France, there was a succession of state economic plans in the post-war era. Like the Japanese plans, they were indicative plans, showing how the French government expected output to rise over the next five year period. Again, like the Japanese, the French government has tended to be openly interventionist, supporting key industries, particularly high technology industries, through tax incentives, subsidies, tariffs and quotas and the giving of many other forms of support. Its ability to pursue interventionist policies was severly curtailed, however, in the 1990s by EU competition policy and increasing globalisation (☞ unit 97).

The UK has a long history of free trade, dating back to its dominance in trade in manufactures in the 19th century. Industrial policy has been pursued in a much less coherent manner and with far less conviction than in many other industrial countries. One important aspect of UK industrial policy has been **regional policy** (☞ unit 38), but this has been implemented far more to redirect industry to particular locations in the UK than to stimulate industrial growth overall. The Labour government of 1964-1970 has possibly been the government most committed to interventionism in the post-war period. In 1965, it produced a National Plan which was made irrelevant within months of its issue because the government decided to deflate the economy in order to resolve an exchange rate crisis. It also created the Industrial Reorganisation Corporation (IRC), which encouraged key companies to merge in

order to be able to exploit economies of scale more fully and be better equipped to compete in international markets. The IRC was abolished by the incoming Conservative administration in the early 1970s. The Labour administration of 1974-1979 created the National Enterprise Board, a holding company for the various relatively small state owned and partially state owned companies in public hands. Lack of funds prevented it from pursuing an aggressive strategy in, for instance, new technologies and it never had a significant impact on the structure of output before it was dissolved by the Conservative administration after 1979. From this evidence, it would be difficult to argue that UK industrial policy has been a key factor in promoting high growth. Advocates of interventionist industrial policy suggest that industrial policy has never really been given a chance to operate in the post-war period in the UK, and this explains its ineffectiveness. Free market economists suggest that it operated but has been ineffective and therefore government intervention in the market should be radically reduced.

South Korea

The management of the South Korean economy

The South Korean economy has been run on interventionist lines for the past 30 years. Key features of the system are:

- a division of the economy into market segments with companies being allocated marget segments in which they can compete by government;
- the fostering of conglomerate companies called *chaebols*; the two largest of these are Samsung and Hyundai;
- state intervention in industry, with the government giving large loans at low rates of interest to chaebols for investment to meet targets for production and exports set by the government;
- a willingness by the state to get South Korean companies to move into areas of manufacturing which are growing; for instance, in the mid-1980s, Samsung entered the semiconductor chip market despite the fact that it had no record of production in the industry and the USA and

Japan had established a technological lead; by 1995 Samsung was the the world's leading producer of memory chips;
- very high protectionist barriers on manufactured goods, whilst at the same time being happy to run current account deficits to import raw materials for manufacturing;
- a willingness by government to penalise *chaebols* which fail to work with the government; between 1992 and 1995, Hyundai lost access to offshore borrowing rights and access to low interest industrial loans from state banks because the founder of the group lost to a rival, President Kim, in the 1992 presidential elections; Hyundai also lost because during the same period its leading rival, Samsung, was allowed to expand into car production, one of the areas of production which had been allocated to Hyundai.

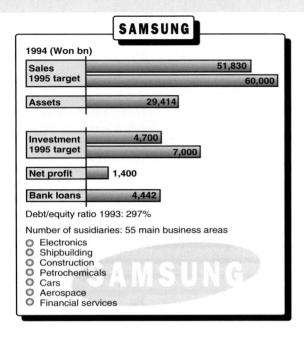

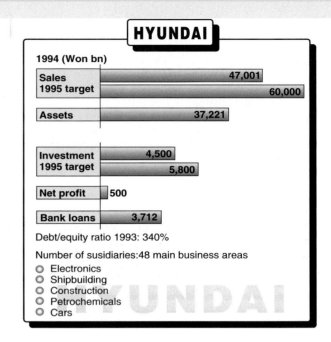

Note: companies in the UK which have a debt to equity ratio of 100 per cent or more are considered to be high risk with the possibility that they might go into bankruptcy.

Figure 91.1 *Performance of the two leading South Korean chaebols*

Table 91.1 *Annual growth in output and exports*

% annual growth

	South Korea			Hong Kong			UK		
	1970-80	1980-90	1990-98	1970-80	1980-92	1990-98	1970-80	1980-92	1990-98
Real GDP	9.6	9.4	6.2	9.2	6.9	4.4	2.0	3.2	2.2
Exports of goods and services	23.5	12.0	15.7	9.7	14.4	9.5	4.4	3.9	5.5

Table 91.2 *Distribution of GDP by output and expenditure*

Percentage of GDP

	South Korea			Hong Kong			UK		
	1970	1980	1998	1970	1980	1998	1970	1980	1998
By expenditure[1]									
Private consumption	75	64	55	62	60	60	62	59	64
Government consumption	10	12	11	7	6	9	18	22	21
Gross domestic investment	25	32	35	21	35	30	20	17	16
Exports of goods and services	14	34	38	92	90	125	21	27	29
Gross domestic savings	15	24	34	25	34	30	21	19	15
By output									
Agriculture	26	15	6	2	1	0	3	2	2
Industry	29	40	43	36	32	15	44	43	31
of which manufacturing	21	28	26	29	24	7	33	27	21
Services	45	45	51	69	67	85	53	55	67

1. GDP = General government consumption plus private consumption plus gross domestic investment plus exports minus imports.

Table 91.3 *Percentage of age group enrolled in education*

	South Korea			Hong Kong			UK		
	1970	1980	1996	1970	1980	1996	1970	1980	1996
Primary	99	104	92	92	95	90	97	100	100
Secondary	42	70	97	36	61	71	73	79	92
Tertiary	16	15	60	11	10	96	20	19	50

Source: adapted from World Bank, *World Development Report*.

The UK

1979 was a watershed in British economic history. Between the end of the Second World War and 1979, UK governments had been moderately interventionist in their running of the UK economy. Significant parts of the economy had been nationalised between 1945 and 1951. In the 1960s and 1970s, governments had encouraged firms to merge, rescued key firms from closure and attempted to influence their location through regional policy. After 1979, with the Conservative government of Margaret Thatcher, the government adopted a radical free market approach to running the economy. Most nationalised industries were privatised. The government stated that it would not intervene in commercial decisions by firms. Deregulation increased competition in some key industries.

The Asian crisis

The Asian crisis of 1998 exposed the financial problems faced by the South Korean economy. The crisis was initially caused by Thailand announcing that it had large amounts of non-performing loans, i.e. loans that were most unlikely to be repaid. Some of this money was owed to foreign lenders. This produced a liquidity crisis as foreign banks virtually stopped lending to Thailand for fear that they would lose more money. The contagion then spread to other countries in East Asia which had borrowed heavily abroad, such as Indonesia and South Korea. The result was a severe downturn in these economies as key firms found it difficult to finance ongoing production and investment. This had a multiplier effect and led to cancelled orders, bankrupt firms and lost jobs throughout these economies. South Korea found that its chaebols were financially bankrupt, having borrowed far more than they could pay back. They were forced to restructure. Subsidiaries were sold off to foreign companies to raise cash whilst others were closed down. By 2000, however, the South Korean

economy was growing strongly again. South Korean firms remain formidable world competitors despite their continued financial problems. However, the days when they had access to seemingly unlimited amounts of money to finance investment and expansion are gone. The government has declared that it will no longer intervene directly to pick winners and influence the investment decisions of individual Korean firms.

Hong Kong

Hong Kong is one of the most free market industrialised economies to be found in the world today. It is one of the 'Tiger economies' of East Asia which has enjoyed spectacular growth over the past 30 years.

1. Compare the growth and structure of the South Korean economy with that of the UK and Hong Kong.
2. Contrast the interventionist approach of the South Korean government to the economy with that of Hong Kong and the UK since 1979.
3. What, if anything, could the UK government learn from the South Korean experience if it wanted to raise its growth rate?

Applied economics

The goals of government policy

The UK government has traditionally had four main economic goals:
- low inflation;
- low unemployment;
- high economic growth;
- equilibrium on the external balance, the current balance of the balance of payments.

These are not necessarily all achievable at a single point in time. For instance, in a boom, unemployment may be falling but inflation may be rising and the external balance may be going into deficit. This happened during the Lawson boom of 1986-89. Alternatively, if there is a sudden shock to the system, such as a large rise in commodity prices or a sudden recession in a major trading partner, it may not be possible to achieve any of these goals. In the mid-1970s, with the oil price shock, UK policy makers found themselves facing rising inflation and unemployment, a growing external deficit and falling economic growth.

This forces governments to make choices about which are the most important goals. In the 1950s and 1960s, governments tended to emphasise the maintenance of full employment and an external balance. Full employment was important because so many workers could remember the depression years of the 1930s when unemployment soared. The external balance was significant because the UK was part of the Bretton Woods system of fixed exchange rates. Significant current account deficits led to selling pressure on the pound. Although in theory the government could devalue the pound, in practice it tended to deflate the economy to reduce imports and bring the current account back into balance.

From the mid 1960s, inflation began to rise significantly and control of inflation assumed much greater importance. By 1975, the then Labour Prime Minister, Jim Callaghan, was prepared to admit that the government could not control both inflation and unemployment at the same time. Governments allowed unemployment to rise and made the control of inflation their first priority.

The external balance also became less important as a government policy objective in the 1970s. In 1971, the UK left the Bretton Woods system and the pound was allowed to float. External deficits tended to lead to falls in the value of the pound, and vice versa. However, so long as governments did not want to maintain a particular exchange rate, these were of little significance. In the mid 1980s, the then Chancellor of the Exchequer, Nigel Lawson, declared that the external balance was no longer of any policy significance. His view was that so long as deficits could be financed, it was not up to governments to decide whether households and firms wanted to borrow money to finance more imports in any one year.

By the 1990s, there was a consensus that the main short term goal of government policy should be the control of inflation. Unemployment might have to rise in the short term and GDP might have to fall to secure this objective. However, in the long term governments should be adopting supply side policies which would bring about a reduction in unemployment and a rise in the growth rate. The external balance was of no policy significance in itself. By 2000, government was beginning to think that full employment rather than just lower unemployment might become a realisable objective once more.

Managing demand

Monetary policy In the 1950s and 1960s, monetary policy took a number of forms. Governments attempted to control credit through rules and regulations about how much building societies, banks and other lenders could loan out. Interest rates too were raised and lowered to manipulate borrowing levels. They were also used to influence the value of the pound. In the 1970s and the 1980s, the emphasis moved to controlling the money supply, but by the mid 1980s it was clear that there was no simple relationship between growth in the money supply and inflation (the quantity theory of money relationship). Control of interest rates then became the policy weapon used. In the 1980s and 1990s, monetary policy was the main way in which governments managed aggregate demand. If inflation threatened to rise, interest rates would be raised, and vice versa. This was referred to as a 'one club' policy - the government only had one weapon at its disposal to steer the economy.

In 1997, the Bank of England was granted independence and given control of the operation of monetary policy. The government set it targets for inflation (e.g. to maintain it at 2.5 per cent or less). There were fears when the Bank of England was given its independence that it would act very cautiously and tend to pursue deflationary policies to achieve its inflation target. This would have meant higher unemployment and lower growth than otherwise might be the case. In practice, the Bank of England has, according to most, attempted to set interest rates which would allow the maximum economic expansion within the constraints of its inflation target.

Fiscal policy Fiscal policy in the 1950s and 1960s was seen as being a more effective way of influencing aggregate demand than monetary policy. Governments would increase budget deficits when the economy was in recession and reduce them when the economy was overheating. In the 1970s, the traditional relationships between inflation and unemployment broke down and by the mid-1970s the economy was experiencing stagflation, high inflation and high unemployment. Traditional fiscal policy was powerless to bring down both inflation and unemployment. So governments broadly abandoned the use of active fiscal policy. However, they have allowed the automatic stabilisers within the system to manage the trade cycle. For instance, in the recession of 1990-92, the PSNCR, the budget deficit, was allowed to rise, and peaked at £43 billion in 1993. The stated aim of the government today is that the budget should be in balance over the trade cycle. In recessions, it will be allowed to go into deficit whilst in booms, there will be a budget surplus. This rule prevents the government from destabilising the economy, from over-inflating it or inducing too severe a recession by the inappropriate use of fiscal policy.

Exchange rate policy Exchange rate policy has, for very brief periods, been used to influence inflation. In 1987-88, Nigel Lawson adopted a policy of shadowing the value of the German currency, the deutschmark. Germany had been throughout the post war period a relatively low inflation economy. The argument was that by linking the pound to the deutschmark, the UK could mirror Germany's low inflation. The policy was abandoned when inflation began to rise in the UK and the Chancellor was forced to raise interest rates sharply to deflate the economy. However, the policy re-emerged in a slightly different form when the UK joined the ERM (the precursor to European Monetary Union) in 1990. The pound at the time was relatively high in value. The argument was that maintaining a high value of the pound would help keep downward pressure on inflation. It proved a costly policy mistake. By September 1990 when the UK joined the ERM, high interest rates had arguably already reduced aggregate demand sufficiently to return the economy to low inflation within 12 months. To maintain a high value of

the pound, the government was forced to keep interest rates much higher that it would otherwise have wanted in 1991 and 1992 as the economy stagnated in a prolonged recession. When the UK was forced out of the ERM in September 1992 and the pound fell around 15 per cent, the government was able to cut interest rates. Both depreciation of the currency and lower interest rates soon helped the economy to come out of recession. Since then, the government has allowed the pound to float freely. However, if and when the UK joins the single currency, it will have to decide on a value for the pound on entry. Too high a value will depress aggregate demand and could lead to a prolonged recession. Too low a value will increase aggregate demand and could lead to inflation in the short term.

Prices and incomes policies In the 1960s and 1970s, government's used prices and incomes policies (☞ unit 90) to suppress cost-push inflationary pressures. Whilst they were successful in the short term in reducing aggregate demand, they failed to address the underlying reasons why aggregate demand was rising so fast. The result was that they had little impact on long run prices.

Influencing aggregate supply

In the 1950s and 1960s, governments concentrated on industrial and regional policy to influence aggregate supply. At the time, it was felt that the UK faced two main problems: lack of competitiveness compared to other countries and regional inequalities with higher unemployment levels outside the south of England and the Midlands. In the 1970s, free market economists coined the term 'supply side economics'. They argued that efficiency could be increased if markets became free markets. In the 1980s, the Conservative government implemented a large number of supply side reforms (☞ unit 38). These included trade union reform, privatisation of state monopolies and deregulation of industries such as the bus industry. Fiscal policy, no longer used actively to influence aggregate demand, was used to influence aggregate supply. For instance, income tax rates were cut whilst tax and benefit incentives were given to those who started up their own businesses. Fiscal policy is still used today as one of the main ways in which governments try to influence aggregate supply. Other ways include further liberalisation of markets, such as telecommunications and air transport, and improvements in value for money in areas such as education and the health service.

Equity

Fiscal policy has been used to redistribute income and wealth in society. In the 1960s and 1970s, Labour governments favoured taxing higher income earners more heavily to gain revenue to increase benefits to those on low incomes. One of the results was a marginal income tax rate on earned income of 83 per cent for the highest earners. If these individuals also enjoyed unearned income, such as bank interest or dividends on shares, the unearned income was taxed at 98 per cent. This led to severe market distortions. High income earners avoided tax by ceasing to work, moving abroad, receiving large fringe benefits or altering their financial assets so that they earned no income but maximised untaxed capital gain. In the 1980s, the Conservative government brought down marginal tax rates on higher income earners and also cut welfare benefits to the poor. The argument was that lowering tax rates would increase incentives to work and take risks, whilst cutting benefits would encourage the poor to take on work or work harder. The result was a significant redistribution of income from the poor to the rich. The Labour government since 1997 has combined elements of both these strategies. It wishes to see fewer inequalities in society. It argued that the way to do this was to encourage the poor to become more self sufficient through the tax and benefit system. So tax breaks were given to raise the income of those in low pay, increasing the incentive for those out of work to take on work. Help with child care facilities was given to encourage low paid parents, particularly women, to carry on working when they had children rather than become welfare dependent. In the long term, the government wants to see most workers have a private pension rather than rely on the state for income in old age.

Free trade and protectionism

UK governments since the Second World War have tended to favour free trade rather than protectionist policies. Since the 1950s, trade barriers have been brought down, particularly through the trade agreements negotiated through GATT, which is now the World Trade Organisation, WTO (☞ unit 40). Britain's membership of the EU in 1973 led to free trade with EU partners and further limited Britain's ability to pursue protectionist policies because such decisions were now taken at EU level.

Control of the economy

The UK government's ability to control the economy is, in many ways, severely limited and is likely to become more rather than less limited over time.

Shocks The government cannot prevent economic shocks destabilising the economy. Arguably the most important shock to hit the UK in the post war period was the rise in oil prices between 1973 and 1981 (☞ unit 8). There have been many others though, including the Korean War in the early 1950s and more recently the Asian crisis in 1998.

Long term shifts in consumption and trading patterns At the start of the twentieth century, one in ten workers were in the textile industry. Agriculture and coal mining were significant employers too. Today, these industries are relatively unimportant in terms of both output and employment. This is just one example of how the economy changes over time. Today, IT industries are booming and the internet is predicted to change the way in which the economy works. Such shifts give governments many opportunities but also leave them with many problems. In the post-war period, it could be argued that the restructuring of British industry was an important supply side constraint and limited the ability of government to influence long term economic growth. When the UK was part of the Bretton Woods system of exchange rates, Britain's lack of international competitiveness caused it recurring exchange rate problems.

International trade The UK has become a relatively more open economy over time. The greater the openness of its economy, the less a government is able to use fiscal or monetary policy to influence aggregate demand. For instance, if the government uses expansionary fiscal policy, the more open the economy, the more leaks out into greater demand for imports and the less is spent domestically. The last time a UK government used fiscal policy to reflate the economy in 1972-73, there was a substantial increase in domestic demand but the current account deficit rose to an unsustainable level.

International treaty obligations The UK is bound by a number of international treaty obligations which limit its ability to pursue independent policies. Trade policies are influenced by both the WTO and the EU. Supply side issues, such as giving aid to individual firms, or working hours for employees, are constrained by EU law. If and when the UK joins the European Single Currency, policy will be further constrained. Monetary policy will be decided not by the Bank of England but the European Central Bank. For fiscal policy purposes, the government will have to keep its budget deficit to a maximum of 3 per cent of GDP and the level of the National Debt will not have to exceed 60 per cent of GDP.

Macroeconomic strategy and prospects

Over the past three decades, the UK economy has exhibited high volatility in output and inflation. Instability has made it hard for individuals and firms to plan and invest and has damaged the long-term growth of the economy.

The government has reformed the framework for macroeconomic policy to promote economic stability. Greater stability will help people and businesses to plan for the long term. Making the the economy more stable will also raise employment and living standards.

The government's reforms to the macroeconomic framework involve both monetary and fiscal policy.

A modern macroeconomic framework Stability is essential for high levels of growth and employment. Maintaining low and stable inflation is the best contribution monetary policy can make to long-term economic and social prosperity.

High and variable inflation involves social costs that are likely to fall particularly hard on those people on lower incomes. By damaging growth, high inflation leads to lower average incomes than otherwise. High inflation and macroeconomic instability can also affect those on low incomes through the impact on the distribution of income.

Lower and stable inflation plays a central role in creating the stable macroeconomic environment which individuals and businesses need to make sound investment and saving decisions. By ensuring that monetary policy focuses on maintaining low inflation, both sharp slowdowns and runaway booms can be avoided.

The government reformed the monetary framework immediately on coming to office to ensure that monetary policy makes the best possible contribution to achieving high and stable levels of growth and employment. The primary objective of monetary policy is price stability. But, subject to that, the Bank of England must also support the government's economic policy objectives, including those of growth and employment. The government's inflation target - reaffirmed in this Budget - is $2\frac{1}{2}$ per cent for the 12-month increase in the Retail Price Index excluding mortgage interest payments (RPIX).

The forward-looking and transparent nature of the new monetary policy framework means interest rates have been changed, when necessary, in a more timely fashion than in the past. This has helped to keep output closer to trend, preventing a repeat of the large boom seen in the late 1980s. With inflation close to target, the UK is now in a better position to steer a course of stability and respond to the current global economic slowdown.

Macroeconomic policies aimed at achieving sustained growth, sound public finances and low inflation should also promote exchange rate stability, consistent with the government's objective of a stable and competitive pound in the medium term.

The fiscal policy framework The government's new fiscal policy framework constitutes the second key element of its strategy to promote economic stability.

The new framework has been designed to tackle head-on a number of key deficiencies:
- fiscal policy objectives were not precise and were subject to change.
- the framework promoted neither the economic stability nor long-term focus vital to economic success.
- current spending often took precedence over capital.
- fiscal decisions did not accurately reflect the impact of current public spending on future generations.

The Code for Fiscal Stability sets out the new fiscal policy framework and gives it a statutory base.

Five principles lie at the heart of the Code - transparency, stability, responsibility, fairness and efficiency.

The government has set two strict fiscal rules to deliver sound public finances:
- the golden rule - on average over the economic cycle, the government will borrow only to invest and not to fund current spending; and
- the sustainable investment rule - public sector net debt as a proportion of GDP will be held over the economic cycle at a stable and prudent level.

Borrowing is permitted to finance public investment. This is because capital spending generates assets that confer benefits to both current and future generations.

High levels of public debt, however, can reduce the government's ability to buffer the economy against major shocks. Debt may also impose other costs.

Source: adapted from HM Treasury in the *Financial Times*, 10.3.1999.

1. Outline the economic problems that the UK economy has faced 'over the past three decades' according to the government.
2. Analyse, using diagrams, how the monetary and fiscal policies described in the data can help solve those economic problems.
3. To what extent could the government avoid major economic problems in the UK if stock markets in the US crashed and the US economy went into a deep and prolonged depression?

Summary

1. The exchange rate is the price at which one currency is convertible into another.
2. The equilibrium exchange rate is established where demand for a currency is equal to its supply.
3. The equilibrium exchange rate will change if there is a change in the value of exports or imports, the value of net long term foreign investment, or the volume or direction of speculative flows.
4. On a day to day basis in a free exchange market, speculation tends to be the dominant influence upon the price of a currency.
5. In the longer term, economic fundamentals relating to exports, imports and long term capital flows tend to determine the exchange rate.
6. The purchasing power parity theory of exchange rates states that exchange rates will in the long run change in line with relative inflation rates between economies.
7. Speculation tends to lead to short term exchange rate instability.

The exchange rate

Different countries use different types of **money** or **currency**. In the UK, goods and services are bought and sold with pounds sterling, in France with the French franc, and in Germany with the German deutschmark.

The rate at which one currency can be converted (i.e. bought or sold) into another currency is known as the **exchange rate**. For instance, a French company may wish to purchase pounds sterling. If it pays 10 million francs to purchase £1 million, then the exchange rate is 10 francs to the pound. A UK household may wish to buy US dollars to take on holiday to Florida. If they receive $2 000 in exchange for £1 000, then the exchange rate is $2 to the pound, or 50p to the dollar.

Question 1

Table 93.1

Original value of the trade weighted index	Change in exchange rate %		New value of the trade weighted index
	Country X	Country Y	
100	+10	+20	
100	+20	+10	
100	-10	+10	
100	+10	-10	
100	- 6	- 6	

Country A trades only with two countries. 60 per cent of its trade is with country X and 40 per cent with country Y.
(a) Complete the table by calculating the new value of the trade weighted index for country A following changes in its exchange rate with countries X and Y.
(b) What would be the values of the trade weighted index if country A had 90 per cent of its trade with country X and 10 per cent with country Y?
(c) Calculate the new values of the trade weighted index in (a) if the original value of the trade weighted index were not 100 but 80.

Exchange rates are normally expressed in terms of the value of one single currency against another single currency - pounds for dollars for instance, or deutschmarks for yen. However, it is possible to calculate the exchange rate of one currency in terms of a group or **basket** of currencies. The EFFECTIVE EXCHANGE RATE (a measure calculated by the International Monetary Fund) and the TRADE WEIGHTED EXCHANGE RATE INDEX (or the EXCHANGE RATE INDEX as it is often called) are two different calculations of the average movement of the exchange rate on the basis of weightings (☞ unit 3) determined by the value of trade undertaken with a country's main trading partners.

To illustrate how the trade weighted index is calculated, assume that the UK trades only with the USA and France. 70 per cent of UK trade is with the USA and 30 per cent is with France. The value of the pound falls by 10 per cent against the dollar and by 20 per cent against the franc (which, incidentally, means the franc has gone up in value against the US dollar). The trade weighted index will now have changed. The fall in the dollar contributes a 7 per cent fall in the exchange rate (10 per cent x 0.7) whilst the fall in the franc contributes a 6 per cent fall (20 per cent x 0.3). The average fall is the sum of these two components (i.e. 13 per cent). If the trade weighted index started off at 100, its new value will be 87.

Equilibrium exchange rates

Foreign exchange is bought and sold on the FOREIGN EXCHANGE MARKETS. Governments may buy and sell currencies in order to influence the price of a currency. Here we will assume that governments do not intervene and that currencies are allowed to find their own price levels through the forces of **demand** and **supply**. There are then three main reasons why foreign exchange is bought and sold.
- International trade in goods and services needs to be financed. Exports create a demand for currency whilst imports create a supply of currency.
- Long term capital movements occur. Inward investment to an economy creates a demand for its currency. Outward investment from an economy

creates a supply.

• There is an enormous amount of speculation in the foreign exchange markets.

The equilibrium exchange rate is established where the demand for the currency is equal to its supply. Figure 93.1 shows the demand and supply of pounds priced in dollars. The market is in equilibrium at an exchange rate of $2 = £1. Buying and selling is equal to £1 000 million each day.

The demand curve is assumed to be downward sloping. If the price of the pound falls against the dollar, then the price of British goods will fall in dollar terms. For instance, if the exchange rate falls from $2 = £1 to $1 = £1, then a British good costing £1 000 will fall in price for Americans from $2 000 to $1 000. Americans should therefore buy more British goods and demand more pounds to pay for them. So a fall in the price of the pound should lead to an increase in quantity demanded of pounds, giving rise to the downward sloping demand curve. Similarly the supply curve is upward sloping because a fall in the value of the pound will increase the price of foreign imports for the British, leading them to reduce their purchases of foreign goods and therefore of foreign exchange.

All other things being equal, a fall in the value of the pound from, say, $2 to $1 is likely to make the pound look cheap and this may attract speculative buying of the pound and discourage speculative selling. This would then produce downward sloping demand curves and upward sloping supply curves for the pound sterling. However, in general on the capital side, it is unclear how buyers and sellers will react to rises and falls in the price of a currency. Given this, the justification for downward sloping demand curves and upward sloping supply curves for foreign exchange tends to rest on arguments about the buying and selling of currency for export and import payments.

Figure 93.2 shows that the exchange rate will change if either the demand or supply curve shifts. Equilibrium is at price OB and output OQ.

• If British exports to the USA increase, American firms will need to buy more pounds than before to pay for them. Hence an increase in the value of UK exports will increase the demand for pounds, shifting the demand curve from D_1 to D_2. The exchange rate will therefore rise from OB to OC.

• If imports from the USA increase, British firms will need to buy more dollars than before to pay for them. They will buy these dollars with pounds. Hence an increase in the value of UK imports will increase the supply of pounds. The supply curve will shift to the right from S_1 to S_2. The equilibrium value of the pound will fall from OB to OA.

• If the rate of interest in the London money markets increases, US savers will switch funds into the UK. This is likely to be short term money or **hot money** which flows from financial centre to financial centre attracted by the highest rate of return. An increase in inflows on the capital account of the balance of payments will increase the demand for pounds, shifting the demand curve from D_1 to D_2, and increasing the value of the pound from OB to OC.

• If there is an inflow of funds for long term investment in the UK, again the demand for pounds will rise. For instance, Japanese investment in car plants in the UK will raise the demand for pounds (and increase the supply of yen) shown by the shift in the demand curve from D_1 to D_2, raising the value of the pound from OB to OC.

• Speculation is the single most important determinant today of the minute by minute price of the pound. If speculators believe that the value of the pound is going to fall against the dollar, they will sell pounds and buy dollars. An increase in the supply of pounds on the market, shown by the shift in the supply curve from S_1 to S_2, will lead to a fall in the price of the pound from OB to OA.

It is difficult to assess the level of speculative activity on the foreign exchange markets. Less than 5 per cent of daily foreign exchange transactions in London is a result of a direct buying or selling order for exports and imports

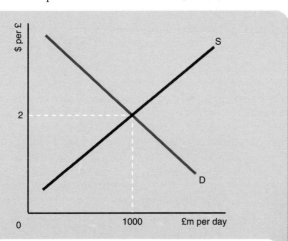

Figure 93.1 *Floating exchange rate systems*
In a free exchange rate market, the price of a currency is determined by demand and supply. Equilibrium price is $2 to the pound whilst equilibrium quantity demanded and supplied is £1 000 million per day.

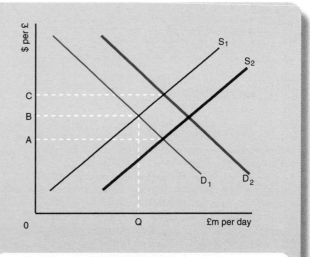

Figure 93.2 *Changes in exchange rates*
The equilibrium value of the pound will change if there is a change in either the demand for or supply of pounds (or both).

or long term capital flows. However, each order tends to result in more than one transaction as foreign exchange dealers cover their exposure to the deal by buying and selling other currencies. Even if every order were to result in an extra three transactions, this would still only account for at most 20 per cent of transactions, which would suggest that speculative deals form the majority of trading on a daily basis.

Thus, in the short term, the value of a currency is dominated by speculative activity in the currency. However, there is evidence to suggest that in the longer term, the value of a currency is determined by economic **fundamentals** - by exports, imports and long term capital movements.

The purchasing power parity theory of exchange rates

If purchasing power parity exists, then a given amount of currency in one country, converted into another currency at the current market exchange rate, will buy the same bundle of goods in both countries. For instance, if £1 = $2, and consumers only buy jeans, then purchasing power parity will exist if a £20 pair of jeans costs $40 in the USA. It won't exist if a pair of jeans priced at £20 in the UK is priced at $50 or $30 in the USA. If there are only two goods in the economy, food and clothing, then purchasing power parity will exist if an identical bundle of food and clothes costs £100 when it costs $200 in the USA, or £500 when it costs $1 000 in the USA.

The PURCHASING POWER PARITY (PPP) THEORY states that exchange rates in the long term change in line with different inflation rates between economies. To understand why exchange rates might change in line with inflation rates, assume that the balance of payments of the UK is in equilibrium with exports equal to imports and capital outflows equal to capital inflows, but it is suffering from a 5 per cent inflation rate (i.e. the prices of goods are rising on average by 5 per cent per year). Assume also that there is no inflation in the rest of world. At the end of one year, the average price of UK exports will be 5 per cent higher than at the beginning. On the other hand, imports will be 5 per cent cheaper than domestically produced goods. At the end of the second year, the gap will be even wider.

Starting from a PPP rate of $2 = £1, this change in relative prices between the UK and the rest of the world will affect the volume of UK exports and imports. UK exports will become steadily less price competitive on world markets. Hence sales of UK exports will fall. Imports into the UK on the other hand will become steadily more price competitive and their sales in the UK will rise. The balance of payments on current account will move into the red.

A fall in the volume of UK exports is likely to lead to a fall in the value of exports (this assumes that exports are **price elastic** ☞ unit 8) and therefore the demand for pounds will fall. A rise in the value of imports will result in a rise in the supply of pounds. A fall in demand and a rise in supply of pounds will result in a fall in its value.

So the purchasing power parity theory argues that in the long run exchange rates will change in line with changes in prices between countries. For instance, if the annual UK inflation rate is 4 per cent higher than that of the USA over a period of time, then the pound will fall in value at an average annual rate of 4 per cent against the dollar over the period. In the long run, exchange rates will be in equilibrium when **purchasing power parities** are equal between countries. This means that the prices of typical bundles of traded goods and services are equal.

The causes of inflation are complex. However, one fundamental reason why economies can become less price competitive over time is **labour productivity** (i.e. output per worker). If output per worker, for instance, increases at a rate of 2 per cent per annum in the UK and 5 per cent per annum in Japan, then it is likely that the UK will become less competitive internationally than Japan over time. Wage costs are the single most important element on average in the final value of a product. In the UK, approximately 70 per cent of national income is made up of wages and salaries. Hence changes in labour productivity are an important component in changes in final costs.

Question 2

Figure 93.3 shows the demand and supply of pounds. D and S are the original demand and supply curves respectively.

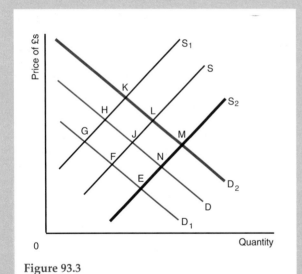

Figure 93.3

(a) At which point (E to N) is the market in equilibrium?
(b) To which point will the market be most likely to move in the short term if there is: (i) an increase in exports; (ii) an increase in imports; (iii) a fall in interest rates in the London money markets; (iv) a rise in takeovers of US companies by British companies; (v) a belief that the value of the deutschmark will rise in the near future; (vi) the discovery of a huge new oil field in the North Sea; (vii) bad summer weather in the UK which sharply increases the number of foreign holidays taken; (viii) a series of prolonged strikes in the UK engineering sector of the economy?

country will tend to depress the exchange rate.

Question 3

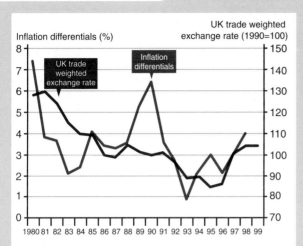

Figure 93.4 *Inflation differentials[1] and the UK trade weighted exchange rate*
1. UK inflation rate minus the average G7 (seven largest OECD countries) inflation rate.
Source: adapted from *Economic Trends Annual Supplement*, Office for National Statistics; OECD, *Economic Outlook*.

(a) Explain why differences in the UK inflation rate and that of other countries might affect the value of the pound.
(b) To what extent is this relationship supported by the data?

Other factors affecting competitiveness

Price is an important factor in determining purchasing decisions, but it is not the only consideration. Other factors include design, quality, reliability or availability for instance. Over long periods of time, countries can become increasingly uncompetitive internationally in one or more of these factors. Indeed it is often argued that the UK has suffered this fate over the past century. What then happens is that the economy finds it more and more difficult to export whilst imports increase. There is therefore a continual downward pressure on the exchange rate. The debate about what makes a country internationally uncompetitive is the same as the debate about why a country grows at a slower rate than other countries (☞ unit 26).

Long term capital movements

During much of the 19th century, the USA was a net capital importer. It financed its development in part by borrowing money from Europe. Countries which are in a position to borrow money will have a higher long term exchange rate than they would otherwise have done. For instance, during the 19th century, Europeans demanded dollars to invest in the USA. This rise in demand led to a rise in the value of the dollar. Similarly, net long term lending by a

Speculation

Day to day exchange rate movements today are affected by speculation or short term flows of capital. Thirty years ago this was different, as nearly all countries imposed a variety of EXCHANGE CONTROLS upon their currency movements. At the most extreme, currency could only be bought and sold through the central bank. In more liberal regimes, purchases could be made on the open market, but individuals and firms often had to seek permission from the central bank to trade in currency. Exchange controls have now largely been swept away in the major industrialised trading nations of the world. Vast sums of money are committed internationally and flows of just a fraction of these across exchanges can lead to large currency fluctuations.

Classical or monetarist economists in the 1960s and 1970s predicted that speculation would dampen exchange rate fluctuations and help stabilise currencies. They argued that the exchange rate in the long term was fixed by economic fundamentals such as the balance between exports and imports. Economic fundamentals only change slowly over time and therefore market expectations of future exchange rates will only change slowly over time too. If the market believes that in two year's time the value of the pound against the dollar will be $2 = £1, and today the value of the pound is $3 = £1, then speculators will sell pounds, driving down the value of the pound towards its longer term value.

The evidence of the 1970s and 1980s suggests that this is not true. In the above example, it is just as likely that the value of the pound will go up as down even if speculators agree that in the long term the pound is overvalued at today's prices. The reason is that speculation by its very nature is short term. Speculators are not very interested in the price of sterling in 2 years' time. They are far more interested in the price of sterling in the next 30 minutes. Large sums of money can be made by buying and selling in the very short term.

It is impossible to pin-point exactly what drives short term exchange rate markets. Certainly markets tend to react in a predictable way to news about changes in economic fundamentals. A bad set of trade figures, for instance, which points to a future fall in the exchange rate, tends to lead to selling pressure today. A rise in domestic interest rates will tend to increase today's exchange rate as speculators anticipate future capital inflows to take advantage of the higher rates of interest. But many exchange rates are inexplicable. Speculators 'lose confidence' or 'gain confidence'. They are very influenced by the opinions of other speculators. Some individuals in the market may be extremely influential. A word spoken in a television interview or written in an article may spark off feverish buying or selling.

Some economists argue that there is no pattern at all to exchange rate movements: that they are on a **random walk** and the market is totally **chaotic**.

Even though speculation can be highly destabilising in the short term, economists tend to believe that economic fundamentals prevail in the long term.

Question 4

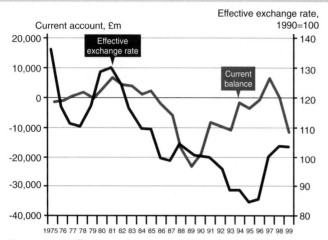

Current account, £m

Effective exchange rate, 1990=100

Figure 93.5 *Effective exchange rate (1990 = 100) and the current balance*

Source: adapted from *Economic Trends Annual Supplement*, *Monthly Digest of Statistics*, Office for National Statistics.

(a) Explain what economic theory predicts is likely to happen to the exchange rate if the current account position deteriorates.

(b) Speculative activity should anticipate changes in economic fundamentals such as changes in the current account position. Do the data provide any evidence for suggesting that currency speculators have correctly anticipated changes in the UK current account position?

Applied economics

The exchange rate, 1978–1981

Between 1978 and 1981, the effective exchange rate (EER) of the pound rose by over twenty five per cent before falling back a little, as can be seen in Table 93.2. There is a number of possible reasons why there should have been such a significant change in the EER.

One important factor was the change in the oil balance on the balance of payments. 1976 had seen the first production of North Sea oil and by the early 1980s production had reached its highest level. The effect was to transform a traditional deficit on trade in oil (with the UK importing all her oil requirements) to a substantial surplus. As Table 93.2 shows, there was a £5 000 million turnaround in the oil balance. The effect of increased production was magnified by the second oil crisis of 1978-9 which increased the price of oil from approximately $15 a barrel in 1978 to $36 a barrel in 1981. Increased exports result in greater demand for pounds and hence a higher value of the pound. So the positive change in the oil balance helped increase the EER.

Table 93.2 *Factors affecting the exchange rate, 1979-1981*

		Effective exchange rate 1985 = 100	Interest rate[1] %	Change in official reserves[2] £million	Current account balance £million	Oil balance £million	Net external assets £billion
1978	Q1	105.0	6½	-46	-146		
	Q2	99.2	9	-2 026	509	-2 129.1	12.0
	Q3	100.1	10	54	151		
	Q4	99.6	12½	-311	422		
1979	Q1	101.6	13½	955	-658		
	Q2	106.9	12	68	4	-1 070.7	11.0
	Q3	111.9	14	152	310		
	Q4	107.7	14	-166	-205		
1980	Q1	113.1	17	457	-96		
	Q2	115.5	17	140	-125	60.5	16.8
	Q3	118.3	16	-223	1143		
	Q4	123.6	16	-83	1 873		
1981	Q1	127.1	14	319	2 888		
	Q2	122.7	12	-1 448	1 932	2 871.9	31.1
	Q3	114.1	12	-1 167	510		
	Q4	112.2	15	-123	1 309		

1. Bank base rate at 15 February, 15 May, 15 August, 15 November.
2. Additions to reserves (+), falls in reserves (-).
Source: adapted from *Economic Trends Annual Supplement*, *Annual Abstract of Statistics*, *United Kingdom National Accounts (Blue Book)*, Office for National Statistics.

Despite the positive change in the oil balance, the current balance (total exports minus imports) deteriorated in 1978-9. This was because the economy was enjoying a boom, and imports were being sucked into the country to satisfy domestic demand. However, by the early part of 1980, the economy was spiralling downwards into deep recession, which was to see a fall of 5 per cent in GDP and nearly 20 per cent in manufacturing output before the bottom in mid-1981. That led to a sharp fall in imports which, together with the effect of North Sea oil, led to a record current account surplus in 1981. This move from deficit in 1979 to record surplus in 1981, a turnaround of approximately £7 000 million on an annual basis, must have contributed to the rise in sterling between 1979 and 1981.

A further factor which is likely to have put upward pressure on the pound was the rise in interest rates. Between 1978 and 1980, bank base rates rose from 6½ per cent to 17 per cent. This increased the interest rate differential between London and other financial centres round the world, attracting speculative flows of money into sterling. Falls in interest rates in 1980 and 1981 were followed by falls in the exchange rate in 1981.

Speculation too must have played a part in sending the EER to record levels. In 1978, there was still grave international concern about the competitiveness of the UK economy and the pound. By 1979, the pound was being seen as a petro currency. It didn't take much to look at what was happening to the oil balance to realise that the UK was likely to be in substantial surplus on current account in the early 1980s. Substantial surpluses would be likely to increase the EER, and therefore speculators bought pounds, which had the effect of further raising the EER.

There were two factors which helped prevent the rise in the pound between 1979 and 1981 being even greater than it was. First, in November 1979, the government abolished exchange controls. These had limited the outflow of money on the capital account, reducing outflows from their free market levels. Following abolition, there was a substantial outflow of capital from the UK, reflected in the increase in net external assets of the UK shown in Table 93.2.

Second, the Bank of England intervened in the foreign exchange markets, on the whole buying foreign currency in exchange for pounds (i.e. the supply of pounds increased). The fact that the Bank of England was intervening like this can be seen from the increase in the official foreign currency reserves of the UK during this period. When the exchange rate began to fall in 1981, the Bank of England reversed its policy. It began to buy pounds with foreign currency. This helped break the fall in the pound, but official foreign currency reserves fell.

The exchange rate, 1995-99

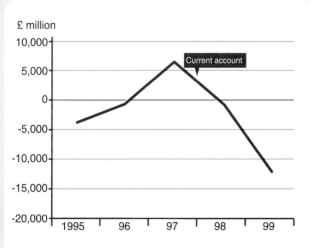

Figure 93.6 *UK, current account*
Source: adapted from *Economic Trends*, Office for National Statistics.

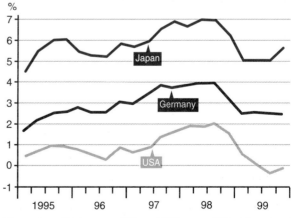

Figure 93.7 *Interest rate differentials[1] between UK and eurozone[2], Japan and USA, %*
1. Difference on 3 month sterling LIBOR.
2. As represented by German 3 month interest rates.
Source: adapted from *Financial Statistics*, Office for National Statistics.

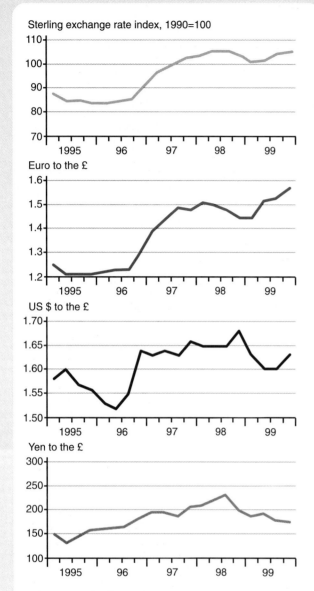

Sterling exchange rate index, 1990=100

Euro to the £

US $ to the £

Yen to the £

Figure 93.8 *Sterling exchange rates*
Source: adapted from *Economic Trends*, Office for National Statistics.

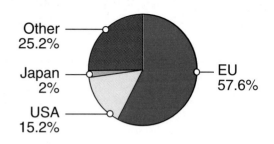

Figure 93.9 *Exports: the UK's main trading partners, 1998*
Source: adapted from *Monthly Digest of Statistics*, Office for National Statistics.

Manufacturers seek change of policy

Since the pound strengthened in 1996, British manufacturers have been complaining that they are under a severe competitive disadvantage. They have been lobbying the Chancellor and the Bank of England to cut interest rates. However, high interest rates are the only weapon the government uses in its fight against inflation. The control of inflation is given higher priority than any problems faced by manufacturing industry.

Source: adapted from the *Financial Times*, 25.1.2000.

1. **Analyse whether the pound was strong or weak in the second half of the 1990s.**
2. **Discuss what might have led to the changes in the value of the pound against other currencies shown in the data.**

Summary

1. There is a number of different types of exchange rate system - mechanisms for determining the conditions of exchange between one currency and another.
2. The Bretton Woods system was an example of an adjustable peg system. In the short term, currencies were fixed in value against each other. In the longer term, currencies could be devalued or revalued. Currencies were fixed in the short term by central bank intervention - the buying and selling of currency using foreign currency reserves.
3. In a floating exchange rate system, the value of a currency is determined, without central bank intervention, by the forces of demand and supply in foreign currency markets.
4. With a managed or dirty float, the price of a currency is determined by free market forces, but occasionally central banks will intervene using their reserves to steady the price of the currency.
5. The Gold Standard was an example of a fixed exchange rate system. Currencies were pegged in value against gold and therefore they could not change in value against each other.

6. The European Monetary System is an example of a currency bloc. A group of currencies maintain fixed exchange rates against each other, but float against other currencies.

Exchange rate systems

An EXCHANGE RATE SYSTEM is any system which determines the conditions under which one currency can be exchanged for another. In unit 93, it was assumed that exchange rates were determined purely by the free market forces of demand and supply. This type of system is known as a free or floating exchange rate system. In contrast fixed exchange rate systems have existed in the past, where currencies have not been allowed to change in value against each other from year to year. In between, there is a variety of adjustable peg systems which combine elements of exchange rate stability in the short term with the possibility of exchange rate movements in the long term.

Adjustable peg systems

An ADJUSTABLE PEG SYSTEM is an exchange rate system where, in the short term, currencies are fixed or pegged against each other and do not change in value, whilst in the longer term the value of a currency can be changed if economic circumstances so dictate. Between the end of the Second World War and the early 1970s, exchange rates were determined by an adjustable peg system. It was known as the BRETTON WOODS SYSTEM after the town in the USA where Allied powers met in 1944 to discuss new international trade arrangements for the post-war era.

How it worked Under the system, each country fixed its exchange rate against other currencies. For instance,

between 1949 and 1967, the pound was valued at US $2.80. This was known as the par value for the currency. The Bank of England guaranteed to maintain prices within a narrow 1 per cent boundary. So the price of the pound could fluctuate on a day to day basis between $2.78 and $2.82. Prices were maintained because central banks bought and sold currency. When the price of pounds threatened to go below $2.78, the Bank of England would intervene in the market and buy pounds. When the price threatened to go over $2.82, the Bank of England would

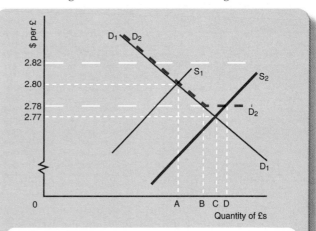

Figure 94.1 *Fixed exchange rate systems*
The pound is pegged at $2.80 but is allowed to fluctuate within a very narrow band from $2.78 to $2.82. If market forces shift the supply curve from S_1 to S_2, the Bank of England will need to buy BD pounds to maintain the minimum price of $2.78.

Question 1

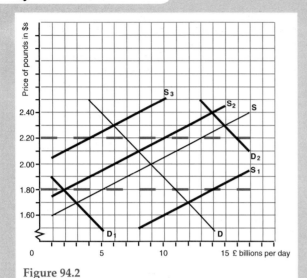

Figure 94.2

D and S are the free market demand and supply curves for pounds in dollars. The Bank of England is committed to keeping the dollar price of sterling between $2.20 and $1.80.

(a) What is the free market price of the pound?
(b) With a demand curve D, how much currency (in £) will the Bank of England have to buy or sell per day if the supply curve shifts from S to: (i) S_1; (ii) S_2; (iii) S_3?
(c) With a supply curve S, how much currency (in £) will the Bank of England have to buy or sell per day if the demand curve shifts from D to: (i) D_1; (ii) D_2?

sell pounds.

This is illustrated in Figure 94.1. The free market demand curve for pounds is $D_1 D_1$. In contrast, the demand curve under an adjustable peg system, $D_2 D_2$, is kinked. Above a price of $2.78, the demand curve is the same as the free market demand curve. But at $2.78, the Bank of England is prepared to buy any amount of foreign currency to maintain the value of the pound at this minimum level. Therefore the demand curve for pounds becomes horizontal (i.e. perfectly elastic) at this price.

Assume that the supply curve is initially S_1, resulting in an equilibrium price of $2.80. OA is bought and sold and the Bank of England does not intervene in the market. Now assume that imports into the UK increase, shifting the supply curve for pounds to the right to, say, S_2. The new free market equilibrium price would be $2.77, below the minimum **intervention price** within the system, with OC currency bought and sold. The Bank of England would react to this by buying pounds with gold or foreign exchange held in its RESERVES. To restore the exchange rate to the minimum $2.78, it has to buy BD pounds, the difference between the OB pounds demanded by the rest of the market at $2.78 and OD, the quantity supplied for sale.

If the value of the pound threatened to rise above the

maximum price of $2.82, the Bank of England would sell pounds on the market, increasing the supply of pounds and thus forcing their price down. Note that in Figure 94.1, the supply curve of sterling under an adjustable peg system would be kinked like the demand curve, becoming horizontal (i.e. perfectly elastic) at a sterling price of $2.82. The Bank of England would be prepared to supply any amount of sterling in exchange for foreign currencies at a price of $2.82.

Adjustment mechanisms Under the Bretton Woods system, countries were committed to two major policy objectives:
● in the short term, to maintaining stable exchange rates;
● in the long term, to maintaining a balance of payments equilibrium (which they would be forced to do anyway by free market forces).

In the short term, exchange rate stability was maintained by buying and selling currencies as explained above. The system was therefore crucially dependent upon the existence of gold and foreign currency reserves held by central banks. In theory, the price of the currency was set at its long term equilibrium level. A run down in reserves caused by the need to buy the domestic currency when the currency was weak would be offset by increases in the reserves at other times when the currency was strong.

However, free market speculation could lead to very rapid depletions of a country's gold and foreign currency reserves. The UK suffered a series of **sterling crises** in the 1950s, 1960s and 1970s as speculators sold pounds believing that the UK government might devalue sterling. Governments had a limited number of options open to them if they wanted to maintain the value of their exchange rate.
● The most likely response to heavy selling pressure on the currency was to raise interest rates. This attracted speculative money from abroad, raising the demand for and therefore the price of the currency. In the medium term, a rise in interest rates would have a deflationary impact via the **transmission mechanism** (☞ unit 89).
● The government could also attempt to prevent a fall in the value of the currency by introducing **currency controls** (☞ unit 93).
● As a last resort, the central bank would turn to the **International Monetary Fund** (IMF). The founders of the system realised that there would be times when an individual country would run out of reserves. So it set up an international fund, the IMF, which would lend money to central banks when needed. Central banks would deposit part of their gold and foreign currency reserves with the IMF and in return would be able to borrow a limited amount of money when in a crisis.

Short term measures were unlikely to satisfy the market for long if speculators were selling a currency because they judged that there was a FUNDAMENTAL DISEQUILIBRIUM on the country's balance of payments. If imports were greater than exports and/or the capital account was in deficit over a long period of time, the central bank of the country would continually be buying its currency and thus running down its reserves. Eventually the reserves, including any money borrowed

from the IMF, would be exhausted and the currency would have to fall in value. Governments could adopt a number of long term policies to prevent this happening (☞ unit 96 for more detail).
● It was intended that governments would officially devalue their currency before markets forced this anyway.
● In practice, governments tended to deflate their economies, reducing imports and thus restoring a current account balance.
● Protectionist measures, such as raising tariffs and quotas, were a possibility but were illegal under WTO rules (☞ unit 40). This severely limited their use by major industrialised countries.
● Supply side policies designed to improve long term competitiveness were also a possibility.

Question 2

In 1952, the ratio of world central bank gold and foreign currency reserves to total world imports stood at 70 per cent. By 1966, this had fallen to 38 per cent.

(a) Suggest reasons why this fall is likely to have contributed to the collapse of the Bretton Woods system in the early 1970s.

Crawling peg systems

A CRAWLING PEG system is a form of adjustable peg system. A country fixes its currency value against another currency within a band. However, there is a mechanism built into the system which allows the band to rise and fall regularly over time. For instance, the band may be moved every three months. The central value could then be based on the average value of the currency in the previous three months. Crawling peg systems allow more flexibility if a country is experiencing different economic circumstances from other countries and in particular those against which its currency is pegged. It makes it much easier to adjust the value of the currency as economic circumstances change.

Floating exchange rate systems

In a pure FLOATING or FREE EXCHANGE RATE SYSTEM, the value of a currency is determined on a minute by minute basis by free market forces. This is the exchange rate system described in detail in unit 93. Governments, through their central banks, are assumed not to intervene in the foreign exchange markets.

In theory there is no need for intervention because the balance of payments must always balance (☞ unit 30). The balance of payments will look after itself. In practice, governments find it impossible not to intervene because changes in exchange rates can lead to significant changes in domestic output, unemployment and inflation.

Moreover, sharp falls in a currency are usually damaging politically and hence governments are tempted at these times to shore up the currency by buying in the market.

A system where the exchange rate is determined by free market forces but governments intervene from time to time to alter the free market price of a currency is known as a MANAGED or DIRTY FLOAT. Governments intervene by buying and selling currency as under the Bretton Woods system explained above. It is 'managed' by governments. It is 'dirty' because it is a deliberate interference with 'pure' forces of demand and supply.

Adjustment mechanisms Since the collapse of the Bretton Woods system in the early 1970s, world trade has been

Question 3

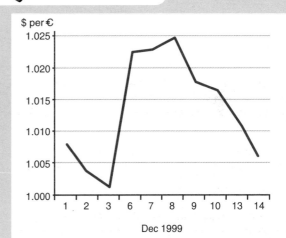

Figure 94.3 *Euro versus the dollar*
1. 4 and 5, 11 and 12 of December were weekends and therefore non-working days.
Source: adapted from Primark Datastream.

Market sentiment suggested that the euro could fall back to parity ($1 = E1) in the near future. 'Parity is definitely back on the cards, and the euro is likely to go a little further through than before' said Chris Furness, senior currency strategist at 4Cast in London. 'But support from central banks below the parity level should prevent it going any further'.

In Tokyo, Eisuke Sakakibara, the former vice finance minister for international affairs, was reported as saying that the Bank of Japan (the Japanese central bank) would intervene substantially in the new year with the aim of driving the dollar-yen value up to Y110.

Source: adapted from the *Financial Times*, 15.12.1999.

(a) At the time the article was written, both the euro and the yen were 'floating freely' against the dollar. What does this mean?
(b) (i) What happened to the value of the euro against the US dollar between 8 and 14 December 1999?
    (ii) What must have been happening in the foreign exchange markets for this to happen?
(c) How could the European Central Bank or the Bank of Japan intervene to support currencies? Explain your answer using a diagram.

regulated not under a pure free exchange system but under a system of managed or dirty floats. Governments have used interest rates and their gold and foreign currency reserves to manipulate the value of their currencies. Depreciation, appreciation and deflation have all been used in an attempt to alter current deficits or surpluses. Governments have found it more difficult to pursue openly protectionist policies because of international pressure for greater free trade. Currency controls too have fallen into disfavour as supply side economics has stressed the value of free markets and deregulation in promoting the international competitiveness of economies.

Fixed exchange rate systems

A FIXED EXCHANGE RATE SYSTEM is one where a currency has a fixed value against another currency or commodity. The best known example of such a system in the past was the GOLD STANDARD, which operated in the 19th and early 20th centuries.

How it worked Under the Gold Standard, the major trading nations made their domestic currencies **convertible** into gold at a fixed rate. For instance, in 1914 a holder of a £1 note could go to the Bank of England and exchange the note for 0.257 ounces of gold. Because French citizens could exchange French francs for a fixed amount of gold, and German citizens the same, and so on, it meant that there was a **fixed exchange rate** between the major trading currencies of the world. The domestic money supply was directly related to the amount of gold held by the central bank. For every extra 0.257 ounces of gold held by the Bank of England, it could issue £1 in paper currency (the currency was backed by gold). On the other hand, a fall in the gold reserves at the Bank of England meant an equivalent fall in the paper money in circulation.

Adjustment mechanisms A deficit on the current account of the balance of payments could not be corrected by devaluation of the currency. By the rules of the Gold standard mechanism, the currency was fixed in value. Imbalances on the current account were corrected instead through deflation and reflation or changes in interest rates.

Assume that the UK is on the Gold Standard and that the current account is in deficit. There is therefore a net outflow of pounds to foreigners. Foreigners have no use for pounds so they will exchange those pounds for gold at the Bank of England. With less gold, the Bank of England will be forced to reduce its issue of notes (the notes handed in by foreigners for gold will effectively be destroyed). The money supply will fall and interest rates will rise. This will produce a deflation in the economy through the **transmission mechanism**. Not only will demand fall, reducing imports, but there will also be a fall in prices (predicted by the **quantity theory of money** ☞ unit 84). Exports will thus become more competitive and imports less competitive. The current account will return to equilibrium. The initial rise in unemployment caused by the fall in demand will be reversed as exports

increase, returning the economy to full employment.

A small but increasing number of small countries are adopting CURRENCY BOARDS. This is a form of fixed exchange rate system where the price of one currency is fixed against another currency. This could be the US dollar, as in the case of Argentina, the German deutschmark and now the euro as in the case of Bulgaria, or the French Franc and now the euro as in the case of some West African countries.

How it works A country fixes the value of its currency, usually against a major international currency such as the US dollar or the euro. The choice of currency is linked to foreign trade. For Argentina, the USA is its most important trading partner and so it chose the US dollar. For Bulgaria, Europe is its most important trading partner and so it chose a European currency. The central bank then prints domestic currency, such as pesos. However, it is only able to print as much domestic currency as it has reserves of its pegged currency. For instance, in 1999, the Argentinean central bank held $15 billion worth of US dollar assets to cover all its peso notes and coins in circulation. It is not allowed to print any more notes and coins without acquiring further dollar assets.

Adjustment mechanisms The adjustment mechanism is the same as with the gold standard. A deficit on the current account will lead to an outflow of dollars, which in turn will reduce the money supply and cause deflation. This leads to lower domestic demand and hence lower imports; and lower domestic prices and hence exports increase as they become more competitive.

Currency blocs

A country may choose to peg its currency against one other currency but allow the currency to fluctuate against all others. This would be a minimal example of a CURRENCY BLOC, a group of currencies fixed in value against each other but floating against all others.

The most important example of a currency bloc in the 1980s and 1990s was the EUROPEAN MONETARY SYSTEM (EMS). This was a system designed to lead onto the creation of a single European currency, the euro. Participant countries agreed to keep their currencies within a band around a central reference point. If a currency threatened to break out of the band, central banks within the EMS would intervene in the market, buying or selling currency to maintain the currency in its band. The country's central bank could also change interest rates to alter its value. The whole bloc, however, floated freely against other world currencies including the dollar and the yen. If the UK is to join the euro, it will have to peg the pound against what is now the euro and show that it can maintain exchange rate stability within this system.

Like the Bretton Woods system, this is an example of a hybrid system, combining elements of fixed and floating exchange rate systems.

Question 4

Argentina is thinking of going one step further from its existing currency board exchange rate system. The government has ordered officials to investigate the advantages and disadvantages of becoming a dollar economy. Under this system, Argentina would no longer have its own currency, the peso. All notes and coins in circulation would have to be bought from the US. Argentineans would then use the exact same dollar to make transactions as people in New York or San Francisco.

One advantage would be that the Argentinean currency could never be devalued against the US dollar. Under the present system, the Argentinean government may one day be tempted to print more pesos than its dollar reserves justify. Dollarisation of the economy would prevent such a temptation. One downside is that Argentina would lose seigniorage, the gain from being able to issue notes and coins. At present, the currency board doesn't hold dollar notes to back up the peso. Instead, it holds US Treasury Bills, loans by the US government on which the US government pays interest. This interest, which is seigniorage, at present amounts to around $750 million (£457 million) a year. If it has to sell these Bills to buy notes and coins, Argentina will lose $750 million, whilst the US government will gain it. Argentina would like the US government to share this seigniorage between the two countries.

Source: adapted from the *Financial Times*, 21.5.1999.

(a) Explain how Argentina fixed its currency to the dollar in May 1999.
(b) Why might Argentina lose $750 million a year if it 'dollarised' its economy?

key terms

Adjustable peg system - an exchange rate system where currencies are fixed in value in the short term but can be devalued or revalued in the longer term.
Bretton Woods system - an adjustable peg exchange rate system which was used in the post-Second World War period until its collapse in the early 1970s.
Crawling peg system - an adjustable peg system of exchange rates where there is an inbuilt mechanism for regular changes in the central value of the currency.
Currency bloc - a group of currencies which are fixed in value against each other but which may float freely against other world currencies.
Currency board system - a fixed exchange rate system where a country fixes the value of its currency to another currency. Notes and coins in the domestic currency can only be printed to the value of assets in the other currency held by the central bank.
European Monetary System - a currency bloc where the participating currencies were fixed against each other within a band and where the bloc as a whole fluctuated freely against other currencies.
Exchange rate system - a system which determines the conditions under which one currency can be exchanged for another.
Free or floating exchange rate system - where the value of a currency is determined by free market forces.
Fixed exchange rate - a rate of exchange between at least two currencies which is constant over a period of time.
Fundamental disequilibrium on the balance of payments - where imports are greater than exports over a long period of time resulting in unsustainable levels of international borrowing.
Gold and foreign currency reserves - gold and foreign currency owned by the central bank of a country and used mainly to change the foreign exchange value of the domestic currency by buying and selling currency on foreign exchanges.
Managed or dirty float - where the exchange rate is determined by free market forces but governments intervene from time to time to alter the free market price of a currency.
The Gold Standard - an exchange rate system under which currencies could be converted into gold at a fixed rate, hence providing a relative price between each currency.

Applied economics

The Bretton Woods system

The Bretton Woods system, first devised in 1944, provided exchange rate stability. Hence, it can be argued that it encouraged the growth of world trade during the 1950s and 1960s.

It was intended that governments could choose how to resolve a current account deficit. They could deflate the economy, creating unemployment, reducing imports and reducing domestic inflation. This was the same adjustment mechanism as present under the Gold Standard. They could also devalue the currency. By changing the relative price of exports and imports, the

economy could be made more internationally competitive without creating unemployment. However, there would be some cost in terms of imported inflation.

In practice, countries tended not to devalue except in a crisis. This was because devaluation, wrongly in the view of many economists, came to be associated with economic failure. Deficit countries tended to use deflation as the main policy weapon to deal with balance of payments problems, negating the flexibility of adjusting relative prices built into the system. The burden of adjustment also fell solely on deficit countries. There was little pressure within the system for surplus countries to reduce their surpluses, for instance by revaluing their currencies. The result was that the system became increasingly brittle. Deficit countries like the UK tended to lurch from one foreign exchange crisis to the next whilst surplus countries like West Germany resisted pressures to take any action to reduce their surpluses.

Problems were compounded by the fall in the value of gold and currency reserves as a ratio of world trade during the 1950s and 1960s. To maintain exchange rate stability, central banks bought and sold currency. So long as the central banks were the main buyers and sellers in the market, they could dictate the price of foreign exchange. However, during the 1950s and 1960s world trade expanded at a much faster rate than gold and foreign currency reserves.

In an attempt to inject greater liquidity into the international financial system, the IMF issued **Special Drawing Rights** (SDRs) to member countries in 1969. SDRs are a form of international currency which can only be used by central banks to settle debts between themselves or with the IMF. When a country needs foreign currency to defend its own currency, it can buy it with the SDRs it holds. Whilst SDRs, effectively a handout of 'free' money, increased liquidity in the system at the time, the IMF failed to allocate further SDRs to member countries. The countries which control the IMF, the industrialised nations of the world, particularly the USA, are afraid that further creation of SDRs would encourage countries, particularly in the Third World, to put off dealing with fundamental balance of payments problems by using newly distributed SDRs to finance their large current account deficits. Today, SDRs account for only about 5 per cent of world reserves.

The Vietnam war from 1965 onwards made matters worse. To finance the war the USA ran a large current account deficit and therefore was a net borrower of money on its capital account. Individuals and firms were quite happy to lend their pounds, francs, deutschmarks and other currencies to the US and in exchange receive dollars because exchange rates were fixed to the dollar and dollars were seen to be as safe as gold itself.

By the late 1960s there was a large amount of money, particularly dollars, being held outside its country of origin. Americans were holding pounds, Japanese were holding deutschmarks, Germans were holding dollars, etc. This provided the base for large speculative activity on the foreign exchanges. It had become obvious that the United States would need to devalue the dollar if it were to return to a balance of payments equilibrium. On the other hand, it was obvious that Germany and Japan, two large surplus countries, would have to revalue their currencies. There was persistent selling pressure on the dollar and buying pressure on the D-mark and yen. Central banks found it more and more difficult to match the speculative waves of buying and selling. In the early 1970s, after some traumatic devaluations and revaluations, one country after another announced that it would float its currency.

The Bretton Woods system provided a long period of exchange rate stability during which there was a significant expansion of world trade. The cost of adjustment to current account deficits was probably less than under the Gold Standard. Although deflation was widely used in response to this problem, countries also devalued their currency, trading off slightly higher imported inflation for less unemployment. However, the system was not sufficiently robust to prevent its collapse in the early 1970s.

The Real

The creation of the Real

In the 1970s, 1980s and early 1990s, Brazil was plagued by constant bouts of hyperinflation. In 1994, the Brazilian government introduced yet another reform package aimed at eliminating inflation. Central to this was the creation of a new Brazilian currency, the Real, which was pegged in value against the US dollar at 1 Real to $1. It was fixed within a 3 per cent band. The reform package was highly successful. Hyperinflation disappeared, the economy began to grow strongly again and international investors were attracted back to what is, potentially, the largest market in the world after the USA, the European Union and China.

The Real, 1994-99

Brazil used an adjustable peg system to determine the value of the Real. It was pegged against the US dollar. When the Real was created, its value against the US dollar was roughly correct in terms of purchasing power parities. However, within the first 18 months of the adjustment programme used to bring down inflation, between the second quarter of 1994 and the end of 1995, prices and wages in Brazil approximately doubled. This meant that the value of the Real was considerably overvalued by 1996. The government responded by allowing a very slow and gradual depreciation of the Real, shown in Figure 94.4.

In the Autumn of 1997, the Real came under fierce selling pressure on the foreign exchange markets. This was connected with the start of the Asian crisis when Thailand announced that much of its financial system was in a state of collapse. The Thai currency, the baht, was itself pegged against the US dollar. Due to heavy selling pressure, the Thai authorities were forced to abandon the peg and allow the baht to float. Foreign exchange speculators then proceeded to attack other weak pegged currencies including the Real. In 1998,

currency speculators forced the Russian rouble off its peg, and in January 1999 another wave of selling forced Brazil to abandon its peg. The Real was devalued immediately by 8 per cent and the central bank announced that in future the Real would be allowed to fluctuate within a wide 9 per cent band against the US dollar at its new rate.

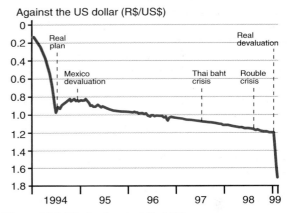

Figure 94.4 *The Real against the US$*
Source: adapted from Primark Datastream.

The Brazilian economy, 1994-99

The Brazilian economy was, in many ways, very successful following the introduction of the Real. Inflation was brought under control, whilst economic growth was strong. Investment increased. However, the economy also faced a number of weaknesses. The most important was the failure of the government to control its finances. The central government of Brazil and its states had borrowed heavily in the previous decades, both at home and overseas, to finance budget deficits. Part of the stabilisation programme of 1994-95 was a commitment to bring these budget deficits under control. In 1997, the budget deficit was 4 per cent of GDP. Following the Thai crisis in late 1997, the government announced that it would adjust its budget to bring down its borrowing to 2 per cent of GDP in 1998. However, it had been forced to raise interest rates to 50 per cent in October 1997 to defend the Real against speculative pressures. Fiscal austerity combined with high interest rates pushed the

economy into recession. Tax revenues fell sharply and the final budget deficit for 1998 was an unsustainable 8 per cent of GDP.

In November 1998, Brazil secured a $41 billion financial package from the IMF. The funds could be borrowed if Brazil needed them to defend the value of the Real. In January 1999, the government of one of Brazil's states announced that it would not be making repayments of its loans owed to the Brazilian central government for the next 90 days. It was a negotiating ploy designed to make the central government agree to easier terms on its loans to the heavily debt-ridden state. But it had the effect of undermining confidence in Brazil's ability to repay its foreign debt. There was a wave of selling of the Real. On 12 January, an estimated net $700 million of Reals were sold by speculators and had to be bought up by the Brazilian central bank to maintain the Real's value. On 13 January, the central bank devalued the Real.

Source: adapted from the *Financial Times* 14.1.1999, 18.1.1999, 22.1.1999.

1. **Explain why the Real came under selling pressure in January 1999.**
2. **What measures did the Brazilian central bank take to defend the Real and how, in theory, should they have helped?**

3. **Discuss whether the Brazilian authorities could have done anything to prevent the devaluation.**

Summary

1. An exchange rate system should encourage world trade, particularly through exchange rate stability. Floating exchange rate systems have proved very poor at providing exchange rate stability.
2. Economic costs of adjustment when the balance of payments of a country is in fundamental disequilibrium should be low. Adjustment mechanisms within fixed exchange rate systems, such as the Gold Standard, and to a lesser extent adjustable peg systems, such as the Bretton Woods system and the EMS, tend to create unemployment because they rely upon deflation of the economy. In contrast, floating exchange rate systems tend to give rise to inflation when currencies depreciate following current account deficits.
3. Fixed exchange rate systems, and to a lesser extent adjustable peg systems, force governments to maintain inflation rates comparable to their industrial competitors.

4. Exchange rate systems should be robust. Free exchange rate systems are the most robust because they require the least government intervention.

Judging between systems

Over the past 200 years, a variety of exchange rate systems has been in operation. This would suggest that no system is without its problems. A number of criteria can be used to judge the relative merits of different exchange rate systems.

Encouragement of world trade

World trade enables countries to specialise in the production of those goods and services in which they have a **comparative advantage** (☞ unit 14). This specialisation increases the total amount of goods available for world consumption. Hence exchange rate systems could be judged upon the extent to which they encourage or discourage world trade.

It has long been argued that exchange rate volatility, such as occurs under free floats or managed floats, discourages trade. If exchange rates fluctuate by large amounts on a day to day basis, exporters and importers will find it impossible to know what price they will receive or have to pay for deliveries in the future. For instance, a UK exporter may agree to sell goods to the US for payment in US dollars in 3 months' time. Built into the $1 million price is a 10 per cent profit margin. Over the 3 months, the pound falls in value against the dollar by 15 per cent. Not only will the exporter lose its planned profit, but it will also make a loss on the contract of about 5 per cent.

There are ways around this problem in a free or managed float regime. **Futures markets** exist, where foreign exchange can be bought at a fixed price for delivery at some point in the future. So the exporter could have bought pounds **forward**. At the time it signs the export agreement, it would have taken out a contract in the foreign exchange markets to buy $1 million worth of pounds in three months' time (which it will pay for using the $1 million gained from the export contract). It now has a guaranteed price in pounds for its contract. Of course the forward price of pounds may be less than the price of pounds today (the spot price). But this is not important in the sense that the UK exporter will have based the export agreement price on the forward rate of the pound, and not on the current spot price. This process of buying currency forward to prevent losses is known as **hedging**.

Unfortunately, futures markets are limited in their scope. It is not possible, for instance, to buy a currency for delivery in 5 years' time. So long term contracts need other forms of insurance. This is often provided by government agencies which guarantee prices in the domestic currency for large long term export contracts. Hedging and insurance cost money and they therefore either discourage trade or raise its cost. Companies that are unable or unwilling to hedge or to insure have to decide whether or not to take the risk of proceeding with the export or import contract.

So, in general, the less volatile the currency movement, the less likely that international trade will be discouraged. Fixed exchange rate systems, such as the Gold Standard, and adjustable peg systems, such as the Bretton Woods system, are on these criteria considered to be 'better' systems than free or managed float systems.

Question 1

Moves towards European monetary union would lift a heavy burden from the backs of Europe's smaller businesses, most of which lack the expertise to deal with the complexities of foreign exchange markets. Smaller businesses pay a high cost for converting small amounts of foreign currencies, says Ms Jane Waters, a foreign exchange consultant. Banks typically charge 1 per cent on small deals of up to $10 000, but only 0.1 per cent on larger amounts.

Van Halteren, a Dutch meat processor with annual sales of £23m, pays about £25 000 each year to hedge the riskier currencies, such as sterling.

Many small businesses are frightened off from using the textbook exchange hedges - forward transactions or currency option arrangements - because of their perceived complexity and cost. They take evasive action. They invoice customers in their own currency; some delay making transfers of funds until currency rates are favourable; others boost prices to cover the currency risk.

All these manoeuvres carry risks. Better by far, smaller owners argue, to establish a foreign exchange framework which allows companies to get on with their business rather than having to watch currency movements.

(a) Explain, using examples from the passage, why exchange rate stability might encourage world trade.

Economic costs of adjustment

A country's balance of payments on current account can move into disequilibrium. Different exchange rate systems have different mechanisms for returning the balance of payments to equilibrium. The movement back to equilibrium may involve economic costs, such as increased unemployment or lower economic growth. The larger these transitional costs, the less attractive the exchange rate system.

The main cost of adjustment within a fixed exchange rate system or an adjustable peg system is likely to be increased unemployment. Under the Gold Standard, a current account deficit was automatically eliminated in the long term through a fall in domestic prices. However, economists disagree about the extent to which money wage rates fall quickly in response to unemployment. Keynesian economists tend to argue that wage rate adjustment is slow. Classical or monetarist economists argue that it is a relatively quick process. The slower the adjustment, the higher the cost in terms of unemployment and lost output. Countries abandoned the Gold Standard in the early 1930s because they felt that floating exchange rates would enable their economies to reduce unemployment at a faster rate than if the exchange rate was linked to gold.

Under the Bretton Woods system, countries tended to avoid devaluing their currencies (☞ unit 94). When current accounts moved into deficit, governments tended to deflate their economies, imposing higher taxes or

reducing government expenditure. Unemployment therefore rose as the rate of economic growth fell.

One of the main criticisms of floating and managed exchange rate systems is that they encourage inflationary behaviour on the part of governments. Assume that an economy has a higher inflation rate than its major trading partners and that, consequently, the current account is in deficit. Under the Bretton Woods system, governments would have been likely to tackle these two problems through deflating the economy. Under the Gold Standard, deflation would have occurred automatically. Rising unemployment and lost output are politically unpopular as well as costly economically. Under a floating exchange rate system, the exchange rate should fall automatically with a current account deficit. This leads to **imported inflation**. A government can avoid tackling domestic inflation and the current account deficit simply by allowing the exchange rate to fall continually. Hence there is no anti-inflation discipline built into the floating exchange rate system.

Moreover, tackling inflation under a floating exchange rate system can be more costly than under fixed exchange rate systems. Assume that the government reduces the money supply and raises interest rates as part of an anti-inflation package. The rise in domestic interest rates will encourage an inflow of speculative funds on the capital account. This will increase the price of the currency. An increase in the exchange rate will make the economy less internationally competitive. Exports will fall and imports will rise, leading to a worsening of the already bad current account deficit. But falling exports and rising imports also lead to a fall in aggregate demand, pushing the economy into recession. This recession is part of the process by which inflation falls and the economy becomes more internationally competitive. The current account will only return to equilibrium when the market exchange rate is approximately equal to the **purchasing power parity rate** (☞ unit 93). It will only stay in equilibrium when the country's inflation rate is equal to that of its trading partners. Lowering inflation is a painful process and will certainly not be politically popular.

Financial disciplines

Today, there are some who argue that inflation is the most important economic problem facing economies and governments. Monetarists argue that inflation is caused by excessive increases in the money supply. Under the Gold Standard, governments are unable to expand the money supply unless stocks of gold in the central bank rise first (although countries did issue a fixed amount of notes which were not backed by gold - the **fiduciary issue** - this did not affect the principle that central banks could not increase notes in circulation without corresponding increases in their stocks of gold). Changes in stocks of gold are unlikely to be very large in the short term. Hence the Gold Standard provides an important check on the ability of governments to generate inflation through the creation of money.

Equally, under an adjustable peg system, such as the Bretton Woods system, governments could not allow their inflation rates to differ greatly from those of their industrial competitors because otherwise they would lose international competitiveness, their current account would go into deficit and they would then be likely to deflate to solve this problem.

However, under a floating exchange rate system, as argued above, governments can always solve problems of

international competitiveness, caused by domestic inflation, by allowing their currencies to fall in value. There is no financial discipline imposed by the system.

Robustness of the system

Some exchange rate systems are extremely robust; that is, they are unlikely to break up when economic conditions are unfavourable. The more likely it is that an exchange rate system will break up under strain, the less attractive the exchange rate system.

Fixed exchange rate systems, or adjustable peg systems, are less robust than free or managed float exchange rate systems. Countries abandoned the Gold Standard in the early 1930s during the Great Depression because they wanted to be able to devalue their currencies in order to gain competitive advantage. By devaluing, they hoped to be able to reduce imports, boost exports and thus reduce domestic unemployment. However, the rest of the 1930s, with a managed float system of exchange rates, saw a series of competitive devaluations with countries trying to export their unemployment. Competitive devaluations are ultimately self-defeating because devaluation by one country, matched by a devaluation by another country simply left exchange rates unchanged.

The unsatisfactory experience of the 1930s led to the creation of the Bretton Woods system. It broke up in the early 1970s, partly because countries failed to devalue and revalue when there was a fundamental disequilibrium on their current accounts and partly because central banks lacked reserves to counter the growing mountain of speculative money which moved so quickly from country, to country.

The managed float system of the 1970s, 1980s and 1990s has had to cope with three oil crises, and in the early 1980s, the worst world slump since the 1930s. Free and managed float systems are extremely robust because governments can allow free market forces to determine the value of the exchange rate without intervening in the market. However, the extreme volatility of exchange rates over the period has led many to advocate a return to some sort of fixed or adjustable peg system. The robustness of the system is less attractive than the exchange rate stability that can be found.

Question 2

Throughout the 1980s the UK exchange rate was determined under a floating exchange rate system, whilst the exchange rate of her main EU trading partners was determined under an adjustable peg system - the ERM. Inflation rates in all EU countries tended to fall in the first half of the 1980s and then remained low till the end of the decade. UK inflation rates tended to be 2-3 per cent higher than those of France and Germany during the period, whilst the value of pound tended to fall. By 1987 the value of the pound was 15 per cent lower against the ECU (the basket or average of European currencies) than in 1980. However, between 1982 and 1988, average annual economic growth in the UK exceeded that of most European countries. In 1988, inflation in the UK began to accelerate again with the UK government responding by doubling interest rates to 15 per cent. The economy began to slow down. Then, in 1990, the UK joined the ERM at the very high central exchange rate of DM2.95, the same rate of exchange as prevailed on average in 1986. To maintain the value of the pound, the UK government was forced to keep interest rates at much higher levels than it probably would have wanted. The UK economy was in a very long prolonged recession between 1990 and 1992, with inflation falling rapidly to levels not seen since the 1960s. In September 1992, speculative pressure forced the pound to be suspended from the ERM. The value of the pound immediately fell over 10 per cent and the government cut interest rates from 10 per cent to 5^1/2 per cent over the next 12 months. Growth in the economy rapidly picked up and the economy came out of recession.

(a) (i) What was true about the UK's inflation rate and rate of economic growth during the period 1982-88 compared to those of her main EU partners?
(ii) With these trends, explain what you would have expected to happen to the UK current account on the balance of payments if the value of the pound had remained constant.
(iii) Some economists and politicians argued at the time that allowing the pound to float downwards was inflationary. Explain this view.
(b) (i) Why might the fact that the UK joined the ERM in 1990 have prolonged the recession of 1990-1992?
(ii) Explain the likely impact of Britain's membership of the ERM on domestic inflation.

Question 3

In the early 1970s, the Bretton Woods system of exchange rates broke up. Explain why the system proved insufficiently robust.

Applied economics

European Monetary Union

History

The debate about European Monetary Union (EMU) has a long history in the the European Union (EU). Different currencies within Europe can be argued to be a major obstacle to trade, in the same way as tariffs or quotas. In 1970, the Werner Report proposed the creation of a European Monetary Union and for a short period in the early 1970s, the 6 member countries of the EU pegged their currencies against each other. However, the inflationary pressures of the time, culminating in the oil crisis of 1973-74, broke the system as one country after another either devalued or revalued.

The late 1970s saw more stable economic conditions and a fresh start was made in 1979 with the creation of the European Monetary System (EMS), the most important component of which was the Exchange Rate Mechanism (ERM). Member countries agreed to peg their currencies within a 2¼ per cent band of a weighted average of European currencies. This weighted average was called the ECU (the European Currency Unit). Between 1979 and 1987, there were 11 **realignments** within the EMS as countries devalued or revalued. In general, the low inflation, current account surplus countries, such as West Germany and Holland, revalued their currencies, whilst higher inflation, current account deficit countries, such as France and Italy, devalued their currencies.

The Maastricht Treaty

In 1989 Jacques Delors, President of the European Commission, presented a radical report suggesting that member countries should move to full European Monetary Union. His proposals formed the basis for the part of the Maastricht Treaty, signed in 1992, which dealt with EMU. A timetable was laid down for the progression to full EMU.

Stage 1 An EU 'Monetary Committee' was to be set up which would advise governments and the European Commission about the steps needed to move onto the next two stages.

Stage 2 During this stage, which in theory started on 1 January 1994, a new 'European Monetary Institute' was to be established which would help countries work towards stage 3. In particular, during stage 2, countries would have to adjust their own domestic policies to achieve 4 **convergence criteria**. These convergence criteria were considered vital to the success of a single currency.

- Inflation. Inflation rates had to be within 1.5 per cent of the average rate in the three lowest inflation countries in the EU. This was because a country with considerably higher inflation than other countries would, in a floating exchange rate mechanism, normally see its currency sink lower against its trading partners as it becomes less and less competitive. It could only maintain purchasing power parity through a falling exchange rate. To maintain a stable exchange rate, it therefore had to align its inflation rate approximately to those its trading partners.

- Interest rates. Long term interest rates were to be no more than two per cent above the average rate in the three lowest interest rate countries in the EU. If long term interest rates were much higher than this in one country, then there would be short term flows of money into that country to take advantage of the higher interest rates. This would then destabilise currency flows, putting pressure on the currency of that country to move upwards. Stable exchange rates could only be maintained if there was little or no incentive to move large sums of short term money from country to country within the EMS.

- Fiscal stance. Governments had to have budget deficits of no more than 3 per cent of GDP (at market prices) and a national debt of less than 60 per cent of GDP (at market prices). Governments which were heavily indebted, or needed to borrow large sums of money in a year would tend to have to offer high rates of interest on the debt being issued. High interest rates on government bonds would tend to attract flows of money from overseas which could destabilise the currency. Equally, there was a danger that governments would find it difficult to finance their debt and as a result foreigners would refuse to lend to the country. This too will tend to destabilise the currency. Hence, for currency stability, there had to be fiscal stability too.

- Durability of convergence. A country's currency had to have been in the narrow band of the ERM for at least two years with no realignments or 'severe tensions'. This was to ensure that there had been at least some history of stability of the currency.

Stage 3 At this stage, there would be a move towards fixed currencies. A new body, what is now the

European Central Bank (ECB), would hold and manage the official reserves of all the member countries. What is now the euro would become an official currency. Unless decided otherwise, Stage 3 would start on 1 January 1999.

The creation of the euro

This timetable was adhered to by the members of the EMS. On 1 January 1999, the euro was launched. Eleven countries participated - France, Germany, Italy, Spain, Portugal, Austria, Belgium, Luxembourg, the Netherlands, the Republic of Ireland and Finland. Greece wanted to join, but it fell far short of meeting the convergence criteria. Sweden and Denmark decided not to join for political reasons. The UK was not eligible to join because it had not pegged its currency against EMS currencies since September 1992.

Between 1 January and 31 December 2001, the currencies of participating countries were locked in at a fixed exchange rate. Control of the key interest rate in the euro-zone, the equivalent of bank base rate in the UK, passed to the European Central Bank (ECB). This institution was now responsible for monetary policy throughout the 11 countries. So the key interest rate was now the same in Germany as it was in Italy, France and Portugal. The ECB was also responsible for exchange rate policy of the euro-zone. It had control of a proportion of the reserves of the central banks of member countries and could, in theory, use these to buy and sell currency to alter the value of the euro against currencies such as the dollar and the yen. In practice, the euro was allowed to float freely on the foreign exchange rate markets.

On 1 January 2002, euro notes and coins would be issued and within months would replace existing national currency notes and coins. Shortly after, national currency notes and coins would cease to be legal tender and the 11 countries would share a common currency.

The advantages of EMU

Reduced exchange rate costs A single currency means that there are no exchange rate costs in making transactions. It is as costless for a French firm based in Calais to buy from a firm in Germany as from a firm in Paris. In contrast, a French firm buying from a British firm will still have the cost of changing currency. This is not just the commission and charges imposed by banks. It is also the costs arising from the risk factor of currencies changing in value from day to day in a floating exchange rate system.

Greater price transparency With 11 national markets and 11 different currencies, customers, whether firms or households, are likely to have imperfect information about prices across the whole area. A single currency makes it easy for customers to compare prices between different countries and buy from the cheapest source. This will make it far more difficult for multinational producers to price discriminate between countries, charging higher prices in some than in others to earn monopoly profits. The result is likely to be lower prices across the euro-zone to the benefit of consumers.

More trade and greater economies of scale Reduced exchange rate costs and greater price transparency are likely to lead to more trade between member countries. There will be greater integration between firms, with those in the traded goods sector becoming larger, supplying across the euro-zone rather than just a single national economy. This in turn will lead to greater economies of scale, further reducing prices to customers. Critics of EMU argue that there is likely to be very little, if any, increase in trade because exchange rates impose few costs on businesses. Euro-sceptics in the UK, for instance, believe that British industry is as competitive outside the euro-zone as it would be inside it.

Inward investment The UK has enjoyed considerable inward investment, for instance from Japanese and US companies. One advantage to them of this strategy is that they avoid tariffs and quotas placed on goods coming from outside the EU. They are also nearer the European market, which gives them advantages when developing new products and in marketing. The creation of a euro-zone with exchange rate stability gives countries outside it an even greater incentive to invest in Europe. But it also means that they are less likely to invest in an EU country, such as the UK, which is outside the euro-zone. They can get greater economic advantages now by locating within the euro-zone itself. Inward investment is usually considered to be positive. It creates both physical capital and new jobs. It can also act as an important catalyst for change. For example, the European motor car industry has, arguably, been transformed for the better over the past 20 years by competition and then investment from Japanese car manufacturers.

Macro-economic management Some countries, such as Germany, were very successful in managing their economies in the post-war period. In particular, they achieved relatively low inflation. Other countries, such as Italy and the UK, were less successful. Italy's public finances, for instance, were unsustainable in the long term. Government spent too much and raised too little in taxes, leading to ever higher amounts of government debt. The creation of EMU led to criteria being laid down for macro-economic management. National governments, for instance, cannot run large budget deficits over a long period. The European Central Bank cannot be manipulated by politicians seeking re-election because it is independent of national government. So macro-economic management is likely to be less driven by short term political considerations than before in the euro-zone. It is more likely to achieve economic stability.

The longer term agenda A single currency is part of a wider move towards greater European integration. The greater the economic integration, the greater the economies of scale and the lower the costs for producers. But there are potentially many other benefits that could be achieved from greater integration. For instance, having 11 national armies is an extremely inefficient way of providing defence for Europe. Ultimately, some would like to see political union as well as economic union. Without a single currency, this would be difficult.

The disadvantages of EMU

Transition costs The creation of a single currency inevitably creates transition costs. For instance, vending machines have to be changed to take the new coins. Some bank employees will lose their jobs because foreign exchange departments will be cut in size. Customers will have to become used to using the new money. However, the short term transition costs are likely to be far lower than the long term economic benefits from change.

Loss of policy independence The UK has long suffered from structural imbalances. The South of England, for instance, might be booming with no unemployment, whilst Wales or the North East of England might be seeing little economic growth and chronic unemployment. In these circumstances, it is difficult for adjust fiscal and monetary policy to accommodate the needs of all regions of the UK. For the South of England, interest rates might need to be high to deflate the economy. For Wales and the North East, interest rates might need to be low to boost aggregate demand. This sort of problem is likely to be worse, the larger the area of the monetary union. In the euro-zone, for instance, interest rates in 1999 needed to be high in the Republic of Ireland to curb a boom, whilst in France they needed to be much lower to stimulate growth and reduce unemployment. Unfortunately, a single currency implies there can only be one set of interest rates across the euro-zone. The European Central Bank therefore has to set interest rates to benefit the greatest number across 11 countries. The advantage of having national currencies is that each country is free to set its own interest rates and therefore in theory macro-economic policies can be tailored to the national interest. In practice, governments of countries with relatively open economies (i.e. ones where exports and imports are a large proportion of GDP) have difficulty operating macro-economic policy independently of their main trading partners. Before 1999, for instance, macro-economic policy in the Netherlands was strongly influenced by policy in Germany. So whilst there is some loss of control of macro-economic management for countries joining the euro-zone, it is not as great as it might at first seem.

Structural problems The 'one size fits all' nature of monetary policy in the euro-zone could lead to severe pockets of recession in some regions. This has happened in the UK over the past 50 years. A regional economy like the North East, which has been hard hit by the decline of mining and heavy manufacturing industry, takes decades to recover. At least in the UK, there are strong flows of money between rich and poor regions. A region in difficulty pays less tax per head than a successful one. It also receives large transfers, for instance from the unemployment benefit system. There are no such mechanisms within the EU. Brussels only receives a small proportion of taxes paid in the EU and pays out relatively little. Much of this goes to farmers anyway. So it could be that the European Central Bank raises interest rates because of inflationary pressures in Germany, but this only makes matters worse for a region in Italy already suffering structural decline. There is then no transfer of resources from Germany to Italy which would help boost aggregate demand in the Italian region and also help deflate the German economy. The solution to this problem is for Brussels to be responsible for far more of what is currently government spending by individual nation states. This implies much more centralisation and loss of national sovereignty, which would be seen as a problem by many.

Loss of political sovereignty Some argue that monetary union represents an unacceptable loss of national sovereignty. At its simplest in the UK, some Euro-sceptics argue that there is a value in keeping the pound sterling as a symbol of 'Britishness'. Others argue that foreigners should not control national economic policy. There is no doubt that the creation of a single currency has led to loss of national sovereignty since control of monetary and exchange rate policy for the 11 member countries has passed to the European Central Bank.

Break up of the euro-zone A single currency can just as well be dissolved as created. If the euro were to fail, for whatever reason, there could be considerable transition costs in the resulting break-up. Single currencies in the past have tended to fail because of the political break up of a country or area. Examples include the Austro-Hungarian empire which collapsed in 1918, the Soviet Union which collapsed in 1990 and Czechoslovakia which split into two countries in 1993. Proponents of the single currency would argue that this shows the need for further economic and political integration towards some sort of indissoluble united states of Europe.

Should Britain join the euro?

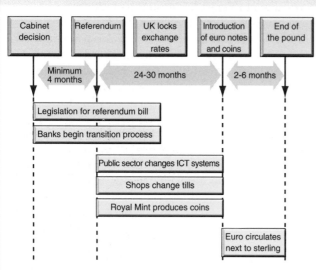

Figure 95.1 *Possible steps to joining a currency*
Source: adapted from the *Financial Times*, 24.5.1999.

EMU will provide a level playing field

Derek Cook is a car dealer. Like most car dealers, he feels that a significant proportion of any price discrepancies between the UK and European car markets can be attributed to fluctuating currency strengths and that a strong pound will always play against car dealers in the UK. 'The introduction of a single currency will make price comparison a more transparent affair. It will become obvious that cars in Germany, say, are cheaper than here.'

Source: adapted from *The Times*, 29.12.1998.

The one obvious and inescapable consequence of Emu membership is the elimination of exchange risk within the zone. But it is wrong to conclude that foreign exchange risk will be eliminated for British business. The UK received just 48.7 per cent of its total credits on the currency from from members of the euro-zone in 1998 (☞ Figure 95.2). It follows that membership of the euro-zone cannot eliminate currency instability. It could even deliver more instability. The euro may well fluctuate more against the dollar and other outside currencies than the D-Mark used to.

Source: adapted from the *Financial Times*, 26.5.1999.

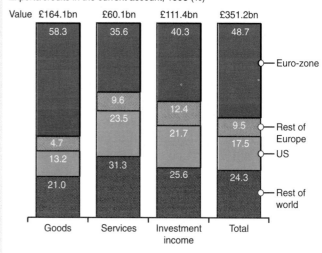

Figure 95.2 *Where the UK earns its money*
Source: adapted from *The Pink Book*, Office for National Statistics.

Volvo warns of cost of euro

Volvo, the Swedish automotive group, yesterday warned that transactions and currency charges associated with the euro could cost the company up to SKr 300 million ($36.9 million) a year. The group, which is urging the Swedish government to join the single currency as soon as possible, said Sweden's decision to abstain from the project meant Volvo would incur higher costs at its car and truck manufacturing plants inside the euro-zone. 'As long as Sweden remains outside the euro, Volvo will suffer from a disadvantage in currency and interest costs, said Lars I. Persson, the executive leading Volvo's euro preparations.

Source: adapted from the *Financial Times*, 30.12.1998.

Toyota threatens to close factories

Britain faces an exodus of foreign money and the loss of more than a million jobs unless the government signs up for the single currency within the next 30 months, leading overseas investors have warned. Toyota, the Japanese car maker which has invested £1.5 billion in Britain where it employs 3 300 staff in Derbyshire and North Wales, yesterday threatened to pull out of the UK unless the government set an early timetable for joining the single currency. Joseph Quinlan, senior global economist at USD investment house Morgan Stanley said: 'The UK has long been viewed by US multinationals ... as a springboard to continental Europe. The UK's decision on whether or not to join (monetary union) will be a key determinant of just how much bounce this springboard has left.'

Source: adapted from *The Guardian*, 18.1.2000.

Loss of sovereignty

'The surrender of British sovereignty is something I am completely opposed to. The whole idea of a single currency is untenable and would lead to instability.'
Big retailer, Midlands.

'I think things will get more expensive than at the moment. At present things can be bought cheaply off the Continent and if the single currency goes ahead things will become more expensive.'
Small construction company, North.

'Sterling is an international currency and has been for many years. Why should we move away towards an obscure bond? If we abolish the pound then we will drift into a weaker currency.'
Medium-sized manufacturer, South.

Source: the *Financial Times*, 28.9.1998.

US study shows benefits of single currency

The boost to trade from a single currency could be much greater than previously estimated. A new report estimates that two countries with the same currency do three times as much trade as they would if they had different currencies. The reasons for this are not clear, but a common currency gives a much bigger boost to trade than having fixed but separate currencies. The economic argument over going in or staying out hinges on whether the benefits of increased trade, bringing greater efficiency and higher growth, are outweighed by the costs of losing exchange rate and interest rate flexibility.

Monetary policy

Emu imposes a one-size-fits-all monetary policy for all its members. This could be a problem for countries with different economic circumstances. For example, the Irish economy is growing more strongly than the other 10 economies in the euro-zone, but Ireland is too small to influence the monetary policy stance of the whole Emu area. The Frankfurt-based European Central Bank, now in charge of monetary policy in the euro-zone, will look at the 11 countries as though they are part of a single economy. It will not pay special attention to individual countries. Countries facing particular pressures - such as Ireland- will have to find other ways to deal with shocks, for example through more labour market flexibility or mobility.

The ECB operates under a legal obligation to maintain price stability in Europe and this limits the degree of freedom to use monetary policy to encourage economic growth. European central bankers believe that unemployment and low growth have little to do with monetary policy anyway but with structural rigidities in the countries themselves. The ECB, however, has said it will not tolerate either inflation or deflation. It defines price stability as an increase in euro-zone inflation of less than 2 per cent.

Source: adapted from the *Financial Times*, 4.1.1999.

The right time to join

The UK needs to find the right time to join the single currency. It must ensure that it is at the same stage of the trade cycle as the rest of Europe. If it entered in a recession when the rest of Europe was in boom, then euro interest rates could be too low for the UK, prolonging its recession. If the contrary happened, too high interest rates in the euro-zone could lead to an even greater but unsustainable boom in the UK. Inflation would rise above that of the euro-zone making British goods uncompetitive. The UK would then have to suffer relative deflation to restore its competitiveness. This could involve high unemployment and negative growth.

The value of the exchange rate too must be right. Nearly all UK commentators agreed that the value of the pound between 1997 and 2000 would be far too high an entry value. The fear is that the UK would suffer a repeat of its experience of 1990-92. In September 1990, it entered the precursor to the single currency, the ERM, at a very high value at a time of recession. Then when the UK wanted to get out of recession, it found that it was caught by too high a rate of interest needed to sustain the value of the pound. The result was a prolongation of a deep recession by possibly one to two years.

Costs of transition

Britain's smaller businesses are facing a £6.2 billion to convert to use the euro. A recent survey by the Allied Irish Bank (GB) showed that conversion costs vary significantly between industries, but on average they can expect to pay £1 685. Retailers are the hardest hit, facing a bill 300 per cent higher than their colleagues in the construction industry.

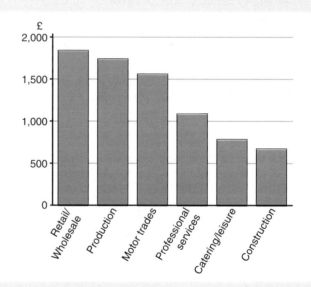

Figure 95.3 *Costs to business of euro conversion*
Source: adapted from *The Guardian*, 20.7.1999.

1. **Discuss whether the UK should join the single currency. Use examples from the data to support your arguments.**

Summary

1. The balance of payments is likely to be in disequilibrium if the value of exports and imports differs over a long period of time.
2. One policy weapon available to governments to tackle a current account deficit is to devalue the currency or allow it to depreciate. The Marshall-Lerner condition states that devaluation will be successful if the combined elasticities of demand for exports and imports exceed unity.
3. In the short term, devaluation is likely to lead to a deterioration in the current account position because of the J curve effect. In the longer term, the competitive benefits of devaluation may be eroded by cost-push inflation.
4. Deflationary policies will act to reduce imports because of the fall in total demand in the economy. Raising interest rates is one way of implementing a deflationary policy.
5. Raising interest rates is also likely to lead to a rise in the value of the currency in the short term as speculative funds are attracted into the country.
6. Protectionist measures can reduce imports but the ability of governments to implement such policies today is severely limited by international agreements.
7. Supply side policies should lead to an increase in international competitiveness over long periods of time.
8. In the short term, a country may choose to impose currency controls, restricting the supply of its currency for use in international transactions.

Balance of payments equilibrium

The balance of payments can be said to be in **equilibrium** when there is no tendency for it to change. This is most likely to occur in the short to medium term if exports are equal to imports and hence both the current and the capital account are in balance. However, equilibrium could also exist if:

● imports are greater than exports and the country is using borrowed foreign money to develop its economy as the USA did in the early part of the 19th century;
● exports are greater than imports and the country is investing the money abroad in order to finance increased imports in the future. It can be argued that Japan is in this position today given that it faces a sharp decline in its workforce and a sharp rise in the number of pensioners in the next 30 years.

In the long term, countries are unlikely to be able to continue as substantial net borrowers because other countries will refuse to lend to countries which get deeper and deeper into debt (as has happened with many Third World countries). In the long term, therefore, equilibrium will occur when exports equal imports.

If the balance of payments is in equilibrium there will be no tendency for the exchange rate to change. If, on the other hand, a country tends to export more than it imports over long periods, its exchange rate will tend to rise. The demand for the country's currency to pay for its exports will continually exceed the supply of currency offered for sale to pay for imports. Speculation may cause the exchange rate to fluctuate randomly in the short term if exchange rates are floating but the exchange rate trend is likely to be upward in the long term. If the country runs a persistent current account deficit, its exchange rate will tend to fall.

If the current account is in persistent deficit (or surplus), what measures can government take to rectify this situation? How can governments keep exchange rates up when there is persistent selling pressure from the markets?

Devaluation and revaluation

One possible way of curing a current account deficit is for the government to DEVALUE the currency. This means that it lowers the value of the currency against other currencies. Devaluation affects exports and imports because it changes their relative prices and thus their international competitiveness. The opposite of devaluation is REVALUATION, an increase in the value of the currency.

Devaluation assumes that the government pegs the value of its currency against other currencies. However, exchange rates may **float**, which means that governments allow free market forces to determine the value of the currency. A fall in the value of the currency is then called a **depreciation** of the currency. The opposite of depreciation is **appreciation** (☞ unit 39) of the currency. In what follows, it will be assumed that the government does control the value of the currency and therefore the term 'devaluation' rather than 'depreciation' will be used. However, devaluation and depreciation have the same effects, as do revaluation and appreciation.

The effects of devaluation

Assume that the pound falls in value against other currencies by 20 per cent. The price of imports will therefore rise in pounds sterling. With an exchange rate of 10F = £1, a French car sold to UK importers for 100 000 francs would have cost £10 000 in pounds sterling. With a 20 per cent devaluation of the pound, the new exchange rate will be 8F = £1. So the cost of a 100 000 franc car will be £12 500. At the new price, demand is likely to fall. The effect on the total value of imports will depend upon the elasticity of demand for French cars. If demand is elastic, the percentage rise in the price of French cars will be more than offset by a percentage fall in the demand for cars. Hence the total sterling value of imported French cars will fall. (This is an application of the relationship between elasticity and revenue ☞ unit 9). If demand is price inelastic, a rise in price will lead to a rise in expenditure on French cars and hence a rise in the sterling value of French car imports.

In summary, a devaluation of the pound will:
- leave the French franc **price** unchanged but increase the sterling price of imported goods;
- result in a fall in **import volumes**;
- lead to a fall in the **total sterling value** of imports assuming that domestic demand for imports is elastic; if demand is inelastic, there will be a rise in the sterling value of imports.

Devaluation of the pound should have no effect on the sterling price of exports. A £10 000 car exported to France will still be £10 000 after devaluation. But the price will have fallen in French francs. If the value of the pound falls from 10F = £1 to 8F = £1, the £10 000 car will fall in price in France from 100 000 francs to 80 000 francs. This should lead to a rise in demand for UK cars.

A devaluation will therefore:
- leave the **sterling price** of exports unchanged but reduce the price in foreign currency terms;
- lead to a rise in **export volumes**;

Question 1

In October 1993, it was reported that exports of steelwork for construction had risen by up to a fifth since sterling left the ERM in September 1992 and the pound had fallen in value by over 10 per cent. Invitations to tender for international contracts had risen even faster, according to a survey of orders received by the 12 largest UK constructional steel producers.
The survey, by British Constructional Steelwork Association, showed that the companies had received international invitations to tender and requests for price quotations involving more than 400 000 tonnes of steel since September 1992, compared to just 20 000 tonnes in the preceding 12 months. Mr Rollo Reid, director of John Reid & Sons in Dorset, said: 'We have been quoting prices up to 25 per cent lower than local German fabricators. We have even been asked, for the first time, to price jobs in Japan.' Mr Joe Lock, managing director of Watson Steel, part of the Amec construction group, said: 'Opportunities to bid for international work have increased considerably following sterling's devaluation.'

Explain, using examples from the passage, what is likely to happen to (a) price, (b) volumes and (c) revenues of exports following a devaluation of a currency.

- increase the **total sterling value** of exports.

Devaluation and elasticity

Overall, devaluation of the pound will increase the sterling value of exports, but may or may not lead to a fall in the value of imports depending upon the elasticity of demand for imports. It is likely that, even if import values increase, export values will increase even more. Hence devaluation will result in an improved current account position. The MARSHALL LERNER condition states that, given very stringent conditions, devaluation will result in an improvement on current account if the combined elasticities of demand for exports and imports are greater than 1. If the combined elasticities for exports and imports are less than 1, then the correct policy response to a current account deficit should be a currency **revaluation**.

Devaluation and pricing strategies

So far it has been assumed that UK exporters will choose to keep the sterling price of the products constant and change the foreign currency price, whilst importers will choose to keep the foreign currency price of their goods the same and change the sterling price. However, exporters and importers may choose a different strategy. Jaguar, for instance, may price a model at $40 000 in the USA. If the value of the pound is $2 = £1, it will receive £20 000 per car. If the pound is now devalued to $1 = £1, Jaguar has a choice of strategies. It could keep the sterling price constant at £20 000 and reduce the dollar price to $20 000. However, a fall in price of a luxury car may give the wrong signals to US car buyers. They may assume that Jaguar cars are no longer luxury cars. They may think that Jaguar is not doing well in the US and is having to reduce prices in order to maintain sales. The fall in the dollar price may generate few extra sales. So Jaguar is likely to hold constant the dollar price of $40 000 and consequently increase its profit margins. When the value of the pound rises against the dollar, Jaguar may again choose to hold constant the dollar price. A rise in the dollar price may lead to large falls in sales if Jaguar is in a competitive market with other luxury car manufacturers.

If both exporters and importers adopt the strategy of leaving the prices they charge to their customers unchanged, devaluation will still improve the current account position. Assume the pound is devalued.
- The sterling value of exports will rise because exporters have chosen to increase the sterling price of exported goods rather than reduce their foreign currency price. Export volumes will remain unchanged because the foreign currency price has remained unchanged. Therefore sterling export values will increase because of the sterling price increase.
- The sterling value of imports will stay the same. Foreign firms have chosen to keep the sterling price of their goods constant. Hence volumes will not change. Neither, therefore, will the sterling value of imports.

With export values increased and import values unchanged, there will be an improvement in the current account position.

Question 2

In the first quarter of 1995, the value of the pound fell sharply against its main trading partners. Mr Malcolm Taylor, managing director of Bridgport Machines, the Leicester-based machine tool maker, said his company intended to use the competitive bonus offered by a lower pound to increase market share in Europe. 'Our strategy will be to let the distributors take the advantage of the currency movement to win more market share', he said. The ambition was to raise exports overall by up to one quarter this year. But some companies were not going to take the same view, according to Mr Richard Brown, deputy director-general of the British Chamber of Commerce: 'They are unlikely to use a temporary change in sterling's value to increase market share and are much more likely to take windfall profits'. China manufacturer, Royal Worcester, which had not yet seen any additional boost to overseas sales because of the fall in the pound, may choose this option. Mr Tim Westbrook, managing director at Royal Worcester, said: 'We will have to see where sterling settles before considering whether to readjust prices. If the weakness is only short-term, we may just see a blip in profit margins.'

(a) Compare the impact on the current account of the balance of payments of the two different reactions to a fall in the value of the pound described in the article.
(b) Why might a machine tool company be more willing to change its prices than a manufacturer of fine china like Royal Worcester?

Problems associated with devaluation

There are two major problems with using devaluation as a policy weapon.

The J curve The current account following devaluation is likely to get worse before it gets better. This is known as the J CURVE EFFECT and it is shown in Figure 96.1.

Assume the UK has a current account deficit and attempts to devalue its currency. In the short run the demand for exports and imports will tend to be inelastic. Although the foreign currency price of UK exports will fall, it takes time before other countries react to the change. Hence, the volume of exports will remain the same in the short term, before increasing in the longer term. This means that in the short term, there will be no increase in sterling export values.

Similarly, although the sterling price of imports rises, in the short term UK buyers may be stuck with import contracts they signed before devaluation. Alternatively, there may be no alternative domestic suppliers and hence firms may have to continue to buy imports. Hence, in the short term, sterling import values will rise. In the longer term, contracts can be revised and domestic producers can increase supply, thus leading to a reduction in import volumes.

Overall, in the short term, import values will rise but

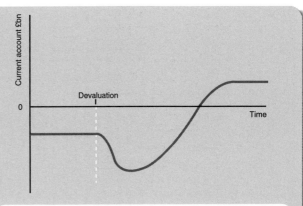

Figure 96.1 *The J curve effect*
Devaluation will initially lead to a deterioration of the current account position before it improves in the longer term.

export values will remain constant, thus producing a deterioration in the current account. In the longer term, export values will rise whilst import values might fall, producing an improvement in the current account position.

Cost-push inflation Devaluation generates imported inflation. This is not serious if there is a once and for all increase in prices. But if it starts up or fuels a cost-push **inflationary spiral**, then the increased competitiveness achieved by the devaluation will be quickly eroded. Keynesian economists have become increasingly sceptical of the value of devaluation as a policy weapon to cure a balance of payments deficit unless it is part of a much wider package of measures designed to increase the competitiveness and performance of a deficit economy.

Question 3

In the first quarter of 1995, the value of the pound fell sharply against its main trading partners. David Walton, UK economist at Goldman Sachs, compared this situation to the one in late 1992 when the pound equally fell in value. He pointed out that: 'The difference between now and 1992 is that inflation was heading down but now it is already rising'. He believed that if sterling's weakness were to be maintained, then it would take inflation outside the government's target range in 1996.

Some companies were already passing on increased costs and others were preparing to do so. Mr Bob Bischoff, chair of Boss Group, the Bedfordshire-based fork lift truck maker which exports 65 per cent of its vehicles, said Boss now had an added competitive edge against its German, Japanese and Scandinavian rivals, but he also bought components from Germany and import costs were already rising. 'If these continue, we will increase our prices,' he warned.

(a) What problems might be associated with a falling value of the pound? Illustrate your answer with examples from the passage.

Deflation

Devaluation results in **expenditure switching**. Foreigners buy more of our exports and less of their own and other countries' production, whilst domestic consumers buy fewer imports and more domestically produced goods. An alternative approach to curing a current account deficit is **deflation**. This is an **expenditure reducing** policy. If the government reduces aggregate demand in the economy, for instance by raising interest rates or increasing taxes, people have less money to spend so they reduce their consumption of domestically produced goods and imported goods. Imports therefore decline. Exports may also rise if domestic firms switch sales from the depressed domestic market to foreign markets.

For the UK, deflation has proved very successful in reducing imports, particularly because the UK has a very high **marginal propensity to import** in manufactured goods. The effect on exports has been less noticeable. Firms may well choose to reduce output in response to a recession in the economy rather than seek export orders.

One important policy advantage of deflation is that it is likely to reduce inflationary pressures in the economy, assuming those pressures come from the demand side of the economy. On the other hand, it also reduces growth and increases unemployment, both undesirable in themselves. In the long term, the economy must increase its international competitiveness unless the economy is to remain permanently below full employment.

Interest rates

Increased interest rates will initially bolster the value of the currency. They attract speculative inflows into the country, raising the demand for the currency. In the longer term, a rise in interest rates which must have been generated by a fall in the supply of money (☞ unit 82) will lead to a fall in aggregate demand through the transmission mechanism. Higher interest rates deflate the economy, leading to a fall in imports and hence an improvement in the current account.

Question 4

In 1988, with a worsening balance of payments situation and rising inflation, the UK government raised interest rates. Bank base rates between 1988 and 1990 rose from $7\frac{1}{2}$ per cent to 15 per cent.

(a) Explain how a rise in domestic interest rates might lead to an improvement in the balance of payments current account position.

Protectionism

Increasing tariffs or quotas or other protectionist measures will reduce imports thus improving the current account position. Tariffs and quotas can both have a significant impact in the short term. However, protectionism is not much favoured by economists. First, the country is likely to find itself becoming even more internationally uncompetitive in the long run as its domestic industries have no incentive to improve their efficiency. Second, protectionism in one country invites retaliation from its trading partners. The country could find that the gains on current account from reduced imports are more than matched by losses of exports as a result of retaliation (☞ unit 40).

Increased protectionist measures are also forbidden except under certain specific circumstances by the WTO (the World Trade Organisation). Membership of a trading bloc like the European Union severely limits the ability of individual countries to limit imports through protectionist policies.

Currency controls

A government may choose to impose or tighten currency controls. These are controls on the purchase of foreign currency by domestic citizens and firms. In the late 1960s, for instance, the UK government limited the amount of currency that could be taken abroad on holiday to £50 per person. Governments could equally restrict finance for investment abroad or even for imports. The government abolished exchange controls in 1979, and today the UK government is unable to impose currency controls because of its membership of the European Union.

Supply side policies

One way of making domestically produced goods more competitive is through devaluation: altering the relative price of exports and imports. However, there are many other ways in which domestic industry can become more competitive internationally. **Supply side policies** (☞ unit 38) aimed at reducing unit labour costs, increasing investment, increasing the skills of the labour force and improving the quality and design of products should lead to increased exports and reduced imports. Supply side policies tend to be long term policies. They cannot cure a current account deficit within, for instance, 12-24 months.

Question 5

In February 1990, the government of Bangladesh, faced with a swelling of the country's current account deficit, tightened its currency controls. Importers were required to provide a 50 per cent cash deposit when opening new letters of credit.

A letter of credit is a type of loan common in the export/import trade. Explain why the government measure outlined in the passage could lead to (a) an improvement in the current account position and (b) a rise in the value of the Bangladesh currency, the Taka.

Applied economics

Government policy

The 1950s and 1960s

For much of the 1950s and 1960s, the balance of payments and the exchange rate posed major problems for the UK government. Whenever the economy went into boom, the current account slipped into deficit. This would tend to be associated with exchange rate crises. Speculators would sell sterling, forcing its price down. At the time the UK was a member of the **Bretton Woods system** (☞ unit 94) of exchange rates, where the pound was fixed in value against other currencies. To keep the pound fixed the government tended to deflate the economy, putting it into recession. This led to falling imports and an improved balance of payments situation. However, by the mid-1960s, it was argued by many that the UK had a structural deficit on its balance of payments (i.e. in the long term deficits would outweigh surpluses and thus there would be a long term deficit on the current account). In 1964, an incoming Labour government under Harold Wilson rejected the policy option of devaluing the pound. His government then spent the next three years dealing with intermittent exchange rate crises and finally, in June 1967, devalued the pound by 15 per cent.

The next nine months saw a sharp deterioration in the current account position - probably the working out of the J curve effect. The government therefore decided that its March 1968 Budget needed to be severely deflationary. The current account rapidly improved and by 1969 was back in surplus. Which was the most important factor in this - the 15 per cent devaluation or the most deflationary Budget since the Second World War - is difficult to judge.

The 1970s

The current account continued in surplus in 1970 and 1971 as the economy went into a recession. The March 1972 Budget was highly reflationary, designed to reduce unemployment. The government recognised that this might have implications for the current account and announced that it was not committed to maintaining the existing exchange rate. In June 1972, following heavy selling of the pound, the UK left the Bretton Woods system and the pound depreciated in value.

The pound fell rapidly. Against the deutschmark, for instance, it fell from DM8.26 in the second quarter of 1972 to DM6.05 in the last quarter of 1973, a 27 per cent depreciation. This should have allowed the current account to remain in balance. However, government policy was so reflationary that the current account moved deeper and deeper into the red. The final twist was the oil crisis of 1973-74, which quadrupled the price of imported oil.

The government's policy response was to continue to allow the pound to float downwards. By the end of 1975, the pound was only worth DM5.30 and by the last quarter of 1976 it was worth only DM3.98, a 52 per cent depreciation against its second quarter 1972 value. Budgets in 1975 and 1976 were deflationary. This did not prevent a major sterling crisis in late 1976 when the government was forced to borrow money from the IMF to prop up its reserves. However, the current account position was already improving by 1975-76 and in 1977 it moved into surplus. Again, it is difficult to judge the extent to which this improvement was due either to depreciation of the currency or to deflationary budgets.

The current account position was then transformed by exports of North Sea oil. The first oil was produced in 1976 and by 1980 oil exports were greater than oil imports. The government produced mildly reflationary Budgets in 1977 and 1978 to stimulate growth and reduce unemployment. Inevitably, the current account position worsened and by 1979 the current account was back in deficit. However, the exchange rate remained broadly stable and, indeed, the pound began to go up in value in 1979 as the foreign currency markets anticipated the effect the North Sea oil bonanza would have on the current account.

1980-1992

In the 1950s, 1960s and 1970s, current account deficits were seen as a problem which demanded a policy response from government. Since 1979, the government has believed that the current account is self correcting and therefore does not demand a policy response. Between 1980 and 1982, the current account benefited from a growing oil surplus and a deep recession in the economy. In contrast, the value of the pound soared. Against the deutschmark, for instance, it rose from DM3.81 in the last quarter of 1979 to DM4.81 in the first quarter of 1981, an appreciation of 26 per cent. But for this appreciation, the current surpluses in 1980-82 would have been even larger.

The appreciation did, however, have the disastrous effect of destroying a sizeable part of UK manufacturing industry. Unable to compete internationally, firms went out of business. Manufacturing output fell 18 per cent between the second quarter of 1979 and the last quarter of 1982. The trade balance on finished manufactures, which had fluctuated between +£2bn to £3bn per annum in the 1970s, plunged to a deficit of £4bn by 1984 and then, after a short period of stabilisation, plunged to a £13bn deficit by 1989. From 1982, the pound began to fall again as it became apparent that much of the increased oil revenues on the current account had been offset by large falls in the trade balance on manufactured goods.

Throughout the 1980s, the main objective of government policy was the control of inflation. The Conservative government elected in 1979 initially was convinced that this could be achieved through control of money supply (☞ unit 85). However, in the first half of the 1980s, the money supply grew in double figures when inflation was less than 5 per cent. It became increasingly disillusioned with money supply control. In the mid-1980s, the then Chancellor, Nigel Lawson, became attracted to the idea that exchange rate policy could help maintain low inflation. In particular, if the pound could become linked to the deutschmark, the UK could enjoy the same low inflation that Germany had achieved during the post-war period. The obvious way to do this was to join the Exchange Rate Mechanism, but the euro-sceptic prime minister, Margaret Thatcher, refused to allow this. So instead, the Chancellor pursued a policy of shadowing the deutschmark. Bank base rates were raised or lowered to maintain a stable exchange rate.

In retrospect, this policy was misguided. Between 1985 and 1987, economic growth accelerated sharply. By 1987-88, at the height of the period known as the Lawson boom, the economy was operating beyond its productive capacity with a positive output gap present. This overheating showed through clearly on the balance of payments. In 1986, the current account recorded a small deficit of £2.3 billion. In 1987, this grew to £5.6 billion. In 1988, it ballooned to £17.5 billion, 3.8 per cent of GDP. In 1989, it was even higher at £23.5 billion, 4.6 per cent of GDP. This was unsustainable in the long term.

The government was too slow to react to this overheating. It had become convinced that the economy could grow above its trend rate because of its supply side reforms. Like any government, it was also reluctant to bring to a stop a boom which saw a growth

in prosperity and rapidly falling unemployment. It took the view that current account deficits were not a problem. It argued that the deficits showed a desire on the part of consumers and firms to borrow abroad to finance spending. If that was what they wanted, then the government should not intervene to prevent from doing so.

However, by mid-1988, it became clear that inflation was beginning to rise despite the shadowing of the deutschmark. The exchange rate policy was abandoned and interest rates were raised from 7.5 per cent in May 1988 to 15 per cent in October 1989. This slowly deflated the economy. The current balance deficit began to fall as demand for imports fell and by 1991 it was £8.4 billion.

Interest rates were slow to act in bringing down inflation. It carried on climbing throughout 1989 despite successive increases in interest rates. RPI growth only peaked in the third quarter of 1990 at 10.4 per cent per annum. At this time, the government was frustrated at the failure of inflation to fall. So it decided to use exchange rate policy to further deflate the economy. In September 1990, it entered the ERM at what most commentators at the time thought was a very high value of the pound of 3 deutschmarks to the pound. This proved to be a mistake.

Almost immediately inflation began to fall, but the economy went into recession with negative economic growth. UK inflation rates were still higher than those of its main trading partners, but the pound couldn't fall sufficiently to restore UK competitiveness because of the UK's membership of the ERM. By 1992, the current account deficit had increased to £10.1 billion as exporters found it difficult to remain price competitive, whilst imports increased despite the fact that the economy was in the longest recession since the 1930s. In 1991 and 1992, with inflation falling rapidly and the economy in recession, the government wanted to cut interest rates quickly. But it couldn't do this because by now the pound was towards the bottom end of its trading band in the ERM. Too large a fall in interest rates threatened to take the pound out of its trading band. The government was convinced a devaluation of the pound would raise inflation again. Politically, it was unacceptable too because it had committed itself both to the UK electorate and to EU governments to remain in the ERM.

In July and August 1992, the foreign exchange rate markets made a number of attacks on weak members of the ERM. The Bank of England was forced to use its foreign currency reserves to buy up pounds in the markets to prevent the pound falling through the floor of its band. On 15 September, 'Black Wednesday', selling pressure became so intense that the Bank of England raised interest rates back to 15 per cent. But the selling continued and the government was forced to announce that it was leaving the ERM. The pound fell 10 per cent immediately. The exact amount of money spent by the Bank of England supporting the pound is not known, but it ran into tens of billions of pounds.

This shows just how much money is available to foreign currency speculators to attack weak currencies which are pegged to other currencies.

1992-2000

Black Wednesday was a key moment in reinforcing euro-sceptic tendencies in the UK. If the UK had remained in the ERM, it would probably have joined the single currency, the euro, starting in 1999. So Black Wednesday had a significant impact on the UK's policy towards the EU.

However, in all other ways, it was arguably beneficial to the UK. Immediately the government began cutting interest rates. This led quickly to economic recovery. The devaluation of the pound also helped improve the current account. Despite strong economic growth between 1993 and 1997, the current account balance improved from a deficit of £10.6 billion to a surplus of £6.6 billion. This illustrates the powerful effect that a significant devaluation can have on the current account.

After Black Wednesday, the government abandoned any attempt to control the value of the pound. It also continued with the view that current account deficits were self-correcting in the long term and therefore not an immediate concern for policy makers.

In 1996, the pound began to appreciate again, particularly against other European currencies. Between the third quarter of 1996 and the first quarter of 1998, the pound appreciated 23 per cent against what is now the euro. One reason for this was that the UK economy at the time was performing well in comparison with many EU countries. Inflation was subdued whilst there was strong economic growth, indicating that the UK was becoming more competitive. At the same time interest rates were higher in the UK than in the euro-zone, which attracted hot money into London. The initial effect of the appreciation was to depress export growth. The current account moved back into deficit. By 2000, however, there was evidence that UK manufacturers had learned to live with a much higher value of the pound and export volumes were increasing again, helping to reduce the current account deficit. However, during the late 1990s, the Bank of England did not bring interest rates down to help reduce the value of the pound despite pressure on it to do so. Interest rates were used solely to maintain low inflation.

At the start of the 21st century, the most important policy decision the government has to make is whether and when to join the euro. Once it joins, it will lose control of both exchange rate policy and interest rate policy. The balance of payments will cease to be of concern because Britain's trade will be included with the rest of the euro-zone, just as the trade of California is simply part of that of the USA.

Depreciation of the pound, 1992–94

Table 96.1 *Current balance 1990-1994*

	£m
1990	- 19 035
1991	- 8 176
1992	- 9 831
1993	- 11 800
1994	- 168

Table 96.2 *Components of the current balance*

£ million

	Visible trade		Invisible trade	
	Oil balance	Non-oil balance	Traded services balance	Other services balance
1990	1 529	- 20 338	3 689	- 3 915
1991	1 208	- 11 492	3 708	- 1 600
1992	1 548	- 14 652	4 089	- 816
1993	2 457	- 15 851	5 213	- 3 619
1994	4 158	- 14 685	4 759	+ 5 600

Table 96.3 *Non-oil visible balance*

1992	£m	1993	£m	1994	£m
Q1	- 3 100	Q1	- 3 893	Q1	- 4 295
Q2	- 3 336	Q2	- 3 972	Q2	- 3 596
Q3	- 3 663	Q3	- 3 945	Q3	- 2 781
Q4	- 4 553	Q4	- 4 041	Q4	- 4 031

Table 96.4 *Volume indices[1] for exports and imports*

1990 = 100

	All goods		Non-oil goods		Services[2]	
	Exports	Imports	Exports	Imports	Exports	Imports
1992						
Q1	101.9	97.0	102.1	97.3	98.6	101.4
Q2	103.9	101.4	104.0	101.4	99.1	100.1
Q3	103.0	101.8	102.5	101.7	97.9	97.6
Q4	105.9	103.5	105.6	103.8	96.9	97.2
1993						
Q1	106.3	104.4	105.7	104.5	100.8	94.4
Q2	104.7	102.3	103.8	102.0	98.5	99.0
Q3	107.2	104.4	105.8	104.4	103.6	97.6
Q4	109.3	107.5	107.4	107.4	105.4	101.9
1994						
Q1	112.1	110.0	110.0	111.0	104.3	105.4
Q2	116.6	108.0	113.8	108.8	102.4	102.9
Q3	120.9	108.9	119.5	109.8	104.9	102.2
Q4	124.0	115.5	122.4	116.8	107.8	108.9

1. Quantity sold, expressed in index number form.
2. Traded services. This does not include 'other services' (i.e. investment income and public sector and private sector transfers).

Table 96.5 *Average prices of exports and imports*

1990 = 100

	All goods		Non-oil goods		Services[1]	
	Exports	Imports	Exports	Imports	Exports	Imports
1992						
Q1	102.4	101.3	104.2	102.4	105.4	103.6
Q2	103.2	100.6	104.7	101.4	106.1	103.0
Q3	102.8	99.8	104.4	100.5	106.3	104.8
Q4	105.4	106.7	106.6	107.2	112.0	111.6
1993						
Q1	114.2	110.1	116.0	110.9	115.4	118.8
Q2	114.2	110.8	115.9	110.8	114.1	115.9
Q3	115.5	111.0	117.7	112.4	116.0	115.7
Q4	115.1	110.7	117.9	112.4	115.8	117.1
1994						
Q1	115.9	111.0	119.2	112.8	116.0	116.5
Q2	117.3	114.8	120.0	116.6	115.5	115.8
Q3	117.7	116.3	120.3	117.7	118.3	116.2
Q4	117.0	115.9	119.7	117.5	118.8	117.6

1. Traded services. This does not include 'other services' (i.e. investment income and public sector and private sector transfers).

Table 96.6 *Exchange rates*

	Sterling exchange rate against deutschmark	Sterling exchange rate index (1985 = 100)
1992		
Q1	2.866	90.5
Q2	2.916	92.3
Q3	2.786	90.9
Q4	2.445	79.8
1993		
Q1	2.414	78.5
Q2	2.484	80.2
Q3	2.522	81.0
Q4	2.510	81.0
1994		
Q1	2.563	81.3
Q2	2.497	80.0
Q3	2.421	79.2
Q4	2.446	80.2

Table 96.7 *Economic growth*

	% change in real GDP on previous 12 months
1990	
Q1	1.0
Q2	0.0
Q3	0.0
Q4	- 1.1
1991	
Q1	- 2.3
Q2	- 3.1
Q3	- 2.6
Q4	- 1.8
1992	
Q1	- 1.7
Q2	- 1.3
Q3	- 0.4
Q4	0.0
1993	
Q1	1.5
Q2	2.0
Q3	2.4
Q4	2.6
1994	
Q1	3.3
Q2	4.1
Q3	4.1
Q4	4.2

Source: adapted from *Economic Trends*, Office for National Statistics.

On 16 September 1992, the government suspended the pound from the ERM. The result was an immediate double digit fall in the value of the pound. The suspension came at a time when the economy was only slowly coming out of a prolonged recession in the economy. In the period following the suspension, the government rapidly cut interest rates in the economy, from 10 per cent to 5¹/₂ per cent in early 1994.

1. Explain, using a diagram, what the J curve model suggests will happen to the current account on the balance of payments (a) in the short term and (b) in the longer term.
2. What would you expect to happen to the current account when an economy comes out of recession?
3. To what extent do your answers to questions 1 and 2 help you understand what happened to the current account on the balance of payments between 1992 and 1994?

Applied economics

Globalisation

In the late 1990s there was a feeling that the world economy was becoming more integrated. This integration was called GLOBALISATION. Goods were increasingly being manufactured abroad, many for the first time in **developing countries** (☞ units 99-104). Trade in services was growing. For instance, growth in tourism was taking large numbers of visitors abroad. Foreign ownership of firms was forever increasing. Brands were increasing their penetration internationally. Coca Cola, Magnum ice creams or Snickers chocolate bars were available in all five continents. International financial flows were also becoming far greater. Countries such as China and Malaysia were financing a significant part of their fast economic growth from inward flows of international capital. Countries such as Russia, Brazil and Thailand were also finding that sudden movements of international financial capital out of the country could destabilise their currencies and cause severe downturns on their domestic economies.

Globalisation was not a phenomenon just of the 1990s. It has been taking place since trade first began thousands of years ago. In Roman times, for instance, goods were traded in Europe which had originated in Africa, India and China. Figure 97.1 shows how UK exports as a percentage of GDP have more than doubled in the post-war period. In 1950, exports were 14.0 per cent of GDP but by 1998 this was 31.2 per cent. Average annual growth of exports over the period 1950-1998 was 4.4 per cent, almost double the annual growth in GDP. However, there is little evidence to suggest that the rate of change of export growth has increased over time. Table 97.1 shows that the average annual rate of growth of exports was faster in the 1960s and 1970s than it was in the 1980s. The 1990s average is only a little above that of the 1960s and 1970s.

Table 97.1 *Average annual percentage increase in exports, UK*

	% annual growth
1950-59	3.63
1960-69	5.13
1970-79	5.13
1980-89	3.00
1990-98	5.52
1950-98	4.46

Source: adapted from *Economic Trends Annual Supplement*, Office for National Statistics.

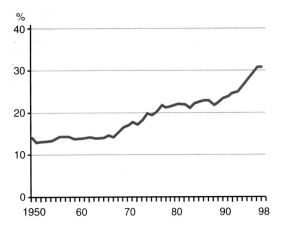

Figure 97.1 *Exports as a percentage of GDP*
Source: adapted from *Economic Trends Annual Supplement*, Office for National Statistics.

The structure of the economy

Globalisation should have an impact on the structure of economies. In the developing world, for instance, it has led to an increase in the share of the manufactured sector of many economies and made them less reliant on agriculture. The structure of the UK economy in 1998 is shown in Figure 97.2. The economy is mainly a service-based economy. Manufacturing only accounted for 19.7 per cent of GDP, whilst services accounted for 69.8 per cent.

However, there have been significant changes in this structure over time. Before the industrial revolution of 1750-1850, output was concentrated in the rural sector of the economy. Production was heavily weighted towards the production of food or household services. This was rather like the economies of many poor developing countries. In Uganda in 1980, for example, 72 per cent of output was accounted for by the agricultural sector, 4 per cent by industry and the remaining 24 per cent by service industries. In 19th century Britain, manufacturing grew as a percentage of total output whilst the relative importance of agriculture declined. By the 1920s, as Figure 97.3 shows, agriculture accounted for only 5 per cent of GDP whilst manufacturing was around 30 per cent. In the immediate post-war period, manufacturing output reached almost 40 per cent of output, stimulated by production of armaments in the second world war. Since then, the share of manufacturing has declined whilst the share of services has grown.

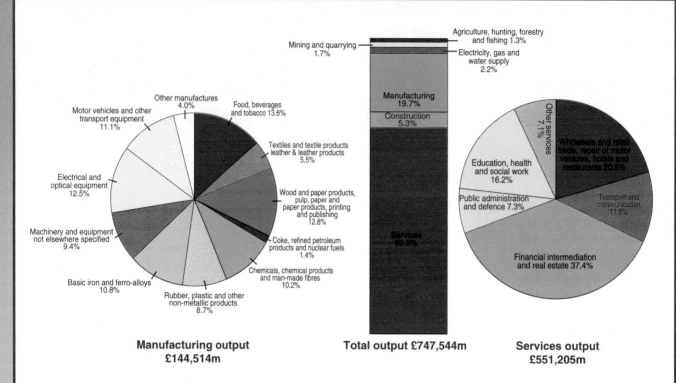

Figure 97.2 *The structure of the UK economy by sector, 1998*
Source: adapted from *Annual Abstract of Statistics*, Office for National Statistics.

Not only has manufacturing declined in relative terms, but at certain times in the post-war period it even declined in absolute terms. Figure 97.4 shows the index of output of manufacturing and services, and of GDP (measured by gross value added at basic cost). Whilst GDP and services show a general upward trend, manufacturing has seen severe declines of 8 per cent between 1973 and 1975, 14 per cent between 1979 and 1981 and another 5 per cent between 1990 and 1992. It wasn't until 1988 that manufacturing output reached

the same levels as those achieved in 1973, and the recession of 1990-92 meant that output was no higher in 1993 than it was in 1988. Over the longer term, manufacturing grew at a faster rate than services in the 1950s and 1960s. Manufacturing output in 1970 was 82 per cent of its 1950 value compared to 60 per cent for services. But manufacturing has performed poorly since then. Manufacturing output in 1998 was only 22 per cent higher than in 1970, whilst services had grown 103 per cent over the same period.

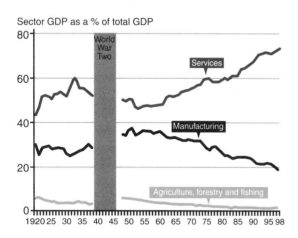

Figure 97.3 *Agriculture, manufacturing and service sector output as a percentage of GDP*
Source: adapted from B R Mitchell, *British Historical Statistics; Annual Abstract of Statistics*, Office for National Statistics.

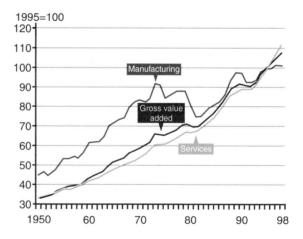

Figure 97.4 *Gross value added, manufacturing and service sector output 1995=100*
Source: adapted from *Economic Trends Annual Supplement*, Office for National Statistics.

Table 97.2 *Manufacturing output by industry at constant gross value added, 1995=100*

	1982	1990	1998
Food, beverages and tobacco	93.0	97.2	102.7
Textiles and leather products	82.8	111.8	88.9
Wood and wood products	64.7	111.6	96.6
Pulp, paper and paper products, publishing and printing	71.8	96.4	98.2
Coke, petroleum products and nuclear fuel	120.7	77.4	88.2
Chemicals, chemical products and man-made fibres	84.4	83.5	103.4
Rubber and plastics products	67.5	88.2	101.1
Other non-metallic mineral products	73.1	109.4	96.8
Basic metals and fabricated metal products	73.0	111.2	98.6
Machinery and equipment not elsewhere classified	80.1	110.6	95.4
Electrical and optical equipment	75.2	80.8	113.3
Transport equipment including motor manufacturing	70.0	108.8	115.3
Manufacturing not elsewhere classified	75.4	112.5	100
Total manufacturing	75.8	97.7	102.1

Source: adapted from *Annual Abstract of Statistics*, Office for National Statistics.

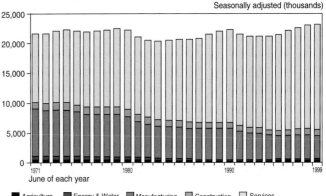

Seasonally adjusted (thousands)

Agriculture, forestry & fishing ■ Energy & Water ■ Manufacturing ▨ Construction □ Services

Figure 97.5 *Employees in employment by industrial sector: Great Britain, 1971-1999*

Source: adapted from *Annual Abstract of Statistics*, *Labour Market Trends*, Office for National Statistics.

Certain manufacturing industries have done better than others. Table 97.2 shows the groupings of manufacturing in the Standard Industrial Classification and the change in output compared to 1995 which is given an index number of 100. In 1982, the economy was just beginning to grow again after a deep recession which particularly hit manufacturing industry. In 1990, most of manufacturing industry was still producing at levels reached in 1988-89 at the height of the Lawson boom. 1998 was another boom year for the UK economy. Table 97.2 shows that all industries except energy saw growth in output between 1982 and 1998. However, some industries performed weakly. Textiles, for instance, continued its relative decline which has been taking place since the start of this century. The UK chemicals and man-made fibre industries have suffered relatively, as too have food, beverages and tobacco. In contrast, transport equipment, which mainly comprises motor manufacturing, has performed strongly. This must be set in the context of the 1970s, however, when motor manufacturing performed disastrously as it faced fierce competition from Japanese and continental manufacturers.

Not surprisingly, the changes in the share of output of the manufacturing and service sectors of the economy have produced changes in the structure and pattern of employment, as can be in Figure 97.5. In 1971, there were 7.1 million workers employed in manufacturing out of a total number of employees in employment of 21.6 million (the self-employed and unemployed are not included). By 1999, employment in manufacturing had

fallen to 3.9 million out of a total of 23.3 million employees. A rise in manufacturing output of 23 per cent was accompanied by a 50 per cent fall in employment. Employment in primary industry had fallen too. On the other hand, service sector employment rose considerably, from 11.4 million employees in 1971 to 17.8 million in 1999, a rise of 56 per cent which accompanied a doubling in total output. Figure 97.6 shows that in 1971 approximately half of all employees worked in service sector industries. By 1999, this had grown to 77 per cent. The share of manufacturing employment, on the other hand, fell from 36 per cent to just 17 per cent.

De-industrialisation

The process of decline in manufacturing industry is known as DE-INDUSTRIALISATION. There is no standard definition of the term, but it has at times been used to describe:
- the absolute decline in output of manufacturing industry;
- a significant decline in the share of manufacturing output in total output;
- the absolute decline in the numbers of workers employed in manufacturing;
- the relative decline in the proportion of all workers employed in manufacturing.

In the case of the UK, there has been an absolute decline in employment in manufacturing industry, from 7.1 million workers in 1971 to 3.9 million workers in 1999. There has also been a relative decline in manufacturing output.

De-industrialisation has been a major cause of changes in employment by region in the UK. Areas which were heavily reliant on manufacturing industry, mainly outside Southern England, experienced higher levels of unemployment as industries declined. For instance, the North East of England has never fully recovered from the decline of traditional heavy

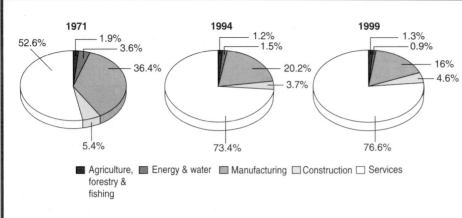

1971

52.6%
1.9%
3.6%
36.4%
5.4%

1994

1.2%
1.5%
20.2%
3.7%
73.4%

1999

1.3%
0.9%
16%
4.6%
76.6%

■ Agriculture, ■ Energy & water ■ Manufacturing □ Construction □ Services
forestry &
fishing

Figure 97.6 *Employment by sector (employees in employment as a percentage of the total), Great Britain, 1971 and 1999*
Source: adapted from *Annual Abstract of Statistics, Labour Market Trends*, Office for National Statistics.

industries, such as shipbuilding and mining which began in the 1930s. The West Midlands experienced a sharp relative jump in unemployment in the 1970s when its traditional metal based manufacturing industries went into decline. In contrast, the service sector in much of Southern England grew strongly enough to make up for the loss of its primary and secondary industries. The result has been the creation since the 1930s of a **North-South divide** in the UK, where regions outside the South of England have performed less well than Southern England. Population has migrated from North to South, putting intense pressure on resources such as housing in many areas of the South. In contrast, some areas in the rest of the UK have suffered a fall in population in a period when the overall UK population has been slowly growing. Liverpool, for instance, has seen a fall in its population over the past 30 years. The waste of resources that has resulted from depopulation, such as unwanted housing or underutilised road systems, has been a drag on the performance of the UK economy.

Changes in international competitiveness

To what extent have these changes in the structure of the economy been caused by changes in international competitiveness? Can these changes be explained solely by shifts in **comparative advantage** (☞ unit 14)?

The major shifts between sectors of the economy are unlikely to have been caused primarily by changes in competitiveness. Much reflects changes in consumer spending patterns. Economic growth has given consumers ever increasing amounts of disposable income to spend. Over time, they have chosen to spend an ever greater proportion of their income on services rather than manufactures (i.e. services have an income elasticity of demand greater than 1 whilst manufactures have an income elasticity of demand of less than 1). This is true not just of the UK but of all major industrialised countries. Table 97.3 shows that manufacturing industry's share of output has fallen in

all G7 economies (the seven largest economies in the world). However, the UK suffered one of the largest falls in manufacturing output amongst the 7 countries between 1960 and 1998, along with Germany.

It is also the case that much of the output of the UK economy cannot be or is unlikely to be traded. For instance, the water industry is in a non-traded sector. So too are many service industries from hairdressing to education to health. So changes in relative spending in the non-traded sector of the economy cannot be explained by international comparative advantage either.

However, within the traded goods and services sector, there are clear indications that individual industries have been considerably affected by issues of competitiveness. For example, the UK motorcycle industry was destroyed by Japanese competition in the 1960s and 1970s. The British motor manufacturing industry became increasingly uncompetitive in the 1970s, but experienced a renaissance in the late 1980s and 1990s, arguably due to Japanese investment in UK motor manufacturing (☞ unit 15). The British coal industry has almost disappeared due to competition from imported coal and North Sea gas. Textile manufacturing has increasingly shifted to cheap labour Third World countries. Growth in UK domestic tourism has been hit because British holiday makers have shown a stronger preference for taking foreign holidays than foreigners coming to the UK. Financial services, on the other hand, have kept their share of the world markets in which they operate.

Table 97.3 *Manufacturing value added as a percentage of GDP in the G7 countries, 1960-1998*

	Output as a percentage of GDP		
	1965	1980	1998
United States	28	22	18
Japan	34	29	24
Germany	40	34	24
France	30	24	19
United Kingdom	34	27	21
Italy	30	28	20
Canada	26	19	17

Source: adapted from World Bank, *World Development Report*.

There is also some evidence that manufactures and other traded goods have suffered more from international competition than services. Table 97.4 shows average annual trade balances as a percentage of GDP for each decade from the 1950s to the 1990s. The balance of trade shows exports of goods minus imports of goods. Traditionally, the UK has imported more goods than it has exported. However, from the 1960s onwards there has been a deterioration in the balance of trade as a percentage of GDP. The 1970s figures are distorted by the oil crisis of 1973-75 which saw the balance of trade plunge to 6 per cent of GDP at its worst in 1974. Even the balance of trade in services, however, has been falling as a percentage of GDP over the 1970s, 1980s and 1990s, indicating a loss of international competitiveness. Overall, the figures would suggest that the UK has been losing international competitiveness over the past three decades. It has paid for overall deficits on traded goods and services either by earning more on its foreign investments than is paid out to foreigners on UK investments (shown by the total net income figures) or it has borrowed the money (shown by deficits on the current account).

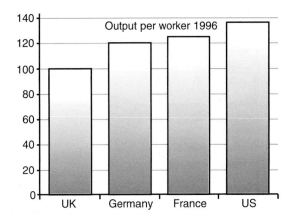

Figure 97.7 *Output per worker, 1996, (UK=100)*
Source: adapted from HM Treasury, the Red Book.

Table 97.4 *Balance of payments components as a percentage of GDP, annual averages*

	Balance of trade	Traded services balance	Balance on traded goods and services	Total net income	Current balance
1950s	-1.1	0.4	-0.7	1.5	1.0
1960s	-0.9	0.2	-0.7	1.0	0.2
1970s	-2.1	1.5	-0.6	0.8	-0.2
1980s	-1.5	1.4	-0.2	0.2	-0.3
1990s	-1.8	1.0	-0.9	0.6	-0.8

Source: adapted from *Economic Trends Annual Supplement*, Office for National Statistics.

Labour productivity

Labour productivity (output per worker) has risen substantially in the post-war period. As Table 97.5 shows, labour productivity in manufacturing has risen faster than for the economy as a whole and in the service sector in particular. This is because large gains can be made in manufacturing in substituting capital for labour. There is less scope for this in service industries, particularly in personal services and tourism where high labour to customer ratios are equated with quality of product.

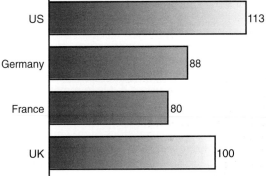
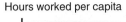

Figure 97.8 *Hours worked per head of population, 1996, (UK=100)*
Source: adapted from NIESR, Adair Turner (CBI).

Table 97.5 *Labour productivity, average annual percentage change, UK*

	Whole economy	Manufacturing
1960s	2.4	3.0
1970s	1.8	2.2
1980s	2.3	4.9
1990s	1.9	2.2

Source: adapted from *Economic Trends Annual Supplement*, Office for National Statistics.

These increases in labour productivity have not improved the UK's international competitiveness because other countries too have seen rising productivity. Figure 97.7 shows how the UK lags behind Germany, France and the USA in output per worker. In 1996, the USA was nearly 40 per cent and Germany 20 per cent more productive than the UK. Comparisons of productivity are complicated, though, by the number of hours worked. In the USA and the UK, a greater percentage of the population are in work, and workers work longer hours per year than in France and Germany as Figure 97.8 shows. If productivity is then measured as GDP per hours worked, as in Figure 97.9, a different ranking occurs. France and Germany are then more productive than the USA. The UK still lags at least 20 per cent behind.

Lower productivity doesn't necessarily make the UK less internationally competitive in itself. If British workers are prepared to accept at least 20 per cent less pay than, say, French, German or US workers, UK firms can remain price competitive. Equally, labour

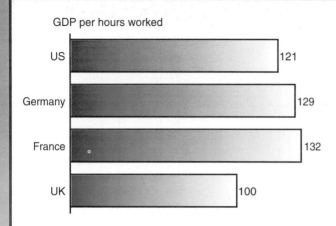

Figure 97.9 *Output per hours worked, 1996 (UK=100)*
Source: adapted from NIESR, Adair Turner (CBI).

productivity is closely linked to the amount of capital stock. Figure 97.10 shows that the UK has considerably less capital stock per hour worked than the USA, France or Germany. This is the result of decades of relative underinvestment by UK firms. By 1995, Germany had accumulated over 50 per cent more capital stock per hour worked than the UK. German workers can therefore produce much more per hour because they are working with far more capital equipment. However, capital is also a cost to industry. The higher the investment of a firm, the higher will be its costs, and the higher will have to be its prices if it is to remain competitive, all other things being equal. The UK and the USA, relatively low investment countries, have traditionally used their capital stock highly intensively to remain competitive and keep down costs. They have employed relatively large amounts of labour and paid them relatively low wages. France and Germany have used their much higher levels of capital stock less intensively. Hours of work are less, a smaller proportion of the population are in employment, but workers receive higher wages.

Low investment, though, is likely to have been a continued drag on Britain's international competitiveness over time however well firms have

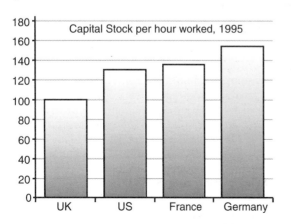

Figure 97.10 *Capital stock per hour worked, 1995 (UK=100)*
Source: adapted from HM Treasury, the Red Book.

managed their capital stock. In low technology manufacturing, the UK has increasingly faced competition from Third World countries where workers earn a fraction of UK wage rates. In high technology traded goods, investment has been key to producing new, high quality, better performing products which can command premium prices. Investment, or the lack of it, has been crucial in determining whether individual industries have survived in the UK. Not surprisingly, government over the past 50 years has continually exhorted British industry to invest more.

Multinational companies

Multinational companies have come to play an increasingly important role in world trade. MULTINATIONAL COMPANIES are companies which have significant production operations in at least two countries. These could be primary product companies such as Gheest or BP. They could be manufacturing companies like Ford or Sony. Or they could be service sector companies like Starbucks, the coffee shop chain, or Cable & Wireless. Some multinationals have outputs which are greater than many countries in the world today. There must therefore be reasons why such large firms exist.

Economies of scale There are many industries where only the largest firms with worldwide access to both production facilities and markets can fully exploit economies of scale. Examples of such industries include the oil and motor manufacturing industries. Typically, the amounts of capital needed are so large that small firms find it difficult to compete.

Knowledge and innovation Many multinational companies are storehouses of accumulated knowledge and powerful players in the field of innovation. For instance, it is difficult to imagine how any enterprise could exploit oil from miles below the sea bed in the deep waters of the North Sea, or produce the technology to put a man on the moon. Genetic engineering or microchips are two examples of where multinationals are in the forefront of bringing new products to the market.

Branding and marketing Some multinational companies use very little technology. Instead, they rely for their world presence on branding and marketing. At some point in the past, they have produced a highly successful product in a local market. This is then rolled out into other national markets. Coca Cola or McDonald's are two examples of this. The brand is protected from competition through patents, and heavy use of advertising and other forms of promotion.

Market and political power Some multinationals exploit market power in individual national markets to create a global business. They might have legitimate patents or copyrights or own key resources. Equally, they may build on these by **anti-competitive practices** (☞ unit 65) which attempt to force existing firms out of the market and prevent new firms from entering it. Multinationals also have a long history of subverting and corrupting governments to achieve their aims. They are so large that they have considerable financial resources to be able to use either in bribing government officials and politicians, or maintaining powerful lobby organisations.

Individual countries gain international competitiveness if they are the national base for a multinational corporation. This is because a disproportionate amount of spending by the multinational will take place in its home country. Moreover, the resources employed are likely to be the most sophisticated within the organisation. For instance, the multinational will almost certainly have its headquarters in its home country. A disproportionate amount of research and development is likely to take place in the home country. It is likely to be used as a production base, with a disproportionate number of production facilities there or with inputs being sourced from other firms in that country. One of the reasons why the developed world has maintained its dominance over world markets is because hardly any developing countries have created successful multinationals. The few countries that have, such as Taiwan or South Korea, have rapidly turned themselves into developed countries.

Some argue that multinationals have a negative impact on the world economy.

Lack of accountability The size of multinationals can make them seem unaccountable to anyone. In practice, multinationals are accountable to many bodies. They are answerable, for instance, to their shareholders. Increasingly, though, they have had to account for their actions to other stakeholders. They have to obey the laws of the countries in which they operate, unless government is so corrupt or weak that multinationals can evade the law. They are also subject to scrutiny by pressure groups, such as environmental groups.

Loss of national identity Multinationals are often accused of leading to lowering living standards by destroying native culture. McDonald's, for instance, has encountered fierce opposition in some countries which see US burgers as a threat to national cuisine and eating habits. Globalisation inevitably means that there is a blurring of national identities as standards are accepted throughout the world. Standards can give rise to considerable benefits, though, because they allow people and firms to use common equipment, common ways of thinking and doing things, as well as helping in the purchase of products.

Footloose capitalism Multinationals have the power to move production from country to country, creating and

destroying jobs and prosperity in their wake. They do this to maximise their profits. For instance, they might close a production facility in a high cost country like the UK or the USA and move it to a low cost country like India or Thailand. Globalisation is inevitably leading to a shifting of production from the First World to the Third World. This is one key way in which developing countries of the world can increase their living standards. However, multinationals are not the prime cause of this shift in production. Rather, they are responding to market forces in exactly the same way that national companies are so doing. Over the past 30 years, domestic UK companies have increasingly sourced goods from overseas to take advantage of better prices. They have closed their own manufacturing operations, or forced previous UK suppliers to close down through loss of orders. Multinationals are part of this trend which is exploiting **comparative advantage** (☞ unit 14).

Destruction of the environment A number of multinationals dominate world extraction industries such as oil or gold mining. These industries are inevitably particularly destructive of the environment. Other multinationals, such as motor manufacturers or even service companies have also been accused of destroying the environment for instance in the way in which they source their raw materials. However, any form of production could be argued to be undesirable from an environmental viewpoint. Moreover, multinational companies often have better environmental records than smaller national companies. They not only have the financial resources to be able to minimise their impact on the environment; they also have the technical knowledge and ability to innovate which can lead to minimising environmental problems.

Multinationals can be easy targets for those who dislike global capitalism. Adam Smith's hidden hand of the market does make individuals relatively powerless when factories are closed and production is shifted thousands of miles away. New products, such as genetically modified food, can also raise important questions about whether such technologies should be exploited. On the other hand, without multinational companies, there would be far less trade and innovation. World output would almost certainly be considerably lower, arguably leading to lower living standards. Free market economists would argue that the focus of any debate about multinationals is not whether they should be allowed to exist but about how government, representing all stakeholders in society, can set up regimes which can regulate the activities of multinationals for the benefit of all.

key terms

De-industrialisation - the process of decline of industry, particularly manufacturing industry, measured for instance by declines in absolute levels of employment and output, or declines in the relative share of employment or output in the economy of manufacturing industry.

Globalisation - the integration of the world's economy into a single international market rather than many national markets.
Multinational companies - companies with significant production operations in at least two countries.

The UK's international competitiveness

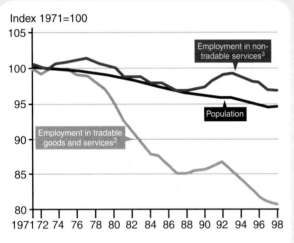

Figure 97.11 *Share of the North[1] in GB employment and population*
Source: adapted from Robert Rowthorn, Cambridge University, Kalecki Memorial Lecture.

1. All regions of Great Britain apart from the South West, South East and East Anglia.
2. Tradable goods and services = agriculture, mining (including oil and gas), manufacturing, external financial and business services and the armed forces.
3. All other services.

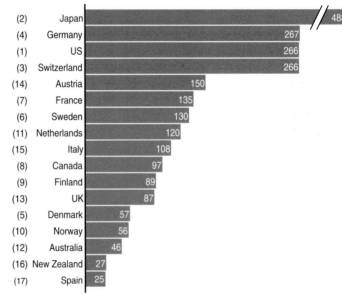

Figure 97.12 *Innovation index 1996*
Source: adapted from Citations and Patents, CHI Research.

Michael Porter, a professor at Harvard Business School and a leading authority on measuring economic performance, uses an unscholarly term to describe Britain's poor showing internationally as a generator of wealth. 'It stinks' is how the professor describes the UK's lowly ranking in most global league tables covering areas such as income per person or industrial competitiveness.

Professor Porter yesterday came out with his own analysis of Britain's shortcomings, which puts the country 13th out of 17 industrial nations in terms of its ability to derive commercial benefits from science and technology. This 'innovation index' is based on such factors as number of patents granted and research and development spending.

He advocates creating a more entrepreneurial culture in the UK by giving 'high powered incentives' to aid entrepreneurship. Large cuts in capital gains tax, for instance, would mean that entrepreneurs could keep most, if not all, of the gains they make by setting up businesses. Allowing any increase in research and development spending to be offset against tax would increase incentives to spend on R&D. Both measures could lead to significant increases in funds for venture capital, money used to back promising new businesses.

Source: adapted from the *Financial Times*, 11.12.1998.

The White Paper on competitiveness published yesterday commits the government to the ambitious aim of reversing a century of relative decline in the UK. It contains a raft of policy announcements, ranging from action to promote science and engineering to financial help for entrepreneurs and limited protection from creditors for small companies in difficulties.

The most important element of the bundle of papers released by the Department of Trade and Industry may be the economic analysis of the role of knowledge in economic growth. The argument put forward is that knowledge is becoming more important as a factor in economic growth because of four mutually reinforcing developments - rapid developments in information and communications technology, the increased speed of scientific and technological advances, greater global competition, and more sophisticated demand patterns caused by growing prosperity.

This is changing the way businesses compete, increasing the importance of innovation and increasing the returns to products with a large knowledge component. These developments lead to a crucial role for entrepreneurs - in identifying and exploiting the economic opportunities presented by rapid change - and for investors - who may find companies' wealth-creating potential increasingly tied up in intangible assets such as the knowledge of the workforce. Generating economic prosperity in future, it says, will require: the capacity to exploit science and technology, enterprise and innovation, people and skills; collaboration between companies operating in networks and clusters; and greater competition to increase innovation and consumer choice. The paper says the UK is in a strong position in many areas of the knowledge economy because of the strength of the media, entertainment and financial services. The composition of UK output is already changing to reflect the importance of knowledge, reflected in increases in knowledge-based employment and exports. However, the analysis blames a relatively low level of gross domestic product per head on a labour productivity gap of between 20 and 40 per cent with the US, France and Germany.

Source: adapted from the *Financial Times*, 17.12.1998.

Figure 97.13 *Knowledge based industries*
Source: adapted from *OECD*, ONS.

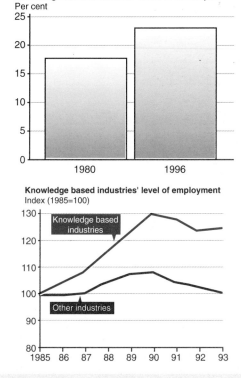

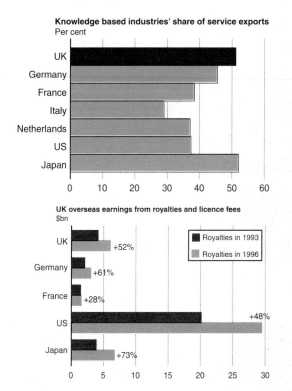

1. **Outline the evidence presented in the data which suggests that the UK lags behind its international rivals in competitiveness.**
2. **Analyse the contribution that knowledge based industries could play in restoring UK international competitiveness.**
3. **Assess whether the most important policy response of government to the problem of lack of competitiveness should be to promote entrepreneurship.**

Summary

1. In a common market, there is free movement of goods and services, and factors of production. Goods and services imported from outside the common market face a common external tariff.
2. Free trade involves harmonisation in a wide range of areas, including product standards and taxation.
3. The formation of a common market will lead to trade creation and trade diversion. The greater the trade creation and the less the trade diversion, the greater will be the welfare benefits to member countries.
4. Dynamic gains from membership include economies of scale in production. Competition is likely to increase in the short run but mergers and takeovers are likely to lessen competition amongst firms in the long run.
5. Common market spending and taxation will lead to a redistribution of resources between member countries. Inevitably some countries will gain and others will lose from the common market budget.
6. Common markets may be the first step towards complete monetary and political union between member countries.

A common market

A COMMON MARKET or CUSTOMS UNION is a group of countries between which there is free trade and which impose a COMMON EXTERNAL TARIFF on imported goods from outside the market. In theory, free trade between member countries involves goods and services as well as the factors of production.

- Land. There should be free trade in natural resources. In Europe, for instance, a British company should be free to buy land in Paris, whilst a French company should be free to own a licence to exploit North Sea oil.
- Labour. Workers should be free to work in any member country. For instance, an Italian should be able to work in London on exactly the same terms as a worker born in Birmingham.
- Capital. Capital should flow freely between countries. Of particular importance is **financial capital**. A Scottish firm should be free to borrow money in Paris to set up a factory in Italy, just as a London based firm could borrow money from a Scottish bank to invest in Wales.

Imports from outside the common market present a problem. For instance, assume that the UK imposes a tariff of 10 per cent on imports of foreign cars whilst France imposes a tariff of 20 per cent. With free trade between France and the UK, foreign importers would ship cars intended for sale in France to the UK, pay the 10 per cent tariff, and then re-export them 'tariff-free' into France. There are two ways to get round this problem.

- One way is to impose a common external tariff. All member countries agree to change their tariff structures so as to impose the same tariff on imported items. In our example, France and the UK would have to change or HARMONISE their tariffs on cars to an agreed European Union (EU) figure.
- The other way is for member countries to impose tariffs on re-exports. In our example France could impose a 10 per cent tariff on the original price of cars imported from non-member countries.

This second solution is a feature of FREE TRADE AREAS. A free trade area differs from a common market partly because of its different approach to dealing with non-member imports. It also differs because member countries are not committed to working towards closer economic integration. In a free trade area, the sole objective is free trade between member countries.

In a common market, the goal is to establish a single market in the same way that there is a single market within an individual economy. Ultimately this involves a large number of changes including:

- no customs posts between countries; just as goods and people are free to travel between Manchester and London, so they should be free to travel between

Question 1

- In 1994, a group of countries, including France, Germany, Holland and Belgium, dismantled all frontier posts between their countries.
- On 1 January 2002, euro notes and coins were issued in 11 countries of the European Union, followed shortly afterwards by the withdrawal of national currencies in those countries.
- Since the 1980s, the EU has suggested that tax rates between member countries should be harmonised (i.e. made the same). This would prevent, for instance, the large scale smuggling of tobacco into the UK from France and Belgium, or the move of manufacturing plants from high labour taxed countries like Germany to low taxed countries like the UK.
- In 1998, the EU conducted an enquiry into mobile phone charging, concerned that mobile phone companies were using their monopoly powers to exploit customers. In some countries, such as Ireland, it forced operators to reduce their prices.
- The Social Charter, part of the Maastricht Treaty of 1991, allows the EU to impose regulations on the use of labour, such as maximum working weeks and holiday entitlement, across European countries.

(a) Explain why each of these illustrates how a common market works.

London and Milan;
- identical product standards between countries; the existence of individual national safety standards on cars, for instance, is a barrier to trade just as it would be if cars sold in London had to meet different safety requirements from cars sold in Bristol;
- harmonisation of taxes; if the tax on the same car is £2 000 more in the UK than in France, then UK residents will buy their cars in France and take them back to England, distorting the pattern of trade; equally if direct taxes on income are an average 15 per cent in France and 30 per cent in the UK, some UK workers may be tempted to go and work in France;
- a common currency; having to buy foreign exchange is a barrier to trade, especially if there are exchange rate movements; hence there should a single common market currency just as there is a single currency in the UK.

A common market becomes an **economic union** when there is a truly integrated single market and when the main macro-economic decisions are decided at community level. For instance, a single currency leads to the creation of a single central bank which makes decisions about monetary and exchange rate policy across the whole union. Economic integration is also likely to lead to some form of central government which controls a significant budget for spending and taxation across the union.

Trade creation and trade diversion

The **theory of comparative advantage** (☞ unit 14) shows that free trade between countries is likely to increase total world production. When a small number of countries form a common market, there will be gainers and losers.

TRADE CREATION is said to take place when a country moves from buying goods from a high cost country to buying them from a lower cost country. For instance, country A might have imposed a 50 per cent tariff on imported cars. As a result, all cars sold in country A were produced domestically. It now joins a customs union. The common external tariff is 50 per cent but cars from member countries can be imported free of the tariff. Country A now buys some cars from common market countries because they are lower priced than those previously produced domestically. Consumers in country A have benefited because they are able to buy cars from a cheaper source.

TRADE DIVERSION takes place when a country moves from buying goods from a low cost producer to buying them from a higher cost producer. For instance, before entry to the European Union, the UK had low or zero

---

Question 2

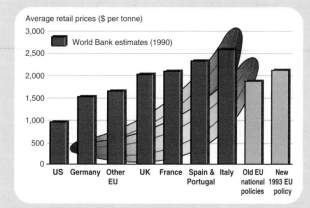

Figure 98.1 *Average retail prices of bananas*
Source: adapted from IMF.

The Single European Market came into existence on 1 January 1993. Its purpose was to abolish the remaining barriers to trade between EU countries. One of its effects was to prevent individual countries from imposing their own trade restrictions on individual products. An example of this was bananas.

Before 1993, some EU countries, notably Germany, had bought their bananas from the cheapest world source. This, in practice, was Latin American countries such as Guatemala. Other countries, notably France and the UK, had imposed tariff barriers on these bananas to allow the import of dearer bananas from ACP (African, Caribbean and Pacific) countries. These are countries which are former colonies of the UK and France. The banana growers are mainly Caribbean countries.
From 1993, the EU imposed a common tariff and quota

policy on all bananas coming into the Union. The result was a rise in prices of bananas in Germany and other countries, with little reduction in price in the UK and France.

A World Bank study published in 1995 estimated that EU consumers were paying $2.3bn a year more for their bananas than if they were bought at lowest world prices. Before 1993, the extra cost of buying higher priced bananas had been only $1.6bn. Average prices in the Union had increased by 12 per cent as a result of the new regime. The World Bank report also pointed out that only $300m of the extra $2.3bn paid for bananas reached the ACP producers. The rest benefits mainly the European companies which market bananas. ACP countries would be better off if the EU abolished its banana policy and gave them direct aid instead. Alternatively, the EU should limit the distortions caused by the scheme by making quotas transferable.

(a) Using examples from the data, distinguish between trade creation and trade diversion.
(b) (i) Using the theory of comparative advantage, explain why the ACP countries might be better off in the long run if they accepted abolition of the banana import policy in return for a guaranteed payment of $300m a year for the next 20 years. (ii) What would be the economic implications if instead of the current policy of giving banana quotas to ACP countries (which allows them to import a fixed amount of bananas into the EU tariff free), the quotas became transferable and tradable? This would mean that any producer, whether in Africa, the Caribbean or Latin America, could buy banana quotas from ACP producers allowing them to import bananas tariff-free into the EU.

tariffs on imported foodstuffs. It bought from the lowest cost producers round the world such as New Zealand and the USA. After entry, the UK had to impose the much higher EU common external tariff. As a result it became cheaper to buy food from other EU countries such as France and Italy. France and Italy are higher cost producers than the USA and New Zealand for many food items.

In general the higher the tariffs imposed by a country before entry to a common market, the more likely it is that trade creation rather than trade diversion will take place. It is also true that the net gains will tend to be larger, the greater the volume of trade between the countries in the common market.

Free trade vs customs unions

Customs unions can be seen as a 'second best' solution in a world where there is protectionism. Economic efficiency would be maximised if there were no barriers to trade between countries. Individual economies would also have perfectly competitive products and free labour and capital markets. In this theoretical world, comparative advantage would determine which countries produced what goods. This would be the 'first best' solution. In the real world, such conditions don't exist. Economic inefficiency arises because relatively high cost producers can shelter behind protective barriers. A customs union brings down these barriers, at least between member states. Member countries may therefore be able to switch buying from a high cost producer to a lower cost producer. However, countries will only benefit if trade creation is greater than trade diversion. Consideration must also be taken of whether there will be dynamic gains or losses from the creation of a customs union.

Economies of scale

Gains from trade creation are **static** gains. They occur once and for all following the creation of, or entry to, a common market. Membership of a common market may also result in **dynamic** gains or losses - gains or losses which occur over a period of time. One important such gain comes from **economies of scale** (☞ unit 49). In a common market, the potential size of the customer market is inevitably larger than in a national market. For instance, the European Union has 300 million inhabitants compared to 59 million for the UK. This means that important economies of scale can be achieved by national companies if they carve out a market for themselves throughout the common market. This is no easy task given that each country is likely to have different consumer preferences. However, there are some products, such as basic chemicals, which are demanded by all countries. Other products, such as cars, are relatively easily sold across national boundaries. Yet other products, such as cosmetics, may need different packaging for different countries, but the basic product is the same.

Economies of scale will be achieved over a period of time as companies expand internally or merge with other foreign companies. The size of the potential gains will be greater, the more homogeneous the tastes of consumers within the market. For instance, the gains are likely to be higher for a market comprising France and the UK than for the UK and Iran. Economies of scale bring benefits to consumers because average costs of production fall, and therefore prices are likely to fall too.

Question 3

The Cecchini Report, published in 1988, argued that there would be a 5.3 per cent increase in national income of the European Union following the creation of the single market from the beginning of 1993. One major gain would arise from economies of scale. For instance, there were 50 tractor manufacturers in the EU fighting over a market similar in size to that served in the US by just 4 manufacturers. Similarly in the US there were 4 producers of domestic appliances compared to 300 in the EU.

(a) Why was there scope for increased economies of scale in the EU following 1992?
(b) (i) What benefits might consumers have received from increased economies of scale?
   (ii) What might have been the costs to workers?
   (iii) What were the implications for merger and monopoly policy in the EU?

Competition

Another possible dynamic gain arises from increased competition between firms. A common market should eliminate restrictions on trade between member countries. Domestic industries will therefore face greater competition than before from firms in other member countries. Competition will encourage innovation, reduce costs of production and reduce prices. There will therefore be gains in productive and allocative efficiency (☞ unit 16).

Although there is likely to be greater competition in the short run, evidence suggests that this competition will be reduced in the long run. Competition will drive the least efficient firms out of the market, as the theory of perfect competition predicts. Other firms will seek to maintain monopoly profits by re-establishing control over their markets. They will do this by merging with or taking over foreign firms within the common market. Over time, the oligopolistic nature of competition in domestic markets will be recreated on a common market level. This may benefit the consumer through economies of scale but it certainly will not bring the benefits that free market economists suggest.

The Austrian school of Economics argues that competition is not necessarily beneficial to the consumer. Large international monopolies, earning considerable abnormal profit, will have the resources to devote to research, development and investment. If they fail to develop products that satisfy consumer wants, their monopoly will be lost through the process of creative destruction. Competitors will break their monopoly by creating new products. This constant development of new products is far more beneficial to consumer welfare than a few per cent off the price of existing products which might result from a perfectly competitive environment.

Transfers of resources

Common markets may differ in the size and power of their institutions. The European Union has a sizeable bureaucracy, a parliament and a large budget. Money is paid into a Union budget by member countries. The money is used to pay for administration and the implementation of Union-wide policies. In the case of the European Union, about 70 per cent of the budget has traditionally been allocated to one area of policy - the **Common Agricultural Policy** (☞ unit 16 and 21). Any budget of any size opens up the possibility that some member countries may pay more into the budget than they receive. There may therefore be a net transfer of resources from one country to another within a common market. These represent static losses and gains (i.e. once and for all losses and gains).

Perhaps more importantly, there can also be transfers of real resources from country to country. Countries in the common market which are particularly dynamic and successful are likely to attract inflows of labour and capital. Countries which have lower growth rates are likely to suffer net capital outflows and lose some of their best workers to other economies. This could heighten regional disparities, making the richer nations relatively even richer.

The process may be magnified if the successful countries are at the geographical centre of the common market whilst the less successful countries are on the fringe. Transport and communication costs tend to be lower for companies sited at the centre and higher for those at the periphery. Hence central countries tend to have a competitive advantage over fringe countries.

Neo-classical economic theory suggests that free market forces would equalise the differences between regions. An unsuccessful region will have cheap labour and cheap land. Firms will be attracted into the region to take advantage of these. In practice, this effect seems to be very weak. Cheap labour economies can easily become branch economies. Firms set up branches in these regions, employing cheap labour to perform low productivity tasks. Tasks which have high value added are completed at headquarters in higher cost areas. The result is growing economic divergence, with poorer regions losing the most skilled of their labour force to the richer regions and being left with less dynamic and less skilled workers to do less well paid jobs.

Monetary and political union

An internal common market where there are different currencies in each country imposes costs upon producers. Therefore a common market implies a move to a common currency. A common currency implies common monetary and fiscal policies. The economic implications of monetary union are discussed further in unit 95.

A common market may eventually lead to political union. Political union inevitably involves a loss of national sovereignty. Decisions which previously were made at national level will now be made at community level. This may have economic implications in that a member country will lose the ability to direct its economic

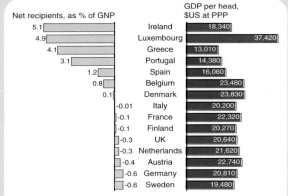

Question 4

Figure 98.2 *Net recipients from the European Union budget and GDP per head ($US at purchasing power parities) 1998*
Source: adapted from *European Commision*, Eurobarometer.

(a) To what extent is there a correlation between low income countries and net receipts (the difference between monies paid out from the EU budget to countries and the contributions they have to make to the EU budget) in the EU?
(b) Explain how the EU budget could be used to equalise living standards between the different regions of the EU.

affairs to its own advantage. On the other hand, it can be argued that any country which is very **open** (i.e. exports a high proportion of its national product) has already lost most of its ability to direct its own economic affairs because so much of its economy depends upon the spending and saving decisions of foreigners.

Applied economics

The European Union

The historical background

At the end of the Second World War, Europe's economies were shattered. It was realised by many western politicians that this was the direct outcome of unwise political decisions made at the end of the First World War when Germany was economically penalised for having lost the war. Huge war reparations and the isolation of Germany politically had given German fascists the chance to gain support and power, which in turn led to the Second World War. Some had a vision of co-operation and a united peaceful Europe. This vision led to the creation of today's European Union (EU).

The first step on the road to today's EU was the formation in 1952 of the European Coal and Steel Community (ECSC) by France, Germany, Italy, Luxembourg, Belgium and the Netherlands. This created a free trade area for coal and steel, at the time crucial industries in those countries. It enabled the six countries to protect their industries more from US competition. Greater output then enabled ECSC producers to reduce costs through greater economies of scale and thus become more competitive.

In 1957, the European Atomic Energy Community was formed by the same six countries to encourage the growth of the peaceful use of nuclear power. By the time the treaty had been signed, negotiations were well under way for the creation of the far more ambitious European Economic Community (EEC) or Common Market. This came into existence on 1 January 1958 after the signing of the Treaty of Rome in 1957.

The Treaty of Rome established a customs union, with provisions for the phased withdrawal of all tariffs between the six member countries and the imposition of a common external tariff on goods coming into the Community. This was finally completed in 1986. The Treaty also contained provisions which would in future allow the free flow not just of goods but also of capital and of labour between countries. Another aspect was the creation of a European policy on competition and restrictive trade practices.

The Treaty of Rome created a number of important institutions.

- The **European Commission**, based in Brussels, is the equivalent of the civil service in the UK. At the top are 17 Commissioners, each with a particular responsibility for an area of community policy. The Commission is responsible for implementing agreed policies and for proposing new policies. It can be a very powerful body, partly because it is responsible for the day to day running of Community policies, but also because it is the main agent of change and progress in policy.

- The **European Council of Ministers** is a powerful body too. It is made up of a ministerial representative from each member state. When agriculture is being discussed, then countries are represented by their agriculture ministers. When broad economic issues are discussed, it will be finance ministers who are present. New policies put forward by the European Commission are either approved or rejected by the Council of Ministers. Hence, the Council of Ministers is the most important decision-making body. In most areas, there has to be a unanimous vote for a policy to be approved. However, in some areas, only a majority vote is needed.

- The **European Parliament**, based in Strasbourg, is made up of elected representatives (MEPs) from the member states. The European Parliament is a relatively weak body. Until recently, it had almost no decision-making powers at all and even since the Treaty of Maastricht (1992), when its powers were increased, it has been able to do little more than rubber stamp decisions made elsewhere. The intention is that the European Parliament will, over time, increase its powers to become more like a national parliament.

- The **European Court of Justice**, which meets in Luxembourg, is another powerful body. It is the ultimate court of law and is responsible for making judgements on EU law. It regularly passes judgements which

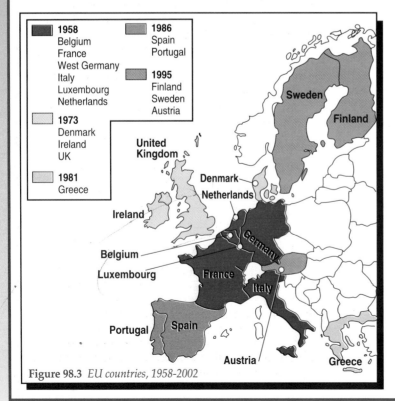

1958
Belgium
France
West Germany
Italy
Luxembourg
Netherlands

1973
Denmark
Ireland
UK

1981
Greece

1986
Spain
Portugal

1995
Finland
Sweden
Austria

Figure 98.3 *EU countries, 1958-2002*

have a significant impact on individual countries or the entire community. For instance, its judgement on equal pension rights in 1992 forced the UK government to move towards equalising the state retiring age for men and women in the UK at 65.

The Treaty of Rome envisaged the creation of a number of common policies. The first of these to be implemented under Article 39 of the Treaty was the **Common Agricultural Policy** (CAP). This was established in 1962 and is discussed in much greater detail in units 76 and 21. Article 85 of the Treaty covers **competition policy**, aspects of which are discussed in units 63 and 65. **Regional policy** has been used to reduce income and wealth differentials between member countries. **Transport policy**, covered in Articles 3 and 74-84 of the Treaty, has been difficult to implement because national governments have been reluctant to cede powers to the Community over transport issues. However, both competition policy and the Single Market have had a considerable impact on national transport policies. **Social Policy**, covered in Articles 117-128 of the Treaty, envisages the creation of a single market for labour where all workers in the community are covered by common laws. Social policy was given a major boost by the signing of the Treaty of Maastricht in 1991 which contained the Social Charter.

The UK had decided not to join the EEC (now the EU) in 1958, feeling that it would turn out to be largely irrelevant in European terms and preferring to maintain strong links with the USA and its colonies and ex-colonies in the Commonwealth. Instead, it helped create the **European Free Trade Association** (EFTA) in 1960 along with Austria, Denmark, Norway, Portugal, Sweden and Switzerland. Finland joined a little later. EFTA was a free trade area rather than a customs union. There was no intention that EFTA would develop into anything more than an association which dealt with trade, unlike the EEC where there was a vision from the start that a united European state could be formed. The UK quickly recognised that it had probably made the wrong decision and in 1962 applied to join the EEC. The French blocked the proposal, fearing that Britain's entry would destroy the dominance of France and Germany. Ten years later, the UK was again negotiating for entry and this time, along with Denmark and Eire, was successful in its application. The three countries joined in 1973, enlarging the community to nine members.

An attempt was made in the 1970s to move the EEC in the direction of a single currency. The turbulent economic conditions at the time meant that little was achieved. However, in 1979, the **European Monetary System** was established which became the framework for the move towards a single currency in the 1980s and 1990s. This is discussed further in unit 95.

The 1980s saw the further enlargement of the Community. Greece joined in 1981 whilst Spain and Portugal joined in 1986. This helped shift the political balance in the Community and increased the relative importance of agriculture. The 1980s also saw the signing of possibly the most important act since the Treaty of Rome. The **Single European Act (SEA)** of 1985, which came into force in 1987, committed member states to take the second step towards the creation of a genuine common market by 1 January 1993. The 1950s and 1960s had seen the removal of tariff and quota barriers on trade in most goods between member countries. The SEA committed governments to removing the many other barriers to trade which still existed. This is discussed in further detail below. The SEA saw a change in the name of the community. To show that the Community was now not just about economic issues, the 'economic' was dropped from EEC and the Community was now officially called the European Community (EC).

In 1989, the European Commission put forward proposals for a **Social Charter** (☞ unit 75) which would guarantee workers' rights. This Social Charter became the Social Chapter in the Maastricht Treaty in 1992. This Treaty was another important stepping stone in the move towards a united Europe. It laid down a timetable for the creation of a single currency. It also established a framework for co-operation in foreign policy between member countries. To signify the move forward by the Treaty, the name of the Community was changed from the European Community to the European Union (EU).

In 1995, three more countries joined the Union, Austria, Finland and Sweden. On 1 January 1999, the currencies of 11 member states which had been part of the EMS became locked in value against each other as the next stage of the process towards monetary union. A new central bank, the European Central Bank, was created. It was responsible for monetary and exchange rate policy throughout the 11 member states - the 'euro-zone' or 'Euroland'. One of its functions was to organise the distribution of notes and coins of the Euro for the launch date of the new currency on 1st January 2002. Shortly afterward, notes and coins of the existing different national currencies will be withdrawn. Households and firms in Paris, Berlin and Rome will then use the same currency, in the same way that households and firms in London and Belfast use one currency at present.

The creation of a single currency was the next large step for the European Union. In the first half of the 21st century, a number of challenges face the EU. The immediate challenge is how to deal with new applicants: nearly all countries in Eastern Europe and the Balkans, together with Turkey, have applied to join. This is discussed in further detail below. Budget reform, particularly reform of CAP, is essential if agriculture is to be made more efficient and if the industry is not to continue securing the largest portion of funds from Brussels. The EU would like to see more funds being made available for regional regeneration to help narrow the gap between the rich and poor regions of the Union. Greater political integration is inevitable as more powers have been transferred from national governments to the EU. One area, for instance, which is likely to see further development is common foreign policy and joint armed forces. There would be considerable economies of scale to be gained if there were a single European armed force rather than 15 armed forces as in 2000. Finally, there remains much work to be done to create a single market. In the first decade of the 21st century, for instance, gas, electricity, telecommunications, water and rail transport markets are being opened up to competition.

The Single Market

Although the removal of tariff and quota barriers between member countries between 1958 and 1968 promoted free trade, there still existed substantial barriers to trade. First, barriers existed in trade in services. For instance, UK insurance companies could not sell most types of insurance in France or Spain. There were legal restrictions on road haulage by foreign transport in domestic markets. Different regulations prevented UK companies borrowing in France, in spite of the fact that French companies might be able to borrow in London. Second, different standards presented a major obstacle to trade in goods. For instance, a tractor manufacturer had to produce a different tractor for sale in each member country because each imposed different safety regulations. Third, governments tended to buy only from domestic companies (government purchases are known as 'public procurement'). The French government would only buy computers from a French manufacturer, whilst the UK tended to buy military equipment only from UK companies. Lastly, everything from customs posts, import and export forms to different VAT rates and corporation taxes imposed heavy administrative costs on companies trading across country boundaries.

In 1985, member countries signed the Single European Act. This committed members to removing all trade obstacles by 31 December 1992. To get round the problems of trying to harmonise 3 000 European product standards, the EU adopted the principle of mutual recognition. This meant that so long as a manufacturer made its products conform to the rules and regulations of one country in the EU, it could be sold throughout the EU even if it did not conform to the rules and regulations of other countries. So a UK tractor manufacturer can sell a British made tractor in Italy even if it does not conform to Italian safety regulations, so long as it conforms to UK safety regulations.

The benefits of a single European market were put forward in the Cecchini Report published by the European Commission in 1988 and are summarised in Table 98.1. Removal of border controls, technical regulations and other administrative hurdles could increase Union GDP by up to 2.7 per cent. Exploitation of greater economies of scale because producers will now be able to sell across the whole European market rather than in just their domestic markets will add up to 2.1 per cent of GDP. The resulting increase in competition, particularly in the area of public

Table 98.1 *EU gains from the internal market*

	% of GDP
Removal of barriers affecting trade	0.2 - 0.3
Removal of barriers affecting overall production	2.0 - 2.4
Total gains from removing barriers	2.2 - 2.7
Exploiting economies of scale more fully	2.1
Gains from intensified competition reducing business ineffectiveness and monopoly profits	1.6
Total gains from market integration	2.1 - 3.7
Total gains	4.3 - 6.4

Source: European Commission.

procurement, would increase GDP by up to 1.6 per cent.

These one-off gains would amount to between 4.2 and 6.4 per cent of GDP. However, the dynamic gains might be even greater. In a study by Richard Baldwin (1989), it was estimated that the gains could be up to four times as great as the Cecchini Report estimated. This was because the static boost in GDP would lead to an investment boom as more capital was needed to produce the extra output created by the 1992 process. This once and for all increase in investment could add another 15 per cent to GDP on top of the extra 5 per cent (a middle estimate of the 4.2 and 6.4 per cent gain) which might be expected from the static gains.

In all this process, there will be gainers and losers. Inefficient national companies which had been protected from international competition by relying upon public procurement contracts would either have to become more efficient or go bankrupt. Either of these would be likely to lead to a loss of jobs. However, overall the Cecchini report estimated that a total of between 1.75 and 5 million extra jobs would be created in the Union in the medium term.

Enlargement of the union

Perhaps the most important reason why the UK joined the Union was a belief that membership would increase the growth rate of the country. In Britain's case, increased prosperity was to come from the benefits of greater trade. However, other applicants have also been aware that there are transfers of resources within the Union and that they might be significant beneficiaries of such transfers. Transfers can come from the EU budget, such as regional grants or subsidies paid to farmers under CAP. There can also be significant transfers of private sector capital as firms set up in a country to take advantage of selling into its markets or to exploit cheap labour or land. It is difficult to establish whether the UK did benefit from joining. However, it is clearer in the case of Spain and Portugal whose growth rates went up in the second half of the 1980s.

These transfers can pose a threat to existing members and in part explain the opposition of some members to the enlargement of the Union. By the mid-1990s, there was a considerable queue of countries wanting to join the EU, including Eastern European countries such as Poland and Hungary, southern European countries such as Albania and Slovenia, and an Asian country, Turkey. The threats to existing members are mirror images of the opportunities to applicant countries.

- Existing members are afraid that their markets will be swamped by cheap imports from these countries. The markets which are most at risk are politically sensitive markets, such as agriculture and textiles, where the EU has traditionally imposed high tariff barriers to protect domestic industries.
- There is a fear that the contributions of rich countries to the EU budget would rise considerably following enlargement. If much poorer countries join the community, and regional and CAP payments are maintained, it is inevitable that there will be large budget transfers to the new members, paid for by existing members.
- Movements of labour and capital can also pose problems. There is a fear that capital would move to newly joined cheap labour countries whilst workers would move in large numbers from these countries to existing member countries, attracted by much higher wages.
- Existing members are concerned that they will lose political power in an enlarged union. Germany and France, for instance, wielded more power and influence when there were only six members of the EU in 1957 than they do today. In particular, they are concerned that it will be easier to force through changes which are not in their economic interest. They also fear that it will be more difficult to

introduce measures and reforms which will deepen the economic integration of the union. For instance, joining member countries will fight hard to maintain generous spending on CAP if their farmers can receive subsidies.

So what might develop is a range of membership or association options. In 1992, the EU signed an agreement with EFTA, the European Free Trade Association (which at the time comprised Switzerland, Iceland, Norway, Liechtenstein, Finland, Sweden and Austria), extending to them EU freedom of movement of goods, services, people and capital. This created a European Economic Area (EEA). Industrial tariffs between EFTA and the EU were already zero but the new agreement further reduced barriers to trade in agricultural goods. So EFTA countries get the benefit of free trade with Europe but without the complications of the next step, a common market.

Enlargement of the EU is inevitable but the pace of enlargement may be much slower than applicant members would wish. There are disagreements between existing members about the timetable for enlargement. Applicant countries themselves are also not necessarily preparing their political, legal, social and economic systems in a way which will earn them early entry. Turkey, for instance, faces major criticisms about human rights abuses over its internal war with Kurdish rebels. Many Eastern European countries are reluctant to open up competition in sectors of the economy traditionally under state control. Necessary legislation to bring national law to conform with EU law can easily be delayed by domestic political considerations. In the long term, however, a united Europe which stretches from the Atlantic to the borders of the Ukraine looks increasingly likely.

Enlarging the EU

The difficulties of enlargement

The enlargement of the European Union is a difficult issue for all concerned. Those preparing for membership, nearly all in Eastern Europe, are having to adapt their economies to conform to EU regulations and law. For instance, their industries will have to abide by EU environmental regulations. Employers will have to abide by EU directives on workers' rights. Governments will have to provide statistics in a format common to the rest of the EU. Markets, such as telecommunications and gas, will have to be open to competition. Television companies will have to show a minimum amount of output produced in the EU.

For existing member countries, there are strong fears about the cost of enlarging the EU. Giving countries such as Poland the same access to CAP funding as existing member countries, for instance, would require a large increase in contributions from countries such as Germany, France and the UK. This would be politically unacceptable. There are also fears that decision making in an enlarged EU will become impossible because there are so many conflicting interests amongst members. Alternatively, existing members fear that they will lose influence in an enlarged EU and be forced to accept decisions which are not in their interests.

Table 98.2 *European countries: selected indicators*

	EU members				First wave applicants					Other EU applicants	
	UK	Spain	Germany	Greece	Poland	Hungary	Czech Republic	Slovenia	Estonia	Lithuania	Romania
Income per head ($US at PPP), 1998	20 640	16 060	20 810	13 010	6 740	-	-	-	-	4 310	3 970
GDP per head ($US), 1998	21 400	14 080	25 850	11 650	3 900	4 510	5 040	9 760	3 390	2 440	1 390
Population (millions), 1998	59	39	82	11	39	10	10	2	1	4	22
Agriculture, % of total GDP, 1998	2	3	1	-	4	6	-	5	5	14	15
Agricultural productivity, $: agricultural value added per agricultural worker, 1998	-	12 022	19 930	12 611	1 647	4 655	-	26 006	3 342	2 907	3 170
Paved roads, % of total, 1998	100	99	99	92	66	43	100	83	51	89	51
Telephone mainlines per thousand people, 1997	540	403	550	516	194	304	318	364	321	41	167
Exports of goods and services as % of GDP, 1998	29	26	27	15	25	45	58	57	76	50	24

Source: adapted from World Bank, *World Development Indicators*.

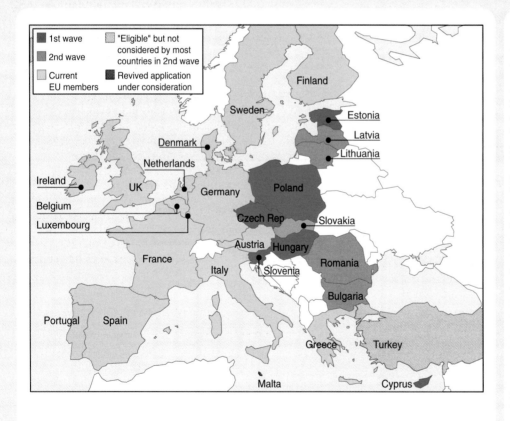

Figure 98.4 *EU countries and applicants, 2000*
Source: adapted from the *Financial Times*, 10.11.1998.

The promised land

Different countries want to become members of the EU for different reasons. For many former Eastern bloc countries, EU membership would cement their membership of a capitalist Europe and put their former Soviet communist past behind them. All applicants aspire to the living standards enjoyed in Western Europe. Greater opportunities for trade, investment and exchange of ideas as well as conformity to legal and regulatory standards set in the EU open the promise of faster growth. There is also the possibility of large inflows of money from the European Union budget to modernise their economies. They want to become like Portugal, Greece and the Republic of Ireland, on a path to equality with France, Germany and the UK.

1. Assess the main differences between the economies of EU countries and those of applicant countries.
2. Analyse the main advantages of EU enlargement for (a) applicant countries and (b) existing EU members.
3. Discuss the difficulties that countries are likely to face as a result of enlargement.

Applied economics

Classification

The world can be divided into groups of countries.

First world countries FIRST WORLD countries are a small group of rich industrialised countries: the United States, Canada, France, Italy, Germany, the UK and Japan (known as the 'G7 countries'), other countries in Western Europe and Australia and New Zealand. Sometimes they are called Western countries, because for the most part they lie in the western hemisphere, as can be seen from Figure 99.1. Sometimes they are called 'North' countries (from the phrase 'North-South divide') because, for the most part they lie in the northern hemisphere, as Figure 99.1 shows. They are also known as DEVELOPED COUNTRIES, indicating that they have reached an advanced stage of economic development.

Second world countries The phrase '**second world**' countries is rarely used today. However, these are the former communist countries of Eastern Europe and the USSR. The move from communism to capitalism resulted in many of these countries seeing large falls in their income in the 1990s. The result was that, according to the World Bank classification of countries by income, only Slovenia was considered a First World country in 1998. Some former republics of the Soviet Union, such as Armenia, Azerbaijan and Moldova, were so poor in 1998 that they were ranked as low income countries - the poorest countries of the world.

Third world countries THIRD WORLD countries are a large group of poor countries in Asia, Africa and Latin America. Most are situated in the southern hemisphere, and hence are known as the 'South' (as in the phrase 'North-South divide'). Sometimes they are called DEVELOPING COUNTRIES (DCs), indicating that their economies are still developing, in contrast with the 'developed' economies of the First World. They are also called LESS DEVELOPED COUNTRIES (LDCs), again contrasted with the 'developed' countries of the North.

   Third world countries differ greatly amongst themselves and hence they are often sub-divided into further groups. For instance, sometimes the poorest are called **Fourth World** countries or **low income countries**, whilst the richer **Third World** countries are known as **middle income countries**. These are subdivided by the World Bank into **lower middle** and **upper middle** income countries. Fast growing **middle income countries,** such as South Korea, Singapore and Mexico, are sometimes called emerging economies, emerging to take their place amongst the developed countries of the world. South Korea, Singapore, Taiwan and others are called **newly industrialised countries (NICs)**, indicating

that their economies now have a strong, Western-style, industrial base or **Tiger economies** indicating fast economic growth. Third World countries are also grouped by region, such as sub-Saharan African countries, or South East Asian countries.

   The World Bank classifies countries according to whether they are low income, lower middle income, upper middle income or high income. Table 99.1 shows the income levels chosen for this classification for 1998 and indicates some countries which fall into these classifications.

   Third World countries are all very different from each other, and therefore in some ways it is dangerous to lump them together and talk about 'the characteristics of Third World countries'. However, there are a number of basic problems which are shared by this group of countries, to a greater or lesser extent. These will now be discussed in turn.

Table 99.1

	GNP per capita US$	Examples of countries
Low income	760 or less	Ethiopia China India Nicaragua
Lower middle income	761 to 3 030	South Africa Albania Peru Egypt
Upper middle income	3 031 to 9 360	Botswana Malaysia Lebanon Mexico
High income	9 361+	Japan Hong Kong Taiwan USA

Source: adapted from the World Bank, *World Development Report.*

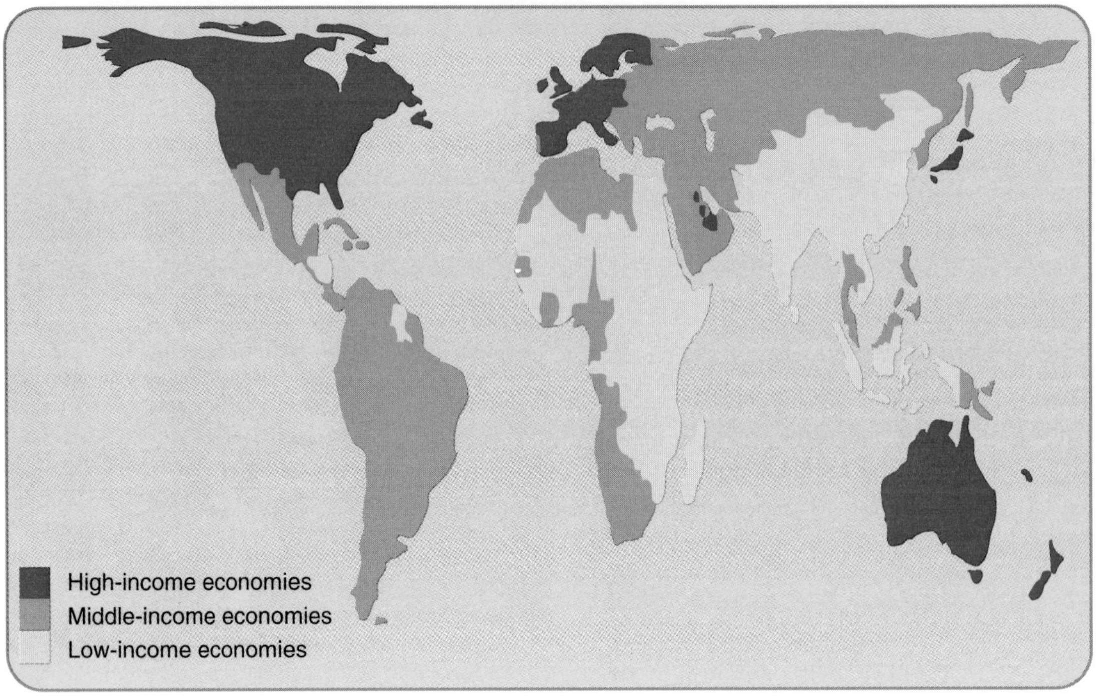

Figure 99.1 *High, middle and low income economies of the world, illustrated on a Peters Projection; a Peters Projection shows the countries of the world with their correct relative areas*

■ High-income economies
■ Middle-income economies
□ Low-income economies

Per capita income

As Table 99.2 shows, 85 per cent of the world's population lived in the Third World in 1998. Yet, the total GNP of the Third World is only 22 per cent of the world's total. The First World, with 15 per cent of the world's population, enjoys 78 per cent of its GNP. Low income Third World countries, with 60 per cent of the world's population, enjoy just 6 per cent of world GNP. The figures in Table 99.2 need, however, to be treated with caution for two reasons (☞ unit 27). First, the poorer the country, the greater will be the proportion of output which is not traded in the market economy. For instance, produce from subsistence farming, building houses and providing entertainment is likely to be either underestimated or not included at all in GNP figures for low income economies.

Second, the figures are in US dollars converted at market exchange rates. A more realistic measure of differences in living standards would be to consider GNP converted at **purchasing power parity** rates (☞ unit 27). These compare different GNPs using exchange rates which take account of differences in the cost of living. For instance, in 1998, it was 2.5 times more costly to buy the same bundle of goods in the USA than in Mozambique, according to World Bank estimates. In this case, Mozambique's GNP needs to be multiplied 2.5 times if a fair standard of living comparison is to be made between the USA and Mozambique. Table 99.3 shows GNP per capita figures in US dollars both at market exchange rates and at purchasing power parity rates. The table shows that there can be significant differences between the two figures.

Adjusting GNP at purchasing power parity rates can significantly alter a country's ranking in world GDP

Table 99.2 *Population and national income, 1998*

	Population millions	GNP US$bn	GNP per capita US$	GNP per capita US$ at PPP rates
World	5 897	28 862	4 890	6 200
Developed world				
High income economies	885	22 599	25 510	23 440
Developing world	5 011	6 263	1 250	3 150
Low income economies	3 515	1 844	520	2 130
excluding China and India	1 296	494	380	1 400
Middle income economies	1 496	4 420	2 950	5 560
Lower middle income	908	1 557	1 710	4 080
Upper middle income	588	2 862	4 860	7 830
East Asia and Pacific	1 817	1 802	990	3 400
Europe and Central Asia	473	1 039	2 190	4 240
Latin America and Caribbean	502	1 978	3 940	6 780
Middle East and North Africa	285	586	2 050	4 220
South Asia	1 305	556	430	1 610
Sub-Saharan Africa	628	304	480	1 430

Source: adapted from the World Bank, *World Development Report.*

league tables. It also considerably reduces the world inequalities in income shown in Table 99.2. Even so, there are still 36 countries which, according to World Bank estimates, have a GNP per capita at purchasing power parities of less than 5 per cent of the US total. Another 72 have a GNP per capita of less than 10 per cent. No middle income country has a GNP per capita of more than one third of that of the USA.

It should be remembered that the figures in Tables 99.2 and 99.3 relate to average incomes for these countries. Rich elites in poor Third World countries can enjoy incomes which are comparable to First World countries.

Table 99.3 *Purchasing power parity estimates of national income per capita for selected countries, 1998*

	Population millions	At market exchange rates		At purchasing power parity rates	
		GDP US$ billions	GNP per capita US$	GNP per capita	
				US$	% of GNP of USA
Mozambique	17.0	3.6	210	312	1.1
Tanzania	32.0	6.7	210	490	1.7
Ethiopia	61.0	6.1	100	500	1.7
Malawi	11.0	2.1	200	730	2.5
Uganda	21.0	6.7	320	1 170	4.0
Pakistan	132.0	63.2	480	1 560	5.3
India	980.0	421.3	430	1 700	5.8
Egypt	61.0	79.2	1 290	3 130	10.7
Jamaica	3.0	4.3	1 680	3 210	10.9
China	1 239	928.9	750	3 220	11.0
Romania	22.0	31.3	1 390	3 970	13.5
Thailand	61.0	134.4	2 200	5 840	19.9
Brazil	166.0	758.0	4 570	6 160	21.0
Poland	39.0	150.8	3 900	6 740	23.0
South Africa	41.0	119.0	2 880	6 990	23.8
Mexico	96.0	380.9	3 970	8 190	27.9
South Korea	46.0	369.9	7 970	12 270	41.8
Chile	15.0	71.3	4 810	12 890	43.9
Portugal	10.0	106.4	10 690	14 380	49.0
New Zealand	4.0	55.8	14 700	15 840	54.0
Spain	39.0	553.7	14 080	16 060	54.7
Hong Kong	7.0	158.3	23 670	22 000	75.0
Switzerland	7.0	284.8	40 080	26 620	90.7
Singapore	3.0	95.1	30 060	28 620	97.5
United States	270.0	7 921.3	29 340	29 340	100.0

Source: adapted from the World Bank, *World Development Report*.

Equally, the poorest 10 per cent of the population of New York have incomes which are comparable to the average of middle income countries. Problems of inequality within countries are discussed further in unit 100.

Question 1

Table 99.4 *Bangladesh, Argentina and the UK: population and GNP, 1998*

	Population, millions	GNP, $ billions	GNP measured at PPP, $billions
Bangladesh	126	44.0	137.7
Argentina	36	324.1	368.5
UK	59	1 263.8	1 218.6

Source: adapted from the World Bank, *World Development Report*.

(a) (i) Compare income per head in Bangladesh, Argentina and the UK.
(ii) What problems are faced by economists in comparing income between countries?
(b) Explain, using Tables 99.1 and 99.4, whether these countries would be classified as low, middle or high income countries.

Physical capital

Third world countries have far less physical capital per capita than First World countries. This includes not just factories, offices and machines, but also infrastructure capital such as roads and railways, as well as schools and hospitals. Communication is an important part of the infrastructure too and so telephone landlines, mobile phones and even radios need to be taken into account.

Table 99.5 shows a variety of infrastructure statistics for different countries. For instance, a country tends to be less developed:
- the fewer the number of telephone mainlines per person;
- the lower the percentage of roads that are paved, although to some extent this also reflects population densities (the fewer the numbers per sq kilometre, the less likely it is be economic to pave roads);
- the fewer the percentage of the population with access to safe water;
- the less agricultural land is irrigated, although this also depends on the cost of irrigation and the crops being grown;
- the fewer the number of radio sets per person.

Table 99.5 *Infrastructure in selected countries*

	Telephone mainlines per thousand persons 1997	Paved roads, % of total	% of population with access to safe water, 1995	Irrigated land % of cropland, 1994-96	Radio sets per 1 000 people, 1997
Mozambique	4.0	19.0	9.0	3.4	39.0
Tanzania	3.0	4.0	49.0	4.6	278
Ethiopia	3.0	15.0	na	1.6	194
Malawi	4.0	19.0	60.0	1.6	256
Uganda	2.0	na	42.0	0.1	123
Pakistan	19.0	58.0	62.0	80.2	92.0
India	19.0	46.0	85.0	32.0	105
Egypt	56.0	78.0	84.0	100	316
Jamaica	140.0	71.0	93.0	14.0	482
China	56.0	na	83.0	37.0	195
Romania	167.0	51.0	62.0	31.4	317
Thailand	80.0	98.0	89.0	23.2	204
Brazil	107.0	9.0	69.0	4.9	435
Poland	194.0	66.0	na	0.7	518
South Africa	107.0	42.0	59.0	8.1	316
Mexico	96.0	37.0	95.0	23.1	324
South Korea	444.0	74.0	83.0	60.7	1 037
Chile	180.0	14.0	91.0	32.6	354
Portugal	402.0	na	82.0	21.7	306
New Zealand	486.0	58.0	90.0	8.9	1 027
Spain	403.0	99.0	99.0	17.7	328
Hong Kong	565.0	100	na	28.6	695
Switzerland	661.0	na	100	5.9	969
Singapore	543.0	97.0	100	na	739
United States	644.0	61.0	100	12.0	2 115

Source: adapted from the World Bank, *World Development Report*.

The table is rank ordered according to GDP per capita at purchasing power parity rates. It can be seen that, in general, the lower the level of GDP per capita, the poorer the infrastructure level of the country. However, there are large differences between countries which have little correlation with GNP levels. For instance, the United States has fewer paved roads as a percentage of its total than Thailand. This is likely to reflect the low densities of population in much of the United States where it is uneconomic to pave roads. Romania has almost as many telephone mainlines as Chile, a richer country. This problem reflects Romania's greater affluence in the 1980s when it was still a communist country. Malawi has almost the same percentage of its population with access to safe water as South Africa despite a much lower GNP per person, probably reflecting better developing strategies in the past.

Physical capital is important because the more physical capital, the greater the productive potential of the economy. If a country is to grow, it must increase its stock of physical capital in order to push out its **production possibility frontier** (☞ unit 1).

Human capital

Developing countries have lower levels of human capital than developed countries. It is difficult to measure levels of human capital. However, educational statistics can provide indicators of present and likely future levels. Table 99.6 gives three measures. The first is of the percentage enrolment in different stages of education. Least developed countries would expect to have the lowest proportions of the total age group enrolled in education. For instance, less than half of all children from the relevant age group are enrolled in primary education in Mozambique, Tanzania and Ethiopia. Only 6 per cent are in secondary schools in Mozambique. These enrolments then have an impact on adult literacy. Low enrolments in the past have led to high illiteracy rates in Mozambique, Ethiopia and Pakistan. On the other hand, relatively high enrolments have led to low illiteracy rates in countries such as China, Brazil and Mexico.

Table 99.6 *Education*

	Percentage of age group enrolled in education[1], 1996		Expected years of schooling, females, 1995	Adult illiteracy, 15 and over, 1997	
	Primary	Secondary		Males	Females
Mozambique	40.0	6.0	3.0	43.0	75.0
Tanzania	48.0	na	na	18.0	38.0
Ethiopia	28.0	na	na	59.0	71.0
Malawi	68.0	na	na	27.0	57.0
Uganda	na	na	na	25.0	47.0
Pakistan	na	ns	ns	45.0	75.0
India	na	na	na	33.0	61.0
Egypt	93.0	68.0	10.0	35.0	60.0
Jamaica	96.0	64.0	11.0	19.0	10.0
China	102.0	na	na	9.0	25.0
Romania	95.0	73.0	11.0	1.0	3.0
Thailand	na	na	na	3.0	7.0
Brazil	90.0	20.0	na	16.0	16.0
Poland	95.0	85.0	13.0	0	0
South Africa	na	51.0	13.0	15.0	17.0
Mexico	101.0	51.0	na	8.0	12.0
South Korea	92.0	93.0	14.0	1.0	4.0
Chile	88.0	58.0	12.0	5.0	5.0
Portugal	104.0	78.0	15.0	6.0	12.0
New Zealand	100.0	97.0	17.0	na	na
Spain	105.0	95.0	16.0	2.0	4.0
Hong Kong	90.0	71.0	13.0	4.0	12.0
Switzerland	na	na	14.0	na	na
Singapore	na	na	na	4.0	13.0
United States	95.0	90.0	16.0	na	na

Source: adapted from the World Bank, *World Development Report.*
1. Figures may total more than 100 per cent. This is because some children are in primary (usually defined as 6-11 year olds) or secondary (usually defined as 11-17 year olds) education who are older or younger than the defined age group. For instance, 105 per cent of Spaniards are enrolled in primary education because some 12 year olds are still in the primary system, defined as being for children up to the age of 11.

Education levels are vital to the ability of countries to grow in the future. Countries which invest today in education, particularly in primary education where research shows that **rates of return** on the investment are highest, are likely to grow faster in the future. South Korea, for instance, one of the Tiger economies of South East Asia, invested heavily in its education system from the 1960s onwards. The result is that today it has minimum levels of illiteracy and a highly trained

Question 2

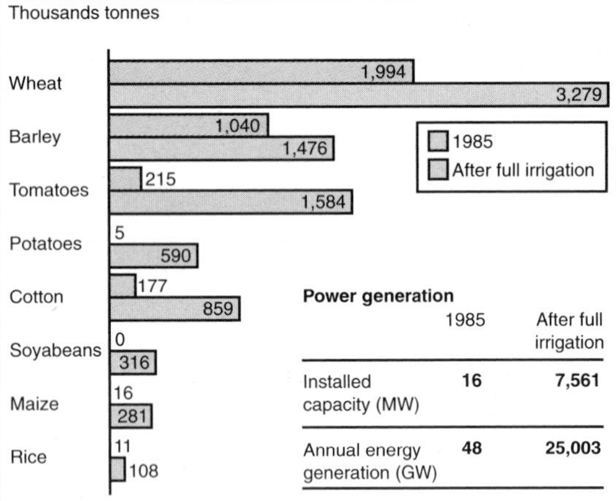

Power generation

	1985	After full irrigation
Installed capacity (MW)	**16**	**7,561**
Annual energy generation (GW)	**48**	**25,003**

Figure 99.2 *Irrigation boosts crop production*
Source: adapted from official figures.

The lives of farmers in south-eastern Anatolia in Turkey have been transformed by irrigation. 'Our life has been good since irrigation. People who had a horse and cart now have a car and tractor, and those who did not have a house have built one', says Mahmut Dincol, a local farmer. The irrigation has been made possible by the building of dams in the area, part of a $32 billion investment programme aimed to narrow the income gap between the region and Turkey's far more prosperous western half.

Source: adapted from the *Financial Times*, 26.2.1999.

(a) Explain, using examples from the data and a production possibility frontier diagram, how investment in infrastructure can increase: (i) output; and (ii) living standards.

workforce. In the United States, with arguably the highest levels of human capital in the world, females on average could expect to have 16 years of education in 1998. Three quarters of tertiary education aged young people were in college in the USA in that year. China, a low income country, has, since the 1949 Revolution, placed a strong emphasis on education. This has been one of the prime reasons why the country has been able to grow at 10 per cent per annum in the 1980s and 1990s.

In recent years, there has been growing interest in female education amongst economists. In developing countries, females are less likely to receive formal education than males. However, it can be argued that the rate of return on educating females is higher than that for males. For a start, a woman who can read and write is far more likely to pass on these skills to her children and grandchildren than a man. Education levels can therefore be raised outside the school system at little cost. Women also have primary responsibility for the nutrition and health care of family units. The ability to read helps education programmes designed to improve the health of individuals. Literate women are more likely to take part in family planning programmes. If governments are concerned about the rate of growth of their populations, it is important to be able to persuade women to take control of this aspect of their lives. Women in many cultures also have important roles outside the home. In agricultural communities, women can often be as important or more important than men in growing food. Women may run their own enterprises, selling home produced goods in a market for instance. Literacy can give an important boost to the success of such ventures. Studies also show that a larger proportion of money earned by women is likely to be spent on nutrition and education of children than of that earned by men.

High population growth

Third World countries have had relatively high rates of population growth compared to First World countries (☞ unit 101 for a fuller discussion). This poses two major problems. First, it means that Third World countries need to invest large amounts in both physical and human capital in order to create the goods and services and jobs needed for their growing populations. However, Third World countries also need to increase their consumption in order to provide a basic standard of living for their populations now. Higher investment to create future prosperity can only be achieved by forgoing consumption now, lowering current prosperity. Some successful Third World countries have avoided this problem by securing large amounts of investment capital from abroad. However, other high growth Third World countries have financed heavy investment by large domestic savings (☞ unit 102).

The second problem that high population growth brings is high dependency ratios. In First World countries, low population growth is causing a crisis because the ratio of retired workers to those in work

will increase substantially over the next 30 years in most countries. In the Third World, it is children who are causing the crisis. In some African countries, half the population is under the age of 15. Not only do these children need education, but they also need to be provided with jobs in the future, both points which reinforce the need for high growth in investment.

Health and mortality

People in the Third World on average enjoy poorer health and are likely to die younger than in First World countries. Poor health and high mortality shown in Table 99.7 are caused by a number of factors. One is the standard of nutrition of individuals. Table 99.7 shows that in the poorest developing countries, malnutrition amongst under-5s is common. In Ethiopia and India, in 1992-97, approximately half of all children under 5 suffered malnutrition. Poor nutrition is a major contributor to ill health and higher mortality rates. For instance, as Table 99.7 shows, that the poorer the country, the higher the under 5 mortality rate and the lower the life expectancy tends to be. Poor nutrition also affects both the physical and mental development of individuals. One of the reasons why individuals are on average taller in First World countries compared to, say, fifty years ago is a better diet. Equally, educational performance is affected by diet.

Another factor is the physical infrastructure of the

Table 99.7 *Health, nutrition and mortality, selected countries*

	Under 5 mortality rate per 1000, 1997	Life expectancy at birth, males, years, 1997	Access to sanitiation % of population 1995	Prevalence of malnutrition, % of children under age 5, 1992-97	Public expenditure on health, % of GDP 1990-97[1]
Mozambique	201.0	44.0	24.0	26.0	4.6
Tanzania	136.0	47.0	49.0	33.0	1.1
Ethiopia	175.0	42.0	26.0	48.0	1.6
Malawi	224.0	43.0	60.0	30.0	2.3
Uganda	162.0	43.0	42.0	26.0	1.9
Pakistan	136.0	61.0	62.0	38.0	0.8
India	88.0	62.0	85.0	53.0	0.7
Egypt	66.0	65.0	84.0	15.0	1.7
Jamaica	14.0	72.0	93.0	10.0	2.5
China	39.0	68.0	83.0	16.0	2.1
Romania	26.0	65.0	62.0	6.0	2.9
Thailand	38.0	66.0	62.0	na	2.0
Brazil	44.0	63.0	69.0	6.0	1.9
Poland	12.0	69.0	na	0.0	4.8
South Africa	65.0	62.0	59.0	9.0	3.6
Mexico	38.0	69.0	95.0	14.0	2.8
South Korea	11.0	69.0	na	na	2.8
Chile	13.0	72.0	91.0	1.0	2.3
Portugal	8.0	71.0	82.0	0.0	4.9
New Zealand	7.0	75.0	90.0	0.0	5.9
Spain	7.0	75.0	100.0	0.0	5.9
Hong Kong	na	76.0	na	na	2.3
Switzerland	6.0	76.0	100.0	0.0	7.1
Singapore	6.0	73.0	100.0	0.0	1.5
United States	na	73.0	100.0	1.0	6.6

1. This is does not include expenditure on private health care.
Source: adapted from the World Bank, *World Development Report*.

country. Access to clean water, shown in Table 99.5, is vital for health. So is access to proper sanitation facilities, shown in Table 99.7. This is particularly true for urban populations. The environment must be healthy too.

Large numbers of people die from diseases such as dysentery or malaria, which are water-born or carried by animals. In First World countries, these diseases have been almost eliminated through proper infrastructure or control of the natural environment.

A third factor is the working environment. People often are forced to work in poor conditions which severely damage their health. If they are agricultural workers, there are many animal carried diseases to which they can be exposed. If they work in industry, poor light, noise, heat and dust can shorten life. Moreover, many start work at a much younger age than in First World countries.

Finally, health care provision is poorer. Table 99.7 shows public (i.e. state) expenditure on health care as a percentage of GDP. The poorer the country, the less tends to be spent as a percentage of GDP. Given that GDP is much lower in poor countries, they spend only a small fraction on health care compared to Western Europe and North America. Healthcare provision can be highly effective even on quite low budgets, as the example of, say, Sri Lanka or China has shown. However, this requires a sound infrastructure of nurses with some basic training, rudimentary clinics and basic medicines along with effective health education.

Unemployment and underemployment

Third World countries tend to have much higher

Table 99.8 *Structure of production*

| | Distribution of gross domestic product[1] (%), 1998 | | |
	Agriculture	Industry	Services
Mozambique	34.0	18.0	48.0
Tanzania	46.0	14.0	40.0
Malawi	39.0	19.0	41.0
Uganda	43.0	18.0	39.0
Pakistan	25.0	25.0	50.0
India	25.0	30.0	45.0
Egypt	17.0	33.0	50.0
Jamaica	7.0	35.0	58.0
China	18.0	49.0	33.0
Romania	15.0	36.0	48.0
Thailand	11.0	40.0	49.0
Brazil	8.0	36.0	56.0
Poland	4.0	26.0	70.0
South Africa	4.0	38.0	57.0
Mexico	5.0	27.0	68.0
South Korea	6.0	43.0	51.0
Chile	18.0	49.0	33.0
Australia	3.0	26.0	71.0
United Kingdom	2.0	31.0	67.0
Germany	1.0	55.0	44.0
Hong Kong	0.0	15.0	85.0
Norway	2.0	32.0	66.0
Singapore	0.0	35.0	65.0
United States	2.0	27.0	71.0

Source: adapted from the World Bank, *World Development Report*.
1. Figures may not add up to 100 per cent due to rounding.

Question 3

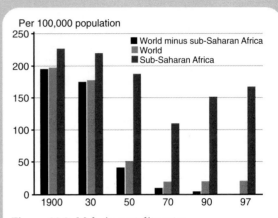

Figure 99.3 *Malaria mortality rates*
Source: adapted from World Health Organisation.

The World Health Organisation (WHO), in its latest annual report, argues that policy makers need to tackle the 'unfinished agenda' of infectious diseases, malnutrition and complications of childbirth which disproportionately affect the poor. For instance, malaria deaths, concentrated among African children, could be halved to 500 000 by spending another $1 billion (£600 million) a year on known prevention and treatment measures.

Source: adapted from the *Financial Times*, 12.5.1999.

(a) Explain the trends in deaths from malaria between 1900 and 1997.
(b) How much would it cost per child to halve malaria deaths according to the WHO?
(c) Suggest why malaria mortality rates are much higher in sub-Saharan Africa (where almost all countries are classified as low income countries) than in Europe and North America.

unemployment and underemployment rates than First World countries. This arises from a number of factors. The most important is a lack of physical capital. Without the machines, factories and offices, workers are **structurally** unemployed (☞ unit 86). However, factors such as poor government economic policies and protectionism in other countries can also play a part. In countries heavily reliant on agriculture, unemployment is highly **seasonal**.

Structure of the economy

Growth and development alters the structure of output in the economy (☞ unit 97). Developed countries have gradually shifted from primary to secondary and then tertiary production over time. An indicator of the level of development of an economy today is therefore the extent to which its output is dependent upon agricultural production and industrial production. Table 99.8, for instance, shows that the poorest

Question 4

Table 99.9 *Structure of output*

	Structure of output, % of GDP		
	Agriculture	Industry	Services
Bangladesh	23.0	28.0	49.0
Argentina	7.0	37.0	56.0
UK	2.0	31.0	67.0

Source: adapted from the World Bank, *World Development Report*.

(a) Explain how the structure of an economy is likely to change as it grows and develops. Use the data to illustrate your answer.

countries, Mozambique, Tanzania and Malawi, have between 34 and 46 per cent of output accounted for by agriculture. In contrast, Germany, Singapore and the USA have 2 per cent or less. The proportion devoted to industry (including manufacturing) at first increases, from, say, Mozambique's 18 per cent to China's 49 per cent. It is then likely to decline as demand for services grows within the country. Amongst developed countries, industry accounted in 1998 for between 27 per cent for the USA and 55 per cent for Germany.

Structure of foreign trade

The structure of the economy tends to mirror the structure of trade. Third World countries are likely to be more reliant on exports of primary commodities, such as rice or copper, than First World countries. Rapid industrialisation in the Third World over the past 20 years has meant that manufactures now account for a much greater proportion of Third World exports. However, many of these manufactures tend to be low technology products such as textiles or footwear. The problems associated with an over-reliance on commodity exports will be discussed in unit 103.

key terms

Developed and developing or less developed countries - developed countries are the rich industrialised nations of Europe, Japan and North America, whilst developing or less developed countries are the other, poorer, less economically developed nations of the world.

First World countries - the rich, developed, nations of Western Europe, Japan and North America.
Third World countries - the developing nations of the world in Africa, South America and Asia.

The Third World

Consider the data in the tables in this unit.
1. Explain why Mozambique would be considered a poor Third World country.
2. Compare Chile and Egypt as developing countries.

3. Discuss the obstacles to development that face Tanzania and Romania.

Applied economics

Economic growth

In economics, development has traditionally been associated with economic growth. Economic growth measures changes in national income, the sum of all traded output in the economy. Countries which produce a great deal are also able to consume at high levels. Hence, a country like the United States, which has the highest GDP in the world (excluding very small countries such as Luxembourg), as well as the highest GDP per capita (measured at purchasing power parity rates), is able to give its citizens a high standard of living. On the other hand, a country like Ethiopia, the poorest country in the world measured in terms of GDP per capita, sees its citizens enjoying a very low standard of living.

It might seem, then, that economic success can be measured in terms of economic growth rates. Countries with high growth rates, such as the Tiger economies of East Asia, are ones which are developing very fast. Countries which have negative growth rates, such as many African countries in the 1980s, are regressing, not developing. Levels of national income were discussed in unit 99. On a GDP measure, Pakistan is 'more developed' than Ethiopia, South Korea more developed than China and the USA more developed than Singapore. In terms of growth, the relative position of

Table 100.1 Growth of real GDP, 1966-1998

	1966-73	1974-90	1991-98
World	**5.1**	**3.0**	**2.4**
High-income	**4.8**	**2.9**	**2.1**
Low and middle-income	**6.9**	**3.5**	**3.3**
East Asia and Pacific	**7.9**	**7.1**	**8.1**
China	8.5	8.2	11.1
Korea, Rep.	11.2	8.5	6.2
Indonesia	6.6	6.1	5.8
South Asia	**3.7**	**4.9**	**5.7**
India	3.7	4.8	6.1
Latin America and the Caribbean	**6.4**	**2.7**	**3.7**
Brazil	9.8	3.6	3.3
Mexico	6.8	3.4	2.5
Argentina	4.3	0.5	5.3
Europe and Central Asia	**7.0**	**3.6**	**-4.3**
Russian Federation[a]	7.1	3.7	-7.0
Turkey	6.1	4.3	4.1
Poland	7.7	1.9	4.5
Middle East and North Africa	**8.5**	**0.7**	**3.0**
Iran, Islamic Rep.	10.6	-0.4	4.0
Algeria	6.3	4.4	1.2
Egypt, Arab Rep.	3.8	7.3	4.2
Sub-Saharan Africa	**4.7**	**2.2**	**2.2**
South Africa	4.7	2.2	1.6
Nigeria	6.5	1.0	2.6

a. Data for years before 1993 refer to the former Soviet Union (FSU).
Source: adapted from World Bank, *Global Economic Prospects and the Developing Countries*.

countries is changing very fast. Table 100.1 shows real annual growth rates for different areas and countries between 1966 and 1998. The world rate of growth has slowed down considerably over the period, from an average of 5.1 per cent in 1966-73 to 2.4 per cent between 1991 and 1998.

However, some areas of the world are growing at a much faster rate than others. East Asia and the Pacific, with countries like China (with one-quarter of the world's population), South Korea and Hong Kong, have grown at over 7 per cent per annum throughout the period. Other areas have performed poorly. Africa's growth performance has been poor in the 1980s and 1990s, with many countries experiencing negative growth for short periods of time. Latin America performed relatively poorly in the 1970s and 1980s, but economic reforms have helped the region's growth performance in the 1990s. In the low and middle income countries of Europe and Central Asia, which were mainly former communist countries of Eastern Europe and the Soviet Union, the break up of the soviet empire around 1990 and the introduction of market reforms led to a mixed economic performance. Overall, the region experienced significant negative growth between 1991 and 1998. The largest country, the Russian Federation, saw GDP fall on average by 7 per cent a year over the period.

Table 100.1 shows annual changes in GDP. However, population growth must be taken into account if GDP is to be a reliable indicator of development. Table 100.2 shows annual changes in GDP per capita for the same countries as in Table 100.1. The scale of the African disaster can now be seen. In Sub-Saharan Africa, real GDP per capita fell at an average annual rate of 0.7 per cent between 1974 and 1990, and 0.8 per cent between 1991 and 1998. On average, sub-Saharan Africans were 15 per cent poorer in GDP terms in 1998 than they were in 1974. On the other hand, in the East Asian countries, with an average growth rate per capita of 6 per cent, citizens had nearly quadrupled their income over the period. This is despite the savage downturn many East Asian countries experienced in 1998 due to the 'Asian crisis' in that year.

Different growth rates have had a dramatic impact on relative incomes between regions and countries. At the start of the 1950s, Asia was poorer than Africa. By the mid-1960s, East Asian countries had caught up with Africa. By 1998, the low and middle income countries of East Asia and the Pacific had a per capita GDP of £3 400 measured at PPPs, compared to $1 430 for sub-Saharan Africa. Nigeria and Indonesia are two specific examples of this. In the 1960s, development economists judged that Nigeria had much brighter prospects for development than Indonesia. In the 1970s, Nigeria

Table 100.2 *Growth of real GDP per capita, 1966-1998*

	1966-73	1974-90	1991-98
World	3.1	1.2	0.8
High-income	3.8	2.2	1.4
Low and middle-income	4.5	1.5	1.5
East Asia and Pacific	5.2	5.4	6.5
China	5.8	6.6	9.8
Korea, Rep.	8.8	7.0	5.0
Indonesia	4.1	3.9	3.8
South Asia	1.3	2.6	3.5
India	1.4	2.6	4.0
Latin America and the Caribbean	3.7	0.5	1.8
Brazil	7.1	1.4	1.7
Mexico	3.5	0.9	0.5
Argentina	2.7	-1.0	3.7
Europe and Central Asia	6.0	2.6	-4.5
Russian Federation[a]	6.5	3.1	-6.9
Turkey	3.5	1.9	2.3
Poland	7.0	1.2	4.3
Middle East and North Africa	5.8	-2.4	0.4
Iran, Islamic Rep.	7.6	-4.2	2.1
Algeria	3.3	1.3	-1.4
Egypt, Arab Rep.	1.7	4.7	1.9
Sub-Saharan Africa	2.0	-0.7	-0.8
South Africa	2.1	-0.3	-0.7
Nigeria	3.8	-1.8	-0.7

a. Data for years before 1993 refer to the former Soviet Union (FSU).
Source: adapted from World Bank, *Global Economic Prospects and the Developing Countries.*

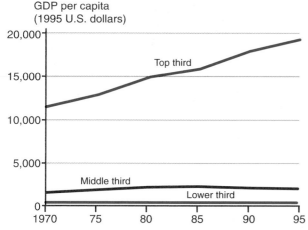

GDP per capita
(1995 U.S. dollars)

Figure 100.1 *Incomes of rich and poor countries*
Source: adapted from World Bank, *World Development Report 1999/2000.*

became rich through its oil production as oil prices soared. Yet Nigeria failed to develop despite its many advantages. By 1998, its GDP per capita at PPPs was $820 compared to $2 790 for Indonesia.

Figure 100.1 illustrates another aspect of development in recent decades. Inequalities have been widening. The income of the upper third of countries by GDP nearly doubled between 1970 and 1995. It increased less than this for the middle third of countries. For the poorest third, it increased hardly at all.

Growth: an inadequate measure

In the 1950s and 1960s, there was an assumption amongst economists that economic growth and economic development were closely linked. High

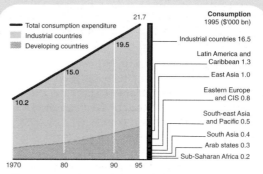
economic growth would lead to fast economic development and vice versa. However, in the 1970s, this assumption was severely questioned. It was correctly pointed out that economic growth only measured growth in a limited number of variables in the economy. It took no account of a large number of other variables, ranging from health, to the environment, to the distribution of resources within the economy. This is part of the debate which was discussed in unit 27. Michael Todaro, a leading economist in the field of development economics, has put forward three objectives of development which will now be discussed in turn.

The provision of basic needs

Economic growth raises the level of goods available for consumption in an economy. It does not necessarily mean, however, that all will have access to those extra goods. The history of economic development since the

Second World War suggests that the benefits of growth are very unevenly spread. For instance, in 1995, 84 per cent of Egyptians had access to safe water. Yet in Morocco, a country with a similar GDP per capita at PPPs, this was true for only 57 per cent of the population. In China, 25 per cent of female adults were illiterate in 1997. In Egypt, again with a similar GDP per capita, the figure was 60 per cent. In 1997, there were 341 television sets per thousand of the population in South Korea. In Greece, with a similar GDP per capita, there were 466. Further examples can be seen in unit 91.

Whilst some in Third World countries enjoy incomes which approximate to those in the First World, the majority are much poorer. The numbers living below the poverty line, defined as $1 or less per day, increased from 1.2 billion in 1987 to 1.5 billion in 2000 and is predicted to rise to 1.9 billion by 2015. Figure 100.3 shows the geographical distribution of the poor. The largest numbers live in South Asia and East Asia, and in particular India and China. South Asia, which includes India, Pakistan and Bangladesh, also has the largest incidence of poverty as a proportion of its population, followed by Sub-Saharan Africa, as shown in Table 100.3.

To reflect the difference between economic development and GDP and economic growth, the United Nations calculates a number of indices of development, the most important of which is the **human development index**. This is an index based on three indicators: longevity, as measured by life expectancy at birth; education attainment, as measured by a combination of adult literacy and the combined first, second and third level gross enrolment ratios (numbers in education divided by population of education age); and standard of living as measured by real GDP per capita at purchasing power parities.

One of the goals of economic development must therefore be the satisfaction of **basic needs** (☞ unit 1) amongst the whole population. Everyone must have access to food and drink and shelter. Good health is a basic need too. Hence, everyone should have access to basic medical care. The eradication of **absolute poverty** (☞ unit 68) in society must therefore be a goal of any development strategy.

Economic systems do not necessarily bring about an increase in welfare for the poor even when fast economic growth is being experienced. In the 1950s and 1960s, it was widely thought that fast increases in income for the better off in society would 'trickle down' to the poor as well. Indeed, this was one of the arguments used by both Ronald Reagan in the United States and Margaret Thatcher in the UK in the 1980s to justify their economic policies which led to sharper inequalities in their societies. However, the experience has been that there is little or no trickle down effect. **Dual economies** can develop. One half of the economy is growing whilst the other half stagnates.

In development terms, two particular groups can be singled out which are most likely to be in absolute poverty. The first are rural dwellers. Many urban dwellers living in slums in large cities are on the edge of absolute poverty. However, electricity, health care,

food and shelter are likely to be more accessible to these than to rural dwellers who may live hundreds of miles away from the nearest town. Moreover, many rural dwellers are engaged in very low productivity subsistence agriculture. Their productivity is even lower than that of many urban slum dwellers.

Table 100.3 *Poverty in the developing world, 1985-2000*

Region	Percentage of the population below the poverty line			Number of poor (millions)		
	1985	1990	2000	1985	1990	2000
All developing countries	30.5	29.7	24.1	1 051	1 133	1 107
South Asia	51.8	49.0	36.9	532	562	511
East Asia	13.2	11.3	4.2	182	169	73
Sub-Saharan Africa	47.6	47.8	49.7	184	216	304
Middle-East and North Africa	30.6	33.1	30.6	60	73	89
Eastern Europe	7.1	7.1	5.8	5	5	4
Latin America and the Caribbean	22.4	25.5	24.9	87	108	126

Source: The World Bank, *World Development Report*.

The second group most at risk is women. In many traditional societies, women have less access to food and education than males. When women find themselves widowed, they have more difficulty surviving than men because female wages are on average lower than male wages. In part this is caused by discrimination. However, it also reflects differences in access to education between genders. Table 100.4 shows that females are more likely to be illiterate than males. This is due to less access to schooling. Table 100.4 also shows differences in life expectancy. In developed countries, females can expect to outlive males by between 5 and 7 years on average. However, this gap is reduced to three years or less in low income countries. In Uganda, females live on average one year less than males.

Raising standards of living

Development is not just about providing basic needs for the whole population. It is also about raising standards of living beyond that of subsistence level. Higher incomes

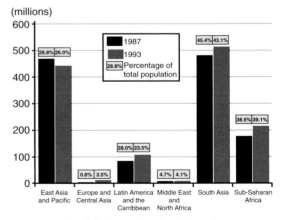

Figure 100.3 *People living on less than $1 per day*
Source: adapted from World Bank, *World Development Report*.

Table 100.4 *Gender comparisons*

	Life expectancy at birth 1997, years		Maternal mortality per 1 000 live births, 1990-97	Adult illiteracy, 15 and over, 1997 %		Proportion of the labour force, 1998 %	
	Males	Females		Males	Females	Male	Female
Mozambique	44	47	11.00	43	75	52	48
Tanzania	47	49	5.30	18	38	51	49
Ethiopia	42	44	14.00	59	71	59	41
Malawi	43	43	6.20	27	57	51	49
Uganda	43	42	5.50	25	47	52	48
Pakistan	61	63	3.40	45	75	72	28
India	62	64	4.40	33	61	68	32
Egypt	65	68	1.70	35	60	70	30
Jamaica	72	77	1.20	19	10	54	46
China	68	71	0.95	9	25	55	45
Romania	65	73	0.41	1	3	56	44
Thailand	66	72	2.00	3	7	54	46
Brazil	63	71	1.60	16	16	65	35
Poland	69	77	0.05	0	0	54	46
South Africa	62	68	2.30	15	17	62	38
Mexico	69	75	1.10	8	12	67	38
South Korea	69	76	0.30	1	4	59	41
Chile	72	78	0.65	5	5	67	33
Portugal	71	79	0.15	6	12	56	44
New Zealand	75	80	0.25	na	na	55	45
Spain	75	82	0.07	2	4	63	37
Hong Kong	76	82	0.07	4	12	63	37
Switzerland	76	82	0.06	na	na	60	40
Singapore	73	79	0.10	4	13	61	39
United States	73	79	0.12	na	na	54	46

Source: adapted from World Bank, *World Development Report*.

currently subject to economic reform programmes imposed by the IMF (International Monetary Fund ☞ unit 104). Whilst these reform programmes may lead to higher economic growth in the future, they are bitterly resented by the countries concerned because they are seen as limiting the freedom to choose how to operate economic policy by the individual country.

At the individual level, economic development is about allowing people to decide what to buy today, rather than being forced to buy basic necessities only. It is about controlling where one works, which implies that there are jobs available in the economy. It is also about political freedoms, such as the right to free speech, or to choose where to live or who to meet. Some of the East Asian countries with particularly high growth rates, such as China and South Korea, have relatively poor human rights records.

are one sign of rising living standards. A whole range of goods then become affordable, from televisions to meals out to travel.

There are, however, many more aspects to the standard of living of an individual. For instance, improved education not only allows the workforce to become more productive. It also increases the ability of individuals to enjoy and appreciate their culture. Access to work not only provides individuals and their dependents with an income. It also provides self-esteem and a sense of purpose. Access to a clean environment not only contributes to today's standard of living but is also an indication that this standard of living is sustainable for one's children.

Rising living standards are also linked to the ability of citizens to participate in society. The poor are often denied that ability because they do not have the income to be able to buy what is considered to be the 'norm' for that society. A key focus of economic development must then be to reduce sharp inequalities in income.

Expanding the range of economic and social choices

Development is about giving societies and individuals within those societies greater choice. Many Third World countries in the past were colonies of First World countries. Independence brought them greater freedom to decide their own national destiny.

Development is also about giving nations greater freedom to decide on their economic objectives. Many Third World countries are

Question 2

Elephantiasis (sometimes known as big foot or big leg) is a crippling disease which affects 120 million people in 80 poor tropical countries. It produces huge swellings in the feet, legs, arms, breasts and male genital organs. If left untreated, the disease also produces massive skin folds, fissures and a weeping cauliflower surface that produces a terrible odour. Not surprisingly, those affected suffer shame, stigma and extreme social exclusion as well as an inability to carry out everyday tasks needed for survival. Vivian Amoah, from Ghana, is lucky because she is able to attend an elephantiasis clinic where she has learned new techniques to control the swellings. Even so, when she contracted the disease, she was training to be a financial assistant. She was forced to leave college, and today she sells maize, grown by her mother, at a road junction.

The World Health Organisation, in partnership with other public and private organisations, has now launched an eradication programme for the disease. It is transmitted by mosquitoes which inject the larva thread like parasitic filarial worms into humans when they feed on human blood. The worms only live in humans. So if the disease is eradicated from humans, the worms will become extinct. The WHO strategy is based on two drugs, taken in tablet form, which must be taken once a year for five years by the whole population of areas affected, not just by sufferers. The tablets kill the worms and their larvae. The programme is ambitious because over 1 billion people need to take the drugs and they are among the poorest people in the world.

Source: adapted from *The Guardian*, 19.1.2000.

(a) Explain why freedom from risk of contracting Elephantiasis is part of the provision of basic needs for a tropical country.
(b) Suggest why eradication is unlikely to come today from the trickling down of wealth from the rich to the poor.
(c) How will eradication of the disease help lift long term growth rates in countries affected?

Question 3

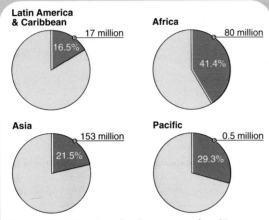

Latin America & Caribbean — 17 million — 16.5%

Africa — 80 million — 41.4%

Asia — 153 million — 21.5%

Pacific — 0.5 million — 29.3%

Figure 100.4 *Number of and percentage of working children between the ages of 5 and 14*
Source: adapted from ILO Bureau of Statistics, Geneva, 1996.

An immediate and universal ban on the worst forms of child labour is expected at this month's annual International Labour Organisation conference in Geneva. 'The nightmarish vision of boys and girls toiling in mines, sold for prostitution and and pornography, enslaved and trafficked like chattels or exposed to hazardous work has pushed child labour to the top of the international agenda', says Juan Somavia, the ILO's director general. 'Ending these exploitative practices is one of the most important issues of our time.' The ILO estimates there are 250 million children aged between 5 and 14 at work in developing countries alone, half of them working full time.

The ban will be difficult to enforce. The Pakistan government told the ILO: 'some of the worst forms of child labour are manifestations deeply rooted in poverty, parental unemployment and parental illiteracy. No society can eliminate them overnight or merely legislate them away even with the best political will. Sometimes action to eradicate child labour can drive children into greater destitution'. However, even many developing countries accept that work which impedes a child's education is one of the worst forms of child labour.

Source: adapted from the *Financial Times*, 8.6.1999.

(a) Outline the extent of the problem of child labour in the world.
(b) Why is the eradication of child labour part of economic development for a country?
(c) What might be (i) the short term losses and (ii) the long term gains for a country of its elimination?

Egypt

Poverty

Egypt's flagship programme to combat poverty, the Social Fund for Development, was launched in 1991. Today, it has a budget of $775 million but finds it difficult to make sizable inroads into the problems that face Egypt's poor today. Despite a government commitment to free health care and education, standards of provision are low. For instance, 51 per cent of pupils drop out of basic education, due both to 'their own poverty as well as the poor equational services they receive' a Ford Foundation study commented. Illiteracy rates for women were 76 per cent in rural areas. Hania Sholkamy, an anthropologist working for the Population Council, believes the most disturbing aspect of being poor in Egypt is not just a low standard of living but the lack of channels through which to demand better services. 'The poor cannot dent a system that is being more and more geared to serve the super-rich' she says.

One of the most startling symbols of social inequality is the estimated 1 million squatters that have been forced, through lack of affordable housing, to turn cemeteries into their living quarters. Long term residents of the City of the Dead are unimpressed by a new road built through the area, claiming that it simply serves to connect Cairo's rings roads to areas outside the city inhabited by the new rich and middle classes.

Imbaba

Egypt faced a major internal threat in the early 1990s when Islamic fundamentalists waged a terrorist war against the state. Problems started in the Imbaba area of Cairo, a poverty stricken area of the city. The government reacted brutally with military force. But Imbaba subsequently was targeted for state assistance. Funds were poured into local schools, hospitals, housing and improved infrastructure. Employment projects were organised to reduce chronic unemployment. NGOs (non-governmental organisations such as aid charities) made low interest loans available for the setting up of small businesses, including those of former prisoners. They also provided a literacy programme to young Egyptian women who have traditionally had less access to education than men.

In the least developed areas of Imbaba, as in other areas of Egypt, some families scrape a living from the garbage, feeding their animals and sometimes themselves on discarded food waste. Children, poorly dressed and unwashed, inhabit the streets rather than the schoolroom. Development still has a long way to go for many Egyptians.

Civil liberties

The government seems to be getting more conservative. Faced with terrorism from Islamic fundamentalists organisations in the 1990s, the army has responded firmly, but at the same time, the government has moved towards the fundamentalist position. For instance, it has banned or is about to ban up to 60 books from the bookshop and course texts of the American University of Cairo (AUC) for offending cultural sensitivities. The effect of the ban is trivial but highly symbolic. AUC is a private university which charges high fees and has relatively few students. But the government has bowed to pressure from a small minority of the students at the AUC, signifying its sympathy with Islamists. More important was its attempts to close the *Cairo Times* in 1998, known for its frank and outspoken reporting of the shortcomings of the state.

The security forces, used to suppress Islamic fundamentalists, act with impunity. For instance, the Egyptian Organisation for Human Rights (EOHR) published a highly critical report of the police handling of an investigation into the murders of two Coptic Christians. Up to 1 200 Copts, among them children and old people, were arrested, with no success at finding the perpetrators. The report concluded that the police were keen to find a Copt guilty of the murder, because to have charged a Moslem may have inflamed sectarian violence. The government responded by arresting the secretary-general of EOHR, who was jailed. The organisation was accused of receiving foreign funds to finance the report as a way of discrediting Egypt.

Source: adapted from the *Financial Times*, 11.5.1999

Table 100.5 *Egypt, Jordan, Morocco and the Philippines, selected development statistics*

	Egypt	Jordan	Morocco	Phillipines
GDP per capita at PPP rates 1998, $	3 130	3 230	3 120	3 540
Real growth in GDP, % per annum				
1965-80	8.8	na	5.7	5.7
1980-90	5.4	2.5	4.2	1.0
1990-98	4.2	5.4	2.1	3.3
Population growth, average annual rate, %				
1965-80	2.1	4.3	2.5	2.8
1980-90	4.1	7.4	3.6	4.4
1990-98	2.3	5.2	2.1	2.6
Percentage share of income, 1991				
Lowest 10 per cent	3.9	2.4	2.8	2.4
Top 10 per cent	26.7	34.7	30.5	33.5
Life expectancy at birth (years), females				
1965	50	52	51	57
1997	68	73	69	70
Infant mortality rate (per thousand live births)				
1965	145	na	145	72
1997	51	29	51	35
Prevalence of child malnutrition, % of children under age 5, 1992-97	15	10	10	30
Adult illiteracy, females, %				
1990	66	30	62	11
1997	60	18	67	6
Access to safe water, % of population				
1982	90	89	32	65
1995	84	98	57	83
Telephone mainlines per 1 000 people,				
1997	56	108	50	29
Annual deforestation 1990-95, %	0	2.5	0.7	3.5
Irrigated land, % of cropland				
1979-81	100	11.0	15.2	14.0
1994-96	100	18.20	13.0	16.7

Source: adapted from the World Bank, *World Development Report*.

Write a report for the World Bank on the extent to which Egypt has achieved genuine development in recent decades. In your report:

- **distinguish between development and economic growth;**
- **assess the extent to which Egypt has achieved economic development (i) from the data provided about the country and (ii) by comparing it to Jordan, Morocco and the Philippines;**
- **discuss what needs to happen if Egypt is to become a 'developed' country.**

Applied economics

The population explosion

The size of the world's population has exploded in the twentieth century, as Figure 101.1 shows. In 1900, the world's population was an estimated 1.6bn. By 1980, it had grown to 4.4 billion and by 1998 was 5.9 billion. By the year 2000, it is projected to be 6.3 billion. The United Nations has predicted that the most likely scenario is that the world's population will stabilise at 12 billion in the 21st century.

The population explosion has been caused by the number of births exceeding the number of deaths. Due to better diet, better housing and sanitation, and access to clean water and health care, people are living longer. However, there has been a lagged response of the birth rate to falls in the death rate. In the developed world, birth rates now roughly equal death rates, so that there is little or no population growth as can be seen in

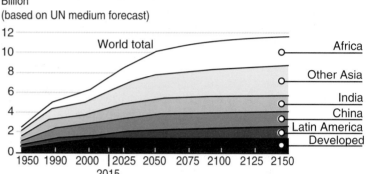

Figure 101.1 *Population projections by region*
Source: adapted from United Nations.

Table 101.1. Indeed, the population of some countries, such as the former West Germany, is actually declining. In the developing world, birth rates are still very high, although in some countries they have been falling

Table 101.1 *Population structures*

	GDP per capita, US$ at purchasing power parity rates	Population millions			Average annual growth in the population %			Age structure of the population, 1997 and 2015		
								% of population aged 0-15	% of population aged 65+	
	1998	1980	1998	2025 projected	1965-80	1980-90	1990-98	1997	1997	2015 projected
Mozambique	312	12	17	40	2.5	3.4	2.6	46.7	4.0	3.3
Tanzania	490	19	32	59	2.9	5.5	3.3	45.2	2.5	2.2
Ethiopia	500	38	61	141	2.7	4.9	2.6	48.0	2.7	2.0
Malawi	730	6	11	21	2.9	5.3	3.1	44.0	2.5	6.0
Uganda	1 170	13	21	45	3.0	4.9	3.5	48.6	2.2	1.4
Pakistan	1 560	83	132	243	3.1	4.6	2.8	40.7	3.1	3.7
India	1 700	687	980	1 016	2.3	3.5	2.0	35.3	4.7	5.9
Egypt	3 130	41	61	86	2.1	4.1	2.3	35.7	4.4	5.5
Jamaica	3 210	2.0	3.0	3.0	1.3	1.9	1.0	30.4	6.4	7.1
China	3 220	981	1 239	1 471	2.2	2.3	1.2	24.5	6.6	8.8
Romania	3 970	22	22	23	1.1	0.1	-0.5	19.0	12.3	14.3
Thailand	5 840	47	61	81	2.9	2.7	1.4	25.9	5.2	7.4
Brazil	6 160	122	166	224	2.4	3.1	1.6	30.9	4.8	6.6
Poland	6 740	36	39	42	0.8	0.8	0.2	18.8	11.4	14.5
South Africa	6 990	28	41	69	2.4	4.0	2.3	32.8	4.8	6.6
Mexico	8 190	68	96	136	3.1	3.5	2.0	31.2	4.4	6.3
South Korea	12 270	38	46	53	2.0	2.0	1.1	22.5	4.8	10.8
Chile	12 890	11	15	23	1.7	2.8	1.8	27.7	6.8	9.8
Portugal	14 380	10	10	10	0.4	0.2	0.1	16.7	16.1	16.6
New Zealand	15 840	3	4	4	1.3	2.0	1.7	19.1	11.3	14.2
Spain	16 060	37	39	69	1.0	0.5	0.2	14.7	15.9	18.6
Hong Kong	22 000	5	7	6	2.0	2.8	2.3	15.2	9.8	13.4
Switzerland	26 620	6	7	7	0.5	1.2	0.8	12.6	14.7	20.7
Singapore	28 620	2	3	4	1.6	3.3	2.2	17.3	6.5	11.3
United States	29 340	227	270	323	1.0	1.7	1.1	19.1	12.3	14.2

Source: adapted from the World Bank, *World Development Report*.

rapidly in recent years due to a complex mix of factors discussed later in the unit. Until birth rates equal death rates in developing countries, the world's population will continue to grow.

Growth in population varies enormously from country to country and continent to continent. Figure 101.1 shows that the largest growth in the world's population is forecast to come from Africa, the world's poorest continent. By the year 2150, one-third of the world's population is predicted to be African. China's population, currently one-fifth that of the world's, will rise by 0.3 billion but shrink to 12 per cent of the world's population by 2150.

The size of the population: is it a problem?

Many argue that the planet is already over-populated with 6 billion inhabitants. Growth to 12 billion will be unsustainable. There is a number of arguments put forward to sustain this proposition.

The food supply and Malthus Malthus was an early nineteenth century British economist who put forward 'the iron law of wages'. He argued that the food supply could only increase arithmetically over time (e.g. 2, 4, 6, 8, 10 ...) whilst the population would grow geometrically (2, 4, 16, 256, ...). The result would inevitably be poverty and starvation with most of the population never getting out of the poverty trap. This was because a rise in wages would lead to more children surviving into adulthood. This would increase the supply of labour, driving down wages, with more children starving to death. In equilibrium, most of the population can only live at subsistence level.

Malthusian economics has proved to be incorrect in the developed world. As was discussed in unit 48, world food supply has more than kept pace with population growth. In the developed world, average daily calorie intake is more than twice what it was 100 years ago. Modern day Malthusians argue that the pace of technological change cannot be kept up. Farmers cannot increase their yields per acre forever by improving the land, applying more fertilizer and developing better strains. There has to be a limit to how much food the planet can grow. Critics of this view say that crop yields in the West have been increasing at about $2^{1/2}$ per cent per annum for 100 years, more than outstripping population growth. Why should this trend not continue? Moreover, the developed countries of the world already have the potential to grow more food than is currently being produced. The objectives of the USA, Canada and the EU are to restrict food production from current levels (☞ unit 16). Food is not a physical problem today, it is a market problem. Starvation occurs because consumers don't have the money to buy food, not because it cannot be produced.

Resource pressures GNP of the developing countries of the world grew at an average annual rate of 3.5 per cent in the 1980s. Yet average population growth over the same period was 3.2 per cent. Growth per capita was therefore only 0.3 per cent. Almost all the developing world's increased resources during this decade were needed to provide for a growth in the population. Is this typical? On Malthusian grounds, it is very much what is to be expected. Increased incomes lead to increased population, leaving the mass of the population at subsistence level. Critics of this view point out that countries do break out of this cycle. France, Germany and the UK all had high population growth in the nineteenth century but economic growth per capita was positive. In the 1990s, the GNP of developing countries grew on average by 3.2 per cent but population growth was only 1.8 per cent. Low income countries performed even better than this, averaging GNP growth of 7.3 per cent whilst population only rose 2 per cent per annum. So high growth per capita is possible with the appropriate policies.

The environment Even if the growth in food production and in production of all other goods exceeds population growth, this is not environmentally sustainable. Giving every household in the world a refrigerator would do irretrievable damage to the ozone layer when those refrigerators were thrown away. Giving every household a car would lead to global warming on a scale not even predicted today. Constant intensive farm production would lead to permanent degradation of farm lands. Pressure for living space would result in the destruction of countless species of plant and animal, reducing bio-diversity, with unpredictable effects on the environment and on the human species.

For these reasons, economists argue that development must be SUSTAINABLE DEVELOPMENT. The 1987 World Commision on Environment and Development stated that development needed to meet 'the needs of the present generation without compromising the needs of future generations'. In economic terms, this means 'maximising the net welfare of economic activities, while maintaining or increasing the stock of economic, ecological and sociocultural assets over time and providing a safety net to meet basic needs and protect the poor' (Mohan Munasingle in *IMF, Finance and Development,* December 1993). Meeting today's needs should not rob the next generation of the ability to grow and develop. Successful efforts by First World countries to reduce greenhouse gas emissions (☞ unit 19), ban CFCs and recycle materials show that sustainable development is possible when threats to the environment are clearly identified.

The age structure of the population

Many argue that the planet is already over-populated with 6 billion inhabitants. Growth to 12 billion inhabitants will bring even greater pressures to bear on the environment. It will require enormous investment

Question 1

Population growth is connected with the success or failure of a sustainable development agenda. Long term projections show that the world's population may level off around the middle of the 21st century. But before it does, the number of people could double. This will lead to problems.

In parts of the world with fragile ecological systems that are already threatened by water stress and land degradation, increased population pressure could lead to environmental catastrophes. Global food supplies will need to double over the next 35 years because of population and economic growth. While food supplies have actually doubled in the last 25 years, agronomists warn that the next doubling will be far more difficult - especially if it is to be environmentally sustainable. In Nepal. for instance, where population growth is reducing average farm size, farmers have been pushed into clearing and cropping hillsides in an attempt to maintain their income, and erosion is becoming an increasingly serious problem.

The doubling of food production will have to occur at a time when 800 million people worldwide are already malnourished, 25 billion tons of topsoil are lost annually, and nearly three-quarters of the ocean's fish stock are over exploited.

Water scarcity also threatens the potential for continued improvements in the quality of life of the world's poorest people. Today, about one-third of the world's population lives under moderate or severe water stress, with at least 19 countries dependent on foreign sources for more than 50 per cent of their surface water. Under conditions of water scarcity, agricultural yields will fall as irrigation supplies dry up, and health will suffer as more people are reduced to using unsafe water sources for drinking and washing.

Source: adapted from the *World Development Report 1999/2000*, The World Bank.

(a) Identify THREE key problems that could arise from the estimated doubling of the world's population by 2150.
(b) Why might unsustainable growth over the next 50 years harm prospects for the world's population in 100 years' time?

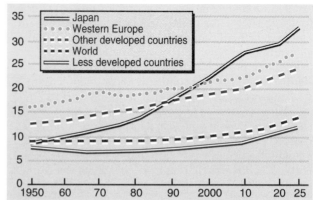

Figure 101.2 *Population aged 60 and over as a percentage of total population*
Source: adapted from United Nations.

population imply a shift in the structure of production. For instance, there will be a greater demand for health care and residential homes (☞ unit 76). However, there are also major implications for the distribution of income.

Dependency ratios, the number of dependants to the number of workers in the population, are predicted to rise substantially over the next 50 years in the developed world. If pensioners are to share in the growing prosperity of their economies, then there must be a shift in the share of total income being received in favour of the pensioner population and away from the working population. For instance, if pensions are provided by the state, then paying for increased pensions to a larger number of pensioners implies that workers will have to pay higher taxes to fund this. The UK government responded to this in the 1980s and early 1990s by cutting back on future pension commitments (i.e. by making future pensioners poorer than they would have been under the state pension arrangements which existed in 1980). Other western governments may well respond over the next 20 years

in physical and human capital. There is also a question mark about whether the planet will be able to feed 12 billion people, discussed below.

However, the process of transition from the 1 billion inhabitants in 1900 to 6 billion in 1998 to 12 billion in 2150 is giving rise to large variations in the age structure of populations of different countries. In First World countries, falling birth rates this century combined with longer life expectancy have led to a gradual increase in the proportion of old people to both the working population and to the total population. Figures 101.2 and 101.3 show that some countries or regions have been worse affected by this trend than others. Increased numbers of old people in the

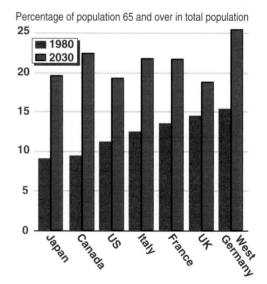

Percentage of population 65 and over in total population

Figure 101.3 *The ageing population of the developed world*
Source: adapted from OECD.

by cutting their commitments too.

In the Third World, the current problem is not with an ageing population but with the very high proportion of the population that is under 15. Of the developing countries shown in Table 101.1, only the two Eastern European countries had more than 6 per cent of their population over the age of 65. In contrast, all the developing countries had at least 25 per cent of their population under the age of 15 and one-third had between 40 and 50 per cent of their population in this age group. This situation is predicted to improve by the year 2025 for middle income countries, but most low income countries of the world are predicted to remain with over 40 per cent of the population below 15.

There are major problems with having a large proportion of the population below the age of 15. Providing for children will impose a heavy burden on workers. Children need to be clothed and fed. They also need health care and education. There is a close link between poverty and low educational attainment.
- Poor countries cannot afford to provide adequate state education systems.
- Many families cannot afford to send their children to school even if education is free. This is because they need children to work, either on their farms or as child labourers working for local businesses. Only by securing an income from their children can these families survive.
- Moreover, the local economy often cannot provide jobs suitable for reasonably educated children. There is then little incentive for families to educate their children for the local job market.

As children pass through into adulthood, they then need jobs to survive. However, poor countries have too little physical capital to provide all workers with jobs. Hence, there is widespread unemployment and underemployment. This, particularly in urban settings, can lead to high levels of crime and drug dependency.

Equally, passage to adulthood implies marriage and the setting up of homes. This means that the economy must provide more homes, more sanitation facilities, more clean water, etc. Even if the birth rate is slowing dramatically, it can take 50 to 60 years for the population to stabilise and for the economic effects of children on the economy to reach some sort of equilibrium.

Government policy and the birth rate

It is generally agreed that there is a link between development and the birth rate. As Table 101.1 shows, the poorer the country, the more likely there is to be a high rate of population growth. The link is arguably biological, social and economic.

Development implies better health with fewer children dying. Either for biological or social reasons, or some combination of the two, people react by having fewer children. For instance, if half of all children die before the age of 15, then a family needs on average to have 4 children for two to survive to adulthood. If

Question 2

The ageing of populations in industrial countries and some industrialising East Asian economies could have significant macro-economic effects. The shifts in the age distribution are dramatic. The median age of the population in northeast Asia will rise from 28 years to 36 years between 1995 and 2015. Just 12.5 per cent of the US population and 11.8 per cent of the Japanese population were over 65 in 1990, proportions that will rise to 18.7 per cent and 26.7 per cent by 2025. Between 1990 and 2025 rapid ageing will raise the share of the 65-plus cohort from 6 to 13.3 per cent in China and from 5 to 15 per cent in the Republic of Korea.

There is a danger that there will be a slump in savings as a smaller middle aged group saves less, whilst the elderly run down their savings to pay for their retirement. This could lead to a severe global capital shortage. With less savings, interest rates will rise and this will reduce investment to bring it into line with savings. Reduced investment will not just affect the developed countries of the world. There will be less investment by First World savers into Third World countries. This could affect their development. A less pessimistic scenario suggests that countries like Japan and South Korea will see their investment rates fall anyway since they invest almost half as much again as the average First World country on a percentage of GDP basis. Middle aged people in First World countries will increase their savings rates as they become more affluent and are able to save more for retirement. In the meantime, savings rates in middle income countries should rise as their fertility rates fall, life expectancy rises and average incomes rise. Some countries in South Asia and Central and South America could even become net capital exporters, like Japan at the moment.

Source: adapted from *World Development Report 1999/2000*, The World Bank.

(a) Explain why developing countries could be affected by the ageing of the population in the developed world.
(b) Why might rising incomes in developing countries help reduce the problems caused by population ageing?

almost all children survive to adulthood, they only need two.

The higher the level of development, the greater the cost of bringing up children. At low levels of development, children eat little and need little looking after. They can quickly be put out to work and become an economic asset. As levels of development increase, children have to spend time in school, reducing their ability to work. The amount of care taken over children also tends to increase, reducing the amount of time adults can spend working. In a developed country, children have to stay in education for most if not all of their teenage years. There is very little expectation on

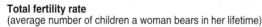

Total fertility rate
(average number of children a woman bears in her lifetime)

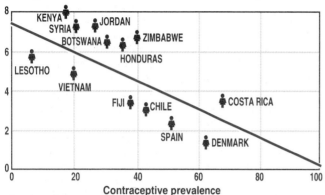

Contraceptive prevalence
(% of married women of reproductive age with access to contraception)

Figure 101.4 *Fertility and contraception availability*
Source: adapted from United Nations.

the part of parents that the children will contribute any wages to the household. The cost of keeping children in terms of university education, food, clothes, etc. rises as parental incomes rise. The opportunity cost, usually for women, of staying away from work to bring up children also increases as average incomes in the economy rise. From being a financial asset to parents in a poor developing country, they become a large financial burden in developed economies. Not surprisingly, birth rates fall.

Government, however, can play a part in altering the rate of change of the birth rate and influencing the long run equilibrium birth rate in a country.

Education Governments can, through health clinics, schools and the media, try to persuade couples to have fewer children. Studies have shown that this is most effective if aimed at women who have to bear most of the time and health cost of bearing and bringing up children.

Family planning Governments can sponsor family planning programmes. Most developing countries have such programmes, although they differ widely in the amount of resources put into the programme and their effectiveness. In general, as Figure 101.4 shows, the greater the number of women with access to contraceptives, the lower the fertility rate. Family planning can run into cultural objections. As with education, the most effective family planning is achieved with the co-operation of women rather than men. However, women deciding how many children they have can be seen as subverting the domination of men in patriarchal societies. Family planning is also condemned by some religious groups as being immoral.

Incentives and disincentives These have been widely used throughout the developed and developing world. Some are **fiscal** (i.e involve government spending or

taxation). France, for instance, which has believed for all of this century that it has too small a population, currently has a generous system of child benefits designed to encourage women to have children. In contrast in Singapore, income tax relief is also only given for the first three children. Other incentives and disincentives are physical, legal, administrative or social. In Singapore, again, no account is made of the number of children in a family when allocating public housing. A family with six children will get the same cramped apartment space as a family with one child. In China, the government introduced a widely disliked policy in the early 1980s allowing parents only to have one child. Women had to get the approval of the local neighbourhood committee or council for permission to get pregnant. Approval was usually denied if the parents already had one child unless that child had a disability. Steep fines were imposed on women who had children without permission. Women with two or more children were refused promotion.

It is difficult to evaluate the effectiveness of such programmes because it is impossible to know what the birth rate would have been in the absence of the programme. However, in those cases where incentives are given for men to have vasectomies (as in India in the 1970s), it seems logical that the programme must have some impact on the birth rate.

Raising the economic status of women Women are the child-bearers in society. If the state can increase the opportunity cost for women of having children, then the number of children being born can be reduced. This can be achieved mainly through increasing employment opportunities for women. If women can earn a reasonable wage, they will be less likely to marry early. For instance, why should a family marry off a daughter at 14 when she could be put out to work to earn money till she was, say, 18? Women can also leave home and set up independently if they can earn a living wage and make their own choice about when and who to marry. Once married, the opportunity cost of staying at home to look after children rises the greater the wage the women could earn in a paid job. The workplace can also be an important place for education. Government agencies may be able to get access to talk to women in the workplace but not in the home. Women may also support each other against more traditional values through the relationships they build up in the workplace.

Migration

Urbanisation, the shift of the population from the countryside into the towns, has been rapid over the past 40 years as Table 101.2 and Figure 101.5 show. In the 1950s and 1960s, the widespread migration of people from rural areas into cities was regarded by economists as beneficial. It was argued that workers in rural areas were engaged in low productivity (often agricultural) occupations. In urban areas their labour

Table 101.2 *Urbanisation*

	Urban population as % of total		
	1970	1980	1998
World	35	39	46
High income countries	74	75	76
Middle income countries	46	55	66
Low income countries	18	21	31
Low and middle income countries *of which*			
Sub-Saharan Africa	19	23	33
East Asia and Pacific	19	22	35
South Asia	19	22	27
Middle East and North Africa	41	48	58
Latin America and Caribbean	57	65	75

Source: adapted from the World Bank, *World Development Report*.

could be transferred into higher productivity manufacturing and service sector jobs. The growth of secondary and tertiary industries, indeed, demanded a growth in the urban population.

In the 1970s and 1980s, however, there was a reversal of opinion and rural-urban migration has come to be seen as having a negative impact on the development of many countries. This is because migrants often fail to find jobs in the cities. From being low productivity rural workers, they become the zero productivity urban unemployed. Moreover, migrants tend to be young, better educated, rural dwellers. Having received some education, they set off for the city to seek their fortune. This drains rural areas of those individuals who could have played a vital role in increasing the productivity of the rural sector in the economy. In the city, migrants contribute to the already difficult environmental and social pressures, which would not necessarily have been present in the rural area they left.

Rural migrants are often aware that urban unemployment is high and that they may leave a job and family security in the countryside to become unemployed in the town. However, rural migrants base their decisions on **expected income**. For instance, assume that they have a one in two chance of becoming unemployed when going to the city, but if they do get a job, their wages will be four times as high as their present rural wage. Then, the average expected urban wage will be twice that of the rural wage. Potential unemployment is not a deterrent to migration if the potential wage to those who do get jobs is large enough. This theory is called the **Todaro model** after Michael Todaro, the economist who first put it forward in the late 1960s.

Measures which aim to improve the standard of living of urban dwellers relative to rural dwellers will only increase migration and increase unemployment in the country. For instance, an anti-poverty campaign in urban areas, with slum dwellers being given help with housing, access to electricity and sanitation and government work programmes and a higher minimum wage, will increase the expected benefits of being a town dweller. This will then attract further migrants who will create new slums

and a new urban poor. There may also be a perverse impact of education programmes on economic development. There is evidence that, as in developed countries, urban employers use qualifications as a rough guide to sorting out applicants for a job. It is the better educated who are most likely to migrate from rural areas into towns. With a fixed number of jobs in the urban job market, employers will be able to increase the educational qualifications of their newest employees by choosing from the now enlarged pool of existing urban workers and the new migrants. Qualification 'inflation' will occur, where success at secondary school level is needed even for quite low productivity jobs. The new workers will be over-qualified for their jobs and the economy will receive a very low rate of return on its investment in education in those individuals. The resources allocated to that investment would have been better used elsewhere to promote development.

The solution to the problem of migration is to improve the economic benefits received by rural dwellers. Prices of agricultural products have often been artificially depressed by governments who have forced farmers to sell part or all of their produce to the state. The difference between the price paid to the farmer and the market price then becomes a tax on the farming community. Raising prices to market levels would increase rural incomes and increase **allocative efficiency** (☞ unit 61) in the economy.

More money could be spent by government on promoting job creation in rural areas. The establishment of labour intensive small scale enterprises would have a number of other benefits, including less of a dependence on the importation of capital-intensive equipment which tends to create a few jobs in city areas. Education policy needs to be changed too. All the evidence suggests that high quality primary education for all children gives a far higher rate of return than primary, secondary and tertiary industry for a few. Investment in primary education in rural areas would give a higher rate of return than, say, investment in secondary schooling in urban areas. It would also reduce education qualification 'inflation' and reduce the attractiveness for future parents of migrating to

Urban population (billions)

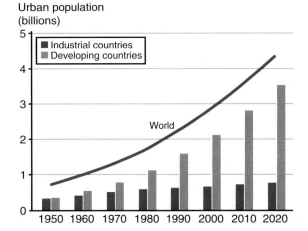

Figure 101.5 *Growth in urbanisation*
Source: adapted from *World Development Report*, World Bank.

urban areas where their children might receive a better education.

The environmental problem

Environmental problems and government policy responses have already been discussed at length in units 19 and 62. Third World countries face similar problems to First World countries, although the poorest billion inhabitants create special environmental difficulties.

Air pollution   In First World countries, industry and the motor car are the main polluters. The same is true in urban areas in the Third World although on a larger scale because environmental controls are laxer. Concentrations of suspended particulate matter in cities in low-income countries have worsened over the past 30 years due to three factors - growth in motorised transport, unregulated emissions from factories and the burning of fossil fuels by households for heat and cooking. Many Third World cities face the same problems that London experienced before the 1955 Clean Air Act dramatically reduced airborne pollution and banished 'smogs'. In rural areas, there is a problem with the burning of biomass fuels, such as manure, straw and wood. When burnt indoors for cooking and heat, these create dangerously high levels of indoor pollution which affect an estimated 400-700 million people, particularly women and children who spend longer indoors. Air pollution is a major cause of respiratory diseases, and results in an estimated 300 000 - 700 000 deaths annually.

Table 101.3 *Annual deforestation, 1990-95*

	Average annual % change
World	0.3
High income countries	-0.2
Middle income countries	0.3
Low income countries	0.7
Low and middle income countries	
of which	
Sub-Saharan Africa	0.7
East Asia and Pacific	0.8
South Asia	0.2
Middle East and North Africa	0.9
Latin America and Caribbean	0.6

Deforestation   The cutting down of the tropical rainforests is widely publicised in the West. Deforestation is caused by three main factors. First, forest is cut to create farming land. Second, trees are cut for timber to be sold, for instance to First World countries. Third, trees are cut for fuel. For the First World, the main problem is that cutting down forests increases the possibility of global warming since trees absorb carbon dioxide. For the Third World, the major problem is degradation of the land and possible desertification. Forests often exist on poor quality land which is unsuited to intensive cultivation. When abandoned after a period of cultivation, the land can become desert or scrub land. Where trees are cut for firewood, the trees can be acting as windbreaks. With

fewer trees in an agricultural area, there is the danger of fast erosion of top soil and a consequent loss of productivity of the land. Table 101.3 shows that the problems of deforestation are particularly acute in Africa. In contrast, the area devoted to forests is growing in the developed world. This implies that development is likely to lead in the long term to a solution to the problem of deforestation.

Soil degradation   Deforestation is only one cause of soil degradation. Over-intensive farming caused by too high population densities in a local area is another. Pressure on land supply also forces some farmers to begin to cultivate poor quality non-forest marginal land, which again within a few years leads to soil degradation.

Water scarcity and pollution   Lack of water and water pollution are major causes of disease in Third World countries. The World Bank, for instance, estimated that at the end of the 1990s, at any given time, half the urban population in developing countries is suffering from one or more water borne diseases. The most life threatening of these are malaria and dengue fever. In the countryside, lack of water affects the ability of farmers to grow food because of lack of irrigation. Water pollution from human activity also affects the environment and crops. The UN Food and Agriculture Organisation, for instance, estimated that 50 per cent of all mangrove forests in Asia disappeared between 1980 and 2000, half of which was caused by the growth in highly polluting shrimp farming. Thailand has placed severe restrictions on shrimp farming to prevent pollution damaging rice crops.

Waste disposal   Problems of the disposal of hazardous waste, such as nuclear waste, are familiar in First World countries. In Third World countries, there is hazardous waste too which can have a considerable impact on local communities. However, the more general problem is disposal of everyday garbage. The World Bank estimated that in the 1990s roughly half of all solid waste in urban areas in the developing world went uncollected, piling up on streets and in drains and contributing to flooding and the spread of disease. Moreover, domestic and industrial effluents were typically being released into waterways with little or no treatment, often affecting the quality of water outside the city. For instance, the La Paz River which flows through La Paz, the capital city of Bolivia, has become so polluted that it has reduced horticultural activity downstream.

Reduction of biodiversity   Each year, species of plants and animals are becoming extinct. Figure 101.6 shows the estimated number of mammal and bird species lost between 1700 and 1987. This, as explained above, leads to a loss of genetic material which might be of use in agriculture and industry. Many also argue that it is immoral for humans to destroy species.

Atmospheric change   Depletion of the ozone layer and global warming are well known. They could affect

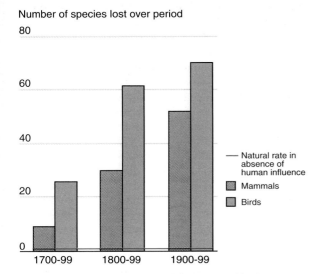

Figure 101.6 *Recorded extinctions of mammals and birds, 1700-1987*
Source: adapted from World Bank, World Development Report.

Third World countries by increasing skin cancers, increasing the possibility of climatic disasters, and causing a disruption in patterns of food production. If sea levels were to rise by 1 metre, approximately 70 million people in Bangladesh (equivalent to 116 per cent of the population of the UK) would be forced to move. The country would lose half its current rice production. Given that Bangladesh is a poor country with much of its population living at subsistence level, this could lead to widespread famine.

Third World policy responses to the environment

In unit 62, it was explained that governments had a variety of instruments which they could use to reduce pollution externalities. These included:
- banning or imposing quantitative controls on polluting activities;
- extending property rights so that pollution becomes 'owned' and allowing free market forces to act to reduce pollution;
- imposing taxes on pollution;
- subsidising activities which would reduce pollution;
- awarding permits to pollute which become tradeable.

However, many pollution problems arise directly from a lack of development. Increase economic development and many of these environmental problems will disappear. Urban pollution, for instance, is much higher in Third World cities than in First World urban areas. Reducing pollution by firms through some of the above strategies can only be one part of a much wider strategy. Elements of a successful strategy are also likely to include the following.

Land reform People will be discouraged from investing in their own infrastructure unless they know that they have rights over their property. In urban slums, for instance, where many houses are illegal,

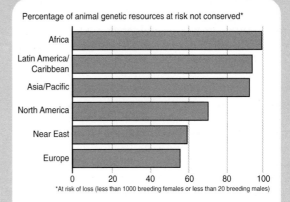

Figure 101.7 *Conservation of domestic animal diversity*
Source: adapted from FAO.

Should we care that there are now fewer than 1 000 Arvana-Kazakh dromedary camels in Kazakhstan, or only 900 Yakut cattle left in Siberia? The Food and Agriculture Organisation (FAO) thinks we should not only care but be alarmed. It points out that 30 per cent of the world's domestic animal breeds are at risk of extinction. Domestic animals, including modern breeds, supply about 30 per cent of the world's total human food requirements. 2 billion people depend at least partly on them for their livelihoods.

Most of the threatened breeds are indigenous to developing countries. They have often been pushed to the margins by the import of 'exotic' breeds from the developed world which promise much higher yields but can be prone to collapse in the different conditions they find. Exotic breeds can also cause problems if there is economic collapse. In Indonesia, farmers have been substituting local breeds of chicken for western breeds for some time. But the western breeds depend on expensive, protein enriched, imported diets. When Indonesia suffered a severe downturn in 1998 during the Asian crisis, a mass slaughter of chickens took place because farmers could no longer afford to buy the feed.

The FAO argues that the loss of animal breeds means that communities will be less able to respond to change. They will have a reduced capability to breed animals for characteristics such as resistance to disease, and have fewer options to respond to changes in consumer preferences. But perhaps the biggest impact of the loss of animal genetic resources and a failure to develop other adapted types is that it reduces overall global food security.

Source: adapted from the *Financial Times*, 15.9.1998.

(a) Explain the link between bio-diversity and global food security.
(b) Discuss the advantages and disadvantages of using exotic breeds in the Third World.

giving occupants official ownership will encourage them to put in proper sanitation and running water and fight to have their waste disposed of properly. In rural areas, where many farmers are tenants, giving tenants right of tenure or redistributing the land to them from large landowners will provide them with a long term incentive to adopt agricultural techniques which will ensure the long term survival of their land.

Working with the local community Evidence suggests that government programmes which provide for local communities are far less successful than programmes which work with local communities. For instance, a government programme to replant trees in a local area is likely to result in local people chopping down those trees for fuel as soon as the programme has been completed and government officials have left. A programme where the government persuades local people to plant trees and helps them find solutions to the problems which underlie the initial deforestation of the area is far more likely to have a permanent impact on the area.

Creating economic opportunities for the poor
Creating new ways in which the poor can earn their living can have an important environmental impact. For instance, creating low technology labour intensive industries in rural areas will relieve pressure to farm marginal land. It will enable people to purchase more environmentally friendly fuels, rather than resorting to collecting bio-mass fuels such as trees from the local environment. They will have more disposable income to provide their own better water and sanitation facilities. Fewer people will migrate to the cities, relieving pollution problems in urban areas. A vital part of any such economic policy must the creation of economic opportunities for women since they play such a key role cooking, farming, collecting water and dealing with sanitation problems.

Pricing which reflects social costs and benefits Prices in Third World countries often benefit urban elites to the disadvantage of the rest of society. For instance, urban elites, who are most able to pay, may be provided with subsidised water whilst urban slum dwellers and rural dwellers have little or no access to clean water. Properly pricing water, to include the benefits of far better health, should lead governments to aim to provide a basic water supply system for as many as possible rather than a high quality supply for a few.

First World policy responses

The First World could be a major loser from environmental degradation in the Third World. For instance, economic actions in the Third World which increase emissions of greenhouse gases and ozone-depleting gases, or which reduce bio-diversity, could lead to large economic costs in the future for the First World. Therefore, many argue that the First World must adopt appropriate policy responses to deal with the problem.

The most important policy response for First World countries could be to help Third World countries increase their rate of development. People in Third World countries do not wish to degrade their soils, use contaminated water or produce greenhouse gases. The higher the level of development, the lower the level of pollution. This is because people place a higher and higher value on the environment as their incomes increase. Consequently, they are prepared to pay higher prices to reduce pollution emissions than when their incomes were lower. As will be discussed in units 102-104, First World countries need to open up their markets more to exports from Third World countries to give those countries greater economic opportunities. They need to forgive debt and increase foreign aid. Inward investment is also vital.

First World countries also need to develop and then disseminate best practice on pollution control. First World countries, with a fraction of the world's population, need further to reduce their own levels of pollution. It would be difficult for First World countries to argue that Third World countries should tackle issues such as global warming when they are the major contributors of greenhouse gas emissions.

There has also been discussion of rewarding Third World countries which comply with environmentally friendly policies. For instance, **debt-for-nature swaps** have been negotiated on a very limited basis, where First World governments forgive debt owed to them by Third World countries if Third World countries comply with a specific conservation programme. Alternatively, it has been suggested that First World countries should pay Third World countries to manage their rain forests. There is a number of problems with these policies. One is that they are difficult to police. Third World governments are likely to receive money from the agreement but it is usually their citizens who are damaging the environment. There is often a lack of political will on the part of the Third World government to stop them doing this. Even if they wanted to, governments often have considerable difficulties enforcing measures. However, the most important drawback is that they can only have a marginal impact on global environmental problems. They are too specific and too small scale to be a significant solution, even though they might attract widespread media publicity in First World countries.

key terms

Sustainable development - development which meets the needs of the present generation without compromising the needs of future generations.

Sustainable development

Senegal fights back against desertification

Sand is the great enemy of farmers who grow the staple crops cassava and millet in the Sahel belt of Senegal, blowing mercilessly over the land, degrading their soil and robbing them of decent yields and incomes. Land degradation has become a worldwide problem, affecting about a quarter of the world's land area according to the United Nations Environment Programme. Income lost by people living in desertified areas amounts to $42 billion a year in lower agricultural production.

Trees can be a powerful weapon in the fight against desertification. In Senegal, under the aid-funded Village Organisation and Management project, sand is being stopped by belts of trees that have been planted around one hectare plots of millet and cassava. In total some 6 000 hectares in the area are being protected. Three years after planting trees, cassava yields have risen from 2 000 kg to 6 000 kg a hectare, and millet yields from 400 kg to 700 kg. The UNEP puts the global cost of anti-desertification measures at between $10 billion and $22 billion a year, and the big question is whether the money raised by international organisations will be anything like enough to help the world's dry-land farmers to stay and make a living amid the sand.

Source: adapted from the *Financial Times*, 16.2.1999.

China to import gas

China has the unenviable record of having nine of the ten worst polluted cities in the world. Part of its problem comes from the operation of thousands of small, coal-fired power stations that rain dust over cities and the countryside. In 2000, the Chinese government gave approval for the first project of its kind in the country to import liquefied gas (LNG) to the southern boom city of Shenzhen. Up to that point, China had felt it necessary for defence and security reasons to be self sufficient in energy. In the long term, there will be significant economic and environmental advantages to be gained through the use of more efficient and cleaner fuels. In the short term, though, problems could be encountered because the cost of imported LNG and the associated $500 million investment in infrastructure is likely to be higher than continued use of cheap coal in power stations that have already been paid for.

Bolivian mining starts cleaning up

Mining in Bolivia is dangerous and dirty, but this will inevitably change. One sign of this is at the Kantuta gold mine, one of the 540 mining co-operatives in the country. They have joined an internationally funded programme to help them boost production and care for their environment and health at the same time. In September 1998, they began to use several thousand dollars worth of machinery designed to drastically cut the amount of mercury used in the recovery of gold. The machinery is low-tech: basic equipment to assist in the concentration process and a retort to keep the mercury in a closed circuit. Instead of the mercury evaporating into the atmosphere, being inhaled by miners or tipped into water sources, it is cooled, recovered and recycled.

Some of Bolivia's small mines use up to 40 kilos of mercury to recover one kilo of gold - a lamentable world record in contamination, says Thomas Hentschel, the project manager for Medmin, the environmental mining project run in Ecuador and Bolivia by Cosude, the Swiss technical co-operation agency. 'Mining is aggressive and destructive by its nature' says Mr Hentschel, 'but with good practices and appropriate technology, its impact on health and the environment can be minimised and miners can improve productivity. It's a win-win situation.' Kantuta miners expect their new equipment to pay for itself within a year through increases in output of up to 20 per cent.

Source: adapted from the *Financial Times*, 15.10.1998.

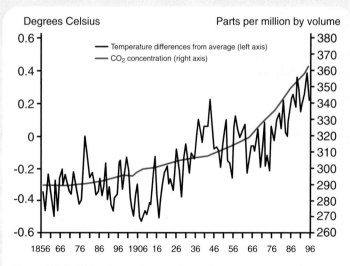

Figure 101.8 *Rising temperatures and greenhouse gas concentrations, 1856-1996*
Source: adapted from *World Development Report*, World Bank.

1. **Outline TWO environmental problems that developing countries face, according to the data.**
2. **Why might these two problems be caused by a failure of markets to include externalities in the resource allocation decisions of consumers and producers?**
3. **Evaluate whether developing countries should ignore the concept of sustainable development if this means that they can boost production of essential goods such as food and clean water now.**

Applied economics

Investment and saving

Development economics has a relatively short history. The first major work in this field of economics was done in the 1950s. The most important question which development economists asked themselves to begin with was 'how can an economy grow,' given that the 'problem' with Third World countries was that they were far poorer than First World countries. As explained in unit 105, growth in GDP rather than a more complex measure of development was assumed to be the yardstick by which countries would be measured.

Development economists initially used a widely accepted growth theory of the time called the **Harrod-Domar** growth model, named after the two economists who developed it in the 1930s (shown in Figure 102.1). This theory stated that investment, saving and technological change were the key variables in determining growth. Increased investment in the economy pushes out the **production possibility** frontier of the economy. So too does the introduction of new capital (machines, factories, equipment, offices) where a unit of the new, technologically advanced capital can produce more output than a unit of the old capital. Savings is important because savings approximately equal investment in an economy.

The Harrod-Domar model can be expressed in simple algebraic terms. Savings (S) is a proportion (s) of national income (Y). So S = sY. Investment (I) is the change in the capital stock (ΔK). The amount of extra capital (ΔK) needed to produce an extra unit of output (ΔY) is called k, the capital-output ratio and is equal to ΔK ÷ ΔY. As already explained, investment is roughly equal to savings in an economy, and so it can be said that S = I.

What then causes economic growth, which is measured by the change in output divided by the original level of output (ΔY ÷ Y)? The top of the fraction, ΔY can be found from the definition of the capital output ratio, k = (ΔK ÷ ΔY). Rearranging this equation gives: ΔY = (ΔK ÷ k). The bottom of the fraction, Y, can be found from the equation S = sY, remembering that S = I and that I = ΔK. This gives us S = I = ΔK = sY. Rearranging the last part of this gives:

$$Y = \Delta K \div sY$$

ΔK can be found on both the top and bottom of this fraction for the growth rate of the economy and therefore cancel each other out. This leaves us with:

$$\text{The rate of growth} = \frac{\Delta Y}{Y} = \frac{s}{k}$$

Figure 102.1 *The Harrod-Domar model of growth*

The policy implications of the Harrod-Domar model are clear. Increasing the rate of growth is a simple matter of either increasing the savings ratio in the economy which will increase the amount of investment, or it is about technological progress which allows more output to be produced from a single unit of that capital.

The insights of the Harrod-Domar model were used by the first important development economist, an American called Walt W Rostow. He said that economies went through five stages.
1. The traditional society, where barter is common and where agriculture is the most important industry.
2. An economy which has the pre-conditions for take-off into self-sustaining growth. Savings are rising to a level of between 15 and 20 per cent of national income.
3. The take-off stage. The economy begins to grow at a positive rate.
4. The drive to maturity. The economy has broken away from the ranks of economies still in stages 1 and 2 of the development process and is marching towards the status of a developed economy.
5. The age of mass consumption. The economy has finally made it, and its citizens are able to enjoy high consumption levels.

For Rostow, savings was the most important element in getting the economy to stages 3 and 4. The theory also used the insights of the Marshall Plan. This transferred large amounts of resources from the USA to Europe in the late 1940s to help Europe rebuild its industries. Foreign saving was added to domestic saving to increase the rate of growth of investment in Europe, thus raising European growth rates. Rostow and his followers similarly argued that Third World prosperity could be increased if First World countries gave foreign aid to Third World countries. This would fill a **savings gap**, the difference between the domestic rate of saving and the rate of investment needed for take off and the drive to maturity.

Economists are widely agreed that increasing savings and investment are vital to secure higher growth rates. The economic success stories of East Asia, from Japan to South Korea to Taiwan and Singapore, are built upon investment ratios to national income of 30 per cent or more compared to, say, the 17 per cent ratio currently being achieved by the UK and the 21-22 per cent being achieved by countries such as France and Germany. Figure 102.2 shows this correlation clearly for the high performance region of East Asia and the Pacific which includes China, Taiwan, South Korea, Thailand, Malaysia, Indonesia, Hong Kong and Singapore.

However, these are not a **sufficient** condition for growth. Investment can be wasted. Building a new steel mill in a Third World country might lead to nothing if workers are not able to run the mill, or if there aren't the ports to import iron ore, or roads to transport the finished product. Savings can be exported, with Third World citizens sending their surpluses to Swiss bank accounts or using it to buy shares on the New York stock exchange (the problem of **capital flight**). Foreign aid has too often in the past been diverted into paying for arms rather than being used for investment. Figure 102.2 shows that rates of investment in Sub-Saharan Africa were very similar to those in South Asia (most of whose population lives in India, Pakistan and Bangladesh) in 1980 and 1998. Yet growth rates differed enormously. Development is, in fact, a far more complex process than that set out in Rostow's stages of growth.

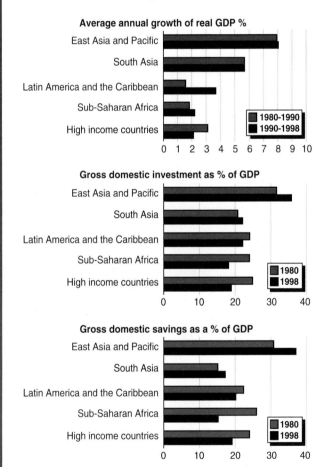

Figure 102.2 *Investment, savings and economic growth*
Source: adapted from *World Development Report*, World Bank

Structural change models

Another economist, W Arthur Lewis, focused on the role of migration in this process of development. He argued that growth could be sustained by the gradual transfer of workers from low productivity agriculture (the **traditional sector**) to higher productivity urban secondary and tertiary industries (the **modern sector**). The **industrialisation** of the economy, therefore, can be seen as an objective of development. He assumed that

Question 1

The Nigerian palm oil industry, once the envy of the world, has fallen on hard times. Lack of investment and a less favourable climate has allowed east Asian producers to assume market dominance. In 1997, Nigeria produced around 700 000 tonnes of palm oil, of which around 5 per cent was exported, compared to Malaysian and Indonesian production of some 9 million and 5 million tonnes respectively.

Good practice is possible. For instance, one recently set up Nigerian palm oil company, Okumu Oil Palm, started out by buying a plantation once renowned for poor management, low production and bad pay. Production has tripled from 30 000 bunches to 90 000 bunches over five years and yields have risen to 17 tonnes a hectare, a Nigerian record, although well below the average 24 tonnes in Malaysia. There is extensive new planting, mostly using seeds from the Ivory Coast which produce higher oil yields. With the help of a $12 million European Investment Bank loan, it bought a mill to process the palm fruits from the plantation.

On a smaller scale, Ganiya Badnus, an engineer, has been developing low-technology, cheap and simple machines that could transform smallholder oil palm processing. At present, smallholders roast fruits over a fire, pound them with a large stick in a pit and hand press them with a large iron screw. The result is that seven people can expect to press half a drum - about 100 kg - of low quality oil in a day. The new machines allow a throughput of between 0.25 and 1.5 tonnes of fruit an hour, produce much higher quality oil and are able to cope with a farm of 100 to 200 hectares. At $8 500 they are too costly for the typical farmer. However, he is currently testing a much cheaper and simpler machine which would cost only $560 and would suit a typical smallholding. He wants to raise $0.5 million to build a manufacturing plant to built his kit. The return to farmers could be enormous. The oil produced by the machines commands prices three times higher than hand-pressed production and with the same amount of manpower can produce 20 times the quantity of oil in a day.

Source: adapted from the *Financial Times*, 12.3.1999.

(a) Explain how investment in the Nigerian palm oil industry can lead to economic growth.
(b) (i) Why are savings necessary for this investment?
    (ii) Where did or where could producers in the industry obtain funds for such investment?

marginal workers in rural areas added nothing to the output of the rural economy (i.e. their marginal productivity was zero). Either they genuinely did no work (i.e. they were unemployed) or the work that they did could have been performed by existing workers with no effect on total output (i.e. there was a large amount of underemployment in the rural economy). Workers could gradually be transferred into the urban higher productivity sector. The rate of transfer depended on the rate of capital accumulation in the modern sector of the economy. The greater the investment, the faster the transfer. Eventually, nearly all workers will have been transferred from the traditional sector to the modern sector and the economy will have become developed.

The Lewis model provided key insights into the development process, and was in part used to explain why developed countries with high rural populations, such as France, grew at a faster rate than those with small rural populations, such as the UK in the 1950s and 1960s (☞ unit 26). However, the model proved highly simplistic. For a start, there is considerable evidence that marginal workers in urban slums in the Third World are far more likely to have zero productivity than marginal workers in rural areas. The model also implies that there will be full employment in urban areas, which is certainly not the case. Other key assumptions or conclusions, such as static urban wages during the period of development, also do not fit with development experience. Table 102.1 shows that the change in population from rural to urban has been very similar across all regions of the developing world, and yet, as Figure 102.2 showed, these regions have very differing growth rates in GNP per capita.

Industrialisation in the Third World has also not necessarily led to economic development. Too often, First World technology has been imported. This has been highly **capital intensive**, requiring little but highly skilled labour. The result has been little job creation in economies where unemployment is very high. In too many cases, highly skilled labour has not been available in the local economy with the result that machinery has been inefficiently used. Economists, such as E.F. Schumacher, have argued that the Third World needs **appropriate technology**, suited to the skills of local workers and which creates jobs. Small scale, rural investment often yields a higher rate of return than large scale, urban factory investment.

Table 102.1 *Urbanisation*

	% of total population living in urban areas	
	1980	1998
Low income countries	21	31
Middle income countries	55	66
High income countries	75	76
Low and middle income countries	32	41
of which		
South Asia	22	27
Sub-Saharan Africa	23	33
East Asia and the Pacific	22	35
Middle East and North Africa	48	58
Latin America and Caribbean	65	75

Source: *World Development Report*, World Bank.

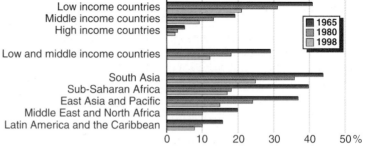

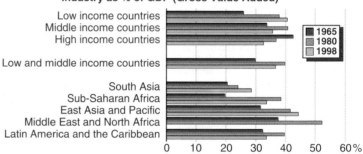

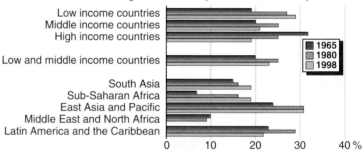

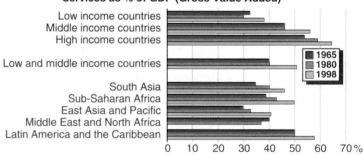

Figure 102.3 *Changing output by sector[1], 1965-1998*

1. Manufacturing output is part of industrial output. Agricultural output + industrial output + services output = 100% total output.

Dependency theory

In the 1970s, economists began to turn their attention to the links between the First World and the Third World and argue that many of the problems of lack of development were caused by First World countries. In these models, a failure to grow was not caused by conditions inside developed countries, such as low savings ratios, but by external forces.

Part of the failure to grow can be attributed to much of

the Third World's colonial past. First World countries exploited their colonies, thus increasing the inequality between themselves and their Third World empires. When the colonies gained independence, they remained tied to First World countries through trade and aid links. Under colonial rule, they had been forced to become exporters of primary commodities. In the post-colonial era, many countries are still highly dependent upon primary commodity exports. With average prices of commodities falling substantially since the 1950s, this trade link is continually impoverishing Third World countries. There is some truth in this argument. Countries such as Zambia or Nigeria have been negatively affected by a reliance on commodity exports. However, as Figure 102.3 shows, development has brought about a shift in output by sector. The more advanced the economy, the less significant is agriculture and the more important is service sector output. The 1970s, 1980s and 1990s also saw an important growth in the manufacturing sector. For many of the better off developing countries today, sales of manufactures far exceed sales of commodities in their export trade. Developing countries are therefore able to escape the problems caused by falling commodity prices if they can develop strong manufacturing industries.

Another argument put forward by some economists of this school is that aid loans to the Third World in the

1960s and 1970s led to the Third World **debt crisis** (☞ unit 104) in the 1980s. This in turn was a major cause of many African and Latin American countries experiencing negative growth rates in that decade as money flowed out of the Third World to pay debts owed to First World banks.

The actions of bodies such as the **IMF** (☞ unit 104) have reinforced dependence of the Third World on the First World. They have consistently given poor advice about how countries should develop and be managed. They have been helped in this by the actions of urban elites in Third World countries. These urban elites have been able, with the help of First World firms, governments and institutions, to enjoy First World living standards. The wealth they enjoy does not 'trickle down' to the rest of society. These urban elites are typically members of the government, the armed forces and key personnel working for or with western companies. Their interests lie with furthering the interests of the First World, not with the Third World people who are their fellow citizens.

The neoclassical revolution

During the 1950s, 1960s and 1970s, most Third World governments had built up economic structures which closely resembled the mixed economies of Western Europe. Key industries were often in state hands.

Governments intervened heavily to promote development. For instance, Rostow's ideas that levels of saving were primary in the development process, together with Lewis's two sector model of development, led to the rural poor being taxed far more heavily than urban dwellers. This was often achieved by forcing farmers to sell produce to state agricultural boards at prices far below the market price. The produce could then be sold at market prices overseas or to towns, with the government taking the surplus as revenue which it could then plough back into investment in the economy. Alternatively, part or all of it could be sold to urban dwellers who could then be paid lower wages by employers. This would reduce costs, increase profits and thus increase investment. Even inequality was sometimes considered to be desirable because of the Keynesian view that the savings ratio of high income earners was higher than that of low income earners (☞ unit 31). Redistributing income from the poor to the rich, for instance through taxes, could therefore increase the national savings ratio.

The 1980s saw an economic revolution in ideas in the First World. 'Reaganomics' and 'Thatcherism' were the political names for a movement in economics which argued that growth could be increased by freeing markets from government constraint (☞ unit 38). Reductions in the size of the state, for instance through **privatisation** (☞ unit 67), would increase efficiency because the state was poor at allocating resources. Moreover, private markets should be **deregulated** (☞ unit 67). Government interference, such as state agricultural boards, should be removed. Low growth, so

Question 2

Steep falls in commodity prices are expected to cut some developing countries' export earnings by as much as a quarter this year and sharply reduce their economic output, according to the United Nations Conference on Trade and Development (UNCTAD). It blames much of the weakness on the economic crisis in Asia, which until recently had been the fastest growing market for agricultural and other primary commodities exports from Latin America and Africa. The harshest economic impact of falling prices will be felt by oil-exporting countries. Angola, Gabon, Iran, Kuwait, Nigeria and Venezuela all face declines of at least a fifth in their export earnings compared with last year. Their loss of economic output is set to range from 4 per cent to 18 per cent. Countries which depend heavily on exports such as copper and wood will also be seriously affected. Export earnings of Burma, Chile, Mongolia, the Solomon Islands and Zambia are set to fall by at least a tenth, and their economic output to shrink by between 2.5 per cent and 12 per cent.

Source: adapted from the *Financial Times*, 17.9.1998.

(a) Explain why countries such as Angola or Zambia are dependent upon other countries for their economic well being.
(b) Discuss whether countries such as Angola, which are highly dependent upon exports of commodities, would be better off if they abandoned production of those commodities.

it was argued, was caused by a failure to pursue free market policies.

The new neoclassical approach called, for instance, for a radical change in policies with regard to multinational companies. The traditional view was that the activities of multinational companies in general were harmful to the Third World. They tended to be engaged in the production of primary commodities, such as bananas or copper. They would pay low wages to their Third World workers and had little regard for health and safety at work. Profits were large and these would be repatriated back to the First World. Hence, the multinational contributed little to the Third World country and were run for the benefit of First World shareholders. Not surprisingly, many Third World countries nationalised the operations of multinational companies. However, nationalisation often proved disastrous in the long run. The Third World countries were unable to afford to keep up the investment required in the operations. The nationalised companies were often inefficiently run and productivity fell following nationalisation. With falling output, export earnings fell putting pressure on the balance of payments. In the new climate of the 1980s and 1990s, multinationals have often been reinvited back to Third World countries to resume their activities. There has been a fundamental reappraisal of the balance of benefit between Third World country and multinational.

Neoclassical theory, in fact, suggests that the liberalisation of markets will attract investment from First World countries into the Third World. First World companies will be attracted by cheap land and labour costs to set up factories in Third World countries. Inward investment will increase growth rates. There is little doubt that governments and state organisations were (and many still are) highly inefficient in the Third World. Their policies were a major part of the problem of lack of development. As will be argued in unit 103, all the evidence suggests that openness to international trade is a crucial element in maintaining growth. Therefore, government policies which limit trade and limit the influence of foreign companies on the domestic market are likely to lead to less growth.

Critics of the neoclassical approach point out that growth and development are different. Policies which promote growth, where the benefits go to the better off in society at the expense of the poor, may lead to a backward shift in economic development. Poverty reduction, pro-women programmes, environmental policies all imply government intervening in the market place. Moreover, some of the greatest success stories of recent years, including Japan, South Korea and Singapore, have been economies where there has been heavy state direction of the economy. The creation of genuine free market economies is obviously not a necessary condition for successful development.

Strategies for successful development

The experience of the last 40 years has shown that the causes of economic development are complex. However,

Question 3

China's sugar industry has finally made it on to the government's reform agenda after racking up losses of more than $1.2 billion in the last four years. Fifty years of command economy have rendered many Chinese state-owned enterprises inefficient, incompetent, debt-ridden and mired in losses. Many of China's 539 sugar refineries are insensitive to market demand, and have churned out more sugar than the country's population could consume as a consequence.

The average annual production capacity of each Chinese sugar mill is 18 000 metric tonnes, but many of them are very old and incapable of producing even 3 000 tonnes. Their costs of production are also high when compared with their internal peers. The average refining cost in China is about $240 a tonne, whilst domestic sugar sells for about $260 a tonne. With sugar trading internationally at around $180 a tonne, Chinese sugar factories face an unsustainable situation.

The State Economic and Trade Commission (SETC), the government body in charge of industry, has promised that within the next 12 months the number of sugar refineries would be cut to 392 and the national capacity would be trimmed from 10.5 million tonnes to 7.5 million tonnes. However, declining sugar prices have not prevented Chinese farmers from planting more sugar cane or beet root crops. China's sugar cane acreage is expected to increase by 1.2 per cent despite a 5 per cent decrease in sugar cane prices and a nationwide campaign by the government to reduce the area planted with the crop. A switch by many farmers from planting early rice, which will no longer be purchased by the state, and an increase in yields due to favourable weather conditions are to blame.

Source: adapted from the *Financial Times*, 5.1.2000.

(a) Explain why the sugar industry under state management was both productively and allocatively inefficient in 2000.
(b) Discuss whether liberalising the sugar industry, including the privatisation of sugar mills, would (i) increase efficiency and (ii) promote economic development.

a number of important lessons can be learnt. High rates of economic growth and development depended upon the simultaneous achievement of three factors.

Accumulation The Harrod-Domar growth model is correct in pointing out that savings and investment are vital for high growth. Investment, however, must be balanced. There must be the right mix of investment in private capital, such as machines and factories; in public infrastructure, such as roads, telecommunications and housing; and in people, developing their education and skills.

Allocation Resources must be allocated efficiently. It is pointless investing in new capital equipment if it lies idle for much of the time. It is futile to educate 5 per cent of

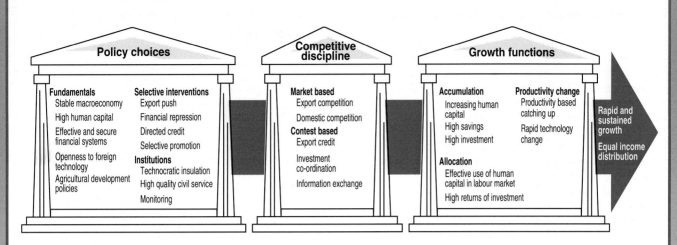

Source: World Bank.

Figure 102.4 *The World Bank theory of growth*

the population to degree standard if the economy only needs 1 per cent of degree standard workers. Equally, resources must be used in a way which maximises rates of return on those resources. Allocating resources into higher education when greater returns could be achieved by using those resources in primary education will lower the rate of growth of the economy. This is probably the most important insight of neo-classical free market economists.

Productivity change Fast growing economies are ones which are constantly changing their methods of production to incorporate the best and most appropriate technology. Increasing the rate of change of resource inputs, both human and physical, to output will increase economic growth.

These are best achieved, for the most part, in the context of competitive markets. The market, as Adam Smith pointed out, brings together information from large numbers of buyers and sellers. The discipline of the market ensures that resources are allocated efficiently. Being **export-orientated** is essential. Third World countries tend to trade with First World countries rather than between themselves. Selling into First World markets means that the successful export-orientated Third World country has to produce to First World standards. They therefore have to learn to buy and use First World technology. This also encourages the flow of information from First World to Third World. The result is an increase in the rate of change of productivity.

Where competitive markets are inappropriate, allocation of resources should be based on contests between producers. For instance, government may provide **export credits** - loans to foreign buyers who purchase exports from the country. There should be an open system in which firms are able to compete for the limited number of export credits, with clear rules as to how they are to be allocated.

It should also be remembered that in some markets,

market failure is so strong that governments have a duty to restrict competition and organise production itself. In education, for instance, a key to success in economic growth, all high growth countries have developed strong publicly funded systems of primary education.

Having decided what determines growth, and discussed the role that free markets can and cannot play in promoting growth, appropriate growth policies of governments can now be discussed. The World Bank, in Figure 102.4, singles out a number of key areas.

Stable macroeconomy The government must provide a stable macroeconomic climate. This means, for instance, containing inflation, securing a balance between exports and imports, and maintaining sound government finances. Macroeconomic stability encourages firms to invest. It also creates a balanced economy which can grow without having to be adjusted because one or more macroeconomic variables is unsustainable in the long term.

High human capital The importance of human capital in the development process has already been discussed.

Effective and secure financial systems The role of the financial system is crucial. The financial system (including banks) is responsible for gathering the savings of individuals and firms in the economy and allocating some of those to firms for investment. Any country wanting to increasing its savings ratio needs to improve the effectiveness of its financial system.

Limiting price distortions Governments must adopt policies which allow the price signals of the market to allocate resources. Governments, in most cases, are poorer at fixing optimal prices than the market mechanism and hence they should reduce market distortions such as government subsidies.

Openness to foreign technology Governments must

encourage domestic firms to use foreign technology. They must also encourage foreign firms to set up in their country, bringing with them technology that can then be copied by domestic firms.

Agricultural development policies With such a large proportion of output and population in the agricultural sector of the economy in the Third World, a failure to develop this sector would lead to lower growth.

Selective intervention The government may choose to intervene to direct the growth of particular industries, for instance by making cheap finance available for investment, or by setting export targets for the industry. Countries such as South Korea and Japan have pursued such intervention in the past. Other equally successful countries, such as Hong Kong, have generally not intervened. So intervention is not a necessary condition of growth.

Institutions A successful economy must have appropriate institutions. For instance, there must be a high quality civil service. Technocrats - those in the civil service, other government agencies and the government itself - must not be open to bribery and must act in the best interests of the nation (the 'technocratic insulation' of Figure 102.4). All economic agents must be monitoring their successes and failures and correcting where necessary.

The International-dependence school of thought are correct in saying that the relationship between the Third World and the First World plays a crucial role in the development process. However, high growth developing countries have tended to use that relationship to import capital and technological knowledge and export goods and services. They have sought to integrate themselves into the world economy. Countries which have had low or negative growth rates have been victims of that relationship, mainly by borrowing money which they had little or no hope of repaying (☞ unit 104). If the world macro-economic framework is hostile to development, it has not been so hostile as to prevent some Third World countries from enjoying spectacular growth rates over the past 20 years.

Development also implies progress in a number of other areas which in turn will feed through to higher economic growth.

Sustainability Development must be sustainable (☞ unit 101). Unsustainable growth today will lead to higher costs and lost opportunities for future generations.

Commitment to preserving indigenous cultures and values Every society needs to share common values if it is to remain stable. These values comes from the past and every society has something to offer to the richness of global culture. Societies where cultural change is too fast, or where a foreign culture (usually a Western one today) is imposed can easily break down, leading to a reversal of the development process.

Gender issues Women in many developed countries find themselves disadvantaged by social, legal and economic systems. They play a vital role in the development process, however. For instance, education enables them to be more productive both in their traditional roles within the home and in the wider world of paid work.

Comparing development

Nigeria and Indonesia

In 1965, Nigeria was regarded as a country with a high potential for growth, whilst Indonesia was being seen as having few prospects. In the 1970s, Nigeria experienced a windfall gain in the form of booming oil prices - Nigeria is a major exporter of oil. It borrowed heavily on the back of oil revenues. The 1980s and 1990s, with falling real oil prices, saw Nigeria getting into difficulties in financing its foreign debt and, in common with many other African countries, it struggled to grow at all. Indonesia, on the other hand, has grown relatively steadily throughout the period.

Table 102.2 *GDP at current prices and population*

	Nigeria		Indonesia	
	1965	1998	1965	1998
Population (millions)	60	121	103	204
GDP (US$ billions)	5.4	36.4	6	138.5
GNP per capita (US$ at market exchange rates)	90	300	58	680
GNP per capita (US$ at purchasing power parity rates)	-	820	-	2 790

1. Compare the change in growth and development of Nigeria and Indonesia over the period 1965 to 1998.
2. (a) Using evidence from the data, suggest what might have caused the difference in development rates between the two countries.
   (b) What other evidence would you need to understand fully the differences in development rates?
3. Discuss TWO policies which Nigeria could adopt to improve its growth and development.

Table 102.3 *Distribution and growth of production*

	Percentage of total GDP				Annual percentage growth					
	Nigeria		Indonesia		Nigeria			Indonesia		
	1965	1998	1965	1998	1965-80	1980-90	1990-98	1965-80	1980-90	1990-98
Agriculture	55	32	51	16	1.7	3.3	2.9	4.3	3.4	2.8
Industry	12	41	13	43	13.1	-1.1	1.2	11.9	6.9	9.9
of which Manufacturing	5	5	8	26	14.6	0.7	1.8	12.0	12.6	10.8
Services	33	27	36	41	5.9	3.7	3.6	7.3	7.0	7.2

Table 102.4 *Structure and growth of demand*

	Percentage of total GDP				Annual percentage growth					
	Nigeria		Indonesia		Nigeria			Indonesia		
	1965	1998	1965	1998	1965-80	1980-90	1990-97	1965-80	1980-90	1990-97
Private consumption	83	77	87	63	6.2	-2.6	-0.8	5.2	5.6	8.1
General government consumption	7	11	5	7	13.9	-3.5	-3.2	11.4	7.7	3.5
Gross domestic investment	15	20	8	31	14.7	-8.5	10.4	16.1	6.7	10.4
Gross domestic saving	10	12	8	31	-	-	-	-	-	-
Exports of goods and services	11	23	5	28	-	-	-	-	-	-

Table 102.5 *Social indicators*

	Nigeria		Indonesia	
	1965	1997	1965	1997
Life expectancy at birth males (years)	40	52	43	63
Total fertility rate[1]	6.9	5.3	5.5	2.8
Infant mortality rate[2]	162	77	128	47
Primary enrolment[3]				
% of age group	32	98	72	115
of which % of female age group	24	83	65	105
Population with access to safe water, % of total[4]	36	50	39	65

1. Number of children born per thousand women of child-bearing age.
2. Number of infants who die before reaching the age of 1 per thousand live births.
3. 1965 and 1996.
4. 1982 and 1995.

Table 102.6 *Total external debt, debt ratios and inflows*

	Nigeria		Indonesia	
	1970	1997	1970	1997
Total external debt $ million[1]	567	28 455	3 097	136 174
% of GNP[2]	10	72	28	62
Total debt service as a % of exports[2]	4.2	7.8	13.9	30.0
Net foreign direct investment, $ million	205	1 539	83	4 677

1. 1970 figures exclude short term debt
2. 1980 and 1997.

Source: adapted from World Bank, *World Development Report.*

Applied economics

Patterns of world trade

World trade is as unevenly distributed as world income. Not surprisingly, most world trade occurs between the rich developed countries of the world. Roughly three quarters of First World exports went to other First World countries in 1998. Developing countries trade mainly not with other developing countries but with the developed world. The rich industrialised nations provide the largest export markets for developing countries given that in 1998, First World countries produced 78 per cent of the world's total GNP.

Since the mid-1980s, trade of developing countries has been growing at a faster rate than that of developed countries, as Figure 103.1 shows. Trade has also grown at different rates in different parts of the developing world. Growth has been most rapid in East Asia and the Pacific which include the Tiger economies such as Taiwan and South Korea. There has been little growth in trade as a percentage of GDP in Sub-Saharan Africa, an indicator of the poor development record of that continent. The Middle East and North Africa has also had a mixed record due to political upheavals and dependence on oil exports.

Composition of world trade

Most world trade is trade in goods rather than services as Table 103.1 shows. Traditionally, developing countries have relied upon the exports of primary commodities to pay for the imports of manufactured goods and services. Even in 1983, 77 per cent of the exports of Sub-Saharan Africa were primary commodities for instance. By 1998, many developing countries had diversified considerably. Countries which before had been reliant on exports of primary commodities were exporting more low and medium technology goods, whilst more advanced developing countries were increasingly exporting high technology goods and services. In East Asia and the Pacific, exports of primary commodities fell from 42.7 per cent of total exports of goods and services in 1983 to 18.4 per cent in 1998. Figure 103.2 further illustrates this trend. Malaysia, for instance, which has seen very rapid GDP growth in the 1980s and 1990s, cut its reliance on commodity exports of goods from 53 per cent to 18 per cent whilst exports of high-technology goods increased from 31 per cent to 60 per cent of exports of goods. It is still true, though, that the poorest countries of the world are still reliant on primary commodities for more than half their export earnings.

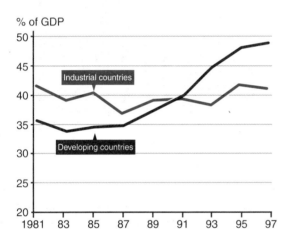

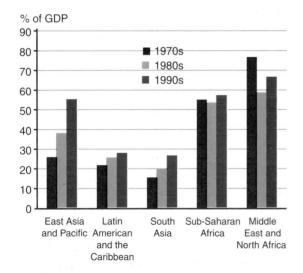

Figure 103.1 *Growth in trade[1] as a percentage of GDP*
Source: adapted from World Bank, *World Development Report*.
1. Exports plus imports.

Table 103.1 *Pattern of world trade in goods and commercial services*

	% of merchandise and commercial services exports					
	Primary commodities		Manufactures		Commercial services	
	1983	1998	1983	1998	1983	1998
World	28.3	16.9	54.9	63.5	16.9	19.7
High income countries	22.8	15.2	58.7	64.6	18.4	20.2
Middle income countries	51.8	29.0	36.0	51.5	12.2	19.5
Low income countries	51.6	21.6	37.4	64.9	11.0	13.4
of which						
Sub-Saharan Africa	77.0	na	10.5	na	12.5	13.3
East Asia and Pacific	42.7	18.4	46.3	65.1	11.0	16.5
South Asia	37.1	20.2	41.8	60.7	21.1	19.0
Middle East and North Africa	na	65.2	na	12.4	11.2	22.4
Latin America and Caribbean	65.7	43.0	21.9	43.0	12.4	14.0

Source: adapted from World Bank, *World Development Report*.

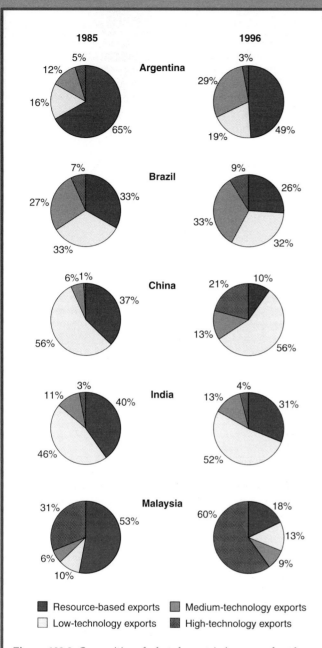

Figure 103.2 *Composition of selected countries' exports of goods*
Source: adapted from World Bank, *World Development Report*.

Commodity prices

Because many Third World countries are crucially dependent for their export earnings on commodities, the price which they receive for them has a considerable impact on GDP and standards of living within the country. Broad commodity price trends can be seen in Figure 103.4. Commodity prices fell during the 1960s but rose sharply in the first half of the 1970s. There was a second sharp increase in oil prices in the late 1970s. In general, however, commodity prices in real terms have tended to decline since the mid-1970s. The sharp rise in the price of oil in 1999-2000 shows that OPEC still has the power to influence the price of oil and maintain its real value. But other commodity exporters are less fortunate. By 1999, average real commodity prices had

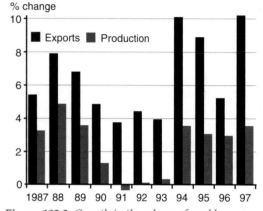

Question 1

Table 103.2 *Growth in the value of world exports by major product groups*

	Value ($bn) 1997	Annual average % change 1990-1997	% change 1995	% change 1996	% change 1997
World merchandise exports	5 300	7.0	19.5	4.5	3.0
Agricultural products	580	5.0	17.0	1.5	-1.0
Mining products	598	3.0	18.0	13.5	1.0
Manufactures	3 927	7.5	19.0	3.5	4.0
World exports of commercial services	1 310	8.0	15.0	6.5	3.0

Source: adapted from *Annual Report*, WTO.

Figure 103.3 *Growth in the volume of world merchandise trade and production*
Source: adapted from *Annual Report*, WTO.

(a) Describe the trends in world trade shown in the data and suggest reasons why these trends might be occurring.
(b) Assess whether these trends in trade are more likely to benefit a poor low income country such as Mozambique or Tanzania, or a middle income country such as Brazil or Thailand.

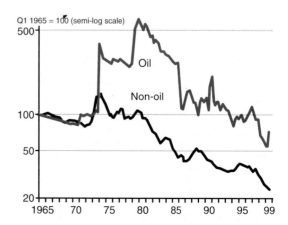

Figure 103.4 *Real commodity prices[1]*
1. Deflated using OECD CPi.
Source: adapted from Primark Datastream.

fallen to nearly 20 per cent of their 1965 values. This means that for every tonne of commodity exported in 1965 to the First World, Third World countries now have to export nearly 5 tonnes to buy the same amount. Not surprisingly, the sharp deterioration in the terms of trade has affected the balance of payments and economic growth rates of developing nations.

Individual commodity prices can fluctuate sharply. It is not unknown for prices to double or halve in the space of 12 months. This is because commodities are relatively inelastic in the short run. If there is a 25 per cent shortfall in this year's coffee crop, First World coffee manufacturers are prepared to pay much higher prices to secure supplies of coffee for their customers. Sharply fluctuating prices add more problems to poor Third World countries dependent upon one or two commodities for most of their export earnings. The only way out in the long term is for the country to develop and become less reliant on one industry.

One solution to the problem of fluctuating and yet also falling prices is for developing countries to form **cartels** to stabilize or raise prices. The oil producing cartel, OPEC has been successful to date in raising the real price of oil from its early 1970s price. However, other commodity cartels, such as those for coffee and tin, collapsed in the 1980s. The world's rubber cartel

collapsed in 1999 (☞ unit 65). As was explained in unit 21, cartels fail because:
- high prices encourage overproduction and cheating on the part of participant countries;
- it is difficult to persuade all producers to join the cartel;
- most commodity schemes (unlike OPEC) require the commodity to be produced and then stored if there is oversupply at the minimum price - a costly process;
- producers are encouraged to set too high a minimum price, which results in overproduction, and eventually the money to buy up surplus produce runs out.

Trade and development

A reliance on primary commodities for the main source of exports has proved to be disastrous for many developing countries. Not only have real prices fallen over the past 30 years, but there have been very sharp fluctuations in price of commodities. Third World countries therefore need to diversify.

During the 1930s, when the world economy was rocked by the Great Depression in the USA and Europe, many Third World countries, like most First World countries, opted for a policy of **protectionism**

Question 2

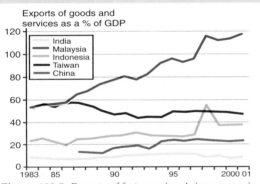

Figure 103.5 *Exports of fast growing Asian economies*
Source: adapted from Primark Datastream.

It has been forecast for some years that India will become one of the tiger economies of Asia. But it may have to do so without the help of the robust record in manufacturing exports which underpinned the rise of the tiger economies of East Asia in the 1980s. India has a long tradition of trade protection. With exports of only around 8 per cent of GDP, India is way behind Asian tigers such as Malaysia and Taiwan.

Some Indian economists argue that exports are not a prerequisite for high growth. China's initial surge of growth under Deng Xiaoping was based on rural reform rather than exporting, while Latin American countries were able to grow strongly during the 1970s without placing much emphasis on exports. But the more recent experience in Asia suggests that exports do play an important role. Both Indonesia and the Philippines lagged behind the other Asian tigers in terms of growth and they were both slow to develop an active manufactured export sector.

But the Indian economy is perhaps not best placed to expand manufactured exports. Its low literacy rate of only about 60 per cent makes it hard to find the skills to compete in manufacturing. Poor quality infrastructure and weak support services in areas such as banking hamper export efforts. At the same time, the country's industrialists have found it hard to shake off the import substitution mindset of the 1960s and 1970s. The country is also so large that many firms see no need to go outside India to expand their markets.

Perhaps India's immediate future lies instead in the export growth of services. This argument is based on the fact that India has a highly educated elite who still have low wage expectations. This gives India a distinct advantage in knowledge-based industries including not only software but also pharmaceuticals. Already, India has a strong world reputation in the software field. According to the National Task Force on IT, software exports could grow as large as $50 billion by 2008 from around $4 billion at present. At that level they would dwarf present exports of goods of only around $35 billion. This kind of growth coupled with some increase in manufactured exports means the economy could expand at an annual rate of 7 per cent in the medium term without putting a strain on the balance of payments.

Source: adapted from the *Financial Times*, 10.12.1999.

(a) Why might India's relatively low growth rate in the 1980s and 1990s compared to tiger economies be explained by low growth in exports?
(b) Discuss whether India, if it wishes to increase its growth rate, should promote manufactured exports rather than service exports or rely on its domestic markets for growth.

(☞ unit 40). It was argued that the best way to protect jobs and promote the growth of domestic industry was to keep foreign goods out. This then led many Third World countries to believe that their own development could best be promoted through a policy of **import substitution**, the deliberate attempt to replace imported goods with domestically produced goods by adopting protectionist measures.

Whilst import substitution policies might create jobs in the short run, as domestic producers replace foreign producers, economic theory would suggest that in the long run output and growth of output will be lower than it would otherwise have been. This is because import substitution denies the country the benefits to be gained from **specialisation**. The theory of comparative advantage (☞ unit 14) shows how countries will gain from trade. Moreover, protectionism leads to dynamic inefficiency. Domestic producers have no incentive from foreign competitors to reduce costs or improve products. Countries which have adopted import substitution strategies have tended to experience lower growth rates than other countries, particularly if they are small countries (the larger the country, the more opportunities there are for specialisation within the country).

The opposite strategy to import substitution is that of **export-led growth**. Rather than becoming less dependent upon world trade, it is argued that growth can be increased by becoming more dependent.

Removing trade barriers will force domestic industry either to close or to become as efficient as any world producer. Resources will be reallocated to those industries that produce goods in which the country has a comparative advantage in production. In a developing country, these are likely to be labour intensive, low technology industries. Countries wishing to diversify from exporting commodities can give short term selective assistance to their manufacturing industries. The newly industrialised nations of Brazil and Mexico, and particularly Hong Kong, South Korea and Singapore, have enjoyed above-average growth by adopting such a strategy.

First World protectionism

Export success for Third World countries has not always been easy. Third World countries in general have a comparative advantage in agriculture and low technology, labour intensive manufactured goods. There is no problem in making computer components in China since the computer industry is very young. However, many goods exported from the Third World find themselves in direct competition with goods made in long established industries in the First World. Not surprisingly, these industries respond by pressing their governments for **protection** against these cheaper imports. For instance, agriculture is highly protected in the First World. The EU even exports farm products to

Question 3

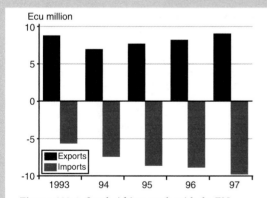

Figure 103.6 *South African trade with the EU*
Source: adapted from European Commission.

Last month, trade talks between the European Union (EU) and South Africa broke down. The two sides have been negotiating a wide ranging trade deal since 1995 which covered products such as steel, textiles, chemicals and cars. The South African negotiators blame the agricultural lobby for the failure. The EU, for the first time in a bilateral trade deal, had been prepared to offer trade concessions on agriculture. On the table was an offer which would allow 62 per cent of South Africa's agricultural exports to enter the EU duty free after ten years. This compares with the present situation where only 18 per cent come in duty free and the remaining 82

per cent are subject to tariffs. In return, South Africa has offered to increase the duty free percentage of its imports from the EU to 86 per cent, whilst lowering tariffs on other products including steel and cars to 15-20 per cent over a 12 year period.

To break the deadlock, the EU has offered to open special 'tariff-quotas' for a limited number of South African farm exports including dairy products, wines and cut flowers, which would allow South Africa to export a limited quantity of these goods to the EU duty free. South Africa wants the facility extended to canned fruit and fruit juices. One immediate cause of the deadlock has been the sudden insistence of the EU that the agreement cover what the South Africans had assumed were completely separate talks on wines, spirits and fisheries. The EU is demanding that South Africa stop describing fortified wine for export as 'port' and 'sherry'. EU officials made it clear that Spain and Portugal would not support any deal without such a concession. Wines and Spirits account for just 0.5 per cent of the EU's $10 billion worth of imports from South Africa.

Source: adapted from the *Financial Times*, 21.10.1998.

(a) Explain how consumers in South Africa and the EU might benefit from a trade deal.
(b) (i) Why might Spain and Portugal have intervened to veto the deal?
    (ii) To what extent would the collapse of the deal have benefited both South Africa and the EU?

the Third World, at hugely subsidiséd prices, completely going against the principle of comparative advantage. Textiles is another industry which has been fiercely protected by First World countries, though to a lesser extent than agriculture.

Despite this protectionism, the volume of trade between First and Third Worlds is growing. The experience of the Tiger economies of East Asia shows that there is a wide range of products which are relatively unprotected by First World countries.

Balance of payments problems

Third World countries are no different from First World countries in experiencing balance of payments problems. However, smaller Third World countries dependent upon exports of primary commodities are particularly vulnerable to sharp changes in their **current account** (☞ unit 30) position.

Assume there is a sharp fall in the price of the country's main commodity export. The country is then faced with a dilemma.

- It may predict that the change in price will be short lived and that the price will return to a long term trend price. It decides not to alter its policy position. If, however, the price remains depressed, the country will then be in serious difficulties. Import revenue will be exceeding export revenue. This will be financed either by borrowing from abroad, which increases the country's indebtedness, or by a run down of the country's foreign currency reserves. In the long term, it will need to replenish these. Either way, the country will have been living beyond its means. Harsh deflationary policies combined possibly with a devaluation of the currency will then be needed to bring the current account back into equilibrium (☞ unit 96). Economic growth and development will falter.
- It may decide that the price is the new long term price. It will then have to respond by cutting imports, through deflationary policies and/or a devaluation of the currency. But if prices bounce back, the country will have lost out on economic growth and will have made its citizens suffer unnecessarily.

The success of the Third World countries in exporting

manufactures, the majority of which go to the First World, has imposed its own difficulties on the balance of payments of First World countries. Increased imports and current account deficits have, in some cases, been blamed on 'unfair' competition from cheap labour Third World countries. This has led to calls for protection from workers and firms hit by these Third World imports. However, the Uruguay Round (☞ unit 40) has led to less protection rather than more protection, particularly in textiles and clothing. In the future, Third World countries will find it easier rather than harder to export manufactured products to the First World.

Tourism

Third World countries are increasing their exports of services over time. One example of a Third World service industry dependent upon the First World is tourism.

- Growth in tourism has been very high since 1970. This is not surprising since tourism has a relatively **high income elasticity of demand** (☞ unit 9).
- Travel receipts account for over a third of all invisible exports for Third World countries, a higher proportion than in the First World. Hence, developing countries are more dependent on the travel industry than First World countries.
- For the top 20 countries which specialise in tourism, the industry accounts for between 60 and 90 per cent of total service exports.

Tourism can be a valuable earner of foreign currency. It is labour intensive and is low technology and is therefore particularly suited to Third World economies. There are criticisms made of the impact of tourism on economic development. It can make local inhabitants feel inferior because they cannot afford the lifestyle on offer in the hotels to First World tourists. It can degrade local people by turning them into characters from a theme park. There may also be a negative impact on the local environment as, for instance, the local shore line is irreparably damaged by the building of hotels. However, on balance, countries which have become tourist destinations have strongly welcomed the opportunity to earn export earnings and diversify their economies.

Tourism

Nevis

These are anxious times for the tiny island of Nevis. The Four Seasons Resort, the island's leading hotel, is being closed because of damage by a hurricane last November. About 720 workers, one out of every five of the island's labour force, will have to find new jobs. Flights to Nevis have been affected, as have local suppliers of goods and services to the hotel. Tax revenues too will be hit since the Resort was the single largest contributor to hotel taxes. However, the island has little alternative but to stay reliant on tourism for its economic prosperity since there is little other economic activity which would generate significant revenues.

Sustainable development in the Caribbean

When approval was given in the late 1980s for the construction of a replica Carib village on the summits of the Pitons - two hills which are the most famous landmarks on the island of St Lucia - there was widespread protest. Llewellyn Xavier, then leader of the opposition and now Prime Minister, said: 'Tourism development should bring maximum benefit to the people who live in an area and not just the foreign firms who make a quick profit and destroy the environment in the process.' In fact, the interests of tourists and local people tend to coincide. If the Caribbean destroys its natural beauty and local resources through over-exploitation, tourists will become disillusioned and the tourist trade will go into decline.

How to protect the environment is a problem. The World Bank and the European Union in a recent report have outlined how increased tax revenues could be used to conserve the environment. The report proposes a new value added tax, an arrivals tax for cruise passengers, a room tax or departure tax and the design of a straight forward and moderate income tax for tourism businesses as well as the elimination of tax holidays for tourism investments. However, there is widespread opposition to these tax revenues going into the general pot of governments' tax revenues. For instance, Kelly Robinson, director of the Caribbean Alliance for Sustainable Tourism, argues that the funds need to kept separate and earmarked for 'the continued conservation and preservation of our natural resources'.

Higher taxes are opposed by the hotel trade. It argues that they will put up prices and discourage visitors from coming to the Caribbean. All governments are aware of the recent problem of Grenada. A World Bank Programme to build sanitary landfills on several islands was financed by the imposition of a US $1.50 environmental tax on all stayover and cruise visitors. In January 2000, Carnival Cruises announced that its ships would no longer be calling at Grenada. The company claimed that this was because of a change in its schedules. However, some governments feared that it reflected the shipping company's unhappiness at the imposition of the environment tax imposed by Grenada two years earlier.

Benefiting from tourism

In the Caribbean, there is a considerable difference between countries in the net income retained from every £1 spent by tourists. It ranges from 85 per cent in the Dominican Republic to an estimated 30 per cent in the Bahamas. Much of this has to do with the ability of the local economy to provide the goods and services which tourism needs.

At one extreme, tourists fly in on a foreign airline, stay in a resort complex which they are not encouraged to leave, eat food which has been imported and where all the key management staff are Europeans or Americans. At the other extreme, tourists stay in hotels staffed entirely by locals, are encouraged to eat out in local restaurants, go on many excursions or take part in activities such as boat trips provided by local firms and eat food which has been grown on the island.

Hotels and cruise companies say they would always prefer to source locally, all other things being equal. However, this can be frustrated by broken delivery schedules, inconsistent quality and uncompetitive prices.

Simon Suarey, President of the Dominican Republic's Tourism Promotion Council, said: 'We have benefited from very strong linkage between tourism and the economy. The linkages with agriculture and industry have had two main effects. Because of what it has done for local hotels, our furniture industry is now exporting to hotels in Cuba and in other Caribbean countries. The linkages have also allowed our tourism to have low operating costs, with the import content of tourism at about 15 to 20 percent, against about 60 per cent in some other countries and this will improve through several initiatives. For example, hoteliers in Play Dorado have constructed a refrigerated warehouse for supplies to hotels from local farmers.'

The Bahamas provides a contrast to this. About half of the islands' workforce is dependent on tourism. However, 'tourists spent an estimated $1.5 billion here last year, but about 70 cents of every tourist dollar turns around and goes back out. There is little agriculture and manufacturing which can gain from tourism', according to James Hepple, the Deputy Director General of Tourism for the Bahamas.

Port Royal

In 1692, a massive earthquake dragged Port Royal, a thriving city at the tip of a peninsula south of Kingston, the capital of Jamaica, into the sea. Four hundred years later, $260 million is to be spent recreating what was once a buccaneers' base. A cruise ship pier will be constructed in the village which is all that remains of Port Royal. This will coincide with the construction of restaurants, museums and shops for the 5 000 cruise ship visitors expected per week. Central to the project will be a park replicating Port Royal in the days of the buccaneers.

The Dominican Republic

Table 103.3 *Development indicators: Dominican Republic compared to lower middle income countries.*

		Dominican Republic	Lower middle income country average
GNP at PPP, per capita US$	1998	4 700	4 080
GDP, annual % growth	1980-90	3.1	2.6
	1990-98	5.5	-1.3
Exports of goods and services, annual % growth	1980-90	4.5	7.0
	1990-98	20.4	2.8
Agriculture, value added, annual % growth	1980-90	0.4	2.5
	1990-98	3.6	-2.2
Industry value added, annual % growth	1980-90	3.6	2.5
	1990-98	6.1	-2.8
Services value added, annual % growth	1980-90	3.5	7.0
	1990-98	5.6	2.8
Annual deforestation, average % change	1990-95	1.6	0.2
Adult illiteracy rate, % of people 15 and above	1997		
	males	17.0	18.0
	females	11.0	18.0
Under-5 mortality rate per thousand	1997	69.0	65.0

Source: adapted from World Bank, *World Development Report.*

The Dominican Republic today is the Caribbean's biggest holiday destination. Over the past 15 years, the island has recorded double digit growth in tourist arrivals and hotel capacity. The expansion in tourism last year contributed significantly to overall economic growth of 8.3 per cent.

Future growth will depend on the development of resorts in areas of the country which are not involved currently involved in tourism. However, the tourist sector requires better infrastructure, including expressways to allow transportation of products needed by the industry. Frank Rainieri, President of the Punta Cana Group, a hotel operator in the country, argues that 'parts of the country where tourism is important should get priority treatment. These regions have the capacity for generating hard currency, employment and social welfare within the country.'

Source: adapted from the *Financial Times* 3.4.2000

1. **Explain the contribution that tourism can make to raising a country's national income. Use examples from the data to illustrate your answer.**
2. **To what extent can expansion of the tourist industry increase the level of economic development in the Caribbean?**
3. **Discuss the potential problems for a country which becomes heavily reliant on tourism for its foreign exchange earnings.**

Applied economics

The colonial experience

From the 16th century onwards, European powers acquired colonial empires throughout most of what we call the Third World today, as well as in North America and Australasia. Colonies were acquired for a variety of reasons, but one major factor was economic gain. In the colonial model of the 19th century, European countries supplied capital to their colonies. They built roads, railways and factories, and invested in agriculture. So there were net **capital flows** to the Third World. However, these capital flows were more than outweighed by the repatriation of **interest, profits and dividends** from Third World colonies back to Europe. After all, there was little point in owning a colony if the colonial power had to pay for the privilege of ownership. Hence, colonial powers could be said to have **exploited** their colonies.

In this unit we will consider whether or not world capital flows continue to flow from Third World to First World countries and the impact of differing capital flows on developing countries.

Types of capital flow

There are four main types of capital flow between countries as shown in Figure 104.1.
- There are **short term bank loans**. These might, for instance, cover imports and exports of goods and services. A UK firm may buy tea from a Kenyan firm. The British firms would expect to receive credit from (i.e. borrow money from) the Kenyan firm in the short term once the tea had been delivered. Terms for payment might, for instance, be one month from delivery of tea. Alternatively, a Kenyan firm might want to import goods from the UK but the UK suppliers want payment before delivery. The Kenyan

company might organise a short term loan with a UK bank to cover the transaction.
- **Long term loans** are mainly long term bank loans. However, Third World countries and their enterprises also issue bonds, another form of long term loan. These loans are used for a variety of purposes. A Third World government may borrow money over ten years to finance the building of a power station for instance.
- **Aid** is the giving of money by First World countries to Third World countries, or is the granting of loans on concessionary terms. In Figure 104.1, aid is divided between ODA (Official Development Assistance) grants and other official flows. ODA grants are gifts of money. Other official flows are loans from First World governments to Third World governments, which may or may not be concessionary loans (i.e. be given at lower rates of interest than commercially available).
- **Foreign direct investment (FDI)** and **portfolio equity flows** are monies which flow from country to country and which are used to buy assets in the receiving country. For instance, Coca Cola may set up a plant in Nigeria to manufacture soft drinks. Money sent from the United States to Nigeria to finance this would be an example of foreign direct investment. The purchase by a US pension fund of shares in Chinese companies would be an example of portfolio equity flows (equities are another name for shares).

Figure 104.1 shows the relative sizes of these net flows (i.e. the difference between capital flowing into the Third World and capital flowing out) between 1975 and 1998. There has been a considerable change in the structure of these flows over the period. In the 1970s and early 1980s, long term loans were the major component of total net capital flows. This led directly to the debt crisis of the 1980s discussed below. From 1983,

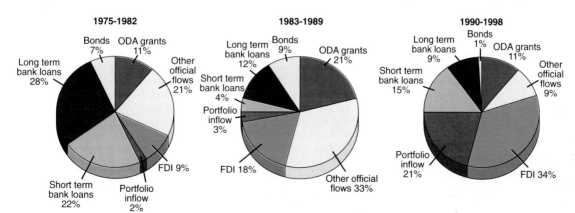

Figure 104.1 *Developing countries: net capital inflow by type of flow 1975-1998, (percentage of aggregate net inflow)*
Source: adapted from *Trade and Development Report 1999*, UNCTAD.

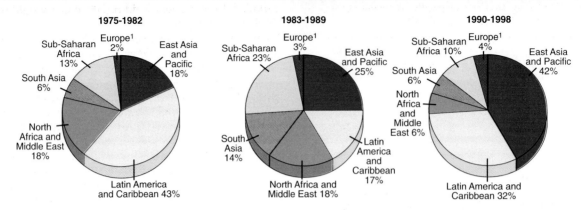

Figure 104.2 *Developing countries: net capital inflow by region, 1975-1998, (percentage of aggregate net inflow)*
Source: adapted from *Trade and Development Report 1999*, UNCTAD.
1. Europe comprises Malta and Turkey only.

foreign aid has assumed a greater role. The 1990s was the decade of foreign direct investment and portfolio investment.

Within the total, there are significant differences between regions, as shown in Figure 104.2. In the 1970s, Latin America received nearly half of all net capital inflows to developing countries. Most of this was in the form of long term loans (either bank loans or bonds). This led directly to the financial crisis of 1982 when Mexico announced that it could no longer afford to pay all its interest payments on government loans. Many countries had, in fact, overborrowed and after 1982 commercial loans from the First World to the Third World fell to a trickle. With private capital transfers much reduced, foreign aid came to account for over half of all transfers in the 1980s. Sub-Saharan Africa, one of the world's poorest regions, was particularly badly affected by the debt crisis and between 1983 and 1989 accounted for nearly one quarter of all net capital transfers as First World governments extended assistance to the region. In the 1990s, with the worst effects of the debt crisis over, private capital flows rapidly increased. This time, the main beneficiaries were East Asian and Pacific countries such as China, South Korea, Taiwan and Malaysia. Latin America, too, benefited with one third of all transfers going to the continent. This helped stimulate

an economic revival in Latin American countries.

Figures 104.3 (a), (b) and (c) give measures of the size of capital inflows to the developing world. Figure 104.3 (a) shows that aggregate net flows in constant US dollars have increased over time. However, the sharp fall in flows following the 1982 Mexican crisis can clearly be seen. In US dollar terms, the size of flows did not return to their 1982 values till the early 1990s. As a percentage of GNP, net capital inflows for much of the 1970s and 1990s were in the 4 to 6 per cent range. Again the effect of the 1982 Mexican crisis can be seen in Figure 104.3 (b), with inflows falling to 3 per cent for most of the 1980s. Figure 104.3 (c) shows the distribution of borrowing between the public and private sectors. Peaks in borrowing occurred in the 1970s and 1990s, with the Mexican crisis causing a slump in the 1980s. However, whereas most borrowing in the 1970s was by governments, by the 1990s the private sector was borrowing as much as government.

Figure 104.3 (b) also shows net transfers. This is net capital inflows minus net interest and profit payments which are made on loans and shares and other asset holdings. Table 104.1 gives a more precise breakdown of this. In the 1970s and 1990s, the Third World was having to repay net around half of the money that it was attracting in capital flows. In the 1980s, however, net

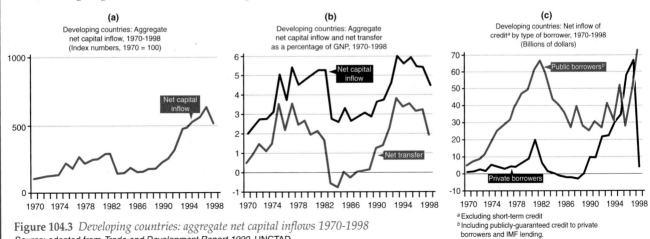

Figure 104.3 *Developing countries: aggregate net capital inflows 1970-1998*
Source: adapted from *Trade and Development Report 1999*, UNCTAD.

Table 104.1 *Developing countries: aggregate net capital inflow and net transfer, 1975-98, (percentage of GNP)*

	1975-82	1983-1989	1990-98
Total net capital inflow	4.91	2.87	5.00
less interest payments	1.49	2.58	1.79
less profit remittances	0.93	0.54	0.56
Net transfer	2.48	-0.26	2.65

Source: adapted from *Trade and Development Report 1999*, UNCTAD.

capital flows halved as a percentage of GNP of developing countries. Interest payments on loans, nearly doubled though. The result was that for much of the 1980s, the poorer developing countries of the world were sending more back to the richer developed world than they were receiving.

The justification for foreign aid

Following the devastation of the Second World War, the Americans gave Marshall Aid to Europe to help in reconstruction. This became a model for later economic development for the Third World. The argument was persuasive.

● The citizens of Third World countries, because they were so poor, would have a very high propensity to consume and a very low propensity to save. Hence, savings would be likely to be below the level of investment needed to generate high economic growth in the economy. Inflows of foreign capital, for instance

supplied through foreign aid programmes, would help fill this **savings gap**.

● Foreign exchange would be extremely scarce. Export revenues would be limited and would be likely to be insufficient to cover imports of machinery and other capital equipment as well as imports of essential raw materials. Foreign aid would help cover this **trade gap**.

● Foreign aid reflects only part of capital flows from the First World to the Third World. However, it can be directed at those countries which are in most need of development assistance. These countries may be very poor or they may find it difficult to attract private capital funding. On the other hand they may be going through temporary difficulties and therefore need assistance at a point in time.

Types of foreign aid

Foreign aid can take a variety of forms.

Grants The most generous form of aid is a grant. A donor country might, for instance, give a sum of money to a Third World country for a development project, it might offer free technical expertise, or it might offer free university education for foreign students in the donor country.

Loans Aid might take the form of a loan. The loan might be at commercial rates of interest, in which case the donor country is giving little if anything to the Third World borrower. Alternatively, the loan might be a **soft loan**, a loan which carries a lower rate of interest than the

Question 1

Table 104.2 *Requirements for poverty reduction in Africa*

	North	West	Central	East	Southern	Sub-Saharan countries	Total average
Number of countries	7	15	7	13	11	46	53
Required GDP growth rate (%)	5.60	7.61	6.70	8.12	6.20	7.16	6.79
Incremental capital output ratio	3.8	4.8	7.3	5.6	6.1	5.8	5.0
Domestic savings rate (%) of GDP	15.9	7.8	15.0	7.7	19.6	14.2	14.9
Required investment /GDP rate (%)	21.3	36.5	48.9	45.5	37.8	40.4	33.0
Required external finance (% of GDP)	5.4	28.7	33.9	37.8	18.2	26.2	18.1
Current ODA[1] flows (% of GDP)	3.8	13.5[2]	7.3	15.6	11.8[3]	12.3	8.9
Residual finance (% of GDP)	1.6	15.2	26.6	22.2	6.4	13.9	9.2

[1]Official develpment assistanc [2]Excluding Nigeria [3]Excluding South Africa
Source: UN, Economic Commission for Africa

International goals to cut African poverty in half by 2015 are unlikely to be achieved, the UN's Economic Commission for Africa (ECA) has warned. According to the organisation, Sub-Saharan Africa faces a financing gap of almost 14 per cent of gross domestic product to achieve annual growth of 7 per cent, the level it estimates is necessary to achieved the poverty reduction target. 'The central message is a simple one' said the ECA. 'Most of the countries of the continent lack the fundamentals for sustained future growth.'

Source: adapted from the *Financial Times*, 10.5.1999.

(a) Which group of countries needs to achieve the highest growth rates to eliminate poverty by 2015 according to the data?

(b) (i) Will domestic saving rates be sufficient to finance the investment needed to achieve this target? Justify your answer from the data.
   (ii) Which countries will then require the highest level of external finance?

(c) (i) What is meant by 'residual finance' in Table 104.2?
   (ii) What sources of finance might be available to African countries to cover this residual?

commercial rate of interest.

Tied aid Grants or loans might only be available if the recipient country was prepared to purchase goods and services with the money from the donor country. For instance, during the 1980s the UK government devoted some of its aid budget to backing British exports. UK loan aid was available if a Third World country awarded a contract to a British company.

Bilateral and multilateral aid Bilateral aid is given directly from one country to another. A UK loan to Kenya would be an example. Multilateral aid describes the situation when donor countries give money to an international agency, such as UNICEF (the United National Children's Fund), and the agency then disperses the aid. The most important multilateral aid agency is the International Bank for Reconstruction and Development (IBRD), more commonly known as the World Bank. Most bilateral aid is tied in one form or another whilst multilateral aid is generally not tied.

An evaluation of foreign aid

Foreign aid has undoubtedly helped millions in the Third World achieve a better standard of living. However, foreign aid has been increasingly criticised by those in both the First World and in the Third World.

- It is implicitly assumed in the economic argument presented above that Third World governments desire to maximise the economic welfare of their citizens. However, this is not the case in most Third World countries. Governments serve the interests of a narrow range of groups in society, often better-off urban dwellers. Foreign aid monies can be diverted into serving the needs of these groups rather than achieving genuine economic development, particularly for the poor in the Third World.
- 'Fashions' in foreign aid projects change over time. In the 1950s, large scale projects, such as dams and steel mills, were seen as important in economic development. Many of these projects failed to yield a sufficiently high rate of return. Many large scale manufacturing plant projects failed because of lack of infrastructure and lack of skilled workers and management. In the 1990s, aid to help large numbers of small scale enterprises, particularly in rural areas, was fashionable. Equally, aid projects increasingly had to pass an environmental audit to prevent large scale ecological disasters which occurred on some previous aid projects. The question that arises is whether Western aid agencies, even now, know what are the best strategies for development.
- Foreign aid which takes the form of subsidised food or consumer goods is likely to be positively harmful to long term Third World development. Food aid in a famine situation can be helpful. However, long term food aid, by increasing the supply of food on the local market, depresses local prices and therefore discourages local production of food. This increases

the dependence of the country on imported food, uses up scarce foreign exchange and results in lower living standards for farmers.
- Tied foreign aid, especially in the form of loans, may result in Third World countries getting a worse 'buy' than if they shopped around internationally for the cheapest product.
- Loans need to be repaid with interest. The repayment of loans has resulted in enormous problems for Third World countries, and it is to this issue that we will now turn.

The Third World debt crisis

Aid has not been the only source of financial capital for Third World countries. They have been free to borrow from banks and on First World money markets. In the 1960s and early 1970s, developing countries used commercial sources of finance to some extent. However, the first oil crisis of 1973-74 proved ruinous for most Third World countries.

Non-oil producing countries were faced with sharply increased bills for imports of oil. An easy way to solve the problem in the short run was to borrow the money to finance increased oil prices.

Oil producing countries, on the other hand, were faced with a sudden inflow of foreign currency. In the very short term, there was no way they could spend this money. In the longer term, countries such as Mexico and Nigeria used the extra revenues to finance investment projects. Others, such as Saudi Arabia and Kuwait, tended to be net exporters of capital, building up financial assets in the developed world.

In 1974 and subsequent years, large numbers of petro-dollars (dollars used to pay for oil) were deposited by oil producing countries in Western banks. The banks needed to lend these out again if they were to make a profit. First World countries responded to the first oil crisis by deflating their economies, with the aim of squeezing inflation and reducing balance of payments deficits. They didn't want to borrow the money. So banks turned to the Third World. Countries are good risks, it was argued, because governments cannot go bankrupt. Loans to Third World countries were marketed aggressively by the banks in the second half of the 1970s.

The 1980s proved disastrous both for Third World countries and for banks. In 1980, Ronald Reagan was elected President of the United States. Quickly, he cut taxes whilst leaving government spending totals unchanged. The result was a huge increase in the US government budget deficit. To finance the deficit, the government had to issue enormous amounts of new government stock, which sent US interest rates soaring. Sharply increased interest rates then increased the value of the dollar, as foreign investors demanded dollars to invest in the US. This hit Third World countries hard:
- increased interest rates meant that repayments on their debt increased sharply;
- the increased value of the dollar meant that they had to sell far more exports to pay back $1 worth of debt;

- developed countries went into a severe recession; this hit exports from Third World countries in the short term; more seriously, it began the long term decline in commodity prices discussed in unit 103, which hit export revenues hard.

In 1982, Mexico precipitated the Third World debt crisis by **defaulting** (i.e. not paying) on part of its loans. Immediately, First World banks and other lenders stopped lending to countries which they believed would follow Mexico's example. The severity of the **debt crisis** can be measured in a number of ways.

Net capital flows As Figure 104.3(c) shows, net private lending to Third World countries collapsed from 1982 and some countries even became net repayers of debt. Between 1977 and 1982, borrowing, mainly by African governments, averaged approximately $13 for each African citizen. Given that average incomes were only approximately $200, this was a sizeable amount. By the 1990s, African countries were repaying on average $5 a year when average incomes were approximately $300.

Net transfers Net capital flows do not include repayments of interest on loans. If these are taken into account, the Third World became a net transferee of money to the First World for much of the 1980s as Table 104.1 shows. What this meant was that the poor in the Third World were sending part of their income to the rich in the First World. Only in the 1990s did the transfer of resources from Third to First World again become favourable to the Third World.

Total Third World debt Third World debt, shown in Table 104.3, increased 25 times between 1973 and 1998. Particularly affected in the short term by the debt crisis were Latin American countries, but in the longer term, it has been Africa which has been hardest hit.

Debt-export ratio The ratio of debt to exports is important because, to repay debt, a country has to earn foreign currency (unless of course it takes out new loans to repay the old ones). Exports are the equivalent of wages for a household that has borrowed a large sum to buy a house.

The value of total debt to exports rose sharply in the 1980s. Partly this was because many Third World

Table 104.3 *External debt of developing countries*

	$bns
1973	97
1982	662
1986	1 032
1990	1 289
1995	1 826
1998	2 465
of which 1997/98	
Africa	311
Asia	936
Latin America	736

Source: adapted from United Nations, *World Economic Outlook, World Economic and Social Survey.*

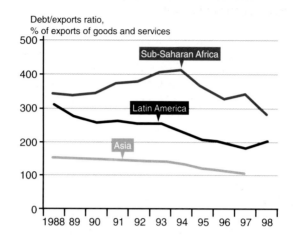

Debt/exports ratio, % of exports of goods and services

Figure 104.4 *Developing countries: debt to export ratio*
Source: adapted from United Nations, *World Economic Outlook; World Economic and Social Survey.*

countries were borrowing to finance the interest payments on their loans. They were becoming more indebted despite not receiving any loan money to spend on development. However, some Third World countries were also keeping up with repayments on debt, reducing debt or able to afford to take on more loans. The value of their exports also increased. The debt crisis was at its worst in the late 1980s when the ratio of debt to exports reached a maximum. In the 1990s, as shown in Figure 104.4, the ratio fell and by 1997 was nearly half its 1988 world value. Sub-Saharan Africa at times, however, was carrying nearly four times as much debt to exports as Asia. This was proving a heavy burden on its development efforts.

Debt-GDP ratio Table 104.4 gives another measure of indebtedness. It shows the proportion of debt to GDP. The picture is very similar to Figure 104.4, with African countries most indebted and Asian least indebted. For the Third World as a whole, the debt to GDP ratio peaked in the late 1980s and by 1998 had fallen to 37.3 per cent.

Table 104.4 *Developing countries: ratio of external debt to GDP*

%

	1973	1977	1980	1988	1993	1997	1998
Developing countries	13.7	24.9	25.7	45.5	41.1	36.9	37.3
of which							
Africa	-	31.4	26.9	73.5	72.8	63.2	-
Asia	-	17.2	16.7	31.4	35.0	34.2	-
Latin America and Caribbean	-	29.0	32.2	55.6	40.5	34.0	36.9

Source: United Nations, *World Economic Outlook, World Economic and Social Survey.*

Debt-service to export ratio Figure 104.5 shows the percentage of exports which have been used to repay debt plus interest. The problems facing Latin America in the 1980s can be seen from the graph. The continent had the highest ratio of debt-service to exports of all the regions and in 1998, it was twice the average for developing countries. At the start of the debt crisis in 1982, Latin American countries were paying half their export earnings to repay debt and interest. This is the equivalent of a household paying half its income in mortgage repayments. Sub-Saharan Africa had a much lower debt-service to export ratio. Even so, levels of around 20 per cent have been crippling to a group of countries which include some of the poorest in the world. Asia, in contrast, has in the 1990s, reduced its debt-service to exports ratio mainly by growing its way out of the problem. Debt service has increased as Asian countries have borrowed. However, exports have grown even faster, allowing the continent to reduce its debt-service to export ratio from 21.6 per cent in 1988 to 13.0 per cent in 1997.

There is a strong parallel between the Third World debt crisis and the mortgage crisis of the early 1990s in the UK. In the late 1980s, many UK households borrowed heavily to buy a house. In the early 1990s, many of those lost their jobs or saw their incomes fall in the recession which followed the Lawson boom. The result was that they failed to keep up repayments on the mortgage. The repayments not made plus continued interest were then added to the size of the original mortgage, so the amount borrowed kept on increasing, making it even more difficult for homeowners to meet the monthly repayment. Homeowners on relatively low incomes who bought at inflated prices in the late 1980s and then lost their jobs were the equivalent of many of the African countries in the 1970s and 1980s. Higher income earners, who borrowed less heavily as a proportion of their income, and who kept on getting pay increases during the 1990-1992 recession, were the equivalent of most of the Asian countries during the period.

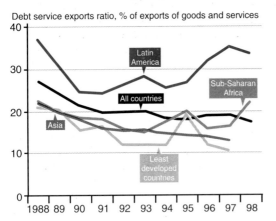

Debt service exports ratio, % of exports of goods and services

Figure 104.5 *Developing countries: debt-service to export ratio*
Source: adapted from United Nations, *World Economic Outlook; World Economic and Social Survey.*

The Asian Crisis of 1997-98

The Mexican default of 1982 was caused by a failure of the Mexican government to repay debts on time. A similar problem occurred at the end of 1997 when it

became apparent that Thailand would be unable to repay all its debts. Western banks responded in exactly the same way as in 1982. They became extremely reluctant to offer new loans to Thai borrowers. They also cut off new loan support from other Asian countries which they now thought might have overborrowed. These countries included South Korea, Indonesia and Malaysia. The crisis spread in late 1998 to Latin America when Brazil came under attack from financial speculators when one of its provincial governments announced that it might not longer be able to make full repayments on debts owed to Brazil's central government. Like the debt crisis of 1982, the Asian crisis was partly caused by countries overborrowing, but it was also caused by Western banks being far too optimistic about the ability of these countries to repay debt. The assumption was that because these countries were very fast growing 'Tiger' economies, they could sustain much higher levels of debt than would be prudent in developed countries.

The result of the crisis was a credit crunch. Without new loans, a number of key firms, including banks, property companies and manufacturers, found that they did not have the cash to continue trading. Others had to be temporarily bailed out by government. Real spending fell sharply by up to 20 per cent. However, Asian countries staged a strong recovery in 1999 and 2000. For the most part, they took quick and strong action to restore the financial health of their economies. They were also helped by large loan packages organised by the International Monetary Fund (IMF) which helped restore the confidence of Western commercial banks to continue lending to these countries. In Latin America, economies were in much better shape than they were in 1982 and again the crisis passed relatively quickly.

The Asian crisis showed, however, that countries and firms can easily overborrow. Loans to Third World countries on the one hand are an important source of finance for development. On the other hand, they can lead to financial ruin and many of the poorest countries of the world are still recovering from the debt crisis which started at the beginning of the 1980s.

Solving the debt crisis

The debt crisis of the 1980s has been resolved for many countries in a number of ways.

Growing out of the problem Many countries have grown out of the problem. This is like the homeowner who gets into difficulties with a mortgage. If the mortgage repayments are £500 a month and the household income is £600, then the debt is too great. If, however, one of the wage earners gets promotion and pushes up the household income to £1 000, then the mortgage is manageable. Asian countries, for instance, have on the whole seen their GDP and exports rise at a fast enough rate for them to be able to service existing debts and indeed take on new debt.

Debt forgiveness A second solution has been debt

forgiveness. Most Third World debt is owed to three main groups: First World governments which have lent money to the Third World as part of their aid programmes; First World banks; multilateral agencies, such as the IBRD, (the International Bank for Reconstruction and Development or World Bank) and the IMF (International Monetary Fund). The poorest Third World countries have argued that all three groups should wipe out much if not all of their debt. They argue, correctly, that if their debts were forgiven, they could afford to buy more imports (remember, unless they secure new capital from abroad, debt repayments plus interest have to come from the money earned from exports). If they bought more imports, then they could raise their standard of living now by buying more consumption goods from abroad; or they could increase their growth rate by importing more investment goods such as machinery.

First World governments have, on the whole, been very reluctant to forgive debts. The United States in particular has argued that to forgive debts now would only encourage Third World countries to borrow more money and then plead with the lenders to forgive the debts again. Third World countries tend to owe money to a variety of governments. If the USA refuses to forgive debt to a Third World country, perhaps not surprisingly other governments which are also owed debt by that country become very reluctant to forgive their portion of the debt. However, European countries in particular have forgiven some debt to Highly Indebted Poor Countries (HIPCs), most of which are in Africa. For instance, in 1999 and 2000 the UK, France and Spain announced they would be writing off billions of dollars of debt to selected HIPCs following a strong campaign by a group of lobbying groups centred round Jubilee 2000. The campaign message was that the year 2000 should be a turning point for HIPCs marked by a forgiveness of their debts. Debt forgiveness has only been very recent, however. For the most part, when countries have had difficulties in repaying debt, they have tended to **reschedule** their debts. This means taking out further loans to make existing loan repayments. In negotiations about rescheduling, lenders try to increase the amount that a country is currently repaying, even if the repayments are nowhere near enough to cover the full amount needed. After all, some money is better than nothing. Borrowers try to negotiate loans, write downs or lower interest payments.

Structural adjustment International agencies, such as the IMF and the World Bank, have also forgiven debt, but have imposed strict conditions on the forgiveness. The IMF and the World Bank have different roles. The World Bank was set up after the Second World War to provide aid to war torn Europe (hence the 'reconstruction' part of the Bank's full IBRD title). Its main work since then has been to provide loans to Third World countries for development, and more recently to Eastern European countries to aid reconstruction. The World Bank is able to make loans because First World countries have agreed to deposit money with the Bank. It also can make new loans with money which is coming in from repayment of existing loans.

The IMF is not a body which is mainly interested in development. Its role is to help maintain a stable economic international trading environment, particularly by maintaining a stable system of exchange rates. Exchange rates come under pressure when a country's balance of payments gets into the red. So it has funds to lend to countries which get into balance of payments difficulties to help them on a short term basis whilst the country sorts out its difficulties. The debt crisis threatened to destabilise the world trading system and it concerned the balance of payments. Hence, the IMF has been heavily involved in trying to sort out the problem.

When countries have sought debt forgiveness from individual First World countries or from multi-lateral aid agencies like the World Bank, a condition of granting forgiveness has usually been that the country must submit to an IMF **structural adjustment programme**. The

Question 2

Many countries and international institutions such as the IMF have long recognised that debt can cripple an economy and have adopted a variety of strategies to relieve debt. In 1996, the IMF announced a new debt relief package aimed at HIPCs (Highly Indebted Poor Countries). If an individual country had conformed to an IMF structural programme for a number of years, it would qualify for debt relief under the HIPC initiative. Uganda was the only country which immediately qualified. However, the HIPC initiative relied on First World donor countries paying funds into the IMF. There were also disputes between donors about which countries should qualify. Uganda began to receive help in 1998, a year later than promised, followed shortly by Bolivia. By 2000, another four countries seemed on the point of receiving help, with another six likely to be eligible shortly afterwards.

Even if countries receive help, they will not necessarily gain much. Uganda, for instance, found that the twelve month delay in receiving aid was very costly. The debt relief was calculated according to export earnings. A large increase in coffee exports in 1997 cut the benefit received by Uganda from $238 million a year, if it had had its application processed on time in 1997, to an actual $30 million a year in 1998. What's more, Uganda had been receiving $40 million a year in grants for debt relief, which stopped when its HIPC relief was given. $10 million a year worse off, the IMF agreed to front load the HIPC relief to a little over $40 million. So the HIPC scheme has given little benefit to one of the poorest countries of the world, which is still paying $120 million a year in debt payments.

Source: adapted from *The Guardian*, 14.6.1999 and the *Financial Times*, 5.4.2000

(a) Why might poor countries need debt relief?
(b) Illustrate the problems that poor countries face in obtaining debt relief.

Reducing food subsidies as part of a structural adjustment programme can increase prices in Third World countries.

IMF is brought in to devise a plan for recovery for the individual Third World country. The main elements of the plan are simple.

- The IMF agrees to lend the country's central bank money to replenish its foreign currency reserves. This then allows the country to carry on importing and exporting.
- The country must increase its exports or reduce its imports to obtain the foreign currency to repay debt. Increased exports are typically achieved by a sharp devaluation of the currency. This also makes imports more expensive, hence cutting them. Foreign investment into the country must also be encouraged, for instance by dismantling curbs on the foreign ownership of firms in the economy.
- The government must increase taxes and cut its spending. This is because the debt is usually owed by the government rather than by individuals or firms. Typically, the government funds its debt by printing money, creating inflation and also, in the process, making its exports less competitive in the absence of a corresponding fall in the exchange rate. By increasing taxes and cutting spending, the government will create the resources needed to fund the debt. Of course, the effect of this is to force its citizens to contribute to paying the debt.
- The IMF also insists on a wide package of measures to promote efficiency in the economy. Examples are removing import controls, making the exchange rate fully convertible, privatisation, cutting of subsidies such as food subsidies and deregulation of markets. In the 1980s and 1990s, the IMF has strongly believed that economic growth can only be achieved through a thorough **supply-side** reform (☞ unit 38) of the economy.

Structural adjustment programmes are very unpopular in the Third World. This is hardly surprising since the aim is to increase the country's resources being used to repay debt and reduce those available for domestic consumption and investment. Countries subject to structural adjustment programmes tend to see their growth rate fall immediately, and many experience falls in GDP. Growth rates can then remain low or negative for

some time. The IMF usually blames this on a failure to implement the programme fully. The individual country blames the IMF for imposing the wrong policies.

Structural adjustment programmes also hit **economic development** (☞ unit 100) very hard. Reducing food subsidies, for instance, increases the price of food. Cutting government spending in general tends to deflate the economy, raising unemployment. Anti-inflation policies which seek to curb wage increases tend to result in falling real wages. All of these help create conditions where the poor eat less, increasing health problems and even leading to malnutrition. Cuts in government spending are also likely to hit education. Without investment in education today, long term growth rates are likely to be reduced. For this reason, programmes have increasingly included new loans from the World Bank designed to allow governments to maintain key health and education programmes.

Opinion is sharply divided about structural adjustment programmes. Critics point out that high economic growth is by far the best way for a country to deal with its debt problem. Structural adjustment programmes, however, in the short term reduce economic growth rates and in the process lead to negative economic development. Advocates say that the alternative of doing nothing would lead to an even worse situation. Past individual structural programmes have made mistakes in not recognising the severity of the downturn in the economy that can be the result of its implementation. Programmes in the 1980s also often coincided with sharp negative shocks for the country, such as dramatic falls in the price of a commodity which was the country's main export earner. The solution is to increase the amount of selective assistance to the country. However, the programme itself will leave the country in a state in which it has the potential to grow in the future.

Direct foreign investment and portfolio capital flows

The debt crisis was caused by large flows of borrowed funds in the 1970s and an inability to repay the borrowings in the 1980s. However, throughout the 1970s, 1980s and 1990s, there was a build up of a very different type of capital flow: investment capital. Table 104.5 shows that direct foreign investment and portfolio capital inflows rose from 8.5 per cent (0.42/4.91) of total net

Table 104.5 *Developing countries: aggregate net capital inflow by type of flow, 1975-98, % of GNP*

	1975-82	1983-1989	1990-98
Official aid flows	1.58	1.57	1.03
Bank and bond loans	2.57	0.49	1.69
Foreign direct investment	0.42	0.53	1.67
Portfolio equity	0.00	0.02	0.54
Total net capital inflow	4.91	2.87	5.00

Source: adapted from United Nations, *World Economic Outlook*; *World Economic and Social Survey*.

A Nestlé factory being built in Nigeria. Investment by multinationals can benefit Third World countries.

inflows as a percentage of GNP in 1975-82, to 19.2 per cent ([0.53+0.02]/2.87) between 1983-89 to 44.2 ([1.67+0.54]/5.0) per cent between 1990 and 1998.

Foreign direct investment (FDI) is the investment by First World companies in Third World countries. Ford setting up a car manufacturing plant in China would be an example. Most FDI, though, is the purchase of existing assets in the Third World by a First World company. For instance, Ford buying a local Chinese car manufacturing company would be FDI. Any purchase of more than 10 per cent of the shares of a Third World company would be classified as FDI. In contrast, portfolio investment includes the purchase of shares in Third World companies of less than 10 per cent of the total. For instance, many First World savers have bought shares in unit trusts or their equivalent which specialise in investing in Third World country shares.

Investment capital is radically different from loan capital.

- A loan has to be repaid even if the investment which is made with the loan is not successful. A Third World government borrowing money to build a power station has to repay the loan whether the power station is built or not. However, if the power station is built and owned by a First World company, then the First World company takes on the risk of failure. If it fails, the Third World country does not owe any money to the First World.

- Investment capital involves the transfer of some sort of knowledge from the First World to the Third World. If it is direct investment, then the Third World company will almost invariably import some machinery and equipment from the First World. But it will also combine that with locally produced investment capital such as buildings. It will train staff. It will create a climate which ensures commercial success. This has large positive spin-offs for the country. Extra goods for domestic consumption and for export will be produced, increasing GDP. Local workers will be able to absorb First World production techniques, leading probably to the establishment of local competing firms. The First World company will also need suppliers in the local economy. There is therefore a **multiplier effect** on investment and output.

- To counterbalance this, the country will lose some of its sovereignty. It will become dependent to some extent

on the activities of foreign firms. However, this is no different from individual countries in the First World. It will also have to allow the repatriation of profits - the equivalent of debt interest. Table 104.6 shows the relationship between profit remittances and FDI and portfolio net capital inflows as a percentage of GDP. In the 1970s, profit remittances where higher than net investment. First World countries were therefore earning more from existing investments in the Third World than they were putting back in the form of new net investment. In contrast, by the 1990s, First World investors were making £4 of new net investments for every £1 they were repatriating in profit payments. Profit rates on capital are typically lower than interest rates on borrowed funds and so FDI investments are a relatively cheap way of acquiring investment capital. What is more, if the investment is relatively unsuccessful, there will be no profit to be repatriated to the First World. The First World firm may also 'exploit' the local economy by setting itself lower safety standards or working its labour force longer hours for lower pay than similar operations in First World countries. However, it should be remembered that one of the main reasons why First World firms are attracted to set up in Third World countries is because of lower costs of production.

FDI flows, though, are unevenly spread geographically. Figure 104.6 shows that two regions, Latin America and East Asia, have accounted for over three quarters of all FDI flows since 1975. In 1975-82, the majority of flows went to Latin America. By the 1990s, this had changed to East Asia. In contrast, the proportion going to poor Sub-

Table 104.6 *Developing countries: aggregate net capital inflow and profit remittances, 1975-1998, % of GNP*

	1975-82	1983-1989	1990-98
Total net capital inflow	4.91	2.87	5.00
Foreign direct investment	0.42	0.53	1.67
Portfolio equity	0.00	0.02	0.54
Total	0.42	0.55	2.21
Profit remittances	0.93	0.54	0.56

Source: adapted from United Nations, *World Economic Outlook*; *World Economic and Social Survey*.

Saharan Africa has fallen. In practice, FDI funds are attracted to high growth regions of the world because this is where it is most likely that share capital will earn a high profit. FDI flows then reinforce existing high growth rates by providing extra funds for investment.

In the 1960s and 1970s, FDI was often viewed with suspicion by Third World countries because they saw it as part of the way in which First World countries could continue to exploit them. By the 1990s, it was obvious that FDI flows could be of enormous benefit to Third World countries. The challenge in the future for many of the world's poorest countries is how to tap into this source of capital.

The activities of multinationals investing directly in Third World countries differ from those of foreign investors buying shares in Third World firms. As with direct investment, the great advantage of this type of investment is that the risk of failure is transferred from the Third World to the First World. Moreover, First World investors may be a little better at picking investment projects that will be successful than, say Third World governments. There will be a loss of sovereignty and profits will have to flow back to the First World. However, most are agreed that the benefits to the Third World far outweigh the disadvantages. The challenge for the rest of this decade is for more investment capital to be attracted to the poorer countries of the world and particularly Africa. Investment capital could be one way in which Africa could escape from its recent history of low or even negative growth.

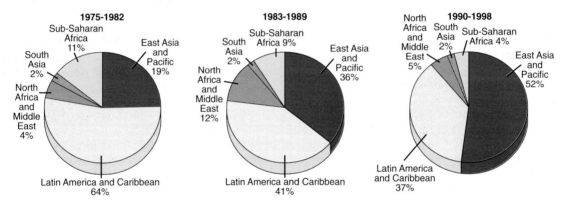

Figure 104.6 *Developing countries: share of different regions in total net inflow of FDI in developing countries, 1975-1998, per cent*
Source: adapted from United Nations, *World Economic Outlook; World Economic and Social Survey.*

Question 3

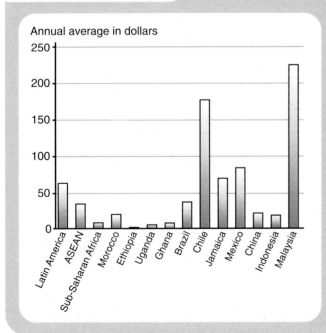

(a) Explain what is meant by 'FDI per capita'.
(b) Name the three countries which, according to the data, have received (i) the highest levels and (b) the lowest levels of FDI per capita in the 1990s.
(c) Explain how FDI inflows might help increase a country's growth rate.

Figure 104.7 *Net inflow of FDI per capita in selected developing regions and countries, 1990-97, (annual average in dollars)*
Source: adapted from United Nations, *World Economic Outlook; World Economic and Social Survey.*

Aid to developing countries

Among least-developed countries, the smallest and most resource poor are the least likely to receive substantial and private capital flows. These countries still need official aid flows to finance investments in health, education, the environment and basic infrastructure. In 1998, net official flows worldwide totalled approximately $51.1 billion.

Aid can be highly effective in promoting growth and reducing poverty. But aid is also a scarce resource that needs to be used well, and using it well requires good decisions by governments and donors alike. Whether aid increases economic growth, for instance, depends on a country's policy and institutional environment. Good macroeconomic management, sound structural policies and public sector administration, and measures that increase equity, are all important. They promote growth themselves, and they support the growth-enhancing effects of development assistance.

Development assistance, like so many other economic inputs, is subject to diminishing returns. Even countries with excellent policies are limited in their capacity to absorb such aid. Once official assistance reaches around 12 per cent of GDP, its potential contribution to growth is usually exhausted. But few countries receive such high levels of aid, so that only a country's policy environment limits its capacity to absorb development assistance.

While the governments of developing countries determine the effectiveness of aid in the growth process, donors determine how effective aid is in global poverty reduction. For it is donors, not recipient governments, that decide which countries receive assistance. In making this decision, donors need to keep in mind two factors.

● The extent to which assistance will raise the growth rate, a factor that depends on the policy and institutional environment and thus differs considerably across countries.
● The existing level and distribution of income in the recipient country, since income growth in a country like Chile, where poverty is low, tends to reduce poverty less than in a country with mass poverty like India.

Three-quarters of the world's poor (those living on less than $2 per day) now live in countries where the policy environments are such that additional aid would raise the growth rate. The challenge is to allocate the assistance available in order to take advantage of the favourable climate for growth.

Source: World Bank, *World Development Report*, 1999/2000.

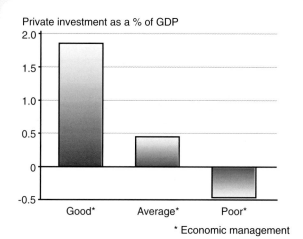

Figure 104.8 *Marginal impact on private investment of 1% of GDP in aid*
Source: adapted from World Bank.

The graph shows the impact of foreign aid on generating additional private investment depending upon the mix of policies pursued by governments in a country. Good economic policies will result in more private investment being generated than average policies.

The amount industrial countries spend on development aid for poor nations fell to a record low in 1997- from $55.4 billion to $48.3 billion. Adjusting for inflation, this represented a fall of 5.8 per cent. As a share of national income, aid spending fell from 0.25 per cent in 1996 to a record low of 0.22 per cent. Development assistance is well down from the historic norm of 0.33 per cent recorded before 1992 and well below the 0.7 per cent United Nations target.

However, the OECD's development assistance committee, presenting the figures, welcomed the fact that many donors were now concentrating development assistance on the achievement of international targets for poverty reduction. Gender equality, improving basic health and education, good governance and environmental sustainability have all become more important priorities.

Source: adapted from the *Financial Times*, 9.2.1999.

1. **What is meant by 'aid to developing countries' and what happened to levels of aid in the late 1990s?**
2. **Explain how aid can help in economic development.**
3. **Analyse the obstacles which limit the effectiveness of aid programmes.**
4. **Discuss whether a substantial increase in aid would be the most effective way of relieving absolute poverty in the world today.**

Study skills

When you start your AS/A Level course, you should try to evaluate whether or not your study and organisational skills are effective. For instance:

- are you always present and on time for classes or lectures?
- do you always hand work in on time?
- is work done to the best of your ability?
- do you work in a suitable environment?
- do you leave time to plan and evaluate your work?
- do you participate in all learning activities in a way which helps you to learn?
- do you listen to advice and act on constructive comments about your work?

Having good study skills does not necessarily mean that work is done well in advance, or that the room where you work at home is tidy. Some students are very organised in what might at first seem chaotic situations. For instance, they might always write their essays close to the time they have to be handed in. Or their study room might look an incredible mess. However, if you work best under pressure of deadlines, and you know what is where in the mess of your room, then it could be argued that in fact you are an organised student!

In class

The core of your study is likely to take place in the classroom or lecture room. Not only will you spend a considerable proportion of your studying time in class, but what you do in the classroom and the instructions you receive there will influence what you do outside. Effective classroom skills are therefore essential. They include the following.

Attending classes regularly and on time Good organisational skills involve attending all lessons unless there are serious reasons for absence. They also involve arranging doctor's and dentist's appointments, driving lessons or holidays outside class time so that work is not missed.

Always being attentive It is important to be attentive at all times and engage in the activities being presented. Participation in class also helps other students to learn.

Making clear and concise notes during lessons Notes can act as a record of what has been said. Taking notes whilst the teacher/lecturer is talking is a form of active learning. It can help some students to focus on what is being said and identify what they don't understand. For other students, though, note taking can get in the way of understanding what the teacher or lecturer is saying. They may prefer to read handouts or notes given out by the teacher or lecturer. You have to decide what is best for you.

Asking questions of the teacher or lecturer It is unlikely that all students will understand everything that goes on in a lesson. Asking questions helps to fill in these gaps. It is also very important to keep you focussed on the lesson. If you are thinking about what you do and don't understand, you will inevitably be participating in that lesson. Formulating questions is also important for developing oral skills, which will be essential in the world outside of school or college.

Participating in classroom discussions Classroom discussions enable you to practice important key learning skills. Some students find they want to contribute more than others. Remember though that in a discussion, listening is as important as talking. All participants must respect the contributions of others. There must be a balance between communication and listening.

Preparing for the next lesson Many schools and colleges issue their students with homework diaries, or encourage them to buy one. They are a useful tool for planning and organising work. They help you to remember what you have to do and structure your out of class activities.

Planning outside the class

Planning is an essential part of good study skills. By keeping a diary, for instance, students can see at a glance what needs to be done and when. They can then mentally allocate time slots for completion of the work. For work which is not structured by the teacher or lecturer, such as coursework or revision, students need to construct a plan. Typically, this will show dates and the work to be done on or by a particular date. It may also show times during the day when work is to be done. Some students find it helpful to discipline themselves by the clock. So they plan to start, say, revision at 9.00 each morning, have a ten minute break each hour on the hour, break for lunch at 1.00, etc.

It may also be helpful to construct precise plans for day to day work outside the classroom. When you start on your AS/A level course, for instance, it might be useful to plan meticulously when you are going to complete work during the first month. This will ensure that work gets done and you have set out on your course with good work habits. Hopefully, you will then be able to relax your planning because you will have got into a sound routine for completing work.

Planning tends to increase in importance:
- the longer the task to be completed:
- the less structure is given by your school or college for its completion.

Organising time

Every student has different preferences about organising time. Some of the key issues are as follows.

Time during the week You have to decide when you want to complete your work during the week. There are likely to be conflicting claims on your time. For instance, you may have a part time job which takes priority at certain times of the week. You may have family or social commitments. You may decide that you will never work on Friday or Saturday nights (except in emergencies!). There are no right or wrong times to study. However, it is essential to build in enough time during the week to study. AS/A level examinations have been developed on the assumption that you are studying full time for 1 to 2 years.

Time during the day Some people work best in the morning, some in the afternoon and some at night. You should know whether you are a 'morning person' or otherwise. Try to work at times of day when you are most likely to learn effectively.

Breaks Breaks are essential to maintain concentration. How frequent and how long your breaks need to be varies from one individual to another. You need to find out what works best for you. Try to be as disciplined as possible in your approach to breaks. It is all too easy for the break to extend itself over the whole period when you planned to work. Get to know what is most likely to stop you from getting back to work. For instance, if you start watching television during your break, do you find that you only go back to work at the end of the programme?

Variety Some students like variety in what they do. So during an hour's work session, they may do a little on three pieces of work. Others find that they cannot cope with such short blocks of time and would rather concentrate on just one piece of work. Longer pieces of work, such as essays or coursework, may need to be broken down and completed in several different work sessions anyway.

Networking and resources

It is important that students make use of all the resources that are available to them. Here are some suggestions about how to find help when completing work.

Ask the teacher/lecturer Make full use of your teacher or lecturer as a resource. If you are stuck on a piece of homework, for instance, ask the teacher or lecturer to help you out. If you frequently need help, it is a good idea to start the homework well in advance of the date it needs to be handed in, so that you can contact the teacher or lecturer.

Network with fellow students Students may find networking with friends helpful. If they have a problem, they can call a friend or see them in school or college. Students who prefer to work in this way should be aware of which students in their teaching group are most likely to give helpful advice. Networking is a valuable tool in the learning process both to the person who receives the help and the person who gives it.

Parents, business people, etc. Parents, family members,

friends or contacts in the business community may all be sources of help in different situations and for different pieces of work.

The textbook Using a textbook effectively will help students to achieve the highest possible marks for their work. Remember that the textbook is there to help you understand a topic. The relevant section should be read before you attempt a piece of work and you are likely to want to refer to the textbook as you write. You may wish to consult a number of textbooks if, for example, you do not understand a particular area in one book.

The library Schools and colleges will have libraries, perhaps even in the classroom or lecture room, of books and other materials which can be borrowed. Reading around a topic is an essential part of preparing any work such as an essay. Libraries will also hopefully carry daily quality newspapers. Economics is about the real world. AS/A level Economics students should be aware of the major economic issues of the day and be able to discuss them.

The internet The internet varies considerably in how useful it can be in the learning process. It is most useful when students are able to use the same site repeatedly. They know what is on the site and how to navigate around it. There may be problems, however, when searching for general information. It requires the same skills and time as going to a large reference library and looking for information. The internet is likely to be very useful to students working on their own in Economics when researching coursework.

The work environment

Your work environment needs to be chosen to maximise learning. Students often work either in a library or study area, or at home in their own room. What is there about these work places which make them effective?

Availability Your work place should be available to you when you want to study. If you like to complete as much work as possible at school or college, and work hard between time-tabled lessons, then the library might be an excellent environment for you. You may prefer to complete homework in your own home. Your bedroom may be the only place where you are guaranteed that you can work uninterrupted. Not only must a place be available but so too must the resources. If you are undertaking research, for instance, you may have to work in a library or at a computer terminal.

Music, television and noise Some students find it easy to concentrate in the midst of chaos. They like distractions and find it easier to work if they know they can also listen to music, stroke the dog or have a conversation. Many students find distractions impossible to cope with. To work effectively, they need relative peace and quiet. They might or might not like background music.

Alone or in groups Some students find that working in a

group is ineffective. One person may start talking about a non-work issue and work is then never resumed. They therefore, prefer to work alone. However, other students who can avoid such distractions find working in groups highly effective. It means they can instantly network with others when they have a problem.

Furniture Furniture can be very important in studying. Some students prefer to read in an armchair and write at a desk. You may find it easier to create work spaces where particular types of work can be done. Make sure that the chair you sit in is comfortable and doesn't give you back problems.

Lighting Experiment with lighting to reduce eye strain. If you find studying makes you tired very quickly, one reason might be inadequate lighting. You can also use lighting to create a mood which encourages you to study.

Movement Your work environment should allow you to move around if you wish. When trying to memorise something, for instance, some students may prefer to walk around, whereas others may prefer to sit.

Preparing for tests and examinations

Different students prepare effectively for tests or examinations in a variety of different ways. You have to find out what is most effective for you. Different methods may also be useful in different circumstances. For instance, you may want to spend most time memorising information for an essay-based examination, but for a multiple-choice examination you may want to spend most time practising past questions.

Written notes Many students use notes in their revision. Notes are useful records of what has been learned either because the student has made them and therefore hopefully can understand them, or because they have been given by the teacher or lecturer and show what material is likely to occur in the examination.

Good note taking is a skilled art. Notes are meant to be a precis, a shortening of what, for instance, might be found in a textbook. So it is important to develop a style of writing notes which does shorten material.
- Miss out common words like 'the' and 'a' which do not affect the meaning.
- Abbreviate words. For example, write 'gov' for 'government', 'C' for consumption, or 'P' for price.

Notes should be clearly laid out using headings and subheadings. Ideally, headings and subheadings should be colour coded to make them easier to skim read. The headings should provide a story in themselves which prompts you to remember the material contained underneath each heading. Highlight key terms within the notes. Star, circle or underline important points.

Some students like to work from notes written on A4 paper. Other students like to transfer notes onto small cards where there is less on each card. Whichever method you use, make sure that the notes are logically ordered and can be referred to instantly.

When memorising material from notes, some students find it helpful to think of the layout of individual pages. This then prompts memory recall of what is on the page.

The textbook Some students dislike revising from notes and prefer to use a textbook. They may find it easier, for instance, to read printed material rather than their own handwriting. They may want to use material collected together rather than a series of handouts or loose pages. Also, notes may be incomplete in places.

Some students rely on both notes and textbooks for revision. Revising from a textbook involves the same skills as revising from notes. The textbook will have chapter or unit headings, and headings and subheadings within these. These provide the skeleton on which the detail should be hung.

Pictures and visual presentations Some students find pictures particularly helpful when revising. Examples of commonly used visual presentations include mind maps, flow charts and family trees, which are illustrated in Figures 105.1 to 105.3. These illustrations summarise the main points in unit 4, The Demand Curve, of this book. Visual presentations work through helping the student see a topic laid out. Places on the page can be visualised and connections clearly identified.

Oral methods Some students like to be 'tested' by another person on a topic to see if they have learnt the material. Repeating words or phrases can be helpful. So too can devising word associations and mnemonics. A word association is linking one word with another. For instance, you may be particularly interested in football, and decide to remember the main components of aggregate demand (consumption, investment, government spending and exports minus imports) by assigning each term to the name of a football club. Remember the football clubs and you remember the components. Alternatively, you may make up a mnemonic, a rhyme or phrase usually associated with the first letter of each word. For instance, you could have Clobber In Gap Extremely Important OR Chelsea In Goal Excitement Incident for consumption, investment, government spending, exports and imports.

Active learning Some students find it difficult just to sit and memorise material. They need to be doing something to help them remember.
- One way is to construct a set of notes, or a mind map. Once written out, the notes may be of little use, but it is in the doing that the learning has taken place.
- You may want to practice past examination questions. Multiple choice question papers, for instance, are best revised for in this way. If you practice essay questions, it is often more useful to spend scarce time writing out essay plans for a wide variety of questions than answering a few essays in detail.
- You may use published materials which give short answer questions on a topic such as 'Define economies of scale', or 'List the costs of unemployment'.
- Some students practice past homework tasks which they have been set and then compare their results with their first marked attempt.

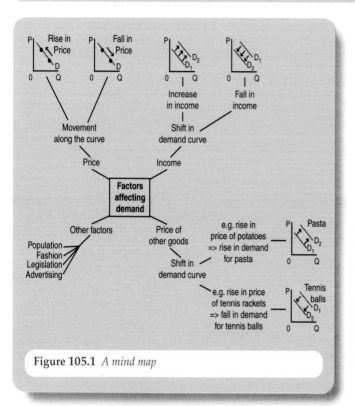

Figure 105.1 *A mind map*

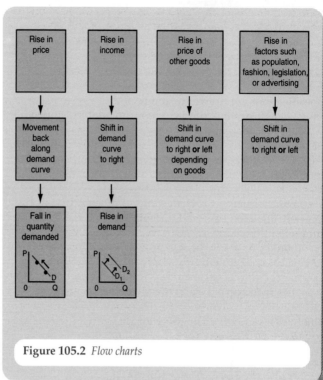

Figure 105.2 *Flow charts*

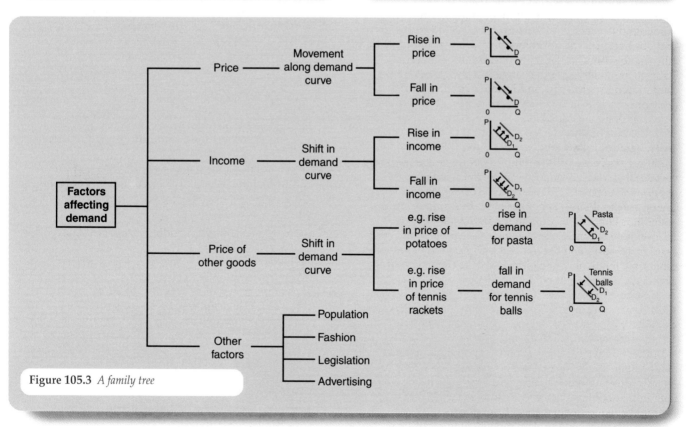

Figure 105.3 *A family tree*

Assessment criteria

Specifications are drawn up and papers are set to test a range of assessment criteria. These are qualities and skills which a candidate must demonstrate to the examiners to gain marks in any form of assessment. In Economics at AS/A level, these assessment criteria are grouped into four areas.

Demonstration of knowledge and understanding of the specified subject content **Knowledge and understanding** requires candidates to show that they can recognise economic concepts and terms and be able to define or explain them. For instance, *Explain what is meant by economies of scale* asks for a definition of economies of scale (knowledge) and a good answer is likely to give examples to demonstrate clear understanding of the term. Knowledge and understanding are also present when economic theories are used. For instance, knowledge is required when drawing a demand and supply diagram. Has the candidate correctly identified the axes? Is the demand curve downward sloping? Is the supply curve upward sloping? Is the candidate using proper conventions by clearly labelling the axes and the demand and supply curves? Another example would be the link between interest rates and inflation. Does a candidate show knowledge of the chain of causality between a change in interest rates, a change in aggregate demand and a change in the equilibrium price level of the economy?

Application of knowledge and critical understanding to economic problems and issues arising from both familiar and unfamiliar situations Knowledge is essential for any economist, but the knowledge must be **applied** to economic problems to be of use. For instance, being able to define economies of scale is of little use if economies of scale at work in motor vehicle manufacturing cannot be recognised. Application is the skill of being able to use knowledge in a wide variety of contexts. Some of these contexts will be familiar. For instance, you might have studied leisure industries during your course and in the examination a question is set on economies of scale in leisure industries. The context may, however, be unfamiliar. For instance, you may have studied the environment as part your course. In the examination, a question on pollution permits in the USA may be set. Pollution permits is part of expected knowledge and understanding but the USA may be an unfamiliar context. Another example of application would be using mathematical formulae to work out answers to problems. Calculating a value for price elasticity of demand is application.

Analyse economic problems and issues **Analysis** is the process of breaking down information into relevant parts and then using this to understand a problem or issue. A simple piece of analysis, for instance, would be to identify a trend from a set of unemployment figures on a graph. The graph might be accompanied by a passage which contains information about why unemployment might be falling. The skill of analysis is needed to link the trend with its causes. Analysis would also be required if a candidate were asked to identify possible government policies to tackle unemployment. The candidate might have to select which policies from a list might be appropriate and justify why these policies might be effective.

Evaluate economic arguments and evidence, making informed judgements **Evaluation** requires candidates to make conclusions and argue which courses of action might be most appropriate in a situation. If a government wanted to reduce unemployment today, which would be the most effective policies for it to pursue? If global warming is to be stopped, what are the most important actions which consumers and firms must take? It is relatively easy to make a simple judgement. At this level, though, examiners expect candidates to be able to justify their answers. It is this justification which tends to carry most marks. To do this, candidates must weigh up the evidence presented to them and judge which is important and which is not. They must consider whether the information presented is reliable and whether or not it is complete enough to come to a decision. If it is not, what other information is required to come to a definitive conclusion? Candidates must also distinguish between fact and opinion.

Candidates are also assessed in Economics AS/A level on the **quality of written communication**. Candidates must:
- select and use a form and style of writing appropriate to purpose and complex subject matter. For instance, candidates must be able to write an essay, or a short answer to a question;
- organise relevant information clearly and coherently, using specialist vocabulary when appropriate. So candidates must, for instance, be able to write in paragraphs and they must be able to use terms like price elasticity or the current balance when these are required;
- ensure writing is legible, and spelling, grammar and punctuation are accurate, so that meaning is clear. Candidates must therefore write clearly, construct proper sentences and spell correctly.

Command, directive or key words

Questions typically start off with command or key words. These words indicate which skills are required when answering the question. It is important for candidates to respond in an appropriate manner. For instance, if candidates are asked to evaluate a problem, but only show knowledge and understanding, then they will lose most of the marks for that question. Command words can be grouped according to what skills will be required in an answer.

Knowledge and understanding

- Define - to give the exact meaning of a term or concept using words or mathematical symbols whose meaning is already understood by the reader, e.g. *Define what is meant by economies of scale.*
- Describe - to give an account of something, e.g. *Describe the costs of inflation.*
- Give - to state or say, e.g. *Give two examples of goods in which Saudi Arabia has a comparative advantage in production.*
- How - to present an account of something, e.g. *How does the government raise taxes?*
- Identify - to single out from other information, e.g. *Identify three factors which cause inflation.*
- Illustrate - to use examples to explain a point, e.g. *Illustrate the way in which monopolists keep out competitors from their markets.*
- List - to state in the briefest form, e.g. *List three factors which affect the demand for a product.*
- Outline - to give a short description of the main aspects or features, e.g. *Outline the arguments used by Greenpeace against genetically modified (GM) crops.*
- State - to give or say, e.g. *State three factors which affect elasticity of supply.*
- Summarise - to bring out the main points from a more complex set of data, e.g. *Summarise the main arguments in favour of government intervention.*
- What - to clarify a point, e.g. *What are the main characteristics of a perfectly competitive industry?*

Application

- Apply - use knowledge of economics to understand a situation, issue or problem, e.g. *Apply the theory of perfect competition to the market for potatoes.*
- Calculate - use mathematics to work out an answer, e.g. *Calculate the price elasticity of demand if price increases from £3 to £4.*
- Distinguish between - identify the characteristics which make two or more ideas, concepts, issues, etc. different, e.g. *Distinguish between price elasticity of demand and income elasticity of demand.*
- Explain - making clear. It is often useful to define terms and give examples in an explanation, e.g. *Explain how prices are determined in a free market.*
- Suggest - give possible reasons or ideas. These must be plausible but not necessarily correct. 'Suggest' may require candidates to analyse a problem and not just apply economic problems, e.g. *Suggest reasons why the firm did not put up its prices.*

Analysis

- Analyse - to break down into constituent parts in order to be able to understand an issue or problem. Analysis involves recognising what is important, and being apply to knowledge and understanding of economics where necessary, e.g. *Analyse the reasons for the firm investing in new machinery.*
- Compare and contrast - to show the similarities and differences between two or more ideas or problems, e.g. *Compare and contrast the performance of the UK and Japanese economies over the past ten years.*
- Examine - to break down an issue or problem to understand it, e.g. *Examine the problems facing the UK economy today.*
- Investigate - to look for evidence to explain and analyse, e.g. *Investigate why the government chose to cut interest rates in May.*

Evaluation

- Assess - to analyse an economic issue or problem and then to weigh up the relative importance of different strands, e.g. *Assess the impact of high interest rates on the UK economy.*
- Comment on - invites the candidate to make their judgements based upon evidence which they have presented, e.g. *Comment on why the Bank of England thought it necessary to raise interest rates in June.*
- Critically analyse - to analyse an issue or problem and then to weigh up the relative importance of part of this analysis, e.g. *Critically analyse the problems facing the industry today.*
- Do you think - invites candidates to put forward their own opinions about an issue or problem. However, the marks will always be awarded for the quality of the arguments put forward and not for any individual opinions, e.g. *Do you think the government should have allowed the motorway to be built?*
- Discuss - to compare a number of possible views about an issue or problem and to weigh up their relative importance. A conclusion is essential, e.g. *Discuss the advantages and disadvantages of fixing rents in the housing market.*
- Evaluate - like discuss, to compare a number of possible views about an issue or problem and weigh up their relative importance. A final judgement is essential, e.g. *Evaluate the policies available to government to reduce unemployment.*
- To what extent - invites candidates to explain and analyse and then to comment upon the relative importance of arguments, e.g. *To what extent should the government rely upon monetary policy to control inflation?*

Levels of response

Questions which test the higher order skills of analysis and evaluation are likely to be marked using a levels of response mark scheme. Rather than giving candidates a mark or several marks for a point made or an argument developed within an answer, the answer is marked holistically (as a whole). It is then compared to descriptions of what answers might look like in terms of the skills displayed. The answer is then put within a level. This level will have a range of marks which the examiner can award depending upon whether it is a good answer within that level or not.

For instance, a levels mark scheme might have three levels and 12 marks are awarded. The level descriptors are as follows.

Level 1

One or more reasons given, but little development of points. The answer lacks coherence and there is no valid analysis or evaluation. 1-3 marks

Level 2

Several reasons given with reasonable analysis. Arguments are expressed with some confidence and coherence. Evaluation, though, is weakly supported by evidence. 4-8 marks

Level 3

A good coverage of the main reasons. Sound analysis with clear links between the issues raised. Arguments for and against have been evaluated and a conclusion reached. 9-12 marks

Mark schemes are available from the awarding bodies. You should become familiar with the levels of response mark schemes used by examiners on the papers you will sit. To gain a mark in the highest level, candidates typically have to give evidence of all four main skills of knowledge, application, analysis and evaluation.

Multiple choice questions

Some awarding bodies use multiple choice questions as a form of assessment. They are used mainly to test lower order skills of knowledge and application. They are also a convenient way of testing breadth. A data response question or an essay is likely to cover only one topic. If there is choice, candidates may be encouraged only to revise part of the course in the hope that they will still be able to answer a full set of questions. A multiple choice test covers the whole course and therefore penalises candidates who are selective in their revision.

Success at multiple choice questions involves being thoroughly familiar with the basics of economics. It also requires skill in answering multiple choice questions, just as essays requires essay writing skills. Practice on questions is therefore very important. Using past question papers from the awarding body can also be very helpful. Not only will it help you familiarise yourself with the style of multiple choice question being used, but past questions may be reused on new papers.

There are two ways in which candidates are likely to get to a correct answer on a multiple choice question.
- Knowing the correct answer.
- Eliminating the wrong answers.

Candidates should make full use of the laws of probability. If the correct answer is not obvious, but two out of four responses can be eliminated, the chances of getting the answer right are improved from 1 in 4 for guessing to 1 in 2. Taken over a whole paper, a strategy of eliminating wrong answers can significantly improve marks.

Some multiple choice tests require candidates not just to give an answer from A to D but also to justify their answers. The written explanation should be short and to the point.

In an examination, do not spend more than the allotted time on any single question but pass over it. For instance, if there are 30 questions to be answered in 30 minutes, there is on average just 1 minute per question. Don't spend 10 minutes working out question 5. Come back at the end to the questions which you have missed out. If you have nearly run out of time, always make sure that there is an answer to every question. You will then have some chance rather than no chance to gain marks. Some candidates prefer to draw a line through incorrect responses (i.e. wrong answers) within a question and visibly isolate the correct answer.

Data response questions

Data response questions are used to test a candidate's ability to apply their knowledge and understanding to familiar or unfamiliar data. They usually also require candidates to display skills of analysis and evaluation as well.

The data presented may be verbal or in numerical form, or a mixture of both. Candidates often find data in verbal form easier to understand and interpret. However, in practice, examiners construct questions so that there is little or no difference in outcome in marks between questions which contain mainly verbal data and those which contain mainly numerical data.

Some awarding bodies only use real data, such as newspaper extracts or statistics from government sources. Others also use hypothetical or imaginary data - data which has been made up by the examiner. In some areas of Economics, it is difficult to obtain real data. Exact figures for price elasticity of demand is one example. Therefore some examiners prefer to use imaginary data for questions.

There is a number of ways in which candidates can improve their performance on data response questions in examinations.
- Read through the material thoroughly.
- Use highlighter pens to mark what you think are important words or passages.
- Highlight the key words in a question.
- Think carefully about what each question is asking of you. In particular, think about the skills you are required to display in a question.
- If there are any numerical calculations, show all your workings carefully. You may get marks for the workings even if you fail to get the final answer correct.
- Have a clear understanding of how long each answer should be. For instance, assume there are 60 marks overall, with the first two questions being awarded 5 marks each, the third question carrying 10 marks, the fourth carrying 15 marks and the last 25 marks. The first question should be roughly one fifth the length of the last question and should take only 5/60 of the time to complete. Many candidates write too much on

questions which carry few marks and too little on questions which carry many marks.

- Be aware of what economic concepts and theories the question is testing.
- Some candidates find it helpful to prepare plans for longer answers.
- Make sure you don't run out of time. It is usually better to abandon one part and move onto the next if you are running out of time rather than attempting to create the perfect answer on that part.
- Last parts of data response questions may expect candidates to write for around 20 minutes. These questions then become small essays and the techniques for writing essays outlined below need to be applied to them.

Sometimes, it is appropriate to use a diagram in a data response question. Some questions, in fact, specifically ask for a diagram to be drawn. There are some easy rules to remember when drawing diagrams.

- Examiners will expect to see standard diagrams which are found in any Economics textbook.
- When drawing diagrams, make sure they are large enough to be read.
- Diagrams are easier to read and look much better if they are drawn with a ruler where appropriate.
- Always label the axes and the lines or curves.
- Always refer to and explain the diagram in your written answer.

Essays

Essays are often used to test higher order skills of analysis and evaluation, although there are likely to be marks for knowledge and application in the mark scheme too. Typically, candidates are expected to write for 35 to 45 minutes on an essay title which is likely to be split into two separate but linked parts.

Essay writing is a skill which needs to be practised and learnt. It requires putting together (or **synthesising**) a number of ideas to form one complete answer. Essays are likely to be marked using levels of response mark schemes.

Candidates can improve their essay writing skills if they can learn the following techniques.

- Before you start writing, have a clear understanding of what the question is asking. In particular, identify the skills which will be required from you to write a successful essay by looking at the command words. Identify too the areas of economics of relevance to the essay. Some candidates also find it useful to highlight the key words in an essay title to focus them on what the question is asking. For instance, take the following question: *Evaluate the policies which a government might adopt to deal with the problem of youth unemployment.* The key words here are *Evaluate* , *government policies* and *youth unemployment*. Evaluate means that you will have to compare the effectiveness of different types of government policy. You will be expected to argue that some might be more useful than others in order to gain the maximum number of marks. Government policies

to deal with unemployment is the main area of economic knowledge. However, especially important is the word *youth*. Your answer must focus on *youth* unemployment if it is to get the higher marks.
- Some candidates find it useful to write out an **essay plan**. This is a brief synopsis of what you will write. It allows you to jot points down and to see how they can be organised to form a coherent whole. Often candidates start their answer and add points to their plan as they go along because writing triggers their memories. This is good practice, but always check that your new points will not unbalance the structure of your answer. Adding new material after you have written your conclusion, for instance, may gain you extra marks but it is unlikely to help you get the highest marks.
- Paragraph your essay properly. Remember that a paragraph should contain material on one idea or one group of ideas. A useful technique to use is to see a paragraph as an opening sentence which makes a point, and the rest of the paragraph as an explanation or elaboration of that point.
- Include diagrams wherever they are appropriate. Advice about the effective use of diagrams is given above.
- Write a concluding paragraph. This is especially important if you are answering an evaluation question. The conclusion gives you the opportunity to draw your points together and to weigh up the arguments put forward.
- With two part questions, ensure that you have allocated your time effectively between the two parts. Don't spend too much time on the first half of the question. It is particularly important to work out how long to spend on each part if the two parts carry very unequal mark weighting.
- Essays are continuous pieces of prose. They should not include bullet points, lists, subheadings, etc.
- Spot the story. Many essay questions are set because they cover a topical issue. Recognising what this topical issue is should help you decide what to stress in your essay. Knowledge of the issue will also give you additional material to introduce into the essay.
- Adapt your material to suit what is required. Don't write out an answer to an essay question you have already answered in class and memorised and which is similar to the essay question set. Equally, don't write 'everything I know about' one or two key words in the essay title. For instance, answering a question about the costs of inflation by writing at length about the causes of inflation is likely to be an inappropriate answer.
- Remember there are likely to be marks for quality of language in the mark scheme. Write in a simple and clear style and pay attention to your spelling.

Coursework

You may be required to write a piece of coursework. You are likely to be given extensive help in doing this by your teacher or lecturer.

Planning One key issue in coursework for the student is time management. Coursework is likely to be carried out over a period of time. It is important that deadlines are not missed because they are weeks or months ahead before the coursework is due to be handed in. It is also important that all work is not left to the end when there may not be enough time to complete it. Planning is therefore very important. Your teacher or lecturer is likely to help you in this, setting goals and helping you to complete the coursework well within the time limit required.

Following specification instructions The examination specification will give detailed instructions about how topics should be chosen, how the coursework should be written up and how marks will be awarded. You should always keep a copy of this with your work. Awarding bodies also publish specification support materials for teachers and lecturers. These too will contain information about coursework which should be made available to you. High marks are usually gained by following what examiners have told candidates to do.

Choice of topic Your first task will be to decide upon a topic to research. This should be an investigation into an economic problem or issue. The choice of topic is vital for two reasons. First, the student must be able to obtain primary and/or secondary data on the topic. Secondary data is data and information which have already been collected by someone else. It is likely to be the main source if not the sole source of data for the investigation. It might, for instance, include newspaper articles, government statistics, or material from web sites on the internet. Primary data is data which have been collected directly by the student and do not come from another source. The results of a questionnaire conducted by the student would be an example. Primary data may not be available for the chosen topic. Primary data may also be of poor quality, for example from a poorly conducted survey. So primary data should only be included when it is reliable and relevant to the chosen topic.

Choice of topic is also important because it will determine whether the candidate can display all the skills required by the examination. This will include both analysis and evaluation. The key is to phrase the coursework title as a problem or issue. 'Is the package tour industry an oligopoly?' may not be a suitable title. It does not give candidates sufficient scope to display skills of evaluation. A title which asked whether the UK or EU competition authorities should allow a merger which is currently being proposed between package tour companies is a more suitable title. Candidates will be able to explore the issue, including commenting on the oligopolistic nature of the package tour industry. They will then have to use this analysis to evaluate a policy decision. This is precisely what economists working for the competition authorities would, of course, also be doing.

Collecting information Collecting information is likely to take a fair amount of time. For instance, doing a newspaper search may take a number of sessions in a library. Gathering statistical information from government publications such as *Economic Trends Annual Supplement* and converting it into a form which is useful in your chosen assignment will take hours and perhaps days. The internet may be equally time consuming. You may have to sift through large amounts of irrelevant information to find something of value.

If you undertake any primary research, you should have a clear understanding of the techniques you are using and what makes them valid as evidence. For instance, if you construct a questionnaire, you should be aware of the issues involved in setting appropriate questions. You should also understand the size and nature of the sample needed to give valid results.

Data is likely to be collected from the following sources:
- books including textbooks;
- newspapers;
- magazines;
- specialist trade journals;
- advertising literature;
- government statistical publications including *Monthly Digest of Statistics, Economic Trends and Economic Trends Annual Supplement, the Annual Abstract of Statistics, Social Trends, Regional Trends, Environmental Statistics and Transport Statistics*;
- web sites on the internet.

When collecting information, seek the help of others where possible. For instance, if you use a library, ask the librarian for help in finding material. If you use the internet, make sure that you understand how best to use a search engine.

Collecting information is time consuming and challenging. Don't underestimate the difficulty of this part of the task.

Structuring the report The awarding body will give clear guidance on how the report should be laid out and what should be included. For instance, awarding bodies may recommend that there should be:
- a contents page;
- an introduction outlining the economic issue or problem to be investigated, framed in the form of either an hypothesis to be tested or a question requiring further investigation;
- a brief outline of economic concepts and theories relevant to the issue or problem, in some cases involving reference to existing literature;
- a brief outline of the technique(s) to be used to collect the relevant data;
- a presentation of the findings related to the hypothesis or the question posed;
- an evaluation of the findings and method of research, with recommendations where appropriate;
- a bibliography of sources.

When writing your report, remember that you are writing about economic theory and presenting the evidence you have collected to arrive at a set of conclusions. It is important to avoid writing everything you can find from textbooks about certain economic theories, or forgetting that the purpose of collecting evidence is to evaluate problems or issues.

Report writing

Students may be required to write a report. The style of a report is different from that of an essay.

- It should begin with a section showing who the report is for, who has written it, the date it was written and the title. If the report is written under examination conditions, this may all be omitted.
- It should be broken down into a number of sections. Each section should address a particular issue. A heading should start each section to help the reader see the structure of the report. In most reports, sections are numbered in sequence.
- A section may be broken down into sub-sections, each with their own headings and their own numbers. For instance, section 3 of the report may have two sub-sections, 3.1 and 3.2.
- The report must be written in complete sentences and not in note form. However, unlike in an essay, it is acceptable to use bullet points to further structure the report.
- Use diagrams wherever appropriate. Diagrams must be part of the argument used in the report. It is important that the reader understands why they have been included.

A report will require you to draw conclusions and make judgements, i.e. show that you can evaluate an issue or problem. The evaluation can be presented at the end of the report, or it can be included in each section of the report. If it is included in each section, a conclusion or summary still needs to be written at the end to bring together what has been said earlier.

The report should also highlight missing information that would have been useful or, perhaps, was essential, to come to reasoned conclusions or recommendations. The reliability or accuracy of the information provided could also be questioned.

If the report is written in examination conditions, as with a data response question, take time at the start to read through the data given. Highlight key ideas or data. It may not be necessary to understand all the data before you start writing as this may waste important time which may be needed to write the report. However, it is important to understand what is required of you before you start writing.

Constructing a plan is essential. A report is a complex piece of writing. Identify the main headings of your report and jot down the main points which you are likely to include under each heading. You may add to your plan as you write your report if you think of new points. In an examination, you are unlikely to have the time to write a number of drafts of the report. However, outside the examination room, it would be useful to produce several drafts.

Index